STRANGERS
IN THE LAND

STRANGERS IN THE LAND

Blacks, Jews, Post-Holocaust America

ERIC J. SUNDQUIST

The Belknap Press of Harvard University Press

Cambridge, Massachusetts · London, England

Printed in the United States of America

First Harvard University Press paperback edition, 2008.

Library of Congress Cataloging-in-Publication Data

Sundquist, Eric J.
Strangers in the land : Blacks, Jews, post-Holocaust America / Eric J. Sundquist.
p.   cm.
Includes bibliographical references (p.) and index
ISBN 978-0-674-01942-3 (cloth : alk. paper)
ISBN 978-0-674-03069-5 (pbk.)
1. African Americans—Relations with Jews. 2. United States—Race
relations—History—20th century. 3. Holocaust, Jewish (1939–1945).
4. Exodus, The. 5. Zionism. 6. Race relations in literature. 7. Racism in literature.
8. Jews in literature. 9. African Americans in literature. 10. American
literature—20th century—History and criticism. I. Title.

E184.36.A34S86   2005
305.892'4073'09045—dc22   2005047033

Contents

List of Illustrations vii

Introduction 1

1. America's Jews 17

2. The Black Nation Israel 95

3. Black Skin, Yellow Star; or, Blues for Atticus Finch 170

4. Exodus 239
 I. A Negro-less World: William Melvin Kelley 239
 II. The Wounding Past: Paule Marshall 269

5. Black Power, Jewish Power 311

6. Bernard Malamud's Dark Ghetto 381

7. Holocaust 435
 I. Never Forgetting 435
 II. Other People's Nightmares 481

8. Spooks 503

Notes 529
Acknowledgments 643
Index 647

Illustrations

Ben Shahn, *Thou Shalt Not Stand Idly By* (1965)   33

Lila Oliver Asher, *Homage to Ben Shahn* (1966)   34

Louis Farrakhan at Madison Square Garden (1985)   89

Jacob Lawrence, "Migration of the Negro, Panel 3,"
    The Migration Series (1941)   98

Abraham Heschel and Martin Luther King, Jr.,
    at Arlington National Cemetery (1968)   108

Moorish Zionist Temple of Moorish Jews,
    New York City (1929)   117

Cover illustration for "Entartete Musik"
    (Degenerate Music) (1938)   185

Cover illustration for *Time* magazine (1969)   349

Judy Chicago, "Arbeit Macht Frei / Work Makes Who Free?"
    from the *Holocaust Project* (1992)   447

Illustration from *The Black Holocaust for Beginners* (1995)   463

Art Spiegelman, Valentine's Day cover illustration
    for the *New Yorker* (1993)   501

STRANGERS
IN THE LAND

Introduction

READING SAUL BELLOW, like reading Ralph Ellison, said the novelist Leon Forrest in 1997, is a means of opening up the "consciousness of the country." "We are all part Jewish," he continued, since to be an American intellectual, you must, at least figuratively, be a Jew. And we have now found that to be an American intellectual, you must also "discover that you are part black."[1]

It happens that Forrest was African American, but he spoke in a decidedly cosmopolitan vein about America's transnational, multiethnic culture. Even though one's particular ethno-racial identity cannot be ignored—his claim about Bellow and Ellison otherwise makes no sense—it must be transcended, by writers and readers alike. In reminding us of the prominent role played by Jews and blacks in American intellectual and cultural life during the twentieth century, however, Forrest underscored the fact that a once vibrant interlocution between two peoples had more or less ceased. A dialogue had become an acrimonious argument, then shouted epithets, then sullen silence, and finally somber reminiscence, in tribute and regret.

In a culture now steeped in ethnic fractionalization and contested identities, the idea that the relationship between blacks and Jews was once thought special—indeed, critical to the cause of civil rights—might seem strange. Yet the importance of blacks for Jews and Jews for blacks in conceiving of themselves as Americans, when both remained outsiders to the rights and privileges of full citizenship, is a matter of voluminous if often perplexing record.[2] Celebrated by idealists, dismissed by cynics, their relationship tells the always tense, often tragic story of race relations in twentieth-century America. It is possible now to attempt a comprehensive study of blacks and Jews not simply because the century has ended but because their special relationship appears to have ended as well.

Separated by color and religion, hardly insignificant considerations in a predominantly "white," Protestant nation, Jews and blacks once found that their day-to-day communal experiences were as intimately connected as their histories were distinct. Those among them who made common cause in the face of anti-Semitism and racism, as well as many commentators since, have described Jews and blacks as "friends," "partners," and most often as "allies," as in references to the "black-Jewish alliance." But contrary metaphors, not to mention racist and anti-Semitic slurs, abound as well, and one is continually forced to wonder whether their equally evident antagonisms do not spring, as Paul Berman has suggested, from instinctive hatred for the person who is "almost the same," not quite the double but rather the false brother.[3]

Or, instead, is their relationship better represented in the bifurcated identity of Philip Roth's protagonist in *The Human Stain*, a light-skinned black man who chooses to pass as a Jew, thus making himself "a heretofore unknown amalgam of the most unalike of America's historic undesirables"?[4] The fractious brotherhood of these "most unalike" of "undesirables" has made their relationship all the more intriguing. Students of the issue have resorted to exotic terminology—"*blackjewishrelations*,"[5] for example—to account for a nebulous conjunction of interests and animosities, while in literary terms the relationship has been seen as both a "conversation" and an "intricate archaeology of hatred and identification."[6] Each description is correct in its way, and catchphrases such as "black-Jewish alliance" and "black-Jewish relations," which recur throughout this book, are an inevitable if inadequate shorthand for something more paradoxical. Recognizing that in the United States there has never been a "Jewish question," as in Europe, though there certainly has been a "black question" (what was once called the "Negro problem"), we might refer instead to the "black-Jewish question."

Thrust into overlapping physical and cultural spaces by their respective histories of racial violence and migration—African Americans in flight from southern segregation, Jews in flight from European and Russian persecution—they met as "strangers" in the Promised Land of America, principally northern, urban America. For Jews, even those whose spiritual home was forever in Palestine (and later Israel), their new nation would in a generation or two become a homeland, a new Zion, with relative ease. For blacks, torn from an African homeland, their new nation, even after being their home for decade upon decade, was still not Zion. Unlike other minorities in America, wrote William Melvin Kelley in 1963, "after six or more generations, the African 'immigrant' remains one."[7]

Jews could not be "melted" into quite the same American shape as other European ethnics, but the rapidity of their acculturation stood in stark contrast to that of blacks, who had long made essential contributions to American economic, cultural, and religious life while continuing to face discrimination at every turn. Nevertheless, said many African Americans, their long residence and measureless sacrifice counted for something. As the black hero of Chester Himes's wartime novel *Lonely Crusade* remarks to his Jewish counterpart, by way of suggesting both his own people's fortitude and their unacknowledged priority as citizens: "The Negro is an American. No matter what happens to him he is still an American. . . . He might be pressed down but he can never be liquidated."[8]

As "America's Jews," to cite a formulation that appears over the course of the century, blacks were far more likely to bear the brunt of racism, a fact that made Jews sympathetic to their predicament if for no other reason than that it reminded them of the European pogroms they had escaped—and might face once again in the United States but for the scapegoat provided by the African American. If blacks were America's Jews, then Jews need not be. Alongside the human bonds expressed often enough in love, sexual passion, and marriage, the moral obligation Jews felt toward blacks, and blacks toward Jews, was in each case sincerely rooted in faith and traditions of compassion. That the offer of brotherhood was also, at times, an opportunistic means for Jews to fight anti-Semitism and for blacks to fight racism should hardly be a surprise. Even its most ardent proponents recognized that it was at best an "uneasy alliance,"[9] one bound to be tempered by ambivalence and self-interest.

My title, meant to capture this intermixture of empathy, anxiety, and hostility, comes from the familiar scripture of Leviticus 19:34, "But the stranger that dwelleth with you shall be unto you as one born among you, and thou shalt love him as thyself; for ye were strangers in the land of Egypt."* Jews and blacks

---

* King James Bible. Compare *Tanakh: The Holy Scriptures* (New York: Jewish Publication Society, 1988), which translates the passage: "The stranger who resides with you shall be to you as one of your citizens; you shall love him as yourself, for you were strangers in the land of Egypt." In the case of the African American scriptural tradition, I generally use the King James Bible; in the case of the Jewish tradition, I generally use *Tanakh*. In some cases, including this one, I have chosen the translation whose language best embraces both perspectives or best expresses my argument.

were both "strangers in the land" of America, yet they experienced very different, if sometimes parallel, dynamics of exclusion and inclusion while "dwelling
with" the dominant white, gentile culture. By virtue of being or becoming
"white," Jews, even recent immigrants, might more quickly be accepted "as one
born among" other Americans, but Judaism and Jewishness would still set
them apart. By virtue of being usually Christian and often generations-long
residents, blacks might lay stronger claim to being "as one born among" other
Americans, but their beginnings in slavery and their blackness would still set
them apart. Jews contemplating blacks and blacks contemplating Jews were
called upon to see "the stranger that dwelleth with you" in a mirror image that
made it at once easy and hard to "love him as thyself."

In some respects, my argument does not diverge markedly from the prevailing historical interpretation that black-Jewish relations suffered serious erosion
over the last half of the twentieth century. The story of bipartisan liberalism
undermined by black radicalism, on the one hand, and Jewish neoconservatism, on the other, takes for granted that there once was a more vital, more ethically responsible, more politically progressive relationship. In each case, it is a
matter of degree. The civil rights alliance, said to tie the two groups together
from the early years of the NAACP forward, was surely never as strong as some
of its more idealistic proponents claimed at the time or later, nor was its disintegration in the postwar decades neatly linear or complete. A broad-brush
treatment of the relationship would reasonably depict a high tide of activist cooperation during the civil rights era of the 1950s through the mid-1960s—cooperation suddenly undone, so it seemed, by the eruption of Black Power. To
be sure, the late 1960s subjected the alliance to a trial by fire, but the divergence
actually began decades earlier. Whatever remained of the structural similarity
between blacks and Jews at the end of World War II—and despite the evident
devotion of many Jews to the cause of black rights in years to come—started to
dissipate as Jews embarked on a rapid ascent of the social and economic ladder,
while African Americans, however much their lives were improved by the
downfall of segregation, began an ascent destined to be far slower and more
erratic.

Although socioeconomic statistics may not be the truest measure of such
a divergence, it is a stunning fact that by 1969 a ranking of the median family income of fifteen ethnic groups in the United States, by percentage of the
national average, placed Jews at the top, at 172 percent, and African Americans next to the bottom, at 62 percent (barely ahead of American Indians, at
60 percent).[10] The divergence was made all the more pronounced when some
Jews objected to race-based compensatory programs—what came to be known

as affirmative action—while some African Americans, adopting a nationalist strategy of racial separatism, openly disdained the support of whites, Jews prominently included. Blacks grew increasingly suspicious of Jews, whose ambiguous whiteness allowed them to find the fruition of liberalism in the provision of "color-blind" equal opportunity while still insisting that they were a persecuted minority. Jews, in turn, suspected that African Americans, having abandoned liberalism for radicalism, could never be true allies.

By the end of the 1960s, the tendency of early African American leaders to cast their relationship with Jews in terms of emulation—of Jewish educational and economic practices, of Zionism, and of the scriptural basis for religious and even political life—had long since bred charges of exploitation and paternalism. Even though the voices that defined the debate then and subsequently were not always representative (in contrast to Black Power ideologues, for example, most African Americans maintained pro-Israel views; in contrast to influential neoconservatives, most Jews maintained liberal views on a range of social justice issues), the increasing stridency of public argument, its tone often set by polemicists in the spotlight, was a fair barometer of a political and cultural divorce that was well on its way to being irreversible.

Although some parts of this story will be familiar to scholars, not to mention more active participants in the dialogue between blacks and Jews, I do not take for granted that a great deal is known to a wider audience, especially in the case of some works of literature under discussion here. Drawing on a broad array of things said or written—speeches, essays, manifestos, memoirs, poems, drama, novels, broadsides, even rumors—*Strangers in the Land* is a study of interdependent self-conceptions in which imitation and revulsion, kinship and alienation are entangled. It is also, for that reason, a study in problems of analogy and equivalence: How are texts, arguments, metaphors, and rhetorical figures set in dynamic relation with one another? What strategies can bend disparate events and experiences toward one another without collapsing into false sameness or comparative victimization?

Two key ideas belonging first of all to Jewish history, *Exodus* and *Holocaust*, are tracked throughout this book, as well as being the focus of sustained comparative analysis at various moments. The refashioning of the Exodus in African American culture, from the slave spirituals through the liberatory leadership of Martin Luther King, Jr., to cite just the two most obvious instances, lies at the heart of the black-Jewish question, and we will reexamine this tradition in some detail. No less important in postwar history, but less well understood, is the African American adaptation of the Holocaust as a conceptual framework for reinterpreting both the ordeal of slavery and its legacy in racial discrimination and violence. In many ways, blacks responded more knowingly to the Holocaust than did other Americans prior to the upsurge in public discussion in the 1960s. In doing so, they set the stage for the eventual proliferation of claims about the "black holocaust," which in turn played no small part in dividing Jews and blacks, rather than uniting them, in subsequent decades.

Instinctively understanding why the Nazis found ideological support for their own racial science in the laws and customs of segregation, African Americans reacted early on to the rise of Adolf Hitler, even as some responded momentarily to the allure of fascism. In the amorphous language of the United Nations Genocide Convention of 1948, which was destined not to be ratified by the United States for four decades, initially because of the bright light it would shine on America's practice of racial discrimination, they likewise discovered a plausible description of their own historical trauma. Yet the effect of the Holocaust on the relationship between African Americans and American Jews was not a simple matter of moral illumination. While black Americans petitioned the United Nations and laid *their* genocide before the court of world opinion, a contrary effect also came into play. The perils faced by blacks and Jews in the United States were not equivalent—the lynching of Leo Frank in 1915 was the exception that proved the rule that anti-Semitism had never posed the same collective danger as anti-black racism—but the Holocaust changed the equation. Suddenly, the threat to Jews as a people, even if those in the United States remained comparatively safe, was devastatingly real, and the threat to blacks might well seem diminished in proportion.

One intention signaled in my subtitle, *Blacks, Jews, Post-Holocaust America*, is to examine the mutual ways in which Jews and blacks have perceived each other—as well as the ways in which the dominant non-Jewish, non-black, and largely Protestant culture has perceived them—with reference to the Holocaust. To put it differently, I intend to explore the means by which the Holocaust became the benchmark of genocide against which at least one other case, African American slavery and its aftermath, has been judged. I choose "post-Holocaust" rather than "postwar" to indicate the near impossibility nowadays of approaching the black-Jewish question outside this highly charged rubric. For related reasons taken up in several chapters, I use the term "Holocaust," rather than "Shoah," precisely because of the complications created by the former term's ubiquitous and often indiscriminate use.

Immediately, of course, a secondary problem in terminology comes into view. The analogical attraction of the Holocaust that began with black reactions to the Genocide Convention gained ground through assertions by black militants in the 1960s that the government was targeting African Americans for extermination, accusations by the Nation of Islam in the 1980s that Jews themselves bore special responsibility for the "holocaust" of slavery and the slave trade, and arguments along the way in favor of black reparations modeled on the those paid to victims of the Nazis. Although claims and counterclaims about the two experiences have produced a considerable body of scholarship and imaginative literature, the very magnitude of the Holocaust and its unique ideological intention—the elimination of an entire "race" from the face of the earth—have also made comparisons to slavery and lynching at best problematic, at worst liable to jealousy and vituperation.

To distinguish African American and other claims from the destruction of the European Jews, I leave the characterization of slavery or other racialized violence as a "holocaust" uncapitalized except where I am quoting from or referring to other sources that capitalize the word. Whether or not one accepts any such usage, this transformation in the symbolic languages of identity was quickly woven into their discourse about each other by both blacks and Jews. Likewise, "genocide" and "survivor" assumed a more contentious presence in the sociocultural language of the last half century. Decade by decade, the prototypical "problem from hell,"[11] to cite the title of Samantha Power's study of modern genocide in the wake of Nazism, became a more pronounced frame of reference in the black-Jewish question, in the process changing the meaning of the initial frame of reference, the biblical Exodus, as much for one group as for the other.

Reinterpreting their history, from Exodus to modernity, in the shadow of the Holocaust required Jews to realign the purpose of Zionism with the post-1948 history of Israel as a final refuge from murderous anti-Semitism. With the establishment of Israel, Jews in the United States did not become less American—in codifying the view of Louis Brandeis that Zionism and patriotism were in no way contradictory, in fact, it may be that they became more American—but their relationship to America and other Americans was consequently altered. Combined with their comparative prosperity in postwar America, Jews' dedication to ensuring their security in a post-Holocaust world in which Israel was their symbolic home—and, for those choosing dual citizenship or making *aliyah*, their literal home—diminished their need for continuing partnership with other ethno-racial groups, blacks in particular.

For African Americans, the change was less obvious but no less telling. Beginning in the late nineteenth century, Zionism had been a key point of departure for blacks' own aspirations to a recovered homeland, whether actual or spiritual, in Africa. Their support for both the principle of Zionism and its practice in Palestine did not cease with the founding of a Jewish nation-state—far from it. Even as Afro-Zionism modulated into black anti-Zionism at mid-century, some Black Power radicals remained divided in their identification between Jews and Arabs, Moses and Pharaoh. Pan-Africanism, said Malcolm X in 1964, echoing W. E. B. Du Bois and others half a century earlier, "will do for the people of African descent all over the world, the same that Zionism has done for Jews all over the world."[12]

At the same time, however, a number of black leaders and writers joined an overarching commitment to leftist anticolonialism and anti-imperialism to a comradely identification with Palestinians and Arabs, a confluence that would hold sway into the next century. In some cases they further recast the Jewish example by declaring, in a domestic application of anticolonial theory, that blacks had to be liberated from the "concentration camp" of the urban "ghetto," where they were still exploited by "Goldberg," the Jewish landlord or merchant. The resulting versions of anti-Zionism were sometimes indistinguishable from anti-Semitism, as when Stokely Carmichael asserted that "the same Zionists that exploit the Arabs also exploit us in this country,"[13] or when Amiri Baraka declared: "I got the extermination blues, jewboy. I got / the hitler syndrome figured."[14]

One difficulty in confronting accusations and expressions of racism and anti-Semitism is that it requires using the language of racists and anti-Semites, thereby according them more attention than they may deserve. Language itself in such cases easily becomes a hyperbolic weapon, lending itself to paranoia and tendentious construction, which in turn has made it a significant factor in the conflict between blacks and Jews. This is especially true for the highly charged question of black anti-Semitism, expressions of which may be hateful, but the rationale for which may be considerably more complex. The same may be said of Jewish racism, which, even if it is less conspicuous—or at least less distinguishable from a more generalized "white" racism—is no less insidious. The fact that attitudes or statements may appear anti-Semitic or racist does not mean either that they necessarily have that intent or that a closer examination of the historical context might not reveal mitigating pressures or explanations. Any such argument, of course, has distinct limits: racists and anti-Semites always have their "reasons."

It may go without saying that my principal terms of analysis—*blacks* and *Jews*—are far from univocal in meaning, and each, on any number of occasions in what follows, might be put in quotation marks to indicate that it is not a person, a people, or their fundamental identity that is described but rather what a representative person or group says or believes, or what is perceived by others to be the case. Here one might bear in mind Berel Lang's warning that the phrase "the Jews"—as in "the Jews killed Jesus," "the Jews control Hollywood"—implies not only that some Jews were responsible but that most or all Jews "acted collectively or in concert, among themselves and as part of a larger whole . . . expressing a common purpose or will."[15] Even if no conspiracy is implied, no less a danger arises in speaking of "Jews" and "blacks" (or "African Americans") holding or acting upon certain beliefs, not least with regard to each other, or in deducing such beliefs from individuals who may not speak, or even intend to speak, for the larger group.

Such risks are compounded by the fact that neither blacks nor Jews are uniform in terms of class, political persuasion, religion, or ethno-national identity. The West Indian blacks and Hasidic Jews set against each other in the Crown Heights violence of 1991, each group atypical of American blacks and Jews, are a case in point. Because of their intertwined migratory experiences dating to 1492, to take another example, Sephardic Jews may see African American or Afro-Caribbean people from a different perspective than do Ashkenazi Jews. And for whom do black Jews speak, not to mention Black Jews, some of whom have believed that they, and they alone, are the true descendants of the ancient Israelites? (The difference between *black Jews* and *Black Jews* is taken up in Chapter 2.) Given the many ways in which both African Americans and American Jews may define themselves—including as *not* black or Jewish, respectively—"blacks" and "Jews" are therefore nebulous terms by themselves, let alone used in dialogue.

In the case of a topic so liable to misunderstanding and so easily inflamed as the relationship between Jews and blacks, where perceptions and imputed motives, as well as the passion and enmity of human interaction, often count for as much as empirical evidence, works of imagination have a special role to play. My hope is to use literature as a lens, at times microscopic, at times telescopic, through which to see this complex relationship. My premise is that the literary works in question were produced in a dynamic, multilayered historical matrix in which the collision and superimposition of time frames—different moments and kinds of exile, of liberation, of genocide—provide the ground for shared spiritual, political, and cultural practices, even those governed by resentment and recrimination. Whether in works distinguished by their artistic merit or in more ephemeral documents that simply register sociopolitical trends, literature's continual engagement with the problem of translating the plots of life into ethno-racial and national narratives makes it an especially valuable resource. To the degree that literary texts reflect the evidentiary uncertainties and psychological sub-currents of human debate, they help to bring the convulsion between Jews and blacks into sharper focus.

Strangers in the Land is a work of cultural history and literary criticism, not a study of politics, sociology, or religion, although arguments drawn from those arenas are often central to my analysis. The book is made up of some chapters in which historical and sociological issues are foregrounded, with literature somewhat subordinated, and others in which the reverse is the case or the balance more even. My approach is generally but not strictly chronological. Several chapters traverse similar ground from different angles of vision or in different degrees of detail in order to describe the motives and events that brought blacks and Jews together and then drove them apart over the course of the twentieth century. Thus, in Chapter 1, I offer a wide-ranging overview of the paradoxical intimacy and estrangement that characterized the relationship between American Jews and "America's Jews," that is, African Americans; in Chapter 2, an investigation of the ways in which blacks have drawn upon Jewish thought in conceptualizing their own Exodus and exile, including the transformation entailed by Zionism and its postwar, post-Holocaust manifestation in the state of Israel; in Chapter 3, a comparative look at the racial ideologies that both jointly defined and clearly differentiated blacks and Jews, from the early twentieth century through the early civil rights era; in Chapter 5, a focus on the public antagonisms of the late 1960s and early 1970s, over both domestic and foreign affairs, with proponents of Black Power and "Jewish Power" embroiled in arguments that reached a harsh crescendo in reaction to the Six-Day War; and in Chapter 7, a consideration of the black holocaust, both its empirical justification and its evolution in popular culture and serious fiction, along with the related question of reparations.

In these chapters I mean to blend cultural, social, and literary history, in a few cases lingering over literary examples that illuminate particular complexities of the black-Jewish relationship, whether the displacement of Jews by blacks in the urban ghetto (Jo Sinclair), for instance, or the belief that blacks are the "true Jews," descended from the ancient Israelites (Gloria Naylor and Jon Michael Spencer), or the argument that the Middle Passage is the prototype for the Holocaust (Toni Morrison). A pointed example from Chapter 5 would be John A. Williams's 1969 novel *Sons of Darkness, Sons of Light* (paired with Saul Bellow's *Mr. Sammler's Planet*). Taking his title from an apocalyptic text among the Dead Sea Scrolls, Williams hypothesizes a coming race war in the United States, carried out by Black Power revolutionaries employing guerrilla tactics. His analogies, however, are drawn not from Algeria or Kenya or

Vietnam, as one might expect, but from the history of Israel. Yet that history, in Williams's calculation, is one in which the anticolonial struggle of the pre-1948 Palestinian Jews for a homeland proves no less compelling a truth about the place of Jews in the modern world—their very right to exist in the modern world—than their post-1967 "occupation" of Arab lands. The resurgence of worldwide anti-Zionism (and, sometimes, anti-Semitism) that has accompanied the tragic, grinding cycle of Palestinian terrorism followed by Israeli reprisal in recent years makes it all the more important to consider the black-Jewish breakdown following the Six-Day War in this broader context.

Where works of literature are the subject of extended attention, my assumption is still that the literature in question cannot be rightly interpreted apart from the constellation of racial theories, religious beliefs, legal decisions, policy arguments, and popular mythologies with which literary modes of representation are entangled. In this respect, for example, the homicidal conflict between Jews and blacks that provides the plot for Bernard Malamud's novel *The Tenants*, the subject of Chapter 6, is a novelistic expression of the polarizing conflicts taken up in Chapter 5. Literature is both a part of and a means to represent the historical story, even when it issues, as more often it does by the last decades of the century, only in strained calculations of racial damage and debt, flights of fantasy, or incongruous mixtures of nostalgia and parody.

As the sequence of terms in my subtitle implies, I place a greater emphasis on how African Americans, over a period of time, have "seen" Jews and reacted to them. This is in part a function of the unequal symbiotic relationship of the two groups and in part a function of the fact that there is a larger body of relevant literature by African American writers that speaks to the question—for instance, the post-Holocaust recalibrations of the Exodus as a philosophical problem in William Melvin Kelley's novel *A Different Drummer* or a problem of intersecting black and Jewish global migrations in *The Chosen Place, the Timeless People* by Paule Marshall (Chapter 4), or as one of communal self-destruction in John Edgar Wideman's *Philadelphia Fire* (Chapter 7).

It will be apparent that the inclusion of *To Kill a Mockingbird*, the centerpiece of Chapter 3, calls into question the boundaries of a book on blacks and Jews. Because my concern is not only with the mutual ways in which blacks and Jews have seen each other but also with how they, as well as the relationship between their histories, have been seen within dominant (non-black, non-Jewish) culture, the case of Harper Lee is instructive. Sitting at the intersection of cultural and historical cross-currents, her famous novel provides a "national" perspective on issues that radiate out from the black-Jewish question—liberalism and the guarantee of rights; the limits of universalism in construing the mean-

ing of genocide; and recognition that in biracial American culture, defined predominantly as the "white" majority in contrast to the "black" (or "colored")
minority though the middle decades of the twentieth century, Jews played an
important mediating role by virtue of belonging neither to one category nor
the other.

In *To Kill a Mockingbird*, a novel whose deceptively simple story encompasses an expansive history, we find the means of judging the core transformation in American life wrought by the superimposition of the rise and fall of
Hitler on the withering of legal discrimination according to race. Because it
is the most widely read novel on the problem of racism in the United States,
and because it makes Nazism a point of reference as important as *Brown v.
Board of Education*, Harper Lee's novel brings into view a wide array of issues
historically and thematically central to pre- and postwar debates about equal
rights. That the novel is read by children as well as adults makes it an especially
valuable window on the formation of cultural attitudes.

The inclusion of Lee raises subsidiary questions about the "house of fiction,"
to cite the metaphor made famous by Henry James that comes prominently
into play in *The Tenants*. Who has the right to a particular literary terrain, the
right to define the terms of representation? How do blacks and Jews compete
against white, gentile, middlebrow writers who manage to command much
larger audiences while working the ground that "belongs" to others? Why does
any topic belong to one group and not another? And to take the issue beyond
literature and literary criticism: If the black-Jewish question does not belong to
the culture at large, why should others care about it?

My answer is that the black-Jewish question is intrinsic to and inextricable
from any understanding of American culture and cultural politics in the postwar decades. Just as both blacks and Jews have played especially formative roles
in American musical culture—jazz, gospel, blues, and hip-hop in the case of
blacks, popular song, musical theater, and classical performance in the case of
Jews—so in literature and intellectual debate each group has had a tense but
creative relationship with the mainstream, telling a story of absorption and resistance, of the aspiration to universalism and the retreat into particularism.
In doing so, they also tell an archetypal American story of the vicissitudes
of pluralism, since for blacks and Jews alike, self-effacing assimilation and
ethnocentric separatism sometimes have been two sides of a coin. As Kenneth
Clark once remarked: "The minority person who seeks desperately to deny his
heritage and his brother who wears his minority status as a severe and inflex-
ible suit of armor have in common the fact that each is seeking in his particular

way to save his personality from the full devastating impact of racial or religious rejection."[16]

Insofar as it provides a key to the ideological interplay between liberalism, radicalism, and neoconservatism that shifted the focus in the quest for equality from opportunities to outcomes, and insofar as it is generative or at least illustrative of the charges of exploitation and paternalism that trouble any social, political, or cultural strategy based on emulation or appropriation, the black-Jewish question may also provide a perspective on other interethnic relations—for example, between blacks and Asian Americans, who in the late twentieth century became, in public perception, the new high-achieving, quiet but persistent "model minority." Or it may help us to understand historical conceptions of other loosely circumscribed ethno-racial groups—for example, American Indians, who in the eyes of many Euro-American immigrants, early or late, were already "black" (by virtue of being a primitive, alien race), were already "Jewish" (by virtue of being, by some accounts, descended from the lost tribes of Israel), and, as indigenous peoples facing their own kind of genocide, were truly the "first" Americans. Such issues are beyond the scope of this study, but my hope is that they may nevertheless be illuminated by it.

African Americans today have more compelling reasons to continue telling what Rogers Smith has called "ethically constitutive stories," those that provide moral affirmation of particular identities as a counterweight to oppression or deficient political and economic power.[17] Over the course of the last century, however, American Jews often had comparable reasons to tell comparable stories, and to do so in conjunction with black Americans. At times a true alliance, at times a marriage of convenience, at times a bitter quarrel, the relationship between blacks and Jews provides a critical measure not just of their respective positions in American society but also of the changing significance of "race," something whose meaning and even whose existence can be debated, and racism, something whose meaning may be debated but whose existence cannot be doubted.

A further exposition of my argument, by way of an added note on terminology, is in order here.

For the most part, I use *black* and *African American* interchangeably, while sometimes preferring the former in those cases where the issue of color and the discrimination based on it are paramount, or where the political context or the common usage by an individual or group requires it, and preferring the latter in those cases where being an African in America, with all its attendant questions of diaporic identity, hyphenation, or hybridity, as well as related issues of pluralism, are more visible. For the most part, I also use *Jew* interchangeably with *American Jew* (or, less frequently, *Jewish American*), while recognizing that *Jew*, like *black*, but for different reasons, refers to the member of a religious or ethno-cultural group with less clearly demarcated national or continental boundaries—a people whose *diaspora* defined the term. In contrast to *Holocaust*, I do not capitalize *diaspora*, except when quoting others who do. Although the term originates as a description of the dispersed Jews—in our own era, those who live outside the homeland of Israel—it has become so broadly used to describe the dispersion of other peoples, and is so much less often deployed tendentiously, that a comparable distinction is not necessary. Likewise, except when quoting others, I do not capitalize *chosen people*, another concept used, in both religious and secular ways, by both Jews and blacks.

The juxtaposition of *black* and *Jew*, as opposed to *African American* and *American Jew*, aside from producing terminology such as "black-Jewish relations" or the "black-Jewish alliance," has the corollary effect, relevant to the argument throughout, that African Americans continue, whether they like it or not, or whether they themselves intend it or not, to be characterized as *people of color*, whereas American Jews, especially as the twentieth century wore on and fewer were defined by their Judaism than by their Jewishness, could more easily be either *Jew* or *white*, or both *Jew* and *white*. Blacks might in some instances, of course, be both *black* and *Jew*. Except in cases of "passing" and the conscious adoption of mixed-race identity, however, they could not be both *black* and *white*. The last chapter of the book, "Spooks," will be an occasion to look specifically, first, at the case of a black man, Julius Lester, whose autobiography details his conversion to Judaism; and, second, at the case of a black man, the protagonist of *The Human Stain*, whose light skin provides him with the necessary disguise to pass as a Jew. Whereas Lester, in a radical act of self-making, discards his blackness as irrelevant to his true identity, Roth's hero, Coleman Silk, qualifies his ability to pass as white with the authenticating (but ultimately deadly) touch of color provided by Jewishness—emphatically when he makes his choice in the early 1950s and even still when he is brought down as a "racist" in the 1990s.

Except among some anti-Semites, *Jew* has stopped being the description of a racial category, as it was in the early decades of the twentieth century, whereas *black* and *African American*, different in connotation but not necessarily in denotation from *Negro*, typically have not. Jews are now *ethnic*, but blacks remain *racial*, not because the idea of race per se has creditable scientific or genetic meaning but because color, whether the communal traits associated with it or the group membership ascribed to it, still trumps all else, notwithstanding widespread agreement that "race" is constructed, contingent, ephemeral, illusionary, or nonexistent. (I use the concepts of ethnicity and race in their conventional ways, though sometimes a more encompassing term, *ethno-racial*, proves useful to describe the shifting spectrum along which individuals and groups are arrayed in sociological, legal, or cultural terms.) The advent of multiracial and/or multiethnic categories in the United States Census and other such official practice, along with the recent trends of highlighting ethnically ambiguous identities in advertising, fashion, popular culture, and academic inquiry, may eventually change these assumptions and practices. For the period of history with which we are concerned here, however, up to and including the early years of the twenty-first century, the category of *black* has continued to correspond, though frequently for contrary reasons advanced by blacks themselves, to the "one-drop" rule promulgated by Jim Crow segregationists.

This difference itself has proved critical to the erosion of the partnership between Jews and blacks. Although Jews and blacks often joined together, at least through the civil rights era, in combating the discrimination that kept both groups on the margins of the democratic nation, their political and social stations in the United States were never the same, and their coalition was eviscerated far less by differing goals than by differing opportunities. Today the very notion of a coalition seems quaint. It may be, as Samuel G. Freedman has written, that the black-Jewish "era," although it can still be studied and celebrated, should "be retired to the realm of history or mythology."[18] Even though memoir, literature, and scholarship aimed at resuscitating the time of alliance, if only through commemoration or longing for what is no more, show no sign of abating, the evidence more often than not suggests that what has been lost, however sincere and effective it may at times have been, was shot through with illusion. As the African American protagonist of Lore Segal's novel *Her First American* remarks to his Jewish immigrant lover, a Holocaust refugee, the experiences of blacks and Jews may well be parallel, but "parallels are two lines that run side by side and never meet except in infinity."[19]

CHAPTER 1

America's Jews

"To a man from Mars, it must seem strange and tragically ironic that the Jewish and Negro peoples on planet Earth are not allies. The Martian observer sees the Jews kicked about in Germany and the Negroes kicked about in Georgia; and yet both Jew and Negro continue to insist upon the privilege of facing their doom separately, whereas together they could stand and fight." So wrote L. D. Reddick in a 1942 essay, "Anti-Semitism among Negroes," which was paired with Louis Harap's "Anti-Negroism among Jews," first in *Negro Quarterly* and soon thereafter in a collection titled *Should Jews and Negroes Unite?* Likewise contending that blacks and Jews in America, galvanized by the rampages of Nazism, must work together, Harap quoted from an editorial in a leading African American newspaper, the *Amsterdam Star-News:* "Without reservation and camouflage Colored and Jewish Americans must unite. The wolves of intolerance are yapping savagely at the heels of both."[1]

The two essays taken together, one by an African American, the other by an American Jew, display the ethical imperative that has often defined the relationship between the two groups in the United States. At the same time, their statements reveal the limitations of any claim made on behalf of a sustaining black-Jewish alliance and forecast the precariousness of analogies later drawn between the devastations of slavery and genocidal anti-Semitism. If blacks and Jews were not united in 1942, one might wonder if they ever did, or ever could, stand together against the wolves of intolerance. If not then, when?

No unequivocal answer is possible, but for twenty-first-century readers the question itself might seem perplexing. Nowadays, what sets blacks and Jews apart appears much more obvious than what binds them—or, rather, what once bound them—together. Like all other ethno-racial groups save American Indians and most pre–Civil War blacks, Jews came to America as immigrants. The pernicious effects of anti-Semitism notwithstanding, the hardships Jews overcame did not differ dramatically from those faced by other immigrant "minorities," but the particular skills, the dedication to learning, and the traits of social and familial cohesion they brought to America suited them for success, over time, in a liberal, capitalist democracy. To make the obvious point, Jews did not arrive in America as slaves, nor did they face, generation after generation, the same degree of debilitating legalized and extralegal racism that, until well into the twentieth century, made comparable success for African Americans very difficult to achieve.

Whatever the liabilities of acculturation to a predominantly Anglo-Saxon, Christian nation, moreover, Jews were sustained by a way of life that was at once a religion and a civilization, and by a sacred language, Hebrew, that survived amidst the accretion of numerous languages and national cultures throughout centuries of exile and persecution. Although the recovery of African beliefs and practices has offered blacks sporadic measures of such an inheritance, the duress of slavery and segregation made them singularly American (and mostly Protestant) by force. The oft-remarked educational and economic achievements of American Jews, well out of proportion to their share of the population, contrast sharply with the educational and economic disadvantages that remain key markers of life for African Americans, also out of proportion to their share of the population.

Such a catalogue of differences could be extended—and yet, the affiliation between blacks and Jews advocated by Reddick and Harap in the midst of World War II was no fantasy. By virtue of sharing the shifting margins of American life, Jews and blacks have shared perspectives on the rewards and dangers of assimilation, the vicissitudes of intermarriage and passing, and the meaning of citizenship in the face of discrimination and racist violence. Both peoples have conceived of themselves as "chosen" and found themselves wandering "in strange lands," their primary identities derived from belonging not to a particular nation-state but instead to a religio-cultural diasporic "nation" with an identifiable set of relations to sacred texts and a lost homeland. In turn, both have found themselves defined, or in some instances have elected to define themselves, negatively—by anti-Semitism or racism. Immigrant and native Jews alike found in blacks a reminder of their centuries-long persecution, most

recently in European and Slavic nations, while Africans in America, beginning
with their immersion in the slaveholder's Christianity and continuing through
the modern civil rights movement, were shaped by a profound identification with the Jews' biblical narrative that found its locus classicus in James
Baldwin's 1948 essay "The Harlem Ghetto":

> The Negro identifies himself almost wholly with the Jew. The more de-
> vout Negro considers that he *is* a Jew, in bondage to a hard taskmaster
> and waiting for a Moses to lead him out of Egypt. The hymns, the texts,
> and the most favored legends of the devout Negro are all Old Testament
> and therefore Jewish in origin: the flight from Egypt, the Hebrew chil-
> dren in the fiery furnace, the terrible jubilee songs of deliverance. . . . The
> covenant God made in the beginning with Abraham and which was to
> extend to his children and to his children's children forever is a covenant
> made with these latter-day exiles also: as Israel was chosen, so are they.
> The birth and death of Jesus, which adds a non-Judaic element, also
> implements this identification. It is the covenant made with Abraham
> again, renewed, signed with his blood. . . . The images of the suffering
> Christ and the suffering Jew are wedded with the image of the suffering
> slave, and they are one: the people that walked in darkness have seen a
> great light.[2]

Brought together by unpredictable and unsought necessity, black and Jewish
activists and intellectuals—from the co-founders of early civil rights organizations such as the National Association for the Advancement of Colored People
(NAACP), to the communist left of the 1930s, to the civil rights vanguard of the
early 1960s and radical left in the late 1960s, and on to the post-counterculture
left of, say, Michael Lerner and Cornel West—have discovered common sustenance in the paradigm of delivery into the Promised Land of democratic citizenship that America might provide.

Their kinship and its potential for painful conflict were made more visible in
the post–World War II years, as African Americans and American Jews experienced in different but related ways a diminishment in long-standing practices
of exclusion. For blacks, the downfall of legal segregation slowly brought about
unprecedented, if still incomplete, equalities of opportunity, while the pressure
of southern resistance to integration, combined with the expanding national
economy, sparked a new exodus from rural South to urban North, the latest in
the series of migrations that had shaped black life—and American culture—
since the end of Reconstruction. For Jews, the postwar transformation in eco-

nomic and educational opportunities, accompanied by their growing social acceptance, represented an acceleration, not a revolution.

By comparison to the persecution faced by Jews in Europe or by blacks under slavery and Jim Crow, what Jews in the United States suffered was far less harsh. American Jews faced punitive immigration laws, employment discrimination, educational quotas, restrictive housing covenants, religious bigotry, and vicious stereotyping, but they were never defined legally as aliens, as in pre-Enlightenment Europe, nor was anti-Semitism ever formalized as a practice of the state, even if it was sometimes expressed by governmental institutions and legal constraints. Likewise, anti-Semitic attitudes among the general populace, while they certainly had consequences for individuals who were rebuffed or violently attacked, seldom translated into sustained action that threatened the common safety of Jews in the United States. Despite discrimination and abuse, Jews generally took their place in a pluralist nation of immigrants where religious tolerance and the separation of church and state protected rather than condemned them, and where anti-Semitism was diminished in significant part by the openness with which Jews were able to combat it.[3]

Following a momentary peak immediately after World War II, anti-Semitism declined markedly in subsequent years.[4] Economic and social barriers fell away almost entirely, and, coupled with the cohesion of Jewish culture, the willing sacrifices made by immigrant generations for their children began to reap clear rewards that would continue over the remainder of the twentieth century in exceptionally high levels of professional achievement. Although Jews became a smaller part of the American population (while blacks became a larger),* they represented, as David Hollinger writes, the most dramatic case in American history in which a once stigmatized ethno-racial group "suddenly became over-represented many times over" in arenas where their progress had previously been inhibited.[5] Distrust and mistreatment of Jews did not disappear, and the decline in discrimination must also be ascribed in part to the vig-

---

* From the war years through the end of the twentieth century, the Jewish population rose slightly but declined as a percentage of the total American population (from 4.8 million, or 3.6 percent, in 1940, to 5.7 million, or 2.8 percent, in 1970, to 6.1 million, or 2.2 percent, in 2000), while the African American population rose more dramatically both in numbers and in percentage of the total (from 12.8 million, or 9.7 percent, in 1940, to 22.5 million, or 11 percent, in 1970, to 35.5 million, or 13 percent in 2000). Some sources put the proportion of Jews in 2000 at 2 percent or less, an index, perhaps, of the increasing ambiguity in Jewish self-identification. See the Jewish Virtual Library and the United States Census on-line: http://www.jewishvirtuallibrary.org/jsource/US-Israel/usjewpop1.html; http://www.census.gov/population/www/socdemo/race/black.html (both accessed April 14, 2004).

ilant actions of Jewish organizations such as the Anti-Defamation League, but it proved unnecessary to mount a civil rights movement for Jews.

Excepting those who emigrated to Israel or who remained so pious as to reject a non-messianic state altogether, American Jews were now more likely than ever to embrace America as the secular Zion that many immigrants and native Jews alike had long proclaimed it to be. The post-Holocaust American Zion, however, was defined even more clearly both by what it was and by what it was not. According to Abba Hillel Silver, writing in 1944, the Holocaust represented the end of American Jewish exceptionalism in that the destruction of the European Jews drew American Jews into the orbit of Old World anti-Semitism and presented them with a special responsibility. Because the United States was "no longer a distant land on the rim of a vast ocean" but now "the center of the world," said Silver, American Jews had come to share "the common and inescapable destiny of their fellow Jews in the rest of the world." One might say as well, however, that the Holocaust proved the case for American exceptionalism. Having been spared the cataclysm of the European genocide, Jews found in America the new "heartland" of the Jewish Western world, in the words of Jacob Agus, where a "vision of the good life, the luminous core of the tradition," could be "cultivated, developed and made fruitful."[6]

Insofar as Jews of the postwar era embraced what Cheryl Greenberg has described as "assimilative pluralism"[7]—structural equality before the law, along with the protection and preservation of cultural differences—they appeared to be, and often were, part of the privileged majority, not the stigmatized minority. Whereas the laws and customs of segregation enclosed African Americans in a community of color and stymied their attempts to translate equal opportunity into equal achievement, access to the valuable property of whiteness— an index of rights, reputation, privilege, and thus the exercise of power[8]—allowed Jews to make the translation more easily even as it contributed to the erosion of their communal identity. As integration into the Promised Land proved more difficult for African Americans than for Jews, difference began to overshadow likeness, and their partnership carried ever stronger undercurrents of distrust and anger.

Although prejudice against blacks continued to decline throughout the postwar years, opinion polling in the early 1960s showed that a majority of whites still held much more pronounced antipathy toward blacks than toward Jews and felt that blacks were going "too far, too fast." As Murray Friedman observed in 1963, "to the Negro demand for 'now,' to which the Deep South replied 'never,' many liberal whites are increasingly responding 'later.'"[9] Even before the major legal victories of the civil rights movement—the Civil Rights Act of 1964 and the Voting Rights Act of 1965—a number of Jews joined other white liberals in distancing themselves from arguments that black equality could be achieved only through economic compensation or other forms of preferential treatment soon to be heralded under the banner of affirmative action.

When demoralizing resistance or setbacks made African Americans skeptical of the integrationist strategy of Martin Luther King, Jr., then aroused them to the color consciousness championed by Black Power, many moved toward a stronger sense of identity, as well as legal entitlement, predicated on race. Rejecting what Christopher Lasch referred to as "the politics of resentment and reparation,"[10] and reacting increasingly as whites to black militancy, Jews moved in the opposite direction. Still disproportionately committed to the cause of racial justice but offended that black militants would challenge their good faith and evict them from civil rights organizations, Jews proved resistant to strategies for integration that awakened memories of the very restrictions they themselves had so recently faced. Especially after the Six-Day War of 1967, when black radicals espoused an anti-Zionism that lapsed at times into overt anti-Semitism, American Jews expressed their own new sense of revitalized ethno-political identity—but they did so within a context of increasing secularization, exogamy, and neoconservatism.

Amidst a rapidly shifting set of historical forces, then, the identification of blacks with the Jewish experience, nurtured by Jewish traditions of sympathy with the oppressed and allied beliefs that the diminution of prejudice against any people is "good for the Jews," became ever more entangled with suspicion on the part of blacks that Jews were ultimately unlike them, even to the point of exploiting them, and suspicion on the part of Jews that blacks were ultimately unlike them, even to the point of reviling them. When Jews held fast to a meritocratic ideal of individual rights, as opposed to group rights in need of compensatory action, blacks perceived them to be abandoning historic commitments to social justice while reaping the rewards of assimilation, further evidence of their conversion to "whiteness." In the eyes of blacks, said Nat Hentoff in 1969, Jews are included among the goyim in America, and the only question is who "among us are the Germans."[11] Slowly pulled further apart as peoples of one nation, blacks wondered how Jews could feel insecure in America, while Jews wondered how blacks could be oblivious to the danger of anti-Semitism, let alone indulge in it themselves.

As black America became more socially and economically divided during the 1970s and 1980s, with the educated and talented climbing the ladder of American prosperity into middle-class status and a large lower class persisting in a state of alienation and despair, historic anti-Semitic typologies erupted with disturbing regularity. Worrisome though they were, such outbursts of black anti-Semitism pointed less to substantial dangers than to the disparate situations of Jews and blacks a generation or more after the Holocaust and the advent of the civil rights movement. The integration of American Jews in the postwar decades was comparatively seamless, while the integration of African Americans was halting and tormented, achieved only after constitutional up-heaval, recurrent social disorder, and bloodshed and imprisonment for a num-ber of courageous individuals. Jews took their place among those individuals, but in doing so they had to face the accusation that their self-interest rivaled their idealism and admit the fact that their suffering in America and that of Af-rican Americans were asymmetrical. "As the real anti-Semites in this country best know," wrote Jacob Cohen in 1966, "the Negro has been and will be Amer-ica's Jew, a fact, an historical condition, which fundamentally alters the situa-tion of Jews in this country."[12]

A Certain Homelessness in the World

Characterizations of blacks as America's Jews were common from the early twentieth century through the civil rights era; indeed, they had a long his-tory among African Americans themselves. Having been literal slaves in what W. E. B. Du Bois referred to as "the Egypt of the Confederacy,"[13] and remaining "strangers in the land of Egypt," South and North alike, long after the end of slavery, blacks found in Jewish experience an imperfect mirror image for un-derstanding and combating their own persecution. For Frederick Douglass, writing with cruel optimism in "The Future of the Negro" (1884), Jews were a model of uplift, an example of the tendency of the age toward racial unifica-tion, not isolation, and the coming erosion of racial classifications: "The Jew was once despised and hated in Europe . . . but he has risen, and is rising to higher consideration, and no man is now degraded by association with him anywhere. In like manner the Negro will rise in [the] social scale."[14] Sixteen years later, with the doctrine of segregation just affirmed in *Plessy v. Ferguson* (1896) destined to be the law of the land for more than half a century to come, Booker T. Washington argued that the suffering of the Jews throughout world history offered blacks an illustration of unity, pride, and love of race: "Unless the Negro learns more and more to imitate the Jew in these matters, to have faith in himself, he cannot expect to have any high degree of success."[15] As the twentieth century wore on and racialized ideologies loomed larger, Alain Locke's words located the kinship within a more unsettling framework: "The Jew has been made international by persecution and forced dispersion, and so, potentially, have we."[16]

Both early and late, it was an open question, of course, whether emulation of Jewish unity, sacrifice, and perseverance was sufficient to protect blacks from American pogroms, and blacks' admiration of Jews' communal and economic power was often mixed with resentment of their paternalism or, worse, their suspected malevolence. Malcolm X thus expressed distinct ambivalence when he admired the Jew because he "never lost his pride in being a Jew," "never ceased to be a man," "never went sitting-in and crawling-in and sliding-in and freedom-riding, like he teaches and helps Negroes to do. The Jews stood up, and stood together, and they used their ultimate power, the economic weapon."[17] But a more complicated kind of envy was also possible. When Louis Armstrong recalled his close relationship as a young boy with the Karnofsky family in New Orleans, circa 1907, his comparative assessment of Jews and blacks, based in part on tales of slavery passed down from his ancestors, was hardly flattering to his own people:

> The Negroes always hated the Jewish people who never *harmed* anybody, but they stuck together. And by doing that, they *had* to have *success*. Negroes *never* did stick together and they *never* will. They hold too much *malice—Jealousy* deep down in their heart for the *few* Negroes who *tries.* But the odds were (are) *against* them. Of course, we are all well aware of the *Congo* Square—*Slavery—Lynchings* and *all* of that *stuff.* Maybe the Jewish people did not go through *All* of those *things,* but they went through *just* as *much. Still* they *stuck together.* Most of the Negroes who went through some of those *tortures,* they *asked* for it. . . .
>
> They [slaves] couldn't keep a secret among themselves. They would make plans among themselves and *one* Negro would double cross them by sneaking back and tell the white man everything they had planned to do. Quite naturally that would make him the Head Nigger. At least for the time being anyway. That's why all of the *Head* whippings was originated—from our own people. Jealousy and Hate. The same as today. That's where that old phrase *Master* or *Marster* came from. From *conniving lazy Niggers. Slavery* was just like Anything else. B. S.

The Jewish People never betrayed their own people. Stick together yes.
I watched the Jewish people take a lot of Abuse in New Orleans ever since
I was *seven* years old. I felt very lucky to get a job working for them. We
suffered Agony right along with them. Only worst. They [whites] did not
Lynch them, but us Negroes, *any*time they got ready.

The other White Nationalities kept the Jewish people with fear constantly. As far as *us* Negroes, well, I don't have to explain anything. . . . So
they get full of their *Mint Julep* or that *bad* whiskey, the poor white Trash
were Guzzling down, like water, then when they get so *Damn* Drunk until they'd go out of their minds—then it's Nigger Hunting time. *Any*
Nigger.[18]

Perhaps this fragmentary memoir should be chalked up to the bitterness,
even dementia, of an old man much resented at this point in his career by some
African Americans as a sellout to white culture. Armstrong's accusation of slave
betrayal, whatever truth it contained, was gratuitous. The recollection is important, instead, for being a tale in miniature, from a single perspective, of the
contentious history of black-Jewish relations. He makes clear that the "nigger
hunting" of lynching was something far worse than simply being kept fearful
by racist intimidation. Like Booker T. Washington before him and Martin Luther King, Jr., in his own day, moreover, Armstrong underscored the family
strength, loyalty, and economic thrift of the Jews as examples to emulate—examples blacks had failed to emulate, in fact, because they remained embroiled
in the catastrophes of their own community, as yet unable to unite effectively
in the face of deeply ingrained racism. Jews may have suffered "abuse" and "agony," Armstrong's idiosyncratic story tells us, but their comparative margin of
safety allowed them to capitalize on the fortitude and habits of self-sacrifice, as
well as the unbroken cultural inheritance and set of beliefs, that they brought
with them to America.

Kinship with blacks, and the ambivalence that sometimes went with it, was
no less keenly experienced by Jews in the early twentieth century. In both the
Yiddish press and the Jewish English-language media, the interest of Jews in
American blacks as brothers in persecution was evident in a significant number
of short stories, poems, and essays, as well as longer works such as a Yiddish
translation of *Uncle Tom's Cabin* (1911), I. J. Schwartz's 1925 epic poem *Kentocki*
(Kentucky), and Dovid Segal's *Der neger in amerike* (1935), a history of the African American experience. In *The Promised Land* (1912), an immigrant autobiography that went through dozens of editions and elicited the praise of national leaders such as Theodore Roosevelt and Louis Brandeis, Mary Antin

took inspiration from the masterpiece of Americanization by the "Negro Moses," Washington's *Up from Slavery* (1901), in making America her Jerusalem ("next year—in America!" she writes of her family's decision to emigrate following yet another outbreak of anti-Semitism in Russia) and, like Washington, declaring herself representative of the destiny of her nation: "I am the youngest of America's children, and into my hands is given her priceless heritage."[19]

The perception that blacks were America's Jews was felt most strongly by those immigrants who had recently fled persecution in eastern Europe and by the first generation born in the United States. Typically less educated and less well off economically than those German Jews who had arrived in the nineteenth century and become more assimilated, the mostly Orthodox, mostly Yiddish-speaking new immigrants settled predominantly in the urban North, where they collided with the newly arrived black "immigrants" from the rural South, who seemed in some respects their mirror image. Among working-class Jews, the epithet "Nigger" was one nickname applied to those whose physiognomy made them appear part black. In Michael Gold's *Jews without Money* (1930), for instance, the protagonist's toughest childhood friend is the ghetto-bred proto-revolutionary "Nigger," so named because of his black hair, his "murky face," his nose "squashed at birth," and his eyes, which have "the contemptuous glare of the criminal and the genius." In another scene, new Jewish immigrants on their first night in America are thrust into a crowded cellar known as the "Nigger House."[20] The visceral connection between the new Jews and the old blacks was well portrayed by the young narrator of Isaac Rosenfeld's *Passage from Home* (1946), set in mid-1930s Chicago:

> What was it like to be a Negro? . . . [W]ithout ever having been able clearly to estimate it, feeling the weight of it and haunted by its presence, I had always carried [the question] with me as a token, both secret and obvious, of my own existence. For as a Jew, I was acquainted, as perhaps a Negro might be, with the alien and the divided aspect of life that passed from sight at the open approach, but lingered, available to thought, ready to reveal itself to anyone who would inquire softly. I had come to know a certain homelessness in the world, and took it for granted as part of nature. . . . We had accepted it unconsciously and without self-pity, as one might accept a sentence that had been passed generations ago, whose terms were still binding though its occasion had long been forgotten.[21]

The burden of exile, their "certain homelessness in the world" passed on generation to generation, was accentuated for Jews and blacks alike by their common heritage of racist violence. Just as they felt the sting of American anti-Semitism more strongly than their predecessors, owing to the upsurge of nativism in the early twentieth century, the new Jews also found in the brutalizing of American blacks a vivid reminder of the anti-Semitic assaults they had fled in Europe and Russia. In Chicago, for example, the *Daily Jewish Courier* compared southern lynchings to Russian pogroms, concluding that in the present-day world "the Jew is treated as a Negro and [the] Negro as a Jew." Likewise, in New York, the Yiddish-language *Forward* compared the demonizing of blacks as rapists to the age-old blood libel—the accusation that Jews drank the blood of slain Christian children, baked it in matzo, or used it otherwise in sacramental rituals—and wrote of the East St. Louis riot of 1917, in which some forty blacks were killed, with reference to the 1903 pogrom in Kishinev, Russia, in which fifty Jews died: "The same brutality, the same wildness, the same human beasts."[22]

Along with other works that took the lynching of blacks as a starting point for thinking about Jewishness in America, Yosef Opatoshu's Yiddish short story "Lintsheray," published in 1915—and thus coincident with the lynching of Leo Frank, which sparked both the revival of the Ku Klux Klan and the creation of the Anti-Defamation League—makes a small-town southern lynching resonate with echoes of Russian pogroms. The story illustrates as well the potential threat to Jews hidden within the promise of Americanization: "Mark my words. If today they lynch a black, tomorrow it will be a Jew."[23] Contemporary fiction by Jews attentive to injustice and violence against African Americans included John Spivak's *Georgia Nigger* (1932), a novelistic exposé of chain gangs, John Sanford's *People from Heaven* (1943), about the camaraderie between a black woman raped by a white racist and the Jewish refugee he also attacks, and Howard Fast's popular novel about the promise of black liberation during Reconstruction, *Freedom Road* (1944). Julius Bloch, Louis Lozowick, Harry Sternberg, and Aaron Goodelman were among the Jewish artists who lent their talents to the campaign against lynching from the 1920s through the 1940s.[24] The poignant lyrics about lynching made famous by Billie Holiday in "Strange Fruit," recorded in 1939—"Black body swinging in the southern breeze, / Strange fruit hanging from the poplar trees"—had been written and published as a poem a few years earlier by the Jewish schoolteacher (and committed communist) Abel Meeropol, writing under the name "Lewis Allen."[25]

Despite discrimination and sporadic violence, Jews did not commonly face vigilante murder, let alone pogroms, in the United States. The lynching of Leo Frank was not the only, but it was certainly the most atrocious, aberration in the general practice of tolerance with respect to Jews and intolerance with respect to blacks. No less than Opatoshu's story, however, Meeropol's poem appeared at a time when the future course of anti-Semitism in the United States was far from predictable. Spurred on by the revival of the Klan and anti-immigration legislation, anti-Semitism in the United States increased from the 1920s through the 1930s. In his company-sponsored newspaper, the *Dearborn Independent,* Henry Ford retailed paranoia about Jews to a substantial readership by reprinting the *Protocols of the Elders of Zion,*[26] a specious fabrication later central to Nazi propaganda, and by serializing a homegrown anti-Semitic classic titled *The International Jew: The World's Foremost Problem.* Exploiting a new and powerful medium, Father Charles Coughlin of Detroit cultivated a large nondenominational radio audience with scurrilous attacks on Jews that by the late 1930s were a mirror image of Hitlerian ideology. Even the mainstream *Saturday Evening Post* undertook a series of articles arguing that Jews were "human parasites," the immigrants most difficult to assimilate because of their "ruthless concentration on self-interest." On the eve of World War II, a majority of the public, according to one poll, found Jews greedy, dishonest, and aggressive, and an even higher percentage rejected raising the immigration quota for German Jewish refugees.[27]

Between evolving theories of racial classification and the war on Nazism itself, however, hard-core anti-Semitism was destined to be driven back to the margins of American opinion, clearly subordinate to anti-black racism. "If Jews have been the great obsession of Christianity, blacks have been the great obsession of Americans," Irving Howe would later write, and so long as the second obsession trumped the first, blacks would serve as a buffer between Jews and racist whites.[28] The warning by Jews that they might be the next victims of programmatic racial violence thus also contained a potential recrimination on the part of blacks that would accompany Jewish involvement in African American civil rights efforts throughout the century. Not only might analogies drawn between black and Jewish experiences of persecution appear spurious, but also, even worse, it might turn out that the comparative safety of Jews in the United States depended to some degree on the continued legal and social degradation of blacks. "If the David Dukes of the world were to achieve their wishes and finish off the blacks, where would they turn next?" asked the Reverend Al Sharpton rhetorically eight decades later. (Sharpton gave credit to Jews' disproportionate numbers among white supporters of black civil rights but noted that Jews, too, benefited from the movement: "A lot of foot soldiers who kicked down the door for Jews were black.") However safe Jews might be now, observed one participant in a contemporary black-Jewish community dialogue—

a black man who had converted to Orthodox Judaism—Jewish success in the United States came in part because "Jews were not the victims of choice."[29]

The suspicion that Jews were using blacks as a shield led inevitably to accusations of paternalism and hypocrisy. For Harold Cruse, Jewish manipulation of blacks stretched over the century. *The Crisis of the Negro Intellectual* (1967) contained a sustained critique of what Cruse portrayed as the overbearing dominance of Jews in their political alliances with blacks, from their early involvement in the NAACP to their acting as spokesmen for Negro interests in the Communist Party to their ascendancy to leadership in the civil rights movement—what Tony Martin would later refer to as Jewish "overseership." Cruse took exception to American Jewish intellectuals who adopt the "martyr's mantle" as their own—"Jews have not suffered in the United States," he said bluntly—and rebuked them for being "pro-integrationist for Negroes and anti-assimilationist for Jews."[30] The poet Haki Madhubuti followed Cruse's lead in arguing that Jews use blacks as a diversion and deploy the charge of anti-Semitism in order to bolster their control of the journalistic and entertainment media. In contrast, said Madhubuti, blacks are "encouraged to suffer as if it is a special badge of liberation." Even simple recognition of the leadership role of Jews on the part of black scholars has sometimes been grudging. "As a narrowly conceived movement against racial discrimination and bigotry," writes Clayborne Carson, "the civil rights movement had attracted substantial Jewish support, but black power militants correctly charged that that conception of the movement was as much a Jewish creation as it was a black one"—a formulation that seems to offer gratitude with one hand and retract it with the other.[31]

It is hardly a surprise, though, that such accidental allies in misfortune would try to use each other to advantage. Advocacy of black civil rights, whether by individuals or by organizations, may have been in keeping with the Jewish tradition of commitment to social justice, David Levering Lewis points out, but it had the added benefit of establishing for Jews another front on which to resist their own mistreatment in America: "By establishing a presence at the center of the civil rights movement with intelligence, money, and influence, elite Jews and their delegates could fight anti-Semitism by remote control."[32] Blacks for their part were no less opportunistic. Taking note of Harvard's decision to curtail black student enrollment in the 1920s, the African American magazine *The Messenger* welcomed the exclusion of Jews along with Negroes. "Hitting the Jew is helping the Negro," said the unnamed columnist, in all likelihood the magazine's editor, A. Philip Randolph. "Negroes have large numbers and small money: Jews have small numbers and large money. To-

gether, the two have large numbers and large money. . . . The Negro has benefited before from fights made in [the] interest of Jews."*

GOD'S GIFT TO AMERICA

Even if Jews took up advocacy of black civil rights in part for reasons of self-
protection, and even if such advocacy was at times paternalistic, their motives
had deeper meaning as well. Whether their inspiration came from the central
lesson of the Passover observance, to remember their own delivery from bondage in Egypt, and the Torah's some three dozen commandments against oppression of the "stranger,"† or from secular traditions of commitment to social
and economic justice in Europe and the United States, American Jewish individuals and agencies were outspoken proponents of African American equality
from the 1910s through the 1960s and beyond.[33] In the black Baptist Church, recalls the poet Yusef Komunyakaa, "the Jewish people were always seen as revolutionary," a people who "always challenged the system's ideas and phobias."[34]

Stressing parallel experiences of suffering and disadvantage, numerous Jews,
including prominent figures such as Louis Marshall, Stephen Wise, and Felix
Frankfurter, were active alongside blacks in early civil rights groups, including
the NAACP, whose founders included Joel Spingarn and his brother Arthur,
who headed its legal vigilance committee, precursor to the Legal Defense Fund.
Wealthy Jews contributed significant sums of money to the NAACP and the
National Urban League—by one estimate, at least one third of the financing for
these two organizations during the 1950s came from Jewish philanthropy[35]—as
well as the United Negro College Fund and many other agencies and institu-

---

* Blacks stood to benefit all the more, said the writer in appealing to a rank stereotype, because "the
Jews control the powerful media for the dissemination of opinion—namely, the press, the screen and
the stage." Of course, if Jews had so much power, one might wonder why they faced discrimination and
restrictive quotas in so many walks of life, including education. "Harvard University and Racial Discrimination," *The Messenger* 4 (August 1922), 459.

† In addition to Leviticus 19:34, the scripture from which my title derives, see, for example, Exodus
22:20 ("You shall not wrong a stranger or oppress him, for you were strangers in the land of Egypt") and
Deuteronomy 10:19 ("You too must befriend the stranger, for you were strangers in Egypt"). Although
the King James Bible, *Tanakh: The Holy Scriptures*, and other major translations of the Books of Moses
use the widely recognized term "stranger," recent translations by Everett Fox and Robert Alter render
the word in all these instances as "sojourner." See Everett Fox, *The Five Books of Moses: A New Translation* (New York: Schocken Books, 1995); and Robert Alter, *The Five Books of Moses: A Translation with
Commentary* (New York: Norton, 2004).

tions. Julius Rosenwald's benefaction, to cite a prominent example, made possible the construction of more than five thousand black schools and colleges in the South.[36] Blacks and Jews drawn by Franklin Roosevelt into the Democratic Party formed a partnership in presidential politics that would persist throughout the century, even though by the 1980s a notable number of influential Jews had aligned themselves with the Republican Party of Ronald Reagan. The Jewish left, including labor leaders affiliated with the Communist Party, advocated on behalf of black rights and black labor during the 1930s and 1940s, supporting A. Philip Randolph and the Brotherhood of Sleeping Car Porters, among others. Such activism was suppressed by the cold war but redirected to some extent into the southern freedom movement, where Jews were prominent to the point of being singled out for contempt and attack. Samuel Leibowitz, as we will see in Chapter 3, provided an ardent defense of the so-called Scottsboro Boys; Jack Greenberg played key roles in the NAACP Legal Defense Fund, in the cases that led to *Brown v. Board of Education,* and later in the Equal Employment Opportunity Commission;[37] and Stanley Levison was one of Martin Luther King, Jr.'s, closest advisers.

The civil rights movement "spoke to the Jewish head," as Jonathan Kaufman writes, "but it also spoke to Jewish hearts."[38] It did so because Jews saw in African Americans not just themselves but also their scriptural obligations. A 1942 cantata titled "What Is Torah?" composed to mark the holiday of Shavuot, which celebrates the giving of the Torah on Mount Sinai, aptly joined the imagery of Jewish life to the cause of black justice: "Torah is the hope of the Negro people, plunged into poverty and despair. . . . In all their tragic years upon this continent, the memory of Israel's struggle has kept their faith alive."[39] Said Israel Goldstein, president of the American Jewish Congress and former president of the Zionist Organization of America, in 1956: "We must defend the rights of the Negro as zealously as we would defend our rights as Jews whenever and wherever these might be threatened."[40]

Many African Americans responded no less empathetically to the spirit of brotherhood they found in Jewish culture. The political activist and performer Paul Robeson, for example, sang "Kaddish" alongside "Go Down, Moses" in concert and declared that "the Jewish sigh and tear are close to me," while Harry Belafonte took pride in his recording of "Hava Nagila!" saying, "To be given an opportunity to popularize this song and to have so many people from diverse backgrounds be touched by it is an honor."[41] When Ben Shahn incorporated scripture in his 1965 lithograph *Thou Shalt Not Stand Idly By,* which commemorated the murders of the civil rights activists James Chaney, Andrew Goodman, and Michael Schwerner during Mississippi Freedom Summer in

1964—an African American and two Jews killed while investigating the burning of a black church in retaliation for voter registration efforts—his image of
blacks and Jews working hand in hand was echoed by the Howard University
artist Lila Oliver Asher, also Jewish, in *Homage to Ben Shahn* (see illustrations).[42] In the wake of rioting in New York and Rochester during 1964, Martin
Luther King, Jr., was pained to learn that a large number of the stores looted
were Jewish-owned, since in his view Jews had demonstrated their commitment to tolerance and brotherhood at great personal sacrifice. It would be impossible, he remarked, "to record the contribution that Jewish people have
made toward the Negro's struggle for freedom—it has been so great."[43]

No doubt Jewish commitment to blacks has sometimes been inordinately
idealized. "Steeped in the prophetic tradition of his people," said Charles
Glicksberg in 1952, the Jewish intellectual is drawn to the problem of anti-black
racism because he is of necessity "a champion of justice for all people."[44] Yet
their own lesser exclusion from the American Dream coincided for many Jews
with their religious and cultural traditions of service and philanthropy. Young
Jews of the New Left, in contrast to the previous generations, may have been
driven somewhat more strongly by secular ideals than by religion (neither Andrew Goodman nor Michael Schwerner had a Jewish burial service), and their
elders may have worried that they had no particular commitment to Judaism
("painfully few of the young men and women who went to Mississippi last
summer [1964] had any understanding that what they were doing was in the
least connected with their Jewishness, or with the teaching of Judaism," remarked Charles Silberman), but their actions were in keeping with Judaism's
commitment to social justice and, in any event, were no less morally deliberate.[45]

One of King's staunchest allies, Rabbi Abraham Heschel, construed the Jew's
obligation to the black stranger in a revealing way. "Seen in the light of our religious tradition," said Heschel in addressing the National Conference on Religion and Race in 1963, *"the Negro problem is God's gift to America,* the test of
our integrity, a magnificent spiritual opportunity." His own irrefutable commitment to black rights allowed him to pose a challenge to fellow Jews: "The
concern for the dignity of the Negro must be an explicit tenet of our creeds. He
who offends a Negro, whether as a landowner or employer, whether as waiter
or salesgirl, is guilty of offending the majesty of God."[46] Notwithstanding the
fact that blacks might have found something other than idealism in Heschel's
formulation of the "Negro problem" as "God's gift," many Jews were attentive
to discrimination against African Americans, active on behalf of black rights,
and especially alert to their own participation in racial persecution. They may

לֹא תַעֲמֹד עַל-דַּם רֵעֶךָ
"THOU SHALT NOT STAND iDLY BY"...

Ben Shahn, Thou Shalt Not Stand Idly By *(1965), photo-offset lithograph in black and burnt siena, 22 x 16.75 inches.*
© Estate of Ben Shahn/Licensed by VAGA, New York.
New Jersey State Museum Collection, Museum Purchase, FA1970.354.1

Lila Oliver Asher, Homage to Ben Shahn *(1966), linoleum block, 13½ x 19½ inches.*
Collection of the artist, courtesy of Lila Oliver Asher.

not have been "foot soldiers in the black Hagannah," in Lenora Berson's melli-
fluous phrase, but their commitment demonstrated that many of these Jews, as
Hasia Diner writes of the earlier generation's race-conscious philanthropy, had
internalized an "American adaptation of the message from Mount Sinai" and
fashioned a social justice version of chosenness.[47]

For the postwar generations, however, the chosenness of the Jews—and therefore any attempt by blacks to borrow from that paradigm—was radically called
into question by the Holocaust, which threw into sharp relief the latent differences between the African American and American Jewish experiences. As we
will see in more detail in this and later chapters, the Nazi genocide highlighted
the vulnerability of Jews *as* Jews even as it offered blacks a new way to understand their own tragic history as one that stood in clear contrast to that of Jews
in America. This is one message of William Gardner Smith's novel *The Stone
Face* (1962), in which post-Holocaust America is made the common testing
ground of racial justice for a black American expatriate and a Jewish survivor
from Poland, he a painter and she an actress. For her, America offers the promise of true emancipation as a Jew—that is to say, emancipation of a kind al-

ready available to American Jews—while for him, it offers recognition that he, too, may find freedom, but only by confronting racism in the land of his birth.[48] Often, the comparison has been even more calculated, as in James Baldwin's neatly formulated comment, with its striking chiasmus of temporality, that the Jew's "Holocaust ends in the New World, where mine begins. My diaspora continues, the end is not in sight."[49]

Andrew Hacker has refined this asymmetry in arguing that the only comparison to the suffering of blacks that introduces "parity" for Jews is the experience of those who actually underwent European persecution and the Holocaust. Even survivors of the death camps, upon their liberation, Hacker remarks, once again became part of the white race, and in the years since 1945 "none of them has known what it is like to be black."[50] Such a distinction is likewise the subject of a brief but compelling scene in Art Spiegelman's *Maus II* (1991). Fast on the heels of recounting his evacuation from Auschwitz to Dachau as the end of the war approached, the narrator's father, Vladek, complains to his son and daughter-in-law about having to pick up a "shvartser" hitchhiker—represented as a black dog in this tale of Jewish mice and Nazi cats—to which his daughter-in-law replies: "How can you of all people be such a racist! You talk about blacks the way the Nazis talked about the Jews!" Juxtaposed to his harrowing account of surviving on crumbs of food, Vladek's fear that the black man will steal their groceries goes beyond irony into a disabling incommensurability. His racism—not unlike that of Bellow's survivor protagonist in *Mr. Sammler's Planet* (1970), to whom we will return in a later chapter—is embarrassing and groundless to his son's generation. Engulfed in the suffocating tide of his Holocaust memories, however, it is also rendered insignificant, as his rejoinder to his daughter-in-law demonstrates: "Ach! . . . It's not even to compare the shvartsers and the Jews."[51] For Vladek, the Holocaust survivor, the racial worlds of Jews and blacks offer no grounds for comparison.

What Vladek suffered at the hands of the Nazis does not mitigate his hostility toward American blacks, but it does put in perspective the limits of American anti-black racism—whether on the part of gentiles or Jews. Hacker's argument, in other words, has an obverse that he neglects: survivors of the Holocaust continued to be Jews who lived with the memory that they might have been annihilated, while in turn, black Americans alive at the time of the Holocaust, whatever racial oppression or violence they may have experienced, never knew slavery, let alone the real risk of wholesale genocide. "No white can understand, [blacks] say. I do, I say," writes Holocaust survivor Ruth Kluger. "But no, you have white skin, they counter." To which Kluger's rejoinder, whether or not it makes any impression, is unassailable: "But I wore a *Juden-stern* to alert other pedestrians that I wasn't really white." (African Americans may be America's Jews, but historically Jews are the world's "niggers," writes Phyllis Chesler.)[52] If postwar American Jews could achieve "parity" neither with European Jews nor with American blacks, many of them, even so, were but a generation or two removed from those Jews, often their own families, who died in the Nazi Judeocide. Instinctively, if vicariously, they felt themselves in greater danger, as a people, than African Americans had ever been.

As we will see in Chapter 3, African Americans were quick to respond to the rise of Nazism not only because of what it meant for Jews in Europe but also because of what it might mean for blacks, as well as Jews, in the United States. "Should America develop its own brand of Fascism, which presumably would be an intensification of much that now exists in the South," wrote Ralph Bunche in 1936, "both the Negro and the Jew would provide handy scapegoats," since one could imagine its being argued that "the Jew controls much wealth that rightfully belongs to the superior Nordic peoples, and that some four million Negroes are holding and competing for jobs which only white men have a right to possess."[53] (Philip Roth imagined one vector of this scenario in his 2004 novel *The Plot against America,* in which anti-Semitism is unleashed after the election of the pro-Nazi isolationist Charles Lindbergh as president in 1940, but he left undramatized the effect on blacks of such a turn in America's history.) For American Jews, the rise of Nazism, even more certainly than their memory of pogroms, likewise awakened apprehensions that the prevalence of racism in the United States, though focused on blacks, might pose a real threat to Jews. By brutalizing the white masses, wrote Moise Katz in 1947, the "lynch-breeding jimcrowism" that afflicts blacks might create the necessary conditions for "a new Hitlerite destruction of the Jews in America."[54] In the event, there was no "Hitlerite destruction" of any kind in the United States. Yet their distance from the Holocaust, combined with their unnerving knowledge that they were "safe" only because of that distance, left American Jews with patterns of grief, guilt, remorse, and relief that were painful enough in their own right but that became even more vexatious when African Americans began to borrow the concept of the Holocaust to explain their own racial tragedy.

Whereas the psychological struggle over ownership of the Holocaust, like full comprehension of the event itself, took more than a decade to become manifest, some lessons of the Jewish genocide were more immediate. However much it challenged Jews' capacity to believe in a just God, let alone one who had chosen them before all other peoples, the rise of Hitler and his attempt to murder all the Jews within Germany's reach made them all the more vigilant about their obligations to the black stranger—obligations that were in no way hypocritical for including an element of self-protection.

For the historian of slavery and abolition Louis Ruchames, speaking in honor of Negro History Week in 1955, the destruction of the Jews offered proof that "no minority group is safe while others are the victims of persecution," a lesson "seared into our minds and hearts through the burning flesh of six million of our brethren in Europe." It demonstrated to Ronald Sanders that it was no more possible to be half Jewish than to be half Negro in America, since "mulattoes get sent to the back of the bus, and half-Jews were made to suffer under the Nazis."[55] In his address at the 1963 March on Washington, Joachim Prinz, president of the American Jewish Congress, invoked the Jewish tradition of obligation to one's neighbor and recalled his time as a rabbi in Berlin under Hitler, when he learned that "the most disgraceful, the most shameful and the most tragic problem is silence" in the face of brutality and in the face of murder. America, he said, must not become a "nation of onlookers."[56] Placing King's civil disobedience within a constitutional framework that transcended states' rights, Jack Greenberg drew a similar lesson from the rise of Nazism. When demonstrators in the South are beaten or jailed for speaking freely and engaging in nonviolent protests, argued Greenberg, they are only guilty of breaking unjust laws much like the Nuremberg Laws, most of which were perfectly legal within the Nazi system. Whereas there was "no redress" in Germany, he added, "here the contrary is true."*

On closer examination, such lessons were not instantaneous, nor were they so easily transposed into the American context. Contemplation of the Holocaust might make possible deeper empathy between Jews and blacks, but it proved, over time, just as likely to confuse their alliance and drag them into ar-

---

* The ironic perils of Jewish liberalism over the course of the century are aptly illustrated by an episode in later years. When Greenberg, the successor to Thurgood Marshall as director of the NAACP's Legal Defense Fund, was invited in 1982 to co-teach a course on civil rights law with a black faculty member, Harvard Law School students, disturbed by the paucity of black faculty, boycotted the course because Greenberg, in his tenure as head of the fund, had been insufficiently radical, and because as a Jew and therefore "white," he was not a "Third World professor" who could "identify with and empathize with the social, cultural, economic, and political experiences of the Third World community." Jack Greenberg and "Letter from the Third World Coalition of Harvard Law School to the Harvard Law School Community, May 1982," quoted in Jonathan Kaufman, *Broken Alliance: The Turbulent Times between Blacks and Jews in America* (1988; rpt. New York: Touchstone, 1995), pp. 104, 118; on Greenberg's career, see pp. 85–123.

guments over comparative victimization. For the American Jew, said Shlomo Katz, the "road to Little Rock is a long one and leads by way of Warsaw and Auschwitz." True sympathy and understanding lie not in parochial ethnocentrism or in the self-glorification of political activism, but rather in the immersion, for Jews and blacks alike, in tragic knowledge. Those who take the "long road" of knowing their own history will be led also to know the other's sorrow, said Katz, and "will not isolate themselves in the belief that their sorrows and hopes are so unique that none can equal them."[57] The Holocaust recast the comparative sufferings of blacks and Jews in the United States, and in doing so redefined their sense of moral obligation—as well as their potential aversion— to each other in ways that would take decades to unfold. More immediately, it sharpened each people's apprehension about their security and identity as Americans.

TWO NATIONS ARE IN THY WOMB

In choosing as the epigraph for her study of black-Jewish relations a passage from Genesis 25:23 concerning the birth of Esau and Jacob—"Two nations are in thy womb / And two people shall be separated / From thy bowels / And one shall be stronger / Than the other people / And the elder shall serve the younger"[58]—Lenora Berson called attention to the awkward fact that the "elder" black Americans, whose slave ancestors helped build the nation at incalculable cost to themselves and their descendants, should nevertheless be left in a position of subservience to a group they at once resembled and resented. Reflecting on the fact that Jewish help was real but nonetheless paternalistic, even colonialist, Albert Vorspan quoted the insight of McGeorge Bundy: "The cause of the American Negro has nourished the self-righteousness of generations of white men who never troubled to understand how destructive it can be to make the uplifting of others the means of one's own self-esteem."[59] The disequilibrium was exacerbated whenever the historical experience that made blacks most "American"—namely, slavery—was ignored by Jews in their own comparative assessments. Speaking to a 1926 NAACP convention, Louis Marshall, president of the American Jewish Committee, noted that he belonged to "a race which has had even longer experience of oppression," dating back thirty centuries to the Israelite Exodus. Subject to mass expulsions and "wholesale massacres, not mere individual lynchings," Jews have been persecuted in every land in which they settled. Most recently in the pogroms of Russia and Poland, he added, Jews have suffered "indignities in comparison to which to sit in a 'Jim Crow' car is to occupy a palace."*

Marshall's one-sided argument reappeared in a more complicated form in Chester Himes's novel *Lonely Crusade* (1947), where the ongoing colloquy between the novel's black protagonist, Lee Gordon, and Abe "Rosie" Rosenberg, Lee's tutor in the brotherly tenets of Marxism, works its way through a host of themes—the histories of anti-Semitism and anti-black racism, the purported exploitation of blacks by Jews in the ghetto, the rights of labor and the virtues of communism—at the center of which are mirroring questions: Are Negroes especially anti-Semitic? Are Jews just as racist as whites?

> "Of all the rotten results of racial prejudice," Rosie said, "anti-Semitism in a Negro is the worst."
>
> "I think the same thing about anti-Negroism in a Jew," Lee retorted. "With Jews being slaughtered in Europe by the hundreds of thousands, brutalized beyond comprehension, you Jews here in America are more prejudiced against Negroes than the gentiles."
>
> "That's silly. Have you ever heard of a Jew in a lynch mob?"
>
> "Only because the white lynchers discriminate against him. He does everything to the Negro short of lynching."

When Lee is unable to produce evidence of such hostility on the part of Jews, falling back on his own distaste for their manners and personality, Abe spells out the dilemma of their relationship:

---

* Julius Rosenwald made a similar point. "If it is any consolation to you," he told a black audience, "I want to say that there are white people who suffer a great deal more. The Jewish race, which dates back thousands of years and like yours dates back to a time when they were known to be in slavery." After his conversion to Judaism, the African American writer and scholar Julius Lester, trying to find the right word to encompass true racial "suffering," rejected a comparison of slavery and segregation to the Holocaust in similar but more intricate terms: "Is there a word strong enough to hold naked bodies stacked in hills beneath a sunny sky? Being forced to ride at the back of a bus is not in the same realm of experience. But Jews had to wear yellow Stars of David on their clothes to be identified as Jews. My star is my skin color. Yet I am alive. Anne Frank is not." Louis Marshall quoted in Hasia Diner, *In the Almost Promised Land: American Jews and Blacks, 1915–1935* (1977; rpt. Baltimore: Johns Hopkins University Press, 1995), pp. 151–52; Rosenwald quoted in David Levering Lewis, *When Harlem Was in Vogue* (1981; New York: Vintage, 1982), p. 102; Julius Lester, "The Stone That Weeps," in David Rosenberg, ed., *Testimony: Contemporary Writers Make the Holocaust Personal* (New York: Random House, 1989), p. 196. The same passage, in a slightly different construction, had already appeared in Lester's autobiographical meditation, *Lovesong* (1988), to which we will return in Chapter 8.

"The Jew has been oppressed, not only today, but for nineteen hundred years; he has been oppressed in practically every nation in which he has wandered, in every historical era through which he has passed. The fact that he has survived is not an accident. The Jew has survived by developing habits of survival. He bears the stamp of his oppression—just as the Negro bears the stamp of his oppression. If this is what you dislike in the Jew, you must also dislike it in yourself."[60]

Or, as James Baldwin would later characterize the logic of black anti-Semitism: the Jew is singled out for black criticism "not because he acts differently from other white men, but because he doesn't." Whatever may have happened to the Jew in Europe during premodern pogroms or the cataclysm of the Holocaust, Baldwin contended, he lives with comparative freedom in America, unfettered by the heritage of racism that the end of slavery did little to diminish. The Jew does not realize that the fact that "he has been despised and slaughtered does not increase the Negro's understanding. It increases the Negro's rage."[61]

If anti-black racism on the part of Jews, real or imagined, allied them with the gentile majority, so too might anti-Semitism on the part of blacks, real or imagined, offer a way for them to claim membership in the white majority. The casual anti-Semitism that Richard Wright recalled as "part of our cultural heritage" in a famous episode of *Black Boy* (1945)—the blacks he grew up with hated Jews "not because they exploited us but because we had been taught at home and in Sunday school that Jews were 'Christ killers'"—was a means both to be, and to make claims on behalf of being, American.[62] By calculations such as this, black anti-Semitism has been seen as an expression of intra-group security meant to "re-inflate deflated self-respect" (Kenneth Clark); a hatred perfected by Christians and handed to blacks "ready made" (Howard Fast); a misguided expression of solidarity with WASP America at just the moment when WASPs were finally discarding their own anti-Semitism (Leslie Fiedler); proof that blacks "can have their cake and eat it: they can dislike white people and simultaneously be copying them" (Joel Carmichael); evidence that black assimilation entails being subjected to the same anti-Semitic cultural imperatives as American whites (Oliver C. Cox); a way of "locating oneself within the national mainstream, indeed of establishing an affinity with whites" (Andrew Hacker); a reflection of the anti-Semitism learned "whenever anyone absorbs without question the values of mainstream white culture, values that are taught via mass media, et cetera" (bell hooks); and the "routine loathing of Jews that comes with being an American" (Dexter Jeffries).[63]

It has also been a means to articulate a grievance so deep and painful as to be otherwise inchoate. An aspect of the Negro's "humiliation whittled down to a manageable size and then transferred" to a convenient target, said a younger Baldwin, anti-Semitism was the best means for the Negro to express "his long record of grievances against his native land." As fragile minorities within a distinctly white, sometimes violently repulsive Christian culture, both blacks and Jews, strangers from within and strangers from without, were trapped in mistaken legends, the Jew having been taught the legend of Negro inferiority, the Negro having been taught the legend of Semitic greed. To the degree that both groups were helpless to throw off these stereotypes, Baldwin wrote, they fell prey to each other, caught in the "crossfire" of American race relations: "Just as every society must have a scapegoat, so hatred must have a symbol. Georgia has the Negro and Harlem has the Jew."*

Harlem had the Jew—or did the Jew have Harlem? Anti-Semitism was also a function of the Negro's physical proximity to the Jew. Because many Jews in the first half of the century, especially recent immigrants, were effectively just one step ahead of African Americans in their economic advancement, their points of contact and abrasion were ever present—a proximity of social station evident in folkloric humor: *Question:* What do you get when you cross a black and a Jew? *Answer:* A janitor, but he owns the building.[64] Wherever blacks and Jews were thrown together in close quarters, especially in the urban North, anti-Semitism gained a strong foothold in black vernacular culture. The Jew "is playing the odds against you all the time," Marcus Garvey warned blacks in the curriculum of his "School of African Philosophy." "He plays with loaded dice, his card is marked, you can never win against him."† In the 1930s, such suspi-

---

* To cite a more recent example that combines Baldwin's two arguments: A visit to the Jewish ghetto in Venice made the West Indian–born Caryl Phillips sympathetically alert to the vengeance forgone by Shylock in *The Merchant of Venice*, an identification he attributes as well to many black Americans, who might turn to anti-Semitism even as they wish, like Shylock, to exact their pound of flesh from their principal oppressors, non-Jewish whites. To the degree that Jews have become "white," so they might also, ironically, have ceased to be the targets of white gentiles and become instead targets of black wrath. What black America may therefore be saying, Phillips concludes, is that for two thousand years "you might have been Europe's niggers, but now you're in America don't pretend you're not pleased to have discovered real ones." James Baldwin, *Notes of a Native Son* (1955; rpt. New York: Bantam, 1979), pp. 57–60; Caryl Phillips, *The European Tribe* (1987; rpt. New York: Vintage, 2000), pp. 53–55.

† Garvey continued: "The policy of the Jew is if he sees a Gentile dying on the pathway and a penny covers his eye, as a hope for recovery, he will take it off and let him die." Blacks must therefore answer fire with fire: "Always try to get something from the Jew because he has always robbed you and your fathers in that he believes he is the chosen of God and as such all other men must pay tribute to him." Blacks

cions were exacerbated by the depression and the simultaneous infusion of Axis propaganda. Sufi Abdul Hamid, a Muslim who claimed to be from Egypt, became known among whites and blacks alike as the "Black Hitler" because his agitation on behalf of black employment in Harlem stores ("Don't Buy Where You Can't Work") was said to be baldly anti-Semitic. For his part, Hamid asserted to Claude McKay that this was a rumor spread by Jewish merchants. Having read *Mein Kampf,* said Hamid, he understood all too well Hitler's view of blacks. To a Harlem proprietor who, when asked to employ blacks, answered evasively that "we are fighting Hitler in Germany," Hamid replied, "There is no Hitler in Harlem."[65]

Whether understood as a place of poverty and squalor, or simply of hardship and enclosure, the concrete representation of black-Jewish proximity and the friction it created was the *ghetto,* a concept whose very meaning and ownership, as we will see further in Chapter 6, underwent a demographic transformation from the early to the mid-twentieth century, gradually becoming the province of blacks rather than Jews. At later moments, different immigrant groups—Asians or Arabs, for example—might fill the role of despised middleman in the black urban ghetto; but throughout much of the century, the figure of the exploiting Jew, a seemingly permanent feature of anti-Semitic lore, has been a persistent feature of African American attitudes.

No doubt some Jews, like members of any group, were greedy, callous, or dishonest, but their "exploitation" of blacks was more often structural than personal. St. Clair Drake's *Black Metropolis* (1938) and Roi Ottley's *New World A-Coming* (1943) were among the studies of black urban life which recognized that anti-Jewish sentiment was effectively *anti-white* sentiment that took on convenient anti-Semitic overtones. Insofar as the flood of early-twentieth-century European immigrants arrived at just the moment when African Americans stood ready to become a critical component of an industrialized workforce and, perhaps, gain the rights of citizens promised them in Reconstruction, anti-Semitism was a means of particularizing black resentment not just generally against all whites but specifically against immigrants who might be seen to have usurped black opportunities for access to employment and modest prosperity. Frequently blacks' main contacts with the white world, Jews became their scapegoats of choice. "Goldberg," the personification of exploitation, has a prominent place in Claude Brown's classic memoir of growing up in

---

must reverse the Jewish propaganda of chosenness: "Let him pay tribute to you if tribute is to be paid." Marcus Garvey, "Lessons from the School of African Philosophy," in *Marcus Garvey: Life and Lessons,* ed. Robert A. Hill (Berkeley: University of California Press, 1987), pp. 204–5.

Harlem, *Manchild in the Promised Land* (1965), for example, and free-floating stereotypes of the gouging merchant, landlord, or artistic agent—and even the charge that Jews perpetuated the ghetto at the expense of blacks—have remained alive even in recent years.*

Anti-Semitism arose most easily in once-Jewish neighborhoods subsequently inhabited by blacks or in workplaces where Jews, who entered civil service or public education when other professional options were closed to them, had risen to managerial positions by the time blacks followed the same path in later generations.[66] It arose, too, because Jews and blacks were also and inevitably economically reliant on each other. After recalling his boyhood in the South, where there was a dependent relationship between Jewish merchants, who had a market among blacks, and blacks, who could only buy from Jews, Himes offered a succinct summary of the conundrum of black anti-Semitism in the ghetto: "Now the gentiles had enslaved the blacks and worked them as beasts, but when they were freed, the gentiles didn't want to have a damn thing to do with them. They left the blacks without food or shelter. They worked them for a pittance and that was all. Whereas the Jew realized that to house and feed the black man was a business, a business that paid off. This paid off better than any other business because where else could the Jews, who were in a ghetto themselves, open up any kind of business and have customers, other than in the black ghetto?" Himes is reflecting on the prewar years, but one may look forward to Bayard Rustin's 1968 speech to the Anti-Defamation League of B'nai B'rith. Blacks in the ghetto see only four kinds of white people, said Rustin, the policeman, the businessman, the teacher, and the welfare worker, and except for the policeman, the majority of the others are Jewish: "Here again is the love-hate syndrome." Added Lenora Berson a few years later: "The stores that will be boycotted, the tenements to be hit by rent strikes, the collection agents to be driven out are mostly Jewish, as are the remaining white politicians; for the only whites left in the ghetto, besides the police, are Jews."[67]

The paradox of such "exploitation," explained Arnold Rose in 1949, is that it

* In David Mamet's film *Homicide* (1991), following the murder of an elderly Jewish woman who still tended her store in a black neighborhood, we see a posted flyer, illustrated with a rat wearing a yarmulke, whose message reads, "Crime is Caused by the Ghetto, the Ghetto is Caused by the Jew." Accusations that Jews have exploited black artistic talent were revived, for example, in Spike Lee's film *Mo' Better Blues* (1990) and Public Enemy's song "Swindler's Lust" (1999), with its repulsive pun on *Schindler's List* and lyrics comparing record producers to Jewish bankers and slave traders designed to show the importance of owning the master recording lest "the master own you." Public Enemy, *There's a Poison Goin' On,* Atomic Pop, 1999; lyrics to "Swindler's Lust" are also posted on Public Enemy's official Web site, www.publicenemy.com.

resulted from the gentile prejudice that constrained Jews' own opportunities, on the one hand, and from Jews' comparative lack of prejudice, on the other: "Jews are willing to exploit Negroes while the more prejudiced white non-Jews are not, because economic exploitation involves economic service and social contact with Negroes." Even so, Jews still had greater opportunities than blacks, and some seeming black anti-Semitism must therefore be understood as a corresponding business strategy. The Jews' advantages in business, said the president of a black businessmen's association in Chicago, consist of reputation, business contacts, control of the best districts, and good training in business, but "the Negro doesn't have those weapons and if he's going to survive and get ahead, then he's got to insist that his people patronize his store, and not the Jew's. After all, the Jew can open up a store outside of the Black Belt, but can the Negro?"[68]

From the 1940s onward, however, the opportunities for such contact decreased, diminishing one kind of friction while augmenting another. As Jews entered the American mainstream, they became associated with migration from the ghetto to the suburbs, the symbol of postwar affluence and mobility. Whereas new federal housing programs allowed Jews and other white ethnics to join a rising economic tide, blacks were often prevented from buying or renovating property even in their own urban neighborhoods, let alone in the suburbs, because of systematic redlining.[69] When they attempted to move into transitional white ethnic neighborhoods, including those which Jews were abandoning, they were shunned, threatened, and sometimes violently attacked. In subsequent years, African Americans would achieve far greater economic mobility, but during the mid-century decades, almost every major midwestern and northeastern American city saw neighborhoods once heavily Jewish become predominantly black, a demographic transformation that exacerbated the potential for exploitation and recrimination.

This symbiosis was taken up in a number of novels, including Vera Caspary's *Thicker Than Water* (1932), Waters Turpin's *O Canaan!* (1939), Carl Ruthven Offord's *The White Face* (1943), David Mark's *The Neighborhood* (1959), Hal Bennett's *The Black Wine* (1968), and Louise Meriwether's *Daddy Was a Number Runner* (1970). Prior to the special case of *The Pawnbroker* (1961) by Edward Wallant, whose suffusion of character and setting with the trauma of the Holocaust we will return to in Chapter 6, the outstanding example was *The Changelings* by Jo Sinclair (pseudonym of Ruth Seid). The novel's original title, "Now Comes the Black," better described Sinclair's study of the postwar displacement of Jews by blacks in the lower-middle-class neighborhood of a midwestern city modeled on Cleveland, and its protracted composition from 1930 to 1955, the year of its publication, had the effect of telescoping broad generational changes into a foreshortened moment of wrenching upheaval, as though several eras were superimposed upon one another. Distinctly subordinating black anti-Semitism to Jewish racism, moreover, Sinclair focused not on the role of Jews as middlemen in a ghetto economy but instead on their fear, as white ethnics, of black encroachment on their protected world.

Sinclair's novel is built around the friendship of the Jewish Judy Vincent and the black Clara Jackson, the post–European immigration, post–southern black migration "changelings" whose color-blind bond and willingness to cross racial boundaries, if they can sustain it, holds the key to the future. The plot follows the two girls' efforts to negotiate adolescence and sexual maturation within a conflicted racial context in which the neighborhood's older Jews compare the coming of "the Black Ones" to Hitler ("next is the crematorium"), one more in the series of disasters Jews have faced throughout history. For the traditional Jews, blacks are associated with sexual promiscuity and the decay of familiar social norms, but the dangers for which they stand are also internal to the community: the corrosive effects of Americanization and upward mobility, the conflict between Orthodoxy and Reform Judaism, and the rising incidence of intermarriage. In reaction to the coming of the blacks, says one character, suddenly "we can see who we are, what we are." The neighborhood's "white, beautiful street," personified throughout the novel as a circumscribed community, places blacks on one side of the nation's color line, Jews on the other, enclosing them within "walled homes" built from fear of "the *schwartze*." The "street" marks boundaries that, if transgressed, lead inexorably to the destruction of the precariously secure communal life sought by the older generation: the street is their "wailing wall." If not transgressed, however, the boundaries recreate the enclosures of the Russian shtetl and the wartime ghetto, imprisoning those of the younger generation who wish to "soar over the wall." A historical way station between the walled enclosures of anti-Semitic Europe and the self-selected, quasi-segregated American suburb, Sinclair's street is the American Jewish ghetto in disintegration, transformed day by day into "a Palestine to the Black Ones," since "every man has his dream of a Homeland." Before Judy finds the courage to prevent her father, Abe Vincent, from committing arson rather than sell his property to blacks, she must imagine herself consumed in the conflagration: "Lit by the roaring flames, she was outlined in some old pattern of ignorance and fear." Like the community's walls, the fire symbolizes change, but with two options: "Either you burn up or you come through—pure, good."[70]

Judy's rescue of the family and its spiritual integrity signals a fragile communion with the future, but Sinclair's ingenious transfiguration of the defining metaphors of modern Jewish persecution—*wall* and *fire*—into American terms leaves them balanced between regression and transcendence, estrangement and empathy. The fires to come will be not in Jewish neighborhoods but in black, with the very term *ghetto,* which originated in the historical sequestering of European Jews, coming within a handful of years to define a seemingly permanent, "pathological" dimension of black American life.

Illustrating a transition common in the postwar decades, the neighborhood shul, by the end of *The Changelings,* has become a black Baptist church,[71] a further sign of the coming estrangement between Judy and Clara.* In the black, says the poem "Die Schwartze," composed by a sensitive young Jew who serves as the novel's conscience, the Jew sees the past metamorphosing into the future: "Now comes The Black / From out the secret dark cell of my heart. / Now comes The Black Enemy, unnamed, unseen, / For I fear his name, his face, / For I will not admit his name is mine, / His face is mine!"[72] But it is a mimesis whose frightening undertones register more strongly than its promise of brotherhood and sisterhood. Imprisoned in their own bigotry, the adult Jews of Sinclair's novel have become the goyim of their own European nightmares—they, too, have become "changelings"—while the blacks have become their Jews: interlopers, destroyers of family and faith, a sexual menace.

Despite her daring overture in making adolescent sexuality the arena in which identity and racial beliefs are most strongly formed and challenged, Sinclair leaves unresolved the most potent threat of assimilation—namely, interracial mixing—but she does so to predict an impasse, a color line, between Jews and blacks in which the paradox of their intimate proximity and repulsive distrust is made all the more prominent. Whereas Jews could aspire to suburban life, African Americans became associated not with middle-class mobility but with the paralyzing poverty of the ghetto—in many cases the very neighborhoods and housing vacated by Jews.

Returning in 1966 to the Harlem of his boyhood, a once lower-middle-class Jewish and Irish neighborhood turned black slum where the apartment that formerly housed his five-member family now housed seventeen, Vernon Bern-

---

* Compare the semi-autobiographical voice of "The Rabbi" by Robert Hayden, who finds in the separation of black and Jewish childhood friends that accompanied the transition of his native neighborhood from Jewish to African American a prophecy of divorce in mutual sympathies and coming recriminations: "But the synagogue became / New Calvary. / The rabbi bore my friends off / in his prayer shawl." Robert Hayden, "The Rabbi," in *Collected Poems,* ed. Frederick Glaysher (New York: Liveright, 1985), p. 9.

stein found in one building, among tens of thousands, a microcosm of the sea change: "I wanted very much to take a complete census of the old building, including the rats . . . [but] there was no need, really."[73] In "The Long-Distance Runner" (1974), a fictional rendering of a Jewish woman's return to her old neighborhood, Grace Paley imagined something closer to recovered community. Yet the bond that is achieved when the protagonist takes up residence for three weeks with the black mother and her four children in the apartment where she used to live in "the white old days," as one of the black characters puts it, is inevitably short-lived, the idiosyncratic narration purposely making it hard to distinguish fantasy from reality. More prosaically, Leslie Fiedler discovered in himself an uncanny effect of the demographic shift. Walking with his mother in a decaying black neighborhood only to have her reveal that she had been born there, Fiedler found in his own surprised voyeurism a compound of relief and guilt: "I could feel the Jew's special rancor at the Negro for permitting himself visibly to become (there is no question of the justice of such a notion, only of its force) the image, the proof of the alien squalor that the white, Gentile imagination finds also in the Jew."[74]

A decade later, Paley created a more profound vehicle for the dialectic between empathy and alienation in "Zagrowsky Tells" (1985), where memory of the Holocaust at first prevents an aging pharmacist from recognizing his own earlier racism but finally provides a bridge for him to come to terms with his half-black grandson, Emanuel, symbolically the messiah of a new racial world. Like Spiegelman's Vladek and Sinclair's Abe Vincent, Izzy (Israel) Zagrowsky, who fears for the hard-earned value of his business as blacks and Hispanics move into the neighborhood, insistently asserts that Jews can never be made white, even in America—that the legacy of the Holocaust trumps assimilation—and that in his prejudice he is not a racist but a pragmatist. Whereas his wife, Nettie, accepts the accusation of a black man who refuses to assist her on the subway that "we" Jews, as whites, "kept them down" for three hundred years, Izzy replies: "We? We? My two sisters and my father were being fried up for Hitler's supper in 1944 and you say we?"[75] When their psychologically disturbed daughter gives birth to a black baby while confined in a mental hospital, however, Izzy must take responsibility for the life of this African American–Jewish American child who embodies, literally, the demographic convergence of two ghettos and the precarious union of two peoples, two strangers in the land who remain strangers to each other.

In the black Jew Emanuel, the "we" expands to embrace not just the necessity of black-Jewish coexistence but also a possible genealogical correlation—one to whose many permutations we will return in the next chapter and one that holds the key to Izzy's recovery of his moral equilibrium. "They tell me long ago we were mostly dark," Izzy muses, while recounting his grandson's circumcision. "Also, now I think of it, I wouldn't mind going over there to Israel. They say there are plenty of black Jews. It's not unusual over there at all. They ought to put out more publicity on it."[76] Out of love for his black grandson, Izzy makes peace with the disruption of his own American dream and remembers his suppressed understanding of the Jew's obligation to the stranger—his obligation, in effect, to himself as a Jew, who was once a stranger in the land of Egypt.

THE DRY BONES OF THE NATION

Jewish suspicion of, or contempt for, blacks with whom they were demographically entangled, and a corresponding vacillation on the part of blacks between anti-Semitic scapegoating and emulation—between "insecurity and compensatory idealization," as Julius Lester would later characterize the encounter[77]—was possible because in their lack of a stable, inherited identity, brought from an "old country" and refashioned through a process of acculturation, African Americans stood in seemingly marked contrast to the unifying religious and historical experience of American Jews. If Louis Marshall's effacement of black slavery and the slave trade as formative historical experiences seems scandalous now, it depended on a combination of then commonplace assumptions, which were shared by many blacks as well: that Africa was a place of superstition and savagery, "the land of childhood, which lying beyond the day of self-conscious history, is enveloped in the dark mantle of Night,"[78] in Hegel's notorious description; that slavery was a historical moment of racial degradation to be transcended; and that blacks' forced migration to the Americas had obliterated their natal connection to a viable African past. If the Negro is a pariah in his own country, said Baldwin, it is because his ties to "ancestral homelands [have been] totally destroyed."[79]

Whether in Harlem Renaissance works such as *The New Negro* (1925), the landmark anthology edited by Alain Locke, or in anthropological studies such as Melville Herskovits's *Myth of the Negro Past* (1941), the recovery of Africa as a cradle of world culture and civilization—or at least as the progenitor of a vital black culture in which African cultural retentions could be detected throughout the Americas—was one of the crucial African American projects of the twentieth century. The reconstruction of an African past had to compete, however, with the more common view, propounded in detail by the black sociologist E. Franklin Frazier in *The Negro Family in the United States* (1939) and reiterated in his later works, that Africans in America had been stripped of their culture by slavery and stamped indelibly with a sense of inferiority. Whereas "other conquered races have continued to worship their household gods within the intimate circle of their kinsmen," Frazier wrote, slavery destroyed those gods and "dissolved the bonds of sympathy and affection between men of the same blood and household." With the few "scraps of memories" left them, African Americans were unlikely to find "in the alien culture of Africa a basis for race pride and racial identification," let alone be able to resurrect reliable memories of their ancestors.[80]

Taking note of the contrasting views of Herskovits and Frazier, Abram Kardiner and Lionel Ovesey sided with the latter in their aptly titled study *The Mark of Oppression* (1951) in order to draw a distinction between the black and Jewish experiences. Unlike Jews, whose life in European ghettos and shtetls permitted—indeed, necessitated—the nourishing and maintenance of their own culture, which was then transferred little diminished to the United States, Africans in slavery and after were left with few resources to sustain them.[81] Jews brought to the New World not religion alone, nor only the particular nations of their nativity, but rather the abiding "nation" of Jewish belief and civilization. Africans, in contrast, were typically deemed people of no nation. Blithe acceptance of Frazier over Herskovits, countered Harold Isaacs, compounded racist associations of blackness with savagery and evil, furthering the "systematic debasement and self-debasement of the Negro in this white world"—what Martin Luther King, Jr., following Frazier, would refer to as the Negro's ingrained "nobodiness"—and proving that the Negro's rejection of Africa is, at bottom, "a rejection of himself."[82] Yet the widespread acceptance of Frazier's view underscored the seeming extremity of Africans' exile in America. Not only were their temples destroyed but also their gods, their sacred stories, their very way of life, leaving them no alternative but to borrow from the essential beliefs and holy books of Jews and Christians.

The full-scale effort to connect the black diaspora to its lost homeland lay a generation in the future, and even then the effort would remain far from conclusive. In the postwar years, the stark contrast between Jewish and black histories drawn by Leslie Fiedler seemed perfectly plausible: whereas the Jew brought to America centuries of learning and civilization, the African American arrived "without a past, out of nowhere—that is to say, out of a world he [was] afraid to remember, perhaps could not even formulate to himself in a language he [had] been forced to learn. Before America, there [was] for him simply nothing." Leo Strauss went so far as to claim that the black struggle for justice, unlike the Jewish, was based entirely on borrowed ethics: "When we Jews fight for something which we may fairly call justice, we appeal to principles ultimately which (if I may say so) were originally our own. When the Negroes fight for justice, they have to appeal to principles which were not their own, their ancestors' in Africa, but which they learned from their oppressors."[83]

Less harshly, Laurence Mordekhai Thomas has argued that it was blacks' acceptance of Christianity that completed their natal alienation from African tradition and rendered them a people without an inherited narrative of their own. Since neither a set of behavioral patterns, nor a vernacular linguistic style, nor skin color can make a narrative to which blacks are heir, contends Thomas, himself black and Jewish, the history of blacks differs fundamentally from that of Jews, canonized in ancient ritual practice and in an enormous theological and philosophical literature. Adapting to the condition of African Americans a version of Jean-Paul Sartre's notorious observation that Jewishness, if not Judaism itself, is sustained by the survival of anti-Semitism, Thomas remarks: "If racism should be eradicated tomorrow, most blacks would have next to no reason to identify with one another qua being black; for there is no narrative, and hence no conception of the good, to which blacks are heir, that the demise of racism would make abundantly evident."[84] By Thomas's account, even the Mosaic story, the great sustaining force from the slave spirituals to the charismatic leadership of Martin Luther King, Jr., because it is a secondhand tradition, is proof of blacks' loss of distinctive cultural origins.

Each of these views in its way discounts the deep interweaving of, and improvisation upon, traditions of Exodus, exile, diaspora, and messianic liberation within the black American experience, a topic to which we will return in more detail in the next chapter. Yet the very fact that an African cultural past had to be pieced together from fragmentary folkloric traditions, scholarly inquiry into early Africa and the slave trade, and new Afrocentric paradigms of knowledge distinguished it, in the first instance, from the Jewish past. Neither the recovery of African cultural inheritances nor the sense of racial identity promulgated by black nationalist movements, including the most distinctive and influential, the Nation of Islam, has to date significantly contravened the fact that the core beliefs of African America principally derive, on the one hand, from democratic liberalism and, on the other, from Christianity, in its foundations a Jewish narrative.

It is possible, however, to see the often pejorative distinctions drawn between Jewish and African American traditions in another light. The blacks in *The Changelings* are migrants from the South, relative newcomers to the urban

North, as are the Russian Jews. But their recent ancestors, going back to slavery, were not migrants. For all the irony of their constitutional status, they were among the most *American* of Americans by reason of longevity, labor, and culture alike.* Writing from the clarifying distance of residence in France, Himes made this difference definitive. Unable to determine whether or not Jews are "white," *Lonely Crusade* leaves the argument between his interlocutors in a stalemate, Lee Gordon unpersuaded that Jews are not racists, Abe Rosenberg unpersuaded that blacks are justified in their anti-Semitism. In their interchange, however, Abe underscores the unusual, if precarious, citizenship of African Americans: "The Negro is an American. No matter what happens to him he is still an American. That's something even [ultra-racist Mississippi senator Theodore] Bilbo can't take from him. He might be pressed down but he can never be liquidated."[85]

Louis Marshall to the contrary, black Americans, whatever their civic marginality, existed profoundly, if paradoxically, at the substratum of the nation's consciousness. Through the ordeal of slavery, an experience without recent parallel and largely irrelevant to the American history of Jews, many of whom were comparatively new citizens, or not citizens at all, African Americans held a position of priority *as Americans*—a priority underscored, for immigrant generations, by the fact that blacks were well versed in the linguistic and religious culture of gentile America. "Some Jews [may] have left their homes in Europe involuntarily," said Martin Luther King, Jr., in a breathtaking understatement intended to demonstrate that solving "the dilemma of Negro America" would call "our beloved nation to a higher destiny," but "they were not in chains when they arrived on these shores," nor has any other immigrant group, whatever its economic and linguistic disadvantages, been enslaved on American soil and "had its family structure deliberately torn apart."[86]

Even early-twentieth-century racial theorists detected a difference that favored the African American's claim to a closer kinship with white Americans. Attempting in 1904 to distinguish between the traits that made Jews and blacks offensive to "Aryans," Nathaniel Shaler fixed upon what he took to be the black's essentially imitative and adaptive nature, which allows him to appear

---

* Needless to say, American Indians had the strongest prior claim as the country's "natives," but they also mediated between blacks and Jews in curious ways. They, too, had been enslaved sporadically and unsuccessfully, though in turn some Indian tribes—the Cherokees, for example—became slaveholders themselves. And just as they were depicted by some as descendants of the lost tribes of Israel, so it has been argued that it is *their* genocide, not that of Africans in America, that in some features most resembles the Holocaust.

more like "us." The Jew's verbal facility and quick wit, as well as his seeming carnality and preoccupation with money, define the essence of "the Hebrew Problem" as it is perceived by Aryans. The greater gulf between Aryan and African may result first of all from the latter's physically repulsive features, as well as his traits of ignorance and licentiousness, argued Shaler, yet because the Jew "cannot imitate our manner of approach to [our Aryan] neighbor or divine his motives just as we do, he remains remote from us, while the Negro, an essential alien, comes easily very near."[87]

At once close and corrosive, the bond of alienation between black and Jew therefore made the black's "Americanness"—something even the most vile segregationist could not take away from him, said Himes—all the more perceptible and ironic. The Negro cannot be considered an alien or a stranger, concluded the sociologist Robert E. Park in 1934, for "he has lived here longer than most of us," whether assimilated or not, and "is more completely a product than anyone of European origin is likely to be of the local conditions under which he was born and bred." The prior claim of African Americans was no less compelling to the next generation of social scientists. Blacks are "old settlers whose presence shaped our Constitution," wrote Nathan Glazer and Daniel Patrick Moynihan in describing blacks' unique American position in their landmark study *Beyond the Melting Pot* (1963). "They were the only group held as slaves, [and] they dominate a good part of American culture and literature."[88]

Even as their own acceptance within the national mainstream surged in the postwar years, Jews might therefore be plagued by lingering doubts about who most belonged to America—the black Christian or the white Jew. Consider Bruce Jay Friedman's comic incorporations of the paradox into *Stern* (1962), a quirky, masterly allegory of postwar assimilation and suburbanization. After a neighbor insults his wife by calling her a "kike" and making an opaque sexual advance, Stern consults his black co-worker, Battleby, attempting to engage him on grounds of shared prejudice ("you probably run into a lot of Negro things like that"). While Stern's fantasy runs wild—he imagines Battleby hiding him in Harlem, providing him with black girls, bringing a gang of thugs to beat up the "kike man"—Battleby, an amateur artist, responds to his overture parabolically: "I've got some crucifixion oils I'd love for you to see." Stern's jarring return to exclusion from a gentile world where even black Americans are more secure members, despite their persecution, is made more poignantly ironic by Battleby's advice that the price of surviving prejudice and the violence it continually portends is a life of virtual anonymity: "You've got to abstract yourself so that you present a faceless picture to society."[89] Crucified though he may

have been throughout United States history, the black American belongs nonetheless to a Christian paradigm from which the Jew can still be excluded, finding no absolution, nor even any temporary fraternity, with his black brother.

Perhaps blacks were not "God's gift to America," as Abraham Heschel
phrased it, but they did set the nation's moral compass, and their prior claim
was argued, time and again, by African Americans themselves. "Would America have been America without her Negro people?" Du Bois asked in *The Souls
of Black Folk* (1903), adding later in an article for *The Crisis:* "There is nothing
so indigenous, so 'made in America' as we. It is as absurd to talk of return to
Africa, merely because that was our home 300 years ago, as it would be to
expect the members of the Caucasian race to return to the fastnesses of the
Caucasus Mountains from which, it is reputed, they sprang."[90] "I am not a
stranger in America," wrote Baldwin half a century later. Borrowing from
Frazier, he found that what made the Negro undeniably *more* American was
the fact that he "arrived at his identity by virtue of the absoluteness of his estrangement from his past," that any Negro wishing to trace his origins in Africa
"will find his journey through time abruptly arrested by the signature on the
bill of sale which served as the entrance paper for his ancestor."[91] In contrast to
the parochial Afrocentrist belief that the authenticity of blackness was left behind in pre-slavery Africa—"the day the slave ship landed in America, our history ended and the white man's history began," writes Maulana Karenga[92]—
Ralph Ellison likewise determined that it was America itself that made blacks
who *they* are, because blacks made America what *it* is. The "jazz-shaped" culture of African Americans had enlivened the "dry bones of the nation," Ellison
wrote at the crest of the civil rights revolution, invoking Ezekiel's prophecy of
the nation of Israel raised up from exile in Babylon. It was they, therefore, who
best defined the nation's political ideals: "By the irony implicit in the dynamics
of American democracy, they symbolize both its most stringent testing and the
possibility of its greatest human freedom."*

---

* Writing in the same year, Ellison's friend Albert Murray made much the same point: "Black Americans, not Americans devoted to whiteness, exemplify the open disposition towards change, diversity, unsettled situations, new structures and experience, that are prerequisite to the highest level of citizenship. . . . It is the non-conforming Negro who now acts like the true descendant of the Founding
Fathers." Both Ellison and Murray may have been drawing here on an essay by Kenneth Clark in *Jewish
Social Service Quarterly* in 1954, the year of *Brown v. Board of Education,* who remarked that "America
can only survive through the strength and the validity of the democratic idea. The guardians and the
barometer of the effectiveness of this idea are America's minorities. Each time that they validate this
idea in terms of their relationship to the rest of the American people, they contribute a stronger bul-
wark of democracy for all." Ralph Ellison, "What America Would Be Like without Blacks" (1970), in

Martin Luther King, Jr., played subtly on this theme when, in speaking to the national convention of the American Jewish Congress in Miami in 1958, two months after a prominent synagogue there had been bombed, he called for Jewish support of black civil rights by pointing to the role played by black Americans in destroying Hitler: "Negroes saw that such hideous racism, though not immediately applied to them, could sooner or later encompass them, and they supported the struggle to achieve his defeat." Jews, in other words, owed black Americans a debt of gratitude, and King, turning the tables on Leo Strauss, was calling for it to be paid. Whatever their premodern or modern European history, King appeared to argue, Jews could play no role in America comparable to the spiritual vocation of blacks, whose "chosenness in America," as Gerald Early would later put it, was "to redeem the nation and thus redeem themselves."[93]

For all their potential priority as Americans, however, blacks were in Babylon. Jews were not. Blacks wore their mark of servitude in the color of their skin. Jews did not.

THE OUTWARD LIFE, THE INWARD SECRET

Green lawns, white Jews . . . The Jewish success story in its heyday, all new and thrilling and funny and fun. Liberated new Jews, normalized Jews, ridiculous and wonderful. The triumph of the untragic. Brenda Patimkin dethrones Anne Frank.

—*Philip Roth,* Operation Shylock

Even if America had not yet "put Jewish history out of its misery" (to anticipate Stephen Whitfield's later observation), less than a week after the Japanese surrender in September 1945, Bess Meyerson, daughter of an immigrant, working-class, Yiddish-speaking family, was crowned Miss America. That same year— the year that Jackie Robinson broke the color barrier with the Brooklyn Dodgers—Hank Greenberg, already an established star, returned from military service to win the American League pennant for the Detroit Tigers with a

---

Going to the Territory (New York: Random House, 1986), pp. 109–12; Albert Murray, *The Omni-Americans: Black Experience and American Culture* (1970; rpt. New York: Da Capo, 1990), p. 37; Kenneth B. Clark, "Jews in Contemporary America: Problems in Identification" (1954), rpt. in Norman Kiell, ed., *The Psychodynamics of American Jewish Life: An Anthology* (New York: Twayne, 1967), p. 126.

ninth-inning grand slam and lead them to victory in the World Series. A little more than a decade later, a *Time* magazine cover story devoted to Herman Wouk's blockbuster *Marjorie Morningstar* (1955) proved to Leslie Fiedler that "on all levels, the Jew is in the process of being mythicized into the representative American." It may be, as Ruth Kluger would write many years later, that American Jews were "running away from themselves" in reaction to "the undigested Holocaust in Europe," but their assimilation, albeit on qualified terms, was achieved in the United States at virtually the same moment it had been radically stamped out in Europe.[94]

Whereas American Jews of the early twentieth century, to borrow chapter titles from Arthur Hertzberg, were "The Children of the Ghetto," their postwar children and grandchildren were engaged in "The Conquest of the Suburbs," first in the urban East and North, eventually in the South and West. The years following the war constituted a "golden decade," even a "golden age," for these "children of the Gilded Ghetto," who at last luxuriated, recalled Philip Roth, in "that wonderful feeling that one was entitled to no less than anyone else, that one could do anything and could be excluded from nothing."[95] During the 1950s, "the Jewish Decade" of American literature,[96] Roth, Saul Bellow, Bernard Malamud, Isaac Bashevis Singer, Norman Mailer, Leon Uris, and Herman Wouk were up-and-coming kingpins of American fiction, while criticism by Fiedler, Lionel Trilling, Philip Rahv, Irving Howe, and Alfred Kazin challenged the New Critics in reshaping the world of American letters. Torn between a drive toward assimilation and survival as a distinctive ethno-religious group, postwar American Jews might prove to be "ambivalent" about "making it" or fret that the American social contract required one to become a "facsimile WASP,"[97] but such anxieties only made their rapid Americanization more startling.

To be sure, becoming WASP-like exacted certain costs. If Jews had been able to come up with a slogan like "Black is Beautiful," says Grace Paley's Mr. Darwin, an elderly man speaking to the black gatekeeper of his retirement home, "it would've saved a lot of noses, believe me."[98] Although Jews would cultivate their own version of Black Power, as we will see, their more reliable path to power lay in preserving their religious and cultural distinction as a people while strategically blending into the majority white culture. But some dissented according to principles they considered more essential to Jewish identity than whether or not to have cosmetic surgery. For radical children coming of age during the war in Vietnam and its resulting war in the streets of America—and sometimes transferring their radicalism to opposition to Israel over the Six-Day War—the assimilation of their parents was the sign of a corrosive immorality. "I do not believe in 'freedom' for the Jews at the expense of Arabs and black people," said Jerry Rubin. "The concentration camp fear of Jews has made them rush to prove themselves to Pig Amerika, and make themselves 'secure' with money and property."[99]

Rubin's countercultural rebuke of his elders warned that acceptance by "Amerika" required Jews to forsake their fundamental beliefs—but with no certainty that they would not still be scorned as Jews. If the best solution offered by liberal society is legal equality accompanied by private discrimination, and the only escape from discrimination is through "ceasing to be recognizable as a Jew," Leo Strauss argued more subtly in 1962, then it was impossible *not* to remain a Jew. To do otherwise would erase one's origins, one's identity.[100] A generation earlier, with the threat of Nazism coming clearly into view, the psychologist Ellis Freeman had worried that too strong an expression of ethnocentrism might amount to the "self-imposed restoration of a spiritual ghetto," perpetuating Jewish distinctiveness in such a way as to play into the hands of the anti-Semite.[101] With Jews free to be Jews (or not) in the postwar era, however, the danger of visibility contended with the danger of invisibility—the danger that Americanization might destroy Jews from within. Roth's heterodox invective in *Portnoy's Complaint* (1967), which, by ridiculing the stereotypes of middle-class Jewish aspiration, confirmed their legitimate claim on identity, could only have appeared—or at least to such great, though certainly not universal, acclaim—once it had become possible to worry about the "Vanishing American Jew," a species created through low birthrates, intermarriage, and the sociocultural absorption of "white" middle-class lifestyles.[102]

When Fiedler delivered a mordant epitaph for assimilation, his own first among equals, the very extremity of his seeking an analogy in the European genocide was a sign of the perceived risk to American Judaism: "To be sure, our 'Holocaust' [our apostasy from Judaism] is not imposed from without by brute force but freely chosen." Unlike the Nazis, said Fiedler, "we unreconstructed assimilationists" seek not to obliterate memory of the Jews but rather "to memorialize in honor the last choice of the Chosen People: their decision to cease to exist in their chosenness for the sake of a united mankind."[103] What, though, was the price of becoming "white"? Having found the ultimate freedom of Jewish emancipation in ceasing to be Jewish, Fiedler was required to conclude that the condition he envisioned might logically end in the Nazi dream of a *judenrein* world.

The price of making it—adopting a dual identity or, worse, cloaking or abandoning a Jewish identity—had long been a point of contention for American Jews. Commenting on Israel Zangwill's popular play *The Melting Pot*

(1908), Judah Magnes feared that Americanization, melting the many peoples of the world into "a new people of freedom," meant "dejudaization," with the Jew asked to give up his identity "in the name of brotherhood and progress." Anticipating the better-known argument of Louis Brandeis by several years, Magnes counseled in a sermon of 1909 that it was not a matter of choosing "America or Zion," as Zangwill would have it, but rather of choosing "America and Zion—America for the thousands who can live as Jews here, Zion for the thousands who must live as Jews there. . . . Zionism is the complement to, the fulfillment of America, not its alternative." In an address of 1915, the year before he was named to the Supreme Court, Brandeis characterized assimilation as "national suicide" and argued that Zionism and American patriotism were perfectly compatible. Whether or not the Jew intends to settle in Palestine, he said, "loyalty to America demands rather that each Jew become a Zionist," for "only through the ennobling effect of [Zionism's] strivings can we develop the best that is in us and give to this country the full benefit of our great inheritance."[104] (On the strength of such advocacy, membership in the Zionist Organization of America rose to 27,000 in 1925, then declined to 8,400 in 1932, owing to the depression and conflicts over British policy in Palestine, before rising thereafter to 300,000 by 1945.[105])

Such a commitment was necessary in part because assimilation animated a question with anti-Semitic undertones: Is the Jew assimilable because he has no true nation, no geographical or political basis for life, or does he have no nation because he has been assimilated? "Is it not just this in the Jewish personality that has piqued and irritated and attracted other peoples, that it is at once so congenial and so alien?" asked Randolph Bourne.[106] For Bourne, however, the ambiguity of the Jew's status suggested a model for his theory of "trans-nationalism," whose "purest pattern," in his view, was the kind of Zionism articulated by Magnes and Brandeis—a theory which could only be tested by the founding of Israel and the questions of allegiance occasioned by its subsequent history, points to which we will return in Chapters 2 and 5. Transnationalism aspired to keep America's "vast reservoir of dispersions" from becoming the deracinating melting pot Bourne feared, "a colorless, tasteless, homogeneous mass" congenial to the Anglo-Saxon ruling class. Even if the cultural pluralism he envisioned as a "weaving" of many fabrics and colors[107]—or what Horace Kallen portrayed as a "symphony of civilization," a metaphor borrowed from Magnes and repeated by John Dewey among others—was utopian, such metaphors better predicted the arc of history than did the homogenized "Kulture Klux Klan" feared by Kallen.[108] "The point about the melting pot," Glazer and Moynihan would later write, "is that it did not happen."[109]

Although Bourne spoke for a dynamic cosmopolitanism and Kallen for the persistence of immigrant cultural inheritances, both found in the Jews—whose nations of origin might hold less meaning for them than did Jewish civilization and the theoretical "nation" of Zionism—the best model of hybrid pluralism in which ethnics could be both American and something else. Neither, however, offered any wisdom about the future assimilation of the Negro. Blacks were simply not part of the nation's beautiful weaving or its harmonious symphony. For them, "Kulture Klux Klan" was destined to be more than a witty figure of speech for decades to come.

In retrospect, the situations of the Jews in America and Germany seem so different as to make perverse any attempt at comparison. Their emergence into post-Enlightenment modernity led European Jews to embrace a promise of assimilation whose deceit showed up with stark brutality in the reversion of the Third Reich to racial categorizations that made Jews subhuman. Seemingly in confirmation of Theodor Herzl's observation that modern anti-Semitism "is a result of the emancipation of the Jews"[110]—an essential part of his argument for a Jewish state—it was precisely the assimilation of Jews, their "whiteness," that made them a virulent danger under the racial regime of Nazism. No comparable catastrophe befell the Jews of the United States, but they did not escape comparable suspicions.

Whatever its origin in Christianity's ancient demonizing of Jews, and whatever grotesque stereotypes of rapaciousness and bestiality were employed to promote anti-Semitism, the immediate source of Nazism's image of the Jew as an "enemy within" lay in the unease and animosity among gentiles stimulated by the increasing integration of Jews into the German economy and way of life. Jews who maintained their traditional identity, through Orthodox observance or appearance, were a reminder of the Jew's alien nature, but charges that Jews zealously guarded their own racial purity while threatening "higher" races with contamination derived just as insidiously from the discrepancy between the assimilated Jew's conventional appearance and his purported alien essence. With the new Jew no longer so easily identified as in the past, his status as a recognizable other was disappearing at the same time that his power, according to anti-Semitic logic, was expanding.[111] Immersion in liberal society and intermarriage might strip Jews of their Judaism and its historic signs—hence, a yellow star was required to fix their identity—but, so the Nuremberg Laws and ultimately the Holocaust proved, nothing could strip them of their Jewishness.

Apprehensions about the danger posed by assimilated Jews were not absent in the United States, even if their configuration, and obviously their consequences, were quite different. In a polyglot nation where physiognomic features per se were likely to be even less indicative of one's identity, uncertainty about their place within the transnational composite still left Jews vulnerable. At the turn of the century, Jews were likely to be seen, in the words of one New York magazine editorial, as a "chameleon race," difficult to assign to one or another racial category. Because their history is one of migration, in the course of which they "have developed connections which have crystallized into what seems to be an international organization," wrote Louis Wirth in 1928, Jews appear to be "not merely ubiquitous but something of a mystery" and are thus targeted in fantasies of conspiratorial anti-Semitism.[112] Although the most rabid anti-Semitism of this kind peaked in the United States in the 1930s and was ended by the confrontation with Nazism, the perceived equivocalness of Jewish identity retained a residual menace. As J. O. Hertzler wrote in 1942, "the Jew is different in ways felt but not always specifically determined." Whereas blacks confront open enmity and visible abuse, said Ben Halpern as late as 1956, Jews are left isolated in an "invisible ghetto," heirs to anti-Jewish attitudes so intimately woven into the fabric of Western civilization that it is not enough for the Jew to "pass." Rather, he must become a Christian before he can become a gentile, and even then the transformation will become complete only in his children's generation or beyond.[113]

But the ambiguous anti-Semitism faced by Jews was likewise a function of the unambiguous racism faced by blacks. In explaining why Jewish assimilation was of no avail in avoiding persecution, Ellis Freeman was forced to look for an analogy in the dilemma of the Negro. In Nazi Germany, either the Jew stands out in his difference and is glaringly reprehensible, or, if he is assimilated, he is charged with "sailing under false colors the better to perform his mischief unmolested." The paradox that racial antipathy may flourish most where the reviled group is neither strange nor threatening but instead familiar, said Freeman, could best be understood by reference to the reactions of white Americans to the behavior of blacks. He chose the example of dress: "If the colors were subdued, the Negro was guilty of denying his 'race'; if they were gaudy, he was guilty of flaunting his barbarism. In either case he was 'guilty' of something."[114] Freeman's analogy said a good deal about the singular vicissitudes of African American life within a purportedly pluralistic society. As an explanation of the American Jewish dilemma, however, it suffered the obvious shortcoming that, except for those African Americans light enough to pass for white, their color itself constituted a kind of permanent clothing that might be modified—cosmetically or genetically—but seldom changed entirely.

In a formulation that was to prove more widely influential for its psycho-

pathological distinction between black and Jewish stereotypes—blacks are stigmatized as agents of sexual excess, Jews as agents of intellectual excess—Frantz
Fanon spoke directly to this problematic issue of the Jew's passing in *Black
Skin, White Masks* (1952), a work widely adapted in subsequent decades by
American theorists of race, blacks in particular. The Jew "can be unknown in
his Jewishness. He is not wholly what he is," wrote Fanon. "He is a white man,
and, apart from some rather debatable characteristics, he can sometimes go
unnoticed." Although Jews may be "hunted down, exterminated, [and] cremated," he added, half tongue-in-cheek, these are "little family quarrels." But in
his own case as a black man, he argued, the object of scorn is clear: "I am given
no chance. I am overdetermined from without. I am the slave not of the 'idea'
that others have of me but of my own appearance." The African American's ancestry and physical traits, said Gunnar Myrdal more succinctly, "are fixed to his
person much more ineffaceably than the yellow star is fixed to the Jew [by]
the Nazi regime in Germany."*

Myrdal's epigrammatic formulation, appearing in his monumental work *An
American Dilemma: The Negro Problem and Modern Democracy* (1944), epitomized the evolution of American racial theories, and the place of Jews in those
theories, over the decades leading up to the war and beyond. Early-twentieth-
century efforts to compose the population of United States society according to
racial classifications, one goal of the eugenics movement, culminated in the

---

* One finds a fictional rendering of Fanon's provocation in John Edgar Wideman's short story
"Valaida" (1989), in which the aged Mr. Cohen, a Holocaust survivor, recalls being saved as a child from
a savage beating in the death camps by the African American jazz musician Valaida Snow, herself a prisoner, who was beaten and sexually abused by the Nazis but refused to sing "in their cage." Intermingled
with his reverie about his agonizing time in the camp and the aftermath of its liberation are sketches of
Cohen's futile efforts to tell the tale of Valaida's rescuing him to his black maid, Clara Jackson, who is intent on finishing her work so she can go home to prepare for Christmas with her family. Despite their
many years together as employer and employee, the two are locked in separate worlds, divided by lingering suspicions and apprehensions, unable to make visible, let alone vital, the history they provisionally
share. In response to Cohen's conclusion of his story, that Valaida was "a dark angel who fell from the
sky and saved me," Clara, as though borrowing from Fanon, thrusts Cohen back across the racial barrier
into his alien, undifferentiated "white" world: "Always thought it was just you people over there doing
those terrible things to each other." Frantz Fanon, *Black Skin, White Masks*, trans. Charles Lam Markmann (New York: Grove Press, 1967), pp. 115–16; Gunnar Myrdal, *An American Dilemma: The Negro
Problem and American Democracy*, 2 vols. (1944; rpt. New Brunswick, N.J.: Transaction Publishers, 1996),
I, 117; John Edgar Wideman, "Valaida," in *Fever: Twelve Stories* (1989; rpt. New York: Penguin, 1990),
pp. 27–40. On Valaida Snow, see Clarence Lusane, *Hitler's Black Victims: The Historical Experiences of
Afro-Germans, European Blacks, Africans, and African Americans in the Nazi Era* (New York: Routledge,
2003), pp. 165–72.

1924 Johnson-Reed Act, which set a quota for each nationality at 2 percent of
the number of foreign-born residents in the United States as of the 1890 census
(the quota was revised in 1927 so as to correspond to each nationality's proportion of the population as of the 1920 census).[115] These provisions effectively
barred immigration from southern and eastern Europe, as well as from Asia,
and sharply curtailed the arrival of European and Slavic Jews at the same moment when black migration to the urban North was increasing. Appealing to
supposedly scientific principles of fitness for government that dated to the
founding of the nation, proponents of the 1924 legislation intended to ensure
the selection of physical types resembling the prevailing racial stock of the nation—a stock in which "Hebrew" was for the time being still a distinct "race."
Nevertheless, the demarcation between Jews and other white ethnics excluded
by the Johnson-Reed Act was not always clear. According to John P. Gavit's
Americans by Choice (1922), the "absence of exclusive racial marks is the distinguishing physical characteristic of the American," for he is the "product of all
races"—an argument that simply ignored blacks, Asians, and other people of
"color" in predicting the amalgamation of European ethnicities, but one that
looked forward, for that same reason, to the comparatively easy absorption of
the "Hebrew" race into the white American polity.[116]

In distinct contrast, blacks in the United States were subject to a racist dynamic that stigmatized them specifically according to color—indeed, according
to a "one-drop" rule in which the mere suspicion of "black blood" made one
a Negro—and then defined them by association with barbarism, libidinous
violence, and sloth. As Edward Reuter outlined the correlative assumptions
of anti-black theory in 1927—assumptions that would persist for decades to
come—"the whole record of the race was one of servile and barbarian status,"
summed up in the distinguishing fact of color, which was taken to be a source
of shame, not pride. Like their folkways and moral customs, the language, arts,
and religion of African Americans were acquired only from whites and "fur-
nished no nucleus for a racial unity," let alone a means of assimilation into the
mainstream of American society.[117] In their influential postwar study *Dynamics
of Prejudice* (1950), Bruno Bettelheim and Morris Janowitz anticipated Fanon
in likewise concluding that characteristics associated with the superego, offensive but not degrading, were projected upon Jews, while those associated with
the id, offensive and degrading both, were projected upon blacks. Thus, Jews
were said to be clannish, preoccupied with money, unscrupulous, out to control everything; blacks were said to be filthy, lazy, immoral, subject to base sexual urges.[118]

Such distinctions were often elided in the racial theory of the Third Reich—

as we will see in Chapter 3, the "blackness" of Jews was one hallmark of Hitlerian thinking—but those stereotypes of Jews that aroused gentile contempt also accounted in part for the apparent ease with which they seized upon the opportunities of modernity. Whereas Jewish immigrants adapted well to the American ethos of liberal individualism, progressivism, and capitalism, George Fredrickson has pointed out, blacks were held back by deeply ingrained beliefs that associated them "in the white mind with the primitive, the backward, or the irredeemably premodern."[119] According to this differentiation, Jews might be rebuked for not assimilating quickly or completely enough, while it might be wondered if blacks could ever be expected to assimilate at all.

Twenty years after the Johnson–Reed Act, in the midst of a war that rapidly accelerated the displacement of scientific racism by social and cultural theories that race is "constructed,"[120] Jews found themselves wedged into a "quasi-caste" position somewhere between those European immigrant groups considered simply to be foreign "ethnics" and those differentiated as subordinate racial castes.[121] As categories such as Celt, Teuton, Mediterranean, Slav, and Hebrew were absorbed into a single dimension, leaving only the three broad "races" of white, black, and Asian (Caucasian, Negroid, Mongoloid), there was a decline in perceived differences among non-Nordic, non-Anglo-Saxon "whites" that allowed Jews to join those immigrants who, unlike blacks, could define their own terms for transformation into Americans. As Matthew Frye Jacobson has shown, the rise of monolithic ethnic whiteness, a transformation that deepened rather than bridged the gulf between white and black, was stimulated by a number of such factors.[122] In the arguments of Ruth Benedict's *Race: Science and Politics* (1940) and Ashley Montagu's *Race: Man's Most Dangerous Myth* (1942), for example, the prevailing belief that race, biologically inherent and constitutive, determined social and historical patterns of behavior gave way to the obverse belief that it was those patterns of behavior that shaped conceptions of race.

To which one can add that the Johnson–Reed Act itself played a role in this process. Although there was some resemblance between the anti-Semitism that arose under European fascism and the antagonism toward Jews that appeared in the United States coincident with the revival of the Ku Klux Klan in the 1920s—"a fear of everything strange, polyglot, and impure," as John Higham once wrote—it was the end of mass immigration, in all likelihood, that curtailed the growth of more pronounced ethnocentrism and prevented the appearance in the United States of a "Jewish question."[123] As the Jews of America and their descendants became predominantly native-born—a fact underscored, tragically, by the government's accepting only a fraction of the Jewish refugees who might otherwise have been saved between 1933 and 1945, and afterward an equally modest number under the postwar Displaced Persons Acts—the emergence of an urbanized national culture, and with it the veneration of individual enterprise and material success, ensured their Americanization, weakened their coalition with blacks, and facilitated their absorption into the white spectrum.

The racial depredations of Nazism secured the downfall of biological explanations of both race and racism, albeit with pointed consequences for the psychological identity of African Americans. As Jews became white, blacks were redefined once again as America's Jews, but now in terms of the Holocaust. Although phenotypical differences might encode race socially and block African American assimilation, argued one wartime study, differences in achievement or aptitude between black and white, as well as black racial "characteristics," had to be understood as the circumstantial result of racial discrimination rather than a justification for it.[124] The "psychology of oppression," that set of reactive social pathologies caused by the reciprocity of domination and subservience originating in slavery—and now defined analogically by the example of European anti-Semitism—might be inherited but was not innate, said Kardiner and Ovesey optimistically, and it would disappear once oppression disappeared.[125] As we will see in Chapter 3, however, theories of racial pathology based on the psychological harm caused by racism quickly became ingrained in scholarly argument and public policy debate. To the extent that influential theorists, both white and black, cited the racial regime of Nazism and its results in the Holocaust, moreover, "damage" to African Americans, whether inflicted in the present day or passed down as a legacy of slavery, often assumed the character of genocidal trauma, further complicating efforts to divorce the idea of racial behavior from that of racial inheritance.

Law and public policy underwent a corresponding realignment. Because Nazi and Japanese propaganda had exploited American racism, black rights became a matter of national security, as well as a matter of "human rights" brought before the new United Nations by Du Bois and others.[126] "In all wars, including the present one," said Myrdal, "the American Creed has been the ideological foundation of national morale." Because it was patently at odds with that creed—a humanistic liberalism grounded equally in Enlightenment philosophy, Christianity, and English law, according to Myrdal—racial prejudice was against the nation's interest, a view given greater impetus by President Harry Truman's desegregation of the armed forces and the progressive report of his Civil Rights Commission, *To Secure These Rights* (1947).[127] Beginning in the 1930s and culminating in *Brown v. Board of Education* (1954), where Chief

Justice Earl Warren's unorthodox appeal to social science declared that racial "inferiority" had no basis in nature but rather was the product of long-standing habits of prejudice, the legal crusade against segregation generated a new analytic language built around the concepts of discrimination, prejudice, and justice, and attuned to the political realities of a nation whose global power flowed from its combined military might, its championship of democracy, and its moral claim to having defeated a nation-state guided by an ideology of pure racism.

Although the splintering of the civil rights movement into competing agendas would eventually displace pluralism with modes of ethnic particularism that re-enshrined "race" as an index of oppression or, in turn, as a cultural birthright, in the immediate postwar years the horrific example of the Holocaust was instrumental in spurring renewed pluralist arguments against any form of racial hierarchy or classification.* The advent of the cold war, Germany having become an ally and the Soviet Union an enemy, dampened but did not deter such arguments over the course of the 1950s and 1960s. Neither the defeat of Nazism nor the civil rights revolution brought about an instantaneous end to anti-Semitism in the United States, of course, and however much blacks might be distinguished as America's Jews, Jews were still subject to prejudice, both subtle and overt.† But the convergence of political idealism and legal ac-

---

* A classic analysis of the day, Will Herberg's *Protestant-Catholic-Jew* (1955), surmised that ethnic identifications had given way to religious ones—an idea that now seems quaint less for its neglect of other religions than for Herberg's failure to foresee the resurgence of secular, tribalistic ethnocentrisms as a mainstay of American intellectual life. As David Hollinger points out, "race" had hardly disappeared in American discourse by the end of the twentieth century, but the "dynamics of prejudice and oppression" did significantly redefine the term's meaning from era to era. Whereas "race" originally referred to deep structural differences among human groups that were both determinative of human character and immutable ("the leopard cannot change his spots"), "race" nowadays is taken to depict the opposite: identities created by human conduct that is changeable and that we would like to see changed, namely, "patterns of unequal treatment according to perceived descent." Prejudice against Jewish Americans is judged today to be less severe and damaging than prejudice against, for example, Latinos, who, "because of [their] greater perceived victimization, are now said to constitute a race." David A. Hollinger, *Postethnic America: Beyond Multiculturalism* (New York: Basic Books, 1995), pp. 38–39.

† A recent fictional re-creation of the place of Jews and the Holocaust in postwar thinking about racial rights and racial prejudice is instructive. Set in Topeka, Kansas, in 1951, against the backdrop of the beginnings of *Brown v. Board of Education* and a summer flood that is given quasi-biblical resonance, Carol Ascher's novel *The Flood* (1981) makes a family of Jewish refugees one means of testing the dynamics of integration. Despite their ordeal under Hitler, the refugees find that, in America, there is a difference between them and blacks that the even Holocaust did not negate. "We were the Negroes" in Ger-

tion with the theoretical collapse of biological racism ultimately, if differentially, benefited all minorities. As Anthony Lewis would later characterize the civil rights revolution of which *Brown v. Board of Education* was the legal center, "after Adolf Hitler the world knew, and the Supreme Court would have been blind not to see, that it was invidious to separate one group in society, whether Negroes, Jews or some others."[128]

The civil rights revolution was not needed to liberate American Jews; nevertheless, it did so. In a transformation that would one day have come about in any event but was accelerated by the Holocaust, the combination of color, secularization, and an embrace of modernity—none of which precluded the tenacious preservation of ethnic heritage but did make it optional—allowed Jews to be "Jewish" or "white" or both. Writing in 1961, Daniel Bell, the secular child of observant immigrants, described himself as one "who has not faith but memory," who was "born in galut [exile]" and accepts, now gladly, though once in pain, "the double burden and the double pleasure of my self-consciousness, the outward life of an American and the inward secret of the Jew. I walk with this sign as a frontlet between my eyes, and it is as visible to some secret others as their sign is to me."[129] His metaphor, so it seems, was borrowed from Du Bois's famous description of African American double consciousness.[130] But whereas Du Bois's doubleness was written in his skin for all to see, Bell's variation on the traditional promise of emancipation—that Jews could be Americans (or Germans, French, whatever) "on the street" and Jews "at home"—started from the privilege of whiteness, which made his doubleness, however strong its inner meaning, a mask to be put on or off.

Combined with their inability to exercise the option available to Bell, the visible success and acceptance of Jews in the postwar decades led some blacks to venture anti-Semitic explanations for Jewish success, while still qualifying the privilege of color on which it appeared to be based. Whereas the Irish, Italians, and Germans had "passed on through" to whiteness with ease, while black attempts to "assimilate" seemed to rhyme only with "hate" and "ANNIHILATE," wrote Haki Madhubuti in his poem "Mainstream of Society" (1966), Jewish as-

---

many, says one character, to which another replies that it was both better and worse under the Nazis: "For one thing, a Jew could disappear into the gentile culture and a Negro can't." By comparison to Germany, the United States allows them even more leeway to be white. To the extent that they admit to being Jewish, however, the family still remains alien to a neighboring family of poor whites, to whom Jews and blacks may as well be lumped together as "Jew-Niggers." Carol Ascher, *The Flood* (Freedom, Calif.: Crossing Press, 1981), pp. 79–80, 186.

similation might still be denigrated as a simple function of money: "Am I not white too? . . . I can buy my way through."[131] Despite slowly expanding opportunities for a black middle class to "buy its way through," Earl Warren's ideal of a color-blind society was not close to being realized; indeed, it remained unfulfilled even at century's end. By force of circumstance, and sometimes by defiant choice, African Americans were still distinctly marked by the "scar" or "stigma" of race.[132] Except in the rantings of white supremacists and neo-Nazis, however, American Jews were now usually characterized by reference to elected religious, cultural, or "ethnic" differences, having long since become "raceless."[133]

THE WHITE NEGRO

Or almost. Whether in the folklore of the street ("A nigger is a Jew turned inside out") or in the acerbic comedy of Lenny Bruce ("Negroes are all Jews"),[134] Jewish identity remained fluid, as Madhubuti surmised. Hewing between the poles of colored and white, race and its absence, Jews were driven to a stronger identification with whiteness by the lingering pressures of anti-Semitism but at the same time were lured, often for the same reason, toward affinity with blacks—not only with their suffering, but also with their uncompromising demand for political power, their artistic invention, their supposed sensuality, or their hipness. "I've been up all night, talking, talking, reading the Kaddish aloud," wrote Allen Ginsberg in "Kaddish" (1959), a representative Beat era fusion of outlaw Jewish and black sensibilities, "listening to Ray Charles blues shout blind on the phonograph."[135] Later in the century, when racial consciousness had again become a coveted indicator of authenticity, raceless Jews might find in their ethical commitment to African Americans a reinvigorating means to dissent, provisionally, from their own privileged whiteness. They might even argue, provocatively, that the erosion of Jewish culture had reversed the hierarchy of emulation, giving them a reason to envy the collective identity of African Americans, inscribed by a unique experience of racism and then compounded as a matter of public policy by race-based compensatory programs. Asks Seth Forman: "Has not the American Jew replaced the Black American as this nation's 'invisible man?'"[136] At mid-century, though, the ambiguities of whiteness provided Jews important psychic and cultural latitude.

On the one hand, the postwar era's archetypal tolerance narrative, Laura Hobson's *Gentleman's Agreement* (1947), argued that Jews really are white—so

long as there is nothing very visibly Jewish in their appearance or behavior.*
On the other, equivocation in the demarcation between "Jew" and "white" underlined anxieties about the means by which Jews, unlike blacks, might throw
off the evidence of race in favor of a new American self. Jews often appeared as
the mediators between black and white in early-twentieth-century narratives of
racial identity and passing such as James Weldon Johnson's *Autobiography of an
Ex-Coloured Man* (1912), Sherwood Anderson's *Dark Laughter* (1925), and Nella
Larsen's *Passing* (1929).[137] In the much-analyzed example of the film *The Jazz
Singer* (1927), Jakie Rabinowitz, the cantor's son played by Al Jolson, achieves
secular fame as a blackface performer, a masquerade that partially liberates him
from Jewish communal identity into a more "American," albeit subordinated,
group, displacing one set of racial markers with another. If the Jew requires
blackface in order to be "alien," to be racial, he becomes by definition white—
or at least whiter. At the same time, however, their identification with African
Americans and their participation in jazz culture, exemplified by blackface performance, allowed Jews, especially recent immigrants from eastern Europe, to
commemorate and retain their historic position as outsiders.[138]

This same ambivalence remained in place during the war when Milton
Mayer, in one installment of a *Negro Digest* series devoted to the theme "If I
Were a Negro," portrayed himself as the incarnation of racial uncertainty. "Say,
brother, I am a Negro," wrote Mayer, addressing himself to a fictive black interlocutor. "I don't take as bad a beating as the rest of the Negroes because I am a

---

* The "agreement" among gentlemen here refers first of all to covenants, rules of exclusion, and unspoken customs that discriminate against Jews, and second to the rules of self-selection that Jews themselves might observe in order to limit their inclusion to the "right kind" of Jews. When the gentile journalist Schuyler Green passes as a Jew in order to publish an exposé of anti-Semitism, "I Was Jewish for
Six Months," his purpose is to demonstrate that there is no difference between Jew and gentile, that
Jews, according to the current anthropological theory cited by Hobson, belong to the Caucasian division
of the human family of races. Not only does Green encounter the expected restrictions in housing, vacation accommodations, employment, and the like, but also some of his own family members turn on
him, as does his fiancée. Schuyler explains to his son that they are temporarily playing a "game" of identifying with people different from them, but the game represents the novel's distinct limitations. Green's
secretary turns out to be a Jew passing for gentile, but her camaraderie with him does little to hide her
resentment of those "other kinds" of Jews she finds loud and pushy—the ones, as she construes it, who
forced her to change her name from Walovsky to Wales. Subordinating tolerance to assimilation, both
Hobson's novel and the popular film based on it confirmed the movement of Jews toward whiteness,
but effectively at the cost of overt Jewishness. Like *Uncle Tom's Cabin*, said James Baldwin, *Gentleman's
Agreement* is governed by a "formula created by the necessity to find a lie more palatable than the truth."
James Baldwin, "Everybody's Protest Novel" (1949), in *Notes of a Native Son* (1955; rpt. New York:
Bantam, 1979), p. 11.

white Negro; in other words, a Jew." Being a "white Negro" enables the Jew to get into some restaurants, hotels, and schools, to hold certain jobs, to be given hope "that [he] can be a white man." But, Mayer added, some of us white Negroes in Germany pretended we were white before Hitler came to power, but to no avail. In the end, Mayer's sketch takes a patriotic turn: he proclaims that he is lucky to be in America, where, even as a second-class citizen, "white or black," he has a chance to fight for freedom.[139]

Mayer's grating claim to be a "Negro" illustrated how Jewish difference from blackness might actually become more evident in the very process of its being denied. That Jews were "niggers" in Germany was meaningful to many African Americans; that American Jews tried to make the same claim was far more problematic. The presumption was all the greater in Norman Mailer's hyperventilating essay of 1957, "The White Negro." Forecasting the shocks of the civil rights and sexual revolutions, Mailer, with uncanny peripheral vision, picked up the triangulation of slavery, Holocaust, and nuclear annihilation that would soon loom large in the critique of modernity. His "white Negro" was a slumming hipster who thrived in the shadows between totalitarianism and democracy by absorbing "the existential synapses of the Negro." Imprisoned within *l'univers concentrationnaire*—a phrase Mailer took from the title of David Rousset's landmark study of the concentration camps (published in France in 1946 and translated as *The Other Kingdom* in 1947)—the white Negro was liberated from the slavery of middle-class repression and sent in quest of the Holy Grail of the "apocalyptic orgasm," which might be channeled as easily into violence as into eros. Adumbrating an equivalence between post-Holocaust trauma and post-slavery trauma, Mailer offered the cool, libidinous Negro, his victimization turned to prophecy, as a liberating model for the un-hip, cerebral Jew.*

---

* Ralph Ellison, for one, was not impressed by Mailer's theory of the hipster as "white Negro." Mailer, said Ellison in a letter to Albert Murray, "thinks all hipsters are cocksmen possessed of great euphoric orgasms and are out to fuck the world into peace, prosperity, and creativity. The same old primitivism crap in a new package." Mailer's relationship to the blackness of hipsterism seemed opportunistic at best. In a "footnote" to "The White Negro" titled "Hipster and Beatnik," he said that the term "hipster" was used "as long ago as 1951 or 1952." In fact, the word had been in popular use for at least a decade longer (the *OED* dates it in print to J. Smiley's *Hash House Lingo* [1941]), though its colloquial use was older, and some recent scholars have argued that its root word, "hip," has an African origin. In any case, it was included by Mezz Mezzrow in his glossary of hip language in *Really the Blues* (1946) and had become so prevalent by 1948 that Anatole Broyard, in a *Partisan Review* essay about which Mailer either was ignorant or pretended to be, found it superannuated and declared it effectively dead: the hipster, no longer "a seer, a hero" who could lay claim to "apocalyptic visions" that made him "so prodigal as to be

A "real sweet ofay cat," said Baldwin of Mailer in a gentle but acid retort to "The White Negro." Fantasizing about life on a social periphery he could not possibly understand—the periphery inhabited by the real black Baldwin— Mailer maligned the "sorely menaced sexuality of Negroes in order to justify the white man's sexual panic."[140] Baldwin might just as well have directed his ire at Seymour Krim, a "soul- as well as penis-starved" human being, who briefly made a name for himself in an essay titled "Ask for a White Cadillac" by setting out to be the greatest Harlem slummer since Carl Van Vechten. Having lost his "girlish, milky notions about the natural greatness of Negroes—a defiant liber- alism and sense of identification stemming in part from my being the unre- ligious modern American Jew who feels only the self-pitying sting of his iden- tity without the faith"—and putting on the mask of hip tough among black hustlers and whores, Krim found his lost manhood in Harlem's paradise of eroticism. As a Jew with a nose job (in an attempt "to gleam like a clean-cut White Protestant beauty"), he felt a kinship with blacks getting their hair straightened; but his writing, in the end, was no less cynical and predatory than Mailer's and his courtship of blackness just as slavish.[141]

Such staged acts of transgressive rebellion on the part of Jews who blacked up figuratively as white Negroes, an existential sideshow of 1950s prosperity, provoked little of the threat that lay in store for John Howard Griffin when he undertook his notorious undercover exposé *Black Like Me* (1961), or even that faced by the fictional protagonist of Sinclair Lewis's *Kingsblood Royal* (1947), based on the life of NAACP president Walter White, in which a middle-class white man chooses to "become" black when he discovers that he has a distant black ancestor.[142] Contrary to their own intentions, however, they drove the wedge between Jews and blacks deeper. Jewishness was the pivot on which

---

invulnerable," had become "a pretentious poet laureate." A decade later, explaining the meaning of Black Power in a *Partisan Review* symposium, Mailer would convert his neo-primitivism into a demeaning Afrocentrism. Because blacks have never been able "to absorb a technological culture," Mailer offered, the "real and natural intent" of Black Power advocates is "not to get better schools, but to find a way to educate their own out of textbooks not yet written," to use "herbs in place of antibiotics, witchcraft for cancer," to calculate not with computers but with "psychic inductions." Norman Mailer, "The White Negro: Superficial Reflections on the Hipster" and "Hipster and Beatnik," in *Advertisements for Myself* (1959; rpt. New York: Signet, 1960), pp. 303–4, 312–14, 334; Ralph Ellison, letter of September 28, 1958, in *Trading Twelves: The Selected Letters of Ralph Ellison and Albert Murray,* ed. Albert Murray and John F. Callahan (New York: Modern Library, 2000), p. 195; Anatole Broyard, "Portrait of the Hipster," *Partisan Review* 15 (June 1948), 726–27; Norman Mailer, "Black Power: A Discussion," *Partisan Review* 35 (Spring 1968), 220.

Mailer's and Krim's minstrelsy turned, but whereas their blackness was an imaginative construct, whiteness remained a physical fact and refuge.

That fundamental difference between the kinds of passing available always to the Jew and seldom to the black was the subject as well of Anatole Broyard's 1950 "Portrait of the Inauthentic Negro," a searching, disturbing essay that largely disappeared from view until its terms were refashioned by Philip Roth in the plot of *The Human Stain* (2000) half a century later. In contrast to the Jew, said Broyard in an argument that echoed Myrdal, the Negro, because of the "stain" of his skin color, normally cannot pass into the inauthenticity of self-contempt. That is, the Jew, if he is willing to pay the price of losing his natal identity, can choose to hide within whiteness, but the Negro cannot. Rather, the "inauthentic Negro" must occupy himself with either affirming or denying by his behavior "what the anti-Negro says about him, until his personality is virtually usurped by a series of maneuvers none of which has any necessary relation to his true self."*

Broyard's essay was prompted by Sartre's *Anti-Semite and Jew* (1946), first published in English two years later as a series of articles in *Commentary,* in which Sartre notoriously argued that the "Jew" is so powerfully a creation of anti-Semitism that Jews can only rarely escape or transcend the inauthenticity of defining themselves in neurotic reaction to hatred and caricature. Refining Sartre's theory in contrasting the black and Jewish experiences, Broyard distinguished authenticity from defensive reaction as a "stubborn adherence to one's essential self, in spite of the distorting pressures of one's situation." Lacking the disguise of whiteness available to most Jews, blacks may be driven submissively to adopt postures of "minstrelization" or, less inimically, distinctive vernacular styles of speech, dress, and humor that at once give rise to stereotypes and correlate with the creation of a separate culture. Worse, white romanticizing of the Negro's cultural exoticism—part of the historical "bestialization" of blacks that caricatures their speech patterns and purported physical aggressiveness and sexual prowess—imprisons him within a rigid role not of his own choosing. "The Negro," wrote Broyard, "is seen by certain misguided whites as a beautiful, exotic creature, oppressed by our society like a handsome black

---

* Quotations in subsequent paragraphs are from Anatole Broyard, "Portrait of the Inauthentic Negro," *Commentary* 10 (July 1950), 56–64. Although he does not develop the comparison sufficiently to make it persuasive, Broyard notes at one point that the self-hatred and sadism evident in the in-group use of the word "nigger" or in playing the dozens, which he characterizes as a game whose inventive insults are demeaning, finds an analogy among Jews in Nazi Germany, where "ironical authoritarian jokes were secretly circulated and served as a release for the repressed minorities."

panther in our cruel zoo." Born into an untenable situation but emancipated by "contemporary liberals" from responsibility and self-determination, the inauthentic black "plays right into the hands of his vigilant enemy, the anti-Negro."

Broyard's penetrating analysis, published several years in advance of "The White Negro" and "Ask for a White Cadillac," preemptively dismissed the exoticizing claims of Mailer and Krim and called equally into question the hypermasculinist seizure of power that would later become a trademark of the Black Panthers, his use of the phrase itself coincidentally predictive. Of course, Broyard's pronouncements are all the more fascinating because he himself, a "black" man born in Louisiana, of generations-long African American ancestry on both sides of his family, was passing for white, not just when "Portrait of the Inauthentic Negro" was published but, indeed, throughout his career. He thus embodied the inauthenticity of self-contempt that he made his subject, and the very terms he employed in a subsequent essay to condemn the stylized and, as he saw it, self-defeating stance of the black hipster might just as well have been applied to himself: "In his withdrawn abstraction, the cool Negro suggests the *stunned* Negro of slavery. The irony is that coolness is self-enslavement."[143]

It would be enticing to think that Broyard's masquerade was somehow proof of Ellison's argument in "Change the Joke and Slip the Yoke" (1958) that the Negro's "masking is motivated not so much by fear as by a profound rejection of the image created to usurp his identity. Sometimes it is for the sheer joy of the joke; sometimes to challenge those who presume, across the psychological distance created by race manners, to know his identity."[144] But even as Broyard's own disguise no doubt gave him special insight into the hazards of inauthenticity, it produced tautology. The inauthentic Negro lives at odds both with whites and with his own people, he argued, immersed in a performance of identity that becomes "his tradition, for he has no other. Unlike the inauthentic Jew, he has no cultural residue to which he can secretly return, or by which he can at least negatively orient himself." Yet these strictures applied with redoubled force in his own case, since Broyard's own act—being a "white" man—was no less a form of degrading minstrelsy, by his definition, than the pathetic darky act of the "inauthentic Negro."

COLORS AND QUOTAS

In 1921 Franz Boas was so pessimistic about the prospect of either blacks or Jews overcoming racial prejudice that he openly advocated racial mixing, contending that the problem of prejudice would not disappear "until the negro blood has been so much diluted that it will no longer be recognized just as anti-Semitism will not disappear until the last vestige of the Jew as a Jew has disappeared."[145] Less than half a century later, the one problem had become virtually moot, while the solution to the other still seemed much as Boas had imagined it. When Norman Podhoretz, echoing Boas and William Faulkner among others, asserted that the "Negro question" could be solved only by a "wholesale merging of the two races" through intermarriage ("let the brutal word come out—miscegenation"), his argument implicated Jews as white rather than nonwhite partners in the solution. Given that Auschwitz proved that the survival of Jews as a distinct group came at an unthinkable cost, Podhoretz wondered why blacks should wish to survive as a separate group, not least since the Negro's "past is a stigma, his color is a stigma, and his vision of the future is the hope of erasing the stigma by making color irrelevant, by making it disappear as a fact of consciousness."[146]

Whether or not Podhoretz meant to accept the Sartrean definition of Jewishness, as his appeal to Auschwitz implied, his prescription for African American survival appeared to offer only a choice between two kinds of "holocaust"—literal or genetic. Failing wholesale racial bleaching of the kind imagined in George Schuyler's satiric fantasy *Black No More* (1931), however, the sexual solution Podhoretz envisioned neglected to account for the fact that any person "partly" black would continue to be tallied in the African American column for many decades to come—and still today. Interpreting the racial stigma of blackness from an opposing perspective, James Farmer astutely isolated the dilemma of black particularism. America will become color-blind, he said, only "when *we* [give] up our color." Insofar as the regime of racial visibility made this impossible, blacks were left with the unhappy bargain—the one set forth by Podhoretz—of achieving some semblance of equality by conceding that "our skins [are] an affliction; that our history is one long humiliation; that we are empty of distinctive traditions and any legitimate source of pride."[147]

Jews might have color on their side, but color was a two-edged sword. Intermarriage with non-Jewish whites did not require Jews to lose the privilege of whiteness, but it posed a threat to communal identity; intermarriage with blacks might or might not pose a threat to Jewish community, depending on the partners' faith and that of their children, but it inevitably required a renunciation of whiteness. For a few renegades, the survival of Jews as a distinct group was itself immoral. Having accused the Israelis of being too "Jewish" and thus expressing the "astonishing mirror image resemblance between [the] Nazi theory of racial superiority and [the] Jewish hang-up as [the] chosen race," Allen Ginsberg asserted in 1963 that the impasse of Jewish liberalism—preaching tolerance but practicing exclusion, as he saw it—could best be broken by crossing the most proscribed racial line: "I think Jews should start making it with Negroes."[148] Such black-Jewish intimacies might prove difficult or not, though in theory they were no more destructive of Jewish community than intermarriage with whites if the outcome in either case was apostasy and non-Jewish progeny.* More deliberately than Podhoretz, however, Ginsberg spoke to the paradox that Jews' devotion to liberalism—of which the right to mix racially, as well as religiously, was a loaded symbolic example, according to *The Changelings* and "Zagrowsky Tells"—carried with it the risk that Jews might not survive, as Jews, in America.

Unlike Roth's Coleman Silk in *The Human Stain*, Anatole Broyard simply let himself be taken for white, not Jewish, which would have preserved a shadow of otherness sufficient, perhaps, to mitigate his betrayal—if betrayal it was. His case, as well as his appeal to Sartre's negative proof, pinpoints the lingering ambiguity of postwar Jewish whiteness. Anti-Semitism, said Arthur A. Cohen, is a way to tell the Jew "he's colorless, not white, surely not black, just Jew."[149] For the "just Jew," whiteness, like assimilation, was at once a convenience and an act of betrayal, a temptation and a curse, and the apparent erosion in Jewish devotion to black rights over the last half of the twentieth century has to be measured against fears that the Jewish community itself was being eroded—some-

---

* Although many black-Jewish marriages and the children they produced have prospered, of course, the tensions and risks are not hard to find, in both fact and fiction. The protestations of his Jewish girlfriend to the contrary, Claude Brown, in *Manchild in the Promised Land,* is proved right about the limits of mid-century Jewish liberalism when her parents send her away for the summer to separate them. (Brown himself professed to have no such illusions about the upshot of their potential marriage: "Can you imagine a kid being born a Jew and a Negro? You've struck out before you even start.") For her part, Hettie Jones, onetime wife of LeRoi Jones (Amiri Baraka), found herself turned into the *white*, not the *Jewish*, mother of "interracial" children: "And white I would be, because I knew the Jews—mine at least—would give me up." In Alice Walker's *Meridian* (1976), when the civil rights activist Lynne Rabinowitz calls her father to tell him that the child she had with a black man is dead, he replies: "So's our daughter. . . . *Nu?* So what else?" Claude Brown, *Manchild in the Promised Land* (1965; rpt. New York: Signet, 1967), p. 358; Hettie Jones, *How I Became Hettie Jones* (New York: E. P. Dutton, 1990), pp. 52–53; Alice Walker, *Meridian* (1976; rpt. New York: Pocket Books, 1977), p. 150. On the codes, practices, and perceptions of interracial unions, in particular between blacks and Jews, see Katya Gibel Azoulay, *Black, Jewish, and Interracial: It's Not the Color of Your Skin, but the Race of Your Kin, and Other Myths of Identity* (Durham: Duke University Press, 1997), pp. 89–177 passim.

times by the very ideals that were necessary to combat racism and promote integration.

Secularization threatened to make Jews "reverse Marranos" who displayed the social surface of Jewishness while lacking the inner core—"lox and bagels rather than Covenant and commandment," as Eugene Borowitz put it—but intermarriage, combined with low birthrates, produced greater alarm. Looking ahead to the tricentennial of 2076, Elihu Bergman ventured the pessimistic prediction that the Jewish population in America would in all likelihood be fewer than 1 million—perhaps as few as ten thousand—a prospect with dire consequences not only for United States Jewry but also for the security of Israel.[150] (The intermarriage rate for Jews, which in the 1940s had been less than 5 percent, reached 57 percent by 1993. By contrast, the rate for blacks had risen by that time to just over 12 percent, a relatively small proportion but a seventeen-fold increase since 1963.)[151] Leaving aside longer-term demographic threats to heritage and community, to be recognized as a Jew remained a constitutive fact of Jewish social and political life in the postwar era, even for Fiedler's "unreconstructed assimilationists." Jews were ambivalently comfortable, or comfortably ambivalent, with their role as "insiders who are outsiders and outsiders who are insiders."[152]

To the extent that they exemplified the new pluralism, however, Jews were bound to be increasingly vexatious partners in the civil rights battle. The pluralist tradition, wrote Talcott Parsons in 1967, is "neither one of separatism—with or without equality—nor of assimilation, but one of full participation combined with the preservation of identity," a status white American Jews and Catholics had generally managed to achieve, while blacks had not. Just as some religious denominations might well remain by this logic "Negro churches," Parsons added, many neighborhoods might well "continue to be mainly Negro, as many today are Jewish."[153] The simple symmetry so hopefully envisioned by Parsons was elegant in theory but proved fractious and unworkable in practice.

Anxious about the challenge of Black Power and, later, multiculturalism to liberal values, a number of Jews attempted to split the difference between assimilation and ethnocentrism by holding to the ideal of color-blindness in the political arena while trying to preserve their own distinctive sociocultural "color." Whereas Jews, like other white ethnics, wanted to preserve distinctive social communities so long as they were guaranteed political and economic equality, Nathan Glazer observed in 1964, the African American demand to abolish all barriers to social as well as political equality constituted a threat to Jewish particularity.[154] A 1965 formulation by Arthur Hertzberg, comparable to that of Podhoretz, reveals the dilemma of the Jewish liberal who stood for equal opportunity, individual rights, and freedom from discrimination, while still expecting to preserve a distinctive Jewish identity and to belong to a distinctive Jewish community. "The Negro has no culture other than the general American one," he argued, and therefore "whatever pertains specifically to him as a Negro will and should disappear in some future generation which will be color blind." For the same reason, though, when Jews fight on behalf of black civil rights, they are also fighting on behalf of their own "entry into the white majority" and thus accelerating the dissolution of Jewish communal identity.[155]

Rather than being paternalistic and opportunistic, Jewish devotion to black civil rights might therefore appear to be at odds with self-protection. Whether it was prejudice or an adherence to traditional liberal values that dictated Jews' conjoined belief in color-blindness and community, the tension, if not the contradiction, was plain to see. As Louis Lomax asked in *The Negro Revolt* (1962): "How do you satisfy a Jew's right to live among other Jews without abrogating my right to rent or buy the house next to his? What modern Solomon can mediate the conflict that arises when I try to rent a store on Harlem's 125th Street from a Jewish landlord who wants another Jew to have the space?"[156]

Even before the earthquake of Black Power, then, the fault line in Jewish liberalism had become visible. The emergence of an aggressive activism on behalf of liberal causes following World War II made Jews a formative influence in American politics and social movements, and their agenda was generally less chauvinistic than some have supposed. (According to a Chicago survey of the late 1950s, for instance, only one fifth of Jews thought it important to support Israel, but two fifths believed it essential to support the Negro struggle.)[157] Despite their activism on behalf of desegregation, however, the national backlash against communism, their own distrust of black militancy, and increasing attention to Israel, especially after the Six-Day War in 1967, gradually fortified a centrist position among American Jews, a seeming retrenchment that may simply have confirmed the inherent limits of their liberalism but in any case prompted a shift from a universalist focus on social action to a more particularist focus on Jewish "reawakening" and renewal of community.[158] Although Jews, in contrast to other white ethnics, did not always vote accordingly—in overwhelmingly favoring a liberal Democratic slate they defied "the laws of sociological gravity," said Albert Vorspan[159]—they had a special stake in preserving the meritocratic standards that had secured their access to educational and economic opportunity, while at the same time preserving the homogeneity guaranteed by religious practice and residential choice.

The prominence of Jews in different aspects of the civil rights movement and the overwhelming Jewish support for its goals, so long as they were framed in terms of equal opportunity and freedom from discrimination, likewise obscured the fact that middle-class suburban Jews in the North were not decidedly different from their non-Jewish counterparts in supporting the principles of *Brown v. Board of Education* but opposing programs of mandatory integration, an opposition that grew proportionately in reaction to the preferential policies of affirmative action. Its mission, said the Anti-Defamation League of B'nai B'rith in the 1950s, was guided by the need "to strike a balance between the 'good citizen' approach, driven by a dedication to the advancement of liberal democracy, and the 'good or bad for the Jews' approach.'" Combined with resistance to aggressive civil rights tactics and fears of resurgent anti-Semitism in groups such as the John Birch Society (or, on the outer fringe, the American Nazi Party), apprehension that assimilation and generational succession was leading to the disintegration of Jewish community had already tilted the balance toward the second approach by the early 1960s. By 1964, the American Jewish Congress concluded that "sadly, even liberals are attracted by the proposition that education can be separate and equal, and all that is required is the upgrading of slum schools."[160] Harold Cruse cuttingly pressed this argument a step further. Like some pre-Hitler German Jews who were "more German than Germans," he remarked, some assimilated American Jews, despite proclaiming themselves "brother-sufferers," are more reactionary than WASPs in their response to black militancy.[161]

The shifting positions of major Jewish organizations over time are instructive. From the 1930s through the 1950s, the American Jewish Congress, along with the American Jewish Committee and the Anti-Defamation League, had been instrumental in implementing studies and policies intended to diminish prejudice against Jews and break down legal and social barriers of discrimination. On the other side of the civil rights revolution, these same groups, along with other "white" ethnic organizations representing Greeks, Italians, and Poles,[162] filed amicus briefs in support of the plaintiff first in *DeFunis v. Odegaard* (1974), in which Marco DeFunis, a white Jewish student, charged that he would have been admitted to the University of Washington Law School but for its preferential policies, and then in *University of California Regents v. Bakke* (1976), the landmark Supreme Court case that upheld affirmative action according to race-based preferences. Whereas most African Americans saw affirmative action, including racial quotas, as a just means of providing access to education and employment, the most effective way to counteract discrimination, many Jews, on the basis of recent experience, remembered racial quotas as a discriminatory means of denying them access to education and employment. Although the intentions were opposed, the effects could not help but be entangled.

"Quotas send shivers down Jewish backs," observed Milton Himmelfarb, writing in *Commentary* in 1969, since the system being introduced is not, as in the universities and professional schools of the 1920s, designed "to keep pushy Jews (greasy grinds) from dispossessing the gentlemen, but to do justice to Negroes." (Subsequent articles in *Commentary*, the leading journal of Jewish neoconservatism—for example, "How Jewish Quotas Began," "Quotas by Any Other Name," "Is It Good for the Jews?"—codified an increasingly vocal Jewish dissent on the question of affirmative action.)[163] Legislation and judicial decisions of the civil rights era abolished social and professional discrimination against Jews, who could now live and vacation where they wished, join fraternities and country clubs, and enter openly into political life, Robert Langbaum pointed out, but equality achieved by numbers raised the fear that "more Blacks must necessarily result in fewer Jews." The change in principle "from discrimination to representation," said Daniel Bell, was a "reversal of radical and humanistic values," one that turned the "denial of a justly earned place to a person on the basis of an unjust group attribute" into a preference on that same basis. A philosophy of equality based on quotas of any kind led to an inevitable question: "And would the number of Jews in most faculties in the country need to be reduced because the Jews are clearly overrepresented in proportion to their number?"[164] Jews in that case might well be better off fading into whiteness.

Such objections had little merit in the eyes of most African Americans. Jews' insistence that affirmative action quotas amounted to reverse discrimination, said Benjamin Hooks, executive director of the NAACP, is "a most perplexing Orwellian perversion of language."[165] Like most whites, Jews generally believed—correctly, as it turned out—that the practices permitted by *Bakke*, however narrowly tailored, made the diversity argument an open door for race-based quotas or their practical equivalent. ("In order to get beyond racism, we must first take account of race. There is no other way. And in order to treat some persons equally, we must treat them differently," wrote Harry Blackmun, borrowing from McGeorge Bundy, in his concurring opinion in *Bakke*.)[166] In contrast, blacks generally scorned Allan Bakke and believed that the Court's action was not far-reaching enough. Jesse Jackson found the decision parsimonious and likened it to Nazis marching in Skokie or the Klan marching in the

South, while John Edgar Wideman looked back on Bakke as "the white minstrel who corks his skin, dons a stevedore's raggedy clothes, jumps on the stage, and dances Jim Crow," acting out "a grotesque parody of a black man."[167]

By the early 1990s, Jews and blacks were more likely than ever to be set in opposition, whether by themselves or others, in matters of educational policy—visibly, for instance, in debates over the appropriate criteria for triggering affirmative action, such as IQ or college admission tests.* Yet the great majority of blacks, a lesser majority of Jews, and a still sizeable number of liberal whites had by then concluded that the ideal of color-blindness was a delusion, just "particularism masquerading as the universal," as the philosopher Charles Taylor puts it.[168] Jewish opposition to affirmative action has been less salient in recent years—the American Jewish Committee, among other Jewish groups, came out in favor of it in *Grutter v. Bollinger* and *Gratz v. Bollinger* (2003), the University of Michigan cases that reaffirmed *Bakke*'s endorsement of limited compensatory treatment on racial grounds—but wherever Jewish opposition has survived, it has had nothing at all to do with the claim of commensurate experiences. Just the opposite: no Jews, observes the black scholar John McWhorter, himself an opponent of affirmative action, would accept having their children made "museum exhibits for gentiles."[169]

Along with the widening gulf between them on educational and economic grounds, their differing interpretations of the meaning of "equal opportunity,"

---

* Despite their implicit diametrical opposition to blacks, Jews made but a single appearance in the notorious 1994 study of race and intelligence by Richard Herrnstein and Charles Murray, *The Bell Curve*—specifically, in the fact that Ashkenazi Jews of European origin test higher than any other ethnic group. Jews, however, were featured more visibly in rejoinders to the book, which noted not only that Jewish immigrants early in the century had tested low, only to rise dramatically over the course of several generations, but also that "scientific" comparisons of Jews with non-Jews had in other contexts led to genocidal disaster. See Richard J. Herrnstein and Charles Murray, *The Bell Curve: Intelligence and Class Structure in American Life* (1994; rpt. New York: Free Press, 1996), p. 275; and the critiques, for example, of Thomas Sowell and Leon Wieseltier in *The Bell Curve Wars: Race, Intelligence, and the Future of America*, ed. Steven Fraser (New York: Basic Books, 1995). See also Sander L. Gilman, *Smart Jews: The Construction of the Image of Jewish Superior Intelligence* (Lincoln: University of Nebraska Press, 1996). On the matter of intelligence, it has also proved possible for Jews antagonistic to racial preferences to affiliate with white nationalists while rejecting their anti-Semitism. The philosopher Michael Levin, author of *Why Race Matters* (1998), which presents a case for the genetic intellectual inferiority of blacks, thus distinguishes the racism of white nationalists from their anti-Semitism in a revealing way: "People who think that whites are genetically more intelligent than blacks don't think that whites are genetically more intelligent than Jews. . . . If anything, they think Jews are too clever, they're too tricky, they take over everything." Carol M. Swain, *The New White Nationalism in America: Its Challenge to Integration* (New York: Cambridge University Press, 2002), pp. 70–71, 235–39, Levin quoted at p. 71.

not to mention "quotas," tell a very clear story about the different postwar trajectories of Jews and blacks in the United States. As Jews moved closer to a white, suburban, middle-class norm, the claim that they shared a contemporary condition of prejudicial treatment with other minorities—even if they did share such a history—became more difficult to sustain, and their insistence on it provoked consternation among blacks. Once Jews ascended to positions of power alongside WASPs and Catholics, said Harold Cruse with his typical acute hostility, they fought for the preservation of group interest by picturing themselves still as outsiders and manipulating the charge of anti-Semitism: "Having gained the cake, there are Jews who are not averse to eating it enjoyably in public; [yet] they would like to pretend that it is not cake but yesterday's bagels."[170] It likewise became more difficult to hold up the Jewish model for black emulation. Writing in *Commentary* in 1965, Bayard Rustin questioned the facile analogy to Jewish assimilation, citing three key differences: the Jewish tradition of literacy (in contrast to slaves, forbidden to read and write), Jewish family stability (in contrast to slavery, which destroyed family structure and with it cultural transmission), and the option for Jews of passing into undifferentiated whiteness. The postwar years, as Oscar Handlin characterized the transformation in law and custom that had taken place up to the civil rights era, witnessed the emergence of a "new racism" that absorbed all but blacks into a murky whiteness, leaving them alone classed as a "single inferior race" positioned beyond a "single impassable line, that created by the color of the black man's skin."[171]

In choosing as a consequence to make blackness the foundation of their community, African Americans did not accept segregation as inevitable, much less embrace inferiority. But they did embrace the value of separatism and, like Jews in at least this respect, gathered up the power of communal identity. Between a "good citizen" approach and a "good or bad for the blacks" approach, they usually tilted, of necessity, toward the latter. Updating *Beyond the Melting Pot* in 1970, Nathan Glazer and Daniel Patrick Moynihan reviewed their earlier conjecture that blacks, in their test case of New York City, might one day be treated as an ethnic rather than a racial group and came to a similar but, to them, worrisome conclusion. Reflecting on the impact of Black Power, they now averred that the valorization of blackness could be a "positive discrimination designed to strengthen and develop a distinctive group" with its own recognizable history and culture. They likewise believed, however, that insofar as the choice facing African Americans was not between assimilation and ethnic identification, as they had originally posited, but between ethnic identification and racial separatism, it was a choice between moderate success and "an unending tragedy."[172] The course of American race relations over the rest of the century would not prove them wrong. Jews might choose to live or not to live in a color-blind nation. Blacks had no choice.

In an eccentric but perceptive essay of 1970, Donald Kaufmann found that the moment of Jewish dominance in American culture was passing and predicted that the influence of Jewish "heart" and "schmaltz" would give way in the coming decade to that of black "soul"—the kind of cross-racialism envisioned by Mailer made bourgeois and corporate. Surveying the effervescence of secular American Jewish culture between *Gentleman's Agreement* and *The Joys of Yiddish,* a best-seller in 1969, Kaufmann decided that "the scars of Dachau and Auschwitz lack relevance for the now generation" and that Jewish influence had just about run its course. The time had come for black culture, inherently emotive, musical, and sexual, to take over the place held by the "people of the Book" and move to the "white center" of American culture through the exploitation of non-print media. Uncannily forecasting the crass pressures of commercialized multiculturalism, moreover, Kaufmann worried that in the 1980s and beyond, the United States would risk running out of "expendable minorities" with which to inject new sensations into popular culture.[173]

Kaufman's analysis took for granted that Jewish writing and social commentary had achieved prominence in the postwar years even as the "ghetto" culture on which its supposed unity of voice and theme was predicated began to disappear, only to return as a subject of nostalgic reconstruction. (Comparing the emergence of American Jewish fiction in the postwar years to the heyday of southern regionalism in the previous generation, Irving Howe noted that in both cases the subculture had found "its voice and its passion at exactly the moment that it approach[ed] disintegration.")[174] Kaufman also took for granted that the gradual displacement of Jews by blacks in old urban neighborhoods was matched, if inexactly, by blacks' rise to prominence in the realm of culture as well—unquestionably in popular music, soon in sports, and eventually in literature, stand-up comedy, film, and other arenas.

After the war, blacks took the place of Jews as the more obvious artistic subjects of racial discrimination, as when Stanley Kramer's film *Home of the Brave* (1949), based on the Arthur Laurents play, replaced the persecuted and combat-shocked Jew of the stage version with an African American ("anti-Semitism's been done").[175] Although he was wildly mistaken about the irrelevance of the Holocaust in American culture, Kaufmann underscored the changing authority of Jewish literary and intellectual voices that took place during the 1960s. Jews produced no less great writing and commentary, but they now did so more often as outsiders who had become insiders. No sooner had Jewish writers found their ethnicity eminently marketable, their alienation providing a "passport into the heart of Gentile American culture," quipped Leslie Fiedler in 1964, than they discovered that the Negro had taken over "the number-one slot among the insulted and the injured."[176]

As more finely tuned calibrations of ethnicity became indispensable to America's cultural life in subsequent decades, the historic leading roles played by blacks and Jews were diminished, the one becoming the polestar of "color," the other getting pushed to its very margin. Jews were white, but enigmatically not quite, so that Jewishness might still, in special circumstances, be the secret partner of blackness, as in Danzy Senna's *Caucasia* (1998), a novel about the fallout from 1960s radicalism. When Birdie, the mixed-race daughter of a middle-class New England WASP turned revolutionary and a militant black intellectual, goes underground with her mother, she assumes the disguise of the half-Jewish "Jesse Goldman," purportedly the daughter of an esteemed classics professor with a Jewish afro. ("When we were alone," writes Birdie in narrating her story, "[my mother] liked to remind me that I wasn't really passing because Jews weren't really white, more like an off-white.")[177] As in *The Human Stain* two years later, Jewishness constitutes an ambiguous zone between color and its absence in which a renegade from whiteness and blackness might provisionally hide.

The disappearance of Jews as minorities, from the end of World War II through the end of the century, was a matter of both choice and circumstance. Jews had been identified as minorities by Truman's Civil Rights Commission, for example, and they were mentioned more often than any other white ethnic group in the committee's final report, *To Secure These Rights*. As early as 1953, however, Steven Marcus had already placed Jews and blacks on contrary historical paths, the Jew "becoming more and more anxious to rediscover that by now elusive quality which makes him Jewish," the Negro "more and more anxious to discover his kinship with the white race and human history." Having left the ghetto, the Jew had lost his separateness; confined to the ghetto, all the black had was the "deadliness of his isolation."[178] By the late 1960s, Marcus was proved only half right. When black groups objected to Jews' being included in the Equal Employment Opportunity Commission's mandated form for employers to report the number of minorities they had hired, neither the Anti-Defamation League nor the American Jewish Congress nor the American Jewish Committee defended the practice, and any inclination to include Jews as minorities in such policy calculations was stymied by contention over the problem of quotas, preferences, and merit.

The "minority rights revolution" of the mid-1960s to mid-1970s was propelled by a combination of legislation, litigation, scholarship, and governmental fiat that spread compensatory programs well beyond their original objective—namely, to right the wrongs done to black Americans by slavery and Jim Crow. In the process, Jews and other white ethnics were squeezed into the first prescribed zone of what David Hollinger has termed the "ethno-racial pentagon," the five hypostatized communities of descent—Euro-American, Native American, African American, Hispanic/Latino, and Asian American—that came to govern much public policy and academic practice, the last two categories substantially augmented by the convergence of affirmative action with mass immigration, so that the children of impoverished Soviet Jews, for example, were denied educational and employment preferences offered to the children of wealthy Chinese professionals.[179] Even if Jews and other white ethnics were excluded from formal participation in the minority rights revolution, however, the institutionalization of multiculturalism, with its veneration of ethno-racial differences as transcendent values, made politicized ethnicity attractive for many groups.

Alongside the rise in Holocaust consciousness and reactions to the Six-Day War, the anti-Zionist posture of Black Power, as we will see in Chapter 5, prompted an affirmation of "Jewish Power," the most clamorous manifestation being the Jewish Defense League, which borrowed directly from the Black Panthers. In the world of popular culture, the 1978 television miniseries *Holocaust*, watched by some 120 million viewers, capitalized on the vogue for ethnic nationhood stimulated by the equally popular 1976 miniseries *Roots*, based on Alex Haley's Pulitzer Prize–winning book.[180] Indeed, some African Americans charged that *Holocaust* was the Jews' way of stealing their spotlight—a reversal of the charge by Jews that blacks "stole the Holocaust" in characterizing slavery.[181] If *Holocaust* cultivated acceptance of Jewishness as an ethnic rather than a religious category by blandly normalizing the Weiss family as assimilated German Jews, much as the American stage play of Anne Frank's life assimilated her Jewishness to a normative humanism,[182] and much as the television version of *Roots* diluted the "blackness" of Haley's original, its unequivocal stand on the question of Jewish resistance, as well as the uniqueness and intentionality of the Final Solution, imprinted the Holocaust on American cultural consciousness with unprecedented success. Two weeks after the miniseries, President Jimmy Carter announced the appointment of a presidential commission to evaluate plans for the United States Holocaust Memorial Museum, which put a conclusive end to any lingering American "silence" about the genocide of the Jews.

The reassertion of Jewishness as an ethno-cultural identity deserving of group recognition (if not governmental protection) was likewise apparent, for example, in the rise of Jewish Studies scholarship and university programs, the popularity of *Fiddler on the Roof* (on stage, 1964; on film, 1971), and acclaim for *The Joys of Yiddish*, "a book about language—more particularly, the English language," which had a mirroring counterpart in *Black English*, a book that likewise aimed to catalogue a vernacular language "in some ways even more American than other varieties of English spoken in the United States."[183] Yet if Jews' embrace of ethnic particularism came over time to rival that of other "people of color," it sometimes did so with more than a hint of parody or by self-consciously rejecting the strictures of Jewish observance, as in the camp iconography of the 1996 exhibition "Too Jewish?," the phenomenon of "The Tattooed Jew," the Holocaust track "Never Again" recorded by Jewish rap artist RemedyRoss, the comic glossary of popular Yiddish and Hebrew terms constituting the dialect of "hebonics," or the branding of the chosen people for generation J: "*Just Jew It.*"[184]

More often, though, Jews disavowed the racial splintering of identity politics and sought to sustain a commitment to pluralism within a commitment to integration.[185] In the bicentennial year 1976, using the catchy title "Liberty, Equality, Fraternity—and Ethnicity," Nathan Glazer, then antagonistic to affirmative action, worried that the rising call to recognize group differences and protect them by government intervention might destroy the co-fraternity necessary to nurture tolerance and establish social cohesion.[186] The public and often acrimonious debate over multiculturalism and diversity that ensued for the next quarter century (and counting) made wider and narrower circles around Glazer's premise without advancing much beyond it. Although some Jewish neoconservatives changed their minds about some kinds of racial preference—Glazer himself, for example*—some Jewish liberals in turn grew estranged

---

* The winding course of Glazer's thinking is especially noteworthy. As noted earlier, he argued in 1964 that the black effort to abolish all barriers to membership in particular social organizations and communities, even if it served the demand for equality, threatened the cohesion of self-selected Jewish life. In the decade leading up to Glazer's 1976 article, it seemed to him that the risk of "color-conscious" policy lay in its attempt to achieve equality by reinstantiating communal identity in the form of preferential treatment based on ethnic differences—that is, to achieve equality of station through inequality of means. In his astutely titled book of 1975, *Affirmative Discrimination*, Glazer argued that in a nation of minorities, "to enshrine some minorities as deserving of special benefits means not to defend minority rights against a discriminating majority but to favor some of those minorities over others," a source of special resentment among white ethnics who felt that they had overcome economic deprivation and discrimination while remaining loyal and grateful to the nation. By the end of the century, Glazer had

from race-based arguments, rejecting the "rapture of marginality,"[187] as Todd
Gitlin has called it, cultivated by many activists and scholars of ethno-cultural
endogamy. When Jews embraced the flourishing of racial and cross-racial, ethnic and cross-ethnic, studies, they were often expected to do so as (white) outsiders, not insiders (of color). In the mid-1960s Malcolm X, with his characteristic sense of the power of racial inversions, had turned the white ethnic merger
upside down by creating a rainbow coalition from which Jews would automatically be excluded: "Black, brown, red, yellow, all are brothers, all are one family.
The white one is a stranger. He's the odd fellow." More than thirty years later,
some Jews would still be trying to find a way back into the rainbow: witness the
1994 editorial in *Tikkun* claiming that "whiteness" must be adduced not from
skin color and the privilege that might go with it but rather from "the degree to
which one has been a victim of Western colonialist oppression," by which measure Jews, having been the "greatest victims" during the past two thousand
years, had earned the status of "people of color."[188]

THE END OF AN ILLUSION

Be that as it may, at key moments and in key arenas the post–civil rights era
saw blacks and Jews become more deeply estranged than ever. Not unlike quotas, the meaning of "black anti-Semitism" frequently became a flashpoint—
Jews, from their point of view, ever vigilant, blacks, from their point of view,
ever alert to Jewish hypersensitivity. ("When the first Jew becomes president of
the United States," Harold Cruse had charged in his 1969 reply to Norman

---

determined that the intractability of black acceptance and assimilation justified some forms of affirmative action and, in any event, explained the racial culture wars of the past quarter century. At each
turn, blacks have been the "storm troops in the battles over multiculturalism," he noted. Their differential experience of discrimination and segregation, including aversion to their intermarriage, has undermined assimilation as the ideal for all Americans. "Multiculturalism is the price America is paying for
its inability or unwillingness to incorporate into its society African Americans, in the same way and to
the same degree it has incorporated so many groups." Nathan Glazer, "Negroes and Jews: The New
Challenge to Pluralism," *Commentary* 38 (December 1964), 29–34; idem, *Affirmative Discrimination:
Ethnic Inequality and Public Policy* (1975; rpt. Cambridge, Mass.: Harvard University Press, 1987), p. 201;
idem, *We Are All Multiculturalists Now* (Cambridge, Mass.: Harvard University Press, 1997), pp. 95, 147.
Shelby Steele has designated this reversal of course the "Glazer trap," by which he means that Glazer's
recantation confused the remedies of affirmative action with the civil rights "mandate that called for
white America to seek redemption through racial reform." Shelby Steele, *A Dream Deferred: The Second
Betrayal of Black Freedom in America* (New York: HarperCollins, 1998), pp. 40–43.

Podhoretz's "My Negro Problem—and Ours," "other Jews will consider every Gentile who voted against him to be an anti-Semite.")[189] But the hypersensitivity of Jews was not really the question. When in 1984 presidential candidate Jesse Jackson referred to Jews as "Hymies" and New York as "Hymietown," declared Zionism a "poisonous weed," and sang "We Shall Overcome" with Yasser Arafat; when Chicago mayoral aide Steve Cokely claimed in 1988 that Jewish doctors were injecting black babies with the AIDS virus;[190] when Tony Martin, the author of several important studies of Marcus Garvey and Garveyism, claimed in The Jewish Onslaught (1993) that Jews were responsible for the curse of Ham, which "killed many millions more than all the anti-Jewish pogroms and holocausts of Europe";* or when Leonard Jeffries, a professor of Black Studies at City College in New York, added to the hackneyed charges that Jews run Hollywood the beguiling thesis that blacks, by virtue of their enhanced melanin, are racially superior "sun people," while whites are inferior, sexually

---

* The curse of the sons of Ham, often identified in the Judeo-Christian tradition with the people of Africa, derived from Genesis 9:25, where Noah curses Ham, as well as his offspring, for looking upon his nakedness: "Cursed be Canaan; a servant of servants shall he be unto his brethren" (King James Bible). Compare: "Cursed be Canaan; the lowest of slaves shall he be to his brothers" (Tanakh: The Holy Scriptures). Just as the Roman Catholic Church in 1975 issued a formal apology for the long-countenanced charge of deicide—that "the Jews" had killed Jesus Christ—so Jews, said Martin, should apologize for their purported invention of the Hamitic myth. Etymologically, Ham does not signify darkness or blackness, but later equations between black Africans and slavery reinforced mistaken etymologies and rabbinic associations, so that the myth of the curse of Ham, as David Goldenberg writes, "legitimized and validated the social order by divine justification," becoming entrenched in proslavery arguments for centuries to come. Even so, the curse's racial mythology was rather nonsensical, since, as George Fredrickson notes, it was said to have fallen on Canaan but not on his brother Cush, who in biblical exegesis inherited from the sixteenth and seventeenth centuries was the progenitor of the African race. Tony Martin, The Jewish Onslaught: Dispatches from the Wellesley Battlefront (Dover, Mass.: Majority Press, 1993), pp. 32–35; David M. Goldenberg, The Curse of Ham: Race and Slavery in Early Judaism, Christianity, and Islam (Princeton: Princeton University Press, 2003), pp. 105–8, 141–77, quotation at p. 177; George M. Fredrickson, Racism: A Short History (Princeton: Princeton University Press, 2002), pp. 29, 43–45, 51–52. For refutations of the notion that the Hamitic myth was a racist invention of Talmudic scholars or that Judaism holds blackness in contempt, see Efraim Isaac, "The Talmud Does Not Teach Racism," afterword to Harold Brackman, Ministry of Lies: The Truth behind the Nation of Islam's "The Secret Relationship between Blacks and Jews" (New York: Four Walls Eight Windows, 1994), pp. 101–4 (Martin had quoted from Brackman's 1977 dissertation in support of his argument); Stephen Howe, Afrocentrism: Mythical Pasts and Imagined Homes (London: Verso, 1998), pp. 277–79; and Marvin Perry and Frederick M. Schweitzer, Antisemitism: Myth and Hate from Antiquity to the Present (New York: Palgrave Macmillan, 2002), pp. 247–48. On Jewish attitudes toward blacks during the first centuries of the slave trade, normal for the era according to the author's argument, see Jonathan Schorsch, Jews and Blacks in the Early Modern World (New York: Cambridge University Press, 2004).

frustrated "ice people," with the Semites among them the "purest" and oldest of such "Neanderthal-Caucasoids"[191]—on such occasions, moral time seemed to march backward.

It did so once again after a black youth was accidentally killed by a car in the motorcade of the Rebbe Menachem Schneerson, leader of the Lubavitcher community in the Crown Heights section of Brooklyn in 1991, an incident that sparked Anna Deavere Smith's innovative one-woman drama *Fires in the Mirror* (1993). Dormant anger and distorted rumors led blacks to attack Hasidic Jews in reprisal, one of them stabbing to death Yankel Rosenbaum, a visitor from Australia. Both on the street and in the media, charges and counter-charges awakened the worst fears of Jews and blacks alike, as though a century of common striving for equal opportunity and acceptance by the nation to which both peoples belonged had come to naught. As Arthur Hertzberg wrote of the Crown Heights violence, "blacks saw ghosts of slavemasters riding into their quarters and not caring whom their horses might trample," while Jews saw the ghosts of "mobs [carrying] out pogroms against Jews while the authorities stood by."[192]

Crown Heights was demographically anomalous but symbolically representative of the deterioration in black-Jewish relations that had occurred by the 1990s, in particular the apprehension among Jews that black anti-Semitism, far from declining, was actually increasing. Even though right-wing anti-Semitism continued to find expression in white supremacist literature such as *The Turner Diaries* (1978) by Andrew Macdonald and in neo-Nazi churches and affiliated organizations such as the Christian Identity movement, whose adherents revile Jews along with other minorities and believe that white Anglo-Saxons are the only true Children of Israel, anti-Semitism in the general population of the United States diminished dramatically in the last decades of the century.[193] During that same period, however, left-wing anti-Zionism sometimes blurred into anti-Semitism among those antagonistic toward Israel's response to terrorism and its policies in the West Bank and Gaza—negative reactions that have made present-day Israel, in the words of Natan Sharansky, "the world's Jew"[194]—and anti-Jewish attitudes in general appeared to become more pronounced in segments of the African American community. As we will see in Chapter 5, the die for such anti-Semitism, as well as its confusion with anti-Zionism, was cast by influential proponents of Black Power in the 1960s, including literary figures such as Amiri Baraka. Granting that surveys of public opinion are often not reliable or conclusive and that a measure of black anti-Semitism must be attributed to the venomous attacks of a small number of public figures, most prominently Nation of Islam leader Louis Farrakhan, its apparent spread and vocal expression among the educated have made it more than a marginal phenomenon.[195]

Adolph Reed, Jr., has coined the word "Blackantisemitism" to describe something that he believes does *not* exist: there are black anti-Semites, to be sure, but the phenomenon of "black anti-Semitism" is a mythic species on the order of "'Africanized' killer bees . . . a racialized fantasy, a projection of white anxieties about dark horrors lurking just beyond the horizon."[196] Even though he does not seek shelter in the untenable argument that blacks, by virtue of their historic oppression and powerlessness, cannot themselves be racists,* Reed's arch objection too easily sets aside the fact that anti-Semitism is itself a racialized fantasy, one with a long and catastrophic history, as well as a continuing allure in black culture. It likewise ignores the fact that racist clichés, in the form of media sound bites, frequently dictate the tenor of contemporary public discourse.

Demagogic anti-Semitism on the part of some blacks may not have been enough to cause an upsurge in anti-Semitism among other Americans,[197] but Ishmael Reed's otherwise cogent argument that the real threat of extremist anti-Semitism and anti-black racism today lies not among blacks and Jews but rather among Protestant white supremacists and neo-Nazis—neither blacks nor Jews have "as much power to destroy each other as their enemies have to destroy them both," Reed remarks[198]—is similarly beside the point. Public debate is carried on not by the grass roots or the silent majority, but rather by elected or self-anointed leaders who purport to speak for the masses and who may gain attention not by the quality of their remarks but by the responsiveness of their audiences. While many blacks felt that the ill-considered and aberrant pronouncements of a few were erroneously made representative by a

---

* The argument that blacks cannot be racist achieved wider academic acceptance in the post–civil rights decades, but one can find intimations of it much earlier, as in a 1954 essay by Kenneth Clark that spoke to the condition of blacks in America by analyzing the position of postwar Jews: "The danger of extreme chauvinistic reactions among oppressed minority groups must be recognized as one of the more insidious consequences of hostility directed against them." The problem is exacerbated by the fact that "chauvinism on the part of the minority is used by the prejudiced majority group as justification for their prejudices and therefore tends to reinforce the initial hostilities. . . . The only difference which emerges between the chauvinism of a dominant group and that of a minority group is that chauvinism of the minority group is chauvinism without the power to oppress and persecute." By the 1990s, however, one of the foremost proponents of "structural racism," the argument's foundation, was disturbed by the sleight of hand through which a theory meant to apply to a group was cited to relieve individuals such as Louis Farrakhan of responsibility for their crude anti-Semitism. Clark, "Jews in Contemporary America," p. 123; Bob Blauner, "That Black-Jewish Thing: What's Going On?" *Tikkun* 9 (September/October, 1994), 29.

zealous media, many Jews felt that blacks were allowed to violate the public etiquette of the "civil rights compact" with near impunity,[199] and were too seldom
held accountable for their public anti-Semitism.

The outstanding example is the acclaim accorded Farrakhan and his depu-
ties, who spoke to enthusiastic audiences, not just among the less educated but
also on a number of college campuses, in the 1980s and 1990s. Farrakhan was
featured as presiding over a "Ministry of Rage" in a 1994 cover story in *Time*
magazine, where his charge that Jews had passed along to Arabs and Koreans
their historic practice of "sucking the lifeblood" out of the black community
did little to temper his economic blood libel.[200] He had already made headlines
by declaring Hitler a "great man"* and reviving odious displays of anti-Semitism that were almost parodies of Nazism. At a well-attended and raucous Savior's Day speech devoted to the theme "Power! At Last, Forever" at Madison
Square Garden in 1985, which concluded a nationwide tour of speaking engage-
ments, he delivered what might be considered the benchmark speech of the
black anti-Semitism that came so publicly to the fore in the late twentieth century (see illustration). As reported in *New York* magazine by Michael Kramer,
Farrakhan charged Jews with a history of chaos and destruction, as well as responsibility for the miseries of black American life, all the while portraying
himself as the persecuted one. "The germ of murder is already sewed into the
hearts of Jews in this country," he said. "Jews, this little black boy is your last
chance, because the Scriptures charge [you] with killing the prophets of God."
If the Jews were to rise up to kill him, however, Farrakhan promised that Allah
would "bring on this generation the blood of the righteous. All of you will be
killed outright. You cannot say 'Never Again' to God, because when He puts
you in the oven, 'Never again' don't mean a thing." In his own account of the

---

* Farrakhan's infamous statement occurred in a 1984 radio speech, during which he was attempting
to defend Jesse Jackson's remarks about "Hymies" and "Hymietown," made off the record during Jackson's presidential campaign that year. After being called Hitler by Jewish detractors, Farrakhan responded: "Here come the Jews [saying they] don't like Farrakhan, so they call me Hitler. Well, that's a
good name. Hitler was a very great man. He wasn't great for me as a black person, but he was a great
German. Now, I'm not proud of Hitler's evils against Jewish people, but that's a matter of record. He
raised Germany up from nothing. Well, in a sense you could say there's a similarity in that we are raising
our people up from nothing. But don't compare me to your wicked killers." The full quotation hardly
exonerates Farrakhan—he harked back to Marcus Garvey in responding to the appeal of fascism—but
it was less repugnant than the inflammatory headlines derived from it. Farrakhan quoted in Mattias
Gardell, *In the Name of Elijah Muhammad: Louis Farrakhan and the Nation of Islam* (Durham: Duke
University Press, 1996), pp. 251–52.

Louis Farrakhan at Madison Square Garden, New York City, October 8, 1985.
Larry C. Morris/The New York Times.

event, Julius Lester, a black convert to Judaism, likened it to a Nuremberg rally and found himself ashamed as a black man and frightened as a Jew.[201]

In subsequent years, Farrakhan has been given to a more conciliatory tone and often presented himself as a minister of interfaith peace and brotherhood, surely a welcome development. At the height of his influence, however, his magnetism served mainly to turn the esoteric ideas of Elijah Muhammad and the more politically calculated nationalism of Malcolm X into infamous Jew-baiting. The culmination of the Nation of Islam's misguided and preposterous campaign of anti-Semitism was *The Secret Relationship between Blacks and Jews* (1991), an incendiary work of pseudo-scholarship that held Jews largely responsible for slavery and the slave trade. (Contrary to the Nation of Islam's diatribe, Jews were responsible for perhaps 2 percent of slaves imported to the New World, made up during the era of American slavery only one tenth of 1 percent of plantation owners, and were outnumbered fifteen to one by free persons of color owning slaves in America.)[202] The book had little merit as scholarship, but it constituted the harshest possible rejection of Jews' interest in black civil rights. "Fact is, brothers and sisters," says a Black Muslim in Jon Michael Spencer's novel *Tribes of Benjamin* (1999), "the Jew participated in the movement for about four decades only because he had a bad conscience after enslaving, exploiting, and making fun of the black man for four centuries."[203]

When present-day black anti-Semites deploy the labels of "bloodsucker" and "interloper"—the one derived from the blood libel, the other from the accusation that Jews, regardless of their longevity in a nation, town, or neighborhood, have deviously intruded into the business affairs of a community—they blindly hark back not just to Henry Ford, the Farrakhan of his day, but to medieval practices.[204] It is instructive, too, that when Henry Louis Gates, Jr., took issue with *The Secret Relationship between Blacks and Jews* and other instances of extremist black anti-Semitism in a *New York Times* op-ed piece of 1992, his calm, judicious statement became controversial in its own right. Gates's willingness to break the ranks of racial uniformity confirmed Earl Raab's earlier insight into anti-Semitism at the height of Black Power. The measure of the survival of anti-Semitism must be not only the level of such beliefs, Raab said, nor even their rhetorical excess, which has been an abiding feature of anti-Semitic expression, but also the degree to which they are resisted or tolerated by those who do not share or express them. Neither is it mitigating, Raab added, to claim that the Jew stands symbolically for black rage against the white man—James Baldwin's thesis—for making one's enemy the Jew, the symbol of generic evil, is in some respects more dangerous than fostering anti-Semitism based on the behavior of individual Jews.[205]

To the extent that black anti-Semitism conveys intimacy bound up with resentment, emulation bound up with hatred, as Baldwin argued, the complexity of African American alignment with, and dissent from, a Jewish model of historical experience is nowhere more evident than in the evolution of the concept of the "black holocaust," to which we will return on several occasions in the chapters that follow. Black civil rights moderates—Martin Luther King, Jr., and other ministers of the Southern Christian Leadership Conference, for example—alluded to Nazism and the Holocaust with caution and awe. But some activists from the 1950s forward, beginning with Du Bois and Paul Robeson and reaching a high pitch in the coruscating rhetoric of Black Power, rich in predictions of imminent black genocide, capitalized quickly on the new rhetorical weapon. Ungenerously, blacks might resent the distant calamity of the Nazi genocide, which took the spotlight off racism in the United States; or compassionately, they might seek, along with those Jews who threw themselves into the cause of black rights, to bridge their differences through a common healing of comparable, if not equivalent, catastrophic experiences. Either way, they joined their historical experience to that of the Jews in ways bound to be provocative.

Attempts to draw an analogy between the Holocaust and slavery—understood in many such arguments to encompass an experience extending from the Middle Passage through the racial violence of Jim Crow—should generally be read as a symptom, not the cause, of a deeper conflict between blacks and Jews; but the reverse has also been true, often simultaneously. Although many Jews did not take it that way, perhaps more empathy than mockery was intended when the mission statement for Farrakhan's 1995 Million Man March, which borrowed from the Jews' most holy day, Yom Kippur, and requested monetary reparations like those paid to Hitler's victims, called on the federal government to atone for its participation in the "Holocaust of African Enslavement" and its subsequent role in "criminalizing a whole people."* But it was clear enough what was intended when the census of Jewish slaveholders and slave traders in *The Secret Relationship between Blacks and Jews* was called "Jews of the Black Holocaust" and when Jews were charged with "monumental culpability in slavery—and the holocaust."[206] The time-honored anti-Semitic sleight of hand that made Jews responsible for their own destruction was also on display when Farrakhan acolyte Khalid Abdul Muhammad, updating the 1964 accusation of Malcolm X that "everyone's wet-eyed over a handful of Jews who brought it [the Holocaust] on themselves," posed the rhetorical question in an address of 1993: "Everybody always talk[s] about Hitler exterminating six million Jews. . . . But doesn't anybody ever ask what did they do to Hitler?"[207]

As though to verify that such views might have merit, a pair of Jewish psychoanalysts offered the groveling recommendation that hate mongers such as Muhammad be invited to group workshops because "psychoanalytically speaking, they represent important communal black affects (especially narcissistic injury and rage), fantasies, and wishes that need to be addressed in terms of improving the overall black-Jewish relationship."[208] Such self-flagellation on

---

* The mission statement, written by Maulana Karenga, called for a "Holy Day of Atonement before the Creator" and asked blacks to atone for "collaborating in our own oppression by embracing ideas, institutions and practices which deny our human dignity, limit our freedom and dim or disguise the spark of divinity in all of us." For his part, Louis Farrakhan further elucidated the borrowing from Yom Kippur in a way that joined it to Passover as well: "Some of our friends in the religious community have said, why should you take atonement? That was for the children of Israel. I say, yes it was. But atonement of the children of Israel prefigured our suffering here in America. Israel was in bondage to Pharaoh 400 years. We've been in America 440 years. They were under affliction. We're under affliction. They were under oppression. We're under oppression." Maulana Karenga, "Mission Statement," and Louis Farrakhan, "Day of Atonement," in Haki R. Madhubuti and Maulana Karenga, eds., *Million Man March / Day of Absence: A Commemorative Anthology* (Chicago: Third World Press, 1996), pp. 143, 145, 17.

the part of Jews has been rare. In the Holocaust-inflected culture of the late twentieth and early twenty-first centuries, however, injuries done on the basis of race can never—nor should they ever—ignore the Holocaust. One argument of this book will be that blacks, for good reason, responded more quickly and intimately than whites to the rise of Nazism and that the revelation of the Jewish genocide changed the African American experience, or at least its public expression, even more than it did the broader American experience. The consequences were not insignificant. As *Holocaust* replaced *Exodus* as the stronger metaphor joining black and Jewish lives, a matrix of suffering, guilt, and the demand for reparations, in both moral and economic terms, threatened to become the ultimate meaning of African American identity, even as it provided irrefutable proof, for its proponents, that blacks were, indeed, America's Jews.

It may be that however dedicated the commitment of spiritual partners such as Martin Luther King, Jr., and Abraham Heschel, and however strong the bonds among grassroots activists, the dynamics of racism were too persistent, and the opportunities of each people too distinct, to prevent the disintegration of the black-Jewish civil rights alliance and the resurgence of vocal, if effectively narcissistic, black anti-Semitism. At the end of the twentieth century, the majority of American Jews were still thought to hold "liberal" beliefs about questions of social justice, but the evidence was far from conclusive. According to a study by Steven M. Cohen and Arnold Eisen, the "strongly universalist, politically progressive, and social-activism-oriented combination" of views that may have been more characteristic of mid-century Jews had declined by the 1990s. A more comprehensive analysis of post-1960s Jewish opinion by Cohen and Charles S. Liebman found, in fact, that some aspects of Jews' vaunted liberalism, including their sympathy for African American causes and its ascription to a universalized compassion stemming from Jewish values, were largely chimerical.[209]

The fracturing of the alliance occurred at a moment of maximum tension, as the heightened radicalism of the civil rights movement, fueled by the rise of Black Power and the assassination of King, collided with the rising prosperity and increased national visibility of Jews—from their overthrowing of quotas and restrictive covenants, to their prominence in intellectual and literary circles, to their increased political clout coinciding with the prestige of Israel following the Six-Day War in 1967. To the extent that the alliance was formally articulated—by groups such as the National Jewish Community Relations Advisory Council and the Southern Christian Leadership Conference, for example—it was mainly an artifact of the postwar years, part myth and part reality, says Arthur Hertzberg, with selfless devotion and high idealism accompanied at every point by friction and suspicion.[210]

By the last decade of the twentieth century, amidst frequent acrimonious charges and countercharges, a few Jewish and black compatriots, occasionally on the neoconservative right but more often on the liberal left, were still pressing forward with strong convictions. At the same time, African American observers across the political spectrum cast serious doubt on the alliance. Maulana Karenga rejected the idea of a black-Jewish alliance as a wholesale fantasy, while Cornel West contended that there was no golden age, only a better age lasting through 1967 but then undermined by Jewish neoconservatism coupled with—indeed, fueled by—black sympathy for the Palestinian cause and resentment of Jewish assimilation and economic success.[211] Julius Lester, in a characteristically contrarian view, argued that there was a working coalition that achieved its purpose in the Civil Rights Act, bringing about the legal end of segregation and an endorsement of voting rights the following year. "The black-Jewish coalition didn't end because it failed; it ended because it succeeded," remarked Lester, having finally brought about equal opportunity under the law. For Glenn Loury, in a more nuanced statement of the same position, the public disintegration of black-Jewish relations in the 1990s represented the inevitable "end of an illusion."[212]

Proving, perhaps, that the black-Jewish relationship is stronger in the life of the mind than in reality, there has been no subsidence in analytic commentary, memoir, and literature—sentimental, ironic, epic, farcical—devoted to the topic. Alongside the symbolism of those public figures who identify themselves as black Jews, or at least black and Jewish—writer Walter Mosley, law professor Lani Guinier, musicians Joshua Redman and Lenny Kravitz, actor Yaphet Kotto, and professional basketball player Jamila Wideman, among others—the lengthening shelf of books by the children or more distant descendants of black and Jewish parents, an issue to which we will return in the last chapter, may be counted as yet another sign that some lingering sense of an unusual, if not unique, kinship still survives. But such narratives, like much contemporary fiction and historiography, often carry a sense of wistfulness for alliances lost, as though only black Jews themselves, observant or not, remain as evidence of an intimate relationship now difficult to imagine and unlikely ever to be revived. It is telling, too, that the magazine *CommonQuest,* launched in 1996 by co-sponsors Howard University and the American Jewish Committee to "offer

African Americans and Jews a fresh opportunity to talk to each other with honesty and decency," ceased publication within a few years.[213]

The chapters that follow represent a more detailed attempt to say why the enigma of the "black-Jewish question" still matters—why a once vital relationship between strangers, now more estranged than ever, is indispensable not only to our understanding of modern American history but also to the future of a nation whose people seem ever in search of common ground.

CHAPTER 2

The Black Nation Israel

By the rivers of Babylon, there we sat down, yea, we wept, when we
* remembered Zion.*
We hanged our harps on the willows in the midst thereof.
For there they that carried us away captive required of us a song; and
* they that wasted us required of us mirth, saying, Sing us one of the*
* songs of Zion.*
How shall we sing the Lord's song in a strange land?
                                        —PSALMS 137

The Children of Israel of the North American captivity are like unto
their fathers in ancient Egypt who did not appreciate the signs and
wonders wrought by Moses.
                          —BEN AMMI [CARTER], *The Messiah*
                          and the End of this World

"AFRICA HAS HER MOUTH ON MOSES," wrote Zora Neale Hurston in *Moses,*
Man of the Mountain (1939), adapting the foundational Jewish narrative to the
culture of the black diaspora. "Wherever the children of Africa have been scattered by slavery, there is the acceptance of Moses as the fountain of mystic powers."[1] Contemporaneous with Freud's similar characterization in *Moses and*
Monotheism, which also appeared in 1939, Hurston's portrait of Moses exploited an ambiguity in his racial identity: Was he Hebrew or Egyptian?[2] A
comparable ambiguity in the meaning of the Exodus appears often in black
renditions and acquired even more pointed political meaning in the late 1960s
when Black Power anti-Zionists sided with Egypt, along with Israel's other ene-

mies. But Hurston's Moses—who led his people out of slavery in Egypt, gave them God's commandments, and in doing so founded the Israelite nation—was otherwise consistent with the widespread and long-standing African American belief that the Jews' liberation provided a model for their own.

Whether in the simple words of the freedom songs created in slavery or in the elaborate rhetorical allegories and, ultimately, the martyrdom of black America's exemplary Moses, Martin Luther King, Jr., the biblical Exodus has been the principal paradigm for the African American passage from bondage to freedom, a signal instance of cultural identity forged from the union of disparate histories. "'Go Down, Moses' is an absorption of certain Jewish religious traditions," Ralph Ellison remarked simply, "and that's my possession; no one can take that away from me." Or, as he said on another occasion, "*all* of us old-fashioned Negroes are Jews." Or, again, in his posthumous novel *Juneteenth,* where the Reverend Alonzo "Daddy" Hickman makes the emancipation of African Americans synonymous with that of the Israelites in his scintillating Juneteenth sermon: "The Hebrew children have their Passover so that they can keep their history alive in their memories—so let us take one more page from their book and, on this great day of deliverance, on this day of emancipation, let's us tell ourselves a story."[3]

Just as the epic story of the journey from Egypt to Canaan became deeply ingrained in Jewish life through the celebration of Passover, "ever imposing itself afresh upon the collective mind and memory" as a permanent symbol of Israelite national consciousness, in the words of Nahum Sarna,[4] so the black Exodus, through continual elaboration and reinvention, became an enduring symbol of African American nationalist consciousness. Other uses of the Bible—the jeremiads of the prophets, for example, or the inspiration of Jesus Christ as a figure not just of salvation but also of militant resistance—have likewise played a recurrent role in black culture, but none rivals the Mosaic paradigm, which became the public property of preachers, politicians, and poets alike.

Adapting the biblical figure to their own purposes, African American portrayals often idealized the leadership of Moses (in the biblical account, God's intervention is decisive, while Moses is a reluctant hero, and hence a marginal figure in the Passover observance) and his delivery of his people into the Promised Land (the biblical Moses did not live to see the conquest of Canaan achieved by Joshua). Some black uses of Moses pay close attention to nuances of the biblical text—Hurston's fictional account and the numerous borrowings by King are good examples—but others simply deploy the story as symbolic shorthand for political resistance and envisioned liberation. Risking her life numerous times to bring more than three hundred fellow slaves to freedom and later leading Union forces on liberating raids into South Carolina, the escaped slave Harriet Tubman thus came to be known as the slaves' Moses. A century and a half later, the stirring cadences of the famous spiritual—"Go down, Moses, / 'Way down in Egypt land, / Tell ole Pharaoh, / To let my people go"—remained very much alive for the Reverend Al Sharpton, who titled his 1996 autobiography *Go and Tell Pharaoh,* just as it did for the Los Angeles newspaper that likened O. J. Simpson defense attorney Johnnie Cochran to "Moses demanding that Pharaoh let God's people go."[5]

Whether figured as escape, flight, or exile, the longing for freedom symbolized by the Exodus also motivated schemes for colonization in Africa and elsewhere, individual acts of expatriation, and periodic mass migrations, as in the post-Reconstruction migration into Kansas of blacks who called themselves "Exodusters." When African Americans have employed the trope of the Promised Land, moreover, they have done so acutely conscious of their position as outsiders to a dream typically achieved within a matter of generations by most immigrants, including European Jews. The Exodus has remained a living necessity in black America because, unlike the Israelites, who left slavery behind in Egypt when they set out for the Promised Land, emancipated African Americans, especially in the South but not only there, endured a century-long regime of apartheid that recreated many features of slavery, making their prior claim to being more American than new immigrants paradoxical and tragic. Although it brought many forms of freedom, the flood tide of migration in the first half of the twentieth century that dispersed many of slavery's descendants to other parts of the nation made painfully evident that the habits of bondage were not confined to slavery or the South.

Described by proponents at the time and historians since as a new Exodus to the Promised Land, the enormous flight of blacks out of the agricultural South to the urban centers of the industrial North, Midwest, and West—some 6.5 million people over the first three quarters of the century—redefined the social, economic, and cultural landscape of America.[6] The Harlem Renaissance and the body of innovative black fiction and poetry that followed from it in subsequent years; the "blackening" of American popular culture as jazz and blues flowed out of the South and into the mainstream of world music; the eventual integration of blacks in education, athletics, and the media; the creation and expansion of legal, political, and social strategies necessary to bring about racial equality—all were results of a migratory transformation depicted at its high point in Jacob Lawrence's sixty-panel *Migration Series* (see illustration) and Richard Wright's documentary *12 Million Black Voices,* both appearing in 1941. If their profound impact on American life gave blacks an even stronger claim to equality and opportunity, many still found themselves stymied by prejudice and sequestered in ghettos, sometimes bound, as we saw in

Jacob Lawrence, "Migration of the Negro, Panel 3," The Migration Series (1941).
© 2005 Gwendolyn Knight Lawrence/Artists Rights Society (ARS), New York.
The Phillips Collection, Washington, D.C.

the previous chapter, in the most ambivalent of brotherhoods with the very people whose story they repeated. In Waters Turpin's *O Canaan!* (1939), for example, the migration of black southerners replicates that of the biblical Israelites until they reach Chicago, where some Jews befriend them while others flee in the face of their invasion of the neighborhood. Although the "black chillun o'God" followed "the sound of Gabriel's horn" when they migrated north "on that long-overdue Judgment Day," wrote Claude Brown in *Manchild in the Promised Land* (1965), "the children of these disillusioned colored pioneers inherited the total lot of their parents—the disappointments, the anger. To add to their misery, they had little hope of deliverance. For where does one run to when he's already in the promised land?"[7]

Richard Wright specifically counted the twentieth-century migration of blacks from South to North as part of slavery's radical dislocation of Africans and their culture to the Americas and argued that blacks, in just three hundred years, had "traversed through swift compulsion" a historical terrain equivalent to two thousand years of European history. "Hurled from our native African homes into the very center of the most complex and highly industrialized civilization the world has ever known," said Wright, "we stand today with a consciousness and memory such as few people possess."[8] Ripped violently from numerous tribal cultures and compelled to adopt new languages and gods, Africans and their descendants were thrust into slavery and subsequent persecution in the very land where their masters found liberty. In the Jews' history, to risk a syllogistic simplification, *Exodus* preceded *Exile*, which ended only after *Holocaust;* for blacks, the sequence was effectively reversed. Those Africans who survived the Middle Passage came not to a Zion but to a land of servitude and torment, while their progeny were left to reenact the quest for liberation generation after generation as though in impossible expiation of white sins.

In coming to consciousness of themselves as a new people, African Americans had to heed the ironic terms of their exile proposed by Derek Walcott, who writes in "The Sea Is History" of slavery's trans-Atlantic transport:

> Then there were the packed cries,
> the shit, the moaning:
>
> Exodus.
> Bone soldered by coral to bone,
> mosaics
> mantled by the benediction of the shark's shadow,
>
> that was the Ark of the Covenant.

In Walcott's puns on "mosaic" and "ark," a Promised Land is invoked in the very act that denies it, deliverance embedded within extermination in a single sequence. A modern mass Exodus under duress, the Middle Passage here transmogrifies the act of liberation into the coralized bone of countless slaves lying at the sea's bottom, while the ark that should hold the Decalogue, carried down from Mount Sinai by Moses, becomes another kind of ark—not Noah's ark of salvation but a slave ship imprisoning its doomed cargo.*

---

* The poem refers as well to Ezekiel's prophecy of the Valley of Dry Bones, based on a vision given him by God, that the dead and dispersed bones will rise again into life, that the nation Israel will be delivered from its exile: "Then [the Lord] said unto me, Son of man, these bones are the whole house of Israel: behold, they say, Our bones are dried, and our hope is lost: we are cut off for our parts. . . . Behold, O my people, I will open your graves, and cause you to come up out of your graves, and bring you into the land of Israel" (Ezekiel 37:11–14). As we will see on several occasions to follow, the Valley of Dry Bones is a staple in the African American sermonic tradition, as well as in literature—for example, in Henry Dumas's "Ark of Bones," where the ark is specifically a ghostly slave ship laden with the bones of millions, and the narrator, recalling Ezekiel's prophecy, is instructed by the ship's captain: "Son, you are in the house of generations. Every African who lives in America has a part of his soul in this ark." Derek Walcott, *Collected Poems, 1948–1984* (New York: Farrar, Straus and Giroux, 1986), p. 364; Henry Dumas, "Ark of Bones," in *Goodbye, Sweetwater: New and Selected Stories,* ed. Eugene B. Redmond (New York: Thunder's Mouth Press, 1988), p. 15.

George Shepperson cautioned in 1982 that only Jews may use the term *diaspora* without a modifier[9]—thus, the "black diaspora" or the "African diaspora"—but the term was by then well on its way to the pervasive use that it enjoys today throughout postcolonial studies. In adopting the vocabulary of exile and interlayering it with the vocabulary of the Exodus, African Americans took for granted that they were a diasporic people whose tragedy had been well expressed early on in the words of a haunting spiritual: "Sometimes I feel like a motherless child, a long ways from home." Unlike Jews, however, blacks were not defined by a distinct, inherited civilization and body of beliefs handed down century after century. They were and were not a single people—"more than an ethnic group, less than a nation," as Wilson Moses has written.[10] Nor, more important, did the twentieth century bring them a national homeland to which they could return. The founding of Israel on May 14, 1948, ended two thousand years of Jewish exile and, in the words of its Declaration of Independence, established "the natural right of the Jewish people to lead, as do all other nations, an independent existence in its sovereign state."[11] The Jewish diaspora did not end, but life in it became a choice rather than a necessity.

For Africans in America, however, no such alternative nation presented itself. Their exile—and their holocaust, some argued—as yet had no end, and they were unable to translate their identification with biblical Zionism into the realized political promise of modern Zionism. With a black Canaan nowhere in sight, indeed, it is possible to conclude that the insistent repetition of the Exodus paradigm has been a confused mistake. Speaking of the rootlessness endemic in twenty-first-century globalism, a condition he finds epitomized in the constant migration of Caribbean peoples, Caryl Phillips thus chose lines from John La Rose's poem "Not from Here" as his epigraph to a book of essays on black diaspora culture: "We were not in the exodus, / there was no Moses / and this is no promised land."[12]

Although some African Americans have wished for territorial sovereignty abroad or at home, the vast majority have desired something simpler, not in contradiction to but in refinement of Phillips's point. Especially as their freedom movement gained momentum in the aftermath of *Brown v. Board of Education,* African Americans reflected with greater degrees of intensity on Hurston's observation in her fictional life of Moses, cast as a parable of black leadership, that the legal downfall of segregation was but the beginning of a revolution in consciousness, for whites and blacks alike. Looking out into the Promised Land and remembering how often he had to fight those who wished to return to Egypt, Hurston's Moses dwells on the central dilemma of democratic liberalism: "Freedom was something internal. . . . All you could do was to give the opportunity for freedom and the man himself must make his own emancipation." Over half a century later, the challenge remained. In his 1995 keynote address on the occasion of the Million Man March, a jeremiad directed simultaneously at black Americans and the white United States as a governmental entity, Nation of Islam leader Louis Farrakhan turned the Exodus in a similar direction in describing a nationalist vision of self-discovery and healing: "Now the word exodus means departure—a going out. A way out. . . . But a way out of something bigger than our affliction." Rather, said Farrakhan, African Americans must "come out from under the mind of a slave . . . self-afflicted with the evil of Black inferiority" inculcated by white supremacy.[13]

It might appear ironic that Farrakhan, widely viewed at the time as the mainspring of contemporary black anti-Semitism, would call upon the master metaphor of Jewish tradition. In fact, the Exodus holds an archetypal force in Nation of Islam ideology dating to the era of Elijah Muhammad, and Farrakhan's simple transformation of it into a psychological and political condition, rather than a matter of recovering or establishing territorial rights to a homeland, is indicative of its evocative but nebulous place in African American history. With the exception of certain strains of Afrocentrism or periodic calls, by both blacks and whites, for black colonization in Africa or elsewhere, the Promised Land envisioned by African Americans has typically been an amalgam of emancipation, equal rights, political representation, and economic justice. "If the Afro-American does not find his salvation in the United States," said Harold Cruse, "he will find it nowhere."[14] If blacks are to achieve the Promised Land, that is to say, they will have to do so in the Egypt of America.

GOD'S CHOSEN PEOPLE

> *i walk on bones*
> *snakes twisting*
> *in my hand*
> *locusts breaking my mouth*
> *an old man*
> *leaving slavery*
> *home is burning in me*
> *like a bush*
> *God got his eye on*
> *—Lucille Clifton, "Moses"*

The chosenness of Jews, Will Herberg once wrote in distinguishing this central tenet of Judaism from other conceptions of racial or religious election, is seldom "an ethnocentric device of self-flattery and self-glorification." The fact that the people Israel are neither a nation nor a religious group alone, but rather a community created by God's covenant, enforces upon them a destiny and an obedience to ancient, transcendent law that has no obvious analogue in black America.[15] Nevertheless, a people may have many motives for deeming themselves chosen, some spurious or inconsequential, some sincere and profound, and the ambiguous imperative inherent in chosenness—its equivocation between favor and contempt, between messianic potential and merciless persecution—has made the trope no less pressing for blacks than for Jews. To recall James Baldwin's formulation, cited at the outset of the previous chapter: just "as Israel was chosen," so must African Americans, "these latter day exiles," be recognized in God's covenant with Abraham and "his children's children forever."[16]

From their earliest adaptations of scripture, African Americans found themselves chosen by virtue of their readiness for God's favor and their longing for liberation. In an 1827 Fourth of July sermon celebrating the abolition of slavery in New York, Nathaniel Paul, pastor of the First African Baptist Society of Albany, looked forward to the appearance of a black Moses, "like to the wise legislator of Israel, who shall take his brethren by the hand, and lead them forth from worse than Egyptian bondage, to the happy Canaan of civil and religious liberty."[17] What Du Bois heard as the slave spirituals' "voice of exile" was their Hebrew message of chosenness, for in the prisonhouse of bondage, said R. Nathaniel Dett, another early analyst of the black spirituals, slaves found in "the story of the children of Israel much in the way of a text that was ready made."[18] More than that, wrote James Weldon Johnson of the beautiful music fashioned by the "black and unknown bards" of slavery, African Americans turned their paradoxical position as slaves in a nation dedicated to democratic freedom into a sign of God's special salvific attention:

> It is not possible to estimate the sustaining influence that the story of the trials and tribulations of the Jews as related in the Old Testament exerted upon the Negro. This story at once caught and fired the imaginations of the Negro bards, and they sang, sang their hungry listeners into a firm faith that as God saved Daniel in the lion's den, so He would save them; as God preserved the Hebrew children in the fiery furnace, so would He preserve them; as God delivered Israel out of bondage in Egypt, so would He deliver them.[19]

Generations later, the story of the Hebrew children, their texts of chosenness and exile, proved no less compelling to the modern-day Chicago street gang the Blackstone Rangers, one of whose leaders graphically depicted the gang's structure, drawn on a piece of cardboard, as a black nationalist "HOUSE OF DAVID" with slogans and named subunits of the gang distributed within different sections of a Star of David, the whole underlined with admonitions to study the biblical prophets, Hebrew, and self-defense, and to recognize that blacks are "God's chosen people."[20]

That blacks might epitomize both the promise of American democracy and its betrayal, both election and exile, was possible because delivery into the Promised Land is, arguably, the dominant *American* trope. "Jerusalem was, New England is, they were, you are, God's own, God's covenant people," said New England minister Samuel Wakeman in an election day sermon published in 1685. "Put but New England's name instead of Jerusalem."[21] Springing from a deep identification with the Israelite experience, the beginnings of the colonial American nation in the Puritan immigration were inscribed within a sacralized narrative of biblical redemption—what Werner Sollors has spoken of as the nation's "typological ethnogenesis."[22] According to Protestant millennialist theory, Americans were the "Chosen Race," the people selected by God to liberate the world from the darkness of unbelief in fulfillment of Christian scripture. As "Israel *redivivus*," the political nation acquired eschatological meaning, and its destiny was made manifest by the absorption of Hebrew biblical patterns into national history, with the scope of its potential conquest extending not just to the borders of the future United States but throughout the entire Western Hemisphere.[23] "Escaped from the house of bondage," as Herman Melville put it in a cogent statement of the nation's post-revolutionary claim on the new Canaan in *White-Jacket* (1850) which quoted from Exodus 20:2, America is "the Israel of our time; we bear the ark of liberties of the world." As "the peculiar, chosen people," wrote Melville, Americans were the long-awaited "political Messiah," to whom God had given, "for a future inheritance, the broad domains of the political pagans, that shall yet come and lie down under the shade of our ark, without bloody hands being lifted."[24]

Although the Puritans, like other Christians from time to time, considered the conversion of the Jews a harbinger of the conversion of all mankind, the more important Americanization of the Jews—and with it the Judaization of America—was initiated early in the post-revolutionary era, if one may extrapolate from the oratory of Rabbi Isaac Mayer Wise. Speaking in 1858, Wise declared the Fourth of July to be a second Passover, the "second redemption of mankind from the hands of their oppressors, the second interposition of Providence in behalf of liberty."[25] Passover's special message for Americans echoed on into the next century, for example, in Mordecai Kaplan's argument that the Exodus offered a rationale for moral action and ritual observance in the Jewish community not unlike the Declaration of Independence.[26] And why not? After all, Thomas Jefferson, in the months following the birth of the new nation, had proposed as inscriptions for the two sides of the Great Seal of the United States "the children of Israel in the wilderness, led by a cloud by day and a pillar of fire by night," on one side, and the Saxon chiefs Hengist and Horsa, "whose political principles and form of government we have assumed," on the other.[27] Exodus and Manifest Destiny were more than compatible; they were synonymous.

For its African slaves and their heirs, however, America's providential mission to bring liberty and the gospel to the world labored under a curse, and their very existence was a reminder that the American Zion was achieved through the destruction or bondage of its own Canaanite peoples. "Born in genocide" in its wars against American Indians, Martin Luther King, Jr., would later say, the nation was further "disfigured" by the practice of slavery, which stamped it with a duplicitous meaning as it threw off British rule while failing to throw off its own brutalizing colonialist practices.[28] For Frederick Douglass, in contrast to Wise, slavery so profoundly stained democratic ideology that no true celebration of the Fourth of July was yet possible. In his famous address "The Meaning of July Fourth for the Negro," delivered on July 5, 1852, Douglass rebuked his audience for celebrating a national day of political freedom, likened to "what the Passover was to the emancipated people of God," and declared it instead a day of mourning for African Americans: "To drag a man in fetters into the grand illuminated temple of liberty, and call upon him to join you in joyous anthems, were inhuman mockery and sacrilegious irony."[29] Delivered not into Canaan but Babylon, blacks were left, to join Douglass in citing the psalm that became widespread in African American and Afro-Caribbean usage, weeping beside the waters for a barely remembered Zion and singing the Lord's song in a strange land.

Through their own typological readings of Exodus, African Americans thus constituted themselves oppositionally as a "nation within a nation"—a nation *held in bondage* within a nation. They created a redemptive framework in which God would deliver them, as he had delivered Israel, from oppression and in which the nation, their Egypt, faced God's wrathful judgment—as envisioned in David Walker's *Appeal to the Coloured Citizens of the World* (1829) or in the conclusion of *Uncle Tom's Cabin* (1850)—unless emancipation and repentance were achieved by fiat or by force of arms. As Walker, Douglass, and other black abolitionists argued, moreover, it was blacks, in their quest for freedom, who were chosen to bear the special burden of repairing the flawed design of the revolutionary fathers, if necessary through violent rebellion,[30] much as Ellison was to argue a century later that it was the African American, in his "tragic knowledge" of democracy, who demands "that there be a closer correlation between the meaning of words and reality, between ideal and conduct, our assertions and our actions."[31]

African Americans began, too, with a further conceptual ambivalence in their adaptation of biblical tradition. Except in the case of black Jews, their deployment of the Exodus derived from what most of them thought of first of all as Christian scripture, not the Hebrew Bible. Compressing historical time into a multilayered, symbol-rich sacred time, the slaves' spirituals spliced together Old and New Testament figures and allegories. Images of the suffering Christ and the suffering Jew were wedded in "the image of the suffering slave," to recall Baldwin's description once more, but by no means was their redeemer a passive martyr. The slaves' Jesus Christ often more resembled an avenging Hebrew prophet than a Christian messiah, a warrior who promised delivery from bondage as well as spiritual liberation.[32] It was in no way contradictory to the tradition of the black Exodus that some verses of "Go Down, Moses," a song with numerous vernacular variations, turn the Israelite liberation in the direction of Christian eschatology: "Oh, let all from bondage flee, / Let my people go, / And let us all in Christ be free, / Let my people go."[33] A chaplain with the Union Army was struck by the degree to which slaves, reversing Christian typology, had folded the redeemer Jesus into the liberator Moses: "There is no part of the Bible with which they are so familiar as the story of the deliverance of the children of Israel. Moses is their *ideal* of all that is high, and noble, and perfect, in man. I think they have been accustomed to regard Christ not so much in the light of a *spiritual* Deliverer, as that of a second Moses who would eventually lead them out of their prison-house of bondage."[34]

This, surely, was the Moses envisioned by the black rebel Denmark Vesey, a former slave who launched an ultimately unsuccessful uprising, when, in 1822, he began preaching to congregants of the African Church of Charleston, South Carolina, that they were the children of Israel awaiting deliverance from bondage. (In some traditional accounts, Vesey was said to have been the inspiration for "Go Down, Moses.")[35] Long after Emancipation and the betrayal of Reconstruction, the same militancy, driven by the same ambivalent adaptation of scriptural models of action, was alive in latter-day vernacular renderings of the Old Testament such as the *Black Bible Chronicles* (1993), advertised as a "survival manual for the streets" and including the stories "Cain Wastes Abel" and

"Abram Kicks Some Butt"; or the more reactionary Black Power fusillade *The Nigger Bible* (1967), whose signifying renditions of familiar scripture ("In the beginning was Not the Word") shows the Bible to be a tool of repression even as it longs for the security of Mosaic leadership: "Oh, but to create a Nigger God like that of the Jews, and a Leader with the guile, mind and spirit of their Moses! You, Nigger Converts, are born inheritors of this very same God and His Commandments."[36]

The radical theology of the Black Power era, assimilating biblical scripture to the worldwide class struggle envisioned by Lenin, Mao, Che Guevara, and other revolutionaries, frequently aligned African Americans with regimes inimical to Jews (as in the case of the Arabs and the Palestinians) and to Judaism (as in the case of communism). But this dimension of the black Exodus was itself a refinement of the right to revolution, at once biblical and secular, implicit in a number of slave spirituals and articulated as ideology by Douglass, Vesey, and others. Modifying both Christian eschatology and the obedience to God's commandments written into the story of the Israelites' liberation, the scripture of freedom adopted by most African Americans put them closer to those revolutionary thinkers in the tradition of English Puritanism or Latin American liberation theology who, as Michael Walzer has put it, "judaize" the messianic narrative by returning it to political history and seeking secular liberation within worldly time.[37] The redemptive, pacifist teachings of Jesus might thus be harmonized with the resort to militant struggle by Moses and the prophets.

The curative force of the Bible within the black political tradition, grounded in the spirituals and the discourse of abolitionism, reached its apex in the biblical republicanism of the Reverend Martin Luther King, Jr., in which the redemptive power of delivery into a Promised Land lay in its realization of democratic ideals.[38] In the event, of course, the power of King's appeal became uncannily bound up with his own martyrdom. Speaking on behalf of striking sanitation workers in Memphis, Tennessee, on April 3, 1968—just before the Passover holiday he was expected to spend with Rabbi Abraham Heschel's family—King offered his most famous, and what proved to be his valedictory, invocation of the Exodus: "I just want to do God's will. And He's allowed me to go up to the mountain. And I've looked over. And I've seen the Promised Land. I may not get there with you. But I want you to know tonight, that we, as a people will get to the Promised Land."[39] The next day, King was assassinated, and many cities were soon in flames.

Here, as elsewhere in his hallmark improvisatory style, King fashioned variations on the Exodus by borrowing from a vast theological literature and an equally rich folk tradition.* Placing himself within a style of religious leadership in which sacred symbology mobilizes community and legitimates resistance, King turned everyday faith into a language of racial justice inspired in equal measure by Christian and Jewish traditions. As Andrew Young recalled of King's organizing efforts in Mississippi:

> Nobody could have ever argued [simply about] segregation and integration and gotten people convinced to do anything about that. But when Martin would talk about leaving the slavery of Egypt and wandering in the wilderness of separate but equal and moving into a promised land, somehow that made sense to folks. . . . It was nobody else's political theory, but it was their grass roots ideology. It was their faith; it was the thing they had been nurtured on. And when they heard that language, they responded. You could go into Mississippi and tell people they needed to get themselves together and get organized. And that didn't make much sense. But if you started preaching to them about dry bones rising again, everybody had sung about dry bones. Everybody knew the language. . . . You had a ready framework around which you could organize people.

In his Memphis speech, King therefore alluded to the "streets flowing with milk and honey," but knowing that the Canaan of true equality might remain elusive for many years to come, he was compelled to remind his audience that "God has commanded us to be concerned about the slums down here, and his children who can't eat three square meals a day." The new Atlanta

---

* A vivid early example within a large repertoire is his sermon "The Death of Evil upon the Seashore," preached on May 17, 1956, in which Egypt is the "symbol of evil in the form of humiliating oppression, ungodly exploitation and crushing domination." With the Israelites symbolizing "goodness, in the form of devotion and dedication to the God of Abraham, Isaac, and Jacob," King develops an extended allegory of freedom and justice, with the forces of oppression and colonialism finally overcome as the Red Sea opens and enslaved peoples win their freedom. In its desegregation decision in *Brown v. Board of Education,* said King, the Supreme Court had awakened the moral conscience of white America and opened the Red Sea, so that it was possible to look back now and see "segregation caught in the rushing waters of historical necessity" and "the evils of colonialism and imperialism dead upon the seashore." Martin Luther King, Jr., "The Death of Evil upon the Seashore," in *The Papers of Martin Luther King, Jr.,* ed. Clayborne Carson et al., 5 vols. to date (Berkeley: University of California Press, 1997), III, 259–61. Although King was hardly alone in the practice, for evidence that substantial portions of "Death of Evil upon the Seashore" were borrowed from "Egyptians Dead upon the Seashore," a sermon by the abolitionist Phillips Brooks, as well as other sources, see Keith D. Miller, *Voice of Deliverance: The Language of Martin Luther King, Jr., and Its Sources* (New York: Free Press, 1992), pp. 13–17, 121–22, 153–58.

Abraham Heschel and Martin Luther King, Jr. (center front), in Vietnam
War protest at Arlington National Cemetery, February 6, 1968. Behind
King on his left is Ralph Abernathy; immediately to King's left, holding
the Torah, is Maurice Eisendrath. © Bettmann/Corbis.

and the new Philadelphia and the new Los Angeles, he argued, were as important to talk about as the new Jerusalem: in fact, they were one and the same.[40]

Not surprisingly, King's references to Jews were always admiring and sympathetic, and his invocations of the Holocaust as a point of reference for the history of African Americans were for the most part careful, even ecumenical. Although he was capable of ironically comparing the "legal" segregation of the South to Hitler's "legal" promulgation of race laws, as he did in "Letter from Birmingham City Jail" (1963), he did not shrink from charging that the growing toleration of violence among black radicals was comparable to the violence of the Third Reich, as he did in *Where Do We Go from Here?* (1967). King and the Southern Christian Leadership Conference enjoyed the support of leading Jewish figures, most prominently Abraham Heschel, a refugee from Nazi Germany with whom King had been brought together at the National Conference on Religion and Race in 1963. On that occasion, Heschel called upon the example of the biblical prophets, who confronted injustice and oppression without losing their faith. The main participants "at the first conference on religion and race" were Pharaoh and Moses, said Heschel, but the modern Exodus was not yet complete, for "it was easier for the children of Israel to cross the Red Sea than for a Negro to cross certain university campuses."[41]

Heschel walked with King in the voting rights march from Selma to Montgomery in 1965—"I felt my legs were praying," Heschel said after the march—and later in protest of the Vietnam War (see illustration), and he joined him in publishing identically titled 1964 essays, "What Happens to Them Happens to Me," devoted to the theme "Am I my brother's keeper?"[42] In turn, King paid frequent tribute to Jewish support for black rights, defended Israel's right to exist, supported the Jewish state during the Six-Day War (while calling for a negotiated settlement in keeping with his advocacy of nonviolence),[43] and on more than one occasion opposed the anti-Zionism then taking increasing hold in the Black Power movement. Although the accuracy of the quotation has been questioned and it became the source of a serious hoax, King is said by Seymour Martin Lipset to have replied to a black student who criticized Zionists at a 1968 dinner: "Don't talk like that! When people criticize Zionists, they mean Jews. You're talking anti-Semitism."*

Even if he spoke for the majority of African Americans, however, King's voice was destined to be drowned out in years following by those delivering a

---

* Eventually, through channels difficult to pin down, this quotation was transformed into a text purportedly by King titled "Letter to an Anti-Zionist Friend," which was said to have appeared in an August 1967 issue of *Saturday Review* and later to have been reprinted in a book titled *This I Believe: Selections from the Writings of Dr. Martin Luther King, Jr.* (1971). The "Letter," as quoted by Marc Schneier, reads in part: "You declare, my friend, that you do not hate Jews, you are merely 'anti-Zionist.' And I say, let the truth ring forth from the high mountain tops, let it echo through the valley of God's green earth: When people criticize Zionism, they mean Jews—this is God's own truth. . . . So know also this: anti-Zionist is inherently anti-Semitic, and ever will be so . . . the anti-Semite must constantly seek new forms and forums for his poison. How he must revel in the new masquerade! He does not hate the Jews, he is just 'anti-Zionist'!" Unfortunately, even though these sentiments are in no way at odds with King's views, there is no such number of the *Saturday Review* and no such volume of King's writings. The "Letter," as its awkward mimicry of King's oratorical style might have suggested, is a hoax, but that did not prevent it from being cited by a number of King scholars, including the editor of the King papers, Clayborne Carson. See Seymour Martin Lipset, *"The Socialism of Fools": The Left, the Jews, and Israel* (New York: Anti-Defamation League of B'nai Brith, 1969), p. 7 (Lipset's article first appeared in *Encounter*, December 1969); Marc Schneier, *Shared Dreams: Martin Luther King, Jr., and the Jewish Community* (Woodstock, Vt.: Jewish Light Publishing, 1999), p. 178; Clayborne Carson, "Black-Jewish Universalism in the Era of Identity Politics," in Jack Salzman and Cornel West, eds., *Struggles in the Promised Land: Toward a History of Black-Jewish Relations in the United States* (New York: Oxford University Press, 1997), p. 190. For corroboration of the hoax, see Lee Green, "Letter by Martin Luther King a Hoax," CAMERA (Committee for Accuracy in Middle East Reporting in America), January 22, 2002, http://www.camera.org/index.asp?x_context=7&x_issue=369&x_article=369; and Fadi Kiblawi and Will Youmans, "Israel's Apologists and the Martin Luther King, Jr., Hoax," *The Electronic Intifada*, January 19, 2004, http://electronicintifada.net/v2/article2356.shtml (accessed March 22, 2004).

less brotherly message. Their inspiration by anticolonialist theory and Third World revolutionary movements, as we will see, divorced a number of black leaders of the younger generation from the "emancipatory liberalism"[44] of King and allied them with a more militant strain of black liberation theology that reached back to the Ethiopianism of Edward Blyden and the Afro-Zionism of Marcus Garvey. Motivated by a different understanding of the Holocaust and expressing solidarity with the Palestinians and Israel's Arab enemies, proponents of Black Power found the biblical story of the Israelites' liberation, as Hurston intuited, open to interpretation as a racially framed narrative of colonial conquest—even one borrowed from Arab or African traditions. Palestinians "had been in Palestine long before Musa [Moses]," said Yasser Arafat in 1992. "He was our guest, when he escaped from Pharaoh . . . and married one of us."[45]

First as slaves and then as post-emancipation exilic people still searching for freedom, if not restoration to a homeland, blacks expressed a pronounced sympathy for modern Zionism. Support for the Jews' return to Palestine played a prominent role in African American thought until at least the 1960s, at which point the anti-Zionism of black radicals, the vanguard of the New Left, turned ambivalence about the model into outright rejection of it. Such oppositional views were in harmony with the "Canaanism" of those mid-century Israeli writers who asserted the existence of an autochthonous Hebrew-Palestinian culture overridden by colonialist Zionism.[46] They were even closer in spirit to the adversarial readings of the Exodus later advanced, for example, by Edward Said and Regina Schwartz, wherein God's injunction to exterminate their Canaanite enemies ("doom them to destruction: grant them no terms and give them no quarter," according to Deuteronomy 7:2) compromises the Israelites' moral imperative, as well as those of later conquering nations who looked to the biblical text for guidance—in particular, the American Puritans, the South African Boers, and the Jews in modern Palestine.[47]

In the anticolonial inversion of Exodus adopted by Black Power, especially after the Six-Day War in 1967, blacks were (still) slaves in the Egypt of America, while the Egypt of Africa, often imaginatively allied not only with Ethiopia but also more generally with pre-1948 Palestine, was said to be their spiritual homeland—a nation at war with Israel and, by extension, with Jews in America. Branches of this black counter-typology, as we will see, can be found in the Nation of Islam; in Black Power theology, which articulated a line of descent from Moses and the Hebrew prophets to a black messianic Jesus Christ; and in the tradition of Black Jews, many of whom claim to be the true descendants of the original Israelites. Each of these alternative genealogies argues variously for a stronger, a more "authentic" lineal relationship between blacks and Jews than between (white) gentiles and Jews; but rather than allying blacks and Jews as God's chosen people, they assert, more radically, that blacks, *not* Jews, are those chosen people—a usurpation that leads, at extremity, to expressions of fascistic anti-Semitism.

Whether in proclaiming themselves the "true Jews" descended from the ancient Israelites and primordial black civilizations in Egypt or Ethiopia, or in identifying politically with the enemies of contemporary Israel symbolized by Egypt, however, blacks nonetheless continued to find in Jewish history, not excluding political Zionism, a seemingly inescapable paradigm for their own unfolding history. Feeling an equal attraction to identification with God's chosen people and with the glories of ancient Egypt—with slaves and slaveholders alike—black Americans, as Wilson Moses has written, wanted and still want "to be children of Pharaoh as well as children of Israel."[48]

ALL GENUINE JEWS ARE BLACK MEN

Why the hell, Sweet Jesus, did you ever leave Egypt and all those spades? Why didn't you stay and lay Pharaoh's second-best daughter and make another Moses? Put your back into it, Jew boy. Act like a white man for once.
                                   —*Ralph Ellison,* Juneteenth

In Gloria Naylor's episodic novel *Bailey's Cafe* (1992), set in 1948, the momentous year of Israeli independence, a mysterious immigrant, the pregnant fourteen-year-old Ethiopian Jew named Mariam, holds herself out as a virgin. Despite her intact hymen, her barely penetrable vagina, and her insistence that she has never had intercourse, she has been deemed shameful and sent into exile from her community. Unwelcome in Israel (for at least another generation), Mariam makes her way to Bailey's Harlem cafe, a kind of crossroads for the various dispossessed migrants whose loosely connected stories constitute Naylor's novel. As a "Keeper of the Commandments," she is perhaps associated with the Commandment Keepers of the Royal Order of Ethiopian Hebrews, one of the nation's earliest congregations of Black Jews,* but Naylor more clearly ascribes her origin to the Falashas of Ethiopia:

* Here and following I use the capitalized term "Black Jews" to refer to congregations or individuals who are not just black Jews but for whom their blackness and Jewishness constitute a specific conjoined identity, much as Black Muslim denotes an adherent of the Nation of Islam rather than a Muslim who happens to be black. In some cases, "Black Jews" or variations such as "Black Hebrews," "Hebrew Israelites," "Ethiopian Hebrews," and so on constitute a congregation's chosen name.

They're outcasts in their own nation and only allowed to be tenants on the land. All prayers turn toward Jerusalem as they spin linen, shape iron, and bake pottery outside their broken hovels. Keepers of the Commandments. Commandments given to ex-slaves. To the dispossessed. It is a poor man's faith, so it has thrived among them well. A faith built on what is always attainable for the poor: prayer, children, and memories. In a nation that time forgot, a nation ringed by mountains, they are hemmed in by huge stone churches but have clung to the God of Abraham and the Law of Moses. They believe they are the last Jews in the world. They are certainly the last to build sanctuaries and anoint a high priest.[49]

Insofar as Naylor's characterization of the Falashas connects them symbolically with the dispossessed ex-slaves of America, another "nation that time forgot," it is appropriate that when Mariam gives birth, her child's godfather is Bailey, an African American, while his "honorary" father is Gabe, a Russian Jewish émigré.

His two fathers contemplate sending their miracle child to Harlem's Rabbi Matthew—the reference is to Rabbi Wentworth Arthur Matthew, who founded the Ethiopian Hebrew Rabbinical College to train leaders for the Commandment Keepers—but the cafe's customers are ignorant and dismissive of Black Jews. "Whoever heard of a colored rabbi? Instead of misleading the Negro people he should bring 'em on to Christ," says one. "There's no such thing as a black Jew. Ain't being one or the other bad enough?" replies another. By the same token, Gabe's dialogues with Bailey purposely undermine any invidious comparison of historical trajectories based on oppression—"who's got the highest pile of bones," as Bailey contemptuously puts it.[50] Their paternal alliance springs instead from a felicitous coincidence: each man's father is named George, so that is the name bestowed on Mariam's savior child.

Because her own name is an amalgam of Mary, the mother of Christ, and Miriam, the sister of Moses, Mariam may be one of the Ethiopian forced converts to Christianity who professed worship of Mary but secretly practiced Judaism. But in Harlem an additional cultural amalgamation is also in play. In taking the name of his new nation's mythic founding father, George Washington, Mariam's son represents not just the potential union of gentile and Jew, even black and Jew; like his mother, he also stands for the utopian promise of democratic inclusion still compromised by racial discrimination,[51] no less in the United States than in the new nation Israel, where Black Jews like Mariam, even more than the Mizrahim—those Arab-descended Sephardic Jews who came to Israel from northern Africa, South Asia, and neighboring Arab nations in 1948 and after—were still unwelcome. Upon Mariam's death in childbirth, in fact, George's Jewish identity dissolves. Despite the circumcision performed by Gabe, which enters him into God's covenant with Abraham, George is destined neither for Israel, which would not yet recognize him under the Law of Return, nor for the Black Jewish congregation of Rabbi Matthew, and his consignment to a homeless shelter disrupts the story's closure, vexing whatever communal redemption the birth of this peculiar messiah might have promised.

The black savior child as homeless orphan has numerous precedents in earlier African American literature, in particular the various Black Christs born to unwed or raped black women in W. E. B. Du Bois's short stories and his generic hybrid *Darkwater* (1920). But Naylor's innovative convergence between Judaism and Christianity, Israel and America, with blackness as the pivotal term, presents Mariam's migration and seeming virgin birth in a striking light. Unlike the Falashas of Ethiopia, the Black Hebrews of Harlem, the Rastafarians of Jamaica, or the Hebrew Israelites of Chicago, who followed their leader Ben Ammi Carter to Israel's Negev desert in 1969, there to remain unrecognized as Jews by the Israeli rabbinate for more than thirty years, Mariam and her child are not said to be descended from the ancient Israelites. Rather, her conception of an apparent messiah subsumes Christianity—black Christianity, no less— into Judaism, not the reverse. In contrast to the normal typological progression whereby Christianity completes Judaism by superseding it in the birth, death, and resurrection of Jesus, George's birth is, in fact, a form of anti-supersession, but one whose potential for salvation and reconciliation disappears into the streets of Harlem along with the newborn messiah himself.

In portraying Mariam's miraculous childbirth as coincident with Israel's own political birth, Naylor made the dilemma of Black Jews historically poignant. If the Law of Return was unable to accommodate the Falashas or the various American sects of Black Jews who claimed descent from the biblical patriarchs, exile was not at an end. Judgments that Black Jews were not Jews at all—let alone the "true Jews"—neither dissuaded them from claiming their rights nor prevented them from setting up corresponding structures of congregational life. Black Jews have often seemed anomalous as Jews, anomalous as blacks, but as Naylor's example suggests, they have a modern-day Zion to match their faith and may also be seen to represent the coherent, if eccentric, reconciliation of one exile with another, one chosenness with another.

Until the early twentieth century, African American identification with biblical Israel and Jewish history was largely metaphoric. Yet some earlier assertions of identity, including long-standing interpretive traditions based on Exodus 2:21

and Numbers 12:1 that identified Moses' wife (or second wife) Zipporah as a Midianite or Kushite, a dark or black woman,[52] were intended to stake a claim of ancestral kinship, or even genealogical priority, regardless of matters of theology or worship. Anticipating later ethnogenetic arguments that Jewish tradition derives from black tradition rather than the reverse, the slave memoirist Olaudah Equiano found that similarities between the Exodus of the Jews and the exile of African slaves, when added to his people's traditions of ritual offerings and purifications, circumcision, and legends of the patriarchs about the "Land of Promise," proved that "the one people had sprung from the other."* Martin Delany similarly claimed a preemptive African past in order to combat a racist order. "Had Moses or the Israelites never lived in Africa," he argued, "the mysteries of the wise men of the East never would have been handed down to us."[53] It was only with the massive early-twentieth-century migrations to the urban North, however, that both Black Jewish congregations and various Afro-Judaic, Afro-Zionist ideologies began to flourish.

As mentor to Elijah Muhammad, founder of the Nation of Islam, Wallace D. Fard (also known as W. Fard Muhammad, according to legend a Syrian or an

---

* Recent scholarly evidence that Equiano was born in South Carolina, and thus never went through the Middle Passage and was never in Africa, may cast doubt on his reference to African customs, although he might well have been told of these customs by family members or fellow slaves. Despite the authority of scripture and rabbinic tradition, circumcision was not universal among early Jews, and according to Herodotus and others, it was widespread among peoples of the Near Eastern and Mediterranean world and is said to have been borrowed in most cases from the Egyptians. In *Moses and Monotheism*, Freud cited Herodotus in confirmation of his own view not only that Moses was an Egyptian but also that the Jews, at his direction, adopted the Egyptian practice of circumcision as part of Jewish law. Correspondences in inherited ritual practice have allowed some Africans to claim a kinship with Jews, while others have mounted an Afrocentric argument that such correspondence proves that Jews borrowed (or stole) their practices from Africa. The pan-Africanist Cheikh Anta Diop, for example, identified circumcision as a Semitic borrowing from Egyptian tradition. Specifically, he said, both Abraham and Moses were circumcised in connection with their marriages to "black" women (Hagar in the case of Abraham, a Midianite in the case of Moses). For Diop, the Judaic practice lacked the cosmological explanation available in ancient African practice. God's covenant with the Jews, in his view otherwise inexplicable, derived from Dogon cosmogony in which both circumcision and female excision (clitoridectomy) suppress androgynous characteristics of male and female children and restore them to sexual difference. Olaudah Equiano, *The Interesting Narrative and Other Writings*, ed. Vincent Carretta (New York: Penguin, 1995), pp. 41–44; Vincent Carretta, "Olaudah Equiano or Gustavus Vassa? New Light on an Eighteenth-Century Question of Identity," *Slavery and Abolition* 20 (December 1999), 96–105; Jonathan Z. Smith, *Imagining Religion: From Babylon to Jonestown* (Chicago: University of Chicago Press, 1982), pp. 9–14; Sigmund Freud, *Moses and Monotheism* (1939), trans. Katherine Jones (New York: Vintage, 1967), pp. 29–30, 40, 54; Cheikh Anta Diop, *The African Origin of Civilization: Myth or Reality*, ed. and trans. Mercer Cook (Chicago, Ill.: Lawrence Hill Books, 1974), pp. 136–37.

Arab from Mecca) inspired one of the most elaborate arguments that blacks in America were the real children of Israel, destined by prophecy to be restored to an earthly kingdom following a series of cataclysmic events. Muhammad's reworking of the Exodus, examined in more detail later in this chapter, borrowed from a medley of Christian, Jewish, and Muslim traditions—not to mention the classic tracts of anti-Semitism. Yet the Black Muslims were hardly alone in saying they were no "Johnny-come-lately-Jews," to cite a favorite Nation of Islam epithet,[54] but literally the chosen people elected to effect God's plan of redemption in the Babylon of America. Whether it was asserted that Judaism originated in Africa—an argument set forth in books such as Joseph Williams's *Hebrewisms of West Africa from the Nile to the Niger with the Jews* (1930) and Allen Godbey's *Lost Tribes: A Myth* (1930), and more recently in Yosef A. A. ben-Jochannan's *We the Black Jews: Witness to the "White Jewish Race" Myth* (1993) and José V. Malcioln's *African Origin of Modern Judaism* (1996)—or that it was carried into Africa by lost tribes in exile, Black Judaism has depended on a belief that blacks are the direct descendants of the ancient Israelites, a lineage said to be confused by the turmoil of tribal warfare or disrupted and suppressed by the ravages of European (and Arab) colonialism and slavery. Stripped of their religion and cultural identity during the transport into slavery, according to Howard Brotz, Black Jews had to recover their true identity by "purg[ing] the Negro of the remnants of the Sambo in the soul." Or, in the more contemporary language of Tudor Parfitt, Black Jews, like other peoples said to descend from the biblical patriarchs or the lost tribes of Israel—American Indians, British Israelites, and New Zealand Maoris, along with a number of Asian and African groups—consequently expressed "a longing for a lost past" and aspired to "oneness with an intellectual, moral and spiritual universe."[55]

Seldom recognized as authentic Jews by rabbinic authorities but sometimes quietly supported by them, early Black Jews in the United States fashioned theologies that often read backwards from the prophet Jesus to a Torah enmeshed in ancient African history and, in some cases, derived from Islam. Noble Drew Ali, founder in 1913 of the Canaanite Temple in Newark, New Jersey, and later the Moorish Science Temple of America, initially in Chicago, taught through his sermons and the Holy Koran of the Moorish Science Temple that Mor͏ was the original homeland of modern blacks and instructed his f·ˑ trace their lineage through Jesus to the ancient Canaanites ·ˑ the earliest inhabitants of Africa.[56] The oldest known sec Church of the Living God, the Pillar and Ground of Tru͏ founded by Prophet F. S. Cherry in Tennessee in 1886 and late͏ delphia, as well as congregations such as the House of Judith,

William A. Lewis, and William S. Crowdy's Church of God and Saints of Christ, emerged out of a tradition of millennial Protestantism in which the restoration of the Jews to Palestine was seen as a prelude to the return of Jesus Christ. Like Ali, they anticipated aspects of Black Muslim thought in contending that blacks, not the "so-called Jews," were the true Hebrews, descended directly from the patriarchs through the lost tribes in Africa and then throughout the black Atlantic.[57]

In Harlem, Marcus Garvey's musical director, Arnold Josiah Ford, a black rabbi originally from Barbados, and his disciple Wentworth Arthur Matthew were among those who established congregations such as the Moorish Zionist Temple of Moorish Jews in Harlem (see illustration) and promulgated a Black Judaism that had a good deal in common with the Black Muslim beliefs soon to be espoused by Elijah Muhammad. Variously said to come from Sierra Leone, Lagos, and Ethiopia, but apparently born in the British West Indies, Matthew, as noted earlier, founded the Ethiopian Hebrew Rabbinical College (later the Israelite Rabbinical Academy) to train leaders for the Commandment Keepers of the Royal Order of Ethiopian Hebrews.* "The black man is a Jew," Matthew explained, because he is a lineal descendant of Abraham, Isaac, Jacob, Moses, and David, and of Solomon, who mated with the Queen of Sheba (also said to be a descendant of Moses). Sheba then returned to Africa, where she bore Solomon a son, known in biblical history as Menelik I, the first emperor of Ethiopia, following whom there had been an "unbroken succession of six hundred and thirteen kings" to the then present-day "King of the Tribe of Judah," emperor of Ethiopia Haile Selassie. "Hence, all genuine Jews are black men."[58]

Like some other Black Jews, Matthew distinguished between "Hebrews," true *black* descendants of the Israelites—specifically, the tribes of Judah and Benjamin, which he said had been driven into Africa—and "Jews," *white* Ash-

---

* Rejected for membership in the New York Board of Rabbis, Matthew nonetheless kept his congregation intact for decades. After his death in 1973, leadership was assumed by Capers Funnye, rabbi of the Beth Shalom B'nai Zaken Ethiopian Hebrew Congregation in Chicago. Backed by the Commandment Keepers, Ford led a group of emigrants to Ethiopia in 1930 to secure a territory among the Falashas for a black Jewish community, but he died without having succeeded in 1934 on the eve of the Italo-Ethiopian war. The alternative story that Ford went to Detroit, where he emerged as the Wallace D. Fard who inspired Elijah Muhammad to found the Nation of Islam, has been discredited. Some accounts have identified Matthew as the congregation's rabbi in James VanDerZee's photograph of members of the Moorish Zionist Temple of Moorish Jews, but James Landing identifies him as Israel Ben Newman (wearing er shawl), with temple president Mordecai Herman on his left. James E. Landing, *Black Judaism: of an American Movement* (Durham, N.C.: Carolina Academic Press, 2002), p. 246.

Moorish Zionist Temple of Moorish Jews, New York City, 1929.
Photo: James VanDerZee. Copyright © Donna Mussenden VanDerZee.

kenazi pretenders to Judaism,[59] a distinction that made its way into popular culture and remained alive in subsequent manifestations of Black Judaism.* In aspiring to develop the Hebrew language among blacks and return them to Ju-

* When the hero's father in Michael Gold's *Jews without Money* (1930) brings a Black Jew home to dinner, the family's surprise turns to resentment when the man proudly proclaims himself an Abyssian Jew descended from King Solomon and the Queen of Sheba, whose people "had kept the faith pure" while the Ashkenazim of Europe (and now America) had "wandered among the Gentiles," making themselves "mere pretenders to the proud title of Jew." The idea reappears in Herbert Tarr's *Heaven Help Us!* (1968). When the novel's well-meaning, socially conscientious hero, Rabbi Gideon Abel, spots the Star of David on one house while passing out Thanksgiving turkeys in a poor black neighborhood, he first assumes it must be the home of the minister of the local Zion A.M.E. (African Methodist Episcopal) Church. Upon discovering that the family is Jewish, he asks them to join his temple, only to be rebuffed by the woman of the house, who insists on a difference between Black Jews and white Jews that transcends color: "But you're not Hebrews. You're all Goldbergs." According to Rabbi Shalomin HaLevi, a leader in a present-day congregation of Hebrew Israelites known as the Israelite Torah Covenant Community, the "Slavery of the Black Hebrews (the worst holocaust)" led to "the true Shemite (Negroid) culture" being replaced with "a Caucasoid Yiddishkite culture," although Ethiopian (Cushite) "Yahudaism" can be traced up to

daism, Matthew also forecast a familiar tenet of the Nation of Islam: "The colored man was a great man as long as he could hold on to his true religion. When he lost it, he developed an inferiority complex and became the slave of the white man."[60]

The Black Jews of Harlem probably numbered no more than one thousand in the 1920s. (By the mid-1980s, according to one count, there were between 25,000 and 40,000 *Black* Jews throughout all of the United States, many of whom would be numbered among the 200,000 *black* Jews estimated to live in the United States by the Alliance of Black Jews a decade later.)[61] Treated to condescension, if not outright racism, they inevitably provoked ambivalence among other Jews, who stood to be tarnished by too close an association with blacks and only reluctantly recognized them as Jews rather than fraudulent pretenders. In 1920 the Yiddish daily *Forward* carried a story on the Black Jews led by Elder Warien Roberson which summarized the congregation's views, bound to be offensive: "The real, the true kosher Jews, are the Blacks, or as they are known, the Negroes. They are the chosen children of God, while you [Jewish readers of the *Forward*] are only his stepchildren, and you needn't hold it against Him if He doesn't treat you [as would] a real father."[62] Not least because of the admixture of Christian and Islamic elements in their eclectic Judaism, the Black Jews constitute a special case of what Leslie Fiedler described as the Jew's historic entrapment between the Christian Negro, for whom he is not spiritually white enough ("not sufficiently washed in the Blood of the Lamb"), and the Black Muslim, for whom he is not mythologically black enough ("not far enough removed from the White Man's God").[63]

Whether they maintain that the ancient Israelites were originally black or became black after intermingling with black Canaanite women,[64] Black Jews have most often defined their true origins by claiming a shared ancestry with the Falashas of Ethiopia, the most prominent, but not the only, group of Africans who say they are descended from the early Israelites.[65] (Arnold Ford thought that all blacks were related to the Falashas, and what Emanuela Trevisan Semi has called the "Falashisation" of the Black Jews of Harlem was

---

the slave trade, at which point blacks were cut off from their Ethiopian Hebrew heritage and their descendants taught Christianity, Islam, or "a Form of Rabbinical/Yiddish white-washed Judaism." Those who go by the name of Jews are not to be confused with those of the "true Hebrew culture," who are Yahweh's Chosen: "An Israelite can be a Jew if he converts to the Jewish religion, but a Jew cannot automatically be a Hebrew unless he is a descendant of one of the twelve tribes." Michael Gold, *Jews without Money* (1930; rpt. New York: Avon Books, 1965), p. 125; Herbert Tarr, *Heaven Help Us!* (New York: Random House, 1968), p. 120; Rabbi Shalomin HaLevi, *Growing Intellectually, Spiritually, and Prophetically in the Hebrew Israelite Culture and Faith* (San Jose, Calif.: Writers Club Press, 2001), pp. 7–8, 12.

prompted by the inquiries of the Polish Zionist Jacques Faitlovitch during the 1910s and 1920s into the possibility that traces of the lost tribes might be found among Matthew's congregation.)[66] Although it may be that their ancestors were Ethiopian Christians whose beliefs and worship derived from the Hebrew Bible, the Falashas, or Beta Israel (House of Israel), also claim descent from Abraham or from Emperor Melenik. They believe that their ancestors came to Ethiopia at the time of the Exodus or the destruction of the Second Temple, or that they were Yemenite Jews who crossed the Red Sea into Ethiopia, or alternatively that they were Egyptian Jews who intermarried with Egyptians. According to another account, a band of Jews fleeing the oppressive rule of the Babylonians sought refuge in Egypt and along the cataracts of the Nile, in time migrating to the deserts of Africa and the highlands of Ethiopia, where they became known as the Falashas—the "emigrants" or "outsiders"—and designated themselves Beta Israel. In some interpretations especially compelling for those who believe that "all genuine Jews are black," the Falashas are the originators of Hebrew monotheism. In all likelihood, however, their origins will remain as mysterious as Mariam's virgin pregnancy in *Bailey's Cafe*.

Ruled in 1971 by the Sephardic chief rabbi of Israel, Ovadia Yossef, to be "descendants of Jewish tribes who moved South to Cush"—descended specifically from the tribe of Dan—the Falashas were made eligible for the Law of Return in 1975.[67] But it was not until 1985, and then again in 1991, faced with civil war and famine in Ethiopia, that Israel mounted Operation Moses and Operation Solomon to rescue them. The fifty thousand who were living in Israel by 1993, including children born there, constituted the remnant of a population once said to number nearly half a million.* Although they are not unique alongside

---

* Responsibility for Israel's protracted decision to accept the Falashas, after many thousands had died, was shared by Haile Selassie, who opposed the emigration for fear that granting them special rights among the various Ethiopian peoples who might want independence or the right to emigrate would threaten the nation's stability. Ethiopia, in fact, was a cornerstone of Israel's Africa policy in the 1950s and 1960s. During the Italian occupation from 1936 to 1941, Haile Selassie had spent the initial part of his exile in Jerusalem, and after his return to power he established a relationship with the Jews of Palestine that resulted in coming decades in strong economic and security ties. Even after the Yom Kippur War, which dissolved Israel's official ties with Ethiopia, along with most other African nations, the relationship remained relatively, if unofficially, strong. One can compare the fate of some other Africans claiming to be Jews. The Abayudaya (or Bayudaya) of Uganda, founded in 1919 by warrior and statesman Semei Kakungulu—after Christian missionaries left translated Bibles with the tribe and, preferring monotheism, they elected to follow the Old Testament texts—practice an evangelical religion blending Judaism, Christianity, Islam, and African tribal beliefs. Although the group has as many as six hundred adherents today, their failure to gain recognition as Jews, and thus become eligible to return to Israel, threatens their survival. The claim of descent from ancient Israel made by the Lemba of South Africa, once thought to have adapted the teachings of white missionaries, appears corroborated by DNA test-

the Mizrahim, whose prejudicial treatment, as we will see in Chapter 5, created a minor eruption of Israeli "Black Power" in the early 1970s, the Falashas and their kindred Black Jews in America stand out because of the special role played by Ethiopia, as well as its emperor, Haile Selassie, in the evolution of American and Caribbean black nationalism.

THE NEGRO HATIKVAH

The Falashas wished only to join other Jews in the homeland of Israel, but the homeland they left behind, Ethiopia, had taken on powerful symbolic associations in African American culture over the course of the early twentieth century and consequently became the closest thing black Americans had to a hoped-for Zion of their own. Not only was its meaning comparable to that of Palestine for early Zionists, but Ethiopia (Abyssinia) also provided a symbolic point of departure for several strains of argument that may properly be called Afro-Zionism, broadly speaking, a mode of pan-Africanism that took its inspiration in significant part from modern Zionism's goal of restoring the Jewish state—the announced aim of Theodor Herzl's *Der Judenstaat* (1896)—by re-populating the land of Palestine.

A Greek translation of the Hebrew word *kush* (or *cush*), meaning "burnt face," Ethiopia came in biblical exegesis to designate black Africa in part or in whole, while Ethiopians consequently stood for black Africans or, more generally, the "dark" or "colored" people associated with parts of Africa. By the late nineteenth century, the term "Ethiopian" had come to refer generically to black-skinned Africans (as in the King James Bible), to blacks in the diaspora (as in the case of Marcus Garvey and others), and more generally to spiritual claims to black racial integrity and territorial sovereignty. Taking its text from Psalms 68:31—"Princes shall come out of Egypt, and Ethiopia shall soon stretch forth her hands to God"—a triumphal song of David reinterpreted to prophesy both the spiritual and the political liberation of African nations,

---

ing, which has shown male sequences nearly identical to those of the *cohanim,* the Jewish priests and their Ashkenazi descendants said to derive from Moses' brother Aaron. See James R. Ross, *Fragile Boundaries: Travels through the Jewish Diaspora* (New York: Riverhead Books, 2000), pp. 15–52; Tudor Parfitt, *Journey to the Vanished City: The Search for a Lost Tribe of Israel* (New York: St. Martin's, 1993), passim; and idem, *The Lost Tribes of Israel: The History of a Myth* (2002; rpt. London: Phoenix, 2003), pp. 205–7, 223–25.

Ethiopianism and the early pan-Africanism of which it was a part, a forerunner of modern-day Afrocentrism, blended biblical teaching with an amorphous black nationalist politics.[68] Its proponents often embraced Christian humanism and civilizationist models of progress even as they borrowed strategically from Jewish belief and history. Ethiopianism was a spur to several important anti-colonial rebellions in sub-Saharan Africa early in the twentieth century and opened into a more far-reaching argument that sought to place American and Caribbean blacks in a continuum with African history.[69] Harking back to Robert Alexander Young's quasi-mystical 1829 jeremiad against slavery and the denial of black rights, "The Ethiopian Manifesto," and cited repeatedly by African and African American leaders from the 1880s through the 1920s, the psalmist's words were said to forecast the providential delivery from bondage of colonized Africans and enslaved blacks in the diaspora, or, more radically, to prophesy black freedom achieved by a millennial redeemer who would arise in Africa or, according to some accounts, in the New World.

Such prophecy was given further impetus by the modern history of Ethiopia, a Christian state that had retained its sovereignty throughout the European colonization of Africa and achieved a surprising military victory over Italy in 1896. Rejecting Italian treaty claims in 1889, the modern emperor Menelik had thus alluded to the psalmist: "Ethiopia has never been conquered and she never shall be. . . . Ethiopia will stretch out her hand only to God."[70] Spurred on by depictions of Ethiopia in fiction such as Pauline Hopkins's *Of One Blood* (1903) and Charles Henry Holmes's *Ethiopia, the Land of Promise* (1917), as well as popular historiography such as John William Morris's *The Ethiopian's Place in History* (1916) and Drusilla Dunjee Houston's *Wonderful Ethiopians of the Ancient Cushite Empire* (1926), the same power of identification was again in evidence during the Italian-Ethiopian war of 1935–36, which stimulated African American boycotts of Italian businesses, petitions to the pope, fundraising for the citizens of Ethiopia, and the organization of volunteer militia, none of which had any effect on the victory by Italian forces but all of which indicated the catalytic power of the Ethiopian example.[71] Said the *Chicago Defender,* unlike American blacks, the Ethiopian "finds virtue in being black. Think about him, read about him, and your thought will be lifted to appreciate his value of manhood."[72] Reconciling contrary forces, the Ethiopia of the psalmist became a revitalized metaphor for Africa generally—its embodiment of a glorious past, both ancient and more recent, waiting to be freed from colonialism and reborn in a glorious future of pan-African political sovereignty. "The Rape of Ethiopia," as Du Bois termed it in *The Negro* (1915) and *Darkwater,* stood for colonialist exploitation not just of geographical Africa but of all pan-Africa, the "colored" peoples who belt the world and await the liberating power of a black redeemer and his revolutionary movement.

Influential in virtually every version of Afro-Zionism, whether literal or figurative, were the views of Edward Blyden, a West Indian Presbyterian missionary educated in Liberia, whose argument that the diaspora provided a means to regenerate Africa was the foremost early instance of Ethiopianist thought. Although his critique of Christianity derived initially from Islam,[73] Blyden turned often to the example of the Jews and Zionism. Distinguished by their service and suffering, wrote Blyden, Africans in the diaspora are like "God's ancient people, the Hebrews, who were known among the Egyptians as the servants of all."[74] The "motherland" of Africa, compressed into the history of Ethiopia, assumed the spiritual qualities of a black Palestine, at once a symbol of exilic longing and a potential site of emigration. There was no need for *all* blacks to settle in Africa, said Blyden in "The Origin and Purpose of African Colonization" (1883), where he cited George Eliot on Zionism. "In a return from exile, in the restoration of a people," Eliot had written, only the worthy few were needed to provide leadership. "Plenty of prosperous Jews remained in Babylon when Ezra marshaled his band of forty thousand, and began a new, glorious epoch in the history of his race."[75]

In "The Jewish Question" (1898), however, Blyden stated a stronger affinity with the tenets of Zionism, recalling his youth in St. Thomas, where he was raised a Christian among many Jews and thus became an "earnest student of the history of God's chosen people." (Judah Benjamin, the pro-slavery senator from Louisiana who was named secretary of state for the Confederacy and aroused alarm among southerners with his proposal to arm slaves to fight against the Union Army, also came from St. Thomas.) The essay expressed Blyden's equation of Zionism and spiritually redemptive pan-Africanism, as well as his belief that Christians and Muslims, no less than Jews, recognize "the claim and right of the Jew to the Holy Land." Because they owe the beginning of their own civilization to the influences of ancient Africa, said Blyden, Jews have been entrusted with propagating monotheism internationally, bringing "men of all races, climes, and countries [to] call upon the one Lord under one Name," and they therefore have a special role to play alongside blacks in rescuing "the civilized from a deadening materialism and the barbarous from a stagnant and degrading superstition."[76]

Blyden's Zionist Ethiopianism was thus forged not simply by an affinity in servitude but more so by a sense of shared history in which Africa had fostered the development of civilization and produced for Jews and blacks, both of them "chosen," a common mission to be the spiritual saviors of the world: "In

Africa, the Hebrew people from three score and ten souls multiplied into millions. In Africa, Moses, the greatest lawgiver the world has ever seen, was born and educated." In his most polemical reading of the Davidic psalm, "Ethiopia Stretching Out Her Hands to God; or, Africa's Service to the World" (1880), Blyden determined that the scripture referred at once to Africa's piety, fidelity, and economic service to the world. "Africa is distinguished as having served and suffered," he wrote. "In this, her lot is not unlike that of God's ancient people, the Hebrews." Whereas in America the "exiled Negro" must surrender his integrity, in the "spiritual conservatory" of Africa "his wings develop, and he soars into an atmosphere of exhaustless truth."[77]

In their focus on the redemptive power of African culture and spiritual life, Blyden's views were more closely akin to the Afro-Zionism of Bishop Henry McNeal Turner, Marcus Garvey, and the West African nationalist J. E. Casely Hayford than to that of the more secular Du Bois, who, alongside his early affinity for German nationalism, found in American Jews a model of community put to political purpose and in Zionism a model of race-based diasporic consciousness. "If the Negroes of the United States want to know what organization is and what it can accomplish along racial lines they should buy the American Jewish Year Book," Du Bois wrote in 1915. Addressing the significance of pan-Africanism four years later, he declared that "the African movement means to us what the Zionist movement must mean to the Jews, the centralization of the race effort and the recognition of a racial fount."[78] Africa might provide a homeland for those blacks in diaspora who choose to settle there, argued Du Bois, but the racial ingathering need not be literal in order to provide the necessary political and spiritual sustenance.

For his part, Turner, a minister in the African Methodist Episcopal Church, advocated a more literal version of Afro-Zionism. Anticipating Marcus Garvey's "African Fundamentalism" by two decades, he instead called for blacks to throw off the enslavement of the diaspora, emigrate to the homeland of Africa, and recreate their own nation and language.[79] Likewise, when Casely Hayford mounted a critique of what he considered to be Du Bois's parochialism and assimilationism in his documentary novel *Ethiopia Unbound* (1911), he too took a different lesson from the Jews and, by implication, from Zionism: "The African in America is in a worse plight than the Hebrew in Egypt. The one preserved his language, his manners and customs, his religion and household gods; the other committed national suicide, and at present it seems as if the dry bones of the vision have no life in them."[80] Whereas the Jewish diaspora remained a "nation" and was on its way to restoration in its homeland—the dry bones in Ezekiel's vision were being bound together and raised up—the African diaspora, so far as Casely Hayford could judge from the American example of Du Bois, held no such promise.

In harmony with Turner, Casely Hayford, and Garvey, and in contrast to Du Bois, Blyden argued in favor of black separatism and against the "suicide" of racial mixing. His conception of "African Personality," influenced by Johan Gottfried von Herder's concept of the *Volkgeist*, held that genuine race development, possible only in Africa, was premised on resistance to the biological and cultural absorption of the black race by the white. Racial separatism was thus a prerequisite to the restoration of psychological and spiritual health. Just as the idea of departure from Egypt "was in the minds of the Hebrews long before Moses was born," so the idea of Africa was innate for blacks if only they could recover it.[81]

This strain of Afro-Zionism culminated, in the United States, in Garvey's creed of "African Fundamentalism," which made a direct appeal to Judaism: "As the Jewish child is born in the world that philosophy is laid before him; he grows in that philosophy, lives and dies in that philosophy."[82] Like Turner before him and the theologians of Black Power after him, however, Garvey preached a hybrid of Zionist Ethiopianism and messianic black Christianity, overlaid in his case with an entrepreneurial philosophy of racial uplift.[83] Of a piece with works such as W. L. Hunter's *Jesus Christ Had Negro Blood in His Veins* (1901) and James Morris Webb's *A Black Man Will Be the Coming Universal King Proved by Biblical Prophecy* (1918), Garvey's black God and black Jesus were the racial obverse of the Christian triumphalism of white supremacists whose support he paradoxically courted,* and his "Declaration of Rights of the Negro Peoples of the World," issued at a 1920 Universal Negro Improvement Association (UNIA) convention, contended that all black people are "free citizens of Africa, the Motherland of all Negroes," and resolved that "Ethiopia, Thou Land of Our Fathers" should be the "anthem of the Negro race."[84]

Garvey's allure both during his lifetime and since prove that the conceptual

---

* In seeking a rapprochement with the Ku Klux Klan and southern racists such as Senator Theodore Bilbo of Mississippi and Earnest Cox, the author of anti-miscegenation, pro-colonization tracts such as *White America* (1923), which was advertised in the Universal Negro Improvement Association's *Negro World,* Garvey created a militant civil religion that E. Franklin Frazier characterized as the "black klan of America." In the late 1930s, Garvey went so far as to endorse a bill sponsored by Bilbo to repatriate black Americans to Africa. E. Franklin Frazier, "Garvey: A Mass Leader," *The Nation* 123 (August 18, 1926), rpt. in John Henrik Clarke, ed., *Marcus Garvey and the Vision of Africa* (New York: Vintage Books, 1974), pp. 236–41; Lawrence W. Levine, "Marcus Garvey and the Politics of Revitalization," in John Hope Franklin and August Meier, eds., *Black Leaders of the Twentieth Century* (Urbana: University of Illinois Press, 1982), p. 132.

messianic dimension of his back-to-Africa movement far exceeded its stillborn pragmatic dimension. His efforts to organize a plan for emigration to Liberia, established as an independent African nation in 1821 by American free blacks and former slaves, foundered not only for lack of resources but also because of considerable official Liberian opposition.[85] For those inclined to see racial oppression through the prism of labor and class, Garvey's promises were futilely utopian. Garveyism proposes no better solution to racial persecution than does Zionism, said A. Philip Randolph, for each offers a dream that draws workers away from the proletarian liberation movement needed to unite workers of color around the world.[86]

Nevertheless, the UNIA's combination of pageantry, catechism, and racial purity had a galvanizing effect on the residents of Harlem, many of them recent migrants from the South. It also foreshadowed the tentative attraction to fascism shown by blacks in the 1930s, as one may witness in Garvey's oft-noted claim to be among the first fascists or in Richard Wright's comments introductory to *Native Son* (1940): "When the Nazis spoke of the necessity of a highly ritualized and symbolized life, I could hear Bigger Thomas on Chicago's South Side saying: 'Man, what we need is a leader like Marcus Garvey. We need a nation, a flag, an army of our own. We colored folks ought to organize into groups and have generals, captains, lieutenants, and so forth. We ought to take Africa and have a national home.'"[87] In warning against racial "suicide," however, Garvey was in the mainstream of the era's pan-racial nationalist arguments, whether those of Blyden, Casely Hayford, Theodore Roosevelt, or, for that matter, Louis Brandeis. It is not their differing theories of Zionism but rather the exclusion of blacks from the channels of Americanization, to which Jews had much greater access, that accounts most for the fact that Brandeis could easily envision dual loyalty while Garvey could not.

Like his pretense to fascism, Garvey's Afro-Zionist emulation of the Jews was nothing if not equivocal. On the one hand, he argued in a 1933 editorial denouncing Nazi intolerance that "the Jew is only persecuted because he has certain qualities of progress that other people have not learnt." On the other, because "the original Pharaohs were black," he offered his followers the chauvinistic lesson that "in dealing with Jews [you should] let them know that they were once your slaves in Egypt."[88] But such advice simply inverted the model from which he derived his principal argument. When he asked "the sons and daughters of Ethiopia everywhere to buckle on [their] armor" and "march 400,000,000 strong toward the destiny of a free and redeemed Africa,"[89] Garvey envisioned not an actual black repatriation on such a massive scale but rather a worldwide dedication to the creation of a homeland to which blacks might in theory return, like Jews to Palestine. His ideology, not surprisingly, resonated with the pro-Zionist Yiddish press, which saw in the UNIA a kindred expression of race nationalism and called "Ethiopia—Thou Land of Our Fathers," an anthem composed by Arnold Ford, "The Negro Hatikvah."[90]

The dissolution of Garvey's movement under charges of fraud and corruption diminished his stature but not necessarily the consequences of his Zionist Ethiopianism, both incidental and more vital. One of his adherents, Grover Redding, contended that it was his biblically ordained mission to lead America's "Ethiopian captives" back to their true homeland. But the promise of his Chicago splinter congregation, known as the Star Order of Ethiopia, came to naught when Redding was put on trial for burning an American flag, a public event apparently intended to spark a riot that would lead to a liberating act of repatriation.[91] Messianic black Zionism in Chicago would await the appearance a generation later of Ben Ammi Carter.

In his native Jamaica, to cite a more lasting legacy, Garvey became a prophetic figure akin to John the Baptist among the Rastafarians, a religious movement dating from the 1920s whose adherents venerate the Ethiopian emperor Haile Selassie, also known by his given name Ras Tafari, who by some accounts fulfilled Christ's promise of return and by others was the Jewish Messiah prophesied in the Hebrew Bible.[92] The most numerous and influential today among those who might very loosely be designated Black Jews, the Rastafarians consider themselves the reincarnation of ancient Israelites, exiled because of past transgressions to slavery in the West Indies, much as the tribes of Israel were scattered, and awaiting restoration to the Zion of Ethiopia as soon as exile in the "Caribbean Babylon" is overcome. Their political ideology features a close identification between the sacred homelands of Ethiopia and Israel, as in the "Ethiopian National Anthem," in which Jehovah speaks both to Israel and to the motherland of Ethiopia, or in the song "Awake, Sleeping Jews, Awake": "Great Ras Tafari, King of Kings / You come to reign. . . . / Can I forget his Covenant / He made with Israel once? / To Jacob's seed for evermore / His Covenant cannot break."[93] But there is this difference: since blacks are the true chosen people of the Bible and the real Jerusalem is in Ethiopia, Israel is a futile error, the so-called Jews are gentiles, not Hebrews, and "anyone outside the black man is not a Jew; he is the anti-Jew."[94]

In Rastafarianism, Christian Ethiopianism was transfused into Black Judaism while taking on a more pronounced anticolonial and black supremacist ideology in which the protest of black captivity and triumphalist transcendence of it coexist. One finds this hybrid ideology, for example, in Bob Marley's album *Exodus* (1977), which reconfigured the biblical Exodus as a spiritual and cultural return to an African Zion, in the process transforming the dead Haile Selassie, who had been overthrown in a coup by Mengistu Haile Mariam in 1974 and died the following year, into a deified African father.[95] Marley's "Movement of Jah People"—that is, the people of God, in that *Jah*, venerated in the messianic figure of Selassie, is a Rastafarian equivalent of *Yahweh* and derived linguistically from *Eli-jah*—concisely portrays the reverse Exodus, the return of exiles to their true homeland, that resides at the heart of Rastafarianism:

> We know where we're going, we know where we're from,
> We're leaving Babylon, we're going to our fatherland.
> Exodus, movement of Jah people,
> Movement of Jah people.
> Send us another Brother Moses gonna cross the Red Sea . . .
> Jah come to break down oppression, rule equality,
> Wipe away transgression, set the captives free.*

At mid-century, however, Rastafarianism was an inchoate movement, and Garvey's example, if not his objective, had more immediate significance for the black freedom movement in the United States. Visiting a shrine to Garvey in Kingston, Jamaica, Martin Luther King, Jr., recognized him as the "first man of color" to lead a mass movement in the United States, the first man "to give millions of Negroes a sense of dignity and destiny and make a Negro feel he was somebody."[96] The invigorating and lasting power of Garvey's Afro-Zionism, as

---

* A staple throughout African American music and vernacular tradition, the exilic locale of Babylon appears as a spur to protest in a number of Marley's songs, including "Babylon System" ("Babylon system is the vampire sucking the blood of the sufferers") and "Chant Down Babylon" ("Come we go burn down Babylon one more time"). Bob Marley and the Wailers, "Exodus," *Exodus* (1977; reissued by The Island Def Jam Music Group, 2001; lyrics as posted on the official Bob Marley Web site, www.bob marley.com (accessed August 21, 2003). In early 2005 plans were announced by his widow for the remains of Marley, who died in 1981 and was buried in Jamaica, to be exhumed and reburied in the Ethiopian community of Shashemene. Marley's fans immediately protested that Jamaica was his proper resting place and that, despite his message of African repatriation, there is no evidence that he wished to settle or be buried in Ethiopia. Beginning in the 1960s, as many as 2,500 Rastafarians emigrated to Shashemene, living on land granted to the returnees by Selassie. Native Ethiopians always considered them foreigners, however, and the number had dwindled to several hundred by the turn of the century. Whatever its effect on the permanent population, the reburial of Marley's remains, though highly unlikely, would no doubt make the community a prominent tourist site. Davan Maharaj, "Rastafarians Struggling to Hold On to African Dream," *Los Angeles Times*, June 8, 2003, A8; Roger Steffens, "Jamaica's the Place When We Think Reggae, Rasta—and Bob," *Los Angeles Times*, January 24, 2005, B9.

well as its inheritance from Ethiopianism, may certainly be detected in King's philosophy, but it appears more prominently in two other strands of black resistance to the American Babylon—the Nation of Islam and Black Power Christianity. In the Nation of Islam, structural elements of Black Judaism, along with conventional apocalyptic, are fitted into a new paradigm of Holocaust consciousness at once profound and incredible. In the liberationist Black Theology of Albert Cleage, Jr., and James Cone, Black Judaism is subordinated to Christianity, but in "blackening" Jesus, they make him a Hebrew prophet bringing a chosen people out of bondage. In each case, however, the borrowings from Judaism were less an occasion for finding affinity with Jews than for diminishing, if not maligning, their example.

I HAVE REMEMBERED MY COVENANT

Few black thinkers presented a more challenging adaptation of the Exodus and the trope of chosenness to the age of genocide than Elijah Muhammad and, following for a time in his footsteps, Malcolm X. Because it feared the coming power of black people in the next millennium, said Muhammad in *Message to the Blackman in America* (1965), America was now plotting the destruction of blacks, much as Nazis dreamed of an empire without Jews. Through a "Birth Control Death Plan"—a regime of contraception, sterilization, and integration, which Muhammad, like Garvey before him, said was meant to destroy the black race—"our enemies, the devils, know and now seek to prevent us from being a nation through our women, as Pharaoh attempted to destroy Israel by killing off the male babies of Israel at birth."[97] In "this wilderness of North America," as Elijah Muhammad and Malcolm X styled it on various occasions, African Americans were the true chosen people, and the risk of assimilation, not to mention race mixing, was that blacks would be making the same "fatal mistake" as Jews in Germany. "Their self-brainwashing had been so complete," Malcolm said of the Jews in his autobiography, "that long after, in the gas chambers, a lot of them were still gasping, 'It can't be true!'"[98]

The etiology of this doctrine lay in lessons Elijah Muhammad had imbibed from his mentor Wallace D. Fard, in whose person he said Allah came to him in 1931 prophesying the fall of America. Fard converted Muhammad, né Elijah Poole, to his belief that black Americans were the "lost-found" tribe of Shabazz, stolen away from their Muslim life in the holy city of Mecca some four hundred years earlier. Variously reputed to be Palestinian, Syrian Druse, black

Jamaican, or Turko-Persian, Fard promised to restore Muslim converts to their true names and identities by revealing the truth of the primacy of blackness covered up by white supremacy.[99] As stated by the minor comic character Jacob 32 in Bernard Malamud's novel *The Tenants* (1971), the Nation of Islam's philosophy is one of inversions—whites are black, and blacks are the true whites: "You see us wrong and you see yourself wrong. If you saw me right you would see me white in the manner in which I see you black. You think I am black because your inside eyes are closed to the true vision of the world."[100] Because intermarriage would eliminate whiteness, white people have a survivalist imperative not just to maintain racial segregation but also to destroy blacks. The present-day threat of genocide is thus a new iteration of the plan through which the white race was created by the renegade black mad scientist Yakub.

The skeleton of the theology promulgated by Elijah Muhammad is this: Blacks are the original people, dating back 66 trillion years. Some six thousand years ago a mad scientist named Mr. Yakub, in revolt against Allah, began a series of genetic experiments through which white people were gradually created. Associated with a panoply of biblical antecedents, including fallen Adam and guilty Cain, Yakub is figured as a dissident member of the original black tribe of Shabazz in the holy city of Mecca. Specifically, he is said to be the biblical Jacob, the father of Judah, which means that Jacob's religion, and that of Isaac and Abraham before him, was not Judaism but Islam; for the same reason, Abraham and his descendants were black. Exiled along with his new race to an island in the Aegean Sea, Yakub perfected his kingdom through a regime of birth control and infanticide. Eugenics is one source of Muhammad's characterization of Yakub: "His aim was to kill and destroy the black nation. He ordered the nurses to kill all black babies that were born among his people, by pricking the brains with a sharp needle as soon as the black child's head is out of the mother." The result was a race of blue-eyed, blond-haired devils marked by weakness, wickedness, and violent propensities. These whites were taught the imperialist science of "tricknology" that would one day allow them to conquer the world. After the race of devils had lived two thousand years in the caves of Europe, Moses was sent by Allah not to Egypt but to Europe, to civilize the white man, and the first whites to accept his teachings were the people now known as Jews. Whites were destined by Yakub to rule the earth for six thousand years, but two thousand years had already been lost. The children of Yakub, through slavery and other depredations, had killed no fewer than 600 million descendants of the tribe of Shabazz. Moses taught that at the end of time a messiah would come to destroy the white race. The Jews, mistaking Christ for that messiah and fearing the end of the white race, killed him.

But they were wrong: the true black Messiah would not come for another two thousand years.*

As it is spelled out in Elijah Muhammad's own works, principally *Message to the Blackman* (1965), coupled with Malcolm X's 1962 address titled "Black Man's History" and fragments of *The Autobiography of Malcolm X* (1965) and other speeches, the foundational legend of Yakub constitutes a remarkable counter-theology to Western tradition. The lineaments of Exodus clearly survive, as does the typological structure of a prophetic delivery into a Promised Land, but they are now immersed in a theory of black genocide that is derived from racial eugenics and recast in the language of apocalypse. Elijah Muhammad at times distinguished Jews favorably among the white devils, as in his teaching that "the Jewish people have a greater sense of justice and humanness than their white gentile brothers" and "have developed a higher sense of ethics, less tainted with the crimes of colonialism, white supremacy and prejudice characterizing the Christians." He also established other parallels with Judaism in his borrowings from the dietary laws of Leviticus and, by one interpretation, in the resemblance of his exegesis of the Hebrew Bible to Midrash.[101] But inversion of typology, not its replacement, was Muhammad's key strategy, and his theology was, among other things, an unpredictable amalgam of Judaism and anti-Judaism (among the books that Fard recommended to him were the Bible, the Qu'ran, and the *Protocols of the Elders of Zion*).[102]

The Yakub myth, a rewriting of Genesis and the Judaic patriarchs carefully crafted to make Jacob the progenitor of the Black Muslims, is thus meant to reveal "The White Race's False Claim to be Divine, Chosen People," to cite the ti-

---

* By one calculation the time for white rule had run out in 1914—and then been extended—but Muhammad prophesied the Fall of America in 1965 or 1966, namely, "the day and time we're living in right now," as Malcolm X put it in his most elaborate expounding of Elijah Muhammad's cosmology. At the apocalypse, the white world would be destroyed through an attack led by a wheel-shaped spaceship known as the Mother Plane, which Elijah Muhammad found to have been forecast in the allegories of Ezekiel and Revelation. Upon the ruins of white civilization, blacks would build a new world, resuming their rightful place as the chosen people. See Elijah Muhammad, *Message to the Blackman in America* (Chicago: Muhammad Mosque of Islam No. 2, 1965), pp. 103–22, quotation at p. 115; Malcolm X, "Black Man's History," in *The End of White World Supremacy: Four Speeches*, ed. Imam Benjamin Karim (1971; New York: Arcade, n.d.), pp. 23–66, quotation at p. 64. On the Mother Plane, see Elijah Muhammad, *The Fall of America* (Chicago: Muhammad's Temple of Islam No. 2, 1973), pp. 236–42; and for Muhammad's theology, see E. U. Essien-Udom, *Black Nationalism: A Search for an Identity in America* (Chicago: University of Chicago Press, 1962), pp. 122–42; Claude Andrew Clegg III, *An Original Man: The Life and Times of Elijah Muhammad* (New York: St. Martin's Press, 1997), pp. 41–73; and Michael Lieb, *Children of Ezekiel: Aliens, UFOs, the Crisis of Race, and the Advent of End Time* (Durham: Duke University Press, 1998), pp. 129–53.

tle of one section of *Message to the Blackman*. The Bible is to be understood as a revelation to the true Jews, namely, black people. "The original scripture called 'The Torah'—revealed to Musa (Moses)—was Holy until the Jews and the Christian scholars started tampering with it," wrote Muhammad. "It is like a 'rattlesnake' in the hands of my people, for they (most of them) do not understand it."[103] Correspondingly, the conventional Christian theology of Martin Luther King, Jr., was also false. In a 1963 speech, "God's Judgment of White America," Malcolm portrayed Elijah Muhammad as the true modern Moses, ensnared by the white Pharaoh of America's leadership, who sets up "puppet-magicians"—here he meant King and his followers—"to parrot his lies and to deceive the Hebrew slaves into thinking that Moses was a hate-teacher, an extremist," when Moses was only trying to "restore unto his people their own lost culture, their lost identity, their lost racial dignity."[104]

Creating a racial world turned upside down, the Nation of Islam provided a kind of "spiritual shock therapy," as Leon Forrest remarked, intended to reclaim the lost tribe of Shabazz wandering in the wilderness of America's ghettos, prisons, and segregated communities.[105] As the civil rights movement fractured and the counterculture waged war on every icon of American tradition, the time was ripe for such an alternative Exodus, with its rituals of purification designed to purge the white rapist's blood from black bodies and the poison of white culture from black minds so as to lead the reclaimed to the Canaan of blackness.

Much of Black Muslim doctrine was congruent with the theology of Black Judaism, but even more was readily adaptable to the tenets of Black Power. Malcolm's homey metaphors—coffee "integrated with white milk" is weak, black is strong; dark sugar is "pure sugar"; bread with the nutrients "bleached out" causes constipation[106]—were a witty way to cultivate black pride by implying, without overtly claiming, the genetic superiority of blackness. More crudely, Amiri Baraka (LeRoi Jones) made the mythology of Yakub the basis for his play *A Black Mass* (1966), in which the prototypical white man is a vomiting, farting beast, a "soulless distortion of humanity," who, in a variation on Shakespeare's Caliban, can only grunt primitive signs of his own grotesque ontology: "White! White! White!" Eldridge Cleaver likewise identified a telling psychological thread when he called Yakub's history "an inversion of the racial death-wish of American Negroes" manifest in bleaching cosmetics and marrying "light." From the premise of genetic assimilation—"that the race problem in America cannot be settled until all traces of the black race are eliminated," as Cleaver put it—comes the prediction of black genocide.[107]

That Malcolm X threw off the trappings of this convoluted counter-racism after his visit to Mecca in 1964 and adoption of traditional Islam did not lessen its potency for those who maintained allegiance to Elijah Muhammad. The Nation's absorption in the organizational secrecy and conspiratorial worldviews typical of fascist movements would reach its eventual nadir in *The Secret Relationship between Blacks and Jews* (1991), whose argument that the Jews were largely responsible for the "black holocaust" of slavery carried Muhammad's theories of genocide to their logical conclusion. Although the Nation of Islam has never gained enough power to constitute a true threat, the group's later ostentatious anti-Semitism lent credence to Alex Haley's characterization of Black Muslim philosophy, on the occasion of his interview of Malcolm X, as an amalgam of Christianity and Islam, "spiked with a black supremacy version of Hitler's Aryan racial theories."[108]

If the anti-Semitism of Louis Farrakhan was a symptom of weakness, not of power, it was also a symptom of the Nation's failure to advance beyond the ideological and imaginative lucidity achieved under Elijah Muhammad. In a jeremiad titled *The Fall of America* (1973), Muhammad quoted equally from the Bible and the Qu'ran while interpreting the political turmoil of the late 1960s and early 1970s as modern-day plagues visited upon the Egypt (or the Babylon) of America. Even as he claimed that concentration camps were being built to sequester black Americans, however, Muhammad depicted them as the chosen people about to be raised up by divine cataclysm: "So strong is Allah's love for us that He now desires nothing but a total destruction of America."[109] In the apocalyptic salvation of blackness prophesied by Muhammad, the internalization of the Exodus and chosenness was complete: white supremacy was replaced by black, one vision of genocide answered by another.

Unlike the Nation of Islam and the leading ideologues of political Black Power, proponents of "Black Theology" seldom referred to conflicts between blacks and Jews in the United States, and modern Israel seldom appeared in their sermons. Although their reading of scripture derived from Ethiopianism and was related in its genealogical assumptions to Black Judaism, they preached a liberation theology that married the biblical rhetoric of Martin Luther King, Jr., to the secular Marxist rhetoric of Black Power and made Jesus Christ an exponent of resistance and revolution. In recasting the salvationist ideologies of Garvey and black preachers such as Father Divine and Daddy Grace,[110] however, they called implicitly on the transformation in Judaism and the Jews wrought by Zionism, the Holocaust, and the creation of Israel so as to heighten the standard comparison of African Americans' four hundred years in America to the Israelites' allegorical forty years in the wilderness and their subsequent history of exile and persecution. The starting point of their Afro-Zionism was the "blackness" of the biblical Israelites; their goal, as for Elijah Muhammad, was the messianic liberation of blacks in the Egypt or Babylon of America; and their messiah was the black Jewish Jesus exhorted by the evangelical Baptist Daddy Hickman in Ralph Ellison's *Juneteenth* to prove his divinity by coming down off the cross: "IF YOU BE THE KING OF THE JEWS AND THE SON OF GOD, JUMP DOWN! JUMP DOWN, BLACK BASTARD, DIRTY JEW, JUMP DOWN!"[111]

Although Cleage and Cone stayed within a Christian eschatology, their neo-Garveyite Zionism nonetheless shared elements of the more radical claim made by the Nation of Islam and some Black Jews that the African diaspora comprised the world's "real Jews." For Cleage, pastor of the Shrine of the Black Madonna in Detroit and the foremost proponent of Black Power Christianity, Moses was a half-Jewish, half-Egyptian—but in any event "unquestionably all non-white"—man married to a Midianite, a black woman, and therefore the father of black children. (His conception of Moses thus bears comparison with Hurston's in *Moses, Man of the Mountain*.) In Cleage's "Epistle to Stokely" (1968)—that is, Student Non-Violent Coordinating Committee leader Stokely Carmichael—Abraham likewise is not white, and the covenant revealed to him in Egypt (rather than in Canaan, as we are told in Genesis 15) is the beginning of the Black Nation. When Israel, after captivity in Egypt, "fought its way into Canaan and mixed with the people of Canaan," and when it endured the captivity in Babylon, said Cleage, there was a further mixing with dark, or black, people, the ancestors of contemporary Egyptians and Arabs. A Jew of the tribe of Judah, Jesus was "a Black Messiah born to a black woman." The Pauline Christianity of slavery perpetuated in King's nonviolence is thus a falsification of scripture and history, Cleage maintained, and black militants are right to disavow this degradation in favor of the true liberation movement founded by the Black Messiah Jesus.[112]

When he argued that the struggle of the oppressed is God's struggle, James Cone quoted from Exodus 6:5–7, "I have heard the groaning of the people of Israel whom the Egyptians hold in bondage and I have remembered my covenant.... 'I will be your God.'" It was neither from introspection nor from mystical meditation, but rather from reading biblical history, argued Cone, that Israel and later the black community came to believe that "the God of the Exodus and of Jesus was struggling to liberate broken humanity to wholeness." The fulfillment of the Hebrew scripture, as well as its lasting value for African peoples, lay precisely in the blackness of Jesus:

He *is* black because he *was* a Jew. The affirmation of the Black Christ can be understood when the significance of his past Jewishness is related dialectically to the significance of his present blackness. On the one hand, the Jewishness of Jesus located him in the context of the Exodus, thereby connecting his appearance in Palestine with God's liberation of oppressed Israelites from Egypt. Unless Jesus were truly from Jewish ancestry, it would make little theological sense to say that he is the fulfillment of God's covenant with Israel. But on the other hand, the blackness of Jesus brings out the soteriological meaning of his Jewishness for our contemporary situation when Jesus' person is understood in the context of the cross and resurrection. Without negating the divine election of Israel, the cross and resurrection are Yahweh's fulfillment of his original intention for Israel to be

> a light to the nations,
> to open the eyes that are blind,
> to bring out the prisoners from the dungeon,
> from the prison those who sit in darkness (Isaiah 42:6–7).[113]

Like their forefathers in the tradition of Ethiopianism, Cone and Cleage borrowed from the example of the Jews and the inspiration of Zionism in turning the message of the slave spirituals—Africans in America are God's people awaiting liberation—into a testament of rebellion. In *Black Theology and Black Power* (1969) Cone harked back to early black militants such as Henry Highland Garnet and cited more recent theorists of liberation such as Frantz Fanon in order to fashion a theology in which *"the black revolution is the work of Christ."* By choosing Israel, said Cone, God chose the oppressed as his allies, and for that reason Black Theology cannot be color-blind: "Christianity is not alien to Black Power; it is Black Power."[114] Like Cone's volume, the Afrocentric sermons collected in Cleage's 1968 volume *The Black Messiah,* a jeremiad for the black nation that no longer believes in itself, also reinterpreted the figurative Exodus of early African Americans to demonstrate that the biblical Jews were truly "the Black Nation Israel" and that contemporary African Americans were beyond question "God's chosen people."[115]

By the time Cleage and Cone were writing, however, it was not just the biblical Israel with which African Americans had to reckon but the state of Israel, a true homeland of the Jews for those who wanted one—and the enemy of Egypt. In blackening the Bible and the people Israel, Cleage and Cone grafted the iconoclastic genealogical assumptions of Black Judaism onto a conventional Christian typology. By collapsing Moses and Christ into a single messianic figure, Black Theology acknowledged an intimate dependence on the foundational beliefs of Judaism while at the same time offering a strident form of Christian supersessionism in keeping with the anti-Zionism of Black Power. Before looking more closely at black American reactions to Zionism and the creation of a modern Jewish homeland, though, we must briefly examine three correlative issues. Jumping forward to the present day, we will consider one instance of speculative fiction whose Afro-Zionism builds on the core beliefs of Ethiopianism and Black Judaism, Tananarive Due's novels *My Soul to Keep* and its sequel *The Living Blood,* and another instance that attempts to unravel the tangled genealogy of Black Judaism and Black Islam, Jon Michael Spencer's *Tribes of Benjamin.* We will then take up the example of Afro-Zionism literalized when Ben Ammi Carter and the Hebrew Israelites of Chicago made *aliyah* in 1969.

Blood Is The Vessel For Life

Tananarive Due's supernatural thrillers tap into a set of contemporary assumptions about the nebulous relationship between race and "blood." In *My Soul to Keep* (1997), we are introduced to the African American jazz scholar David Wolde, a resident of Miami who in reality is Dawit, a five-hundred-year-old Ethiopian, one of fifty-nine brothers of the "Life Blood" who have been given immortality through blood so infused with magical "supercells" that no diseases or injuries, no matter how severe or how agonizing the pain, can destroy them. In his past life as an American slave, for example, David lived through a lynching. Because members of the Life Blood watch family and friends die while they themselves live on, generation after generation, they hold themselves aloof from emotional attachment to mortals lest they be tempted to reveal their secret, and they must likewise kill, as David has on several occasions, to protect their power. But David makes the fatal error of becoming too enmeshed in the lives of his wife, Jessica, and his daughter Kira, and at the end of *My Soul to Keep,* he kills them both so that they may join him in eternal life. Although he succeeds in making Jessica immortal by infusing his Living Blood into her open wound, he fails to resurrect Kira before being gunned down by the police.

In *The Living Blood* (2001) we find Jessica and her second daughter, Fana, with whom she was pregnant when David killed her, and who was therefore born with his immortal blood, living in Botswana. Jessica runs a clinic where she heals children with AIDS, sickle-cell anemia, and other incurable blood diseases by surreptitiously transfusing them with her own Living Blood. Meanwhile, David has been captured by the Life Brothers and returned to Lalibela, Ethiopia, his place of birth, where he is recovering from having been burned alive in punishment for making Jessica immortal. As word of the clinic's miracle cures gets out, Jessica becomes the target of a Florida doctor seeking help for his leukemia-stricken son, drug company mercenaries pursuing the clinic's magic blood, and Life Brothers determined to destroy the illegitimate immortals. Much of the plot is devoted to the spectacular effects of Fana's supernatural powers (she reads minds, alters memories, causes hurricanes, and kills by mentally telegraphing heart attacks and morbid "exsanguinations," the effects of which resemble the bloodletting of the Ebola virus). By the conclusion of *The Living Blood*, Jessica and Fana have been reunited with David, new members have been added to the Life Brothers, and the novel's characters are settled on a Washington commune, where health specialists and alternative medicine gurus have been summoned to hear about the healing properties of the Living Blood.

It is not the garish, sci-fi action of the novels, however, but their religious substructure that is of interest here. In one sense, Due renders the Living Blood in universalist terms, for when David makes Jessica immortal, he defies "God, or Allah, or Yahweh, the Life Force who made the blood live." But the specific links to Judaism are many, beginning with the role of blood as a sacrificial substance central to the Hebrew Bible's understanding of life itself: "For the life of the flesh is in the blood: and I have assigned it to you for making expiation for your lives upon the altar" (Leviticus 17:11). We are told that David in his contemporary life bears the "Hebrew variation of the name his mother had given him in his first language, so long ago." In performing the Ritual of Life for the Living Blood, David recites an incantation in Hebrew: "The blood is the vessel for Life. The blood flows without end, as a river through the Valley of Death." In returning to Lalibela, he returns to a city likened to Jerusalem. And the topos of Ethiopia as the home of the original Black Jews is further underscored in the Rastafarian chant that Due chooses as the epigraph to the chapter of *The Living Blood* in which Jessica and Fana, crossing a stream called "the river Jordan," travel to Lalibela in search of enlightenment about their immortality and Fana's telekinetic powers:

> Zion me wan go home,
> Zion me wan go home,
> Oh, oh,
> Zion me wan go home.[116]

In locating the gifts of higher consciousness and the secret of immortality among an ancient Ethiopian sect, Due recalls the Ethiopianism of Edward Blyden, as well as its modern manifestation in the Rastafarian veneration of Haile Selassie, both of which adapt Christian scripture to an Afro-Zionist paradigm. As in *Bailey's Cafe*, Ethiopia is both a sacred black homeland and the source of messianic salvation.

Not just the "true Jews," however, these Ethiopians are held out as something better, for their immortality has been achieved through a sacrificial rite derived from the very essence of Christianity. In performing the Ritual of Life for the Living Blood, David also betrays "the Covenant," the Life Brothers' agreement to protect their sacred kinship, which in turn springs from their leader, Khaldun, whose original immortality was achieved by means of a sacrificial infusion of blood stolen from the crucified Jesus Christ. As Khaldun explains to Jessica, the first Life Brother was therefore the light-skinned black Jesus Christ, the "first to awaken after he died . . . the first to Rise."[117] (For the Life Brothers, "Rising" is a Buddhist-like higher form of consciousness achieved only after much study and meditation.) The Zionist thrust of Due's Ethiopianism is thus displaced—superseded, one should say—by a Christian eschatology that more resembles James Cone's liberationist argument, cited earlier, that Jesus "*is* black because he *was* a Jew," that it is his Jewishness, indeed, that truly makes him "the fulfillment of God's covenant with Israel." The fact that the Living Blood derives from the resurrected Christ might be deemed blasphemous, but the typology of Christian supersession, in particular one issuing in a Black Christ, is in no way foreign to Ethiopianism. But another aspect of Due's premise is more unsettling.

The use of the stolen blood of the resurrected Jesus Christ also invokes, whether by design or not, the historic blood libel at the heart of Christian anti-Semitism. The nefarious accusation that Jews drain the blood of Christians, children in particular, for use in Passover matzo or other ritual purposes has been responsible for persecution and pogroms two thousand years in duration. Although it is by no means confined to Christians—in modern times it has been very much alive among Islamic anti-Semites in the Middle East—the blood libel logically derives from Christianity itself. Some interpretations have identified the blood libel with the charge of deicide—that the Jews killed Christ—but the symbolism of violent sacrifice and consumed blood is more intricate. Because the idea of collecting blood from the body of a slain Christian child resembles the legendary iconography of Joseph of Arimathea using the chalice of the Holy Grail to collect the blood of the crucified Christ, as Alan Dundes has pointed out, the belief that Jews use Christian blood in the Passover meal may also be seen as a perversion of transubstantiation whereby Jews, by devouring the blood of Christ, would presume to achieve immortality. The bloody matzo is thus a version of the bread and wine that purport in communion to be the body and blood of Christ. Whereas the Hebrew Bible prohibits the eating of blood (Genesis 9:4; Leviticus 3:17, 17:12), however, the Christian New Testament in effect commands it in the words of Jesus (John 6:53–56); the blood libel may therefore be seen as an inverted transference to Jews of Christians' guilt over partaking of the Eucharist, over their own blood libel. Instead of Christians devouring a Jew (Christ), Jews are devouring a Christian.[118]

The ritual of immortality on which the plots of My Soul to Keep and The Living Blood are built need not be understood as an instance of either deicide or blood libel per se. In awakening these undercurrents, however, Due places the metaphor of blood, central to African American culture, in a volatile historical context. African Americans, as we will see in Chapter 7, have feared genocide in the guise of medical research, whether in the real case of the "bad blood" left untreated in unknowing subjects in the Tuskegee syphilis experiments of 1932 or the more recent conspiratorial fantasy that AIDS is either the product of germ warfare tests or a plague invented to wipe out the black community (or, in an especially scandalous variation, a lethal germ injected into black babies by Jewish doctors). Conversely, as a slang term for Africans in the diaspora, "blood" connotes kinship and shared bloodlines,[119] or more loosely a sense of community or figurative family, as in Bloods, the title of Wallace Terry's oral history of black soldiers in Vietnam, or the Los Angeles–based gang known as the "Bloods."

Such usage, a sign of brotherhood and belonging, stands in psychological counterpoint to the history of anti-black racism where "black blood" carries the threat of contamination, whether in the "mongrel" hybridity produced by miscegenation or in the polluting "blackness" of Jews in Nazi Germany. Conscious of the negative meaning attributed to their own blood by racists, blacks might understandably wish in turn that they could cleanse their blood of the white infection that is the legacy of interracial rape during slavery and Jim Crow. A purified bloodline was what Malcolm X, referring to his white grandfather as "that raping, red-headed devil," wished for: "If I could drain away his blood that pollutes my body, and pollutes my complexion, I'd do it. Because I hate every drop of the rapist's blood in me."[120]

Conspiracy theories and nationalist rhetoric aside, AIDS has devastated Africa, and African Americans have suffered the stigma of "black" blood from slavery onward, all the while being subjected to the devastating communal and individual consequences of "one-drop" racism. Due's location of the single source of pure, immortal blood in Africa is a way of transcending the contamination of white racism by positing an original, vital, life-giving African prehistory standing free from enslavement and its legacy. The fact that her biomedical Afrocentrism depends on both the core belief of the West, Christ's death and resurrection, and the corruption of that belief purveyed by anti-Semites in the blood libel only makes it more haunting and magnetic. Due speaks directly to the religious life histories of African Americans, overwhelmingly steeped in evangelical Christianity. Yet in making her Jesus black, while hinting at the diabolism of the Jews, she turns the Living Blood into a remarkable, but disturbingly compromised, figure of racial redemption.

In drawing together several genealogical strains of Black Judaism, Ethiopia plays an even more catalytic role in Jon Michael Spencer's *Tribes of Benjamin* (1999), whose title is drawn from the enigmatic words uttered by its dying hero, Nation of Islam minister Benjamin Muhammad, after he is gunned down by fellow Muslims who suspect him of apostasy and betrayal. Whereas in Due's novels Christianity is the vehicle for discovering the latent priority of Judaism in black culture, in Spencer's novel that vehicle is, unexpectedly, the Islam of American Black Muslims. Specifically, it is the Black Muslims' argument that they, through the prophecy of Muhammad and the teaching of the Qu'ran, are the inheritors of the black biblical patriarchs, a true Semitic people, while the "so-called Jews" of Europe, Israel, and the United States are illegitimate latecomers to the tribe of Judah. (Those who call me an anti-Semite, Louis Farrakhan once remarked, "are not Semites themselves" but "Jews that adopted the faith of Judaism up in Europe; they're called *Ashkenazi* Jews. They have nothing to do with the Middle East—they're Europeans . . . not Semitic people. Their origin is *not* Palestine.")[121] In Spencer's novel of ideas, set in the late 1980s, Black Judaism finally takes precedence over Black Islam, but it does so by recourse to an equally unorthodox interpretation of modern-day Jewish identity.

Born the son of Rachel Schwartz, the observant daughter of Holocaust survivors living in Israel, and Jack MacDonald, a black man steeped in readings about Garvey, the Nation of Islam, and Rastafarianism, Benjamin inherits two intertwined histories of slavery, Exodus, Zionism, and survival that nonetheless pit his parents against each other in the matter of his faith, his father arguing that *"Ethiopia would stretch forth her hand"* to Benjamin, his mother arguing that, as a Jewish child, *"he would be called to the House of the God of Jacob."* Raised secretly by Rachel as a Jew, a kind of black Brooklyn Marrano, and then openly once Jack abandons his family, Benjamin is tormented by other children as "a nigger and a kike, a kigger and a nikker and a nike," his confused identity, as in *Bailey's Cafe*, one index of the volatile conjunction of "black" and "Jew" in the United States. At his bar mitzvah, he speaks on the subject of prophecy enunciated by Maimonides (whose family was forced to practice Judaism secretly in twelfth-century Islamic Spain). After being swept up by black nationalism in college, however, Benjamin is converted to the Nation of Islam by one Jeremiah X, a black man whose form is "sublime and holy, beautiful like Solomon, a beauty repeated by Ethiopia's young Ras Tafari," and he adopts the Nation's anti-Semitism as his own.[122] It seems, in short, as though his renunciation of his mother and his Jewishness could hardly be more complete.

In Jeremiah X's resemblance to Ras Tafari, however, we have one clue among others that the Nation of Islam, despite its virulent anti-Semitism, is not so alien to Judaism as it may appear. It is no accident that early in their marriage Jack seems to be the "dark shadow of [Rachel's] Jewish self."[123] Not only does it turn out that Rachel's Polish ancestors were, in fact, Sephardic Jews—her last name is said to be an index of the family's original "blackness"—but also Jack, for his part, turns out to be the son of an Ethiopian Jew who hid his identity after fleeing to the United States during the Italian occupation. Having joined a Brooklyn offshoot of Wentworth Matthew's congregation of Ethiopian Hebrews, Jack's father furtively passed on elements of his learning to his son, much as Rachel has raised Benjamin as a Jew. The mysterious fragments of Judaism bequeathed to Jack never coalesce into a structure of belief in his case, but they do predispose him to accept the allied belief structures of the Rastafarians and the Black Muslims. Both father and son, we are told, independently come to the conclusion that being a Muslim is the only way to be black and Jewish in America.

To be a contemporary Black Muslim, however, is to be no Jew at all—certainly not in the heyday of Nation of Islam anti-Semitism during which the novel is set. Benjamin's anguished efforts to reconcile the faith in which he was nurtured and the one he has adopted—the world of his mother and what he thinks is the world of his father—lead him to unravel the secret of his paternal ancestry among Ethiopian Jews, now living in Israel after their *aliyah* among an early wave of immigrants in 1976. In doing so he discovers, moreover, that Jeremiah X is actually his own cousin and that the words he spoke in converting Benjamin—"your way of thinking is pleasing to the Creator but not your way of acting"—were a coded message that the Nation of Islam's genealogical descent from Black Judaism, *not* its anti-Semitism, is its unrecognized foundation, "the Qur'an being at heart but a confirmation of the books of Moses."[124] At the time of his assassination, Benjamin is suspected by those who plot against him not just of reverting to Judaism but of being an adherent of the

Doenmeh, a sect of Turkish Jews posing as Muslims and spiritually descended from the Shabbetai Tzevi, a seventeenth-century self-styled messianic figure who was forcibly converted to Islam but secretly remained a Jew. The import of this clue, like Benjamin's study of Maimonides, is to underscore the historic presence of crypto-Jews within Islam, the very crime for which Benjamin is condemned by his fellow Black Muslims.

In knitting together the strands of belief and genealogical assumption held in common by the Nation of Islam, the Rastafarians, the Falashas, and American Black Jews such as the Commandment Keepers, *Tribes of Benjamin* presents an ingenious, rather surreal argument on behalf of the groups' collective claims to be the "true Jews" or their direct descendants. At least as a fictive history of ideas, it may be read as corroboration of Rudolph Windsor's 1969 counsel that Ezekiel's Valley of Dry Bones represents the enslavement and oppression of the Black Hebrews, now scattered throughout Africa and the black Atlantic, including the United States, but ready to be raised up and restored to nationhood.[125] The claims, taken one by one, may range from the suspect to the incredible, but their sociological and spiritual value cannot be discounted. Nor can the scripture that gives voice to their aspirations to liberation, repatriation, and political sovereignty. The black "theological investigator" who solves the mysteries of Benjamin's death and lost identity concludes, enigmatically, that it is not the message of Jeremiah X to which we must look for understanding but rather the (unquoted) text of Jeremiah 51, a prophecy of redemption for blacks enslaved in the Babylon of the New World: "Thus said the Lord: See, I am arousing a destructive wind against Babylon. . . . For this is a time of vengeance for the Lord, He will deal retribution to her."

THE DOOR OF NO RETURN

Spencer's intricate scheme for making the Torah the basis for the Nation of Islam would be quite enough for any novel to digest. As Jeremiah's menacing prophecy suggests, however, there is more. *Tribes of Benjamin* is constructed as a detective novel whose secrets are unlocked by the theological investigator in conversation with Benjamin's parents, but the exact nature of their son's spiritual discovery dies with him. We are left instead with another piece of the novel's strange puzzle—namely, Benjamin's determination that the only American blacks who have discovered their lost identity are the so-called Hebrew Israelites attached to Ben Ammi Carter, who turns out to be a parallel source of Jeremiah X's elliptical message. When properly parsed, we are told, Benjamin's dying utterance, "tribes of Benjamin," is really "tribes of Ben Ammi." Nevertheless, if one lesson of *Tribes of Benjamin* is that membership in the Nation of Islam is only an imperfect (and certainly ironic) way of being black and Jewish in America, the lesson of the Hebrew Israelites is that membership in Ben Ammi Carter's congregation has been only an imperfect way of being black and Jewish in Israel.

Under the leadership of Carter, who became a rabbi of the Original Hebrew Israelite Nation in the early 1960s and soon thereafter adopted a messianic posture, the Hebrew Israelites, also known as the Black Hebrews or the African Hebrew Israelites, set themselves up as true Jews based on their belief that Israel was once part of Africa and that black slavery in the New World was adumbrated in the "second Exodus" of Deuteronomy 28:68 ("And the Lord shall bring thee into Egypt again with ships . . . and there ye shall be sold unto your enemies for bondmen and bondwomen, and no man shall buy you"). Against the backdrop of race riots which seemed to Carter the sign of a coming apocalypse that would destroy the United States, he announced in 1966 that a message from God had instructed him, beginning on Passover in 1967, to lead his people to the Promised Land. His prophecy was off by a few months, but in November 1967 about 160 members of his congregation followed him first to Liberia—a two-year sojourn, Carter would later say, meant only as a "stopover to rid ourselves of our negrotism, our slave thoughts, so we could start a new life as our ancestors did when Joshua led them across the Jordan River"[126]—and then in 1969 to the community of Dimona, in Israel's Negev desert.

Unable to prove they were born of Jewish mothers and otherwise isolated from the heritage of Judaism—they followed the laws of the Torah but did not believe other books of the Bible—the Hebrew Israelites failed to qualify as Jews under the Law of Return but were admitted to Israel as tourists, a temporary measure that stretched, in the event, into decades, largely because Israel did not wish to appear racist in expelling them. Refusing to allow his followers to convert to Judaism, which would have settled the matter, Carter and other Hebrew Israelites issued a series of arcane but ominous proclamations—asserting that when Theodor Herzl founded the Zionist movement, black Americans had been raised up from the dead to preach that they were the true descendants of the ancient Israelites; claiming that the United Nations had given Israel to the wrong people in 1947; and prophesying a war of Armageddon in 1977, when 2 million of his followers would come from the United States to fulfill Carter's vision that "the Lord personally ordered me to take possession of Israel" and liberate the nation from the "false Jews," the "white Israeli racists."[127]

In a later published work, *The Messiah and the End of This World* (1991), Ben Ammi—or Ben Ammi Ben Israel, as he came to be called—would go so far as to claim that his act of repatriation was "the spiritual force behind the success of the Six Day War because the unification of Jerusalem was a prerequisite for the establishing of the Kingdom of God and the beginning of the Messianic Process of Deliverance for all men from the yoke of Euro-gentile economic and social strangulation." Most Jews, not excepting Israelis, were part of these "satanic forces" that had to be overthrown prior to the Black Hebrews' "purification of the earth."[128] Striking a middle ground between the civilizationist argument sometimes advanced by Booker T. Washington and other post-Reconstruction black leaders (slavery, despite its cruelties, had raised up black people from savagery and superstition) and the redemptive theology of the Nation of Islam (slaves to whiteness, black people must be rescued from their state of fallenness), Ben Ammi averred in another publication that blacks had lost "dominion of the world" and favor with God because of their disobedience to His laws, but the "Euro-gentile" reign was soon to end. "The African Hebrews (Children of Israel)," he maintained, "underwent a chastisement (slavery) that caused them to descend to the lowest ebb of existence among the people of the world. However, the spirit of Jacob (the African Hebrew) is now resurrected and is contesting the spirit of Esau (Euro-gentile). The return of Jacob denotes the downfall of Esau."[129]

Despite his devotion to restoring blacks to their true lost homeland, Ben Ammi kept one eye on the United States. Not surprisingly, given the implicit affiliation between Black Hebrews and Black Muslims, he cultivated ties with the Nation of Islam and, like Louis Farrakhan, charged that Jewish slave merchants and slaveholders had become rich at the expense of blacks. (After Farrakahn visited Ben Ammi in 1978, he explained that their respective followers had been chosen by God as the cornerstones of a new world government, "but they're coming at it from the point of view of the Torah and we're coming at it from the point of view of the Koran.")[130] Responding to one among a number of threats of deportation, Ben Ammi warned in the early 1970s that growing "anti-Jewish resentment" among black Americans could lead to civil chaos, owing to the potential for disruption among the nation's purported "two million Hebrew Israelites."[131] In the estrangement of blacks and Jews in the United States, however, the plight of the Hebrew Israelites and Ben Ammi's delirious pronouncements played virtually no role. He could only dream of having his views taken as seriously in the United States as those of Farrakhan, if only as acts of provocation.

Ben Ammi no longer claims that blacks are the only true Jews but simply that blacks and Jews share a common heritage and, more specifically, that all Israelites are Africans, not Europeans. But given their marginality in the United States, where small congregations survive in Chicago, St. Louis, Washington, D.C., and other cities, and their ostracism in Israel, the "tribes of Ben Ammi" do not offer a very promising model for the reconciliation of "black" and "Jew" as political, let alone ontological, categories. In an epilogue to *The Atlantic Sound* (2000) titled "Exodus," Caryl Phillips records his encounter with the Hebrew Israelites during their "New World Passover," marking the thirty-second anniversary of their "departure from the great captivity." Whatever the community's achievement for its adherents—a chosen people living according to Torah but enlivened by the music of Marvin Gaye, double-Dutch contests, and black English—the Hebrew Israelites, in Phillips's view, represent a cul-de-sac in diasporic philosophy, a marginal and possibly doomed community fruitlessly stranded between America and Israel. Ben Ammi's reversal of the Exodus, he concludes, was a misguided attempt to erase the massive history written by the Middle Passage, not just for blacks but certainly for them first of all: "There were no round-trip tickets in your part of the ship. Exodus. It is futile to walk into the face of history. As futile as trying to keep the dust from one's eyes in the desert."[132]

In philosophical terms Phillips may be right. In the everyday life of Israel, however, he has been proved wrong. Enduring government neglect, as well as hostility from Israelis and other immigrants on account of their abrasive behavior, their practice of polygamy, and their flouting of Jewish observance—the newly arrived Meir Kahane, founder of the Jewish Defense League, traveled to Dimona in 1971 to attack Ben Ammi and his followers as psychopaths, anti-Semites, and con men—the community, numbering some two thousand by the turn of the twenty-first century, has nevertheless survived. Protracted legal arguments about their legitimacy led at length to the Hebrew Israelites' being granted temporary residency in 1992 and permanent resident status in 2003, which allows them to serve in the Israeli military, establish their own residential communities, and eventually acquire full citizenship.[133] In January 2002, however, the Hebrew Israelites had already become Israeli in a sad but definitive way: the first of them to be born in Israel, Aharon Ben-Yisrael Elis, was also the first to fall to Palestinian terror, in an attack on a bat mitzvah celebration.[134]

Phillips's encounter with the Hebrew Israelites, just one episode among many in his books devoted to the intertwined global histories of blacks and Jews,* is all the more instructive because *The Atlantic Sound* also records his encounter with another community of Black Jews among the dilapidated slave forts of the Ghana coast, now a principal tourist attraction for African Americans. "These are holocaust sites for those in the diaspora," a Ghanaian academic tells Phillips during his visit. They constitute *"your* history"—that is, the history of the black diaspora—and their dilapidation is not the fault of Africans: "The Jews would never have let their holocaust shrines become places that can crumble to the ground."[135]

The keeper of black memory in this case turns out to be a Black Jew named Kohain Halevi. Inspired in part by his father's Garveyism, Kohain (as Phillips refers to him, recognizing Kohain's claim of descent from the priestly class of *cohanim*) studied traditional Judaism for a year before embarking on a seven-year study for the priesthood in the African American "House of David House of Study," after which he formed his own congregation within the Hebrew Israelite tradition. Rebuffed by Israel in his attempt to establish his congregation in the Negev, following Ben Ammi, Kohain instead settled in Ghana in 1991. Rec-

---

* Although Phillips belongs to this study only in an expansive interpretation of "American" culture, his continued inventiveness about the lessons of Jewish history for the memorialization of black history and its own holocaust is unparalleled in recent literature and commentary. Growing up in England, a country where Jews were at the time the only minority group discussed with reference to racism and exploitation, Phillips reports that he vicariously channeled his own hurt and frustration through the Jewish experience. Always remember Fanon's words in *Black Skin, White Masks*, he counsels in *The European Tribe* (1987): "Whenever you hear anyone abuse the Jews, pay attention, because he is talking about you." By the same token, Phillips's nearly relentless pursuit of metaphors of synonymity betrays a kind of blockage, as though his dramatization of one black-Jewish scenario after another were an attempt not to probe the analogical relation more deeply but, instead, to escape its compulsive repetition. In *Higher Ground* (1989), for example, the triangulated history of the slave trade and its late-twentieth-century filtering through the Holocaust animates three juxtaposed tales: the confessional story of an African collaborator in late-nineteenth-century slavery, set in a coastal slave garrison; the account of a Polish Jew in postwar England who lives with the indelible memory of her wartime life in a Nazi ghetto; and the epistolary autobiography of a neo-Garveyite black nationalist jailed in the 1960s, for whom America is Babylon, prison at once a plantation and a concentration camp, the guards Gestapo, and the religious tradition of Christian black America "slavish worship of a white faggot woodsman with long hippy hair who messed with the Jews and got what was coming to him." In *The Nature of Blood* (1997), first-person stories of concentration camp survivors are similarly interwoven with three further narratives: the story of fifteenth-century Venetian Jews accused of the ritual sacrifice of a Christian boy; a fictionalized version of Othello's race-saturated consciousness and his trajectory of destruction, including his engagement of a Jew as his intermediary with Desdemona; and the search for Jewish identity in Israel by an immigrant Falasha nurse. Caryl Phillips, *The European Tribe* (1987; rpt. New York: Vintage, 2000), p. 54; idem, *Higher Ground* (New York: Viking Penguin, 1989), p. 172.

reating the Hebraic traditions that he believes to have been practiced in Africa prior to the slave trade, Kohain's "Returning African Descendants Community" is guided by the principle that black Americans, having arrived in the Americas through the gateway of Ghana, should return by the same route. His movement, therefore, is called Hashuvah, "the return." Congruent with the Hebrew Israelite belief that slavery was God's punishment of those who disobeyed his commandments, Kohain proposes to establish sanctified places of pilgrimage at the former slave castles on the coast, places of "cleansing" akin to Mecca for Muslims and the Western Wall for Jews, but ones that include programs of "sensitization" like those found at Auschwitz.[136]

The Kohain community's contribution to the so-called Panafest, a government-sponsored cultural festival meant to cultivate tourism to the sites of slave embarkation, is a ceremony held at Cape Coast Castle titled "Thru the Door of No Return," whose purpose is to call black diasporans back to the homeland and to true spiritual wholeness. In his account of the festival, Phillips sidesteps the complicity of Africans in the slave trade, both prior to and after the onset of European trading in the late sixteenth century. He nevertheless makes clear his weariness with the therapeutic remedies of both the African hosts and the African American and Caribbean pilgrims who have returned to the motherland in search of a curative experience. The Panafest ceremony features a bathetic program of manic drumming; feeble poetry delivered by a Jamaican who claims to bring greetings from the patron deity of Rastafarianism, the long-dead Haile Selassie; and crude invocations of Nazism by one of the Kohain expatriates, who asserts that "the African holocaust of one hundred million merits a ceremony on at least the same level, and with the same degree of seriousness with which our Semitic brothers celebrate the loss of their six million."[137]

Whereas pilgrimage to the slave castles of West Africa ought to inspire some degree of awe and reverential respect for the dead, in the Black Jews of Ghana Phillips finds only a dismally compromised instance of Afro-Zionism and a destitute exposition of the black holocaust. His jaded account of the spiritual meaning the slave forts might hold for the black diaspora need not be considered dispositive—no more so than the account of a Jewish visitor who rejected the spiritual meaning of Auschwitz—but it is a telling index of the difference between the memorialization of slavery and the memorialization of the Holocaust. For Jews, the Exodus led them out of slavery; for blacks, their first Exodus led them into slavery, and their second remains uncompleted. For Jews, Zionism led them back to an ancient homeland; for blacks, the model of Zionism has provided no comparable return to an African nation—and for Black Jews like the Hebrew Israelites a return to Eretz Yisrael only as second-class residents, not citizens at all. For Jews, the calamity of their Holocaust entered into the world's memory as a warning against genocide for all time to come; for blacks, their holocaust has yet to be acknowledged in anything resembling equal terms.

Phillips's withering portrait is hardly the last word on the matter of the Holocaust and slavery, a subject to which we will return, but "Thru the Door of No Return" finds the grounds of comparison between the tragic histories of Jews and blacks distinctly asymmetrical. As the point of origin for a vast migration in which horrible suffering accompanied a far-reaching economic and cultural global transformation, but in which the purpose was not to extinguish an entire people and its way of life, Cape Coast Castle is no Auschwitz, nor can it ever be; but it is surely a site of profound meaning that deserves reverential commemoration. It is quite unlikely, even so, that it will ever truly be a place of return, the doorway of black repatriation to a lost homeland. Although Phillips, in his degree of skepticism, does not distinguish between Ben Ammi Carter and Kohain Halevi, it is clear that the former, however exotic and inimitable, has found his people's Zion, while the latter, wandering still in a strange land that is Africa itself, has not.

OUR JERUSALEM

I knew about Israel; I knew about Marcus Garvey too, and I didn't have the heart to hear about Garvey's dream coming true in another man's world.

—*Walter Mosley,* Fearless Jones

Recounting his 1962 colloquy with Elijah Muhammad, who commented that a people's ability to command respect depends on their possession of a land to call their own, James Baldwin agreed that this set the American Negro apart: "For everyone else has, is, a nation, with a specific location and a flag—even, these days, the Jew."[138] As in the case of the Exodus, the example of Israel provided blacks with an equivocal model of national identity in a restored homeland—an inspiring symbol unlike any they could ever claim as their own. African independence movements were without a doubt a potent source of unifying inspiration to civil rights leaders across the political spectrum. As NAACP director Roy Wilkins wrote to Kwame Nkrumah and the All-African People's Conference in 1958, "The rise of the African peoples to the status of free nations has inspired Americans of African descent and others of our fellow citizens who love freedom for freedom's sake."[139] Yet despite the demise of colonial rule—in 1960 alone, declared the "Year of Africa" by the United Nations, seventeen countries achieved independence and a dozen new African members were admitted to UN membership[140]—only a small number of American blacks emigrated to Ghana, Liberia, and other countries (or, like Eldridge Cleaver in Algeria, sought asylum from the United States justice system). A massive, heterogeneous continent of many tribes, cultures, and languages, most of whose modern nations were alien and inhospitable to even the most resolute immigrants, provided nothing like the concrete, singular reality of the new Jewish state.

Born of genocidal catastrophe, sanctioned by the United Nations, and won through its own bloody anticolonial revolt against British rule and multi-nation Arab antagonism, Israel was a "nation, with a specific location and a flag," not just for the Jews of Palestine but, by moral intent and legal design under the Law of Return, for the Jews of the world—both the remnant in Europe and all others who sought a homeland where they would be free from persecution. It was quickly evident what such a nation offered in the way of example to American blacks—more evident, perhaps, than what it offered to highly assimilated American Jews.

Prior to Israel, the Jew was "an *absolute foreigner*," said Albert Memmi, distinguished from other oppressed peoples in being at home nowhere and unable to return anywhere.[141] For the Nazis, indeed, exile and diaspora were conditions of Jewish identity that created one pretext for their destruction. Because the Jews' irremediable homelessness prevented them from engaging in the normal commerce and conflict among nations and left them to seek power clandestinely, said Hitler in turning persecution on its head in a routine anti-Semitic gesture, they were a particularly sinister enemy that had to be destroyed.[142] Instead, the Holocaust spurred the recovery of an ancient homeland through the creation of a new nation with powerful political and military allies. ("The Reich begat Israel," says George Steiner's fictional Hitler in a grotesque epitaph. "These are my last words. The last words of a dying man against the last words of those who suffered.")[143] An Israeli state not in Palestine—for example, in Uganda, as Herzl proposed*—might have avoided a generations-long

---

* Uganda was a provisional goal of late-nineteenth-century Zionists as an alternative to Palestine. At the Sixth Zionist Congress in Basel in 1903, Herzl managed to obtain a favorable vote for sending an investigative commission to Uganda to explore the possibility of emigration. Opposition from east European Jews, from which the major emigration was to come, would probably have killed the plan in any case, but Herzl's death in 1904 eliminated it from serious consideration.

armed conflict with hostile Arab neighbors, but it would have failed to fulfill the desirable condition of returning a chosen people to their Promised Land and reversing a two-thousand-year history of exile.

Israel's 1948 War of Independence bred an updated idealization of Zionism's "new man"—a secular, combative figure epitomized by the sabra, the native-born Palestinian Jew, and standing for national sovereignty in opposition to the trauma of the Holocaust and the degenerate condition of the diaspora.[144] From the beginnings of the Zionist movement, the pathos of life in the diaspora had been contrasted to the robust authenticity of life in Palestine. Writing in 1914, for example, Jacob Klatzkin, editor of the World Zionist Organization's official organ *Die Welt*, contended that diasporic life created Jews "disfigured in both body and soul," maintaining them "in a state of national impurity and breed[ing] some sort of outlandish creature in an environment of disintegration of cultures and of darkening spiritual horizons."[145] In the initial postwar decades, Israeli leaders frequently referred to such views in presenting emigration, on which the future strength and security of the nation depended, as a moral obligation. "Whoever dwells outside the Land of Israel is unclean," said Prime Minister David Ben-Gurion, quoting the Talmud in an address to the World Zionist Congress in 1960. The later prime minister Golda Meir was equally blunt: "Whoever becomes assimilated [in the diaspora] no longer exists for us."[146] But the vast majority of America's 5 million Jews, a population more than twice that of postwar Israel, agreed with the view subsequently expressed by a character in Philip Roth's *Operation Shylock* (1993)—that "the Diaspora is the normal condition and Zionism the abnormality."[147] Emigration was for them voluntary, and warnings that they must make *aliyah* or vanish into inauthenticity held little authority.

Nevertheless, the very existence of Israel threw into painful relief the fact that the national homes to which most American Jews or their immediate ancestors might lay claim were the wasted nations of European Jewry or those of the Soviet Union, now engulfed by anti-Semitic totalitarian rule, a fact that magnified the significance of Israel. Contemporary Jews are the first "in two millennia to exist simultaneously with the homeland," wrote Cynthia Ozick in 1970, but "we do not yet know what the full consequence of this simultaneity will be."[148] One consequence was certain. Although they dismissed the Israeli view that disapora life was degenerate and showed little interest in emigrating to a nation whose official language was known to them, if at all, only as a liturgical language,[149] the great majority of American Jews were dedicated in principle to the unconditional guarantee of Israel's survival. There would be no—there *could* be no—second genocide of the Jews.

As members of the world's largest Jewish population, Mordecai Kaplan had insisted as early in 1948, those who chose life in the United States were not "cultural parasites." Like African Americans, whose "Double Victory" campaign entailed fighting fascism abroad in order to achieve racial equality at home, Jews were engaged in a comparable battle but with the added challenge that the *"the Jewish problem in the Diaspoa and the Jewish problem in Eretz Yisrael are one."* Despite their distance from the land in which "the Jewish spirit is being reborn," said Kaplan, the founder of Reconstructionism, American Jews could achieve in their way "as great and lasting a contribution to human values as [the Jews of Palestine] are achieving in theirs." Zionism had to be redefined, he added in *A New Zionism* (1955), "so as to assure a permanent place for Diaspora Judaism," especially the Judaism of those Americans unwilling to forsake their own Zion.[150] A decade later, on the eve of the Six-Day War, Marshall Sklare's well-known study of Jews in the midwestern suburb of "Lakeville" found a strong sense of pride, protectiveness, and philanthropic devotion to Israel. (Said one resident: "Every person should have a flag or a country that they can call their own. Israel has given the American Jew a place in the world.") Yet in the previous year only 8 percent of respondents had tried to learn Hebrew, and only 2 percent had attended any study groups, courses, or lectures about Israel.[151] American advocates of emigration such as Hillel Halkin, who published *Letters to an American Jewish Friend* (1977) as a goad to others to join him in Israel, likewise did more to underwrite Israel's security than to prompt a deep interest in Israel, let alone in emigration.* As subsequent history would prove, however, the number of Americans making *aliyah* was not the right measure of the meaning of Israel.

---

* Halkin illuminated the demographic conundrum. On the one hand, Israel was faced with being slowly engulfed by its Arab population owing to a large discrepancy in birthrates; on the other, the Jewish diaspora, taken altogether, was shrinking in numbers and resources, like a planet "atmospherically exhausted, on its way to becoming as dead as the moon." If the Jewish leadership of the United States or a significant fraction of its population were to emigrate to Israel, moreover, the state's principal economic and military guarantor might be undermined. The issue, in any case, was moot. Only some five thousand to seven thousand Americans emigrated during the first twelve years of statehood, and by 1967 the number had grown only to about ten thousand, a rate embarrassing to Israelis. Near the century's end just 15 percent of American Jews indicated that they had ever even thought about settling in Israel. Hillel Halkin, *Letters to an American Jewish Friend: A Zionist's Polemic* (Philadelphia: Jewish Publication Society of America, 1977), pp. 71–73; 218–25, quotation at p. 71; Melvin I. Urofsky, *We Are One! American Jewry and Israel* (Garden City, N.Y.: Doubleday, 1978), pp. 255–77; Steven T. Rosenthal, *Irreconcilable Differences?: The Waning of the American Jewish Love Affair with Israel* (Hanover, N.H.: Brandeis University Press, 2001), p. 27; Charles S. Liebman and Steven M. Cohen, *Two Worlds of Judaism: The Israeli and American Experiences* (New Haven: Yale University Press, 1990), p. 85.

Insofar as it embodied the ideals—if not always the practices—of democracy, social justice, and liberty that were congruent with American values, Israel offered those disenchanted with the traditional beliefs and practices of Judaism an alternative sacred mission to revivify their lives as Jews and to engage indirectly in the nation's defense.[152] Israel would make them better Jews, and they, in turn, would strengthen Israel and Judaism by their philosophical and material support. As Louis Brandeis had envisioned early in the century, the United States would be both their *home* and the legitimating agent of their new *homeland*, a point made by the popularity of Chaim Potok's novel *The Chosen* (1967). Published coincidentally with the Six-Day War, the novel handily reconciles Old World spiritualism with New World pragmatism, and support for the state of Israel with life in the American diaspora.[153] In time, the attitudes of American Jews toward the nation of Israel would prove more complex. For African Americans, that complexity emerged quickly.

Just as Israel's existence as a nation, along with the United States' apparent guarantee of its continued existence, altered the identity of American Jews, so it altered black-Jewish relations by providing a vivid point of reference for the different strands of Afro-Zionism, from the Ethiopianism of Blyden through the actual emigration of Ben Ammi Carter's Hebrew Israelites. The fulfillment of Zionism in 1948, whether or not it offered a political (not to mention a military) model that blacks could emulate, inevitably changed their conception of racial nationhood. One sees this, for example, in the comments of the great African American singer Marian Anderson—best known for her Easter 1939 concert at the Lincoln Memorial after she had been forbidden by Jim Crow laws to sing in Constitution Hall—following a visit to the new state of Israel. Impressed by the special character of her Israeli audiences, in particular those who had found "a refuge and home" on two kibbutzim, Anderson understood anew how "the Negro made images out of the Bible that were as vaulting as his aspirations." The translation of biblical history into the realized political dream of a Jewish state constituted for Anderson "an act of liberation" that equally well expressed the "deepest necessities of [blacks'] human predicament."[154]

Anderson was hardly alone in recognizing the kinship alive in the example of Israel or the longing for it. Paul Robeson had argued as early as 1934, in an essay titled "I Want to Be African," that in forging their own culture, blacks must consider the parallel case of the Jews, who, "like a vast proportion of Negroes, are a race without a nation." In contrast to blacks, who do not recognize the "survivals of the earliest African religions" in their own syncretic Christianity, said Robeson, Jews, though far from Palestine, "are indissolubly bound [together] by their ancient religious practices." An acknowledgment of their common origin, interests, and attitudes "binds Jew to Jew," and a similar acknowledgment, he hoped, would one day "bind Negro to Negro."[155] Twenty years later, in "Bonds of Brotherhood," an essay written for *Jewish Life*, Robeson found more concrete evidence linking Jews and blacks in a common struggle in the translation of "Go Down, Moses" into Hebrew for Israeli audiences and, in turn, the inclusion of Jewish songs in the contemporary black repertoire:

> If it has been true that the Jewish people, like so many other national groups for whom I have sung, have warmly understood and loved the songs of my people, it has also been true that Negro audiences have been moved by songs of the Jewish people. The Hassidic Chant, for example, has a profound impact on the Negro listener not only for its content—a powerful protest against an age-old persecution—but also because of its form: the phrasing and rhythm have counterparts in traditional Negro sermon-song. And here, too, is a bond that can be traced back through the centuries to a common heritage.[156]

Israel, for Robeson, realized a nationalist imperative in which the remnants of a dispersed and persecuted people, along with their religion and culture, were gathered up and restored to their homeland. No longer were they "a race without a nation."

Although pro-Arab political sympathies and cultivation of the idea of a black holocaust eventually complicated the meaning of Israel for many African Americans, they initially responded passionately to the moral example of a movement that called a people in exile to return home and achieved a nation by overthrowing colonial rule and repelling invading enemies. Not long before partition, George W. Harris, president of the Ethiopian World Federation, an emigrationist organization dating to the Italian-Ethiopian war, stated in a letter to Du Bois that blacks, without a nation-state of their own like Israel, were destined to remain the "Topsy of Christendom," incapable of achieving either "self respect [and] racial pride" or "economic and civic parity."[157] Embracing Israel not just as a historical necessity but as an example of progressivist liberation, Du Bois pointed to what Jewish immigrants to Palestine had already accomplished in "bringing a new civilization into an old land and building up that land out of [the] ignorance, disease, and poverty into which it had fallen; and by democratic methods erecting a new and peculiarly fateful modern state." His opinion would shock later anti-Zionists, but Du Bois was in the African American mainstream in the immediate postwar years. Welcoming Israel into "the family of nations," the NAACP adopted a resolution at its 1948 annual conference proclaiming that "the valiant struggle of the people of Israel for independence serves as an inspiration to all persecuted people throughout the world."[158]

Such unalloyed commendation was not long-lived. A turning point for Israel's image among blacks was the 1955 Afro-Asian Conference in Bandung, Indonesia. Providing a forum for decolonized nations of Africa, Asia, and the Middle East to speak against the polarization and nuclear threat of the cold war, the conference led to the Movement of Non-Aligned Countries, formalized in 1961, which sought to position itself between the superpowers while adumbrating an anti-Zionist alliance of Third World nations that was to acquire increasing political power in coming decades. The conference galvanized the black left in the United States, at once introducing it into the network of pan-African, pan-Asian debates on decolonization and anti-imperialism that preceded the surge of independence movements in sub-Saharan Africa and sending a strong signal of the rising hostility toward Israel among the Nation of Islam and other dissident blacks. The exclusion of Israel from Bandung ensured easy passage of a resolution in support of Palestinian rights, but it was an index of the general support still enjoyed by Israel among most African Americans that Marguerite Cartwright, reporting on the conference in a series of articles for *Negro History Bulletin,* condemned Israel's exclusion as a pretext for Arab representatives to plot the destruction of the Jews that had eluded them in 1948.[159]

Bandung also provided the occasion for the initiation of a Soviet arms deal that consolidated Egyptian president Gamal Abdel Nasser's prestige as the exponent of pan-Arabism and prompted him to nationalize the Suez Canal the following year. In reaction, France and Britain bombed and captured the waterway itself, while Israel, acting to preserve its rights of passage through the canal and to stifle ongoing Egyptian guerrilla raids at its borders, quickly conquered all of the Sinai. Although it counted as a military victory for Israel, the Suez war was a greater ideological triumph for Nasser and Arab nationalism, which swept through the Middle East and emboldened Egypt and other nations to seek another opportunity to eliminate the Zionist enemy. As Nasser wrote to King Hussein of Jordan: "We believe that the evil introduced into the heart of the Arab world must be uprooted."[160] Long a proponent of global solidarity against colonial rule—"the color line belts the world," declared the title of a 1906 essay—Du Bois now sided with those who were quick to criticize Israel for its role in the military offensive against Egypt. In doing so, he took his cue from the Soviet Union, which had joined the United States in advocating

the establishment of Israel but in 1954 renounced its support in favor of alliance with those Arab nations, Egypt in particular, arrayed against "imperialist"
Zionism. In providing the "shock troops of two knaves," Britain and France,
who "steal the Negros' land," Du Bois wrote in his poem "Suez," Israel had betrayed the "murdered" of the Holocaust and revealed itself as a pawn of Western imperialism.[161]

Because the cold war broke the linkages between anticolonialism and the
battle against segregation, with liberal anticommunists supporting American
foreign policy as one means to secure a domestic civil rights agenda,[162] such denunciations had a small audience. (Unrepentant in his allegiance to the Soviet
Union and China, and harassed by the United States government, the aged
Du Bois in 1961 renounced his citizenship, joined the Communist Party, and
moved to Ghana, where he died two years later.) More noteworthy, though no
less problematic, in Du Bois's statement was his portrayal of Egypt as "the
Negros' land," a figurative construction that forecast the coalition, as well as the
imagined genealogical connection, between decolonized Arab and African nations that was to have a pronounced place in Black Power and set its leaders at
odds with the historic African American support for Zionism. Because Israel's
independence was the result of "anticolonial" revolt against British rule, however, many African Americans, along with many Africans, found in the Jewish
restoration of 1948 a prototype of their own pan-Africanist aspirations. Before
the late 1960s, the view that Zionism was an imperialist ideology and Israel a
colonial power—hallmarks of both Arab and Black Power anti-Zionism—
gained little acceptance among African Americans, and even some of the most
ardent anti-Zionists, we will see, continued to find strength of purpose in Zionism and even "racial" solidarity with Israelis.

For some African Americans, however, it was not clear that Israel offered any
practical lesson at all. Given black America's isolation from Africa—let alone
from a single black nation united by religion and ideology, brought into existence by United Nations mandate, and supported economically and militarily
by a world superpower—the nationalist argument that Africa, or some part of
it, could hold the same meaning for blacks that Israel held for Jews was met
with general skepticism on the part of some moderate integrationists. Appeals
to Africa may offer "temporary props to a sagging ego," said Kenneth Clark, but
the American Negro is no more African than he is Danish or Irish.[163] For Clark
and others, both the Holocaust and the creation of Israel held special meaning
with respect to the guarantee of human rights, including the particular case of
civil rights in the United States, but not as a conduit for redefining black racial
identity. Writing in 1974, Roger Wilkins recognized that slavery imposed a dif-

ference, rather than a similarity, on the experience of blacks and Jews: "Neither the yearning for a promised land nor Hitler's European bloodbath" has a clear parallel in the black American experience. "My 'old country' is Mississippi," said Wilkins, borrowing from James Baldwin, "and I can trace the trail only three generations back, to Holly Springs, where it seems to peter out. Slavery broke the link with Africa. Our first American experience was to be de-Africanized and made into chattel." By this argument, Africa was at best a "theoretical" motherland, and the enemies of Africa, unlike the enemies of Israel, said Wilkins, were "as elusive as the continent itself."[164]

In contrast to nationalists of all stripes, Albert Murray went even further in casting a cold eye on the African "homeland," but he used the example of Zionism and the Jews quite differently. If Americanization stripped blacks of their African culture, it also equipped them, ironically, to reclaim the heritage of Africa through the power of literacy, named by Murray as a particular blessing of Western tradition. Vernacular culture has been a source of great strength to Africans in America, he remarked, but the absence of documentary histories of Africa cannot be blamed on slave traders and colonial rule. In fact, "white archeologists and anthropologists have been instrumental in stimulating contemporary Africans to develop a European-type concern with the documentation and glorification of the past." The process of Americanization undergone by blacks, as well as other immigrants, therefore also exposed an advantage available in the "painstaking documentation" of Talmudic culture and the traditional Jewish orientation toward education.[165] What blacks might learn from the highly literate culture of the "people of the Book," that is, had little to do with nationalist dreams of lost homelands.

Murray was mistaken in thinking that Africa had no tradition of literacy (the Islamic tradition has proved to be significant), just as Roger Wilkins was mistaken in his characterization of the yearning among blacks for a territorially sovereign Promised Land, whether in Africa, the Caribbean, or the United States itself, a point to which we will return in Chapter 4. They were right to question the stability of the analogy between liberationist pan-Africanism and Zionism, but they overlooked its emotional power. Hence the epigraph to this section, taken from Walter Mosley's *Fearless Jones* (2001), set in 1954, in which the narrator, when confronted with an Israeli who speaks proudly of the Jews having "made our own nation," thinks despondently of Garvey's failure.[166] As the actor Ossie Davis would remark in 1969, in a tribute honoring the prominent Zionist Avraham Schenker on his emigration to Israel: "Think of the pathos of men who stand on the corner and dream of free Southern States that they want to call their own. Think of the sorrow and sadness of men who stand on a ladder in Harlem and preach of the desirability of returning to Africa some day because they will never find in this country what it is that will make them complete men." Reminding his Jewish audience that "you were Jews longer than we were," that "you have set before you a shining flame to which you can dedicate the whole totality of your being," he asked them to recognize that "we, too, seek our Jerusalem."[167]

The Lord Will Scatter You

The passionate longing for "our Jerusalem" notwithstanding, it remained the case, as James Alan McPherson would later put it, that "we [black Americans] have no distant homeland preparing an ingathering."[168] No fact better differentiates the black and Jewish diasporas. The principal historic term from which the concept of diaspora derives, the Hebrew *galut,* signifies forced displacement, subjection to alien authority, and a condition of perennial homelessness and longing for restoration to a homeland: it signifies, and is best translated as, exile. A more decidedly religious term, *galut* refers to the Babylonian exile of Israel following the destruction of the First Temple in 586 BCE and, next and principally, to the expulsion of Israel following the destruction of the Second Temple in 70 CE, after which exile became the rule, rather than the exception, in Jewish life, thus marking religious and cultural life with a sense of violent dislocation.[169] Rather than the blessings that will be theirs if Jews uphold God's covenant, pledged at Sinai, this understanding of exile is expressed scripturally as punishment for failing to do so: for example, "the Lord will scatter you among all the peoples from one end of the earth to the other, and there you shall serve other gods, wood and stone, whom neither you nor your ancestors have experienced" (Deuteronomy 28:64); or, "you I will scatter among the nations, and I will unsheathe the sword against you. Your land shall become a desolation, and your cities a ruin" (Leviticus 26:33). Other scripture implies that exile will at some point be followed by restoration—for example, "He who scattered Israel will gather them, / And will guard them as a shepherd his flock" (Jeremiah 31:10)[170]—but for the devout, only the coming of the Messiah, not a program of political settlement and conquest, can bring about the true ingathering of the Jews.[171] Modernity offered a secular solution in Emancipation; when Emancipation failed, it offered a further solution in Zionism, and at midcentury it remained to be seen if Zionism would succeed.

By stimulating a reclamation in both the political present and the reimagined past, says David Roskies, Zionism set a revolutionary goal of realizing "a covenantal space that marks the end of exile."[172] The ground having been laid by the secularization of the Enlightenment and subsequently by the Zionist settlement and cultivation of the *land* of Israel, the political realization of the *state* of Israel made it possible to say that Jews in Israel were no longer in *galut*. With the creation of Israel, the text-centered rabbinic culture that had shaped centuries of exile was displaced to a significant degree by allegiance to political identity, and God's discourse was conflated with the discourse of political modernity.[173] Tel Aviv University thus became the home not to a "museum of Jewish exile" but to the Nahum Goldmann Museum of the Jewish Diaspora (in Hebrew, Beth Hatefutsoth).[174] No Jew was forced to live in exile; any Jew could choose to live in the diaspora.

The different exilic configuration of Africans in the New World is readily apparent. For the modern-day black diaspora, the specificity of an actual national homeland is typically overridden by migratory, circum-Atlantic cultural formations that no longer connote a life of deracination but rather the vitality of multicultural, multi-diasporic national identity—a black "counterculture of modernity," in Paul Gilroy's phrase, rebuilt over the slave trade's triangulation of Europe, the Americas, and Africa. In the postcolonialist usage characterized by the now widespread pun on "roots"/"routes," whereby the correlation between one's place of residence and one's consciousness of belonging to a "nation" is severed, diaspora signifies a politico-cultural ethos of transnationalism, hybridity, and creolization, and consequently nourishes identities that are incompatible with racial essentialism and absolutist modes of ethnic nationalism. The empowering paradox of diaspora, writes James Clifford, "is that dwelling here assumes a solidarity and connection there. But there is not necessarily a single place or an exclusivist nation."[175] Nothing excludes the contemporary Jewish diaspora from such a characterization, of course, but the direction of influence might be substantially reversed, with black culture providing the model for Jewish culture, exile being accepted as a dynamic, even redemptive condition, and the state of Israel seen less as a place of homecoming than a point of continuing return and departure. Insofar as postmodernism values just those qualities of dispossession, fragmentation, uncertainty, and marginality that life in exile demands, Eva Hoffman observes, tribal life lived within an ever-shifting and reforming diaspora has become "sexy, glamorous, interesting."[176]

As it was revived by political pan-Africanism in the 1950s and 1960s, the concept of an African diaspora oscillated between the historic Jewish and postcolonial interpretations, though its roots lay in the Ethiopianism of Blyden and the different Afro-Zionisms of Garvey, Casely Hayford, and Du Bois. Even if the terminology was new, the idea was not—in fact, its association with the Jewish diaspora can be traced at least to William Mayor's *History of the Dispersion of the Jews; of Modern Egypt; and of Other African Nations* (1802)[177]—and in this respect the American dialogue between black and Jewish traditions of exile had already tempered the sense of Jewish priority brought to the fore by the success of Zionism. In mid-century usage, the concept of an African diaspora sometimes consciously drew attention to the similarities between Jewish exile and the coerced dispersion of blacks in the slave trade. George Shepperson, for example, began his landmark article on the African diaspora—initially presented at an International Congress of African Historians meeting in Dar es Salaam in October 1965, when the term had yet to gain wide use in a scholarly context—by citing the King James version of Deuteronomy 28:25, "Thou shall be removed into all the kingdoms of the earth."[178]

The scripture, as it continues, bears closer examination: "The Lord shall cause thee to be smitten before thine enemies: thou shalt go out one way against them, and flee seven ways before them: and shalt be removed unto all the kingdoms of the earth." (Or, in the version of *Tanakh:* "The Lord will put you to rout before your enemies; you shall march out against them by a single road, but flee from them by many roads; and you shall become a horror to all the kingdoms of the earth.") Confirming Moses' admonition that curses and all manner of affliction will befall the Israelites if they are disobedient, diaspora is associated in subsequent passages of Deuteronomy with madness, illness, blindness, military vanquishing, and removal or terrified flight from God's sight and protection.[179] The fuller passage thus brings the African experience, as Shepperson introduces it, much closer to the Jewish. The ambiguity within Jewish tradition introduced by the Septuagint translation of *galut* and related terms as "diaspora," rather than as "exile," is made all the more prominent in the postcolonial adaptations of recent years. In the Greek translation that carries over into English, etymological implications of *diaspeirein*—to scatter or sow, as in the cognates "disperse," "spore," "sperm," and "spread"—that are not present in the Hebrew Bible become constitutive.[180] As in the "scattering" evident in the scriptural passages just cited, "removal" carries for the Deuteronomist the negative implication of forced exile with which the post-Sinai generation is threatened. In much postcolonial practice, however, the force of dispersal is considerably counteracted by the "inseminating" significance of diaspora as the locus of transnational cultural vitality.

The idea of a black diaspora articulated by modern pan-Africanism, at least through the era of Black Power, retained the force of natal alienation and suffering in exile—what E. Franklin Frazier, echoing Casely Hayford and others, spoke of as the "household gods" effaced by slavery[181]—while lacking a readily identifiable Palestine, let alone an Israel. Absent such a homeland, its meaning sustained by the Torah and centuries of commentary on God's laws, and absent a modern nation-state in which that scriptural history has been redeemed, blacks in the African diaspora were left in a far more nebulous position than Jews either before or after 1948. Formed by the confluence of scores of cultural traditions and many colonial contexts, there was not a single African diaspora in the New World but many,[182] and Africans found themselves dispersed into a Babel of languages from which there was no return, as for the Jew, to a monolingual sacred language like Hebrew or even a transnational secular language like Yiddish or Ladino.

One solution was to turn Zionism on its head, accepting its theoretical base but rejecting its political realization in the state of Israel. Depicting Africans in the diaspora in the early 1920s, Marcus Garvey had issued a forthright Zionist challenge: "The Negro needs a nation and a country of his own, where he can best show evidence of his own ability in the art of human progress. [Being] scattered as an unmixed and unrecognized part of alien nations and civilizations [serves] but to demonstrate his imbecility, and point him out as an unworthy derelict, fit neither for the society of Greek, Jew nor Gentile." Later generations, however, saw the model in a different, oppositional light. When he counseled that "we are Africans . . . scattered all over the Western Hemisphere" and must pledge racial unity and vow "never [to] fight another African," Stokely Carmichael borrowed terms from his progenitor, yet his Zion was no longer the Palestine of the Jews but that of the Arabs and other "African" antagonists dedicated to Israel's destruction.[183]

The notion of a "scattered" people reappears throughout various strains of African American discourse, ranging from the allegorical usage of Zora Neale Hurston, quoted at the outset of this chapter, to the democratic liberalism of Ralph Ellison, to the quasi-mystical therapies of Afrocentrism.* In the anti-Zi-

---

* Ellison's most elaborate deployment of the metaphor of the "scattered" people appears in the brilliant exposition of diasporic dispossession that constitutes the Juneteenth sermon in *Juneteenth*, where the antiphonal call and response between the Reverend Daddy Hickman and his protégé Bliss builds through a crescendo of incantation into an allegory of Ezekiel's Valley of Dry Bones in which the Negro people, "scattered around this land," are raised up from captivity in the Babylon of America: "Ah, but though divided and scattered, ground down and battered into the earth . . . deep in the womb of this land, we began to stir! . . . Ah, we sprang together and walked around. All clacking together and clicking into place. All moving in time! Do! I said, Dooooo—these dry bones live!" In Ellison's usage, the Old Testament takes precedence over the American Protestant tradition inaugurated by John Winthrop in "A Model of Christian Charity" (1630), where the love of Christ "gathers together these scattered bones, of perfect old man Adam, and knits them together into one body again in Christ, whereby man is be-

onist calculations of leftist postcolonialism, it even becomes a finger of accusation pointed at the Jews of Israel, as when Stuart Hall privileges the black diaspora as one arising from the heterogeneous, hybrid cultural forms of the black Atlantic rather than the imperialist, hegemonic forms of those "scattered tribes whose identity can only be secured in relation to some sacred homeland to which they must return at all costs, even if it means pushing other people into the sea."[184] In deriding an essential component of Jewish historical identity, Hall's inversion of the frequently announced goal of Arab anti-Zionism—namely, to push the Jews into the sea—demonstrates the ease with which the emulation of the Jewish example could be spun into its opposite.

By the time of the Six-Day War, Israel's image as a model of anticolonial liberation—one that made it a prominent partner of black African nations throughout the 1950s and early 1960s—had been almost completely superseded by its image as an imperial tyrant. David had become Goliath, according to a common cliché. Black Power pan-Africanists such as Carmichael, as we will see in more detail in Chapter 5, were driven by camaraderie with Israel's Third World enemies, Egypt in particular, a political variation on the Afrocentric metonymy in which the land of the pharaohs is taken for the whole of Africa.[185] This shift in allegiances grew as much from Black Power's domestic agenda as from its response to America's support for Israel, but it also had an abstract psychological dimension. Insofar as a heritage of bondage and powerlessness was part of the foundation of black nationalism and its liberationist ethos, the very existence of the state of Israel, which ended Jewish exile, diminished its value as a model. The demonstration that Jews were no longer powerless—indeed, were a military power allied with and armed by the United States—diminished it further still.

It is important to note, nevertheless, that even those blacks who now read

---

come again a living soul." But his notion of a black diaspora does not entail racially or religiously determined identity. The peoples "of partially African origin now scattered throughout the world," Ellison wrote in 1958, are bound together not by an inherited African culture, still less by "pigmentation," but rather by "an identity of passions" rooted in hatred of their "alienation, colonization, and enslavement." Yet this identity is shared by most nonwhite peoples, he went on to say, so that "while it has political value of great potency, its cultural value is almost nil." Molefi Asante, in contrast, speaks of "overseas Africans . . . who have been scattered over the globe" and hypothesizes a force of consciousness acting to rescue the "children of Africa" who have become "doubly lost, zombies in the midst of stone and steel cities of the Americas," and restore them to a sense of identity with the culture of the homeland. Ralph Ellison, *Juneteenth: A Novel*, ed. John F. Callahan (New York: Random House, 1999), pp. 124–27; idem, "Some Questions and Some Answers" (1958), in *Shadow and Act* (1964; rpt. New York: Vintage, 1972), pp. 263–64; Molefi Kete Asante, *Afrocentricity* (Trenton, N.J.: Africa World Press, 1988), p. 106.

the modern Exodus as a story of colonial conquest continued to find in Zionism a compelling version of national liberation. Although he was to be better known for his anti-Semitism, none other than Malcolm X predicted a black spiritual, if not a physical, ingathering to the homeland that borrowed from the example of the Jews. Placing himself in the tradition of Afro-Zionism that included Washington, Blyden, Du Bois, and Garvey, Malcolm contended in 1964 that blacks have much to learn from American Jews, whose cultural, philosophical, and psychological ties to Israel take the place of actual emigration: "Pan Africanism will do for the people of African descent all over the world, the same that Zionism has done for Jews all over the world."[186] The example of Zionism thus included turning to force of arms as a means to create a homeland. Malcolm was "only speaking the truth," argued Baldwin in *The Fire Next Time* (1963), when he pointed out that protests against the use of violence were not raised when Israelis fought for their independence but only when "black men indicate that they will fight for *their* rights."[187]

Seeking an ideological ground for the Black Panther Party's combined dedication to armed struggle and community service activities—its slogan was "nationalist in form, socialist in action"—Eldridge Cleaver, the Panthers' minister of information, found the example of Zionism equally instructive. At the time of Herzl, he wrote, Jews "had no homeland and were dispersed around the world, cooped up in the ghettos of Europe." Responding to devastating pogroms and driven to common action, the Zionist movement was, in effect, "a government in exile for a people in exile." For the same reason, political movements such as Malcolm X's Organization of Afro-American Unity and the Black Panthers were instrumental to promoting a black revolutionary consciousness that will either "sweep the people forward into nationhood" or else end in a "catastrophe of unprecedented proportions."*

Further probing the Afro-Zionism of Malcolm and Cleaver in the context of Black Power, Haki Madhubuti (Don L. Lee) contended in 1970 that black nationalists must look not just to Israel's example but also to that of American

---

* Cleaver was neither disingenuous nor mistaken in citing Herzl. Whether or not Cleaver knew it, the father of the Zionist movement had made the same connection. In his futuristic 1902 novel *Altneuland (Old-New-Land)*, Herzl's idealistic Zionist Professor Steineck proposes to address the problem of black slavery and its aftermath of displacement and discrimination by helping to open the way for blacks to return to Africa: "Now that I have lived to see the return of the Jews, I wish I could help to prepare the way for the return of the Negroes. . . . All men should have a homeland. Then they will be kinder towards each other. They will understand each other better and love their brethren better." Eldridge Cleaver, "The Land Question and Black Liberation" (1968), in *Post-prison Writings and Speeches*, ed. Robert Scheer (New York: Random House, 1969), pp. 67–69; Theodor Herzl, *Altneuland (Old-New-Land)*, trans. Paula Arnold (Haifa: Haifa Publishing Co., 1960), pp. 129–30.

Jews, who "have developed a *nationalist consciousness* that is interwoven with their *religious identity.*" They are a "nation within a nation," which in turn is guaranteed by the survival of an external nation-state. A few years later, in "We Are an Afrikan People," Madhubuti added that the danger of assimilation—the danger of a population's not considering themselves a "people" in the face of persecution—was proved by the Holocaust and then again by the threat to Israel's survival in the Six-Day War. Jews know that "they have to fight 365 days a year wherever they are in the world, to remain Jews and to keep Israel as a Jewish homeland." Lest it require "Afrikan pogroms" to bring about a similar political awareness among blacks, they must develop the "frame of reference" prerequisite to survival as a nation, however dispersed around the globe they may be.[188]

As Madhubuti's combative language indicates, the Six-Day War proved a stark moment of reckoning in black-Jewish relations. For a significant number of African American intellectuals, the Israelis were enemies of the Third World, puppets of American power, while the Arabs stood for resistance to the forces of colonialism—standard-bearers for "a world of color that fights for its liberation from Mozambique to Mississippi," as Richard Gibson phrased it in 1967.[189] In the revision of the Exodus promulgated by Black Power, the delivery of blacks into the Egypt of American slavery was to be reversed by symbolic kinship with the Egypt of Africa, which, like Ethiopia before it, became a repository of ancestral black civilization and a perceived political ally of Black Power. Not single nations alone, however, but the entirety of the black diaspora was the object of struggle. The liberation of Africans worldwide, said Amiri Baraka, would be underwritten by a "*Black Value System*" of African philosophical principles uniting blacks in a "continental African state." Just as Jews from around the world came to Israel's assistance in 1967, asserted Stokely Carmichael, blacks must now do the same, with Ghana the starting point for the pan-African "ingathering" of the world's blacks in exile.[190]

There would be no ingathering of the African diaspora, and none was needed to ensure the continued vitality of syncretic cultures throughout the black Atlantic. But the failure of Afro-Zionism did not lessen the longing for a lost homeland; it only made it more poignant.

WHERE COULD I GO?

When mid-century proponents of cultural nationalism called for the rediscovery of a lost African past, they sought to counter the prevalent view of Frazier and others that African Americans had been severed from African culture by the trauma of slavery. In doing so, they harked back to an earlier historiography that delineated a continuum between African civilization and the Harlem Renaissance. The Black Arts anthology *Black Fire* (1968), for example, included John Henrik Clarke's "Reclaiming the Lost African Heritage," an essay that revived an Afrocentric (and reparative) argument first articulated in works such as Du Bois's *The Negro* (1915); Arthur Schomburg's "The Negro Digs Up His Past," his contribution to Alain Locke's landmark collection *The New Negro* (1925); and Nancy Cunard's *Negro: An Anthology* (1934). The study of African culture, Schomburg contended, would allow the Negro to discover his ennobling future in the study of the past: "History must restore what slavery took away, for it is the social damage of slavery that the present generation must repair and offset."[191] The psychological repair and, by extension, the political empowerment that would issue from recovery of an African past were even more pronounced aspects of the ideology and aesthetic of Black Power. "There is no 'Negroland,'" argued Richard B. Moore in trying to dislodge the denigrating misnomer "Negro," only a continent whose "record of history bears out a glorious past and a mighty history of achievement for the peoples of Africa."[192] Seeking to overturn the derogatory images of Africa long promulgated by the enemies of "our homeland," Malcolm X remarked concisely that "you can't hate the roots of the tree without hating the tree."[193]

It was not necessary to return to Africa, of course, in order to cultivate an African identity, any more than it was necessary for Jews to return to Israel. Well before the creation of Israel, the repeated dispersal and re-grounding of Jewish culture, its repeated "rediasporization," as Jonathan Boyarin points out, had made it "commemorative."[194] From the folktales and spirituals of slavery through the Harlem Renaissance and on through contemporary Afrocentrism, African Americans have likewise sought to fashion a culture of "remembered" history, making commemoration of the past and political action in the present part of the same nationalist strategy. Black Americans must recognize their obligation to cultivate an African heritage as part of a coherent black culture, said Renee Neblett, an African American teacher who settled in Ghana, lest they "end up like other tribes, and that is extinct as a cultural entity." Does the "New York Jew" feel apologetic about supporting Israel? she asked rhetorically. Even though American Jews might be ambivalent about Israeli politics, she pointed out to black Americans, "it's still your family."[195]

As it entered the mainstream of African American life in the third decade of the civil rights era, pluralist Afrocentrism, an Americanized dilution of pan-Africanism, offered blacks a means to replicate the ethnic fraternity of European immigrants, Jews in particular. Writing in the bicentennial year 1976 and

sounding very much like Louis Brandeis when he proclaimed the easy amalgamation of Zionism and American patriotism, Margaret Walker, author of the
best-selling slavery novel *Jubilee* (1966), struck a bland compromise between
Afrocentrism and Americanism when she chose words of aspiration that might
have belonged to any number of Irish Americans or Asian Americans or Jewish
Americans: "To understand and reclaim our ancient African past as a heritage—to acknowledge our American nationhood as our new horizon—these
are the first steps toward our great future and spiritual destiny in a world of the
twenty-first century, which we are building for our children."[196]

As it evolved in the later twentieth century, however, the populist, conspiratorial version of Afrocentrism propagated by some black academics and itinerant speakers—what Stephen Howe refers to as "wild Afrocentrism"[197]—owed
more to the psychotherapeutic effects envisioned by Frantz Fanon when he
said that the anticolonial intellectual struggle was animated by "the secret hope
of discovering beyond the misery of today, beyond self-contempt, resignation
and abjuration, some very beautiful and splendid era whose existence rehabili-
tates us both in regard to ourselves and others."[198] Like other ethnocentric
nationalisms, Afrocentrism in this vein combines ancestral practice with customs invented in the United States or borrowed from other traditions in a mixture of authenticity and kitsch, with Jewish models in this case once again
much in evidence. To take the most conspicuous example, the now popular
Kwanzaa, a neo-African harvest festival invented by Maulana Karenga in 1966,
borrows elements from the Passover seder. Celebrated in late December, however, it is closer in purpose to Hanukkah, an otherwise minor Jewish holiday that, like Kwanzaa, has undergone commodification in competition with
Christmas. The likeness between the African American and Jewish holidays is
underscored by the fact that each remains subordinated in public recognition
and ritual practice to the normative beliefs of the white gentile community.*

---

* Despite the resemblance of Kwanzaa to Hanukkah, Karenga has advised against using a menorah in
place of the required candelabrum since it would represent "a culturally incompatible and aesthetically
dissonant intrusion in the context of an African motif." In his January 2, 2001, installment of "The
Boondocks," syndicated black cartoonist Aaron McGruder depicted his middle-class character Tom Du
Bois deriding Kwanzaa as a "low-budget Hanukkah." Like any holiday, Kwanzaa is subject to many interpretations, from politically radical to commercially superficial. (The U.S. Postal Service issued a
Kwanzaa stamp in 1997.) To the extent that its resemblance to Hanukkah is a sign of cultural imitation, however, it is also a sign of a telling identification between outsiders. As a manifestation of
Afrocentrism, argues Gerald Early, Kwanzaa is a "holiday of compensation" whose refutation of the
"whiteness" of Christmas describes a trajectory of decline from a mythic yesterday to a today of marginality and second-class citizenship. But Hanukkah, too, refutes the "whiteness" of Christmas in the sense

In keeping with the nationalist essentialism of Black Power—Ethiopianist by inspiration and anti-Zionist by implication—the most chauvinistic models of Afrocentrism posit a precolonial "blackness," derived from the glories of an ancient homeland in pharaonic Egypt, as the foundation of African American identity. Slavery and the slave trade are erased through the recovery of primal African consciousness, with historical time frozen at a point anterior to modernity, while the apparent futility of the Mosaic paradigm is set aside in favor of claims to the effect that North Africans, not Greeks, were the originators of Western civilization—in particular, that Egypt was a "black civilization" from which all of Western thought and culture have flowed. In the colorful simile offered by Afrocentrist educator Wade Nobles, the purported Greek theft of Egyptian knowledge is "like someone drinking some good stuff, vomiting it, and then we have to catch the vomit and drink it ourselves."[199]

The important corrective influence of some Afrocentric scholarship—the best known being Martin Bernal's critique of the "Aryan" model of research that divorced Egypt from the western tradition because it was African or, if its importance was granted, proceeded as though it were not a part of Africa—has been overshadowed by extravagant claims notable more for their promotion of racialist self-esteem than for their contribution to scholarly knowledge.[200] For the Nation of Islam, whose core mythology I examined earlier, Africa and the Middle East usually constitute a single geo-theological entity, the native home of the Afro-Asiatic black people now living in exile in America—what Elijah Muhammad had in mind when he spoke of the "so-called Negroes" as the tribe of Shabazz, which purportedly came to earth 66 trillion years ago and discovered "the best part of our planet to live on," the "rich Nile Valley of Egypt and the present seat of the Holy City, Mecca."[201] Somewhat less extravagant, the "afrology" of Molefi Asante is an airy blend of Africanist spiritualism and pop psychotherapy intended to counter the "suicide" of black minds by restoring in them the conviction that "the original idea for culture and civilization first went down the Nile from the interior of Africa."[202]

By leaving its most exaggerated claims open to ridicule, the pseudo-scholar-

---

that, like Kwanzaa, it sits on the margin of the majority American experience, signaling an assimilation that remains partial in cultural terms even if it is substantial in economic, political, and social terms. Perhaps the ambivalence of Jewish assimilation is best represented in "White Christmas," an archetypal expression of the dominant culture written by the Jewish Irving Berlin. Maulana Karenga quoted in David K. Shipler, *A Country of Strangers: Blacks and Whites in America* (New York: Alfred A. Knopf, 1997), pp. 202–3; Aaron McGruder, "The Boondocks," *Chicago Tribune*, January 2, 2001, sec. 5, p. 7; Gerald Early, "Dreaming of a Black Christmas," *Harper's Magazine* 294 (January 1997), 58–61.

ship of extremist Afrocentrism—perhaps the most notorious among the up-surge in Afrocentric teachings during the 1990s was Leonard Jeffries's conten-tion, noted earlier, that the racial superiority of blacks, the "sun people," is produced by the secret powers of melanin denied to whites, the "ice people"—runs the risk of creating more racism than it refutes.[203] Yet the Afrocentric dismissal of legitimate scholarly methods as inherently racist (because they are "white") and the substitution of symbolism for historical proof runs the greater risk of erecting blood-based, fascist mythologies of ethnic supremacy.[204] When Cheikh Anta Diop revived earlier arguments that the origins of civiliza-tion were to be found in black Egypt, he meant to offer a vehicle for psychic liberation from colonial rule and, at the same time, to warn against the dangers of ideological fanaticism: "The Black man must become able to restore the continuity of his national historic past, to draw from it the moral advantage needed to reconquer his place in the modern world, without falling into the ex-cess of Nazism in reverse."[205] But more than a few Afrocentric heirs of Black Power and Black Arts, observes Stanley Crouch, have simply created an inver-sion of Jim Crow, in effect replicating the doctrine of white supremacy by pos-iting an "inviolate way of life" whose prototype is the Third Reich's fusion of culture and genetic destiny.[206]

Such radical revisions of the black Exodus appear not just in scholarship and polemic but also in popular music, from jazz to reggae to hip-hop. The avant-garde musician Sun Ra, for example, elicited a cult following, as well as a sub-stantial body of commentary, based on a theory of black origins that infused paradigmatic beliefs of the Black Jews and the Nation of Islam with a Holo-caust-inflected utopianism. Widely read in Egyptology and Afrocentric history, George G. M. James's *Stolen Legacy* in particular, and taking his name from the sun god of ancient Egypt, Sun Ra developed the theory that African Americans, because they were forced to identify with the ancient Israelites and to revere Moses rather than Pharaoh, have lived with a corrupt sense of their own his-tory, cut off from the Egyptian fount of beauty. The ethos of the civil rights movement is thus no more redemptive than modern-day soul and gospel mu-sic, the denigrating heritage of those songs that slaves were permitted to sing "in the concentration-camp universe of 18th C America."* Racial redemption,

---

* In borrowing from Elijah Muhammad's salvationist vision of a great wheel-like spaceship that will come to destroy white supremacy and institute the divine reign of black people, and even more so in proclaiming Saturn as his true home, one cosmologically prior to Egypt, Sun Ra took the slave spiritu-als' trope of flying "home" to Africa to a new level of imagination and transformed alienation, literally, into a supernatural identity. Like the Nation of Islam, he turned Exodus upside down. Blacks are the

according to Sun Ra's argument, lies not just on the other side of the holocaust of slavery but on the other side of the false model of the Jews' Exodus.

Its most vocal skeptics have dismissed Afrocentrism and the racialist ideology on which it is based as so much bogus mysticism—a species of "blood magic and blood thinking" (Ralph Ellison), guided by the "totalitarian groupthink" of "Afromessianism" (Clarence Walker), in which the real, blues-inflected history of Africans in America is replaced by "Afrocentric wonderlands" and salvific therapies leaving blacks "wrapped in the piety of our victimization and the holiness of our ethnicity" (Gerald Early).[207] Even the most ardent skeptics of Afrocentrism, however, have understood its power to promote ethnic solidarity, a principal way of finding one's place in America, no less for blacks than for Italians, Poles, Chicanos, Jews, and others. Pointing to Leo Strauss's 1963 address to the Hillel Foundation of the University of Chicago, "Why We Remain Jews," in which Strauss argued that, in the face of the destructive pressures of mono-cultural assimilation, any other course would be dishonorable, the economist Glenn Loury adds, "It seems odd that many defend Strauss's impulse while repudiating blacks for believing essentially the same thing." When he came a few years later to explain his conversion from neoconservatism to the liberal mainstream of black politics, Loury played more affectingly yet upon the theme of longing for an identifiable homeland: "There came a point when I couldn't look my own people in the face. Everyone else had a place to go. Some would go to Jerusalem. Others would go to Dublin. You see the metaphor. Where could I go?"[208]

Not to Africa, it seems. Those who have hoped to discover their primordial identity and a true homeland in Africa have frequently found their illusions shattered, as we may see in two testimonies from the 1990s. In *Native Stranger* (1992), a text of return located tonally midway between Alex Haley and

true chosen people, the true Jews of biblical prophecy, whereas those who call themselves Jews are the usurpers, whose Talmudic scholars fabricated the curse of Ham to enslave black people. As Sun Ra remarked in a 1990 interview, "the world's in the condition it is today because of Moses, not because of Pharaoh. . . . They talk about Hitler, the worst dictator was Moses." Kodwo Eshun, *More Brilliant Than the Sun: Adventures in Sonic Fiction* (London: Quartet Books, 1998), pp. 154–56, quotation at p. 155; Graham Lock, *Blutopia: Visions of the Future and Revisions of the Past in the Work of Sun Ra, Duke Ellington, and Anthony Braxton* (Durham: Duke University Press, 1999), pp. 28–74, quotation at pp. 20–21; John F. Szwed, *Space Is the Place: The Lives and Times of Sun Ra* (1997; rpt. New York: Da Capo Press, 1998), pp. 62–73; Robin D. G. Kelley, *Freedom Dreams: The Black Radical Imagination* (Boston: Beacon Press, 2002), pp. 29–35.

Thomas Wolfe, Eddy Harris identifies Africa as a motherland, a source of black pride and a place of black dignity, while at the same time he determines that his estrangement from Africa leaves him "an orphan, a waif without a home." "Blackamericans" differ from white Americans, who, not marked by color, have two distinct advantages: they "can hide inside American society in ways we cannot. And they have access to their homelands in ways that we have been denied. Proximity, money, cultural awareness." Somewhere "deep in the hidden reaches of my being, Africa beats in my blood and shows itself in my hair, my skin, my eyes," Harris concludes, but the "land of my ancestors" cannot be home "simply because of an accident of birth. I am not one of them."[209]

In visiting Goree Island in Senegal, a transit point for African slaves bound for America, the journalist Keith Richburg hoped a few years later for even more—but found even less. Standing where his ancestors began their forced migration, he feels revulsion at the crime of slavery comparable to the revulsion he felt when he once visited Auschwitz, he notes. The experience produces a reminder that past atrocities must not be forgotten—but he feels no "spiritual connection," no "emotional frame of reference," no kinship with those destroyed. Having traveled extensively in Zaire, Kenya, Nigeria, and other countries, and having covered wars in Somalia and Rwanda as Africa bureau chief for the *Washington Post*, moreover, Richburg reaches a conclusion utterly at odds with the romance of Afrocentrism. The continent's squalor, political chaos, and especially its abuse of human rights in manifold civil wars confirms for him the irrefutable truth of national identity: "Thank God my ancestor got out, because, now, I am not one of them. In short, thank God I am an American."[210]

In the face of such sobering experiences, it is no surprise that contemporary Afrocentrism rarely calls for repatriation. Rather, Kelefa Sanneh points out, Africa thrives best as an elusive metaphor, living on "in the black American imagination as a dream, as something so ethereal that it can't possibly disappoint"[211]—in short, the Egypt of Molefi Asante or Sun Ra and the Ethiopia of the Rastafarians or the Brothers of the Living Blood.

This is the hard lesson of Derrick Bell's conceptualization of an elusive Afro-Zionism in his story "The Afrolantica Awakening," which takes the form of a parable of the discovery of the lost Atlantis—with the unique twist that only blacks can inhabit this mythic land. In Bell's rewriting of the Exodus, blacks interpret the island that suddenly appears on the horizon as, at last, their Promised Land. Following a debate over reparations in the form of a subsidy for those who wish to emigrate, the "Afrolantica Armada" sets sail, a thousand ships that are carrying just the first wave of several hundred thousand anticipated settlers. But no sooner does the fleet approach than the black Atlantis sinks back into the ocean—a cruel hoax and confirmation that African Americans "are preordained to their victimized, outcast state." Emboldened by their efforts, however, the people recognize that they themselves possess the qualities of liberation they had hoped to realize in their new homeland. True Americans now, they experience "a liberation—not of place, but of mind."[212]

The point of Bell's parable, of course, is that no repatriation to Africa, no reversion to an uncontaminated state of blackness, will sustain the people, but only self-making in exile, on the qualified terms offered by America. Yet the liberation "not of place, but of mind"—coming out "from under the mind of a slave," as Farrakhan put it at the Million Man March—might likewise be an illusion. As Black Power waned, it was possible to configure the dead end of the Exodus myth as a delightful conundrum, as in Fran Ross's 1974 curiosity *Oreo*, a satirical puncturing of univocal racial identity. The novel traces the picaresque search by its eponymous biracial heroine, Christine "Oreo" Clark, for her white Jewish father and the Jewish side of her identity, plotting her story as a contemporary version of Theseus' journey into the labyrinth, which in her usage clearly stands in favorable contrast to the linear reductiveness of Exodus as a genealogical plot.[213]

Yet Ross's figure of the labyrinth also carries another implication. For all its resourceful use in the tradition of black ministerial and political leadership or as a descriptive account of patterns of black migration, the sheer repetition of the Exodus paradigm leaves it subject to enervating circularity. However profoundly American they become, that is to say, African Americans might still fear a condition of perpetual wandering, ever in pursuit of the mirage of Canaan, as Langston Hughes portrayed it with exquisite economy:

> The Promised Land
> Is always just ahead.
> You will not reach it
> Ere you're dead.

> But your children's children
> By their children will be led
> To a spot from which the Land—
> Still lies ahead.[214]

CHAPTER 3

Black Skin, Yellow Star;
or, Blues for Atticus Finch

"IN THIS DAY OF MASS RAPE of white women who are not morons, why is it that you young Jewish authors seek to whitewash the situation?" So asked one irate reader, addressing Harper Lee in a letter to the editor published in *Newsweek* in January 1961. The magazine reported that Lee, author of *To Kill a Mockingbird* and kin to Robert E. Lee, was planning a tongue-in-cheek reply to be signed "Harper Levy."[1] Leaving aside the letter's implication that raping "morons" might be acceptable, the anonymous writer managed to express two modes of bigotry that remained intimately entangled in the postwar years even as the dynamic relationship between blacks and Jews underwent rapid changes. The same page of the magazine displayed the weekly national best-seller list, with Lee's novel in fourth place among works of fiction. Topping the nonfiction list was *The Rise and Fall of the Third Reich* by William Shirer, one of the first books, and for many years the foremost, to bring the depredations of Nazi Germany before a wide American audience, while in tenth place on the fiction list was a translation of André Schwartz-Bart's Holocaust novel *The Last of the Just*.

The simultaneous popularity of these three books, all destined to become classics, might be written off as a coincidence. Not so the angry letter writer's charge that Lee, taken to be Jewish, was whitewashing the purported threat to white women at the hands of black rapists. In America it was blacks, not Jews, who were accused of racial "pollution," and even though Jews were attacked for abetting the cause of black civil rights, they were not often said to be contaminating agents or to be contaminated by "blackness" themselves, as they were in Nazi Germany. But postwar consciousness about the Holocaust cast a new light on the racial policies that led to segregation in the United States, and it forms a strong subliminal undercurrent in Lee's quasi-autobiographical story of a young white girl, the daughter of an idealistic attorney, coming of age in the segregated South of the 1930s.[2] Offering an anatomy of American segregation at the moment of its legal destruction, *To Kill a Mockingbird* presents a peculiar combination of didactic simplicity and moral ambiguity, its lessons about African American equality both transparent and oblique. Owing to Lee's cunning references to Nazism, it also illuminates the distinction between genocidal anti-Semitism—what happened in Germany—and tragic but not genocidal racism—what happened in the United States.

Published in 1960 and quickly issued as a *Reader's Digest* condensed book and featured as a Book-of-the-Month Club selection, Lee's novel went on to win the Brotherhood Award of the National Conference of Christians and Jews in 1961, and generations of American children, continuing into the twenty-first century, have read it at least once before leaving secondary school. Like Mark Twain's *Adventures of Huckleberry Finn,* the novel has sometimes been the subject of misguided suppression in public schools because it contains the word "nigger" or it is alleged that young black readers are incapable of coming to terms with the normative racial attitudes of another era. Yet in 2001, at just the same moment that Muskogee High School in Oklahoma, with a majority African American population, removed the novel from its required reading list for freshmen because of Lee's purportedly derogatory and racist language, the city of Chicago, with one of the nation's largest African American populations, selected *To Kill a Mockingbird* as the novel that everyone in the city was to read as part of its highly successful "One City, One Book" civic project.

Doubtless, the book's immense popularity at the time of its publication, as well as its enduring hold on both adolescent and adult readers ever since, may be ascribed in part to the magnetic power of its young heroine's righteousness. Diane McWhorter, author of a Pulitzer Prize–winning study of civil rights clashes during 1963 in Birmingham, Alabama, her hometown, recalls that she and her fellow fifth-grade friends wept "clandestinely" and championed the liberalism of Lee's heroine, Scout Finch, at matinees of the equally famous film adaptation of *To Kill a Mockingbird* before their mothers, alarmed at the city's growing racial conflict, stopped them from attending the downtown the-

ater. Decades later, in arguing against the neo-Confederate iconography of the
Georgia state flag, Governor Zell Miller cited the famous scene in which Scout's
banter disperses the mob come to lynch Tom Robinson as a model for his appeal to the state assembly as "fathers and mothers, neighbors and friends" who
had been taught in Sunday school to do the right thing.[3] Even if Lee aimed first
to change the hearts and minds of a recalcitrant white South, however, the
novel also had a strong impact on readers whose experience of racial discrimination was more visceral. In his memoir of the civil rights movement, James
Farmer, head of the Congress of Racial Equality, recalled that in the spring of
1961, while he was under arrest with other Freedom Riders in Jackson, Mississippi, Roy Wilkins brought in two books "to help me pass the prison hours,"
one of them *To Kill a Mockingbird*.[4]

Although it was written, and subsequently read, in the atmosphere of
mounting tension that followed the Supreme Court's ruling against school segregation in *Brown v. Board of Education* (1954) and the advent of the civil rights
movement, the novel's action is set in the 1930s, implying that its dramatized
miscarriage of justice belongs to a bygone era. By cultivating a naïve yet knowing narrative voice that looks back to another time—when "people moved
slowly . . . took their time about everything," when "there was no hurry, for
there was nowhere to go"—and writing retrospectively of events after "enough
years had gone by to enable us to look back on them,"[5] Lee moved the mounting crisis over desegregation into an arena of seemingly safer contemplation. If
it shared few of their reactionary messages, *To Kill a Mockingbird* nevertheless
had tonal elements in common with other nostalgic evasions of racial realities,
whether coincident with its setting, such as *Gone With the Wind*, published in
1936 and adapted for the screen in the landmark color film of 1939, or with its
publication, such as *The Andy Griffith Show*, which premiered in 1960, ran for
eight successful seasons that coincided with the increasing radicalization of the
civil rights movement, and yet never gave any indication of taking place in a
world of marked racial inequality and vigilante justice. Like Sheriff Andy Taylor's idyllic Mayberry, which evoked a tranquil, static southern world impervi-
ous to change,[6] Lee's fictional setting of Maycomb, based on her hometown of
Monroeville, Alabama, became an "Everytown" of the South, if not the nation,
its quiet order perturbed but not yet smashed.

The backward-looking time frame of *To Kill a Mockingbird* and the nostalgic
tenor of Lee's fictive autobiographical voice reflect her minor share in the
southern tradition of reactionary antimodernism, in which mourning is com-
mingled with defiance. They also reflect the fact that key civil rights legislative
and judicial policy dates from the 1930s and early 1940s, even though southern

segregation, enforced at times by brazen courtroom injustice or mob rule, remained largely untouched.[7] Indeed, the novel is nearly a recapitulatory tribute
to liberal exposés of southern racism that appeared in those same years—
works such as Arthur Raper's *The Tragedy of Lynching* (1933), Charles Johnson's
Shadow of the Plantation (1934), John Dollard's *Caste and Class in a Southern
Town* (1937), Wilbur Cash's *The Mind of the South* (1941), and Gunnar Myrdal's
An American Dilemma (1944). Because segregation was still the custom, if not
the law, in the early 1960s, Scout Finch's reminders that we are reading a tale of
the depression-era South have the effect of holding the reader in suspension,
alert to Myrdal's observation that "the Negro problem is not only America's
greatest failure but also America's incomparably great opportunity for the future."[8] By recreating the aura of time standing still, the novel immerses us in an
allegory of the white South's philosophy of race relations—"go slow"—exploiting the notorious ambiguity in *Brown*'s 1955 decree of implementation, which
required southern schools to desegregate "with all deliberate speed." (Ruling on
a desegregation case that came before the Supreme Court in 1964, by which
date fewer than 2 percent of southern black children attended majority white
schools, justice Hugo Black wrote, "There has been entirely too much deliberation and not enough speed.")[9]

A further effect of Lee's temporal displacement, however, is to locate her
story of racial crisis within a world witnessing the rise of European fascism.
"The Jewish people and the Negro people both know the meaning of Nordic
supremacy," said Langston Hughes near the end of World War II. "We have
both looked into the eyes of terror."[10] In the United States it was African Americans about whom defenders of southern honor and white supremacy were typically speaking when they warned their neighbors to beware the desecration of
"a noble and unique living creature, given to the earth by God's grace," when
"these black parasites of the nation defile our inexperienced young blond
girls and thereby destroy something which can no longer be replaced in this
world."[11] That these words, from Hitler's *Mein Kampf* (1925), might have been
uttered or written by any number of white Americans, notably but by no
means exclusively defenders of segregation in the Deep South, indicates the uncomfortable proximity between the regime of Jim Crow and the racial underpinnings of Nazism, whose end point was so much more catastrophic. In casting back to the 1930s, Lee was also casting back to the high tide of racial
ideology both at home and abroad, a fact she uses with subtlety and indirection
to measure the ordeal of desegregation in the South while carefully separating
the course of United States history from that of Nazi Germany.

Constrained by its ultimate allegiance to the genre of the children's story, *To*

Kill a Mockingbird nevertheless offers a good prism through which to see refracted the entangled practices of anti-black racism and anti-Semitism over the first half of the twentieth century, including the emergence of a new vocabulary of racial damage and genocide. Coyly subverting the romantic archetypes of southern "breeding" and partially concealing her condemnation of southern racial mores in a puzzle of pious half-truths and ritualized games and pageants, Lee forecast the impending destruction of a white southern way of life while acknowledging the strength of the racial supremacism and vigilantism that still protected it. American racism paled by comparison to the destruction of the Jews, said Lee, but the war against Nazism should have awakened the nation, the South in particular, to the disconcerting truth divined by Hugo Black, who had briefly joined the Alabama Ku Klux Klan in the 1920s but by the 1950s strongly supported the ruling in *Brown,* despite the fierce backlash against it which he had rightly predicted. The creed of the South, said Black, was "Hitler's creed."[12]

THE MASTER RACE

The jolting power of *To Kill a Mockingbird* lies in Lee's cautious but direct confrontation of the "race-sex-sin spiral" that drove the South, in Lillian Smith's words, to superimpose the semiotics of segregation upon the white female body: "Now, parts of your body are segregated areas which you must stay away from and keep others away from. These areas you touch only when necessary. In other words, you cannot associate freely with them any more than you can associate freely with colored children." Smith's acerbic description of the ethos of segregation brings together the two strong vectors of Lee's novel—its focus on childhood, the battleground of desegregation, and the hyper-idealization of white southern womanhood. Enclosed in a "pink cotton penitentiary" by a "disease" that makes "reasonable people go stark raving mad," white women were the weapons of choice in arguments that political equality would bring about social equality and, as a consequence, racial defilement. As a portrait of the South of the 1930s, the novel is a confirmation of the hoary defense of lynching offered in the United States Senate by Alabama's J. Thomas Heflin: "Whenever a negro crosses this dead line between the white and negro races and lays his black hand on a white woman he deserves to die."[13]

The legal enforcement of segregation in the decades following *Plessy v. Ferguson* (1896) brought the South and much of the nation to an almost total commitment to "one-drop" rule, whereby virtually any admixture of "black blood" was sufficient to make a person "Negro," and stimulated demagogic race-baiting and a rabid popular literature about the dangers of miscegenation.[14] Sexual white supremacy was celebrated in several genres—in Jim Crow screeds predicting the atavistic destruction of the white race through intermarriage, such as Charles Carroll's *The Negro: A Beast* (1900) and R. W. Shufeldt's *America's Great Problem: The Negro* (1915); in D. W. Griffith's famous pro–Ku Klux Klan film *The Birth of a Nation* (1915), inspired by the popular novels of Thomas Dixon; and in neo-Confederate historiography such as *The Tragic Era* (1929), Claude Bowers's study of the post–Civil War years that portrayed rape by Negroes as the "foul daughter of Reconstruction" and contended that it was not until the original Klan began to ride that white women regained a sense of security.[15] The mixed-race William Hannibal Thomas, citing the degenerate characteristics of blacks, warned in 1901 that "a mass of white negroes" would merely compound the danger since "the variegated freedman would still be a negro in mind, soul, and body," while in *Can the White Race Survive?* (1929), James D. Sayers turned the castration and mutilation that often accompanied lynching into a political metaphor, pleading that the "frightful cancer" of miscegenation must be excised from the white body politic, as with a surgeon's knife, "vigorously and with a steady hand."[16]

The mid-century struggle for black civil rights proved quickly that hysteria over miscegenation had hardly disappeared. *The Birth of a Nation* enjoyed renewed popularity in the South, and the rallying cry of massive resistance to desegregation was "mongrelization," reborn in postwar protests such as segregationist judge Tom P. Brady's broadside *Black Monday*—so called for the day *Brown v. Board of Education* was announced—in which the court's misguided intervention in the southern way of life is ascribed to communism and charged with authorizing the violation of "the loveliest and the purest of God's creatures . . . a well-bred, cultured Southern white woman or her blue-eyed, golden-haired little girl."[17] Just a year before *To Kill a Mockingbird* was published, an Alabama state legislator who objected to a children's book titled *The Rabbit's Wedding*, in which a white rabbit marries a black rabbit, succeeded not only in banning the subversive book from state libraries but in having copies burned as well.[18] Such a reaction was not ludicrous but predictable at a time when anti-miscegenation laws still existed in twenty-two states, including Alabama, with such unions considered void *ab initio*. Thus, the trial judge who convicted Richard Loving and Mildred Jeter of violating Virginia's anti-miscegenation law in 1958 proclaimed his belief in distinct races and their place in a divinely ordained order: "Almighty God created the races white, black, yellow, malay and red, and he placed them on separate continents . . . [showing] that he did not intend for the races to mix."[19]

Although anti-miscegenation laws were patently unconstitutional, hostility to intermarriage was so great that the Supreme Court was unwilling to strike them down until 1967, when *Loving v. Commonwealth of Virginia* finally overturned *Pace v. Alabama* (1882), which had upheld an anti-miscegenation law that punished interracial fornication and adultery more severely than similar crimes in which race was not a factor on the grounds that the law applied equally to both races.* In this respect *Loving*'s key holding—that anti-miscegenation laws violated the equal protection clause of the Fourteenth Amendment and were designed mainly to uphold white supremacy—attacked *Pace* much as *Brown v. Board of Education* had attacked *Plessy v. Ferguson* and its predecessors, which had likewise argued speciously that segregation laws were applied "equally" to both races.[20] (In *Loving*, unlike *Brown*, the Court did not appeal directly to social science, a tactic that might more easily have dismantled the argument that there were biological grounds on which to proscribe racial mixing, but instead hewed closely to interpreting the Fourteenth Amendment.) Although *Loving* concerned consenting adults, while *Brown* concerned nonconsenting children, the cases were related by the purported danger of racial pollution.

In many ways, however, southern public opinion simply reflected, in more strident form, national opinion. The South is in accord with nature in its preference for racial separation, asserted Herbert Ravenel Sass, writing in the mainstream *Atlantic Monthly* in 1956. Nowhere else in the world has a "helpless, backward people of another color" been so uplifted by the dominant race as in the South, he said, but with the ironic result that amalgamation now "lurks in ambush." Schools, warned Sass, would be the battleground: "If the South fails

---

* By Alabama statute, dating from the late nineteenth century and reaffirmed in 1940, sexual relations between black and white, within marriage or not, were punishable by a prison sentence of two to seven years, comparable to statutes in other southern states. Although it typically punished the parties only when a white married someone of one-eighth or greater admixture, Alabama was among the sixteen states that still had anti-intermarriage laws when *Loving* was decided in 1967. The Lovings were a white man and a "colored" woman. Though married in Washington, D.C., which had no anti-miscegenation law, they were arrested in 1958 for living in Virginia, where their marriage violated the "Act to Preserve Racial Integrity," enacted in 1924. Their sentence was suspended on the condition that they leave the state, but after living in Washington for five years, they decided to appeal their conviction. Because the Virginia law prohibited only interracial marriages involving whites, it was self-evident that the law and its enforcement, regardless of claims that blacks and whites faced the same punishment, were "designed to maintain White Supremacy." *Loving v. Commonwealth of Virginia*, 388 U.S. 12 (1967).

to defend its young children who are not yet capable of defending themselves, if it permits their wholesale impregnation by a propaganda persuasive and by them unanswerable, the salutary instinct of race preference which keeps the races separate, as in Nature, will be destroyed before it develops and the barriers against racial amalgamation will go down."[21] As Sass's pun on "impregnation" implied, the doctrine announced in *Brown* was tantamount to the sexual violation of defenseless white schoolgirls like Scout Finch, who stands in *To Kill a Mockingbird* at the threshold of puberty.

It is possible that Lee's Tom Robinson was inspired by the 1930 death sentence given a black Alabama man of the same name for his part in defending his family from a lynch mob, a story recounted in Raper's *Tragedy of Lynching*.[22] But closer analogues, contemporary with both the novel's historical setting and its moment of publication, were available to prove that the types of justice administered by southern mobs and southern courts were often indistinguishable.

The capital rape case of Tom Robinson tried by Atticus Finch occurs in 1935, set in a small-town Alabama courtroom that would inevitably have been reverberating with the impact of the ongoing trials of the young black men known as the Scottsboro Boys. Perhaps the most important modern criminal trial in which racial injustice quickly overshadowed the facts at issue, the ordeal of the young men prosecuted for the rape of two white women in a sequence of trials lasting from 1931 to 1937, to which we will return, put the South under sensational national scrutiny matched only by that aroused by the lynchings of Emmett Till in 1955 and Mack Charles Parker in 1959.[23] Lee capitalized on the fact that the Till and Parker cases were Scottsboro revisited—atavistic eruptions of the South's "rape complex," in Wilbur Cash's artful phrase,[24] which should have resulted in the conviction of the white killers. Instead, the killers in both cases went free, as did nearly all of those responsible for the approximately five thousand lynchings, the vast majority of victims being African Americans in the South, that had occurred in the United States since 1861.[25]

Emmett Till was a fourteen-year-old Chicago boy visiting relatives near Money, Mississippi, when he purportedly made lewd adolescent remarks or "wolf whistled" at a white woman, Carolyn Bryant. Roy Bryant, the woman's husband, and his half-brother, J. W. Milam, beat Till, shot him in the head, tied a cotton gin fan around his neck with barbed wire, and dumped his body in the Tallahatchie River. The heinous miscarriage of justice that led to the murderers' acquittal (in a cold-blooded display of defiance, the murderers were defended by every attorney in the county, and the jury drank soda pop to pass the time before announcing their unanimous verdict of not guilty) was matched by the gruesome publicity of the violence done to Till (his mother demanded an open casket at his Chicago funeral, attended by some fifty thousand people, and photos of the disfigured corpse ran in *Jet* magazine and the *Chicago Defender*). In a famous 1957 interview conducted by William Bradford Huie for *Look* magazine, Till's murderers freely admitted killing the boy and explained their actions by calling up the specter of miscegenation. Milam argued that he and Bryant had only intended to pistol-whip Till and send him back to Chicago, but when Till supposedly bragged about his white girlfriends in the North, Milam did the only thing he could: "I counted pictures o' three white gals in his pocketbook [wallet] before I burned it. What else could I do [but kill him]? No use lettin' him get no bigger!"[26]

Although Parker was almost certainly guilty of raping a pregnant white woman, his lynching occurred while he was in legal custody. With the complicity of the jailer, Parker was beaten, abducted by men in disguise, and driven out of Poplarville, Mississippi, where he was shot to death and his body dumped in the Pearl River. Despite widespread knowledge about the identity of the lynchers (among them a former deputy sheriff who would be elected sheriff in 1963), an FBI investigation that provided ample evidence of their guilt, and national publicity highlighted by a *Look* article depicting Poplarville as a world-wide symbol of race violence, both a county grand jury (in November 1959) and later a federal grand jury (in January 1960) failed to bring indictments against any of the men. As in the Till case, local southern support for the lynchers was perhaps less a defense of lynching per se than an expression of defiance against hostile national press coverage,[27] but the line between lawlessness and honor, as Lee makes clear in the jury trial and subsequent killing of Tom Robinson during his attempt to escape from prison, was rendered effectively invisible.

Even though they proved to be the endgame of southern vigilantism, the Till and Parker lynchings indicated that the obsession with racial purity on which segregation was predicated, despite the lesson of the Nazi genocide that rested on a similar predicate, had not disappeared from American life. As Roi Ottley wrote of Mississippi and the Till trial: "Few places in the world can be as savage and inhuman. Few people nowadays remember that back in the 1930s Adolf [sic] Hitler sent a mission to the U.S. to study the South's treatment of the Negroes, so that he could more efficiently terrorize the Jews."[28]

The Till lynching in particular galvanized young blacks coming of age during the early years of the civil rights movement and became a reiterated point of reference in confrontations with sexualized racism. Two thousand miles away from the world of Emmett Till, Mack Parker, and Tom Robinson,

Eldridge Cleaver, minister of information for the Black Panthers, composed a harsh, violent refutation of the white South's racial fantasies when he recalled his 1955 breakdown in Soledad Prison on learning of Emmett Till's lynching. His rage against the perversion of justice, said Cleaver, was the catalyst for his new philosophy that rape could be made into an "insurrectionary act," one explicable in the lines from his poem "To a White Girl":

> Your white meat
> Is nightmare food.
> White is
> The skin of Evil.
> You're my Moby Dick,
> White Witch,
> Symbol of the rope and hanging tree,
> Of the burning cross.[29]

The theory of rape Cleaver enunciated in *Soul on Ice* (1968)—the white woman, like Melville's white whale, is at once godlike and demonic, magnetically alluring and dangerously destructive—was abhorrent. No doubt he meant to pander to the desire of a "masochistic white bourgeoisie for prurient titillation," as Wilson Moses remarks, thus reinforcing its own paranoid fantasies. Yet his militant seizure of the historical myth of black sexuality, in verse that is an amalgam of lynching poems by James Weldon Johnson, Jean Toomer, Langston Hughes, and others, was also an effort to hold accountable the "Master Race psychology" that in Cleaver's view linked the slave trade and its aftermath, the slaughter of the European Jews, and the atomic bombing of Japan.[30]

An equally assertive evocation of Till in terms of Nazism, and likewise a counterpoint to Lee, had already appeared in James Baldwin's 1964 play *Blues for Mister Charlie,* whose open confrontation of the barbarities of lynching and the sexual dynamics of white racism, said one critic, "plowed deep into the very psyche of white America."[31] Baldwin's Till character is no cringing, humble victim but a smart-talking black man, born in the South but with a racial aggressiveness sharpened by life in the North, a character whose brash reveling in the mythology of black potency mocks the white man's sexual anxiety: "The master race! You let me in that tired white chick's drawers, she'll know who's the master race!"[32] Providing a bridge from Bigger Thomas to the Black Panthers, from impotent rage to the threat of orchestrated black revolution, Baldwin capitalized on postwar arguments that slavery and segregation were the moral, if not the literal, equivalents of the genocide of the Jews and offered an easy identification of the "master race" of southern white supremacy with the regime of Aryan racial supremacy.

By the mid-1960s, the restraint associated with Martin Luther King, Jr., and the rule of law epitomized by *Brown* had given way to the militancy of Black Power, among whose proponents appropriation of the language of Nazism and the trauma of the Holocaust, we will see in later chapters, drew even more deeply on an African American tradition with roots in the 1930s. As the moderate civil rights agenda congenial to white liberalism was displaced by the ultimatums of black radicalism, cautionary tales such as *To Kill a Mockingbird* were pushed to one end of the moral spectrum. Citing the impotence of assimilated middle-class Jews in prewar Germany and their resulting mass murder, Amiri Baraka (LeRoi Jones) contended that, since middle-class black leaders in the United States had already sold their souls and betrayed their people, the younger generation must be ready to abandon the failed tactics of nonviolence.[33] Although her strategy was more subtle, Harper Lee was no less concerned to expose and overturn the South's master race psychology. In registering the reappearance of the South's rape complex in the Till and Parker cases, even as she banished it to the bygone days of Scottsboro, a nightmare past from which the South might yet awake, she too turned directly to the lessons of the Holocaust.

WASHIN' ALL THE FEEBLE-MINDED

> *How many times*
> *Do a Führer's claws*
> *Dig up dry bones*
> *Of the gray Lost Cause?*
> —*Melvin B. Tolson, "The Idols*
> *of the Tribe"*

Because he is disabled, his left arm shriveled from a cotton gin accident, Tom Robinson cannot have produced Mayella Ewell's injuries. In the accusation of black-on-white sexual assault around which the plot of *To Kill a Mockingbird* turns, there may be a particular allusion to the Scottsboro Boys here in that evidence brought forth in proof of the young men's innocence included the fact that one was crippled by syphilis to the point of sexual incapacity and retardation, while another was nearly blind. All were poorly educated, and four of the nine were said to be mentally impaired. None of this necessarily counted against a charge of rape. As the United States Supreme Court reiterated in *Powell v. Alabama* (1932), however, it counted significantly in the rationale for right to counsel as a part of due process, for the physical or mental deficiency of the defendants was made a key part of the appeals in *Powell* both to undermine the probability of guilt and to bolster the constitutional argument.[34] More important, the question of physical and mental deficiency bears on the novel's own representation of blackness and its guarded but nonetheless pointed analogies to the rise of Nazism. It is not enough for Tom to be innocent, a "quiet, respectable, humble Negro." He must be pathetically innocent— a victim of Mayella's desperate loneliness and abuse, a strong man but emotionally incapable of resistance or violence. He must be comparable, as the novel's central metaphor puts it, to innocent songbirds whose only job is to "make music for us to enjoy . . . [to] sing their hearts out for us," and his death must be capable of being likened both to the "senseless slaughter of songbirds" and to the murder of impaired humans: "It was a sin to kill cripples, be they standing, sitting, or escaping."[35]

Tom's characterization as an innocent and a cripple has the specific burden of explaining the purpose of Lee's most explicit reference to the Holocaust, the grade school current events lesson presented to Scout's class when the children return to school the autumn after Tom Robinson's death. When his turn comes, one student produces a fair summary of the effects of Nazi anti-Jewish measures: "Old Adolf Hitler has been after the Jews and he's puttin' 'em in prisons and he's taking away all their property and he won't let any of 'em out of the country and he's washin' all the feeble-minded and—." The first point of the scene, of course, is to render an ironic reflection on Alabama law in particular and American racial justice in general, both in the 1930s and in the early 1960s. "I mean how can Hitler just put a lot of folks in a pen like that, looks like the govamint'd stop him," one student remarks, while another wonders why the Jews can be persecuted, since they are "white." Not satisfied with her teacher's counsel that American democracy precludes the persecution of people on account of prejudice, Scout later asks her brother, Jem, "How can you hate Hitler so bad an' then turn around and be ugly about folks right at home—."[36] As the book makes clear, however, it is "folks right at home" about whom one needs to be most concerned, and the differences between southern anti-black racism and Nazi racism, starting with "washin' all the feeble-minded," were less apparent in 1935 than they would be a quarter century later.

The medicalization of anti-Semitism—the association of Jews with disease, parasitism, and racial pollution—had deep roots in European history but took effective policy form with a sterilization law, the Law for the Prevention of Progeny with Hereditary Diseases, that went into effect in 1933.[37] The first of the nine categories of "illness" for which individuals could be sterilized, if so directed by the Hereditary Health Court, was congenital feeblemindedness (mental retardation), an initial step in a program of racial genocide that cloaked murder in euphemisms such as "special treatment," "disinfection," and "cleansing," and utilized stationary gas chambers disguised as shower rooms. Public awareness of the new racial science was promoted by the Office of Racial Enlightenment (its name was changed in 1934 to the Office of Racial Policies), which carried out a wide-ranging campaign to make Germans "eugenically ed- ucated" (in the language of Joseph Goebbels, Hitler's minister of propaganda) through programs in theaters, schools, and doctors' offices, and on radio. Even- tually, 400,000 people were sterilized in the Third Reich.*

The year 1935 witnessed a notable increase in anti-Jewish agitation, moti- vated in part by the rancid anti-Semitism of Julius Streicher's periodical *Der Stürmer* and by relentless propaganda denouncing the biological and cultural menace to German racial purity posed by Jews. On September 15 of that year, the same year in which *To Kill a Mockingbird* is set, Hitler called a special ses- sion of the Reichstag to ratify those measures that came to be known as the Nuremberg Laws. In addition to the Hereditary Diseases measure, they in- cluded the Reich Citizenship Law, which distinguished between "citizens" and "residents," the former being predominantly Germans classified by blood and national allegiance; the Law for the Protection of the Genetic Health of the German People, which required couples to submit to medical examination be-

---

* Although sterilization for feeblemindedness began in 1933, it was only in 1939, through an order signed by Hitler in October but backdated to September 1 to coincide with onset of war, that murder be- came a formal instrument of public health. Initiated under the obfuscating name of the Reich Commit- tee for the Scientific Registry of Severe Hereditary Ailments, the program set in motion by Hitler's order selected adults with a variety of physical disabilities and psychological disorders for elimination at kill- ing centers. Before the program was halted in 1941, on the eve of the formulation of the Final Solution, more than seventy thousand Germans deemed examples of "lives not worth living" had already been killed in gas "showers," their bodies destroyed in crematoria. From the beginning, Jews were viewed as a group apart who did not have to meet ordinary criteria for killing such as mental deficiency or physical deformity. They were "deficient" by virtue of being Jews. Among the many statements that could be cited, one succinct example may stand for the rest. The Jew, said Goebbels at a 1937 Nuremberg rally of the Nazi Party, was "the world's enemy, the destroyer of civilizations, the parasite among the peoples, the son of Chaos, the incarnation of evil, the ferment of decomposition, the demon who brings about the degeneration of mankind." Goebbels quoted in Norman Cohn, *Warrant for Genocide: The Myth of the Jewish World Conspiracy and the Protocols of the Elders of Zion* (1967; rpt. London: Serif, 1996), p. 225.

fore marriage so that the German nation could avoid suffering "racial damage" and "genetic infirmities"; and the Law for the Protection of German Blood and German Honor, which forbade marriage and sexual relations between Jews and "state members of German or cognate blood," and declared "the purity of the German blood" a "pre-requisite for the future existence of the German People." The sexual menace of the Jew, historically a minor aspect of anti-Semitism, became pronounced in Nazi propaganda. Combining the Jew as rapist with the blood libel, to take a shocking example, one Nazi illustration depicted a naked Aryan woman crucified by a crouching, diabolically drawn Jew who had, according to the caption, raped her while blood flowed from her wounds.[38]

However different their ultimate outcomes, both the South's—or, to be more accurate, the nation's—rape complex and the one-drop rule of its racial policy had their counterparts in Germany, where assimilation and even conversion could not diminish the threat of pollution. Jewishness, said one contemporary, "is like a concentrated dye: a minute quantity suffices to give a specific character—or, at least some traces of it—to an incomparably greater mass."[39] Although the Nuremberg Laws might be traced circuitously to the anti-Semitism of medieval and early modern Europe, the perversions and predatory behavior ascribed to Jews by Nazism were derived more directly from works of nineteenth-century racial science that tended to group Jews and blacks together in their proscription of miscegenation. Jews were deemed a dangerous mongrel race, carriers of pestilence and disease, including tuberculosis and syphilis, and their propensity for hybridization, resulting in pathological "blackness," was said to derive from an intermixture of Negro blood or their descent from African tribes.[40]

In the aftermath of World War I, German anti-Semitism built also on resentment of the "Rhineland mulattoes" or "Rhineland bastards"—offspring of the French occupation of the Rhineland by African colonial troops after World War I and interracial children returned to Germany after the nation lost its colonies in Africa—who were among the first persons to be subjected to the Nazi sterilization program. (Between 1935 and 1937 at least 385 Rhineland children were sterilized. German sterilization and medical experiments on racial subjects had also taken place in colonial German South-West Africa [Namibia] following the suppression of the Herero uprising in 1904.)[41] To this were added accusations that in the aftermath of World War I, occupying black troops, both American and French, had engaged in Kulturschade ("rape of culture"), with Jews held responsible for promoting these acts of rape and thus waging a "Negro-Jewish war" on Germany, an issue that would reappear in a new guise with the post–World War II American occupation. The violation of German women, and, more broadly, the figurative ravishing of pure German blood, was condemned in both analytic works such as Edmund Morel's *Black Horror on the Rhine* (1920) and Hitler's *Mein Kampf,* the genre's masterpiece, and novels such as *The Sin against the Blood* (1918) and *The Black Insult, a Novel of a Ravished Germany* (1922),[42] the German equivalents to Thomas Dixon's anti-miscegenation, pro–Ku Klux Klan novels in the United States.

The small number of blacks in Germany, some twenty to twenty-five thousand at the rise of Nazism, made moot a genocide that might conceivably have rivaled that of the European Jews.* But the pernicious influence of blacks on American culture, despite segregation, was held up as evidence of the mongrelism that threatened Germany. As part of the attempt to purge the Rhineland of its mixed-race population coincident with the Nuremberg Laws, Joseph Goebbels issued an order, largely futile in practice, banning jazz from German airwaves, and the damaging cultural influence of blacks and Jews was summed up in the propaganda campaign against degenerate "Nigger-Jew jazz" (see illustration). In the United States, Henry Ford did his part, railing against the insidious menace of "Jewish Jazz," which carried the African bestiality of Negro music to an even lower level. "The mush, slush, the sly suggestion, the abandoned sensuousness of sliding notes," said Ford, "are of Jewish origin."[43]

Although in Hitler's usage "black parasites" referred first of all to Jews, he included both "races" when he described their debilitating influence on the economic and social structure of post–World War I Germany as a "sin against one's blood," or when he railed that "in a bastardized and niggerized world all concepts of the humanly beautiful and sublime, as well as all ideas of an idealized future of our humanity, would be lost forever." The two subhuman races conspired to corrupt Aryan blood and destroy the state. It is the Jews who bring Negroes into the Rhineland, Hitler contended, "always with the secret

---

* Although it has been estimated that some two thousand died in concentration camps, black Germans were never collectively persecuted or defined as aliens, let alone targeted for extermination. And even though American segregation was one model for the Nuremberg Laws, blacks were not named in those laws, perhaps because Germans, ironically, sought to contrast their treatment of blacks with that of the United States. Black American POWs during World War II were sometimes treated more harshly and on some occasions summarily executed, but, in contrast, some Afro-Germans served in the military or in groups such as Hitler Youth. See Rosemarie K. Lester, "Blacks in Germany and German Blacks: A Little-Known Aspect of Black History," in Reinhold Grimm and Jost Hermand, eds., *Blacks in German Culture* (Madison: University of Wisconsin Press, 1986), pp. 113–34; Robert W. Kesting, "Forgotten Victims: Blacks in the Holocaust," *Journal of Negro History 77* (Winter 1992), 30–36; and Clarence Lusane, *Hitler's Black Victims: The Historical Experiences of Afro-Germans, European Blacks, Africans, and African Americans in the Nazi Era* (New York: Routledge, 2003), pp. 98–107, 112–13, 147–55.

Cover illustration for the brochure "Entartete Musik" (Degenerate Music)
by H. S. Ziegler, to accompany the 1938 exhibition "Entartete Kunst"
(Degenerate Art) in Düsseldorf, Germany.
United States Holocaust Memorial Museum,
Courtesy of Bildarchiv Preussischer Kulturbesitz.

thought and clear aim of ruining the hated white race by the necessarily result-ing bastardization."[44]

The "sin against one's blood," as a concept if not a locution, was hardly unfa-miliar in the United States. By many accounts, in fact, the ideology of Nazism was nurtured by reference to the laws and customs of Jim Crow. Even though ties between the German-American Bund and the Ku Klux Klan were of only marginal benefit to the Nazi cause and were quickly broken off upon America's entry into the war, the Klan was frequently equated with Hitlerism by liberal commentators, south and north alike, and its fascist image reflected a correla-tion between the racial theories underlying America's anti-immigration and segregation laws and those of the Third Reich. "You tell me that Hitler is a mighty bad man. / I guess he took lessons from the Ku Klux Klan," rhymed Langston Hughes.[45] He also took lessons from the American eugenics move-ment.

Prior to the Nuremberg Laws and the advent of Nazi programs of euthana-sia, American research on eugenic selection for hereditary traits and the scien-tific potential for creating a "master race" was closely studied by the Germans, among others. Carried out by respected organizations such as the Carnegie In-stitution and the American Breeders Association, as well as peripheral groups such as the Race Betterment Foundation and the Eugenics Research Associa-tion, the eugenics movement in the United States sought during the early de-cades of the twentieth century to formulate protocols that would multiply genetically desirable bloodlines while cutting off, through birth control and sterilization, anti-immigration measures, and, in extreme cases, euthanasia, those likely to issue in "defective" human beings—the diseased, the deformed, the mentally retarded, or racially inferior "mongrels." Although the goals of the American Eugenics Society were promoted by a number of Protestant minis-ters, as well as some priests and rabbis, as a progressive cause aimed at improv-ing the quality of American life, the movement's "scientific" basis was racist. According to the theories touted in American works such as Alfred A. Schultz's *Race or Mongrel* (1908), Madison Grant's *Passing of the Great Race* (1916), Lothrop Stoddard's *Rising Tide of Color against White World-Supremacy* (1920) and *The Revolt against Civilization: The Menace of the Under Man* (1922), and Burton J. Hendrick's *Jews in America* (1923), both blacks and Jews were capable of causing the degeneration of the white race since, according to the one-drop rule, hybridization always subsumed whiteness within the lesser race. Stoddard was among the American eugenicists who visited Germany in order to report on the elimination of "bad stock" from the Aryan population, while Hitler proclaimed Grant's book his "Bible" and one defendant in the 1946 Nuremberg doctors' trial cited it in mitigation of his guilt.[46]

American eugenics did not originate in the Deep South—California, in fact, saw earlier advocacy of theories of selective breeding—but anxiety about apparent increases in insanity, mental retardation, and degenerative illnesses led in the South of the 1920s to statutory definitions of feeblemindedness, designed for the "protection of the race," which allowed for institutionalization and eventually sterilization. For the most part, such policies applied to whites rather than blacks, who were housed in segregated facilities, if they were treated at all. By definition mentally deficient and already subjugated by the laws of segregation, blacks were generally not expected to perform more than servile labor or otherwise contribute to the progress of society and therefore could in no way contribute to the nation's eugenic elevation. As South Carolinian Benjamin O. Whitten, president of the American Association for the Study of Feeble-Mindedness, remarked in a 1937 address: "The Negro is the beneficiary of a civilization to which he contributed little and from which he derives much. He is supported in many aspects of his life by institutions which he did not originate and which he can not, by himself, support."[47]

Because American eugenics was a matter of state rather than federal policy and gained only sporadic acceptance, Germany quickly surpassed the United States during the 1930s in creating a world governed by strict racial regulations and plans for a eugenically improved Aryan people. Even if it was opportunistic, however, it was not illogical that German propagandists announced their ideological affinity with American eugenicists and segregationists, exploiting the cruel practices authorized by the spurious notion of "separate but equal" and pointing out that southern miscegenation laws were more strict than Nazi policies forbidding racial pollution.[48] The mirror images grew more and more distorted, but they were mirror images nonetheless.

White southerners for the most part condemned Nazism and rejected comparisons between the persecution of German Jews and the lynching of blacks. In this they were little different from the majority of white Americans. But such a rejection required that they ignore the fact that the defense of white southern womanhood provided ammunition for the defense of Aryan racial purity, just as, in later years, the neo-Confederate defense of the Lost Cause, whether or not it meant to be racist, provided ammunition for German neo-Nazis.* Not

---

* Traveling at century's end in the "*judenrein*" new Germany with Paul Beatty and other participants in the Spoken Poets project, Alan Kaufman found that neo-Nazism had warped into a brand of Old

surprisingly, the more than sixty Jewish refugee scholars who accepted teaching positions at black colleges in the segregated South felt a close bond with their students, who in turn recognized their kinship with the Jews as "colored folks," while the enmity of the white community—the teachers were sometimes threatened and even jailed for fraternizing with black families—reminded them of the Nuremberg Laws they had left behind in Germany.[49] Nothing in Lee's novel suggests that the prewar South's obsession with "breeding" or its hysteria about miscegenation might have had the same consequences, but the parallels with Jim Crow custom were unmistakable.*

Nazi anti-Semitism casts a dark and unnerving cloud over *To Kill a Mockingbird,* since, even though American racism did *not* issue in a comparable catastrophic conclusion, at the time of the book's action the logic of the one genocide could not have been unerringly distinguished from the potential for the other. "Old Adolf Hitler," as Scout's classmate calls him, is an epithet that makes little sense in 1935, but it is in keeping with Harper Lee's strategy of projecting the novel's action into a dim past, illuminating postwar events even as they are conveniently screened by the strategy of retrospect. The student's uncomprehending reference to Hitler "washing" the feebleminded is deliberately anachronistic in the sense that the genocide to which it led would have been clearly comprehensible to Lee's readers in 1960 but not to her juvenile characters in 1935. By telescoping events—"washing" (sterilizing or killing) the feebleminded and putting the Jews in "pens" (work camps and death camps)—Lee reminds her audience of the trajectory of European history while challenging them to grapple with the trajectory of American race law and the case of Tom Robinson—or, one could say, the many Tom Robinsons of American history—

South racism among contemporary European skinheads, for whom Confederate flags had replaced outlawed swastikas. In chilling counterpoint to the common cause made by the Freedom Riders of the civil rights movement, reported Kaufman, present-day blacks and Jews working together found the ghosts of Mississippi brought back to life in the reunified Germany. Alan Kaufman, *Jew Boy* (New York: Fromm International, 2000), pp. 458–59.

* In a provision notable for its parallel to instances of the South's hair-trigger understanding of "rape," whereby a black man's merely looking at a white woman might prompt prosecution or violence—a legal nicety later satirized by Ishmael Reed in *Reckless Eyeballing* (1986)—the Law for the Protection of German Blood and Honor did not require an overt sexual act in order to result in criminal charges. As Raul Hilberg writes: "Sexual gratification of one of the persons in the presence of another was sufficient. Touching or even looking might be enough. The reasoning in these cases was that the law covered not only blood but also honor, and a German, specifically a German woman, was dishonored if a Jew made advances toward her or exploited her sexually in any way." Raul Hilberg, *Perpetrators, Victims, Bystanders: The Jewish Catastrophe, 1933–1945* (New York: HarperCollins, 1992), p. 72.

within the newly revealed discourse of genocide in which black Americans, perhaps even more instinctively than American Jews, found their own history explained.

Tom is placed in a deadly trap when he must either give in to Mayella Ewell's sexual advances or resist her, and then when he must either recant his story or accuse a white woman of lying. Driven to the impudence of declaring his fear that, no matter what he does, he will end up sacrificed to a judicial system in which mobs and juries are indistinguishable—"scared I'd hafta face up to what I didn't do," he replies to the prosecutor—Tom is the personification of the daily apprehension that John Dollard found typical of black southerners in 1937: "Every Negro in the South knows that he is under a kind of sentence of death; he does not know when his turn will come, it may never come, but it may also be at any time."[50] The danger of mortal violence with which African Americans lived daily in the Jim Crow South was reflected almost perfectly in the language of the Austrian Holocaust survivor Jean Améry. Remarking that he later found his psychological self-analysis confirmed when he read about the behavior of colonized peoples in Frantz Fanon's *Wretched of the Earth*, Améry recalled his sudden understanding, on reading the Nuremberg Laws, of the "death threat" under which he was living as a Jew: "To be a Jew, that meant for me, from this moment on, to be a dead man on leave, someone to be murdered, who only by chance was not yet where he properly belonged."[51] Tom Robinson lives under such a sentence of death, and finally he dies from it.

Before looking more closely at his fate as a racial subject, however, we need first to consider the perilous position of Jews in the South and two related instances of southern injustice, each revealing the interplay between racism and anti-Semitism, against which Tom's case must be measured.

MISSISSIPPI MARRANOS

On the subject of anti-Semitism in the United States, *To Kill a Mockingbird* adopts an evasive posture, as when Atticus disingenuously contends that the Ku Klux Klan is a thing of the past ("way back about nineteen-twenty"), a burlesque show of cowards easily humiliated by the Jewish merchant, Sam Levy, whom they attempt to intimidate by dressing up in sheets purchased from Levy himself.[52] To be sure, anti-Semitism was far less pronounced than anti-black racism. Apropos Atticus's remark, it could even have a comic aspect. During the Little Rock school integration crisis of 1957, a member of the White Citizens' Council declared that one of its leaders should be expelled for his anti-Semitism: "We can't afford to be seen as an anti-Jewish organization. Why, we are having trouble enough just being anti-Negro!"[53] Whether in 1920 or 1957, however, history tells a more complex story about the lives of Jews in the South.

Because of his "universal refusal to be assimilated," argued Wilbur Cash of the early-twentieth-century climate, the Jew "is everywhere the eternal Alien," and in the South, "where any difference [stands] out with great vividness," it is natural that he would seem "a sort of evil harbinger and incarnation of all the menaces [southerners] feared and hated—external and internal, real and imaginary." It was not clear that things were much changed half a century later. According to one analysis, postwar anti-black prejudice in the South declined more quickly than anti-Semitism, to the point that by the early 1960s, the South was somewhat more anti-Semitic than the rest of the nation, reversing a prewar tendency to the contrary.[54] "One can hardly hail from two more historically losing causes than the South and Judaism," Edward Cohen wryly notes in recalling his ambivalence as a young man growing up in Jackson, Mississippi, trying to reconcile the ethics of Judaism with the norms of white southern Christianity. "We might've been strangers in the land of Egypt, but we were in many ways strangers in the South, too, welcomed but very aware that our welcome could easily be revoked."*

By the same token, what made Jews alien in some ways made them familiar. If an Old Testament–based tradition of philo-Semitism in the South meant that Jews were traditionally less subject to anti-Semitism than in other parts of country, the fellowship they found depended on their adherence to communal norms and their renouncing, or at least concealing, support for racial equality. William Styron was surely right that Jews were able to find fellowship in the South because their Protestant brethren already "possessed another, darker sacrificial lamb."[55] Yet the ebb and flow of anti-Jewish prejudice, hard to predict in any case, was everywhere perturbed by its volatile relationship with anti-black prejudice and the role played by Jews, actual or perceived, in the battle over desegregation.

---

* Edward Cohen, *The Peddler's Grandson: Growing Up Jewish in Mississippi* (1999; rpt. New York: Dell, 2002), pp. xi, 155–56. For a depiction of Jewish experience in a small southern town more like Harper Lee's Maycomb, compare Stella Suberman's memoir *The Jew Store* (1998), which recounts her parents' establishment during the 1920s of a dry goods store in a Tennessee town named, fictively, Concordia. In Suberman's story, her immigrant parents, as New York Jews, are as exotic as if they had come directly from the shtetls of Russia. But the mild anti-Semitism that they encounter, even in a community with an active Ku Klux Klan, is easily overshadowed by the decency and acceptance displayed by the townspeople, just as Atticus Finch might have predicted.

Although some 30 percent of northern whites on the Freedom Rides were Jewish, as were up to 90 percent of the civil rights attorneys working in Mississippi during the 1960s—among them future New York mayor Ed Koch, whose experience defending civil rights activists left him feeling that the state of Mississippi was "a police state rivaling Nazi Germany"[56]—most southern Jews, unlike those able to return to northern homes after a season of protest, kept a low profile during the fight over desegregation. The difference between national image and local practice was apparent in the interviews that Robert Penn Warrren conducted and published in the 1965 volume *Who Speaks for the Negro?* Roy Wilkins, national president of the NAACP, told Warren that the vast majority of Negroes "have never forgotten, wherever they've been, the Jews who helped them," even in the Deep South, where they know that "Jews have been vulnerable, too." In contrast, Aaron Henry, a pharmacist and president of the local NAACP in Clarksdale, Mississippi, regretted that the reputation of the Jew as a friend of the Negro had not been translated into action by southern Jews. "Frankly," he said, "some of our oppressors are found in the Jewish community." He agreed with Warren that Jews in Mississippi might be even more susceptible to social pressure on the race question than gentiles, but he wondered why their vulnerability produced antipathy rather than sympathy: "I would think they would know that once the white man clubs or clobbers the Negro into submission, the Jew is probably next."*

It was just that vulnerability, however, that exposed southern Jews to both danger and contempt. The outspoken integrationist Jacob Rothschild, rabbi of the Temple, Atlanta's oldest synagogue, observed two years before it was torn apart by a bomb in 1958: "If white Christians are fearful, the Jew is panic-stricken. He prefers to take on the protective coloring of his environment, to

---

* Earlier accusations of Jewish complicity may also be found. In *The Marrow of Tradition* (1901), for example, Charles Chesnutt's fictionalized account of the Wilmington, North Carolina, race "riot" of 1898—a white pogrom meant to suppress black political power in which dozens of blacks were killed and thousands driven from the city—the narrator is distressed that a Jewish merchant who sides with the whites "had so forgotten twenty centuries of history as to join in the persecution of another oppressed race!" In that era, southern blacks shared with southern white gentiles many of the same prejudices against Jews: they were conniving, greedy, responsible for killing Jesus Christ. Like Booker T. Washington and other black leaders of the day, however, they also admired Jews for their social cohesion, their racial consciousness, and their persistence despite a legacy of persecution. Roy Wilkins and Aaron Henry interviewed by Robert Penn Warren in *Who Speaks for the Negro?* (New York: Vintage, 1965), pp. 152–53, 83; Charles Chesnutt, *The Marrow of Tradition* (1901; rpt. Ann Arbor: University of Michigan Press, 1969), pp. 289–90; Arnold Shankman, "Friend or Foe: Southern Blacks View the Jew, 1880–1935," in Nathan M. Kagaroff and Melvin I. Urofsky, eds., *"Turn to the South": Essays on Southern Jewry* (Charlottesville: University Press of Virginia, 1979), pp. 105–23.

hide his head in the cotton patch in the dual hope that he won't be noticed and the problem will go away."[57] Dependent on the goodwill of their neighbors and subject to pressure from White Citizens' Councils, the Ku Klux Klan, and local police, southern Jews were understandably reluctant to risk ostracism or violence. Their assimilation to local customs or fear of being associated with northern "radicals"—"the niggers and the Jews of New York are working hand in hand," fulminated Mississippi senator Theodore Bilbo in 1945—sometimes included pressuring national civil rights organizations to stay out of the South.[58] In anticipation of Martin Luther King, Jr.'s, 1963 campaign in Birmingham, a local Jewish organization demanded that "outside" Jewish agencies, specifically the Anti-Defamation League, stay away—in this case "Miami Jews" who put local Jews at risk without being willing to move permanently to parts of the South where their activism might have more meaning. Targeted for protest by black activists who recognized their potential vulnerability to moral pressure, intimidated by TWK ("Trade with Klansmen") signs displayed by gentile merchants, and at the same time eager to distance themselves from "outside agitators," some Birmingham Jews took the position that desegregation was a "Christian problem" to be worked out between "whites" and Negroes.[59]

The ambiguous status of Jews within the sacred community of southern whiteness, the subject in whole or in part of a number of novels,[60] was captured well in *Meridian* (1976) by Alice Walker, who drew upon her own marriage to a northern Jewish civil rights attorney working in the South when she portrayed civil rights worker Lynne Rabinowitz confronting frightened southern Jews in their delicatessen: "They made her conscious, heavily, of her Jewishness, when, in fact, they wanted to make her feel her whiteness. And, beyond her whiteness, the whiteness that now engulfed this family (originally, she had heard, from New York) like a shroud."[61] When he remarked in a provocative essay titled "Mississippi Marranos" that "Mississippi in 1964 is like Germany in 1934," Marvin Braiterman meant not that southern Jews faced anything like the Inquisition or Nazism but that, in the face of potential hostility, Jews hid both their Jewishness and their sympathy with blacks.[62] Rather than "New Christians," as forced converts in early modern Spain were called, however, these Marranos were, so to speak, "New Whites"—the kind later portrayed by Alfred Uhry in *Driving Miss Daisy* (1987) in the title character's son, Boolie, who celebrates Christmas and refuses to attend a United Jewish Appeal dinner for Martin Luther King, Jr., because it would be bad for business.

But anti-Semitism on the part of the Klan or less formally organized racists escalated during the civil rights movement, and Jewish fears were hardly groundless. Ten percent of bombings in the South between 1954 and 1959 were directed at synagogues, Jewish community centers, or the homes of rabbis; in 1957 and 1958 alone, in addition to the Temple in Atlanta, synagogues and other Jewish properties were targeted in Nashville, Jacksonville, Miami, Charlotte, and Birmingham, where the perpetrators declared the temple a "center of integration." (In Uhry's play, Miss Daisy is shocked by the bombing of the Atlanta Temple, certain that those responsible must have meant to strike an Orthodox synagogue. But her black chauffeur and interlocutor, Hoke, thinks otherwise: "A Jew is a Jew to them folks. Jes' like light or dark we all the same nigger.") Nor had the long-standing associations that made "communist" a code word for "Jew" disappeared. In a trial in which the defense played upon this code, the men indicted in the Atlanta bombing either were acquitted or had the charges dropped, and when Attorney General Robert Kennedy went to Birmingham at the height of civil rights tension, his entourage was greeted by Klan protesters carrying signs such as "Kosher Team: Kennedy, Kastro, Krushev [sic]" and leaflets advertising "The Giant, Jew-Communist Race Mixing TRAINED NIGGERS Road Show and Travelling Circus."[63] A Klan member caught by FBI surveillance in 1968 while planning the bombing of another synagogue, whose congregation would have included children, mimicked the crude sensibilities of Emmett Till's killers: "Little Jew bastards grow up to be big Jew devils. Kill 'em while they're young."[64]

Atticus Finch's characterization of the Klan and its anti-Semitism as a kind of buffoonery is disingenuous in a further way. Although blacks occupied a distinctive place on the bottom rung in the world of Jim Crow, and Jews were rarely subjected to the same degree of exclusion and persecution, the prospect of anti-Semitic violence was always present. The evolution of racial theories over the first half of the century, as we saw in Chapter 1, increasingly grouped Jews with other "whites," but their place remained indefinite. To a lesser degree than blacks, and with none of the disastrous consequences that befell them in Europe, Jews were often still viewed as unassimilable aliens prone to introducing a degenerate "blood chaos" into white society, as in Arthur T. Abernathy's 1910 book arguing that Jews were descended from Africans, *The Jew a Negro* (perhaps a deliberate echo of Carroll's *The Negro a Beast*).[65] In one frightening instance, the lynching of Leo Frank in 1915, the threat of anti-Semitic violence contained within such suspicions was made all too real. Although the case of the Scottsboro Boys and their defense by Samuel Leibowitz is more immediate to the action of Lee's novel, Frank's murder, the most heinous act of anti-

Semitism in American history, more completely elided the difference between black and Jew and gives the lie to Atticus's casual dismissal of southern anti-Semitism.

JEW LANGUAGE

After a thirteen-year-old employee named Mary Phagan was found murdered in an Atlanta pencil factory at which he was a supervisor, Leo Frank became a suspect when prosecutors failed to make a quick case against the black custo-dian, Jim Conley.[66] The best evidence at the time and every investigation since have proved that Conley was almost certainly guilty, but attention shifted to Frank, a Jew born in Texas but raised in the North, when witnesses charged that he had indulged in lewdness and sexual "perversions"—including oral sodomy, a capital offense—with other factory workers or local prostitutes, and when Conley's drummed-up testimony against Frank was made credible by aggres-sive prosecutors. Accused of murder and rape, despite the fact that no evidence of rape was ever presented, Frank served the need for a villain who would sat-isfy the blood lust of those Georgians whose racism was strongly inflected with populist antagonism toward wealthy industrialists wielding power over local working "girls."

Principal among those creating the narrative about Frank over the course of a two-year trial was the demagogue Tom Watson, former Georgia congressman and vice presidential and presidential nominee of the Populist Party, who used his magazine, *Watson's Monthly*, and his weekly, *The Jeffersonian*, to inflame his readers with relentless denunciations of Frank as "a Yankee Jew," "a Jew pervert," a "Jew Sodomite," a "Hebrew libertine," and so on. Watson's anti-Semitism was first of all a tool of reactionary politics, but it had roots in the kind of Populist anti-Semitism peddled by Ignatius Donnelly, who likewise de-ployed the image of the lecherous Jewish businessman pursuing and defiling the golden gentile.[67] Although the lecherous Jew was a comparatively periph-eral figure in early-twentieth-century American racism—a minor example ap-peared in Ben Hecht's novel of Jewish self-loathing, *A Jew in Love* (1931), where the hero, Jo Boshere, is said to take the "niggerish delight of the Jew in the blond"[68]—the hysterical anti-Semitism that enveloped Frank exploited a com-bination of racial and sexual ambiguity. To some observers his thick lips and bulging eyes revealed a Negroid physiognomy and typed him as innately lasciv-ious; but the imputation of sexual perversion was sealed by Conley's testimony that Frank, in asking Conley to help him dispose of Mary's body, had told him, "You know I ain't built like other men." It remains unclear whether this statement, if it was in any way accurate, referred merely to Frank's being circumcised (as the governor who commuted Frank's death sentence concluded) or rather to some genital impairment that made him likely to seek oral gratification. A physical exam revealed that Frank was normal, to all appearances, but the implication of a physiological or racial basis for his Jewish "perversion"— what David Mamet, in his novelistic account of the case, *The Old Religion* (1997), refers to as Frank's "deformity"—quickly became part of the charges against him.[69]

In keeping with the symbolic presentation of the white maiden pursued by a bestial black in *The Birth of a Nation*, released in early 1915,[70] Mary Phagan, like Mayella Ewell and like the accusers of the Scottsboro Boys, was a lower-class white woman suddenly made respectable and pure by her murder and purported rape—an archetype that Mamet underscores by having his fictional Frank castrated as well as lynched. Frank's defense was racist in turn, attacking Conley as a "dirty nigger" whose testimony against Frank had been rigged by the prosecution and depicting him in the stereotypical guise of the black brute. In this one instance, however, the Jew exceeded the Negro as a symbol of predatory lust. Born of luxurious corruption and bound up with circumcision or not, Frank's perversion made him more alien, more menacingly degenerate. Said Watson: "The negro is naturally lustful and will take a female, even a beast, if it costs his life, but he never *takes a woman UNNATURALLY*." Frank's case appeared to demonstrate that Jews were only provisionally white, that their hybridity, their hidden "blackness," was potentially more dangerous than the overt threat of blacks. The Jew in this construction, as Mamet puts it, was a "nigger to the nth degree."[71]

In the political melodrama that unfolded in Watson's publications and local news coverage, Frank, president of the local B'nai B'rith, became representative of a Jewish upper class preying upon the gentile working class, his sexual proclivities of a piece with his parasitic living off the labor of poor southern girls. In the words of a local attorney who spoke at Frank's commutation hearing: "Mary Phagan was a poor factory girl. What show would she have against Jew money?"[72] Frank was made to stand for everything alien to the South and its traditional values. (Both Alfred Uhry's 1998 musical version of the Frank case, *Parade,* and Mamet's play highlight the symbolic significance of the fact that Mary Phagan was murdered on Confederate Memorial Day, as though Frank had compounded his crime by profaning a sacred day.) The pastor of the Phagan family's Baptist church felt that "one old negro" such as Jim Conley would be "poor atonement" for Mary's murder, but with the arrest of "a Yankee Jew," he felt natural satisfaction "that here would be a victim worthy to pay for the crime."[73]

As in the Scottsboro cases, the charge that Mary Phagan had been raped and killed by Frank, rather than robbed and killed by Conley, likewise ignored (or covered up) the evidence that she was already sexually active. Forecasting the Scottsboro prosecution, Watson attacked questions about her chastity as scandalous affronts to her family and community. According to the resolution passed by one Atlanta union, Mary Phagan was the "priceless jewel of virtue"; for the United Confederate Veterans in her hometown of Marietta, who set out to build a monument to her, she was "a symbol of the purity of the little virgin"; and in Watson's caustic rhetoric she was the epitome of white southern womanhood: "Our Little Girl—ours by the Eternal God—has been pursued to a hideous death and bloody grave by this filthy perverted Jew of New York."[74]

During Frank's appeal and commutation hearing, Louis Marshall, president of the American Jewish Committee, helped design the strategy of his defense and organized financial contributions from prominent New York Jews. Frank's trial gave birth to the Anti-Defamation League and indirectly helped to catalyze Jewish support for black civil rights, but publicity about the case in northern papers at the same time fanned the fire of southern fanaticism and created a pretext for Watson and others to lash out at coverage of the case in "Jewowned" northern newspapers and the support for Frank's defense by "big Hebrew money."[75] (For its part, the northern black press supported Frank but rejected theories of Conley's guilt and maintained that the white press was making him a scapegoat.)[76] The commutation of Frank's sentence by the governor brought on a further outburst of anti-Semitism in Marietta and other towns, culminating in his lynching on August 16, 1915. Frank's killers, the selfproclaimed "Knights of Mary Phagan," were hardly the riffraff who lynched Emmett Till or who come for Tom Robinson in *To Kill a Mockingbird;* they included a clergyman, two former Superior Court judges, and a former sheriff. Their widely publicized act proved the political value of Jew-baiting: Frank's original prosecutor, Hugh Dorsey, won a landslide victory in the 1916 gubernatorial race, and Tom Watson was elected to the Senate in 1920. More important, it led directly to the post–World War I revival of the Ku Klux Klan, which Watson trumpeted as a means to restore "home rule" in the South and which quickly became a national phenomenon, reaching its peak of popularity in the mid-1920s with mass rallies, cross-burnings, and parades, including grandiose marches down Pennsylvania Avenue in Washington, D.C.[77]

Although Leo Frank was a sacrificial surrogate on whom Georgians focused their hostility toward industrialization and the intrusion of northern capital, his lynching proved to be exceptional. Notwithstanding the fact that his trial created a momentary preoccupation with "the Jew" as an agent of racial pollution, anti-Semitism in subsequent decades was not appreciably stronger in the South than in other regions of the country, and it certainly never rivaled anti-black racism. Yet the fluidity of the racial boundary between black and Jew in Frank's case underscored the precarious "whiteness" of Jews and, absent blacks as the more obvious target of racism, the ease with which they might, at some moments in American history, slide into a different racial classification. The Frank case vividly illustrated the danger of "home rule" in the Jim Crow South, but an equally strong illustration, one likewise predicated on an association between anti-black racism and anti-Semitism, and more pertinent to the era in which Harper Lee set her story, lies in the Scottsboro trials.

Tom Robinson's case, like the Scottsboro and Till cases, magnifies the innocent question put to Atticus by Scout: "What's rape?"[78] Atticus gives what to Scout is a bafflingly legalistic answer, one of the several occasions on which his own dicta for truth and plain-speaking are violated. Both the novel and Scottsboro asked, however, what meaning "rape" might have if it were only a rhetorical justification for lynching and lesser forms of prejudice, or for sectional resistance to the nationalization of constitutional rights, all predicated on the purported threat of miscegenation and racial pollution. Past a certain stage in each case, no one could doubt the defendants' innocence. The question, rather, was the interpretation of "rape" and the methods of adjudication employed to find a predetermined guilt. It is notable that the speedy procedure of the initial Scottsboro trial at once averted mob rule, created various abridgments of due process, ultimately resulted in key Supreme Court guarantees of criminal and civil rights—principally in *Powell v. Alabama*—and yet brought justice to none of the accused.

The Scottsboro cases are central to the novel not simply because Tom Robinson's trial is perforce set in their context, to the point that the atmosphere at his trial, like the festivity that surrounded the Scottsboro trials, resembles a "Roman carnival," a "gala occasion" for picnics and socializing on the part of white townspeople;[79] and not simply because the similarities between the accusations by, and cross-examinations of, the respective complaining white women, Victoria Price and Mayella Ewell, are of similar special note. More important, the decision in *Powell v. Alabama*, which guaranteed right to counsel in certain capital cases as a matter of due process, brings into view several important dimensions of Lee's legal drama. Although the restrictions of *Powell* would not be entirely erased until *Gideon v. Wainwright* in 1963, the Court's opinion initiated a federal dismantling of previously insulated procedures of state criminal law and started a gradual revolution in constitutional restraints based on the Fourteenth Amendment which would continue throughout the century.[80] In the realm of criminal law, *Powell* therefore nationalized rights under the Fourteenth Amendment in a way comparable to the education cases, beginning with *Missouri ex rel. Gaines v. Canada* in 1938, that led to *Brown v. Board of Education* and finally destroyed the states' capacity to maintain a legal regime of Jim Crow.[81]

As Atticus's futile defense of Tom Robinson implies, however, the beneficial effects of *Powell v. Alabama* were not immediately evident in the courtrooms of Alabama. Although the facts of *Powell* might have arisen in any number of criminal cases, black-on-white rape cases in some parts of the Deep South were virtual guarantees of the denial of due process—if the accused even got to arraignment and trial. As in the Till case two decades later, the court was anxious to preserve the appearance of due process and, in this instance, avert vigilante justice, but the Scottsboro judgments were reached in an atmosphere of mob hysteria. As the anti-lynching crusader Jessie Ames noted, a lynching of the defendants was avoided only "at the expense of the integrity of the law."[82]

The trials of the Scottsboro Boys were moving toward their moment of greatest publicity, in 1933, at a time when northern newspapers were paying increasing attention to the racial doctrine and depredations of the Third Reich, and news coverage of Scottsboro thus brought southern racism and Nazi racism into close proximity. Just as Nazi Germany borrowed from the racial ideology of the Jim Crow South, so African Americans and their allies turned the tables in making Nazi racial policy a mirror of Jim Crow. The week of Haywood Patterson's trial, the *New York Evening Post* ran a series on Nazi Germany which told readers that they might best understand the meaning of Hitlerism by imagining a takeover of the United States by the Ku Klux Klan.[83] But in the Scottsboro case, as in the Leo Frank case, it was not the Jews of Germany but the Jews of New York who most aroused the passionate defenders of one-drop rule. In this respect, too, the resemblance between Tom Robinson's case and that of the Scottsboro Boys is worth closer attention.

Vilified as a personification of the "Jew money from New York" that one prosecutor, at trial, claimed was bankrolling the representation of the Scottsboro defendants by the NAACP and the Communist Party,[84] the flamboyant defense attorney Samuel Leibowitz came into the case in 1933, after its most significant development. His appearance as counsel was predicated on the remanding of the case against Clarence Powell back to Alabama following the

Supreme Court's reversal of the initial verdict in *Powell*. Leibowitz outraged the Alabama courtroom audience, the southern press, and several judges by his evisceration of the testimony of Victoria Price, the principal witness after Ruby Bates recanted her story, supposedly tricked by Jews. (Bates, said one prosecutor, had been contaminated as a witness when, apparently remorseful over her perjured testimony, she confessed to a New York minister: "Ruby Bates couldn't understand the things they told her in New York because it was in Jew language.")[85] His tactics of cross-examination, alien to the southern court, called into question Price's virtue (he presented evidence that she had been a prostitute), impeached her account of her sexual experiences at the time in question (he showed that she had had voluntary intercourse with a white man less than twenty-four hours before the purported gang rape), and tore apart the state's medical evidence (he forced examining doctors to admit that there were no motile sperm, no semen on her clothing, no vaginal injuries, and no scratches on her back despite her claim of having been raped by six men while lying barebacked in a train car loaded with chert). For her part, Victoria Price, who at first took apparent pleasure in a chatty recounting of the events, became increasingly sullen and vituperative in response to Leibowitz's grilling, not least when he feigned politeness.[86]

Leibowitz miscalculated the effect of his rhetoric when he belittled the prosecution's summation as tantamount to urging the jury to "lick this Jew from New York. Stick it to him! We're among home folks." He also failed to grasp that the trial, in the end, was about the South's right, as one prosecutor put it, to "protect the sacred secret parts of . . . the fair womanhood of this great State." In the course of the first round of appeals, the justices of the Alabama State Supreme Court rejected the adduction of Victoria Price's reputation as a prostitute, just as they rejected the appeal on the right-to-counsel and jury composition issues as well. If the court observed a distinction important to women's rights, however, it too put the South's rape complex on display. Dismissing the appellants' complaint about the undue speed of the trial, the court applauded swift justice and, taking a page from the novels of Thomas Dixon, contended that "some things may happen to one worse than death . . . and, if the evidence is to be believed, one of these things happened to this defenseless woman, Victoria Price." Or, as another prosecutor had responded in the second trial when Leibowitz objected to his ranting about "niggers" and rape: "I ain't said nothin' wrong. Your Honor knows I always make the same speech in every nigger rape case." The judge in question concurred; and when he gave his instructions to the jury in a subsequent trial, he snarled out the word "r-r-rapist" in a gruesome tone.[87]

Leibowitz miscalculated as well the degree to which anticommunism, anti-Semitism, and anti-black racism were easily merged in the ritual scenario of violated southern womanhood. Throughout the trial, the southern press condemned the defense as an instance of communist interference in local affairs. The demonization of Leibowitz and Joseph Brodsky, the other principal attorney hired by the International Labor Defense, sprang from a facile association between Jews and communism that depended on the willingness of southerners in some instances to attach even greater stigma to a northern Jew than to a southern black, a possibility already evident in the lynching of Leo Frank.[88] Vanderbilt University historian Frank Owsley identified the northern intrusion into the sacred body of the South prompted by Scottsboro with the previous infamies of abolitionism and Reconstruction, when radical whites had encouraged black men "to commit universal pillage, murder and rape." The Alabama American Legion likewise deplored the horde of communists who had descended on the South to incite riot among African Americans by their defense of "negro rapists," while a leaflet issued by the Birmingham White Legion in 1934 asked, "How would you like to awaken one morning to find your wife or daughter attacked by a Negro or a Communist?" The ongoing anti-Semitic outbursts against Leibowitz (ignoring the fact that he was not a Communist Party member) included threats of lynching parties and the peddling of incendiary broadsides such as the one titled "Kill the Jew from New York."[89]

Atticus Finch, often studied by attorneys for the quality of his character,[90] is a good lawyer and a gentleman, but, unlike Samuel Leibowitz, he is not a crusader. He takes Tom Robinson's case because he is appointed counsel (as specified by statute in Alabama capital cases), is a man of professional ethics, and appears, moreover, to believe in defending Tom, even though he has no illusions about winning a rape case involving a black man and a white woman. Scout puts it best: "Tom was a dead man the minute Mayella Ewell opened her mouth and screamed."[91] Without taking any of Leibowitz's personal pride in the task, Atticus Finch politely but thoroughly humiliates Mayella Ewell on the stand, shredding her testimony, proving that she has been beaten (and probably raped) by her father, Bob Ewell, and in the process laying the ground for an appeal even as he virtually guarantees his client's conviction by the local jury.

Atticus does not characterize the verdict as "spitting on the tomb of Abraham Lincoln," as did Leibowitz, nor does he say of the jury, "If you ever saw those lantern-jawed creatures, those bigots whose mouths are slits in their faces, whose eyes pop out like a frog's, whose chins drip tobacco juice, bewhiskered and filthy, you would not ask how they can do it."[92] Neither does Atticus call into question Mayella's veracity by undermining her reputation for chastity. Instead, he takes the greater risk—for which Tom must pay the heavier price—of making evident her own attempt to seduce a black man. It is necessary to the novel's excruciating effect that Mayella Ewell be a more sympathetic victim and a more compelling witness than Victoria Price; but it is necessary, too, that she lie in order to shield her father and to uphold the sacred honor of white womanhood. In Mayella's case, fittingly, there can be no medical evidence of rape since no doctor was called, although Atticus uses the evidence of her beating to show that Robert E. Lee Ewell (to cite her father's legal name), not Tom Robinson, is guilty. As in the Scottsboro cases, however, neither evidence nor argument matters.

Standing in contrast to bad southern "fathers" such as segregationist governors Ross Barnett, George Wallace, and Orval Faubus, Atticus Finch appears as a paternalistic hero to the book's black community, played to great effect on film by Gregory Peck. (It is noteworthy that Peck, whose role made him the embodiment of postwar racial liberalism, had previously starred in the 1947 film adaptation of Laura Hobson's best-seller *Gentleman's Agreement,* in which, as noted in Chapter 1, the gentile journalist Schuyler Green undertakes to write a series of articles on anti-Semitism by posing as a Jew.) But Atticus is also a man of the South, an insider whose sense of justice transcends prejudice without causing him to repudiate his roots. How else could he function as the symbolic conscience of the white townspeople, those "with background" who privately "say that fair play is not marked White Only," who wish him to do the right thing on their behalf but publicly scorn him as a "nigger-lover," who excuse themselves from jury duty, thus turning the decision over to "white trash," and who uphold at terrible human cost the grandiose myth of racial purity? Unlike Leibowitz, who taunted the prosecution about the nature of Alabama justice—"Stick it to [the Jew]! We're among home folks"—Atticus admonishes his daughter, who seeks to defend him from the scorn of town and family alike: "This time we aren't fighting the Yankees, we're fighting our friends. But remember this, no matter how bitter things get, they're still our friends and this is still our home."[93]

Though on a significantly less horrendous scale, *To Kill a Mockingbird* portrays Maycomb's otherwise decent "home folks" in the same light as those everyday Germans who kept quiet, failed to protest, followed orders, and eventually, in varying degrees, consented to genocide. The literature on the moral culpability of "bystanders" in Nazi Germany, as well as in other nations, defines a wide array of complicit acts and failures to act, both personal and institutional, which made the Holocaust possible.[94] Understanding well enough the difference between genocide and lynching, Harper Lee nonetheless dwelled on the role of "home folks" in order to show that those who committed acts of racial violence and those who kept quiet or exonerated the perpetrators in court—whether in the case of Leo Frank or that of Emmett Till—had to be located along the same spectrum of moral responsibility.

Tom Robinson, technically, is not lynched, but his conviction and killing take place against the backdrop of shameful vigilante justice that was familiar enough to many of Lee's readers. Sometimes openly advertised as "Negro barbeques," lynchings up through the 1930s were frequently marked by large crowds, carnivalesque festivity, and the collection of souvenirs amidst a sacrificial atmosphere—indications that the moral enormity of the crimes had been effaced by their absorption into the local culture of ingrained racism, where the difference between those who carried out murder and those who condoned murder by their witness or their silence might be hard to ascertain.[95] Parallels between American racial violence and the Nazi persecution of the Jews have prompted Orlando Patterson, interpreting lynch law within the context of Nazism and reading both as perversions of Christianity, to ask: "What is it about the cross that so easily turns people on to genocide? That so frequently makes bloodthirsty brutes and cannibals of ordinary men and women?"* Although

---

* The epidemic of lynchings between the 1880s and the 1940s, argues Patterson, proves that Christianity is nothing less than a violent, two-thousand-year betrayal of Jesus' teachings that reached its apex in the American South. The combined ritual festivity and solemnity testified to by participants bears out that lynching sometimes had the character of sacrifice "to a Southern Christian God." But it is another matter to consent to Patterson's view that the smell of burnt offerings in Leviticus, the prevalence of barbeque in the South, and Claude Lévi-Strauss's theory of the "raw and the cooked" can together explain why lynching was a form of southern "cannibalism" whereby the "cooked Negro, properly roasted, has been tamed and culturally transformed" into something that can be communally consumed. It is no doubt possible to demonstrate that the burning cross of the Ku Klux Klan—an image inspired by Thomas Dixon's novel *The Clansman: An Historical Romance of the Ku Klux Klan* (1905)—psychically displaced the Christlike "sacrificed Negro" with a brand of white supremacy grounded in terror and the communal shedding of Negro blood. After all, African American literature and commentary of the period is suffused with images of the "black Christ" as lynching victim, while in turn the racist literature of the day, led by Dixon's novels and epitomized in *The Birth of a Nation,* explicitly associated racial purity with religious fervor. But Patterson goes further, suggesting that only the advent of African American Christianity, culminating in the leadership of Martin Luther King, Jr., redeemed the radical gospel preached by Jesus and rescued it from white supremacist abominations. King's liberation theology was inspired, to be sure, but it was hardly "the first time since the death of Jesus" that the message of Jesus found a true community of believers. A potentially more useful approach through ritual action was

black and white writers were quick to discover the synonymity of lynching and crucifixion—the long list would include, for example, Jean Toomer's *Cane* (1923), Countee Cullen's "Black Christ" (1929), William Faulkner's *Light in August* (1932), and Lillian Smith's *Strange Fruit* (1944)—Patterson fails to find an adequate theological motive for lynching. Yet his focus on the sins of ordinary men and women illuminates the culpability of local bystanders in *To Kill a Mockingbird*—friends, neighbors, community leaders, and by implication the entire way of life that supports an apparatus of segregation, winks at vigilantism, and, in a wrenching moment of innocence lost, mitigates the heartbreak Scout feels after Tom's conviction when she explains that, after all, "he's just a Negro."[96]

Upon losing Tom's case, Atticus suffers personal anguish and bitterness, but he reminds the children on this occasion, as on others, that both juries and mobs are composed of "people you know," of "reasonable men in everyday life," of "folks right at home," of "our friends."[97] Racial injustice, that is to say, is a southern problem that must be solved from within by right-thinking white people. But no less than the "home rule" reasserted in the lynching of Leo Frank or the "home folks" version of justice visited upon the Scottsboro defendants in one trial after another, in *To Kill a Mockingbird* "our friends" include both those few who trust Atticus "to do right," even as they themselves do not, and those many who defiantly uphold states' rights and the racial regime of Jim Crow. The full import of Lee's introduction of the moral responsibility of bystanders is apparent, however, only when we reflect further on reactions to the rise of Nazism during the era in which *To Kill a Mockingbird* is set, the state of public consciousness about the Holocaust at the time the novel appeared, and the evolution of thinking about racism and genocide during the years in between.

---

once adumbrated by Ralph Ellison. Although he did not refer to Nazism, his account of the symbolic meaning of lynching brought him close to a description of acts of anti-Semitic (or other forms of) terror that targeted individuals purposely or randomly with an ulterior purpose in view. In propitiating the "insatiable god of whiteness," Ellison remarked, lynching is not so different from a car bomb detonated in a crowded public place, for "both car bomb and lynch rope are savagely efficient ways of destroying distinctions between the members of a hated group while rendering quite meaningless any moral questioning that might arise regarding the method used. For the ultimate goal of lynchers is that of achieving ritual purification through destroying the lynchers' identification with the basic *humanity* of their victims." See Orlando Patterson, *Rituals of Blood: Consequences of Slavery in Two American Centuries* (Washington, D.C.: Civitas, 1998), pp. xv, 188–202, 215–18, 230–32; Ralph Ellison, "An Extravagance of Laughter," in *Going to the Territory* (New York: Random House, 1986), p. 178.

To Speak of the Unspeakable

*That is the real soul-sickness, the spear in the side, the drag by the neck
through the mob-angry town, the Grand Inquisition, the embrace of the
Maiden, the rip in the belly with the guts spilling out, the trip to the chamber with the deadly gas that ends in an oven so hygienically clean—only
it's worse because you continue stupidly to live.*
                                        —*Ralph Ellison,* Invisible Man

Although it would be another two decades before African American culture
began to be pervaded by representations of the Holocaust, Ellison's almost casual 1952 deployment of the gas chamber and the crematorium to describe his
protagonist's racial anguish in *Invisible Man* is one index of the visceral imme-
diacy with which many blacks had reacted to the Holocaust from the 1940s onward—a phenomenon all the more striking when it is considered within the
context of the much-noted "silence" about the Holocaust in the first decade or
more of its aftermath. The dimensions of that silence, as Michael Staub argues,[98] have frequently been overstated, for Jews, among others, could not help
but grapple with and refer to so incomprehensible an instance of mass murder,
and it immediately shaped their perspectives on a range of social and political
issues such as desegregation, Zionism, and women's rights. Even though images
from the liberated concentration camps had a sobering effect on all who saw
them, however, the facts on which scholarly analysis and judgments, as well as
artistic exploration, might be based were slow to come into view, making the
worlds of the sealed ghetto, the transport, and the death camp at once terrible
and obscure.

The scale of the Holocaust was not widely understood, nor was it immediately seen as a distinctive kind of racial murder set apart from the other atrocities of the war; neither was it clear whether Jews were unique victims of the
ravages of totalitarianism. William Shirer devoted only 2–3 percent of *The Rise
and Fall of the Third Reich,* an 1,100-page book, to an account of the Holocaust,
while in *Judgment at Nuremberg* (1961), the first American film to bring the
mechanism of the Nazi genocide before a popular audience, Jews were portrayed as but one group among many victims, and the only Jews in the film
were those in documentary footage from the concentration camps liberated in
1945.[99] Both abroad and in the United States, eyewitness accounts, especially in

English, only began to appear in any numbers in the late 1950s and early 1960s—notably, Primo Levi's *Survival in Auschwitz* (1959), Elie Wiesel's *Night* (1960), Alexander Donat's *Holocaust Kingdom* (1963), Joseph Bor's *Terezin Requiem* (1963), and Chaim Kaplan's *Scroll of Agony* (1965).

Reticence about the Holocaust, even after its magnitude began to be comprehended, was also a function of its horror, before which historians, philosophers, theologians, and novelists seemed awestruck. "Our images of God, man, and the moral order have been permanently impaired," said Richard Rubinstein, adapting Nietzsche's admonition about the death of God to the post-Holocaust order. "The first reaction to such a wounding must be shock and numbness." Where once we experienced God's presence, now we find "Holy Nothingness."[100] In order to confront an event seemingly without precedent, one might need to resort to radical indirection, as in the case of *The Slave* (serialized in Yiddish in 1960–61 and translated into English in 1962), where Isaac Bashevis Singer employed a historical narrative set against anti-Semitic violence of the seventeenth century to explore the millennial upheaval of the Holocaust and its aftermath,[101] or *The Fixer* (1966), where, as we will see in Chapter 6, Bernard Malamud's fictionalization of the Mendel Beilis blood libel of 1911 included an allegory of Jewish resistance to state-sponsored anti-Semitism. By some accounts, any attempt to approach the Holocaust in words might, in fact, do damage to the fabric of language itself. "The world of Auschwitz lies outside speech as it lies outside reason," wrote George Steiner in 1963. "To speak of the *unspeakable* is to risk the survivance of language as creator and bearer of humane, rational truth."[102]

American reticence about the Holocaust up through the 1960s was motivated less by such abstractions, however, than by anxiety about incommensurate experiences. The relative insulation of American Jews from the Nazi menace and the postwar suburban security to which many aspired simply could not be reconciled with the unfathomable destruction of nearly 6 million European Jews. Insofar as any pretense of explanation was bound to seem inconsequential, "a mere trifling with categories in the face of the unspeakable," said Irving Howe, adopting Steiner's language, postwar American Jews lived with historical dissociation, inwardly tormented about the disaster they had not been able to prevent, publicly silent about an event they wished to make alien to Judaism as they knew it.*

---

* In a symposium, "The Condition of Jewish Belief," conducted by *Commentary* in 1961, the editors posed a series of questions to young intellectuals about Jewish values, Americanism, conversion, the so-

In the United States, moreover, recognition was hindered by several factors—by Jews' fears of being identified with the wrong side in the cold war,
where Germany was the new ally against the Soviet Union and the exposure of
former Jewish sympathies or affiliations with the Communist Party was dangerous; by the advice given refugee survivors to forget their past and look forward to their rebirth in America, the land of plenty; and by an apprehension
that the very act of speaking about the Holocaust would make American Jews
stand out *as* Jews at just the moment when they were achieving notable acceptance and assimilation.[103] This last argument had already been the subject of
Philip Roth's short story "Eli, the Fanatic" (1959), with its lacerating portrait of
suburban Jews thrown into a frenzy of embarrassment when Orthodox refugees establish a yeshiva in the town. Roth's contrast between the immigrants,
some of them Holocaust survivors, and the Americanized Jews, for whom the
refugees constitute a threat to the town's "peace and safety—what civilization
had been working toward for centuries," precisely illuminated the sometimes
subtle, sometimes stark line between "Jew" and "American."[104]

In a now familiar story, it was only with the publication of Raul Hilberg's
monumental book *The Destruction of the European Jews* (1961) and that same
year the televised trial of Adolf Eichmann, the subject of numerous studies by
journalists, pollsters, and scholars, that the American silence was finally broken. (In Israel, the Eichmann trial, whose principal purpose was to strengthen
national unity and Israel's claim to represent world Jewry, also set in motion
a wave of reevaluation in which shame for the Holocaust and its survivors
was replaced with a degree of identification with them, an effect that changed
substantially the nation's educational and commemorative practices.)[105] Like
Hilberg's work, Hannah Arendt's *Eichmann in Jerusalem* (1963), the most noto-

---

cialism of the previous generation, and Israel's claim on American Jewish sympathies. Yet, as many
scholars have noticed, there were no questions specifically about the Holocaust, and relatively few of the
thirty-one participants spoke about it even in passing. Likewise, the subject was missing from a 1961
symposium of Jewish intellectuals, "My Jewish Affirmation," in *Judaism,* where respondents who were
asked questions such as "What do you regard as centrally significant in Jewish tradition and presently
viable?" made no reference to the Holocaust. As late as 1962, Rabbi Irving Greenberg was refused permission to teach a course on the Holocaust at Yeshiva University. Irving Howe, *World of Our Fathers:
The Journey of the East European Jews to America and the Life They Found and Made* (New York: Simon
and Schuster, 1976), pp. 626–27; "Jewishness and the Younger Intellectuals: A Symposium," *Commentary*
31 (April 1961), 306–63; "My Jewish Affirmation—A Symposium," *Judaism* 10 (Fall 1961), 291–352; Stuart
E. Eizenstat, *Imperfect Justice: Looted Assets, Slave Labor, and the Unfinished Business of World War II*
(New York: Public Affairs, 2003), p. 13.

rious analysis of the trial, was shocking in particular for its imputation of weakness and complicity to European Jews in the ghettos and death camps.* Even as they may have awakened the guilt of American Jews over their insufficient protest against Nazism or their insufficient identification with European Jews, such claims prompted furious debate and rebuttals that would reach a crescendo during the Six-Day War, when Israel appeared to be threatened by a "second Holocaust" at the hands of Arab enemies.[106]

The decades since have witnessed a massive outpouring of scholarship on Nazism and the Holocaust, as well as a flood of horrifying but necessary testimony by survivors. (Although the purpose of Hitler's Third Reich was to deprive Jews of an identity and history, to erase their subjectivity and peoplehood, as Ruth Wisse has remarked, the vast collection of first-person testimony left by both survivors and those who perished has enlarged, rather than diminished, the Jews' prominence in history.)[107] Study of the Holocaust has been accompanied by intensive memorialization of the event—in literature and art, in museums and public commemorative sites, and even in the core theology of Judaism. Supplementing the argument advanced by Elie Wiesel and others that the Holocaust was equal in magnitude to God's revelation at Sinai, for example, Emil Fackenheim, in the aftermath of the Six-Day War, presented an admonition fashioned into a "614th Commandment" (the Torah has

---

* Arendt's book, initially serialized in the New Yorker, focused on the genocidal capabilities of the modern state rather than on anti-Semitism per se. Her provocative suggestion that the Nazi regime had a numbingly mundane and bureaucratic quality that made Eichmann little more than a "cog" in a massive machine—an argument reflected in the book's subtitle, A Report on the Banality of Evil—was hardly meant to exonerate anyone of genocide, but her detailed, if flawed, account of the progress toward extermination in Germany, Poland, and other countries was overshadowed by her foregrounding of moral ambiguity. It was especially her attention, shared by Hilberg, to the participation of Jews themselves in the bureaucracy of the Holocaust—facts undeniable in the roles of Jewish ghetto councils and concentration camp Kapos but highly questionable as generalizations about Jewish behavior—that aroused the greatest anguish and rage at Arendt for promulgating a negative image of the European Jew and carrying the painful argument too much into the public sphere. The concept of the "banality of evil" was inevitably an invitation to misinterpretation. When Gershom Scholem took her to task for the "flippancy" of her tone and for abandoning her "eloquent and erudite witness" in The Origins of Totalitarianism (1951) in favor of such a "slogan," Arendt replied that she had, indeed, changed her mind. Evil, she said, "possesses neither depth nor any demonic dimension. It can overgrow and lay waste the whole world precisely because it spreads like a fungus on the surface." Only good "has depth and can be radical"; in attempting to grapple with evil, thought "is frustrated because there is nothing." Exchange of letters of 1963 between Scholem and Arendt in Hannah Arendt, The Jew as Pariah: Jewish Identity and Politics in the Modern Age, ed. Ron H. Feldman (New York: Grove Press, 1978), pp. 242–51.

613 commandments, observed by the most devout Jews) that Jews "are forbidden to grant posthumous victories to Hitler" and "commanded to remember the victims of Auschwitz, lest their memory perish."[108]

As the Holocaust entered Jewish remembrance and liturgy, the story of liberation told in Exodus became bound to the story of destruction in the death camps. Just as the memory of bondage in Egypt and the euphoria of freedom are central to the evolution of consciousness of nationhood among the Israelites, and every Jew must be made present at Sinai in the observance of Passover because *all* Jews were led from bondage and given God's covenant, now the Holocaust and the new nation of modern Israel must enter into sacral memory, with every Jew made present at the Holocaust because *all* Jews were the intended victims of the Nazi genocide: every Jew is a survivor.[109]

But commemoration of the kind required by an event of such cataclysmic scale presented its own problems. "No one becomes a survivor either by virtue of being a Jew or by the intensity of their absorption in the history and literature of the Shoah," cautions Michael André Bernstein.[110] The initial risk was that the wound of the Holocaust would be left to fester unexamined by a secular generation of assimilated American Jews—its unconscious pain emerging, if at all, with sudden destructive force, as in Roth's *Zuckerman Unbound* (1981), when Nathan Zuckerman's terminally ill mother cannot write her own name on a piece of paper but instead writes the single word "Holocaust." An equal risk, however, was that the Judeocide would become a means of shoring up faltering community and cashing in on the vogue for ethnicity;[111] or an ideological vehicle for the "postgenocidal" generation to achieve solidarity with "the earth's damned";[112] or, worse, the centerpiece of a perverse kind of chosenness, a "surrogate Judaism," in Jacob Neusner's phrase, in which preoccupation with the Nazi genocide overshadows the traditional observances of Jewish religious life and gives credence to the view that the survival of Judaism depends on the survival of anti-Semitism.[113]

The percentage of American Jews who identified anti-Semitism as a serious problem in the United States, including the vague threat that a Holocaust could happen "again," rose by the late 1980s to 80 percent,[114] a fact attributable in part to the persecution (and rescue) of Soviet Jews and in part to Arab threats to the security of Israel and its increasing ostracism in the United Nations and elsewhere, but equally to more and more finely grained attention to the Nazi genocide. Despite making his heroine a Polish Catholic anti-Semite who survives Auschwitz only to be dragged by a deranged American Jew into a relationship of chaotic sadomasochism ending in their double suicide, William Styron managed with *Sophie's Choice* (1979) to bring the Holocaust into mainstream

American fiction without outraging Jews nearly as much as he had outraged blacks with *The Confessions of Nat Turner* (1967). In the quotidian discourse of television, the Jewish melodrama *Holocaust* capitalized on the prior success of the black melodrama *Roots*, while the proliferation of Holocaust historiography was such that the hero of Don DeLillo's satiric novel *White Noise* (1986), a liberal arts professor at a small midwestern college, could take credit for a new discipline in American higher education: "I invented Hitler studies in North America in March of 1968."[115] The timidity of earlier generations gave way to bold confrontation, writes Melvin Jules Bukiet, the child of Holocaust survivors: "Now, we are strident. Now, we rub the world's nose in our misery. Go to our museums. Go see our movies. Go read our books. Look at what you did. Behold." In a 1990 forward to her 1969 novel *Touching Evil*, which portrayed the reaction of non-Jewish Americans to the Holocaust, Norma Rosen nicely measured the transformation in Jewish, and more broadly American, consciousness of the Holocaust over those two decades: "As safe Americans we were not there. Since then, in imagination, we are seldom anywhere else."[116]

It is easy to forget that what is now common knowledge was once inchoate. Although it is ubiquitous today, use of the term "Holocaust" to designate the genocide of the European Jews only became widespread (and began to appear in dictionaries) after it was adopted as the appropriate translation of the Hebrew *shoah* at Yad Vashem, Israel's museum and study center on the Holocaust, as well as in the English edition of Elie Wiesel's *Night* (1959) and then again during the Eichmann trial. In earlier usage, *shoah* or its cognate term *churban* were typically translated as "great disaster" or "catastrophe," although more complex meanings were occasionally sought in awkward phrases such as "permanent pogrom." *The New Jewish Encyclopedia*, published in 1962, had no separate entry on the Holocaust, and Raul Hilberg did not use the term in *The Destruction of the European Jews*, although by 1968 the Library of Congress had created an entry card for "Holocaust—Jewish, 1939–1945."[117] Despite its current usage, the term itself remains surrounded by ambiguity and debate,* all the

---

* A few scholars have opted for the Hebrew *churban,* used characteristically in reference to the historical destruction of the First and Second Temples. More common is the Hebrew *shoah,* which also has a biblical resonance but is not linked to specific precedents. Omer Bartov has made the point that the different names employed for the Holocaust signify understandable confusion as to its essence, fear and anxiety about naming what it really is. For each nation, the name chosen represents its psychological relation to the event: *shoah* in Hebrew; *génocide* in French; *Judenvernichtung* (destruction of the Jews) in German. The English word Holocaust derives from the Greek *holokaustos* (wholly burnt), the Septuagint translation of the Hebrew *olah,* which refers to the burnt sacrificial offering dedicated to God (for example, in Leviticus 1:9 and 1 Samuel 7:9), thus creating problematic connotations of worship or obe-

more so because it has become enveloped in arguments about what other instances of genocide, if any, may be rightly compared to the Holocaust, or, for
that matter, what actually constitutes an act of genocide. In a 2002 call for papers, for instance, the prospective editors of a "Critical Holocaust Anthology"
proposed a volume devoted to "decentering" the Holocaust, questioning its
"supposed uniqueness" and "hyper-visibility."[118] Indeed, sanctification of the
Holocaust proved less of a problem than the inexorable progression whereby
other instances of actual or potential genocide, as well as all manner of politicized death and injury, from abortion and AIDS to the use of animals in
medical research and the disfigurement caused by breast implants (a "silicone
holocaust," according to a contemporary Web site), became, by analogy, "holocausts."

Such progression has, of course, not gone unchallenged. Despite Hiroshima
and Nagasaki, the Soviet Gulags, the Cambodian genocide, and other atrocities,
Primo Levi argued, the Nazi concentration camp system "still remains a uni-
cum, both in its extent and quality. At no other time has one seen a phenomenon so unexpected and so complex: never have so many lives been extin-
guished in so short a time, and with so lucid a combination of technological
ingenuity, fanaticism, and cruelty."[119] Levi's insistence on the "uniqueness" of
the Holocaust, a problem to which we will return in Chapter 7, has produced a
voluminous literature devoted to two key issues: Were Jews distinct among the
intended victims of Nazism, and was the Nazi Holocaust distinctive as an
instance of genocide? Although the exhaustive attention paid to the moral ab-
solutism of Germany's guilt has created in that nation an "eleventh command-

---

dience. Especially in its association with the Christian crucifixion, Ruth Wisse has written, "Holocaust"
implies a secular version of the crucifixion in which Jews are cast as sacrificial figures "in a denational-
ized saga of evil and innocence." The problem is compounded by the fact that "holocaust" in its medieval origin was used in a specifically anti-Semitic fashion to characterize the massacre of Jews, so that its
modern-day revival implies a disturbing equation between crematoria and altars. On the one hand,
such associations may lead to disabling semantic ambivalence. On the other, notes Bartov, they may be
appropriate in a nation such as the United States, which experienced the events from afar and remains
intolerant of the inexplicable or the non-redemptive. Numerous, equivocal terms may, indeed, be necessary in order to encompass a "multi-named hell" that, for all its facticity, remains inexplicable, unthinkable. See James E. Young, *Writing and Rewriting the Holocaust: Narrative and the Consequences of Interpretation* (Bloomington: Indiana University Press, 1988), pp. 85–89; Ruth R. Wisse, *The Modern Jewish
Canon: A Journey through Language and Culture* (New York: Free Press, 2000), p. 197; Giorgio Agamben,
Remnants of Auschwitz: The Witness and the Archive, trans. Daniel Heller-Roazen (New York: Zone
Books, 1999), p. 30; and Omer Bartov, *Murder in Our Midst: The Holocaust, Industrial Killing, and Repre-
sentation* (New York: Oxford University Press, 1996), pp. 57–58.

ment: Thou shalt not compare,"[120] says Henryk Broder, the issue of comparability remains very much alive elsewhere, nowhere more evidently than in the case of American slavery.

"Is the South fascist?" asked Gunnar Myrdal in *An American Dilemma*. His answer was negative,[121] but no sooner had the genocide of the European Jews begun to be written into the millennia-long genre that David Roskies has called the "literature of destruction"[122] than blacks began to reinterpret their American experience, as well as the literatures of slavery and racial assault, through the lens of the Nazi genocide. Indeed, the grounds for comparison were set forth by African Americans even before the event that became the Holocaust had happened.

We Charge Genocide

Seeing in Nazi Germany a reflection of homegrown racism and in European Jews a potential reflection of themselves, African Americans had every reason to be alert to the rise of Nazism, sympathetic to its victims, and wary of, even cynical about, white Americans' denunciations of Hitler. Black Jews, indeed, might be expected to feel the threat viscerally. "We are fighting barbarism of all kinds on two fronts," wrote Wentworth Matthew, leader of the Commandment Keepers, in 1934. "One is the Hitler terror and the other is the wave of lynching of colored folks that has swept the South."[123]

But blacks hardly needed to be Jewish to see something familiar in Hitler's menace. As an editorialist for the Baltimore newspaper the *Afro-American* observed in 1936, although the Constitution kept the South from passing its own Nuremberg Laws against blacks, "by indirection, by force and terrorism, the South and Nazi Germany are mental brothers."[124] Leading black intellectuals such as Kelly Miller and George Schuyler drew parallels between the American South and Hitler's Germany, or identified the South as one source of Nazi racial ideas.[125] Although black fears of genocide failed to materialize, the power of southerners to carry out racial violence with near impunity in the era of Jim Crow was not in question. A white race riot in Columbia, Tennessee, in 1946, said the *New York Times*, went beyond a simple case of lynching and more resembled "the pattern of Nazi terror against the Jews." The *Times* headlined its editorial "Pogrom in Tennessee," while the *Crisis* captioned its photo of the event "Kristallnacht." As Roy Wilkins, editor of the *Crisis*, wrote in 1938, "The South approaches more nearly than any other section of the United States the

Nazi idea of government by a 'master race' without any interference from any democratic process."[126]

Nor was the analogy applicable only to the South. Melvin Tolson's poem "The Idols of the Tribe" (included in his 1944 collection *Rendezvous with America*) took its epigraph from *Mein Kampf* and argued for the parallel between fascism in Europe and nationwide state-sponsored racism in the United States, while Langston Hughes wondered what the nation proposed to do about those who "segregate Negroes as the Nazis ghettoized Jews in Europe" and force "our Red Cross to mark Negro blood AA—*Afro-American*—as things Jewish are labeled *Yude* in Germany."[127] Attempts on the part of whites to turn the analogy on its head by blaming race riots on Hitler's inflammatory rhetoric about American racial policies only increased the consternation of blacks. "This trick of getting Negroes chasing after Hitler as the cause of the race riots and tension," said A. Philip Randolph, "diverts Negroes' attention from the true source of the riots which is America." Said one rioter smashing windows during the Harlem riot of 1943, when challenged by a policeman, "Shoot me, I would rather die here for my people than in Germany."[128]

Such sentiment indicates that black response to the threat of Nazism did not automatically translate into increased sympathy for Jews, American Jews in particular. Although Jews and Negroes "are being slowly strangled in the grip of the same octopus," lamented S. A. Haynes in 1934, "the chasm between them continues to widen."[129] At the same time that they exploited the rise of Nazism in order to attack white racism in the United States, in fact, a few blacks were inclined secretly, and at times openly, to applaud Hitler or his persecution of the Jews. Part of the appeal lay in the nationalist promise of fascism for a disfranchised racial group. Like Du Bois in the 1920s, who found something to admire in the early accomplishments of Hitler, Marcus Garvey, as we have already seen, responded instinctively to his magnetism. Writing in *Negro World* from Berlin in 1928, Garvey ignored German colonialism in order to find inspiration in Teutonic nationalism: "Africa must be redeemed; Africa must become a great nation of blacks; therefore I am inspiring you to work as the Germans have worked, to carve out of the scattered tribes in Africa and elsewhere a united racial empire."[130] Black sympathy with Nazi propaganda sometimes took the form of declaring the European conflict a "Jewish war" in which Negroes would be foolish to fight for the kinsmen of the landlords and merchants who abused them, and black anti-Semites found inspiration in the doctrines of the Third Reich. The Chicago tabloid *Dynamite* opined in 1936, "What America needs is a Hitler and what the Chicago Black Belt needs is a purge of the exploiting Jew."[131]

Although it would later become apparent that white Americans, both gentile and Jew, had failed to react quickly enough to the rise of Nazism and that the United States government had thwarted Jewish refugees and turned a blind eye to the Holocaust,[132] for a number of blacks, American reaction to the persecution of the Jews simply diverted attention from racist laws and Jim Crow violence in the United States. George Schuyler declared that he would be willing to "wail a lot louder" about Hitler if he thought Jews and other whites showed comparable signs of concern about blacks. When Secretary of State Cordell Hull invited twenty-nine nations to provide safe haven for German Jewish refugees in March 1938, NAACP secretary Walter White cabled Hull that blacks applauded the action but "would be even more enthusiastic if our government could be equally indignant at the lynching, burning alive and torture" of African Americans, which had shamed America "for a much longer time than persecution under Hitler." Others believed that the plight of the Jews would awaken such indignation. Du Bois, who would one day speak with much greater sympathy for the Jews under Nazism and in open favor of the founding of Israel, confessed in September 1933 to being filled with "unholy glee" by Hitler's outrages: "When the only 'inferior' peoples were 'niggers' it was hard to get the attention of the *New York Times* for little matters of race, lynching and mobs. But now that the damned included the owner of the *Times,* moral indignation is perking up."[133] The same sentiment lingered after the war. Writing in the *Pittsburgh Courier* in 1947, Joseph D. Bibb found an unfortunate contrast in the concern shown by white Americans for the displaced persons of Europe—predominantly survivors of the Holocaust and their relatives—while the nation, at the same time, seemed "unconcerned, untouched and unperturbed by the pathetic plight of hundreds of thousands of displaced and uprooted colored Americans"[134]

In both the suffering and the perseverance of the Jews, however, most African Americans found consoling fraternity and, sometimes, inspiration. Congressman Adam Clayton Powell, Jr., writing in the *Amsterdam News* in 1938, denounced Hitler and warned that anti-Semitism is "a deadly virus in the American bloodstream" about which African Americans, of all people, could not afford to be apathetic. Near the war's end, Powell protested in *Marching Blacks* (1945) that "America does not belong to Bilbo"—longtime Mississippi senator and governor Theodore Bilbo, who opposed miscegenation ardently enough to prefer nuclear annihilation and whose hobby horse was that all blacks should be repatriated to Africa—but rather to "all the people, the people who fled Europe" and those "who were brought here in chains."[135] Black sympathy also found its way into foreign policy. During the negotiations that led to the 1949 armistice between Arabs and Israelis, for which he received the Nobel Peace Prize, Ralph Bunche had clandestine meetings with Menachem Begin, leader of the paramilitary Irgun, who recalled that Bunche shook his hand and exclaimed: "I can understand you. I am also a member of a persecuted minority."[136]

The full complexity of black responses to Nazism appears in the fictional example of Zora Neale Hurston's *Moses, Man of the Mountain* (1939), which seems uncannily marked by a post-Holocaust understanding of the Exodus. Although her Moses is a master of conjure and a sermonizing exhorter who rallies his backsliding people and attempts to make a nation of them, he is also very much a modern-day warrior, seeming to reflect both the struggle for black rights at home and the imminent conflict between fascist and democratic powers. Insofar as he forms an authoritarian and racially exclusive state based on charismatic leadership and proceeds on his mission to take the Promised Land by force, Hurston pointed to the allure of fascism as a model for black cultural nationalism. But she showed its dangers as well. The ambiguity of Moses' own "blood" and Pharaoh's marking of Hebrew male babies for extinction evoke a clear parallel between the racial classifications of Jim Crow and the more ominous results of the Nuremberg Laws.[137] Telling the story of black liberation with reference to both the Jews' ancient liberation and their contemporary persecution, *Moses, Man of the Mountain* thus sits at the watershed beyond which future black rewritings of the Exodus would be ineluctably haunted by the prospect of a people's extermination.

Despite their sporadic attraction to aspects of Nazism, African Americans' actual encounter with its victims typically had a harrowing effect, whether for soldiers abroad or observers at home. In *Devil in a Blue Dress* (1990), to cite a literary re-creation of post-Holocaust black views set in 1948, Walter Mosley's detective Easy Rawlins recalls his participation in the Allied liberation of the concentration camps: "I remembered the Jews. Nothing more than skeletons, bleeding from their rectums and begging for food. I remembered them waving their weak hands in front of themselves, trying to keep modest; then dropping dead right before my eyes. . . . That was why the Jews back then understood the American Negro; in Europe the Jew had been a Negro for more than a thousand years."*

---

* A far stranger and more disturbing instance of such confession, in fictional form, appears in Leslie Epstein's *San Remo Drive* (2003), where the narrator, a young Jewish boy, discovers puberty in a scene of sexual initiation at the hands, literally, of a black former GI. In an episode set in 1948 and titled "Negroes," a black plumber working at his family's house fondles the boy's erect penis while his co-worker

Real recollections were no less sobering and self-reflexive. Confronted with the "the walking dead" of Buchenwald, the body parts left from medical experiments, and "mounds of little children's clothing," black GI Leon Bass found his resentment of the United States tempered: "I came into that camp an angry black soldier. Angry at my country and justifiably so. Angry because they were treating me as though I was not good enough. But [that day] I came to the realization that human suffering is not relegated to me and mine." Yet the devastation of the Jews reminds him, too, that blacks went unprotected from lynching for decades in some parts of the United States. "If this could happen here, it could happen anywhere," he added. "It could happen to me. It could happen to black folks in America." Likewise, after conversing at Dachau with an emaciated rabbi, who explained to him that Jews were killed simply because they were Jews, Paul Parks tried to understand by comparing the death camps to slavery, where "there were no laws against killing you and destroying your family." The "close parallel between the history of my people in America and what's happened to the Jews in Europe," said Parks, stimulated him to fight for civil rights upon his return to the United States.*

Others, however, were less certain that the situations were comparable. The artist John Biggers recalled that his mentor at Hampton Institute, the refugee

---

tells of the man's experience as a death camp liberator, where he saw the "living dead," "bones that was moving," digging through a pile of their own excrement in search of "corn kernels, maybe, that had not been digested; or seeds; or a crust of bread." Although the sexual encounter is interrupted before climax, the story the boy hears is more terrible than anything he has seen in *Life* magazine's coverage of the Holocaust and provokes in him more pity for the man who had to witness it than for the Jewish victims themselves, who remain distant and abstract. Walter Mosley, *Devil in a Blue Dress* (1990; rpt. New York: Washington Square Press, 2002), pp. 184–85; Leslie Epstein, *San Remo Drive: A Novel from Memory* (New York: Handsel Books, 2003), pp. 142–43.

* Leon Bass and Paul Parks quoted in Lou Potter, William Miles, and Nina Rosenbaum, *Liberators: Fighting on Two Fronts in World War II* (New York: Harcourt Brace Jovanovich, 1992), pp. 207, 219, 242. The PBS film on which the book was based showed that foregrounding African American patriotism in relation to the Holocaust could prove problematic. Like the book, the film *Liberators* focused in part on the role played by two all–African American army units in liberating Buchenwald and Dachau, but it was attacked for having falsely inflated that role and being turned into a tendentious catalyst for black-Jewish unity at a moment of great tension between the two communities. Veracity aside, the premise of the film itself was rife with tension. In setting out to demonstrate that the bravery and patriotism of African Americans were every bit the equal of those of white Americans, Jeffrey Shandler notes, *Liberators* awkwardly made the Holocaust, an event of such catastrophic loss for the Jewish world as to seem beyond appropriation to other purposes, into a moment of triumph for black soldiers. See Jeffrey Shandler, *While America Watches: Televising the Holocaust* (New York: Oxford University Press, 1999), pp. 219–29.

Viktor Lowenfeld, read to him a letter from the State Department conveying the news that members of Lowenfeld's family had perished in a Nazi death camp. Said Biggers, I had heard of neighbors whose family members had been lynched, "but I realized that [our] race and color might not have any meaning at all when it comes to terrifying experiences in this world."[138] Du Bois, too, modified his point of view. In *Dusk of Dawn*, published in 1940, he had predicted that the advancement of black rights and economic power might produce a backlash: "We may be expelled from the United States as the Jew is being expelled from Germany." Even after the war, writing in *The World and Africa* (1947), he contended that "there was no Nazi atrocity—concentration camps, wholesale maiming and murder, defilement of women or ghastly blasphemy of childhood—which the Christian civilization of Europe had not long been practicing against colored folk in all parts of the world in the name of and for the defense of a Superior Race born to rule the world."[139] By the time he visited the liquidated Warsaw Ghetto in 1949, however, Du Bois made no attempt to draw a comparison. Nothing in his memory of the Atlanta race riots or the march of the Ku Klux Klan—indeed, he said, nothing in his "wildest imagination"—prepared him for the ruin he described in a sobering essay, "The Negro and the Warsaw Ghetto," published in *Jewish Life*.[140] (In a 1953 reissue of *The Souls of Black Folk*, admitting that his earlier charges were based on hearsay, Du Bois also revised a number of original passages that had accused carpetbagger Jews of exploiting poor southern blacks so that they referred simply to corrupt "whites.")

The calamity of the Holocaust thus provided both the seeds of resentment that African American suffering would be diminished by comparison to that of the Jews, as well as the grounds for reconceiving black history in ways that proved necessary but not entirely salutary. In either case, the most telling, and in the end the most enduring, sign of blacks' identification with the modern Jewish experience lay in their ready adaptation of the lessons of the Holocaust to the history of Africans in America.

Consider the "Petition to the United Nations for Relief from a Crime of the United States Government against the Negro People," an appeal presented to the United Nations by the Civil Rights Congress, an advocacy group from the United States (the United Nations did not respond). The petition referred to the 1948 "Convention on the Prevention and Punishment of the Crime of Genocide," an ancillary provision of the "Universal Declaration of Human Rights" issued by the United Nations in 1947 and from whose ratification the United States abstained. The American objection lay in the ambiguity of the term "genocide," coined by Raphael Lemkin in his *Axis Rule in Occupied Eu-*

rope (1944) and introduced into the trial of Nazi war criminals at Nuremberg. (Lemkin's neologism apparently came in response to his hearing Winston Churchill in a radio address describe the destruction of the Jews, which included seventy-two of seventy-four members of Lemkin's own family, as "this crime without a name.")[141] Equivocation in Lemkin's definition of genocide allowed for both a radical denationalization through mass murder, which might leave many or most of those constituting the group alive, and the intended complete erasure of the group. Lemkin's equivocation was based in part on his conviction that the Nazis' murder of Poles, Serbs, Russians, and others, while perhaps different in precision and scale from their murder of Jews, nonetheless included the intention, at least in principle, to destroy those peoples as national groups. His language, instrumental in the deliberations of the United Nations, produced a linguistic gray area in the Genocide Convention, where the phrase "acts committed with the intent to destroy, in whole or in part, a national, ethnical or religious group, as such" left considerable latitude for interpretation under a set of expansive headings in Article II: "(a) Killing members of the group; (b) Causing bodily or mental harm to members of the group; (c) Deliberately inflicting upon the group conditions of life calculated to bring about its physical destruction in whole or in part; (d) Imposing measures intended to prevent births within the group; (e) Forcibly transferring children of the group to another group."[142]

The same articles that prompted the United States to abstain were cited in the 1951 petition by the Civil Rights Congress, led by William L. Patterson and Paul Robeson, as evidence that segregation and continued racial violence in the United States qualified as acts of genocide under the new United Nations rubric, specifically Article II.* Issued as a book in the same year under the title *We*

---

* The Genocide Convention was subject to four decades of acrimonious argument before it became binding upon the United States following a Senate resolution in 1986 and subsequent congressional legislation in 1988. Of particular concern was the key phrase in Article II describing "acts committed with the intent to destroy, in whole or in part, a national, ethnical, racial, or religious group." Ambiguity as to what constituted a "part" of a group—a fraction of what size? a single individual? destroy in what mannner?—left critics to wonder if individual racial crimes such as lynchings might be prosecuted as instances of genocide. Likewise, it was argued, not without justification, that the phrases "mental harm" and "conditions of life calculated to bring about [a group's] physical destruction" could be construed to include segregation laws and thus become an instrument of the civil rights struggle. At a later point, during the Vietnam War, the phrase "killing members of groups" became controversial insofar as Article I considers genocide a crime "whether committed in time of peace or in time of war," thus opening the door to charges against United States military personnel in combat. In a different manner, the exclusion of political groups from protection under Article II was open to criticism for failing to account for victims of a totalitarian regime that might choose to liquidate whole classes of people on charges that

Charge Genocide: The Crime of Government against the Negro People (and then reissued in 1970 as Black Power reached its zenith), the petition comprised a catalogue of race crimes and injustice in the United States from 1945 to 1951 but also reached back to Reconstruction to find the origins of contemporary racist conditions. The Congress petitioned as "American patriots" mindful of "Hitler's demonstration that genocide at home can become wider massacre abroad, that domestic genocide develops into the larger genocide that is predatory war." Describing "the lifelong terror of thousands on thousands of Negroes forced to live under the menace of official violence, mob law and the Ku Klux Klan," and erecting its arguments about "mental harm" and destructive "group conditions" on some of the same social science research employed in civil rights litigation, especially in *Brown v. Board of Education,* the petition demanded that the United Nations declare the United States guilty of the crimes charged and prevent their recurrence.[143] Casting back to Justice John Marshall Harlan's famous dissent in *Plessy v. Ferguson* excoriating the doctrine of "separate but equal"—a dissent soon to be famous because of its redemption in the reversal of *Plessy* by *Brown*—the petition's principal author, William Patterson, also charged that the United States had violated all the provisions of law cited by presiding Justice Robert Jackson at the Nuremberg trial of Nazi war criminals and agreed with Jackson that "silence in the face of such crimes would make us a partner to them."[144]

It is notable that Raphael Lemkin himself rejected extending the meaning of "genocide" to cover the oppression of blacks in America: "In the Negro problem the intent is to preserve the group on a different level of existence but not to destroy it."[145] In the immediate postwar years, however, when unpunished racist violence, including lynching, was still much in evidence, the analogy remained potent. Promoting ratification of the Genocide Convention in a 1952 column titled "Genocide Stalks the U.S.A.," Robeson stated a moral equivalency that would gain greater currency in some circles as the century wore on

---

they were a threat to state security—for example, in Stalin's Soviet Union or Mao's China. In view of these ambiguities, many would agree with Steven Katz, who at once broadens the scope of victims and narrows the conception of intentionality behind genocide to mean "the actualization of the intent, however successfully carried out, to murder in its totality any national, ethnic, religious, political, social, gender or economic group, as these groups are defined by the perpetrator, by whatever means." Stephen T. Katz, *The Holocaust in Historical Context: The Holocaust and Mass Death before the Modern Age* (New York: Oxford University Press, 1994), pp. 125–39. Cf. Berel Lang, *The Future of the Holocaust: Between History and Memory* (Ithaca, N.Y.: Cornell University Press, 1999), pp. 19–21, 41–44.

when he contended that, insofar as the purpose of the Genocide Convention is "to prevent the destruction of a people," one must recall the "tens of millions sacrificed in the slave ships and on the plantations," as well as the "terror" still inflicted by law and custom on African Americans under Jim Crow. To live with the constant threat and periodic reality of lynching was to live in a state of perpetual fear that now, with the example of the death camps seared into the world's memory, inexorably assumed the shape of extermination. "The history of Nazi thought," said Robeson, proved that the Nazis "had learned much from the South, that a straight line led from Mississippi, South Carolina, Georgia, [and] Alabama to the Berlin and Dachau of Hitler. I stood in Dachau in 1945 and saw the ashes and bones of departed victims. I might have seen the ashes of some of my brothers in Groveland, Florida, just the other day—or in Martinsville [Virginia] a few months back."[146]

The petition of the Civil Rights Congress took its place among similar, but less extensive, appeals to the United Nations made by Du Bois (on behalf of the NAACP)[147] and Malcolm X (on behalf of the Organization of Afro-American Unity),[148] both of which sought redress for the violation not of the civil rights but of the "human rights" of black Americans during centuries of oppression and racial violence. By 1969, when the Black Panthers petitioned the United Nations to apply the Genocide Convention to "savage police activities" and vigilante violence, and to provide reparations for the 40 million people of color in the United States "who have suffered the damages of racist and genocidal practices," the concept of genocide had been considerably diluted by indiscriminate use. In his preface to the 1970 edition of We Charge Genocide, Ossie Davis warned: "History has taught us prudence—we do not need to wait until the Dachaus and Belsens and the Buchenwalds are built to know that we are dying. We live with that death and it is ours; death not so obvious as Hitler's ovens—not yet. But who can tell?"[149]

Davis's speculation was in keeping with Black Power's frequently graphic rhetoric of annihilation, but even Martin Luther King, Jr., in a characteristically more moderate vein, blurred the distinction between Jews and blacks in borrowing from the amorphous language of the Genocide Convention. Hitler "carried the logic of racism to its ultimate tragic conclusions," said King, and although America "has not literally sought to eliminate the Negro in this final sense," it has sanctioned a system of segregation that substitutes "a subtle reduction of life by means of deprivation" and inflicts on blacks a form of "spiritual or physical homicide."[150] Such a characterization, as we will see in later chapters, gained wider acceptance in subsequent decades. It depended, however, on the stipulation not simply that African Americans had suffered grievous harm in the past but, more tellingly, that such harm—such "damage," to use the concept that became nearly a term of art—was inherited and perpetual.

CONDEMNED FOR BEING A CRIPPLE

Tom Robinson is not a candidate for euthanasia, let alone a member of a racial group selected for extermination. Still, his pathos depends on Lee's emotive triggering of correlative paradigms of racial deprivation: the "feebleminded" or otherwise damaged person deemed unworthy of citizenship and, ultimately, of life, and the black man who lives with an impending "sentence of death" simply by virtue of being black, and who is likely to be deemed guilty of racial crime no matter how fraudulent the evidence brought against him. Although Scout inadvertently prevents his lynching and Atticus provides him an expert defense, all the more stirring for its futility, Tom suffers an unjust death that absorbs legal punishment into vigilantism. In his trial, Tom's crippled arm provides his legal exoneration, but it is also a metonym for the racial category to which he belongs. The platitudinous figures of songbird and cripple through which Lee conveys Tom's impending fate, as well as her novel's moral lesson, create a sensation of simultaneous sympathy and revulsion for readers of a later era. In depicting Tom as crippled, Harper Lee not only proves his innocence and accentuates the pathos of his victimization but also identifies him with disturbing stereotypes—a modern-day Uncle Tom, the racial inferior ever on the verge, like the mockingbird, of natural minstrelsy.

Like Harriet Beecher Stowe's notorious hero, Tom Robinson is meant to be strong, vital, and stoic, his pathos springing from the historic brutalization that made him but cannot corrupt him. In his ingrained passivity, however, he cannot help but bear the lingering marks of slavery. He is more a "thing" than a "man"—to borrow Stowe's language—a figure defined, again like Uncle Tom, by a mode of paternalist sentimentalism in which Lee, like Stowe, found her enduring power. In this respect, Tom is a bridge figure not just from the Scottsboro Boys to Emmett Till but likewise from the racialist theology of Stowe and the pseudoscience of Jim Crow to the social theories of racial pathology and damage that governed legal decisions and liberal public policy on race in the postwar era. According to these theories, as we saw in Chapter 1, it is not race but racism, not inherent characteristics but constructed stigma, that creates and perpetuates inequality. The downfall of Jim Crow was set in motion by sociological and legal arguments that gained ground in the 1930s, although without the events of the world war—its acceleration of economic and social forces that favored integration, its globalizing of consciousness about totalitarianism, and most of all its terrible refinement of the meaning of racism by way of the Nazi genocide—the end of segregation would have been harder to predict and surely slower to come.

In the immediate postwar period there was perhaps no more critical venue for the elucidation and application of theories of racial damage than Chief Justice Earl Warren's bold, iconoclastic opinion in *Brown v. Board of Education.* To legitimize his heterodox appeal to social science rather than constitutional jurisprudence and to set aside the long capitulation of federal rule to local southern practice, Warren noted in his ruling that "we cannot turn the clock back to 1868 when the [Fourteenth] Amendment was adopted, or even to 1896 when *Plessy v. Ferguson* was written." Warren's manipulation of temporality sought to justify the Court's dismissing previous interpretations of the Fourteenth Amendment as inconclusive and thus to pave the way, not for a carefully reasoned refutation of "separate but equal" as a legal doctrine, but instead for a clean break with the constitutional past. *Brown* dealt with the racist underpinnings of *Plessy* by declaring that contemporary knowledge of racism and the formation of racial identity rendered the ruling inapplicable to the moral life of the postwar, post-Holocaust United States. Warren's opinion in *Brown,* like his opinion overturning anti-miscegenation laws in *Loving v. Commonwealth of Virginia* a decade later, rejected as a subterfuge the rationale that segregationist laws were color-blind, applied equally to both races. Built on specious theories of innate black deficiency designed to maintain white supremacy, the doctrine of separate but equal, he wrote, had a psychologically devastating impact, especially on children, creating in them "a lasting feeling of inferiority as to their status in the community that may affect their hearts and minds in a way unlikely ever to be undone."[151] Like *To Kill a Mockingbird,* Warren's *Brown* opinion started from the simple premise that today's children are tomorrow's adults.

Warren's reasoning reflected the influence in America of works supported by the American Jewish Committee such as Theodor Adorno's massive study *The Authoritarian Personality* (1950), *Dynamics of Prejudice* by Bruno Bettleheim and Morris Janowitz (1950), and *Anti-Semitism and Emotional Disorder* by Nathan Ackerman and Marie Jahoda (1950), which sought to define the origins of, and the means to combat, intolerance, racism, and the susceptibility to fascism, and which generally explained prejudice as a pathological condition with psychological rather than socioeconomic roots.[152] But Warren's reasoning derived more immediately from the scholarship of American social scientists who, from the 1930s forward through succeeding decades—and strongly in reaction to Nazism—focused increasingly on race as a social and cultural, not a biological, phenomenon and characterized the effects of racism in terms of its psychological, as well as its physical and economic, damage. In the words of a representative study of the early 1970s titled *Black Psyche*, mid-century social science found in the "modal personality" of African Americans a means of assessing the impact of discrimination and revealing the "psychological damage that racism has caused."[153]

In crafting the language of *Brown*, Warren was influenced most of all by the work of the African American sociologist Kenneth Clark, whose studies of black children sought to demonstrate the easy inculcation of patterns of racial self-hatred and inferiority, and whose findings in a 1951 report for a White House conference on children, later elaborated in *Prejudice and Your Child* (1955), buttressed Warren's effort to overthrow segregation by means of the therapeutic ethos of social science rather than the parsing of legal precedent.[154] Both whites and blacks can be damaged by racism, of course, but differentially—whites because it demeans them morally and twists them psychologically, blacks because it subjects them to physical deprivation, if not bodily harm, and a humiliating sense of inferiority based on their being typed as "things," beasts, or, at best, lifelong children. The essence of the damage thesis was articulated by Clark in 1954, the same year as *Brown*. "No nation can afford to subject groups of individuals to the psychological crippling and distortion which are the consequences of chronic racism," he wrote. "The damaging consequences of racial and religious prejudices are found not only in the personality distortions which are imposed upon the victims but also in the more insidious psychological damage which infects the members of the so-called dominant or privileged groups."[155]

The language of damage and inferiority was no less central in other arenas of the civil rights revolution. One finds its assumptions reflected, for example, in King's famous 1963 "Letter from Birmingham City Jail," in which he points out the damage caused by a young black girl's first experience of racial discrimination, when she will "see the depressing clouds of inferiority begin to form in her little mental sky, and . . . begin to distort her little personality by unconsciously developing a bitterness toward white people," or in his more pointed argument four years later in *Where Do We Go from Here?*:

> No Negro escapes this cycle of modern slavery. . . . It means being a part of the company of the bruised, the battered, the scarred, and the defeated. Being a Negro in America means trying to smile when you want to cry. It means trying to hold on to physical life amid psychological

death. It means the pain of watching your children grow up with clouds of inferiority in their mental skies. It means having your legs cut off, and then being condemned for being a cripple. It means seeing your mother and father spiritually murdered by the slings and arrows of daily exploitation, and then being hated for being an orphan.[156]

By then, in fact, King's assumptions, if not quite his rhetoric, had been inscribed into national policy by President Lyndon Johnson in his landmark speech "To Fulfill These Rights," delivered as a Howard University commencement address in 1965: "You do not take a person who, for years, has been hobbled by chains and liberate him, bring him up to the starting line of a race and then say, 'you are free to compete with all the others,' and still justly believe that you have been completely fair. Thus it is not enough just to open the gates of opportunity. All our citizens must have the ability to walk through those gates." In the span of a very short speech soon to be cited by proponents of affirmative action, Johnson, along with words such as "twisted," "battered," "stunted," "wounded," and "trapped," used the word "crippled" (or "cripple") four times, most characteristically in his assertion that a breakdown in the black family dating from slavery created a "circle of despair and deprivation" in which both African Americans and the nation are put at risk: "When the family collapses it is the children that are usually damaged. When it happens on a massive scale the community itself is crippled."[157]

Johnson's policy statement had other iterations to which we will return, but the exponent of damage theory most pertinent to *To Kill a Mockingbird* was Stanley Elkins, whose controversial study *Slavery: A Problem in American Institutional and Intellectual Life* appeared in 1959, the year before Lee's novel, and went through several expanded editions in subsequent decades. Although it is highly unlikely that Elkins had any influence on Harper Lee, his argument was not an aberration within but rather one culmination of a tradition of social theory incarnate in her rendering of Tom Robinson. Elkins's notorious comparison of plantation slavery to a concentration camp, both of them examples of "total institutions" in which individual autonomy vanished under conditions of duress and rigid discipline, was daring but no more so than his fundamental characterization of American slavery. Docile beings severed from any sustaining African culture and rendered incapable of rebellion by the exigencies of capture, the Middle Passage, and the brutality of the plantation, Africans in America, said Elkins, were infantilized by a regime so oppressive that the slave was turned into "Sambo," a "perpetual child" incapable of maturity or significant resistance. Like the concentration camp, the plantation thus functioned as a "perverted patriarchy," instilling in slaves such humiliating dependence that they came to identify with their masters, much as prisoners in the death camps were said in extremity to identify with their Nazi masters.[158]

Perhaps the Jewish Elkins hoped that coming to terms with slavery would make the catastrophe of the Holocaust comprehensible. In any case, even though his "Sambo" was not so far removed from the "darky" of neo-Confederate plantation fiction and historiography, his provocative analogy between slavery and Nazism set him apart both from Ulrich Phillips, the leading early-twentieth-century scholar of American slavery, for whom plantation slavery, economically and politically wise or not, was benign and nurturing, and from Kenneth Stampp, whose revisionist work *The Peculiar Institution* (1956) soundly refuted the Phillips school and rejected the view that plantation slavery was a closed system with its own social psychology, benign or not. For Stampp, pathology implied inferiority and was discredited; for Elkins, inferiority sprang from pathology and was to be treated not as a moral problem but as a psychological one.[159]

The apparent innovation of the Elkins thesis grew to some degree from the fact that, for the reasons noted earlier, he was writing in a virtual vacuum of scholarly commentary about the Holocaust. His problematic analogy derived in part from Hannah Arendt's opinion that the concentration camps were an experiment in "total domination" in which the inmates were transformed into beings whose reactions could be closely calculated even as they were led to certain death, "laboratories in training people to become bundles of reactions,"[160] and in greater part from the work of the psychologist Bruno Bettelheim. The purported survivor of a short imprisonment in Buchenwald and Dachau at the outset of the war—his autobiographical claims would later be called into question[161]—Bettelheim became famous for his 1943 paper "Individual and Mass Behavior in Extreme Situations," later elaborated in *The Informed Heart* (1960), which idealized active resistance and rebuked victims of the Holocaust for what he took to be a collective failure of will that invited collective disaster.[162] In a mitigating countercurrent initially even less palatable than his charge of Jewish complicity, however, Bettelheim also contended that the death camps induced in prisoners a loss of autonomy so exacting as to produce mass dehumanization, even a deranged mimetic identification with SS guards and the Nazi regime itself. The specific goal of the concentration camp, said Bettelheim, was to subject the autonomy not just of free men but especially of ardent enemies to "the process of disintegration" and "produce in their subjects childlike attitudes and childlike dependency on the will of the leaders."[163]

Elkins was taken to task by those who thought his assumptions about human behavior under extreme hardship facile or parochial. Orlando Patterson pointed out that "Sambo" was a trait found in all slaves at all times, not an artifact of American conditions, let alone African personality. "But the Ancients were neither so foolish, nor so clouded in their perception by half-digested psychological theories," he added. "It was Seneca who said it all in one of the most succinct and telling remarks ever made about slavery: *'Quot servi, tot hostes'* ('As many slaves, so many enemies')."[164] Others thought that the differences between blacks and Jews were not diminished but rather enhanced by speculation about the worst conditions in each people's history. Commenting on *The Burden of Race*, a 1967 collection of essays edited by Gilbert Osofsky, Albert Murray remarked, "Negroes already have enough burdens without being saddled with any more cliché-nourished, Stanley M. Elkins—oriented theorists who insist on confusing them with Jews."[165]

As Jews and blacks began by the mid-1960s to diverge even more sharply in their views on the goals and strategies of the civil rights movement, reactions to Elkins's work did not always break down along racial lines, but often, and tellingly, they did. In a 1965 address in which he argued that the real need of black Americans was for power, not just desegregation, the Jewish liberal Charles Silberman accepted Elkins's theory of infantilization but reminded his audience that "this never happened to the Jews; neither slavery nor persecution destroyed our history, or religion, or our culture."[166] For Amiri Baraka, however, such advice was Jewish paternalism at its most offensive. Elkins, for him, raised brutal questions of power. In one exchange in his incendiary play *Dutchman* (1964), set aboard a New York subway, Baraka appeared to mock both the Phillips school and the Elkins thesis. As the play's cross-racial sexual taunting rises toward its final homicidal confrontation, the white woman Lula, who will soon stab to death the black man Clay, calls him an "escaped nigger" who has "crawled through the wire" around the plantation, to which he responds: "You must be Jewish. All you can think about is wire. Plantations didn't have any wire. Plantations were big open whitewashed places like heaven, and everybody on 'em was grooved to be there. Just strummin' and hummin' all day."[167]

Yet Elkins's fundamental characterization of the psychological and sociological damage done to African Americans by slaveholding and segregation, whose premises he traced to the literature of abolition, was in no way at odds with the reasoning underlying *Brown*. His book set off an intense, fertile debate about slavery not just in jurisprudence and historiography but also in fiction, as one may see in the firestorm over *The Confessions of Nat Turner*, in which William Styron, depicting Turner as driven to rebellion by religious lunacy and lascivious desire for white women, effectively accepted Elkins's view that Turner was an exception to the general rule of slave degradation and infantilism. No less than Styron's Turner, Elkins's theory of slave personality quickly became anathema to many African American readers. Generalized as an account of American slavery, it soon merged with public policy in the equally controversial formulation of racial damage articulated in Assistant Secretary of Labor Daniel Patrick Moynihan's report "The Negro Family: The Case for National Action," which extended Lyndon Johnson's Howard University address in arguing at greater length that African Americans, especially the urban underclass, were enmeshed, generation after generation, in a "tangle of pathology" that had its origins in slavery.[168]

Vilified soon after its appearance as much as the Elkins thesis, the Moynihan Report, as it came to be known, appeared at the very moment when Black Power posed an increasing challenge to the integrationist agenda associated with *Brown* and with the strategies of Martin Luther King, Jr. For all its neglected virtues as social analysis, the report unavoidably ran up against the fact that younger black activists found in the black community the wellsprings of separatist solidarity and revolutionary resistance. But Elkins and Moynihan were hardly the first—and they would be far from the last—to adapt the course of the Nazi genocide to an analysis of black oppression, to define the trajectory of black identity by a historical regime of extreme deprivation, or to dwell upon the enervating effects of a culture preoccupied with legal and illegal codes of racial purity and pollution. Moynihan's report was much indebted to E. Franklin Frazier, and its conclusions were accepted not only by moderates such as King but also by the Nation of Islam, which found that Moynihan substantiated Elijah Muhammad's claims about black social disintegration and thus corroborated his philosophy of self-help and community-building.[169] To the degree that they shared the assumptions of racial damage theory and appealed to the language of black "pathology," however, contrary ideological positions might simply collapse into one another. When white sociologists and "welfarists" vied with black analysts of communal breakdown, charged George Schuyler, both did so in tones reminiscent of the "Negrophobic propaganda" of Thomas Dixon's era.[170]

Offended by Moynihan's focus on a stifling black matriarchy that supposedly "crushed male spirit and arrested masculine development,"[171] leaving the community beholden to the welfare state, black nationalists did not so much reject the damage thesis as insist that whites were not able—were not permitted—to articulate its ideology. "The black man today is at one end of a psychological continuum which reaches back in time to his enslaved ancestors," wrote the authors of *Black Rage*, a popular 1968 psychological profile of African Americans (regularly reprinted on into the next century) that promulgated a picture of black psyches deformed and distorted by a culture of infantilizing dependence and inferiority passed on from generation to generation.[172] At the same time, revisionist studies of slavery rebutted the notion that African culture had not survived transplantation, documented a propensity for resistance among slaves, and sought to locate in slavery the foundations of modern African American culture, as in Herbert Gutman's contention that in its extended, if sometimes fragmented, kinship ties, the black "family" in slavery and after was more stable than Moynihan and others had acknowledged.[173]

The Moynihan thesis, along with the concept of racial damage on which it was based, was not conclusively rebutted so much as it was ridiculed and suppressed, waxing and waning according to the ideological needs of the day—liberal in the post-*Brown* era, moving to the other side of the ledger in accord with neoconservative arguments about the damage inflicted by race-based policies, before once more swinging to the left with the rise of multiculturalism.[174] By the late 1960s, the historiography of African American life—including Elkins's own revisions of his classic work—had shifted to the recovery and sustenance of African culture in America, and the celebration, not the denigration, of "blackness"; but at the time *To Kill a Mockingbird* was published, the metaphoric conception of blacks as damaged or crippled—no longer by inherent racial characteristics, but rather by external racism—remained pervasive. "If he had been whole," says Scout, Tom "would have been a fine specimen of a man." But Tom, as a black man, can never be whole; indeed, in Maycomb he will always be a "boy," a word that even Atticus uses in reference to him.[175] The maturation of the black American from child to adult, from "boy" to man, was also a maturation, in the iconography of the nation's racial culture, from partial, stunted personhood to a figuration of legal and political wholeness. At the time Harper Lee was writing, however, no one could forecast accurately when that day would come.

You Children's Time

After the miscarriage of justice that leads to Tom Robinson's death, Atticus estimates the future for Scout and Jem in a pragmatic way: "Don't fool yourselves—it's all adding up and one of these days we're going to pay the bill for it. I hope it's not in you children's time."[176] The novel thus contains the unsettling prediction that the solution to the "Negro problem" lies far in the future, that the white southern children of the 1930s will have grown up into the still recalcitrant white southern parents of the 1950s and 1960s—supporters of interposition and massive resistance, members of the White Citizens' Councils, those who spit on the Little Rock students or mobbed Autherine Lucy when she integrated the University of Alabama and James Meredith at the University of Mississippi. Because Scout and Jem are, respectively, eight and twelve years old in 1935, they would be thirty-three and thirty-seven in 1960, in all likelihood parents faced with the decision whether to support or resist school desegregation. The Supreme Court ruling had detractors well beyond the South, to be sure, but the South was the bloody battleground on which the war was first to be fought, and children, both black and white, were often on the front lines, a fact resonant throughout *To Kill a Mockingbird* despite its action being set twenty-five years earlier.* The novel's beguiling proposition that juries, police forces,

---

* As he grudgingly acted to assist in the implementation of *Brown*, President Dwight Eisenhower did not hide his feelings: "It's all very well to talk about school integration—if you remember that you may also be talking about social disintegration. Feelings are deep on this, especially where children are involved." Although she distinguished public facilities as an appropriate target and criticized *Brown* for not striking down laws against interracial marriage, Hannah Arendt stubbornly argued that school segregation involved ambiguous private social spheres where "no human and no basic political right is at stake" and insisted that the Supreme Court wrongly made children fight the battle for equal rights. Arendt prefaced her controversial article by saying, "Since what I wrote may shock good people and be misused by bad ones, I should like to make it clear that as a Jew I take my sympathy for the cause of the Negroes as for all oppressed or under-privileged peoples for granted and should appreciate it if the reader did likewise." Writing in *Jewish Frontier* in 1964, Marie Syrkin took a different tack, but one equally reflective of Jewish self-interest, when she argued that legally mandated desegregation of schools and neighborhoods made no more sense than mandating legally that restaurants always create an integrated dining experience. The desire for complete desegregation introduced a logic of self-hatred to which blacks, like Jews, should be especially attentive: "A minority may justly oppose the quality of housing, schooling or job opportunities available to it, but with what grace can it object to a preponderance of its own people?" Blacks were almost, but not completely, of an opposite mind. Although her view was idiosyncratic, Zora Neale Hurston attacked the "forcible association" required by *Brown v. Board of Education* as insulting to blacks. Of Autherine Lucy she remarked, "I would rather go to some school where I would be welcome." Ralph Ellison was more representative when he dismantled Arendt's argument that black children were being exploited by their parents in the battle for desegregation. "She has absolutely no conception of what goes on in the minds of Negro parents when they send their kids through those lines of hostile people," he told Robert Penn Warren. As many parents see it, "the child is expected to face the terror and contain his fear and anger precisely because he is a Negro American. Thus, he's required to master the inner tensions created by his racial situation, and if he gets hurt—then his is one more sacrifice. It is a harsh requirement, but if he fails this basic test, his life will be even harsher." Dwight D. Eisenhower quoted in James T. Patterson, *Brown v. Board of Education: A Civil*

and whole communities of sympathetic children would make for a more just world, and, most famously, Scout's naïve routing of the lynch mob that has come to drag Tom Robinson from jail—all are calculated to substantiate the ethical authority driving *Brown v. Board of Education,* whose effects, good and ill alike, were to be felt primarily by a younger generation.

In manifold ways, the novel dwells on education, its relationship to the force of law, and the Finch children's assimilation to a network of southern social codes,[177] including the all-encompassing code of states' rights. Everywhere present is the contest between region and nation, state law and federal authority, played out as the South attempted to preserve school segregation through "freedom of choice" laws that gave parents and authorities the means to subvert federal mandates and forestall the racial defilement they were sure would accompany the collapse of Jim Crow. In federalizing the social practice of education and setting in motion the sequence of judicial and legislative actions that led at length to affirmative action and the backlash against it, the unanimous opinion written by Earl Warren stated that equal education was "the very foundation of good citizenship . . . a principal instrument in awakening the child to cultural values, in preparing him for later professional training, and in helping him to adjust normally to his environment."[178] Harper Lee renders Alabama's compulsory attendance in the mediocre segregated school attended by Scout and Jem a farce not just to ironize anxiety about desegregation but also to estimate the nation's legitimate interest in the future citizenship of children, the only hope for a post-Holocaust, post-*Brown* world of racial justice.

It was Lee's brilliant insight to create a narrator who speaks with the wisdom of an adult in something like the voice of a girl, filtering her mature, retrospective knowledge of southern race relations through her younger self's childish prejudice and dawning recognition that she is immersed in a world of social

---

Rights Milestone and Its Troubled Legacy (New York: Oxford University Press, 2001), p. 82; Hannah Arendt, "Reflections on Little Rock," Dissent 6 (Winter 1959), 50, 54–56, 46; Marie Syrkin quoted in Michael E. Staub, *Torn at the Roots: The Crisis of Jewish Liberalism in Postwar America* (New York: Columbia University Press, 2002), p. 107; Valerie Boyd, *Wrapped in Rainbows: The Life of Zora Neale Hurston* (New York: Scribner, 2003), pp. 423–24; *Zora Neale Hurston: A Life in Letters,* ed. Cora Kaplan (New York: Doubleday, 2002), p. 747; Ralph Ellison interviewed by Robert Penn Warren in *Who Speaks for the Negro?* (New York: Vintage, 1965), p. 344. On Arendt's heterodox argument, see also Elizabeth Young-Bruehl, *Hannah Arendt: For Love of the World* (New Haven: Yale University Press, 1982), pp. 318–22; and Werner Sollors, "Of Mules and Mares in a Land of Difference; or, Quadrupeds All?" *American Quarterly* 42 (June 1990), 173–77.

pretense and sanctimony. The compelling power of that ambivalence is inseparable, however, from the fact that To Kill a Mockingbird is, in the end, a "children's book"—complex enough to transcend its genre but nonetheless constrained by it, a fact nowhere more visible than in the tendentiously cute
framework of the Boo Radley plot. Like the "morphodite" snowman, of mixed
gender and race, that Scout and Jem create, or Dolphus Raymond pretending
to be an alcoholic so people will have an explanation for his choosing to have a
black wife and children, or Mrs. Dubose overcoming her morphine addiction
so that she can die "free," or Atticus's shooting of the mad dog, meant to prove
that courage is more than "a man with a gun in his hand,"[179] Boo's rescue of the
children belongs to this panoply of plot devices meant to enforce the moral lesson about Tom Robinson. It is patently allegorical, yet it is also semantically indeterminate.

As the agent of racial justice, Boo Radley is intended as a counterweight to
the most prominent of Lillian Smith's "ghost stories" of southern racism, the
ritual killing of the black man accused of raping a white woman: "If one had
tried to dramatize the inward suspicion and guilt and fear that still gnaws on
the white southerner's mind, it could not have been done more vividly than
the Ku Klux Klan has done it for us. Pictorially, the Klan presents this Return of
the Repressed in a stunning manner. White pillow case and sheet . . . the face
covered . . . identity disappears and with it the conscience."[180] At the same time,
Boo's slaying of Bob Ewell, although it saves Scout and Jem, pointedly does
nothing for Tom Robinson, who has already been shot dead while attempting to escape his unjust prison sentence. Laden with symbolic value, Boo's
wraithlike appearance might suggest a phantasmal projection of racial hybridity comparable to Faulkner's "white nigger," Joe Christmas, in Light in August
or a philosophical projection of the color-blind ideal enunciated in the jurisprudence of Earl Warren and the political moralism of King's "I Have a Dream"
speech. But his name is still the pretend scare in a children's game, and his role
in the plot, climaxing on Halloween, concludes when the "malevolent phantom" the children think him to be turns out to be a savior much like the "grey
ghost" of the soothing tale Atticus is reading to Scout in the closing scene of the
novel ("when they finally saw him, why he hadn't done any of those things . . .
he was real nice").[181]

Although he is perfectly suited to the fairy-tale substructure that governs the
novel, it remains an open question whether Boo Radley is an adequate surrogate for the exorcism of the racial "nightmare" with which Scout and her novel
are concerned.[182] To judge better what To Kill a Mockingbird can and cannot do,
it is useful to consider briefly a few other books, also devoted to the moral lives

of children in racially charged circumstances, which appeared at about the same moment.

Set during Hitler's rise, Scout's recollection of time past was published just as her postwar readers were coming to greater consciousness of the Holocaust. The floodtide of historical assessments lay in the future, and survivors' memoirs in English translation of the kind noted earlier were likewise little known or still to come. Not least because it is rendered through the recreated consciousness of a young girl and feels at times like a kind of diary, however, *To Kill a Mockingbird* bears comparison to one girl's narrative that, both at the time and in subsequent decades, rivaled it in popularity and influence—Anne Frank's *Diary of a Young Girl*. First published in Holland in 1947 and in English translation in 1952, the *Diary* has sold more than 20 million copies worldwide and, like *To Kill a Mockingbird*, has been read by several generations of schoolchildren as a representative indictment of modern racism. Also like Lee's novel, Frank's *Diary* has been dismissed as sentimental pabulum, a work famous only by happenstance and important only because it became invested with symbolic power far beyond its literary merit.

It is not incidental, however, that the best-known voice of Holocaust testimony should be that of a child coming to adolescence in the face of moral brutality, for the voice of the child may be made to carry an exceptional moral authority, at once grounded in authentic eyewitness experience—in which the absence of cynicism or covert design may be assumed but in which simple ignorance cannot be discounted—and offering a challenge to our own innocence reborn in every generation. To take another contemporaneous example, Elie Wiesel's *Night*, second only to Anne Frank's *Diary* in its impact on American readers, was published first in Yiddish and then in a significantly shortened version in French before appearing in English the same year as *To Kill a Mockingbird*. Although it was a memoir rather than a contemporaneous record, Wiesel's autobiographical account of his transport and imprisonment in Auschwitz and Buchenwald, stripped to the rawest emotions and simplest metaphors, made the trauma of one young boy and his family stand for millions. That *Night* is not only a primary act of testimony but also a complex piece of literature—one in which, for example, key scriptural sources and ritual structures of Jewish belief are ironically deformed by subjection to Nazism—has in no way subverted the authenticity of its narrative voice.

In other cases, however, the desire to believe in the authenticity of the child witness, whose words promise an unmediated record of trauma, has led readers to place their faith in enchanting prevarications. An extreme case of daring that threw into relief the blurred relationship between autobiography and fiction, between documentary and speculation, was Jerzy Kosinski's novel *The Painted Bird,* which in the years after its publication in 1965 became a standard literary text in American courses on the Holocaust and for close to twenty years continued to be hailed by Wiesel and others as a remarkable instance of testimony, fiction grounded in autobiographical experience. With confirmation that the series of grotesque abuses and deprivations to which its child protagonist is subjected is meant only to *simulate* the ravages of the Holocaust, that the book's incidents are fabricated, and that Kosinski's own family hid safely from the Nazis (and may even have acted as collaborators), the novel became a kind of anti-witness, a text that, having posed as quasi-documentary, must forever live with this act of authorial invention as part of its meaning. The surprise is that the book, surely influenced by the theories of Bettelheim and perhaps Elkins as well, would ever have been read as true autobiography, for its adaptation of the terrifying logic of dream and fairy tale to a first-person narrative seems meant to lay bare the problematic nature of bearing witness to genocide. Insofar as Kosinski went on to become a media celebrity in the United States, a figure whose mysterious, deliberately fabricated public identity was of a piece with the equally exotic, covert heroes of his novels, *The Painted Bird* may be interpreted as a kind of fictive performance piece wherein the key themes of an emergent Holocaust literature—victimization, degradation, complicity, witness, testimony, survival—were set before an American audience in hyperbolic form.*

The controversy surrounding Anne Frank's *Diary,* however, is of a different order. Whether as a book, a stage play, or a film, the *Diary* was for many Americans their first—and perhaps their only—exposure to a voice from the Holocaust, its power derived not from the survival of devastating trauma but rather from the peculiar normalcy of Anne's recorded adolescence. With the death by starvation and illness awaiting Anne at Bergen-Belsen placed beyond the boundaries of her narrative, the voice recorded in the *Diary* never entirely sur-

---

* Comparable problems arose later in the case of Binjamin Wilkomirski's *Fragments* (1995), which recounts the story of Wilkomirski's purported survival of the Birkenau and Majdanek death camps and life in postwar orphanages. When it was revealed that Wilkomirski is actually Bruno Grosjean, an illegitimate child of no known Jewish ancestry raised in foster homes, his pen name borrowed from the violinist Wanda Wilkomirski and his knowledge of the death camps picked up from visits as a tourist, *Fragments* went from being a revelation to being a scandal. That *Fragments* elicited moving, seemingly corroborative testimony from survivors, who recognized the fundamental "truth" of their horrific experience, underscores both the ambiguity of remembered witness and, among the reading public, a seemingly insatiable passion for Holocaust testimony.

renders its girlish charm. Her daily communication with "Dear Kitty" proved to the writer Daphne Merkin, in her own adolescence, that you could be "right in the eye of the Nazi storm and still take your own little angst seriously. Better yet, you could emerge from the Holocaust a literary heroine!"[183]

Like *Uncle Tom's Cabin* in its day, the *Diary* has become an archetype of suffering, the poignant sentimentality of Anne's budding passions elevated into the cloying iconography of victimhood in numerous editions of her diary, stage plays and films, scores of biographical studies and documentaries, chamber music adaptations, and related memorabilia. ("About the only thing we haven't seen so far is Anne Frank on Ice," remarked Ian Buruma after a 1998 Broadway revival.)[184] Despite the book's inevitable paucity of information about the Holocaust as such, it is influential enough to have been condemned as inauthentic by Holocaust deniers.[185] As numerous commentators have argued, however, it was not the *Diary* alone but the 1955 American stage version and the 1959 film adaptation that truly made Anne Frank a sentimental heroine. Their excision of important reflections on Judaism and Nazi anti-Semitism, on the nightmare closing in upon the Frank family, and on Anne's sexuality left the play and film deracinated even as they ensured its embrace by an audience eager for an expurgated version of the Holocaust, one summed up in Anne's lines spoken immediately before the Franks are arrested and deported: "In spite of everything, I still believe that people are really good at heart."[186]

Constrained to impose some kind of resolution on a narrative in which no concluding episodes will be narrated, both the play and the film, unsurprisingly, make Anne a symbolic spokesperson against oppression of all kinds, including racial discrimination in the United States: "We're not the only people that've had to suffer . . . sometimes one race . . . sometimes another." As Yehuda Bauer notes, such "kitsch and distortions" may be a necessary prelude to arriving at "authentic interpretations of the Holocaust." The diminishing of Anne's recognition of the coming genocide and of her Jewish particularity, a strategy consonant with the assimilationist ethos of the 1950s, created of the biographical girl a beatified figure who speaks less to the power of evil than to the triumph of the human spirit. In doing so, however, it also drove home the sobering lesson unaltered even in *The Ghost Writer* (1979), Philip Roth's brilliant dissection of Anne Frank hagiography—that the assimilated Frank family, no less than their most "alien" brethren, would be sent to gas chambers "just for being Jews"—and raised American consciousness about less terrible but nonetheless pressing issues of racism closer to home, including those detailed in *To Kill a Mockingbird*.[187]

The relative absence of recorded reactions to Anne Frank's *Diary* among

black readers suggests not their inattention or lack of sympathy but their reasonable preoccupation with their own murdered children. Anne's brief comparison of the Jews being rounded up for transport in Holland to the "slave
hunts of olden times"[188]—in all likelihood a recollection of *Uncle Tom's Cabin,*
widely read and redramatized the world over during the twentieth century as
a representation of slavery—does not provide sufficient basis for analogical
thought. But Nikki Giovanni had no trouble turning Anne's life into a harbinger of American genocide when she warned timid "negroes," facing the wrath
of white reaction to Black Power, that "Anne Frank didn't put cheese and bread
away for you / Because she knew it would be different this time."* Although
America was not a Nazi state and blacks were not facing a Holocaust, homegrown racism had already spurred a tradition of black protest writing devoted
to the nation's Emmett Tills—to racism's physical and psychological destruction of young black lives—that took the analogy as a given. Before we return to
Harper Lee, it is therefore worth reflecting on a very different kind of child's
narrative that appeared at the same time as the American adaptation of Anne
Frank's life and death.

At the height of southern resistance to desegregation, the most exhaustive
literary portrayal of the damage inflicted on the young by segregation and racial prejudice was Richard Wright's 1958 novel *The Long Dream,* a coming-of-
age story in which the aftermath of slavery—the enervating effects of a culture
preoccupied with legal and illegal codes of racial purity and pollution; the random, unpunished violence of lynching and lesser crimes; the debilitating effect
of economic deprivation generation after generation—is made so traumatic
and the inculcation of racial violence so constant and baroque as to constitute
a kind of treatise. Like *Blues for Mister Charlie* and *Soul on Ice, The Long Dream*
must be interpreted as a reaction to the lynching of Emmett Till and the persistence of racial injustice that, in some parts of the South, overrode the rule of
law. Wright wrote as though in a trance of depravity meant to summarize the

---

* Two later reactions may also be recorded. Her own adolescent reading of the *Diary* instilled in Alice
Walker's daughter, half black and half Jewish, a fear that, when the Gestapo came, her father would be
no more able to protect her than was Anne's father, while the black British writer Caryl Phillips recalled
wondering, after seeing a documentary about the Nazi occupation of Anne Frank's Holland, "If white
people could do that to white people, then what the hell would they do to me?" (He wondered, too, why
the Jews complied in wearing the yellow star, since they were by color not distinguishable from their oppressors.) Nikki Giovanni, "Poem (No Name No. 3)" (1968), in *Black Feeling, Black Talk, Black Judgment*
(New York: Morrow Quill, 1979), p. 24; Rebecca Walker, *Black, White, and Jewish: Autobiography of a
Shifting Self* (New York: Riverhead Books, 2001), p. 89; Caryl Phillips, *The European Tribe* (1987; rpt. New
York: Vintage, 2000), pp. 66–67.

destruction of black life from the Middle Passage onward. Originally titled "Mississippi," *The Long Dream* follows the maturation of Fishbelly Tucker as he is drawn by his father, Tyree, into a quasi-criminal life of dealing in "hot meat, cold meat, and houses"[189]—prostitution, undertaking, and rent collection for white slumlords. In a mode somewhere between nightmare and allegory, Wright subjects the adolescent Fishbelly to a barrage of traumatic experiences, most often circling around the terrible consequences of interracial sexuality. Every move in the plot, until Fish, as a young man, improbably escapes to France at the novel's end, is designed to show his acculturation to a process of racial annihilation—Orlando Patterson's "social death"[190] taken close to the limits of human possibility.

Reviewers complained that Wright the expatriate was oblivious to civil rights advances in the wake of *Brown v. Board of Education*. In his unrelenting indictment of southern racism, remarked *Time* magazine, Wright acts as if nothing had changed since he grew up in Mississippi.[191] Perhaps Wright would have seemed to middlebrow readers within the bounds of plausibility had he, like Harper Lee, set his narrative in the 1930s, or had he, like the handlers of Anne Frank's memory, found reason to introduce uplifting messages of universal hope into his dark book. But the lynching of Emmet Till and the exoneration of his killers proved to Wright that the racial customs of his native Mississippi, where more than six hundred blacks were lynched between 1880 and 1945,[192] had not vanished in the decade of *Brown*. Neither the finely honed, literate protest of James Baldwin nor the undiluted outrage of Eldridge Cleaver came near to the deep well of primordial horror plumbed by Wright in *The Long Dream*, and his novel was at once anachronistic and paradigmatic as a novel of Jim Crow. A kaleidoscope of scenes of mutilation, mass immolation, and sexual terror in which nightmare and reality can barely be distinguished, Wright's novel construes mid-century racial damage theory as a state of permanent and grotesque derangement.

Which is also to say that *The Long Dream* was written under the shadow of the Holocaust, both its calculated mass murder and revelations of the scientific torture that accompanied it.[193] Ralph Ellison, responsive to Bettelheim and anticipating Elkins, would have found an even better basis in *The Long Dream* than in *Black Boy* (1945), his example in "Richard Wright's Blues," for his surmise, borrowing from Edward Bland, that southern blacks in Wright's world live in a "pre-individual state induced artificially, like the regression to primitive states noted among cultured inmates of Nazi prisons."[194] (Indeed, had Elkins himself wished to find a contemporary illustration of his thesis that the ethos of racism was designed to reduce African Americans to impotent docility, he would have done better to look to Wright's dreamscape of wretchedness than to the plantations of the Old South.) In a posthumously published essay on the cold war written about the same time as *The Long Dream*, Wright linked Europe's confrontation with the terror of Nazism with its own postwar embrace of black culture; but he also speculated that depression or war within the United States, more readily than in Germany, could lead to a program of genocide. Since blacks in the United States do not hold economic positions comparable to those held by prewar Jews in Germany, he observed, it would be far easier for whites "to take the Negro as a scapegoat than it was for Germans to accept Jews as such."[195]

The perpetual humiliation and instances of random, unprovoked violence of Wright's southern world read like a series of pogroms built on black protest literature's recurrent design of symbolic and real threats of castration.[196] "When you [are] in the presence of a white woman," Fish's father warns him, "remember she means *death!*" After a young black man is lynched for his relationship with a white woman, Tyree and his partner, Dr. Bruce, ready the body for burial, speaking in the neutral, crude language of autopsy: "Seems like [the ear] was scraped, sheered off. Could have been eaten away by the friction of asphalt against the side of the head." "I'd say the genitals were pulled out by a pair of pliers or some like instrument." This scene, like the novel in its entirety, was surely inspired in part by the gruesome photos of Emmett Till's corpse published in *Jet* magazine and the *Chicago Defender*.[197] But Tyree and Dr. Bruce speculate about racial violence in a manner also calculated to evoke Nazi medical experiments: "We've been tortured by whites for three hundred years, and nobody has learned anything from it. If they'd tortured us as a scientific experiment, maybe we'd know more about human reactions under pressure. But they tortured us for their own special, morbid reasons."[198]

The language of autopsy, however, invokes not only those who orchestrate death for scientific purposes but also those who have made the most extreme accommodation with horror, internalizing and becoming instruments of the brutality of their own masters. Following in his father the undertaker's footsteps and "living parasitically upon the vast body of a white organism" of which he can never be a part, Fish learns to survive by making his living "gitting *black* dreams ready for burial."[199] In their complicity in the destruction of the black community, that is to say, Fishbelly and his father bear a deliberate psychological resemblance to the *Sonderkommandos,* those prisoners in the concentration camps, mostly Jews, who among other tasks were employed to direct new prisoners selected for extermination to their deaths without revealing what was to happen. Their further task was to dispose of the bodies—to take them from the gas chambers after washing away the blood and feces exuded in death; to extract their gold teeth; to sort the clothes and remove the valuables; to place the corpses in the crematoria; and to shovel out the ashes. Inhabiting the "gray zone" of complicity between Auschwitz victim and Nazi perpetrator, the *Sonderkommandos*, in Primo Levi's estimate, were Nazism's "most demonic crime," the creation of a damned race by shifting the burden of guilt to complicit victims, as though to say: "We have embraced you, corrupted you, dragged you to the bottom with us. . . . You too, like us and like Cain, have killed the brother."[200]

To Kill a Mockingbird is a long way from either Anne Frank's heartbreaking account of one Jewish girl's passage into genocide or Wright's scalding depiction of one black boy's life as the embodiment of something very much akin to genocide and complicity in it. Scout, moreover, is a witness, not a victim: she is the gentile white woman in protection of whose honor black men are lynched; she is the Aryan bystander, not the Jew. But the reference points of Anne Frank and Fishbelly locate more precisely both the power and the limits of Scout's narrative of awakening to moral vision in the midst of racial nightmare.

Even though its concluding reassurance that most people, when one finally sees them, are "real nice" is on the same didactic plane as the Americanized Anne Frank's belief that "people are really good at heart," Lee's novel, in its exposition of the child hero as a moral agent, is closer in tone to the abolitionist sentiments of an earlier era—Little Eva's pietistic testimony, say, or Huck Finn's secular crisis of conscience. As the embodiment of innocence diminishing and idealism shattered, each heroine or hero is compelled to contain a complex historical experience within a succinct formula of emotions. The reiterated moral of *To Kill a Mockingbird*—to understand a person you must stand in his shoes or, better yet, "climb into his skin and walk around in it"[201]—is unimpeachable but innocuous. It is undermined, moreover, by the novel's principal strategy of representation, the absorption of Tom Robinson's nearly inaudible black voice into Atticus's sacrosanct white voice. But Atticus's voice was heard, while Richard Wright's was not.

Harper Lee's compromise, eschewing Fishbelly's horror while accepting the risk of pious sentimentality, gave her indictment of American racism a vast audience. Jews barely appear in Lee's novel, and blacks are secondary actors on the stage of white conscience. No doubt this played a role in the book's popularity, but its power, certainly in its own day and even still today, lies in Lee's warning, through indirection and metaphoric suggestion, that the nation had come closer than it yet admitted to the mistakes of Nazism. Neither the land-mark court cases that overthrew legal discrimination, nor the heroic acts of protest that empowered the civil rights movement, nor the groundbreaking elucidations of African American life in terms of the Holocaust were made possible by *To Kill a Mockingbird*. Yet it is hard to imagine a single cultural doc-ument, let alone one more widely familiar, that better tells the story of these momentous mid-century transformations in the laws and customs governing race and racism in the United States.

CHAPTER 4

Exodus

I. A NEGRO-LESS WORLD: WILLIAM MELVIN KELLEY

So, I thought, you ask for sympathy and you get a riddle.
—RALPH ELLISON, *"The Little Man
at Chehaw Station"*

BY 1967 WILLIAM MELVIN KELLEY counted himself among those African American intellectuals who had turned the corner into radicalism. The splintering of the civil rights movement, the assassination of Malcolm X, and the appearance of the Black Panthers, among other forces, had sparked increased denunciation of the integrationist goals identified with Martin Luther King, Jr. Color consciousness surmounted the faltering ideal of color-blindness, and Kelley joined those who argued that King's strategy required an untenable contradiction. The black integrationist, he wrote in an essay titled "On Racism, Exploitation, and the White Liberal," concedes that "to the extent he is black, the black man is not a human being . . . because of his black skin, he can never be more than almost human." Proof that the liberalism of integrationists was doomed lay in the logic of Nazism: "The German liberal, frustrated in his attempts to Germanize the Jew, saw the salvation of his dream of uniformity in Hitler's call for the extermination of the Jews. Only when there were no more Jews would everybody be truly German." We cannot risk discovering what white liberals will do, said Kelley, when they find out that their "dream of American uniformity" cannot be realized "as long as black people exist in America."[1] Among those liberals were many Jews whose commitment to pluralism *and* integration, tempered by their acute awareness of the Nazi genocide, was facing a severe test.

Kelley's invocation of the specter of genocide was hardly original in 1967, no more so than his turn to separatism or expatriation as responses to discrimination. His reference to the delusion of Jewish assimilation in Nazi Germany, accompanied by his charge that the stance of Jews toward African Americans was one of exploitation, put Kelley in the mainstream of Black Power. Few writers of the day surpassed his ability to layer realism with dense abstraction, and it would have been no surprise had he written a novel like *The Tenants,* by Bernard Malamud, whose lacerating portrait of the crisis between blacks and Jews, mediated by the rhetoric of the Holocaust, is rendered in the form of a hyperbolic allegory. But his later experimental novels—*dem* (1967) is a piercing satire on racial mixing, *Dumsfords Travels Everywheres* (1970) a postmodern work inspired by *Finnegans Wake*—failed to win a significant audience, while his first and finest novel, *A Different Drummer* (1962), faded from view after brief acclaim. Unlike the reveling in genocidal consciousness through which Richard Wright refined black despair in *The Long Dream,* the angry separatism and appeal to Nazi Germany to which Kelley felt driven by 1967 are only latent in *A Different Drummer.* No less urgently, however, Kelley's distinctly African American narrative registered the precarious uncertainties of black freedom in the early 1960s.

Although the Holocaust had begun to impinge strongly upon African American consciousness for reasons noted in the preceding chapter, the paradigms of Exodus and exile still dominated black reflection on the example of Jewish history. In *The Chosen Place, the Timeless People,* as we will see, the confluence between African and Jewish diasporas—historical experiences of modern exile with twin points of origin in the fifteenth century—form the backdrop for Paule Marshall's dramatization of the increasingly contentious political alliance and cultural affiliation between blacks and Jews. In *A Different Drummer,* exile is presented not as a problem of epic global migrations but rather as a philosophical conundrum to be teased out on a local scale. For all that entry into the Promised Land held forth by the life and sacrifice of Martin Luther King, Jr., seems in retrospect to have been on the horizon at the time when Kelley was writing, *A Different Drummer,* even more than *To Kill a Mockingbird,* peers speculatively into a blank future. Arrested in a state of longing, Kelley's Afro-Zionism identifies a Moses but questions his leadership and destination; it calls for the recovery of a lost homeland but predicts none will be found; it launches an Exodus but implies that the result may be no different from genocide.

MARCHING BLACKS

If we style freedom first of all a revolution in consciousness, there is no more exhilarating variation on the Exodus than that incorporated into *A Different Drummer*, whose action is set in May 1957 and therefore situated on the rising tide of the civil rights movement. Kelley's novel is a spectacular meditation on the trope of migration, the psychology of apartheid, the tenuousness of minority leadership, and the illusions of nationhood. Its premise—the disappearance of all African Americans from a region of the American South—represents the inversion of the proposal periodically advanced by the Communist Party, the Nation of Islam, and others that a separate black republic be created within the borders of the United States. Kelley imagines instead the utopian fulfillment of the black Exodus, a super-migration and erasure of black life from an imaginary state situated between Tennessee, Alabama, Mississippi, and the Gulf of Mexico, produced when, all at once, the state's African Americans simply rise up and leave, confronting the white population with a mock enactment of the racial supremacy that has underlain their laws and social philosophy for more than three centuries. The result is an abrupt negativity.

The migration that leaves the state without any black population is sparked by Tucker Caliban, a fifth-generation descendant of the novel's original, un-named African, a statuesque maroon whose legendary resistance to enslavement sets in motion the deep historical action of the book when he is hunted down and killed by his would-be owner, Dewitt Willson, at an unspecified date in the early nineteenth century. Suddenly one day in 1957, Tucker Caliban, who has not long before purchased from Willson's great-grandson the parcel of land on which his African ancestor was slain, abandons his apparent intention to farm the land. Tucker salts his fields, slaughters his animals, destroys his furniture, and burns his house to the ground before setting out with his wife and child on a journey apparently to the North. Within a matter of days, the entire black population of the state, inspired by Tucker's strange act of prophecy and revolt, follows him in what one white observer calls a "strategic withdrawal," leaving the whites in a bizarre quandary: "It was like attempting to picture Nothing, something that no one had ever considered. None of them had a reference point on which to fix the concept of a Negro-less world."[2]

Carrying to its ultimate conclusion the Hegelian thesis of the master's dependence on his slave, the ironic bondage that Orlando Patterson has represented as a kind of inverted parasitism,[3] Kelley creates a world in which the racialization of America—not just of the South—stands forth in striking clarity. Without blacks, what is left of white thought, white culture itself? The novel's rich play on the long African American tradition of anonymity and invisibility—from the nameless storytellers and singers of slave culture to the comedy of Bert Williams to the fiction of James Weldon Johnson and Ralph Ellison—comes to rest in Tucker Caliban's corroboration of James Baldwin's contention that "the black man has functioned in the white man's world as a fixed star, as an immovable pillar: and as he moves out of his place, heaven and earth are shaken to their foundations."[4]

Tucker Caliban's revolt symbolically recapitulates the Exodus narrative ingrained in African American history, whether in escapes from slavery, periodic mass migrations, nationalist schemes for colonization in Africa and Central America, or voluntary expatriation, as in the case of intellectuals such as Richard Wright, Chester Himes, Baldwin, and Kelley himself.[5] In particular, it abstracts into a single symbolic action the immense migration of blacks from the rural South to the urban North over the first three quarters of the twentieth century, a movement that redefined the nation's social and political landscape and profoundly altered its artistic record. Although some white southerners fought desperately, through economic intimidation and violence, to keep their cheap pool of labor from dwindling, others welcomed the departure of blacks. Epitomizing the wrenching paradox of black nationalism, Kelley's imagined mass migration thus inadvertently fulfills the dream of white racists that African Americans should be set apart from the national polity and, if possible, driven from the land altogether.[6]

The disappearance of blacks from Kelley's imaginary state is voluntary and falls short even of preliminary Nazi schemes to make Germany *judenrein* through mass deportation (to Madagascar or elsewhere) rather than mass extermination. At the same time, the novel's action is a vivid reminder of a counterfactual world that might have been—even in the United States. Referring to the proposals of a German article advocating that the United States "wipe out" Negroes, said to constitute a threat to Nordic supremacy, Ralph Bunche had pointed out in *A World View of Race* (1936) that if the United States were to "put its destiny in the hands of an American Hitler," the certain abrogation of the Fourteenth and Fifteenth Amendments would give southern states a free hand in dealing with the race question and lead the nation to "a plan of emigration whereby Negroes would be systematically shipped out of the country."[7] By hypothesizing a complete rupture with the world of slavery and segregation, Kelley's totalizing migration creates a white South that is, so to speak, *negrorein*. In doing so at the very moment when America's confrontation with the Holocaust began to assume a public dimension, Kelley threw the modern meaning of the Exodus into mesmerizing relief.

The compass of Kelley's vision is evident in the title of the opening chapter, "The State," which provides an almanac history of the anonymous territory from which the Exodus is enacted. In addition to the allusion to Henry David Thoreau's own private resistance to the "State"—evident first of all in the novel's title, drawn from a well-known passage in *Walden*—Kelley's evocative phrase sums up the battle for African American equality. Not just the hypothetical southern state of the novel's primary action is encoded here but other tropes as well: the actual or virtual state of slavery from which African Americans had migrated in multiple reenactments of the journey to the Promised Land; the nation-state from which black Americans, in varying degrees, had long been politically and culturally excluded; the jurisprudential conception of the state as an entity lying outside federal oversight, a problem which had been at the heart of interpretations of the constitutional reach of the Fourteenth Amendment from *Plessy v. Ferguson* through *Brown v. Board of Education;* and the imagined territory of nationalist aspirations by which a subject people might hope to define itself.

In the case of African America, such a "state" might also comprise the diasporic geography coextensive with the history of slavery specified so vividly by Kelley's naming, in Tucker Caliban, *The Tempest* as a master source. Although Caliban's anticolonial dimensions are more pronounced in the roles he plays for Paule Marshall and John Edgar Wideman, Kelley's circumspect introduction of Shakespeare's play, by way of his main character, places his novel among the numerous reworkings by Caribbean, African, and African American writers from the late 1950s through the early 1970s, which emphasized the rebellious energy, as well as the peculiar eloquence, of Caliban—a prototype of the slave, the colonial subject, and, at length, the revolutionary firebrand standing in opposition to imperial culture.[8] Although the radical fervor of Kelley's later pronouncements is muted in *A Different Drummer,* the revolt inspired by his Caliban, however vague its teleology, still constitutes a decided renunciation of the enslaving past.

Tucker Caliban has no announced philosophy. Not just in its title and epigraph but also in its dramatization of "a movement . . . started from within . . . at the grass roots,"[9] however, *A Different Drummer* makes no secret of its appeal to another master text, Thoreau's *Walden* and its companion essay "Resistance to Civil Government" (popularly known as "Civil Disobedience"). One of the most famous passages in "Civil Disobedience" is a prescription for the univocal rebellion of a Tucker Caliban: "If *one* HONEST man, in this State of Massachusetts, *ceasing to hold slaves,* were actually to withdraw from this copartnership, and be locked up in the county jail therefor, it would be the abolition of slavery in America."[10] The uncertain utility of Tucker's act also illustrates the double-edged meaning of Thoreau's example.

On the one hand, Thoreau became a celebrated (and astutely marketed) catalyst to 1960s activism, in the civil rights movement and the counterculture in general. King's inspiration by Thoreau became legendary. Witness his reflection on his organization of the 1955 Montgomery bus boycott, in which he expressed his conviction that the boycott was true to Thoreau's argument in "Civil Disobedience": "We were simply saying to the white community, 'We can no longer lend our cooperation to an evil system.'" Or, consider John Lewis's instructions to activists preparing for the historic 1960 Nashville sit-ins, which he concluded with this admonition: "Remember the teachings of Jesus, Gandhi, Thoreau, and Martin Luther King, Jr." Such modest but heroic resolve is illustrated in Kelley's portrait of the common folk gathered at the bus depot to head into exile, this time by design, or at least by choice rather than through captivity and enslavement: "A few sang hymns and spirituals, but most stood quietly, inching forward, thoughtful, triumphant, knowing they couldn't be stopped."[11]

On the other hand, Thoreau's exhortations were abstract to the point of futility, a limitation brought home by one strain of Stanley Elkins's argument in his landmark book *Slavery.* Overshadowed by his notorious use of the Nazi concentration camp as an analogue to southern slaveholding, Elkins's chapter on the politics of antislavery was equally provocative. The Transcendentalists' focus on individual conscience and moral abstraction threatened to drain antislavery of its ethical meaning, said Elkins, leaving each man, like Thoreau, privately at war with a state—indeed, a nation—whose very leniency protected his right to protest that the state had no authority over him whatsoever.

The trope of "marching" to a "different drummer," borrowed from Thoreau and resonant throughout Kelley's novel, places its rendering of protest as a "movement" within a rich symbolic history, dating in the modern era from Robert Abbott's 1917 exhortation in the *Chicago Defender* that southern blacks must begin "The Flight Out of Egypt" (within two years some 65,000 had moved to Chicago).[12] The march toward the Promised Land might be staged as an allegory of allegiance to the powerful leader, as in the equivocal militancy of Zora Neale Hurston's Moses in *Moses, Man of the Mountain* (1939) or the unequivocal militancy of the Rastafarian Malaku Bayen's pamphlet *The March of Black Men* (1939). It might also encompass literal flight to the geographic

North, as in Adam Clayton Powell, Jr.'s, book *Marching Blacks* (1945): "As soon as World War II is over millions of marching blacks of the southland must pack up and move. Freedom road is no longer an unmarked trail in the wilderness. It is a highway." Although the North is not yet Canaan, said Powell, the South is ruled by "Der Fuehrer, King Lynch," and those who have been "suckled with the milk of freedom" must turn their backs on the Egypt of the South and renew the "American Exodus."[13] Soon after Kelley's novel appeared, the power of the protest march as political theater on a grand scale would be evident in King's 1963 March on Washington, an event first envisioned in the early 1940s by A. Philip Randolph and later reiterated in Louis Farrakhan's 1995 Million Man March, an impressive achievement in mobilization marked otherwise by the stark contrast between the memorable oratory of King and Farrakhan's meandering jeremiad, with its weird excursions into numerology and demands for national atonement.

Given the subconsciously militarized atmosphere of Kelley's novel, its enigmatic command to march to a different drummer, the movement stimulated by Tucker Caliban's radical act of departure is also a story about the power of a state over a subject people, in particular the escalating counterpoint between federal authority and the claim of states' rights in the battle over desegregation. Well beyond World War II, the South was not simply an alliance of states bound together by their resistance to federal authority but, for that same reason, a kind of "State" in its own right. The latitude afforded racist politicians in the South, said Langston Hughes, allowed Dixie to speak "with the brazen frankness of Hitler's *Mein Kampf*."[14] Although black predictions of actual genocide have usually been strategic—ranging from the rhetorically instrumental to the patently implausible—the power of the southern "State" to authorize and conceal racial violence in the era of Jim Crow was hardly in question. The insertion of Thoreau's pacifism—or, more accurately, his eccentric libertarianism—into this setting underscores the tensions that were growing unbearable as the nonviolence of King and the Southern Christian Leadership Conference (SCLC) advanced in the 1960s on a collision course with the varying strands of black militancy represented by the Student Non-Violent Coordinating Committee (SNCC), the Nation of Islam, and the Black Panthers.

At the time Kelley was writing, civil rights activism did not typically take the form of calling upon blacks to abandon the fascist South or establish their own independent nation. The historic marches of the civil rights movement—the March on Washington, the 1965 voting rights march from Selma to Montgomery, James Meredith's 1966 "March Against Fear," among others—recapitulated but at the same time redirected previous calls to enact a black Exodus from the South. In this respect, they were marches in which *flight* to a new homeland was superimposed on reclamation of *rights* to a homeland—namely, the constitutionally guaranteed rights of the United States. They were a kind of Exodus in place, an Exodus transmuted into Zionist reclamation, in which the homeland was here and now, if only the marchers—as southern activist Lillian Smith said in reflecting on the Freedom Rides, launched in 1961 to test the Interstate Commerce Commission's order to desegregate southern buses and bus stations—had the courage to "climb into the unknown."[15]

After a few years of aggressive but nonviolent protest, Henry Dumas's short story "The Marchers," a parable of futility, called such strategies into doubt. Marching upon the "white-domed city" of state power, the oppressed multitude of Dumas's vision becomes a "great nation traveling in a circle" (Dumas in this respect anticipates the futile, circular migration dominant in John Edgar Wideman's *Fatheralong)* and finally a fickle mob whose momentary achievement of freedom disintegrates into renewed imprisonment.[16] Although he would later share Dumas's dark pessimism, in 1962 Kelley remained warily skeptical. At just the moment when African Americans were challenged to march into an indiscernible and potentially violent future, *A Different Drummer* contemplated the movement's uncertain prospects and the querulous dissent with which civil rights leaders would have to contend.

Thrust into prominence by the Montgomery, Alabama, bus boycott of 1956, Martin Luther King, Jr., had emerged as the recognized spokesman for the southern civil rights movement, but it remained to be seen whether his leadership could unite the impatient voices of a younger generation, for whom 1960 proved to be a year of particular ferment. After four black college students quietly, politely launched the sit-in movement by attempting to integrate the lunch counter of a Greensboro, North Carolina, Woolworth's, their grassroots action quickly spread throughout the segregated South, so that by April students were involved in lunch counter sit-ins in some seventy southern cities. (One of the Greensboro students, Franklin McLain, later said he had gained his manhood and self-respect that day: "If it's possible to know what it means to have your soul cleansed, I felt pretty clean at that time.") As thousands of black students at southern colleges joined forces with King's movement, they strengthened its organizational base but also sowed the seeds of dissent by catalyzing SNCC and the future Black Power movement. Even King's allies worried about the movement's becoming too dependent on the magnetism of a single leader. Ella Baker, longtime NAACP activist and executive director of the SCLC, recognized the danger that a leader's power might be spent in holding the lime-light, even to the point of subverting the popular engagement on which libera-tion movements depend: "People have to be made to understand that they can-not look for salvation anywhere but to themselves."[17]

Distrust of the charismatic leader and his strategies, however, was also part of the Exodus paradigm with which King himself worked. To achieve the Promised Land in America, he said, blacks had to maintain their unity and bear in mind a central lesson to be learned from the leadership of Moses: "You know, whenever Pharaoh wanted to prolong the period of slavery in Egypt, he had a favorite formula for doing it. . . . He kept the slaves fighting among themselves." Here King referred most immediately to the splintering of black leadership that plagued the civil rights movement from the start but became pernicious when radicals mocked him as the "Reverend Dr. Chickenwing" or branded him a "house Negro" used by Jews to refute the criticism of black mili-tants. SNCC's dissent from his strategy of nonviolence and the emergence of "Black Power" as the rallying cry of a new generation, a point to which we will return in Chapter 5, illustrated to King that "every revolutionary movement has its peaks of united activity and its valleys of debate and internal confu-sion."[18] Here, as elsewhere in his speeches and writings, King introduced a basic narrative device of the Exodus—namely, the halting, episodic delivery from bondage brought on by continual counterrevolutionary uprisings and strug-gles for power within the ranks by those sniping at the powerful leader, doubt-ing his wisdom or seeking to tear him down.

King was hardly alone among black leaders in warning against such counter-revolutionary tendencies. The Reverend C. L. Franklin, sometimes called "the Rabbi" of Detroit's New Bethel Baptist Church and widely known for his dy-namic radio broadcasts and recordings in the 1950s and 1960s, counseled in "Moses at the Red Sea," one of his published sermons, "If you'll read the history of this exodus of these people, every time they ran into difficulty on the road to nationhood, they looked back toward the fleshpots and the disfranchisement of Egypt." Albert Cleage, proponent of Black Theology and a black Jesus Christ, argued that backsliding is the sign of a "slave mentality," the privilege of not having to make any decisions: "You'll have your little garbage to eat three times a day. The white man will put some kind of rags on your back. He'll tell you what to do, how long to work, when to quit. He'll tell you how many children to have. You won't have a thing to worry about. So, in a sense, it was better back in Egypt. In a sense, it's always better to be a slave." The Promised Land, he added, is not a specific place but "the way you are."* But King's command of the metaphoric structure of the Exodus—which reached its oratorical climax in his "Promised Land" speech on the eve of his assassination—both reflected and heightened his own identity as a Mosaic figure. In his most sustained examination of the hard road to freedom, the 1967 volume *Where Do We Go from Here?*, King called the United States a "later chapter" in the Mosaic narrative of liberation, but he cautioned as well that "the line of progress is never straight," that the "final victory" will be achieved only after the movement has worked through periods of "inevitable counterrevolution," when blacks will become "competitive, carping and, in an expression of self-hate, suspicious and intolerant of each other." Only after African Americans overcome the "divide-and-conquer technique" of the Pharaohs and the former slaves are transformed into a disciplined nation, King contended, will "the Red Seas of history open and the Egypts of slavery crumble."[19]

In this respect, the whole of King's work was an example of the repetition at the heart of the biblical Exodus and more so its political adaptations in the literature of revolution. In appealing to the archetypal story of a rebellion and release from bondage followed by a journey to Canaan, King recognized, in Michael Walzer's words, "that the Exodus did not happen once and for all, that liberation is no guarantee of liberty." Virtually all the aspects of the biblical Exodus that Walzer identifies in its characteristic narrative shape—the retrograde longing for the "fleshpots of Egypt" as the journey goes on and deprivations increase; the fear that freedom itself entails a harsh discipline, a new covenant in some respects more burdensome than slavery; the ritual remembrance of

---

* Criticism of backsliders applied not just to blacks. King's ally Abraham Heschel, for whom the centrality of the Exodus in the civil rights movement was a sign of Christian theological affirmation of Jewish tradition, used images of infighting and backsliding to rebuke Jews just as King did blacks. Characterizing southern racists as a minority who simply filled a moral vacuum, James Baldwin even suggested, optimistically, that the recalcitrance of the white majority arose less from racism than from fear of freedom's ordeal: "Most people assume the position, in a way, of the Jews in Egypt, who really wished to get to the Promised Land but were afraid of the rigors of the journey; and, of course, when you embark on a journey the terrors of whatever may overtake you on that journey live in the imagination and paralyze you. It was through Moses, according to legend, that they discovered, by undertaking this journey, how much they could endure." C. L. Franklin, *Give Me This Mountain: Life History and Selected Sermons*, ed. Jeff Todd Titon (Urbana: University of Illinois Press, 1989), pp. vii, 108; Albert B. Cleage, Jr., "The Promised Land," in *The Black Messiah* (New York: Sheed and Ward, 1968), pp. 256–57, 262; Susannah Heschel, "Theological Affinities in the Writings of Abraham Joshua Heschel and Martin Luther King, Jr.," in Yvonne Chireau and Nathaniel Deutsch, eds., *Black Zion: African American Religious Encounters with Judaism* (New York: Oxford University Press, 2000), pp. 168–86; James Baldwin, "In Search of a Majority: An Address," in *Nobody Knows My Name* (1961; rpt. New York: Dell, 1963), p. 108.

Egyptian slavery as a crucial feature of nationalist consciousness; the sense that Canaan itself, failing to be the Promised Land, will lead to further wanderings in the wilderness; and perhaps most important the frequent "murmurings" against the leadership of Moses, the eruptions of counterrevolutionary dissent that threaten to derail the march toward liberty—all these can be found throughout the post-emancipation African American tradition epitomized by King's proclamations.[20]

In elaborating the vicissitudes of the Exodus, King thus extended the tradition of the black jeremiad, which renders a judgment not just upon the oppressor but also upon those whose deviation from the cause of freedom might subvert its purpose and bring down God's wrath. If blacks wish to be God's chosen people, he contended, they must act like God's chosen people. But insofar as King's black jeremiad was a kind of epic folktale, empowered by an ever elusive sacred mission[21] in which the redeemer nation was Egypt, not Canaan, it was inherent in his leadership that its goals be transcendent and their realization utterly in doubt. His public marches were a performance of liberation in which the history of exile and migration that had defined African American life for centuries was made metaphysical, the Exodus transformed from a flight toward freedom into a pitched battle to change Egypt into Canaan. In breaking down the segregation of black from white, King would bring all Americans, South and North, into the Promised Land of one nation.

For the young dissidents imbued with the urgencies of Black Power, however, integration was a false promise, and liberation would be achieved only with the creation of sovereign black space, their own nation. As LeRoi Jones (Amiri Baraka) wrote in 1962, the same year as *A Different Drummer:* "The black man has been separated and made to live in his own country of color. If you are black the only roads into the mainland of American life are through subservience, cowardice, and loss of manhood. Those are the white man's roads. It is time we built our own."[22] Tucker Caliban's march into the unknown stands poised midway between the idealism of King and the utopianism of Black Power, between the liberal dream of a colorless world and the radical dream of a black world elsewhere.

BACK TO OUR OWN HOMELAND

As though to verify that Tucker's private war against the state and the Exodus it initiates can lead nowhere and yet has no alternative, *A Different Drummer* depicts floundering on both sides of the color line. The puerile philosophy of white segregationists, the stagnation of left progressivism, and the entire range of activist black leadership associated with the NAACP, Marcus Garvey, Father Divine, the Nation of Islam, and the SCLC are implicitly held up to suspicion in Kelley's novel.

With respect to the efforts by the National Society for Colored Affairs (read NAACP), in which his wife is involved, to achieve desegregation through legal means, Tucker retorts: "Ain't none of my battles being fought in no courts. I'm fighting all my battles myself." The "men on the porch," a white choric group called to witness the migration but otherwise inactive until their manic outburst in a hateful lynching at the end of the novel, follow the sophistic dictates of Mister Harper, a failed military man whose despair has reduced him to a self-willed paralytic life in "a wheel chair as old and awkward as a throne."[23] (Harper is distinctly reminiscent of the homegrown fascist Percy Grimm in Faulkner's *Light in August,* of whom the author said that he had "created a Nazi" before Hitler did.[24] He also looks forward to Dr. Strangelove, the mad German émigré scientist, bound to his wheelchair, in Stanley Kubrick's 1964 film.) David Willson, the onetime socialist renegade of the patriarchal white family, sacrifices the ideals formed during the depression through his friendship at Harvard with the West Indian black nationalist Bennett Bradshaw and becomes a self-loathing rent collector for the family's sharecropping properties. And Bradshaw himself, following an early flirtation with the National Society for Colored Affairs, from which he is purged because of his communist leanings (much as Du Bois was driven away from the NAACP), becomes a well-heeled religious showman. Having allied himself with the black salvationist ideologies of the Garveyites and other religious nationalists, including Father Divine and Daddy Grace, Bradshaw has made himself one of the "black gods of the metropolis," in Arthur Huff Fauset's phrase, cultivating a mixture of nationalism and populism in which allegiance to color ostentatiously mimicked the privileges of whiteness—"god in a Rolls Royce," as one biographer described Father Divine. Founder in 1951 of the Resurrected Church of the Black Jesus Christ of America, Inc., Bradshaw offers a familiar litany of anti-Semitic lore and models the doctrine of his church on a mix of "Mein Kampf, Das Kapital, and the Bible."[25]

By tracking the narrated lives of the modern-day Willson family and Bennett Bradshaw back to the radical politics of the 1930s, *A Different Drummer* reminds us of the animating effects of totalitarian orthodoxy on some civil rights leaders. More specifically, it reminds us of the modern beginnings of black territorial separatism in the Communist Party's ill-fated "49th State Movement," which envisioned that southern counties with a majority black population could be banded together and converted into a southern Black Belt republic[26]—a concept that showed up, for example, in the "black republic" envisioned in Wright's "Bright and Morning Star" by a black-white coalition of communists brutally suppressed by legally sanctioned violence.* Neither George Schuyler's ridicule of what he called the "Separate State Hokum" nor the suppression of communism entirely put to rest this "cartographic fantasy" of a black republic, as Eric Hobsbawm has labeled it,[27] for other motives and models were equally strong.

Just as the Afro-Zionism of Edward Blyden, Garvey, and other blacks of the early twentieth century took inspiration from the Zionist emigration to Palestine, so the concept of a separate homeland was made palpable for postwar African Americans in the sovereign nation-state of Israel, a homeland for the world's Jews—and later by its opposite in Black Power's anticolonial support for the dispossessed Palestinians and Israel's Arab enemies, now conceived of as African. The search for a black homeland predated Zionism, reaching back to the colonization of Liberia in 1821, for example, or to Martin Delany's proposals of the 1850s for a separate state in Nicaragua or the Niger Valley of Africa. But in the twentieth century it was redirected far more often into a search for territorial sovereignty within the United States, the actualization of a "nation within a nation."[28]

For the Nation of Islam, to take the most prominent example, the idea of a utopian homeland, prevalent in many social protest movements, was a constant, however mutable its articulations. By definition a kind of self-proclaimed nation-state, one possible result of the radical migration hypothesized in *A Different Drummer,* the Nation of Islam joined a philosophy of separatism to reiterated calls for territorial integrity. Elijah Muhammad objected that Ralph Bunche ignored his own people's need for a homeland while advocating nationhood for the Jews—an act of disloyalty made all the more ironic since, in Muhammad's view, it was blacks, not Jews, whom the Bible depicts as enduring four hundred years of slavery. If Bunche could displace Palestinians to create a homeland for Jews, Muhammad maintained, surely he could remove white

---

* Wright's story dramatizes the fact that communist organizing in the South, as well as the North, included a significant, and dangerous, coalition of Jews and blacks. "He busted a Jew boy tha [sic] way once," drawls a member of his posse as the sheriff, attempting to extract information by torture, splits the eardrums of one would-be black revolutionary. In point of fact, neither black nor white American communists had actually called for a Black Belt republic. The theory rose and fell within party propaganda according to the whims of Moscow rather than the needs of the American Communist Party, and by 1958, in the face of continued black migration to the urban North and the rise of the civil rights movement, the party officially abandoned any remaining interest in a separate state. Richard Wright, "Bright and Morning Star," in *Uncle Tom's Children* (1940; rpt. New York: Perennial, 1965), p. 209.

people from four or five southern states to create a homeland for the people Muhammad styled the "Blackstone Nation."[29] In a 1959 speech, delivered in the aftermath of the lynching of Mack Parker, Muhammad proclaimed that "politics will not solve the problem of the Negroes any more than it did for the Hebrews of Israel in Egypt" and insisted that, if whites refuse to grant equal rights, they must provide instead sufficient land to establish a Black Republic, "a home on this earth we can call our own." "We have earned whatever they give us," he added. "If they give us twenty-five states, we have earned them." Speaking for Muhammad at Harvard two years later, Malcolm X called upon the United States government to "just give us a portion of this country that we can call our own. Put us in it. Then give us everything we need to start our own civilization—that is, support us for twenty to twenty-five years, until we are able to go for ourselves." Malcolm called this scheme "God's solution" and just compensation for America's crimes against black people: "A cup of tea in a white restaurant is not sufficient compensation for three hundred ten years of slave labor."[30]

Like Garvey, Elijah Muhammad was even willing to make common cause with white racists in order to achieve his territorial dream. Malcolm later recalled that in 1960, while at the home of a Nation of Islam minister in Atlanta, he sat with members of the Ku Klux Klan who were at that time trying to make a deal with Muhammad to provide a county-sized tract of land where the Nation could establish a segregated state.[31] Sometimes the Nation's imagined homeland, in a revival of colonizationist plans from the past, entailed the return of America's "twenty-two million ex-slaves *back to our own homeland*" or to a separate territory somewhere in the Western Hemisphere.* Almost always, however, an underlying chord of Muslim thought was struck—that the Fall of America was coming, either as a literalization of Elijah Muhammad's prophe-

---

* In a later revival of the colonizationist vision, Louis Farrakhan brought together the plans tendered by Abraham Lincoln to repatriate blacks to Africa or build an alternative colony in Central America and the modern creation of Israel as a homeland for the Jews. If Africans were to carve out a territory in which blacks in the diaspora could be resettled (since Africans had a hand in "the Holocaust of slavery," Farrakhan admitted, they should "have a hand in our redemption"), and the Nation of Islam were allowed to go into America's prisons and educate black inmates, Farrakhan argued that the $18,000 spent annually on each inmate could better be used to build this new African colony, where those repatriated could be granted the same kind of dual citizenship available to American Jews in Israel. In the early twenty-first century, the Nation of Islam Web site still posted "The Muslim Program" of Elijah Muhammad, which included the following demand: "We want our people in America whose parents or grandparents were descendants from slaves, to be allowed to establish a separate state or territory of their own—either on this continent or elsewhere. We believe that our former slave masters are obligated to provide such land and that the area must be fertile and minerally rich. We believe that our former slave

cies or, in a more conventional mode, as God's judgment on the nation for its racial sins: "If America waits for Almighty God Himself to step in and force her into a just settlement, God will take this entire continent away from her; and she will cease to exist as a nation."[32]

Other plans for black sovereignty were no less majestic. In April 1968 the National Black Government Conference, a radical caucus convened in Detroit, rejected emigration to Africa and instead promulgated plans for the "Republic of New Africa."* Featured in an *Esquire* magazine article titled "We Want Georgia, South Carolina, Louisiana, Mississippi, and Alabama—Right Now . . . We Also

---

masters are obligated to maintain and supply our needs in this separate territory for the next 20 to 25 years—until we are able to produce and supply our own needs." Louis Farrakhan, *A Torchlight for America* (Chicago: FCN Publishing, 1993), pp. 116–20; "The Muslim Program," Nation of Islam Web site, http://www.noi.org/program.html (accessed August 28, 2003).

* The Republic of New Africa was an outgrowth of the Revolutionary Action Movement, which originated in 1963 under the Garveyite motto "One Purpose, One Aim, One Destiny." Identified in *Life* magazine in 1964 as one of the radical groups "Plotting a War on Whitey," the Revolutionary Action Movement, taking inspiration from Harold Cruse's 1962 essay "Revolutionary Nationalism and the Afro-American," offered a philosophy mixing Marxism and Malcolm X that was adopted by the Republic of New Africa, which played a role among nationalist splinter groups for years to come. After advocating a plebiscite, to be supervised by the United Nations, that would allow blacks to determine if they wished to secede from the United States and form an independent nation, the Black Panthers diverged from the Republic of New Africa on the matter of territorial separation. Writing to the Republic's president, Robert F. Williams, Huey Newton averred that a separate black nation within the United States "would suffer imperialism and colonialism even more so than the Third World" and argued instead for the revolutionary overthrow of white supremacy. The power of the Republic's separatist vision was diminished but still evident at the end of the century. In prison, Los Angeles gang member Sanyika Shakur (Monster Kody Scott) replaced his gang affiliation with allegiance to the now updated and slightly renamed Republic of New Afrika. By the same token, however, the Republic became the butt of Afrocentric slapstick in Paul Beatty's *White-Boy Shuffle,* where the protagonist, Gunnar Kaufman, is put to the racialist test by the "all-albino brothers and sisters" of NAPPY (New African Politicized Pedantic Yahoos), which prophesies "the founding of a New Africa, a glorious day when the United States government [will] turn over five southern states to legions of turbaned pink-eyed heliocentrists." See Dean E. Robinson, *Black Nationalism in American Politics and Thought* (New York: Cambridge University Press, 2001), pp. 60–63; Robin D. G. Kelley, *Freedom Dreams: The Black Radical Imagination* (Boston: Beacon Press, 2002), pp. 70–94; Huey P. Newton, "To the Republic of New Africa" (September 13, 1969), in *To Die for the People: The Writings of Huey P. Newton* (1972; rpt. Writers and Readers, 1999), p. 98; Sanyika Shakur, *Monster: The Autobiography of an L. A. Gang Member* (New York: Atlantic Monthly Press, 1993), p. vii; Léon Bing, *Do or Die* (New York: HarperCollins, 1993), p. 240; Paul Beatty, *The White-Boy Shuffle* (1996; rpt. New York: Picador, 2001), p. 96. The Republic of New Africa has continued to press the case for reparations. A petition presented to Congress in 1993 appears in Chokwe Lumumba, Imari Abubakari Obadele, and Nkechi Taifa, *Reparations Yes!* (1993), reprinted in William L. Van Deburg, ed., *Modern Black Nationalism: From Marcus Garvey to Louis Farrakhan* (New York: New York University Press, 1997), pp. 333–41.

Want Four Hundred Billion Dollars Back Pay," the Republic of New Africa envisioned a sovereign land comprising these five southern states, which were to
be ceded by the United States government along with monetary reparations,
one model being Tanzania but another Israeli kibbutzim. "Like the Jews moving into Israel," said the Republic's vice president, Milton R. Henry, "we will
start to organize along the lines of cooperative and collective farms." An outline
of the program was delivered to the State Department in May 1968, whereupon members waited futilely to begin negotiations between the two "nations."
Should the government fail to provide what was demanded, the Republic was
prepared to begin purchasing Mississippi, county by county, like Palestine, with
"Malcolm X land certificates" worth $100 each, thus giving members a secure
position, like the Jews before the creation of Israel, from which they could demand sovereignty for their nation, to be named El Malik in honor of Malcolm
X. Should the government contemplate hostilities to thwart the Republic's
aims, there would be a people's war on two fronts. The New African Security
Force would wage war in the white South, while urban guerrillas would divide
the territories of the North, attempting to bring about its economic collapse. If
necessary to secure the new state, armed guerrillas and nuclear weapons acquired from China would be deployed.[33]

The bizarre unreality of such a scheme obscured the abiding power of separatist fantasies in the African American imagination. Such a temptation led
Sutton Griggs to envision a secret black republic in Texas in his 1899 novel *Imperio in Imperio*, a book, like *A Different Drummer*, also concerned with the
inability of the federal government to enforce the Fourteenth Amendment. It
led Cyril V. Briggs, founder of the African Blood Brotherhood, whose inaugural manifesto in 1920 proclaimed it "the first Negro *secret* organization to be ef-
fected in the Western world, having as its sole purpose the liberation of Africa
and the redemption of the Negro race," to call for a "colored autonomous state"
in the American West. It led Communist Party member James Allen to speculate, in *The Negro Question in the United States* (1936), that the creation of a
"Negro Republic" would give southern blacks, as in the Soviet Union—so he
imagined—"the right to choose freely between complete independence as a
separate state and federation with a state or group of states." It led Robert S.
Browne and Robert Vernon, citing the example of Israel—a "national homeland for a people who have no homeland," a place where Jews could "[run] the
show"—to issue a broadside titled *Should the U.S. Be Partitioned into Two Separate and Independent Nations—One a Homeland for White Americans and the
Other a Homeland for Black Americans?* (1968). And it led Nelson Peery, in full-
dress neo-Marxism in *The Negro National Colonial Question* (1972), to look for-

ward to a network of state farms and cooperatives brought about by Soviet-style land redistribution: "The Negro national colonial question can only be solved by a return of the land to the people who have toiled over it for centuries." (In Peery's idiosyncratic variation, however, the Black Belt of the South is a "Negro," not a black, nation, and one in which southern whites, because they share with blacks a common language and culture in all its Euro-African hybridity, would be included as a protected minority within that nation.)[34]

So long as political freedom and economic justice remained chimeras, the intense longing for a homeland, anywhere, would be registered even in unlikely corners of African American culture. Compensatory reparations played a modest and not entirely irrational role in Amiri Baraka's call for the creation of a sovereign territory in Harlem through the "nationalization of all properties and resources belonging to white people, within the boundaries of the Black Nation."[35] But even sovereignty for Harlem, perhaps the closest thing there was in the United States to a black "nation," might not provide an adequate solution. In *Cotton Comes to Harlem* (1965), the best known of Chester Himes's detective stories, the con man Reverend Deke O'Malley's neo-Garveyite Back-to-Africa scam, which preys on the pent-up frustration of Harlem residents aching to leave their exile ("Look how long it took the Jews to get out of Egypt"), vies with the neo-Confederate Colonel Calhoun's Back-to-the-Southland Movement, which is hiring Harlem residents to pick cotton in the South, an alternative homeland to war-torn, famine-ridden Africa. Whereas Jews have made their peace with America—a minor subplot in the novel involves the junkman Goodman, who contemplates emigration to Israel but determines that he is better off in America, where "every man is free"—the position of African Americans, according to the expatriate Himes, writing in France, can never be comparable:

> These people were seeking a home—just the same as the Pilgrim Fathers. Harlem is a city of the homeless. These people had deserted the South because it could never be considered their home. Many had been sent north by the white southerners in revenge for the desegregation ruling. Others had fled, thinking the North was better. But they had not found a home in the North. They had not found a home in America. So they looked across the sea to Africa, where other black people were both the ruled and the rulers. Africa to them was a big free land which they could proudly call home, for there were buried the bones of their ancestors, there lay the roots of their families, and it was inhabited by the descendants of those same ancestors—which made them related by blood and

race. Everyone has to believe in something; and the white people of America had left them nothing to believe in.[36]

No plan for repatriation is offered in *A Different Drummer* either, but in his refusal to name a destination for the Exodus led by Tucker Caliban, Kelley came close in spirit to the comic despair of *Cotton Comes to Harlem*. Conceivably, his novel remained silent on the question of the Promised Land's location because he found or anticipated it to be a bankrupt illusion, a mere redesigning of the space of segregation in urban terms that had already been well imagined, for example, in works such as Richard Wright's *Native Son* (1940) and *The Street* by Ann Petry (1946), and that Kelley himself had already portrayed in several of the short stories later collected in *Dancers on the Shore* (1964), where the Promised Land for some of his characters turns out to be the Black Belt of Chicago. Or the black world elsewhere might prove to be even more surreal.

Begun while Kelley was a student in John Hawkes's writing class at Harvard, *A Different Drummer* was almost certainly inspired by an episode in Ray Bradbury's *Martian Chronicles* (1950) titled "Way in the Middle of the Air." Set in 2003, Bradbury's story begins with the conversation among white men on the porch of a hardware store in the South, a tableau, just like Kelley's, that might on the face of it be set at any time within the previous hundred years. But Bradbury's conversation concerns the shocking exodus of all the "niggers," who have secretly saved their money and built rockets to take them to Mars. Like the episode's title, which echoes a black spiritual, the names ascribed to the rockets by a taunting white man—*Elijah and the Chariot, The Big Wheel,* and *Over Jordan* among them—underscore the biblical meaning of this delivery to the Promised Land in outer space. (The story also echoes Elijah Muhammad's teaching that Mars was inhabited by a colored race and his enduring prophecy that the reign of a new black civilization would begin, after an apocalyptic destruction of white people, with the arrival of the celestial Mother Plane adumbrated biblically in Ezekiel's Wheel.)* Paying one another's debts, maintain-

---

* "Way in the Middle of the Air," also known as "Ezekiel Saw the Wheel," was collected in various anthologies of black spirituals, including James Weldon Johnson's *American Negro Spirituals*. Elijah Muhammad's interpretation of Ezekiel's vision, which bore the influence of contemporary science fiction, including Orson Welles's radio adaptation of *War of the Worlds* in 1938, as well as cold war preoccupations with invaders from outer space, is spelled out in three brief chapters of *Message to the Blackman in America*, "Battle in the Sky Is Near," "The Great Decisive Battle in the Sky," and "The Battle in the Sky." In one characterization, the Mother Plane is "a small human planet made for the purpose of destroying the present world of the enemies of Allah" by unleashing a fleet of 1,500 bombers to attack the earth. Af-

ing an unfailing courtesy to the white folks, and abandoning their possessions in neat piles along the road, a vast "black tide" of the South's African Americans disappear "straight up into the blue heavens," leaving the white men to contemplate life without a cheap black labor force and the night-riding pleasures of the Ku Klux Klan: "The men on the porch sat down, looked at each other, looked at the yellow rope piled neat on the store shelves, glanced at the gun shells glinting shiny brass in their cartons, saw the silver pistols and long black metal shotguns hung high and quiet in the shadows. Somebody put a straw in his mouth. Somebody else drew a figure in the dust."[37]

Comparable plots would later reappear in Douglas Turner Ward's 1965 stage farce *A Day of Absence* and then again in Derrick Bell's 1992 parable of black expulsion, "Space Traders."* But Bradbury's prescient story set a high creative

---

ter this millennial deliverance, "we are Allah's choice to give life and we will be put on top of civilization." Ezekiel's vision was also associated with Exodus in various writings and speeches by Elijah Muhammad and later by Louis Farrakhan—for example, in *Torchlight for America*, where it is connected to the original seal of the United States and typologically derived from Exodus 13:21–22, "a cloud by day and a pillar of fire by night." For Farrakhan, who continued to promulgate the prophecy of the Mother Plane and the destruction of America well into the 1990s, America is the Pharaoh that has held blacks captive for more than four hundred years. Since he is a man of exile who never returns to the homeland, however, Ezekiel may also be said to transfigure the Exodus into a permanent state of exile congruent with the African American condition. See Elijah Muhammad, *Message to the Blackman in America* (Chicago: Muhummad Mosque No. 2, 1965), pp. 290–94; Farrakhan, *Torchlight for America*, p. 158; Allen Dwight Callahan, "Remembering Nehemiah: A Note on Biblical Theology," in Chireau and Deutsch, *Black Zion*, p. 158. See also Michael Lieb, *Children of Ezekiel: Aliens, UFOs, the Crisis of Race, and the Advent of End Time* (Durham: Duke University Press, 1998), pp. 155–77; Claude Andrew Clegg III, *An Original Man: The Life and Times of Elijah Muhammad* (New York: St. Martin's, 1997), pp. 42–67; Edward E. Curtis IV, *Islam in Black America: Identity, Liberation, and Difference in African-American Islamic Thought* (Albany: State University of New York Press, 2002), p. 77.

* *A Day of Absence* was inspired equally by Jean Genet's long-running Broadway play *The Blacks*, in which Ward participated as a cast member, and by the Montgomery bus boycott, during which buses drove their routes emptied of the usual crowd of black passengers. Staged by a black cast in whiteface and costumed in red, white, and blue, the action depicts the chaos in a southern community that "has always been glued together by the uninterrupted presence of its darkies" following the sudden, unexplained exodus of the African American population. Economic paralysis is followed by near social disintegration when it is revealed that some prominent white citizens who have been passing are also missing—among them city council members, a college football star, and the chairwoman of the Daughters of the Confederate Rebellion. The mayor's televised passionate appeal to the missing blacks to honor their "sacred" obligations to the Jim Crow South dissolves into a white riot; but the next morning all the blacks are back, as though they had never been gone and nothing has changed—except, presumably, the consciousness of the white townspeople. "Space Traders" is an allegory of exile set in the year 2000. An extraterrestrial power offers the United States gold to pay its debts, chemicals to clean its toxic environ-

standard by blending a utopian Garveyite migration, revitalized by civil rights militancy, with the aftermath of the Holocaust—the complete removal of a people as though they had disappeared into the blue heavens. At the same time, it posited a planetary homeland that would presumably afford African Americans the rights denied them on earth, much as post-Holocaust Jews were afforded a homeland only after their tortuous emigration, most famously aboard the refugee ship *Exodus,* to a new nation born of one war and secured by another.

Kelley's strange abridgment of Tucker Caliban's revolt registers this ambiguity in its particular historical moment. As "America's Jews," blacks had long since adopted the Exodus as their foundational narrative, and they were increasingly prone, whether in sympathy or in a twisted contest, to claim that slavery forged their closer kinship with those who had suffered the Holocaust. Yet the absence of a national state to which African Americans could make *aliyah* under a Law of Return granting them immediate citizenship and cultural identity pinpointed the transforming power not of the Holocaust alone, but particularly of the creation of the sovereign Jewish state. African nations to which American blacks had emigrated in the modern era, such as Liberia and Ghana, remained tenuous outposts bearing no resemblance in their economic and military relations with the United States to those of Israel. Jews could be at home either in America or in Israel; by comparison, blacks were at home nei-

---

ment, and a safe nuclear energy source in exchange for removing all African Americans from the nation. Refusing to let the trade be the "final solution" for blacks in America, Jews organize in protest, promising to hide blacks away according to plans drawn up by the Anne Frank Committee; an unarticulated concern is that, in the absence of blacks, Jews will become the nation's principal scapegoats. Ultimately, a constitutional amendment allowing the trade passes with 70 percent of the vote. On Martin Luther King, Jr., Day, all African Americans are forced to leave: "Heads bowed, arms now linked by slender chains, black people left the New World as their forebears had arrived." A sequel to "Space Traders" produces greater ambiguity. When America's acceptance of the trade turns out to have provoked the scorn of other nations, which break off diplomatic and economic ties, a reversal of the action is contemplated. The extraterrestrials allow the black emigrants to vote on whether to remain in their new exile or return to the American Egypt they left behind. The vote appears to favor returning, but this installment of the parable ends on the ambiguous note of "Amazing Grace." Composed by John Newton, a former slave ship captain, the melody seems to emanate "from the sounds of sorrow and strength rising from the holds of Newton's ship," thus suggesting that the Middle Passage of African American life will never end. See Douglas Turner Ward, *Happy Ending and A Day of Absence: Two Plays* (New York: Dramatists Play Service, 1966), p. 51; Derrick Bell, *Faces at the Bottom of the Well: The Permanence of Racism* (New York: Basic Books, 1992), p. 194; Derrick Bell, "Redemption Deferred: Back to the Space Traders," in *Gospel Choirs: Psalms of Survival in an Alien Land Called Home* (New York: Basic Books, 1996), pp. 17–28.

ther in America nor in Africa. "Unlike Zionists who after 2,000 years of wandering in the wilderness have found their home," wrote Lenora Berson a few years later, "the Black Nationalists have only just begun their odyssey."[38]

For African Americans, therefore, the "State" that mattered most remained the United States. Although it did not grant them territorial sovereignty, the draining of power by *Brown v. Board of Education* from states long accustomed to ruling by legal and customary codes of racism did initiate a profound change, for blacks and whites alike, in the meaning of both states' rights and the power of the nation-state. As Kelley's dwelling on the white reaction to Tucker Caliban's rebellion suggests, desegregation would have to throw off both the state of servitude to a racial ethos and the white delusion of black faithfulness, the fantasized agreement to segregation integral to supremacist thought. Whereas Exodus logically implies the exchange of one state for another, however, *A Different Drummer* has nothing to say about the imagined future of its black characters. Appearing at a time when the consequences of the civil rights movement could not yet be envisioned—when barely 1 percent of black children in the South attended school with whites,[39] when the Civil Rights Act was still in the future, when a peculiar extremist named Malcolm X, catapulted into the national consciousness by the 1959 television documentary *The Hate That Hate Produced,* appeared more often on network news than Martin Luther King, Jr.—Kelley's novel was a startling but mystifying exercise of the teleological imagination.

Endorsing neither liberalist integration nor nationalist separatism, it depicts instead a state of utter liminality, in which temporal and spatial motion alike are left in jeopardy. A description of the migrating blacks by a white bus driver, who carries them to the depot in New Marsails, whereupon they disappear from view, is instructive: "They come running out of the woods and wave me down and get on and move to the back [of the bus]. Back there it looks like it's jammed up with black sardines—with suitcases."[40] This subtle but remarkable image fuses the segregation of southern transportation with an archetype of the horror of the Middle Passage, Africans crammed side by side, even one atop another, in the suffocating stench of the ship's hold. Tucker Caliban's liberating migration offers hope that the traumatic exile of the Middle Passage might be, if not reversed, at least superseded by realized nationalist aspirations. But the novel does not say where, when, or how, and the new journey, it appears, might be just another passage into slavery.

Kelley wrote paradoxically in a prophetic mode but without prophecy. For whites and blacks alike, thinking of a world without segregation was beyond contemplation, "like attempting to picture Nothing." Envisioning no future land of milk and honey—that is, initiating a mass resettlement but identifying no sought-for homeland—Kelley exaggerated the pain of the continuing black diaspora, as though to situate Tucker's act within the tradition of Western messianism whose signal feature, as Michael Walzer has written, "is the apparent endlessness of the Exodus march."[41] Severed economically, psychologically, and culturally from a true natal home, *A Different Drummer* suggests, African Americans may be left in a never-ending search for freedom whose mirage is "always just ahead," as Langston Hughes said, and which Ralph Ellison wrote neatly into Dr. Bledsoe's letter of recommendation for Invisible Man, designed to sabotage his career: "I beg of you, sir, to help him continue in the direction of that promise which, like the horizon, recedes ever brightly and distantly beyond the hopeful traveler."[42]

CALL ME X

The conflict between integration and nationalism that reverberates throughout Kelley's novel may also be interpreted in light of his autobiographical representations of black identity. Kelley was a native of New York City, the son of an editor of Harlem's *Amsterdam News* and a young man of relative privilege, educated at the mostly white Fieldston School and later at Harvard. David Bradley calls attention to the searching irony in the fact that, while the nine black students who integrated Central High School in Little Rock were being cursed and spat upon in the fall of 1957—*A Different Drummer* is set a few months earlier, in the spring of 1957—Kelley matriculated into a very different September world. In the words of Kelley's revealing 1963 *Esquire* essay "The Ivy League Negro," the world of Harvard Yard was one where "the leaves on the trees were dark green; the grass too was green and I remember thinking that it looked like the view in an Easter egg."[43]

A bittersweet reflection on the combined, but asymmetrical, racial and class alienation likely to be experienced by a black student at Harvard in the late 1950s, "The Ivy League Negro" also affords a different but no less demanding calculation of the metaphors of state and nationhood at the center of *A Different Drummer*. Several elements of Kelley's schooling, as desultory as Thoreau's at Harvard, are echoed in the novel. The autobiographical fate of the black intellectual described in Kelley's essay involves nowhere near so cruel a revelation of racism as the lynching of the West Indian nationalist Bennett Bradshaw that concludes *A Different Drummer*—the Bradshaw character was vaguely modeled on one of Kelley's friends at Harvard—but the world from which Kelley the student finds himself excluded and to which he finds his identity sacrificed is no less a reincarnation of the authority of the master. Whereas his privilege and isolation within a very small world of black university students estrange Kelley from what he calls "Negro consciousness" and the race pride it might imply, his color leaves him stranded between Africa and America, between "a race he feels he has grown away from and a [white] class which will not fully accept him."[44]

The essay's poignancy is less striking, however, than its meditation on African American alienation. For the other strong vector in the novel, closely allied with the radical *migration* initiated by Tucker Caliban, concerns the question of *immigration*—the question whether, as the title of a 1966 article by Irving Kristol put it, "The Negro Today Is Like the Immigrant of Yesterday."[45] Kelley's answer decisively excluded African Americans from the pattern of ethnic American assimilation. Unlike other minorities in America, Kelley writes, "after six or more generations, the African 'immigrant' remains one." In composing his variation on the common African American theme of double consciousness made famous by Du Bois, Kelley explicitly echoed Langston Hughes, who wrote in "My America" (1944), "This is my land, America. Naturally, I love it—it is home," but who lamented the fact that his fourth-generation American family had fewer rights than European immigrants just off the boat.[46]

Whatever priority they had as Americans, blacks were still black, defined by the liability of race rather than the assimilative potentiality of ethnicity. In this respect, Kelley anticipated the psychology of alienation diagnosed in *Black Rage* (1968), which argued that African Americans, unlike other immigrant groups, had been denied a culture of their own. Whereas the Jew may look to religious and cultural tradition for sustenance, the "black man stands alone," wrote William Grier and Price Cobbs, "forbidden to be an African and never allowed to be an American." Couched in the assumptions of racial damage theory, *Black Rage* ignored African retentions and slave culture so as to enforce the African American's existential predicament. Richard Wright had put the matter more viciously in "the dozens" played by Fishbelly and his friend Sam in *The Long Dream*: "You can't live like no American, 'cause you ain't no American! And you ain't African neither! So what is you? Nothing! Just *nothing!* . . . When you a nigger, you's *all* nigger and there ain't *nothing* left over."[47]

Like the authors of *Black Rage*, Wright described a psychological state rather than a cultural fact, strategically ignoring the riches of black music, literature, religion, and intellectual life, as well as their partially recoverable African origins. But he accurately gauged the dominating ethos of the day, in which segregation, theories of racial inferiority, and disbelief that African inheritances could have any coherent meaning still provided the public framework for much commentary on black existence in America. As Melville Herskovits argued in his classic study *The Myth of the Negro Past* (1940), a number of myths have validated the concept of Negro inferiority—that Negroes are naturally of childlike character; that only the less intelligent Africans were captured for enslavement; that the diversity of African tribal customs eliminated the possibility of a common cultural denominator; that Africans inevitably gave up their savage customs in favor of the superior practices of Euro-American culture. But the culminating mistaken myth is that the Negro is "a man without a past." Kelley, however, came closer to E. Franklin Frazier's contrary view that the Negro in America, "consistent with civilized modes of behavior," had "sloughed off completely the African heritage." Indeed, Kelley's argument that "the Negro was so completely cut loose from Africa that next to nothing is left of it in his culture" sounds like nothing so much as the contention of U. B. Phillips that African Americans were "as completely broken from their tribal stems as if they had been brought from Mars."[48] Even if one takes Kelley's statement as a rhetorical ploy, it remains a fair indication of his haunting construction of "Negro consciousness" in *A Different Drummer*.

By the time he embraced the separatist philosophy of Black Power, Kelley had set aside any remaining ambivalence about the source of his alienation. In rejecting the politics and aesthetics of integration—and in denouncing older black writers, except Wright, for working too much in a Western rather than an African literary tradition—he also condemned his former self as "one of the most integrated people that the society has produced. . . . I was one of the most messed up mentally, one of the most brainwashed. All the private school and Harvard education I've had is something I've had to get over." But in the early 1960s, Kelley was writing against a backdrop of personal educational privilege very much in tune with *The Black Bourgeoisie* (1957), in which Frazier described middle-class blacks who, in their desire to forget the Negro past, had become "exaggerated Americans" inhabiting a world of intense ambivalence about their emulation of whites, a world of deep-seated inferiority and make-believe that strands them between two worlds, "in the process of becoming NOBODY."[49]

In a 1962 preface to his best-selling book, Frazier noted that his Jewish friends found that his portrayal of black alienation within a "white" world described their experience as well.[50] Unlike Jews, however, African Americans in the late 1950s had not yet reached the point at which appeals to an African cultural past could shore up, much less embolden, a sense of transnational diasporic identity. One of the most famous—later one of the most infamous—

reflections on black America by a prominent American Jew, Norman Pod-horetz's essay "My Negro Problem—and Ours" (1963), asked why blacks should wish for pluralistic survival as a distinct group when, unlike Jews, they were not bound by "a memory of past glory and a dream of imminent redemption." Expressing the growing anxiety about black militancy among Jews sympathetic to the civil rights movement, said Podhoretz in a passage cited in Chapter 1, the Negro is bound instead by the fact that "his past is a stigma, his color is a stigma, and his vision of the future is the hope of erasing the stigma by making color irrelevant, by making it disappear as a fact of consciousness."[51]

Podhoretz to the contrary, the necessity not just of integration but of assimilation would soon become anathema to many African Americans. In creating a memory of past African glory, they would dream their own "dream of imminent redemption." In the era of "The Ivy-League Negro," however, the erasure of color and its historic stigma was a far greater challenge than the post-Holocaust dismantling of anti-Jewish quotas and legal covenants. A telling remark by Harvard president A. Lawrence Lowell, responsible for establishing a quota for Jewish enrollment at Harvard College in 1922, remained relevant in Kelley's day: "Cambridge could make a Jew indistinguishable from an Anglo-Saxon; but not even Harvard could make a black man white."[52]

To be a Negro in such a nation, wrote Martin Luther King, Jr., employing a metaphor that reappears throughout his writing and speeches, means "[being] harried by day and haunted by night by a nagging sense of nobodiness." To be a Negro in America, concluded Kelley, alluding to the Liberty Paints episode in *Invisible Man,* is "to be a man waking up in a hospital bed with amnesia," willing to accept any name "because it is better to have a name, even one which holds no meaning, than to have no name at all." No doubt *A Different Drummer* reflects Kelley's own middle-class alienation from an "authentic" blackness, his immersion in the world of "exaggerated Americans" described by Frazier, but it also reflects the glimmer of a new moment of consciousness among African Americans. Writing at a time when some black nationalists argued for casting off the slave names of the past in favor of African names—or for canceling out the master's name altogether in a cryptic signature X, symbolizing the forced illiteracy of their ancestors—Kelley's portrayal of the consciousness of nationhood had to balance his rejection of the Black Muslims ("who have turned the American Nightmare of irrational prejudice on its head and made it a Faith") against his unnerving invocation of African American historical amnesia.[53]

Although Tucker Caliban professes no political platform and in no overt way self-consciously invokes his recalcitrant namesake, an emblem of the depredations of Euro-American colonialism, he anticipates the rewriting of Shakespeare's native rebel later undertaken by Aimé Césaire in his 1969 version of *The Tempest*. Césaire's Caliban, relegated to a filthy cave, a "ghetto," is an exponent of liberation, and his ongoing dialogue with his master, Prospero, offers at every turn a critique of colonial rule and a forecast of its eventual overthrow. "Call me X. That would be best. Like a man without a name. Or, to be more precise, a man whose name has been stolen," Césaire's Caliban says. "Every time you summon me it reminds me of a basic fact, the fact that you've stolen everything from me, even my identity."[54] Unlike Césaire's rebel slave, cast in the mold of anticolonial hero and bluntly orating about his oppression, Kelley's Caliban speaks through voiceless actions. But the impossibility of his overthrowing his masters or returning to a consciously remembered homeland makes his dispossession and amnesia all the more moving and urgent.

A Different Drummer records this struggle in its fragmentary recovery of a black past. The legend of the African maroon from whom Tucker Caliban is descended stands in counterpoint to the almanac's history of the state's most famous citizen, General Dewey Willson, the son of Dewitt Willson, a Confederate hero, and the archetypal southern patriarch. Yet the importance of the African as a heroic liberator, an alternative to white history, is hedged by his betrayal from within by a seeming compatriot ("I'm an American; I'm no savage," the slave traitor says), and his murder by a white man before he can prevent his infant son from being enslaved.[55] Named First Caliban by Dewitt, a reader of Shakespeare, the black child raised by slave masters in the New World breeds a race enslaved by law and custom until Tucker's singular revolution undoes Caliban's curse and reverses the design of slavery's empire. In a variation on the misguided attempt by Gavin Stevens in Faulkner's *Light in August* to account for Joe Christmas's homicidal spree ("it was the black blood which swept him . . . up into that ecstasy out of a black jungle where life has already ceased"), Mister Harper ascribes Tucker's revolt to the "blood" of the African acting in him.[56] The novel, however, understands blood not as biology but as a figure for the achievement of cultural consciousness. Tucker Caliban's act, though its practical outcome remains unimagined in the novel, is thus a true "revolution." To the extent possible, it turns full circle, through the amnesia of history, back to the moment at which the African family lost its own name and accepted the name of Caliban.

When he buys back the land on which his African ancestor was slain, Tucker is given a mystic white stone recovered from the site where the dying African had tried and failed to murder his infant son in order to prevent his enslavement—a stone held in trust by the Willsons, so it seems, as a symbol of mutual dependence and bondage, an enigma to be grappled with generation after generation until such time as enslavement might end. But Tucker finds that property is not identity, that he has nonetheless "lost something." Or, as Bradshaw more accurately puts it, "I think he meant that he had been robbed of something but had never known it because he never even knew he owned what had been taken from him."[57]

As Bradshaw's convoluted proposition suggests, A Different Drummer places itself on the horizon of a future that is also a past. Tucker Caliban's act of renunciation, like Thoreau's temporary migration to Walden Pond, and even more like Ike McCaslin's renunciation in Faulkner's Mosaic saga Go Down, Moses (1942), places a premium on the relation between property and identity. Whereas Thoreau sought to describe a geography of the self in which complete sovereignty might be imagined, if never achieved, Tucker's self-dispossession maps, for African America, a comparable space of sovereignty in fittingly negative terms. By buying and then destroying and abandoning his property, Tucker declares that what has been taken from these long-exiled Africans can never be given back.[58]

Like "The Ivy-League Negro," the novel implicitly argues that consciousness of African identity among American blacks is predicated upon inventing a collective memory—an invention rendered at once intense and precarious by the fact that slavery threatens forever to differentiate African Americans from other immigrants. They have neither a specific historical nation left behind nor a restored homeland, like Israel, to put an end to their exile. The paradox, notes Gerald Early, is that African Americans are "bound by the prison of self-consciousness about the meaning of their once having been African, while realizing that they can never be African again." Indeed, so far as the novel tells us, Tucker Caliban does not discard his name. His act instead creates a blank domain of historical mourning, a space that may be provisionally filled by legend and memory but never fully healed, no more than the life and possessions stripped away in centuries of enslavement and racism can be fully returned or a rootedness in Africa entirely recovered. Whereas his purchase of the land brings an "end" to work for the white man, marking a rejection of the racist pastoral promulgated by white southerners and constituting a clear break with the sharecropping past, it does not, as he discovers, permit him and his family to "free ourselves."[59]

Among the possessions that Tucker destroys is an antique grandfather clock taken off the slave ship by Dewitt Willson along with the first African and eventually given to the Caliban family as a reward for service. When Tucker chops up the clock with an axe, he annihilates both the time of bondage and the false recompense of property. He also provides a fitting figure for the novel's stymied journey from amnesia to memory, its struggle to narrate the temporal plot of African American life in a way commensurate with a history of estrangement that cannot be undone either by Tucker's revolt or by Kelley's storytelling. Time—Nation Time, as Black Power would say—is not recovered in Kelley's novel but rather suspended. Egypt is no more, but Canaan is nowhere in sight.

OUR LAST NIGGER, EVER

"The fantasy of an America free of blacks is at least as old as the dream of creating a truly democratic society," wrote Ralph Ellison in his brilliant 1970 essay "What America Would Be Like without Blacks." Fruitless schemes to banish blacks "from the nation's bloodstream, from its social structure, and from its conscience and historical consciousness," Ellison argued, were a kind of "primitive reflex" born not simply of persistent racism but rather of "moral fatigue." Their inverse, equally naïve and racist in its way, was the "illusion of secession" to a world elsewhere, the territorial fantasy nursed by radical nationalists as the only antidote to segregation and prejudice. For Ellison, writing in the face of dismissals of his integrationist idealism as some kind of Uncle Tom act, the nation could not survive the absence of blacks because, as noted earlier, they symbolize democracy's "most stringent testing and the possibility of its greatest freedom."[60]

Kelley was not so sure. Tucker's action points to a world without segregation, but the paradoxical underside of this dream, the "Negro-less world" left behind in the white state when segregation is taken to its logical end point, is perfectly portrayed in the mirroring action that ends the novel, the lynching of Bennett Bradshaw. The original African is killed by Dewitt Willson because he cannot be possessed, will not become part of the white man's property, like his clock, and live in his time. Bradshaw, in contrast, is killed by the men on the porch as an outside agitator mistakenly thought responsible for instigating the migration. But most of all he is killed as what the men perceive to be "our last nigger, ever. There won't be no more after this, and no more singing and dancing and laughing." Whereas the African had seen something akin to a look of masculine respect in the gaze of Dewitt Willson before Willson shot him, Bradshaw sees, as though in a short circuit to the historical present, paternalism degenerated into racist fury—a stare that is "completely blank, that very blankness a sign of the renunciation of alternatives, of tenderness or brutality, of pleasure or pain, of understanding or ignorance, of belief or disbelief, of compassion or intolerance, of reason or unswerving fanaticism; it was a gaze which signals the flicking off of the switch which controls the mechanism making a man a human being."[61]

Incorporating the totality of victimhood, as though the eliminationist philosophy of the Holocaust were contained in a single murdered Jew, Bradshaw at once depletes the reservoir of sacrificial victims and inaugurates an age of paternalist nostalgia. Kelley's scenario is distinctly reminiscent of George Schuyler's *Black No More* (1931), in which the disappearance of the nation's blacks through a skin-bleaching technology, imported from Germany, leaves the desperate members of a southern community with "nothing left to stimulate them but the old time religion and . . . clandestine sex orgies," until they discover one last pair of bleached Negroes, whose mutilation and burning provide a final act of communal gratification. If Tucker Caliban's revolutionary act of exile reveals the metaphysical trauma of whiteness deprived of blackness, Bradshaw, as the white community's "last nigger, ever," reveals its underpinnings in the pornography of racial violence. It was "like having a naked girl in arm's reach and not doing nothing about it," says one of the lynch mob of their initial failure to prevent Bradshaw from advocating the black Exodus, as they mistakenly surmise he meant to do.[62] Scapegoat for a community in crisis, Bradshaw is the epitome of what Lillian Smith referred to as the "Sign" of a way of life on the edge of self-destruction, "not [just] an object that must die but a receptacle for every man's dammed-up hate, and a receptacle for every man's forbidden [sexual] feelings."[63]

One could say that these southern killers are "ordinary men," that lynch mobs, as Christopher Browning, and more recently Daniel Jonah Goldhagen, have argued of the Germans under Nazism, were composed of common people wrenched by circumstance into a capacity, even a lust, for diabolical acts.[64] Whatever *A Different Drummer* tells us about the continuum between casual racism and the genocidal capabilities lodged in the white segregationist psyche, however, Kelley's rendering of black consciousness is terrible and sobering because even its annihilation is contained within white consciousness. After his driver, like the original African's black compatriots, deserts him, Bradshaw is forced to dance and sing a grotesque minstrel tune before being hauled off in his own limousine to an undescribed ritual death, narratively rendered only by its distant screams, on Tucker Caliban's abandoned property. The peculiar night sounds of the lynching are registered in the consciousness of a young white boy, Mister Leland, who is the novel's hope for a better racial future—a boy whose name reflects the artificial "manhood" with which he is endowed by virtue of being white, while black men around him are "boys," and who comes to consciousness, like other southern children, with his sleep disturbed by distant, unnamable sounds of fury and sacrifice. ("So hard to see Something swinging from a limb—because you never saw it," wrote Lillian Smith. "You only heard the whispers, saw the horror of it in the dark faces you loved.")[65] Rather than ritual murder, however, Mister Leland imagines a festive party prompted by Tucker's return, a disjunction in perception that closes the novel on a harrowing note. Black consciousness remains in eclipse; time is momentarily frozen on the brink of a revolution that cannot be enacted; and the white men's killing of Bradshaw suggests that, once one people becomes accustomed to the elimination of another, exile and murder draw closer together.

Exodus cannot be fully conceptualized in *A Different Drummer,* not because there are no models available—black American history is replete with models—but because, in 1962, Kelley could not see where this new march toward freedom would lead. Year by year as he was writing, the liberation of African nations from colonial rule inspired the civil rights movement in the United States. Beginning with Ghana in 1957, more than a dozen former colonies had achieved independence by the time Kelley's novel appeared, but these historic events did not yet provide a foundation on which blacks in America could build a pan-African ideology of liberation, let alone a workable strategy of repatriation. Any Jew in the world could return to the homeland of Israel, immediately granted citizenship by the Law of Return, but there was no such African nation to which all blacks might commonly aspire to belong, no black homeland preparing for an ingathering, no Jerusalem which African Americans could call their own.

A Different Drummer appeared at virtually the same moment as *To Kill a Mockingbird*—a moment of racial crisis whose resolution had already been postponed by a century—and both novels describe a world in which the power of the masters has begun to give way to something new. White consciousness dominates both books, but whereas Lee hypothesized another version of the white Moses—Atticus Finch, the liberal savior—pointing the way to the Promised Land, Kelley hypothesized a revolutionary act in which white identity, stripped of its black fetishes, would be cut down in ironic negation. Both hypotheses, one could say, were true to the experiential history of the early civil rights era. What Lee spoke of as "you children's time" had come, with whites left fighting to preserve a way of life that could not be imagined otherwise and African Americans poised on the edge of Nation Time, searching for an unrecoverable past and longing for a future not yet visible. William Melvin Kelley the writer might retreat to Harvard Yard, if not to Walden Pond, but for William Melvin Kelley the African American, there was as yet no Exodus.

II. THE WOUNDING PAST: PAULE MARSHALL

Written during the years 1963 through 1968, *The Chosen Place, the Timeless People* is a compendium of themes in the dialogue between blacks and Jews, as its evocative puns on "chosenness" and "timelessness" tell us from the start. Over the years of its composition, ideas now taken for granted first came to prominence—analogies between the Holocaust, nuclear war, and slavery, for example, or the emergence of the black Atlantic "diaspora," a concept until then associated almost exclusively in American consciousness with dispersion of the Jews. At the same time, whatever alliance may have existed between African Americans and American Jews in the early years of the civil rights movement had given way to alienation and recrimination. The full scope of that change will become apparent in the next chapter, but Marshall's novel, begun at a moment of comparative political promise and concluded at a moment of spiraling national violence over Vietnam and black rights—more specifically, Black Power—presents one writer's effort to hold the relationship, even the intimacy, of blacks and Jews in place.

Paule Marshall conceived of *The Chosen Place, the Timeless People* as the second part of a trilogy begun with *Brown Girl, Brownstones* (1959), whose American protagonist travels to the Caribbean at the novel's end, determined to discover in her parents' birthplace the source of her own identity. At the end of *The Chosen Place, the Timeless People,* this novel's unrelated protagonist, Merle Kibona, descendant of a white planter and his black lover, sets out for Africa in search of her lost daughter and her lost African soul, "on another leg of the journey back into the historical self." The third novel of the trilogy, which eventually became *Praisesong for the Widow* (1983), was "to be in some way concerned with Africa," said Marshall, the three books together "describing, in reverse, the slave trade's triangular route back to the motherland, the source."[1] One of the most acute novelistic expositions of the African diaspora,[2] *Praisesong for the Widow,* which had yet another set of characters, is not, in fact, set in Africa. Instead, the novel remains rooted in the island culture of the Caribbean, including its immigrant manifestations in the United States, as though Marshall had discovered not just that the black Americas were ontologically part of Africa but also that the black diaspora *was* her nation, that the tragedy of slavery could not be escaped but only plumbed more deeply on home ground.

The grander historical panorama of *The Chosen Place, the Timeless People* predicts as much, not least because the novel's intersection between African American and American Jewish histories comes at a moment when both blacks and Jews in the United States, for different but related reasons, were intensely engaged in defining the "nation" to which they belonged. Those histories are not exactly parallel in the novel, but in juxtaposing the stories of Merle Kibona, an Afro-Caribbean *obeah* woman—a sage and storyteller—and Saul Amron, a Jewish American anthropologist, Marshall casts backwards from the conflicted brotherhood of blacks and Jews in the United States to explore their common life narratives of destruction and survival as diasporic peoples.

From the outset, Merle and Saul are staged as characters moving toward collision and embrace. The undercurrent of antagonism in their relationship heightens its simmering eroticism, and their affair, when it happens, appears as a kind of supercharged coupling of the mid-twentieth-century global folkways of Africans and Jews. Just as their physical traits reflect a crossing—Saul's Semitic features include his "nigger hair," while Merle's shrug of her shoulders seems to Saul "the gesture of a Jew"[3]—so their stories are meant to reveal each other's secrets and to bring them together at the crossroads of modernity, much as the African New World portrayed in Marshall's mythical Caribbean island, now independent but entrenched in neocolonial rule, is itself a cultural and spiritual crossroads of the black Atlantic.

Marking "the eastern boundary of the entire continent," Marshall's fictional setting of Bourne Island, modeled loosely on Barbados, is at once an outpost facing the "colossus of Africa," Merle's homeland, and a symbolic stop on the way of Saul's Sephardic ancestors, who fled the Inquisition and "slowly, over the generations, journeyed north through the countries of the Americas and the Caribbean."[4] In this conjunction of two people's destinies, Marshall returns to the originating moment of 1492, when virtually simultaneously the Jews, as well as the Moors, were expelled from Spain, the most dramatic in a series of expulsions both before and after, and the Columbian voyages set in motion the making of the "New World," built on the foundation of black slavery. Emma Lazarus had represented only half of the equation in her 1883 poem "1492" when she wrote: "Thou two-faced year, Mother of Change and Fate, / Didst weep when Spain cast forth with flaming sword, / The children of the Prophets of the Lord . . . Hounded from sea to sea, from state to state."[5] If the Jews of the modern age, Sephardic as well as Ashkenazi, found partial refuge in the United

States, by the time of Marshall's novel their comparative ease in the new Zion stood in sharp contrast with the continued obstacles faced by slavery's descendants, still seeking freedom after four centuries.

Although Marshall once professed a fascination with Thomas Mann's *Buddenbrooks,* dynastic sweep is present in *The Chosen Place, the Timeless People* mainly by implication. The patriarchal prowess of Merle's white ancestor Duncan Vaughn—who "sired" forty children with the black women working on his estate[6]—is anecdotal; likewise, the lives of Merle's mother and other Bourne Island blacks of earlier generations are not portrayed in the novel. Comparison to a work such as Faulkner's *Absalom, Absalom!* would not be revealing either for formal reasons—the narrative form of Marshall's novel is quite conventional—or for understanding the intricate passions, the mixed-race layerings of love and hatred that mark the history of slavery, to which Marshall pays relatively little attention. Her novel is instead unquestionably didactic, its characters, events, and topography weighed down with the task of personifying the streams of history arrested in Bourne Island, as the heirs of slavery await the second coming of a mythic slave rebel.

If genealogy is subordinated to ideology, however, the novel's epic scope is well suited to conveying a sense of archaeological time alive with messianic anticipation. By playing upon but inverting the idea of the Jews as the "chosen people" now able to return, with the founding of Israel, to the "timeless place" of their historical origin, Marshall signals a further entwining of diasporic destinies, while signaling as well that blacks' Promised Land lies still in the New World, made over in African terms. With Israel's victory in the Six-Day War, perhaps even more certainly than in the creation of the Jewish state two decades earlier, Jews found crystallized the meaning of nationhood. At the same moment, by embracing slavery as both a living heritage and a "holocaust" in its own right, postwar African Americans transposed their historical immersion in biblical Zionism into the political terms of modern Zionism and found the rudiments of their own symbolic return to a lost homeland.

AN AVALANCHE OF MURDERS

Decked, stacked, pillaged from
their homes
packed bodies on bodies rock in the belly
of death.

sea blood. sea blood churns
production for the West's dying machine.
commodities for profit stuffed empires
with spices . . .

—*Larry Neal, "The Middle Passage*
and After"

In his sprawling, eccentric study *The Crisis of the Negro Intellectual* (1967), Harold Cruse called attention to a "fateful triangular tension" between Anglo-Saxons, Negroes, and Jews. Deep within the social consciousness of these groups, Cruse contended, lay three nationalist ideologies—Anglo-Saxon (Christian) nationalism, black nationalism, and Jewish nationalism (Zionism). The first was overt, dominant in the American tradition, the second vocal but poorly organized, and the third "the most sophisticated, scholarly and intellectual, with the most highly refined propaganda techniques."[7] Cruse's lamentations about the intellectual betrayal of blacks by Jews and the failure of black leadership do not play a direct role in *The Chosen Place, the Timeless People,* but his triangulation of ideologies is represented in the novel's three main characters, who act out assigned parts on a world-historical stage even grander than the one Cruse had in mind.

Marshall does not by any means make Saul Amron a spokesman for Zionism, but her dramatization of his relationship with Merle Kibona, by probing the deeper diasporic subcurrents of their lives, illuminates the anxiety African Americans might feel in looking to the Jewish example for the nationalist identity denied them by Anglo-Saxonism; and the novel's caricature of Saul's wife, Harriet Shippen, as the heiress to the same Anglo-Saxon imperial ambitions, is a transparent device for portraying emergent global capitalism as inherently predatory. Even though Cruse attacked the politics of Zionism ("can one fight necolonialism in Africa today without fighting Israel?") and argued that the battle for black civil rights was too much under the sway of Jews, he recognized a shared "yearning for national redemption through regaining a 'homeland' that was lost" and averred that blacks could learn from Jews the "art of survival against all odds," as well as the art of using research and propaganda to promote their own brand of cultural nationalism.[8] Marshall's three characters are more than mouthpieces of ideology, but their correspondence to Cruse's triangulation of nationalisms also extends to other triangulated structures that govern the convergence of racial destinies in the novel.

Merle Kibona is the great-great-granddaughter of Duncan Vaughn, a white patriarch of the colonial era, and daughter of the wealthy planter Ashton

Vaughn and his sixteen-year-old black lover, a weeder on his estate, who was shot and killed in 1926 by Vaughn's vengeful wife when Merle was two years old. Raised with the privileges of a mulatta child of a white patriarch, Merle is sent to London to be educated. Her sojourn in the metropole scars her when, after the failure of her marriage to Ketu, an African economist, she resumes a lesbian love affair previously broken off and Ketu responds by fleeing with their daughter to his homeland of Uganda. (When he meets Merle, Ketu is taking a further degree in agricultural economics, with the intention of returning to Uganda to improve the lives of his people, a feature that allies him with Saul.) Shamed and psychologically devastated, Merle returns to Bourne Island, which is run by an elite class of neocolonial administrators, some of them white and some black—"but black that for the most part had been passed through the white prism of their history and been endlessly refracted there, altered, alloyed"—a class to which Merle might lay claim by virtue of her own elite heritage. Instead, she shuns them in favor of life among the black people of Bournehills, the "timeless people" of Marshall's title, whose deep poverty, devotion to native culture, and continual thwarting of neocolonial development schemes make their region of the island seem like "someplace out of the Dark Ages."[9]

Bournehills is saturated in slavery, both because the contemporary economy of sugar cane cutting and processing is little different from the forced labor of previous generations and because the people still live intensely within the memory of a momentary black heroic age, situated at an indeterminate time in the eighteenth or early nineteenth century, when the slave Cuffee Ned raised a rebellion. After setting fire to the estate of Percy Bryam, one of the island's largest planters, Cuffee Ned's force of slave rebels burned the surrounding cane fields, yoked Bryam to the mill wheel at Cane Vale and tortured him to death, stormed an arsenal, drove back government forces in a fierce battle, and for two years sustained an independent maroon state. Ultimately, the insurrection was put down and Cuffee killed, his head placed on a pike in the traditional warning to other slaves.

The Pyre Hill Revolt—so named because the fire started by Cuffee Ned purportedly burned for five years, its destruction still evident, as sacral meaning and millennial forewarning, in the present time of the novel—is emblematic of the historical moment in which the "timeless people" live, still arguing to the present day about the valor of Cuffee's rebels and the question of his prophesied return. "Tough, stubborn, sustained by their sense of history," writes Marshall, the people of Bournehills will hold out "until the sweeping revolutionary change initiated by Cuffee Ned long ago can be achieved." Having lost her job as a schoolteacher when she insisted on instructing students about the rebellion, Merle Kibona lives in the island's historical margin, apparently trying in her weird hybridity of dress and affect "to recover something in herself that had been lost"—not just Cuffee's promise of liberation but, at bottom, the black identity stripped away in the shock of transport into slavery and its consequent radical estrangements of kinship, tribal authority, and language.[10]

From the moment he arrives on Bourne Island, Saul Amron feels mysteriously drawn to the island's black cultural resonances, and he is compelled to penetrate the secret of his strong identification with local history. When the neocolonials mock the people of Bournehills for their resistance to modernization and their absorption in the legend of Cuffee Ned, Saul is stung by a deep-seated shame with more than one source. His descent from the Sephardic Jews of Iberia, and hence his ancestral family's experience of expulsion from a modern as well as an ancient homeland, links him symbolically with Africans in the Americas. More particularly, Saul is shamed by the recollection that he, too, once rejected his "brothers" when, as a youth, he took pride in his "large, straight-shouldered build" while despising the "sallow, long-nosed look, sloping shoulders and side curls" of neighborhood Ashkenazim, the descendants of northern and eastern European Jews, who also "were his people after all." A terrain of persecution and yearning, "Sweet Beulah Land" to Merle, Bournehills also evokes for Saul all his previous fieldwork in places such as Guatemala, Bolivia, Honduras, and Chiapas—"every place that had been wantonly used, its substance stripped away, and then abandoned"—but more, it "could have been a troubled region within himself to which he had unwittingly returned." A "professional wanderer," a kind of wandering Jew who has become a "symbol of Western man's alienation and disaffection," Saul is most at home in the remote sites of colonial ravaging and most himself when he discovers in Merle Kibona a kinship of racial marginality and spiritual exile unavailable to him in the land of his birth.[11]

In the wake of one of Merle's nativist outbursts, when she castigates Lyle Hutson, a leading barrister and senator, for the local government's plan to sell the island into the neo-slavery of tourism and gambling—"Who says the auction block isn't still with us?" she asks—Saul is perplexed by something "hidden," "subliminal," "nebulous" about the island that he cannot quite fathom. Merle declares to Lyle, the archetype of the native turned neocolonial administrator, that Bournehills will stay "the way it is for a reason," a statement initially opaque to Saul, except that it prompts his memory of a melange of incidents: his earlier fieldwork in Mexico and Peru, his killing a German soldier in combat, his visit to the death camps of Poland after the war, his mother's tale of the

family's migration, and most of all the agony of his first wife, Sosha, a Holocaust survivor who died in childbirth, her body weakened by the first ordeal
only to succumb to the second because Saul had subjected her to year after
year of his grueling fieldwork.[12] Midway into the novel, that is to say, Saul's
secret tragedy and his guilt have been fully revealed to the reader; but it remains for him to discover what it is in the living history of Bournehills and the
folk memory of Cuffee Ned's legendary revolt that brings forth such painful
memories.

Except for a few pointed passages in reference to racial violence and civil rights
politics, Marshall's novel has little to say about the contemporary United States.
In a concluding conversation with Saul, as she is about to set out for Africa,
Merle doubts that she would ever wish to visit the United States. Having
learned quite enough about Anglo-European racial attitudes in England, she
rejects life in a place "where they treat the black people, the very ones who
made the bloody country rich in the first place, so badly," where they kill little
children in church bombings—she refers to the 1963 bombing of Birmingham's
Sixteenth Street Baptist Church—and where "every time you look around,
they're warring against some poor, half-hungry country somewhere in the
world."[13]

   If the contemporary United States is distant, however, the imperialist, neocolonial ideology for which it stands in Marshall's eyes is very much present.
Saul is a pioneer in the field of applied anthropology, and there is no question
of his well-meant intentions to improve the economic and social lives of the
people of Bournehills. But as the architect of a developmental research project
with dubious prospects for success, and thus the embodiment of Marshall's critique of the discourse of progressivist modernism,[14] Saul represents also the
likelihood that social science and public policy are meager weapons for ending
three centuries of oppression. Worse, they might themselves be instruments of
empire, or at any rate diversions from more urgent needs at home. What good
is the "benevolent colonialism" of the Peace Corps and other such agencies,
asked Malcolm X, "when you're hanging black people in Mississippi?"[15]

   Funded by the Center for Applied Social Research (CASR), Saul's project is a
puppet play of global capitalism, with roots in the wealth produced by slavery.
So as to leave no question that Saul's work risks futility because it is born of
corruption, Marshall depicts CASR as a creation of the Philadelphia Research
Institute, itself controlled by Unicor, a vast conglomerate originating in the old
money of prominent Philadelphia families, including that of Saul's second
wife, Harriet Shippen. Linked with other industrial conglomerates such as

Kingsley and Sons, Ltd., which operates the Cane Vale sugar factory on Bourne Island, Unicor is part of an ominous network of monopoly trade. Early in its history, Unicor controlled the export of staples such as cornmeal, salted fish, lumber, and cloth to colonial outposts like Bourne Island, thus engrossing the production of paper, oil, uranium, and especially sugar, the commodity that links past to present and defines the long shadow of slavery in the novel. Just as the plot, unfolding in the span of a single year, is keyed to the fortunes of the sugar factory and the prospects for the year's harvest, one tableau after another illustrates the history of the Anglo-American sugar empire,[16] rehearsing the place of Caribbean slavery in the triangular trade between Europe, Africa, and the Americas.

As part of the trade that "formed a perfect circle," in the words of Du Bois,[17] slavery and slaveholding were the launching point of modernity, creating global markets in which racialized labor forces were central to the production of commodities on a world scale and the accumulation of great wealth for families such as the Shippens. Harriet's family fortune derives from shares in a sloop that shipped staples from Philadelphia to Africa, there picking up slaves for transport to the West Indies, where the slaves were sold and sugar, rum, and molasses purchased for sale in the United States. Within the economy of the day, American traders also shipped rum to Africa and picked up slaves for sale in the West Indies, where molasses was purchased for export to the American colonies, there to make more rum. The rival British triangular trade sent finished goods from Britain to Africa, slaves to the Americas, and American commodities, especially sugar, back to the mother country and its neighbors. In all cases, slaves were the middle term in the triangle, "consumed in the creation of wealth," as Sidney Mintz writes. Over the course of the seventeenth and eighteenth centuries, Barbados, Jamaica, and the Leeward Islands—Bourne Island is imagined to lie among this constellation, most resembling Barbados—received close to 1.5 million slaves, maximizing sugar production for a world market that grew from 245,000 tons in 1800 to 6 million tons by 1890 through grueling labor, harsh discipline, and the rapid depletion and replenishment of black human capital. Perhaps the closest instance in the history of black slavery to the withering slave labor of Nazi camps, the grinding of human capital into a commodity that had begun as a luxury and become a necessity of the civilized world more than justified the chilling Cuban aphorism "sugar is made with blood."[18]

Heir to a blood-stained fortune that flows from investment in this triangulated Atlantic slave trade, Harriet Shippen is a dilettante of racial liberalism—mouthing the right clichés, working as a volunteer when the Research Institute opens a recreation center in a Philadelphia ghetto, fondly remembering her mother's black maid, convulsing in disgust at the impoverished conditions of Bournehills, and defensively citing evolving desegregation laws and new poverty programs when the islanders criticize the United States. Her sentimental liberalism is doomed, of course, and her eventual suicide is no surprise when it comes. As though her pedigree and naïveté were not burden enough, Harriet is recently divorced from a passionless nuclear physicist—Marshall archly incriminates "Western man" in his very name, Andrew Westerman—whose career induced in her nightmares of nuclear destruction: she awakens one morning to realize that it is not Andrew's hand alone "on the lever which triggered the holocaust, that mass suicide in which its creators would be the first to go, but that her hand was also there, resting lightly on his, guiding it."[19]

Marshall's plot tends toward heavy-handed pastiche, as these details of Harriet's characterization suggest, but her appeal to nuclear "holocaust" brings into view a further dimension of the novel's triangulations. As Harriet, Saul, and Merle gaze out into the Atlantic, the sea sounds of history toll differently for each. For Harriet, the crashing waves recall the "terrifying explosion" of nuclear destruction that troubled her sleep with Andrew Westerman; for Saul, they provoke memories of bombs striking during his combat, as an American Jew, in World War II; and for Merle, they sound like "the combined voices of the drowned raised in a loud unceasing lament—all those, the nine million and more it is said, who in their enforced exile, their Diaspora, had gone down between this point and the homeland lying out of sight to the east."[20] By encompassing the two other "holocausts" within the Middle Passage, while explicitly appropriating the term "Diaspora" to Afro-Caribbean and African American usage—her capitalization underscores her borrowing from the Jewish Diaspora—Marshall positioned black history alongside Jewish history while allying herself with those for whom the threat of nuclear annihilation offered a new paradigm for interpreting other instances of genocide.

As the potential for nuclear attack pressed increasingly into American consciousness at the height of the cold war, some writers, like A. Alvarez, saw the Holocaust as a "small-scale trial" for nuclear war or, like Robert Jay Lifton, discovered an ethical conjunction in their scholarly calling: "My writing about Hiroshima is affected, and I hope informed, by my relationship as a Jew to the Nazi persecutions—and my comparison of the two holocausts becomes an imperative personal task as well as a logical intellectual one."[21] American exploitation of blacks, stretching from the Middle Passage through Jim Crow and beyond, completed the triad of genocides. "We will never be able to determine the psychic havoc of the concentration camps and the atom bomb upon the unconscious mind of almost everyone alive in these years," wrote Norman Mailer in "The White Negro" (1957), which, as we have seen, presented the Negro, whose survival in America necessitated an outlaw culture, as the nihilistic herald of a post-Holocaust, post-Hiroshima world. A year later Richard Wright challenged the West to accept Goethe and Hitler as contradictory manifestations of a single historical development. Confronted on the one hand with communism and on the other with "a billion and a half colored people gripped by surging tides of nationalist fanaticism," the Western white man, Wright feared, will think that "only a vengeful unleashing of atom and hydrogen bombs can make him feel secure."[22] Carrying this line of thought into the arena of Black Power, Eldridge Cleaver grouped those responsible for slavery, the Holocaust, and Hiroshima under the same savage mentality and numbered their days: "The white heroes, their hands dripping with blood, are dead."*

Marshall's examination of such equations is no more subtle than Wright's or Cleaver's, but her introduction of the figure of "nine million and more" slaves dead in the Middle Passage, although it is surely inflated, is a reminder that what in later years sometimes seemed a contest of suffering between blacks and Jews had its origins in rhetorical gambits that began in the immediate aftermath of the Holocaust but escalated in the late 1960s.[23] Marshall does not set out to scale the culpability for genocide to massive body counts, and numbers alone, which grew exponentially hyperbolic in some estimates, are a meaningless measure. What is notable is that a large number is named—a number larger than 6 million—and that the Holocaust, as well as the nuclear bombing of Japan, emerges as an appropriate lens through which to read the history of African American slavery.

The relationship between imperialism and Nazism develops at several removes in *The Chosen Place, the Timeless People,* but the theoretical framework for Marshall's schematic understanding of slavery's empire—interpreted now in light of both the trajectory of Jewish exile and destruction, and the penchant for annihilating weapons displayed by "Western man"—had already been provided by Frantz Fanon, whose spirit presides over the novel. Published in 1961 and translated into English in 1965, Fanon's *Wretched of the Earth* became a

---

* But compare Julius Lester's novel *And All Our Wounds Forgiven* (1994). Whereas Auschwitz and Hiroshima at first ignited a passionate humanitarianism in the civil rights movement, says the novel's hero, a politically moderate civil rights leader, black militants allowed themselves to be "swallowed alive by the idolization of race" and chose instead a "passion for death . . . ignited in the extermination camps, and at hiroshima and nagasaki." Eldridge Cleaver, *Soul on Ice* (New York: McGraw-Hill, 1968), p. 82; Julius Lester, *And All Our Wounds Forgiven* (1994; rpt. San Diego: Harvest Books, 1996), p. 8.

foundational text of Third World and postcolonial studies. More immediately, it was scripture for rebels around the world, from Algeria to Vietnam to the West Bank of the Jordan to the United States. Its initial chapter, "Concerning Violence," summoned up a glamorous view of anticolonial violence. Decolonization, wrote Fanon, "brings a natural rhythm into existence, introduced by new men, and with it a new language and new humanity. . . . [T]he naked truth of decolonization evokes for us the searing bullets and bloodstained knives which emanate from it."[24] After Du Bois and C. L. R. James, Fanon was also the foremost early proponent of the view that modern Europe and the Americas were forged from the slave labor of colonial countries—"Europe is literally the creation of the Third World. The wealth which smothers her is that which was stolen from the under-developed peoples," said Fanon—and he was also among the first to outline a correlation between the Holocaust and nuclear war, and to articulate a moral tie between the blood money of empire and the compensation paid to Jews by Germany in the aftermath of the Holocaust.* Anticipating the argument of Richard Rubenstein and William Styron, who sought to portray Nazism as slavery in extremis, Fanon pointed out that Nazism "transformed the whole of Europe into a veritable colony." For centuries, he added in a facile leap, capitalists have behaved in the colonial world like "war criminals."[25]

Despite the fact that he professed skepticism about the motives of African nationalists and took *négritude* not as the end point of identity but as a stage on the way toward a truly raceless universalism,[26] Fanon's message proved eas-

---

* The essential linkage had been given ready-made to Fanon, as he recalled when quoting from a 1945 radio address by Aimé Césaire: "When I turn on my radio, when I hear that Negroes have been lynched in America, I say that we have been lied to: Hitler is not dead. . . . [Or when] I turn on my radio and hear that in Africa forced labor has been inaugurated and legalized, I say that we have certainly been lied to: Hitler is not dead." Césaire argued in *Discourse on Colonialism* (1955) that each step in the process of colonialism paves the way to genocide. Brutalizing not just the colonized but also the colonizer, numbing him to the pain he inflicts and awakening his own instincts of race hatred, "a universal regression takes place, a gangrene sets in, a center of infection begins to spread." One day the bourgeoisie wakes up to find that "the gestapos are busy, the prisons [filling] up." To understand the etiology of the Nazi genocide, Césaire contended, was to understand its origins in the instincts of colonialism: "Yes, it would be worthwhile to study clinically, in detail, the steps taken by Hitler and Hitlerism to reveal to the very distinguished, very humanistic, very Christian bourgeois of the twentieth century that without his being aware of it, he has a Hitler inside him, that Hitler *inhabits* him." The demonizing of Jews and other races by Hitler, said Césaire, was the voice of the "Western humanist." "At the end of capitalism, which is eager to outlive its day, there is Hitler." Frantz Fanon, *Black Skin, White Masks*, trans. Charles Lam Markmann (1952; rpt. New York: Grove Press, 1967), p. 90; Aimé Césaire, *Discourse on Colonialism*, trans. Joan Pinkham (1955; rpt. New York: Monthly Review Press, 1972), pp. 13–15.

ily adaptable to anticolonial strategies in both the Caribbean and the United States. His language had the cachet of revolution, and from his synthesis of psychology, philosophy, and politics there grew up an Afro-Caribbean revolutionary tradition that "de-Calibanized blackness,"[27] making it a locus of cultural energy and ideological resistance. "What is our history, what is our culture, if not the history and culture of Caliban," wrote Roberto Fernández Retamar, who set the stage for his Marxist critique of colonialism by adducing, side by side, the decimation of American Indian tribes in the United States and the Nazi genocide, an unacknowledged equivalence that led some "to stigmatize in Hitler what they applauded as a healthy Sunday diversion in westerns and Tarzan films."[28]

In the United States, not only the Black Panthers but also, for example, Roy Innis of the Congress of Racial Equality, Stokely Carmichael and James Forman of the Student Non-Violent Coordinating Committee, theologians such as James Cone, and cultural nationalists such as Larry Neal and Maulana Karenga all found inspiration in Fanon's argument that revolutionary violence was required to bring psychological cleansing and redemption to the oppressed. Eldridge Cleaver called *The Wretched of the Earth* the "Black Bible" of the black liberation movement, and by 1970 the book had sold some 750,000 copies in the United States, where its indictment of slavery and colonialism as crimes comparable to the Holocaust was at once shocking and exciting.[29] The corruption of Enlightenment ideals did not start with the Holocaust, said Fanon, and the search for such ideals, past or present, yielded only "an avalanche of murders." He counseled abandoning faith in Europe, "where they are never done talking of Man, yet murder men everywhere they find them . . . in all corners of the globe." For centuries, the Europeans have oppressed all of humanity in the name of a so-called spiritual doctrine, but "look at them today swaying between atomic and spiritual disintegration." The United States, for its part, was but an appalling extension of Europe—a "monster."[30]

Fanon's anti-Western invective is familiar to the point of quaintness half a century later, but it was formative for Marshall. In a revealing essay about her novelistic aims, "Shaping the World of My Art," she quotes this passage from *The Wretched of the Earth*, specifically the line about "atomic and spiritual disintegration," in contending that *The Chosen Place, the Timeless People* projects a future "which sees the rise through revolutionary struggle of the darker peoples of the world and, as a necessary corollary, the decline and eclipse of America and the West."[31] (One also hears in the title of Marshall's essay an echo of the pseudo-subtitle emblazoned on the widely read Grove Press paperback of Fanon's classic: "The Handbook for the Black Revolution that is Changing the Shape of the World.") In the novel's intersection between African and Jewish historical trajectories, Euro-America is thus the middle term to be discarded, its moral imperative corrupted by the triple sins of slavery, the Holocaust, and nuclear destruction. The white West, in sum, incarnates genocide, while the people of Bournehills, steeped still in the diasporic culture of the island's first Africans, stand as its moral antidote.

A Jew-Man, a Kaffir-Man

Writing in *Negro Digest* in 1968, Wilfred Cartey found the poet-prophets of Zionism such as Hayyim Bialik and those of *négritude* such as Aimé Césaire animated by a single desire to give a "new rhythm" to "historical chaos," creating pathways "back to the homeland." Cartey cited the pungent lines from Césaire's *Cahier d'un retour au pays natal* (Notebook of a Return to the Native Land):

> As there are hyena-men and panther-men, I would be a jew-man
> a Kaffir-man . . .
> the famine man, the insult-man, the torture man you can grab anytime,
>   beat up, kill—no joke, kill—without having to account to anyone, with-
>   out having to make excuses to anyone
> a jew-man
> a pogrom-man . . .

In doing so he drew the "chosen people" and the "wretched of the earth" into a single diasporic figuration. Just as return to Israel made possible for Jews a "vital continuum" with ancestors and a healing of the open wounds of the Holocaust, so for blacks return to Africa, wrote Cartey, would be an "ingathering, a return" to the lost homeland.[32]

Cartey's intriguing analogy built on a lengthy tradition of identification of blacks with the biblical Israel and, after 1948, with the modern state of Israel as a recovered homeland. As we saw in Chapter 2 and will explore in more detail in Chapter 5, the African American appeal to the example of Judaism intensified during the 1960s, becoming more complex and fractious before reaching a crisis after the Six-Day War. Although neither Saul nor Merle reflects consciously at any point on the meaning of Israel, Marshall's understanding of the respective diasporas to which her characters belong appears to take for granted the new nation's significance. The black liberation movements of Africa, combined with the radicalization of the civil rights movement at home, created for African Americans a new exilic typology in which Africa figured as their longed-for homeland, at the very moment when the young Jewish state, facing its gravest challenge, drew Jews of the diaspora to its support with unprecedented passion. The implications of the Six-Day War for the escalating domestic crisis between blacks and Jews are registered with more immediate intensity in Jewish fiction such as Bellow's *Mr. Sammler's Planet* (1970) and Malamud's *The Tenants* (1971), and among black writers in John A. Williams's *Sons of Darkness, Sons of Light* (1969), but they appear in grand, if less direct, form in *The Chosen Place, the Timeless People,* where the dual consciousness of nationhood pressing upon both Jews and blacks in the late 1960s is personified in the dialogue, both sexual and intellectual, through which Saul Amron and Merle Kibona come to know and share each other's racial lives. Saul's education in the history of black modernity begins with his own spiritual entitlement—that Jews, wherever they may be on the globe, have an imposing historical narrative through which to establish their post-Holocaust place as a nation. In turn, Merle's education, a version of Marshall's authorial perspective, requires that the concept of black nationhood—understood not as a literal territory or polity but as the diasporic community of black people descended from slavery—be passed through the screen of post-Holocaust Jewish history, at once conforming to the anticolonialism of Fanon and reconceiving the traditional story of delivery into a Promised Land in what would today be thought of as global, exilic terms.

In placing the history of Africans in the Americas within the postwar discourse of genocide, Marshall also anticipated by just a few years Derek Walcott's eloquent rendering of the black Mosaic paradigm in his well-known 1974 essay "The Muse of History." The New World epic of slavery's descendants, wrote Walcott, springs from the tribal origins of the West in its "identification with Hebraic suffering, the migration, the hope of deliverance from bondage"—but with this difference, that "the passage over our Red Sea was not from bondage to freedom but its opposite, so that the tribes arrived at their New Canaan chained," estranged from their past and their gods, and left "wailing by strange waters for a lost home." Their Zion, in short, was Babylon, a characterization made prominent by the Black Panthers and the Nation of Islam, among others, in the postwar decades. This much in Walcott's formulation is commonplace, but not so his regret that the epic poet, finding no grand ruins among West Indian islands on which to base his craft, must celebrate instead "the rusted slave wheel of the sugar factory, cannon, and chains, the crusted amphora of cutthroats, all the paraphernalia of degradation and cruelty which we exhibit as history, not as masochism," as if the Jews and the Japanese were asked to make Auschwitz and Hiroshima into "temples of the race."[33]

Walcott's frequent return to the Holocaust as a point of departure for understanding slavery does not lead him, any more than it does Marshall, to claim an
exact equivalence. Rather, his claim is that analogical thought, pursued with
nuance and care, is a spur to the moral imagination. In "North and South"
(1981), for example, Walcott, "like any child of the Diaspora," reflects on the
common heritage of Jews and blacks by situating the memorialization of slavery within the superannuating metaphors of the Holocaust:

> Under the blue sky of winter in Virginia
> the brick chimneys flute white smoke through skeletal lindens,
> as a spaniel churns up a pyre of blood-rusted leaves;
> there is no memorial here to their Treblinka—
> as a van delivers from the ovens loaves
> as warm as flesh, its brakes jaggedly screech
> like the square wheel of a swastika. The mania
> of history veils even the clearest air,
> the sickly sweet taste of ash, of something burning.[34]

That the plantations of Virginia were no death camps, that the practitioners of
slavery did not set out to exterminate a people, does not erode the haunting effect of Walcott's interlaced metaphors. Precisely because there are yet no fitting
memorials to the "Treblinkas" of slavery, the lens of the Holocaust presents itself insistently as one way of knowing, one way of remembering.

It is thus appropriate that Marshall's point of entry into the strange temporality of Bournehills, "where one felt that other time existing intact, still alive,"
is Saul Amron, the flawed representative of Western ideology but also the damaged representative of an ancient people whose twentieth-century cataclysm
provides a frame of reference for knowing the equal cataclysm of slavery. As he
goes about initiating his research, more and more drawn into the mysteries of
Bourne Island and imbibing the grinding oppression of the sugar factory and
labor in the cane fields, where the workers gaze back with the look of people
asleep or dead, Saul feels like a "voyeur looking on from the immunity of his
peephole at another's debasement." But his own legacy of persecution disrupts
that immunity and produces an epiphanic "vertigo." As if "hurled, blinded,
back into his past, into those memories that served as his reference to the
world," Saul remembers his Sephardic mother, a rarity among the Ashkenazim
of New York, as she retells the story of his family's centuries-long exile and migration, in the aftermath of the Inquisition, through Latin America and the Caribbean until they found a home in New York.[35]

Marshall gives us few specifics about Saul's history, but his family trajectory of persecution, forced exile, and wandering in alien lands parallels that of Merle's African ancestors. The family story told by Saul's mother would date from the fourteenth- and fifteenth-century campaigns of anti-Semitism on the Iberian peninsula, when Jews, according to the doctrine of *limpieza de sangre* ("purity" or "cleanliness of blood"), were excluded from public life, deprived of economic and social rights, and subjected to pogroms and forced conversions. What originated as a religious or social exclusion came to have a more determined racial meaning first in the Spanish encounter with the Moors and then again in the encounter with blacks and Indians in the Americas, where the anti-Semitic purges of the Inquisition were intermittently revived.[36] The fifteenth-century campaigns culminated in the Edict of Expulsion, which drove more than 200,000 Sephardic Jews from Spain in 1492, followed by a further expulsion from Portugal four years later. The only Jews remaining were converted "New Christians" or "Marranos" ("swine," "pigs"), as those suspected of being clandestine Jews came derogatorily to be called, although the converted were likewise subject to continued persecution by the Inquisition in its effort to root out secret Judaizers.[37] The Sephardic exiles settled in other parts of Europe, notably Holland, and some, like Saul's ancestors, came eventually to the New World. In particular, the Dutch West Indies, as well as Barbados and Jamaica, both then British colonies, became central areas of Jewish life from 1650 through 1810 and later on points of departure for the settlement of Jews in the North American colonies.*

---

* The Inquisition continued to persecute Marranos in Latin America, and autos-da-fé were common up until the late seventeenth century, especially in Mexico, Brazil, and Peru. When the Dutch conquered territories in Brazil, Marranos living there could return openly to Judaism; but when the Portuguese reconquered Recife in the 1650s, most Marranos fled to various Caribbean islands, including Curaçao, Martinique, and Barbados. Jews in Barbados were subject to a special tax and excluded from political rights, landholding, and certain economic activities, but their population grew over the seventeenth and eighteenth centuries, and they encountered less anti-Semitism than in surrounding countries. Not incidentally, those who settled in Curaçao in the mid-seventeenth century arrived at about the same time as African slaves and joined them in creating the national language of Papamiento, a combination of Portuguese, Dutch, English, and African tribal languages. Because some of them traded in slaves, as well as other commodities, it is significant, as David Brion Davis writes, that Jews thus "found the threshold of liberation in a region dependent upon black slavery." See Seymour B. Liebman, *New World Jewry, 1493–1825: Requiem for the Forgotten* (New York: KTAV Publishing, 1982), pp. 169–91; Cecil Roth, *A History of the Marranos* (1932), rev. ed. (Philadelphia: Jewish Publication Society of America, 1947), p. 290; David Brion Davis, "Jews in the Slave Trade," in Jack Salzman and Cornel West, eds., *Struggles in the Promised Land: Toward a History of Black-Jewish Relations in the United States* (New York: Oxford University Press, 1997), p. 70.

Scholars have speculated about a further entanglement between the expulsion of the Jews and the European conquest and settlement of the New World in the possibility that Columbus himself, even though he congratulated his benefactors Ferdinand and Isabella on their military defeat of the Moors and the edict against the Jews, might have been a New Christian and that his voyage may have been largely a Jewish enterprise, owing to financing and participation among the crew by Marranos.[38] Such fragments of historical knowledge, coupled with the fact that there were, indeed, some Jewish slave traders and some Jewish planters in both Latin American and North American colonies, would lead by the late twentieth century to the sulfurous charges on the part of the Nation of Islam and others that Jews controlled the slave trade and were therefore responsible for the misery and exploitation of Africans in the Americas. Marshall presents no argument about Columbus and no such absurd conspiracy theories. For her, rather, the entanglement of Inquisition and Middle Passage, Jewish exile and African slavery, leads not to scapegoating but to kinship—but kinship in which empathy and conflict have equal shares.

Although the young Saul ceased to be impressed by his mother's tale of their ancestors' "ancient flight, privation and wandering," and even doubted the veracity of her unproven claim that there were "tombstones bearing the family name on the island of Jamaica," it came nevertheless to stand "in his child's mind for the entire two-thousand year history of exile and trial, including the Nazi horror which was still to come when he was a boy." His vertiginous insight also puts him in mind of an observant old man from his childhood who "turned every day into Yom Kippur," atoning not just for his own sins but also for those of the world. Set alongside the epochal reach of slavery's empire, Saul's "double memory" of exile and atonement provides a racial consciousness through which he intuitively understands why the Cane Vale sugar factory is like the "deep hold of a ship" and the workers "disembodied forms: ghosts they might have been from some long sea voyage taken centuries ago."[39] Or, as Marshall said in commenting on her novel: "They might have been the rebel slaves who refused to die. They might have been the original Africans who survived the crossing."[40] In his access to the diasporic mysticism of Bournehills, Saul is meant to provide a measure of cross-cultural sympathy, and possibly a measure of atonement as well, for the ghosts of the plantation who live on in the labor of the twentieth century.

In telling the story of the black Atlantic diaspora from the Columbian voyages to the neocolonial present, Marshall also means to interrogate the founding typology of Saul's and Harriet's nation, the United States, in which the providential mission to settle a New Israel, the sign of God's covenant, was corrupted by slavery. In their own new reading of Exodus, white proponents of African American civil rights attempted to atone for the sins of the past by creating a redemptive counter-typology of deliverance at long last realized as national policy. "It is the glorious opportunity of this generation to end the one huge wrong of the American Nation and, in so doing, to find America for ourselves, with the same immense thrill of discovery which gripped those who first began to realize that here, at last, was a home for freedom," said President Lyndon Johnson in his Howard University address of 1965, a cornerstone, as we have seen, of subsequent governmental policy on racial equality.[41]

Although Marshall does not contradict Johnson's vision, her displacement of the novel's action to the Caribbean suggests not only that the economic stratification of the United States was inseparable from the history of slavery and colonial rule throughout the Americas, but also that the polarizing "one-drop" rule of Jim Crow stood in contrast to the more fluid racial culture of the Caribbean. She wrote at a time when, in counterpoint to Johnson's vision, the alternative redeemer nation envisioned by Black Power, whether in the quest for a symbolic motherland in Africa, support for Third World anticolonial revolution, or more generally in the embrace of black vernacular culture, made nationalist consciousness an axiomatic response to segregation for many African Americans. The end of their exile entailed believing that the resources of liberation were ready at hand and that they came from blackness itself, a belief hard to reconcile with the color-blind strategies being pursued by the civil rights establishment and the slow, painful pace of desegregation.

Even as Johnson spoke of the new redeemer nation, riots and racial violence tore through America's cities. For a number of blacks who came of age during the upheavals of the 1960s, it seemed that armed insurrection might be necessary to counter America's history of oppression and restore them to their true homeland—not in Africa but in a United States freed from domestic colonialism. Liberatory violence of the kind advocated by Fanon would make "new" black men—the discourse was, of course, stridently masculinist—with a new language and humanity, and in doing so it would forestall the homegrown genocide allegedly being prepared for African Americans by the government. Here, too, as we will see in more detail in subsequent chapters, the Jewish experience provided a point of departure. Huey Newton charged that the concentration camps that once held Japanese Americans during World War II were being "renovated and expanded" to hold blacks in anticipation of massive roundups. Only a concerted revolution among African Americans, he contended, could halt "a trend that leads inevitably to their total destruction." The poet Don L. Lee (Haki Madhubuti) envisioned World War III, the "u ass" versus the Third World, resulting in "30 million niggers in / concentration camps / (formerly called public housing)."[42]

Less implausibly, Eldridge Cleaver revisited the historical course of Zionism for lessons pertinent to the black revolution. Taking his cue from Theodor Herzl, patriarch of modern Zionism, Cleaver noted in "The Land Question and Black Liberation" (1968) that Jews on the eve of the twentieth century, like blacks at mid-century, were dispersed around the globe, subjected to murderous pogroms, confined to ghettos in Europe, and left to contemplate colonization schemes in such places as Argentina and Uganda. "Functionally," Cleaver argued, "a return to Israel seemed as impractical as obtaining a homeland for Afro-America now seems." Rather than spell out a neo-Zionist plan for storming a homeland in Africa, however, Cleaver veered off into an endorsement of the Black Panthers' call for a plebiscite in the ghettos of the United States, to be supervised by the United Nations. Forcing a black popular vote on the question of separate nationhood was an appendix, or rather an alternative, to the Panthers' pleas for reparations under the United Nations Genocide Convention. Failing the plebiscite, Cleaver called for black urban guerrillas, heirs of Nat Turner and Denmark Vesey, to break "the power of the mother country over the black colony" through violent uprising.[43]

Despite the resort to arms and bold public challenges to urban police power that were a hallmark of the Black Panthers, it was obvious, even to party leaders, that actual rebellion was doomed to swift suppression (hence the accompanying charges of imminent genocide) and the display of weapons largely an agonistic mode of street theater. One thing that Jews knew was that no homeland was possible amidst the persecution and pogroms of Europe. Insofar as Cleaver and others within Black Power typically rejected emigration to Africa, while construing white America not as a foreign power but as the metropole of the black colony, the invocation of Zionism seemed off target and the desire for independent black nationhood consequently fantastic.[44] But the Black Power equation between "colony" and "nation" was not entirely built upon a contradiction. The domestic black sovereignty that Cleaver called for might not be forthcoming—and despite the various programmatic demands of the Nation of Islam, the Republic of New Africa, and others for territorial statehood, black freedom in the United States would never resemble the independent nationhood of liberated African or Caribbean countries. But the unity of blacks as a revolutionary people, however tenuous, did not require that they establish a literal nation within a nation, much less repatriate to their own Israel, but only that they establish identity as a "people," a "nation," integral with respect to political rights but separate with respect to cultural and spiritual integrity, much as they assumed the Palestinians wished to do—and much, for that matter, as postwar American Jews, balanced on a razor's edge between absorption and ethnicity, had managed to do.

By transporting the theories of Black Power to a true colonial setting, Marshall sought to demonstrate that the slave ancestors and their heirs were the carriers of black culture and that it was their history, not some hypothesized African past, that had to be recaptured and celebrated. Along with C. L. R. James, she argued that Africans in the Caribbean derived an articulated desire for liberty not from Euro-American ideology but rather from the experience of slavery. "Liberty means something to us which is very unusual," said James, for it instantly stamped black identity. "When we made the Middle Passage and came to the Caribbean we went straight into a modern industry—the sugar plantation—and there we saw that to be a slave was the result of our being black," an experience issuing in the ever present, dominating "desire, sometimes expressed, sometimes unexpressed, but always there, the desire for liberty; the ridding oneself of the particular burden which is the special inheritance of the black skin." Passing through the furnace of slavery, observed James, made us "the most rebellious people in history."[45]

A BLACK SANCTUM LANGUAGE

"Jews already had the Torah; blacks waited for Alex Haley to write *Roots*," Taylor Branch has said of the post-1967 exfoliation of black nationalist culture.[46] Branch's comparison is inept, but it speaks to the need of black Americans to compose a narrative of "Nation Time" that was concretely historical yet derived from the most profound resources of soul—the transcendent pain of the spirituals reborn in the activist language of Black Power.

Rabbi Alan W. Miller identified the essence of such nationalism when he predicted that black cultural heroes and political leaders would be canonized in black civil religion the way Abraham, Jacob, and Herzl are in Jewish tradition, or Washington, Jefferson, and Lincoln in American. Just as African Americans hunger for a homeland and for their own *aliyah* even if they choose not to return, said Miller, the need for "a black sanctum language" is just as powerful and rational as "the need of Jews for modern Hebrew."[47] (Pierre Vidal-Naquet turned the lesson around in a 1970 essay on the rationale for Palestinian nationalism, in which he observed that Zionism, as an affirmation of the need for

"Jewish power" in the world, was psychologically comparable to the demand for Black Power. Those who mock the idea of restoring Hebrew as Israel's national language, he added, "ought to ask themselves why Swahili is being taught in New York City.")[48] Miller reached easily across the political chasm developing between blacks and Jews because he instinctively understood that the cultural transformation produced by Black Power was in key ways akin to the spirit of Zionism. By embedding their borrowings from the Judeo-Christian tradition within an Africanist context—as in Black Theology, which created a typology of descent from Moses and the Hebrew prophets to a black messianic Jesus Christ, or in the racial inversions of the Nation of Islam, a kind of Torah turned upside down—African Americans made the slave masters' foundational texts and sacred language the vehicle of anticolonial liberation and nationalist collectivity.

"What I needed," Marshall once wrote in recalling the liabilities of her education, "what all the kids—West Indian and native black American alike—with whom I grew up needed, was an equivalent of the Jewish *shul*," a place to go after school "to read works by those like ourselves and learn about our history."[49] In place of *shul*, Marshall had her mother's kitchen, and the legend of Cuffee Ned is in part a tribute to the stories Marshall heard as a young girl around the kitchen table from her mother and the other women employed as domestics, principally for the Jewish housewives of Brooklyn. "The auction block was still very real for them," said Marshall, and they used the "whiplash of their tongues" in therapeutic rap sessions to perform a "kind of magic rite, a form of juju" that would "exorcise the day's humiliations and restore them to themselves" as they told stories of family and nation. Whether recounting homeland tales of *obeah* (conjure, mojo, juju), their sometimes fractious interactions with American blacks (who called the West Indians "Black Jews"), or the daily grind of "scrubbing the Jew floor," the women transformed English, the master's language, into their own idiom, reinvigorating a "tradition as ancient as Africa, [a] centuries old oral mode by which the culture and history, the wisdom of the race had been transmitted."[50]

The colloquial idiom of the black women employed in New York's early-twentieth-century "slave markets," where black women congregated on street corners awaiting the offer of day work as domestics, frequently in Jewish households, described labor, said Claude Brown, not far removed from plantations of the South: "Before the soreness of the cotton fields had left Mama's back, her knees were getting sore from scrubbing 'Goldberg's' floor." Harlem agitators of the 1930s made the Bronx Slave Markets "Exhibit A of Jewish exploitation," said Roi Ottley.[51] But it would be erroneous to conclude that "scrubbing the Jew floor," at least in Marshall's usage, was expressly anti-Semitic. Jews appear peripherally in *Brown Girl, Brownstones* as ambivalent models of material or cultural aspiration for the immigrant West Indians.* Coupled with her composition of a biracial diasporic narrative in *The Chosen Place, the Timeless People,* moreover, Marshall's longing for a black version of the Jewish *shul* resonates with her admiration for the power of Jewish educational and memorial tradition—specifically, its sustaining a coherent way of life, a civilization, in the face of persecution and genocide. Entwining the immigrant histories of Jews and blacks was a way to identify the African American nationhood created by storytelling and the cultivation of a sacred memorial language.

As much as her mother's actual stories, Marshall recalled something more visceral and abstract that entered her as if through her blood—the "mysterious elements . . . resonating behind the words," a quality that derived from "the emotional core deep at the center of Black life, and which perhaps has its source in our archetypal African memory."[52] The black language of West Indian Brooklyn was ancestral not just because it was her mother's language but because her mother's language drew, in whatever fragmentary ways, on the primordial black resources carried through slavery into the Caribbean "meta-archipelago" that reached from the Amazon through the Mississippi delta and on to New York City.[53] "Nigger feeling," Marshall called it, quoting from a poem by Amiri Baraka about his own mother titled "Leroy," which would later supply the epigraph for Marshall's *Praisesong for the Widow:* "there were black angels / straining above her head, carrying life from the ancestors, / and knowledge, and the strong nigger feeling." Designating the *obeah* of her mother's stories a transhistorical, mystical force that called forth "those qualities which Black people possess no matter where you find them in the hemisphere—and which to my mind make us one people," Marshall set herself within the ideology of

---

* The tentative cross-racial intimacy that might evolve between employer and employed, or between neighbors, is also apparent in Hilton Als's 1996 memoir, *The Women.* Narrating the story of his transformation into a "Negress," a feminized and desirous black homosexual, Als recalls his mother telling him about working as a young Barbadian immigrant in the daily domestic "slave trade" for Jewish matrons—"'We called ourselves Daily Woikers,' my mother said, in a Yiddish-American accent, laughing"—and taking him shopping on Delancey Street, where she is comfortable with "the Jews." But Als felt an even stronger affinity because of his affection for an elderly Jewish couple, the Schwartzes, who lived in the apartment above them: "I marveled at the orderliness of Mr. and Mrs. Schwartz's home, the strange smells, the candles that burned on Friday nights. . . . I loved them. I wanted to be a Jew." Hilton Als, *The Women* (New York: Farrar, Straus, Giroux, 1996), pp. 23–24. Upon learning that Als wants to be "a *writer*," Mrs. Schwartz gives him a typewriter that had belonged to her son, "the *Doctor.*"

négritude proposed by Fanon. The emotional antithesis of colonial culture, said Fanon, *négritude* spread outward from its African origin, defining a diaspora consciousness while drawing "scattered Ethiopia" (to recall Garvey's phrase) back to the motherland: "The poets of negritude will not stop at the limits of the [African] continent. From America, black voices will take up the hymn with fuller unison."[54]

The surge of black historiography and literature in the 1960s and 1970s, of which Marshall's epic novel is a significant part, testifies to the precious heritage that lives outside of books, as in the oral history of Nat Turner passed down in folklore and song. The polemics of the Black Arts movement, for all their rhetoric of Marxist revolution, were suffused as well with the effort to locate a poetics capable of capturing the voices of ancestors and through them discovering a symbolic route to mother Africa. Thus, Larry Neal set down the schematic outline of a future essay whose elliptical annotations amounted to a chronology of modern black consciousness: "RACE MEMORY (Africa, Middle Passage); MIDDLE PASSAGE (Diaspora); TRANSMUTATION AND SYNTHESIS; BLUES GOD/TONE AS MEANING AND MEMORY; BLACK ARTS MOVEMENT/BLACK ARTS AESTHETIC." Each category would be filled out with explorations of African religious and cultural forms as they were transfigured over time into the syncretism of an African American neo-mythology demonstrating the survival of African cultural practices in the New World. The category of RACE MEMORY, for example, is annotated in a way relevant to Marshall's *Praisesong for the Widow*: "Rhythm as an expression of race memory . . . creative force as vector of existence. Swinging." The category of MIDDLE PASSAGE combines the historical exile of slavery with its contemporary neocolonial manifestations: "terror, landlessness, claustrophobia: 'America as prison . . .' Malcolm X."[55]

Whereas the task of American Jewish writers in the post-Holocaust world, said Arthur Cohen, was to re-devise "the narrative condition of the people of Israel and the Jewish people,"[56] the task of black writers coming to terms with their own catastrophic past was to enter into Nation Time, to place themselves within a continuum through which blacks might determine their own fate and write their own history. Because black American writers seeking a "sanctum language" and striving to identify the heroes of a black nation-state had few ready-made epochal events to dramatize, the rediscovery of an African American past and the acquisition of a commemorative language was all the more painstaking. Knowing the black past, "carrying life from the ancestors" to the present generations, would have to overcome the antipathy of traditional scholarship and seeming perversions such as William Styron's rendering of Nat Turner. And it would have to acknowledge, as Edward Glissant has argued, the difference between a people transplanted by a history of exile and a people transplanted by the slave trade. The one continued to survive with the core of its culture functionally intact; the other, through the "metamorphosis" of creolization, became another people.*

In their flight from Egypt, as reconstructed in a long tradition of exegesis and commentary, and throughout subsequent centuries of exile, Jews retained their Judaic identity, even as they fit it to disparate social, political, and linguistic circumstances. Study of the Torah and the Talmud, deeply ingrained with traditions of ritual observance and storytelling, bound Jews together across great reaches of time and geography. In the Atlantic world of slavery, Africans of many tribal origins found themselves thrust into a Babel of languages and cultures, only some fragments of which survived as intact communal property after a few generations. Post-emancipation blacks, not to mention their modern-day descendants, had comparatively few ways to revert to a lost African culture, much as they might despise the suffocating colonial culture in which they were immersed, whether in the United States or the Caribbean. Within the creole culture of the Americas, however, blacks found their own sanctum language and created their own chronicle of resistance to the duress of slavery. At times illegible, always subject to distortion, it was a story, of necessity, in which vernacular traditions had as much credibility as written records. Marshall's story of the slave rebel Cuffee Ned, a figure of Mosaic liberation, is arguably the best illustration of this in all of American literature.

A NATION APART

In [Toussaint L'Ouverture], born a slave and a leader of slaves, the concrete realization of liberty, equality, and fraternity was the womb of ideas and the springs of power, which overflowed their narrow environment and embraced the whole of the world. But for the revolution, this extraordinary man and his band of gifted associates would have lived their lives as slaves, serving the commonplace creatures who owned them, standing barefooted

---

* Glissant suggests, however, that the existence of Israel, by making return to the homeland at once possible and unnecessary, "may ultimately *dry up* Judaism, by exhausting progressively the impulse towards return (the demand for true origins)." Edouard Glissant, "Reversion and Diversion," in *Caribbean Discourse: Selected Essays*, trans. J. Michael Dash (Charlottesville: University Press of Virginia, 1989), pp. 14–18.

and in rags to watch inflated little governors and mediocre officials from
Europe pass by, as many a talented African stands in Africa today.
 —C. L. R. James, The Black Jacobins

Bourne Island is mythical, but in size and geography it resembles Barbados, the easternmost island of the Lesser Antilles, which was colonized by the British in 1627.[57] The first of the islands to produce sugar on a large scale, Barbados was in the mid-seventeenth century England's most populous and wealthiest colony, where the planter class first took shape in the Americas. Coincident with the upsurge and consolidation of sugar production, the ratio of slaves to white landowners in Barbados went from three whites for every slave in 1645 to eighteen slaves for every white by 1667. At the end of the century it had a slave population of more than fifty thousand, whereas the British and French colonies of North America, taken together, had fewer than thirty thousand. Nevertheless, Barbados did not experience any truly successful slave revolt, most likely because it was too small and lacked an interior that would sustain a maroon colony and guerrilla warfare. A 1675 insurrection that intended to install an aged Coromantee named Cuffee as king was put down after betrayal from within. Tried by a court-martial, thirty-five slaves were executed, including six burned alive and eleven beheaded and dragged through the streets as a warning. Several other insurrections in Barbados likewise failed, but one in 1816—prompted by a free mulatto aptly named Washington Franklin, who circulated news of Toussaint L'Ouverture's revolution in Saint-Domingue (Haiti)—led to a significant uprising crushed only at great loss of life among the slaves.

Where there were large-scale revolts, as in Jamaica, Saint-Domingue, the Guyanas, and Cuba, slaves not only had strength of numbers but also tended to be concentrated in proximate plantations, though even on a smaller scale the Caribbean experienced much more frequent slave uprisings than did North America.* By the mid-eighteenth century, Jamaica, where in 1670 the slave

---

* Although it plays no direct part in Marshall's novel, one might note the position of Jews in some of the Caribbean colonies where slave revolts took place. Maroons were restricted to trading with those on the periphery of slaveholding society, including Jews, and there is some evidence that, in addition to stealing arms and powder from plantations, rebels were able to purchase powder from some whites, in particular from Jews. In one of a number of allied Jamaican conspiracies, a woman slave named Cubah belonging to a Jewish woman was elevated to the rank of queen of Kingston (based on an Ashanti practice), an event that promoted special distrust of Jews on the part of Christian slaveholders. In the perhaps apocryphal conversation between a captured slave rebel and a Jewish militiaman reported by Edward Long, the potential alliance between blacks and Jews that would be repeated in later centuries was visible. According to Long's account, the slave proposed creation of a decolonized Jamaica ruled by

population already surpassed that of the masters, had replaced Barbados as
the largest sugar producer, just as Saint-Domingue had replaced Martinique
among French colonies. Jamaica's slave rebellions climaxed in the Christmas
rising of 1831, in which hundreds of sugar estates and properties were burned
and some five hundred slaves killed or executed. Like the Haitian revolution
and the suppressed insurrections led by Gabriel Prosser, Denmark Vesey, and
Nat Turner in the United States, the Jamaican revolt of 1831 took inspiration
from the democratic ideology of the French and American revolutions, as well
as related debates over abolition.

Bearing a name common among Akan-speaking people of Ghana, the
Cuffee Ned of Marshall's novel refers not to any particular slave rebel, such as
the Barbadian would-be king, but, by implication, to a number of them.* The
ideology of Marshall's hero is revealed only in its contemporary echoes. As in
the case of other slave rebels, however, it was surely a simple matter of freedom
and autonomy. Indeed, the ultimate failure of Cuffee Ned's rebellion does not
negate its expression of the longing for liberty and the capacity for rebellion,

---

blacks, with Jews as the trading middlemen: "You Jews . . . and our nation (meaning the Coromantins),
ought to consider ourselves as one people. You differ from the rest of the Whites, and they hate you.
Surely then it is best for us to join in one common interest, drive them out of the country, and hold possession of it to ourselves." Michael Craton, *Testing the Chains: Resistance to Slavery in the British West Indies* (Ithaca, N.Y.: Cornell University Press, 1982), p. 65; Mavis B. Campbell, *The Maroons of Jamaica,
1655–1796: A History of Resistance, Collaboration, and Betrayal* (Granby, Mass.: Bergin and Garvey, 1988),
p. 73; Edward Long, *The History of Jamaica* (1774), quoted in Craton, *Testing the Chains*, pp. 132–33.

* Its somewhat less repressive slave codes and favorable terrain made Jamaica subject to revolts and
guerrilla warfare throughout its slaveholding history, including a year-long rebellion in 1685–86 that assumed the form of a maroon state surviving for nine months under the leadership of a different Cuffee.
Still another Cuffee, a stern disciplinarian, appeared among the maroon rebels who carried out continuing resistance to Jamaican slavery in the 1720s. The territory of Berbice, within Guyana, witnessed numerous uprisings in the mid-eighteenth century, including a massive revolt involving half the colony's
slaves in 1763–64 led by one more Cuffee, whose aims appear to have anticipated Toussaint's dream of
an autonomous black empire and whose followers controlled the colony for more than a year. This
Cuffee negotiated with the Dutch governor as an equal and at first demanded cession of the entire colony; faced with dissent among the rebels and the arrival of Dutch reinforcements, Cuffee then proposed
division of the colony into an independent black federation of different African ethnic groups, on the
one hand, and a slave plantation colony ruled by whites, on the other. When a rival Coromantee rebel
pressed for all-out war, the rebellion fell apart, with Cuffee committing suicide and other leaders capitu-
lating to planter military force. Orlando Patterson, "Slavery and Slave Revolts: A Sociohistorical Analysis of the First Maroon War, 1665–1740," in Richard Price, ed., *Maroon Societies: Rebel Slave Communities
in the Americas* (1973; rpt. Baltimore: Johns Hopkins University Press, 1979), pp. 256–57, 261; Eugene
Genovese, *From Rebellion to Revolution: Afro-American Slave Revolts in the Making of the New World*
(1979; rpt. New York: Vintage, 1981), p. 34; Craton, *Testing the Chains*, pp. 270–72.

any more than in the case of the millenarian insurgency of Nat Turner, and it is precisely his success in founding an independent colony, if only for a period of years, that defines his mythic power and makes the novel alive with messianic anticipation.

Within the history of slaveholding, maroon states stood as living proof of the aspiration to "nationhood," at least in provisional form, and *marronage*—the creation and sustenance of maroon political and social life—struck at the foundations of the plantation system, undermining the mythology of the docile, incapable slave through a demonstration of skills in guerrilla warfare and the beginnings of military organization and governance. By the 1730s, for example, Jamaican maroons numbered in the thousands, some of them inspired by an African *obeah* woman named Nanny, of whom legend said she could catch cannonballs in her buttocks and fart them back at her enemies.[58] Marshall's Cuffee Ned, renowned as a rebel leader and as a maroon statesman, does not rise to the level of the Guyanan Cuffee, let alone Toussaint, but he clearly surpasses the best known of American slave rebels in the apparent scope, coherence, and longevity of the revolt he led. In the end, however, what matters most is that Cuffee Ned symbolizes the treasures of freedom, physical and spiritual, and assumes immortal, iconographic status in the ritual life of Bournehills.

In "Caliban Orders History" (1960), the Barbadian writer George Lamming remarked that C. L. R. James's epic account of Toussaint L'Ouverture and the Haitian revolution, *The Black Jacobins* (1938), should be "Bible-reading" for every young person, for James shows us "Caliban as Prospero had never known him: a slave who was a great soldier in battle, an incomparable administrator in public affairs; full of paradox but never without compassion, a humane leader of men."[59] The responsibility of Afro-Caribbean people to celebrate the life of Toussaint is one model for Merle's teaching about Cuffee Ned, her Caliban, as well as Marshall's literary treatment of his ritual celebration during Carnival. Both masque and novel, though fictive, are rejoinders to the colonialist history that suppresses knowledge of such black leaders just as their rebellions were once suppressed. The history of the West Indies puts Merle in mind of Stephen Dedalus's famous dictum in *Portrait of the Artist as a Young Man*: "History is a nightmare from which I am trying to awaken." In this detail, too, Marshall echoed Lamming, who chose Joyce's aphorism as the epigraph for his study of the conditions of authorship for the West Indian writer, *The Pleasures of Exile* (1960).[60] (The passage would appear yet again as the epigraph for Derek Walcott's "Muse of History.")

But whereas Lamming judged the Caribbean's proximity to America to be an

advantage—"the America that started in the womb of promise, the America
that started as an alternative to the old and privileged Prospero"[61]—for Marshall the nightmare of history persisted in the legacy of slavery that contra-
dicted, at every turn, the promise of America. Although Lamming's artistic exile in England resembles Merle's sojourn in London, Marshall, writing of the
Caribbean from the vantage point of her residence in the United States, more
resembles Joyce when he stood outside Irish tradition, first in order to portray
the artist, Stephen Dedalus, as an embodiment of exilic consciousness, and
next to follow Leopold Bloom, a Jew wandering among a people, the Irish, who
also sometimes saw themselves as children of Israel enslaved by English pharaohs.[62] In Marshall's interpretation of *The Tempest*, Prospero's magic—his
technology, his wealth, even the beneficence of his political liberalism, all of
them reworked in the characters of Saul and Harriet—is an instrument of exploitation only more sophisticated in its neocolonial form than in its initial
manifestation in slavery and the slave trade. Bournehills, meanwhile, longs for
the second coming of its Caliban, Cuffee Ned.

Because she was writing at the mid-century flood tide of new renderings of
slavery in the Atlantic world, Marshall's characterization of her maroon hero
joined contemporary debates, in historiography and fiction alike, about the
character of slave societies, including slave revolts and their frequency. In addition to arguments about the role of slavery in the economic development of the
Atlantic world and the character of slave rebellions, scholarship in the wake of
Kenneth Stampp and Stanley Elkins—each of whom significantly redirected
the field, Stampp by paying close attention to slave culture and Elkins by adducing a complex, if misguided, psychological substratum in slaveholding and
slave consciousness—recovered the coherent ideational foundations of black
American culture, including their fragmentary African origins, and consequently redefined black slavery as an event formative of modern American culture. John Blassingame, Vincent Harding, Eugene Genovese, Lawrence Levine,
and Sterling Stuckey were among the historians whose re-creation of slave culture extended Stampp's findings and rebutted Elkins's contentions that African
culture had not survived transplantation to the New World and that American
slaves were marked by docility and degradation rather than dignity and a propensity for resistance.[63]

Marshall's choice to depict the legacy of a slave rebellion in the Caribbean
rather than the United States might conceivably be read as confirmation of
the thesis that Latin American slavery was more conducive to rebellion. More
certainly, however, her novel stands within the body of writing that scorned
Elkins's "Sambo" theory and what was widely taken to be its exemplary literary

realization, *The Confessions of Nat Turner* (1967). The controversy surrounding Styron's novel, with white and black scholars trading blows in reviews and commentary, was a symptom of the cultural struggle for control of "blackness," evident in the fact that Styron was frequently lacerated for having appropriated a tradition that he knew nothing about—by which was meant a tradition he *could* know nothing about because he was white.* "You've Taken My Nat and Gone" was the title of Vincent Harding's contribution to *Ten Black Writers Respond*, the well-known anthology of rebuttals. Only when blacks themselves have told their story can it be shared by whites, said Harding: "There can be no common history until we have first fleshed out the lineaments of our own, for no one else can speak out of the bittersweet bowels of our blackness."[64]

Whereas Styron mostly ignored the vernacular tradition that kept Nat Turner's story alive among African Americans, Marshall placed the vernacular tradition, in the form of the Carnival masque and the ornate legends of Cuffee Ned, at the center of her narrative. Although *The Chosen Place, the Timeless People* is not a literal reply to Styron—it was published less than a year later than his novel—Marshall's portrayal of Cuffee Ned clearly constitutes a rejection of Elkins's view that Turner was unusual in his precocious literacy and his capacity to conceive a rebellion, a view if not embraced, at least dramatized by Styron. Preserved in vernacular tradition until it is called upon to shape the world of written art, as Marshall might say, the transcript of racial memory is a mode of *marronage* whereby a communal culture, by cultivating the arts of liberation as though in guerrilla warfare, is drawn together, on the basis of race, into a nationalist formation.[65] By setting her novel in the Caribbean, Marshall anchored the freedom struggle of twentieth-century black people in a culture whose Africanist dimension remained palpable and therefore took from syncretic vernacular traditions the "bittersweet" lineaments of their own history.

If Merle's teaching about Cuffee Ned, like C. L. R. James's biography of Toussaint, and like Marshall's novel itself, creates the prototype of a nationalist

---

* Whatever other errors he made, it was not contradictory for Styron to preserve the core of the historical record that portrayed Turner as a religious "lunatic" and to link it to revolutionary ardor. Turner's published 1831 "confession," an enigmatic but purposeful jeremiad whose scriptural properties extended his "meat-ripping holocaust" (to borrow Larry Neal's acute phrase) into the future, transcended Thomas Gray's attempt to contain it within a legalistic framework and put the ethos of democratic revolution on a religious plane that was not at odds with slave culture but rather one of its signal expressions. Larry Neal, "Fragments from the Narrative of the Black Magicians," in *Hoodoo Hollerin' Bebop Ghosts* (1968; rpt. Washington, D.C.: Howard University Press, 1974), p. 35; Eric J. Sundquist, *To Wake the Nations: Race in the Making of American Literature* (Cambridge, Mass.: Harvard University Press, 1992), pp. 36–83.

hero, it also does something more: it records and stabilizes the *memory* of a national hero, canonizing him through ritual remembrance like the heroes of Jewish or American tradition. To become fully meaningful, the history of a Cuffee Ned—or a Toussaint or a Nat Turner—must not only be accurately entered into the archive of world events and written into history books but must also be made the subject of commemoration. The people's colloquial debate about Cuffee Ned and prophecy of his return goes on throughout the year. Beginning with Carnival and continuing through Lent, however, Bournehills engages in ritual veneration of Cuffee and the world that produced him. It is within this highly stylized context that Marshall's dramatized relationship between Merle and Saul reaches its climax, and the entanglement between black and Jewish histories becomes at once intimate and dangerous.

Amidst the gaudy, commodified displays of the other parade bands participating in Carnival, the Pyre Hill crew, devoted to recreating Cuffee's revolt and its legacy, must rescue and preserve the core meaning of black ancestral identity. In contrast to the colorful attire of the other crews—a motley assortment of themes such as Cleopatra's Egypt, the Garden of Eden, Hiroshima, Life on the Moon, and the Fall of the Roman Empire—those enacting the Pyre Hill Revolt dress in identical costumes, somber blue-and-white-striped cotton garments common at the time of the rebellion. As unchanged as their costumes is the action of the masque, every year accompanied by the drumming of a steel band and the shuffling two-step of the marchers:

> It was an awesome sound—the measured tread of those countless feet in the dust and the loud report of the bracelets, a sombre counterpoint to the gay carnival celebration. It conjured up in the bright afternoon sunshine dark alien images of legions marching bound together over a vast tract, iron fitted into dank stone walls, chains—like those to an anchor—rattling in the deep holds of ships, and exile in an inhospitable land—an exile bitter and irreversible in which all memory of the former life and of the self as it had once been had been destroyed.
>
> . . . It didn't appear that [the marchers] would ever again be able to lift their heads or bring their bowed backs into line. The bones that served as the props to their spirit might have been broken. . . . It was almost as if—perhaps because they had performed the masque for so many years—they had actually become those they were depicting, or had been them all along, so that every detail of that long march and stern exile (all the horror of it) was still with them.

The ghostly spell of slavery that hangs over the march is broken once the revolt is reenacted—Cuffee Ned cutting the throat of Percy Bryam, Pyre Hill
set ablaze, the battle for freedom joined. The highlight of the performance,
though, is the narration in song and dance of maroon life, an idealized com-
munitarian moment when the rebel slaves had lived as "a nation apart," when
they had been a people!" As the pageant is repeated over the length of the parade route, eventually the theatrical elements fall away, and all that remains is
the "soaring tribute in song and dance to Cuffee, his victory on the hill and life
in Bournehills during his reign."[66]

Like other such mock rebellions staged during Carnival throughout the New
World, the reenactment of Cuffee Ned's revolt provides a representation of
utopia, the image of a future state in which the rights of a people are achieved
and in which a collectivity momentarily coalesces, expressing what cannot otherwise be said and articulating a future otherwise not visible.[67] The people's
two-step shuffle here looks forward to Marshall's *Praisesong for the Widow,*
where Avey is swept up in the Carricou Tramp. A "shuffle designed to stay the
course of history," the ritual of the Carricou Tramp collects the "burnt-out
ends" of African culture—"a few names of what they called nations . . . the
fragments of a dozen or so songs, the shadowy forms of long-ago dances"—
and forges them into a reenactment of the tribulation of the Middle Passage.
Purged of the accreted filth of Western culture and carried by the wail of the
drumming, "like the distillation of a thousand sorrow songs," Avey crosses
over, passing backward into mystical union with the ancestors, "the bruised
still-bleeding innermost chamber of the collective heart."[68] The performance of
Cuffee Ned's revolt likewise carries the celebrants back into mystical union
with the ancestors, as though they "had actually become those they were depicting, or had been them all along." The slave masque is equivalent to living
marronage, both an action of memorialization and, as such, a template for resistance to neocolonialism. In the masque's cycle of repetition, the timeless
people of Bournehills are fused with Cuffee's rebels, each revival of the events
predicting, by performing, the return of the sacred, messianic moment.

As the Pyre Hill crew traverses the parade route, the crowd of spectators
along the way, composed of all Bourne Island's classes, is itself caught up in
Cuffee Ned's celebration. They forget their aversion to the ragtag Bournehills
people and their repetitious saga, and marchers from other bands as well as onlookers are drawn into the frenzy. Among them is Harriet Shippen, who, in attempting to get away from the "riotous song and dance celebrating Cuffee," is
engulfed by the mob. Driven along the street at the mercy of the ecstatic revel-
ers, as though trapped in a "swarm of flies," Harriet is battered and bruised,

seized "by a revulsion and rage that was almost sexual in its force," as she feels herself disappearing into what Marshall depicts as a maelstrom of Third World revolutionary energy, brought face to face with a primordial terror of cultural, racial negation: "In her slowly drowning mind there appeared to be no end of them. She would never have believed there were so many—all with the same young, set black faces and farseeing eyes—on the island, in the world."[69]

Harriet's climactic experience of Carnival, emblematic of her alienation from the island and her doom as a character, is paralleled by the consummation of Merle's and Saul's increasingly erotic relationship. Repugnant to some black nationalist readers of the day, their affair is a bridge, a momentary bond, between traditions and peoples vociferously set against each other in so many forums of the 1960s. Yet however much it represented the most profound intimacy of blacks and Jews, their sexual union is less important than their consummation in words. Merle draws from Saul the story of Sosha's miscarriage and death—her surviving Auschwitz-Birkenau only to die in childbirth in Honduras, a pregnancy she feared would not be possible because of "certain experiments that Germans had carried out on her"[70]—and his consequent wracking guilt. In turn, Saul draws from Merle the story of her shame at having been the kept lover of a woman in London and her failed marriage to Ketu, who fled to Uganda with their daughter when he discovered that she had resumed the lesbian relationship.

Ash Wednesday dawns with Merle and Saul having completed in their sexual relationship the communion of souls as well as the catharsis of mourning that their mutual storytelling brings. In drawing their confessions of personal tragedy from each other, each of them a story of families sundered and generation forestalled, Merle and Saul also cross cultural identities. Merle identifies Saul as something of a juju man, an *obeah* man, while proclaiming that she, too, is a Jew because she is "waiting on a messiah. No Jesus meek and mild though," but another Cuffee. Marshall's pun on "Jew"/"juju" is hardly incidental. Rather, it symbolizes an exchange of power between these two displaced, marginalized persons for both of whom the horror of the "long march and stern exile" is still very much a living history. The lesson of the slave masque, Saul says to Merle, is that people "who've truly been wronged—like yours, like mine all those thousands of years—must at some point, if they mean to come into their own, start using their history to their advantage."[71]

Saul here speaks clearly for Marshall, who argued, in assessing her novelistic aims, that the oppressed cannot control their lives until they have a truthful picture of the past and "begin to use their history creatively," as Jews have been doing for thousands of years[72]—most recently by rereading the promise of scripture through their experience of a traumatic genocide. By recasting their story as one of exile, enslavement, and "holocaust," blacks, like Jews, could likewise redefine themselves, if not as a chosen people, nonetheless as one whose tragedy is recognized as formative of modern history.

Once a Great Wrong Has Been Done

Even though it represents the deep reservoir of history to which Africans in the diaspora must turn as one means of countering, if not quite reversing, their exile in the Babylon of the New World, the masque of Cuffee Ned's revolt is not the conclusion of the book's moral action. Set against the backdrop of a crisis in the sugar cane harvest when the Cane Vale factory breaks down and the people's economic survival is threatened, the action that takes place during Whitsun (Pentecost), not Lent, marks the high point of the novel's triangulation of cultural forces. When neither the factory owners nor the trade unions care enough about the plight of the peasant workers to solve the problem of the harvest, Saul helps devise a plan for laboriously hauling the cane to a distant factory, thus salvaging the people's fragile economy. The effort momentarily restores the Bournehills people to an earlier age, one closer to "that time long ago when Bournehills, under Cuffee, had been a nation and its people a proper People."[73]

The action of the harvest, however, is more important as a stage for resolving the unsustainable relationship between Saul and Merle. Distraught that Saul, the representative of technology, is powerless to fix the cane rollers, Merle frenetically lashes out at him and falls into a cataleptic state that leaves her similar to Sosha in her helplessness. On his way to visit her, Saul experiences a second moment of visionary vertigo. "Besieged by revelations and visions," Saul sees opened before him an abyss of self-understanding, "as if he had been struck down and temporarily blinded so that he might see in another, deeper, way."[74] Saul's epiphany is patently meant to recall the biblical conversion of Paul, known initially by the Hebrew name Saul, who was struck blind on the road to Damascus. An opponent of Christianity, Paul was pursuing Christianized Jews into Syria when he was engulfed by a holy aura ("suddenly there shined round about him a light from heaven") and heard the voice of Jesus calling upon him to desist in his persecutions and become a missionary of Christianity (Acts 9). Paul is representative of the spread of Jesus' gospel, a supersessionist homogeneity in faith that he took to be the fulfillment of Judaism in the universal body of Christ,* and his scripture became a central tenet of proslavery argument: "Servants, be obedient to them that are your masters" (Ephesians 6:5).

Although Marshall's Saul neither converts nor proselytizes, his vision does lead him effectively to renounce his missionary calling as a fieldworker, at least to the extent of recognizing that the people of Bournehills are bound to continue "resisting, defying all efforts, all the halfway measures, including his," to redeem them.[75] His realization leads as well to the culmination of the novel's triangulated plot. Confronted by Harriet about his affair with Merle, Saul detects that the worst part for Harriet is that Merle is black. But some could ask, he continues, "how is it that you, a Philadelphia blue-blood, could bear to have me, a long-nosed Jew, touch you." Harriet's attempt to bribe Merle to return to England fails, as does her plan to get Saul back by secretly using her influence with CASR to have him relieved of his duties. Abandoned by Saul when he discovers her treachery—"as I've heard people here say," he tells her, "you come like a stranger to me from now on"—Harriet walks into the sea and drowns herself, dragged down in punishment of the corruption for which she stands. For his part, Saul returns to the United States, planning no more fieldwork, no more "odysseys," while Merle departs for Africa—not to stay, but to see her daughter, flying the southern route from Recife, early home of Sephardic Jews in flight from the Inquisition, "where the great arm of the hemisphere reaches out toward the massive shoulder of Africa as though yearning to be joined to it as it had surely been in the beginning."[76] The triangle of characters and the triangle of ideologies—the world-historical forces of Americanism, Zionism, and Africanism, as it were—split apart without resolution, leaving only a residue of symbolic gestures indicative of the hard work still ahead if lasting change is to be brought to Bourne Island.

Surrounded in Merle's room by the paraphernalia of colonial rule—the furniture of Duncan Vaughn's estate, prints and drawings of old plantation life and the slave trade, the confused memorabilia of Merle's African heritage mixed in with that of her student days in London—Saul feels as if he has entered a museum, as though Bournehills had been chosen to be "the repository

---

* A comparable instance of Christian supersession reappears in Toni Morrison's *Beloved* (1987), whose second epigraph—following upon its more famous first epigraph, "Sixty Million and more," naming the hypothetical death toll of the black holocaust—is from Paul's epistle to the Romans: "I will call them my people, which were not my people; and her beloved, which was not my beloved" (Romans 9:25). Paul's message about conversion appears in the context of his argument that God has fulfilled his promise to the chosen people by offering them salvation through faith in Jesus Christ: "For this *is* my covenant unto them, when I shall take away their sins" (Romans 11:27). It is a point of hermeneutic ambiguity, however, whether God has chosen the elect from the beginning of time or whether election may, indeed, be freely chosen. In any case, Christian election supersedes the commandments of Hebrew law.

of the history which reached beyond it to include the hemisphere north and south."[77] Merle's catatonic state may be taken as a manifestation of the paralyzing mental disorders that Fanon diagnosed as symptomatic of colonial subjugation in *Wretched of the Earth* or that the authors of the popular book *Black Rage* found among black women in a society pervaded by stigmatizing white looks and behaviors.[78] Whatever the exact cause of Merle's debilitation, her powers as an *obeah* woman appear to have been damaged, if not destroyed.

Variously derived from the Twi word *obayi* or *obeye*, or from the Ashanti word *obayifo*, *obeah* signifies a system of beliefs grounded in the supernatural and the practice of magic, including putting on or taking off the spirits of the dead. More specifically, it was a form of witchcraft employed, among other purposes, to punish crimes and avenge injuries.[79] The association of *obeah* with slave rebellions and the insurgency of West Indian maroons—it was thought by some to provide an immunizing power to the rebels—lent the creolized religion a particularly potent meaning among the British Romantics as a reflection of their anxieties about colonial rule. The *obeah* woman (or man) correspondingly played a prominent role in the slave societies of West Indian sugar plantations as a repository of ancestral culture, a community leader, and, at times, a prophet of insurrection. By implication, then, Merle has the latent powers of such figures, either one of the historic slave rebels whose collective portrait appears in Cuffee Ned or the celebrated *obeah* woman Nanny, sister of the Jamaican maroon rebel Cudjoe, who became revered in the twentieth century as the mother of Jamaican independence,[80] renowned for her leadership in the maroon war of 1734–1739 and, as noted earlier, for the supernatural powers sometimes attributed to slave rebels.* Merle teaches Cuffee Ned's history, and she is the medium for Saul's vision of the slave past, just as her empathy for his own

---

* Nanny's spirit remains important in present-day constructions of Jamaican national consciousness. Michelle Cliff's novel *Abeng* (1983), for example, bears comparison with *The Chosen Place, the Timeless People* both for its illumination of inherited revolutionary consciousness and for its perfunctory but nonetheless intriguing use of Sephardic Jewish history and the Holocaust as comparative points of reference. *Abeng* is set in 1958, when Cliff's adolescent heroine, Clare Savage, the mixed-race descendant of both the maroon leader Nanny and a brutal planter who burned one hundred of his slaves to death rather than see them emancipated, undertakes a personal study of the Holocaust for what it will teach her about the suffering and sacrifice of Africans in the Americas. Other than her mildly interesting identification with Anne Frank and brief speculation about the kinship of black Jamaicans with Sephardic Jews (and the possible Jewishness of Columbus), however, the analogy gives way to a pat denunciation, no doubt indebted to Fanon, of a personified European "heart of darkness," whose "fantasies" of conquest infected Native Americans with smallpox, destroyed the language of the Mayans and Incas, "brought Africans in chains to the New World and worked them to death," and "killed nine million people, including six million Jews, in the death camps of Europe." Michelle Cliff, *Abeng* (1984; rpt. New York: Plume, 1995), p. 79.

tragic life stimulates her search for her lost daughter and submerged African self. But her *obeah,* like the remembered rebellion of the ancestors, otherwise appears dormant.

For the same reason, perhaps, the authority of Africa is opaque in *The Chosen Place, the Timeless People.* It remains to be seen what sense of selfhood, let alone nationhood, Merle will discover in her voyage to Uganda, the nation once contemplated by Herzl as a Zionist homeland. At first glance, Marshall's appeal to *négritude,* the mystical "nigger feeling" transmitted by those who survived the reverse Exodus of the Middle Passage, bears comparison to the argument of reparative Afrocentrism that white supremacy has created among "Afrikans" a "pathological normalcy" of historical amnesia in which the trauma of slavery is repressed—covered over by a "mythological" Eurocentric history.[81] In this account, slavery produced trauma so severe that the historical identity of blacks, generation after generation, has been one of devastation that no therapeutic acts, moral or material, can heal. The refuge provided by Afrocentricism envisions a past in which black modernity—slavery, colonialism, and their legacy—is an aberration within the story of univocal greatness told by African history. At least in this novel, however, Marshall evinces little confidence that blacks in the diaspora will discover their true identity in some pristine Afrocentric past. Her Bournehills is closer to the black Atlantic world described by Paul Gilroy, which features neither an idealized lost past nor a culture of compensation but instead one of fluid hybridization arising as much from the transformation of Africa *by* diaspora culture as from the affiliation of diaspora culture *to* Africa.[82] Rather than surrender to the amnesia of colonialism or the mystifications of Afrocentrism, Marshall seeks to establish a memorial consciousness that places blacks, as heroic actors, not brutalized objects, within the rupture of African history created by slavery.

Merle's paralytic state, a psychological inversion of Saul's epiphany, deepens her exilic communion with him and his with her. Given emblematic meaning in the tableau of slavery and its colonial aftermath that unfolds before his eyes in Merle's darkened sickroom, Saul's visionary moment thus has transcendent, if not exactly prophetic, significance.

Pentecost, the seventh Sunday after Easter, in Christian tradition commemorates the descent of the Holy Spirit upon the disciples ("and there appeared unto them cloven tongues like as of fire, and it sat upon them") and their speaking in tongues, which Paul presents as a portent of the spread of the gospel and which also has a vivid presence in the syncretic Christianity of the West Indies (Acts 2).[83] In Jewish tradition, Pentecost is Shavuot, the fiftieth day after Passover. Celebrated originally as a period of thanksgiving for the wheat har-

vest, according to the Torah, Shavuot came over time to commemorate the revelation of the Law on Mount Sinai (the Decalogue is read in synagogue on
the first day of Shavuot; likewise, the Book of Ruth for its story of harvest
and Ruth's conversion to Judaism). Whereas Passover celebrates the liberation
of the people Israel, Shavuot celebrates the creation of nationhood in the people's acceptance of written law. Even though his intervention does help to
save the sugar cane harvest, nothing in Saul's vision suggests that he should
be likened to Moses on Mount Sinai—just the reverse. Upon arriving at Merle's
bedside after her collapse and his own epiphanic experience, Saul finds in
"her empty stare and lifeless form" a simulacrum of Sosha's death, "the faces
merging, becoming one, before his eyes," both of them a rebuke to his ego-
tism and his "puffed-up image of [him]self as a latter-day Moses come to
deliver the poor and suffering of the world," as Sosha had charged on her
deathbed.[84]

Saul's new knowledge, the fruit of his intimacy with Merle, and the atonement for Sosha's death that it initiates in the Pentecost sequence also help to
explain an otherwise enigmatic episode earlier in the novel when Saul joins
some Bournehills men in a "pigsticking," a regular Sunday event given special
significance on the eve of the Carnival parade, when a huge old sow is chosen
for slaughter. Were the setting Haiti, we might suspect an association with
Toussaint's revolution, since legend has it that the uprising began with a ceremony led by the voodoo priest Boukman that included the sacrifice of a black
pig, its smoking blood said to have been drunk by slaves swearing their allegiance to Toussaint and Haitian liberation.[85] Marshall's scene is more complex
and ambiguous. Even though the sow is endowed with quasi-human powers of
understanding, both the slaughter and the feast that follows appear to be more
mundane than ritualistic, and yet in Marshall's details they take on the manifold significance of sacrificial drama.

Saul's uneasy sense of cultural exclusion from the event—symbolized by the
"German" knife used to probe for the pig's heart and cut its throat, by the men's
joking comparison of the ritual to the sacrifice of Christ ("My God, my God,
why hast thou forsaken me?" says one of them), and by his gagging on a piece
of pork, which reminds him of the old Jew of his childhood weeping "at the fall
of yet another son of Israel"—tells him he will always be "a stranger" in
Bournehills, "someone from Away." It may be that Saul's alienation from the
native rite of brotherhood and community is to be explained by his association
with the tools of Western technology,[86] yet the syncretism of the scene suggests
that Saul himself is also associated with the scene's sacrificial meaning. Although Saul's willingness to eat pork, forbidden by the commandments of

Leviticus (as well as by the Nation of Islam),* alienates him from his own people, it only provisionally allies him with the men of Bournehills. Their satiric
recitation of Christ's dying words and the moon overhead appearing as a
"substanceless eucharistic host"[87] make the scene a representation of the Passion by way of blasphemy—all the more so in that it calls into view the reflexive
relationship between the Eucharist and the blood libel, the accusation that Jews
used the blood of slain Christian children for ritual purposes. Whether Saul is
an outsider or an insider in the mock ritual cannot be resolved, for in truth he
occupies a liminal position in between.

The men's mockery tells us something about their own dissent from the colonial Christian ethos of the island, but it also implicates Saul in the rites of
sacrifice, not as communicant but as object, whether as a Jew guilty of the traditional charge of deicide, or as a Jew guilty of the blood libel, or as a Judaizing
Marrano, a "pig," or as a Jew condemned to death, for no other reason than being a Jew, by the "German" knife. Although Saul is openly Jewish, his Sephardic
ancestors, as noted earlier, most likely came to Latin America as Marranos,
forced converts to Christianity who practiced Judaism secretly and who at
times became subject to the autos-da-fé of the Inquisition in the New World.
In eating the pig, in other words, Saul is made to be the pig. In this context, the
ritual action to which Marshall subjects Saul effectively makes him reenact the
forced conversion of Jews, whether in Europe or the Americas, while also making him take on the horror endured by Sosha, for whom conversion was no option at all when she came under the German knife in medical experiments at
Auschwitz-Birkenau. Set alongside his contrived resemblance to the apostle
Paul, the scene of the pig slaughter thus comes close to stripping Saul of his
identity and beliefs as a Jew.

Even so, Marshall's scene also contains a very different but equally unsettling
set of symbolic associations in its allusion to syncretic Easter week rituals com-

---

* "And the swine, though he divide the hoof, and be clovenfooted, yet he cheweth not the cud; he *is*
unclean to you" (Leviticus 11:7). It seems to play no direct role in Marshall's scene, except as an ironic
aside, but Elijah Muhammad's elucidation of the proscription of pork in racial terms is worth noting:
"The hog is dirty, brutal, quarrelsome, greedy, ugly, foul, a scavenger which thrives on filth. It is a parasite to all other animals. It will even kill and eat its own young. . . . In short, the hog has all the characteristics of a white man." Malcolm X recalled that his swearing off pork in prison, as he began his conversion to the Nation of Islam, startled the other inmates and contravened the stereotype of blacks as
lovers of pork. In the parlance of Black Power and the counterculture, of course, the "white man" was
variously a racist, imperialist, or fascist "pig." Elijah Muhammad quoted in Martha F. Lee, *The Nation of
Islam: An American Millenarian Movement* (Syracuse: Syracuse University Press, 1996), p. 30; Malcolm
X, with Alex Haley, *The Autobiography of Malcolm X* (1965; rpt. New York: Grove Press, 1966), p. 156.

mon among practitioners of Haitian Vodou. Those practices pointedly include symbolism carried over from medieval Europe, as well as more recent moments in history, in which Semitism vies with anti-Semitism, as when the pig, an animal sometimes sacrificed in Vodou religious ceremony, is called a "Jew" by the *lwa* (spirit) Papa Gede, in all likelihood a derivative of the terminology for Marranos.[88] Modern Vodou's ritualistic demonizing of the "Jew" probably dates to the Inquisition and New World instantiations of Passion plays by early Jesuit missionaries, who spread the idea of Jews as the killers of Christ. In the Rara, an Afro-Creole festival that coincides with Lent and features music, dance, street theater, and ritual invocation of Vodou spirits, even as it plays upon the Christian narrative of redemption climaxing on Easter, an effigy of the "Jew," typically in the guise of Judas Iscariot, is thus erected at the beginning of Lent and then burned on Good Friday in ritual retaliation for the betrayal of Jesus.

In these same practices, however, the "Jew" is sometimes, or at the same time, revered as an ancestral figure, much as in the black Baptist tradition Moses is a snake-controlling conjurer,[89] or in Zora Neale Hurston's *Moses, Man of the Mountian* and *Mules and Men* a Vodou spirit associated with magic. (The Wandering Jew of Carnival sometimes resembles Haitian lithographic portrayals of Moses or Saint Patrick, both recognized in Vodou as iterations of the god Damballah.) The very charges of superstition, sorcery, desecration of the host, and even ritual murder that were once the truck of European anti-Semitism have also been leveled at the black practitioners of Vodou, uniting them with Jews as brothers in persecution and pointing, as in the case of the Jamaican Rastafarians, to an underlying assumption of descent from the ancient Israelites. This paradoxical combination of demonization and veneration, says Elizabeth McAlister, suggests that in their ambivalent identification with Jews, black Vodou celebrants take on "the mantle of denigration as a kind of psychic resistance," symbolically opposing the powers of the Catholic elite who have persecuted them just as they have historically persecuted the Jews.[90]

In this revised context, then, the pig slaughter proves structurally ambivalent. Laden with associations that verge on a reenactment of anti-Semitic persecution, the scene is meant, nevertheless, to discover the remnants of common resistance among Jews and blacks. If Saul himself symbolizes the forbidden, perhaps the diabolical within Judaism, the imputation also joins him in spirit with the Africans of the black diaspora, likewise associated with the diabolical, the unclean, the danger of polluting blood. In the same way that the celebration of Cuffee Ned's rebellion exists within the constraining framework of Carnival, temporarily transgressing the boundaries of Bourne Island's religious and political authorities, and defining a vibrant but controlled counter-narrative to colonial rule, so the slaughter of the pig serves to define the only communion that Saul can achieve with the people of Bournehills—one that is both transgressive and regressive, one in which blood brotherhood and scapegoating are combined. Saul finds "beneath the violence of the act an affirmation of something age-old, a sense of renewal" that leaves him exhilarated; and when Merle says that his ability to find meaning in the Sunday rite of the pigsticking indicates that he is close to being "real people"—that is to say, akin to Bournehills people—she attributes this to his being a Jew, someone whose "people have caught hell far longer than mine,"[91] and whose Holocaust, made dramatically tragic in the life and death of Sosha, is the means by which Saul, as much as Merle, reads the meaning and legacy of African slavery in the Americas.

As Saul sees it, Merle's liberation from the colonial past, if it ever occurs, will be of a piece with that of her people: "Only an act on the scale of Cuffee's could redeem them. And only then would Bournehills itself, its mission fulfilled, perhaps forgo that wounding past and take on the present, the future."[92] The "wounding past" to be healed in *The Chosen Place, the Timeless People* is nothing less than "the hemorrhage of a continent," in Keorapetse Kgositsile's memorable phrase[93]—the monstrous wrong of slavery which no people, let alone a single man such as Saul, can fully repair. In taking on the burden of atonement, Saul Amron achieves a measure of introspective wisdom and therefore acts as a translator of Merle Kibona's experience. As a figure of hybridity—a bridge between white and black, between the United States and the black Caribbean, between economic modernity and the creolized remnants of slave culture, and between Judaism and black Christianity—Saul assumes the classic role of the Jew as middleman or broker. In providing a pathway through the amnesia of Afro-Caribbean history, however, he also suggests how one people's wounding past can provide sustenance for another's.

Marshall's epigraph to *The Chosen Place, the Timeless People,* derived from the Tiv of West Africa, is an injunction to remember the cataclysm of a "wounding past" such as Marshall dramatizes, while recognizing as well that the wound may never be healed: "Once a great wrong has been done, it never dies. People speak the words of peace, but their hearts do not forgive. Generations perform ceremonies of reconciliation but there is no end." In looking to the ancestral traditions and contemporary tragedy of Saul Amron to explain those of Merle Kibona, Marshall admitted that the "great wrong" of African dispossession might never be healed, the ceremonies of reconciliation might never end."

Marshall speaks deliberately not of the "wound of the past" but of the "wounding past," reminding us that the trauma continues. Even though the wound is perpetually opened and probed, however, pain and guilt might still be assuaged, and history must be written so as to memorialize justly those who gave their lives in labor and in rebellion.

In Saul's and Merle's awakening to the fact that their respective genocides may have points of comparison while remaining distinctive, Marshall meant not to appropriate another people's tragedy, let alone compete with it. Not only might the exhilarating freedom of the people Israel remembered in the Passover, and now reborn in the Israeli nationhood, serve in its way to sustain blacks, but also the Holocaust might become a source of reconciliation, not envy and resentment. Just as memory of the Holocaust must be joined to memory of bondage in Egypt in the memory of Jews—in the modern-day Passover observance, for example, or in Emil Fackenheim's 614th Commandment, that the victims of the Holocaust be forever remembered lest Hitler be granted a posthumous victory—Marshall's entering of the Middle Passage and slavery, as well as the rebellion against it, into African Americans' cultural discourse represented an attempt to resolve the conflicting paradigms of Exodus and Holocaust, and to find redemption in their history of resistance, much as postwar Jews were doing.

A political version of Marshall's perspective was ably stated by Wole Soyinka when he asserted the need for a correction to the exclusionist worldview that the Holocaust was an exceptional betrayal of the tradition of European humanism. It was not the Holocaust that first called into question the moral claims of European humanism, said Soyinka, echoing Fanon. Rather, the failure occurred at the inception of the African slave trade, which transported—in Soyinka's estimate—some 20 million people across the Atlantic "under conditions of brutality that have yet to be beggared by any other encounter between races." Soyinka rejected time's annulment of distinctions between human rights crimes committed against blacks and those committed against Jews, noting that if the Spanish government, in the final years of the twentieth century, could address the expulsion of the Jews in 1492 with a formal apology, then surely atonement and restitution for more recent crimes against Africa are in order.[94]

As we will see in later chapters, there are unambiguous differences between slavery and the Holocaust, from which one might extrapolate to differences between 1492 in the history of Jews and 1492 in the history of African Americans. But *The Chosen Place, the Timeless People* stands out among arguments in favor of the analogy for the scope of its historical understanding and the sincerity of its compassion. The momentary communion between Saul and Merle, before they are pulled apart by the irreconcilable trajectories of their lives, is therefore emblematic of the larger one between Jews and blacks once thought possible, but put under exceptional strain during the very years when Marshall was writing her novel. The very terms of her endeavor, the creation of sacral memory from two potentially comparable instances of Zionism, two potentially comparable instances of slavery and Exodus, and two potentially comparable kinds of genocide, were destined to become an additional source of strain, but for those who still believed in the black-Jewish alliance, and those, like Marshall, who still looked to Jewish culture in a spirit of brother- and sisterhood, some kind of communion seemed possible.

CHAPTER 5

Black Power, Jewish Power

AMERICA IS NOT CAPABLE of exterminating blacks, as Germany did the Jews, observed Chester Himes in 1970, for the armed uprising brought about by any such campaign would destroy the nation. The alternative was therefore to grant blacks equality. Of course, there was a sizeable middle ground between equality and genocide—even thirty years later when Orlando Patterson found reason to echo Himes, in the process questioning the character of Jewish resistance prior to the Holocaust: "It is depressing to have to say it, but had the Jews of interwar Germany possessed one-twentieth of the guns and exhibited one-tenth of the aggressiveness of the Afro-American underclass, millions of those six million precious lives might have been saved, since the cost to the Germans of exterminating them would have been too high," just as great as the cost to America "to get rid of the million Afro-Americans who constitute the despised Afro-American underclass."[1]

Himes's fanciful proposition, as well as Patterson's updating of it, was possible because the radicalization of the civil rights movement was accompanied by a fast ratcheting up in expressed fears of black genocide that may be traced to several sources: government efforts to crush black militants, especially the Black Panthers; renewed attention on the part of black activists to the United Nations Genocide Convention; the rise of public Holocaust consciousness; and a concomitant new historiography that drew attention to the indeterminable but unquestionably larger number of Africans who perished in the Middle Passage and other depredations during slavery and Jim Crow, an issue to which we will return in Chapter 7. Evolving black attitudes also played a role. As we have already seen, African Americans evinced a strong historic commitment to Zionism and the creation of Israel; but to the extent that they shifted their allegiance from Zionism to its opposite by the late 1960s, the example of the genocide of the Jews, the apparent threat of which was renewed in the Six-Day War and then again in the Yom Kippur War, took on more complex meaning. Alignment with Arab anti-Zionism or the ideology and tactics of the Palestine Liberation Organization (PLO) by definition committed Black Power to a rejectionist stance toward Israel in which resentment of Jews abroad became entangled with resentment of Jews at home and in which the lessons of the Holocaust were put to very different use.

Whether such anti-Zionism was anti-Semitic is a matter of context and perspective—at times it was, but certainly not always—yet the ideological shift and its debilitating consequences for the black-Jewish question in both political and cultural terms is beyond dispute. The commitment to social justice, one hallmark of Jewish liberalism, led a minority of Jews faced with the demands of Black Power to embrace black separatism and the anti-Zionism that often went with it. For the majority, however, black radicalism prompted increased support for an emerging conservative agenda that was pro-Israel, antagonistic to racial quotas, and vigilant about black anti-Semitism. In the case of a different minority of Jews further to the right, radicalized in their own way by the Six-Day War, Black Power was best answered by Jewish Power—by the unqualified repudiation of both black militancy and the notion of Jewish weakness and passivity on which an argument such as Patterson's rested.

Across the ideological spectrum, blacks and Jews alike withdrew the hand of brotherhood, sought to protect their own communal interests, and reverted at times to ugly stereotypes. Literature played a role in adjudicating these conflicts—my principal examples later in the chapter are Saul Bellow's *Mr. Sammler's Planet* (1970) and John A. Williams's *Sons of Darkness, Sons of Light* (1969), and, in the next chapter, Bernard Malamud's *The Tenants* (1971)—but debate was carried on most ardently in essays, speeches, and polemics in a variety of genres. More often than not, however, it was not a debate, much less a dialogue, but an angry shouting match.

BLACK FOLKS AIN'T GOING TO PLAY JEWS

By the time Martin Luther King, Jr., was assassinated, on April 4, 1968, the civil rights–era alliance between blacks and Jews, fragile in any event, had begun to collapse. Passage of the Civil Rights Act and the Voting Rights Act, in 1964 and 1965, respectively, proved to be the political high point of the integrationist agenda for which King gave his life. Soon after these major legal victories, many whites dedicated to civil rights, Jews included, began to distance themselves from plans for black equality that depended on outcomes rather than opportunities, on rights that would be accompanied by compensation, reparations, or preferential treatment, or that adopted philosophies of separatism and violence. No less than Jews and other whites, African Americans were divided over the best strategy for achieving racial justice. For the vast majority, the goal was equality reached through reform, not armed revolution, through integration, not separatism. But it also seemed to many that the legal achievement of equal protection would address neither long-standing inequalities in education and employment nor the more desperate conditions of the urban ghetto. Integration, said Robert S. Browne, was simply "painless genocide."[2]

Between 1964 and 1968 there were some three hundred racially motivated outbreaks of community violence in the United States, the most prominent being those in New York and several New Jersey cities in 1964; Los Angeles (Watts) in 1965; Chicago in 1966; Newark, Detroit, and many others in 1967; and then multiple cities once again following King's murder. The best-selling report on the 1967 riots by the National Advisory Commission on Civil Disorders, published the same month that King was assassinated, warned that the nation was moving toward "two societies, one black and one white—separate and unequal." Blaming white racism and rejecting the term "riot"—in subsequent years the left showed an increasing preference for the term "uprising"— the commission concluded that such violence was viewed by most African Americans as the logical culmination of the sit-ins, marches, boycotts, and legislation that to date had failed to achieve racial equality. The recurrent urban violence, said the commission, did not presage a large-scale revolution but was a protest "rooted in the basic values of American society, seeking not their destruction but their fulfillment."[3]

Whether it was designated an uprising or a riot, the violence that wracked a number of black communities in the 1960s was one expression of Black Power, an amorphous movement comprising a range of social, political, and artistic efforts among African Americans to find pride, not humiliation, in their aspirations and beauty, not caricature, in their public images. Casting back to Du Bois, Larry Neal defined Black Power invitingly as "a synthesis of all the nationalistic ideas embedded within the double consciousness of black America . . . a kind of emotional response to one's history."[4] In what follows, "Black Power" refers to a constellation of beliefs—a cultivation of black nationalist separatism, militant resistance to "white power," and solidarity with other "colonized" people of color and the nations of the Third World (for our purposes, in particular, the Palestinians and their Arab allies). Although few cared to adopt the austere regime demanded by the Nation of Islam, the natural and most influential exponent of Black Power was Malcolm X, whose confrontational strategy rejected liberalism as antithetical to black interests and adopted resistance to racial subjugation "by any means necessary," in his trademark phrase, as the fundamental category of social, political, and aesthetic analysis. In announcing the organization of his own mosque after his excommunication by Elijah Muhammad in 1964, Malcolm made the nationalist ideology at the heart of Black Power the basis for his personal "Declaration of Independence": "Whites can help us, but they can't join us. There can be no black-white unity until there is first some black unity."[5]

Political Black Power might be traced to many points of origin—most immediately, the Watts riot of 1965, which occurred only a few days after the passage of the Voting Rights Act—but it coalesced into an organized movement a year later when the Student Non-Violent Coordinating Committee (SNCC), formed in 1960 to advance activism in the South, adopted a strident ideology of confrontation with the power structure of "white America," as well as with those African Americans deemed too accommodationist in their tactics, including Martin Luther King, Jr., and the Southern Christian Leadership Conference (SCLC). Published in August 1966, SNCC's "Position Paper on Black Power" was a blueprint for separatism. Rejecting the interference, intimidation, and subversion by whites that they said had characterized biracial civil rights movements from the early NAACP forward, and taking inspiration from Third World anticolonial revolutions, the paper's authors, principally Stokely Carmichael and H. Rap Brown, asserted that "if we are to proceed toward true liberation, we must cut ourselves off from white people." Only when African Americans are free from manipulation by the "white liberal establishment" and the "white power complex," said SNCC, can they confront the fundamental question of their identity: "Who are black people, what are black people; what is their relationship to America and the world?"[6]

The ideology to which Carmichael and Brown gave voice had taken shape publicly and decisively in Greenwood, Mississippi, two months earlier. When James Meredith, who had integrated the University of Mississippi in 1962, was shot during his solo "March Against Fear" from Memphis to Jackson in June 1966, the SCLC, SNCC, and the Congress of Racial Equality (CORE) agreed in a unified effort to resume the march where Meredith was shot. Quickly, however, there was dissent on the part of younger activists who wanted it to be a blacks-only march and were impatient with King's nonviolence (in singing the civil rights anthem "We Shall Overcome," they changed the line to "We Shall

Overrun"). On the tenth day of the march, upon reaching Greenwood, where SNCC had engaged in grassroots organizing for several years, Carmichael mounted a platform and roused a responsive audience with his famous proclamation, "What we need is black power!" When King tried unsuccessfully to dissuade the splinter group from adopting such a divisive approach, Carmichael summoned the example of the Irish and the Jews, who adopted positions of ethnic pride in order to consolidate their power. As King recounted the incident, accepting part but not all of Carmichael's analogy, he replied: "That is just the point. No one has ever heard the Jews publicly chant a slogan of Jewish power, but they have power. Through group unity, determination and creative endeavor, they have earned it."*

Whereas King's mention of Jews at Greenwood was one way of paying tribute to their support, Carmichael's was the harbinger of something different. In view of the disproportionate involvement of Jews in the southern civil rights movement (as noted in Chapter 3, nearly a third of northern whites on the Freedom Rides were Jewish, as were nine out of ten civil rights attorneys active in Mississippi), the eviction of whites from leadership roles in organizations such as SNCC and CORE, accompanied by a shift in those organizations from a reformist strategy predicated on ethnic pluralism to a revolutionary model of national liberation from colonial rule, hastened the white liberal retreat from a compensatory agenda;[7] it also set in motion what proved to be an irreversible deterioration in black-Jewish relations.

Even so, Jews remained divided in their reactions to black militancy. As early as a 1966 *Midstream* symposium on the topic, Shlomo Katz observed that Jews were right to be offended at being singled out for special hostility by blacks, since Jews themselves had been "the victims of the greatest racist crime in human history, perpetrated in their own time, by white nations."[8] Others, how-

---

* The "Black Power" response for which Carmichael became famous was first orchestrated at an earlier rally by Willie Ricks, but the slogan had already gained attention through its use in a graduation address by Adam Clayton Powell, Jr., at Howard University in May 1966: "To demand [our] God-given rights is to seek black power—the power to build black institutions of splendid achievement." *Black Power* was also the title of a 1954 work by Richard Wright concerned with the transition to independence of the Gold Coast (Ghana), but other than the title and the ideal of African freedom from colonial rule, there was little in Wright's book to anticipate the tactical meaning given the phrase by Powell or SNCC. See Martin Luther King, Jr., *Where Do We Go from Here: Chaos or Community?* (Boston: Beacon Press, 1967), pp. 23–32; Hugh Pearson, *The Shadow of the Panther: Huey Newton and the Price of Black Power in America* (Cambridge, Mass.: Perseus, 1994), pp. 90–91; Stokely Carmichael and Ekueme Michael Thelwell, *Ready for Revolution: The Life and Struggles of Stokely Carmichael* (New York: Scribner, 2003), pp. 507, 574; Powell quoted in Gayraud S. Wilmore, *Black Religion and Black Radicalism: An Interpretation of the Religious History of Afro-American People*, rev. ed. (Maryknoll, N.Y.: Orbis, 1983), p. 180.

ever, were prepared to bend in the face of black animosity. Some accepted Kenneth Clark's contention that white liberals had to forsake the illusion of color-blindness and be prepared for rejection even among black friends, while a few even argued, as did the national committee of the Students for a Democratic Society (SDS), that "we must not simply tolerate this 'black consciousness,' we should encourage it."[9] *Jewish Currents* editorialized that it was important for Jews, "who are so alert to the dangers of racism as it affects them, to avoid misjudging an idealistic, heroic movement like SNCC, which is dedicated consciously to abolishing racism." It was unfortunate that Jews, the people "best able to understand the rhetoric of Black Power," said Arthur Hertzberg, were nevertheless most directly "on the firing line of its attack." But properly understood, he added, Stokely Carmichael was really "the most radical kind of Negro Zionist," his language of rage comparable to that of Jews who spoke out against the good people "who stood aside" while Hitler rose to power. Such tolerance and encomia, especially on the part of Jews, were bound to seem perverse by 1970, when Carmichael could be found declaring, "I have never admired a White man, but the greatest of them, to my mind, was Hitler."[10]

Despite the overt rejection of white Jewish participation by leading advocates of Black Power, Jews and Jewish history, both ancient and recent, remained a constant point of reference in the black nationalist agenda, though one more than a little paradoxical, as Hertzberg's own analogy indicated. Even the exclusion of Jews from the brotherhood of justice might rely on a recasting of the Exodus paradigm. In counseling a Jewish colleague that, although his scholarly contributions might be welcome and citations of his own people's persecution sincere, Addison Gayle, Jr., took an ethnocentric approach in rejecting the man's participation in the political efforts of black intellectuals. Just as the job of leading the Israelites out of Egypt went not to an Egyptian but to a Jew, said Gayle, so "the necessary qualification for participation in [the Black Power] dialogue is a black skin."[11]

The case of Carmichael, whom James Baldwin found by 1968 to be more akin than King to the Hebrew prophets, is especially instructive. At the outset of his leadership of SNCC, Carmichael favorably quoted variations on Rabbi Hillel's famous aphorism: "If I am not for myself, who is for me? And when I am for myself, what am I? And if not now, when?"* Citing African Americans'

---

* Among other uses of Hillel's aphorism at the time, see Ben Shahn's quotation of the words, in Hebrew script, in his 1968 tempera painting *Identity*, in which five pairs of raised hands are variously clasped to themselves or to others, or in one case closed into fists, suggesting the tension for Jews, as well as others, between reaching out to the stranger and turning back into one's own community.

"deep religious bond with Judaism, one that springs from the Hebrew scriptures of the Old Testament," he would later recall singing "Hava Nagila" and dancing the hora as a student at Bronx High School of Science, and he averred that Isaac Bashevis Singer had been among his favorite writers at the time.[12] Precisely because his early activism had been significantly inspired by friendship with Jews and other whites, however, Carmichael may have felt constrained to prove his leadership by acceding to the separatist demands of the racial left,[13] legitimating his revolutionary ideology by trips to Havana and Hanoi, and adopting a stance of anti-Zionism that veered at times toward open anti-Semitism and was, in any event, interpreted that way by many Jews.*

The view that black liberation might require armed insurrection was accompanied by a radicalization in language that adapted the previous generation's empathetic identification with Hitler's victims to new purpose. As Rap Brown succinctly proclaimed, "We see America for what it is: the Fourth Reich."[14] In conscious contrast to Jews' counsel of moderation in civil rights protest, black militants gravitated toward a strategy that played off the negative example of Jews' purported lack of resistance to anti-Semitism. Later influential for groups such as the Revolutionary Action Movement, the Republic of New Africa, and the Black Panthers—who promoted armed confrontation with the state, the police in particular, through an intimidating public display of loaded rifles and shotguns—the Marxist manifesto of Robert F. Williams, titled *Negroes with*

---

* In his posthumously published memoirs, Carmichael sought to downplay the difference between his views and those of King, and to clarify his anti-Zionist, pro-Palestinian beliefs. His position, he said, was the fruit of SNCC's deep reading in the literature of the Israeli-Arab conflict and his conviction that Israel, like South Africa, was a colonial power inflicting on the Palestinians a form of apartheid. Rebuking the "Zionist thought police," who believe that any criticism of Israel is anti-Semitism, he insisted on telling the world: "I am not now, have never been, nor can ever be anti-Semitic or anti-Judaic. However, I am, and will be unto death, anti-Zionist." Carmichael and Thelwell, *Ready for Revolution*, p. 563. Carmichael was replaced as chairman of SNCC in the summer of 1967 by H. Rap Brown. After traveling to various Third World countries, he became prime minister of the Black Panther Party, newly merged with SNCC, a position he held until the summer of 1969, when he moved to Guinea and took the name Kwame Ture. In periodic speaking tours of the United States, Ture adopted a more pan-African but still stridently anti-Zionist rhetoric, as in his warm-up speech for Louis Farrakhan at a 1985 Nation of Islam event at Madison Square Garden, noted in Chapter 1. Brown took the name Jamil Abdullah Al-Amin after his conversion to Islam while serving a prison term for robbery from 1971 to 1976 and went on to become the leader of one of the nation's largest African American Muslim groups, the National Ummah, which by the end of the 1990s had some three dozen mosques. In 2002, although he claimed to have been framed by the federal government as part of a long attempt to silence him politically, Al-Amin was convicted of the murder of a (black) Atlanta policeman attempting to serve him with a warrant in connection with a car theft.

Guns (1962), thus included one chapter called "Self-Defense Prevents a Po-grom."[15]

Carmichael, however, advanced a far more provocative and influential ver-sion of the argument. Bolstering his call for identification with anticolonial re-sistance in the Third World, he borrowed from David Rousset's pathbreaking study of the Nazi death camps, *L' Univers concentrationnaire* (published in Eng-lish as *The Other Kingdom*), in asserting that the passivity of the Jews had aided the "Storm Troopers" of Germany: "There is nothing more terrible than these processions of human beings going to their death like zombies. I'm afraid that blacks in America cannot afford to march to the gallows the way the Jews did. If white America decides to play Nazi, we're going to let them know that black people are not Jews." Or, in Rap Brown's variation, "We put America on notice: IF WHITE FOLKS WANT TO PLAY NAZIS, BLACK FOLKS AIN'T GOING TO PLAY JEWS."*

If blacks were not going to play the part of America's Jews, however, neither were Jews going to play Jews; that is to say, they would not conform to false stereotypes or submit meekly to attacks by the black American allies of Israel's enemies. The electric American Jewish response to the Six-Day War, wrote Norman Podhoretz in 1971, expressed the Jewish remnant's "recovery, after a long and uncertain convalescence," from the "grievous and nearly fatal psychic and spiritual wounds" of the Holocaust. Apprehension about Jewish vulnera-bility in Israel was intermixed with a sense of vulnerability at home, he went on to say in an acute formulation, and the "passion of solidarity" that American Jews felt for Israel prompted them to fight against black anti-Semitism, racial quotas, and the radical left, collectively the "enemy of liberal values" and a

---

* Margaret Walker among others added her voice to this refrain, writing that "we Black people are truly your [white America's] metaphor. . . . We do not expect to walk quietly into crematories or into concentration camps. Do not say it cannot happen . . . because it did! But the whole world was not watching Germany on television. The Black minority, tragic though its lot may be, is not willing to suc-cumb quietly to genocide." Stokely Carmichael, "The Dialectics of Liberation" (1967), in *Stokely Speaks: Black Power Back to Pan-Africanism* (New York: Random House, 1971), pp. 93–94; H. Rap Brown, *Die Nigger Die!* (New York: Dial, 1969), p. 139; Margaret Walker, "The Humanistic Tradition of Black Litera-ture" (1970), in *How I Wrote Jubilee and Other Essays on Life and Literature*, ed. Maryemma Graham (New York: Feminist Press, 1990), p. 129. Compare David Rousset: "The triumph of the SS demands that the tortured victim allow himself to be led to the noose without protesting, that he renounce and aban-don himself to the point of ceasing to affirm his identity. . . . Nothing is more terrible than these proces-sions of human beings going like dummies to their death." Carmichael's actual source may have been Hannah Arendt, who cited the same passage in *The Origins of Totalitarianism*, which had just appeared in a new edition in 1968. See David Rousset, *The Other Kingdom*, trans. Ramon Guthrie (New York: Reynal and Hitchcock, 1947), p. 525; and Hannah Arendt, *The Origins of Totalitarianism*, 2nd ed. (1968; rpt. New York: Harcourt Brace and Co., 1979), p. 455.

threat to Jewish security.[16] That the "enemies" of liberalism and the Jewish community were in retrospect not so strong, let alone so organized, as Podhoretz's rhetoric made them sound does not lessen the danger felt by some Jews—a danger all the more worrisome since those enemies also included a sizeable number of Jews on the left.

A politically effective coalition might have survived the tempestuous course of Black Power so long as Jews believed that views such as those expressed by Carmichael and Brown were part of the war for Third World liberation rather than a war against Jews. By the time Podhoretz was writing, however, the distinction was no longer clear. For many African Americans, galvanized by anti-colonial struggles in Africa, Asia, and Latin America, the image of Israel underwent a transformation after the Six-Day War, so that, as Pierre Vidal-Naquet has observed, "the victims [became the] executioners."[17] A comparable inversion in perceptions, on the part of blacks and Jews alike, took place at home. From seeing the United States as the "Fourth Reich," it was for blacks but a short step to confusing American Jews with Israeli colonizers and accusing them of Nazism. For Jews, it was almost as short a step from seeing blacks as fellow sufferers under the yoke of racial persecution to accusing them of Hitlerite anti-Semitism. Such a devolution in black-Jewish relations might have happened in any case, but the Six-Day War set the antagonistic course for political allegiances and animosities for decades to come. Because the rift between Jews and blacks in the United States cannot be understood apart from this context, we need first to look more closely at the war and its consequences before returning to the motives and meaning of the transition in Black Power from Afro-Zionism to anti-Zionism.

SONS OF LIGHT, SONS OF CATASTROPHE

The Six-Day War* codified a permanent change in the world's image of "the Jew." Even though it did not dramatically alter the ambivalence of American Jews about adopting Israel as their homeland—there was a sharp but brief acceleration in emigration—it did intensify their devotion to Israel's survival, re-

---

* The honor of naming the war went to then chief of staff Yitzhak Rabin. Notes Michael Oren: "Among the titles proposed—The War of Daring, the War of Salvation, the War of the Sons of Light—Rabin chose the least ostentatious, the Six-Day War, evoking the days of creation." Michael B. Oren, *Six Days of War: June 1967 and the Making of the Modern Middle East* (New York: Oxford University Press, 2002), p. 309. We will return to "Sons of Light," a phrase occurring in, among other places, an apocalyptic text discovered among the Dead Sea Scrolls.

sulting in mass study missions, phenomenal fund-raising, and a renewed spirit of unity captured in the slogan "We Are One!"

The 1948 War of Independence had laid the groundwork for the modern-day construction of a heroic Israeli past, as in the revival of the national myth surrounding the siege of Masada in 73 CE, when Jewish militants in revolt against the Roman Empire committed suicide rather than surrender.[18] It also produced its own mythic heroes—for example, the dashing Ari Ben Canaan in Leon Uris's novel *Exodus* (1958), played on screen by Paul Newman. "As a piece of propaganda," said Prime Minister David Ben-Gurion of Uris's eighty-week best-seller, "it's the greatest thing ever written about Israel."[19] Whereas the Six-Day War appeared once again to threaten Israel's destruction, possibly a second Jewish Holocaust—Hafiz al-Assad, then Syria's defense minister (and later president), asserted, "I, as a military man, believe the time has come to enter into a battle of annihilation"[20]—the nation's military strategists knew otherwise. In contrast to the 1948 war, the costliest in casualties of all Israeli wars, the 1967 conflict concluded in short order with Israel's triumphant emergence as an acknowledged modern military power. Having conquered 42,000 square miles of territory—the remainder of pre-1948 Palestine, the West Bank and Gaza Strip, as well as the Sinai and the Golan Heights—Israel was enlarged to three and a half times its original size, while inflicting a 25-to-1 ratio of casualties on its enemies.[21] With the return of access to the Western Wall and other holy sites in Jerusalem, Hebron, and elsewhere, closed to Jews since 1948, the spirit of Zionism was reenergized—and with it a new, more virulent spirit of anti-Zionism.

The swift and decisive victory by the Israeli Defense Forces (IDF), among whom were survivors of the European genocide, appeared to some to provide redemption from the lingering anxiety that the Jews of Europe had gone to their deaths like "sheep to the slaughter," and even some measure of vengeance on behalf of those who had died. Uri Ramon, a soldier visiting a Ghetto Fighters Museum at a kibbutz, described the connection: "I felt clearly that our war began there, in the crematoriums, in the camps, in the ghettos, and in the forests." No longer "the frightened victim, to be destroyed, abandoned, pitied, or rescued," in the words of Bernard Lewis, the Jew was now a warrior fighting ferociously to his death—or better, to the death of his enemy.[22] In both Israeli and American culture, history's caricature of the Jew as meek and weak, a man of the book, not the gun, gave way to the "muscle Jew,"* as the early Zionist

---

* The concept of the muscle Jew derives from Max Nordau's *Muskeljuden*. In rejecting the prevailing image of passive Jews, whose "fear of constant persecution turned our powerful voices into frightened whispers, which rose in a crescendo only when our martyrs on the stakes cried out their dying prayers

hero, the sabra, was reincarnated in fearless soldiers, adherents of the Jewish Defense League, espionage agents, and, later, Entebbe commandos, all of them to one degree or another avengers of Auschwitz.[23] Shedding the fearfulness and victimhood on which traditional anti-Semitism had partly fed, Arthur Miller would write, Jews were "suddenly comprehensible as one of the world's dangerous peoples."[24]

The coincidental 1967 serialization in *Look* magazine of Arthur Morse's *While Six Million Died,* which exposed the American government's suppression of information about the Holocaust until millions of Jews had already been murdered, underscored the danger of another kind of passivity in the face of threatened genocide.[25] Erasing any remaining reticence about the Holocaust and producing euphoric pro-Israel militancy among the great majority of American Jews, the 1967 war appeared to vindicate the view that Zionism and American patriotism were not just compatible but strategically inseparable. Jews in particular poured forth moral and financial support and in some cases elected *aliyah,* facilitated fortuitously on the eve of the war by the Supreme Court decision in *Efroyin v. Rusk* (1967), which legalized dual citizenship. Although it had an earlier history in the Israeli motto "Never again shall Masada fall!" and represented a variation on *zakhor,* the traditional injunction to "Remember"—for example, "Remember what Amalek did to you on your journey, after you left Egypt. . . . In the land that the Lord your God is giving you as a hereditary portion, you shall blot out the memory of Amalek from under heaven. Do not forget!" (Deuteronomy 25:17–19)—the slogan "Never again!" became a powerful organizing tool and an effective instrument of philanthropic appeal.[26] The wound of the Holocaust, tentatively opened by the trial of Adolf Eichmann, now lay gaping.

Even as the Six-Day War represented for Israelis the culmination of post-statehood Zionism, however, it immediately posed the dilemma of "occupation," which in turn spurred the further radicalization of Israel's enemies—their increasing resort to maximalism and anti-Semitism in place of diplomacy, and guerrilla warfare and terrorism in place of negotiation. The elation of victory was accompanied by a strong consensus among Israelis not to return to the pre-1967 Green Line—the 1949 Armistice Line, or what Israeli foreign minister Abba Eban famously referred to as the "Auschwitz" line—and certainly

---

in the face of their executioners," Nordau exhorted the Second Zionist Congress in 1898 to adopt a muscular philosophy of resistance: "Let us once more become deep-chested, sturdy, sharp-eyed men." Max Nordau, "Jewry of Muscle" (1903), trans. J. Hessing, in Paul Mendes-Flohr and Jehuda Reinharz, eds., *The Jew in the Modern World: A Documentary History,* 2nd ed. (New York: Oxford University Press, 1995), p. 547.

not without recognition of Israel's right to exist and convincing guarantees that Arab nations and the PLO were ready to pursue a lasting peace, including the suppression of terrorism. Whatever Israeli inclination to trade "land for peace" may have existed was undercut by the "No's of Khartoum"—"no recognition, no negotiation, no peace"—declared by Arab nations at a September 1967 summit and by stalement over the meaning and practicability of United Nations Resolution 242, passed in November and destined to govern Israeli-Palestinian discourse and conflict into the next century.*

The sudden expansion of Israeli territory, moreover, emboldened those bent on settling "Greater Israel." For Israel's religious nationalists—specifically for Gush Emunim (Bloc of the Faithful), a messianic movement founded in 1974 in which religious orthodoxy and territorial expansion were combined—the war was seen as divine redemption of the Jews' incontestable right, under God's covenant, to settle all of Judea and Samaria (the West Bank), beliefs that the ideology of the Herut (Freedom) Party and its successor Likud translated into realpolitik.[27] In the words of Rabbi Yehuda Amital, writing in 1974, the purpose of settling "Eretz Israel through the ingathering of her sons . . . is not the normalization of the people of Israel—to be a nation like all other nations—but to be a holy people, a people of a living God."[28] By 1973 there were seventeen Jewish settlements in the West Bank; by 1977, when Menachem Begin came to power, there were thirty-six; and by 2002 there were as many as two hundred, with a total population, including Jerusalem's surrounding neighborhoods, of some 400,000 Israelis.[29] For many settlers, their existence was then and remains today a manifestation of God's will, the negation of exile, and a symbol of militant Jewish strength after two millennia of fear and flight.†

---

* In its interpretation of the provisions of Resolution 242, Israel focused on the necessity of an Arab commitment to recognize its "sovereignty, territorial integrity and political independence" and its "right to live in peace within secure and recognized boundaries free from threats or acts of force," a condition to be achieved through "a peaceful and accepted settlement"—in short, its right to exist. The Arabs focused on "the inadmissibility of the acquisition of territory by war" and "a just settlement of the refugee problem," which to them meant the right of return for *all* refugees (and their descendants) from 1948 onward. Whereas Israel dwelt on the ambiguity of the requirement for its withdrawal "from territories occupied in the recent conflict"—the absence of a qualifying "all" or "the" made the scope of withdrawal hard to specify and fit with their willingness to give up only the Golan Heights and the Sinai—the Arabs insisted on the unconditional withdrawal from *all* territories, a peculiar and unprecedented demand by a defeated aggressor, in Israel's view, and in any case one unacceptable to it as a unilateral step. "Security Council Resolution on the Middle East" (November 22, 1967), in Walter Laqueur and Barry Rubin, eds., *The Israel-Arab Reader: A Documentary History of the Middle East Conflict*, 6th ed. (New York: Penguin, 2001), p. 116.

† Some immigrant settlers from the United States have found an even more specific reminder of former Jewish vulnerability. "We were raised in a very Jewish area [of Brooklyn]," said Rachel Saperstein, a

Had Israel chosen to relinquish some or all of the territory gained in the Six-Day War and to preclude or limit settlements in the West Bank and Gaza, actions it might more easily have contemplated had hostile Arab nations, as well as the Palestinians themselves, recognized Israel's right to exist and cooperated in the establishment of a Palestinian state, rather than repeatedly rejecting a two-state solution and futilely demanding an all-inclusive right of return for those displaced in 1948 and their descendants, fifty years of bloodshed (and counting) might have been avoided. As David Ben-Gurion said as far back as 1936, however, the Arabs see "exactly the opposite of what we see."[30]

The Six-Day War devastated not only Arab armies but also Arab power, in particular the pan-Arab aspirations of Egyptian president Gamal Abdel Nasser. Into the vacuum of power created by the debacle of the war and the demise of Arab nationalism slipped Yasser Arafat's "Fatah"—a reverse acronym for the Palestine National Liberation Movement meaning "opening" or "conquest"—which revitalized Palestinian nationalism, debilitated and quiescent since the Nakba, "the Disaster" or "the Catastrophe" of 1948. (Arafat later instituted Nakba Day, a day of mourning coinciding with Israel's Independence Day on May 5.) Transferring its operations to the occupied territories and taking advantage of the post-1967 chaos to recruit among the additional Palestinian refugees created by the war, Fatah engaged in a campaign of sabotage and ambush, and in the process solidified its effective control of the PLO.[31] Consciously placing itself in the revolutionary tradition of Frantz Fanon, Mao Zedong, and Che Guevara, and adopting a strategy designed both to block any peace agreement ("peaceful settlements can have only one meaning—surrender," said Arafat), Fatah targeted Israeli troops, Israeli civilians, and Arabs seeking work in Israel ("civilians or military, they're all equally guilty of wanting to destroy our people," said Arafat).[32] Once Arafat was elected chairman in 1969, the aims of the PLO, as articulated in its 1964 Covenant, and the methods of Fatah—guerrilla warfare and terrorism carried out by *fedayeen,* "the men who sacrifice themselves"—converged. Declaring that the Jews do not and cannot

---

resident of Neveh Dekalim in Gaza, one of the settlements slated for demolition by Prime Minister Ariel Sharon as part of his plan for Israeli disengagement from Gaza. "Then the blacks came in and the Jews ran. . . . Everybody went to Crown Heights. I don't want to run away. I always see Jews running and running." One settler opposed to Sharon's plan, Pinchas Wallerstein, appealed to American history in an even more striking, if convoluted, way when he contended, "Were Martin Luther King to be alive today to witness the singling out of Jewish residents for expulsion from their homes," he would find it comparable to the exclusion of blacks under segregation. Rachel Saperstein quoted in Jeffrey Goldberg, "Among the Settlers," *New Yorker* 80 (May 31, 2004), 54; Pinchas Wallerstein quoted in David Remnick, "Checkpoint," *New Yorker* 80 (February 7, 2005), 65.

constitute a nation, the PLO's Covenant reiterated the habitual Arab demand for the elimination of Israel as a state—a demand for the restoration of "Greater Palestine" that would remain standard until at least the ill-fated Oslo Agreement of 1993—and legitimated Fatah's adoption of armed struggle as an appropriate means to secure the Palestinians' "liberation of their country and their return to it."*

Nineteen sixty-seven provided Fatah and eventually the PLO with an unexpected world stage. It was also, ironically, the first time since 1948 that the three substantial segments of the Palestinian people—those in the West Bank and in Gaza, and Arabs in Israel proper—were united, albeit now under the "colonial" rule of the Israelis rather than that of the British.[33] The 1948 war had produced some 700,000 Palestinian refugees, half of whom settled in Jordan and the West Bank annexed by Jordan, 200,000 in the Gaza Strip occupied by Egypt, 100,000 in Lebanon, and 60,000 in Syria. Unlike the 500,000 Jews driven from Arab nations soon after 1948, with another 300,000 to follow by 1972, two thirds of whom were absorbed by Israel, the Palestinians were refused citizenship, except in Jordan, and half of the total landed in United Nations refugee camps that were destined to be their homes, and their children's and grandchildren's homes, for years to come. The 1967 war displaced another 200,000 or more from Gaza and the West Bank. By the early twenty-first century, owing to natural increase, some 3.9 million Palestinians lived in the West Bank, Gaza, and neighboring Arab nations, according to UN figures, one third of them still in refugee camps. When added to Israel's Arab population of more than 1 million, such numbers predicted that the Jewish population, fewer than 5 million, would be overwhelmed and the Jewish state destroyed by demographic fiat

---

* Drafted in 1964 and adopted by the Palestinian National Council in 1968, the Palestinian Covenant (or Charter) made the Palestine of the British Mandate an indivisible unit, a "homeland" for all its Arab inhabitants, as well as their descendants, regardless of their current domicile; declared that the Zionist "invasion" dated to 1917 (the year of the Balfour Declaration, which authorized the formation of a Jewish National Home in Palestine, now "deemed null and void"); defined any Jews living in Palestine prior to this date as "Palestinians" and all others Zionist colonizers and aliens; rejected the United Nations partition of 1947 as "entirely illegal" and "contrary to the will of the Palestinian people and to their natural right in their homeland"; asserted that any call for a separate Palestinian state in the West Bank and Gaza was a Zionist plot; and called Zionism "racist and fanatic in its nature, aggressive, expansionist and colonialist in its aims, and fascist in its methods" (a different translation reads, "Its methods are those of the Fascists and the Nazis"). The PLO demanded that the borders be rolled back not to pre-1967 but to pre-1948, whereupon Jews could remain in "Palestine" as a subject minority once Israel as a nation was destroyed. "The Palestinian National Charter: Resolutions of the Palestine National Council," in Laqueur and Rubin, *Israeli-Arab Reader*, pp. 117–21; cf. alternative translation in Yehoshafat Harkabi, *The Palestinian Covenant and Its Meaning*, 2nd ed. (London: Valentine, Mitchell, 1981), p. 123.

should a bi-national state be established or a comprehensive right of return be granted to Palestinians.*

Although the Palestinians' exilic status came about during the 1948 war (we will consider later in this chapter whether they fled or were expelled), their generations-long immiserization owed as much or more to despotic, manipulative Arab governments. Witness, in this regard, a broadcast on Cairo radio that proclaimed the Palestinian refugees "the cornerstone in the Arab struggle against Israel" and "the armaments of the Arabs and Arab nationalism," or the less sanguine testimony of Khalid al-Azm, former prime minister of Syria, who said in his 1972 memoirs that it was Arab nations that "dispossessed" the Palestinians, "accustomed them to begging," and "exploited them in executing crimes of murder, arson, and throwing bombs . . . in service of political purposes."[34] A minute percentage of the approximately 60 million refugees counted around the world in the aftermath of World War II, the Palestinians, virtually alone among them, were not resettled in surrounding nations. (In a century that has seen millions "put to flight, transported, enslaved, stampeded over the borders, left to starve," observed Saul Bellow, only the case of the Palestinians has been held permanently open.)[35] As Mahmoud Abbas (Abu Mazen)—who would be elected president of the Palestinian Authority in January 2005 after the death of Arafat—remarked in 1976: "The Arab armies entered Palestine to protect the Palestinians from the Zionist tyranny but, instead, they abandoned them, forced them to emigrate and to leave their homeland, and threw them into prisons similar to the ghettos in which Jews used to live."[36]

In rejecting the UN plan for partition in 1947 and vowing to stop it by force, then in failing to stop it, then in failing to provide the Palestinians a permanent home, members of the Arab League betrayed the very people they had vowed to protect. What Rashid Khalidi has observed of 1948 is no less applicable to

* It has remained an intense point of debate whether or not the right of return would mean the subjugation or eradication of the Jewish people. When he spoke of a "just, comprehensive, and durable peace—a peace of the brave—in this holy land and in the entire region" on May 15, 2004, the fifty-sixth anniversary of the Nakba, Yasser Arafat characterized the right of return in terms that appeared to promise reconquest either through force of arms or through the demographic force inherent in any plan for a bi-national state: "From the heart of the fiery furnace in Palestine, in confrontation with the Israeli evil, aggression, occupation, settlements, and arrogance, I bless you, oh my beloved, oh sons of Palestine, in the homeland, in the diaspora and in forced exile. I say to you: Palestine is your homeland, whether sooner or later." Yasser Arafat, speech of May 15, 2004, "No One in This World Has the Right to Concede the Refugees' Right of Return to Their Homeland; The Palestinian Heroes Will Fight for This Right," *Middle East Media Research Institute*, http://memri.org/bin/opener_latest.cgi?ID=SD71704 (accessed May 23, 2004).

1967 and decades following: the incipient Palestinian nationalism that might have afforded the basis for a separate state, as envisioned in the UN partition, had been "strangled at birth, victim of the total failure of the Palestinians, the military triumph of the new Jewish state, and the collusion of a number of Arab leaders."[37]

Palestinian nationalism arose not just in reaction to partition and the 1948 war;[38] but in constructing a collective historical memory as part of their post-1967 armature of resistance, the Palestinians found it all the more necessary to prove the existence of a distinctive national consciousness, preceding Zionism and separate from pan-Arabism. By depicting the biblical Israelites as nomadic and inconsequential Semites who usurped Canaanite Arab lands, and by using their own rejection by Arab nations to foster a distinctive Palestinian identity and an idyllic view of pre-1948 village life, Palestinians in effect turned Zionist historiography on its head. In particular, Fatah used its principal organ, *Our Palestine—the Call to Life*, to cultivate from dispossession a powerful sense of national identity. What Palestinians faced after 1948, said Fatah co-founder Abu Jihad (Khalil al-Wazir), was the "elimination of Palestine, suppression of Palestinian identity, [and] the eradication of Palestinian character."[39] The emergence of generations born in exile and relentlessly imbued with a sense of Israel's illegitimacy facilitated belief in an integral union between the Palestinian people and what the 1988 Declaration of Independence later spoke of as their "patrimonial Land." The right to return to that land, moreover, mirrored Israel's Law of Return—"the State of Palestine is the state of Palestinians wherever they may be"—and the al-Aqsa *intifada,* initiated in 2000, similarly came to be known in Palestinian internal discourse as the "War of Independence and Return"—return not to pre-1967 but to pre-1948 Palestine.[40]

Well before the Six-Day War, that is to say, a mystique of "the Return" permeated Palestinian culture, especially in the refugee camps, with a lost (still-to-be-realized) sovereign Palestine conceived as a bride awaiting her husband or a mother waiting for her "sons" to return—but to return in a violent vanquishing. "The feeling of being stateless, without a homeland," wrote the Palestinian guerrilla Leila Khaled, "is a feeling that can only be obliterated by the return." The Zionists have "raped my true Mother Palestine."[41] According to Nasir ad-Din an-Nashashibi's 1962 narrative *Return Ticket,* the promise of return combined emotive, romantically rendered longings for the lost homeland with calls to avenge previous military defeats—or, as the Palestinians saw it, war crimes by the Jews: "I want [our soldiers] to wash away the disaster of 1948 with the blood of those who prevent them from entering their land. . . . We'll smash Tel Aviv with axes, guns, hands, fingernails and teeth, while singing the songs of

Qibiya, Deir Yassin and Nasir as-Din,"[42] locations renowned for alleged massacres of Arabs by Jews.

The ferocity of Nashashibi's tone forecast an alteration in strategy that accompanied the consolidation of competing splinter groups under the banner of the PLO—namely, dependence on increasingly spectacular instances of terrorism. Inspired by the war against colonial rule waged over two decades by the Vietcong and by the 1962 uprising against the French in Algeria, and sometimes linking their struggle to the Mau Mau rebellion in Kenya or even to black radicalism in the United States, Fatah borrowed from Fanon the view that revolutionary violence could have a cleansing effect on the psyches of the oppressed and thus break through the resignation of the refugees.[43]

Because there was no imperial home such as France, Britain, or the United States to which Israeli forces could withdraw, the PLO's appeal to anticolonialism was misguided but nonetheless rhetorically effective, as would be proved by the subsequent endorsement by many on the Western left of the proposition that the Jewish state had been established "in order to secure continued imperialist robbery and exploitation of our country" (to cite Fatah's 1980 platform). For a people who live "humiliated in the lands of exile, without a homeland, without dignity, without leadership, without hope, without weapons, without direction," said one of the movement's founding documents, *Structure of Revolutionary Construction*, revolution will "put an end to this bitter surrender, this terrifying reality that the children of the Catastrophe experience everywhere."[44]

Guerrilla warfare by Palestinian Arabs against Palestinian Jews preceded Fatah by decades, but the seeming invincibility of the state of Israel after the Six-Day War necessitated an augmentation in methods of violence. Whereas Fatah initially confined its actions to Israel and the direct liberation of Palestine, one rival faction, the Popular Front for the Liberation of Palestine (PFLP), announced in its inaugural statement in 1967 that "the only language which the enemy understands is that of revolutionary violence."[45] The PFLP immediately turned to terrorism—airline hijackings, bombings, assassinations—on an international scale, a campaign in which the PLO and its splinter group Black September soon joined.[46] The PLO's adoption of terror, anywhere and anytime—between 1969 and 1985 the PLO undertook eight thousand terrorist acts, more than four hundred of them abroad[47]—grew from frustration with the ineffectiveness of conventional guerrilla warfare. At the same time, it served to forestall efforts at negotiated settlement that might have led to a Palestinian state in the West Bank, "for if ever such a state is established," said Arafat after Fatah's suppression in Jordan, "it will spell the end of the whole Palestinian cause," namely, the elimination of Israel and its replacement by an Arabic

Greater Palestine.[48] The corresponding policy of Israel to seek out terrorists anywhere and anytime, suppressing them by raids on Lebanon and Syria and establishing punitive control over the West Bank and Gaza Strip, set in motion the cycle of attack and counterattack, now ebbing, now flowing, that would paralyze prospects for Israeli-Palestinian peace for decades to come.

Arafat failed to ignite a popular war of liberation, but victory was never to be measured on the battlefield alone, a fact not lost on the Palestinians' foreign sympathizers in the 1960s. When the IDF struck back hard, rooting out Fatah by blowing up houses and confiscating property, it strengthened Arafat's hand, as witnessed in his oft-quoted remark: "Thank God for [IDF chief of staff Moshe] Dayan. He provides the daily proof of the expansionist nature of Zionism."[49] Terrorism prompted suppression, which in turn fueled a war of words in which the PLO found powerful allies.

The PLO's ideology of revolution was abetted by the anti-Zionism that broke out with renewed intensity among Arabs after their humiliation in the Six-Day War. Hand in hand with the Soviet Union, which embarked on its own anti-Zionist campaign and began regularly to equate Israeli policies with those of Hitler,[50] Arab nations waged a more vociferous propaganda war frequently carried out in anti-Semitic terms. There was a resurgence of the equation between "world Jewry" and "world Zionism"; the blood libel and Holocaust denial flourished; and the *Protocols of the Elders of Zion,* which had already been published in numerous editions in the postwar years and would subsequently be inscribed into the charter of Hamas (the Islamic Resistance Movement), became a best-seller, as did Hitler's *Mein Kampf.* In a 1968 work titled *The Great Plot and the Fateful Struggle,* the prime minister of Jordan, Sa'ad Jum'a, explained the Israeli victory on the basis of the deceit and conspiratorial designs ascribed to Jews in the *Protocols.*[51] Coupled with the (false) charge that Israel had imperial designs on neighboring nations, Arab rejection of Israel's right to exist became enveloped in anti-Semitism that rivaled the previous output of the Nazis and that pointedly employed Holocaust denial as one means among others to assert that Zionism was *worse* than Nazism.[52] Unable to achieve victory on the field of battle or through terrorism, Israel's enemies found greater success in a fusillade of propaganda designed to change world opinion.

Anti-Zionism was not confined to the Palestinians and Arabs or their sympathizers abroad. Terror and its suppression led also to a division among Israelis (and Jews elsewhere) over the moral character of the Jewish state. For many, the Six-Day War fulfilled the Zionist dream, but for others it inaugurated a countervailing "post-Zionism." Influential figures among the new generation of historians and commentators not only agonized over Israeli conduct in the West Bank and Gaza but also replaced the metaphysical interpretation of the War of Independence as an act of unquestioned historical justice with attention to the morality of military conduct and the consequences of the Israeli victory for Palestinian refugees.[53] Once seen as the solution to life in the ghetto, Israel itself had now been fortified, its critics charged, into "a massive, armed ghetto," turning Masada, in the words of writer A. B. Yehoshua, into a fatalistic, "self-fulfilling metaphor."[54]

More disturbing was the charge among Jews themselves that Jews, once the victims of the Holocaust, were now perpetrating a new one. Israeli post-Zionists and their American Jewish counterparts were not anti-Semitic, of course, but their dissent struck at the very meaning of the state. Although Israel won a limited military victory in the Yom Kippur War of 1973, the brokered cease-fire, as well as the high cost in lives lost and expenditure, left it a bitter experience for the nation, marked by recriminations that were very nearly the opposite of the post-1967 elation. As the dialectic of Palestinian terror and Israeli repression continued, some post-Zionists accused the government of engaging in a species of "Judeo-Nazism" and manipulating memory of the Holocaust in order to justify colonial rule.[55] Hebrew University philosopher Yeshayahu Leibowitz predicted in 1979 that Israel would soon be "setting up concentration camps" to accommodate the "mass expulsion and slaughter of the Arab population." In reaction to the Sabra and Shatilla massacre during the 1982 war in Lebanon, said Nicholas Von Hoffman, some Americans had likewise started to believe that the Israeli government was "pounding the Star of David into a swastika."[56] Whether or not they accepted such an inversion of roles, a number of Israeli Jews, along with Jews elsewhere, were sympathetic to the Palestinian self-portrait as "the victim of the victims of the Nazis," in the words of Raja Shehadeh: "Fate has agreed that I also pay the price of the Holocaust; fate— through nightmares, through the great subconscious—has decreed that I inherit the memory, the fear, and the horror of Auschwitz. . . . [The Israeli] acts, and I dream the dreams that he should have."[57]

The 1948 roots of post-Zionism were further revealed in the advent of more vocal protest among the Mizrahim—the "Eastern Ones" (or "Oriental Jews"), Arab-descended Sephardic Jews who had come to Israel since 1948, principally from Morocco, Algeria, Egypt, Iran, Iraq, and India, only to find themselves, like Israeli Arabs, second-class citizens in the otherwise democratic state. Although the borrowings from their United States counterpart were more symbolic than substantial, a Mizrahi protest movement launched in 1971 adopted the name "Black Panthers." Claiming several thousand followers at the height of their notoriety, the Israeli Black Panthers sought an end to discrimination in jobs, education, and housing at the hands of the Ashkenazim who dominated the major national institutions and political leadership of Israel. While evincing little of the anti-Zionism of their American namesake, the Black Panthers protested the "colonial" status of the Mizrahim, advocated "Sephardi Pride" as an antidote to being made ashamed of their darker skin and alien customs, and were among the first Israelis to meet with the PLO and to call for a Palestinian state.[58] Just as African Americans have nurtured an identity based on the strength of the black community and descent from African origins, learning "American history from the point of view of the victim," said the poet Sami Shalom Shitrit, so the Jews of Arab descent in Israel must confront their oppression in order to assert their own rightful identities.*

The PLO occasionally sought to link itself with black radicalism in the United States—Arafat sounded suspiciously like Malcolm X when he declared in 1969 that his goal was "the liberation of our fatherland by any means necessary"[59]—and they certainly welcomed anti-Zionism wherever it might be found. What is more certain is that both the Sephardic Black Panthers and Israelis sympathetic to Arafat's version of Palestinian nationhood had natural allies among blacks in the United States. Although most African Americans supported Israel and still looked to Zionism for inspiration in their own struggle for equal rights, an influential, highly vocal minority who defined the terms of public debate reciprocated Shitrit's desire to tell history from "the point of view of the victim"—by which they, like their ideological descendants in generations to come, meant the point of view of the dispossessed Palestinians and the anti-Zionism of the PLO.

Egypt Is Our Motherland

"We have got to be for the Arabs," said Stokely Carmichael in an effort to rally African Americans after the Six-Day War, for "we are Africans wherever we

---

* The rights of Arab Israelis have been expressed in terms of the American civil rights movement in other contexts as well. In a landmark ruling in 2002 that an Arab family must be allowed to purchase property in a communal settlement restricted to Jews, Chief Justice Aharon Barak of the Israeli Supreme Court referred to the refutation of the doctrine of "separate but equal" in *Brown v. Board of Education*: "There is no contradiction between the values of the State of Israel as a Jewish and democratic state and complete equality among its citizens." Shitrit and Barak quoted in Tom Segev, *Elvis in Jerusalem: Post-Zionism and the Americanization of Israel*, trans. Haim Watzman (New York: Metropolitan, 2002), pp. 51, 75–77.

are." Israel "is moving to take over Egypt. Egypt is our motherland—it's in Africa. . . . Egypt belongs to us since four thousand years ago, and we sit here supporting the Zionists."[60] Black rejection of the state of Israel dated back to the moment of its creation—for example, George Schuyler's scalding 1947 opinion that the partition and War of Independence proved that the Bible is the "Jewish *Mein Kampf*"[61]—but neither Schuyler in his day nor Carmichael in his spoke for all African Americans.

Although attitudes began to change by the late 1970s and early 1980s, polls conducted among the general population of African Americans over the previous decade yielded mixed results but revealed no deep-seated anti-Semitism or even anti-Zionism. A major study published in 1967 showed that, even though African Americans held stronger anti-Semitic views than whites with respect to economic stereotypes, they had views on immigration, discrimination, Jewish support of civil rights, and Israel that showed them to be less anti-Semitic than whites. Broadly representative of African American opinion was Martin Luther King, Jr. As noted earlier, King repeatedly acknowledged support for black rights from Jewish leaders and organizations, just as he repeatedly affirmed Israel's territorial integrity and right to exist. Speaking before the Rabbinical Assembly (of Conservative Judaism) just a week prior to his death, he went so far as to declare that the Jewish state was "one of the great outposts of democracy in the world . . . an oasis of brotherhood and democracy." According to surveys taken between 1970 and 1977, blacks continued even after the Six-Day War and the Yom Kippur War to be generally pro-Israel, if somewhat less so than whites, and Israel enjoyed the continuous support of the Congressional Black Caucus. In 1975 a group of black public figures from various professions led by Bayard Rustin formed BASIC, Black Americans In Support of Israel, which affirmed Israel's right to statehood, condemned Palestinian terrorism, repudiated the United Nations resolution equating Zionism with racism, and adopted as one of its founding principles the fact that "only in Israel, among the nations of the Middle East, are political freedoms and civil liberties secure." Blacks, in their struggle for freedom in the United States, and Jews, in their struggle to preserve a homeland, said Rustin in a speech before the Anti-Defamation League in 1980, are two peoples joined in "the international party of human rights."[62]

Especially from the late 1960s through the 1970s, however, it was the opinions of those openly antagonistic to King, who inevitably gained a greater voice after his assassination, as well as the volatile reactions of Jews, which set the tone. Whether in Carmichael's appeal for an "ingathering" of the world's blacks in exile or Cleaver's hope that the Black Panthers, like the early Zionists, would "sweep the people forward into nationhood," proponents of Black Power, as we saw in Chapter 2, continued to find in Zionism a model of nationalist sovereignty. At the very same time, though, they found in contemporary Israel an imperialist handmaiden of the United States. Carmichael's support of the Arab and Palestinian cause was foregrounded by an ill-conceived SNCC newsletter that accused the Israelis of tactics of terror and massacre. Alongside an article charging that the Six-Day War was a legitimate effort on the part of Arabs to regain territory conquered by Israel in 1948, one photograph that supposedly portrayed an Israeli firing squad executing Arabs—in 1956, during the Suez crisis—was titled "This is Gaza Strip, Palestine, not Dachau, Germany." (Objections to the newsletter proved to Julius Lester only that Jews "are still Hitler's victims, both here and in Israel," trading upon the ghosts of 6 million dead.)[63] Speaking as the minister of defense for the Black Panthers, Huey Newton acknowledged Israel's right of self-defense but concluded, more ominously, that "the Jewish people have a right to survive as long as they solely exist to [put] down the reactionary expansionist Israeli Government."[64]

In Black Power's opposition to Israel, pan-Africanist liberation was keyed in particular to symbolic identification with the "black" homeland of Egypt, now portrayed as invaded and occupied because of the Israeli capture of the Sinai in the Six-Day War. More categorically than Carmichael, Shirley Graham Du Bois asserted in the wake of the Yom Kippur War that *"Egypt is Africa."* Comparing the discrimination faced in Israel by Arabs and Mizrahi Jews to that faced by African Americans in the United States, and taking note of the lack of acceptance accorded immigrant Black Jews, Du Bois denounced the Israelis, "surrounded as they are by an ocean of sun-tanned peoples," for repeatedly and arrogantly asserting their "superior 'whiteness'" in the region.* The whole of Palestine, by this argument, belonged not to the Jews but to a hypothesized alliance of Arabs and Africans. "With the help of Christians in America and Europe," Malcolm X had claimed nearly a decade earlier, the Jews "drove our Muslim brothers out of their homeland, where they had been settled for centuries, and took over the land for themselves."[65]

Black Power's Marxist-inspired anti-Zionism thus aligned itself with the

---

* The same polarizing, racialist color scheme making Jews "white" and Arabs "black" remained in place in 2003 when Nelson Mandela condemned President George W. Bush and Prime Minister Tony Blair of Great Britain for waging war against Iraq. Whereas there was no evidence of weapons of mass destruction in Iraq, but "we know that Israel has weapons of mass destruction," Mandela wanted to know "why should there be one standard for one country, especially because it is black, and another one for another country, Israel, that is white." Shirley Graham Du Bois, "Confrontation in the Middle East," *Black Scholar* 5 (November 1973), 32–33; Nelson Mandela quoted in Yaacov Lozowick, *Right to Exist: A Moral Defense of Israel's Wars* (New York: Doubleday, 2003), pp. 182–83.

rhetoric of Nasser, who, during Egypt's buildup of Soviet arms prior to the 1956 Suez war, declared that "vengeance is Israel's death" and called upon "the disciples of Pharaoh and the sons of Islam" to "cleanse the land of Palestine."[66] Rap Brown's avowal that blacks would not "play Jews" in Nazi America echoed the Arab charge that Israel was repeating the sins of the Nazis, even that Israel was determined to exterminate the Arabs. ("Zionism ought to realize that it can never attain the strength of Nazi Germany," read a Syrian newspaper commentary in 1977, and "neither will the Arabs in Israel ever assume the status of Jews in Germany.")[67] And when Carmichael charged that "the so-called State of Israel" was an "unjust and certainly an immoral state," he did more than adapt the Nation of Islam's denigrating phrase "so-called Jews" to political purpose. He unerringly echoed the Arab view, repeated in the core doctrine of the PLO, that Israel was no state at all but an illegal colonialist excrescence—hence the common epithet "Zionist entity"—imposed on a long-resident Palestinian people by the imperialist West. Carmichael also berated the early Zionists for considering emigration to Uganda—"they were going to give to the Jews a part of Africa!" he exclaimed—and argued that since "a hundred million niggers [had] been killed during the trip from Africa to America," African Americans had a greater right than the Jews to a homeland. His further proposal that Zionists "should take the land for their home state from Germany, since it was Germany who fought them," was either grossly ignorant or disingenuous but in any event started from a preposterous premise, namely, that the Germans "fought" the Jews, as though in a contest of military opponents.[68]

Like SNCC, the Black Panthers insisted that they were not anti-Semitic but only anti-Zionist, a distinction their rhetoric at times made it hard to discern. Anticipating the syllogistic logic of the United Nations, the international coordinator of the Black Panther Party, Connie Matthews, found in the decay of support among whites for the Black Panthers evidence that "a large portion of these people are Zionists and are therefore racists."[69] More specifically, the Panthers openly supported Fatah as "part of the historic process of the liberation of the oppressed peoples" of Asia, Latin America, and Africa, and endorsed its 1969 manifesto, the "Seven Points," whose call for freedom from "Zionist colonization" and the creation of a Palestinian state as part of the "Arab fatherland" declared a distinction between anti-Zionism and anti-Semitism that it immediately began to elide: "*Fatah*, the Palestine National Liberation Movement, is not struggling against the Jews as an ethnic and religious community. It is struggling against Israel as the expression of colonisation based on a theocratic, racist and expansionist system and of Zionism and colonialism."[70]

Having escaped from prison and fled to Algeria, Black Panther minister of information Eldridge Cleaver appeared at a Fatah rally alongside Yasser Arafat. Citing "American capitalist imperialism" as their common enemy and announcing an agreement whereby black Americans would be trained in Fatah camps, Cleaver in exile now found the PLO, not Israel, the proper model for African Americans. (Although other Panthers visited Jordan between 1968 and 1970, as guests of Fatah and the PLO, no guerrilla training seems to have taken place.) Despite suffering genocide in Europe, Cleaver argued, the Jews of Palestine "committed the crucial and historic error of trying to solve their problems at the expense of another people. The same thing happened to [the Palestinians] as happened to the Black people in America." A *Black Panther* headline of 1969 reduced the argument to simple arithmetic: "Zionism (Kosher Nationalism) + Imperialism = Fascism."[71]

In view of the galvanizing, if sometimes abstract, effect on black Americans of the African liberation movements and the anticolonial ideologies they inspired, opposition to Israel, even its demonization, was inevitable. Brotherhood with the Palestinians and identification with Egypt—in a political variation on the Afrocentric metonymy wherein the land of the pharaohs is taken for the whole of Africa—provided a kind of psychological bridge to identification with African wars of liberation and the symbolic recovery of an African homeland. Ironically, however, it constituted a reversal of Israel's own recent status as a model for newly decolonized nations on the road to modernization.

In the late 1950s and early 1960s, Israel had supported African independence movements and provided economic, technical, and educational aid to some thirty-one African countries.[72] For some Israelis, reflecting a view that dated back at least to Herzl, such activities had a redemptive spiritual value, though they were just as certainly a pragmatic means of acquiring influence in opposition to hostile Arab nations. In the wake of the Yom Kippur War, however, twenty-one African nations broke off relations with Israel, following eight others that had already done so after the 1967 war. Although most Africans continued to accept Zionism as a legitimate nationalist movement,[73] they were persuaded that Israel's incursion across the Suez Canal into Egypt was a sign of its imperial adventurism (the fact that this was a counterattack to Egypt's incursion into the Sinai was deemed irrelevant).

American proponents of Black Power who joined in the African condemnation of Israel generally ignored contemporary Arab wars with black Africa, as well as the history of Arab enslavement of black Africans.[74] They likewise made few distinctions among Arab nations' conflicting views of Israel and paid little attention to their manipulation of the Palestinians. It was not lost on them, however, that African colonialism—wherein race as a principle of political organization and bureaucracy as a principle of domination were polished, as Hannah Arendt noted—was one crucible of German fascism.[75] For the same reason, they were particularly sensitive to Israel's partnership with South Africa, which, in the words of John Henrik Clarke, placed Israel in an "unholy alliance" against "black people" and made it a pariah among black African and other Third World countries.[76]

But neither black African rejection of Israel nor Black Power's disapprobation arose in a vacuum. The oil price revolution of the early 1970s provided Arab nations with massive funds for rearmament and for financing terrorism and anti-Zionist, anti-Semitic propaganda, a campaign particularly evident in the "motherland" of Egypt.[77] It also increased their leverage with western Europe, Japan, and Third World nations, including many of those African nations with which Israel had once enjoyed profitable and friendly partnerships. Aligning themselves with the Soviet Union, oil-rich Arab nations, and the Organization of African Unity (OAU), whose influence had been gathering force since its formation in 1963—sometimes through military or economic inducements, sometimes through overt threats—Israel's former black African allies lent their voices to the now nearly unanimous Third World condemnation of the Jewish state.[78] Holding Israel responsible for the Yom Kippur War, the council of OAU ministers in November 1973 expressed the nations' collective will to fight the "power politics of imperialism, colonialism and Zionism," epitomized by Israel's "expansionist policy of aggression against the Arab countries."[79]

New UN membership for a number of Third World nations aligned with the Arabs had two short-term results. The first was an invitation to Yasser Arafat to address the General Assembly in 1974.[80] The second was the ideological justification for that invitation advanced by a coalition of Arab, Soviet bloc, and African countries and codified in the infamous 1975 United Nations Resolution 3379, "Elimination of All Forms of Racial Discrimination," to the effect that "Zionism is a form of racism and racial discrimination" (the vote was taken, as it happened, on the thirty-seventh anniversary of Kristallnacht). Among the black African nations voting on the resolution, most of them Israel's former trade and diplomatic partners, nineteen voted yes, five no, and eleven abstained.[81] Although the United Nations repealed the resolution in 1991, its record of anti-Zionism remained largely intact throughout the century,[82] putting supporters of Israel, American Jews in particular, continually at odds with the leftist Third World coalition toward which many African American intellectuals were sympathetic. The UN was once more the site of controversy in 1979, when the United States ambassador, the African American Andrew Young, was forced to resign his post for conducting unauthorized secret meetings with the PLO. The event quickly broke down into invective between blacks, who thought that "the Jews" had forced Young out, and Jews, who thought that both Young's conduct and his defense of it amounted to Israel-bashing, if not anti-Semitism.

Far from repairing the damage done to black-Jewish relations in the previous decade, the 1970s thus deepened the rift, as anti-Zionism and advocacy of racial preferences became more prominent features of African American opinion. Between their support for Israel, increasingly seen by many on the international as well as the American left as a "pariah state," and their opposition to race-based compensatory actions, observed Nathan Glazer, American Jews were now "doubly exposed" to the potential contempt of African Americans.[83] If one adds the growing willingness among African Americans to interpret slavery and Jim Crow as a centuries-long "holocaust," Jews were, in fact, triply exposed.

HERE IN BABYLON

When Black Power activists drew upon anti-imperial, anticolonial rhetoric to condemn Zionism, the target was seldom Israel alone. It was also those responsible for the "colonized" enclaves of blacks in the United States, and they built, in this respect, on a substantial body of postwar black nationalist theory—indeed, on a theory that dated back to the advent of colonialism. How can Americans condemn in Germany, Belgium, or other colonial powers for whom the world's "'darkies' are born beasts of burden," Du Bois asked in *Darkwater* (1920), the same practices that the United States carries out, "just as brutally, within her own borders"—in Chicago, in St. Louis, in Memphis, in Washington, D.C.? "From the beginning," said Harold Cruse in a more contemporaneous essay that sought to connect Black Power to anticolonial movements in Africa, Asia, Latin America, and Cuba, "the American Negro has existed as a colonial being. His enslavement coincided with the colonial expansion of European powers and was nothing more or less than a condition of domestic colonialism."[84] Even though the black critique of domestic colonialism was motivated by the desire for inclusion within the national polity, rather than by the delusion that black rule might be established in the United States, Fanon's anticolonial studies *The Wretched of the Earth* (translated in 1965) and *Black Skin, White Masks* (translated in 1967), as we have seen, became textbooks for Black Power, as did the 1965 American edition of Albert Memmi's *The Colo-*

nizer and the Colonized, which was dedicated "to the American Negro, also colonized." Because he showed black people "the way to harness their forces," said Cleaver, Fanon proved that the French in Algeria, the British in Kenya, and the Portuguese in Angola were no different from "Yankee Doodle" in Watts.[85]

Perceptions that Israel was no longer the colonized, but now the colonizer, entered directly into the critique of exploitation in the black American ghetto. Mixing black pride, anticolonialism, and anti-Zionism, works ranging from a staid academic study such as Kenneth Clark's *Dark Ghetto* (1965) to the benchmark of liberationist writing, *Black Power* (1967), by Stokely Carmichael and Charles Hamilton, were infused with the twin arguments that African Americans were a colonized people and that, learning from the tragic passivity of the Jews under Hitler and now the Israelis' oppression of the Palestinians, they must resist racist oppression by all available means. If the Jews of Israel and the Jews of the United States could no longer be emulated, they could be scorned. Enemies abroad thus merged with enemies at home, and Jewish support for Israel was subjected to a classic typology. Resurrecting anti-Semitic stereotypes of price gouging by Jewish merchants and landlords dating back to the 1930s, Malcolm X charged that Jews "sap the very life-blood of the so-called Negroes [in America] to maintain the state of Israel," keeping its military in a state of aggression against "our brothers in the East," while Carmichael found that "the same Zionists that exploit the Arabs also exploit us in this country." For the Black Panthers, cops in the ghetto and Israeli troops in the West Bank were cut from the same imperialist cloth, since Zionist expansionism was comparable to exploitation "here in Babylon" at the hands of the Jewish "bandit merchants and greedy slumlords that operate in our communities."[86]

Insofar as the black ghettos of the United States were also likened to the wartime ghettos of Europe, the conduct of the Jews under Hitler became a point of contempt. "Check out the difference between us and the Jews when the Nazis started to commit genocide against them," said Carmichael. "They got the Jews to cooperate with them . . . and the Jews were the ones carrying out the orders so the Nazis could say it's not us, it's the Jews, and then they pulled the Uncle Tom Jews up." When he charged that the elected black leaders of Cleveland and Washington, D.C., were "puppet governments" in league with the white man, Rap Brown pointed to the example of the *Judenräte,* the Jewish counsels through which the Nazis controlled wartime ghettos: "Remember, it was Jews who began to remove other Jews for Hitler."[87] American Jews in positions of authority were likely to be held in equal contempt. The fact that Judge Monroe Friedman's relatives had perished in the Warsaw Ghetto, far from seeming to endow him with insight into racial oppression, made him a special target for

Eldridge Cleaver's wrath during the trial of Huey Newton for murdering an Oakland police officer. "Here he is with his funky ass, sitting on a bench, disgracing the very name of justice," said Cleaver, "presiding over the final solution to the Negro problem here in Babylon." In its commentary on Newton's trial and that of the "Chicago Eight," charged with inciting to riot at the 1968 Democratic National Convention, *The Black Panther* collapsed the distinction between Jews and Israelis: "It was a Zionist judge, Judge Freedman [sic], who sentenced Huey P. Newton to fifteen years in jail. It was a Zionist judge, Judge [Julius] Hoffman, who allowed the other Zionists to go free but has kept Bobby Seale in jail."[88]

Even worse than a Jew conspiring with the white man in the justice system's "final solution" was an African American so estranged from his true being as actually to become a Jew. Haki Maduhubti (Don L. Lee) thus mocked Sammy Davis, Jr., as a "jewishnegro" trapped in his Judaism and stripped of his resources as a "Blackman," as though he himself were colonized by an enemy race. ("See Sammy Davis Run in the Wrong Direction," which played wittily on Bud Schulberg's 1941 novel about Jewish Hollywood, *What Makes Sammy Run?*, was dedicated to a group of "negro editors" who had visited "occupied *Palestine.*") Alienated from nation and family alike, in Maduhubti's rendering, Davis finds only a false home in Israel, betraying both his descent from a black mother and the brotherhood with oppressed Palestinians that Madhubuti makes his racial obligation:

> kissing the wailing wall
> in the forgotten occupied country.
> his top lip stuck
> & in a strange land he hollered for his momma
> not being jewish
> naturally
> she was off some place   being herself.[89]

It was easy to joke about Sammy Davis, Jr.; he was the most popular Negro among Jews but the most unpopular Jew among Negroes, quipped William Stringfellow.* But Madhubuti's poem put significant aesthetic effects—the fig-

---

* Although he ascribed his conversion to Judaism to God's intervention in a failed suicide attempt, Davis found purpose, too, in the affinity between Jews and blacks, in "their oppressions, their enslavements—despised, rejected, searching for a home, for equality and human dignity." Davis recalled that he regularly carried a mezuzah, a present from Eddie Cantor, as a good luck charm, except for the day a car

urative interplay of conflicting modes of estrangement, colonial occupation, and natal identity is quite inventive—in the service of disgusting sentiments. Ridiculing the religious beliefs of black Jews and prescribing for true "blackness" a univocal, unalterable set of allegiances, the poem, like some instances of Black Power rhetoric, turned protest into caricature.

Black Power's propensity simultaneously to depict blacks as figurative Jews and to condemn real Jews was perhaps most apparent in demands for reparations. In a proposition that followed naturally from its vision of the black ghetto as a colony, a wartime Jewish ghetto, or a concentration camp, and otherwise threatening revolution, the 1966 platform of the Black Panther Party demanded government compensation for the "slaughter of over fifty million black people."[90] The case for black reparations had a disjointed history going back to Reconstruction, but it was given new energy by the payments provided Holocaust survivors by Germany beginning in 1952. As we have seen in earlier chapters, reparations were implicit in African American demands for redress under the United Nations Genocide Convention and for land in which to found a sovereign black state. The idea was taken up once more by Whitney Young when he assumed leadership of the National Urban League in 1961. His proposal for a ten-year domestic Marshall Plan, which would consist of private initiatives and $20 billion in government spending to counteract generations of deprivation, was soon endorsed by James Farmer, head of CORE, who asked in 1963 for up to $3 billion a year for five to ten years in remediation for the black community. "The wounds inflicted by 350 years of deprivation," said Farmer, "will not be erased automatically."[91]

More elaborate was the "Black Manifesto" addressed to "The White Christian Churches and the Jewish Synagogues in the United States of America and All Other Racist Institutions." Unveiled by James Forman, international affairs director of SNCC, at a 1969 event sponsored by the multi-denominational Interreligious Foundation for Community Organization (Forman soon thereafter publicized it by disrupting a service at Riverside Church in New York), the

---

accident cost him an eye. On the way to the operating room, Janet Leigh gave him a Star of David, which he clutched so hard it cut a "stigmata" into the palm of his hand. When he married the white (Swedish) actress Mai Britt in 1960, Davis was faced with bomb threats, picketing by American neo-Nazis, and ridicule as a "kosher coon." William Stringfellow in "Negro-Jewish Relations in America: A Symposium," *Midstream* 12 (December 1966), 76; Sammy Davis, Jr., interview with Alex Haley (1966), in Alex Haley, *The Playboy Interviews,* ed. Murray Fisher (New York: Ballantine, 1993), pp. 253–54; Sammy Davis, Jr., with Jane and Burt Boyar, *Why Me? The Sammy Davis, Jr., Story* (New York: Farrar, Straus and Giroux), p. 95.

"Black Manifesto" began with the Du Boisian premise that "racist white America has exploited our resources, our minds, our bodies, our labor" and forced us "to live as colonized people" while building "the most industrialized country in the world." In formulating the rationale for the manifesto, however, Forman was obliged to take his lead from the influence of the American Jewish lobby. "We are an African people," he argued. "We sit back and watch the Jews in this country make Israel a powerful conservative state in the Middle East, but we are not concerned about the plight of our brothers in Africa." With Africa in political disarray, undermined by Western corruption and infiltration by the CIA, he argued, African Americans should forget back-to-Africa dreams and arm themselves to bring down the government. As an alternative to insurrection, the manifesto went on to demand from white churches and synagogues, deemed to be part and parcel of the nation's complex of racism and capitalism, reparations of $500 million, since "fifteen dollars a nigger is not a large sum of money." Among the projects to be funded by this sum was a southern land bank to support cooperative farms; black-owned publishing houses and television networks that would counteract the brainwashing carried out by racist media; training centers for various crafts; an improved welfare system; a labor strike and defense fund; a black university in the South; and the International Black Appeal, one of whose goals would be the creation of a "Black Anti-Defamation League."[92]

Such mimicry of their organizations may have been offensive, perhaps deliberately so, to American Jews (the American Jewish Committee withdrew from the Interreligious Foundation for Community Organization over Forman's manifesto),[93] but it also pointed up a sad discrepancy between the resources of American blacks and those of American Jews, yet another indication of the growing estrangement between allies who had become antagonists.

By the late 1960s, the Anti-Defamation League, the United Jewish Appeal (UJA), and the American Israel Public Affairs Committee, a lobbying group, had emerged as major forces in shaping public policy and public opinion, less well known to a broad public but in all likelihood more influential than comparable black organizations, including the NAACP. As part of the outpouring of support for Israel during the Six-Day War, the UJA raised $100 million in a period of three weeks and $241 million (plus another $190 million in Israeli bonds) in the calendar year 1967, up from $64 million the year before. (One Dallas businessman, after donating $250,000, said that he would give whatever was needed: "You can have everything I own, for if anything happened to Israel what I had left would be meaningless.") In the year following the Yom Kippur War, when the mass destruction of Jews had seemed even more likely than in

1967, bond sales reached $500 million, while UJA contributions to Israel approached $660 million.[94] Had black Americans been capable of contributing even remotely comparable sums to African (or Arab) nations, it is unlikely that they could have counted on the official government support or public acquiescence that aided American Jewish efforts during 1947–48 and again, more abundantly, during the Six-Day and Yom Kippur wars.[95]

Frustration with their comparative lack of power and prestige undoubtedly exacerbated black radicals' tendency to blur the distinction between anti-Zionism and anti-Semitism, even if it aggravated divisions within the black community itself. Roy Wilkins, for instance, charged that Black Power was anti-white to the point of being "a reverse Hitler, a reverse Ku Klux Klan," while Whitney Young likened such views to those of the American Nazi Party.[96] Many African Americans, indeed, shared the view of most Jews that it was not the Israelis but their adversaries who were the true inheritors of Nazism. Roy Innis, director of CORE in the 1970s, saw American Jews held hostage by Arab skyjackers as "a symbolic and frightening reminder of a disease which too many people ignored in Germany and a reminder of the days when slave families were similarly separated."[97] Nevertheless, radical voices dominated the dialogue and were certainly the ones heard most clearly by many Jews.

Although no American black nationalist has ever gained a significant political constituency, let alone commanded a fascist movement—the only conceivable exception would be the Nation of Islam, whose cult of charisma and demonizing of Jews have a few elements in common with the racial pageantry of German or Italian fascism and whose quasi-military Fruit of Islam reminded one black observer of "jackbooted Nazi stormtroopers"[98]—attribution of fascist tendencies to some proponents of Black Power was not entirely misguided. The disintegration of the Mosaic analogy led in extremity to black identification not just with the *jihad* of Arab nations but with an exterminationist mentality. In the aftermath of the assassination of Malcolm X, Amiri Baraka (LeRoi Jones) thus gave Malcolm's vision of political sovereignty for black urban enclaves a grotesque twist. Beyond expelling white politicians and property owners from such black "lands," he called for autonomy recognized by "treaties, agreements, laws" and adopted the racial logic of Nazism. "In order for the Black Man to survive," said Baraka, he must take steps to ensure that he has "what the Germans call *Lebensraum* ('living room') literally space in which to exist and develop." Only a united black consciousness, Baraka went on to say, can save black people from annihilation, and "there is only one people on the planet who can slay the white man. The people who know him best. His ex-slaves."[99] The drift into a species of pan-African fascism reached its nadir in

1974, when Marcus Garvey's son translated an Afro-Zionist motto signifying the hoped-for sovereignty of the black diaspora into an ominous prophecy. The "children of the Black God of Africa," decreeded the younger Garvey, will soon cleave together in a single revolutionary body, whereupon the world will face "the Black cry for an African 'Anchluss' and the resolute demand for African 'Lebensraum.' One God, One Aim, One Destiny for our glorious African race."[100]

In order not to be "America's Jews," it seemed, blacks must instead act like "America's Nazis." On such occasions, said Lucy Dawidowicz, it was hard "to distinguish Black Power from Black Shirts."[101]

THE JEW BOY AND THE IRON WALL

In December 1968 an anonymous black student's poem, titled "Anti-Semitism" (later attributed to Thea Behran), was read on Julius Lester's radio program on WBAI-FM in New York, "The Great Proletarian Cultural Revolution." A litany of clichés concerning the Holocaust, black Jews, and Jewish accommodation to white supremacy, the poem struck to the core of black resentment of Jewish assimilation:

> Hey, Jew Boy, with that yarmulka on your head
> You, pale-faced Jew boy—I wish you were dead. . . .
> Hitler's reign lasted for only fifteen years
> For that period of time you shed crocodile tears
> My suffering lasted for over 400 years, Jew boy. . . .
> Guess you know, Jew boy, there's only one reason you made it
> You had a clean white face, colorless, and faded
> I hated you, Jew boy, because your hangup was the Torah
> And my only hangup was my color.[102]

Lester later came to regard his own position as anti-Semitic and looked back on the events as a turning point in his conversion to Judaism.* At the time,

---

* After the uproar caused by the incident, Lester left the station for a time but returned in 1971 with a show that he now called "Uncle Tom's Cabin." "I wake listeners with the sounds of whales singing, Bach cantatas, Gregorian chants, and on occasion, John Philip Sousa marches," Lester later wrote. "I read the *New York Times* on the air and talk about the news with sacred irreverence." This strange medley of

however, he defended himself in a subsequent broadcast by arguing that there could be no meaningful equation drawn between black anti-Semitism in the United States and anti-Semitism in Europe: "In America it is we who are the Jews. It is we who are surrounded by a hostile majority. . . . There is no need for black people to wear yellow Stars of David on their sleeves; that Star of David is all over us. And the greatest irony of all is that it is the Jews who are in the position of being Germans."[103]

The context for the blow-up over Behran's poem was a strike in the Ocean Hill–Brownsville section of Brooklyn by public school teachers, many of them Jewish, in response to the Board of Education's decision to grant greater authority over the schools to community boards composed of residents and parents, most of them black. When the new community board attempted to transfer a number of teachers and administrators, and began to screen teachers according to their apparent sensitivity to the cultural needs of black children, while ignoring standard measures of seniority and merit, a strike was called by Albert Shanker, the leader of the United Federation of Teachers. Against the backdrop of recent minor incidents that briefly flared into major crises—as when a local CORE official in Mount Vernon, New York, said of Jewish teachers that "Hitler made a mistake when he did not kill enough of you," or when a black teacher named John Hatchett charged that black schoolchildren were being "educationally castrated" and "mentally poisoned" by the Jews in charge of New York public schools—heated rhetoric flourished during the three-month series of walkouts.[104]

Euro-American cultural artifacts, decidedly not the new canon of Black Power, suggests that the sacred irreverence of which Lester spoke included an indulgence in stereotypes meant mockingly to deny them. But in Lester's case it is not entirely clear that he was signifying, for his invocation of *Uncle Tom's Cabin* also set up a different kind of irreverence, one ultimately directed at the constraining requirements of color dictated by Black Power. At the same moment he launched his new show, Lester was in the midst of the crisis of faith that would ultimately carry him back to his true ancestral roots, not as a African American but rather as a Jew (a topic to which I will return in Chapter 8): "I stare at my name on the spines of the nine books I have published and wonder who Julius Lester is and what all those words are that he has written. . . . I have written books that, while not false, are not wholly true. I have lived the life others needed me to live. By doing so I have sold my birthright and I never knew what it was." Who he is, after conversion, circumcision, and bar mitzvah, is a cantor: "At long last I know what my voice was meant to sing. All those years I sang folk songs, spirituals, blues, work songs, and always knew that something was absent, that as much as I loved spirituals, I was not wholly present when I sang them." In converting, renouncing his former militant self, and daring to rebuke James Baldwin, among others, for what he took to be instances of anti-Semitic speech, Lester dissented from political pieties and considered the Nazi genocide, not slavery, his real ancestral experience. Julius Lester, *Lovesong: Becoming a Jew* (New York: Arcade, 1988), pp. 73–74.

The Ocean Hill–Brownsville conflict is important less for the scope of its consequences than for the fact that, in media-saturated New York City, it assumed at the time, and has assumed since, an inordinate symbolic power. Blacks charged Jews with trying to control the local economy, as they purportedly had in Germany, distributed leaflets that referred to Jewish teachers as "the Middle-East murderers of colored people" and "bloodsucking exploiters and murderers," and carried signs with slogans such as "You will all make good lampshades" and "Jews get out of Palistine [sic]. It's not your home anyway! Moses was the first traitor and Hitler was the Messiah!!!"[105] The militant group Republic of Africa proposed elections in Ocean Hill–Brownsville in an attempt to consolidate black ghettos into a self-governing federation free from municipal oversight and union control. For their part, Shanker and other Jewish leaders responded with accusations of reverse racism and depicted the transfer of Jewish teachers as a form of Nazism.

Although their own actions were far from noble, Lester and others were not mistaken in charging that the union strategically cultivated fears of black anti-Semitism.[106] By quoting from the Behran poem, distributing an anonymous anti-Semitic broadside to all teachers, using an effective campaign of hecklers, and leafleting in Jewish neighborhoods, Shanker and the union sought to change the calculus from racial quotas and community control to black attitudes toward Jews.* In the end, control of the kind envisioned by black leaders was effectively quashed, but at the expense of driving blacks and Jews further apart at the very moment when their alliance was most needed. Alienated by the argument of those favoring community control that "black values" were fundamentally different from those of middle-class whites, Jerald Podair has concluded, Jews used the crisis to complete "their journey to unambiguous white identity, the last group of Caucasians in New York to do so."[107]

The strike had local causes, but it brought to a very visible, public climax

---

* An ancillary response was satire. Thus, the Jewish Defense League demanded that the New York Mets hire enough Jews to make up 26.2 percent of their roster, what they estimated to be the percentage of Jews in New York City, while high school students in Minneapolis played upon the Brooklyn crisis in setting forth a list of mock demands that aped the tenets of Black Power: school books must be read right to left; only kosher food could be served in the cafeteria; additional Jewish teachers and special counselors for Jews must be hired; Jewish history and culture will be taught in all grades; the Jewish community of Minneapolis will have the right to interview teaching applicants with the stipulation that "no assimilated Jews shall be hired." Meir Kahane, *The Story of the Jewish Defense League* (1975; rpt. Institute for the Publication of the Writings of Meir Kahane, 2000), p. 115; Jonathan Kaufman, *Broken Alliance: The Turbulent Times between Blacks and Jews in America* (1985; New York: Touchstone, 1988), pp. 202–3.

tensions over black education and the study of black culture that reached back several decades. Gunnar Myrdal opened *An American Dilemma* in 1944, for example, by noting that "Negro genius is imprisoned in the Negro problem," a problem he glossed by contrasting the dynamic presence of Jews in American intellectual life: "A Jewish economist is not expected to be a specialist in Jewish labor. A Jewish sociologist is not assumed to confine himself always to studying the Ghetto. A Jewish singer is not doomed eternally to perform Jewish folk songs."[108] Despite its tragic consequences in Europe, the "Jewish question" occupied a small domain in the racial topography of the United States. Not so the "Negro question," which had a hundred-year history of adjudication mainly by white scholars and political demagogues that largely excluded the contributions even of major black scholars such as Du Bois. Referring to a 1945 meeting devoted to "The Negro in the United States," organized by the Commission on Justice and Peace of the Central Conference of American Rabbis, Kenneth Clark pointedly asked, "What would Jews . . . think if a conference of Negro leaders were to devote a round table to the problem of 'The Jews in the United States?'"[109]

It may be, as Clark saw it eight years later, that study of the Negro problem reflected an effort on the part of Jews "to reconcile the conflict between their assimilationist tendencies—their unconscious identification with privileged whites—and their latent anxieties about their own minority status,"[110] but the underlying assumptions that prompted his intemperance were little changed even in the 1960s. Harold Cruse, whose *Crisis of the Negro Intellectual* (1967) dwelled at length on the purported economic and political manipulation of blacks by Jews, regretted the fact that Herbert Aptheker and other Jewish communists made themselves spokespersons for Negro affairs, thus "burying the Negro radical potential deeper and deeper in the slough of white intellectual paternalism." Larry Neal resented the sociological study of blacks carried out by Aptheker and Melville Herskovits, among others, the music criticism of Nat Hentoff, and the cultural commentary of Leslie Fiedler and Norman Podhoretz, "money hungry leeches playing hip."[111] Blacks were in no mood to be instructed about the virtues of Jewish humanism by Irving Kristol in his archly titled essay "A Few Kind Words for Uncle Tom"* or to be told by

---

* Against the backdrop of renewed attention to American slave revolts and, after Hannah Arendt, to Jewish resistance (or the lack of it) to Nazism, Kristol advised blacks to choose the path of liberalist aspiration rather than that of militant retribution. Pointing to the differing legacies of Simeon Bar Kokhba, who led the revolt against Rome that brought about the destruction of the Second Temple (a kind of "Jewish equivalent of Nat Turner"), and Rabbi Akiba, who negotiated with the Romans in order

Joel Carmichael that the quest for roots in Africa was "simply pathetic, especially since the only prop of such a quest can never be more than anthropological erudition, provided, very often, by Jewish anthropologists!"[112] Such counsel corroborated the fear that Jewish scholarship on blacks was a special instance of perfidy, as Nation of Islam member Jeremiah X claimed in 1965: "Unlike other whites, Jews make it a practice to study Negroes," using "the knowledge thus obtained to get close to the Negro, thereby being in a position to stab him with a knife."*

Over time, situational black anti-Semitism, at first based largely on the interactions of two peoples occupying overlapping ghettos, took on a more distinctive cultural dimension. When Jewish agents and producers promoted black musicians, when Jewish writers and artists found a fresh energy of liberation in black culture, or when Jewish scholars emerged among the most eminent historians of the African American experience, they might be charged with stealing or perverting black talent. According to one Black Muslim interviewed by C. Eric Lincoln, Jewish liberalism was a deceitful drug. Invited to dinner, allowed to shake hands with the Jew's wife, and assured that everyone is equal, the man said, the favored Negro taken into the Jew's confidence "gets so

---

to preserve a "saving remnant," Kristol found much to recommend in the second model, closer in spirit to Booker T. Washington or Stowe's Uncle Tom. The black protagonists in the contemporary civil rights struggle, said Kristol, would do well to recognize that "what is most valuable and memorable in this history—Jewish piety, Jewish humanism, Jewish survival itself—derives relatively little from a series of acts of rebellion, and very much from a series of acts of accommodation which transcended all daily indignities while achieving a serenity of spirit that is a permanent legacy to the human race." Irving Kristol, "A Few Kind Words for Uncle Tom," *Harper's Magazine* 230 (February 1965), 97.

* The problem was no less evident three decades later. Says the black nationalist playwright Randy Shank in Ishmael Reed's *Reckless Eyeballing* (1986), whites allow Jews to be white so long as they "serve the white man by keeping an eye on us, monitoring us, providing him with statistics about us, and interpreting us." "A lot of Jewish academics," observed Andrew Hacker, "have made good careers by passing black people through mathematical models and churning them into columns of statistics." Gerald Early pointed out that contemporary academic and intellectual experience too often shows that "Jews can be experts on anything; blacks only on themselves." To the extent that blacks may resent or envy Jews on this account, one manifestation appears in conspiracy theories that depict the Jew as a "secret insider," the "demon that the white gentiles say he is." The culmination of such tendencies, said Early, was the Nation of Islam's fantastic diatribe *The Secret Relationship between Blacks and Jews* (1991), which "offers intellectual revenge against the Jew who has always been among the leading experts on blacks and their experience." Jeremiah X quoted in Horace Mann Bond, "Negro Attitudes toward Jews," *Jewish Social Studies* 27 (January 1965), 8; Ishmael Reed, *Reckless Eyeballing* (New York: St. Martin's, 1986), p. 67; Andrew Hacker, "Jewish Racism, Black Anti-Semitism," *Reconstruction* 1 (1992), 23; Gerald Early, "Who Is the Jew? A Question of African-American Identity," *CommonQuest* (Spring 1996), 44.

'hopped up' he will not only go out and organize a campaign against [any] Negro the Jew doesn't like, but he will kill his own mother if she gets in the way before that 'fix' he got by being invited out by the white folks wears off."[113] Not for nothing did Bernard Malamud, in *The Tenants*, title the unfinished novel on which his Jewish protagonist works *The Promised End*. The promise of interracial cooperation evident in the early civil rights movement, at least in some quarters, now seemed headed toward the kind of homicidal apocalypse with which Malamud's novel concludes.

The disintegration of the black-Jewish alliance, as well as its underlying demographic change, was captured well three decades later by Philip Roth in *American Pastoral* (1997), set in the Newark of the turbulent late 1960s, where once-Jewish neighborhoods had given way to burned-out black slums. After Seymour "Swede" Levov's middle-class life turns to chaos when his teenage daughter, Merry, bombs the local post office in Old Rimrock, Swede tries to grasp the meaning of her rebellion through a fantasized conversation with Angela Davis, then on trial for murder and conspiracy:*

> [Davis] praises his daughter, whom she calls "a soldier of freedom, a pioneer in the great struggle against repression." He should take pride in her political boldness, she says. The antiwar movement is an anti-imperialist movement, and by lodging a protest in the only way America understands, Merry, at sixteen, is in the forefront of the movement, a Joan of Arc of the movement. His daughter is the spearhead of the popular resistance to a fascist government and its terrorist suppression of dissent. What she did was criminal only inasmuch as it is defined as criminal by a state that is itself criminal and will commit ruthless aggression anywhere in the world to preserve the unequal distribution of wealth and the oppressive institutions of class domination.

---

* A former UCLA philosophy instructor, fired by Governor Ronald Reagan for being an outspoken member of the Communist Party, Davis was tried and acquitted as a co-conspirator in murder charges stemming from the botched 1970 attempt by Jonathan Jackson, brother of Soledad prisoner and political activist George Jackson, to free another prisoner on trial in the Marin County Courthouse (Jonathan Jackson apparently expected his brother would be appearing in court as well). After he took hostages and demanded the release of his brother and other prisoners, Jackson, two prisoners, and the judge were killed in the ensuing gunfire. Davis, who purchased the guns used by Jackson, was acquitted on the grounds that they had been taken without her permission. George Jackson, author of the prison memoir and analysis of black oppression *Soledad Brother* (1970), was killed the following year by prison guards in what was said to be an escape attempt.

Having inherited management of his father's glove company, Newark Maid, Swede refuses to move the company, despite the city's decay, and continues to believe in the magnanimity of his employment of black workers and their loyalty to him, as previously to his father, who is now retired in Florida. Juxtaposed to the imagined voice of Angela Davis is his father's real voice:

> A whole business is going down the drain because of that son-of-a-bitch LeRoi Jones [Amiri Baraka], that Peek-A-Boo-Boopy-Do, whatever the hell he calls himself in that goddamned hat. I built this [company] with my hands! With my blood! They think somebody gave it to me? Who? Who gave it to me? Who gave me anything, ever? Nobody! What I have I built! With work—w-o-r-k! . . . I'm by the pool and my wonderful friends look up from the paper and they tell me they ought to take out the schvartzes and line 'em up and shoot 'em, and I'm the one who has to remind them that's what Hitler did to the Jews.[114]

The mutual antagonism orchestrated in the voices of Angela Davis and Swede's father, the one the epitome of black radicalism, the other the epitome of Jewish liberalism turning toward neoconservatism, corresponds perfectly to the *Time* magazine cover story of 1969 that displayed the headline "BLACK vs. JEW: A Tragic Confrontation" above an illustration of Jewish and black leaders representing three generations, all men, glaring angrily at one another (see illustration). As Malamud would spell out in greater detail, *Time*'s story surveyed the devolution of black-Jewish comradeship into bitter warfare. After calling for an appreciation of pluralism and the right of both groups to "assert their own identity," the *Time* writers ended on a sermonizing note, counseling Jews to practice the forbearance in which their history had steeped them—"the black is just beginning the course [of entry into the democratic polity], and it is unfortunate that part of the cost of his tuition must be paid by Jewish tolerance"—and predicting fancifully that black anti-Semitism would be eliminated by the victory of the civil rights movement: "When that is achieved, the alliance of the two communities, now near the breaking point, should be stronger than ever."[115]

In the heyday of the counterculture some Jews of the Old Left, such as I. F. Stone, remained ready to exercise such forbearance: "It will not hurt us Jews to swallow a few insults from overwrought Blacks."[116] For some on the New Left, black militancy was the vanguard of political fashion, as in the chic 1969 dinner party at which Leonard Bernstein hosted members of the Black Panthers, who

Cover illustration for Time *magazine, January 31, 1969.*

© 1969 Time Inc. Reprinted by permission.

by that point were being regularly harassed by the FBI and torn apart by internal conflicts. (Outlaw magnetism, wrote Tom Wolfe, ran through the party like a "rogue hormone.")[117] A cohort of the younger New Left, however, went further than voguish accommodation, reviving the Jewish radicalism of the 1930s that had been suppressed by McCarthyism. "Jewish kids who are tired of tomming to the *goyim*," said J. J. Goldberg, were learning from pro-Palestinian Israelis, from blacks, and from the Vietnamese "that it's better to extend the hand in solidarity than in charity." Michael Lerner, later the editor of *Tikkun*, was unequivocal in his opinion that black anti-Semitism was "earned" by Jewish oppression of blacks in the ghetto, and that the Jewish community was "racist, internally corrupt, and an apologist for the worst aspects of American capitalism and imperialism." Identifying Huey Newton as the new Moses for activist Jews, Lerner endorsed the Palestinian cause and maintained that major Jewish writers such as Malamud and Bellow, owing to their materialism, their cynicism about social movements, and their abandonment of the "revolutionary perspective built into Judaism," were part of the problem to be overcome, by revolutionary action if necessary.[118]

Taking Mailer's idea of the "white Negro" in a more anarchic direction, Jerry Rubin extolled an alliance between the Black Panthers and the Yippies (the "Youth International Party," a free-floating protest movement given to psychedelic drugs and political street theater). "Amerika declared war on humanity when she exiled Eldridge [Cleaver]," he wrote in *Do It! Scenarios of the Revolution* (1970), which featured an introduction by Cleaver. "The pigs fired the first shot. But we, the white and black niggers, will fire the last."[119] In becoming a Yippie, said Rubin, he had "dropped out of the White Race and the Amerikan nation," while Abbie Hoffman declared that all hippies were "white niggers" and runaway youth participants in a new "slave revolt."[120] But Jews in particular were obligated to resist the fascism of whiteness. "It is the Jew who should always be on the side of the poor, the oppressed, the underdog, the wretched of the earth," said Rubin in his next book, written from Cook County Jail. "And thousands of young ex-Amerikan ex-Jews are. Three of the kids killed at Kent State were Jews. An unusually high proportion of hippies and revolutionaries are Jews." As one of the Chicago Eight charged with inciting to riot at the 1968 Democratic National Convention, Rubin characterized the trial as a "Jewish morality play," since not only were he, Abbie Hoffman, and Lee Weiner Jewish, but so were their attorneys, the prosecutor, and the judge, Julius Hoffman, who was nothing more than a "Shanda for the Goyem" ("Front Man for the Wasp Power Structure," in Rubin's loose translation), if not a "Nazi" out to destroy his own people.[121]

Jewish ritual also became a vehicle of countercultural dissent. Arthur Waskow's *Freedom Seder* (1970), prompted by King's assassination and initially published in *Ramparts,* wove into canonical texts of the Haggadah not just passages from King, Martin Buber, and the midrash for Exodus, but also "Go Down, Moses," Bob Dylan's "The Times They Are A-Changin'," and prophetic excerpts from "Ginsberg the Tzaddik," "rabbi Thoreau," "rabbi Hannah Arendt," and "the shofet Eldridge Cleaver (who went into exile like Moses)"— where, in fact, Cleaver embraced the PLO and called for the destruction of Israel. (After his conversion to evangelical Christianity, however, Cleaver became a fervent Zionist, declaring in 1976 that Arabs were "among the most racist people on earth," while Jews "have done more than any other people in history to expose and condemn racism.") Making Arab anti-Zionism paramount in the Passover observance, *The Freedom Seder* included a poem by Marilyn Lowen calling upon Jews to "remember the / Egyptian people also in bondage" and asking the Lord to "deliver us back into Egypt / that we may join with our / brothers / until we ALL SHALL BE FREE / next year in the Third World."[122] An early instance of Jewish multiculturalism—his Haggadah, said Waskow, was neither universalist nor particularist but "multiparticularist"—*The Freedom Seder* meant to celebrate the "Passover of the Messianic Age, the Passover of the liberation of all the nations," especially the blacks of the United States, truly America's Jews.*

The fact that most Israelis saw Jewish New Left militants as a product of the diaspora, neurotic and faddish in their enthusiasm for revolutionary ideolo-

---

* In a 1967 address titled "How to Prevent a Pogrom," Waskow found the summer riots of that year, like precursor riots in East St. Louis in 1917 and more recently in Watts in 1965, to be a "pogrom" against blacks on the part of police and the nation itself, which had "herded" blacks into ghettos. Jews in the ghettos of Europe had endured repressive state violence carried out by men mounted on horseback "with swords swinging," but not "mounted on tanks and helicopters, machine-guns firing." The repression of blacks, moreover, had a parallel in Israel's repression of the Palestinians: "Imagine the whole encounter over again, but this time in Giant dress, and in hostility and danger the equivalent of about forty years further along the vicious spiral—and this time conducted on the nation-state level." Waskow was a founding member of Breira, a short-lived group critical of Israeli policy that advocated Palestinian autonomy and met privately with members of the PLO touring the United States under the sponsorship of the American Friends Committee. Arthur I. Waskow, "Judaism and Revolution Today," *Judaism* (Fall 1971), rpt. in Jack Nusan Porter and Peter Dreier, eds., *Jewish Radicalism: A Selected Anthology* (New York: Grove Press, 1973), p. 25; Arthur Waskow, "How to Prevent a Pogrom," 1967 address reprinted as a pamphlet produced by the Southern Student Organizing Committee (Nashville, 1968), p. 1; Arthur Waskow, *The Bush Is Burning! Radical Judaism Faces the Pharaohs of the Superstate* (New York: Macmillan, 1971), p. 93; Michael E. Staub, *Torn at the Roots: The Crisis of Jewish Liberalism in Postwar America* (New York: Columbia University Press, 2002), pp. 299–307.

gies,[123] was unlikely to dissuade them. It was plausible to see their radicalism, like that of the counterculture generally, as a reaction against middle-class affluence and the perceived hypocrisy of liberalism—against those suburban bourgeois agents of racially oppressive capitalism, charged Arnold Jacob Wolf, whose support of integration was limited to holding "art fairs for civil rights organizations." In one quasi-psychoanalytic interpretation, such radicalism was taken to be the younger generation's rejection of the assimilationist weakness of Jewish fathers and the suffocating protection of Jewish mothers, à la Alex Portnoy. Their allegiance to Black Power's anti-Zionism might thus be part of a family drama in which Israel, observed Seymour Martin Lipset, "seems to be behaving like their parents."[124]

Be that as it may, turning against Israel, not to mention condoning anti-Semitism, was a step few Jews were willing to take. Although opposition to Israel might compensate black leaders for their humiliation by Jewish dominance in the civil rights movement, wrote Ben Halpern, there was no demand more unpalatable than that Jews should "spit in the face of Jewish nationalism." Norman Podhoretz placed *The Freedom Seder* in the genre of Jewish self-hatred, written against the Jews' "right to exist, to live and not to die," while Max Geltman said New Left Jews were "helping to bring on massive pogroms against the Jews of America." Likewise, Nathan Glazer accused leftist Jewish intellectuals of sacrificing the values of rationality and tolerance that had secured their own precarious freedom, and inflaming militant attacks on the middle class that, if realized, would place Jews themselves at "the head of the column marked for liquidation." Citing a list of prominent Jewish intellectuals, including Noam Chomsky, Norman Mailer, Nat Hentoff, and Robert Silvers, who had appeared in a recent issue of *The Black Panther* as part of the "International Committee to Support Eldridge Cleaver," Glazer condemned those who have "taught violence, justified violence, [and] rationalized violence," of which anti-Semitism was a necessary consequence. If Jews themselves have given up on the promise of American democracy, he added, they cannot fight black anti-Semitism: "All they can do is give the blacks guns, and allow themselves to become the first victims."[125]

Surely the most unsettling critique of prostrate Jewish liberalism appeared in Richard Elman's ironically titled short story "Law 'N Order Day" (1969), which played upon Black Power predictions that blacks were about to be rounded up by the government and exterminated. Elman, however, took a very different tack on the prospect for genocide. In his futuristic story, set in a section of Los Angeles known as Freedom City, black revolution has been contained by being channeled into periodically prescribed Law 'N Order Days, during which Jewish businesses or Jews themselves are targeted for destruction. On the day of the story's action, the city having just about run out of Jewish stores to burn after the climactic pogroms known as the "Big Massacres," a group of Jewish schoolteachers is arrested and burned to death by a corps of trained killers. One of them, aptly named "Burner," dresses in a protective suit with a bandolier of Molotov cocktails across his chest, carries a "Black Power trident," and sports "a strand of bronze *ushujaa* bells around his neck which made him tinkle when he walked." The ritual is overseen by the city's Justice Committee, condoned by the president of the United States, now located in Los Angeles ("my administration is as Black Power as the next guy's"), organized by its police and firemen, and planned by Blauveldt, a Jew who teaches Caucasian Studies at night and during the day works as a Consultant to the Pigs, "dreaming up ways to 'legitimate' [black] anger."[126] Realizing the logic of his own role in the destruction of the city's Jews, Blauveldt proclaims that he (and the president) will have to be burned next. Only then will Freedom City be *judenrein.*

Elman's brutal parody of the extortions of Black Power wrings the last element of liberal Jewish anguish out of the counterculture. Blauveldt is in league with a corrupt power structure that is slowly passing from white to black and is so debased in his appeasement of radical black anger as to oversee the annihilation of his own people—a farcical realization of Lipset's observation that "one of the payments the Jews would [one day have to] make to the Left for having liberated them would be to disappear." By design, it seems, he resembles Chaim Rumkowski, ostentatious leader of the Lodz Ghetto, who undertook one act of accommodation after another in the hopes of saving all, then some, then a few of "his" Jews from Nazi extermination, until at last, the ghetto having been liquidated, he too was taken to Auschwitz and gassed—"a mad Jewish King presiding over the death of half a million people," as Saul Bellow described him in *Mr. Sammler's Planet.*[127] Elman's future, an outlandish send-up of the threat to the Jewish community described by Glazer, literalized events that presumably could never come to pass—except, of course, that the Jews of Lodz must once have thought the same thing.

For the Jewish New Left, Israel proved to be a more complicated matter than the United States. "If Moses were alive today, he'd be an Arab guerrilla," wrote Rubin in *We Are Everywhere* (1971), a Yippie manifesto that featured pictures of Leila Khaled, along with other Palestinian and Arab guerrillas implicitly in solidarity with blacks, Latinos, and those "non-white" white renegades who stood in opposition to "Amerika" and Israel.[128] While a number of Jews affiliated with New Left groups such as the Young Socialist Alliance and the Progressive Labor Party endorsed anti-Zionism, and even the maximalism of the PLO, others, including those who organized the Radical Zionist Alliance and launched the *Jewish Liberation Journal* and *The Jewish Radical,* rejected anti-Zionism and resented blacks' failure to reciprocate their support. The Black Panthers have become "caricatures of mindless Stalinists," said Itzhak Epstein after Cleaver's endorsement of Fatah. Writing in *Ramparts,* Sol Stern recognized that the Palestine envisioned by the PLO would be an Arab state in which a Jewish religious minority would be "tolerated" only so long as it renounced statehood—in which Zionism, in simple terms, would be a crime; in which, that is to say, there would be no Israel. Seeking to split the difference between "the Fatah-supporting S.D.S. and the ultra-middle-class lox-and-bagel breakfast club Hillel society," M. J. Rosenberg embraced black nationalism while refusing to surrender allegiance to Israel. The call for an end to the Jewish state, he reasoned, admitted of no negotiation: "There is no such thing as 'progressive' anti-Semitism."[129]

Despite their rejection of anti-Zionism, these Jews nevertheless found a welcome antidote in the ethnocentrism of Black Power. Today's "Uncle Tom," wrote Rosenberg in a widely cited essay, is the self-hating Jew who joins radical causes as a white, not as a Jew, and denies his own destiny by condoning black condemnation of Israel. He "scrapes along ashamed of his identity and yet is obsessed with it." Desirous of flagellation, he is truly the "invisible man," wandering in a no-man's land.[130] Accepting the argument that blacks should be enabled to create a separate community with its own power base—in lieu of integration achieved by quotas, which would inevitably come at the expense of Jews—Richard Rubinstein was among those reevaluating post-Holocaust Judaism who concluded that Black Power must be countered by Jewish power of the kind exercised by Israel during the Six-Day War. Tsvi Bisk, an American Jew who had emigrated to Israel, likewise maintained in "Uncle Jake, Come Home!," published in the 1969 founding issue of the *Jewish Liberation Journal,* that Black Power inadvertently offered Jews a cure for their "ghetto neurosis." By purging their inferiority complex and rescuing Jews from a counterproductive involvement in the civil rights movement, said Bisk, Black Power may have "saved Jewish identity" by blocking the radical Jew's "escape" into black causes "making ethnic identity once again fashionable." Black Power, argued Jewish Theological Seminary director Ismar Schorsch, more grandly, would help Jews redress the psychological price paid for emancipation, the agreement not to identify as Jews and "to suppress every public display of Jewishness."[131]

The most controversial rejoinder to ghetto weakness and self-loathing was offered by the Jewish Defense League (JDL), which began in 1968 partly as a response to the apprehensions of lower-middle-class and poor Jews, many of them Orthodox, when blacks moved into their neighborhoods in Queens and Brooklyn. The JDL, which came to prominence during the Ocean Hill–Brownsville crisis, was a thorn in the side of moderates. Its members picketed the radio station where the Behran poem had been read with signs reading "No Auschwitz Here." When it was rumored that James Forman was ready to make the same demands for black reparations at Temple Emanu-El that he had made at Riverside Church, a JDL group armed with pipes, bats, and chains arrived (uninvited) to stop him, a theatrical show of Jewish power that soon thereafter became the basis for a display ad in the *New York Times* whose caption was "Question: Is This Any Way for Nice Jewish Boys to Behave?" Accompanied by a photo of somewhat less threatening looking young men—but attired and posed in a way meant nevertheless to mimic black militants—the question was answered:

> Maybe. Maybe there are times when there is no other way to get across to the extremist that the Jew is not quite the patsy some think he is.
>
> Maybe there is only one way to get across a clear response to people who threaten seizure of synagogues and extortion of money. Maybe nice Jewish boys do not always get through to people who threaten to carry teachers out in pine boxes and to burn down merchants' stores.
>
> Maybe some people and organizations are too nice. Maybe in times of crisis, Jewish boys should not be that nice. Maybe—just maybe—nice people build their own road to Auschwitz.

Although its extremism and its sometimes violent tactics were condemned by mainstream Jewish leaders and organizations, much as the Black Panthers were condemned by mainstream blacks, by 1972 the JDL boasted a membership of fifteen thousand.[132]

The JDL was led by Rabbi Meir Kahane, a former anticommunist, pro–Vietnam War activist who condemned assimilated American Jews as "insecure, full of complexes," the epitome of diaspora inauthenticity. "We'd like to bury that new Jew and resurrect the old one," he proclaimed,[133] by which he meant a Jew less likely to be found in the United States than among the early European Zionists or, better, in Palestine and Israel—in short, a "muscle Jew." Kahane reinterpreted the Holocaust as a source of redemptive strength: "We see a different Jew arising from the ashes and decay of Auschwitz. It is a Jew who pauses to look the world in the eye; to stare directly at those who, for centuries, burned and stabbed and drowned and hanged and gassed us; to softly say: Up against the wall, world." No more suffering and martyrdom, said Kahane, no more mourners' prayers and kaddish. With the strong Jews of Israel, we have "looked into the burning and soul-searing eyes" of Holocaust ghosts and "heard them say: 'Never again. Promise us, *never again.*'"[134]

Kahane's idol was Vladimir (Ze'ev) Jabotinsky, about whom a few words are necessary here since we will shortly see his ideas reflected in *Mr. Sammler's Planet* and *Sons of Darkness, Sons of Light.* A former playwright, novelist, and opera critic, and more important a Russian Zionist who had persuaded the British to form a Jewish regiment for service in Palestine in World War I, Jabotinsky carried his postwar militarism into a passionate defense of Jews and the need for a Jewish state. Sentenced to fifteen years in prison (but soon pardoned) for his role in defending Jews in Jerusalem during the 1920 Arab riots, he became a founder and first commander of the Irgun and the father of the Revisionist movement, whose philosophy would later inform Menachem Begin's post-1948 Herut Party and in turn the Likud bloc that brought Begin into office as prime minister in 1977. The Revisionists pressed for mass colonization to achieve a Jewish majority in a Jewish commonwealth (or state) envisioned to include not only Palestine but also Transjordan. Rome's chief rabbi, David Prato, said of Jabotinsky in 1935: "For Zionism to succeed you need to have a Jewish state with a Jewish flag and a Jewish language. The man who really understands this is your Fascist, Jabotinsky." Even though his youth movement, Betar, had some of the symbolic trappings of fascism, and the clash between the Revisionists and Labor Zionism was so severe that David Ben-Gurion referred to him as "Vladimir Hitler," Jabotinsky's models were not Mussolini or Hitler but democratic nationalists such as Mazzini and Garibaldi.[135]

Jabotinsky eschewed idealism in favor of pragmatic recognition that the survival of the Jewish National Home, eventually the state of Israel, was a matter of power. His program of armed resistance, as Alain Dieckhoff has written, "ensured the psychological conversion of the Jew from being sickly, craven and humiliated to being robust, bold and proud," and sought to transform "providential Zionism," which awaited reparation in the messianic age, into a "Promethean activism" through which Jews would forge their own destiny.[136] Jabotinsky's principles were evident even in the gradualism of Ben-Gurion himself, and all the more visible in Moshe Dayan's policy of deterrence through reprisal or, in later years, Benjamin Netanyahu's certainty that continued Israeli control of the West Bank was a necessary condition for national security.[137] In two 1923 articles, "On the Iron Wall (We and the Arabs)" and "The Morality of the Iron Wall," Jabotinsky developed the view that no voluntary agreement with Palestinian Arabs was conceivable, since they would naturally resist alien settlers, and that security was a prerequisite to peaceful coexistence, which would be possible only when Jewish settlement had been placed "behind an iron wall which [the Arabs] will be powerless to break down." If the cause of Zionism is not moral, he argued, then it should be renounced; if it is moral, then the means to its triumph must be provided: "A sacred truth, whose realization requires the use of force, does not cease thereby to be a sacred truth. This is the basis of our stand toward Arab resistance; and we shall talk of a settlement only when they are ready to discuss it."[138]

Jabotinsky's ideology, with variations, has been a guiding principle for most Israeli leaders up to and including Prime Minister Ariel Sharon,* and it was key to the more radical views of Kahane, who called for Jews of "iron and steel" and adopted as one of the tenets of the JDL the characteristic of *barzel*, Hebrew for "iron," signifying "a physically strong, a fearless and a courageous Jew who fights back."[139] After emigrating to Israel in 1971, Kahane quickly moved to the far right, where his ultimate legacy was an uncompromising version of the "iron wall" that authorized extremist anti-Arab violence. Elected to the Knesset in 1984, he advocated the "transfer" of Palestinians, even Israeli Arabs, and introduced bills designed to strip non-Jews of political rights and establish a form of apartheid, including the Law to Prevent Assimilation, which, like the Nuremberg Laws, would have prohibited marriage and sexual relations between Jews and non-Jews.[140]

The genesis of Kahane's chauvinism was no doubt complex, but it had been nurtured in the JDL's confrontation with Black Power in the late 1960s. He lashed out at white liberal tolerance for black anti-Semitism, based on pity, as the worst kind of racism: "If a Jew is kicked in the teeth and, smiling, declares that he understands the reasons and the motives for the 'unfortunate' attack, he is either a coward or a condescending racist." Abhorring the very thought of forbearance, Kahane lamented the "inexplicable, masochistic drive that sends liberal Jews sprawling at the feet of black intellectuals to be berated, insulted, and spat upon."[141]

Kahane's views were all the more remarkable for being borrowed directly from the same black nationalism the JDL meant to oppose. The paperback jacket of Kahane's *Never Again!* (1971), an exposition of JDL militancy, rightly compared the book to Cleaver's *Soul on Ice* and *The Autobiography of Malcolm*

---

* Sharon's government literalized the principle of the "iron wall" by constructing a security barrier—a combination of walls, fences, trenches, and checkpoints—placed more or less along the Green Line, the border provisionally established by the 1967 war, but at key points carving deeper into the West Bank for security purposes and to protect Israeli settlements and thus expropriating land deemed rightly theirs by Palestinians.

X. The JDL's symbol, a clenched fist issuing from a Star of David, mirrored the clenched fist of Black Power. Consciously styling themselves "Jewish Panthers," members undertook armed community patrols—at one point the JDL promoted a self-defense campaign under the slogan "Every Jew a .22"—and an apprentice's bomb detonated in 1970 at Camp Jedel, a JDL youth camp in the Catskills, was constructed according to instructions in a Black Panther manual. Underscoring the parallel, Kahane declared that the JDL did not differ from the Panthers in wanting to instill self-assurance and pride in young people or in believing that "after asking for 300 years for things from the government—federal or local—it [may become] necessary to use unorthodox or outrageous ways." Where we do differ, he argued, is where "nationalism crosses the boundary line and becomes Nazism."[142]

When they advocated racism or resorted to vigilante action, both the Black Panthers and the JDL lapsed into gangsterism, but their cultivation of ethnoracial empowerment had an obvious allure for those in search of communal identity.* In the face of Black Power's demand that Jews acquiesce to policies inimical to their own interests, and wary of their precarious position in a nation still for the most part ruled by a Protestant elite, many Jews may well have felt hemmed in by the "politics of powerlessness," to quote the title of an intriguing but unconvincing essay by Richard Rubenstein.† But the JDL made a different response equally compelling. Citing the way Kahane played skillfully

---

* As though to corroborate that the power of the marginalized is everywhere girded by extremism and violence, former Los Angeles gang member Sanyika Shakur (Monster Kody Scott) offered a disturbing perspective on the fortuitous appeal of ideology: "If I had been born in '53 instead of '63, I would have been a Black Panther. If I had been born in Germany in the early thirties, I would probably have joined the National Socialist Party. If I had been born Jewish, I would have joined the Jewish Defense League. Because I have the energy, the vitality to be part of something with 'power.' Either constructive or destructive. And because there was a destructive element around me when I was growing up, I went into the Crips." Sanyika Shakur quoted in Léon Bing, Do or Die (New York: HarperCollins, 1993), p. 237.

† Offering a further variation on the view that African Americans have a peculiar, if unrewarded, priority as Americans, Rubenstein called attention to the resemblance between Jews and blacks in their search for "power" in WASP America. "Had Jews wanted to be imitation Anglo-Saxons in larger numbers," he pointed out, their cultural and religious life would have been impoverished. "Like the Black Power Negro, self-respecting Jews want 'to do their own thing.'" By the same token, he argued that Jews, because they constitute a "highly visible minority near the top of the economic ladder without real power," may paradoxically be less secure than African Americans, whose "menial" position is a matter of long historical practice. Since Jews "are by training and disposition incapable of utilizing violence to gain a social objective," and since gentiles are unwilling to take anti-Semitic violence seriously and are more likely to appease blacks than Jews, the Jew becomes an especially attractive target for blacks. Richard L. Rubenstein, "The Politics of Powerlessness," Reconstructionist 34 (May 17, 1968), 11–13.

upon an "odd combustion of feelings of superiority and inferiority" in order to provoke young, post-Holocaust Jews to feel simultaneously more powerless and more powerful than they actually were, Leon Wieseltier recalls telling his parents that Eldridge Cleaver "was making me a better Jew."[143]

METAPHOR FOR A TANK

In this highly volatile atmosphere, literature that took up the conflict between blacks and Jews was not likely to be tranquil. To address adequately its combined promise and pain, no action would be too improbable, no language too hyperbolic. Lowbrow fiction took its own tack in promoting the hazards of racial injustice and interracial reconciliation. In Donald Goines's *Never Die Alone* (1974), the pulp writer Paul Pawlowski, a Polish Holocaust survivor, is asked by his editor to "toss a little crap in" about how "the Jews up this way [the North] are constantly causing the niggers to try and be more than they are."[144] Pawlowski spits in the man's face and subsequently demonstrates his color-blind compassion by taking a dying black drug kingpin named King David, whom he finds wounded on the street, to the hospital. An even more improbable plot governs *Shaft among the Jews* (1972). Fighting Israeli agents on one side and New York cops on the other, Ernest Tidyman's hard-boiled black private eye dons the garb of an Orthodox Jew to track down a renegade Israeli physicist who has learned how to craft synthetic diamonds so pure that they threaten to throw the world economy and Israel's security into turmoil. In pursuit of his prey, of course, Shaft is required to sleep with the physicist's beautiful daughter: "She was clawing at his back and gasping words against his mouth in a language he didn't know and yet understood so well."[145]

In a different but no less sensational register, *The Slave Stealer* (1968) turned the faltering black-Jewish alliance into an occasion for interracial smut. In Boyd Upchurch's pseudo-abolitionist narrative, the real purpose appears to be the exposition of sexual stereotypes in the persons of Solomon Villaricca, an Orthodox Jewish trader from Ohio who steals slaves for the Underground Railroad, and Melinda, the coquettish slave he steals in order to unite her with the Irish saloon owner who claims to love her but intends to set her up as a prostitute. The picaresque plot, very much in tune with the sexual revolution, finds Solomon and Melinda embroiled in adventures with German abolitionists, Gypsy con artists, and southern fundamentalists, while Solomon's belief that Moses married an Ethiopian provides the basis for their own affair, rendered in quasi-pornographic detail (a black servant in the house from which he is to steal Melinda concurs with Solomon's observations about Hebrew eroticism: "Them Children of Israel, they sho must like they's poontang"). As a Jew, Solomon is predictably shown to be as interested in profit as in ethics; but after Melinda ultimately escapes to Canada and Solomon returns to his pregnant wife, he is given a telling, if absurd, narrative peroration: "Caught in a rising abstraction of grief, he wept for their two peoples, one scorned and enslaved, the other doomed to an unending exodus toward an ever-receding Promised Land."[146] The paperback jacket of *The Slave Stealer,* with a sultry, voluptuous Melinda and a dashing, decidely un-Orthodox-looking Solomon, accurately advertises a tale "in the pulsating tradition of Mandingo."

Highbrow fiction was often no less exotic—whether intellectually or pruriently. *The Suicide Academy* (1968) by Daniel Stern debated which stigma, Jewishness or blackness, more logically courted a genocidal response. Dedicated to Elie Wiesel, Stern's novel begins with a bizarre premise—that voluntary euthanasia might be arranged according to a set of rituals carried out in a macabre, faux total institution that is half resort, half prison house, as though Nazism had become a bourgeois American therapy. The novel operates on a number of levels, but the running verbal combat between Wolf Walker, the Jewish impresario of this strange metaphysical institution, and his black assistant Gilliat, his philosophical antagonist and "punisher of [his] Jewishness," suggests that blacks and Jews alike, because of their parallel experiences of persecution, have a keen, even competitive appreciation of the need to exercise control over death. Gilliat's disquisition on blackness as a color loaded with negative connotations in the Western tradition—a condition that cannot be "chosen" but need not be rejected—is answered by Wolf's reply that the Jew is born into an ongoing drama of historical anti-Semitism with higher stakes. The Jew is made responsible for "everything: wars, unexplainable deaths, plagues, depressions, revolutions—the murder of God, Himself," in contrast to which racism based on color alone is explicable and therefore strangely reassuring. At least your blackness is an absolute, he replies to Gilliat, so that "you know in what name you're being destroyed."[147]

Existential nihilism, with blacks and Jews set against each other in highly charged symbolic struggle, likewise marks Hal Bennett's *Lord of Dark Places* (1970), which reads like a cross between Hubert Selby and Flannery O'Connor. After coming of age in a perverse world of sexually demented fundamentalism in rural Virginia, where he and his outsized manhood are the prime exhibit in the "Church of the Naked Disciple," the debauched protagonist Joe Market moves to Newark, a city torn by race riots and sunk in decay. Enveloping himself in drugs and fetishizing his penis, he makes his living hustling homosexuals, marries, survives a tour in Vietnam, returns home, and immediately kills his infant son to save him from the life of squalor Joe foresees unfolding in his future. Joe's undoing comes when it turns out that an elderly Jewish shopkeeper known as Cheap Mary, one of the last white holdouts in the black slum, has witnessed the murder. The price of her silence is that Joe must dress in her negligee and perform cunnilingus: "Like ecstatic horns of Satan, [her] gray suede shoes dug into his butt."[148]

Crippled by political murders and civil violence, late 1968 America is no longer "a seductive white bitch" but a tired and ghastly woman like Mary herself, thinks Joe, and black-Jewish conflict is just one act in the psychotic drama being played out on the streets of America as the nation careens toward apocalypse. Purporting to save himself and her, Joe murders Mary, with her desirous acquiescence, by raping her—just as his own father had murdered Joe's mother—with the weapon of his prodigious penis. The fact that Mary dies as a white woman rather than specifically as a Jew is in keeping with the twisted evangelism of Joe's act. Their names are resonant with Christ's nativity, and in their moment of deadly sexual rapture, as Mary makes the "ultimate sacrifice," Joe is consumed by divinity: "A terrible, flaming spirit entered his being, almost stifling his breath with the onslaught of its coming. *I am the Holy Ghost, I have come to redeem the world.*"[149]

Except in these key scenes, the novel has little to do with blacks and Jews—far less, for example, than Bennett's more pedestrian novel *The Black Wine* (1968), in which a black domestic's affair with her Jewish employer, likewise set against the racial turmoil of Newark, leads to tragic complications but finally to cross-racial resolution. As the work of an African American writer, *Lord of Dark Places* is almost unbearably self-lacerating. As a satiric snapshot of the pathology of a black neighborhood that was once the first American home of immigrant Jews, however, it distills into chilling symbolic form a drama of urban displacement alternating between guilt and sadism. Archetypal violence against the Jew is compounded by Mary's caricature as a slut whose nickname, "Cheap," has both vulgar and anti-Semitic connotations; by her association with Satan; by her complicity in Joe's enactment of the mythology of the black beast rapist ("Call me nigger, you white bitch," he commands Mary as he penetrates her);[150] and by her own apostasy and whitening. Whatever kind of Jew Cheap Mary was, with her death, at once a murder and a suicide, the ghetto is cleansed of Jews, with the black migrant fulfilled in his role as usurper and Christian, while at the same time he is delivered into utter degradation.

As these few examples indicate, the fiction of the late 1960s and early 1970s devoted to the black-Jewish question, whether on the margin or in the mainstream, shot out in every direction at once. We have seen already in Paule Marshall's *The Chosen Place, the Timeless People* an example of civil rights–era fiction that held out sincere hope for sustaining a sympathetic alliance between blacks and Jews, and we will see depicted in turn its acrimonious disintegration in Bernard Malamud's *The Tenants,* which carried to its logical extreme the breakdown of relations depicted in other urban novels of the period such as Nat Hentoff's *Call the Keeper* (1966), Ed Lacy's *In Black and Whitey* (1967), and Victor Wartofsky's *Meeting the Pieman* (1971). Of particular importance with respect to the confrontation between Black Power and "Jewish Power" are those novels that introduce the problem of Israel as a distinctive mediating term. Like the extremist black nationalism of which it is a mirror image, the maximalist brand of "iron wall" Zionism espoused by Kahane found cultural expression mainly in essays and manifestos; but it also features in at least two novelistic examples very much worth our attention, both set principally in New York—Saul Bellow's *Mr. Sammler's Planet* (1970) and John A. Williams's *Sons of Darkness, Sons of Light* (1969).

Although he had other targets as well, the abasement of Jewish liberals before Black Power was implicit in Bellow's infamous portrayal of the confrontation between Artur Sammler, a Polish Holocaust survivor, and a slick black pickpocket who, in a "serenely masterful" act of racial intimidation, displays to Sammler the archetype of black potency, his "great oval testicles" and his penis, "a large tan-and-purple uncircumcised thing—a tube, a snake," on which Sammler is "required to gaze."[151] Only William Styron's portrayal of Nat Turner has in recent decades elicited more regular condemnation than Bellow's portrayal of the pickpocket. Even admirers of Bellow's novel routinely feel compelled to apologize for his "racism" before proceeding to deal with his post-Holocaust critique of the Enlightment or other matters. *Mr. Sammler's Planet* is not centrally about the Jewish confrontation with Black Power, but the novel cannot be read outside that context, nor outside the countervailing context of Jewish Power. By calling our attention to the polyglot culture of the United States—by means of the Hispanic women Sammler's survivor friend Walter Bruch makes the object of his lascivious desire, for example, or the Indian, Govinda Lal, with whom Sammler carries on a cerebral dialogue about H. G. Wells—Bellow escapes the white/black, Jewish/black binary even as he is insistently drawn back to it. As though the pickpocket's performance were argument enough that the seemingly irrefutable moral stature of the Holocaust survivor is of no consequence in 1960s America, Bellow's cunning scene literalizes the sexual threat of "the Negro" that Black Power had seized upon as a rhetorical asset. In subjecting the pickpocket to a merciless beating at the hands of Sammler's Israeli son-in-law, however, Bellow introduced a crucial triangulating term into the stalemated domestic argument between Jews and blacks.

Like Bernard Malamud soon after him, Bellow parodied, in the pickpocket's scene of exposure, Frantz Fanon's well-known psychiatric judgment that, whereas the Jew is associated with "intellectual danger and the desire to "own the wealth or take over the positions of power," the Negro is "only biological." Personified as the Jew's utter other, argued Fanon, the Negro "is turned into a penis. He *is* a penis."[152] Again like Malamud, however, Bellow also had frames of reference closer to home.

To be a black American male, said James Baldwin in his 1961 essay "The Black Boy Looks at the White Boy," is to be "a kind of walking phallic symbol." The white boy Baldwin was looking at, very much askance, was Norman Mailer, who contended in "The White Negro" that blacks deploy the "art of the primitive" as a survival tactic, from which he—the white hipster passing as "black," the psychopathic outlaw—learned the necessity of being a "wise primitive in a giant jungle" and elaborating a "morality of the bottom" in his pursuit of "absolute sexual freedom." Ushering in a time of hysteria, violence, and rebellion, said Mailer, the Negro's equality and emergence as a cultural force will "tear a profound shift into the psychology, the sexuality, and the moral imagination of every white alive."[153] Less flamboyantly, but no less notoriously, Norman Podhoretz likewise made the black male body a site of Jewish fascination and anxiety in his landmark confessional essay "My Negro Problem—and Ours." Unlike Mailer, as we saw in Chapter 1, Podhoretz was far from celebrating Black Power, and he held out the fragile hope that race mixing might one day break the political impasse, not bring on a psychic apocalypse. Yet his chastisement of white liberals for adopting toward militant blacks a double standard of moral judgment was accompanied by an admission that his childhood apprehension about the "superior masculinity" of black boys had been translated into his adult admiration of their "superior physical grace and beauty."[154]

Male envy is not so evident in Podhoretz's essay as in Mailer's, but it was quickly read that way by Eldridge Cleaver, who cited Podhoretz in one of several essays in *Soul on Ice* that took up the question of biologized racism. Extending Fanon's paradigmatic distinction between Jewish intelligence and black physicality, Cleaver outlined a vicious dialectic between the white (Jewish) brain, personified as the "Omnipotent Administrator," and the black body, personified as the "Supermasculine Menial," whose every attempt "to heal his wound and reclaim his mind will be viewed as a malignant desire to transcend the laws of nature by mixing, 'mongrelizing,' miscegenating." The black man's threat to the white man, said Cleaver, lies in the fact that he presents to the white woman "an image of masculinity capable of penetrating into the psychic depths where the treasure of her orgasm lies buried." Huey Newton borrowed Cleaver's terms in presenting his own version of the irreconcilable opposition between the intellectual power of the Omnipotent Administrator and the sexual power of the Supermasculine Menial. Because the white man "doesn't have a body, doesn't have a penis, he psychologically wants to castrate the black man," argued Newton, but he cannot "gain his manhood, cannot unite with the body because the body is black. The body is symbolic of slavery and strength."[155]

As Malamud would do a year later, Bellow imported this highly stylized psychodrama directly into his plot, less to give it credence than to satirize the ruthless terms of contemporary debate. As in *The Tenants,* so in *Mr. Sammler's Planet,* victimhood issues in strength; domination issues in impotence. In Europe, circumcision identified Sammler as the dangerous other, the non-white —specifically, the non-Aryan—racial defiler; in America, his otherness is diminished and overshadowed by the exemplary non-white. The uncircumcised black man, a figure of hyperbolic power, stands now in contrast to the emasculated Jew. ("Why do you listen to this effete old shit?" shouts a heckler when Sammler lectures at Columbia. "His balls are dry. He's dead. He can't come." What a woman wants, says Sammler's dissolute grandniece, is "a Jew brain, a black cock, a Nordic beauty.")[156] Like Bellow's pickpocket, Black Power militants wanted whites, Jewish liberals in particular, to gaze upon their demonstration of masculinity, by which they took possession of the destructive stereotype of the oversexed beast that had haunted black men for more than a century and turned released rage into a mode of racial authenticity.[157]

Were the display of black sexual prowess his only function, the pickpocket would be just a prop in the war of ideas on which Sammler spends his benighted time—a surreal illustration of the counterculture's liberating, self-absorbed "sexual niggerhood."[158] What Philip Roth has referred to as Sammler's "Swiftian revulsion"[159] toward the biological excess of the 1960s registers disdain for precisely the orgiastic forces celebrated by Mailer and others.* But

---

* Other aspects of *Mr. Sammler's Planet* can likewise be counted in Bellow's extended debate with Mailer. Sammler's fascination with H. G. Wells and lunar colonization may be read as a rejection of Mailer's speculation in *Of a Fire on the Moon* (1970) that Nazism reached its delayed culmination in the Apollo astronauts, "Waspitude" incarnate. The function of "Waspitude" had not been simply to create Protestantism, capitalism, and the corporation, or to fight communism, asserted Mailer. Rather, the

that revulsion is also resonantly historical. In the presence of the pickpocket, Sammler feels "the breath of wartime Poland passing over the damaged tissues" of his nervous system, a reminder not only of his vulnerability as an old man and a Jew, but also of the untenable choice between the ruined Europe of his memories and "the barbarous world of color" erupting from beneath the surface of New York's corrupt civilization.[160] Neither philosophy nor family, neither his memoir of H. G. Wells nor his speculation about colonization of the moon, affords refuge.

Artur Sammler's planet is resolutely this earth, but not the degraded jungle of New York City, or even the inhospitable, war-torn terrain of Israel, where he briefly ventures to report on the Six-Day War. Rather, his planet is what Israeli Holocaust survivor and author K. Zetnick, among others, referred to as the "other planet Auschwitz," where neither time, nor family relations and genealogy, nor elementary physical survival, nor even death itself occurs "according to the laws of this world."[161] The humanism on which Sammler had staked his intellectual life betrayed him by turning the Jew into the biological nadir—a germ culture to be exterminated in the death camps or by their precursors, killing squads such as the one responsible for the pit of murdered Jews out of which Sammler, though not his wife, crawls to face the remainder of his life. His inexplicable escape and survival have made him alert to the "metaphysical messages" of the post-Holocaust world and turned him into a "symbolic character" for friends and family—but "of what was he a symbol? He didn't even know."[162] Sammler remains locked in a distorted, obsessive world of "explanations" that fail to cohere and explain, let alone save.

"Death is the Messiah. That's the real truth,"[163] says one character in a fa-

---

WASP had "emerged from human history in order to take us to the stars," completing the interrupted program of the Third Reich. At once heartless and noble, primitive and "vertiginously advanced," Nazism had been "an assault upon the cosmos," an attempt to raise civilization to a new plane: "Was space its amputated limb, its philosophy in orbit?" Sammler likewise disdains the new currents of barbarity that Mailer the proto-racialist finds so alluring. Black Power, Mailer contended, was part of the Third World's resistance of "technological man," born of the same primordial force that drives anticolonial independence movements ("a war of liberation converts the energies of criminality, assassination, religious orgy, voodoo, and the dance into the determined artful phalanxes of bold guerrilla armies") and turns the African American into a racial exemplar. Uprooted from his native Africa and forced to live in the "fluorescent nightmare of shabby garish electric ghettos," the "primitive jungle of the slums" overlaid with technology, the black American has not simply survived but discovered that he is "black, beautiful, and secretly superior." Norman Mailer, *Of a Fire on the Moon* (1970; rpt. New York: Signet, 1971), pp. 76, 279–80; idem, "Looking for the Meat and Potatoes—Thoughts on Black Power," *Look* magazine (January 7, 1969), rpt. in *Existential Errands* (Boston: Little, Brown, 1972), pp. 287–304.

mous passage near the end of Isaac Bashevis Singer's multigenerational Warsaw novel *The Family Moskat* (1950), which concludes with the onset of the
Nazi invasion of Poland. Neither the emancipated nor the pious will be saved,
says Singer, only the Zionists and the Americans. *Mr. Sammler's Planet*, it might
be said, begins where Singer's novel leaves off. The same truth about death is
the sum total of Sammler's obsessive cogitation, leading to the novel's famously
ambiguous ending: "For that is the truth of it—that we all know, God, that we
know, that we know, we know, we know."[164] Standing for the nearly annihilated
European remnant, Sammler lives on as proof, as Bellow wrote elsewhere,
that the "humanistic civilized moral imagination" is inadequate to confront
the "metaphysical demonstration" of the Holocaust—the refutation of Jewish
emancipation that should separate Sammler from Americans and join him to
Israelis,[165] if only in showing the anxious dislocation of American Jewish life
from the hell of Jewish modernity.

The decay of American liberalism into black anti-Semitism is, transparently,
not equivalent to the decay of Enlightenment humanism into totalitarian
genocide. The repetition of Sammler's European tragedy as American farce
nevertheless takes a jarring turn with the intervention of his Israeli son-in-law,
Eisen, whose merciless beating of the black pickpocket in the novel's culminating scene, says Stanley Crouch, is a metaphor for the rift between black leaders
"who made their money ripping off or intimidating middle-class whites, and
the outraged Jews of the late sixties who reacted to the separatism of black
power by going into Zionism."[166] Crouch's foreshortened insight is true as far as
it goes: the paralysis of the Jew in the face of black radicalism is countered only
by the realpolitik of the new warrior culture of the "muscle Jew" emboldened
to defend itself against deadly aggression in Israel and racial intimidation in
the United States—a parallel that Jews both on the left (such as M. J. Rosenberg) and on the right (such as Norman Podhoretz) had wrenched into place
in response to the anti-Zionist proclamations of Black Power.

The scene of Eisen's violence presents a stylized triangulation of symbolic
forces[167] which reinserts potentially redemptive historic meaning into a sequence of otherwise mundane events. At Sammler's request, Eisen intervenes
to prevent the pickpocket from killing Lionel Feffer, a Columbia student caught
trying to photograph him at his trade. Eisen's very appearance on the scene,
however, raises it to allegorical significance. His name is Yiddish (and German)
for "iron," and the medallions with which he beats the pickpocket are fashioned out of iron pyrite from the Dead Sea, inscribed with Stars of David,
scrolls, rams' horns, and God's command to Joshua before the battle of Jericho,
Hazak! ("Strengthen thyself!"). Having been crippled by Russian anti-Semites

who treated him no better than did the Nazis, but strengthened by life in Israel after his trek across war-ravaged Europe, Eisen has become an artist, but one with a purpose: "Twenty-five years ago I came to the Eretz a broken man. But I wouldn't die. I couldn't shut my eyes—not before I did something like a human being, something important, beautiful." Eisen's claim to humanity, even to art, is not disingenuous but presents the unflinching face of Israel's necessary contradiction. The salvation of modern Jewry through the iron-willed nationhood for which Eisen's rudimentary art stands has, indeed, been beautiful; but it has been achieved and, in 1967, preserved at further great cost in lives and moral abrasion. "Metaphor for a tank," Eisen explains to Sammler of one of his sculpted figures. "Nothing is literal in my work."[168] In this metaphor tenor and vehicle are virtually identical, however, and Eisen's admonition seems to apply better to the scene in which his art becomes a literal weapon.

It is not Eisen but Sammler, the Holocaust survivor and partisan who once killed a German soldier in cold blood, for whom that scene resonates with moral ambiguity. In the face of "bystanders" united by a "beatitude of presence," Sammler feels the horror of his powerlessness as the pickpocket assaults Feffer. But once Eisen attacks, wielding his bag of Israeli icons like a "homicidal maniac," Sammler feels sickening shock: "Everything went into that blow, discipline, murderousness, everything." Against Sammler's protest Eisen replies: "You can't hit a man like this just once. When you hit him you must really hit him. Otherwise he'll kill you. You know. We both fought in the war." Eisen's actions, as well as his words, are a virtual demonstration of Kahane's dictum: "Not only is the Jew who knows how to fight back hard and expertly saved from a beating, but his smashing of the hoodlum who attacked him will guarantee that the latter will think much more carefully about attacking a Jew the next time."[169]

For the same reason, Eisen stands resolutely for one feature of the maximalist Zionism of Jabotinsky and Kahane, first translated into practice by the Irgun and then the Haganah in 1948, and ingrained in the military conduct of the IDF ever since, not least in the Six-Day War—namely, that attacks on Jews must be met with swift and unmistakable reprisals. He stands, too, for the moral clarity that Bellow, like Sammler, discovered among Israelis during the Six-Day War. Sammler's inchoate need to participate in the war as a journalist—his need "to be there, to send reports, to do something, perhaps to die in the massacre," his "old Polish nerves raging"—reflects Bellow's brief stint as a journalist during the campaign. In his own reporting, Bellow was taken aback by the contrast between the amenities of his luxury hotel and the corpse of an Egyptian soldier, "black and stinking in the desert sun" beside a burned-out

Soviet tank. "But these puzzling contrasts will not affect an Israeli at this moment," he added. "To him the questions are clear. His existence was threatened, and he defended himself."[170]

Sammler is sobered, but not persuaded, by Eisen's logic, and his ethical quandary remains unresolved in the novel. He feels viscerally the culpability of remaining a "bystander," just as he feels viscerally the madness of applying the ideology of the "iron wall" on the streets of New York. If Eisen's action symbolically encompasses Israeli survivalism and the militancy of the JDL, so Sammler's moral anguish reflects the American Jewish community's reassessment of their own role and that of their nation as bystanders during the rise of Nazism.* That reassessment would have come about in any case, but the Six-Day War brought it strongly to the fore, though now with the added complexity that Israel had itself become a military power obliged to deal with the consequences of conquest. In the aftermath of 1967 it became evident that neither achieving military supremacy nor securing defensible borders made peace-making easier. At times, indeed, the events of ensuing decades appeared to argue just the reverse.

AN EYE FOR AN EYE

Whereas Bellow's depiction of the triangulating force of muscle Zionism is only one aspect of his novel, and a highly abstract one at that, in *Sons of Darkness, Sons of Light*, John A. Williams places the contrary forces of Zionism and anti-Zionism, each of them dialectically a part of Black Power's promise of nationalist liberation, at the very center of his examination of the black-Jewish conflict of the late 1960s. Williams had already taken up the tortured relationships between blacks and Jews in *The Angry Ones* (1960), in which the black protagonist's affair with a Jewish refugee is for him an indirect means to attack white people and for her a means to rebel against her Orthodox mother, and

---

* Bellow's depiction of the Columbia student radicals who dismiss Sammler looked forward to the observation of Marie Syrkin, an ardent Zionist, who would later confess that "since the sixties, young students with memories of civil rights protests have often asked me pointedly why American Jews were so craven. Why did we not rage in the streets when the [German refugee vessel] *St. Louis* . . . moved along our shores in 1939 and no country offered sanctuary? . . . Why did we not stage sit-ins in the halls of Congress to demand the lifting of immigration restrictions?" Marie Syrkin, "What American Jews Did during the Holocaust" (1982), quoted in Howard M. Sachar, *A History of the Jews in America* (New York: Random House, 1992), p. 842.

The Man Who Cried I Am (1967), in which black and Jewish friends remain bound together in the face of racism. He would do so again in *!Click Song* (1982), in which the Holocaust is at once a unifying symbol and the ultimate example of the threat held out against blacks, and then again in *Clifford's Blues* (1999), the story of a gay black American jazz musician imprisoned in Dachau. In *Sons of Darkness, Sons of Light*, however, Williams found in the escalating racial violence of the 1960s and the radicalism of Black Power the potential for another kind of cataclysmic race war—the novel's subtitle is *A Novel of Some Probability*—but one in which the lesson of the Holocaust and post-1948 Zionism proves to be anything but predictable.

Set prospectively in 1973—a year in which Black September was to carry out no fewer than sixty attacks[171]—the novel's action revolves around the counterpointed stories of two characters: on the one hand, Eugene Browning, the middle-class black leader of an entity called the Institute for Racial Justice, who is radicalized by the nation's failure to deliver on the promise of racial justice; and on the other, Itzhak Hod, an Israeli who in his youth had been the leader of a Jewish resistance group in Poland, had fled to Palestine in 1939 with his parents, fought Italians in Ethiopia with a commando unit, and joined the paramilitary Irgun in its participation in Israel's 1948 War of Independence, before ultimately becoming a Nazi hunter and contract killer. Tired of working fruitlessly within a system that suppresses activism and rewards corruption, and driven to despair following the killing of a black youth by an Irish policeman, Browning hires the Mafia to assassinate the policeman; the Mafia in turn contracts with Hod, whose assassination of the policeman sets in motion a race war between the black community and the police. Accompanied by demands for reparations (ten acres of land, a car, and $5,000 for every head of a black family; ten years of tax relief; educational and social service benefits), the black uprising in New York City awakens a consciousness of resistance based on both dignity and retribution, as in the case of Browning's act of vengeance. The lesson of modern Jewish history and the Holocaust for African Americans is simple: "Something became etched in the minds of an oppressed people, something it never could forget when it witnessed the systematic world-approved destruction of still another oppressed people."[172]

Williams was dismissive of his novel, and not entirely without reason. The plot is a tissue of contrivance, and its anatomy of black radicalism and Jewish liberalism is far less interesting than its more nuanced exposition of pro- and anti-Zionist ideologies. Among the black characters we get a medley of types ranging from accommodationist bureaucrats to self-serving southern politicians to exploited athletes and entertainers to militant nationalists. Among the

Jews, we get Mickey, an idealistic young woman ready to make *aliyah,* her bourgeois assimilated parents, a cynical immigration recruiter, and Mickey's fiancée, Hod, the Israeli mercenary, who acts as a foil for the "whitening" of American Jews. As Mickey explains to Hod, her parents are the incarnation of degenerate diaspora consciousness. They are "Americans pretending to be Jews," whereas she longs "to go somewhere where there's still a promise. Israel." Her father's generous wedding gift to the couple is, in her view, a guilt offering to the ravaging and redemption of modern Jewry. "What camp did he ever have to go to?" Mickey asks. "What Arabs did he ever have to fight?"[173]

In contrast to her parents' conservatism, moreover, Mickey's idealism places her, along with Hod, on the side of radicalism in support of African American rights. "America is a disease that many Jews've caught," she says. "They feel like other white people, the goyim, about the blacks. They ask: 'What in the hell do they want?'" Williams assigns Hod the shopworn reply that Jews had better help blacks "because it's clear that if it were not for the blacks, it'd be the Jews who'd be doing the suffering." A recognizable statement of the black "buffer" theory, this is no pat sentiment on Hod's part, however, for at just the moment when American Jews appear to be retreating from the front lines of the struggle for black rights, Hod is willing to take real action. Although his killing of the policeman is work for hire, when he becomes disgusted by the racial injustice of the United States, he determines, secretly, to kill Herman Mahler, a celebrated southern white supremacist responsible for the bombing murder of three black college students. In undertaking to kill Mahler, Hod disguises himself as a German, playing upon his perception of the kinship between Germans and Americans: what had "led to the camps and ovens could be buried in the American psyche somewhere, too." Lest we miss the point, Mahler is compared to Adolf Eichmann. "Evil *is* ordinary," thinks Hod, paraphrasing Hannah Arendt. "Maybe that was the difference between Israel and America."[174] That glibly mentioned difference, however, constitutes the novel's center of gravity and its significance in the late 1960s war of ideas.

Along with the title, the epigraph for Williams's novel is drawn from an early apocalyptic text known as *The Scroll of the War of the Sons of Light against the Sons of Darkness:* "After they have withdrawn from the slain towards the encampment, they shall all together sing the hymn of return. In the morning they shall launder their garments, wash themselves of the blood of the guilty cadavers, and return to the place where they had stood, where they had arrayed the line before the falling of the enemy's slain." Part of the wealth of documents excavated at and around Khirbet Qumran since 1947, popularly called the Dead Sea Scrolls, the *War Scroll*—also known as the *War Rule,* in that it was modeled on Greco-Roman tactical manuals on the conduct of war—depicts an apoca-lyptic conflict waged by the sons of Levi, Judah, and Benjamin, and the rest of the tribes of Israel (assisted by the powers of light and justice, and the angels appointed over them) against their enemies the "Kittim" (assisted by the pow-ers of evil and darkness commanded by Belial). Identified with a sect known as the Essenes, but in all likelihood derived from a document contemporaneous with the earlier Book of Daniel, the *War Scroll* was probably composed be-tween 50 BCE and 50 CE, before the destruction of the Second Temple, by writ-ers who saw themselves living in the final generation before the coming of the Messiah or end times that would destroy their enemies. (The text bears a direct relation to other apocalyptic texts of the Hebrew Bible and the Apocrypha, and some scholars have concluded, in fact, that Revelation is a "Christian War Scroll" modeled on the Qumran document.) After a series of battles lasting forty years, "so that wickedness [shall] be subdued without a remnant and none shall escape," says the chronicle, God will intervene on the side of the Sons of Light in a "battle of annihilation" against the Sons of Darkness, gener-ally understood to be the Romans or perhaps the Greeks, but identified in the scroll as well with enemy armies in Assyria and Egypt.[175]

In view of the eschatological message of the *War Scroll*, it is pertinent that Williams's epigraph ignores the intervention of God on the side of Israel, which we see in the lines directly following those he quotes: "In that place they shall bless all together the God of Israel and exalt His name in joyful unison, and shall solemnly declare: Blessed be the God of Israel, Who preserveth mercy for His covenant and times ordained for salvation for the people to be re-deemed by Him."[176] In secularizing the apocalyptic battle depicted in the *War Scroll*, Williams's selection from the text fittingly glosses a modern-day race war whose outcome we do not witness but which is not left very much in doubt. It also secularizes Williams's first frame of reference, the 1948 war in Pal-estine, which would appear to have issued, if not in God's intervention on the side of the Zionists, at least in a victory—one that could not necessarily have been predicted—decisive enough to confirm the Jews' historic right to a home-land in Palestine.

Given its publication in 1969 and its action set in 1973, however, the novel's second frame of reference is, of course, the Six-Day War, one of whose pro-posed official names, as noted earlier, was the "War of the Sons of Light." Hod's name in Hebrew means "majesty" or "glory," and Williams may even intention-ally have alluded to Major-General Mordechai Hod, commander of the Israeli Air Force (IAF) and architect of Israel's obliteration of Egypt's vaunted Soviet-supplied air force in the opening hours of the war.[177] Whether or not he intended such a reference, Williams appears at first glance to turn away from a judgment about Israel's stunning battlefield victory and its momentous consequences. In Itzhak Hod's life course and his career with the Irgun—a fighting force, says Williams, composed of the "remains from a thousand ghettos during two thousand years . . . the survivors of a holocaust the earth had never been witness to before"[178]—our attention is directed first of all to the analogous relationship between the aims of Black Power and the Zionists' anticolonial war of liberation in 1947–48. It is not the *Arab* Palestinians, that is to say, but the *Jewish* Palestinians who are made equivalent to American blacks, each oppressed by a colonizer. The American police, Black Power's antagonists, are like the British military before the partition of Palestine, while blacks, as Mickey sees it, are "the Sterns and the Irgun," the radical nationalists governed, we are repeatedly told in the novel, by the scripture of reprisal, "an eye for an eye."[179]

The principal and more moderate military force in Jewish Palestine, the Haganah, shifted from a policy of restraint to a policy of "aggressive defense" and retaliation during the Arab revolt of the late 1930s, setting a pattern for the conduct of the IDF in later years.[180] But the policy was considerably extended by those in the Revisionist movement's armed unit that took the name Irgun Z'vai Leumi (National Military Organization), led during the 1940s by the Polish immigrant Menachem Begin. Its symbol a hand holding a rifle over the map of Palestine, including Transjordan, with the motto "Rak Kach" (Only Thus),[181] Irgun adopted Jabotinsky's teachings: every Jew had a right to enter Palestine; only active retaliation would deter Arab assaults; and only an armed Jewish force, an "iron wall" of deterrence, could guarantee the survival of the Jewish National Home and, later, the Jewish state. Along with a breakout faction of revolutionary socialists known as Lohamei Herut Israel (Fighters for the Freedom of Israel)—also known as Lehi, or the Stern Gang, so called for its leader, Avraham Stern, also a Polish-born Jew, who had studied in Florence and been influenced by Mussolini in his antipathy to Britain[182]—the Irgun believed that raising the cost to the British, whose policies were designed to appease the Arabs, was the shortest road to independence and security. Palestinian Jews were united in believing that they were fighting for liberation from colonial rule, but whereas the Haganah concentrated on the sabotage of British assets and circumventing the British blockade of Holocaust refugees seeking to enter Palestine, Irgun and Stern forces sometimes attacked targets that included civilians, as in the 1946 bombing of the British headquarters at the King David Hotel. Their actions peaked, not coincidentally, with the UNSCOP (United Nations Special Committee on Palestine) hearings in the summer of 1947. After the kidnapping and hanging of two British officers in retaliation for the hangings of Irgun men, Begin commented simply, "We repaid our enemy in kind."[183]

Williams's reference to the *War Scroll*, his identification of Hod with Israeli military supremacy and the philosophy of the "iron wall," and his seeming approval of the tactics of the Irgun and Stern Gang all point to a clear lesson for African Americans in the saga of Jewish liberation. But Williams points at the same time in another direction. Lying in wait to assassinate Mahler in his Montgomery, Alabama, home, Hod is surprised by Leonard Trotman, a member of the black nationalist faction and the brother of one of the slain students, who is bent on a similar mission of vengeance. Hod recognizes Trotman's prior right and allows him to kill Mahler, but he also recognizes something more revealing of the ambivalence in Williams's analogy between black nationalism and Zionism: "Hod looked at the Negro's eyes and understood. Once he himself had stood like the Negro—at Deir Yassin, it was—so intent on slaughtering that nothing else mattered."[184] As a veteran of Deir Yassin, Hod represents a legendary moment of reckoning in the Israeli national conscience *and* in the creation of revolutionary consciousness among Palestinian Arabs.

Now the location of Jerusalem's main psychiatric hospital, as well as the site of memorials by Palestinian and Israeli peace activists, Deir Yassin in April 1948 was an Arab village lying near the northwest entrance to the city. During the civil war preceding independence, the Haganah adopted Plan Dalet (Plan D), a strategy of conquest as well as survival that aimed to capture Arab villages so as to control critical areas designated for Jewish statehood that were soon to be evacuated by the British. Even though Plan D did not specifically call for the expulsion of Arabs, it has remained a subject of intense controversy whether and to what degree a plan of expulsion—what some post-Zionists have referred to as Israel's "original sin"—was premeditated before or during the 1948 war.[185] Combined with Jewish trepidation about leaving a hostile population behind advancing lines and later having to administer a substantial Arab population while attacks on Jews in surrounding nations were escalating, the idea of expulsion appears at least to have grown more acceptable after Israel's declaration of independence in May 1948 and the concerted attack of five Arab nations. In the event, a mixture of fear, rumor, and false hope among fleeing Palestinians became woven fortuitously into Israeli strategy.

Against the backdrop of the international community's apparent second thoughts about partition, and reacting to a series of Arab ambushes of convoys carrying troops and supplies to the 100,000-person Jewish community in Jerusalem, which had also been hit hard by Arab bombings, Jewish forces undertook Operation Nachshon in April. The goal was to open a corridor between

Tel Aviv and Jerusalem, which would otherwise be isolated within territory al-
lotted to the Palestinian Arabs in the partition, an action deemed indispensable
in defining and protecting the Jewish state, as well as the Jews of Jerusalem,
from the invasion by Arab armies certain to occur once independence was declared the following month. If the Arabs could not be defeated on the roads,
then they had to be attacked in the villages along the corridor that housed their
fighters, Deir Yassin among them.[186]

Within the Irgun and Lehi, which had been entrusted by the Haganah with
taking the village, there were varying views as to the tactics needed to break
Arab resistance in Deir Yassin. In the aftermath of the battle, there were varying
accounts of why the operation went awry. For one thing, a truck carrying a
loudspeaker ordering villagers to flee the Jewish advance got stuck in a ditch, its
message unheard; for another, perhaps as a result, more resistance than expected was encountered. What ensued, in any case, was a hard-fought house-
to-house battle that evolved into what most accounts speak of as a massacre of
civilians. Using hand grenades, dynamite, guns, and sabers, Irgun and Lehi
troops killed 254 men, women, and children, according to initial reports, in
some cases raping the women before killing them, or so it was charged, in others mutilating victims alive or dead.

Although recent investigations have revised that number downward closer
to one hundred, discredited the charges of rape, and revealed that some women
may have been killed because Arab men were themselves dressed as women, the
number killed and the degree of atrocity are less important than the use to
which the bloodshed was put by Jews and Arabs alike. Whether or not the massacre was intended—at least some dimension of it, such as killing all the men
of the village, apparently had been discussed—remains a vexed question. In
some post-Zionist interpretations it has been seen as part of a strategic plan to
secure all of Palestine and to bring about, by design or collateral effect, the
"transfer" of Palestinian Arabs that hard-line Zionists believed was necessary to
the survival of a Jewish state.[187] At the outset of independence, Begin had attacked partition as "a crime, a blasphemy, an abortion"—a view that might
seem to suggest a design among some Jews to make the whole of Palestine their
nation by driving Arabs out—but in *The Revolt* (1951), his account of the
founding of Israel, he contended only that the events at Deir Yassin turned into
an adjunct to battlefield operations. The attempt to warn civilians denied the
Irgun the element of surprise, Begin pointed out, and he emphasized the grave
risk from "murderous fire" directed against outmanned and principled Jewish
fighters: "We never broke [the laws of war] unless the enemy first did so and
thus forced us, in accordance with the accepted custom of war, to apply repri-

sals." Although he claimed further that it was not atrocities at Deir Yassin but Arab propaganda "designed to besmirch our name" that caused the panicked flight of Arabs, Begin's self-aggrandizing account also turned this to advantage. Supplementing the fighting prowess of the Irgun, he said, "What was invented about Deir Yassin helped to carve the way to our decisive victories on the battlefield."[188]

Whatever the explanation for the killings at Deir Yassin, there is little doubt that the Palestinian Jews, soon to be Israelis, used the threat of other Deir Yassins, coupled with less fearsome raids on individual villages, as psychological warfare. If the killings led to wild rumors about Jewish determination to exterminate Arabs, however, such rumors were made credible less because of the way Jews conceived of the war than because of the way a number of Arabs did. Ahmed Shukeiry, aide to the Mufti of Jerusalem, Haj Amin al-Husseini, envisioned "the elimination of the Jewish state," while Abd al-Rahman Azzam Pasha, the secretary general of the Arab League, looked forward to "a war of extermination and momentous massacre" and declared that "it does not matter how many [Jews] there are. We will sweep them into the sea."[189] Joined with other factors—the early flight of the wealthy elite, Arab calls for women and children to evacuate, and the dissolution of Palestinian military leadership— fears that Israelis were bent on waging such a war, a mirror image of the declarations of Arab leaders, were a decisive factor in the momentous outflow of Arab refugees in months to come.

Responding to concerted attacks by five Arab nations bent on destroying the Jewish state, Israel captured some 30 percent more territory than it had been granted by the United Nations. With the exodus of Arabs, a Jewish majority was created. So, too, was the "Palestinian problem," the approximately 700,000 Arabs who fled or were expelled from their homes in Palestine, most expecting to return after Arab nations had driven out the Jews or, in later years, once their right to return had been negotiated, but whose ultimate fate would plague the region and the world on into the next century and whose rallying cry would forever include remembrance of the April 1948 battle for Deir Yassin. With the rise of the PLO as a revolutionary movement, Deir Yassin became suffused with the iconography of loss and retribution. At the height of post-1967 international terror, for example, an assault on Ben-Gurion Airport carried out jointly by the PFLP and Japanese Red Army took the code name "Operation Deir Yassin," while Black September was extolled in one Beirut newspaper for at last having "come round to the methods of the Irgun and Lehi. Can we blame them for seeking to avenge Deir Yassin?"[190] In later years, even more than when Williams was writing, Deir Yassin, in the words of Sharif Kanaana, became "a sym-

bol of everything that happened to Palestinians, a symbol of the Palestinian village, a symbol of people who have been driven out. It seems to represent the
whole nation destroyed."[191]

In *Sons of Darkness, Sons of Light,* as I have noted, Mickey identifies American blacks with the Irgun and the Stern Gang—an identification Williams
might have borrowed from Harold Cruse, who had forecast a day of reckoning
in comparable terms, although his target was Jews in particular, not whites in
general. (Jews conveniently forget that the Irgun and Stern Gang were "racists
and extremists," Cruse offered, and one day terrorist tactics will be used in Harlem against white-owned businesses by a nationalist faction, whereupon "the
Jews will certainly call it anti-Semitism.")[192] In the very same scene, however,
Mickey counters this analogy with an opposing one. Let us say that the Israeli
Arabs were "cut off from other Arabs by a large ocean and couldn't wait for the
Zionists to be pushed into the sea," and let us say that "they wanted to be complete citizens of Israel in every respect that the Jew is," she remarks. "They'd be
doing the same thing Negroes in this country are doing," namely, rising up in
violent protest.[193] Mickey's formulation is meant to highlight the similarity
between Israeli Arabs and American blacks as second-class citizens, while suggesting in contrast that the geographical isolation of American blacks from potential allies in Africa or the black diaspora puts them at an even greater disadvantage than the displaced Palestinians in contemplating armed rebellion. Her
seeming assimilation of Palestinian nationalism to pan-Arabism makes her argument neater, but her reference to the novel's black nationalists, who have at
last resorted to guerrilla warfare and terror, brings the maximalism of the PLO
quickly into the foreground. And it does so by revealing an opposing vector in
the novel's title, one signaled by Williams's reversal of the terms Sons of Light
and Sons of Darkness.

Frequently calling upon them to avenge Deir Yassin, Fatah's *Our Palestine*
addressed its readers as "Children of the Catastrophe," nothing but "jetsam and
flotsam . . . dispersed to every corner," and more specifically, with respect to
Palestine's warriors, as "Sons of the Catastrophe."[194] Like other foundational
Palestinian documents then and since, it identified the Palestinians, in other
words, as the true Sons of Light, those who would liberate their lost homeland
from the Zionist infidel—the usurper, the occupier.* Having emerged from the

---

* The conceit remained very much alive in later years. When the PLO appeared to be ready to negotiate with Israel during the 1988 *intifada*, Hamas called upon the "sons" of Deir Yassin to renounce
Arafat's claim to represent the Palestinian people: "Let any hand be cut off that signs [away] a grain of
sand in Palestine in favor of the enemies of God . . . who have seized . . . the blessed land." Two years af-

second catastrophe of the Six-Day War as not just the Palestinians' only hope but also, for the moment, the Arab nations' only weapon of war, Fatah and the PLO, which had effectively become one by 1969—the year Arafat was elected chairman of the PLO, the year Williams's novel was published—became the embodiment of nascent Palestinian nationalism and with it radical anti-Zionism. As Williams divined, the Sons of Light and the Sons of Darkness, the Israelis and the Arabs—or was it the other way around?—stood in an irresolvable mirroring relationship from the moment of partition, if not from time immemorial. Was the "hymn of return" spoken of in Williams's quotation from the *War Scroll* meant to allude to the return of victorious Jews to Eretz Yisrael after two thousand years of exile, or to the return of displaced Palestinians, reversing the Nakba, in some hypothetical history to come? Who, in 1969 or 1973, were the Sons of Light?

In Hod's valor and clarity of purpose in 1948, upon which rested nothing less than the security and survival of Israel, Williams appears to say, one finds also the beginnings of a dilemma not solved in 1967 but, indeed, made all the more intractable. In Deir Yassin lay the paradox of statehood, as well as the paradox of Black Power anti-Zionism—its approbation of the Jews' right to a homeland, their right to exist, alongside its disapprobation of the Jews' right to defend their homeland against enemies who refused to recognize their right to exist, surely one way to locate the point at which anti-Zionism slips into anti-Semitism.

In returning to Israel, Hod goes "home," there to join the search for "a way" out of the post-1967 dilemma. Although peace with the Palestinians and Arabs is in his view a necessary goal, the stakes of the battle are no less clear: "Fight or be driven into the sea. Develop or be swamped in the Arabic miasma of European-style middle-age feudalism."[195] When the newlyweds emigrate, Hod tells Mickey's parents that he will be opening a jewelry business. Although Mickey knows this is a ruse, what she does not know is that his reason for settling in the Negev, where she believes he will be engaged in a project on "Arid Zone Research," is to protect the clandestine development of nuclear weapons at the

---

ter the Palestinian Authority had assumed administrative control over the West Bank in 1996, a poem broadcast by its television station at the opening of a summer youth camp called for martyrdom in familiar terms: "We are your boys, O Palestine / We will flood you with our blood . . . / Fan the flames of fire, O son of Canaan, for your people are rising up." Shaul Mishal, "Intifada Discourse: The Hamas and UNL Leaflets," in Avraham Sela and Moshe Ma'oz, eds., *The PLO and Israel: From Armed Conflict to Political Solution, 1964–1994* (New York: St. Martin's, 1997), pp. 200, 204; Efraim Karsh, *Arafat's War: The Man and His Battle for Israeli Conquest* (New York: Grove Press, 2003), p. 101.

Dimona reactor, the very symbol of the brinksmanship that characterized the onset of the Six-Day War and that would define, in coming years, Israel's ultimate means of deterrence.[196]

The most important lesson for blacks in the Jewish experience, it occurs to Hod, may lie in the Holocaust and the Jews' insistence that it "never again" be permitted to happen. With some "one hundred million" Africans killed in slavery and the slave trade over the centuries—Williams uses the inflated number favored by Du Bois, Black Power, and the Nation of Islam—blacks, says Hod, "should not forget or permit anyone *else* to forget."[197] Placed within Hod's reflections on the history of Israel's security and his future role at Dimona, however, Williams's invocation of the black "holocaust" reminds his readers that after partition and then again in 1967, it was Arab nations that were determined to annihilate the Jewish state, not the other way around. Here as elsewhere in his fluctuating alignment of black-Jewish and Arab-Israeli perspectives, Williams appeared to corroborate Moshe Dayan's well-known 1968 remarks about Israel's "creation of facts." Anyone "who adheres to the formula whereby the facts we create [through military victory and political reality] will bring the other side to accept us," said Dayan to graduates of the Israel Army Staff and Command College, "can just as well point to significant facts on the Arab side the moment he steps into the Arabs' shoes"—a phenomenon that Benny Morris would later refer to as the "crude and brutalizing perceptional symmetry" of the Israeli-Arab conflict.[198]

Such symmetry has only sharpened the lesson of the Holocaust for the state of Israel and the world's Jews. "To consider Israel fairly," Hod ruminates, "you had to consider the Arabs and if you considered *them* fairly, would you then have an Israel? They stood in such great, great numbers, overwhelming numbers, at the very gates of the nation." Hod refers not just to the military threat of hostile Arab nations, a constant since 1947—indeed, since at least the Balfour Declaration in 1917—but also to the demographic threat embodied in the Palestinian argument for the right of return, which was inscribed in the PLO's Covenant as an alternative way to eliminate the "Zionist entity" by rolling back the borders not to pre-1967 but to pre-1948, absorbing Israel into Greater Palestine. As Egypt's foreign minister, Muhammad Salah al-Din, had put it in 1949: "It is well known and understood that the Arabs, in demanding the return of the refugees to Palestine, mean their return as masters of the Homeland, and not as slaves. With greater clarity, they mean the liquidation of Israel."[199]

In their short and volatile history, the Israelis, in the eyes of some, had gone from victim to aggressor. Measured in terms of their security, however, they were far from having established a sincerely recognized claim to nationhood,

let alone peaceful coexistence with their neighbors, and the claim that the Palestinians were victims of colonial rule, nearly a truism more than three decades
after the Six-Day War, was far more ambiguous at the time Williams was writing. The very question, as Williams's novel means to suggest, raised a prior
question about Israel's own escape from colonial rule and its consequent right
to exist.[200] When he was younger, Hod continues in his rumination, he thought
he could "kill them all. He undoubtedly would have to kill them again, but one
thing was clear: you couldn't kill them *all*."[201] The War Scroll foresees the victory of the Sons of Light over the Sons of Darkness, but history told a different
story for the Jews in the Roman conquest of Jerusalem during the Great Revolt,
the destruction of the Second Temple, and the martyrdom at Masada, not to
mention the Jews of modern Europe. In 1969 it remained to be seen what history had in store for the generations after Hod's. Israel's victory in the Six-Day
War, however much it strengthened the nation, not only failed to eliminate external threats but also, in some respects, created a more dangerous one for Jews
within (and beyond) its new, uncertain borders.

Williams was evidently aware of the fact that the Six-Day War was being interpreted in some quarters, by Jews and Christians alike, as a quasi-apocalyptic
sign of the coming—or the second coming—of the Messiah, a point to which
we will return in the next chapter. If he did not predict literal end times, a true
war between the Sons of Light and the Sons of Darkness, Williams tried plausi-
bly to imagine the anarchy that might ensue were black Americans willing and
able to undertake the kind of terrorism then being exported by the PFLP, the
PLO, and their splinter groups. The novel diagnosed the usurpation and near
destruction of the civil rights coalition by Black Power—insofar as the Sons of
Light will wage war also upon those Jews who have offended against the Covenant, the vengeance of Black Power against the Uncle Toms of accommodation
is also implied in Williams's use of the *War Scroll*—but black nationalists were
neither the Irgun nor the PLO. They were not about to achieve their own state,
let alone drive white America "into the sea." For all the insurrectionary pos-
turing of the Black Panthers and other militants, and for all the anguish expressed by whites, especially Jews, about the dangers of Black Power, the asym-
metries of power and privilege were too pronounced to admit of radical
change. Revolutionary action confined to the ghetto was self-destructive, said
Fred Powledge in 1967, but its spread to white, middle-class neighborhoods
would bring on a "near-genocide" directed not just at radicals but at "everyone
with a black skin." At the novel's end, it appears to Browning that the black
populace he had been trying to save is "being slaughtered after all."[202]

Like Bellow, Williams approached the vociferous argument between radicalism and liberalism from the vantage point of modern Israel, but in doing so he left us with an ideological and epistemological puzzle. If the reading of history that found in Zionism a model for anticolonial liberation was simplistic, so was Black Power's counter-reading of Zionism as imperialism. Although Hod does not speak for Williams, and although Williams makes the Palestinian counter-point to Zionism evident enough, even the coherent expression of a pro-Israeli point of view within a novel that otherwise expounded a black nationalist agenda complicated, if it did not refute, Black Power orthodoxy. Reaching well beyond the sphere of domestic politics, Williams crystallized one key aspect of the deteriorating relationship between blacks and Jews in the United States, and he did so by pinpointing problems that would define the tragic course of Israeli-Palestinian relations on into the twenty-first century. By virtue of its canny response to contemporary events, we are required to read *Sons of Darkness, Sons of Light* as fictive historiography; by virtue of its uncanny intuition, we are required to read this "novel of some probability" as prophetic.

Williams left the tension between Zionism and anti-Zionism unresolved, just as he left ambiguous the potentially genocidal outcome of the violence raging in New York and other American cities by the novel's end. Although he took a different tack, more abstract and philosophical, it remained for Bernard Malamud to renew the investigation of the potential for a race-based apocalyptic war, this one more specifically between Jew and black on American soil.

CHAPTER 6

Bernard Malamud's Dark Ghetto

The Jew and I: Since I was not satisfied to be racialized, by a lucky turn of fate I was humanized. I joined the Jew, my brother in misery. . . . I was answerable in my body and in my heart for what was done to my brother.

—FRANTZ FANON, *Black Skin,*
White Masks

Hatred remains blind by its very nature; one can hate only part of a being. Whoever sees a whole being and must reject it, is no longer in the dominion of hatred but in the human limitation of the capacity to say You. . . . Yet whoever hates directly is closer to a relation than those who are without love and hate.

—MARTIN BUBER, *I and Thou*

TWENTY-FIRST-CENTURY READERS of *The Tenants* might assume that Bernard Malamud greatly exaggerated the bitterness of black-Jewish conflict in the late 1960s. Although his novel ends on a note of potential reconciliation, that moment rises from the ashes of hatred, as the two protagonists, the black writer Willie Spearmint and the Jewish writer Harry Lesser, square off with mirroring crude epithets—

"Bloodsuckin Jew Niggerhater."
"Anti-Semitic Ape."

—before Malamud envisions a visceral enactment of their hatred: "Lesser felt his jagged axe sink through bone and brain as the groaning black's razor-sharp sabre, in a single boiling stabbing slash, cut the white's balls from the rest of him."[1]

The startling scene is realistic neither in the sense that it purports to be the culmination of a sequence of actions within the novel, nor in the sense that it allegorizes contemporary events, as when the Jewish Defense League borrowed its language and iconography of militancy from the Black Panthers, nor even in the sense that it is a fantasy ascribed to one or both characters. Rather, the hallucinatory tableau is purely novelistic in that it is presented as the writer Lesser's version of how the novel—or the novel within the novel that he is writing—might end. Which is also to say that it is Malamud's version, since he is provisionally identified with his Jewish protagonist throughout *The Tenants*, not in any simple autobiographical sense but as a presiding consciousness more or less coincident with Lesser's.

Malamud's climactic violence is a parodic inversion of Frantz Fanon's well-known psychiatric judgment that in the discourse of racism the black, associated with "biological danger," is attacked with castration ("the penis, the symbol of manhood, is annihilated"), whereas the Jew, associated with "intellectual danger," is attacked in his religious or historical identity by being sterilized or killed. Ignoring the foundation of Nazism's attempted Judeocide in biological theories of racial pollution, Fanon's aphoristic judgment makes a neat division that is too clever by half, but the stereotypes have nonetheless been common and persistent. Witness Leslie Fiedler's assessment, indebted to Fanon, that in racial mythologies the Negro represents "the primitive and the instinctive, the life of impulse," while the Jew stands for "the uses and abuses of intelligence, for icy legalism or equally cold vengefulness."[2] By depicting violence that goes against type, Malamud heightened the artifice of such classifications while drawing his protagonists into a horrific mutuality. Although the book begins in solipsism—"Lesser catching sight of himself in his lonely glass wakes to finish his book"—the mirror images that proliferate in the novel continually drive the black and the Jew into a bond at once sympathetic and destructive. "Each, thought the writer, feels the anguish of the other," the narrator/writer says following this gruesome scene of racial mayhem.[3]

The Tenants is situated at a watershed in the relationship between blacks and Jews when it seemed less and less possible to find common ground, and likewise at a divide within the Jewish intellectual community in which the anti-Semitism of some Black Power proponents, as we have seen, played a pivotal role. Like the Ocean Hill–Brownsville school crisis of 1968, which Malamud would later say was a catalyst for his novel,[4] *The Tenants* is about the control of discourse—in the street, in the classroom, on the airwaves, in literature. It is concerned equally with the desire of African Americans, even at the cost of renouncing their longtime allies, to direct their own affairs, and with the necessity for American Jews, in a still ambivalent gentile nation, and facing increasing African American anger, never again to be assaulted without fighting back or to leave hostility toward Israel unanswered.

In our own day, when race-baiting has moved generally to the far edges of the social and political landscape, the linguistic violence of Malamud's brilliant novel is shocking. At the time of its publication in 1971, however, *The Tenants* accurately reflected the decay of liberal aspirations for egalitarian racial justice and the coalescence of various trends: rising black resentment of Jewish participation in the civil rights movement; differences over affirmative action and quotas; and charges that white scholars, Jews prominent among them, had tried to control the education of, and discourse about, African Americans, even to the point of elevating their own history of persecution at the expense of black suffering. Brazen race hatred erupted in arguments over discrimination and reverse discrimination in education, housing, and employment, and vocal epithets such as "Jew Pig!" and "Nigger Lover!" were heard in public confrontations.[5]

The rhetoric of rage already animating much countercultural discourse took on a decidedly racialized cast when some advocates of Black Power openly allied themselves with Israel's Arab enemies and traded in timeworn anti-Semitic stereotypes, as in an anonymous 1967 poem about "Jew-Land" that appeared in the short-lived publication *Black Power:*

> Now dig, the Jews have stolen all our bread
> Their filthy women tricked our men into bed
> So I won't rest until the Jews are dead
> In Jew-Land, Nailing Rabbis to a cross
> Really, Don't you think that would be boss . . .
> We're gonna burn their towns and that ain't all
> We're gonna piss upon the Wailing Wall.[6]

Not all anti-Israel positions were anti-Semitic, and not all African American criticisms of Jews or Israel were anti-Semitic; but in an atmosphere of extreme tension, every utterance was searched for hidden meanings. Asked what his novel might contribute to the increasingly acrid conflict, Malamud replied laconically, "I thought I'd say a word." The concluding incantation of the novel, "mercy mercy mercy," repeated 117 times, might be that word, and it gives credence to Malamud's further statement that he conceived of the ending as providing "reconciliation before it is too late."[7] Yet the burden of his narrative, steeped in recriminations and driving toward racial conflagration, says otherwise.

The Tenants is also an extended inquiry into art, literature in particular, as the highest expression of culture and civilization. Or, as the anticolonial aesthetic of Willie Spearmint would have it, it is an inquiry into the likelihood that prevailing concepts of culture and civilization are bankrupt expressions of racism, colonialism, and genocide. Apostrophized throughout the novel as the "writer," Harry Lesser lives in solitude, supported by royalties from his previous books and devoted to perfecting his novelistic craft—a parody of Flaubert at Croisset or Proust in his cork-lined room or Joyce "in his exile of silence and cunning creating a great work in the smithy of his soul," as Alvin Kernan notes.[8] His writerly interrogation of aesthetic form is clearly akin to Malamud's, and his fears and prejudices, as well as his faltering novel-in-progress, *The Promised End,* represent the author's apprehensions about the state of fiction in a time of spiraling social crisis. Harry's antagonist, Willie Spearmint, is not a biographical figure but a composite voice for the Black Arts aesthetic expounded by Amiri Baraka, Larry Neal, and others. Living off a small grant from the Black Writing Project in Harlem, Willie sees art not as craft but as pure ideology: "Art can kiss my juicy ass. You want to know what's really art? I am art. Willie Spearmint, *black man.* My form is *myself.*"[9]

In both its central subject and its formal devices, *The Tenants* makes fiction writing stand for culture at large: Who creates it? Who possesses it? Is a common culture even possible? And is it possible, in particular, for two peoples of such radically different heritages as Jews and blacks? The novel's unstable point of view and narrative fragmentation, with no fewer than three alternative but inconclusive endings inserted almost randomly into the action, reflect the precarious role of literature in mediating the Jewish response to black radicalism.*

---

* Malamud had already written effectively about black-Jewish relations in a number of short stories, including "Angel Levine" (1955), in which the Job-like sufferings of Manischevitz the tailor are mitigated by the intervention of an angel appearing as a black Jew; "The Jewbird" (1963), a parable of obligation to the stranger in which a talking blackbird, reminiscent of Poe's raven but assuming the guise of a Jew who takes the name Schwartz, is given temporary shelter by the family of Harry Cohen, only to be scorned and driven to its death when its personality and habits make it unwelcome; and "Black Is My Favorite Color" (1963), in which the heartbreaking efforts of the lonely Jewish bachelor Nathan Lime to court a black woman are thwarted by her bigoted community. In each instance Malamud probed the complex dynamics between individuals whose shared aspirations are unsettled by inherited communal

The standoff between universalism and ethnic particularism was not a new concern for Malamud. But however well it might characterize his earlier stories or novels such as *The Assistant* (1957) or *The Fixer* (1966), Malamud's theory that the Jew might be represented novelistically as universal man, owing to the Jews' historical dispersion and their intellectual wedding with various cultures,[10] is of questionable relevance here. Saturated in the traumatic dislocation of worldwide Jewry at mid-century, as well as the more immediate challenge of Black Power to American Jewish liberalism, *The Tenants*, in Philip Roth's words, is informed by a mood of "baffled, claustrophobic struggle."[11]

THE HOUSE OF BONDAGE

Thus said the Lord of Hosts, the God of Israel, to the whole community which I exiled from Jerusalem to Babylon: Build houses and live in them, plant gardens and eat their fruit. . . . And seek the welfare of the city to which I have exiled you and pray to the Lord in its behalf; for in its prosperity you shall prosper.

—*Jeremiah 29:5–7*

The action of *The Tenants* unfolds at a specific location in New York City—a building at the corner of Thirty-first Street and Third Avenue and the neighborhood around it—but both building and neighborhood stand for historical experiences of migration and sequestering superimposed upon each other, Jews in Europe, blacks in America. At once a *ghetto*, a *house of bondage*, and an ethno-cultural *homeland*, the nearly abandoned tenement in which Lesser and Spearmint live represents the psycho-historical ethos of black-Jewish relations in terms comparable to the trope used by James Baldwin when he subtitled one section of *The Fire Next Time* "Letter from a Region in My Mind." But insofar as the tenement embodies the epistemological space of Malamud's novel, coex-

---

animosities, but perhaps "Black Is My Favorite Color" most closely anticipates *The Tenants*. Nathan Lime's efforts to persuade a group of black toughs that they are all "brothers," that his intentions are honorable, and that he is not just a "Jew landlord" out for "black pussy," as one of them puts it, are violently rebuffed. His goodness appears to demonstrate the futility of Jewish liberalism: "I give my heart and they kick me in the teeth." Bernard Malamud, "Black Is My Favorite Color," in *The Complete Stories* (New York: Noonday Press, 1997), pp. 338–39.

tensive with Lesser's, it is also a trope for fictional space itself, as in the "house of fiction" that Henry James held forth as the embodiment of authorial craft.

For Lesser, "home is where my book is," a testament that undergirds his ten-year labor on a novel about love, a writing act laden with muted implications of devotion to Judaic scholarship and abstraction from the literal homelessness that for centuries had been the lot of Jews, "people of the Book," in the diaspora. But Malamud proceeds from this passage immediately to qualify the meaning of the home to which Lesser returns: "In front of the decaying brown-painted tenement, once a decent house, Lesser's pleasure dome, he gave it spirit—stood a single dented ash can containing mostly his crap, thousands of torn-up screaming words and rotting apple cores, coffee grinds, and broken eggshells, a literary rubbish can, the garbage of language become the language of garbage." Until Willie Spearmint takes up illegal residence, Lesser's tenement is inhabited only by transient drunks, bums, and junkies, "a zoo of homeless selves," its stairways and apartments spattered with wine, vomit, and waste, and disfigured by graffiti—a cartoon of a transsexual Hitler and an elaborate jungle motif including a "gorilla with handheld penis erectus." The last of the building's tenants after his landlord Levenspiel "decreed Exodus," Lesser lives as a kind of "Robinson Crusoe" on the sixth floor, the building on one side torn down for a parking lot, the building on the other ("Mark Twain lived there?") scheduled for the same fate. From the ruins of a roof garden, whose appurtenances have been "disassembled, kidnapped, stolen," Lesser observes the "soiled sky" and thinks of Wordsworth. Added to the allusions to Coleridge (the "pleasure dome" of "Kubbla Khan"), Blake, Defoe, Twain, and Eliot, we have a tableau of Western culture in collapse. In Malamud's stark allegory of the confrontation between art and politics, the integuments of romantic humanism have contracted into trashy stagnation and the house of culture has become an abode of "booming emptiness" where "strangers came not to stay, but to not stay, a sad fate for an old house."[12]

Recurring throughout the novel, the figure of the "stranger" refers first of all to the evolving positions of Jews and blacks as aliens in the Promised Land of America. But who is the stranger? As true anti-Semites in the United States understand, wrote Jacob Cohen in a statement cited in the early pages of this book, "the Negro has been and will be America's Jew," a fact that "fundamentally alters the situation of Jews in this country." In America, as Leslie Fiedler put it more precisely, the Negro was the Jew's "shadow, his improbable caricature," and his function in relation to Jews was to occupy "a ghetto which might otherwise be theirs and [bear] the pogroms which might otherwise be directed at them." In such an intense symbiosis, however, if the Jew pretends that in fighting for black equality he is not also fighting for himself, he also risks making himself "indistinguishable from a *goy.*"[13] The displacement of Jew by black as America's preeminent stranger, as Fiedler recognized, was not complete, and the ascendance of Jews might come not just at the expense of blacks but also at their own, insofar as it might entail the sacrifice of identifiable religious and cultural traits.

Without discounting the broad-based commitment of American Jews to African American equality and civil rights, owing both to their historic traditions of working for social justice and to their specific consciousness of Nazi persecution, *The Tenants* probes the limits of Jewish assimilation and Jewish altruism alongside the black backlash that defined those limits. Willie is apostrophized not only as "the black" but also on several occasions as "the stranger," and he thus offers to Lesser a special challenge in observance of the commandments of the Torah against oppression of the stranger—in this case the blacks whose ancestors may have been resident in the land many generations longer than those of the Jews. Lesser's tenuous hold on his obligation derives from the fact that he too remains a stranger—to others and to himself. Pictured strolling alone in Harlem, Lesser is greeted derisively by passersby as a "showoff cracker," an "ofay spy," or "Goldberg hisself," to which he responds, "A stranger is a man who is called stranger," a tautological formulation that echoes Sartre's notorious negative definition of Jewishness as a reaction to anti-Semitism: "The Jew is one whom other men consider a Jew . . . the stranger, the intruder, the unassimilated at the very heart of our society."[14] Because the passage turns out to be a reverie that has interrupted his writing, it confirms Lesser's own deracinated secularism—only anti-Semitism makes him a Jew—but it does nothing to mitigate the pervasive fear, suspicion, and secret gratitude in the failure of each other that defines his relationship with Willie and that likewise defined the black-Jewish dialogue at its nadir.

At the bottom of one of his manuscripts Willie Spearmint has scrawled a significant addendum: "It isn't that I hate the Jews. But if I do, it's not because I invented it myself but I was born in the good old U.S. of A. . . . The way to black freedom is against them."[15] In order not to be "America's Jews," says the logic of scapegoating, blacks must hate and attack America's real Jews. Malamud here invokes a signal line of argument in discussions of black anti-Semitism that we have seen before—namely, that the process of Americanization subjects blacks to the same anti-Semitic cultural imperatives as whites.*

---

* A peculiar instance, one which Malamud surely had in mind as he wrote, arose in the controversy surrounding the introduction to a catalogue for an innovative historical exhibition about Harlem culture mounted in 1968 at the Metropolitan Museum of Art under the title "Cultural Capital of Black America, 1900–1968." The show itself proved controversial because it was perceived by some blacks to be

Desperate for anything to fight their own oppression, blacks are gentiles in a gentile America, anti-Semitic in an anti-Semitic America. But there is a paradoxical reason simultaneously at work. In the defining formulation of James Baldwin's landmark 1967 essay, cited earlier, "Negroes Are Anti-Semitic Because They're Anti-White." The Negro condemns the Jew "for having become an American white man—for having become, in effect, a Christian," Baldwin contended, but the Jew does not realize that the fact that "he has been despised and slaughtered does not increase the Negro's understanding. It increases the Negro's rage." To the degree that Jews have ceased to be persecuted minorities, black empathy is distorted by black envy. Whereas Jews found refuge from European persecution in America and their assimilation had been comparatively rapid, said Baldwin, America *is* "the house of bondage for the Negro, and no country can rescue him. What happens to the Negro here happens to him because he is an American."[16]

At the moment Malamud published *The Tenants,* however, Jewish empathy might be similarly distorted. Their "betrayal" by blacks, said Arthur Cohen, revived Jews' experience of having been betrayed by the nations of Europe in their capitulation to Nazism. Jews could not afford to be passive twice in a generation: "Slaughtered once, symbolically slaughtered a second time by the oppression of the Negro, there is a kind of ritual identification and horror that the slaughter should happen again." The fact that the Jew fights for blacks as a Jew, not as a white man, makes the rejection all the harder to take, Cohen pointed out, for grief over the Holocaust is "not yet deep or profound enough to cover the American Negro"[17]—by which he meant that Jews had not yet sufficiently worked through their grief over the Holocaust to encompass African Americans in their compassion while being subjected to black animus.

As Jews looked at blacks looking back at them across the deepening racial

---

controlled by white sensibilities and white prestige. Titled *Harlem on My Mind,* the catalogue aroused an additional and more pointed furor because of the introduction contributed by a black high school student, Candy Van Ellison, who was a participant in the Ghetto Arts Corps, a youth program sponsored by the New York State Council on the Arts. In her introduction, derived from a school term paper, Van Ellison maintained that "psychologically, Blacks may find that anti-Jewish sentiments place them, for once, within a majority. Thus, our contempt for the Jew makes us feel more completely American in sharing a national prejudice." The attack on Van Ellison by the Anti-Defamation League, among others, dwarfed the breakthrough subject matter of the exhibition—until it was revealed that her remarks were, in fact, virtually a quotation from a well-known work of scholarship, *Beyond the Melting Pot* (1967) by Daniel Patrick Moynihan and Nathan Glazer, which was controversial but hardly anti-Semitic. See Candy Van Ellison, introduction to Allon Schoener, ed., *Harlem on My Mind* (1968; rpt. New York: New Press, 1995), unpaginated.

divide of the 1960s, many came to feel that Baldwin was right. Regardless of their own history of persecution, ancient and more recent, they would simply be classed as whites, inherently racist, as in Jacob Glatstein's 1960s poem "Mayn rasistishe biografye" ("My racist biography"), a poem sharp with irony and despair. In reaction to a chance street encounter with a black man in a "Black Panther hat," who sizes him up as a racist on the basis of his color, the poem's speaker fantasizes that his great-grandparents in Poland secretly harbored a black slave woman whom they tormented for pleasure: "Do not ask how the slave trade / came to Lublin. / If you are predisposed to torturing blacks / you look for them in the farthest corners."[18]

This post-Holocaust inflection in their symbiotic relationship was registered even more vividly, from a black perspective, in James A. Randall, Jr.'s, 1971 poem "Jew":

> Somewhere in the flesh mirror
> I saw myself.
> And after the silent promise
> I, feeling something heavier
> Than the tortured face,
> Felt the bewilderment of one
> Who has recalled his murdering.[19]

Here the black narrator confronts an elderly Jew, apparently a Holocaust survivor, and sees in the tortured face of his "flesh mirror" the visage of his own history, his own "murdering." And yet Randall's ambiguous pronominal construction leaves open two other possibilities: that the narrator recalls the Jew's murdering, as though he were witness to the Holocaust, or that he recalls his own murdering *of the Jew,* as though he were a perpetrator, a present-date anti-Semite.

The mirroring images of Randall's poem, which recall those of "Die Schwartze" in *The Changelings,* are a fitting gloss on *The Tenants,* where the failing alliance of blacks and Jews, and more broadly the social obligation not to oppress the stranger, is presented more often in images of tormented mimesis. "Who's hiring Willie Spearmint to be my dybbuk?" asks Lesser, underscoring their hostile spiritual unity and the Jew's ethical imperative.* However pro-

---

* *Dybbuk* (or *dibbuk*) is Hebrew for "one who cleaves," in Kabbalah a usually malignant transmigrating soul that has been unable to fulfill its function in one lifetime and inhabits a person left vulnerable by sin and takes over his personality, in some cases speaking curses and blasphemy from his mouth. In

nounced its aesthetic dimension, then, the region of Malamud's mind figured metaphorically as homelessness is, for all its solipsism, one of profound moral scope and urgency in which one's obligation to the stranger, as to one's neighbor, is paramount. It is Israel's having been both slave and stranger in Egypt that scripturally prescribes Jewish dedication to social action, without which, by one construction of tradition, there can be no piety.[20] *The Tenants*, however, appears also to share the famous skepticism about the commandments concerning the stranger and the neighbor expressed by Freud in *Civilization and Its Discontents*.* And what social action, what piety, is possible if the stranger himself, as in the case of Willie Spearmint, hates Jews and is mastered by vengeance?

The more far-reaching danger to the "old house" of Malamud's novel is that the world itself, post-Holocaust and unanchored, offers no refuge to its countless strangers. Like the world it describes, the book is permeated by exile and the foreboding of end times:

> Home is where, if you get there, you won't be murdered; if you are it isn't home. The world is full of invisible people stalking people they don't know. More homeless strangers around than ever before. God since the dawn of man should have made it his business to call out names: Jacob meet Ishmael. "I am not my brother's brother." Who says. Back in his study [Lesser] wrote hurriedly, as though he had heard the end of the world falling in the pit of time and hoped to get his last word written before then.[21]

---

one interpretation, the *dybbuk* represents the suppressed bitterness and resentment of Jews at having been condemned by God to centuries of suffering and exile. The best-known literary exposition is the play *The Dybbuk* by S. Ansky [Shloyme Zanvl Rappoport], written first in Russian, then rewritten in Yiddish, and first performed in 1920. Bernard Malamud, *The Tenants* (1971; rpt. New York: Penguin 1972), p. 125; Raphael Patai, *The Jewish Mind* (Detroit: Wayne State University Press, 1977), pp. 199–200.

* Freud refers specifically to Leviticus 19:18, "Thou shalt love thy neighbor as thyself." But, he continues, if my neighbor "is a stranger to me and if he cannot attract me by any worth of his own or any significance that he may already have acquired for my emotional life, it will be hard for me to love him. Indeed, I should be wrong to do so, for my love is valued by all my own people as a sign of my preferring them, and it is an injustice to them if I put a stranger on a par with them. . . . Not merely is this stranger in general unworthy of my love; I must honestly confess that he has more claim to my hostility and even my hatred. He seems not to have the least trace of love for me and shows me not the slightest consideration." Sigmund Freud, *Civilization and Its Discontents* (1930), trans. and ed. James Strachey (New York: Norton, 1961), pp. 55–56.

"Home," in this usage, is closer to what Martin Luther King, Jr., had in mind when he used the metaphor of the "world house" to describe the global crisis of race, thereby extending the archetype of the Exodus to anticolonial movements in Africa, Asia, South America, and the Caribbean, and creating a new diasporic typology of black, brown, and yellow "brothers" moving "with a great sense of urgency toward the promised land of racial justice."[22]

In making the abrasive brotherhood of Harry and Willie his focus, Malamud narrowed the fate of the world to the fate of blacks and Jews in the United States. But, in contrast to the mutual promise made in 1964 by Rabbi Abraham Heschel and Reverend King when they wrote mirroring essays devoted to the theme "Am I my brother's keeper?"[23] Malamud also let the mutual failure of Harry and Willie to be "my brother's brother" stand for the tragic condition of a world of homeless strangers, displaced "tenants" wandering in exile and pursued by unknown, invisible enemies.

Debate over the appropriation of cultural domains was perhaps nowhere more visible in the postwar decades than in the effective transference of the concept of the *ghetto* from Jews to African Americans, which awakened resentment on economic as well as cultural grounds of the kind dramatized throughout *The Tenants*.[24] A term as palpably physical as it is acutely psychological, the ghetto became indissolubly tied in the 1960s to the life course of an urban black underclass, the emblem and result of chronic racial discrimination. Being Negro in America, said King, "means being herded in ghettoes, or reservations, being constantly ignored and made to feel invisible. You long to be seen, to be heard, to be respected." In his anatomy of the ghetto, King went on to quote from a famous passage in Du Bois's *Dusk of Dawn* (1940) which had made the psychological effects of segregation equivalent to imprisonment behind "some thick sheet of invisible but horribly tangible plate glass" that prevents blacks, no matter their gesticulations and screams, from ever being heard and able only occasionally to "break through in blood and disfigurement."[25]

Both the cause and the arena of the urban race riots of the 1960s, the ghetto appeared to be a permanent fact of African American life, an extension of the house of bondage into a damaged way of life at once material and psychological. As the journalist Tom Wicker wrote in his introduction to the report of the National Advisory Commission on Civil Disorders, "the brutal fact is that for millions of Negroes now living, and perhaps for some unborn, the ghetto is all they are ever going to know." The black ghetto was defined by both physical and mental violence, which translated economic deprivation into a web of symbolic devaluation, said Kenneth Clark. But conceptually, it also bound whites and blacks together, like Hegel's master and slave, in a parasitic, if unequal, union. The centuries-long pathology of racism, wrote Clark in *Dark Ghetto* (1965), for many years the authoritative study of the debilitating conditions of African American urban life, was "a reflection of the ghetto in which the white [too] lives imprisoned."[26]

The very notion of the black ghetto, as Clark himself noted, originated in the sixteenth-century Jewish ghetto in Venice. For reasons surveyed in Chapter 1, Jews and blacks were intimately connected by their respective experiences of the ghetto, and Malamud's use of the setting, at once literal and figurative, reflected a complex layering of historical experiences and cultural traditions. American Jews were affluent and mobile enough by the early 1960s that traditional conceptualizations of the Jewish ghetto derived from a long history of sequesterings—in Frankfurt, Cologne, Vienna, Rome, Prague, Madrid, and the Russian Pale of Settlement, along with Venice and others—perforce assumed a measure of abstraction. If they less and less often felt the same degree of confinement as blacks, however, echoes from the past could nonetheless be detected in the realities of the present.

It seemed something of a stretch to argue that the exclusion of Jews by "gentlemen's agreements" amounted to restriction to a new kind of ghetto, or that in their postwar migration from city enclaves to suburbs they had recreated a familiar, albeit more comfortable, mode of enclosure, where "the ghetto gates, real or imagined, close[d] at 5:00 P.M."[27] But quotas and residential covenants were only then beginning to dissolve, and the constricting image of the ghetto typified by Louis Wirth's 1928 study *The Ghetto*—where it was an enclosure of discrimination, both physical and social, best escaped by means of assimilation—was still very much alive. Assimilation itself had costs, and anti-Semitism, though fading demonstrably among white gentiles, was hardly a historically remote experience, even if, unlike anti-black racism, it was more likely to be free-floating and indirect. In passing for "white," said Ben Halpern at mid-century, the Jew must both lose his religion and hate his very self, internalizing a bias, hidden but real, that places him in an "invisible ghetto."[28]

Even so, with the hardship and persecution suffered by earlier immigrant generations overcome through favorable political and economic changes in the postwar years, the American Jewish ghetto was well on its way to becoming a historical artifact by the time of Malamud's novel. Whether in memoirs such as Alfred Kazin's *Walker in the City,* (1969), films such as *Hester Street* (1975), or scholarship, where a representative collection of essays was titled *The Ghetto and Beyond* (1969),[29] the American Jewish ghetto had already become subject to nostalgic reconstruction.

More important, however, there were two models of the remembered Jewish ghetto simultaneously at play in American culture—one from the streets of Brooklyn, another from the streets of Warsaw. As survivors of the Holocaust continued to settle in the United States, and as the motives, means, and results of the European genocide were brought to light, the Jewish experience of hardship in the ghetto in America was quickly overshadowed by harrowing images of genocidal destruction in the ghetto abroad. With the near annihilation of European Jewry, images of the lost folk life of the shtetl, the Jewish village, along with those of urban Jewish life of prewar Europe, were melded into labor camps and, then, death camps.[30] The destroyed shtetl might be reborn as a lost covenantal homeland, a reservoir of *yiddishkeit,* as David Roskies notes,[31] but virtually every Jewish community of Europe, emptied of centuries of Jewish life by an unprecedented act of mass murder, would henceforth bear a terrible doubleness of meaning, no less for American Jews than for those in Europe and in Israel.

A population driven into exile may be destined to live thereafter in "other people's houses," to borrow the title of Lore Segal's 1963 memoir of her life as a young Holocaust refugee. For survivors transplanted to America and told to put the past behind them, moreover, memory of the Holocaust might become its own terrible ghetto, as in Edward Wallant's novel *The Pawnbroker* (1961), which we should pause to consider. A former Krakow university professor whose pawnshop launders money for a local gangster, Wallant's title character, Holocaust survivor Sol Nazerman, lives off the impoverishment and despair of Harlem while remaining trapped in a far more terrible enclosure of shocked dehumanization and paralyzed moral sensibility. In assuming the role of "bloodsuckin' Sheeny" bequeathed to him by a history of persecution and exile, Sol stands at the center of numerous analogies, metaphors, and structural devices through which two radically unlike experiences of the ghetto, two unlike experiences of racial damage, are superimposed on each other. Wallant carefully reminds us why the Holocaust constitutes "misery on a different scale" (himself the victim of Nazi medical experiments, Sol once watched helplessly as his son choked in a pool of excrement and vomit, was forced to witness his wife's oral rape by a camp guard, and worked as a *Sonderkommando* throwing corpses into the crematorium), and he makes the phantasmagoric, subhuman world surrounding Sol a mimetic function of his own Holocaust-induced derangement (at extremity, the deformed souls who bring him their sad treasures and sadder stories seem to be "cells multiplying and decaying, strange mutations . . . [A]ll excuses for life had been gone for a long time"). Nevertheless, *The Pawnbroker* suggests in manifold ways that these two diasporas and their conditions of life have something in common, and that the lesson of the Holocaust must be brought to bear on the problem of racism in the United States, though in what way remains to be seen. Indeed, the novel's prescient self-consciousness about the problem of comparing historic trajectories is well stated by Sol's Afro-Hispanic assistant, Jesus Ortiz, who suspects that Jews have somehow cashed in on their catastrophe at the expense of blacks: "Niggers suffer like animals. They ain't caught on. Oh yeah, Jews suffer. But they do it big, they shake up the worl' with they sufferin'."[32]

Sol Nazerman plays the middleman not only as a modern incarnation of the Jews' "mercantile heritage" but also as a bridge between the slaughterhouse of the Jews' last European ghetto and the de-Judaized life of his sister's family, who, having left both Europe and the last American ghetto behind, provide him with a fashionable suburban home—but one made possible by the addition of Sol's illicit income. Harlem is thus the charged ground on which we see acted out one pivotal episode in a century-long story of demographic transformation, an earlier episode of which we saw in *The Changelings*. Through fierce acts of repression, Sol keeps his horrid memories at bay and inhabits his pawnbroker's cage as though it were an extension of Dachau until, propositioned by Jesus's girlfriend, a prostitute in whose desperation Sol sees reflected the agony of his wife, he recognizes that he has internalized the corruption of the camps. In a moment of stylized transfiguration that accompanies the book's climactic scene, an attempted robbery, Sol realizes that the "nigger smell" of his assailants is, in fact, emanating from within himself. As he cradles the dying Jesus, killed during the crime in which he had colluded when he takes the bullet meant for the pawnbroker, Sol achieves a degree of absolution and transcendence. "He was crying for all his dead now," Wallant writes, "all the dammed-up weeping had been released by the loss of one irreplaceable Negro."[33]

Although Sol's story has distinct elements of Christian redemption ("Jesus" dies for him), it is the pawnbroker himself whom Wallant more clearly endows with potentially salvific power. In prayerful contemplation prior to the robbery, to take just one conspicuous example, Jesus envisions Sol "awkwardly transfixed on a cross, a man with blue, cryptic numbers on his arm." In addition to sacralizing the enigma of "numbers" that haunts the novel—Sol's tattoo, once the mark of his radical dehumanization, has come to signify his consequent belief not in God but only in money—the representation of Sol the Jew as Jesus the Jew normalizes the meaning of the Holocaust for a largely gentile readership by underscoring implications of martyrdom and holy sacrifice, that is, of "holocaust." At the same time, and for that very reason, however, it inevitably carries with it the history of Christian anti-Semitism, leaving Sol an arrestingly ambivalent figure.[34] To what end Sol is redeemed, other than that of his own re-covered humanity, remains as much a mystery as the "secret" he is repeatedly said to bear, whether as a witness to the Holocaust or simply as a Jew. Although the novel's ending allows for reconciliation, Sol's equal alienation from the blacks of Harlem and the Jews of Westchester portends instead a rift that would only grow wider and deeper by the end of the decade.

Harry Lesser bears little resemblance to Sol, but his imprisonment in a house not his own and a ghetto he does not recognize is no less severe, and his abso-lution and transcendence are even less certain. Inhabiting a deracinated world in which the Holocaust is pervasive, though invisible, in which Jewish culture, whether philosophical, literary, or folkloric, has been displaced by ragtag frag-ments of Anglo-American writing, and in which Judaism has been diluted into a set of feeble, barely remembered gestures, Lesser lives in undefined exile, in space layered with Jewish ghettos long gone and more recent, and shared now with the black anti-Semite Willie Spearmint.

Even if the Jew's escape from the ghetto was precarious, however, his Ameri-can experience, as Clark, King, and others pointed out, was markedly different from the African American's. Unlike the ghettos inhabited by American Jews and other white ethnic immigrants, mid-century black ghettos appeared not to be springboards to prosperity in which the sacrifice of one generation would be rewarded in the next, but domains of despair in which a culture of poverty had become so deeply ingrained that it might never be escaped.[35] Rather than being the last of the century's "immigrant" groups to find refuge and opportu-nity, argued Nathan Glazer the year *The Tenants* was published, blacks might be domestic aliens destined to remain unassimilable. On top of which, to quote an accusatory 1947 analysis that was still thought to explain black hardship when it was cited in *The Negro American,* a highly regarded mid-1960s collec-tion, "the Jew" continued to inhabit the black ghetto in a particularly visible way: "A Negro can hardly rent a store for business in his own neighborhood because the Jew has thought ahead of him. When the Jew sees the drift of the Negro population he steps in and buys up the strategic corners and spots for the Jew. . . . He supplies every Jew store in the Negro belt from his wholesale houses."[36]

The literal replacement of Jews by migrating southern African Americans in urban enclaves, along with the economic entanglement that went with it, provoked anti-black hostility among Jews (as Sinclair had dramatized in *The*

Changelings) and anti-Semitic hostility among blacks, for whom "the Jew" was a convenient scapegoat. Stereotypes of the exploitative landlord and merchant preying upon blacks in the "colonized" ghetto, as we saw in the previous chapter, were revived in Black Power's identification of racial enemies both abroad and at home. The metaphor of the "bloodsucker," a perennial favorite of western and eastern European anti-Semites that had cropped up in populist American anti-Semitism and then among urban blacks, became a staple of Nation of Islam rhetoric. Malcolm X lamented black "brothers entwining themselves in the economic clutches" of the Jewish merchant who leaves every night "with another bag of money drained out of the ghetto," while Amiri Baraka spoke of Newark as a black colony where the "Official Jew" sells "poison wine to the slaves."[37] In *The Tenants,* the landlord Levenspiel, who wants to evict Lesser so that he can tear down the tenement and put up a new apartment building, is thus characterized by Willie as a "fartn Jew slumlord"—Levenspiel in turn considers Willie a "gorilla" and a "nigger"—and the archetypal figure of "Goldberg," the gouging Jew, appears in one of Willie's manuscripts, stalking a hallucinatory landscape of anti-Semitic riot, murder, and cannibalism.[38]

In this startling scene, to which we will return, Willie's indulgence in obscene stereotypes that threaten to escalate into bloody action conflates two experiences of the ghetto, black and Jewish. In making his ghetto a palimpsest of historical convergence, Malamud surely condemned black anti-Semitism, but he also found in the black experience of the ghetto a difference to which American Jews, given their own deep psychological investment in transcending discriminatory confinement, might well be blind. When Jews deprecated blacks' experience of ghettoization by comparison to their own ("Is a Slum a Ghetto?" asked Max Geltman in a pointed chapter title)[39] or charged that African Americans "stole" the concept of the ghetto for their own purposes (a variation on the charge that they have "stolen the Holocaust" in characterizing slavery), they no doubt had in mind the discrepancy between pogroms, labor camps, and genocide, on the one hand, and segregation, economic deprivation, and sporadic racist violence, on the other. By the same token, Jews might be inclined to overlook a countervailing but equally important discrepancy in the different moral values ascribed to Jewish and black ghetto life.

At mid-century the black ghetto was the subject of groundbreaking work in American sociology. Contemporary studies appearing along with Clark's *Dark Ghetto* included a new edition of St. Clair Drake's and Horace R. Cayton's *Black Metropolis* (1962; originally published in 1945), Gilbert Osofsky's *Harlem: The Making of a Ghetto* (1966), Elliott Liebow's *Tally's Corner: A Study of Negro Streetcorner Men* (1967), and Ulf Hannerz's *Soulside: Inquiries into Ghetto Cul-*

ture and Community (1970). Likewise, the black ghetto had already been the setting for landmark works of American literature—Richard Wright's *Native Son* (1940), Ann Petry's *The Street* (1946), James Baldwin's *Go Tell It on the Mountain* (1952), and Claude Brown's *Manchild in the Promised Land* (1965), to name a few. Yet even if such scholarship and fiction proved the black American ghetto to be a rich repository of folkways and vernacular culture transplanted from the rural South and refashioned under urban pressures, they proved at the same time that it was far from affording a covenantal rediscovery of homeland.

Nor was the black ghetto sanctified, as in the recent history of the Jews, among the general population as the ground for heroic, life-preserving struggle, much less martyrdom, however much black leaders from the 1930s forward may sometimes have depicted participants in urban riots as engaged in righteous resistance. (Of those who rioted in Harlem in 1943, Adam Clayton Powell, Sr., said that they were driven to madness by race-baiting, just as "Moses was mad when he beat upon the rocks.")[40] Baldwin made the telling point that the black uprisings of the 1960s showed that whereas the Jew's suffering had been accepted as an identifiable episode in the world's moral history, the black's as yet had not: "The uprising in the Warsaw ghetto was not described as a riot, nor were the participants maligned as hoodlums."[41]

And yet the Holocaust, the Jews' ultimate tragedy of ghettoization, had in one critical way already become a defining factor in liberal conceptualizations of black American life. It was neither the sequestering of Jews in the European shtetl (which might find a corollary in the rural black South, a site of both precious cultural inheritances and racial pogroms) nor the up-by-the-bootstraps story of American Jews (shared by other prewar European immigrants but seldom by African Americans) that provided Kenneth Clark his point of departure in *Dark Ghetto*. Rather, it was the apotheosis of the walled ghettos in which Nazi-era European Jews were held to die by starvation and disease, or to await transport to sites of industrialized murder, to which Clark looked in arguing that the black ghetto was similarly a zone of "engulfing pathology." Citing studies of the Holocaust by Bruno Bettelheim and Victor Frankl, Clark found that the "institutionalized pathology" of the ghetto was "chronic, self-perpetuating," and capable of inflicting long-term personality damage, to which violent uprising, as in the ghettos of Nazism, should be considered a justifiable reaction.[42]

Some Jews might object, as did Elie Wiesel, that such claims about the causes and meaning of the black ghetto trespassed on sacred ground. Look at the words that blacks, ungrateful for our spiritual inspiration and political support, bandy about, he exclaimed in a 1970 interview: "Genocide, mass murder. They aren't Jews!"[43] As the reaction of a Holocaust survivor, Wiesel's objection was understandable, but he was out of step with a prominent strain of sociological theory that had by then been absorbed into public discourse, most notoriously in the 1965 Moynihan Report on the state of the black family, which it effectively identified as synonymous with the ghetto in concluding that epidemic black unemployment, alcohol and drug addiction, the failure of school integration, the magnetic attraction of the Nation of Islam's separatist philosophy, and the decay of inner cities pointed to a simple conclusion: "The tangle of pathology is tightening."*

Clark's abiding metaphors of concentration camp and prison were exemplary of the damage thesis prevalent in the social science of race throughout the twentieth century. As we saw in Chapter 3, theories of racialized damage were stimulated in part by Stanley Elkins's *Slavery*, with its controversial argument that both plantation slavery and the Nazi death camps were instances of total institutions whose disciplinary regimes were so severe as to annihilate personality. The analogy of Nazism quickly entered into perspectives on the black ghetto in mainstream social thought. Thus Leslie Fiedler: "We affect surprise at how 'invisible' the German concentration camps were to many Germans; but precisely as 'invisible' are the Negro ghettos of New York and Chicago to those who never walk that way; for to be thus 'invisible' is precisely the point of their existence."[44] Martin Luther King, Jr., initially rejected Black Power as a "nihilistic philosophy" that amounted to a "belief in the infinitude of the ghetto," but as he increasingly turned his attention to the conditions of black life beyond the segregated South so as to address the double urban enemy of "oppression without" and "pathology within," he became more attuned to the lessons of the Nazi genocide. Influenced by the theories promulgated by Clark, as well as by Frantz Fanon's argument that psychological patterns of black "inferiority" and white "superiority" degenerated over time into neurotic forms of self-enslavement, King concluded that, although the United States had never produced a Hitler, American racism nevertheless partook of the central features of Nazism. It resulted in a "total estrangement" that separates not only

---

* Among the many replies to the report, Laura Carper boldly, but not ironically, brought forth the example of Hassidic life in the shtetl, where Jews succeeded in a task at which the Negro had purportedly failed: placing a positive value on the husband's personal withdrawal and his desertion of his family. As Carper put it, "pathology is in the eye of the beholder." Lee Rainwater and William L. Yancey, eds., *The Moynihan Report and the Politics of Controversy* (Cambridge, Mass.: MIT Press, 1967), pp. 91, 472.

bodies but also "minds and spirits," at length inflicting "spiritual or physical homicide on the out-group."[45]

Not everyone accepted the notion that the ghetto represented the truest paradigm for African American life. Ralph Ellison repudiated the pathological interpretations of the Moynihan Report and averred that the writer who dwells on the ghetto—"piss in the halls and blood on the stairs"—as African America's principal creative terrain "will never master the art of fiction." Arguing, in addition, that the differences between segregated housing in the United States and the confinement of Jews in European ghettos made the experiences utterly incommensurate, Albert Murray excoriated the Clark-Moynihan school for filing "survey-safari reports on Ghettoland" and trafficking in accounts of "black wretchedness" that exceeded those "written by *white racists to justify segregation.*"[46]

For a time, however, Clark's argument proved compelling to the new generation of black activists who adapted damage theory to more overt political purposes. In their landmark volume *Black Power* (1967), Stokely Carmichael and Charles Hamilton began with a epigraph from *Dark Ghetto* that characterized ghettos as "economic colonies" whose inhabitants are "subject peoples" living in "fear of their masters," and they repeatedly quoted Clark in building their case that institutional racism is a form of colonialism that must be resisted through race pride, self-affirmation, and a readiness to employ violence as a political tool. In turning the ghetto into an arena of liberation, *Black Power* reflected the evolving liberal and black consensus that the "riots" of the 1960s were in fact "uprisings," legitimate political acts born of anger and frustration in which violence was an indispensable language of protest. The emasculation of black men had reached the point, said psychologist Alvin Poussaint, that no more lies, psychological tricks, dreams, or opiates of patience could stave off the coming apocalypse: "No more reason. Only a welling tide risen out of all these terrible years of grief, now a tidal wave of fury and rage, and all black, black as night."[47]

In their explanations of ghetto uprisings, proponents of Black Power thus departed from the view that African Americans were irremediably scarred and crippled. Endowing victimization with transcendent meaning, they promoted instead an ideology of resistance that eventually achieved iconographic status in black popular culture.[48] Grounded in the moral right to rebel against oppression, the nationalist strategy expressed by Willie Spearmint would permit blacks to remake themselves as a nation by reclaiming history, by renegotiating linguistic usage, and by liberating themselves from white cultural terrorism. In his contribution to the Black Arts anthology *Black Fire,* Nathan Hare accepted Elkins's theory about the equivalence between the plantation and the concentration camp, as well as its derivation from Erving Goffman's account of "total institutions" as arenas of complete subjugation of the inmate to the will of the master, in this case the cultural incarceration of black subjectivity. But he also made the "brainwashing" of blacks by white supremacy the starting point for his rejection of the "ridiculous and appalling farce" of nonviolence and, consequently, for his inculcation of a revolutionary black identity.[49]

Much as the European Jewish ghetto prior to Nazism, or the early-twentieth-century American Jewish ghetto, had allowed the flourishing of a rich philosophical and literary tradition, the black ghetto could in this interpretation be construed as the cradle of liberation and cultural self-affirmation. No longer an emblem of imprisoning segregation and defeat, the new house of bondage was a staging ground for rebellion and for a radical aesthetic in which African Americans would seize control of their own historical narrative. Whether or not they had in mind the example of the Warsaw Ghetto, as did Baldwin, some Jews concurred. "The ethnic and tribal sense of self-value which preserved the Jew from inner deterioration in the ghetto," said Alan W. Miller, "is now being created by the black man to save his own sense of self-value"[50]—even if that expression of black "self-value" now sometimes came, quite publicly, at the expense of Jews.

THE BLOOD OF YOUR NEIGHBOR

Although the action of Malamud's novel is contained within a precise contemporary moment captured in the fraternal but finally homicidal relationship of Harry Lesser and Willie Spearmint, it rehearses the history of black-Jewish brotherhood over the previous several decades. For example, the companion pieces by Louis Harap ("Anti-Negroism among Jews") and L. D. Reddick ("Anti-Semitism among Negroes") published in the 1943 volume *Should Negroes and Jews Unite?* depicted blacks and Jews in a close relationship of deprivation and prejudice. (Reddick's characterization of the discrimination that kept blacks confined within a ghetto was a reminder of how recently Jews had faced the same conditions. "The pressure of the steady stream of migrants demands expansion of the 'Negro neighborhood,'" he wrote. "Like rats trapped in a cellar, the mass of black humanity is thrown back upon itself again and again as it seeks to escape.")[51] Thurgood Marshall and Jack Greenberg, his successor as director of the NAACP's Legal Defense Fund, were longtime comrades in the cause of black civil rights. And at key moments in the 1960s, as we have already seen, Martin Luther King, Jr., was paired in brotherhood with Abraham Heschel, whether in protest marches or in their companion essays, both titled "What Happens to Them Happens to Me." In his contribution to the dialogue, Heschel concerned himself with the Jew's obligation to the stranger, to the neighbor and brother, and cited the Torah: "You shall not stand by the blood of your neighbor" (Leviticus 19:16). King agreed, longing for the visionary pluralist moment when "we will be able to transform the jangling discords of our nation into a beautiful symphony of brotherhood."*

But less harmonious pairings were also in evidence—and not just in the borrowings of the Jewish Defense League from the Black Panthers or in the Ocean Hill–Brownsville crisis, where the standoff between Albert Shanker, the Jewish leader of the teachers' union, and Rhody McCoy, the black head of the school district, was one spark for Malamud's fire.

Norman Podhoretz, editor of *Commentary,* had commissioned Baldwin to write an essay on the Black Muslims only to have Baldwin—unethically, so it seemed—submit his essay to the *New Yorker* instead. When Podhoretz confronted Baldwin with the charge that only a Negro could get away with such an act because white liberal guilt would protect him, and went on to narrate to Baldwin his own resentments dating to his childhood in 1930s Brooklyn, Baldwin urged Podhoretz to set down his thoughts in writing. The result was the seminal 1963 polemic "My Negro Problem—and Ours," which Podhoretz considered first of all a critique of the unrealistic assumptions driving the integrationist strategy.[52] At once alert to, and imbued with, racial clichés—blacks are "free, independent, reckless, brave, masculine, erotic"—Podhoretz's essay, based on his recollection of harassment by blacks, was a blunt confession of his fear and antagonism: "As in a nightmare, I am trapped." It also set

---

* To Heschel's version of the scripture, compare *Tanakh:* "Do not profit by the blood of your fellow." As in the usage by Ben Shahn and Lila Oliver Asher, who worked from the text "neither shalt thou stand against the blood of thy neighbor" (see Chapter 1), Heschel's more common version is normally taken to mean "do not stand idly by when your neighbor is hurt or wronged." Meir Kahane cited the same passage and its Talmudic commentary in the Sanhedrin, but for the purpose of promoting Jewish Power and aggressive self-protection. Abraham J. Heschel and Martin Luther King, Jr., "What Happens to Them Happens to Me," in Jack Salzman, ed., *Bridges and Boundaries: African Americans and American Jews* (New York: George Braziller, 1992), pp. 86, 90; Meir Kahane, *The Story of the Jewish Defense League* (1975; rpt. New York: Institute for the Publication of the Writings of Meir Kahane, 2000), p. 73.

the course for a coming neoconservative reaction against black radicalism as Podhoretz rebuked white liberals "who permit Negroes to blackmail them into adopting a double standard of moral judgment."*

Having already castigated the Jews for their attempts to monopolize black rights issues in *The Crisis of the Negro Intellectual*, Harold Cruse, in a mirroring reply to Podhoretz titled "My Jewish Problem and Theirs," reiterated his objection to Jewish control of the black agenda, whether in the Communist Party, the civil rights movement, or historiography, and condemned what he took to be the contradiction between Jewish nationalism in the form of Zionism and Jewish rejection of black nationalism, which, Cruse said, gets labeled anti-Semitic when it challenges Jews in economic or educational realms. Mimicking Podhoretz, Cruse attempted to adduce the "Jewish personality" on the basis of childhood incidents and, again like Podhoretz, argued that his antipathy grew not from anti-Semitism but from "black ambivalence toward the Jew." The sympathy of Jews for Negroes, he added, is clouded by their own conventional white racism and their need to use blacks to their own advantage: "The problem here is that the American Jew has a very thin skin, and believes that because of his European heritage of religious persecution he is preternaturally free of all sin in his relationship with other peoples."[53]

Baldwin was the catalyst for another flare-up when he daringly—one could say recklessly—invoked the Holocaust while describing Angela Davis on trial for her alleged role in the Jonathan Jackson shoot-out of 1970. "You look exceedingly alone, say, as the Jewish housewife in the boxcar headed for Dachau," he wrote in an essay for the *New York Review of Books* titled "My Sister, Miss

---

* In a 1993 postscript Podhoretz stated that the passing of time had only strengthened his rejection of the "diseased mutation of integrationism" into the quota systems of affirmative action and protested that the "abdication of black responsibility and the commensurately total dependence on government engendered by so obsessive and exclusive a fixation on white racism has been calamitous" for race relations and black economic and political progress. In his own coming-of-age memoir, *Jew Boy* (2000), Alan Kaufman updated Podhoretz in recounting his strained, and finally broken, adolescent friendship with two blacks, one of whom, in a wrenching episode, he recalls having ridiculed for being gay. Rebuked by the other, a boy named Gregory, for his privileged whiteness and his inability to grasp the pain of black exclusion, Kaufman feels that his own exclusion as a "Jew-boy" and a "kike" is little different from Gregory's debasement by the epithets of "nigger, coon, jiggaboo." But whatever sense of kinship he summons with his black companion ("I felt myself able to step into his skin"), Kaufman finds the curtain of color descend as Gregory, "suicidally convinced that no pain existed in the world but his own," steels himself with an "inner stoical numbness" and enters "a hell of his own making for which I [Kaufman] could not be blamed." Norman Podhoretz, "My Negro Problem—and Ours," in Paul Berman, ed., *Blacks and Jews: Alliances and Arguments* (New York: Delacorte, 1994), pp. 84, 79, 87, 93–94; Alan Kaufman, *Jew Boy* (New York: Fromm International, 2000), pp. 203–4.

Angela Davis." Shlomo Katz, editor of *Midstream,* rightly objected that the analogy by itself was scandalous. Taken in legal terms alone, Davis's trial, whatever her actual culpability in supplying guns for the disastrous attempt to liberate George Jackson and other black convicts, had been scrutinized by the world and carried out in a nation whose liberal judicial system bore no resemblance to Nazism or to contemporary show trials of Soviet Jews, condemned for no other crime than wishing to emigrate to Israel. Baldwin debased the genocide of the Jews in his metaphoric martyring of Davis, said Katz: this crown can be earned only "in one way—the way of the chimneys of Dachau." In reply, Baldwin rejected Katz's facile assumption that blacks were well protected by the legal machinery of the United States, as well as his privileging of the Holocaust: "Your assumption means, brutally, that you wish me to stand in awe of your experience, but that you have no respect for mine." There are plenty of martyrs here in America, as at Dachau, Baldwin continued, some of them perishing "in prisons and in hovels, as I write; their blood and their bones nourish the earth of my country."[54] Katz replied once again to Baldwin, refuting him point by point and expressing his anxiety in the face of Baldwin's apparent growing anti-Semitism.

The debate could have ground on endlessly, blow after blow, so illustrative was it of the seemingly omnipresent internecine dialogue between blacks and Jews that Malamud made his subject in *The Tenants.** It might be superficial to depict the Baldwin-Katz argument as the endgame in a war for "victim status," but John Murray Cuddihy was correct to read it, like Malamud's novel, as part of the *Kulturkampf* raging between black and Jewish intellectuals for cultural priority.[55] Like other such quarrels, that between Baldwin and Katz was the sign of a mirroring relationship irreparably shattered. For most Jews, with most educational, economic, social, and even political opportunities now open to them, America was more than ever their Promised Land. For many blacks, with

---

* A further instance of strained relations that may have been on Malamud's mind occurred at a 1965 forum on the arts held at the Village Vanguard in New York City, whose participants included Amiri Baraka (LeRoi Jones), the (black) jazz musician Archie Shepp, and the (Jewish) artist Larry Rivers, who had designed sets for two of Baraka's plays. By Rivers's account, the conversation soon focused on race and became heated. When Shepp commented on the number of Africans killed by the slave trade and Belgian colonialism in the Congo, and Rivers responded by reminding the audience of the Jews who had perished in the Holocaust, Shepp retorted, "There you go again, always bringing up the fucking Jews." Baraka added, "You're like the others [whites], except for the cover story." Larry Rivers, with Arnold Weinstein, *What Did I Do? The Unauthorized Autobiography* (New York: HarperCollins, 1992), p. 431; Harold Cruse, *The Crisis of the Negro Intellectual: A Historical Analysis of the Failure of Black Leadership* (1967; rpt. New York: Quill, 1984), p. 486.

Martin Luther King, Jr., dead, their neighborhoods on fire, and anti-Zionism becoming vociferous, the Exodus seemed a time-worn, inadequate paradigm for salvation. Despite the legal victories of the civil rights movement, many felt no less "like rats trapped in a cellar" than when Reddick used those words a quarter century earlier. The United States was, after all, the "house of captivity" out of which Ben Ammi Carter said he was leading his Hebrew Israelite congregation when they emigrated first to Liberia in 1967 and then to Israel in 1969.[56]

Such a literal Exodus was available to few black Americans, however, and the more pressing question was whether and how they would ever belong to the nation at all. "Do I really *want* to be integrated into a burning house?" Baldwin had asked in *The Fire Next Time,* nearly two decades before Malamud's novel. Baldwin's updating of Abraham Lincoln's "house divided" speech—another metaphoric structure resonant in Malamud's tenement—suggested that persistence in thinking of itself as a "white nation" would condemn America to "sterility and decay." Regardless of the "psychic or social risk," said Baldwin, the Negro was the key to the nation's future and must be embraced. By 1972, however, Baldwin considered the American house of bondage a "vast, howling orphanage" equivalent to a death camp: "The blacks are the slaughtered children of the great western house—nameless and unnameable bastards." One of his epigraphs for *No Name in the Street* came from a slave song that identifies the destructive rage of black rebellion with that of the blinded Samson:

> If I had-a- my way
> I'd tear this building down.
> Great God, then, if I had-a- my way
> If I had-a- my way, little children,
> I'd tear this building down.[57]

Both the house of bondage, the nation's incarcerating history of prejudice, and the house of fiction, the nation's incarcerating culture of racial exclusion, would be torn down and rebuilt in the black revolution portended by Baldwin and Willie Spearmint. Who, if anyone—what Jews, if any—would not "stand idly by" the blood of the black neighbor on the day of revolution?

Strident militancy did not lack for black critics, whether Derek Walcott, who considered it a form of separate-but-equal theater more akin to the "laughter of the minstrel," or Addison Gayle, Jr., who warned that Black Power was passing into black fascism as "professional nationalists" adopted self-serving totalitarian poses while failing to secure any pragmatic political power.[58] The poet

Welton Smith ridiculed the armchair rebels of black New York as "deranged slobbering punks lapping in the / ass of a beast" who were incapable of going beyond the futility of words:

> you are jive revolutionaries
> who will never tear this house down
> you are too terrified of cold
> too lazy to build another house . . .[59]

By the time the eloquent precision of Baldwin's early work gave way to wandering jeremiads, the best of Black Arts work had come and gone. But Malamud wrote at a time when Baldwin's prophecy had a significant audience, when the stability of American society seemed very much at risk, and when virulent Jew-baiting emerged in one artistic wing of Black Power.

THE EXTERMINATION BLUES

> *White Boy,*
> Buchenwald *is a melismatic song*
> *whose single syllable is sung to blues notes*
> *to dark wayfarers who listen for the gong*
> *at the crack of doom along*
> *. . . that Lonesome Road . . .*
> *before they travel on.*
>
> —*Melvin B. Tolson, "Harlem Gallery"*

To Willie's slyly mocking question, upon discovering that Lesser has a Bessie Smith record, "Are you an expert of black experience?" Lesser responds, "I am an expert of writing." Down to the perfect detail of the mangled grammar, this vignette of colliding vectors—on the one hand, the African American's belief that because Lesser's "brain is white" he cannot comprehend any part of black culture; on the other, the Jew's subordination of the political to the cerebral—subsumes long-standing anxieties about control over the social and educational policies meant to remediate African American disadvantage.[60] In exact contrast to the Black Arts movement's insistence on a highly politicized aesthetic and its cultivation of what the Ocean Hill–Brownsville debate defined as communal "black values" inaccessible to whites, the aesthetic of "the writer" is neither white nor Jewish but, in principle, universal, representing the cosmo-politanism and detachment from ideology favored by the mid-century New York intellectuals whose aesthetic Harry Lesser reflects.[61] Lesser's identity is subsumed tautologically into the role of author—"Lesser writes his book and his book writes Lesser"—even to the point of haunting personification wherein the author evaporates and the house of fiction itself assumes authorial con-sciousness: "There's his abandoned book on his desk being read by the room." In the case of Willie, in counterpoint, the house of fiction is enveloped in the ghetto not only as a concrete demographic entity but also as the imprisoning force of racism—including the "rat-brained Jews" who rejected his manuscript for publication.[62]

In this respect, both Willie's anti-Semitism and Harry's racism are attributes of their artistic beliefs rather than the reverse. In the sporadic camaraderie of writing, black and Jew are brought into postures of complementarity, where they "embrace like brothers," only to be quickly torn apart by fierce antago-nism. Malamud's subtle entanglement of their two consciousnesses creates a stylistic equivalent of the psychology of colonialism, whereby the colonized, in-ternalizing the habits of the colonizer—seeking "to resemble him to the point of disappearing in him," writes Albert Memmi—becomes trapped in a vicious, self-annihilating process that produces Negrophobia in blacks and anti-Semi-tism in Jews.[63] In Malamud's variation on the mimetic, parasitic bond between master and slave, Willie depends on Harry's beneficence even as he despises it, while Harry, Malamud's authorial conscience, depends on Willie's anti-Semi-tism and crudely politicized art to prove his aesthetic superiority. As action and reverie slide in and out of each other, the narrator subtly extricates himself from Lesser's point of view even as he colludes in imprisoning Willie within Lesser's consciousness, as though to personify the white ghetto—more spe-cifically, the Jewish ghetto, to hear black anti-Semites tell it—within which black radicalism was both nurtured and trapped.[64]

Acutely aware of his own artistic predispositions, Malamud simultaneously offers a compelling exposition and a compelling critique of the Black Arts aesthetic. Willie is a deliberately outsized exponent of militant sensibility, but Malamud takes his theory of writing seriously, even as the question of au-thorial intention, as well as the cultural prejudice that might go with it, remains deliberately unresolved in *The Tenants*. Being a minority can be a kind of "lucky break" for a writer, said Malamud, since his subject matter comes to him "'hot,' surcharged—call it the emotionalization of history." The collective expe-rience of blacks might be an advantage for fiction, as it once was for Jews, he argued, yet the risk for young black writers is that they will produce "little more than agit-propaganda." Placing Ralph Ellison at one end of the aesthetic spectrum and James Baldwin somewhere in the middle, Malamud asked about Amiri Baraka, "What has he accomplished by hating half the human race?"[65] The same, of course, is asked about Willie Spearmint in the novel.

Over the course of *The Tenants*, Willie's manuscripts undergo several transformations, but rather than coming closer to the universalist aesthetic that Harry's tutelage offers him, Willie plunges into ultra-nationalist caricature. The first of his manuscripts that Harry reads is a novelistic work variously titled *A Nigger Ain't Shit, Missing Life,* and finally *Black Writer,* partly a seeming autobiography and partly a set of short stories. His life story, as written, is a mélange of Richard Wright, Claude Brown, and Malcolm X, among others; themes of sexual violence, the transcendence of self-hatred, and liberation from the imprisonment of illiteracy dominate the work. The inversion of genres in Willie's writing—his purported autobiography turns out to be fiction while his short stories are drawn from his life—reflects the dominance of life writing in the mid-century black renaissance, with its deeply felt allegiance to the "old slave narratives," its internal dynamics of bondage and freedom, and its premium placed on racial authentication. The "bloody fable" of Willie's "black art," the "soul writin of black people cryin out we are still slaves in this fuckn country," is an antidote to the failed universalism of Lesser's cult of high art: "You have had your day and now we are gonna have *ours.*"[66]

It is no accident that Willie Spearmint's autobiographical work places his call to authorship in prison. Incorporating miscellaneous fragments of Black Power philosophies—the Black Panthers, the Black Liberation Front, the Republic of New Africa, Maulana Karenga's US organization, whose conflict with the Black Panthers erupted in street warfare—Willie's writing is inspired as well by Malcolm X and more generally the worldview of Elijah Muhammad, for both of whom prison was a chronotrope of the black man's colonization in the ghetto, his incarceration in the "total institution" of the United States, as it would be later for John Edgar Wideman. But prison was also the site of a countervailing immersion in blackness in which the metaphysical, the political, and the aesthetic might be channeled into a single plane of being.

In declaring "my form is *myself,*" Willie proclaims an unmediated guerrilla aesthetic, a pure expression of Black Power resistance to the total institution of white culture. The concluding chapter of Carmichael and Hamilton's *Black Power* was titled "The Search for New Forms"—new economic and political coalitions that would escape the corruption and despair of the ghetto and combat the crippling of black children by dysfunctional educational systems—and we likewise see in that usage the overarching way in which Willie Spearmint, like most leading figures of the Black Arts movement, conceives of ideology as inseparable from the formal questions governing his fiction. "The dead forms taught most writers in the white man's schools will have to be destroyed," said Larry Neal. The artist and the political activist are one, they are "warriors, priests, lovers and destroyers." At this point in his career, Neal rejected the inspiration of Ellison's *Invisible Man* ("we are not Kafkaesque creatures stumbling through a white light of confusion and absurdity") in favor of Wright and Fanon, the first goal of the black revolution being the eradication of Du Boisian "double-consciousness" in the souls of today's black folk.[67] Since elite art is morally bankrupt, argued Baraka, one must instead celebrate "Garvey the artist. Malcolm the artist. Touré the artist. Nyerere the artist." Adopting a mode of racial purification not unlike adherence to the tenets of the Nation of Islam, the Black Aesthetic demanded stark polarizations. "The Negro artist who is not a nationalist at this late date," Baraka asserted, "is a white artist, even without knowing it."[68]

As it reaches its most vengeful forms, as nationalism mutates into fascism, Willie's writing appears inspired most of all by Baraka, whose rejection of pluralism led him over the course of the 1960s to a more race-based and frequently anti-Semitic aesthetic. In his 1963 essay "What Does Non-violence Mean?" (first published in the Jewish journal *Midstream*), Baraka lamented the myopia of those Negroes who believed they were Americans, much as German Jews believed they were, and could remain, German when Hitler came to power. Doubting but not yet completely rejecting liberalism, Baraka feared a Nazi-like white suppression of black resistance. Soon, however, he embraced rhetorical pseudo-Nazism as a legitimate form of black insurgence, declaring that the black artist's role in America is to "aid in the destruction of America as he knows it," reporting so precisely the nature of the society that white men will "tremble, curse, and go mad, because they will be drenched with the filth of their evil." To create the black nation is comparable to building the *Luftwaffe*, he said. "We are creators and destroyers. . . . Bomb throwers and takers of heads. Let the fire burn higher, and the heat rage outta sight." Only when blacks, like the Nazis, commanded *Lebensraum* "in which to exist and develop" would the healing energy of black revolutionary art find its mature expression.[69]

Melvin Tolson's notes to the stanza from "Harlem Gallery" (1965) quoted in the epigraph to this section say that his argument is not that America is engaged in the moral equivalent of Nazi genocide but that the name Buchenwald, "whether [as] metaphor or warning, gives shape and the force of presence to the pervasive dread that haunts American black people." Lurking just beyond the control of reason, the specter of Buchenwald instigates "fearful dreams wherein the precarious balance of racial roles is lost, and everything collapses into a vacant whiteness."[70] Tolson's implication is that once the Holocaust had occurred, it became possible to repeat and thus necessary to accommodate to the psychic landscape of black people, whose history of oppression and racial violence left them understandably vulnerable to fears of genocide.

Although the nation's embrace of black music, black history, and black language was a more enlightening result of the Black Power movement,[71] the language of liberation, as we saw in Chapter 5 and will see again in Chapter 7, was more than incidentally dependent on the shock language of anti-Zionism, anti-Semitism, and Jewish genocide. Black appropriation of the Holocaust, while hardly new in the mid-1960s, acquired a scurrilous ease and suppleness in the political arguments of Stokely Carmichael, Malcolm X, and others. The same was no less true in select key works by black writers. Poet Nikki Giovanni read the Israelis' response to Arab attack and Lyndon Johnson's "Great Society" agenda as equal instances of Nazism:

> Can't you hear [the naziboots] when Arab women die from
> exposure to israelijews
> You hear them while you die from exposure to wine
> and poverty programs . . .[72]

Even as he admired the culture of the Jews for the "nationalist consciousness" that was "interwoven with their religious reality" and sustained their educational and professional institutions, Haki Madhubuti (Don L. Lee) envisioned in his miniature millennialist epic "For Black People" an urban hell in which a black mother must "spread her legs, in hatred, for her landlord—paul goldstein" so that "her children will eat tonight." In their exploitation of black labor, said Madhubuti, Jews were engaged in an American species of genocide:

> chicago became known as negro-butcher to the world &
>   no one believed it would happen, except the jews—the
>   ones who helped plan it.
> forgetting their own past—they were americans now.[73]

Malamud's novel locked onto the fact that the anti-Semitism of some Black Arts writing rendered abhorrent its most powerful effects. In any debate as to whether the rhetoric of hatred can lead to writing of aesthetic achievement, Baraka's *Black Magic* (1969), the work most deliberately echoed in the pronouncements and artistry of Willie Spearmint, would be a featured exhibit. A trenchant articulation of the Black Arts aesthetic that deserves to be read and remembered for its command of free verse lyric, Baraka's volume is nevertheless laced with differing degrees of anti-Semitism—for example, in "Citizen Cain," where Baraka prophesies that he too will "be herded off like a common jew, and roasted in my teary / denunciations," or in "Black Art," where he speaks of the need for "dagger poems in the slimy bellies / of the owner-jews," poems like "cracking / steel knuckles in a jewlady's mouth," and wishes to see "the Liberal / Spokesman for the jews clutch his throat / & puke himself into eternity." In some poems, the linguistic sophistication obscures the crudeness of the epithets, but it was plainly anti-Semitic when Baraka spoke in "The Black Man Is Making New Gods" of "atheist jews" as "robots," "arty bastards," "pricks," "Dangerous Germ Culture," and "double crossers" who "stole our secrets" and gave us Jesus, "The Fag's Death," to worship:

> the empty jew
> betrays us, as he does
> hanging stupidly
> from a cross, in an oven, the pantomime
> of our torture . . .[74]

In his "Confessions of a Former Anti-Semite" (1980), Baraka repudiated this particular poem, while ascribing others deemed anti-Semitic to a "stance rather than a reality," an effort to use the denunciatory power of art to counter the success of writers such as Mailer, Roth, Bellow, and Malamud, who, despite their ancestral history of oppression, "have been able to pass over into the Promised Land of American privilege."* Regardless of Baraka's intentions,

---

* Baraka attributed his "descent into the wasteland of anti-Semitism" to estrangement (and divorce) from his Jewish wife, Hettie Cohen Jones, which was cruelly memorialized in "For Tom Postell, Dead Black Poet" ("shacked up with a fat Jew girl . . . Jews talked through my mouth") and which, by his account, coincided with his despair over the assassination of Malcolm X. Because anti-Semitism could not sustain his "craving for clarity and freedom," Baraka said, he turned to a pan-Africanist revolutionary philosophy, whose overarching anti-imperialism considered Zionism, white racism, and anti-Semitism to be equally culpable. For her part, Cohen made the breakup a metonym for the larger dissolution of black-white alliances: "I couldn't bear his guilt at being with me. . . . But I viewed as crucial the collective release of black anger" after the assassination of Malcolm X and the rising violence of the civil rights movement in the South. The original title of Baraka's essay was "A Personal View of Anti-Semitism," and he said the purpose of the piece was less to "confess" to his own anti-Semitism than to differentiate a critique of Zionism from anti-Semitism, an issue that flared up once again in 2002, when, having been

"The Black Man Is Making New Gods" remains an important gauge of the moment at which Malamud's novel was written. Quoting from the poem, Rabbi Jay Kaufmann scorned the indulgence of those white and Jewish liberals who remained "silent in the face of this suicidal nihilism." Taking his title from the Torah—"Thou shalt not hate thy brother in thy heart, thou shalt surely rebuke thy neighbor" (Leviticus 19:17)—Kaufmann contended that self-abnegation in the face of black racism was not only humiliating and dangerous but ultimately destructive of black interests as well.[75] Baraka's view was just the reverse: that self-abnegation in the face of liberal Jewish paternalism, not to mention neoconservatism, was humiliating and dangerous. At stake in Malamud's novel is white America's—in particular, Jewish America's—capability to confront Willie's black aesthetic, anti-Semitism and all. Baraka's poem is, in fact, nuanced and demanding, and the force of its fusion of Jewish, Christian, and African American traditions (in figures of Holocaust, crucifixion, and slavery) cannot be dismissed. But the poem's formal and historical accomplishment no more mitigates its repugnant message in the case of Baraka than it does in the case of, say, T. S. Eliot or Ezra Pound. Artful bigotry is bigotry nevertheless.

"I got the extermination blues, jewboy. I got / the hitler syndrome figured," Baraka wrote in "For Tom Postell, Dead Black Poet," a less successful poem than "The Black Man Is Making New Gods," but one even more caustically anti-Semitic.[76] No doubt such lines express misery and longing, as well as resentment and hate. Whereas the destruction of the European Jews resulted in worldwide recognition of the moral calamity, as well as swift American support for the defense of the Israeli homeland when it was threatened in 1967 with a

---

named poet laureate of New Jersey, Baraka took the occasion of his inaugural reading to profess in his poem on the September 11 terrorist attack on the World Trade Center, "Somebody Blew Up America," that four thousand Israelis who worked there had been tipped off in advance and stayed home. This canard was repeated by Baraka in other venues, where he defended it as evidence that the attack was part of a worldwide "white supremacist" conspiracy, asserted that his sources included Israeli media, and derided those who attacked him for attempting to repress his free speech. Amiri Baraka, "Confessions of a Former Anti-Semite," *Village Voice* 25 (December 17–23, 1980), 1, 21–23; D. H. Melhem, *Heroism in the New Black Poetry: Introductions and Interviews* (Lexington: University Press of Kentucky, 1990), pp. 237–38; LeRoi Jones [Amiri Baraka], "For Tom Postell, Dead Black Poet," in *Black Magic Poetry, 1961–1967* (Indianapolis: Bobbs-Merrill, 1969), p. 153; Hettie Jones, *How I Became Hettie Jones* (New York: E. P. Dutton, 1990), pp. 223–27; Jerry Gafio Watts, *Amiri Baraka: The Politics and Art of a Black Intellectual* (New York: New York University Press, 2001), pp. 141–56. For contemporaneous comments on "Somebody Blew Up America," see, for example, *New Yorker* 78 (October 14 and 21, 2002), 66–67. Both the poem and an impassioned (anti-Zionist) defense of it were available as of December 2003 on Baraka's personal Web site: www.amiribaraka.com.

new Holocaust, the anticolonial struggles of black Africa found comparatively little non-black support in the United States, even as the march toward racial justice in America had broken into riots, assassinations, and white political backlash. Singing the "extermination blues," a black poet might give passionate voice to African American suffering and exile, even write into the vernacular record a plea that black "genocide" is worthy of notice. But in turning on the "jewboy" and ridiculing his "hitler syndrome"—or in calculating one's own power by embracing that of Hitler, as the line also suggests—Baraka built a depraved and immoral aesthetic upon monstrous evil, as does Willie Spearmint.

An Unpolitical Man

It is of special interest that Malamud's previous novel, *The Fixer* (1966), was undertaken after he cast about for a subject with the original intention of treating injustice on the American scene: "I had hoped to portray an American experience, possibly concerned with a Negro protagonist, but that didn't work out into a plausible plan for a long fiction." Considering, then discarding, the anarchists Nicola Sacco and Bartolomeo Vanzetti, condemned murderer Caryl Chessman, and finally Alfred Dreyfus, the archetypal victim of state anti-Semitism, Malamud at last remembered Mendel Beilis, a handyman charged with the ritual murder of a Christian child in Kiev in 1911, whose story his father had told him as a boy.[77] Although the blood libel—the accusation that Jews used the blood of sacrificed Christian children to make matzo for Passover or other ritual purposes—was not unknown in United States history,[78] an event in tsarist Russia seemed a peculiar way to get at the question of American racial injustice. In adapting the story of Beilis, however, previously treated in Sholem Aleichem's *The Bloody Hoax* (1923) and Franz Kafka's *The Trial* (1925), Malamud created both an analogy and a context for an American audience still struggling to grasp the meaning of the Holocaust. The historical displacement served two purposes: it gave scope to the violent tradition of anti-Semitism that had marked European and Russian culture for centuries before the rise of Nazism; and it underlined the double difficulty faced by an American writer seeking an appropriate narrative form in which to contain the concept of genocide.

By highlighting the blood libel and exaggerating the nightmare of Beilis's two-year incarceration, Malamud did not falsify the story but revealed its rootedness in a political and psychological substructure of demonization.

Within two decades the premise of the Beilis case and the history of pogroms of which it was a part would be carried by Hitler so far beyond the bounds of the moral imagination that only a novel which recast history in the oblique story of a single victim could begin to fathom race hatred on so massive a scale. Malamud associated *The Fixer* with an array of anti-Semitic acts rather than with the Beilis case alone, suggesting "how recurrent, almost without thought, almost ritualistic, some of our unfortunate historical experiences are," and he intentionally shaped the whole to convey "the quality of the afflictions of the Jews under Hitler."[79] On several occasions the novel openly forecasts the advent of Hitler and Nazism, and Malamud emphasized those aspects of the case, and of Tsar Nicholas II's contemplation of pogroms on a grand scale, that align the persecution of one man with the coming destruction of millions.*

Against the potential complacency of Jews in affluent postwar America, *The Fixer* highlighted the contingency of postwar Jewishness. In changing the historical Beilis from a married man with five children to the childless loner Yakov Bok, Malamud emphasized his estrangement from Judaism and society at large—in this respect he resembles Harry Lesser—and made him a solitary existential figure in whose consciousness the fury of racial scapegoating is played out. Subject to the paradoxical logic in which his guilt is proved merely by the fact that he is suspected, much as the guilt of all Jews "must be inferred from the very frequency of the accusations against the Jews," the evidence against them being nothing less than "the evidence of history," Yakov Bok becomes a representative victim of totalitarian repression, blurring the regimes of Hitler and Stalin.[80] In the postwar crisis of conscience about what Jews, whether victims or bystanders, might have done to prevent the Holocaust, he also figured as one ambiguous answer to charges of Jewish complicity leveled by Hannah Arendt during the Eichmann trial.

Having worked through his deepest despair and resignation—"What was

---

* Malamud quite freely adapted Beilis's story to the greater rhetorical purpose of exposing the ideological origins of the Holocaust. Whereas the novel depicts its hero, Yakov Bok, to be enclosed on all sides by anti-Semites, to have virtually no ally when he is charged with the blood libel, and to offer the perfect chance for the tsarist state to exercise its most extreme repression, Beilis's case in fact proved the weakness, or at least the unpredictability, of official anti-Semitism in tsarist Russia. Because he was respected in his neighborhood and allowed to live openly in a gentile area through the help of his employer, the police had significant difficulty obtaining any hostile testimony against Beilis. It was revealed in court that the principal expert witness for the prosecution, the defrocked priest Father Pramaitis, had such an unintelligible and far-fetched understanding of the Talmud as to make his testimony a sham. In the end, Beilis became something of a national hero, his acquittal welcomed by Kiev and Russia at large as a proper rebuke to the corrupt administration of the tsar.

being a Jew but an everlasting curse? He was sick of their history, destiny, blood guilt," Malamud writes—Bok reaches his transforming moment when, despite the threat of further pogroms, he refuses to sign a fabricated confession betraying other Jews and denouncing a world Jewish conspiracy. Whereas the real Beilis, after his acquittal, emigrated first to Palestine in 1916 and then to America in 1922, Yakov Bok's story ends with him, on his way to trial, contemplating the assassination of the tsar and commiting himself to personal resistance and revolution against the state. "There's no such thing as an unpolitical man," he thinks. "You can't sit still and see yourself destroyed."[81]

Bok's words are almost a quotation from *The Slave* by Isaac Bashevis Singer, another novel that found in historical pogroms a prefiguration of post-Holocaust Jewish heroism, and *The Fixer* has to be read first of all in similar terms. Despite having abandoned the idea of a novel with a black protagonist and an American setting, however, Malamud still believed that *The Fixer* had important resonance for the American experience. "Injustice is injustice," he remarked.[82] More than that, the novel rehearsed a set of themes that were to reappear—sometimes in the crudest of epithets, sometimes as theoretical abstractions—in *The Tenants*. Even though its failed form is best understood as a structural device, one might also conclude that the tale of Harry Lesser and Willie Spearmint failed to cohere into a "plausible plan for a long fiction." In the battle between black and Jew, Malamud was once again searching his moral inventory for the starting point to address the question of injustice, which in the century following the Beilis incident assumed epic size under Hitler, Stalin, and Mao. Insofar as American Jews were even more likely in 1971 than in 1966 to accept Bok's dictum against sitting still for one's own destruction, Harry Lesser, as his name transparently implies, is in key respects the "lesser" man in his contest with Willie, not necessarily as an artist, but perhaps as a man of conscience and self-awareness. Without granting him an equivalent moral ascendancy or qualifying his recourse to crude anti-Semitism, Malamud created in Willie Spearmint a version of the "political man," a Yakov Bok blackened and made militant by the mythology of racial defilement in which the lives of his people are imprisoned. His Jew, by contrast, struggles in his aesthetic snare to find a guiding ethical vision.

The Nazi war against the Jews had many dimensions, but the principal substratum, laid out with numbing insistence in *Mein Kampf* and all manner of anti-Semitic propaganda, was the biological war against the Jews as a source of racial pollution. The Holocaust was both a pogrom and a modern, biomedical form of blood libel on a scale hitherto unimagined. Although the outcomes

were very different, the Nuremberg Laws, as we saw in an earlier chapter, nevertheless had in common with less severe but kindred racial laws levied especially
against blacks in the early-twentieth-century United States the abiding fear of
miscegenation. America's version of the blood libel was the century-long sexual demonization of African Americans, accompanied by a bloody history of
lynching and lesser crimes against black men for their purported lasciviousness
and threat to the sanctity of white womanhood.

Black Power reveled in this myth and in so doing sought to explode it. The
emasculating power of white supremacy, both literal and figurative, might be
answered with comic outrage, as when H. Rap Brown cackled that "Lyndon
Johnson is Hitler's illegitimate child and J. Edgar Hoover is his half-sister," or
when a writer for *The Black Panther* fulminated against the "Southern cracker
[George] Wallace with cancer of the mouth that he got from his dead witch's
uterus."[83] The hyperbole of pulp fiction was likewise well suited to answer-
ing racism with loathsome tableaux of sexualized defiance. The white woman
might offer her "compassionate white bosom in penance" to black men, wrote
Iceberg Slim (Robert Beck), but she remained a "pale, deadly symbol that can
trigger a ghastly montage of gouged out black sex organs, crushed, charred
corpses swinging from crooked necks and purple tongues lolled out of lipless,
madly staring deathheads." However damaging to the interests of black women
and black gay men, the militant assertion of black masculinity was, in some instances, a response to perceived genocidal assault, as in Chester Himes's *Plan B*,
a posthumously published novel dating from the late 1960s whose title refers to
a plot by blacks to launch their own cataclysmic race war. In response to "Black
Hunts" carried out by white vigilantes, whose purpose is to bag "a big dangerous buck and [cut] off his testicles to have them mounted in the trophy room,"
the plot's leader, Tomsson Black (son of Uncle Tom, a radical "black" inversion
of the "Negro"), intends to issue an ultimatum to white America: "Grant us
equality or kill us as a race."[84]

The ultra-masculine poses of Black Power, whether or not they achieved
their purpose, meant to turn the blood libel of black sexual predation upside down by arguing—to state collectively the representative views of Fanon,
Baraka, and Calvin Hernton—that the sexual potency of the Negro is a hallucination reflecting the white man's anxiety about his inferior virility. The Jim
Crow archetype of the black man as a personified penis is a projection of the
white man's desire to ravish the sacred white goddess of his own fantasies, so
that lynching and castration are a form of worship, a primitive "divination
rite," in which white men extol the black phallus in the act of destroying it.[85]
One need not stipulate that any such psychoanalytic interpretations are correct

in order to recognize that *The Tenants* is steeped in the myths of racial virility and that Willie, like Bellow's black pickpocket, functions as a parodic foil for white (Jewish) emasculation.

The contest between Willie and Harry over Irene Bell (née Belinsky), issuing at length in a fistfight poised to escalate into homocide when it is interrupted by Levenspiel at a moment of close combat—"They broke, grabbed, and were once more locked together, head to bloodied head"—continues their argument over the racial politics of art on a sexual plane. More than a mere contest of masculinity, the sexual triangle places the problems of racial pollution and genocide in a dramatic human context while underscoring the theory of genealogical kinship between blacks and Jews—one potential source of alliance that instead became a source of bitter antagonism. In a variation on the scriptural interpretations of Black Jews, Garveyites, or Albert Cleage's Black Power theology—in which black Abraham mixed his seed with Egypt in his marriage to Hagar and the captivity in Babylon produced further interracial marriage ensuring that "Israel was a mixed-blood, non-white nation"—Willie attributes to Jews descent from an ancient instance of miscegenation: "In the Babylonian past a black slave socks it to a white bitch from the Land of Israel?"[86]

No less than Harry, however, Irene enjoys the privilege of whiteness, and it is as a deracinated, assimilated white Jew that she functions as a token of sexual possession and racially charged regeneration in the plot. Irene is peripherally representative of the precarious role of white women, especially Jews, in the black liberation movement. Her relationship with Willie no doubt alludes to the Greenwich Village marriage and very public breakup of Amiri Baraka and Hettie Cohen, noted earlier, though in its degree of violence it also looks forward several years to the searing triangulation of black men, black women, and white Jewish women in Alice Walker's *Meridian* (1976), where the guilty forbearance of white liberalism in the face of black nationalism is played out in the sexual humiliation and rape of a Jewish civil rights worker by a crippled, belligerent black militant. But Malamud grants Irene little in the way of consciousness. At best a tissue of typecast traits—minor career as a actress, episodes of psychoanalysis, dyed-blond "shiksa" hair, sleeping with a militant black writer, eventually recovering some semblance of her ethnic self—she is a pawn in the race struggle, for Willie a sign of achieved revenge, for Harry of the failed possibility of recovering something "lost in the past," both hers and his own.[87]

Despite its repeated implication of the two men in a sexual competition that also conceals a homoerotic bond, the love triangle is less a source of character development than a formal element in Malamud's allegory of racial annihilation. After Harry achieves his fantasy of sleeping with a black woman, Mary Kettlesmith—whose boyfriend spies on them through a keyhole, crying—he is challenged by Willie for transgressing the same racial boundary that Willie himself has transgressed with Irene. The challenge takes the form of a game of "the dozens," the black verbal sparring match in which victory is marked by superiority in creative insults and epithets. (Having determined that Shakespeare was a racist and a "faggot," said H. Rap Brown, he found his true education on the street in the "mental exercise" of the dozens, admittedly a "mean game because what you try to do is totally destroy somebody else.")[88] Lesser is inept. His insults are stilted parodies of vernacular beholden to highbrow literature ("Willie, your mouth is a place of excrement"), and he refuses to see the value of the game ("What good is a contest of imprecation?"). Challenged to proceed, Lesser calls Spearmint a "filthy prick" and then, goaded by him, revises it to "filthy nigger prick," an alteration made "because I know you want to hear it." Having had the stakes raised as high as they can go for a black man in their game of "naked words," Willie is free to call Lesser a "fartn shiteater faggot whore kike apeshit thieven Jew." With Willie's friends buoyed up by his performance, Lesser, the "white spook," concedes the game: "That's my last word."[89] Even though Malamud's mimicry of black vernacular displays a kind of artistic brotherhood through mimesis, the scene could only prove that until Jews and blacks no longer look at each other as potential scapegoats or substitute victims, there can be no last word and no conclusive end to the story.

The episode of the dozens puts in vernacular form the contest of masculinity that appears throughout the two writers' argument about aesthetics. In one of their several hallucinatory conversations about writing, this time heightened by marijuana, Harry argues for the primacy of aesthetic value, while Willie is interested only in commercial success. Harry proclaims the verity of art's "sacred cathedral," while Willie wants only "green power . . . money to stuff up my black ass and white bitch's cunt." To Harry's further insistence that "art is the glory and only a schmuck thinks otherwise," Willie responds with a vicious condemnation of artistic idealism:

Lesser, don't bug me with that Jewword. Don't work your roots on me. I know what you talkin about, don't think I don't. I know you trying to steal my manhood. I don't go for that circumcise schmuck stuff. The Jews got to keep us bloods stayin weak so you can take everything for yourself. Jewgirls are the best whores and are tryin to cut the bloods down by makin us go get circumcise, and the Jewdoctors do the job because they are fraid if they don't we gon take over the whole goddamn country and wipe you out. That's what they afraid. I had a friend of mine once and he got circumcise for his Jewbitch and now he ain't no good in his sex any more, a true fag because he lost his pullin power. He is no good in a woman without his pullin power. He sit in his room afraid of his prick. None of that crap on me, Lesser, you Jewbastard, we tired of you fuckn us over.

A number of themes come together in Willie's shocking reply: warring stereotypes of black and Jewish sexuality and manhood; perverse conceptions of Jewish covenantal law; fears of domestic genocide; and the contest for position between two minorities within a dominant white, Christian culture. Willie ironically captures Harry's "roots" within his own tradition—as black magic, juju—while Harry drives home his argument that the language of art opens onto universality, not ethnic particularity, by deploying once again the ultimate epithet: "If you're an artist you can't be a nigger, Willie."[90]

Willie's fear about the loss of his "pullin power" and his association of writing with the fear of castration—when he faces his typewriter, it seems "like the keys are teeth raised to take a bite out of my personal meat"—are specific to his anxieties as an aspiring writer. But his fear represents as well the history of emasculation that Black Power rhetoric and Black Arts writing, in seemingly endless variations, sought to overcome by turning sexual prowess into a weapon of intimidation.* Following sex with Irene, Lesser's sleep is disturbed

---

* For Baraka, white liberalism "de-testicled" the black man with promises of a slow progress to justice ("We will let your balls grow back . . . one day! Just be cool!") because American white men, themselves "trained to be fags," can control the threat of black masculinity only by literal emasculation, as in lynching, or psychological emasculation: "Trying to strangle a man with his own sex organs, his own manhood: that is what white America has always tried to do to the black man." If he can only "recapture his mind, recapture his balls," said Huey Newton, combining the terms of Fanon's polarity between Jew and black, "then he will lose all fear and will be free to determine his destiny." Ridicule of homosexuality as the negation of black manhood, a commonplace from the Nation of Islam and the Black Arts movement through contemporary Afrocentrism, provided a further way to combat emasculation. For Eldridge Cleaver, who glorified the black rapist of white women as a revolutionary hero, black homosexuals had been psychically castrated by the white man to the point that they acquiesced in a contorted racial death wish, "outraged and frustrated because in their sickness they are unable to have a baby by the white man." As Michelle Wallace rudely remarked in a famous rejoinder to Black Power's cult of masculinity, "when the black man went as far as the adoration of his own genitals could carry him, his revolution stopped. A big Afro, a rifle, and a penis in good working order were not enough to lick the white man's world after all." But it may be that Cleaver and Wallace were both caught in the same racial trap. Reflecting on the propensity of the mainstream press to venerate anything black so long as it contains the proper degree of degradation, Stanley Crouch observed that *Ms.* magazine, which published an

by a dream rendered in the form of a narrative poem that is in effect a "white" version of the dozens. Although the diction and syntax are black, the nightmare fantasy is his own. His writing "island" racked by a storm, he envisions someone in the cellar with a leg amputated and runs to tell Willie, who is gnawing on a "white bone":

> What are you eatin, Mr Bones?
> Don't shit me, Lester,
> I know your real voice,
> What are you eating, Bill?
> Breast of chicken,
> White meat part,
> Honest to God?
> Looks like a big bone,
> It's pig's foot, boy,
> Kosher meat, wanna bite?

The voices of the poem flow in and out of each other, with Harry called out by Willie for trying to talk black even as the displacing punctuation fuses the voices into a single lyric. Irene's sexuality is reduced to soul food, forbidden pork mocked as kosher by Willie, whose blues song preceding this poem—"I got you in bed with nothin on you / You gonna eat my meat"—is nominally about Willie and Irene but is rightly read as a recriminating assault on Harry's manhood, anticipating his homoerotic nightmare, where it is his kosher "big bone," not Irene's white breast, that is to be eaten.[91] The fusion of the voices, first in the black dozens and then in this variation as lyric poetry, turns the sexual combat in a literary direction, but within the framework of a novel that doubts whether there could be such a thing as an unpolitical man, aesthetic questions are always pertinent to a people's regenerative survival.

---

early excerpt from Wallace's book, would not have been so quick to lionize a book titled *American Jewish Macho Identification with Israel and the Myth of the Yenta*. LeRoi Jones [Amiri Baraka], "American Sexual Reference: Black Male," in *Home: Social Essays* (New York: William Morrow, 1966), pp. 216, 221, 230; Huey Newton, "Huey Newton Talks to the Movement," in Philip S. Foner, ed., *The Black Panthers Speak* (New York: Da Capo Press, 1995), pp. 58–59; Eldridge Cleaver, *Soul on Ice* (New York: McGraw-Hill, 1968), p. 102–3; Michelle Wallace, *Black Macho and the Myth of the Superwoman* (1979; rpt. New York: Verso, 1990), p. 69; Stanley Crouch, "Aunt Jemima Don't Like Uncle Ben," in *Notes of a Hanging Judge: Essays and Reviews, 1979–1989* (New York: Oxford University Press, 1990), p. 30. On the black phallus and power, see also Susan Gubar, *Racechanges: White Skin, Black Face in American Culture* (New York: Oxford University Press, 1997), pp. 169–89.

Like Willie's violence, says Malamud, his anti-Semitism is a counterthrust to his emasculation, an extorting demand in which economic and social power, because it cannot be achieved, is restated as symbolic sexual power, which can be achieved. A good contemporaneous illustration appears in Henry Dumas's poem "Cuttin Down to Size," where a Jewish merchant's tape measure turns into a lynching rope, but when the merchant starts "measuring near my balls," says the black narrator, he knifes the "faggot," leaving the Jew's black assistant to be charged with the murder.[92] In rejecting all that "circumcise schmuck stuff" his "Jewbitch" wants to force on him, Willie Spearmint declares that his writing, eminently political, is also, as in the Dumas poem, a form of retributive sexual power, and his craving of the white man's approbation a weakness to be expunged: "I ought to be hung on a hook till some kind brother cuts off my white balls."[93]

Because emasculation was historically more than an idle threat to black men, Malamud's placing it in tandem with circumcision was deliberately provocative to blacks and Jews both. In equating the castration of black men with the sign of God's covenant with Israel—"You shall circumcise the flesh of your foreskin, and that shall be the sign of the covenant between Me and you. . . . Thus shall My covenant be marked in your flesh as an everlasting pact" (Genesis 17:11–13)—Willie says that Jewish men, too, are castrated victims, likewise unable to command true "pullin power." But he also says that Jews, as provisional whites, simply hide behind the cloak of paternalistic liberalism and that they, too, are castrating masters. And not men alone: Leslie Fiedler reported reading in 1966 that a "Negro poet" married to a Jewish woman—surely his unstated reference was to Baraka—had declared that "Jewish girls only married Negroes in order to emasculate them."[94] Either way, the threat to Willie's manhood is the same.

According to Maimonides, one purpose of circumcision is to "weaken the organ of generation as far as possible," thus counteracting "excessive lust." Such an interpretation would set the Jewish man apart from the mythically hyperpotent black man as sexually disadvantaged but morally more pure. Equally important, though, circumcision provides a "common bodily sign, so that it is impossible for any one that is a stranger" to insinuate himself into the community "in order to make some attack upon the Jews."[95] As the sign of belonging, of chosenness, circumcision thus bears an important ambivalence, controlling the Jew's generative impulses, his "lust," while at the same time setting him apart, in God's covenant, and protecting him from harm at the hands of the gentile "stranger"—a stranger who may be either white or black. To the extent that it is a form of "emasculation," circumcision may feminize the Jewish male, diminishing him beside the uncircumcised;* but because of its covenantal meaning, the "circumcise schmuck stuff" that Willie fears Irene will inflict on him sexually, or Lesser on him aesthetically, suggests that Jews command a position of privilege that elevates them above blacks and whites both.

The depiction of Willie's sexuality may be fantastic and grotesque, like that of the black pickpocket in *Mr. Sammler's Planet* ("a large tan-and-purple uncircumsized thing—a tube, a snake"), but for Lesser, as for Sammler—or, as noted earlier, for the young Norman Podhoretz reacting to the intimidating allure of black masculinity—the black's manhood offers a lesson in the form of a threat. The betrayal of their ideals—Enlightenment liberalism in the case of Sammler and Podhoretz, art for art's sake in the case of Lesser—leads each partially to misread the sexual intimidation exercised by Black Power, which was first of all an assertion of *manhood* on the part of those tired of being *boys*. Whereas Bellow's Jewish hero finds nothing redemptive in the wasteland of America's counterculture, least of all the free-love ideology he caricatures as "sexual niggerhood,"[96] Malamud's Jewish hero, because his interlocutor is not a simple thug but a man of conviction, is bound to see in Willie, as though in a mirror, some part of the man he himself should be. Alienated from the covenant symbolized by the "common bodily sign" of circumcision, Harry Lesser is not just unprotected from the black stranger but drawn futilely to his commanding phallic power.

"No Jew can treat me like a man," says Willie, as though to insist, with Harold Cruse, that black manhood will not be gained through the condescending *mitzvot* of liberal Jews. "You think you are the Chosen People. Well, you are wrong on that. We are the Chosen People from as of now on. You gonna find that out soon enough, you gonna lose your fuckn pride."[97] The black appropriation of chosenness leads, in Willie's case, not just to mimetic inversion, as in the Nation of Islam or the Black Theology of Albert Cleage, but to his proclamation of a Nazi aesthetic. Like Baraka, Willie chooses to express his manhood—a hyperbolic masculinity set in opposition to castration and circumcision—through anti-Semitism. The challenge for Harry Lesser is to understand the motivation for Willie's ideology while at the same time accepting its conse-

---

* Insofar as the circumcised Jewish penis is emasculated, feminized, writes Daniel Boyarin in elaborating on Fanon's argument, it symbolically resembles the woman's clitoris: "The black man is a penis; the male Jew is a clitoris. Neither has the [white gentile's] phallus," the signifier of power. Daniel Boyarin, "What Does a Jew Want? or, The Political Meaning of the Phallus," in Christopher Lane, ed., *The Psychoanalysis of Race* (New York: Columbia University Press, 1998), p. 224.

quences for his own instinctive liberalism. Abhorrent though such an aesthetic may be, Harry's contrary attempt to dissociate art from ideology, his attempt to be an unpolitical man, is not simply misguided but dangerous. Embracing Enlightenment ideals and emancipated from Jewishness, Lesser is left to be defined as a Jew by those who would destroy him—not Russian tsarists or Nazis now, but a black American. In the transcendence of the political by the aesthetic that he makes his guiding principle, symbolized here by the duplicitous sign of circumcision, lies the potential for his annihilation as a Jew.

THE PROMISED END

When I was very young, and was dealing with my buddies in those wine- and urine-stained hallways, something in me wondered, What will happen to all that beauty? . . . And when I sat at Elijah [Muhammad]'s table and watched the baby, the women, and the men, and we talked about God's— or Allah's—vengeance, I wondered, when that vengeance was achieved, What will happen to all that beauty? . . . If we—and now I mean the relatively conscious whites and the relatively conscious blacks, who must, like lovers, insist on, or create, the consciousness of others—do not falter in our duty now, we may be able, handful that we are, to end the racial nightmare, and achieve our country, and change the history of the world. If we do not now dare everything, the fulfillment of that prophecy, recreated from the Bible in song by a slave, is upon us: God gave Noah the rainbow sign, No more water, the fire next time!

                —*James Baldwin,* The Fire Next Time

Perhaps the central pair of "brother" figures among the many to whom Malamud alludes in *The Tenants*—surpassing King and Heschel, or Cruse and Podhoretz, or Baldwin and Katz—are the artistic brothers Ralph Ellison and Irving Howe. As Emily Budick has demonstrated in an indispensable analysis, their famous debate about the nature of African American fiction, set off by Howe's notorious defense in "Black Boys and Native Sons" of Richard Wright's politicized naturalism as the only authentic black aesthetic, directly informs the arguments of Willie Spearmint and Harry Lesser.

    Inspired by the leftist radicalism that Ellison had disavowed after an early flirtation, Howe thought it inevitable that the black writer would be motivated by a "pain and ferocity that nothing could remove," causing him to speak "from the black wrath of retribution." "How could a Negro put pen to paper, how could he so much as think or breathe," Howe wondered, "without some impulsion to protest?" Ellison's rejoinder in "The World and the Jug" (1964), which combines two separately published pieces, along with a response by Howe, made it clear that segregation might assume forms that Howe had not anticipated: "I found it far less painful to have to move to the back of a Southern bus . . . than to tolerate concepts which distorted the actual reality of my situation or my reactions to it." Ellison took Howe to task for assuming that black art could be nothing but the "abstract embodiment of living hell" or that black writers could not spring from the classic Western tradition that had also been an inspiration for Jewish writers. "It requires real poverty of imagination" to think that the Negro writer must appeal only to his own condition of deprivation, especially "after the performance of the slaves in re-creating themselves, in good part, out of the images and myths of the Old Testament Jews."[98]

If Howe insisted that Ellison write as a black, Ellison added, then Howe must write as a Jew. In identifying Howe as a Jewish critic, Ellison at once cunningly undermined his assumption of membership in a universalist artistic tradition and thrust him into kinship with dominant white society, his racial guilt a sign of having identified with the culture of assimilation and power. At the same time, Ellison maintained the distinction between white and Jew in order to maintain a distinction between black and white: "If I would know who I am and preserve who I am, then I must see others distinctly whether they see me so or no. Thus, I feel uncomfortable whenever I discover Jewish intellectuals writing as though *they* were guilty of enslaving my grandparents, or as though the *Jews* were responsible for the system of segregation." Although it ends with the hope that Howe will view the exchange as an act of "antagonistic cooperation," Ellison's eviscerating reply, a long and eloquent defense of the complex sources of African American art, left enough tension in the air to imply no reconciliation but only a truce. Cynthia Ozick has aptly described the argument as a "war of manhood" that took on the character of a tragic parable in that the relatively genteel form of the antagonists' debate, in retrospect, prophesied the "savage future" of Malamud's novel. To articulate this future required Malamud to employ caricature—Willie is a "totem" of the black man in whom absolute politics has subsumed art into itself, remarks Ozick, while his militancy is expressed through classic anti-Semitism—and to make his theme the inevitability of pogrom, played out in a claustrophobic racialized world.[99]

Ellison's dwelling on Howe's Jewishnesss was also a reminder that blacks, brought to America as slaves, who immediately set about reshaping the nation's linguistic, musical, and religious resources, preceded Jews on the American cultural scene. Denounced by Black Arts theorists such as Baraka and Neal for eschewing an openly black aesthetic, Ellison rejected race as the legitimate foundation of artistic principles. He insisted, nevertheless, that to be black and to be American was by no means a contradiction, either for a writer or for a citizen. As Budick has pointed out in her reading of the exchange—and here we return to a pattern encountered often in the relationship between blacks and Jews—Ellison is in effect telling Howe that *he* is the stranger in this land, that America cannot be his Promised Land, and therefore that Ellison, not Howe, speaks for America and its inheritance of Western culture, while Howe, at least in "Black Boys and Native Sons," speaks for a diminished, compromised aesthetic.[100]

In *The Tenants* the Ellison and Howe roles are partially reversed: it is Willie Spearmint who carries to its logical extreme Howe's aesthetic of black authenticity, while Harry Lesser espouses an enfeebled version of Ellison's (and Malamud's) universalism, even as, in some particulars of characterization, he resembles Baldwin.[101] Malamud's purposeful confusion of the ideological roles spoofed the Howe-Ellison debate even as it brought him closer to Ellison's careful defense of the writer's resources and craft.* In a coda to his debate with Howe, appearing as part of a 1967 interview, Ellison drew a different distinction between the ancestral resources of the Jewish writer and those of the African American, recognizing the primacy of Jewish culture within the Western tradition and thus more accurately forecasting the polarized argument of *The Tenants*. As a "people of the Book," he said, Jewish writers are more familiar with literature as a medium of expression. They had learned more from modernist masters such as Eliot and Hemingway because in taking possession of that which could be used to express their own sense of reality, regardless of their

---

* On the occasion of his presenting his friend Malamud the Gold Medal for Fiction from the American Academy of Arts and Letters in 1983, Ellison spoke of him, a fellow "minority" artist, in terms that are resonant for *The Tenants*, as well as for Ellison's own authorial self-conception: "If in a general sense we are brothers, in specific relationships we can be so uncertain that the slightest disagreement can transform us into hostile strangers. . . . [W]hile remaining true to his own group's unique perception of experience, [the minority writer] is also goaded to add his individual voice to the futuristic effort of fulfilling the democratic ideal. He too acts to describe a nation to itself, and sometimes in making his own segment of experience available to all he manages to reduce our social confusion to forms of lucid insight. . . . By speaking resonantly for himself he speaks the truth in different accents. This is his answer to the mystery of how, in a nation of minorities, the last becomes first and outstanding among equals." Ralph Ellison, "Presentation to Bernard Malamud of the Gold Medal for Fiction" (1983), in *The Collected Essays of Ralph Ellison*, ed. John F. Callahan (New York: Modern Library, 1995), pp. 465–67.

disdain for those writers' racial or political beliefs, they made art, as Harry Lesser would argue, their overriding consideration. Black writers, "exiled in our own land" and failing to grasp this process of acculturation, have too often denigrated technique and form, and been in such haste "to express our anger and our pain" as to allow "the single tree of race to obscure our view of the magic forest of art."[102]

More than a stalking horse for a congenial aesthetic, however, Ellison raised for Malamud a primordial question about the purpose of fiction in an age of racial crisis. "If I would know who I am and preserve who I am, then I must see others distinctly whether they see me so or no." In this evocative aperçu, Ellison punned on his own rendition in *Invisible Man* of Yahweh's mystic, tautological revelation of Himself to Moses in Exodus. His protagonist's "I yam what I yam"[103] is a folkloric distillation of Exodus 3:14: "And God said unto Moses, I AM THAT I AM: and he said, Thus shalt thou say unto the children of Israel, I AM hath sent me unto you." Ellison, as Malamud recognized, alluded at the same time to *King Lear.* So does Harry Lesser when he not only quotes the relevant line, slightly inaccurately, as the epigraph to his unfinished novel about love—"Who is it who can tell me who I am?"[104]—but also takes the novel's title, *The Promised End,* from Shakespeare's play and secondarily from the title of a collection of essays by Stanley Edgar Hyman, Malamud's onetime colleague at Bennington College and another of Ellison's critical interlocutors.* The passage supplying the epigraph comes in the scene where Lear, challenged by the insolent Goneril and goaded by the Fool to recognize the deterioration of his authority and mental state, questions the meaning of his own identity: "Does any here know me? . . . Who is it that can tell me who I am?" (1.4.226–30), while

* Malamud was therefore also drawing, as Budick demonstrates, on the less heated quarrel between Ellison and Hyman, whose essay "American Negro Literature and the Folk Tradition" appeared first along with Ellison's reply, "Change the Joke and Slip the Yoke," in the *Partisan Review* in 1958, and then in his collection *The Promised End* (1963). (Hyman quotes the exchange between Kent and Edgar as an epigraph to his book.) Ellison appreciated Hyman's interpretation of black vernacular culture—the blues, the dozens, and folktales—but felt it told only half the story and misread the "darky act" of black culture. Often, said Ellison, the Negro's "masking is motivated not so much by fear as by a profound rejection of the image created to usurp his identity." And that masking might have sources other than black folklore: "I knew the trickster Ulysses just as early as I knew the wily rabbit of Negro American lore." See Stanley Edgar Hyman, "American Negro Literature and the Folk Tradition," in *The Promised End: Essays and Reviews, 1942–1962* (Cleveland: World Publishing Co., 1963), pp. 295–315; Ralph Ellison, "Change the Joke and Slip the Yoke" (1958), in *Shadow and Act* (1964; rpt. New York: Vintage, 1971), pp. 55, 58.

the title of Lesser's novel comes from an exchange that follows Lear's entrance with the dead Cordelia in his arms, howling in his grief and madness:

> KENT: Is this the promised end?
> EDGAR: Or image of that horror? (5.3.263–64)

In this welter of allusions Malamud spliced ultimate beginnings into ultimate endings, the meaning of birth into the terror of death, the origins of nations into their real or potential destructions, God's revelation at Sinai into His eclipse at the Holocaust.

Although it is Harry Lesser who borrows from *King Lear* for the title of his novel, there is, of course, an equally strong identification in this allusion with Willie Spearmint himself, who adopts the writing names "Bill Spear" and "Blind Willie Shakespear." Like the frayed inversion of the Ellison and Howe roles, this ambivalence is strategic. In the antagonistic brotherhood of Harry and Willie, Malamud found, in occasional bursts of fraternity, the best hope for a symbolic reconciliation of Jews and blacks. The instability of that reconciliation, however, and finally its disintegration, is vividly registered in the novel's search for an ending amidst its structural chaos. In his effort to resolve the conflict between universalism and particularism, assimilation and neo-ethnicity, aestheticism and polemic, Malamud finds no conclusion, no end to the argument. Even though he feels himself to be closing in, "proceeding within a mystery to its revelation," Lesser does not know how to end his own book, while Malamud supplies no fewer than three formal endings for his, the last of them collapsing into bloodshed.[105]

In addition to the tentative formal conclusions that appear more or less arbitrarily in the novel, a longing for endings pervades *The Tenants*. The second of the novel's two epigraphs is from a song by Bessie Smith: "I got to make it, I got to find the end"; in his last offer to buy Lesser out of his lease, Levenspiel declares, "This is the end"; and Lesser fears he will be mugged without finishing his book, whereupon Levenspiel will have the building demolished: "End of book, era, civilization?"[106] *King Lear* itself is in part a play about the cataclysmic end of time. No less so is *The Tenants* about end times, when social bonds, political authority, cultural inheritances, and the representational capacities of language have all been brought to the brink of dissolution.

If *King Lear* is "an image of the promised end," Frank Kermode wrote in *The Sense of an Ending* (1967), a book likely to have influenced Malamud, "so is Buchenwald; and both stand under the accusation of being horrible, rootless fantasies, the one no more true or more false than the other, so that the best you can say is that *King Lear* does less harm." For Kermode, each illustrates a false apocalypse, though with two differences: anti-Semitism is a fiction of escape that "tells you nothing of death but projects it onto others; whereas *King Lear* is a fiction that inescapably involves an encounter with oneself, and the image of one's end." Unlike a stage play (or a novel), anti-Semitism degenerates into myth because it is not consciously held to be fictive; it is a degenerate fiction, reduced to a set of rituals and gestures that presuppose a total explanation of things as they are, calling for absolute assent.[107] One might say, more succinctly, that whereas *King Lear* is a *fiction* about end times, anti-Semitism, at least in the form practiced by Nazism, is an *ideology* about end times— that is, a belief system in which the erasure of Jews from the world would bring about the millennialist thousand-year Reich. The very attempt to draw an analogy between the "fictions" authorized by Shakespeare's play and Hitler's holy war against the Jews may seem tendentious, but Kermode's precarious exegesis of *King Lear* by way of the Holocaust puts at center stage the problem of Malamud's own "fiction" of end times.

The second epigraph for *The Tenants* is drawn from the *Tetralogies* of the fifth-century Sophist Antiphon: "Alive and with his eyes open he calls us his murderers." The passage in question comes from the third Tetralogy, in which a young man is charged with killing an older man in a drunken quarrel. The young man not only denies his guilt and charges that the older man provoked the fight, but also argues that the doctor who treated the older man's injuries before his death is, in fact, responsible for the death. Because the defendant goes into exile before the arguments of the case are concluded, commentators have assumed that Antiphon intended this fact to signal the weakness of his case. The quotation in the epigraph is drawn from one speech by the prosecutor, who rebuts the young defendant's argument that he was provoked into the blows that led to the older man's death: "He agrees he struck the blows that led to his death, but he says he's not the victim's murderer; instead, though he lives and breathes, he accuses us [those who seek justice] of being his murderer, though we seek only revenge."[108]

Since there is no actual murder in *The Tenants*—only the cataclysmic simulation of a mutual double murder—it would be hard to assign to Harry and Willie roles that match those of the antagonists in the third Tetralogy. Each could be the accuser, each the murderer; each, seeking vengeance, could claim to be seeking justice. Rather than individual prototypes, however, Malamud seems to have drawn formal devices from the example of Antiphon. The *Tetralogies* are themselves instances of imaginary forensic argument concerning homicide, not actual cases, and Antiphon therefore reduced narrative to bare essentials, excluded the testimony of witnesses, and matched the rhetorical arguments of prosecution and defense against each other point for point in a manner unrealistic within a court of law. In addition, the issue of "pollution" plays a prominent role in each of the Tetralogies, with each side arguing that the killer's pollution will infect the city unless the right man is convicted.[109] Just so, *The Tenants* is in effect an imaginary combat between antagonists, played out on a spare stage and forensic in character (though not only witnesses but also attorneys are excluded); arguments are matched blow for blow until we reach a stylized ending, which brings no certainty as to guilt and innocence, and therefore no redemption from the pollution that threatens to infect and then destroy the city-state.

According to Malamud, writing in another context, the "symbolic drama of Jewish experience" consists of two acts: first, the breaking of the covenant with God and subjection to exile; and second, the diaspora, in which history, rather than God, is the antagonist. The secularization of tragedy in the second act raises the possibility that worldly time may be ended without the intervention of God and the appearance of messianic time or, alternatively, that there will be no end to worldly time, only a steady, tragic march into a limitless future. "The end may never be reached, never fulfilled," Malamud continued, "but the drama, in human terms, is made more poignant because it offers this possibility." Although his statements were opaque, Malamud went on to note that the drama of "suffering, expiation, and renewal" that constitutes Jewish history might thus be said to prefigure the "American experience."[110]

The breaking of America's covenant with God surely occurred when, first as a colony and then more decidedly as a nation, it built its prosperity on the foundation of African slavery, leaving "a horrible serpent . . . coiled up in [the] nation's bosom," as Frederick Douglass put it.[111] Because *The Tenants* finds only imperfect vocabularies for the expression of injustice, let alone its eradication, the question raised by Malamud's formulation—will the end of exile and suffering never be reached, or instead will a cataclysmic drama of expiation and renewal bring redemption?—is not conclusively answered. If there is any "possibility" of reaching an "end," however, his novel appears to predict that doing so will entail first traversing some harrowing event—an American Holocaust.

Like *The Fixer* before it, but self-conscious nearly to the point of parody, *The Tenants* belongs to the historical literature of persecution and pogrom, culminating in the Holocaust, that is one strain of Jewish literary history. But, looking forward as well as backward, it belongs also to the literature of prophecy. In

Malamud's obsession with endings, with temporal and narrative closure, Elisa New has suggested, one finds a "hypertrophied but still recognizable version of a Jewish messianism." Lesser may thus be seen as a kind of Talmudic scholar for whom there is nothing outside the text, a man who lives in the mystic's time, though in his case closure has been internalized in regression and sterility.[112] The severe attenuation of Lesser's consciousness as a Jew is of course apposite. The utopian overtones of political Zionism, not to mention its fulfillment, said Gershom Scholem, introduced sharp disequilibrium and uncertainty into the messianic idea, which, over centuries of exile, had corresponded not to a secular redemption but to the "endless powerlessness" of "a life lived in deferment," the profound anti-existentialism of the unredeemed living always in the "blazing landscape of redemption" still to come.[113] Without presuming to hint at the exact nature of a world to come, Malamud nevertheless composed a novel suffused with the aura of apocalypse and alert to the transforming effect of the Holocaust and the creation of modern Israel on the messianic idea within Judaism itself.

Malamud's setting is America, not Israel, but *The Tenants* just as strongly reverberates with populist expressions of the destruction that precedes messianic redemption. As Malamud was writing, in the wake of the Six-Day War, increased attention to the Holocaust after Israel's survival of a new threat of destruction was accompanied in the United States by a fascination with popular prophecy about end times in the Holy Land. Whereas liberal Protestant churches, especially those espousing the liberation theology of the Third World and the cause of Palestinian refugees, were cool toward Israel,[114] the conflict was seen by some millennialist Jews and evangelical Christians as a sign of impending messianic deliverance—the spur, for example, for Hal Lindsey's *Late Great Planet Earth* (1970), the most popular work of apocalyptic in the twentieth century, but quite likely to be surpassed in the twenty-first by the multivolume "Left Behind" series by Tim LaHaye and Jerry Jenkins, which dramatizes end times in the contemporary Middle East and has sold more than 60 million copies. Christian evangelical prophecy about Israel, which flared up after the 1967 war—and then again with the al-Aqsa *intifada* and the post-9/11 "war on terror"—has always been supportive of the modern state, if only because the return of the Jews to Palestine, climaxing in their resettlement of Judea and Samaria (the West Bank), as well as their rebuilding of the Temple, has been seen as the precondition of Christ's return.*

---

* Christian belief in the mass conversion of the Jews derives from Romans 11:26–31, where Paul says that "all Israel shall be saved" before the Second Coming. The establishment of Israel in 1948 and the re-

Alongside the expectation of Christian apocalypse that such interpretations imposed on biblical Israel, there had also arisen prophecy of a black apocalypse, whether the Fall of America predicted by Elijah Muhammad, which situated the "true Jews" of the Nation of Islam within an imminent end time of racialized Judgment[115]—completely biblical in its identification of whites with serpents, devils, and the beast of Revelation, and the wicked city of Babylon as a typological prefiguring of the United States—or what Baldwin, adapting the lesson of his visit with Elijah Muhammad to a less theological paradigm, predicted as "the fire next time." Confirmation that Malamud responded to a moment of American racial upheaval rife with apocalyptic forebodings of its own can likewise be found closer to the mainstream, as when Herbert Weiner invoked Abraham Isaac Kook, first chief rabbi of Palestine, in order to describe the messianic promise of Black Power: "Particularly do [these souls] reveal themselves in an end of days' kind of period, a time which precedes the remaking of the world."[116]

The first ending of *The Tenants*—"END OF NOVEL," barely twenty pages into the book—finds Lesser the writer, oblivious to the destruction around him, consumed in a conflagration started by Levenspiel, "resembling mysterious stranger if not heart of darkness."[117] The allusions to Twain and Conrad sum-

---

taking of Jerusalem in the Six-Day War are in this view part of a divine history wherein religious and political doctrine have coalesced. Thus, in *Armageddon* (2003), by LaHaye and Jenkins, we find Tsion ben-Judah, a former rabbinical scholar and Israeli statesman who preaches weekly to a vast cyberspace audience, converting Jews by the thousands at the Western Wall in anticipation of the return of Christ. Messianic Christians and Jews overlap in their beliefs that, once the Jews are returned to their homeland, the End of Days might be close at hand, and extensive Jewish settlements in Judea and Samaria are thus part of the necessary preparation. Evangelical prophecy also includes a sub-current of more overtly anti-Semitic writings that warn Israel of imminent destruction for its failure to accept Christ as the Messiah, what Paul Boyer has characterized as "the final chastisement of the Chosen." Some have foreseen an end time when a wave of anti-Semitism will sweep over the earth, while others, such as the Christian evangelical writer Arthur Bloomfield, have interpreted Hitler as a typological prefiguration of the destruction of Israel at the hands of the Antichrist: "It took Hitler to turn the Jews toward Palestine. It will take a greater Hitler to turn them to God. . . . Hitler used gas chambers; he got rid of six million Jews, but Antichrist's purpose will be to do away with all Jews of all nations." The Six-Day War also set in motion an Islamic version of apocalypse, though one in which Israel's victory was demonic, in one instance of which, combining Christian messianism and anti-Semitic tracts such as the *Protocols of the Elders of Zion*, the Antichrist represents a Jewish conspiracy operating throughout history and incarnate in the late twentieth century in Israel and the United States. See Paul Boyer, *When Time Shall Be No More: Prophecy Belief in Modern American Culture* (Cambridge, Mass.: Harvard University Press, 1992), pp. 181–224, Bloomfield quoted at p. 216; and Gershom Gorenberg, *The End of Days: Fundamentalism and the Struggle for the Temple Mount* (New York: Free Press, 2000), pp. 14–15, 52–58, 111, 186–88.

mon dark quasi-apocalyptic visions out of canonical literature which resonate with the core themes of *The Tenants* but provide no more aesthetic closure than the other literary debris that blows through the novel as though through the tenement itself. Still, an ending, if only one harnessed to negation, must be imagined: the teleology of narrative, as of human experience, demands it.

As Malamud's parody of William Blake suggests, apocalypse might come in a spoof of the romantic sublime: "Nigger, nigger, shining bright / In the forest of the night." Like Melville's white whale, Blake's "Tyger! Tyger! burning bright / In the forests of the night" ("The Tyger") was the indiscriminate power of the universe, awful and evil in its potential for destruction, incarnate in a beast; Lesser's caricature of that power as "nigger" rather than tiger contains both the end point of degenerative primitivism and its obverse, the Black God of African American revolutionary messianism. Thus, the fragmentary poem, "Manifested Destiny," which Harry retrieves from Willie's garbage along with his anti-Semitic manuscripts:

> black, white, black, white, black, white, black, white
> (go to bottom of page) . . .
> BLACKBLACKBLACKBLACKBLACKBLACKBLACKBLACK
> (make five pages of this) . . .
> BLACKNESSBLACKNESSBLACKNESSBLACKNESS
> (This is the rest of the book). . . .[118]

Alluding to the riff by Ellison's preacher in the prologue of *Invisible Man*—"Brothers and sisters, my text this morning is the 'Blackness of Blackness'"[119]—Malamud reduces the black aesthetic, rooted for Ellison in the galvanizing voice of the African American sermonic tradition, to its purest form of tribalism. In Willie's incantation of the holy word BLACK, differentiations made possible by language are stripped down to monotonal paralysis, and the question of identity, communal as well as individual, is sent cascading into semantic darkness.

Lesser's version of an ending—the ending of his own love novel, if he dared, he tells Irene—is a dreamlike cross-racial double wedding presided over by an African chief and a rabbi. Lesser weds Mary, and Willie weds Irene; the parents of both couples are unhappy and ashamed of the mixed marriages, but the rabbi tells them that the wedding covenant is a reminder of Abraham's covenant with God and a symbol of the hope that someday God will "bring together Ishmael and Israel to live as one people": "THE END."[120] In his putative cross-racial marriage sequence, Malamud offers a variation on Leslie Fiedler's advocacy in an essay collected in *Waiting for the End* (1964) of a "new Edenic ideal" that imagines not only "joining with the Indian or Negro in pseudo-matrimony, or being adopted by some colored foster-father, but being reborn as Indian or Negro, *becoming the other*," the point being to achieve "the strange fruit not of the physical miscegenation so long feared by white supremacists, but of the innocent union of Huck and Jim on the raft." But *The Tenants* quickly sets aside this "resolution we scarcely dared hope for in actual life, however often we imagined it in books,"[121] and Malamud's burlesque ringing down of the curtain tells us that the rabbi's hope is as fruitless as the wedding is fantastic.

The plotted action of the third ending, coincident with the ending of the published novel we are reading, is set in motion when Lesser retrieves from the garbage the last fragments of Willie's manuscripts, which include "Four Deaths of a Pig," in which black men gun down a black cop; "The Goldberg Blues," a protest song against Jewish merchants; and "The First Pogrom of the U.S. of A.," in which an American pogrom against Jews dispenses with the niceties of the Gestapo—"There is none of that Hitler shit of smashing store windows, forcing Zionists to scrub sidewalks, or rubbing their faces in dog crap"—and proceeds immediately to the execution of Jews, as well as their loyal black employees. In "Goldberg Exits Harlem," a "Jew slumlord in a fur-collar coat" collecting his "bloodmoney rents" is stabbed to death by three old men and a Jamaican woman, who then toy with the idea of cannibalizing him before going late at night to a synagogue, where they "make Yid noises" and "dance hasidically," spiritual identifications made the object of scornful besmirching.[122]

The subliminal, if perverse, resemblance between Willie's discarded manuscripts and the clandestine manuscripts left as an archive of life in the Warsaw Ghetto[123] reinforces our sense that the superimposed ghettos of the novel also contain superimposed Holocausts. Malamud's novel itself reads like an inchoate jumble of rescued testimony, but there is grim irony in the fact that it is Willie's anti-Semitic text that Harry retrieves from the garbage—and publishes, so to speak, in the novel we are reading. In the mirroring relationship between Willie and Harry, each secretly coveting the other's work, each assaulting the other as a racial enemy, such an analogy exploits incommensurability, turning resemblance into grotesquerie and making metaphor itself a vehicle of annihilation.

Insofar as the very action of the novel is intimately bound to its ongoing argument over narrative form, yet another climax, an even more conclusive harbinger of end times, occurs when Willie breaks into Harry's apartment and destroys his manuscript. The onslaught, depicted as a reverie within the writer-narrator's imagination, is constructed as a peculiar hybrid of tribal primitivism and Nazi savagery. Willie appears as the "Headman Minister," while his accomplices are missionaries who arrive on Lesser's "accursed island" in a war canoe and proceed to smash his jazz records, pull down his bookshelves, and stomp his books with "leather boots" before burning them. Finally, his friend Sam challenges Willie to destroy Harry's precious current writing, "on account of this cat stole your white bitch and pissed up your black book. . . . Must feel like you been castrated, don't it?" The burning of the manuscript is itself a simulacrum of the Holocaust: "The hot ashes stink of human flesh." From the ashes, Willie smears a message on the wall: "REVOLUTION IS THE REAL ART. NONE OF THAT FORM SHIT. I AM THE RIGHT FORM."[124] If Malamud's analogy between the destruction of Lesser's manuscript and the destruction of the Jews is a grotesque trivialization of the latter, it is for that same reason a cogent expression of one of the novel's central questions: how to render in fiction the terrible repercussions of a plan to end another people's existence.

With his retrieval of Willie's anti-Semitic tracts from the garbage, Lesser's writing experience becomes increasingly hallucinatory. He is fearful of the tenement house, which seems haunted by inexplicable accidents, spatial distortions, and "weird sad sea music": "familiar things are touched with strangeness," as though the alienation of personhood has contaminated his entire world. Lesser's own writing merges into Malamud's, his mind at once engulfed by the annihilating hatred of Willie's venomous writing and displaced by the writer-narrator's consciousness: "Rereading the words he sees scenes he hasn't written, or thinks he hasn't," scenes such as Willie's arson attack on the building. Engulfed by "spark-filled plumes of smoke, horns of glowing ashes," and "a muted roaring, screaming, sobbing," Lesser wonders: "Who cries there? Who dies there? Riot? Pogrom? Civil War?" Left with an unending compulsion to write but the certainty that he will never be able to rewrite his destroyed manuscript, Lesser sees himself sitting in his room forever trying to finish his book. Frantic and miserable, he steals into Willie's room and chops up his typewriter with an axe "till it was mangled junk. It bled black ink." At each step throughout this scene, Lesser becomes more and more a replica of Malamud projected into the novel, at a loss to conceive any ending for *The Tenants* other than cataclysmic violence between Harry and Willie: "Each, thought the writer, feels the anguish of the other. THE END"—followed by the searing plea of "mercy mercy mercy . . ."[125]

Malamud's own explanation of the novel's three endings in an interview of 1974 was glib enough: "Because one wouldn't do." Refusing to predict the outcome of the black-Jewish conflict, however, he suggested that a price might need to be paid in order to "redress the balance" for the history of prejudice against blacks. "Those who want [something] for others must expect to give something up. What we get in return is the affirmation of what we believe in."[126] This assessment, bordering on mysticism, is not necessarily at odds with the deadly polemics of *The Tenants*. In the aura of apocalypse that suffuses the novel, Malamud found that the moral obligations of brotherhood, of stranger to stranger, nonetheless bound black and Jew together in the house of bondage. Neither could escape without the other, and they would meet their promised end together.

CHAPTER 7

Holocaust

I. NEVER FORGETTING

Rotting family we
ghost ate
three
A people flattened chained
bathed & degraded
in their own hysterical waste . . .

Blue blood hole into which blueness
is the terror, massacre, torture
& original western
holocaust . . .
—AMIRI BARAKA,
"So the King Sold the Farmer #39"

THE RISK OF the *reductio ad Hitler,* Philip Lopate has said, is that it introduces a shrill dictum that "dead-ends all intelligent discourse."[1] Once it became routine to attach the epithet "Hitler" to any person deemed despicable and "Holocaust" to any act deemed genocidal in at least someone's definition, the serious question of how African American slavery and its violent aftermath might be said to resemble the Holocaust became harder, not easier, to answer. Some assertions of equivalence are rendered ridiculous by hyperbole. When the American Civil Liberties Union of Hawaii invited Supreme Court Justice Clarence

Thomas to debate the question of affirmative action, one board member, alarmed by Thomas's dissent on the matter of racial preferences, objected that giving him a platform would be no different from "inviting Hitler to come speak on the rights of Jews." Indeed, the entire tradition of democratic liberalism might be suspect. For black reparations advocate Randall Robinson, the fact that Thomas Jefferson owned slaves and fathered children with his slave Sally Hemmings led to the conclusion that he was no more or less a "man of his time" than was Lenin, Mao, or Hitler.[2]

When they were a curiosity rather than a commonplace, analogical appeals to the Holocaust were undoubtedly provocative. Betty Friedan's assertion in *The Feminine Mystique* (1963) that "women who 'adjust' as housewives . . . are in as much danger as the millions who walked to their own death in the concentration camps—and the millions more who refused to believe that the concentration camps existed" was insulting on its face. But the idiosyncrasy of the claim—apparent in Friedan's own qualification: "not as far-fetched as it sounds"—had a shock value that served its purpose.[3] Likewise, it still seemed iconoclastic when Rabbi Alan W. Miller maintained in 1969 that, in contrast to the destruction of the European Jews, the black man's "holocaust has been spread over centuries," or when Black Panther David Hilliard argued that the Nazis did not create genocidal fascism, since "black people were enslaved and killed in the millions before Hitler even came on the scene."[4] But as "the Holocaust" became more purely representational, referring less to an event with particular factual dimensions than to a specter of annihilation haunting modernity,[5] it began to exercise an eerie, enthralling power in which a people's identity might be codified only in their destruction, nowhere more insistently than in African American culture.

Some version of the "damage" thesis—the belief that black Americans have been irremediably scarred, crippled, stripped of ancestral resources, and condemned to pathological behaviors by slavery and its legacy—would have played a role in legal and public policy decisions of the postwar era regardless of the Holocaust. An argument for black reparations might also have emerged absent the Jewish example. It is highly unlikely, however, that the strain of genocidal thinking that runs through the Nation of Islam's cosmology and rhetoric, that shaped Black Power speeches and manifestos, and that came to characterize a sizable portion of late-twentieth-century African American literature would have been so prominent without the surge of survivor testimony, scholarly inquiry, and artistic representation that brought the Holocaust to light and, in painful detail, fixed it in the world's consciousness.

The United Nations Genocide Convention, as we have seen, stretched Raphael Lemkin's neologism into a semantic gray area such that genocide might not require a people's elimination, as in the Nazis' attempted Judeocide, but only their diminishment or cultural erasure, a capacious definition that gained favor with many African Americans in subsequent years. The civil rights revolution, which might logically have been expected to diminish black fears, instead heightened them by shining the light of radicalized consciousness on a past history of abuses, whether the vigilantism of lynching, the "Nuremberg" laws of Jim Crow, or slavery itself, all of which were now subject to being remembered as the collective destiny of a people marked for destruction.

We have already seen how pointedly the Holocaust impinged upon black thought and writing in the early postwar decades—as an analogue for oppression and self-destruction in *The Long Dream;* as a reference point for a South "cleansed" of Negroes in *A Different Drummer;* and as one possible means to delineate a community of commemoration for blacks and Jews in *The Chosen Place, the Timeless People.* As the splintering of black-Jewish relations over the Six-Day War, Black Power, racial quotas, and other hotly contested issues intersected with the surge in Holocaust scholarship and literature in the 1970s and 1980s, the genocide of the Jews was employed more and more frequently as a means to conceptualize the seeming "death sentence," to recall John Dollard's characterization, under which many African Americans and their ancestors had lived. The fact that the black holocaust was the product of a brutal, inhumane labor system based on race, rather than the result of an ideological plan to murder all members of a single group based on race, in no way diminished its moral or spiritual claim. Insistence on the part of Jews that their tragedy was "unique," or their objection to blacks' borrowing the language of the Holocaust, only exacerbated the conflict and became a further source of bitter disagreement.

No doubt comparisons between slavery and the Holocaust have been prompted in part by jealousy—or simply painful awareness—of the undeniable fact that Jewish suffering is publicly acknowledged and memorialized in ways that black suffering is not.[6] But acknowledgment and commemoration may come at a price. As the Holocaust began to be featured in prayer books, holy day liturgies, school curricula, museums, memorials, and other means of public remembrance, not to mention literature, art, film, television, and other forms of popular culture, some Jews feared being enveloped in a kind of "Holocaustomania," as Jacob Neusner put it, wherein catastrophic suffering, the survival of genocide, would be their only source of moral authority.[7] The danger is no less serious for African Americans. In their case, however, the risk is further complicated by the fact that the "black holocaust," like the "black diaspora," requires a modifier, so that the capture and transport of Africans, their generations of slave labor, and the violence and degradation that followed for a century or more after emancipation always carries with it an implied "as if" and unavoidable implications of emulation, envy, and enmity. Strained efforts to match, let alone compete with, another people's tragedy may lead not to sympathy but to animosity, producing a kind of "Victimization Olympics," in Peter Novick's phrase,[8] and devolving into alluring but ultimately futile rhetoric. It is possible to isolate historical phases of the black holocaust—for example, the Black Holocaust Museum in Milwaukee and a contemporary Web site titled "African American Holocaust" are both devoted to the history of lynching—but most accounts run from slavery through Jim Crow and beyond, and many invocations are virtually open-ended. Challenges to affirmative action at the University of California thus left poet June Jordan to "wonder if Nazi Germany's night skies ever beheld a really big moon . . . a useless, huge light above our perishing reasons for hope," while Toni Morrison, in characterizing contemporary discrimination against African Americans, stepped blithely onto the slippery slope of genocide: "Let us be reminded that before there is a final solution, there must be a first solution, and a second one, even a third. The move toward a final solution is not a jump. It takes one step, then another, then another."[9]

And yet, of course, failed analogies never fail completely. At once lamenting the "worldwide museum culture of the Shoah" and insisting on the uniqueness of the event, Ruth Kluger reminds us that comparisons form the "bridges" from one life to another: "In our hearts we all know that some aspects of the Shoah have been repeated elsewhere, today and yesterday, and will return in a new guise tomorrow." Similarities between Jim Crow racial science and Nazism are not negated by their divergent outcomes; the differing deployments of slave labor in the South and the Third Reich inevitably have telling points of contact; and the cruelties inflicted on Africans before, during, and after the Middle Passage may be shown to resemble, in some features, the destruction of the European Jews. In reflecting on the human condition, in "deducing from ourselves to others," to cite Kluger again, "what tools are left if we don't compare?"[10]

The two parts of this chapter are devoted, first, to prominent examples of post-1960s African American literature and cultural commentary that dramatize the emergence of the idea of the black holocaust, along with the related subject of black reparations, in the cultural mainstream; and second, to a group of writers, some African American, some Jewish, whose works represent the cul-de-sac in which the black-Jewish question—specifically, the exhausted problem of the black holocaust—was left by the end of the twentieth century. Although most writers who portray the black holocaust do not set out to debate the prior claims of the Jewish Holocaust, let alone parse ideological differences, they do write against the backdrop of two distinctive histories whose differences, already partially set forth in the previous chapters, must be brought into sharper focus. Essential though moral and spiritual arguments may be, it is imperative that they, as well as the metaphoric constructions that sustain them, not be mistaken for factual ones.

DEAD PEOPLE DO NOT MAKE GOOD SLAVES

We may begin by noticing, and then setting aside, the crude issue of respective death tolls. Contemporary scholarship places the number of Jews killed in the Holocaust at just under 6 million (of a total of some 11 million murdered by the Nazis), while the number of Africans who died during capture and transport in the slave trade, or from brutal treatment during slavery, is certainly higher, though by a factor nearly impossible to determine.* By the same token, more than a few claims made about the number of African American deaths in the slave trade and slavery, in seeking to make the event unique in its magnitude, have raised the number to dizzying heights: no mere 6 million or even 60 million but as many as 6 *billion*.† The outsized numbers purveyed in some ar-

---

* The most reliable estimates suggest that from the early 1500s to the 1860s somewhere between 9.5 million and 15 million Africans were transported to the Americas as slaves. No doubt a large number of those seized in Africa in the earlier stages of attempted enslavement died, perhaps up to 7 million, bringing the general depopulation through slavery to roughly 21 million over a period of several centuries. Following on the preliminary work of Philip Curtin, Basil Davidson and Stephen Katz place deaths in the Middle Passage between 1.2 and 2.6 million (the low and high percentages of the low and high transport numbers). More recently Hugh Thomas has argued that of approximately 11 million slaves shipped to New World, perhaps 2 million perished at sea. Harold Brackman estimates that for every slave who survived to live a normal lifespan, perhaps two or three others died through enslavement, thus producing between 10 and 20 million deaths over the centuries of the slave trade and its immediate aftermath. There is no way to calculate accurately how many transported slaves later died of brutality rather than "natural causes," and the fate of subsequent generations born in the Americas would, of course, add to the complexity of those numbers. See Philip Curtin, *The Atlantic Slave Trade: A Census* (Madison: University of Wisconsin Press, 1969), pp. 3–13, 265–86; Basil Davidson, *The African Slave Trade*, rev ed. (Boston: Little, Brown, 1980), pp. 95–98, 271–73; Hugh Thomas, *The Slave Trade: The Story of the Atlantic Slave Trade, 1440–1870* (1997; rpt. New York: Touchstone, 1999), pp. 804–5, 861–62; Harold Brackman, *Ministry of Lies: The Truth behind the Nation of Islam's "The Secret Relationship between Blacks and Jews"* (New York: Four Walls Eight Windows, 1994), pp. 95–98.

† Offended by Jews' invocation of the Holocaust in arguments about the effects of racism ("Black people *did not* build or operate the labor camps; Black people *did not* build or operate concentration camps and Black people *did not* build or operate the gas ovens in Germany"), Eddie Ellis referred to the 20 million "Black people (a conservative estimate) who were butchered and murdered" in slavery and slave trading. The demand for reparations in the 1966 Black Panther Party platform spoke of "the

guments amount to special pleading that produces a result exactly the opposite of that intended—contempt rather than compassion.

Leaving aside the motive for such expostulations, any census of the dead tells very little of the story. The proclivity to blur together the slave trade and Middle Passage, the multitude of North American and Latin American slave-holding regimes spread over several hundred years, and the subsequent history of legal segregation and vigilante violence makes such comparisons difficult, if not fruitless. The problem of comparability, in any event, is more usefully framed in terms of ideology or intention. In this respect, it is not difficult to enumerate differences between black slavery in the Americas, the United States in particular, and the Nazi destruction of the Jews—between "le racisme d'exploitation" and "le racisme d'extermination," to cite the distinction of Pierre-André Taguieff (which George Fredrickson glosses, less sharply, as a "racism of inclusion" and a "racism of exclusion").[11]

---

slaughter of over fifty million black people," a number that would reappear in various speeches by Panther members. In his *Autobiography,* Malcolm X asserted that 100 million blacks had been murdered in slavery, and this number reappears frequently in Nation of Islam texts—for example, in the speeches of Louis Farrakhan and in the Nation of Islam diatribe *The Secret Relationship between Blacks and Jews* (1991). In all likelihood, this figure comes down from W. E. B. Du Bois, who wrote in *Darkwater* (1920) that the slave trade "robbed black Africa of a hundred million human beings." S. E. Anderson likewise refers to "the slaughter of over 100 million African men, women, and children" and the "enslavement of millions of others" in *The Black Holocaust for Beginners* (1995), while Haki Madhubuti's *Enemies: The Clash of Races* (1978) is dedicated to "the Memory of the 250,000,000 and more Black men, women and children murdered by white people during the Euro-Asian trade in Afrikan slaves" (the figure reappears, situated against the standard Holocaust figure of 6 million, at the opening of a chapter titled "Blackvision: History and Destiny"). At the furthest reaches of sanity one finds José Malcioln's *African Origin of Modern Judaism* (1996), one in the genre of books devoted to proving that the biblical Hebrews were African, which provides a neat illustration of the sleight of hand that can be used when the card of unimaginable genocide is played: "Hitler unjustifiably murdered approximately six million Jews and Gentiles. The slavers murdered, mistreated, mutilated, enslaved, lynched, and still exploit over six billion blacks, and other people of color." Readers took notice when Toni Morrison chose a number ten-fold that of the Holocaust in her epigraph to *Beloved* (1987), but Malcioln's changing of *million* to *billion* seems designed to dispense once and for all with rational comparison. See Eddie Ellis, "Semitism in the Ghetto," *Liberator* 6 (February 1966), 15; "Black Panther Party Platform," in Philip S. Foner, ed., *The Black Panthers Speak* (1970; rpt. New York: Da Capo Press, 1995), p. 2; Malcolm X, with Alex Haley, *The Autobiography of Malcolm X* (1965; rpt. New York: Grove Press, 1966), p. 212; Nation of Islam, *The Secret Relationship between Blacks and Jews* (Boston: Historical Research Department of the Nation of Islam, 1991), p. 178; W. E. B. Du Bois, *Darkwater: Voices from within the Veil* (1920; rpt. New York: Schocken, 1969), p. 57; S. E. Anderson, *The Black Holocaust for Beginners* (New York: Writers and Readers Publishing, 1995), p. 160; Haki R. Madhubuti, *Enemies: The Clash of Races* (Chicago: Third World Press, 1978), p. 13; and José Malcioln, *The African Origin of Modern Judaism: From Hebrews to Jews* (Trenton, N.J.: Africa World Press, 1996), pp. 68–69.

The ultimate deployment of Africans as slaves in the Americas, as Seymour Drescher writes, "was a residual result of centuries of experimentation with various African and non-African groups, not the outcome of an imagined racial selection before the beginning of the Atlantic slave trade."[12] In addition, Africans themselves were partners in slavery, while in turn thousands of free blacks lived in the United States, North and South alike—indeed, some of them were slaveholders themselves—so the correlation between race and slavery was hardly exact. In the case of the Holocaust, by contrast, the linkage between race and extermination was quite clear. The Nazis saw Jews not simply as racial inferiors to be domesticated, like animals, and put to work (as they did Slavs, for example), but rather as an internal enemy upon whose eradication rested the purity of the Aryan blood line and the fate of civilization itself. Defined as a parasitic "germ culture" to be wiped off the face of the earth according to a scientific plan of racial "hygiene," Jews were targeted for destruction as a biological group not confined to a particular geographic area or identified by specific political affiliations or economic connections.* Rather, the group as such would be destroyed, wherever its members might be, with confinement in ghettos or slave labor camps providing only a temporary respite. A sentimental Nazi literature attesting to the Reich's benevolent treatment of Jews, corresponding to the South's voluminous literature in defense of slavery, is inconceivable.

Unlike slaveholding in the Americas, the slavery practiced as an economic feature of Nazism was an adjunct to genocidal racism. Although the Final Solution of the Jewish Question was periodically deferred in recognition of the temporary need for wartime labor, the ultimate ideological goal of annihilation was never superseded; there was tension but never a breach between exploita-

---

* The question of the singularity or "uniqueness" of the Holocaust in comparison with other instances of racial or political genocide has, of course, engendered an enormous historical and critical literature. As David Stannard points out in a study generally in harmony with the capacious language of the United Nations Genocide Convention, to take just one relevant example, it is important to ensure that commensurability in groups, as well as in methods and goals, is evaluated. "A traditional Eurocentric bias that lumps undifferentiated masses of 'Africans' into one single category and undifferentiated 'Indians' into another, while making fine distinctions among the different populations of Europe," he writes, "permits the ignoring of cases in which genocide against Africans and American Indians has resulted in the *total* extermination—purposefully carried out—of entire cultural, social, religious, and ethnic groups." Of course, Stannard's argument is open to the obvious rejoinder with respect to the Holocaust that the Nazis sought to kill all the world's Jews—certainly all those in Europe and other lands they aspired to conquer—regardless of nationality. David E. Stannard, *American Holocaust: Columbus and the Conquest of the New World* (New York: Oxford University Press, 1992), p. 151.

tion and extermination. The policy adopted toward Jewish laborers was one of *Vernichtung durch Arbeit,* "destruction through work," and work was thus no more than a suspended death sentence. In this respect, Benjamin Ferencz has suggested, use of the term "slave" is appropriate only because English has no precise word to describe the status of workers earmarked for certain destruction, just as it has no good equivalent for *verbraucht* (used up), the term applied to such workers at the point when their utility was gone and they had to be gassed and incinerated. Less than slaves, less than humans, Jews were, in death camp parlance, *Stücke* or *Figuren,* "pieces" or "figures,"[13] and the Nazis profited, both materially and ideologically, from killing as many as possible.

Whereas there was no hope or expectation that Jews would internalize Nazi ideals—conversion, implausible in any case, would not save them—Christian values were taught to slaves, however hypocritically, leaving an indelible stamp on their culture both before and after emancipation. Insofar as slaves were property that their masters wished to preserve, moreover, they were generally subject to a particular, if unpredictable, kind of visibility and care as human beings, whereas the death camp inmate had no price, no identity but a tattooed number, and was always being replaced. "Nobody knows to whom he belongs," Hannah Arendt wrote early on, "because he is never seen." The prisoner did not belong to his masters, adds Wolfgang Sofsky, but was at the mercy of a capricious, diffuse, and irrational institutional power through which he was, if not murdered outright, reduced to a corpse-like "bundle of reactions" before finally being killed.[14]

Even though it was based on an insidious scheme of racial classification and sent untold millions to heartless, sometimes brutal deaths in Africa, the Middle Passage, and the plantations of the New World, black slavery was "unique" in none of the senses that the destruction of the European Jews was unique, nor was it unique in the history of labor. It was a "peculiar" institution, in the famous phrase, as Thomas Sowell argues, for being at odds with the democratic principles of the United States, not with widespread and long-standing practices.[15] Because slaves were valuable—deemed inferior but nonetheless integral to an economic and social system defended at the cost of a devastating war—their subordination in labor was tempered by their masters' interest in keeping them alive, which amounted to wealth in its own right and increased the potential for future wealth. The most wasting slave regimes—for example, the sugar plantations of the eighteenth- and nineteenth-century Caribbean—might in extremity come to resemble ontologically the labor camps of Nazism, since working slaves to death and then buying new ones might have been deemed more profitable by some planters than working them less harshly and caring for them as they declined. No matter how expendable they might seem as a workforce constantly replenished by new shipments from Africa, however, slaves had to be purchased at a market price and kept capable of working as long as possible, and it was not the intent of the slaveholders to destroy them, let alone extinguish distinctive tribal nations or all the world's Africans. A disequilibrium that Michael Walzer notes in blacks' adoption of the Exodus applies as well to their adoption of the Holocaust. The Jews of modern Europe, like the Israelites enslaved by Pharaoh, were "not victims of the market, but of the state." Or, in Laurence Mordekhai Thomas's useful epigram, "Dead people do not make good slaves."[16]

Such incommensurate experiences are only marginally illuminated by the arguments of Stanley Elkins and others that the plantation was a precursor to the concentration camp. However important Elkins's work was to theories of slave psychology as well as the evolution of racial damage theory, his insights were done no justice at all by William Styron's fatuous contention, borrowed from Richard Rubenstein and elaborated in *Sophie's Choice,* that "the institution of chattel slavery as it was practiced by the great nations of the West" reached "its despotic apotheosis at Auschwitz." Rubenstein's idiosyncratic contribution to the historiography of the Holocaust lay in his claim, appealing to Styron, that the death camps were the "end product" of a long political and cultural "developmental continuum within Western civilization," wherein the Nazis resolved slavery's contradiction between person and "thing" by eliminating it. In the kingdom of Auschwitz was created something worse than mass killing, says Rubenstein in passages quoted by Styron: "The death-camp system became a society of total domination only when healthy inmates were kept alive and forced to become slaves rather than killed outright. . . . An extermination center can only manufacture corpses; a society of total domination creates a world of the living dead."[17] Styron and Rubenstein cited the Nazi practice of slavery in extremis for differing purposes,* and neither argued that American

---

* In the influence of Elkins on Rubenstein, Styron found a retrospective bridge from his portrayal of chattel slavery in *The Confessions of Nat Turner* to the destruction of the European Jews—or, rather, to the Nazi destruction of millions of people, since a principal argument of *Sophie's Choice* is that the Holocaust was an act of totalitarian terror that swept up Jews and non-Jews alike. As one of his characters, a member of the Polish resistance, remarks, "it is surprisingly difficult for many Jews to see beyond the consecrated nature of the Nazis' genocidal fury" and to recognize that "multitudes of non-Jews" were also "swallowed up in the apparatus of the camps, perishing just as surely as the Jews, though sometimes only less methodically." The anti-Semitism of Styron's Polish Catholic heroine makes this opinion tortuous with irony, and it is a fine question, though perverse in either case, whether he meant "consecration" to explain a quality in Jewish memory or a quality in Nazi conscience. For Rubenstein, although he

slavery truly resembled the Holocaust, but both failed to see that slave labor was simply ancillary to Hitler's plans to exterminate the Jews.

Like the racial theories on which it was based, post-Reconstruction violence against African Americans, which can legitimately be compared to the violence against Jews that preceded the Holocaust, is subject to similar qualifications. If the barbarism of lynching and *white* race riots such as those in Wilmington, North Carolina (1898), East St. Louis, Missouri (1919), Tulsa, Oklahoma (1921), or Rosewood, Florida (1923), had close counterparts in the anti-Semitic pogroms against European and Russian Jews, in each case the rage driving a mob, albeit intense and destructive, was episodic and subject to betrayal, shame, and some degree of legal constraint. In the Holocaust, however, the anti-Semitic rage of the mob was made obedient to state authority and functionally subsumed into a bureaucracy and a technology capable of carrying out mass murder on an unprecedented scale.[18] "One child cremated is the sum total of all evil," argued Alan W. Miller in 1969, at the height of acrimony between blacks and Jews. "One black man lynched likewise."[19] Still, there remains an essential qualitative distinction between vigilantism winked at by local and state governments, and vigilantism made an instrument of national policy.

Whatever the degree of one's allegiance to such distinctions, however, the now pervasive application of the term "holocaust" to other instances of genocide—or to sustained actions of inhumanity that have some characteristics of genocide, such as African American slavery—need not deny the historical singularity of the Jewish Holocaust. Indeed, the very act of thinking about comparability, as Christopher Browning remarks, affirms that the Holocaust was an "unprecedented, watershed event" that required the invention of new terminology to denote modes of human behavior for which no exact analogy appeared to exist in the earlier historical record.[20] Even though it may prompt anxiety or indignation, such borrowing does not diminish the Holocaust of the Jews but instead magnifies its significance.

What if the terms of comparison are turned upside down? On the one hand,

---

does not share the Christian triumphalism on which Styron's novel rests, the idea of the Holocaust is even more capacious. The subtitle of his book when it first appeared was "Mass Death and the American Future," and it was Rubenstein's conviction that the Jews "were the first to perish in the ultimate city of Western civilization, Necropolis, the new city of the dead that the Germans built and maintained at Auschwitz." William Styron, *Sophie's Choice* (1979; rpt. New York: Vintage, 1992), p. 237; Richard L. Rubenstein, *The Cunning of History: The Holocaust and the American Future* (New York: Harper and Row, 1975), p. 94.

Jews were never enslaved in the United States, and anti-Semitism has seldom escalated into sustained violence. We looked earlier at the case of Leo Frank, the exception that proved the rule that Jews did not live under the same "death sentence" as blacks. On the other hand, as I have noted, blacks were considered a source of racial pollution and were persecuted for it in Nazi Germany, even if they were marginal victims by comparison to Jews, and even if many Afro-Germans were left alone or, in some cases, even served in the Nazi regime. Although it is to date a minor subgenre in the literature of comparability, the recent concentration of new scholarship on the fate of blacks in Nazi Germany has been accompanied by at least one intriguing, if rather inconclusive, portrait in fiction, John A. Williams's novel *Clifford's Blues* (1999).

Dedicated "to those without memorial or monument," Williams's novel takes the form of the fictive diary of a gay black jazz pianist, Clifford Pepperidge, recounting his relative freedom in Berlin prior to the war and his imprisonment at Dachau, where he survives through the support of a sexually abusive patron and by playing in a band that performs for SS officers. As an account of blacks in concentration camps and of the role played by jazz musicians—notwithstanding the Nazi proscription of "Nigger-Jew jazz"—*Clifford's Blues* is a valuable addition to Holocaust literature. As a meditation on the respective treatment of blacks and Jews, however, its argument is less consistently useful. The diary's purported discoverer, whose brief commentary frames the book, compares it to James Howard Jones's *Bad Blood* (1981), which concerns the disgraceful 1932 Tuskegee syphilis experiments that left four hundred blacks to suffer untreated for the disease, and asks: *"How different are we, then, from the Germans from whom we got so much? As you know, one of the German defenses at Nuremberg was that a lot of their crazy experiments were conducted here* [in the United States] *first."* Pepperidge reflects on the sterilization of the "Rhineland Bastards," the mixed-race children of French colonial African and black American soldiers who occupied Germany after World War I, and he adduces a number of similarities between Nazism and white supremacy in the South: the Nuremberg Laws are said to be written by someone "studying with some of those crackers like Bilbo and Vardaman and Ben Tilman"; Kristallnacht reminds Pepperidge of a southern lynch mob; and the deportation of Jews to Poland is likened, hypothetically, to sending blacks from New York and Chicago to Mississippi.[21]

Williams does not claim too much in his comparisons, but neither does he sufficiently pull apart their implications, and the cumulative effect is an overreaching that finally makes the analogy ring false:

"Wer ist an unserem Ungluck schuld?" the Jewish capo shouts. "Who caused all our misery?" The guards watch, smiling, as the Jews march out to work, and later march back. The marching call is always the same. The marching Jews, in step, shout back, *"Die Juden! Die Juden!"* (Left, right, left.) Sometimes I think I can hear a strange echo, when the answer could be "The Negro! The Negro!" Then the Jewish columns run into SS guards, whose day isn't complete until they shout *"Dir gefallt es hier? Was?"* The guards ask because the Jews have insisted on living. "Do you like it here?" In other words, "Aren't you dead yet? Damn you, die!" Then I think of a long broken column of men who are Negroes.

Williams's characterization is reminiscent of those black GIs, noted in Chapter 3, who found among the liberated prisoners of Buchenwald and Dachau a reminder of slavery and Jim Crow in the United States—a reminder that "it could happen to black folks in America." Yet it better demonstrates the contrary. Jews may be "the niggers of Dachau,"[22] but this formulation proves also that blacks are not—and, more to the point, that there was no Dachau of any kind in the United States.

Closer examination, then, leads one to unresolvable problems of parity, a dilemma nicely illustrated by "Arbeit Macht Frei / Work Makes Who Free?," one of the works encompassed in Judy Chicago's multidimensional *Holocaust Project: From Darkness into Light* (1993). Proposing that punishment and labor under the two regimes are comparable, if not equivalent, Chicago presents three pairs of scenes in counterpoint—labor on a cotton plantation and in the concentration camp; a southern cotillion and a Viennese pastry shop; and the Ku Klux Klan and Nazi troopers—and emblazons her title on a metal sign supported by two wooden standards, one a plantation column, the other a gatepost at Auschwitz (see illustration). Chicago's comments on her research and process of composition describe, but also qualify, the utility of the comparison. "Now that I've begun to do research on slavery," Chicago wrote, "I'm embarrassed to admit how little time I've spent studying this shameful part of American history. And when people protest—and many do—that as wretched as slavery was, African Americans weren't 'exterminated' in a systematic program, I now realize that although that's true, there are many parallels between the Nazi slave-labor campaign and how African Americans were treated here and in Latin America."[23] Events that are parallel, however, need not be governed by the same ideology or carried out with the same intentions, let alone reach the same outcomes. Chicago's powerful, regimented design shows us worlds that

Judy Chicago, "Arbeit Macht Frei/Work Makes Who Free?"
detail from the Holocaust Project
© 1992 Judy Chicago with Donald Woodman.
Sprayed acrylic, oil, and photography on photolinen and canvas,
welded metal, and wood. Photo: Donald Woodman.

may be set side by side but made to seem truly similar only if wrenched out of
their respective times and places.

Unspeakable Thoughts

"So incomparable in one sense yet so suffused with the boundless mandate of
never forgetting," writes legal scholar Patricia Williams of the Holocaust and
the Middle Passage.[24] But what is it that one is to "never forget" and why? In
setting slavery alongside the Holocaust, it is not so much the events themselves
that can be profitably compared but rather their interpretations and memory—both the communal access to the "remembered" knowledge of slavery

that the storytelling of historical reconstruction can provide and the national "memory" that public recognition and memorialization might secure.

Consider a dream reported by Williams. After receiving from her sister a National Archives property listing that provides evidence documenting the life of their great-great-grandmother, a slave, Williams dreams of paintings by a Holocaust survivor she had once seen, every one of whose brightly colored landscapes left an unpainted white patch in the shape of a person, depicting the Holocaust's erasure of individuated humanity. In Williams's dream, her ancestor appears in those paintings, filling the unpainted space as though with a supernatural presence, so that Williams suddenly "knew exactly who she was— every pore, every hair, every angle of her face. I would know her everywhere."[25] Knowing the slave ancestors, those once excised from genealogical memory, means by implication knowing as well that they were destroyed by a force seemingly as rapacious and consciously directed as Nazism. To know and remember the ancestors now is to awaken their lost testimony.

A comparable strategy of memorial recovery had already been employed in Octavia Butler's time-travel novel *Kindred*, set and published in the bicentennial year 1976. Butler's protagonist, Dana Franklin, finds herself suddenly and mysteriously transported from Los Angeles back to a Maryland plantation in 1815, where she has been called by Rufus Weylin, whom she rescues from drowning and must keep alive until, as a mature planter, he conceives with his slave mistress the child Hagar, Dana's own ancestor. The "back to the future" scenario is not just a mechanical piece of science fiction, however, but a means of locating the origins of modern African American culture in the trauma of slavery. Dana returns both "to insure my family's survival, my own birth," and to place herself at the beginning of the black American genealogy recorded in her family Bible, "so many relatives that I had never known, would never know." Books about slavery, whether nonfiction or fiction, says Butler, have so far failed to capture the experience of slavery as effectively as the recollections of concentration camp survivors have captured the experience of Nazism: "Stories of beatings, starvation, filth, disease, torture, every possible degradation. As though the Germans had been trying to do in only a few years what the Americans had worked at for nearly two hundred." Given the large volume of eyewitness accounts—journals of Atlantic slavers and other documents of the Middle Passage, slave narratives, abolitionist speeches and essays, antislavery and proslavery documents, plantation records, testimonies taken from former slaves—many of which recorded the brutality of slavery, Butler's claim was mistaken, if not tendentious. But her invocation of the Holocaust modified the historical record for a purpose: to name the many ancestors one "would never know" and to discover by implication a demonic design that the documentary record of slavery would yield less readily.[26]

The exemplary instance of such African American "remembering" is undoubtedly Toni Morrison's *Beloved,* one the most widely read and studied novels of the late twentieth century. Morrison famously entered the comparability fray by choosing as an epigraph the provoking phrase "Sixty Million and more," which traded upon Paule Marshall's putatively factual estimate of deaths in the Middle Passage in *The Chosen Place, the Timeless People,* "nine million and more it is said," but raised the stakes with its exponential challenge to the Holocaust. By the time Morrison's novel appeared, however, routine appeals to genocide's touchstone had nearly drained it of meaning, so that Stanley Crouch's indignation—he declared *Beloved* a "blackface holocaust novel," Morrison's entry of "American slavery into the big-time martyr ratings contest"[27]—was no more outrageous than her epigraph.

"Sixty Million and more" had ceased to be shocking not just because of the ubiquity of the Holocaust but, specifically, because of the ubiquity of the *black* holocaust, both in popular culture and in more serious literature and inquiry. Morrison's premise recapitulated assumptions that had been gathering force ever since Lemkin's invention of the term "genocide" and that became more heated and accusatory in the era of Black Power. America is "just as capable of building gas ovens for Black people as Hitler's society was," said Malcolm X in 1965. The coordinated "mass removal of Blacks from the streets," H. Rap Brown maintained soon thereafter, was the first stage in the coming African American genocide, while James Forman catalogued the array of new weapons the federal government was testing—from Mace to tranquilizing darts to superglues to armored vehicles—with the aim of carrying out "the partial or complete genocide of Black people."[28] The revolutionaries in John A. Williams's *Sons of Darkness, Sons of Light* feared a backlash ending in black genocide, but Williams was not alone in such speculations. Basing his liberationist philosophy on lines slightly misquoted from Arna Bontemps's "Nocturne at Bethesda"—"Is there something we have forgotten? / Something we have lost wandering in strange lands?"—ex-CIA operative Don Freeman, the instigator of a nationwide black rebellion in Sam Greenlee's novel *The Spook Who Sat by the Door* (1969), warns that the revolution will run up against "whitey's" propensity for genocide: "He could go all the way: barbed wire, concentration camps, gas ovens; a 'final solution' of the Negro problem."[29]

It was not necessary to speak of death camps, however, for more subtle laws of racial selection seemed already to be operating. Because it intersected with the sexual revolution and countercultural apprehension about a world popula-

tion explosion, Black Power's rejection of integrationist strategies reawakened
old suspicions about family planning in the black community. In Ben Caldwell's play *Top Secret or a Few Million After B.C.* (1968), federal authorities, de-
ciding that concentration camps and the bombing of Harlem are steps too
rash, adopt "Operation Pre-Kill" to market inexpensive birth control pills that
will "kill the nigger babies before they're born! Fast as them black bucks can
shoot 'em out!"[30] Birth control was just a "more subtle" Holocaust, said Dick
Gregory,[31] while the political scientist Ronald Walters, contending that birth
control counseling and after-school programs targeting at-risk children were
"genocidal," cited the so-called King Alfred plan, a blueprint for fascist state
control of the black population that he borrowed from a work of fiction, John
A. Williams's 1967 novel *The Man Who Cried I Am*.* By the 1990s, the grounds
of conspiratorial thinking had shifted to the belief, prevalent among African

---

* In Williams's inventive novel, a memo to the National Security Agency advises that post–*Brown v.
Board of Education* discord and violence put the nation in jeopardy. Because African Americans have
adopted an "almost military posture" to gain their objectives, "racial war must be considered inevitable."
When the war comes, the KING ALFRED plan can be put into effect at the discretion of the president.
Targeting black leaders and militant groups, the plan calls for a coordinated assault by all governmental
agencies "to terminate, once and for all, the Minority threat to the whole of American society, and, indeed, the Free World," and it culminates in a reference to seeming genocide: "We suggest that vaporiza-
tion techniques be employed to overcome the Production problems inherent in KING ALFRED." Williams, whose middle name is Alfred, apparently photocopied sections of his novel dealing with the King
Alfred plan and left them in New York subway cars as a way of stimulating rumors among the black
population about the plan. The King Alfred plan retains a life today among African American conspiracy theorists. It was cited, for example, on Black Liberation Radio in 1992 by commentator Zears Miles
as a scheme that originated in the National Security Council of the Johnson administration and became
the prototype for Global 2000, an actual Carter administration study of global population that Miles
and others interpreted as a blueprint for the destruction of the planet's black population. And it crops
up in writer-activist Del Jones's neo-nationalist essay *Invasion of 'de Body Snatchers* (1996). Citing an updating of the plan said to have been undertaken initially in the Orwellian year 1984 by Oliver North,
deputy national security adviser to President Ronald Reagan, Jones envisions the New World Order as a
white fascist conspiracy designed to carry out the "Afrikan Holocaust" through a shadowy regime of
drugs (both street drugs and pharmaceuticals), vaccines, bar codes, AIDS, integration, and birth control. The FBI assault on the Branch Davidians at Waco is adduced as evidence that the government's
eradication of black culture, setting up concentration camps and "using healthy Afrikan people as medical spare parts," has begun: "Our culture is ripped to shreds and hung up on meat hooks in European
freezers." Ronald Walters, "Population Control and the Black Community," *The Black Scholar* 15 (May
1974), 46–49; John A. Williams, *The Man Who Cried I Am* (1967; rpt. New York: Thunder's Mouth Press,
1985), pp. 371–76; Herb Boyd, "The Man and the Plan: Conspiracy Theories and Paranoia in Our Culture," *Black Issues Book Review* 4 (March–April 2002), 39; John Fiske, *Media Matters: Race and Gender in
U.S. Politics*, rev. ed. (Minneapolis: University of Minnesota Press, 1996), pp. 206–7; Del Jones, *Invasion
of 'de Body Snatchers: Hi-Tech Barbarians* (Philadelphia: Hikeka Communications, 1996), pp. 10–14, 33.

Americans, that AIDS was the by-product of germ warfare experiments, even a secret weapon deliberately introduced into the black community—"genocide, 1990s style," according to San Francisco's Reverend Cecil Williams.[32] For her part, psychiatrist Frances Cress Welsing cited Raul Hilberg on the Holocaust in arguing that AIDS was a stratagem to destroy the world's black population: "Anyone who has not mastered an understanding of Germany under Adolf Hitler's leadership and the holocaust of the Semites, cannot possibly understand the AIDS holocaust of 1980–1991, wherein 50,000,000 to 75,000,000 deaths of Black people on the continent of Africa and elsewhere have been planned."*

Such fantasies, as Charles Johnson once said of the King Alfred hoax, respond to blacks' "deep-seated fear of a racial holocaust, the nagging, gut-pinching terror that they can never be safe in the white world because there is a *design* behind the horrible statistics of black life . . . and all that is lacking is the Aryan Ur-text or blueprint" necessary to explain it.[33] How else to account for the persistence of similar beliefs not just among crackpots but even among the African American elite? Unless it was saved by multiracial coalition politics, said Cornel West in his public dialogue with Michael Lerner (during the presidency of Bill Clinton, not George H. W. Bush or George W. Bush), America was headed for a violent race war that would begin with "quarantining Black communities, arresting progressive Black spokespersons like myself. That's quite imaginable in this society." For West's Harvard colleague, law professor Derrick Bell, the simple act of reading a student term paper on the history of American race riots set in motion his speculation about racial violence escalating into a full-scale pogrom against blacks, in which building after building in New York

---

* Best known for her symbol-laden pseudo-Freudian conspiracy theories based on associative symbol patterns in which Nazi swastika = Christian cross = black man's genitals = castration/lynching = black Holocaust, Welsing argued in a 1980 essay that the Holocaust is but one instance of whites' reaction to the perceived threat of "genetic annihilation" at the hands of people of color, whether Semites or Hamites (that is, Jews or blacks, according to Welsing's racial construction), and, in a prefatory note to her collected essays, advised all non-whites to view a documentary about the Wannsee Conference, where the Final Solution was outlined, in order to see how a white supremacist government "calmly sits and plans the destruction of a people that it classifies as non-white." The persecution of the Jews, said Welsing, was simply an omen of subsequent far-reaching assaults on other people of color. The first lesson of the Holocaust is therefore that Jews were the people "chosen" to teach the moral lesson that neither intermarriage, nor assimilation, nor cultural achievement, nor economic success can stave off destruction within a regime of white supremacy. Frances Cress Welsing, "The White Supremacy System, the White Supremacy Mind-Set, and the AIDS Holocaust" (1988), "The Cress Theory of the Holocaust" (1980), and "Dedication," in *The Isis Papers: The Keys to the Colors* (Chicago: Third World Press, 1991), pp. 294, 218–19.

City is emptied and posted with the sign "Nigger Free." Arising from white resentment of black middle-class integration, and assisted by the police, this contemporary Kristallnacht turns "free"—the single most powerful linguistic sign-
post in African American history—into something more frightening than its
opposite. Not segregation, not slavery, but extermination—"niggerrein" rather
than *judenrein*—is forecast.[34]

Bell's daydream is a parable, of course, not a prediction, but the same cannot
be said of the late work of James Baldwin, for whom the promise of the civil
rights movement gradually gave way to the threat of neo-fascism. Although
Baldwin was mocked by Harold Cruse as an "apologist for the Jews," true to the
tradition of the black ex-preacher steeped "in Hebrew biblical lore and all that
deep-river-waters-of-Jordan history,"[35] his views were anything but predictable.
Published in 1963, coincident not only with the March on Washington and the
centenary of the Emancipation Proclamation but also with the surge in American Holocaust consciousness occasioned by the trial of Adolf Eichmann, *The
Fire Next Time* promised the nation the fire of apocalypse if the rainbow of
God's covenant were not accepted—"no more water but the fire next time"—
but its divination of end times established a template for invocations of the
Holocaust that was to become pervasive. Recalling his own astonishment at the
"world's indifference" to the Holocaust, Baldwin argued that, although the racial theories of Nazi Germany may have astounded white Americans, to black
people their "only originality lay in the means they used."[36] The year 1967 saw
an important transformation in his vision, however, and over the remainder of
his career Baldwin moved from being a prophet of post-ethnicity who foresaw
America transforming racial essentialism into cosmopolitan nationalism[37] to
being the prophet of a racial apocalypse in which Jews were less likely to be allies than envied antagonists and the Holocaust almost an affront to the more
horrendous suffering of blacks.

Following the Six-Day War, in which he took the Arab side, Baldwin's displacement of the Exodus with the Holocaust became more pronounced, and
his rhetorical associations between the United States and German fascism increasingly shrill. Responding to an essay by Eddie Ellis that retailed standard
anti-Semitic stereotypes of gouging Jewish merchants, Baldwin rejected Ellis's
"ancient and barbaric" canard of blaming Harlem on the Jew; but, between
the war in Vietnam and the race war at home, Baldwin observed, America
was responsible for its own "holocaust."[38] Although his own early career had
been richly nourished by Jewish editors and publishers, he soon included Jews
within his caustic accusations. In his published conversation with Margaret
Mead, *A Rap on Race* (1971), Baldwin declared that Harlem was a concentration

camp, that Israel was the cynical creation of the United States and Britain to use Jews to do the dirty work of imperialism, and that his own bitterness arose from the fact that "I have been, in America, the Arab at the hands of the Jews."[39] A year later he asserted that young activists in the civil rights movement were now "paying for [the] holocaust" of American racism, and he likened the black students who integrated Little Rock schools in 1956 to Jewish children who might have "insisted on getting a German education in order to overthrow the Third Reich." Likewise, after a visit to Haight-Ashbury in San Francisco, Baldwin echoed a common Black Power sentiment: just as the Third Reich had to destroy political opposition before exterminating the Jews, so America's "Fourth Reich" would be "forced to plow under the flower children—in all their variations—before getting around to the blacks and then the rest of the world." The election of Ronald Reagan a decade later, Baldwin concluded, had been blacks' last opportunity "to outwit the Final Solution."[40]

As this résumé suggests, Baldwin's use of the Holocaust became indiscriminate. His displacement of analysis with fancy climaxed in *Evidence of Things Not Seen* (1985), an eccentric monograph on the serial killings of black children in Atlanta whose title toyed sardonically with the Pauline definition of faith (Hebrews 11:1). Thought initially to be racial hate crimes carried out by white supremacists before a black man was arrested and convicted,* the menacing

---

* Beginning in the summer of 1979 and concluding in May 1981 with the arrest of a black man named Wayne Williams, a small-time musical talent scout, the Atlanta youth murders resulted in twenty-nine dead, all but two of them boys, including a few in their twenties. (Williams used his position as a talent scout to lure at least some of the children, his only apparent motive being hatred of poor black children—in effect, a form of self-loathing.) When the pattern of a serial killer was recognized in 1980, the "City Too Busy to Hate" became a city consumed by racial fears and accusations, its chilling drama subject to nationwide coverage by major newspapers and network media. Tensions grew to the breaking point when every few weeks another black youth disappeared, only to be found stabbed, beaten, or, most often, strangled to death. At the height of the trauma, much of Atlanta's black population assumed that the killer was white, and many evolved elaborate theories about the involvement of the Ku Klux Klan, the FBI, and the CIA. Rallies were held outside Atlanta, including one at the Lincoln Memorial in Washington, D.C., where Jesse Jackson charged that "it is open season on black people" and suggested that the murders could be "understood only in the context of [the attack on] affirmative action and Ronald Reagan's conservative politics." Although the killings stopped once Williams was arrested, many blacks were hard-pressed to believe that Williams—rather than whites engaged in a racist conspiracy— was guilty, despite the fact that forensic evidence linked him to twenty-three of the murders. Camille Bell, mother of one victim and the head of a parents task force, averred that with Williams's conviction he became "the 30th victim of the Atlanta slayings." Bernard Headley, *The Atlanta Youth Murders and the Politics of Race* (Carbondale: Southern Illinois University Press, 1998); Jackson and Bell quoted in Tamar Jacoby, *Someone Else's House: America's Unfinished Struggle for Integration* (New York: Free Press, 1998), pp. 372–76. In addition to Baldwin's polemic, originally published in *Playboy,* the killings pro-

pattern of the Atlanta child murders allowed Baldwin to cultivate an atmosphere of conspiracy in which the "banality" of "slaughtered Black children," purportedly of no interest to white Atlanta, let alone the nation at large, was the sign of an escalating black holocaust. The "compulsive hacking off" of the black man's genitals and the "enforced sterilization" of black women, said Baldwin, were part of the national "contract" governing black life: white people's "dream of safety can reach culmination or climax only in the nightmare orgasm of genocide." However they accommodate or fail to remember the destruction through which they have lived, all African Americans "bear the inexorable guilt of the survivor."[41]

Against the backdrop of recent revelations about the Tuskegee syphilis experiments carried out by the Public Health Service, a forerunner of the Centers for Disease Control (CDC),[42] some blacks propounded the view that the Atlanta child murders were the work of the FBI, said to be providing body parts to the CDC for medical experiments involving the anti-cancer drug Interferon. As the case unfolded, theories of a far-reaching racist plot linking the FBI, the CDC, and the Ku Klux Klan gained popular credence, leading to outlandish accusations such as Dick Gregory's notion that the CDC was harvesting black penises for the anti-cancer agent contained in their tips, a bizarre kind of circumcision. As an inverse variant of the blood libel common throughout Jewish history, the idea that black body parts, genitalia in particular, were being collected by whites for mysterious uses—this was one source for Del Jones's scenario in *Invasion of 'de Body Snatchers*—carried the grim history of black men being castrated before or after they were lynched to a higher plane of conspiratorial thought. Without explicitly assenting to such theories, Baldwin portrayed a mysterious campaign of "Terror" in which what is *not* seen, what is *not* remembered, could be shadowed forth by evidence of any kind whatsoever. "My memory stammers: but my soul is a witness," he wrote in his preface.[43] In Baldwin's racial paradigm, every African American is the "survivor" of a horrific past and, in all probability, a present no less chilling.

Baldwin does not rank the late-twentieth-century black predicament in America with that of the Jews in Nazi Germany, which for him marked the end of the moral authority of the Western world and the Judeo-Christian ethic. But he argues nevertheless that the difference between the two cases conceals a crucial likeness. It was a shock for European Jews to find that their whiteness, in

---

duced major treatments in the form of an ABC television docudrama, "Atlanta Child Murders" (1985), and a posthumous novel by Toni Cade Bambara titled *Those Bones Are Not My Child* (1999), which left unsettled the question of Williams's guilt.

particular their national allegiance as Germans, did nothing to save them when the social contract that had emancipated Jews was viciously broken: "*Mene, mene, tekel, upharsin* had not yet translated itself into so unspeakable a confrontation between the Chosen People and the Master Race."* Unable because of their color even to contemplate assimilation, blacks have endured a longer, never-ending genocide: "The auction block is the platform on which I entered the Civilized World. Nothing that has happened since, from South Africa to El Salvador, indicates that the Western world has any real quarrel with slavery." The auction block, that is to say, compares to the selection platform on which Jews debarked at the death camps. The West (from which Baldwin separates Germany in this idiosyncratic formulation) understood the concept of *Lebensraum* quite well, and it went to war against Germany for reasons of self-defense alone, to thwart "the monster" it had created. That African Americans have never been systematically slaughtered, as were Jews in Nazi Germany, matters little in Baldwin's view, for blacks are victims of the "most brutal" of human diasporas and have lived in virtual death camps from the outset of their time in the New World.[44]

Because he was an expatriate living in France at the time, it might be argued that Baldwin, like Richard Wright when he wrote *The Long Dream,* used his distance from the American scene to compose a deliberately phantasmagoric indictment of racism in his homeland. Whereas Wright wrote a novel, however, Baldwin purported to offer social commentary. In contrast to the elegant argu-

---

* Baldwin's purpose in quoting the mysterious handwriting on the wall in the Book of Daniel is obscure. A descendant of David renowned during the Babylonian exile for his interpretation of dreams and his apocalyptic visions, Daniel read the inscription that forecasts Belshazzar's downfall—"God hath numbered thy kingdom and finished it. . . . Thou art weighed in the balances, and art found wanting" (Daniel 5:24–27). Whereas it is Daniel, the devout Jew, who prophesies the downfall of Belshazzar and the division of his kingdom, Baldwin appears to invert the passage, or read it ironically, as a gloss on the Master Race's destruction of the Chosen People. Both Baldwin and John Edgar Wideman, who alludes to the same passage in *Philadelphia Fire,* a work that also refers to the Atlanta murders, may have had in mind Melvin Tolson's more conventional rendering of the scene in "Babylon," part of his narrative poem *Rendezvous with America* (1944):

> Babylon, O Babylon,
> Here Israel drinks the captive's scum of gall,
> And here Belshazzar's soul knots with chagrin
> As Daniel translates doom upon the wall:
>   *Mene, mene, tekel upharsin.*

Melvin B. Tolson, *Rendezvous with America,* in *"Harlem Gallery" and Other Poems,* ed. Raymond Nelson (Charlottesville: University Press of Virginia, 1999), p. 93.

mentation of his early essays, *Evidence of Things Not Seen*—which Baldwin improvidently told Caryl Phillips would constitute his "comeback" as a writer[45]—is flaccid, and its portrayal of opaque terror as the salient quality of African American life strips black memory of any oppositional dignity and cultural vitality. What he remembered of his childhood in America, Baldwin asserts, is simply the "terror of being destroyed"—a terror that has made memory's perilous uncertainty all the more awful: "What one does not remember is the serpent in the garden of one's dreams." The lost content of either an individual's or a people's history is thus posited to lie within an originating event whose trauma—"what one does not remember"—conceals something at once enticing, repulsive, and unrecoverable. What cannot actually be known in the case of the Atlanta child murders is, for the same reason, the very key to Baldwin's representation of the events: "And what I am trying to suggest by what *one imagines oneself to be able to remember* is that terror cannot be remembered."[46]

Although Baldwin trumpets his refusal "to speak from the perspective of the victim" in *Evidence of Things Not Seen*, it is hard to locate an alternative point of view.[47] Engulfed in a paranoid state in which the unknown is known and the unremembered is memory, his conception of the "survivor" is drained of any real meaning; it, too, is epiphenomenal "evidence of things not seen." Or, as Toni Morrison said of Baldwin, "You gave me a language to dwell in, a gift so perfect it seems my own invention." The most pertinent among the several styles Baldwin offered was that of racial terror, a language that was "unspeakable."*

Although the scope of *Beloved* is not epic, its highly stylized tragedy produces an effect that is undeniably monumental. Morrison in this respect offered an interesting account of the novel's reason for being:

> There is no place you or I can go, to think about or not think about, to summon the presences of, or recollect the absences of slaves; nothing

---

* "For the horrors of the American Negro's life there has been almost no language," Baldwin wrote in *The Fire Next Time*. "It does indeed mean something—something unspeakable—to be born, in a white country, an Anglo-Teutonic, antisexual country, black. You very soon, without knowing it, give up all hope of communion." Morrison in all likelihood also had in mind George Steiner's remarks on language and the Holocaust, noted in Chapter 3: "To speak of the *unspeakable* is to risk the survivance of language as creator and bearer of humane, rational truth." Toni Morrison, "Life in His Language," in Quincy Troupe, ed., *James Baldwin: The Legacy* (New York: Touchstone, 1989), p. 76; James Baldwin, *The Fire Next Time* (1963; New York: Dell, 1964), pp. 95, 45; George Steiner, "K" (1963), in *Language and Silence: Essays on Language, Literature, and the Inhuman* (New York: Atheneum, 1966), p. 123.

that reminds us of the ones who made the journey and of those who did not make it. There is no suitable memorial or plaque or wreath or wall or park or skyscraper lobby. There's no 300 foot tower. There's no small bench by the road. There is not even a tree scored, an initial that I can visit or you can visit in Charleston or Savannah or New York or Providence or, better still, on the banks of the Mississippi. And because such a place does not exist (that I know of), the book had to.[48]

A number of African American novels, of course, had already attempted to fill out the unwritten record of those who "made the journey" and those who did not. Margaret Walker's *Jubilee* (1966), Ernest Gaines's *Autobiography of Miss Jane Pittman* (1971), Alex Haley's *Roots* (1976), and David Bradley's *Chaneysville Incident* (1981), to name just a few, addressed slavery, slave resistance, and their legacy. Morrison's subject, however, is not slavery per se but rather the transmission of memories grounded in horrific experiences that are nearly beyond representation—"unspeakable thoughts, unspoken," to cite her well-known phrase.[49] *Beloved* thus has more in common with Cynthia Ozick's Holocaust novella *The Shawl* (1990),[50] and the missing commemorative site whose place is filled by the novel is not a museum of the African American experience but specifically a museum of the African American holocaust—an as yet unrealized equivalent, that is to say, of the United States Holocaust Memorial Museum, which had been authorized in 1978 and which opened in 1993.

Inspired by the 1856 case of an escaped slave, Margaret Garner, who cut the throat of her two-year-old daughter and was about to kill her other three children when she was seized by slave catchers,[51] Morrison embeds a similar realistic scenario within a haunting, sometimes beautiful meditation on broken slave bodies, broken slave families, and the broken genealogies that perforce typify most every African American's latent identity. Tracked down by her owner, the escaped slave Sethe murders one daughter and is bent on killing her other three children before she is stopped. After serving a jail sentence for destroying the white man's property and driving away her two terrified sons, Sethe lives on with her remaining daughter, Denver, haunted by the dead daughter's vengeful ghost. Seemingly banished by Sethe's lover, a former fellow slave named Paul D, the ghost materializes as a strange young woman, Beloved, who becomes the daughter-sister-lover conduit for the three characters' respective confrontations with the trauma of their previous enslavement. At length, Beloved's strangling grip on Sethe's household must be broken by an exorcising choric chant of community women, after which Sethe, Denver, and Paul D can be restored to the semblance of a family.

The figure of Beloved is construed by Morrison in such a way as to float among several identities. She is first of all the embodied ghost of Sethe's murdered daughter. But she also takes on other guises as well: Sethe's own mother, as though she had survived the Middle Passage rather than, after being multiply raped aboard the slave ship bringing her to the New World, committing suicide or being killed and thrown into the ocean; the murdered children of those rapes ("she threw them all away but you"); and, more broadly, the many victims of white men's sexual abuse and the children they may have carried (and perhaps murdered) as a result. The core of the novel, like the birthright of its title character, lies therefore not in its present-day action, set in the decades before and after the Civil War, compelling though that is, but instead in the fragmentary, timeless moment of the Middle Passage, as narrated in the Samuel Beckett–like testimony of Beloved:

> some who eat nasty themselves   I do not eat   the men without skin bring us their morning water to drink   we have none   at night I cannot see the dead man on my face   daylight comes through the cracks and I can see his locked eyes   I am not big   small rats do not wait for us to sleep   someone is thrashing but there is no room to do it in   if we had more to drink we could make tears. . . . it is hard to make yourself die forever   you sleep short and then return in the beginning we could vomit   now we do not. . . . those who are able to die are in a pile   I cannot find my man . . . the men without skin push them through with poles   the woman is there with the face I want   the face that is mine   they fall into the sea that is the color of bread. . . . now there is room to crouch and watch the crouching others. . . . the woman with my face is in the sea[52]

Starvation, dysentery, vomiting, drinking urine, being gnawed by rats, the torment of loved ones and strangers, longing for death: here is the Middle Passage as the black Auschwitz, *anus mundi.*[53]

In her ghostly witness to the destruction of a family made emblematic of a people, from an idyllic African beginning to a regime of whipping, branding, torture, rape, and murder, Beloved is an archetype of the "survivor" envisioned by Baldwin, the African American who has passed through the "unspeakable" trials of the American holocaust. But she is more. A phantasm made flesh, Beloved personifies Primo Levi's belief that it is not the survivors whose testimony is recorded who are "the complete witnesses" but rather the "drowned," those who embody the living death of the concentration camp, "who saw the

Gorgon [and] have not returned to tell about it or have returned mute."[54] As a memorial to the centuries-long black holocaust, the "drowned" Beloved, like *Beloved* the novel, bears witness to a liminal modality between life and death that simulates all the terrors of slavery and the racial violence that lived on in its wake.

In its purest state, the reconstituted "memory" of the Middle Passage is a sublime consciousness in which present-day survivors become one with lost ancestors and their pain. As imprisoned "Soledad Brother" George Jackson wrote to his attorney, Fay Stender, in 1970: "I've lived through the [Middle] passage, died on the passage, lain in the unmarked, shallow graves of the millions who fertilized the Amerikan soil with their corpses; cotton and corn growing out of my chest, 'unto the third and fourth generation,' the tenth, the hundredth. My mind ranges back and forth through the uncounted generations, and I feel all that they ever felt, but double."[55] Vicariously knowing slavery by being inhabited by the dead, contemporary African Americans may engage in a hyper-extended version of "postmemory"—in Holocaust literature the genre of retrospective witnessing on the part of second or third generations in which the original trauma is adopted as one's own[56]—and commune not just with those who made the journey but also, even more reverentially, with those "who did not make it," those who "have not returned to tell about it."

Haley's more expository version of the Middle Passage in *Roots* was the outstanding example prior to *Beloved*, though Morrison's setting and plot also bear comparison in some details, including a mother's act of infanticide, to Amiri Baraka's 1967 play *Slave Ship: A Historical Pageant*, in which the part of the play set in the Middle Passage is dominated by a gallery of African voices, including excruciating screams that pierce a stage set in darkness and rendered authentic by sounds of the sea and an odor of filth.[57] But *Beloved*'s notorious epigraph—"Sixty Million and more"—stridently confronted readers with a singular frame of reference, coming as the novel did fast on the heels of a two-decade outpouring of scholarship, survivor testimony, and literature about the Holocaust. The epigraph not only claimed victims ten times as numerous but also gave Africans priority over Jews in shaping the course of modern history. (Although she did not say whom she consulted, Morrison reported that the figure of 60 million was the lowest estimate she got, with some of her sources estimating slave deaths as high as 200 million.)[58] Whereas many historians have been inclined to interpret the Holocaust as the defining event of modernity—an instance of social engineering by means of racial selection, Zygmunt Bauman writes, "meant to bring about a social order conforming to the design of the perfect society"[59]—Morrison provided a proof text for Paul Gilroy's alternative argument that the "concentrated intensity of the slave experience" marks blacks as the first truly modern people, the bearers of an experience that requires writing defined by its "imaginative proximity to forms of terror that surpass understanding and lead back from contemporary racial violence, through lynching, towards the temporal and ontological rupture of the middle passage."[60]

"Modern life begins with slavery," Morrison told Gilroy, more succinctly, in an interview. In subjecting black people to the pathological predation of Western ideology at its most inhumanely refined, in her conception, "slavery broke the world in half, broke it in every way," leaving blacks forever severed from their original nations—what U. B. Phillips called their "tribal stems" and what E. Franklin Frazier called their "household gods." "We have no nation, no language," Morrison contended on another occasion. "No sense that we have existed within historical time."[61] By this account, black exile and black annihilation, not the exile and annihilation of the Jews, is the defining tragedy of modernity. As the *zakhor* ("Remember!") of African Americans, says Geoffrey Hartman, *Beloved* treats their presumed near destruction and their fractured genealogy, like the whipping scars criss-crossed on Sethe's back in the figure of a chokecherry tree, with tender solicitude. What can be known is never the ancestor but only her ghost, never the wound but only the scar, never the event but only the "rememory" of it.[62] As in Baldwin's phantasmic memory of "terror," what can be known is not simply a past subject to the vicissitudes of forgetting and distortion that afflict any history. It is a past discoverable only through an ineffable language of enduring, unspeakable pain, transformed through the act of "rememorying" into the essence of racial identity.*

* Insofar as the ghosts of *Beloved* are figures for the transformation of history into memory, and memory into identity, Walter Michaels argues, Morrison's strategy is consonant with contemporary Holocaust remembrance, which responds to the anxiety that people will cease, not to know about, but to "remember" the events as something transmitted to them by previous generations. The goal in literature and testimony alike is thus, by a performative experience, to allow nonparticipants to "survive" an event that never ends. In Michaels's account, Holocaust remembrance creates an anti-essential Jewishness such that it is possible "to define the Jew not as someone who has Jewish blood or who believes in Judaism but as someone who, having experienced the Holocaust, can—even if he or she was never there—acknowledge it as part of his or her history." This alteration in the meaning of genocide makes possible the obverse view that Jews who forget their Jewishness—who assimilate to the point of complete apostasy and stop thinking of themselves as Jews—are therefore collaborators in the work of Hitler. Cultural genocide thus becomes equivalent to physical genocide, and Hitler's opposition to a race and blood equivalent to opposition to a set of cultural practices. In theory, therefore, it would be possible to define as African American someone—even if he or she was never there—who acknowledges slavery as part of his or her history. Walter Benn Michaels, "'You who never was there': Slavery and the New Historicism,

Seen from this vantage point, *Beloved* differs not in purpose but only in genre and artistic accomplishment from a pop culture work such as S. E. Anderson's *Black Holocaust for Beginners* (1995). Presenting a heavily illustrated collage of testimony, historiography, statistics, and vignettes of suffering, Anderson's book aims both to recover "the stolen cultural and political heritage buried in the complex and beastly acts of the Slave Trade" and to provide indelible reasons for "never forgetting" the originating "unimaginable experience" of Africans in America.[63]

Following a group of slaves from their capture in Africa to their sale in the New World, the narrative takes as a representative experience during the Middle Passage the ordeal of Sister Translator (so named because she is able to translate between several African languages). Having been raped by members of the crew, Sister Translator resists medical treatment by the ship's surgeon by kicking him in the groin. In retribution, she is hanged from the mainmast by a giant hook shoved through her tongue and the roof of her mouth. And worse:

> As you look down from her once beautiful, now monstrous face, you see her stomach was crudely ripped open to show not only her bowels and intestines but also to show an African fetus dangling on her umbilical cord. You want to turn away and throw up but you can't. Something is forcing you to take in every detail, every swing of her body, every sound, every silence. There are many other Sisters—girls and women—who are just as transfixed. Who are REMEMBERING. Who are NEVER FORGETTING.

This scene is followed a few pages later by the comparable brutalization of an African man—bullet-ridden, castrated, likewise hanged by his tongue, and once again gazed upon by a stunned audience "Who are REMEMBERING. Who are NEVER FORGETTING."* Accompanied by vividly detailed line drawings of

---

Deconstruction and the Holocaust," *Narrative* 4 (January 1996), 8–13. A later version of this argument, less focused on Morrison, appears in Walter Benn Michaels, *The Shape of the Signifier* (Princeton: Princeton University Press, 2004), pp. 135–49.

* The injunction to "always remember," Anderson proposes, should be enforced by observance of the copyrighted "MiddlePassage Commemoration," a ceremony of prayer and libation conducted during the "so-called 'Thanksgiving' weekend." In its commandment to remember and "never again" permit such a tragedy to happen to one's people, this ironic counter-Thanksgiving bears obvious comparison to the now widely recognized Yom Hashoah (Holocaust Remembrance Day, celebrated in April). There is no evidence to date, however, that Anderson's proposal has achieved similar recognition. S. E. Anderson, *The Black Holocaust for Beginners* (New York: Writers and Readers Publishing, 1995), pp. 112–13, 161–64.

these gruesome punishments—the prototypes, particularly in the case of the man, are lynching photographs, for blacks the closest visual analogue to the horrific photographic and film record of the Holocaust made by liberators of the camps and others—the text transfixes the reader with grotesque emblems of slavery's barbarism (see illustration).

As a representation of the horrors of the Black Holocaust, the story of Sister Translator is indisputably powerful—wrenching, not just shocking—and its message is clear enough. Her ghastly disembowelment, with her fetus hanging by its umbilical cord, as though lynched, calls our attention to the fact that both black Atlantic slavery and the Holocaust carried out radical assaults on maternity and reproduction. Yet the analogy is partial at best. Whereas the Nazis sought the utter destruction of Jewish reproduction, as well as the corresponding enhancement of Aryan reproduction, slave traders and slaveholders, however predatory their sexual abuse, and despite their deliberate splintering of African families, meant to control and increase reproduction to their economic benefit. But Sister Translator's story is not, of course, a contribution to the historiography of slavery. Whether such horrifying mutilation was typical of the Middle Passage, let alone slaveholding in any part of the Americas, is beside the point of its commemorative purpose.

Like *Beloved, The Black Holocaust for Beginners* starts from the premise that to remember—to "never forget"— who they are, blacks must commune with their dead, as well as with those who murdered them. Underlying such arguments, whether Morrison's complex, nuanced narrative or Anderson's programmatic melodrama, is the assumption that black life, and therefore black memory, is characterized not peripherally but centrally by a heritage of psychic and cultural destruction—what Randall Robinson, in his brief for reparations, speaks of as "the most heinous human rights crime visited upon any group of people in the world over the last five hundred years," a crime which destroyed "every artifact of the victims' past cultures, every custom, every ritual, every god, every language, every trace element of a people's whole hereditary identity, wrenched from them and ground into a sharp choking dust," and thus produced victims *"ad infinitum."*[64] The Black Muslim psychologist Na'im Akbar makes the supersession of the Jews' destruction even more explicit. Whereas "the Nazi atrocities at Auschwitz . . . were fleeting and direct, destroying bodies, but essentially leaving the collective mind intact," writes Akbar, slavery's infliction on blacks of multiple pathologies that have lasted for generations makes it the most traumatizing event in the history of the world. Measured by such benchmarks, *The Secret Relationship between Blacks and Jews* simply added the

As you look down from her once beautiful, now monstrous face, you see her stomach was crudely ripped opened to show not only her bowels and intestines but also to show an African fetus dangling on her umbilical chord.

You want to turn away and throw up but you can't. Something is forcing you to take in every detail, every swing of her body, every sound, every silence. There are many other Sisters — girls and women— who are just as transfixed.

Who are REMEMBERING. Who are

NEVER FORGETTING.

Illustration from The Black Holocaust for Beginners, *by S. E. Anderson; illustrated by Cro-Maat Collective and Vanessa Holley.*
© 1995, The Cro-Maat Collective; Vanessa Holley. Used by permission of Writers and Readers Publishing/Benay Enterprises, Inc.

ugly absurdity that it was Jews themselves who were principally responsible for the "Black African Holocaust."[65]

FATHER SON AND HOLOCAUST

The age of genocide, writes Terrence Des Pres in his study of the Nazi death camps, created the survivor as an indispensable type, his testimony evidence that "the moral self can resurrect itself from the inhuman depths through which it must pass."[66] That today's African American "survivor" lives with only a simulation of slavery's "unspeakable" memory does not disprove but rather verifies commensurability, according to Baldwin and Morrison, for not only are all African Americans survivors of slavery—just as all Jews are survivors of the Holocaust, symbolically present in the death camps—but they are also survivors of the continuing holocaust of American racism. Any two black people meeting in the street, in John Edgar Wideman's formulation, are instantly joined in a "shared sense of identity" formed by "the bloody secrets" of slavery and segregation: "To our everlasting shame and glory what we may recognize first is something we are not"—namely, not white, or perhaps Wideman means, in fact, not truly "American"—and because of that "something we are: survivors, carrying on."[67]

No writer has drawn more awful energy from this conception of black history than Wideman, and it is no surprise that his book most saturated in the rhetoric and imagery of genocide, *Philadelphia Fire* (1990), preceded *Fatheralong* (1994), a book that exhausted the paradigm of the black Exodus in recounting Wideman's journey back to his ancestral beginnings in the fortuitously named hamlet of Promised Land, South Carolina. Despite its endlessly inventive meditation on the themes of migration, exile, homeland, and the African roots of black consciousness, *Fatheralong* cannot escape the overhanging shadow of *Philadelphia Fire,* a fact evident in its opening assertion that the "brutal threshing" of the Middle Passage delivered Africans into an American Auschwitz: "I recall the archetypical scene of German officers in their greatcoats and shining boots processing long lines of Jews stumbling from trains that have transported them from every corner of Europe to the death camps."[68] Typologically subsuming Exodus into Holocaust—overlaying the example of the Jews going out of bondage with their going into ghettos, death camps, and crematoria—Wideman presents the most systematic renunciation of Mosaic deliverance in all of African American literature.

The framework for *Philadelphia Fire* was provided by the city's 1985 police action against MOVE, short for "the Movement," a black urban commune founded in the late 1960s by the magnetic cult figure John Africa, who espoused an arcane philosophy of vegetarianism, animal rights, Rastafarianism, and civil disobedience spelled out in an eight hundred–page typescript known as "The Guidelines." MOVE's conflicts with the neighboring community and city authorities led at length to a police assault on the group's fortified compound that left eleven members, including six children, dead and over two hundred homeless.[69] In a collage of narrative remnants—myriad allusions and puns spliced together, flights of Joycean, Ellisonian improvisation erupting out of nowhere—*Philadelphia Fire* builds an allegory of the incarceration of the black underclass around a skeletal story of the MOVE conflagration. Wideman employs two principal narrative voices to get inside this urban black holocaust—the cultured, if rueful, voice of the university-educated, quasi-autobiographical Cudjoe and the vernacular voice of his alter ego, the homeless J. B., a signifying avatar of John Africa and Shakespeare's Caliban, "exiled, dispossessed, [a] stranger in his own land."[70]

At the novel's center is the elliptical story of the child Simba Muntu,[71] rumored to have survived the conflagration. The metaphysical "black boy" Richard Wright made of himself, hardened by torment and despair, Simba is also a figuration of Wideman's son Jacob (Jake)—son of an African American man and a white Jewish American woman—who at age sixteen, for no apparent reason, stabbed to death Eric Kane, a Jewish companion of the same age, a crime for which he was sentenced to life in prison, his tragedy a near replica of the life sentence being served by Wideman's brother, Robert (Robby), a story told to great acclaim by Wideman in *Brothers and Keepers* (1984). As "the only survivor of the holocaust on Osage Avenue, the child who is brother, son, a lost limb haunting [Cudjoe]," Simba quickly assumes charismatic significance. The rumor of his survival—"Like Hitler's escape from the bunker. Like the Second Coming . . . the boy was last seen naked *skin melting, melting*"[72]—turns the psychodramatic tragedy of John Wideman, brother of a lost brother, father of a lost son, into an ungainly allegory of black persecution and redemption so as to signify what might yet be saved from the ruins of America's black ghettos and to prophesy the fiery end times that will otherwise be forthcoming.

From E. Franklin Frazier to Kenneth Clark to Orlando Patterson, missing fathers and abandoned sons have been central to critiques of the black family that portray it as wracked by inherited patterns of psychic damage and irresponsibility, enmeshed in a "tangle of pathology," as the Moynihan Report put it. Reflecting only a narrow statistical band of the underclass, behaviors associated with the "total institution" of the ghetto and what Clark referred to as the "engulfing pathology" of black American life are heavily inflected by the post-Holocaust understandings of racial victimization Wideman brings to bear in *Philadelphia Fire.** The archetype of filial relationship in this world, as Wideman writes in *Fatheralong,* is "the child visiting prison, speaking to his incarcerated father through a baffle in a filthy Plexiglas screen"—or, in his case, the father visiting the incarcerated son.[73]

It is instructive to place Wideman, in whose family a male of every recent generation has been imprisoned, more precisely within this tradition. In the oratory of Black Power and a subgenre of the Black Arts movement, prison was often portrayed either as a neo–slave plantation or as the prelude to the eliminationist design of white supremacists.[74] A microcosm of "Amerika's black colonies" as theorized by Eldridge Cleaver and Huey Newton, said George Jackson, American prisons "have always borne a certain resemblance to Dachau and Buchenwald, places for the big niggers, Mexicans, and poor whites." A counterpoint may be found in Elijah Muhammad and Malcolm X, for both of whom prison was also the site of religious enlightenment and purification in blackness. Wideman, however, identifies no such path to redemption. "I am a descendant of a special class of immigrants—Africans—for whom arrival in

---

* Building on the theoretical correlation between slavery and Nazism adduced by Stanley Elkins, studies of the psychological effects of the Holocaust by survivors Bruno Bettelheim and Victor Frankl, and the theory of "total institutions" advanced by Erving Goffman in *Asylums* (1961), Kenneth Clark's landmark study *Dark Ghetto,* as we saw in the previous chapter, argued that the black ghetto was a zone of "institutionalized pathology" not unlike the concentration camp. "Chronic, self-perpetuating," and therefore capable of inflicting long-term personality damage, said Clark, the pathology of the ghetto also posed a danger to those who sought to study it, a view that bears directly on Wideman's position in *Philadelphia Fire* as an observer at once detached from his subject and implicated in it. Explaining the methodology of *Dark Ghetto,* Clark noted that the risk to the "involved observer" is "distortion of vision and confusion." Questioning the "cult of objectivity" in social science, however, Clark also averred that anger and revulsion had a place in scholarship on the ghetto. After all, no one would worry that a scholar of the Nazi concentration camps who felt revolted by the evidence was lacking in objectivity; if he was not revolted, in fact, one would "fear for his sanity and moral sensitivity." It is notable, moreover, that Clark's statement comes on the heels of his reflections on Earl Warren's opinion in *Brown v. Board of Education,* which broke through legal technicalities and the equivocations of academic jargon to present a clear statement about "the inevitable anguish of rejected and stigmatized human beings." Clark's perspective on objectivity may also owe something to Justice Robert Jackson's opening address at the Nuremberg trials: "If I should recite these horrors in words of my own, you would think me intemperate and unreliable." Kenneth B. Clark, *Dark Ghetto: Dilemmas of Social Power,* 2nd ed. (1965; rpt. Hanover, N.H.: Wesleyan University Press, 1989), pp. xxxi, 76–80; Robert Jackson, *Nazi Conspiracy and Aggression,* 8 vols. (Washington, D.C.: United States Government, 1946), I, 140.

America was a life sentence in the prison of slavery," he says, and doing time is just one of the ways black men are kept captive in a nation that looks to "white-coated technocrats and bottom-line bureaucrats for efficient final solutions."[75] Standing in precarious opposition to the "genocidal fantasy of integration," Wideman's black nation is a "vast orphanage" ever on the brink of eradication, as in the devastation of MOVE, and the end point of black filiation is prison, the one total institution standing for others—slavery, the ghetto, the colonized nation, the concentration camp.[76]

Here is no "world of our fathers"[77] in which the devotion and sacrifice of ancestors, along with their rise from the ghetto, is lovingly memorialized. Here Simba's gang, the deracinated offspring of Black Power, rule the street according to an ideology stripped of purpose but still animated by historic archetypes of scapegoating and recrimination. Portending "the fire next time unless all [their] negative energy and anger are somehow transformed to useful purposes," as Wideman later commented, Simba's gangsters spray their mark in "rainbow signs"—is it "vandalism or tribal art or the handwriting on the wall"?—and terrorize a neighborhood of ghosts where once the intimately intertwined fate of Jews and blacks was played out. In a conglomeration of disjointed metaphors, a Jewish storekeeper, like a manic version of *The Great Gatsby*'s God-manqué, Dr. T. J. Eckleburg, has been transfigured into a police helicopter's panoptic surveillance: "the ghost of him outside the ghost of his store, old four-eyed Jew above you in the black sky who psyches you into looking up a minute so he can look down on you and say, Shame, shame, on you, boys. His bald helicopter head. Light on steel rims of his specs rotoring . . . on patrol in the air over top of where his store used to be." The gang members' vicious, impersonal violence may be seen as sullen, nihilistic hatred of the ghetto and all the racial deprivations for which it stands, but in attacking "the Jew," conjoined with their sexual assault on random white women, they also avenge their own emasculated fathers, assailing the family and community they have never had: "We the fist. Rammed up their giggies. The hard black fist. . . . Nothing you got is yours anyway. You know you stole it. . . . Mine now. My fingers in her silky hair and silky panties. My hand in your money box, Mr. Markowitz, hymie motherfucker."[78] For the ultra-masculine black "fist," the white girl's "giggie" and the Jew's money box are one in the same.

As the latter-day jeremiad of adolescent survivors, however, Simba's rap lyrics are driven by more than misogyny and Jew-baiting, and Wideman's appeal to Jewish history, whether biblical or modern, is carefully balanced between identification and repudiation:

In the park called Clark we rule the dark
Live like Noah in his ark
They tried to shoot us, bomb us
Drown us burn us
They brought us here, but they can't return us.
We the youth, the truth
. . . we was born in hell
Cooked lean and mean in the fiery furnace . . .
We own the night, gonna rule the day
You brought us here and we're here to stay.[79]

The variegated sociological, autobiographical, and biblical sources from which Wideman constructs this sample of Simba's language, a tale of slavery and its heritage derived from the "fiery furnace" in the Book of Daniel and *The Fire Next Time,** make for a scattershot attempt to interpret the murder and incarceration of black males that had reached seemingly epidemic proportions by the early 1990s, along with drug wars and the glamorization of gang culture. Yet it is not the early Baldwin whose spirit most presides over *Philadelphia Fire*—a text pervaded by false rainbows and even more by figures of fire and ash—but rather the later Baldwin, for whom the promise of the post–*Brown v. Board of Education* years had given way to a regime of American neo-Nazism.

At one point Cudjoe recounts to his friend Timbo a nightmare in which his faith in the message of civil rights anthems fades into his witness of a boy lynched from a basketball rim: "A kid hanging there with his neck broken and drawers droopy and caked with shit and piss. It's me and every black boy I've ever seen running up and down playing ball." Cudjoe's nightmare compresses

---

* Although "the park called Clark" is a real locale near Osage Avenue, the richly signifying Wideman may have intended an allusion to Kenneth Clark. The fiery furnace, like the handwriting on the wall, comes from the Book of Daniel, a book of apocalyptic filled with dream visions and enigmatic symbolism, but Wideman may have borrowed more immediately from the well-known episode in Baldwin's book in which he recounts revealing to his father that he has a Jewish friend. His cold reply to his intolerant father, who asks him whether his friend is saved—"No. He's Jewish."—elicits a whopping slap and underscores both Baldwin's apostasy and his hatred of his father. Until that time, the only Jews Baldwin had encountered were the prophets of the Old Testament, and he can find no connection between the boys he knows and the Jewish pawnbrokers in the ghetto, both of whom seem far removed from Egypt and "the fiery furnace" (Daniel 3). But the torments of hell that his father expects will be visited upon an unconverted Jew remind Baldwin instead of the Jews in another Christian nation, Germany, and the "fiery furnace" made real for them in the Nazi genocide. James Baldwin, *The Fire Next Time* (1963; rpt. New York: Dell, 1964), p. 55.

the history of Jim Crow violence, the MOVE assault, and the fruitless blandish-
ments of welfare into a campaign of state-endorsed genocide. ("People said"
the ghetto's basketball courts, erected, starting in the 1960s, with "four high
metal sides" and cyclone fencing, were "part of the final solution.") Insisting
that there is more to the dream than the death of a single boy, Timbo goads
Cudjoe to expand upon his story: "You're talking miniseries. Child murders. . . .
Cops. KKK." KKK stands here not just for Ku Klux Klan but also for "Kaliban's
Kiddie Korps," Simba's new generation of disfranchised and abandoned black
youth roaming the streets and plotting bloody hip-hop insurrection.[80] In referring to the Atlanta child murders, moreover, Timbo points specifically to *Evidence of Things Not Seen*, for which Wideman, perhaps foreshadowing his willing adoption of Baldwin's mantle, provided a generous, perhaps self-reflexive
blurb: "Baldwin's way of seeing, his clarity, precision, and eloquence, are
unique. . . . He speaks as great Gospel music speaks, through metaphor, parable, rhythm."[81]

For Baldwin, the Atlanta murders typified a nation where the FBI and the Ku
Klux Klan might be in league to slaughter a new generation of black boys; for
Wideman, Philadephia's MOVE catastrophe typifies a nation where the police
are the military arm of a fascist government eager to lay waste an outlaw cult
masquerading as a sovereign black state: "City in flames crackling against the
horizon. . . . Loud pops of automatic weapons fire scything down naked bodies
lined up against walls and fences . . . the hot wind of fire storms smashing
whole city blocks. . . . Walls are tumbling, burning-hot walls on tender babies. . . . Best to let it burn. All of it burn."[82] Realizing the prophecy pronounced
upon the Negro when he migrated from the rural South to what Baldwin, following E. Franklin Frazier, called the North's "cities of destruction,"[83] *Philadelphia Fire* makes "Burn, Baby, Burn," once a slogan of resistance, its epitaph for
a ghetto turned crematorium.

Joshua's conquest of Jericho, commemorated in a famous African American
spiritual to which Wideman refers several times, and later in Bob Marley's
"Jump Nyabinghi" ("It remind me of the days in Jericho / When we trodding
down Jericho walls . . . We keep on trodding until Babylon falls"),[84] is one prototype for Wideman's vision of Philadelphia under siege. So is Jerusalem and
its captive Jews saved by Nehemiah, in which Glenn Loury found a template for
rescuing the black underclass captive within the decayed walls of urban America: "The remnant that are left of the captivity there in the province are in great
affliction and reproach: the wall of Jerusalem also is broken down, and the
gates thereof are burned with fire" (Nehemiah 1:3). But Wideman's Philadelphia, envisioned by William Penn as "a greene Country Towne, which will

never be burnt, and always be wholesome,"[85] is destroyed, not saved, and it finally has more in common with the wicked Babylon portrayed in Elijah Muhammad's *Fall of America*, destined for destruction because the nation will not repent.

It is hard to discriminate among the different planes of moral action in *Philadelphia Fire*, where black kinship with Jews coexists with anti-Semitic revulsion; where Caliban is at once a dreadlocked revolutionary and an Auschwitz *Muselmann*, picking curses out of the language taught him "like starving prisoners in concentration camps straining kernels of corn from do do";[86] and where governmental firebombing converges with black uprising, each the spark for imminent end times in which Revelation and the Holocaust have an equal share. Wideman's seemingly deliberate confusion of purpose extends finally to the very idea of a "black holocaust," as may be seen in the final roles assigned to his two storytellers, J. B. and Cudjoe.

Having morphed into an itinerant arsonist, J. B. searches for a job that will pay his bills and feed his wife and children, even though he has ceased to believe they are alive. In this world, the homeless men whose families are held hostage in an "electrified, poison-staked stockade" constitute a maroon community who "refuse to return from the jungle and work the rubber plantations." In this world, where the plantation, the concentration camp, and the ghetto coexist in historical layers, the black overseer has become the black prison guard, the black ghetto cop, the black *Kapo*. In this world, a police roundup of the homeless glides into a surreal reenactment of the Final Solution, which calls up the suffocating ship's hold of the Middle Passage and the castration that often accompanied lynching, turning the black man's head into a penis that does not bear the sign of the covenant but is nevertheless marked for extermination:

> The noose slips silently over their unwashed uncircumcised necks. They cry like babies. Cops herd them with cattle prods into the holds of unmarked vans. Black Marias with fake shower heads in their airtight rear compartments, a secret button under the dash. Zyklon B drifts down quietly, casually as the net. Don't know what hit you till you're coughing and gagging and puking and everybody in a funky black stew rolling around on the floor.[87]

His life comprising the long penal history of black America, J. B. himself is finally doused in kerosene and set on fire by prankster white kids who steal his briefcase containing the "Book of Life"—Wideman's version of "The Guide-lines"—with its deranged utopian promises.

In "playing father son and holocaust to the kids running wild in streets and vacant lots,"[88] J. B. becomes a sacrificial figure—literally a "holocaust," a "burnt offering"—without becoming a savior. Signifying on "Holy Ghost"/"Holocaust," Wideman asserts an equivalence between the redemptive suffer-ing narrated throughout black Christianity—the spirituals, the sermonic tradi-tion, the poetry of the Black Christ, and their adaptations in the latter-day scripture of James Baldwin or Martin Luther King, Jr.—and the destruction of the European Jews. In the grating dissonance of his assertion that the Christian Trinity may illuminate the Holocaust—that the sacrificial drama of Christ's crucifixion and resurrection may illuminate the Nazis' attempt to kill the world's Jews—Wideman signifies as well on objections that the term "Holo-caust" inevitably, and wrongly, implies that the mass murder of Jews could be redemptive, that it could signify in any way a sacrificial offering.

Insofar as Wideman's focus here is on perpetrators, not victims, his disturb-ing play on words is appropriate to that distinction. Although the Holocaust was a German, not specifically a Christian, act of genocide, the racial mysti-cism of Nazism turned the traditional anti-Semitic charges of blood libel and deicide into a biological principle of human stratification in which the Holy Ghost might be worshipped through murder. The Reich would be made ra-cially pure, and those who purportedly killed Christ and supped on the blood of Christian children would be eliminated in a war of holy purpose. In the spectacular if blasphemous terms of Wideman's Passion play, J. B. could there-fore be said to incarnate the "father son and holocaust," a symbolic victim sacrificed to cleanse the Fourth Reich of America, much as John Africa and his followers, in Wideman's view, were purged to cleanse Philadelphia. More cer-tainly, J. B. is one culmination of the African American dialogue with Jewish history, a perfect recasting of the savior of Black Theology—the Black Jesus Christ, the "true Jew"—as Holocaust victim. In his identification with Cudjoe, however, Wideman created for himself an even more challenging role, also bor-rowed from the Jews, that of a witness with the potential, or at least the fantasy, of preserving the world's fragile humanity.

After a hard game of basketball, drinking, and walking the city at night, an exhausted Cudjoe imagines he will fall asleep and be found frozen like "one of the Lamed-Vov, the thirty-six Just Men, God's hostages who must thaw a thou-sand years after they've done their turn of suffering on earth."[89] According to Talmudic legend, there are in the world at any given time thirty-six righteous men, unknown to one another and those around them, on whom the continued existence of the world depends. A *Lamed-Vav Tzaddik* (or, in Yiddish, *Lamed-Vovnik*) has the mystical power to avert disasters, as during a pogrom or other threat to Jews, after which he returns to anonymity (in some accounts he will emerge as the Messiah, if the age proves worthy). Wideman's usage appears to have been influenced by André Schwarz-Bart's widely read Holocaust novel *The Last of the Just* (1959), in which a single family, generation after generation since the Middle Ages, has contained a *Lamed-Vovnik,* all the way up to Ernie Levy, who perishes with his family in Auschwitz as a compassionate witness to the precipitating events leading to a fiery disaster he can do nothing to avert.

The title of the final chapter of *The Last of the Just,* "Never Again," has a double meaning, referring at once to the post-Holocaust admonition against any future Judeocide and to the fact that these millions of Jews, and this representative family, will never again live and will have perished in an event whose intent was that Jews would never again appear on earth. Both these meanings, no doubt resonant for Wideman, are conveyed by Schwarz-Bart, the only one of his own family to survive the Holocaust, in a chapter whose power comes from its calm recitation of the Levy family's envelopment in the Nazis' "*Vernichtungswissenschaft*—the science of massacre, the art of extermination"—in a setting commensurate with the fiery end times of Wideman's novel. Within a scene of industrialized killing dominated by images of fire, Schwarz-Bart situates Jews dying in the gas chamber reciting the *Shema,** the verse "that through the smoke of fires and above the funeral pyres of history the Jews . . . had traced in letters of blood," and he recounts the legend of Rabbi Chanina ben Teradion, who was wrapped in the flaming scrolls of the Torah when burned to death by the Romans and whose final words become Ernie's when he succumbs: *"Ah, yes, the letters are taking wing."*[90]

Perhaps Wideman intends no specific allusion to Schwarz-Bart, but in an alternative version of the scene in which the "Book of Life" is stolen by the boys who set J. B. on fire, Wideman has him instead watch as the Book, with its message of revolutionary redemption, is consumed in flames: "The book he's singing from snaps shut. Is smoke in his hands. Ashes. He beats down flames on the crackling pages." No allusion need be present, however, for us to recognize the role of the *Lamed-Vav* in *Philadelphia Fire.* The MOVE memorial service at-

---

* "Hear, O Israel! The Lord is our God, the Lord alone" (Deuteronomy 6:4) is the opening line of morning and evening prayers that affirms monotheism, the love of God, and a willingness to live by the commandments. The prayer is recited by the dying and is especially commemorated, as Schwartz-Bart uses it, as the final words of martyrs.

tended by Cudjoe draws only a ragtag crowd to hear miscellaneous speakers, among them a dreadlocked man, perhaps a surviving J. B., who chants a "hymn to death and rebirth by fire," and prophesies "more fire next time." Although the organizers of the event promise to heal the city's wounds through "observance, atonement, education, and cultural expression," the memorial provides Cudjoe no catharsis but instead prompts his hallucination of a mob coming for him: "He'd known them all his life. *Never again. Never again.*"[91]

The Last of the Just runs the risk that Jewish history, even Judaism itself, will be reduced to martyrdom. But the *Lamed-Vav* of the Levy family stand as well for acts of redemption, or at least consolation, and the last Just Man's role as savior, because he cannot prevent the Nazi genocide, is subordinate to his role as witness: "He senses all the evil rampant on earth, and he takes it into his heart."[92] Throughout *Philadelphia Fire*, Wideman, too, subordinates his role as savior to his role as witness, but in the genocidal world of black America that he portrays, there is no recitation of the *Shema*, no redemption, no language of transcendence—no rainbows, only the fire this time. "Father son and holocaust" have become interchangeable terms in a new trinity of racial destruction and the Exodus an endless death march.

Just as Jews have worried that Holocaust commemoration might supplant the covenantal meaning of Exodus in Jewish life and liturgy, however, so African Americans might well worry about black life, during slavery and after, being turned into a catalogue of atrocities, its transcendent and triumphant cultural legacy subordinated to measureless suffering and incalculable damage. This hazard is nowhere more evident than in the contemporary reparations movement, which ranges in its public expressions from concrete, pragmatic attempts to achieve restitution for specific, remediable harms to wild-eyed accusations that blacks have been the victims of a genocidal catastrophe beyond all human understanding.

WHAT YOU OWE ME

Numerous individuals and groups, from Marcus Garvey through the Black Panthers, have called for monetary reparations or, in the case of Elijah Muhammad, the Communist Party, the Republic of New Africa, and others, for the allocation of large areas of contiguous territory in which a black nation might be established. James Forman's "Black Manifesto," discussed in Chapter 5, was the best-known demand for reparations in the civil rights era. More than three decades later, a report prepared for the 2001 United Nations–sponsored World Conference against Racism in Durban, South Africa, recommended lavishly that the UN establish an International Compensation Scheme "for victims of the slave trade, as well as victims of any other transnationalist racist policies and acts," and a Development Reparation Fund to provide resources for "countries affected by colonialism."[93] All such proposals have taken inspiration from the Federal Indemnification Laws through which Germany, starting in 1952, has paid more than $60 billion to some 500,000 Holocaust survivors in Israel and other countries, and then again from the $8 billion paid in 1999 to Jewish and non-Jewish victims by German, French, Austrian, and Swiss companies enriched by their slave labor and stolen assets. Demands for reparations for black Americans have looked as well to the restitution paid by the United States government in recent decades to various American Indian tribes and in 1988 to Japanese Americans interned during World War II.

To date, the most successful African American claimants have been those harmed by specific acts of twentieth-century racial violence, as in Rosewood, Florida, and Tulsa, Oklahoma,[94] and the most promising, though as yet unproven, strategy to emerge is litigation directed at businesses or other institutions that can be proved to have profited from slavery.[95] Otherwise, the contemporary reparations movement is represented by an eclectic range of proponents, from Michigan representative John Conyers, who every year from 1989 on introduced a congressional bill to study reparations,[96] to the group of whites affiliated with the Nation of Islam known as CURE (Caucasians United for Reparations and Emancipation), which seeks reparations while abasing itself before the spiritually superior power of blackness.[97] The ideological case for restitution, reminiscent of Du Bois, has been ably stated by Clarence Munford: "Our unpaid forced labor laid the foundations of the western capitalist order, and no other. Our enslavement alone enabled European civilization to snare the western hemisphere, appropriate its resources, and anchor white wealth and might in the Americas."[98] (But compare the caustic answer from David Horowitz: because of the antislavery movement, the outcome of the Civil War, long-term American dedication to the principle of equality, and the nation's high standard of living, African Americans "enjoy the greatest freedoms and the most thoroughly protected individual rights anywhere. Where is the acknowledgment of black America and its leaders for those gifts?")[99] A narrower claim holds that all blacks who are the descendants of slaves have been injured because slavery took away property that would eventually have been theirs, in however derivative a form, and that countless individuals, whether or not they were directly involved in the use of slave labor or in financing slavery, profited in some way from uncompensated African American labor, as have their descendants.

It is not slavery alone, however, that is at issue. A century or more of discrimination, often enforced by vigilantism, increased rather than decreased the debt owed to African Americans, as blacks were harmed by exclusion from employment opportunities and union membership, by redlining in federal housing and other loan programs, by segregated and substandard schooling, and by other racially discriminatory practices. Prompted by Forman's "Black Manifesto," Boris I. Bittker's *Case for Black Reparations* (1973), one of the earliest briefs for reparations based on constitutional argument, outlined a plan wherein reparations would be limited to those able to prove damage sustained under the laws of segregation. Bittker excluded the harm done by slavery since the damages would be far harder to substantiate, but he offered a philosophical rationale as well. Egypt has not had to provide "compensation for what Pharaoh did to the ancient Hebrews," said Bittker. (Indeed, just the opposite case, presumably a hoax, has been made against the world's Jews on behalf of the pharaohs.)[100] More seriously, he pointed out that Germany instituted reparations only for Holocaust victims and their families, not for the descendants of victims of previous pogroms or those confined in medieval ghettos and the Russian Pale of Settlement, where they may, in fact, have benefited from the "intense communal life, free from the values of the outside world," forced on them by state-mandated anti-Semitism. Bittker recognized that compensation to African Americans based on segregation was itself fraught with problems, especially when forced segregation began to mix with nationalist self-segregation, but such an approach at least presented a chronological delineation that made the calculation of "profit and loss" somewhat more reliable.[101]

The exact cost of removing blacks "from dependence on others (the government, and the descendants of slave owners and colonizers)," says the National Coalition of Blacks for Reparations in America (N'COBRA), one of the movement's leading forces, remains to be determined. N'COBRA declared itself willing to leave things open-ended: "Once we know how much damage has been done to us, and what is required to repair the damage, we will know how much is owed." In contrast to "the four year internment of Japanese in America, or the five year holocaust of Jewish people in Europe," however, a different set of remedies may be necessary for "the 500 years holocaust of Africans in America," and thus compensation of a very different magnitude.[102] By David Horowitz's calculation, means-tested poverty programs launched by the War on Poverty have been responsible for a transfer of $1.3 trillion to African Americans,[103] but reparations proponents counter that the benefits of equal op-

portunity programs, welfare, affirmative action, and other compensatory programs directed to date at blacks cannot possibly equal the assets accumulated
and the advantages accrued by whites since the end of slavery, not counting the
wealth produced by slavery itself. N'COBRA tentatively offers a figure of $8
trillion, and figures running from billions to trillions of dollars have been calculated by all manner of formulas.* Justice, by this argument, will be achieved
only by a massive redistribution of white wealth.

Once such reparations are paid, surmises Robert Westley, who has proposed
a trust financed by funds drawn from the general revenue of the United States

---

* Although he meant only to venture one rough means of calculating the cost, Bittker suggested multiplying the 1969 gap between black and white per capita income ($1,510) by the number of blacks (22.5
million), thus producing an annual reparations cost of $34 billion, which would need to be sustained for
a decade or two. Less precise rationales have inevitably produced less precise—and usually more extravagant—estimates. Just an educational program aimed at repairing the damage to psyches and recon-
necting black children to their African identities through "a reafrikanization process of the mind," says
Yaa Asantewa Nzingha, will cost $128.1 billion. In presenting to Congress its 1987 plan for "An Act to
Stimulate Economic Growth in the United States and Compensate, in part, for the Grievous Wrongs of
Slavery and Unjust Enrichment which Accrued to the United States Therefrom," N'COBRA asked for $3
billion annually, with no end date indicated, to be divided among direct support to black families, the
elected government of the Republic of New Africa, and a National Congress of Organizations, including
churches and community groups, committed to ending "the scourge of drugs and crime in New Afrikan
communities" and advancing economic, educational, social, and cultural opportunities. One economist's inflation-adjusted estimate of the unpaid net wages before emancipation, without interest, was
$1.4 trillion, while the Republic of New Africa has argued for $4.1 trillion. Impatient with such piddling
efforts to monetize black damage, Haki Madhubuti rendered in verse form what America owed blacks
and American Indians together: "Count the stars in all of the galaxies and multiply in / dollars by 100
billion, / For a reflective start." Beginning in 1993, the IRS was besieged annually by reparation claims
springing from L. G. Sherrod's article in *Essence* asserting that blacks were owed a rebate of $43,209 (she
determined that this difference between the median wealth of whites and blacks, according to the 1990
census, was the modern-day equivalent of "forty acres and a mule"), as well as from a scam by the so-
called Legal Defense Fund, which asked for a $4,000 fee for alerting claimants to the money purportedly
owed them by the IRS. Although several people were sent to prison for preparing false returns for clients
or proposing to do so, the larger problem did not disappear. In 2001, as many as eighty thousand reparations claims, seeking more than $2 billion, were filed with the IRS. Boris I. Bittker, *The Case for Black
Reparations* (New York: Random House, 1973), p. 131; Yaa Asantewa Nzingha, "Reparations + Education
= The Pass to Freedom," in Raymond A. Winbush, ed., *Should America Pay? Slavery and the Raging De-
bate on Reparations* (New York: HarperCollins, 2003), pp. 312–13; Robin D. G. Kelley, *Freedom Dreams:
The Black Radical Imagination* (Boston: Beacon Press, 2002), p. 127; Christopher Hitchens, "Debt of
Honor," *Vanity Fair* 490 (June 2001), 88; Elazar Barkan, *The Guilt of Nations: Restitution and Negotiating
Historical Injustices* (New York: W. W. Norton, 2000), pp. 289–91; Haki Madhubuti, "The United States'
Debt Owed to Black People," in Winbush, *Should America Pay?*, p. 285; Clarence Page, "Reparation Rip-
Offs Exploit Dreams," *Chicago Tribune*, February 6, 2002, sec. 1, 19.

annually for a ten-year period, blacks will "function within American society on a footing of absolute equality," their "chance for public happiness" the same as that of any white citizen. Yet no other programs of reparation, certainly not those directed at Holocaust survivors, have ever rested on such an untenable premise. Aspirations of repair, remarks Martha Minow, will be defeated by any suggestion that after restitution it will be "as if the violations never occurred," by any attempt to sidestep continuing responsibility for "the enormity of what was done."[104] As it happens, however, Minow's qualification is also the very essence of objections to reparations. The demand for reparations is based "on a paradigm of black existence rooted in shame," in which self-advancement can occur only through demeaning self-abnegation, says John McWhorter, and it thus perpetuates the very damages it seeks to redress. In contrast to Minow and to Mari Matsuda, who argues that the lack of legal redress compounds historical injuries by signifying the "political nonpersonhood of the victims," McWhorter emphasizes the compound harm done to blacks by imprisoning them in an identity defined forever by suffering—creating, one might say instead, a "nonpersonhood" of perpetual victimhood. The memory of oppression far outlives oppression itself—"the scar does the work of the wound," as Leon Wieseltier has written—and pain becomes a tradition in its own right.[105]

Absent a concrete application, one that reaches beyond local cases of specific injury such as those in Rosewood and Tulsa, it is hard to test such objections. Reparations, by definition, do not restore what has been lost—certainly not in the sense of the Latin root of *repatriare*, to go back to one's home country—but only "repair" incompletely, even inconclusively, what has been damaged. African Americans who seek healing through reparations would do well to bear in mind Dan Pagis's "Draft of a Reparations Agreement," a wrenching post-Holocaust poem that, in its deliberately absurd promise, reveals what will *not* be restored through monetary compensation:

> Everything will be returned to its place,
> paragraph after paragraph.
> The scream back into the throat.
> The gold teeth back into the gums.
> The terror.
> The smoke back to the tin chimney and further on and inside
> back to the hollow of the bones,
> and already you will be covered with skin and sinews and you will live,
> look, you will have your lives back . . .[106]

A symbolic national apology is likely to be of little consequence.* But without at least the semblance of reparations—the planned National Museum of African American History and Culture will surely be the most widely accepted and effective[107]—imprisonment in an identity defined by suffering will persist. Theories of "post-traumatic slave syndrome," the "traumatic psychological and emotional injury" sustained by blacks as a direct result of slavery and later policies of "inequality, racism, and oppression," will continue to gain ground.[108] And overstated comparisons between the black holocaust and the Jewish Holocaust will remain a standard component of the latter-day civil rights agenda.

The foregrounding of reparations in African American responses to the example of the Holocaust has also had a further, less elevating consequence. If reparations are justified not simply as the recompense owed by whites (or the Western world) to Africans in the diapora (or to Africans generally) but specifically as what Jews owe to African Americans, then the stakes of invidious comparison are considerably raised. "Getting pulled over by the cops is the black boy's Bar Mitzvah," says a character in Bebe Moore Campbell's *What You Owe Me* (2001),[109] a novel, as the title suggests, devoted to the question of what is due to blacks, both monetarily and spiritually, for their historical exploitation and suffering. But those who owe in this case are not the millions upon millions of white Americans who might be said to have profited directly or indirectly at the

---

* The quasi-Lincolnesque speech of President George W. Bush on Goree Island, Senegal, in July 2003 had the air of an apology, but culpability was quickly absorbed into a drama of guilt and redemption in which slaves played the role of saviors. "At this place, liberty and life were stolen and sold," said Bush. "Human beings were delivered and sorted, and weighed, and branded with the marks of commercial enterprises, and loaded as cargo on a voyage without return." Although Bush recognized that "years of unpunished brutality and bullying and rape produced a dullness and hardness of conscience that harmed slaveholders as well as slaves," making Christian men and women "blind to the clearest commands of their faith," and making "one of the largest migrations of history . . . one of the greatest crimes of history," he also undercut any claim to reparations by raising the whole episode to a trans-historic level in which compensation of the victims of slavery appeared to come through their being recognized as moral exemplars. In America, said Bush, "enslaved Africans learned the story of the exodus from Egypt" and were likewise inspired by faith in the savior Jesus and the Declaration of Independence, which they demanded must apply to them as well. Somewhat in the manner of Ellison, Bush attributed to African Americans themselves, who "have upheld the ideals of America by exposing laws and habits contradicting those ideals," the task and reward of redeeming the promise of democracy: "By a plan known only to Providence, the stolen sons and daughters of Africa helped to awaken the conscience of America. The very people traded into slavery helped to set America free." "President Bush Speaks at Goree Island in Senegal," July 8, 2003, http://www.whitehouse.gov/news/releases/2003/07/print/20030708–1.html (accessed July 15, 2003).

expense of blacks, but one individual Jew. The argument that the Jews in particular owe reparations to blacks has mainly been the province of the Nation of Islam and others on the anti-Semitic fringe. (After singling out Jews for their purported central role in slavery and the slave trade, Tony Martin cited German reparations as a model for the "moral profit" to be gained by Jews in offering their own monetary restitution to blacks.)[110] Campbell by no means belongs in that category, but despite its qualifying complications, *What You Owe Me* is a prescription for the recovery of the black-Jewish alliance that depends on consenting to the beliefs that Jews are "white" and that it is their custom to exploit blacks.

Campbell's black protagonist, Hosanna Clark, befriends the Holocaust survivor Gilda Rosenstein in 1948. Together they establish a cosmetics business, but Gilda, for reasons of a family crisis explained later in the novel, disappears with their money and then makes only halfhearted efforts in subsequent years to find and repay Hosanna. Both women's businesses are ultimately successful, but Gilda's much more so. As the novel unfolds, we discover that the Rosenstein family's fortune was seized by the Nazis, that the rest of the family perished, and that Gilda was the victim of concentration camp medical experiments; for Hosanna's part, her family's land in Texas was stolen in the 1940s and her sister brutally raped by a gang of white men. Gilda collects $8 million in Swiss reparations, while the Clark family joins a class-action lawsuit filed by descendants of the black Texans who lost their land fifty years earlier. Because of her Holocaust survivor's guilt, mixed with shame over her treatment of Hosanna, Gilda has supported the development of black businesses, and fifty years later we find Hosanna's daughter Matriece Carter, unbeknownst to Gilda, working for Gilda's glamorous company and making her own mark by launching a line of beauty products marketed to African American women. Once she discovers Matriece's identity, Gilda makes final restitution to Hosanna and her descendants by selling her company to Matriece and her backers at a very favorable discount.

On the face of it, *What You Owe Me* concludes on a high moral note of forgiveness and reconciliation. Based on the fictional test case of two families, the novel suggests that the postwar partnership between Jews and blacks, which fell into acrimony over a period of four decades, can somehow be restored. The wounds of the past can be healed, and each people can achieve justice. Just as Jews harmed by genocidal anti-Semitism or their descendants have been able to recover some measure of financial and moral recompense, so African Americans might now hope to do the same. To be sure, black reparations, whatever form they may take in the future, have not yet been achieved: "There are bones in the earth that cry out for both vengeance and peace. Unsettled spirits still roam."[111] The kind of class-action lawsuit joined by the Clarks, Campbell implies, therefore offers the best hope of achieving a comparable recompense. Like the Rosewood and Tulsa cases, and unlike the amorphous harm done to slaves in times long past, such losses can be more or less accurately estimated and reparations paid.

A multigenerational romantic saga, *What You Owe Me* features a panoply of family estrangements, conflicts, and reunions on both sides of the racial divide, but the central conflict between black and Jew remains unresolved because of the very way in which the problem is posed. Campbell places Gilda in the archetypal role of the Jewish immigrant who, once she sees that her whiteness conceals her otherness, is willing to leave her black partner behind. "No, she didn't look like those blond, blue-eyed beauties in the movies with their thin, turned-up noses," says Hosanna of Gilda's racial ambiguity, "but she didn't look like me. America loved her better. All she had to do was spread her wings and fly. She got more out of being here than I did, and she hadn't been here as long or worked as hard." Or, as Gilda says to Matriece in her moment of confession: "Black people in this country had to suffer, and if I chose to be with one I would suffer as well. And, my dear, I had suffered enough. I could be white if I separated from your mother."[112]

Blacks are too forgiving, says the man whose barbeque business provides the launching point for Hosanna's success after Gilda steals her money: "You think Jews forgave Hitler? You think they go to Germany for vacation and spend their money there?"[113] The residual implication that the black is a guileless, forgiving victim and the Jew dishonest and unforgiving trades on base stereotypes, even if it does so in a softened manner that, in the individual characters and action portrayed, remains dramatically plausible. Gilda is a figure to be emulated for her business acumen and for the recompense awarded her on account of her own racial suffering; but, as her name seems to connate, Gilda is also a version of "Goldberg," the archetype of Jewish exploitation of blacks in the ghetto* or otherwise. It might be argued that the debt she owes Hosanna's family is purely

---

* Many blacks, of course, have remembered not exploitation but assistance. To cite one autobiographical account that appeared at about the same time as Campbell's novel, University of California regent and affirmative action opponent Ward Connerly recalled the job he held as a teenager, in early 1950s Sacramento, in Manny Schwartz's fabric store, one of several Jewish businesses that actively sought to hire young black men. Although he was not "pampered," Connerly writes, he surely was not exploited, for "the Schwartzes arranged their needs to fit with my part-time availability because they wanted to help me." Ward Connerly, *Creating Equal: My Fight against Race Preferences* (San Francisco: Encounter Books, 2000), pp. 52–53.

a function of Jews' whiteness (Gilda may not be blond and blue-eyed, but she certainly is not "black"), just as it might be argued that the Holocaust reparations paid to Gilda herself are no less than what *she* is owed for suffering far more horrible than losing one's land or being cheated by a business partner. It is, however, in the conjunction of these two arguments—Jews have been repaid for their tragedy, while blacks have not; not only have Jews made it in America, while blacks have not, but they have done so at the expense of blacks—that Campbell's novel moves uncomfortably close to reaffirming the rancorous allegations she presumably means to overcome.

The very title of the novel, of course, carries the further implication that it is not just Gilda who owes restitution to Hosanna or her descendants for what was stolen from them, but that somehow these individuals stand symbolically for what Jews as a people owe blacks. By making a Holocaust survivor her representative Jew, Campbell grafted the problem of comparability onto the breakdown of the black-Jewish alliance by means of the mediating but precisely targeted concept of reparations—"what I am owed" translated into "what you owe me." Whatever Gilda offers to Hosanna's descendants in recompense or renewed partnership, the novel seems to say, it is Gilda's betrayal, the betrayal of the black by the Jew, that must be forgiven, just as it is Hosanna's forgiveness, the forgiveness of the Jew by the black, that must be earned if blacks and Jews are to be reconciled. By the time Campbell was writing, neither seemed likely.

II. OTHER PEOPLE'S NIGHTMARES

The black-Jewish dialogue taken on the road to college campuses and community organizations during the mid-1990s by Michael Lerner and Cornel West was meant, along with their co-authored book, *Jews and Blacks* (1995), to show the possibility of reconciliation, at least on the left side of the political spectrum. Like other commentaries of the day—Jonathan Kaufman's *Broken Alliance*, (1988), Jack Salzman's *Bridges and Boundaries*, (1992), Paul Berman's *Blacks and Jews*, (1994), and Murray Friedman's *What Went Wrong?* (1995), to name just a few—their dialogue and their book addressed a rift created in the postwar era by the increasing educational, economic, and social divergence of the two groups and subsequently exacerbated by emblematic conflicts easily catalogued: Black Power; Israel and the Palestinians; Ocean Hill–Brownsville; quotas; "Hymietown"; "Sixty Million and more"; Crown Heights; *The Secret*

Relationship between Blacks and Jews. Lerner and West were hardly alone in supposing that there once was a true and meaningful alliance—after all, how could something that never existed generate such passionate reexamination?— or in believing that it could be revived, but their effort seemed in some respects sadly superannuated.

The same might be observed of literary efforts. A large audience welcomed the sentimental version of the alliance symbolically recreated in *Driving Miss Daisy,* Alfred Uhry's Pulitzer Prize–winning play (1987) and Academy Award– winning film (1989) about the initially abrasive but ultimately tender relation- ship between a southern Jewish matron, Miss Daisy, and her black chauffeur, Hoke. As it unfolds from 1948 to 1973, *Driving Miss Daisy* tells a story of black, rather than Jewish, tutelage and of acquired commonalities, a kind of *To Kill a Mockingbird* redux ("How you know the way I see, 'less you lookin' outta my eyes," Hoke asks Daisy).[1] Set against the backdrop of an evolving South in which Jews become whiter and blacks become freer, but carefully framed to recognize the customs of segregation, Uhry's play and film portrayed an inter- racial romance devoid of sexual threat. His alliance was at once moving and sterile—thrust from the vantage point of 1987 back into a moment of friend- ship briefly achieved but likely to disappear altogether, it is implied, with the coming deaths of Daisy and Hoke.

Although he traversed not just twenty-five years but much of the century in an epic novel devoted to the high idealism shared by a Jewish immigrant and his African American wife, Richard Powers pointed to a future no more prom- ising. *The Time of Our Singing* (2003), a beautifully crafted interracial drama stretching from Marian Anderson's 1939 concert at the Lincoln Memorial through the 1963 March on Washington and on to the Million Man March in 1995, holds out the hope, stated and restated elegantly throughout the novel but destined to be unfulfilled, that America—Jews and blacks in this test case—can somehow go "beyond race."

Seeing that chosenness ends in racial annihilation for his own family and millions of others, David Strom, a German émigré, Columbia professor, and Manhattan Project scientist, proposes that he and his wife, Delia Daley, an as- piring concert singer, make such a new world. Based on his life's work in nu- clear physics and their mutual love of music, David envisions a world beyond conventional time in which their hypothetical children will be "charter citizens of the postrace place, both races, no races, *race* itself: blending unblended, like notes stacked up in a chord." Their three actual children, matured in the caul- dron of the 1960s, test the proposition. Jonah and Joseph, prodigiously tal- ented, choose the universalist path of music, while Ruth, convinced that a fire which takes the life of their mother was an act of racially motivated arson, chooses the particularist path of radical activism and becomes a Black Panther. Pointing to the liaisons of Abraham, Joseph, and Solomon with black or Egyptian women, David insists to his militant daughter, "I am not a white man; I'm a Jew." In Ruth's eyes, however, her father is deluded, and in any event Jews cannot help blacks, because "it's not their fight."[2]

The novel's epic scale, as well as its contrapuntal narration, with time frames woven into one another and reenforced by the repetition of themes, habits, scenes, and motifs, unfolds on the model of David's scientific work, which concerns "closed timelike loops . . . curves in time [in which] events can move continuously into their own local future while turning back into their own past." It concludes, suitably, in a patchwork familial reconciliation, with Joseph, Ruth, and her sons—Ruth's husband having been gunned down by the police and Jonah having died as a bystander in the Los Angeles riot of 1992—coming together at the Million Man March. But the Day of Atonement called by Louis Farrakhan celebrated not a "postrace" world but one of racial grievance, and the remnants of the Strom family—black, not Jewish—live still under the sober objection to the marriage of David and Delia raised decades earlier by her father, who doubted at every turn that David's theory could survive empirical test. Worse, its implication, according to a history that David himself should have been the first to appreciate, was tantamount to genocide: "*Beyond color means hide the black man. Wipe him out. Means everybody play the one annihilating game white's been playing since—*."[3] The unfinished sentence spoken by Delia's father, one still resonant at the end of the novel and the end of the century, seems an advance epitaph for the hope that the nation might one day get "beyond race" or that Jews could still play a special role in getting there.

Treating a relationship that has always existed as much in idealized longing as in fact, *Driving Miss Daisy* and *The Time of Our Singing* stand virtually alone in their comparatively sanguine, if bittersweet, tones. More frequently, contemporary literature has portrayed not the potential for a black-Jewish alliance or, conversely, the tragic cost of its brutal conflicts but rather its implosion or strange irrelevance. The subtle allegory of *To Kill a Mockingbird*, the philosophical meditation of *A Different Drummer*, the diasporic panorama of *The Chosen Place, the Timeless People*, the personal combat of *Mr. Sammler's Planet* and *The Tenants*, or the hard-edged politics of *Sons of Darkness, Sons of Light*—these kinds of challenging but nonetheless clear-cut dramatizations gave way to raucous burlesque, postmodern puzzles, and polarizing stalemate.

As the language of genocide and ethnic cleansing became a normal part of the world's vocabulary, the problem of hyper-victimization inserted itself into the black-Jewish question at virtually every turn. Whether in the ranting of Farrakhan, the speculation of Baldwin, or the mainstream fiction of Morrison, Campbell, and Wideman, slavery and Jim Crow, as well as more recent manifestations of racism, could barely be imagined outside the assumption that the African American experience bore a surpassing resemblance to the genocide of the Jews. Even so, analogies between slavery and the Holocaust have ultimately proved to be as enigmatic as the relationship between blacks and Jews, and every attempt to explore the analogy in fiction has shown that it is as hard as it is inevitable to live within what Lore Segal called "other people's nightmares."

SHALOM, MOTHERFUCKER

Once the Holocaust had become the property of all aggrieved people, high tragedy of the kind intended by Morrison and Wideman was a no more necessary outcome than low farce—the genre of Ishmael Reed's *Reckless Eyeballing* (1986). Set in the back-biting, ultra–politically correct world of contemporary theater, Reed's wildly episodic tale rehearses the whole range of contentious issues in the black-Jewish conflict—Jewish exploitation of blacks, black emulation of Jews, black anti-Semitism, blacks as the "true Jews," the erosion of Jewish liberalism, the whiteness of Jews, point and counterpoint on slavery and the Holocaust, and so on—by assigning inconclusive strands of argument almost indiscriminately to various characters. But all this takes a back seat to the novel's more outlandish accusation that, just as the German media demonized Jews, so the United States media and black women have been duped by white feminists, Jews in particular, into promulgating a new "blood libel" against black men.[4] Were it only an indictment of quasi-fascist feminism, *Reckless Eyeballing* would be the rambunctious, if somewhat silly, parody many reviewers took it to be. The three stage plays around which its rickety plot is constructed, however, make the question of parody especially acute.

In the first play, the Jewish director Jim Minsk, having been invited to lecture at the southern "Mary Phegan [sic] College," named in homage to Mary Phagan, is required to watch a Leo Frank play depicting the Jew as a satanic, blood-sucking Dracula who assaults and murders a southern Christian maiden. Minsk's host professor, an African American passing for white, dons blackface to play Jim Conley, the real Mary Phagan's likely murderer and Frank's accuser. ("She had such a pretty face, that Mary Phegan," says the blackface Conley, "kind of looked like Jesus' mother must have looked when she was a little girl.")[5] As the audience is roused to a racist frenzy in tune with the rabidly anti-Semitic preaching Minsk hears on the local fundamentalist radio stations, it becomes apparent that he has been brought to campus not to lecture but to be lynched in an elaborate ritual sacrifice.

In the second play, whose premise is a cunning variation on Philip Roth's novella *The Ghost Writer* (1979), it is revealed that Eva Braun was responsible for killing Hitler and that she survived to marry a Jew and fund a play that will tell her side of the story. (Enough of "that little k—Jewish girl, Anne Frank," she declares.) In *Eva's Honeymoon* the worst crime of Nazism turns out to be its sexism, and Braun herself is portrayed as an "innocent bystander," a triumphant anti-male heroine who "epitomizes women's universal suffering."[6]

But the most elaborate of the three plays, the one from which the novel takes its title, turns feminism itself into a latter-day Nazism. Having enraged feminists with the sexism of his first play, the black author Ian Ball has decided to make amends with *Reckless Eyeballing*, which equates the suppression of women with the lynching of blacks but does so by justifying the latter. Although Ball is really a double agent in the novel—disguised as the "Flower Phantom," he assaults feminists, shaves their heads, and leaves a chrysanthemum as his calling card—his play turns the legal injustice and violent vigilantism of the Jim Crow era into just punishment for the mere "eye-rape"[7] of women. The white female lead, Cora Mae, now a radical lesbian, has the corpse of Ham Hill, the black man lynched for "reckless eyeballing" her twenty years earlier, exhumed and placed on trial in order to erase any doubts that he was just as guilty as those who lynched him or suspicions that she in any way invited his attention. When last we hear, *Reckless Eyeballing* is bound for a Broadway opening.

In each of the three plays, repeating tragedy as farce, Reed asks at what point the virus of racial hatred becomes available to burlesque. Like anti-Semitic Passion plays—the most famous being those performed annually in the Bavarian village of Oberammergau, originating as early as 1634, Nazified in 1934, and finally expurgated and reformed in the late twentieth century[8]—the sacrifice of Jim Minsk suggests that the myths of Jewish deicide and blood libel that were awakened in the lynching of Leo Frank are barely suppressed within some contemporary strains of Christian fundamentalism. Similarly, the fantasy that Eva Braun might have survived is no more or less bizarre than the abiding fantasy that Hitler might have survived, as in George Steiner's *Portage to San Cristobal of A. H.* (1981), or that his DNA might have been preserved to create a new race of Hitlers, as in Ira Levin's thriller *The Boys from Brazil* (1976). As an offshoot of the Hitler industry, both scholarly and popular, whereby every conceivable aspect of the tyrant's life and psychology has been subject to scrutiny, the idea that Eva Braun might have emerged as a proponent of women's rights, bent into a new form of Nazism, is hardly less far-fetched.

Like Ian Ball's play, Reed's novel mocks the corrosive scapegoating of identity politics. But the mockery has a sharp edge. The name Ham Hill combines reference to Emmett Till, murdered for adolescent sass to a Mississippi white woman, with the curse of Ham—not just the passage from Genesis said in traditional interpretations to authorize servitude, but more specifically the attribution to the Talmud of a justification for the servitude of blacks to Jews. Racial purity made iconographic in white (Aryan) womanhood is the common element in the Jim Minsk, Eva Braun, and Ham Hill plays, in each case the dead coming to life to witness to the fact that the reverential protection of white womanhood is justified at all costs. But Reed's burlesque was conceivable because, by the 1980s, slavery and Jim Crow had been fully absorbed into the cultural language of the Holocaust, as likely to produce crass victimization as noble tragedy.

Reed went a long way in trying to empty out America's "rape complex," to recall Wilber Cash's biting phrase, but it was possible to go further—much further. In his scathing 1992 satire *Negrophobia: An Urban Parable*, written in the form of a mock screenplay, Darius James required his readers to send up the most sacred of civil rights iconography and to indulge in the most grotesque whimsies of racial defilement.

Portraying a genocidal paramilitary campaign in the second decade of the twenty-first century, James splices futuristic Americana into a World War II–era documentary of Nuremberg rallies and Gestapo raids, so that the image of Mickey Mouse is superimposed upon representations of Hitler and swastika armbands.* As the theme song from the *Mickey Mouse Club* plays under the crowd's alternate roars of "Sieg heil!" and "Yea, Mickey!" we see white supremacist pictorial propaganda in the Disney style, intercut with the liquidation of the Warsaw Ghetto, depicting racial demonization in classic terms of sexual assault: "Caricatures of sweating Blacks rip off Snow White's bodice and pinch her rosy nipples, a ring of Jews ejaculate jets of sperm on a fluttering Tinkerbell

---

* James may have been inspired by the epigraph to *Maus II*, drawn from a German newspaper article of the mid-1930s: "Mickey Mouse is the most miserable ideal ever revealed. . . . Healthy emotions tell every independent young man and every honorable youth that the dirty and filth-covered vermin, the greatest bacteria carrier in the animal kingdom, cannot be the ideal type of animal. . . . Away with Jewish brutalization of the people! Down with Mickey Mouse! Wear the Swastika Cross!" Art Spiegelman, *Maus II: A Survivor's Tale* (New York: Pantheon, 1991), unpaginated.

in [a] competitive circle jerk, slit-eyed Asians sodomize Cinderella with a glass slipper and oily Hispanics gang-bang Sleeping Beauty."[9] The Final Solution, undertaken for the "White Christian good," is documented through a montage of Auschwitz footage shot inside the gas chambers. James thus harks back to World War II newsreels such as "Nazi Murder Mills" and "History's Most Shocking Record," which displayed the charred human remains inside crematoria and other gruesome images,[10] but in this case the writhing figures of Jews are "blotted over with blobs of minstrel black," and the entire sequence leads to a shot of the crematorium door emblazoned with a sign: "FOR COLORED ONLY." Accompanied by the theme song "When You Wish Upon a Star," a BBC voice-over incants, "As in the words of that old Negro spiritual, the white man finally laid his burden down." On screen the crematorium door swings open to reveal a pile of ash and charred bone pouring from the oven to the floor, crowned by a toothless skull, and the title appears: "THE ROCKY-HORROR NEGRO SHOW."

Within this fantasia of a Second Civil War, which has "reduced the nation to a vast boneyard of ruinated cities and extirpated lives," Walt Disney, propelled by a fusion of Disney corporatism and Third Reich pageantry, has become president for life, while blacks are reduced to a ragged band of guerrilla fighters. Disney's presidential oration begins by celebrating the shot that killed Martin Luther King, Jr., a half century earlier, a shot which "rang out as a foreboding death knell to millions of Negroes living happy as hogs on the tax dollars of hardworking Christian white folks like you and I." The end of the affliction of Negro culture upon America—the end of "the blues," the end of "jellied pig-foot knuckles," the end of the Negro's complaint that he is "sadly crippled by the chains of discrimination" and an "exile in his own land," the end of his "mount[ing] our naïve and trusting daughters, who offered up the golden down of their loins in an act of misguided compassion, impregnating her with his evil seed"—brought the nation closer to the racial purity of which Disney had always dreamed. "I wished upon a star—that one day this nation would rise up and live out the true meaning of its creed: 'Hang the nigger and burn the Jew!,'" his oration continues, modulating into an extended parody of King's "I Have a Dream" speech, devoted here to burning Negroes on hilltops throughout the land and concluding: "Gone at last! Gone at last! Thank God Almighty, them niggers is gone at last!"

However vicious its vision of the future, indiscriminately stringing together racist and heroic clichés, James's satire, even more certainly than Reed's, returns to the notion that blacks and Jews share common ground—but only in their prospects for annihilation. Corporate America's lithe ability to co-opt diversity and minority discourse as marketing devices is made preposterous in

James's vision of Disney as the new Führer, but both *Reckless Eyeballing* and *Negrophobia* take seriously the historical persecution that first thrust Jews and blacks together and that might, in some hypothesized future, reunite them again in the kinship of victimhood—albeit in a culture awash in victims and their demands for redress. Arguably more representative of the tenuousness of even that kind of kinship is the fiction of Paul Beatty, in which tropes of emulation and unity in suffering are conjured up like clues to an unstated but ugly riddle.

When Gunnar Kaufman, the black adolescent protagonist of *The White-Boy Shuffle* (1996), moves from multiethnic middle-class Santa Monica to black South Central Los Angeles, he leaves behind his best friend, David Joshua Schoenfeld, with whom he sniffed airplane glue and played World War II, debating "who Hitler would kill first, David the diabolical Jew or me the subhuman Negroid." Gunnar's letter of farewell pays heartfelt but cynical tribute: "David, somehow through being with you I learned I was black and that being black meant something, though I've never learned exactly what. *Barukh atah Adonai.* Shalom, motherfucker. Gunnar."[11] In Beatty's *Tuff* (2000), when Winston "Tuffy" Foshay, a three hundred–pound New York gangbanger without a gang, sets his sights on election to the city council, his advisers include his former Big Brother, the black rabbi Spencer Throckmorton, who reads Talmudic aphorisms from his *Tiny Tome of Jewish Enlightenment* (in response, Tuffy reads from *The Little Black Book of Sophisms: Fucked Up Things Jews Say About Blacks*), and the pseudo–Black Muslim Fariq, who declares that the Jew is "a circling vulture, an egg-stealing muskrat, a germ-infested, night-crawling parasite" and advises, it seems by extension, that blacks must "keep everything in the community—lie black, die black, and buy black. Emulate the Jew." Alluding to a much-publicized incident in which black schoolchildren in Oakland, California, taken to a screening of *Schindler's List,* laughed during a scene in which Nazis were shooting Jews, Tuffy says he does not need Steven Spielberg's film to prove to him the limits of human depravity: "I seen niggers set motherfuckers on fire. I seen niggers hold a gun to a mother's head and piss on her babies because her man didn't pay on time for some consignment rock."[12]

For Beatty, as for Reed and James, the black-Jewish question has become a quixotic gesture, clearly positioned in history and yet completely emptied of it. Which is not to say that Jewish authors have necessarily found grounds for comparison that are more ennobling or coherent. In Thane Rosenbaum's *Second Hand Smoke* (1999), for example, we find the aged, dying Holocaust survivor Mila Katz telling her life story and shameful secrets not to her one son, an estranged Nazi hunter, or the other, whom she abandoned as an infant in post-war Poland (after tattooing him with her own camp number), but to her three black nurses. Although the nurses say kaddish for Mila—incomprehensible words of a prayer that, as they pronounce it, rhymes with "radish"—and at novel's end make up a strange *minyan* with her sons, come finally to mourn at their mother's grave years after her death, the lesson to be deduced about the interchange of compassion between Jews and blacks remains nebulous at best.

Nor has embedding the question in history rendered in epochal, even messianic terms, provided any guarantee of a different outcome. In *Angels in America* (1993–94), his searching, multifaceted meditation on the age of AIDS and Ronald Reagan, Tony Kushner made the gay "holocaust" the setting for a confrontation between Jew and black as tormented as it is passionate. As he lies dying, Roy Cohn converses with his nurse, Belize, Cohn's querulous comments passing from ridicule of the black-Jewish liberal coalition ("we all held hands and rode the bus to Selma") to keen dissection of the prewar friction, at once ideological and religious, that divided Jews and blacks at just the moment when they might best have united in common struggle ("the thing about the American Negro is, he never went Communist. Loser Jews did. But you people had Jesus so the reds never got you"). The degree to which the black Belize is the Jewish Cohn's "negation"—a negation which also includes the difference between a closeted Republican ideologue and a former drag queen for whom heaven is a dance palace of "racial impurity and gender confusion"—finds its harshest, but implicitly most honest, terms as they argue over Cohn's illicit stash of the AIDS drug AZT:

> ROY: Move your nigger cunt spade faggot lackey ass out of my room.
> BELIZE: *(Overlapping starting on "spade"):* Shit-for-brains filthy-mouthed
>   selfish motherfucking cowardly cock-sucking cloven-hoofed pig.
> ROY: *(Overlapping):* Mongrel. Dinge. Slave. Ape.
> BELIZE: Kike.
> ROY: *Now* you're talking!
> BELIZE: Greedy kike.
> ROY: Now you can have a bottle. But only one.[13]

Whereupon Belize takes three bottles. Within days, Cohn is dead, haunted by the ghost of Ethel Rosenberg singing to him in Yiddish.

Although the exchange between Cohn and Belize reads like a parody of *The*

Tenants, Kushner assuredly presents the black-Jewish question with great tragic depth.* Yet even those literary works that confront the question with the seriousness it deserves have found moral intensity matched by fearful stalemate. In two of the most incisive portrayals, Lore Segal's novel *Her First American* (1985) and Anna Deavere Smith's one-woman play *Fires in the Mirror: Crown Heights, Brooklyn, and Other Identities* (1993), neither parallel lives, nor storytelling, nor even the shared prospect of genocide offers hope for common ground.

THEY HAVE STOLEN OUR GARMENT

Segal's underappreciated novel is carefully poised between realism and postmodern comedy. Ilka Weissnix, a Jewish refugee from Vienna, arrives in 1950s America at age twenty-one. Her father is dead, killed by the Nazis, and her mother, still to be located and brought to America, is living on a kibbutz in Israel. After getting tentatively established in New York by her cousin and sponsor Fishgobbel—her first job in America is collecting door-to-door for the United Negro College Fund—Ilka sets out on a train trip to the West to discover the real America. The nation she finds, in a Nevada bar, appears in the person of Carter Bayoux, an African American alcoholic whose wit, charm, intellectual prowess, and storytelling brilliance, in a familiar American racial tragedy, have not been enough to save him from descent into pathology and despair. Once the special adviser on race relations to the United States ambassador to the United Nations and the acquaintance of figures such as Paul Robeson, Duke Ellington, Billie Holiday, and Gertrude Stein, Carter has been reduced to working as a sometime journalist for the *Harlem Herald,* estranged from his family and tolerated by his friends. The story of Ilka's acculturation to

---

* Kushner has also worked for a number of years on a play devoted to Henry Box Brown, the slave who shipped himself to freedom in a packing crate and went on to become a well-known abolitionist. In 2003 he debuted the musical *Caroline, or Change,* a story of black tutelage structurally closer to the relationship between Scout and the Finch family maid, Calpurnia, in *To Kill a Mockingbird* than to the coy irony of *Driving Miss Daisy.* Set in 1963 Louisiana, the opera's principals include the title character, a black maid, and her Jewish employer's young stepson, Noah, whose personal relationship is inflected by the convulsive political and racial upheavals of the period. The friction between Noah and Caroline is punctuated by Noah's plaintive question when Caroline returns after a period of alienation from the family: "Will we be friends then?" To which her reply, "Weren't never friends," answers a question about blacks and Jews larger than this staged encounter. Tony Kushner, *Caroline, or Change* (New York: Theatre Communications Group, 2004), p. 123.

America unfolds over an undated period of about fifteen years, during which her relationship with Carter blossoms into a difficult love affair and then into an even more difficult friendship.

The peculiarity of Ilka's taking Carter for a "real American"—of the "second-class," he quickly adds—is made ironic in predictable ways. As her immigrant habits, like her initially crude English, are gradually melted in the pot of American culture, Ilka's assimilation underscores Carter's continued subjugation by the color line in 1950s America. Carter's preoccupation with "protocol," a concept featured in numerous diverse contexts over the course of the novel, codifies in one dimension the many written and unwritten rules—legal, linguistic, cultural, ceremonial, diplomatic, even conspiratorial, as in the *Protocols of the Elders of Zion*—that constitute his own attempt to define an acceptable mode of life and to instruct Ilka about her new nation's racial hierarchy. Ilka's lessons in racial protocol prepare her to think in the categorical terms that are as destructively constraining to Carter in America as they were to her in Europe. As soon as Carter explains to her that a particular black woman is actually Puerto Rican, for example, Ilka "acquired the word by which to distinguish this group of people from other groups of people, with the concomitant loss of the likelihood that she would henceforth distinguish any member within the group from any other."[14]

Carter's last name derives from his father's owner, and his multinational ancestral pedigree—Benin, Liberia, Mexico, Scotland—is by law and custom reduced to a single strain of "black" blood, trumped at every turn by the color Ilka brings with her to the United States. (Carter reveals to Ilka both the presence of anti-Semitism in her new nation and its comparative inconsequence when he recalls hiding near a "little sooty synagogue" with childhood friends, daring to make a Jew come out and "do whatever Jews did to little black Christian boys—cut their balls off at the very least." Although they saw people come and go all the time, especially on Saturday, says Carter, they "never ever got to see a Jew.")[15] Whatever tragedy befell Ilka's family in Europe and continues to haunt her in America is radically diminished, if not canceled out, in comparison to Carter's ruin. Their passion is charged with constant tension as Ilka struggles to understand "the American dilemma," in Gunnar Myrdal's contemporaneous phrase, and Carter struggles to explain to her why she will end up "white" and, inevitably, abandon him.

At the same time, however, this classic scenario of the Jewish immigrant set against the native-born African American has an obverse that we have seen before. Segal met the original "Carter" in a writing class she took soon after arriving in New York in 1951 as an Austrian war refugee, an experience recounted in her novel-memoir *Other People's Houses* (1963).* Although it is not imported directly into *Her First American,* one anecdote from Segal's friendship with the original Carter defines a subtler irony at work in the novel. As her first Thanksgiving in the United States approaches, Segal remarks to Carter that she has no holidays to celebrate—no Christmas because she is Jewish, no Jewish holiday because she is an assimilated Jew, no Austrian holidays because she was thrown out of Austria for being a Jew, and no American holidays because "we haven't acquired the American holidays yet." Carter's offer to celebrate Thanksgiving with her is charged with the ambivalent meaning of citizenship that also becomes central to the relationship between Ilka and the fictive Carter. "You thought that because I'm a Negro and write bitter stories, you and I were going to sit here and make snide remarks about Thanksgiving together," says the real Carter. "I'm an American, you know. At any rate, there's nothing else I am," he continues. I have not "lost my culture, nor, like you, my country. My isolation is peculiarly American."[16]

Like Lee Gordon in Himes's *Lonely Crusade* or like Ralph Ellison in his acerbic reply to Irving Howe, to cite just two versions of a familiar paradox, Carter tells Segal, as the fictive Carter demonstrates to Ilka in a number of his parables about American racial etiquette, that for all his persecution he is still fundamentally the "first" American. But his qualifier—"at any rate, there's nothing else I am"—magnifies the pathos and instability of his claim. The racial classifications to which Carter has been subjected throughout his life pale by comparison to those that issued in the Holocaust, but they are sufficient to deny him true membership in the nation he claims as his own.

As Segal recognized, the Holocaust refugee presents a special case of the white ethnic immigrant, and Carter's "Americanness," highlighting the priority of his sad but generic story over Ilka's generic but more catastrophic story, is presented in wrenching terms that call into question the very utility of the comparison. Her father murdered, her mother given to constant nightmares, and she herself, like Segal, conditioned by the "Kristallnacht in my head," Ilka has lost not only her culture and her country but also the essence of her identity. Upon returning with her mother to a childhood Vienna neighborhood in

---

* Following the Nazi invasion of Austria in 1938, the ten-year-old Segal was taken by the *Kindertransport,* a program to rescue Jewish children, to the comparative safety of England, where she lived for eight years with foster families. Her parents also fled to England but had to live apart from her, working in domestic service. After her father died in 1945, Segal and her mother emigrated initially to a Jewish agricultural community in the Dominican Republic and then to the United States. *Other People's Houses* was serialized in the *New Yorker* in 1961, the year of the Adolf Eichmann trial.

search of their home, Ilka "remembered what she did not remember, as if she had reentered a childhood tale,"[17] but the novel offers little certainty that they have found the right apartment or the right spot on the road where Ilka's mother last saw her husband alive. "My own exodus gave me a strength that exacted a price," said Segal of her wartime experience. "Cut yourself off, at ten years old, from feelings that can't otherwise be mastered and it takes decades to become reattached."[18]

We might expect Carter's past, in contrast, to be more visibly intact, less subject to invention. But even though pieces of his biography come into view—his relatively privileged upbringing, his failed marriages, his strained relationship with a brother who refuses any longer to bail him out financially or emotionally—Carter's identity, as Ilka sees it, is characterized by self-pitying, self-destructive behavior that gives his occasional capacity for selfless love a bitter taste. Unlike the Holocaust refugee, Carter may not have lost his country, but, plagued by insomnia and amnesia, he suffers periodic losses of memory that stand as well for forms of cultural destruction that make his priority as an American sorrowful to contemplate. "The best Jew of you all is nothing but a first-generation drunk," says Carter. At one point, disoriented and desperate, he interrupts a Passover seder to ask Ilka to take him to the hospital. Those gathered at the table are in the midst of an argument over God's punishment of the Egyptians. Yet Ilka's sympathy for the Egyptians, like her care for Carter, a latter-day "stranger," only underlines his estrangement and mental deterioration. "When we would lose our things mother made us remember everywhere that we had been," Carter tells Ilka, trying to account for his whereabouts during his most recent blackout. "I can't remember where I've been! There is no picture in my mind. It's the booze [that] has destroyed my brain cells."[19]

While being treated for his alcoholism in the hospital, Carter is taught Talmud by a fellow patient, Wolff Samovicz, who has lost his wife and child in the Holocaust. Weighed down by grief after emigrating to America, Wolff tries to kill himself by putting his head in a gas oven. But "he survived all over again," says Carter, as he might say of himself after one of his binges. The Talmud, says Wolff, teaches that "when a people—a whole race—is systematically humiliated, it is tantamount to genocide." Unlike the loss of property, "there are losses [from which] one does not recover. There are other losses." To which Carter, perhaps alluding to Artur Sammler in the cadence of his voice, replies, "I know. I know there are. I know there are."[20]

The transparent suggestion of the scene—that the Jewish Holocaust and the black holocaust are legitimately comparable—is driven home by the fact that Carter's former role as an adviser on race relations at the United Nations places him squarely within the postwar campaign for black civil rights as a matter of international *human* rights. Typified, as we have seen, by the petitions to the United Nations made by the Civil Rights Congress, Du Bois, Malcolm X, and later the Black Panthers, the framing of African American persecution within the fluid legacy of the United Nations Genocide Convention recast the meaning of slavery and Jim Crow in terms of the Holocaust and established a rationale for reparations, but in the end frequently divided, rather than united, Jews and blacks in their difficult search for common ground.

Despite the seeming camaraderie of Carter and Wolff as they search the Talmud for consolation, the final effect of such scenes, as Segal devises them, is to demonstrate that similarly poignant emotions do not guarantee true comparability of historical experiences. The scene between Carter and Wolff is followed immediately by a vignette in which, during a Thanksgiving conversation, Ilka ventures that the experiences of blacks and Jews are parallel. Carter agrees but points out that "parallels are two lines that run side by side and never meet except in infinity." And a subsequent conversation about education between Fishgoppel and Carter's friend Ebony quickly degenerates into an angry competition:

> Fishgoppel said, "Jews care enough about their children to give them an education."
> Ebony said, "Negroes were lynched if they learned the alphabet."
> "We had pogroms," said Fishgoppel.
> "Slavery," said Ebony.
> "Holocaust!" cried Fishgoppel
> "Are there no griefs that aren't racist or anti-Semitic!" shouted Ilka.[21]

Not a shared history, not a shared genocide, but only their parallel stories are what Ilka and Carter have in common. Like the *midrashim* to which they are compared, Carter's parabolic tales present problems for interpretation that are part exegesis, part invention, and they prove to Fishgobbel that Carter has a Jewish mind.[22] The original Carter, writes Segal in an epigraph to *Other People's Houses,* once told her a story from his childhood: "When he had finished, I said, 'I knew just where your autobiography stopped and fiction began.' He said. 'Then you knew more than I.'" Carter's rejoinder applies in obvious ways to Segal's own memoir and less overtly to *Her First American,* where it points up the inherent fictionality of memory while reminding us, too, that storytellers and listeners are suspended in a tangle of motives. "She loved me for the dangers I had passed, and I loved her that she did pity them," says the perspicacious Carter, quoting Othello's recognition that his enchantment of Desdemona elicits racial condescension alongside sympathy. Fishgobbel cannot get enough of Ilka's mother's "Hitler stories," while Carter's first wife, he reports, "used to *love* my dad's slave stories." But people do not really want to hear "other people's nightmares," adds Fishgobbel. "They have their own stories . . . they don't need our nightmares."[23]

At a memorial service for Carter after his death at an unspecified date in the late 1960s or early 1970s, Ilka attempts to join in the reminiscences of a group of black university students Carter had taught after enjoying a brief renaissance of his career during the era of Black Power. Yet her recollection of Carter's comment on her name—"I told Carter Weissnix means 'Knownothing,' but Carter said it meant 'Notwhite,' because I am a Jew"—holds no meaning for the young black men, who "turned back into their circle and went on with what they had been going to say before Ilka interrupted."[24] Because the trajectory of her novel runs from the early 1950s to the late 1960s, Segal ends where Malamud begins in *The Tenants,* though the story of Ilka and Carter concludes not in mortal combat but in sad estrangement. Her futile attempt to enter into the conversation at the memorial service does not prove that Ilka is white rather than "Notwhite"; it proves that she does not matter at all.

Just as the Holocaust may be seen as an interruption of black history, an unwelcome trumping of black persecution, even as it provided a compelling metaphor for that persecution, so Jews themselves, Segal seems to say, might be seen as interlopers in African American history—a bold, empathetic group who played a welcome role for a time but no longer. Their friendship became paternalism, which in turn became antagonism, and at last an irrelevance. *Her First American* tells us that "Hitler stories" and "slave stories," however desperate the urge to tell or hear them together, are ultimately incompatible. Yet Carter's *midrashim* and his Talmudic dialogue with Wolff also imply that it is only in storytelling, only in the joint narration of parallel lives destined never to meet except in infinity, that Jews and blacks will find what remains of their shared history.

"The young black possessed of rage, stomping on the old Jewish merchant, smashing his glasses and calling him a 'mother fucker,' is getting back at the white world," wrote Lenora Berson of a black youth's assault on a Jewish shopkeeper in the 1960s. "To the old Jew, this crazed creature is not a victim but a tormentor, a persecutor, a dark reincarnation of the Cossack and Polish pogromchik. The difference is that this time the law and force of society are on the old Jew's side. For in the end, he is a white man, and that's what counts in America."[25]

Berson's words, up to a point, might have been written in the wake of the racial violence that erupted in the Crown Heights section of Brooklyn in August 1991 after a car carrying the Lubavitcher Rebbe Menachem Schneerson accidentally struck and killed a nine-year-old black boy, Gavin Cato. In a random act of reprisal, Lemrick Nelson, Jr., a Trinidadian American, stabbed and killed Yankel Rosenbaum, a Jewish visitor from Australia.[26] Four days of rioting, firebombing, looting, marching, name-calling, and media frenzy ensued, the very name Crown Heights becoming a resonant symbol of accumulated tensions and recriminations—the end point of a devolution that began in the 1960s. (In Wendy Wasserstein's 1998 play *An American Daughter,* the Jewish African-American oncologist Judith Kaufman, daughter of a black Alabama piano teacher and a "Freedom Rider Jew," is dubbed a "walking Crown Heights.")[27] An elderly Russian woman, fearing a pogrom, jumped to her death from her apartment window, and dozens of residents and police were injured in what some observers were quick to call Brooklyn's "Kristallnacht."

Partly because it took place in Brooklyn, where black-Jewish conflict and commentary about it have a rich history, the Ocean Hill–Brownsville crisis of 1968 being the most prominent example, and partly because it coincided with a seeming upsurge in black anti-Semitism, the Crown Heights violence, as I noted in Chapter 1, became paradigmatic in the 1990s. It did so despite the fact that its main participants, Lubavitcher Hasidim, including a number of Holocaust survivors, and West Indian blacks, including a number of recent immigrants, were atypical Jewish and black communities—sidelocks, black hats, and *tzitzit* on one side, dreadlocks and the Rasta colors red, black, and green on the other. Focusing on instances of ostentatious racism, media coverage further polarized the complex interethnic and class tensions of the neighborhood while exacerbating the misinformation, rumors, political grandstanding, and race-baiting that characterized much of the "dialogue" during and after the violence.[28] According to the blacks, the Lubavitchers (along with Koreans) exploited the neighborhood economically[29] and enjoyed privileges and protection that were of a piece with the police brutality and corrupt justice system blacks felt they faced on a daily basis; according to the Jews, the blacks were ignorant, largely criminal people who preyed on Jews, engaged in anti-Semitic harassment, and refused to leave the Hasidic community, highly exclusive by design, in peace. Living on top of each other in a neighborhood whose psychogeographical boundaries resemble those of a ghetto, Ethan Goffman points out, each group tended to perceive history as "a closed system continually repeating itself in which their people are victimized and abused by ubiquitous outside forces."[30]

This, at any rate, was the point of departure for Anna Deavere Smith's solo theater piece, which showed with concentrated intensity the near impossibility of reconciliation and brought the slavery-Holocaust debate to a point of bitter stalemate. Smith's twenty-nine monologues, distilled from some six hundred interviews conducted two months after the violence with community members and outside observers, both the anonymous and the famous—the latter including Al Sharpton, Ntozake Shange, and Angela Davis—represent one cut at making sense of what happened and why. Although sustained narratives do appear sporadically, meaning emerges from Smith's play not in a linear way but instead through a jigsaw pattern of discordant voices speaking, sometimes shouting, commandments from the Torah, Afrocentric conspiracy theories, Holocaust tales, insults and accusations—using words misunderstood, tangled up, tendentiously distorted.

By her own account, Smith meant to get behind the media coverage and take a "photograph of what was unseen." As a documentary artist, she meant to "inhabit the speech pattern of another, and walk in the speech of another." The monologues of *Fires in the Mirror* therefore retain the stutters, pauses, and syntactical confusion of everyday speech, a technique that supplements Smith's further effort to discover the essence of the nation's complicated interethnic character, which "lives not in one place or the other, but in the gap between the places, and in our struggle to be together in our differences. It lives not in what has been fully articulated . . . but in the very moment that smooth-sounding words fail us."[31]

In the metaphor of the gap, a physical as well as linguistic borderland, Smith found a resonant description of the pluralist paradox of neighbors united principally by their estrangement from one another. Everything from hairstyles and slang to the observance of holy law demonstrates the near impossibility of tolerating, let alone bridging, differences. Precisely because *Fires in the Mirror* is staged as a set of monologues, moreover, no dialogue, no actual human interaction, can occur. Smith's dramaturgy might stand as a critique of multiculturalism generally—of the illusion that "diversity" issues in understanding or, even more improbably, that it elides rather than preserves suspicion and contempt. Insofar as Jews awkwardly straddle the line between "white" and "color," while blacks have remained the nation's benchmark of "color," the illusion is even starker in *Fires in the Mirror*. No matter what minor variations in the "text" may be introduced in live performance, the characters acted out ventriloquistically by Smith inevitably talk past one another.

The pluralist dilemma is nowhere more vivid than when the Holocaust becomes the play's frame of reference. In this respect, one monologue that stands out for its subject matter as well as for its stylistic difference from the rest of the play is that of the writer Letty Cottin Pogrebin. Because a significant portion of her monologue consists of a story read by Pogrebin from her book *Deborah, Golda, and Me* (1991), hers is the only transcript reproduced verbatim, of necessity, in Smith's performances. Staged as speaking on the phone, as she did when Smith recorded her testimony, Pogrebin introduces her monologue by worrying that "we're trotting out our Holocaust stories / too regularly and that we're going to inure each other to the truth of / them." But she goes on, nevertheless, to read aloud her own personal Holocaust tale, the story of her mother's cousin Isaac.

Blond-haired and blue-eyed, Isaac had been instructed by his town's Jewish council to do anything in his power to survive the Holocaust so that its story could be told to the world. Survival in his case turned out to entail herding his own townspeople, his wife and children included, into the gas chambers in order to convince the Nazis that his forged identity papers were authentic. In the United States, he tells his story to audience after audience:

> For months he talked,
> speaking the unspeakable.
> Describing a horror
> that American Jews had suspected but could not conceive.
> A monstrous tale
> that dwarfed the demonology of legend
> and gave me the nightmare I still dream to this day.

Prematurely aged far beyond his forty years, Isaac seems to grow older and older in telling his story until one night, after "telling everything he knew," he dies.[32]

Pogrebin's monologue, with its story within a story, is a searing tale in her book and no less searing in Smith's reproduction of it in her play. Here, however, it gains much of its significance from its juxtaposition to the preceding monologue of the Black Muslim Conrad Mohammad, for whom the Holocaust is predictably eclipsed by slavery:

This [slavery] is a crime of tremendous proportion.
In fact,
no crime in the history of humanity
has before or since
equaled that crime.
The Holocaust did not equal it
Oh, absolutely not.
First of all,
that was a horrible crime
and that is something that is a disgrace in the eyes of civilized
people.
That, uh, crime also stinks
in the nostrils of God.
But it in no way compares with the slavery of our people
because we lost over a hundred
and some say two hundred and fifty,
million
in the middle passage
coming from Africa
to America.

Mohammad goes on to enumerate various acts of physical violence and torture inflicted on slaves, but the greatest crime lies in the fact that slaveholders "cut off all knowledge from us" and stripped away blacks' dignity, pride, names, and ancestral memory. The criminals in question here, however, have a very specific identity:

They have stolen
our garment.
Stolen our identity.
The Honorable Louis Farrakhan
teaches us
that *we* are the chosen of God.
We are those people
that almighty God Allah
has selected as his chosen,
and they are masquerading in our garment—
the Jews.
We don't have an identity today . . .[33]

Set against Pogrebin's heart-wrenching story of Isaac "speaking the unspeakable"—an arch return of Toni Morrison's phrase to its origins in the initial Jewish confrontation of the Holocaust—Conrad Mohammad's standard-issue Nation of Islam anti-Semitism is crude. Yet the dissonance takes on a different value when his speech is set against another portion of Pogrebin's monologue that precedes Mohammad's in the text. There she charges that whereas blacks are scapegoating Jews, it is only Jews who show empathy and respect toward blacks:

> Only *Jews* listen,
> only *Jews* take Blacks seriously,
> only *Jews* view Blacks as full human beings that you
> should address
> in their rage
> and, um,
> people don't seem to notice that. . . .
> when they,
> when they have anything to say about the dominant culture
> nobody listens! Nobody reacts!
> To get a headline,
> to get on the evening news
> you have to attack a Jew.[34]

The two monologues taken together represent the Crown Heights "dialogue," like the late-twentieth-century dialogue between blacks and Jews generally, at its most explosive and clichéd, Mohammad orating hyperbolically on the black holocaust, Pogrebin pleading that no one appreciates the forbearance of Jews. Although Smith's stark polarizations were the perfect dramatic vehicle for Crown Heights and arguably a fitting end point to the black-Jewish question in the 1990s, the most controversial artistic response was not *Fires in the Mirror* but Art Spiegelman's cover illustration for the 1993 Valentine's Day issue of the *New Yorker,* featuring a Hasidic man kissing a black woman (see illustration). One version of reconciliation in the wake of Crown Heights, Spiegelman's tender portrait depicted transgressions offensive to many people on either side of the argument while at the same time it offered an irrefutable observance of the commandment to "love the stranger as yourself." Perhaps a more candid assessment of the possibilities for pluralist tolerance, and one more in keeping with the irresolvable tensions of Smith's play, was expressed by a member of the Lubavitcher community's counsel of brotherhood. "And now

Art Spiegelman, Valentine's Day cover illustration for the New Yorker, 1993.
New Yorker cover copyright © 1993 Condé Nast Publications Inc.
Reprinted by permission. All rights reserved.
Original artwork by Art Spiegelman © Art Spiegelman;
reprinted with the permission of the Wylie Agency Inc.

I am supposed to go explain myself to people who don't like me because I am different," he said. "Fuck you! We're *supposed* to be different. If you want to understand me, read the Bible. I should explain my Sukkot to you so you won't kill me?"[35]

In performance, *Fires in the Mirror* powerfully demonstrates how the ideal of togetherness remains overshadowed by the dilemma of difference. But the published version of the play conveys the dilemma in a further important dimension. As should be apparent from the sample quoted here, the published play, in which Smith prints the monologues not in the blocks of prose one might expect but rather in free verse, stands as a virtual refutation of the play's documentary surface. Rhetorically formalizing the speech that elsewhere in *Fires in the Mirror* is more colloquial, the voices of Pogrebin and Mohammad, as we see them on the page, call our attention to the strange artifice of Smith's whole enterprise. Even as it reproduces the cadences of everyday speech, her language, as it is displayed in published form, disrupts the illusion of reportage. Whatever aesthetic values might be ascribed to her rendering interview testimony as a kind of poetry, it expresses formally the near impossibility of reconciliation and communion.

In simulating a divided community in the literary artifact of her collected voices, Smith also simulates a divided nation—one reduced by example to the acrimonious verbal battles, punctuated by fleeting moments of communion, between two peoples living out the tail end of the century's racial catastrophes in their increasingly separate and unequal worlds. Whereas Lore Segal was able to imagine a relationship that began in love, even if it ended in estrangement, Smith found the mirroring images of black and Jew, like the mirroring fires of their respective ghetto histories, alike but irreconcilable. Neither the stranger's nightmare nor the stranger's memory, says Smith's play, can ever be truly our own.

CHAPTER 8

Spooks

MY TITLE IS BORROWED from Philip Roth's sensational novel *The Human Stain* (2000), a masquerade of identity that takes to its limit the always ambiguous, often paradoxical relationship between blacks and Jews as "people of color." "Spooks," the seeming racial epithet whose utterance undoes Roth's Coleman Silk, a black man passing as a Jew, provides a fitting summation of a relationship frequently split, over the course of the twentieth century, between fantasy and recrimination. But it speaks also to the compelling human desire, perhaps expressed more often by blacks than by Jews, to trade one identity for another.

Jews may cease to be Jewish—by ignorance of their ancestry, by apostasy and conversion, or simply by the slow erosion of assimilation, leaving them Jewish in name only. Or not even in name, since many Jews' names have been de-Judaized by mistake, by marriage, or by design. Yet however sympathetic to African American rights or immersed in African American culture, however much they might willingly give away the property of whiteness granted them in the United States, Jews can be black only vicariously. Blacks, to turn it around, can easily be Jews—by birth, by study and conversion, or, if they are light-skinned enough, by passing into the "off-white" secular world chosen by Coleman Silk. Having doubled their chances of persecution, they may take delight in one or another variation on an old joke. An elderly Jew, riding the subway, sees a Negro reading the Yiddish *Forward*. Unable to contain his curiosity, the

Jew asks the Negro if he is Jewish, whereupon he lowers his paper in disgust: "That's all I need *noch!*"[1]

Alert to the difficulty, as well as the potential comedy, of their marginally marginal positions, the narratives of black Jews, as well as Jews with a close or familial affinity for black life, speak with a special authority to the conflict that the writers themselves embody.* As a final way of reframing the black-Jewish question, I conclude with two such examples—one the autobiographical story of a black man who finds his true self in Judaism (with a parenthetical look at the companion story of a man who might have been a black Jew but for his mother's apostasy), the other Roth's fictional story of a man whose escape from blackness into pretended Jewishness ends in ironic tragedy, the last word in a century-long dialogue.

---

* One could include here, for example, *Bulletproof Diva: Tales of Race, Sex, and Hair* (1994), by Lisa Jones, daughter of Amiri Baraka (LeRoi Jones) and Hettie Cohen Jones; Jane Lazarre, *Beyond the Whiteness of Whiteness: Memoir of a White Mother of Black Sons* (1996); Katya Gibel Azoulay's *Black, Jewish, and Interracial: It's Not the Color of Your Skin, but the Race of Your Kin, and Other Myths of Identity* (1997), a scholarly study punctuated by reflections on her hybrid black-Jewish identity; *Black, White, and Jewish: Autobiography of a Shifting Self* (2001), by Rebecca Walker, daughter of writer Alice Walker and civil rights attorney Mel Leventhal; the autobiographical one-woman variety show *Fried Chicken & Latkas* (2003) by Rain Pryor, the Jewish and black daughter of actor Richard Pryor ("Rain's diverse backgrounds," says the playbill, "are signified by her grandma Bernice's potato latkas, and Mamma's fried chicken and collard greens—the two cultures that helped her triumph over racial lines and stereotypes"); Dexter Jeffries's *Triple Exposure: Black, Jewish, and Red in the 1950s* (2003), the autobiography of a man born to a black father and a "Jewish but not Jewish" mother, both Communist Party members; and Willis Barnstone's *We Jews and Blacks: Memoir with Poems* (2004), a mix of commentary, poetry, and memoir that reflects on his coming of age when prejudice against and restrictions on Jews made their experiences closer to those of African Americans. *Bulletproof Diva* is only incidentally, or perhaps subliminally, a black-Jewish autobiography. Dedicating the book to her mother and to female relatives on both sides of her family, Jones takes note of her rejection by her Jewish grandparents and her father's desertion of the family as he plunged into a period of overt anti-Semitism. Lazarre, the white Jewish mother of black sons, realizes after a visit to Yad Vashem that the United States cannot be understood without understanding slavery—more specifically, that the repugnance she would feel were modern Germany to celebrate Nazi generals is what her sons must feel in reaction to the southern glorification of Robert E. Lee. Not black enough for some, rarely Jewish enough for others, Rebecca Walker growing up is simply the "yellow bitch." The mature Walker insists on telling people about her invisible Slavic Jewish ancestry: "I get a strange, sadistic pleasure from watching their faces contort as they reconsider the woman who was more easily dismissible as Puerto Rican or Arab. On the subway, surrounded by Hasidim crouched xenophobically over their Bibles, I have to sit on my hands and bite my tongue to keep from shouting out, 'I know your story!'" Rebecca Walker, *Black, White, and Jewish: Autobiography of a Shifting Self* (New York: Riverhead Books, 2001), pp. 106, 36–37.

WHO I AM

In view of his previous identity as a Black Power militant, an antagonist to the Jews in the Ocean Hill–Brownsville school crisis of 1968, the conversion narrative of Julius Lester, *Lovesong: Becoming a Jew* (1988), is a stunning document, but Lester tells us that his choice to be a Jew was no sudden decision. Early on in his autobiography, Lester recalls the uncanny sensation he felt as young boy in 1940s Kansas City while playing an untitled composition out of a piano practice book: "When I stop playing there is a painful yearning in my stomach, a wishing for something I have never had and thus do not know what it is, or a wishing for something which I had once and have forgotten what it is."[2] The song, he later learns, is "Kol Nidre," the annulment of vows recited or sung on the eve of Yom Kippur.* After his mother gives him an edition of Shakespeare for Christmas, recommending that he begin with *The Merchant of Venice*, it is in Shylock, rather than in Du Bois, Robeson, Hughes, or other famous black men, that Lester sees himself reflected. In English literature's most famous Jew, Lester finds a "model of suffering, someone to reflect a child's pain and confusion at being condemned because of the race into which I was born," and proof as well that it is not only blacks "who must ponder in their flesh the meaning of meaningless suffering."[3]

No doubt such moments of self-discovery have been significantly modulated by the process of remembering, as Lester's identity, searched and scrutinized, is established ex post facto. But *Lovesong* is full of moments when he probes his recollections for early clues to the transformation he underwent on the way to conversion to Judaism in 1983. Present and past are cunningly woven together in the narrative, a strategy enforced by Lester's writing of his former self in the present tense and by his penchant for merging temporal planes through semi-mystical self-descriptions: "I have become who I am. I am who I always was. I am no longer deceived by the black face which stares at me from the mirror. I am a Jew." The visible part of his genealogy is set aside in favor of the part that is hidden from view. As he reconstructs his own descent from Jewish ancestors,

---

* "Let all our vows and oaths, all the promises we make and the obligations we incur to You, O God, between this Yom Kippur and the next, be null and void should we, after honest effort, find ourselves unable to fulfill them. Then may we be absolved of them." *Gates of Repentence: The New Union Prayerbook for the Days of Awe* (New York: Central Conference of American Rabbis, 1978), p. 252.

Lester quizzes *his* mother about *her* mother's memorialization of *her* father's death. Told that his grandmother lit a candle once a year, Lester realizes that it was a *yahrzeit* candle, a ritual practice of Jewish remembrance whose family meaning has long ago slipped away: "Momma remembered Grandmomma's remembering without knowing what she was remembering. If I can ever find the date of Great-grandfather's death, I will remember that of which I have no memory."[4] It is hard to imagine, on the individual level, a more striking proof of the observation of Yosef Yerushalmi that the "memory" of a people is a psychological metaphor for the process by which a "past" has been accepted and internalized by the present generation as a meaningful account of their origins.[5]

Lester does discover Adolph Altschul's date of death and can therefore light his *yahrzeit* candle, yet the fact that this single great-grandfather, out of his many intervening ancestors, was Jewish is by itself a weak explanation for Lester's nearly supernatural preoccupation with Jewishness as the singular explanation of who he is. A childhood taunt based on his name—"Ju! Ju! Jew! Jew!"—seems in retrospect a kind of forewarning; at age thirty-six he finds himself responding to "nocturnal messages from unknown parts of my soul"; and after reading about witnesses to the Holocaust he is overcome by visceral dreams: "In the night I have wandered among naked bodies piled atop one another; I shovel bodies into ovens and I am the Jew closing the oven door and the Jew inside; I am smoke and flame spewing from smokestacks; I am particles of ash and soul seeking my burying place in cloud and sky." He awakens reciting the *Shema,* his lips moving with the unknown yet familiar words, "*Sh'ma Yisrael Adonai Elohenu Adonai Ehad. . . .* Hear O Israel. The Lord our God, the Lord is One."[6]

This eerie identification with the Holocaust dead is for good reason distinctly reminiscent of Walt Whitman's identification with slaves and the fallen soldiers of the Civil War—"I am the hounded slave, I wince at the bite of the dogs" ("Song of Myself"); "Yet I think I could not refuse this moment to die for you, if that would save you" ("The Wound-Dresser")—for Lester's change of identity requires that the Holocaust become his Civil War, so to speak. It requires that the genocide of the Jews, not the Middle Passage, slavery, and Jim Crow, become his racial point of reference. It requires, too, that he stand outside the governing Christian narrative of African American life, which, however much it was shaped by the paradigm of the Exodus and given political force by the exhortations of the Hebrew prophets, is ultimately defined by faith in the redeemer Jesus Christ and His promise of salvation today. In order to measure how strongly Lester turned against the tide of African American culture in choosing Judaism, it is worth pausing to consider the contrary example of James McBride, son of a Jewish mother and an African American father, who, had he lived a different life, might have told a story similar to Lester's in his best-selling memoir *The Color of Water* (1996).

The choice of life, as McBride tells it, was not his to make. It was his mother, Ruth, with whom he narrates his life story in a dialogue of alternating chapters, whose marriage to a black minister and conversion to Christianity ensured that her son's story would be just the opposite of Lester's. With two black husbands (she remarried after James's father died, before James was born) Ruth raised twelve children, all of them educated, successful, by customary definition black —and Christian. Although his book begins as a story of Jews and blacks, its subtitle, *A Black Man's Tribute to His White Mother*, prepares us in advance for a story in which Jewishness will be absorbed into whiteness, with only a slight residue left to mediate between the two poles of the biracial nation represented by Ruth and her husbands, and physically embodied in their children.

Born in Poland in 1921, the daughter of Orthodox Jews, Ruth Shilsky McBride was raised in Suffolk, Virginia, where her immigrant parents had settled in 1929 after living for several years in New York and Massachusetts. Ruth's father, a traveling rabbi who preached in the local synagogue and ran a grocery store, was a cold, harsh man who abused her sexually when she was a young girl; her mother, crippled by polio, put up with her miserable lot in a contract marriage. Fishel Shilsky hated the "shvartses" who shopped in his store and was pleased to exploit them, and when Ruth married a black man, Andrew ("Dennis") McBride, soon after her mother's death in 1942, her father and other relatives said the kaddish and sat shiva for her. After she came to America, Ruchel Dwajra Zylska became Rachel Deborah Shilsky. When her classmates in school called her "Christ killer," "Jew baby," and "dirty Jew," Rachel chose to go by a name that "didn't sound so Jewish," but now Ruth effectively sits shiva for herself as well. Whereas her parents got rid of her Polish name, Ruth herself gets rid of the rest of her Jewish self when she leaves Suffolk for New York in 1939 and definitively when she marries Dennis McBride and takes his name: "Rachel Shilsky is dead as far as I'm concerned. She had to die in order for me, the rest of me, to live." Or, as she later puts it in describing her conversion: "I started to become a Christian and the Jew in me began to die. The Jew in me was dying anyway, but it truly died when my mother died."[7]

The Jew in her may have died, but it does not disappear. Ruth haggles with shopkeepers on the Lower East Side ("the Jews have the deals") and sends her "black" children to "Jewish" schools because of their superior academics. She talks about whites in the third person, considers them "implicitly evil toward blacks," and distinguishes them from Jews without telling anyone that she herself is Jewish. Although it is less freighted with mythologies of sacred white womanhood, her color is no less a marker of racial obligation in New York than in Suffolk. In the South, her Jewishness, when measured by the archetypal standard of interracial sexuality, does not keep her from being white, for when she becomes pregnant by a secret black boyfriend, he is sure that he will be lynched if it is discovered. (Her mother, the only one who knows of her pregnancy, sends her to her grandmother in New York for an abortion.) When the mature Ruth transgresses the racial line in the North, her husband will not be lynched, but she will still be a pariah. To passersby on the streets and subways of New York, she is a now a "white bitch" with her "little niggers." In her own mind, however, Ruth has gone beyond race and lives, if only in her own imagination, in the idealized "postrace place" envisioned by David Strom in *The Time of Our Singing*. Neither white, nor black, nor Jewish, she refuses to identify with her color. When her son asks if she is white, she says only that she is "light-skinned" or that she, like God, is "the color of water."[8]

If Ruth's story is one of ethnic renunciation, her son's is perforce one of ethnic recovery. On his own trip to Virginia in search of his Jewish roots, James discovers "old southern crackers who talked with southern twangs and wore straw hats, [who] seemed to believe that [Judaism's] covenants went beyond the color of one's skin." He understands as well, however, that blacks and Jews, taken altogether, are neither more nor less capable than any other people of transcending their communal prejudices. Among his Jewish teachers and classmates in New York he remembers some who were "truly kind, genuine, and sensitive, others who could not hide their distaste for my black face." If he lives with the fact of his color and the reactions it provokes, however, his awareness is leavened by a qualifying sense of another otherness, secondary to the first. "My view of the world is not merely that of a black man but that of a black man with something of a Jewish soul," he writes. "I don't consider myself Jewish, but when I look at Holocaust photographs of Jewish women whose children have been wrenched from them by Nazi soldiers, the women look like my own mother and I think to myself, *There but for the grace of God goes my mother—and by extension, myself.*"[9]

The grace of God, however, has a double meaning here. But for his mother's apostasy James would have been born a Jew under Jewish law, yet he knows his mother not as a Jew but as a Christian. The book's last image is a poignant one of Ruth lingering at a synagogue entrance after attending the wedding of one of James's Jewish friends. "You know that could have been me," she says somewhat wistfully. But the book's overriding message is that it could not—that America gave her the freedom not to be Jewish, even if what she chose to be, the wife of black men and the mother of "black" children, was decidedly ironic by America's racial standards. Whereas her own family rejected her for marrying men both not Jewish and not white, their African American families accepted her warmly, and the overall impression of Jews left by the book is that those "covenants" that might appear to transcend skin color belong nevertheless to a superstitious, rigid, and bigoted people. "There are probably a hundred reasons why Ruthie should have stayed on the Jewish side," says her son, "and I'm sure the Old Testament lists them all, but I'm glad she came over to the African-American side." And so, indeed, is she. Dennis McBride "taught me about a God who lifted me up and forgave me and made me new," says Ruth, describing her recovery of the capacity to love after the abuse and trauma of her childhood. "I was reborn in Christ."[10]

The Color of Water is a remarkable, well-crafted story of interracial marriages that stand as a microcosm of the transformation in American values over two generations. In the entwined family histories of Jewish immigration to America, black migration from South to North, and finally ascendance from the housing projects of Brooklyn to the New Jersey suburbs, we leave behind bigotry and insularity to enter, by the story's end, a utopian space of tolerance, but one in which "the Jewish side" and "the African-American side" stand in clear opposition. All of Ruth's dozen children are "extraordinary people, most of them leaders in their own right," and their dozens and dozens of spouses, children, and grandchildren range from "dark-skinned to light-skinned; from black kinky hair to blond hair and blue eyes." Thus, "in running from her past, Mommy created her own nation," McBride writes, "a rainbow coalition that descends on her house every Christmas and Thanksgiving"[11]—but not, it goes without saying, on Passover or Rosh Hashanah.

In the end, *The Color of Water* is, par excellence, an Americanization narrative in which Christianity supersedes Jewishness, a story as old as the Puritan errand into the wilderness of the New Jerusalem, but also one in which blackness supersedes Jewishness, a story as old as the slavery from which it derives. The authorizing topos, and surely one key to the book's popularity, is made explicit in McBride's acknowledgments, which appear at the end of the book: "My mother and I would like to thank the Lord Jesus Christ for His love and faithfulness to all generations."[12] Whether or not McBride, like Ellison and Himes, among others, means to suggest that to be black is to be more "original," more truly American, than immigrant Jews or their descendants, the more important corollary, and the lesson of the Jewish Ruth's having come over to "the African-American side," seems to be that in order to be an American, one is indeed better off having come over to the Christian side.

Measured against the example of Ruth and James McBride, then, the path chosen by Julius Lester is all the more striking. Willingly both black and Jewish in a nation still far from a "postrace" ideal and perhaps doubly the target of black anti-Semites, Lester tells the more profound story of self-invention. He cannot erase his color, but he can choose that it not forever dictate his political opinions and religious beliefs. It is his story, not McBride's, that is, in fact, the more striking expression of American freedom in all its complex ironies—the freedom to substitute one set of opinions and beliefs, as well as one history of racial persecution, for another.

Over and over *Lovesong* is cast as a search for a lost self that can render Lester's blackness a coincidence of birth. He wants to stand outside the requirements of racial identity—"to make our primary definition the color of our skin is to imitate white people, not to be free of them," Lester writes—yet in choosing the dangers of one kind of racism over those of another, Lester reminds us of their intimate correlation. Jewishness is presented, accordingly, as one way to escape the most hateful stereotypes and primordial fears of black life. The specter of interracial sexuality in the South, Lester writes, created an "ontological terror of non-existence."[13] For a black man seemingly preoccupied with glamorous white women—Peggy Fleming, Raquel Welch, Cher, and Angie Dickinson all figure in his reported erotic fantasies—to be *not* black but *just* Jewish might thus provide a shield against stereotypical accusations of dangerous black libido.[14] As Lester realizes, however, the Holocaust propagated its own "ontological terror of non-existence" through an even more highly refined ideological principle of racial stereotyping. Following a lecture about Anne Frank when he was a student at Fisk University in 1960, Lester recalls, he conversed with faculty member Robert Hayden about the differences between black and Jewish suffering. Lester finds his vocabulary of comparison inadequate to respond to the indelible images of "naked bodies stacked in hills beneath sunny skies" which loom up before him as though in a historical memory he has yet to make his own. "Being forced to ride at the back of a bus is not in the same realm of human experience." However true it is that "my yellow star is in my skin" as a permanent marker of American racial inferiority, Lester writes, "I am alive . . . and Anne Frank is not."[15]

We may or may not take on faith that Lester consciously formulated such a distinction in 1960, but his displacement of a black self with a Jewish self does demand that he account for his radicalism of the late 1960s and the contrary perspectives on blacks and Jews that went with it. Thinking back to his role in the Ocean Hill–Brownsville confrontation, which I examined in Chapter 5, Lester avers that black anti-Semitism was not and never has been a serious problem in the United States, for Jews have never truly suffered at the hands of

African Americans. In fact, the reverse is true, said Lester in the *Look Out, Whitey! Black Power's Gon' Get Your Mama!* phase of his life he now recounts.

Repeating the words of an essay he contributed in 1969 to Nat Hentoff's *Black Anti-Semitism and Jewish Racism,* Lester writes in *Lovesong:* "In America, it is we who are the Jews. It is we who are surrounded by a hostile majority. It is we who are constantly under attack. There is no need for black people to wear yellow Stars of David on their sleeves; that Star of David is all over us. And the greatest irony of all is that it is the Jews who are in the position of being Germans."[16] Twenty years later, Lester is on the other side of the fence. He now berates black intellectuals for defending Jesse Jackson and Andrew Young when they are accused of anti-Semitism or acting against Jewish interests, and finds himself frightened and appalled by the racial self-glorification of the audience at a Nation of Islam rally, whom he judges the first African Americans "to wear suffering as if it were the divine right of kings . . . as if it gives them exemption from moral and ethical responsibility to the rest of humanity."[17]

The slippage between the Lester of today and the Lester of the radical 1960s is not resolved in *Lovesong* because it cannot be resolved. Whatever adumbrations of Judaism he now finds in his former self, the Lester of today, the Jew, is distinctly different from the Lester on whose Brooklyn radio program a black high school student read a rabidly anti-Semitic poem. Squaring the passionate Judaism of his present-day remembering with his former Black Power self produces in Lester an unavoidable psychological contortion. Looking back on a person who, he now says, simply spoke in the "collective black voice" required by the times, he contends that "that Julius Lester [was] the creation of a History sweeping across the American landscape like a band of cossacks galloping down the steppes."[18] But was it white supremacy or Black Power that swept across the American landscape like anti-Semitic marauders galloping down the steppes? The sentence points to the latter construction. If so, however, then it is the radicalism of the left, the black left in particular, that Lester now identifies as an outlaw threat to Jews. In this, too, he has become a late-twentieth-century American Jew.

Lovesong renders such a sincere story of Lester's journey to Judaism that it really cannot be gainsaid. In his invention of an alternative genealogy and alternative racial history, Lester means to suppress the imprisoning "double-consciousness" in which Du Bois found African Americans trapped in favor of the liberating Zionism that Brandeis said should be both the right and the pluralist aspiration of American Jews. Echoing a familiar distinction in black and Jewish reactions to the concrete reality of a recovered homeland, Lester, upon seeing Jews collecting money in the wake of the Six-Day War, says he was "overcome by anger and jealousy that I did not have a country in which to exult." Simply reading *Exodus,* a love story not only between Ari Ben Canaan and Kitty Fremont, Jew and gentile, but also between "a people and a God and a land," prompted him to "feel a part of that love."[19] The Jewish self Lester deduces from such recollected moments seems to give credence to the belief, as we have seen it expressed by his fellow black Jew Laurence Mordechai Thomas, that Jews have a narrative of their own, while blacks do not.

Lester observes that in his love of music, exemplified in the Kol Nidre, "the centuries of black suffering merge with the millennia of Jewish suffering as my voice weaves the two into a seamless oneness." But such claims are few and his attempts to join blackness and Jewishness effectively rendered moot by the choice he has made. The Kol Nidre that haunted Lester as a boy has led him as a man to be absolved of his obligation to be black—it is "null and void"—as he takes on his obligation to be a Jew. "Emptied of who I was" at a Yom Kippur service, he is linked by the sound of the shofar to his ancestors in Germany and to Moses in the wilderness. Once he becomes a "master of prayer," one who leads the congregation in praying in song, Lester realizes that it is not the folk songs, blues, work songs, and spirituals of his black self, much as he loves them, that his voice "was meant to sing." Rather, it is the music he heard at the piano at age seven, the hymns of Judaism: "I know now who I am. I am a Jew and I am a lovesong to the God of Abraham, Isaac and Jacob, a praisesong to the God of Sarah, Rebecca, Rachel and Leah." Emptied of blackness, he is Julius Lester in name only. Truly, in the Hebrew name he chooses, he is Yaacov Daniel ben Avraham v'Sarah, his first name, Jacob, being the name, as he learns in unraveling his Jewish genealogy, of his great-great-great-great-grandfather.[20]

In choosing to be a Jew, Lester finds both a spiritual home in Israel and a more welcome ethnic home in America. Even if he would like, however, he cannot choose to adopt "the outward life of an American and the inward secret of the Jew," to recall Daniel Bell's self-description,[21] nor trade away the color of his skin. The nation in which he lives will allow him to be a Jew, but it will not allow him not to be black.

THE SECRET TO HIS SECRET

"What wouldn't you give to be a white man?" . . . I judge that every intelligent Negro in the United States has met [this question] in one form or another. And it is most likely that all of us have at some time toyed with the

Arabian Nights–like thought of the magical change of race. As for myself, I
find that I do not wish to be anyone but myself. . . . [But] if the jinny
should say, "I have come to carry out an inexorable command to change
you into a member of another race; make your choice!" I should answer,
probably, "Make me a Jew."

—James Weldon Johnson, Along This Way

The last half century's strange entanglements between blacks and Jews—political, psychological, material, symbolic—are nowhere more visible, so to say,
than in the tragedy of Philip Roth's protagonist in *The Human Stain* (2000).
Coleman Silk, an aging classics professor and former dean of the faculty at a
small New England college, is brought to ruin by an innocent query about students absent from his class—"Does anyone know these people? Do they exist
or are they spooks?"[22] It turns out that the students, unbeknownst to Silk, are
black. Condemned by his colleagues, Silk is driven from his job for an insult he
could not have intended. Following the death of his wife, which he attributes to
his persecution, he is hounded further by a vindictive feminist colleague who
exposes his affair with Faunia Farley, a college cleaning woman less than half
his age. Ultimately, Silk and Faunia are killed when their car is forced off the
road by Faunia's former husband, a deranged Vietnam veteran.

Were *The Human Stain* only a satire on the inquisitorial pseudo-morality of
contemporary academia, its success might be measured solely in comic terms.
But since Silk himself turns out to be a very light-skinned black man masquerading as a Jew, his use of the word "spooks" takes on a self-referential irony, as
well as the suggestion of subconscious self-exposure, that very much deepens
Roth's inquiry into the politics of identity. (Since "spook" was originally used
by blacks to refer to whites as ghostlike, the epithet itself is built on a psychological inversion.) As first seen by the novel's narrator, Nathan Zuckerman, Silk
appears to be "one of those crimp-haired Jews of a light yellowish skin pigmentation who possess something of the ambiguous aura of the pale blacks who
are sometimes taken for white,"[23] and it is Zuckerman, to whom Silk's sister reveals his secret after his death, who attempts to fathom the relationship between the taunting masquerade of Silk's life and his ignoble death.

Silk might simply have passed for white, but his more nuanced choice to
present himself as a Jew allows Roth to recalculate the faltering relationship between blacks and Jews in terms appropriate to the late twentieth century. For
the young Coleman's hardworking, lower-middle-class family in 1940s Newark,
Jews were the "Indian scouts, shrewd people showing the outsider his way in,
showing the social possibility, showing an intelligent colored family how it

might be done." When Silk, as a student at New York University, elects in 1953 to take on "the ersatz prestige of an aggressively thinking, self-analytic, irreverent American Jew," he short-circuits this historical process, turning black emulation of Jews into a virtual parody of them. (In the process he also exacts a measure of revenge on the Jewish dentist who had asked him to take a dive on his high school exams so that his own son could be valedictorian.) By means of his marriage to the "non-Jewish Jew" Iris, a left-wing artist whose hair and coloring, he calculates, will help provide the physiognomic mask for any dark shadow that might emerge in their offspring, Silk also preserves the semblance of "colored" authenticity. Her faint otherness, added to his own, leaves "the secret to his secret," the irony within his irony, "flavored with just a drop of the ridiculous." Believing that he can "play his skin however he wanted, color himself just as he chose," Coleman Silk, in short order, makes himself into a person whose meaning requires, in Nathan's description, a tortuous prose commensurate with his elegant, oxymoronic name: "As a heretofore unknown amalgam of the most unalike of America's historic undesirables, he now made sense."[24]

Silk's choice might include a sly allusion to Harry Lesser, the "white spook" of Malamud's *The Tenants,* but more certainly it may be seen as a retort to Mailer's contemporaneous cultivation of the persona of the "white Negro," an act of fantasized transgression mired in racial essentialism. Silk flips Mailer upside down, but his transgression is more profound. In adopting the ambiguous whiteness of postwar Jewishness as his own, says Nathan, Silk purports not to undertake a revolutionary act, "unless it is revolutionary to believe that disregarding prescriptive society's most restrictive demarcations and asserting independently a free personal choice that is well within the law was something other than a basic human choice." In refusing to accept "the contract drawn up for [his] signature at birth," Silk must pay the price of being utterly rejected by his own family—you think "like a slave," says his bewildered and devastated mother—but he does so, by all appearances, quite willingly. Unlike the protagonist of James Weldon Johnson's *Autobiography of an Ex-Coloured Man,* whose passing leads to despairing self-condemnation for having "sold [his] birthright for a mess of pottage," Silk is resolute in the wisdom of his choice.[25] Unlike Faulkner's Joe Christmas, who sleeps with white women and then tells them he is a Negro, courting his own eventual lynching and castration, Silk chooses the path of disguised miscegenation without apparent torment.

On the face of it, Coleman Silk blithely replicates, as a black man, Roth's desire, as he once told Joyce Carol Oates, to experience not being Jewish "after having spent a lifetime as a Jew." He meant, he added, not just "skin-deep conversions" or the mistaken identity that Arthur Miller explored in *Focus* (1945), in which an anti-Semite "is taken by the world for the very thing he hates," but rather "magically becoming totally the other, all the while retaining knowledge of what it was to have been one's original self, wearing one's original badges of identity."[26]

Silk magically becomes the other, but with this difference: he retains the knowledge of having been black, while renouncing the history, both individual and communal, that goes with it. Yet he is able to do so only because he does not, in fact, wear on his skin the "original badges of identity" that would show him to be a trickster and a fraud. In choosing to pass not simply as white but as a Jew, Silk—or, we might rather say, Roth by means of Silk—exposes the comparative ease with which Jews might pass, whether by design or the happenstance of assimilation, while at the same time demarcating the near impossibility of blacks doing so. To hark back to Julius Lester and to his likely source, Gunnar Myrdal, the African American's badge of identity is "fixed to his person much more ineffaceably than the yellow star [was] fixed to the Jew during the Nazi regime in Germany."[27]

In Silk's fatal classroom query, Roth no doubt also had in mind the opening of *Invisible Man*, which appeared the year before Coleman Silk chose to be seen as not black: "I am an invisible man. No, I am not a spook like those who haunted Edgar Allan Poe; nor am I one of your Hollywood-movie ectoplasms. I am a man of substance, of flesh and bone, fiber and liquids—and I might even be said to possess a mind." In choosing to pass, Silk makes himself invisible as an African American and claims unquestioned access to an intellect as well as a body. (Silk's act of passing, which precedes *Brown v. Board of Education* by one year and the lynching of Emmett Till by two years, also follows by one year Fanon's famous attribution in *Black Skin, White Masks* of "biological danger" to blacks and "intellectual danger" to Jews.) By passing as a Jew, he thus counters, without completely canceling, the dilemma of Ellison's protagonist, who lives as though "surrounded by mirrors of hard, distorting glass" so that others see only "my surroundings, themselves, or figments of their imagination—indeed, everything and anything except me."[28]

Roth's implied tribute to Ellison can also be traced to his early career, when he, like Ellison, had been attacked for not toeing the line of racial chauvinism in the stories collected in *Goodbye, Columbus* (1959). Grilled by an audience at Yeshiva University in 1962 for having depicted characters, said his critics, who confirmed anti-Semitic stereotypes, the young Roth was pleased to find himself defended by fellow panelist Ellison, who instructed the audience "through examples drawn from *Invisible Man* and the ambiguous relationship that novel had established with some vocal members of his own race."* Roth responded sympathetically to Ellison's desire to be free of communal prescriptions of racial identity, just as he no doubt responded to Ellison's lesson in "Change the Joke and Slip the Yoke" that "the Negro's masking," very much "in the American grain," was motivated "not so much by fear as by a profound rejection of the image created to usurp our identity."[29] Self-masking and self-making, said Ellison on a number of occasions, were the high art of American individualism—liberalism in its purest form.

Unlike Ellison's Invisible Man, or Ellison himself, however, Coleman Silk has the option of the particular kind of masking likewise available to Anatole Broyard, who, at about the same moment, chose the mask of whiteness even though his immediate ancestors were, by law and custom, black. Like Silk, he wore the disguise of the cosmopolitan intellectual, and though his secret may have been the subject of speculation among friends and acquaintances, he never confronted it publicly or even revealed it openly to his children. Broyard's racial disguise, as we saw in Chapter 1, was made especially bittersweet in view of his 1950 essay "Portrait of the Inauthentic Negro," a text of confession whose hidden meaning, like that of Coleman Silk's life, would only be discovered years later.

Prompted by Sartre's argument that the Jew cannot easily transcend the inauthenticity of having always to define himself in reaction to anti-Semitism, in effect proving the anti-Semite's accusations "by devoting much of his efforts to guiltily dissociating himself from any semblance of Jewishness," Broyard in turn defined racial authenticity as a "stubborn adherence to one's essential self, in spite of the distorting pressures of one's situation." Because the Negro, unlike the Jew, is normally marked by his color, he cannot even pass into the inauthenticity of self-contempt. He necessarily reacts to racism, to definitions of himself invented by others, "until his personality is virtually usurped by a series of maneuvers none of which has any necessary relation to his true self." Without the disguise of whiteness available to most Jews, the inauthentic Negro lives trapped in modes of minstrelsy and self-denigration. Whereas the

---

* To the rabbi who had castigated him for "informing on the Jews" in *Goodbye, Columbus,* Roth replied the following year, as Ellison might have, that if the rabbi had learned nothing from the Holocaust except "how to remain a victim in a country where he does not have to live like one if he chooses," then it was *his* timidity and paranoia, not Roth's purported sacrilege, that was "an insult to the dead." Philip Roth, *The Facts: A Novelist's Autobiography* (1988; rpt. New York: Penguin, 1989), pp. 128–30; idem, "Writing about Jews" (1963), in *Reading Myself and Others,* new ed. (New York: Penguin, 1985), pp. 217–23.

inauthentic Jew has a "cultural residue to which he can secretly return, or by which he can at least negatively orient himself," wrote Broyard, the inauthentic Negro's "only common bond is that of *not being* anything else." Though it is a matter not of instinct but of social proscription, prejudice based on color cannot be escaped: "this stain doggedly endures," even though the absurdity of such physiognomic discrimination "becomes immediately apparent when we realize that thousands of Negroes with 'typical' features are accepted as whites merely because of light complexion."[30]

Broyard, as Henry Louis Gates, Jr., has remarked, was "a virtuoso of ambiguity and equivocation." Coyly failing to name himself among the "thousands of Negroes" who pass unnoticed as white, he adopted the most extreme form of inauthenticity without choosing to recognize it as such—or, it may be, without having the courage to confess his betrayal, except in the coded language of his essay. Within his decision lay a desire to escape the prison house of racial preconception that could be seen to have closed around Wright, Baldwin, and Ellison, among others.[31] But unlike Roth, who famously stated early in his career that he wished to be "not a Jewish writer" but rather "a writer who is a Jew,"[32] Broyard went further: he wished to be recognized as an intellectual and writer who could write knowingly about black culture without claiming it as his own. If he escaped the "stain" of racist stigmatization, of "not being anything else" but Negro, one cannot help but think that Broyard did not escape the stain of self-betrayal. Coleman Silk, at any rate, does not escape it. Before we look further at the nature of his tragedy, however, other Roth characters in masquerade, especially the ones passing as Amy Bellette and "Franz Kafka," deserve brief attention.

Appearing in 1979, one year after the television miniseries *Holocaust* and the announcement of plans for the United States Holocaust Memorial Museum, *The Ghost Writer* epitomized Roth's zest for tarnishing Jewish idols and desacralizing Holocaust sentimentality. Because it is set two decades earlier, as Jonathan Freedman reminds us, the novel "commemorates the world of Jewish intellectuals at their apogee"—figures such as Bernard Malamud, Saul Bellow, Lionel Trilling, Irving Howe, Leslie Fiedler, and Norman Mailer, among others—the same vital world that called into question the ability of William Styron's postwar alter ego, Stingo, to compete with "a pounding fast-footed horde of Bellows and Schwartzes and Levys and Mandelbaums" and into whose periphery Coleman Silk passes in 1953.[33] A self-contained tour de force, the tale uses Nathan Zuckerman's pilgrimage to meet with the famous New England Jewish writer E. I. Lonoff (usually taken to be a version of Malamud, perhaps with aspects of Isaac Bashevis Singer and J. D. Salinger thrown in) as an occasion for Roth to answer, again, the detractors of *Goodbye, Columbus,* and the even greater hostility that greeted *Portnoy's Complaint* (1969)—"the book for which all anti-Semites have been praying," as Gershom Scholem wrote.[34]

In reaction, Roth hit upon a brilliant conceit: that Lonoff's houseguest and onetime lover, a young refugee named Amy Bellette, is actually the surviving Anne Frank, and that by marrying her Zuckerman/Roth can atone for his sins against Jewish sensibilities. Of course, in making Anne Frank the burlesque object of Nathan's affections, Roth simply magnified his offense by laying unclean hands upon the premiere Jewish icon of American popular culture. In this fantasy of betrothal to the ultimate "Holocaust Jew,"[35] however, it was not Anne Frank the diarist that Roth subverted but the award-winning version of Anne Frank produced on Broadway in 1955—an Anne Frank, as we have seen earlier, made the mouthpiece of platitudes about irrepressible hope and the prevailing goodness of man, and one no less alluring in 1979 than in her heyday on stage and screen in the 1950s.[36] The terms of Marie Syrkin's overheated attack on *Portnoy's Complaint* as "racial defilement" straight out of the Nazism of Joseph Goebbels and Julius Streicher thus reappear in the letter written to Zuckerman by a prominent local Jewish judge who advises Zuckerman to see the stage production of Anne Frank's life. Freed from the high elegiac tone of hagiography that Roth said he had to overcome,[37] Zuckerman/Roth redeemed Anne Frank from Holocaust deniers and Holocaust idolators alike, even as he declared the artist's supremacy, or at least his momentary victory, over philistinism.

Like Kafka, says Dan Isaac, Roth placed himself on trial in response to his critics.[38] Yet to judge from the short story embedded within Roth's 1973 essay "'I Always Wanted You to Admire My Fasting'; or, Looking at Kafka," Kafka had already forecast Roth's authorial strategies to come. Here Kafka is alive in 1942 Newark, a fifty-nine-year-old Hebrew school teacher rooming with an elderly Jewish lady in a neighborhood where "the poorest of Newark's Negroes shuffle meekly up and down the street, for all they seem to know, still back in Mississippi,"[39] and about to be married to the narrator's maiden aunt. As in *The Ghost Writer,* the key masquerade is not the imagined betrothal but Kafka's putatively having chosen not to be Kafka, just as Anne Frank putatively chose to be Amy Bellette. In this case, too, the love story dead-ends; the engagement is broken off and Kafka disappears.

The bulk of Roth's essay, however, consists of his analysis of Kafka's scenarios of entrapment, in particular the enigmatic story "The Burrow," in which a mole-like creature—endowed with consciousness and the capacity for first-person narration but only vaguely human—laboriously builds his subterranean enclosure and guards it from mysterious, threatening intruders. Whatever else the story may reveal about the suppression of the individual in the proto-fascist state, Roth rightly found in this strange allegory of thinking and writing an expression of Kafka's "insanely defended ego."[40] Roth's fictive Kafka, like his fictive Anne Frank, illustrates his own penchant for disguises, impersonation, and the fabrication of selves, as in his longtime writerly personae of Nathan Zuckerman and David Kepesh, or the "Philip Roth" of *Operation Shylock,* in each of whom Roth's guarding his fictive burrows from hostile intruders plays a prominent role. Coleman Silk is a further variation in this sequence, combining Roth's early interest in the willing betrayal of one's communal identity with his ongoing investigation of the ego straining against imprisoning barriers while at the same time enclosing itself in protective fictions. As imagined by Roth, Anne Frank and Franz Kafka escape, if just for a fictional moment, the imprisoning identities given them by history. Coleman Silk proposes to escape for a lifetime—if only, as in the case of Julius Lester, by substituting one racial history for another.

In making himself a Jew, Silk leaps beyond the prison of identity bequeathed him by the circumstance of birth, attempting to stand outside "the coercive, inclusive, historical, inescapable moral we with its insidious *E pluribus unum*" and to celebrate instead "the raw I with all its agility."[41] Like Roth's Anne Frank and Kafka, however, he also enacts a fiction that finally cannot be sustained. His canny self-making, what Ross Posnock refers to as his "lethal fantasy of autogenesis," is undone by an unintended, out-of-date pun. Because his crime "exceeded anything and everything [his colleagues] wanted to lay on him," Zuckerman realizes, to destroy Silk for the faux pas of "spooks" is "to banalize everything—the elaborate clockwork of his lie, the beautiful calibration of his deceit, *everything.*"[42] But the beauty of his deceit and the banality of his destruction are not opposed; they are as intimately related as Silk's false Jewishness and his concealed blackness. One may stipulate that Silk, wracked by secret guilt, subconsciously speaks the word that sets in motion his tragic destruction, but it hardly matters. His downfall is certain. For his hubris in presuming to reveal "race" as a mere sign, purely connotative, not a denotative thing, Silk must be sacrificed according to the "rite of purification" announced in Roth's epigraph from *Oedipus Rex:* "By banishing a man, or expiation of blood by blood."

Or race by race. According to the parable of the crow from which Roth's title comes—a crow raised by humans and therefore stained by species contamination momentarily escapes into the wild, whereupon he is attacked by other crows—the "human stain" is the ineradicable "imprint" of human "impurity, cruelty, abuse, error, excrement, semen" that we leave in the wake of our living. The stain of being human, according to Roth's parable, has nothing to do with grace or salvation or redemption, for it "*precedes* disobedience . . . *encompasses* disobedience and perplexes all explanation and understanding*,*" making all efforts at "cleansing . . . a joke."[43] One may also stipulate, as Roth argues, that the fantasy of prelapsarian purity is false and appalling. But in shifting the question of purity from the behavioral domain of illicit sex, highlighted by the Bill Clinton–Monica Lewinsky imbroglio that provides the novel's backdrop, to the ontological domain of illicit race, Roth places the problems of "purity" and "cleansing" into a far more volatile context and initiates a far more complex expiation of "blood by blood."

In a simple sense, the parable of the crow explains why Coleman Silk, a black man who ventured beyond his given racial boundaries, is attacked and finally killed for having tempted fate. The premonitory case of Anatole Broyard, however, enlarges the parable's meaning. For Broyard, the "stain" he sought to escape by passing was not really race—in his case it could not have been color per se, the visible stain of race—but racism, the imputation to an individual of characteristics on the basis of beliefs codified by the "one-drop" rule of racial identity. Coleman Silk, as conceived by Roth, would likewise transcend the stain of racism, even at the cost of renouncing his black family and substituting a Jewish one in succeeding generations. Despite his academic accomplishments in high school and later at Howard University—where, rather than being "a nigger and nothing else . . . he was a *Negro* and nothing else"[44]—Silk, looking into the future, foresaw the difficulty he would encounter in being taken seriously as a classics scholar, not just a *Negro* classics scholar. He might also have foreseen that one day, inevitably, it would fall to him to introduce the college's first Black Studies course and, willy-nilly, be a role model and mentor for all black students—and then, if he refused his racial role, to be branded a race traitor, if not a bootlicking Uncle Tom. Why not, in the face of such a future, trade the stereotype of the black as body, the biological danger, for the stereotype of the Jew as mind, the intellectual danger?

The years that witnessed the Americanization of millions of Jewish immigrants and refugees, the slaughter of millions more in Europe, and the establishment of a defiant Jewish state, Roth once wrote, also produced a novelistic enterprise among American Jews of "imagining Jews *being* imagined," by themselves and others.[45] Jews were not the "danger" in the United States that they were in Germany, but neither were they free from "being imagined" invidiously. For Roth, the metafictional strategies a novelist might employ in response were manifest in his awareness that Jews may be trapped not only in anti-Semitic images when imagined by others, but also, as the instinctive recoil of his early Jewish detractors proved, in the *anti*-anti-Semitic images of their own community, a dilemma that drove Roth, one might say, to write *anti-anti-anti*-Semitic fiction. "Not making Jews invisible"[46] entailed making them hyper-visible, whether through Alex Portnoy's outrageous confession or Nathan Zuckerman's fantasy of making Anne Frank his bride.

In the case of Coleman Silk, who seeks to escape the dilemma of "blacks being imagined," Roth chose an inverse strategy. Rather than making Silk hyper-visible, he made him hyper-invisible—almost. Like the concentration camp number tattooed on those people he joins by passing as a Jew, the sign of what Silk would always secretly be, the sign of the indivisibility of his "heroism and [his] disgrace," is the light blue "U.S. Navy" tattoo he gets the night he is tossed out of a Norfolk whorehouse after being detected as black—"a tattoo being the very emblem of what cannot be removed."[47] Jewishness could be hidden in Nazi Germany, but not removed; once detected, it was marked with the yellow star and the blue number. Silk's blackness can be hidden, but not removed; although it is not literally detected in the novel's present-day action, except by Zuckerman, it is nonetheless figuratively revealed by force of circumstance and marked by his disgrace and death.

In the irony of his downfall over "spooks," we see that the racism Silk wished to escape has come full circle. His condemnation for the incident is preordained by the inquisitorial environment in which he makes his living, an environment in which the condemnation requires no logic or rationale—"only a label is required. The label is the motive. The label is the evidence. The label is the logic." The "stranglehold of history" in which Silk is caught thus offers a kind of poetic justice, not just because Silk himself is a "spook" in disguise but, more important, because his original act of passing was by itself, a lifetime in advance, a radical renunciation of the shibboleths of affirmative action, multiculturalism, and diversity, which now rise up to destroy him. Whereas Zuckerman says of Silk, "It's the secret that's his magnetism," the fact that there is a "blank" in his identity, the "label" is the antithesis of the "blank" on which Silk's birth has written "black," on which he instead writes "Jew," and on which his myopic community finally writes "racist."[48]

Over the course of Silk's academic career, the liberating energy of the 1960s has become the identitarian straitjacket of the 1990s, the logic of diversity, from *Bakke* onward, having been inexorably to make race and ethnicity categorical proxies for intellectual and ideological diversity.[49] The young man Silk thought to free himself from one kind of racism; the old man Silk, having learned that "freedom is dangerous," is struck down by another kind of racism—what his sister, upon hearing from Zuckerman about the "spooks" incident, refers to as "buffoonery."[50]

Seen from one angle of vision, passing is an expression of self-hatred, a form of self-reflexive racism (or, in the case of a Jew, a self-reflexive anti-Semitism). Silk, in this case, gets what he deserves. What of his creator, a man preoccupied with masquerade and self-making? Attributing Silk's motives to Roth, one might assume Roth is acknowledging that, were he black, he would wish not to be. In depicting a black man who wishes to be not black but Jewish, however, Roth leaves Silk open to a different form of suspicion and persecution. A singular problem of Silk's "impersonation," his attempt to escape racism, Zuckerman realizes, is that he was not only "buried as a Jew" but also "killed as a Jew" by Faunia's former husband, for whom Silk's Jewishness is just as provoking as his blackness would have been.[51] In choosing an identity that allows (or requires) him not to pass completely and leaves him the target of a man in whom anti-Semitism registers as strongly as anti-black racism, Silk imposes a self-selected moral marking, a "stain," on his whiteness. He thus does more than choose intellect over body, more than cover his tracks should his children turn out a little "darker" than his own crimped hair and yellowish pigmentation. Even as he renounces blackness and its liabilities, he inadvertently exposes the illusion that Jews are safe, white enough to escape the rage of nativist racists. In Coleman Silk's charade, the fates of black and Jew remain bound together as tightly, as fatally, as ever—the expiation of blood by blood, race by race.

The irony of Silk's death, however, does not undo the moral choice on which he bases his life. Not proving but instead subverting Jews' historic commitment to pluralism and especially to African American rights, Coleman Silk selects an identity destined over time—as Roth knew, writing in the 1990s, whether or not we are to imagine that Silk did in 1953—to make him not more like but more *unlike* his past self, not an ally but a *stranger* to the person he might have been. That is, he makes himself precisely the thing some blacks, whether those who rejected Jewish liberalism as exploitative paternalism or those who, in extremity, held Jews responsible for the enormities of both slavery and their own Holocaust, might most resent—namely, a Jew. "As a heretofore unknown amalgam of the most unalike of America's historic undesirables, he now made sense."[52] Coleman Silk contains the whole history of the twentieth-century black-Jewish question—its paradoxical intimacies, as well as its ever-accumulating differences and animosities—in one liberatingly invented but ultimately tragic life.

OUR RESPECTIVE EXILES

In what ways will the idiosyncratic Julius Lester and the irascible Philip Roth speak to readers of the twenty-first century? *Lovesong* and *The Human Stain*, by my account, make a provocative epilogue to the black-Jewish question in the twentieth century in that they propose two means of escape from constraining identities, though certainly not from the problem of racialized identity. In each case, black emulation of Jews is painfully literalized, as blackness is left behind—at least in principle—in favor of the unpredictable but nonetheless perceptible advantages of Jewishness. Blackness is pervasive enough in the national culture to create its own kinds of emulation, of course, but the disadvantages of being African American in the United States remain self-evident. If Jews were once the "Indian scouts" for blacks, "shrewd people showing the outsider his way in," in Roth's words, blacks are still the "miner's canary," in the metaphor of Lani Guinier and Gerald Torres, the people whose symptoms of distress signal social problems that put the whole nation at risk.[53]

Such metaphors are hardly univocal. In arguing that the cultural models available for adoption in an ethnically diverse society are more numerous than theorists of assimilation admit, Lawrence Levine recalls that in African American jazz he and his childhood friends, Jewish boys from immigrant families, "not only found an art that touched us, we also saw the possibility of functioning in the outside society while retaining our individual and ethnic personas."[54] Blacks, that is to say, might show Jews the way in by showing them how to thrive in the margins of American culture. And, as Roth's novel reminds us, Jews today may be comfortable without being entirely secure. Indeed, the resurgence of anti-Semitism in the twenty-first century says that Jews, even if they are comparatively safe in the United States, are still the "miner's canary" in many parts of the world.

The dissolution of the ethno-racial pentagon and other schemes for identifying people according to color-coded ancestry may eventually bring us fresh ways of moving from the outside in or the inside out. Purged of tribalistic incentives, multiculturalism might actually work. But, given the persistence of some kinds of prejudice, ancient and mystical, one may still fear, to hark back to Franz Boas, that anti-black racism will not disappear "until the negro blood has been so much diluted that it will no longer be recognized just as anti-Semitism will not disappear until the last vestige of the Jew as a Jew has disappeared."[55] Who, then, will be the new blacks, the new Jews?

A man from Mars would surely find it "strange and tragically ironic that the Jewish and Negro peoples on planet Earth are not allies," L. D. Reddick observed in 1942. Writing at a time when the full scope of the Holocaust was unknown, Reddick, as we saw earlier, could be pardoned for thinking the situations of Jews in Europe and blacks in the United States were closely comparable; but his urgent plea made sense to those Jews and blacks who already had been, who were then, and who would later become allies. So did the challenge issued by Sanford Goldner, writing a decade later and with "the deaths of six million of our fellow Jews" in mind, to recognize that the fight for Negro rights was one way "to know fully the meaning . . . of our own survival."[56]

No sooner had Jews and blacks brought their strategies for achieving equality and acceptance into close alignment, however, than they began to split apart. Aspirations that might have united them turned into antagonistic contraries: Jews became White, while Negroes became Black; Afro-Zionism became anti-Zionism; quotas that excluded became quotas that included; "6 million" had to compete with "Sixty Million and more." Just another decade after Goldner's plea, indeed, it may have been only in the counterfactual world of science fiction that the perils faced by the two groups could still be thought similar. Years before his futuristic parables made him a cult figure, Philip Dick imagined in *The Man in the High Castle* (1962) that Germany and Japan had won the war and divided the United States into protectorates. In the future that might have been, black slavery is once again legal—indeed, it is mandatory—and, with death camps and Nuremberg Laws operative in New York, Jews have fled to other parts of the country to lead clandestine lives. Japan is bogged down conquering South America, while Germany, having carried out in fifteen years a shadowy but thorough genocide in Africa ("wiped out to make a land of—what? Who knew? Maybe even the master architects in Berlin did not know"), has begun the colonization of space.*

---

* If Germany had lost the war, the populace believes, Jews would be running the world from Moscow and Wall Street. In a 1964 essay Dick rejected racial categories and the notion of collective responsibilities, whether one speaks of "Germans," "Jews," or "whites." But he also avowed that all people have a propensity for Nazism, even Jews, and gave the example of Zionists, the "arrogant nationalists" who "drove one million Arabs out of Israel," as he saw it, the "greatest single lot of displaced persons on earth today." Philip K. Dick, *The Man in the High Castle* (1962; rpt. New York: Vintage, 1992), p. 11; idem, "Na-

The triumph of Hitler, now unthinkable, would have brought a future no less horrendous, one in which neither Jews nor blacks could have expected anything but slavery and death. In this respect, Dick's fantasy remains compelling as a reminder of how like yet unlike blacks and Jews were by the early 1960s. In the mirror of history, each people saw both themselves and their exact opposites. Jews had not come as slaves to America, had never faced the same degree of discrimination as blacks, and were on their way to the suburbs, even as their fellow Jews in Europe had nearly been annihilated. Only the distant ancestors of contemporary blacks had been slaves, nor had there ever been an attempt, let alone one so recent, to wipe them off the face of the earth, yet massive civil disobedience and sporadic violence were required to bring them out of their long servitude to Jim Crow. For some Jews, blacks continued to provide a test of their morality and courage, while for others they were dangerous anti-Semites; for some blacks, Jews continued to be brothers in the struggle for racial justice, while for others they were as white as the Ku Klux Klan. The story of blacks and Jews over the course of the twentieth century is a story of the coalescence of minority interests and then their disintegration, the raveling and the unraveling.

What would Reddick's man from Mars see today? Four decades after the civil rights victories marking the high point of the black-Jewish alliance, and despite their undeniable integration and their success in numerous professions, the promise of inclusion remains vexingly unfulfilled for many blacks—witness their disproportionate confinement in a culture of poverty and crime, for example, or the outpouring of doubt about the effectiveness or even the wisdom of *Brown v. Board of Education* on the its fiftieth anniversary in 2004— while for Jews the promise was generally fulfilled long ago. Unlike blacks, Jews have "made it" in America. They have found the point of equilibrium at which they can be Jews or not. If they choose to be Jews—the sobering lesson of Coleman Silk's murder notwithstanding—they can generally do so without fear of discrimination or attack. By choice and by cultivation of a distinctive religion (for those who practice it), a distinctive language (for those schooled in it), and a distinctive culture (for everyone else), they may indeed be separate *and* equal. Whatever Jewish Studies or the colorless rainbow of "whiteness studies" may claim for them as an ethnic minority rather than part of the nonethnic majority, and however much they may sometimes use their marginality to strategic advantage, Jews cannot easily claim to be outsiders.

zism and The High Castle" (1964), in *The Shifting Realities of Philip K. Dick: Selected Literary and Philosophical Writings*, ed. Lawrence Sutin (New York: Vintage, 1995), pp. 115–16.

In contrast, even though the minority rights revolution brought other ethno-racial groups—Latinos and Asians in particular—into the negotiations, African Americans, despite their economic and political gains, have generally retained their position as the most disadvantaged outsiders. Standing in the invigorating, oppositional relationship to the broader American culture that was once the case for Jews, blacks have continued to be at once the most and the least American of Americans. At the dawn of the transnational, potentially post-race, post-ethnic twenty-first century, blacks are still "America's Jews," first and foremost the "keeper of the nation's sense of democratic achievement," as Ellison said in the bicentennial year 1976, "and the human scale by which would be measured its painfully slow advance toward true equality."[57] Despite their singular modern tragedy and continued threats against them worldwide, Jews are not "America's Negroes."

No doubt there are still individual blacks and Jews ardently working together on issues of common interest. Cornel West, Michael Lerner, Susannah Heschel, and others have joined together to work on behalf of various Israeli-Palestinian peace initiatives. In New York City, where blacks and Jews railed at each other during the school crisis in 1968 and resorted to violence during the Crown Heights crisis in 1991, radio station WWRL-AM in Queens played host beginning in 2002 to a morning talk show featuring the African American Peter Noel and the Orthodox rabbi Shmuley Boteach interviewing guests across the political spectrum and debating issues of race in America.[58] In Los Angeles, Cookie Lommel, an African American labor activist, became the executive director of the Jewish Labor Committee for the western United States. Inspired by Operation Solomon, the second of Israel's major airlifts of Ethiopian Jews to Israel, and with the support of both black and Jewish civic leaders, as well as major Jewish philanthropists, in 1992 she established Operation Unity, which takes inner-city black and Latino youth to Israel for two months of life on a kibbutz. "I have never been accepted in America as I was in Israel," Lommel has remarked.[59]

Such examples could be multiplied, but no matter what the measure, the time has come and gone when many Jews and blacks had obvious reasons to join hands. As fellow victims of persecution, and mindful of "our respective exiles," said Elie Wiesel in a birthday tribute to Bayard Rustin in 1987, blacks and Jews, "each with [their] own language and tradition, must create their own community, their own fraternity."[60] At one time thrust together in a common cause for which there remains no compelling motivation, Wiesel seemed to say, Jews and blacks might best go forward not as allies but as separate peoples attending to their own needs.

Whatever its future, however, the black-Jewish question remains central to the history of the United States in the twentieth century. Through their contrasting ways of cultivating identity and community in exile, and through their differing opportunities to do so, American Jews and African Americans established distinctive bulwarks against exclusion and victimization that may inform our understanding of how other minority cultures and the alliances between them are formed or fail to form. Although the points of disagreement were and remain intense, their dialogue created a profound sense that the shadow of the Holocaust not only stretched forward and backward, forever a confirmation of Jews' precarious existence, but also reached out to encompass other acts of genocide and racial violence, in purpose or effect. As activists, polemicists, and writers, they reset the course of American liberalism—its promise that all could belong to the nation, as well as the seeming demise of the idea of one nation to which all could belong; its promise of equality, as well as the failure even to find a definition of equality on which all could agree. Caught in the "stranglehold of history," as Roth put it, blacks and Jews finally went their separate ways. But even then they could not escape the ambiguous brotherhood that once defined them as strangers in the land of America.

Notes

Introduction

1. Leon Forrest, "Leon Forrest at the University of Kentucky," in John G. Cawelti, ed., *Leon Forrest: Introductions and Interpretations* (Bowling Green, Ohio: Bowling Green State University Popular Press, 1997), p. 298.

2. Studies of black-Jewish relations include Nat Hentoff, ed., *Black Anti-Semitism and Jewish Racism* (New York: Richard W. Baron, 1969); Robert G. Weisbord and Arthur Stein, *Bittersweet Encounter: The Afro-American and the American Jew* (Westport, Conn.: Negro Universities Press, 1970); Lenora Berson, *The Negroes and the Jews* (New York: Random House, 1971); Ben Halpern, *Jews and Blacks: The Classic American Minorities* (New York: Herder and Herder, 1971); Hasia Diner, *In the Almost Promised Land: American Jews and Blacks, 1915–1935* (1977; rpt. Johns Hopkins University Press, 1995); Joseph R. Washington, Jr., ed., *Jews in Black Perspectives: A Dialogue* (Cranbury, N.J.: Associated Universities Press, 1984); Robert G. Weisbord and Richard Kazarian, Jr., *Israel in the Black American Perspective* (Westport, Conn.: Greenwood Press, 1985); Jonathan Kaufman, *Broken Alliance: The Turbulent Times between Blacks and Jews in America* (1988; rpt. New York: Touchstone, 1995); William M. Phillips, *An Unillustrious Alliance: The African American and Jewish American Communities* (New York: Garland, 1991); Jack Salzman, ed., *Bridges and Boundaries: African Americans and American Jews* (New York: George Braziller, 1992); Paul Berman, ed., *Blacks and Jews: Alliances and Arguments* (New York: Delacorte, 1994); Hubert G. Locke, *The Black Anti-Semitism Controversy: Protestant Views and Perspectives* (Selinsgrove, Pa.: Susquehanna University Press, 1994); Murray Friedman, *What Went Wrong? The Creation and Collapse of the Black-Jewish Alliance* (New York: Free Press, 1995); Jack Salzman and Cornel West, eds., *Struggles in the Promised Land: Toward a History of Black-Jewish Relations in the United States* (New York: Oxford University Press, 1997); Katya Gibel Azoulay, *Black, Jewish, and Interracial: It's Not the Color of Your Skin, but the Race of Your Kin, and Other Myths of Identity* (Durham, N.C.: Duke University Press, 1997); Seth Forman, *Blacks in the Jewish Mind: A Crisis of Liberalism* (New York: New York University Press, 1998); V. P. Franklin et al., eds., *African Americans and Jews in the Twentieth Century: Studies in Convergence and Conflict* (Columbia: University of Missouri Press, 1998); Alan Heimrich and Paul Marcus, eds., *Blacks and Jews on the Couch: Psychoanalytic Reflections on Black-Jewish Conflict* (Westport, Conn.: Praeger, 1998); Maurianne Adams and John Bracey, eds., *Strangers and Neighbors: Relations between Blacks and Jews in the United States* (Amherst: University of Massachusetts Press, 1999); Robert Philipson, *The Identity Question: Blacks and Jews in Europe and America* (Jackson: University of Mississippi Press, 2000); Yvonne Chireau and Nathaniel Deutsch, eds., *Black Zion: African American Religious Encounters with Judaism* (New York: Oxford University Press, 2000).

Books that feature substantial discussion of the relationship include Arnold Foster and Benjamin R. Epstein, *The New Anti-Semitism* (New York: McGraw-Hill, 1974); Elly Bulkin, Minnie Bruce Pratt, and Barbara Smith, *Yours in Struggle: Three Feminist Perspectives on Anti-Semitism and Racism* (Brooklyn, N.Y.: Long Haul Press, 1984); Benjamin Ginsberg, *The Fatal Embrace: Jews and the State* (Chicago: University of Chicago Press, 1993); Leonard Dinnerstein, *Anti-Semitism in America* (New York: Oxford University Press, 1994); Stuart Svonkin, *Jews against Prejudice: American Jews and the Fight for Civil Liberties* (New York: Columbia University Press, 1997); David Biale, Michael Galchinsky, and Susannah Heschel, eds., *Insider/Outsider: American Jews and Multiculturalism,* (Berkeley: University of California Press, 1998); Marc Dollinger, *Quest for Inclusion: Jews and Liberalism in Modern America* (Princeton: Princeton University Press, 2000); and Michael E. Staub, *Torn at the Roots: The Crisis of Jewish Liberalism in Postwar America* (New York: Columbia University Press, 2002). Studies of the relationship in literature are cited elsewhere. For an excellent bibliographical guide, see Adam Meyer, *Black-Jewish Relations in African American and Jewish American Fiction: An Annotated Bibliography* (Lanham, Md.: Scarecrow Press, 2002).

3. Berman, introduction to *Blacks and Jews,* p. 5.
4. Philip Roth, *The Human Stain* (Boston: Houghton Mifflin, 2000), p. 132.
5. Adam Zachary Newton, *Facing Black and Jew: Literature as Public Space in Twentieth-Century America* (New York: Cambridge University Press, 1999), p. 10.
6. Emily Miller Budick, *Blacks and Jews in Literary Conversation* (New York: Cambridge University Press, 1998); Ethan Goffman, *Imagining Each Other: Blacks and Jews in Contemporary American Literature* (Albany: State University of New York Press, 2000), p. 13.
7. William Melvin Kelley, "The Ivy League Negro," *Esquire* 60 (August 1963), 54.
8. Chester Himes, *Lonely Crusade* (New York: Alfred A. Knopf, 1947), p. 159.
9. Douglas Greenberg, "An Uneasy Alliance," *Chicago History* 20 (Fall 1994), 5–19.
10. Thomas Sowell, *The Economics and Politics of Race* (New York: Morrow, 1983), p. 187.
11. Samantha Power, *"A Problem from Hell": America and the Age of Genocide* (New York: Basic Books, 2002).
12. Malcolm X, letter to *Amsterdam News,* May 10, 1964, quoted in Azoulay, *Black, Jewish, and Interracial,* p. 136n.
13. Stokely Carmichael, "The Black American and Palestinian Revolutions" (1968), in *Stokely Speaks: Black Power Back to Pan-Africanism* (New York: Random House, 1971), pp. 137–138.
14. Amiri Baraka [LeRoi Jones], "For Tom Postell, Dead Black Poet," in *Black Magic: Collected Poetry, 1961–1967* (Indianapolis: Bobbs-Merrill, 1969), p. 154.
15. Berel Lang, "On the 'the' in 'the Jews': or, From Grammar to Anti-Semitism," *Midstream* 49 (May/June 2003), 9–11.
16. Kenneth B. Clark, "Jews in Contemporary America: Problems in Identification" (1954), rpt. in Norman Kiell, ed., *The Psychodynamics of American Jewish Life: An Anthology* (New York: Twayne, 1967), p. 113.
17. Rogers M. Smith, *Stories of Peoplehood: The Politics and Morals of Political Membership* (New York: Cambridge University Press, 2003), pp. 102–3.
18. Samuel G. Freedman, "A Relationship That's Past Its Prime," *New York Times,* May 17, 2003, A17.
19. Lore Segal, *Her First American* (1985; rpt. New York: New Press, 1990), p. 263.

1. America's Jews

1. L. D. Reddick, "Anti-Semitism among Negroes," and Louis Harap, "Anti-Negroism among Jews," both in Jack Salzman, ed., *Bridges and Boundaries: African Americans and American Jews* (New York: George Braziller, 1992), pp. 79, 77.
2. James Baldwin, "The Harlem Ghetto" (1948), in *Notes of a Native Son* (1955; rpt. New York: Bantam, 1979), pp. 55–56.
3. Jerome A. Chanes, "Antisemitism and Jewish Security in Contemporary America," in Roberta Rosenberg Farber and Chaim I. Waxman, eds., *Jews in America: A Contemporary Reader* (Hanover, N.H.: Brandeis University Press, 1999), pp. 124–50; Jonathan D. Sarna, "American Anti-Semitism," in David Berger, ed., *History and Hate: The Dimensions of Anti-Semitism* (Philadelphia: Jewish Publication Society, 1986), pp. 115–28.
4. During the war, one poll showed that two thirds of Americans believed that Jews had too much influence, half would sympathize with an anti-Semitic campaign, and fewer than a third opposed such a campaign. Although some forms of anti-Semitism reached a high point immediately after the war, public recognition of anti-Semitism as a historical problem was accompanied by a significant, if somewhat erratic, decrease in perception of objectionable "Jewish traits"—vulgarity, dishonesty, pushiness, lack of refinement—between the late 1930s and the early 1960s. A survey conducted by *Fortune* magazine in 1947 showed that more than one third of Americans polled believed that Jews had too much economic power, while one fifth thought they had too much political power. In answer to its own question "Do Jews have too much power?" the Anti-Defamation League found that 56 percent answered affirmatively at the end of World War II, while the number dropped to 13 percent in 1964 and 10 percent in 1981. C. Bezalel Sherman, *The Jew within American Society: A Study in Ethnic Individuality* (Detroit: Wayne State University Press, 1961), p. 143; Charles Herbert Stember et al., eds., *Jews in the Mind of America* (New York: Basic Books, 1966), pp. 7–10, 48–75, 208–18; Howard M. Sachar, *A History of the Jews in America* (New York: Random House, 1992), p. 791.
5. By 1972, a Census Bureau survey by ethnic group showed that Jews had the highest median family income, the highest percentage of high school and college graduates, and the highest percentage of white-collar workers, while a similar survey by religious group likewise showed Jews to be the best educated and earning comparably higher salaries. By 1970, Jews constituted nearly one fifth of the professorate in elite colleges and universities, and in Ivy League schools they made up one quarter of the faculty hired since the end of World War II. In the last quarter of the twentieth century, when the African American population of the United States outnumbered the Jewish by a ratio of about 5 to 1 and Jews made up only 3 percent of the population, Jews likewise accounted for 50 percent of the top two hundred intellectuals (according to Charles Kadushin's 1974 book *The American Intellectual Elite*), 40 percent of American Nobel Prize winners in economics and science, more than 25 percent of the *Forbes* list of the richest four hundred Americans, and 40 percent of the partners in the leading law firms of Washington, D.C., and New York. Among college-age Jews, 87 percent were enrolled in institutions of higher education, more than twice the enrollment of the general population. David A. Hollinger, "Rich, Powerful, and Smart: Jewish Over-representation Should Be Explained Instead of Avoided or Mystified," *Jewish Quarterly Review* 94 (Fall 2004), 595–602; Milton R. Konvitz, "The Quest for Equality and the

Jewish Experience," in Gladys Rosen, ed., *Jewish Life in America: Historical Perspectives* (New York: Institute of Human Relations Press of the American Jewish Committee, 1978), pp. 33–36; Seymour Martin Lipset and Earl Raab, *Jews and the New American Scene* (Cambridge, Mass.: Harvard University Press, 1995), pp. 26–27; and Stephan Thernstrom and Abigail Thernstrom, *America in Black and White: One Nation, Indivisible* (New York: Simon and Schuster, 1997), p. 541.

6. Abba Hillel Silver, American Jewry in the War and After" (1944), in Arthur Hertzberg, ed., *The Zionist Idea: A Historical Analysis and Reader* (1959; rpt. Jewish Publication Society, 1997), p. 601; Jacob B. Agus in "The Meaning of *Galut* in America Today: A Symposium," *Midstream* 9 (1963), 6.

7. Cheryl Greenberg, "Pluralism and Its Discontents," in David Biale, Michael Galchinsky, and Susannah Heschel, eds., *Insider/Outsider: American Jews and Multiculturalism* (Berkeley: University of California Press, 1998), pp. 62–65.

8. See, for example, Cheryl I. Harris, "Whiteness as Property," in Kimberle Crenshaw et al., eds., *Critical Race Theory: The Key Writings That Formed the Movement* (New York: New Press, 1995), pp. 276–91.

9. Thomas F. Pettigrew, "Parallel and Distinctive Changes in Anti-Semitic and Anti-Negro Attitudes," in Stember et al., *Jews in the Mind of America*, pp. 384, 389–90; Murray Friedman, "The White Liberal's Retreat," *Atlantic Monthly* 211 (January 1963), 46.

10. Christopher Lasch, *The True and Only Heaven: Progress and Its Critics* (New York: W. W. Norton, 1991), pp. 407–11.

11. Introduction to Nat Hentoff, ed., *Black Anti-Semitism and Jewish Racism* (New York: Richard W. Baron, 1969), p. xvii.

12. Jacob Cohen in "Negro-Jewish Relations in America: A Symposium," *Midstream* 12 (December 1966), 12. The *Midstream* symposium, cited on a number of occasions throughout this book, was reprinted as Shlomo Katz, ed., *Negro and Jew: An Encounter* (New York: Macmillan, 1967). Contemporary with Cohen, Alan W. Miller came to a nearly identical conclusion: "[The black] is the one who, on the American scene, has been the persecuted. He is, in truth, the American 'Jew.'" Alan W. Miller, "Black Anti-Semitism—Jewish Racism," in Hentoff, *Black Anti-Semitism and Jewish Racism*, p. 101.

13. W. E. B. Du Bois, *The Souls of Black Folk* (1903; rpt. New York: Penguin, 1989), p. 100.

14. Frederick Douglass, "The Future of the Negro" (1884), in *The Life and Writings of Frederick Douglass*, ed. Philip S. Foner, 5 vols. (1955; rpt. New York: International Publishers, 1975), IV, 412.

15. Booker T. Washington, *The Future of the American Negro* (1900; rpt. New York: Negro Universities Press, 1969), pp. 181–83.

16. Alain Locke, "Apropos of Africa," *Opportunity* 2 (1924), 40.

17. Malcolm X, interview with the *Village Voice*, February 1965, in Malcolm X, *The Final Speeches*, ed. Steve Clark (New York: Pathfinder, 1992), p. 241; Malcolm X, 1963 interview with Alex Haley, in Alex Haley, The *Playboy Interviews*, ed. Murray Fisher (New York: Ballantine, 1993), p. 31.

18. Louis Armstrong, "Louis Armstrong + the Jewish Family in New Orleans, the Year of 1907" (memoir written 1969–70), in *Louis Armstrong in His Own Words: Selected Writings*, ed. Thomas Brothers (New York: Oxford University Press, 1999), pp. 9, 16–17. The grammar and strange orthography are Armstrong's, but the ellipses and bracketed clarifications are mine.

19. Booker T. Washington, *Up from Slavery* (1901; rpt. New York Penguin, 1986), p. 238. Mary Antin, *The Promised Land: The Autobiography of a Russian Immigrant* (1912; rpt. Princeton: Princeton University Press, 1985), pp. 141, 364. The phrase "Negro Moses"

appeared in an admiring newspaper account of Washington's famous Atlanta Exposition Address that he reprints in order to accredit his accommodationist positions.

20. Hasia Diner, *In the Almost Promised Land: American Jews and Blacks, 1915–1935* (1977; rpt. Baltimore: John Hopkins University Press, 1995), p. 74; Jeffrey Melnick, *A Right to Sing the Blues: African Americans, Jews, and American Popular Song* (Cambridge, Mass.: Harvard University Press, 1999), pp. 98–102; Michael Gold, *Jews without Money* (1930; rpt. New York: Avon Books, 1965), pp. 26, 113. On Gold's novel and related writings, see William J. Maxwell, *New Negro, Old Left: African-American Writing and Communism between the Wars* (New York: Columbia University Press, 1999), pp. 104–12.

21. Isaac Rosenfeld, *Passage from Home* (1946; rpt. New York: Markus Wiener, 1988), pp. 117–18.

22. *Daily Jewish Courier* quoted in David R. Roediger, *Colored White: Transcending the Racial Past* (Berkeley: University of California Press, 2002), p. 165; *Forward* quoted in Diner, *In the Almost Promised Land*, pp. 74–75.

23. Yosef Opatoshu, "Lintsheray," cited by Justin D. Cammy in an unpublished paper, "Oykh ikh zing amerike" (the title is from a Yiddish translation of Langston Hughes's "I too sing America"), used by permission.

24. See Milly Heyd, *Mutual Reflections: Jews and Blacks in American Art* (New Brunswick, N.J.: Rutgers University Press), pp. 86–116.

25. David Margolick, *Strange Fruit: Billie Holiday, Café Society, and an Early Cry for Civil Rights* (Philadelphia: Running Press, 2000), pp. 25–6, 37. Not surprisingly, singers and listeners have often assumed that the songwriter was black.

26. Derived from an 1864 French novel by Maurice Joly, the *Protocols* originated as a work of the Russian secret police in the 1890s and was later deployed by White Russians during the 1917 Revolution to advance the view that the Revolution was part of a Jewish plot of world domination. See, in particular, Norman Cohn, *Warrant for Genocide: The Myth of the Jewish World Conspiracy and the Protocols of the Elders of Zion* (1967; rpt. London: Serif, 1996), pp. 187–237; and Stephen Eric Bronner, *A Rumor about the Jews: Antisemitism, Conspiracy, and the Protocols of Zion* (New York: Oxford University Press, 2000).

27. David S. Wyman, "The United States," in David S. Wyman, ed., *The World Reacts to the Holocaust* (Baltimore: Johns Hopkins University Press, 1996), p. 700; Sachar, *History of Jews in America*, pp. 311, 321; Neil Baldwin, *Henry Ford and the Jews: The Mass Production of Hate* (New York: Public Affairs, 2001), pp. 144–51, 237–40; Leonard Dinnerstein, *Anti-Semitism in America* (New York: Oxford University Press, 1994), pp. 94–95, 109–24.

28. Irving Howe, *World of Our Fathers: The Journey of the East European Jews to America and the Life They Found and Made* (New York: Simon and Schuster, 1976), p. 631.

29. Al Sharpton and Anthony Walton, *Go and Tell Pharaoh: The Autobiography of the Reverend Al Sharpton* (New York: Doubleday, 1996), p. 204; Chaim Frazer quoted in David K. Shipler, *A Country of Strangers: Blacks and Whites in America* (New York: Alfred A. Knopf, 1997), p. 471.

30. Harold Cruse, *The Crisis of the Negro Intellectual: A Historical Analysis of the Failure of Black Leadership* (1967; rpt. New York: Quill, 1984), pp. 482–83; idem, "Negroes and Jews—The Two Nationalisms and the Bloc(ked) Plurality," in Salzman, *Bridges and Boundaries*, p. 130; Tony Martin, *The Jewish Onslaught: Despatches from the Wellesley Battlefront* (Dover, Mass.: Majority Press, 1993), p. 75. Enhancing and complicating, but nonetheless reviving, the myth of the conspiratorial Jew, Cruse, notes Ethan Goffman, finds in Jews "a unified explanation of Black paralysis." Ethan Goffman,

Imagining Each Other: Blacks and Jews in Contemporary American Literature (Albany: State University of New York Press, 2000), p. 98.

31. Haki Madhubuti, "Anti-Semitism as Weapon and the Jewish Mis-use of Blacks in Their Struggle for Power and Maximum Development," *Black Books Bulletin* 5 (Winter 1977), 73; Clayborne Carson, "The Politics of Relations between African-Americans and Jews," in Paul Berman, ed., *Blacks and Jews: Alliances and Arguments* (New York: Delacorte, 1994), p. 140.

32. David Levering Lewis, "Parallels and Divergences: Assimilationist Strategies of Afro-American and Jewish Elites from 1910 to the Early 1930s," in Salzman, *Bridges and Boundaries*, p. 25. See also Philip Foner, "Black-Jewish Relations in the Opening Years of the Twentieth Century," *Phylon* 36 (Winter 1975), 359–67.

33. See, for example, Milton R. Konvitz, "Jews and Civil Rights," in Peter I. Rose, ed., *The Ghetto and Beyond: Essays on Jewish Life in America* (New York: Random House, 1969), pp. 270–89; Nancy J. Weiss, "Long-Distance Runners of the Civil Rights Movement: The Contributions of Jews to the NAACP and the National Urban League in the Early Twentieth Century," Cheryl Greenberg, "Negotiating Coalition: Black and Jewish Civil Rights Agencies in the Twentieth Century," and Clayborne Carson, "Black-Jewish Universalism in the Era of Identity Politics," all in Jack Salzman and Cornel West, eds., *Struggles in the Promised Land: Toward a History of Black-Jewish Relations in the United States* (New York: Oxford University Press, 1997), pp. 123–52, 153–75, 177–96.

34. Yusef Komunyakaa quoted in Willis Barnstone, *We Jews and Blacks: Memoir with Poems* (Bloomington: Indiana University Press, 2004), p. 205.

35. Arthur Hertzberg, *The Jews in America: Four Centuries of an Uneasy Encounter* (New York: Columbia University Press, 1997), p. 327. For the role of Jews in the NAACP and the National Urban League in the early twentieth century, see Weiss, "Long-Distance Runners of the Civil Rights Movement," pp. 123–52; and Greenberg, "Negotiating Coalition," pp. 153–75.

36. Sachar, *History of the Jews in America*, p. 337.

37. Murray Friedman, *What Went Wrong? The Creation and Collapse of the Black-Jewish Alliance* (New York: Free Press, 1995), pp. 309–12.

38. Jonathan Kaufman, *Broken Alliance: The Turbulent Times between Blacks and Jews in America* (1988; rpt. New York: Touchstone, 1995), p. 101.

39. "What Is Torah?" quoted in Hasia R. Diner, "Jews and Blacks in America, 1880–1935," in Salzman and West, *Struggles in the Promised Land*, p. 91.

40. Israel Goldstein quoted in Michael E. Staub, *Torn at the Roots: The Crisis of Jewish Liberalism in Postwar America* (New York: Columbia University Press, 2002), p. 49.

41. Friedman, *What Went Wrong?* p. 119; Robeson quoted in Diner, *In the Almost Promised Land*, p. 68; Harry Belafonte quoted on back cover of Sheldon Feinberg, *Hava Nagila! The World's Most Famous Song of Joy* (New York: Shapolsky Publishers, 1988).

42. See Heyd, *Mutual Reflections*, pp. 120–24, 134–35. Shahn interpreted the ambiguous text of Leviticus 19:16—"neither shalt thou stand against the blood of thy neighbor"—to mean that people of conscience should not stand by idly while African Americans suffered and struggled for their rights. For another use of the scripture, see Chapter 6.

43. Martin Luther King, Jr., quoted in Milton R. Konvitz, "Jews and Civil Rights," in Rose, *The Ghetto and Beyond*, p. 283.

44. Charles Glicksberg quoted in Hertzberg, *The Jews in America*, pp. 326–27.

45. Clayborne Carson, "Black-Jewish Universalism in the Era of Identity Politics," in

Salzman, *Struggles in the Promised Land,* pp. 177–96; Silberman quoted in Milton R. Konvitz, "Jews and Civil Rights," in Rose, *The Ghetto and Beyond,* p. 285; Douglass Rushkoff, *Nothing Sacred: The Truth about Judaism* (New York: Crown, 2003), pp. 36–43.

46. Abraham Joshua Heschel, "Race and Religion" (1963), in *The Insecurity of Freedom* (New York: Farrar, Straus and Giroux, 1963), pp. 97–98.

47. Lenora Berson, *The Negroes and the Jews* (New York: Random House, 1971), pp. 112–27; Diner, *In the Almost Promised Land,* p. 237.

48. In Smith's earlier novel *The Last of the Conquerors* (1948), an anatomy of the equally unattractive racial regimes of the United States and Germany is offered from the perspective of African American soldiers in postwar occupied Germany who face three options—expatriatism in Europe, return to the United States, or defection to the Soviet Union. For a treatment of Smith's novels, see Paul Gilroy, *Against Race: Imagining Political Culture beyond the Color Line* (Cambridge, Mass.: Harvard University Press, 2000), pp. 308–24.

49. James Baldwin, introduction to *The Price of the Ticket: Collected Non-fiction, 1948–1985* (New York: St. Martin's, 1985), p. xix. Baldwin actually wrote that the Jew "makes the mistake of believing that his Holocaust ends in the New World, where mine begins," but the gist of the essay, as indeed of this passage otherwise, is to suggest a stark contrast.

50. Andrew Hacker, "Jewish Racism, Black Anti-Semitism" (1991), rpt. in Berman, *Blacks and Jews,* p. 161.

51. Art Spiegelman, *Maus II: A Survivor's Tale* (New York: Pantheon, 1991), p. 99.

52. Ruth Kluger, *Still Alive: A Holocaust Girlhood Remembered* (New York: Feminist Press, 2001), pp. 22–23; Phyllis Chesler, *The New Anti-Semitism: The Current Crisis and What We Must Do about It* (San Francisco: Josey-Bass, 2003), p. 78.

53. Ralph Bunche, *A World View of Race* (1936; rpt. Port Washington, N.Y.: Kennikat Press, 1968), p. 93.

54. Moise Katz quoted in Staub, *Torn at the Roots,,* p. 32.

55. Louis Ruchames, "Parallels of Jewish and Negro History," *Negro History Bulletin* 19 (December 1955), 63; Ronald Sanders in "The Meaning of *Galut* in America Today," 33.

56. Joachim Prinz, "The Issue Is Silence," in Nahum N. Glatzer, ed., *The Dynamics of Emancipation: The Jew in the Modern Age* (Boston: Beacon Press, 1965), pp. 252–53.

57. Shlomo Katz, "Notes in Midstream," *Midstream* 8 (September 1962), 62.

58. Berson, *The Negroes and the Jews,* unpaginated.

59. Albert Vorspan, "Blacks and Jews," in Hentoff, *Black Anti-Semitism and Jewish Racism,* p. 209.

60. Chester Himes, *Lonely Crusade* (New York: Alfred A. Knopf, 1947), pp. 152, 160.

61. James Baldwin, "Negroes Are Anti-Semitic Because They're Anti-White" (1967), in *The Price of the Ticket,* pp. 430–31.

62. Richard Wright, *Black Boy: A Record of Childhood and Youth* (1945; rpt. New York: Perennial, 1966), pp. 70–71.

63. Kenneth B. Clark, "Candor about Negro-Jewish Relations," in Salzman, *Bridges and Boundaries,* p. 97; Howard Fast in "Negro-Jewish Relations in America: A Symposium," *Midstream* 12 (December 1966), 18; Leslie Fiedler in "Negro-Jewish Relations in America," 24; Joel Carmichael in "Negro-Jewish Relations in America," 5; Oliver C. Cox, "Jewish Self-Interest in 'Black Pluralism,'" *Sociological Quarterly* 15 (Spring 1974), 195; Andrew Hacker, "Jewish Racism, Black Anti-Semitism," in Berman, *Blacks and*

Jews, p. 155; bell hooks, "Keeping a Legacy of Shared Struggle," in Berman, *Blacks and Jews,* p. 235; Dexter Jeffries, *Triple Exposure: Black, Jewish, and Red in the 1950s* (New York: Dafina Books, 2003), p. 339.

64. Alan Dundes, "A Study of Ethnic Slurs: The Jew and the Polack in the United States," *Journal of American Folklore* 84 (1971), 194.

65. Sufi Abdul Hamid quoted in Claude McKay, "Harlem Runs Wild," *The Nation* 140 (April 3, 1935), 383. See also Roi Ottley, *"New World A-Coming": Inside Black America* (New York: New World Publishing, 1943), pp. 116–19; and Winston C. McDowell, "Keeping Them 'In the Same Boat Together'? Sufi Abdul Hamid, African Americans, Jews, and the Harlem Jobs Boycotts," in V. P. Franklin et al., eds., *African Americans and Jews in the Twentieth Century: Studies in Convergence and Conflict* (Columbia: University of Missouri Press, 1998), pp. 208–36.

66. Dinnerstein, *Anti-Semitism in America,* pp. 201–7.

67. John A. Williams, "My Man Himes: An Interview with Chester Himes," in John A. Williams and Charles F. Harris, eds., *Amistad 1* (New York: Vintage, 1970), pp. 83–84; Bayard Rustin, "The Anatomy of Frustration," in *Down the Line: The Collected Writings of Bayard Rustin* (Chicago: Quadrangle Books, 1971), p. 233; Berson, *The Negroes and the Jews,* p. 145.

68. Arnold M. Rose, *The Negro's Morale: Group Identification and Protest* (Minneapolis: University of Minnesota Press, 1949), pp. 129–32. Rose draws here on Harold L. Sheppard, "The Negro Merchant: A Study of Negro Anti-Semitism," *American Journal of Sociology* 53 (September 1947), 96–99.

69. Karen Brodkin, *How Jews Became White Folks and What That Says about Race in America* (New Brunswick, N.J.: Rutgers University Press, 1998), pp. 46–50; Robin D. G. Kelley, *Yo' Mama's Disfunktional: Fighting the Culture Wars in Urban America* (Boston: Beacon Press, 1997), pp. 92–93.

70. Jo Sinclair, *The Changelings* (1955; rpt. New York: Feminist Press, 1983), pp. 266, 169, 114, 109–10, 234, 280–81, 268, 304–5.

71. The trend was repeated throughout the 1950s and 1960s. In 1966 alone, as blacks moved in, some seventy-five Orthodox synagogues were abandoned or sold in once heavily Jewish neighborhoods of New York City such as Brownsville, Crown Heights, Williamsburg, and the South Bronx. Sachar, *History of the Jews in America,* p. 817. For a representative broader study, see Wendell Pritchett, *Brownsville, Brooklyn: Blacks, Jews, and the Changing Face of the Ghetto* (Chicago: University of Chicago Press, 2002); on Cleveland in particular, see Kenneth Kusmer, *A Ghetto Takes Shape: Black Cleveland, 1870–1930* (Urbana: University of Illinois Press, 1976).

72. Sinclair, *The Changelings,* pp. 32–33.

73. Vernon H. Bernstein, "Why Negroes Are Still Angry" (originally in *Redbook,* July 1966), in Melvin Drimmer, ed., *Black History: A Reappraisal* (Garden City, N.Y.: Doubleday, 1968), p. 517.

74. Grace Paley, "The Long-Distance Runner" (1974), in *The Collected Stories* (New York: Farrar Straus Giroux, 1994), p. 244; Leslie Fiedler, "Negro and Jews: Encounter in America," in *No! in Thunder: Essays on Myth and Literature* (Boston: Beacon Press, 1960), p. 242.

75. Grace Paley, "Zagrowsky Tells" (1985), in *Later the Same Day* (1985; rpt. New York: Penguin, 1986), p. 159.

76. Ibid., p. 171.

77. Julius Lester, "The Outsiders: Blacks and Jews and the Soul of America," *Transition* 68 (Winter 1995), 73–74.

78. See, for example, Michael McCarthy, *Dark Continent: Africa as Seen by Americans*

(Westport, Conn.: Greenwood Press, 1983), pp. 59–119; Georg W. F. Hegel, *The Philosophy of History* (ca. 1825), trans. John Sibree (Amherst, N.Y.: Prometheus Books, 1991), p. 91.

79. Baldwin, "Negroes Are Anti-Semitic Because They're Anti-White," p. 431.

80. E. Franklin Frazier, *The Negro Family in the United States* (Chicago: University of Chicago Press, 1939), pp. 21–22.

81. Abram Kardiner and Lionel Ovesey, *The Mark of Oppression: Explorations in the Personality of the American Negro* (New York: World Publishing, 1951), pp. 38–41. On Herskovits and Frazier, see also Albert J. Raboteau, *Slave Religion: The "Invisible Institution" in the Antebellum South* (New York: Oxford University Press, 1978), pp. 7–16; and Wilson Jeremiah Moses, *Black Messiahs and Uncle Toms: Social and Literary Manipulations of a Religious Myth*, rev. ed. (University Park: Pennsylvania State University Press, 1993), pp. 22–25.

82. Harold R. Isaacs, "The American Negro and Africa: Some Notes," *Phylon* 20 (Fall 1959), 219–33. Although it might not count as a comparable instance of self-rejection, further evidence of the unequal "racialization" of blacks and Jews may be detected in the fact that Herskovits's immersion in the survivals of the African diaspora, meant to establish the legacy of distinctive traits of African culture in the New World, was not matched, in his own case, by an equal recognition of diasporic Jewish identity, which he took to be a cultural choice. See Walter Jackson, "Melville Herskovits and the Search for Afro-American Culture," in George W. Stocking, Jr., ed., *Malinowski, Rivers, Benedict, and Others: Essays on Culture and Personality* (Madison: University of Wisconsin Press, 1986), pp. 95–126; and Katya Gibel Azoulay, *Black, Jewish, and Interracial: It's Not the Color of Your Skin, but the Race of Your Kin, and Other Myths of Identity* (Durham,: Duke University Press, 1997), pp. 51–52.

83. Fiedler, "Negro and Jews: Encounter in America," pp. 231–32; Leo Strauss, "Why We Remain Jews" (1962), in *Jewish Philosophy and the Crisis of Modernity: Essays and Lectures in Modern Jewish Thought*, ed. Kenneth Hart Green (Albany: State University of New York Press, 1997), pp. 315–17.

84. Laurence Mordekhai Thomas, *Vessels of Evil: American Slavery and the Holocaust* (Philadelphia: Temple University Press, 1993), pp. 159, 202.

85. Himes, *Lonely Crusade*, p. 159.

86. Martin Luther King, Jr., *Where Do We Go From Here: Chaos or Community?* (Boston: Beacon Press, 1967), pp. 102–3, 133.

87. N. S. Shaler, *The Neighbor: The Natural History of Human Contacts* (Boston: Houghton Mifflin, 1904), pp. 123–24. Said James Weldon Johnson of Shaler, writing in the *New York Age* in 1916: "He went so far as to say that he knew Negroes of whom he was extremely fond, but that all Jewish persons, for some unexplainable reason, were positively repulsive to him." Johnson quoted in Daniel Itzkovitz, "Passing Like Me," *South Atlantic Quarterly* 98 (Winter/Spring 1999), 48.

88. Robert E. Park, introduction to Charles S. Johnson, *The Shadow of the Plantation* (1934; rpt. Chicago: University of Chicago Press, 1969), pp. xx–xxi; Nathan Glazer and Daniel Patrick Moynihan, *Beyond the Melting Pot: The Negroes, Puerto Ricans, Jews, Italians, and Irish of New York City*, 2nd ed. (1963; Cambridge, Mass.: MIT Press, 1970), pp. xiii. This remark appears in the introduction to the 1970 edition.

89. Bruce Jay Friedman, *Stern* (1962; rpt. New York: Atlantic Monthly Press, 1990), p. 97.

90. Du Bois, *Souls of Black Folk*, p. 215; W. E. B. Du Bois, *The Crisis* 17 (February 1919), rpt. as "Africa, Colonialism, and Zionism," in *The Oxford W. E. B. Du Bois*, ed. Eric J. Sundquist (New York: Oxford University Press, 1996), p. 639.

91. James Baldwin, "Stranger in the Village" (1953), in *Notes of a Native Son* (1955; rpt. New York: Bantam, 1979), pp. 143–44, 148.

92. Maulana Karenga quoted in Clarence E. Walker, *We Can't Go Home Again: An Argument about Afrocentrism* (New York: Oxford University Press, 2001), p. 60. Karenga, now a professor of Black Studies, was the founder of the Los Angeles–based US organization—meaning both "us" and, intended ironically, "U.S." Before it was disabled by a battle for power with the Black Panthers and by Karenga's conviction and four-year prison sentence for assault against a woman co-worker, US promoted holidays such as Kwanzaa, Malcolm X's birthday (Kuzaliwa), and the anniversary of the August 1965 Watts riot (Uhuru Day).

93. King quoted in Staub, *Torn at the Roots,* p. 20; Gerald Early, "Who Is the Jew? A Question of African-American Identity," *CommonQuest* (Spring 1996), 45.

94. Stephen J. Whitfield, "Why America Has Not Seemed Like Exile," *Michigan Quarterly Review* 41 (Fall 2002), 686; Edward S. Shapiro, *A Time for Healing: American Jewry since World War II* (Baltimore: Johns Hopkins University Press, 1992), pp. 9–10; Leslie Fiedler, "Saul Bellow" (1957), in *To the Gentiles* (New York: Stein and Day, 1972), p. 58; Kluger, *Still Alive,* pp. 196–97.

95. Hertzberg, *The Jews in America,* pp. 242, 304; Lucy Dawidowicz, *On Equal Terms: Jews in America, 1881–1981* (New York: Holt, Rinehart, and Winston, 1982), pp. 125–46; Arthur A. Goren, *The Politics and Public Culture of American Jews* (Bloomington: Indiana University Press, 1999), pp. 186–204; Judith R. Kramer and Seymour Leventman, *Children of the Gilded Ghetto: Conflict Resolutions of Three Generations of American Jews* (New Haven: Yale University Press, 1961); Philip Roth, *The Facts: A Novelist's Autobiography* (1988; rpt. New York: Penguin, 1989), p. 123. For representative studies of Jews and suburbanization, see also Albert A. Gordon, *Jews in Suburbia* (Boston: Beacon Press, 1959); Deborah Dash Moore, *To the Golden Cities: Pursuing the American Jewish Dream in Miami and L.A.* (New York: Free Press, 1994); and Irving Cutler, *The Jews of Chicago: From Shtetl to Suburb* (Urbana: University of Illinois Press, 1996).

96. Louis Harap, *In the Mainstream: The Jewish Presence in Twentieth-Century American Literature, 1950s–1980s* (New York: Greenwood Press, 1987), pp. 21–51; Sachar, *History of the Jews in America,* pp. 748–87.

97. Charles S. Liebman, *The Ambivalent American Jew: Politics, Religion, and Family in American Jewish Life* (Philadelphia: Jewish Publication Society of America, 1973); Norman Podhoretz, *Making It* (New York: Random House, 1967), p. 68.

98. Grace Paley, "Dreamer in a Dead Language" (1977), in *Later the Same Day,* p. 16.

99. Jerry Rubin, *We Are Everywhere* (New York: Harper and Row, 1971), pp. 75–76.

100. Strauss, "Why We Remain Jews," pp. 315–17.

101. It is noteworthy that Freeman, in explaining the risk, pointed to the racial ideology of South African prime minister Jan Christiaan Smuts, who urged that African native culture be preserved intact and set visibly apart as a way of marking and protecting the racial superiority of white South African culture. Ellis Freeman, "The Motivation of the Jew-Gentile Relationship," in Isacque Graeber and Steuart Henderson Britt, eds., *Jews in a Gentile World: The Problem of Anti-Semitism* (New York: Macmillan, 1942), pp. 176–77.

102. Thomas B. Morgan, "The Vanishing American Jew," *Look* 28 (May 5, 1964), 42–46.

103. Leslie Fiedler, "In Every Generation: A Meditation on the Two Holocausts," in David Rosenberg, ed., *Testimony: Contemporary Writers Make the Holocaust Personal* (New York: Random House, 1989), p. 229. On assimilation perceived to be a "silent" or "bloodless" Holocaust, see Peter Novick, *The Holocaust in American Life* (Boston: Houghton Mifflin, 1999), p. 185; and for a critique of several of the essays in *Testi-*

mony, including Fiedler's, see Edward Alexander, *The Holocaust and the War of Ideas* (New Brunswick, N.J.: Transaction, 1994), pp. 61–65.

104. Judah Magnes, "The Melting Pot" (1909), in *Dissenter in Zion: From the Writings of Judah L. Magnes,* ed. Arthur A. Goren (Cambridge, Mass.: Harvard University Press, 1982), pp. 101–6; Louis Brandeis, "The Jewish Problem, How to Solve It," in *Brandeis on Zionism: A Collection of Addresses and Statements by Louis D. Brandeis* (Washington, D.C.: Zionist Organization of America, 1942), pp. 28–30. On Zangwill and the early influence of his metaphor, see Philip Gleason, "The Melting Pot: Symbol of Fusion or Confusion?" *American Quarterly* 16 (Spring 1974), 20–46.

105. Steven T. Rosenthal, *Irreconcilable Differences? The Waning of the American Jewish Love Affair with Israel* (Hanover, N.H.: Brandeis University Press, 2001), pp. 15–18.

106. Randolph S. Bourne, "The Jew and Trans-national America" (1916), in *War and the Intellectuals: Collected Essays, 1915–1919,* ed. Carl Resek (New York: Harper and Row, 1964), p. 128.

107. Ibid., pp. 124, 127. Writing during the breakdown of an illusory national unity during World War I, Bourne worried that a false insistence on disintegrating the various "nuclei" of other cultures that held immigrant or ethnic groups together meant creating people "without a spiritual country, cultural outlaws, without taste, without standards but those of the mob." It was important to recognize figurative if not literal dual citizenship so as to preserve the "threads of living and potent cultures, blindly striving to weave themselves into a novel international nation." Any movement that attempts to "thwart this weaving, or to dye the fabric any one color, or disentangle the threads of the strands, is false to this cosmopolitan vision." Randolph S. Bourne, "Trans-national America," *Atlantic Monthly* 118 (1916), 90, 96–97.

108. Kallen, too, turned to the model of the Jews as the key to pluralist Americanization. Precisely as they become Americanized, less foreign, they learn or recall "the spiritual heritage of their nationality" and develop more cultural pride: "Once the wolf is driven from the door and the Jewish immigrant takes his place in American society a free man (as American *mores* establish freedom) and an American," he is at liberty to become more of a Jew. Horace M. Kallen, "Democracy vs. the Melting Pot" (1915), in *Culture and Democracy in the United States* (New York: Boni and Liveright, 1924), pp. 106, 112–13, 125; idem, "Culture and the Ku Klux Klan," ibid., p. 43. I am indebted here and subsequently to Werner Sollors, *Beyond Ethnicity: Consent and Descent in American Culture* (New York: Oxford University Press, 1986), pp. 181–86, and "A Critique of Pure Pluralism," in Sacvan Bercovitch, ed., *Reconstructing American Literary Studies* (Cambridge, Mass.: Harvard University Press, 1986), pp. 258–73; Sachar, *History of Jews in America,* pp. 377, 426–27; and David A. Hollinger, *Postethnic America: Beyond Multiculturalism* (New York: Basic Books, 1995), pp. 93–94.

109. Glazer and Moynihan, *Beyond the Melting Pot,* pp. xcvii. On proponents and opponents of the melting pot, see Sollors, *Beyond Ethnicity,* pp. 66–101.

110. Theodor Herzl, *The Jewish State* (1896), trans. Sylvie d'Avigdor and Jacob M. Alkow (New York: Dover, 1988), p. 89.

111. Omer Bartov, *Mirrors of Destruction: War, Genocide, and Modern Identity* (New York: Oxford University Press, 2000), pp. 104–11. As the Inquisition had determined that *conversos* were still Jews, subject to torment or death, Bartov notes, so the "nihilistic dynamics" of Nazism grew from the belief that destruction of the European Jews might have no end, that there would always be hidden Jews to root out and destroy.

112. *M'lle NY* editorial quoted in Itzkovitz, "Passing Like Me," 38; Louis Wirth, *The Ghetto* (1928; rpt. Chicago: University of Chicago Press, 1956), p. 291.

113. Somewhat paradoxically, Halpern recognized that because the history of American

Jews, the "youngest of Jewries," was effectively coincident with the post-emancipation entrance into modernity, Abraham Cahan's classic formulation of 1890 remained apropos more than half a century later: "We have no Jewish question in America. The only question we recognize is the question of how to prevent the emergence of 'Jewish questions' here." J. O. Hertzler, "The Sociology of Anti-Semitism through History," in Graeber and Britt, *Jews in a Gentile World,* pp. 82–83; Ben Halpern, *The American Jew: A Zionist Analysis* (1956; rpt. New York: Schocken, 1983), pp. 48–49, 58–59, 13–14.

114. Ellis Freeman, "The Motivation of Jew-Gentile Relationship," in Graeber and Britt, *Jews in a Gentile World,* pp. 149–50.

115. Leonard Dinnerstein and David M. Reimers, *Ethnic Americans: A History of Immigration,* 4th ed. (New York: Columbia University Press, 1999), p. 222.

116. Matthew Frye Jacobson, *Whiteness of a Different Color: European Immigrants and the Alchemy of Race* (Cambridge, Mass.: Harvard University Press, 1998), pp. 87–88; Gavit quoted in Nathan Glazer, *We Are All Multiculturalists Now* (Cambridge, Mass.: Harvard University Press, 1997), p. 105.

117. Edward B. Reuter, *The American Race Problem* (1927; rpt. New York: Thomas Y. Crowell, 1970), pp. 364–65.

118. Bruno Bettelheim and Morris Janowitz, *Dynamics of Prejudice: A Psychological and Sociological Study of Veterans* (New York: Harper and Brothers, 1950), pp. 32–47; Pettigrew, "Parallel and Distinctive Changes in Anti-Semitic and Anti-Negro Attitudes," pp. 385–86.

119. Fredrickson adds: "If the relative weakness of antimodernism in the United States promoted the toleration of Jews, it had the effect of exacerbating the disdain for blacks. The relation of the two groups to America's commitment to the modern seems to me a better explanation for the relative weakness of American anti-Semitism than the conventional theory that Jews were not needed as universal scapegoats because blacks already performed that function." George M. Fredrickson, *Racism: A Short History* (Princeton: Princeton University Press, 2002), pp. 94–95.

120. "Racism had developed into such a contradictory mass of the unprovable and the emotional," wrote Thomas Gossett, "that the serious students eventually recognized that as a source of explanation for mental and temperamental traits of a people it was worthless. Once this point was accepted, the top-heavy intellectual structures of racism began to topple, one after another." Thomas F. Gossett, *Race: The History of an Idea in America* (1963; New York: Schocken, 1969), pp. 409–30, quotation at p. 430.

121. Raymond Kennedy, "The Position and Future of the Jews in America," in Graeber and Britt, *Jews in a Gentile World,* pp. 418–32.

122. Jacobson, *Whiteness of a Different Color,* pp. 91–135, 188.

123. John Higham, *Send These to Me: Jews and Other Immigrants in Urban America* (New York: Atheneum, 1975), pp. 174–95, quotation at p. 176.

124. Otto Klineberg, ed., *The Characteristics of the American Negro* (New York: Harper and Row, 1944). The volume was part of the "Study of the Negro in America" project for the Carnegie Corporation, directed by Gunnar Myrdal, of which *An American Dilemma* was a part.

125. Kardiner and Ovesey, *The Mark of Oppression,* pp. v, 387.

126. John D. Skrentny, *The Minority Rights Revolution* (Cambridge, Mass.: Harvard University Press, 2002), pp. 23–37.

127. Myrdal, *American Dilemma,* I, 5–12; Fredrickson, *Racism,* pp. 128–32, 166–67. For accounts of the social and legal theories underpinning desegregation, see also, for example, Richard Kluger, *Simple Justice: The History of Brown v. Board of Education and Black America's Struggle for Equality* (New York: Random House, 1975); Harvard

Sitkoff, *A New Deal for Blacks: The Emergence of Civil Rights as a National Issue* (New York: Oxford University Press, 1978), pp. 190–243; Mark V. Tushnet, *Making Civil Rights Law: Thurgood Marshall and the Supreme Court, 1936–1961* (New York: Oxford University Press, 1994); and James T. Patterson, *Brown v. Board of Education: A Civil Rights Milestone and Its Troubled Legacy* (New York: Oxford University Press, 2001).

128. Staub, *Torn at the Roots,* pp. 19–57 passim; Anthony Lewis, *Portrait of a Decade: The Second American Revolution* (New York: Random House, 1964), p. 30. Cf. Nathan Glazer: "[Hitler] proclaimed that one race, one people, was superior and should be dominant, he spread hatred of Jews and Negroes, and we were at war with him, so it was in the interest of the war effort to teach the opposite: All peoples were equal, and tolerance should be extended to all." Glazer, *We Are All Multiculturalists Now,* pp. 88, 112–14.

129. Daniel Bell, "Reflections on Jewish Identity," *Commentary* (June 1961), rpt. in Rose, *The Ghetto and Beyond,* p. 475.

130. At once African and American, forever balancing "two souls, two thoughts, two un-reconciled strivings; two warring ideals in one dark body," the African American, said Du Bois, is "born with a veil, and gifted with second-sight in this American world—a world which yields him no true self-consciousness, but only lets him see himself" through the eyes of others and measure his soul "by the tape of a world that looks on in amused contempt and pity." Du Bois, *Souls of Black Folk,* p. 5.

131. Haki R. Madhubuti, "Mainstream of Society," originally in *Think Black!* (1966), rpt. in *Groundwork: New and Selected Poems from 1966–1996* (Chicago: Third World Press, 1996), p. 14.

132. Paul M. Sniderman and Thomas Piazza, *The Scar of Race* (Cambridge, Mass.: Harvard University Press, 1993). Taking his lead from Erving Goffman, Glenn C. Loury has de-fined racial stigma as "dishonorable meanings socially inscribed on arbitrary bodily marks," indicative of "spoiled collective identities." Race, according to Loury, becomes a self-confirming stereotype, an ingrained cognitive stance formed in reaction to rac-ist practices that leads to a perpetual stigmatization. On the other side of the ideologi-cal divide, Shelby Steele avers that it is now the "culture of preference" associated with affirmative action and other compensatory programs that creates racial stigma. Glenn C. Loury, *The Anatomy of Racial Inequality* (Cambridge, Mass.: Harvard University Press, 2002), pp. 20–23, 43–46, 57–73, 103–7; Shelby Steele, *A Dream Deferred: The Second Betrayal of Black Freedom in America* (New York: HarperCollins, 1998), pp. 144–45.

133. Jennifer L. Hochschild, *Facing Up to the American Dream: Race, Class, and the Soul of the Nation* (Princeton: Princeton University Press, 1995), pp. 225–49.

134. Nathan Hurvitz, "Blacks and Jews in American Folklore," *Western Folklore* 33 (Octo-ber 1974), 307; Bruce quoted in Stephen J. Whitfield, *In Search of Jewish Culture* (Hanover, N.H.: Brandeis University Press, 1999), p. 143.

135. Allen Ginsberg, "Kaddish," in *Collected Poems, 1947–1980* (New York: Harper and Row, 1984), p. 209.

136. Emily Miller Budick, "The African American and Israeli 'Other' in the Construction of Jewish American Identity," in Emily Miller Budick, ed., *Ideology and Jewish Identity in Israeli and American Literature* (Albany: State University of New York Press, 2001), pp. 205–6, 210; Seth Forman, *Blacks in the Jewish Mind: A Crisis of Liberalism* (New York: New York University Press, 1998), p. 20.

137. Itzkovitz, "Passing Like Me," pp. 35–57.

138. Whereas Irving Howe saw the film's use of blackface as a kindred "mask for Jewish ex-pressiveness," a means for Jewish performers to reach a spontaneity and assertiveness

in the declaration of their Jewish selves," more recent critics have detected a bicultural conflation of cantorial and jazz singing (what Jeffrey Melnick terms the "sacralization" of Jewish music by blacks and black music by Jews) and a more complex parable in which the triumph of American assimilation is accompanied by a sentimental longing for a lost home and identity that registers as emotive identification with America's foremost racial outcast. As though purging Jewishness by momentarily descending lower and then being reborn as "white," argues Michael Rogin, Jolson leaves Jewishness behind by becoming black. Jewish stereotypes are subsumed and discarded in blackness, such that the Jew becomes "white," paradoxically, by playing "black," a figure with cultural priority, despite his extreme political and social subjugation. Michael Alexander dissents from this line of thinking and argues that it was not their failure to become American but rather their success that led Jews in secular America to identify with the marginalized—with the outsiders that they had once been. Blackface was thus an elaborately constructed vision of American blackness undertaken not in order to be white but to preserve their longing for ethnic identity. Blackface is a "symptom of confusion about Jewish identity in America," but confusion "is not tantamount to abandonment." Andrea Most likewise emphasizes the ways in which Jakie's double role is "a means to acknowledge the divisive, racially determined impulses that motivate him," allowing him to be both American and Jewish. Howe, *World of Our Fathers*, p. 563; Melnick, *A Right to Sing the Blues*, pp. 103–14, 165–96; Michael Rogin, *Blackface, White Noise: Jewish Immigrants in the Hollywood Melting Pot* (Berkeley: University of California Press, 1996), pp. 81–112; Michael Alexander, *Jazz Age Jews* (Princeton: Princeton University Press, 2001), pp. 7–8, 167–79, 181–82; Andrea Most, *Making Americans: Jews and the Broadway Musical* (Cambridge, Mass.: Harvard University Press, 2004), p. 39. See also Jacobson, *Whiteness of a Different Color*, pp. 120–21, and Linda Williams, *Playing the Race Card: Melodramas of Black and White from Uncle Tom to O. J. Simpson* (Princeton: Princeton University Press, 2001), pp. 141–58. One could pursue the same line of interpretation in the case of Sophie Tucker, who broke into show business only after blacking up as the "World Renowned Coon Shouter." See Sophie Tucker, *The Autobiography of Sophie Tucker* (New York: Doubleday, 1945), p. 35.

139. Milton Mayer, "If I Were a Negro," *Negro Digest* 2 (March 1944), 21–23.

140. James Baldwin, "The Black Boy Looks at the White Boy" (1961), in *Nobody Knows My Name* (1961; rpt. New York: Dell, 1963), pp. 175, 181.

141. Seymour Krim, "Ask for a White Cadillac" (1959), in *Views of a Nearsighted Cannoneer* (New York: E. P. Dutton, 1968), pp. 88–104. On Mailer's minstrelsy, see Eric Lott, "White Like Me: Racial Cross-dressing and the Construction of American Whiteness," in Amy Kaplan and Donald E. Pease, eds., *Cultures of United States Imperialism* (Durham: Duke University Press, 1993), pp. 483–84; and on Mailer and Krim, see also Forman, *Blacks in the Jewish Mind*, pp. 105–9.

142. Jacobson, *Whiteness of a Different Color*, pp. 265–71. On the place of Lewis's novel within the postwar genre of tolerance narratives, see Jennifer Dixon, "Before the White Negro: Sin and Salvation in *Kingsblood Royal*," *American Literary History* 15 (Summer 2003), 311–33.

143. Anatole Broyard, "Keep It Cool, Man," *Commentary* (April 1951), 362.

144. Ralph Ellison, "Change the Joke, Slip the Yoke" (1958), in *Shadow and Act* (1964; rpt. New York: Vintage, 1972), p. 55.

145. Franz Boas, "The Problem of the American Negro," *Yale Review* 10 (1921), 395.

146. Norman Podhoretz, "My Negro Problem—and Ours" (1963), rpt. in Berman, *Blacks and Jews*, p. 91.

147. James Farmer, *Freedom—When?* (New York: Random House, 1965), p. 87.

148. Allen Ginsberg, "Statement to *The Burning Bush*" (November 1963), in *Deliberate Prose: Selected Essays, 1952–1995*, ed. Bill Morgan (New York: HarperCollins, 2000), pp. 58–59.

149. Arthur A. Cohen in "Negro-Jewish Relations in America," p. 10.

150. Eugene Borowitz, *The Mask Jews Wear: The Self-Deceptions of American Jewry* (New York: Simon and Schuster, 1973), pp. 40, 124–25; Arnold M. Eisen, *The Chosen People in America: A Study in Jewish Religious Ideology* (Bloomington: Indiana University Press, 1983), pp. 140–41; Elihu Bergman, "The American Jewish Population Erosion," *Midstream* 23 (October 1977), 9–19.

151. Glazer, *We Are All Multiculturalists Now*, p. 129; Thernstrom and Thernstrom, *America in Black and White*, p. 526. The intermarriage rate in New York City, where approximately 40 percent of American Jews lived in the first half of the twentieth century, went from about 1 percent in 1908 to 3 percent by 1940 and over 17 percent by 1965. See Arthur Goren, "Jews," in *Harvard Encyclopedia of American Ethnic Groups* (Cambridge, Mass.: Harvard University Press, 1980), p. 596. According to a United Jewish Communities study released in 2003, whose results have not gone unchallenged, the number of children per woman required for population replacement in the United States was 2.1, whereas the current Jewish average is less than 1.9. "American Jews See Population, Birthrate Drop," *Los Angeles Times*, September 11, 2003, A13.

152. David Biale, Michael Galchinsky, and Susannah Heschel, introduction to Biale, Galchinsky, and Heschel, *Insider/Outsider*, p. 5.

153. Talcott Parsons, "Full Citizenship for the Negro Americans? A Sociological Problem," in Talcott Parsons and Kenneth B. Clark, eds., *The Negro American* (Boston: Beacon Press, 1967), p. 750. Parsons's essay first appeared in *Daedalus* 94 (Fall 1965).

154. Nathan Glazer, "Negroes and Jews: The New Challenge to Pluralism," *Commentary* 38 (December 1964), 29–34.

155. Hertzberg quoted in Staub, *Torn at the Roots*, p. 95. Staub also points out Hertzberg's echo of Podhoretz.

156. Louis E. Lomax, *The Negro Revolt* (New York: Harper and Brothers, 1962), pp. 184–86.

157. See Taylor Branch, "Blacks and Jews: The Uncivil War," in Salzman, *Bridges and Boundaries*, p. 56.

158. B. Z. Sobel and May L. Sobel, "Negroes and Jews: American Minority Groups in Conflict," *Judaism* 15 (Winter 1966), 3–22; Goren, *Politics and Public Culture of American Jews*, pp. 190–201; Jonathan D. Sarna, *American Judaism: A History* (New Haven: Yale University Press, 2004), pp. 306–23. On the decline of liberalism in the Jewish community, see also Staub, *Torn at the Roots*, pp. 8–10, 15–17, 33–36, 50–52, 64–69, 76–82; Staub's precursor essay, "'Negroes are not Jews': Race, Holocaust Consciousness, and the Rise of Jewish Neoconservatism," *Radical History Review* 75 (Fall 1999), 3–27; and Robert Philipson, *The Identity Question: Blacks and Jews in Europe and America* (Jackson: University of Mississippi Press, 2000), pp. 189–220.

159. Albert Vorspan, "Blacks and Jews," in Hentoff, *Black Anti-Semitism and Jewish Racism*, p. 205.

160. Stuart Svonkin, *Jews against Prejudice: American Jews and the Fight for Civil Rights* (New York: Columbia University Press, 1997), pp. 9–112 passim, 178–88, Anti-Defamation League quoted at p. 178; Forman, *Blacks in the Jewish Mind*, pp. 57–64; Marc Dollinger, *Quest for Inclusion: Jews and Liberalism in Modern America* (Princeton: Princeton University Press, 2000), pp. 183–90, 203–13; [American Jewish] *Congress Bi-Weekly* 31 (September 14, 1964), quoted p. 188.

161. Cruse, *Crisis of the Negro Intellectual,* pp. 476, 483.

162. Friedman, *What Went Wrong?* p. 313.

163. Milton Himmelfarb, "Is American Jewry in Crisis?" *Commentary* 47 (March 1969), 35; Stephen Steinberg, "How Jewish Quotas Began," *Commentary* 52 (September 1971), 67–76; Earl Raab, "Quotas by Any Other Name," *Commentary* 53 (January 1972), 41–45; Norman Podhoretz, "Is It Good for the Jews?" *Commentary* 53 (February 1972), 7–12. Since Jews constituted only 3 percent of the population, Podhoretz reasoned, they "must inevitably be harmed by any move in the direction of a system of proportional representation according to group." See also Stephen Steinberg, "The Liberal Retreat from Race during the Post–Civil Rights Era," in Wahneema Lubiano, ed., *The House That Race Built: Black Americans, U.S. Terrain* (New York: Pantheon Books, 1997), pp. 13–47; B. Z. Sobel and May L. Sobel, "Negroes and Jews: American Minority Groups in Conflict," in Rose, *The Ghetto and Beyond,* pp. 384–408; and Jerome A. Chanes, "Affirmative Action: Jewish Ideals, Jewish Interests," in Salzman and West, *Struggles in the Promised Land,* pp. 295–314.

164. Robert Langbaum, "Where Do I Stand Now—A Symposium," *Judaism* 92 (Fall 1974), 439; Daniel Bell, "On Meritocracy and Equality," *Public Interest* 27 (Summer 1972), 37–39.

165. Benjamin Hooks quoted in Marc Stein, "Affirmative Action, the Law, and the Jews," in William Frankel, ed., *Survey of Jewish Affairs* (Cambridge, Mass.: Institute for Jewish Affairs, 1990), p. 156.

166. *University of California Regents v. Bakke,* 438 U.S. 265 (1978). Cf. Bundy: "Still, it seems clear that to take race into account today is better than to let the door swing almost shut because of the head start of others. . . . To get past racism, we must here take account of race. There is no other present way." McGeorge Bundy, "The Issue before the Court: Who Gets Ahead in America?" *Atlantic Monthly* 240 (November 1977), 54. Among the numerous successive arguments that the "color-blind" ideal of liberal individualism fails to take account of group deprivation, one might note the view of the black economist Glenn Loury, a late convert from neoconservative opposition to affirmative action. Given the deeply ingrained stigmatization of inequality carried by race, specifically by blackness, in the United States, Loury writes, "it is often the case that violating race-blindness can powerfully abet the pursuit of racial equality." Loury, *Anatomy of Racial Inequality,* p. 132.

167. Friedman, *What Went Wrong?* p. 314; John Edgar Wideman, *Fatheralong* (New York: Random House, 1994), p. xx.

168. Charles Taylor, "The Politics of Recognition," in Amy Gutman, ed., *Multiculturalism: Examining the Politics of Recognition* (Princeton: Princeton University Press, 1994), pp. 43–44.

169. John McWhorter, *Authentically Black: Essays for the Black Silent Majority* (New York: Gotham Books, 2003), p. 152.

170. Harold Cruse, "My Jewish Problem and Theirs," in Hentoff, *Black Anti-Semitism and Jewish Racism,* p. 178.

171. Bayard Rustin, "From Protest to Politics: The Future of the Civil Rights Movement," *Commentary* 39 (February 1965); rpt. in Francis L. Broderick and August Meier, *Negro Protest Thought in the Twentieth Century* (Indianapolis: Bobbs-Merrill, 1965), pp. 408–9; Oscar Handlin, *Fire-Bell in the Night: The Crisis in Civil Rights* (Boston: Little, Brown, 1964), pp. 73–74.

172. Glazer and Moynihan, introduction to 1970 edition of *Beyond the Melting Pot,* pp. xxxix–xl.

173. Donald L. Kaufmann, "Soul Pass Over: Jews, Blacks, and Beyond," *Midstream* 16 (May 1970), 30–37.

174. Howe, *The World of Our Fathers*, p. 586.

175. Donald Bogle, *Toms, Coons, Mulattoes, Mammies, and Bucks: An Interpretive History of Blacks in American Films*, 4th ed. (New York: Continuum, 2002), p. 144; Thomas Cripps, *Making Movies Black: The Hollywood Message Movie from World War II to the Civil Rights Era* (New York: Oxford University Press, 1993), p. 222.

176. Leslie A. Fiedler, *Waiting for the End* (New York: Stein and Day, 1964), pp. 65–67.

177. Danzy Senna, *Caucasia* (New York: Riverhead, 1998), p. 140.

178. Steven Marcus, "The American Negro in Search of Identity," *Commentary* 16 (November 1953), 462.

179. Hollinger, *Postethnic America*, pp. 97–98; Skrentny, *The Minority Rights Revolution*, pp. 281–85; Hugh Davis Graham, *Collision Course: The Strange Convergence of Affirmative Action and Immigration Policy in America* (New York: Oxford University Press, 2002), pp. 65–200 passim; David A. Hollinger, "Amalgamation and Hypodescent: The Question of Ethnoracial Mixture in the History of the United States," *American Historical Review* 108 (December 2003), 1381–84.

180. The Anti-Defamation League distributed 10 million copies of its tabloid to publicize *Holocaust*, which aired the week before Passover and coincident with the thirty-fifth anniversary of the Warsaw Ghetto uprising; the American Jewish Committee distributed millions of study guides; excerpts from Gerald Green's novelization of his teleplay were serialized in many newspapers; and publicity by NBC and cooperating religious groups caused the entire day the opening episode aired to be proclaimed "Holocaust Sunday." See Judith E. Doneson, *The Holocaust in American Film* (Philadelphia: Jewish Publication Society, 1987), pp. 145, 188–89; Peter Novick, *The Holocaust in American Life* (Boston: Houghton Mifflin, 1999), pp. 209–14; Jeffrey Shandler, *While America Watches: Televising the Holocaust* (New York: Oxford University Press, 1999), pp. 155–78; and Tim Cole, *Selling the Holocaust: From Auschwitz to Schindler, How History Is Bought, Packaged, and Sold* (New York: Routledge, 1999), pp. 12–13. *Roots*, which attracted 130 million viewers and won nine Emmys, combined docudrama and soap opera in a script carefully paced to meet the demands of the television format and altered to appeal more readily to white viewers. The novel's Afrocentric tilt was softened by using recognized stars and focusing more on heroic black resistance to oppression in and after slavery. See Donald Bogle, *Primetime Blues: African Americans on Network Television* (New York: Farrar, Straus and Giroux, 2001), pp. 239–46; and Williams, *Playing the Race Card*, pp. 238–51.

181. Letty Cottin Pogrebin, *Deborah, Golda, and Me: Being Jewish and Female in America* (New York: Crown, 1991), p. 225; Novick, *The Holocaust in American Life*, p. 195.

182. Ruth R. Wisse, "The Anxious American Jew," *Commentary* 66 (September 1978), 47–50.

183. Leo Rosten, *The Joys of Yiddish* (New York: Simon and Schuster, 1968), p. ix; J. L. Dillard, *Black English: Its History and Usage in the United States* (New York: Random House, 1972), p. ix.

184. Norman L. Kleeblatt, ed., *Too Jewish? Challenging Traditional Identities* (New York: Jewish Museum, 1996); Dora Apel, *Memory Effects: The Holocaust and the Art of Secondary Witnessing* (New Brunswick, N.J.: Rutgers University Press, 2002), pp. 163–86; *Remedy: The Genuine Article*, Fifth Angel Recordings, 2001; Jennifer Traig and Victoria Traig, *Judaiokitsch: Tchotchkes, Schmattes, and Nosherei* (San Francisco: Chronicle Books, 2002), p. 118; Lisa Schiffman, *Generation J* (San Francisco: Harper, 1999), p. 74.

185. See, for example, Arthur Mann, *The One and the Many: Reflections on the American Identity* (Chicago: University of Chicago Press, 1979), pp. 119–45; and Goren, *Politics and Public Culture of American Jews,* pp. 205–23.

186. Nathan Glazer, "Liberty, Equality, Fraternity—and Ethnicity" (1976), in *Ethnic Dilemmas, 1964–1982* (Cambridge, Mass.: Harvard University Press, 1983), pp. 209–29.

187. Todd Gitlin, *The Twilight of Common Dreams: Why America Is Wracked by Culture Wars* (New York: Henry Holt, 1995), p. 149.

188. Malcolm X, 1963 interview with Alex Haley, in Haley, *The Playboy Interviews,* p. 33; "Farrakhan's Jewish Problem," *Tikkun* 9 (March/April 1994), 10.

189. Cruse, "My Jewish Problem and Theirs," p. 174.

190. Friedman, *What Went Wrong?* pp. 329–30; Rosenthal, *Irreconcilable Differences?,* p. 53. Cokely's theory was defended by Louis Farrakhan; only three of Chicago's eighteen black aldermen condemned him; and it took Mayor Eugene Sawyer a week to ask for his resignation. See Dinnerstein, *Anti-Semitism in America,* p. 221.

191. James Traub, "The Hearts and Minds of City College," *New Yorker* 69 (June 7, 1993), 42–53; Jim Sleeper, "The Battle for Enlightenment at City College," in Berman, *Blacks and Jews,* pp. 239–53. Jeffries's theory derived from Michael Bradley, *The Iceman Inheritance: Prehistoric Sources of Western Man's Racism, Sexism, and Aggression* (New York: Kayode Publications, 1991). See Stephen Howe, *Afrocentrism: Mythical Pasts and Imagined Homes* (London: Verso, 1998), pp. 270–73; and Marek Kohn, *The Race Gallery: The Return of Racial Science* (London: Jonathan Cape, 1995), pp. 161–62.

192. Arthur Hertzberg quoted in Shipler, *A Country of Strangers,* pp. 465–66.

193. Sniderman and Piazza, *The Scar of Race,* pp. 167–68; Shapiro, *A Time for Healing,* pp. 46–48. According to a 2002 survey of American attitudes toward religion conducted by the Pew Research Center for the People and the Press, Protestants, Catholics, and Jews had identical "favorable" ratings of 74 percent among the Americans polled; Protestants, at 8 percent, had a slightly better "unfavorable" rating than Jews, at 9 percent, and both were exceeded by Catholics (13 percent), evangelical Christians (18 percent), and Muslims (29 percent). "Americans Struggle with Religion's Role at Home and Abroad," Pew Research Center for the People and the Press (March 20, 2002), http://people-press.org/reports/display.php3?PageID=385 (accessed September 25, 2003).

194. Natan Sharansky, "On Hating the Jews," *Commentary* 116 (November 2003), 28, 32. For overviews of the turn-of-the-century resurgence of anti-Semitism, particularly in reaction to Israeli policies, see Chesler, *The New Anti-Semitism;* Abraham H. Foxman, *Never Again? The Threat of the New Anti-Semitism* (San Francisco: Harper Collins, 2003); and Gabriel Schoenfeld, *The Return of Anti-Semitism* (San Francisco: Encounter Books, 2004).

195. A survey of black attitudes sponsored by the Anti-Defamation League in the early 1990s showed that 41 percent of blacks, as opposed to 20 percent of Americans as a whole, agreed with six or more of a list of eleven anti-Semitic stereotypes. On closer examination, the surveys on which such conclusions are based tend to show a decided mix in attitudes among blacks, so that some traits they identified with Jews were, in fact, admired rather than despised, and evidence of black anti-Semitism generally declined in proportion to education. Some surveys, however, have revealed a contrary trend. A 1978 Louis Harris poll showed anti-Semitism to be twice as high among a sample of fifty-three black leaders than among the general population of blacks, although such differences could be ascribed to the use of anti-Semitism by some black leaders as a tactic of confrontation. Some shifts in attitude are likely to be short-lived.

A rise in African American belief that Jews were responsible for the crucifixion of Christ from 21 percent in 1997 to 42 percent in 2004, for example, was probably occasioned in part by response to Mel Gibson's controversial film *The Passion of the Christ* and publicity about it. See Shipler, *A Country of Strangers*, p. 464; Gary E. Rubin, "How Should We Think about Black Antisemitism?" in Jerome A. Chanes, ed., *Antisemitism in America Today: Outspoken Experts Explode the Myths* (New York: Birch Lane Press, 1995), pp. 150–70; Charles E. Silberman, A *Certain People: American Jews and Their Lives Today* (New York: Summit Books, 1985), p. 339; "Belief That Jews Were Responsible for Christ's Death Increases," Pew Research Center for the People and the Press (April 2, 2004), http://people-press.org/reports/display.php3?ReportID=209(accessed April 28, 2004).

196. Adolph Reed, Jr., "What Color Is Anti-Semitism," *Village Voice*, December 26, 1995, rpt. in Maurianne Adams and John Bracey, eds., *Strangers and Neighbors: Relations between Blacks and Jews in the United States* (Amherst: University of Massachusetts Press, 1999), p. 24.

197. See the rather convoluted argument of Charles S. Liebman that because African Americans occupy the lowly position of Jews in other cultures, their own anti-Semitism may, in fact, legitimate hostility toward Jews on the part of other Americans. Charles S. Liebman, "Jewish Survival, Antisemitism, and Negotiation with the Tradition," in Robert M. Seltzer and Norman J. Cohen, eds., *The Americanization of the Jews* (New York: New York University Press, 1995), p. 438.

198. Ishmael Reed, "Is There a Black-Jewish Feud?" in *Airing Dirty Laundry* (New York: Addison Wesley, 1994), p. 36.

199. Lawrence H. Fuchs, *The American Kaleidoscope: Race, Ethnicity, and the Civic Culture* (Cambridge, Mass.: Harvard University Press, 1993), pp. 401–2.

200. Louis Farrakhan quoted in William A. Henry III, "Pride and Prejudice," *Time* 143 (February 28, 1994), 25. The article also contained responses to the Farrakhan phenomenon by Leon Wieseltier, Thulani Davis, Midge Decter, Cornel West, Michael Lerner, and Randall Kennedy.

201. Vilbert L. White, *Inside the Nation of Islam: A Historical and Personal Testimony by a Black Muslim* (Gainesville: University of Florida Press, 2001), p. 109; Michael Kramer, "Loud and Clear: Farrakhan's Anti-Semitism," *New York* 18 (October 21, 1985), 22; Julius Lester, "The Time Has Come," *New Republic* 193 (October 28, 1985), 11–12; Friedman, *What Went Wrong?* pp. 333–34. On Farrakhan's anti-Semitism, see also Robert A. Rockaway, *"The Jews Cannot Defeat Me": The Anti-Jewish Campaign of Louis Farrakhan and the Nation of Islam* (Tel Aviv: Tel Aviv University Press, 1995), passim; and Mattias Gardell, *In the Name of Elijah Muhammad: Louis Farrakhan and the Nation of Islam* (Durham: Duke University Press, 1996), pp. 246–74.

202. Paul Berman, "Introduction: The Other and the Almost the Same," in Berman, *Blacks and Jews*, p. 9; David Brion Davis, "Jews in the Slave Trade," in Salzman and West, *Struggles in the Promised Land*, pp. 65–72; Harold Brackman, *Ministry of Lies: The Truth behind the Nation of Islam's "The Secret Relationship between Blacks and Jews"* (New York: Four Walls Eight Windows, 1994), pp. 28–29, 75. See also Stephen J. Whitfield, "An Anatomy of Black Anti-Semitism," *Judaism* 43 (Fall 1994), 345–50; Marc Kaplan, *Jew-Hatred as History: An Analysis of the Nation of Islam's "The Secret Relationship between Blacks and Jews"* (New York: Anti-Defamation League, 1997); Eli Faber, *Jews, Slaves, and the Slave Trade: Setting the Record Straight* (New York: New York University Press, 1998); Saul S. Friedman, *Jews and the Slave Trade* (New Brunswick, N.J.: Transaction Publishers, 1998); Seymour Drescher, "The Role of Jews in the

Atlantic Slave Trade," in Adams and Bracey, *Strangers and Neighbors,* pp. 105–15; Bertram Wallace Korn, "Jews and Negro Slavery in the Old South, 1789–1865," in Adams and Bracey, *Strangers and Neighbors,* pp. 147–82; and Marvin Perry and Frederick M. Schweitzer, *Antisemitism: Myth and Hate from Antiquity to the Present* (New York: Palgrave Macmillan, 2002), pp. 223–57 passim.

203. Jon Michael Spencer, *Tribes of Benjamin* (Richmond, Va.: Harriet Tubman Press, 1999), p. 138.

204. Paul Berman, "Medieval New York," *New Yorker* 71 (January 15, 1996), 5–6.

205. Henry Louis Gates, Jr., "Black Demagogues and Pseudo-Scholars," *New York Times,* July 20, 1992, rpt. as "The Uses of Anti-Semitism" in Berman, *Blacks and Jews,* pp. 217–23; Earl Raab, "The Black Revolution and the Jewish Question," *Commentary* 47 (January 1969), 26–29.

206. *The Secret Relationship between Blacks and Jews* (Boston: Nation of Islam Historical Research Department, 1991), pp. 213–311, 178.

207. Muhammad continued: "They [the Jews] went there, in Germany, the way they do everywhere they go, and they supplanted, they usurped. . . . They undermined the very fabric of society. Now, he was [an] arrogant, no good devil bastard, Hitler, no question about it. . . . He used his greatness for evil and wickedness but they [the Jews] are wickedly great, too, brother. Everywhere they go and they always do it and hide their head." Malcolm X, quoted in Peter Goldman, *The Death and Life of Malcolm X* (Urbana: University of Illinois Press, 1979), p. 15; Khalid Muhammad quoted in White, *Inside the Nation of Islam,* p. 120.

208. Alan Heimrich and Paul Marcus, "Some Practical Psychoanalytically Informed Suggestions for Communal Leaders for Improving Black-Jewish Relations," in Alan Heimrich and Paul Marcus, eds., *Blacks and Jews on the Couch: Psychoanalytic Reflections on Black-Jewish Conflict* (Westport, Conn.: Praeger, 1998), p. 215.

209. In a study published in 2000, Cohen and Eisen found that only 9 percent of Jews surveyed believed that it was essential in order to be a good Jew to "work for social justice causes," while 41 percent thought it desirable and 45 percent thought it did not matter; only 3 percent believed it essential to be "a liberal on political issues," while 21 percent thought it desirable and 65 percent thought it did not matter. From the amalgamated results of twenty national surveys from 1972 to 1994, Cohen and Liebman found that, although Jews surpassed non-Jews in their political self-identification as liberals (47 versus 28 percent) or Democrats (72 versus 52 percent), and in their support of civil liberties for atheists, communists, and homosexuals (81 versus 60 percent), they were only somewhat more liberal than non-Jews (African Americans excluded) in their acceptance of blacks and support for policies on their behalf (70 versus 58 percent). This difference was less pronounced than in the case of social issues such as school prayer, gender and sexuality (women's rights, abortion, pornography), and domestic spending, and it narrowed to insignificance when other variables were held constant. Steven M. Cohen and Arnold M. Eisen, *The Jew Within: Self, Family, and Community in America* (Bloomington: Indiana University Press, 2000), pp. 129, 215; Steven M. Cohen and Charles S. Liebman, "American Jewish Liberalism: Unraveling the Strands," *Public Opinion Quarterly* 61 (Fall 1997), 405–30.

210. Hertzberg summarized the evolution thus: the "alliance" went from a "comradeship of excluded peoples" in the 1940s and early 1950s, to Jewish paternalistic concern for the less fortunate in the late 1950s, to a pragmatic recognition in the 1960s that, because there was "no elite to which blacks would defer," Jews must acquire what power they could and secure their own place in American society. Hertzberg, *The Jews in*

America, pp. 334–41, quotation at p. 329. See also Friedman, *What Went Wrong?* pp. 213–33.

211. Cornel West, *Race Matters* (Boston: Beacon Press, 1993), pp. 71–79. In Karenga's view, set forth in his popular Afrocentric textbook, the black-Jewish coalition was based on three myths—that Jews are blacks' closest allies (which is true only of selected individuals); that there exists a moral affinity based on shared suffering (which bases a supposed unity of interest on a false premise); and that Jews are not white (which "seeks to redefine Jews into the Third World . . . through a contrived similarity"). Maulana Karenga, *Introduction to Black Studies,* 2nd ed. (Los Angeles: University of Sankore Press, 1993), p. 340.

212. Julius Lester, "The Outsiders," 86; Glenn C. Loury, *One by One from the Inside Out: Essays and Reviews on Race and Responsibility in America* (New York: Free Press, 1995), pp. 83–92.

213. Introductory statement by Robert S. Rifkind, president, American Jewish Committee, *CommonQuest* 1 (Spring 1996), title page overleaf.

2. THE BLACK NATION ISRAEL

1. Zora Neale Hurston, *Moses, Man of the Mountain* (1939; rpt. New York: Harper Perennial, 1991), pp. xxiii–xxiv.

2. Both *Moses, Man of the Mountain* and *Moses and Monotheism* conceive of Judaism and Jewishness as arising in a context of the politicized articulation of differences, as well as borrowings, from another originating tradition. See, for example, Char Miller, "Go Down, Moses: Zora Neale Hurston and Sigmund Freud on Race, Nation, and Political Representation," in Reynolds J. Scott-Childress, ed., *Race and the Production of Modern American Nationalism* (New York: Garland, 1999), pp. 247–71. In Freud's interpretation, chosenness, moreover, springs from the speculation that the Jews murdered Moses, and knowledge of that fact occurs in later generations as the return of the repressed, with unconscious force. In the face of this fact the Jews were chosen, incomprehensibly, to survive, and the separation from the father, in the murder, is repeated in later instances of violence against the Jews. For Freud, writes Cathy Caruth, "the history of chosenness, as the history of survival, thus takes the form of an unending confrontation with the returning violence of the past." Cathy Caruth, *Unclaimed Experience: Trauma, Narrative, and History* (Baltimore: Johns Hopkins University Press, 1996), pp. 68–69. On the idea of Moses' Egyptian origins, see Jan Assmann, *Moses the Egyptian: The Memory of Egypt in Western Monotheism* (Cambridge, Mass.: Harvard University Press, 1997).

3. Ralph Ellison, interview with Howard Sage (1976), quoted in Emily Miller Budick, *Blacks and Jews in Literary Conversation* (New York: Cambridge University Press, 1998), p. 56; James Alan McPherson, "Indivisible Man" (1970), in *Conversations with Ralph Ellison,* ed. Maryemma Graham and Amritjit Singh (Jackson: University Press of Mississippi, 1995), p. 180; Ralph Ellison, *Juneteenth,* ed. John F. Callahan (New York: Random House, 1999), p. 117. On Juneteenth, celebrated on June 19, African Americans commemorate the day in 1865 when Texas slaves, more than two years after the Emancipation Proclamation, learned from Union soldiers that they were free.

4. Nahum M. Sarna, *Exploring Exodus: The Origins of Biblical Israel* (1986; rpt. New York: Schocken, 1996), pp. 2–3.

5. *L.A. Watts Times,* quoted in Justin Driver, "Why Johnnie Can't Lead," *New Republic* 228 (February 17, 2003), 39.

6. Five million of that number migrated after 1940, as cotton farming became mechanized. In 1940 black America was 77 percent southern (49 percent rural southern), but by 1970 it was only half southern and less than a quarter rural. Between 1950 and 1960 alone the nation's twelve largest cities lost more than 2 million white residents and gained more than 2 million black. Lenora Berson, *The Negroes and the Jews* (New York: Random House, 1971), p. 223; Nicholas Leman, *The Promised Land: The Great Black Migration and How It Changed America* (New York: Random House, 1991), p. 6. At times the term "Great Migration" is used to describe this entire period, but it more often refers to the migration during and soon after World War I, when the combination of a depression in the South, a labor shortage in the urban North caused by a decline in immigration from Europe, and continued racial injustice caused an unprecedented acceleration in migration. For representative studies, see George W. Groh, *The Black Migration: The Journey to Urban America* (New York: Weybright and Talley, 1972); Carole Marks, *Farewell—We're Good and Gone: The Great Black Migration* (Bloomington: Indiana University Press, 1989); Alferdteen Harrison, *Black Exodus: The Great Migration from the American South* (Jackson: University of Mississippi Press, 1991). On the literature of the Great Migration, see, for example, Farah Jasmine Griffin, *"Who Set You Flowin'?": The African-American Migration Narrative* (New York: Oxford University Press, 1995); and Lawrence R. Rodgers, *Canaan Bound: The African-American Great Migration Novel* (Urbana: University of Illinois Press, 1997).

7. Claude Brown, *Manchild in the Promised Land* (1965; rpt. New York: Signet, 1967), pp. vii–viii.

8. Richard Wright, *12 Million Black Voices* (1941; rpt. New York: Thunder's Mouth Press, 1988), pp. 145–46.

9. George Shepperson, "African Diaspora: Concept and Context," in Joseph E. Harris, ed., *Global Dimensions of the African Diaspora* (Washington, D.C.: Howard University Press, 1982), p. 51. In the same volume, see also Elliott P. Skinner, "The Dialectic between Diasporas and Homelands," pp. 17–45.

10. Wilson Jeremiah Moses, *The Wings of Ethiopia: Studies in African-American Life and Letters* (Ames: Iowa State University Press, 1990), pp. 27–41.

11. "State of Israel Proclamation of Independence," in *The Israel-Arab Reader: A Documentary History of the Middle East Conflict,* ed. Walter Laqueur and Barry Rubin, 5th ed. (New York: Penguin, 1995), p. 108.

12. Caryl Phillips, *New World Order: Essays* (New York: Vintage, 2002), unpaginated.

13. Hurston, *Moses, Man of the Mountain,* p. 282; Louis Farrakhan "Day of Atonement," in Haki R. Madhubuti and Maulana Karenga, eds., *Million Man March / Day of Absence: A Commemorative Anthology* (Chicago: Third World Press, 1996), p. 20.

14. Harold Cruse, *The Crisis of the Negro Intellectual: A Historical Analysis of the Failure of Black Leadership* (1967; rpt. New York: Quill, 1984), p. 344.

15. Because Jewishness is not tied to state or territory, to culture or nation, but is always "suprahistorical," Herberg adds, "the Jew has always found a home in the Covenant whenever he has been at odds with the world, for it is the Covenant that is his true 'fatherland,' and the world that confronts him with the need for redemption." Will Herberg, "The 'Chosenness' of Israel and the Jew of Today," *Midstream* 1 (Autumn 1955), 89–91.

16. James Baldwin, "The Harlem Ghetto" (1948), in *Notes of a Native Son* (1955; rpt. New York: Bantam, 1979), p. 55.

17. Nathaniel Paul, "An Address Delivered on the Celebration of the Abolition of Slavery

in the State of New-York" (July 5, 1827), in Dorothy Porter, ed., *Negro Protest Pamphlets: A Compendium* (New York: Arno Press, 1969), p. 22.

18. W. E. B. Du Bois, *The Souls of Black Folk* (1903; rpt. New York: Penguin, 1989), p. 208; Lawrence W. Levine, *Black Culture and Black Consciousness* (New York: Oxford University Press, 1977), pp. 30–55; R. Nathaniel Dett, ed., *Religious Folk-Songs of the Negro as Sung at Hampton Institute* (Hampton, Va.: Hampton Institute Press, 1927), p. xiii. On the Exodus tradition in early African American religion, see Albert J. Raboteau, *A Fire in the Bones: Reflections on African-American Religious History* (Boston: Beacon Press, 1995), pp. 29–36; and Eddie S. Glaude, Jr., *Exodus! Religion, Race, and Nation in Early-Nineteenth-Century Black America* (Chicago: University of Chicago Press, 2000), pp. 44–81.

19. James Weldon Johnson and J. Rosamond Johnson, *The Books of American Negro Spirituals,* 2 vols. in 1 (1925, 1926; rpt. New York: Da Capo, 1969), I, 20–21.

20. R. T. Sale, *The Blackstone Rangers* (New York: Random House, 1971), pp. 77–78.

21. Samuel Wakeman quoted in Arthur Hertzberg, "The New England Puritans and the Jews," in Shalom Goldman, ed., *Hebrew and the Bible in America: The First Two Centuries* (Hanover, N.H.: University Press of New England, 1993), p. 115. The sermon was included in Wakeman's *Sound Repentence* (1685).

22. Werner Sollors, *Beyond Ethnicity: Consent and Descent in American Culture* (New York: Oxford University Press, 1986), pp. 40–65.

23. Sacvan Bercovitch, *The American Jeremiad* (Madison: University of Wisconsin Press, 1978), pp. 73–83, quotation at p. 75. See also Ernest Lee Tuveson, *Redeemer Nation: The Idea of America's Millennial Role* (1968; rpt. Chicago: University of Chicago Press, 1980), pp. 137–74; and Sacvan Bercovitch, *The Rites of Assent: Transformations in the Symbolic Construction of America* (New York: Routledge, 1993), pp. 75–82.

24. Herman Melville, *White-Jacket; or, the World in a Man-of-War,* ed. Harrison Hayford et al. (Evanston, Ill.: Northwestern University Press, 1970), pp. 150–51.

25. Isaac Mayer Wise quoted in Ruth R. Wisse, review of *Jewish American Literature: A Norton Anthology,* in *New Republic* 224 (April 2, 2001), 36.

26. Susannah Heschel, "Imagining Judaism in America," in Hana Wirth-Nesher and Michael P. Kramer, eds., *The Cambridge Companion to Jewish American Literature* (New York: Cambridge University Press, 2003), p. 38. Heschel cites Mel Scult, *Judaism Faces the Twentieth Century: A Biography of Mordecai M. Kaplan* (Detroit: Wayne State University Press, 1993), p. 252.

27. Jefferson's proposal was described by John Adams in a letter to his wife, August 1776, quoted in Reginald Horsman, *Race and Manifest Destiny: The Origins of American Racial Anglo-Saxonism* (Cambridge, Mass.: Harvard University Press, 1981), p. 22.

28. Martin Luther King, Jr., *Why We Can't Wait* (New York: Harper and Row, 1964), pp. 130–31.

29. Frederick Douglass, "The Meaning of July Fourth for the Negro" (speech of July 5, 1852), in Philip S. Foner, ed., *The Life and Writings of Frederick Douglass,* 5 vols. (New York: International Publishers, 1950), II, 189. The oration of Nathaniel Paul, cited in n. 17, was also delivered on July 5.

30. See Wilson Jeremiah Moses, *Black Messiahs and Uncle Toms: Social and Literary Manipulations of a Religious Myth,* rev. ed. (University Park: Pennsylvania State University Press, 1993), pp. 17–48; and Eric J. Sundquist, *To Wake the Nations: Race in the Making of American Literature* (Cambridge, Mass.: Harvard University Press, 1992), pp. 27–134 passim.

31. Ralph Ellison, "What America Would Be Like without Blacks" (1970), in *Going to the Territory* (New York: Random House, 1986), p. 111.

32. Baldwin, "The Harlem Ghetto," p. 56; Keith D. Miller, *Voice of Deliverance: The Language of Martin Luther King, Jr., and Its Sources* (New York: Free Press, 1992), p. 20; Levine, *Black Culture and Black Consciousness*, pp. 30–55, 136–89.

33. See, for example, Gwendolyn Simms Warren, *Ev'ry Time I Feel the Spirit: 101 Best-Loved Psalms, Gospel Hymns, and Spiritual Songs of the African-American Church* (New York: Henry Holt, 1997), p. 42. On the origins of "Go Down, Moses," see Dena J. Epstein, *Sinful Tunes and Spirituals: Black Folk Music to the Civil War* (Urbana: University of Illinois Press, 1977), pp. 244–50.

34. W. G. Kiphant quoted in Albert J. Raboteau, *Slave Religion: The "Invisible Institution" in the Antebellum South* (New York: Oxford University Press, 1978), pp. 311–12.

35. Vincent Harding, *There Is a River: The Black Struggle for Freedom in America* (1981; rpt. New York: Vintage, 1983), p. 69.

36. P. K. McCary, *Black Bible Chronicles, Book One: From Genesis to the Promised Land* (New York: African American Family Press, 1993); Robert H. deCoy, *The Nigger Bible* (1967; rpt. Los Angeles: Holloway House, 1987), p. 43. As the paradigm of delivery into a Promised Land became inextricably enmeshed in an anticolonial critique, it also fell into rather random usage, as in Gil Scott-Heron's protest novel *The Nigger Factory* (1972), where the expulsion of radical students by the president of a black college in Virginia is styled an "Exodus." The militant students belong to MJUMBE (Swahili for "messenger"), Members of Justice United for Meaningful Black Education. Like the author, they call for replacement of the Western educational curriculum with Afrocentric Third World thought and "will not be satisfied with Bullshit Degrees or Nigger Educations." Gil Scott-Heron, *The Nigger Factory* and *The Vulture* (1972; rpt. Edinburgh: Payback Press, 1999), p. 246, 460–69.

37. Michael Walzer, *Exodus and Revolution* (New York: Basic Books, 1985), pp. 123, 134, 149. See also Jon Levenson, who refers to a theology of "liberationist supersessionism" standing in marked contrast to the Israelite Exodus, which concludes not with political freedom per se but rather with liberation that exchanges "degrading bondage for the endless service of the God who remembers his covenant, redeems from exile and oppression, and gives commandments through which the chosen community is sanctified." Levenson's objection that the Exodus "is not an instance of liberation in the [modern] sense of a social revolution in pursuit of equality and solidarity" is well taken, but the freedom achieved in the biblical text may nevertheless be construed as political. Jon D. Levenson, "Exodus and Liberation," in *The Hebrew Bible, the Old Testament, and Historical Criticism: Jews and Christians in Biblical Studies* (Louisville, Ky.: Westminster/John Knox, 1993), pp. 127–59, quotations at pp. 157, 159.

38. Theophus H. Smith, *Conjuring Culture: Biblical Formations of Black America* (New York: Oxford University Press, 1994), p. 106; Charles P. Henry, *Culture and African American Politics* (Bloomington: Indiana University Press, 1990), pp. 60–73.

39. Martin Luther King, Jr., "I See the Promised Land," in *A Testament of Hope: The Essential Writings and Speeches of Martin Luther King, Jr.*, ed. James M. Washington (San Francisco: Harper, 1986), p. 286.

40. Charles V. Hamilton, *The Black Preacher in America* (New York: William Marrow, 1972); pp. 112–47; Fredrick C. Harris, *Something Within: Religion and African-American Political Activism* (New York: Oxford University Press, 1999), pp. 27–37, 65–68, 145–53; Andrew Young quoted in Hamilton, *The Black Preacher in America*, pp. 132–33; King, "I See the Promised Land," pp. 280–82. On King's preaching, see, for example, Miller, *Voice of Deliverance*; and Richard Lischer, *The Preacher King: Martin Luther King, Jr., and the Word That Moved America* (New York: Oxford University Press, 1995). On King's use of Jewish tradition and his relationship with Jews, see especially

Marc Schneier, *Shared Dreams: Martin Luther King, Jr., and the Jewish Community* (Woodstock, Vt.: Jewish Lights Publishing, 1999).

41. Martin Luther King, Jr., "Letter from Birmingham City Jail," in *A Testament of Hope,* pp. 294–95; idem, *Where Do We Go from Here: Chaos or Community?* (Boston: Beacon Press, 1967), p. 63; Abraham Joshua Heschel, "Religion and Race" (1963), in *The Insecurity of Freedom* (New York: Farrar, Straus and Giroux, 1966), p. 85. On King and Heschel, see also Taylor Branch, *Pillar of Fire: America in the King Years, 1963–65* (New York: Simon and Schuster, 1998), pp. 21–32; Schneier, *Shared Dreams,* pp. 133–43; and Susannah Heschel, "Theological Affinities in the Writings of Abraham Joshua Heschel and Martin Luther King, Jr.," in Yvonne Chireau and Nathaniel Deutsch, eds., *Black Zion: African American Religious Encounters with Judaism* (New York: Oxford University Press, 2000), pp. 168–86.

42. Abraham Heschel quoted in introduction to Abraham Joshua Heschel, *Moral Grandeur and Spiritual Audacity: Essays,* ed. Susannah Heschel (New York: Farrar, Straus and Giroux, 1996), p. vii; Clayborne Carson, "Black-Jewish Universalism in the Era of Identity Politics," in Jack Salzman and Cornel West, eds., *Struggles in the Promised Land: Toward a History of Black-Jewish Relations in the United States* (New York: Oxford University Press, 1997), pp. 180–81; Abraham J. Heschel and Martin Luther King, Jr., "What Happens to Them Happens to Me," in *United Synagogue Review* 16 (Winter 1964), rpt. in Jack Salzman, ed., *Bridges and Boundaries: African Americans and American Jews* (New York: George Braziller, 1992), pp. 86–90.

43. Murray Friedman, *What Went Wrong? The Creation and Collapse of the Black-Jewish Alliance* (New York: Free Press, 1995), pp. 250–53.

44. Paul Berman, "Introduction: The Other and Almost the Same," in Paul Berman, ed., *Blacks and Jews: Alliances and Arguments* (New York: Delacorte, 1994), pp. 15, 28.

45. Yasser Arafat quoted in Meir Litvak, "A Palestinian Past: National Construction and Reconstruction," *History and Memory* 6 (Fall/Winter 1994), 24.

46. The "Canaanites" adopted the view that the new nation in Palestine was a "Hebrew" rather than a "Jewish" nation, by which they meant that it had no relation to the modern diaspora but found its true roots in a territory that preceded ancient Israelite and Arab conquest and settlement and should, in the contemporary world, equally embrace Muslims and Christians as part of the "Hebrew" nation. The Canaanites' founder, Yonathan Ratosh, argued that "anyone coming from the Jewish Diaspora is a Jew and not a Hebrew and cannot be anything but a Jew—bad or good, proud or cowardly, he is still a Jew. The Jew and the Hebrew cannot be identical and he who is a Jew cannot become a Hebrew." Many Canaanites advocated an alliance with the Palestinian Arabs as a step toward abolishing the distinction between Jew and Arab. See James S. Diamond, *Homeland or Holy Land? The "Canaanite" Critique of Israel* (Bloomington: Indiana University Press, 1986); and Derek Jonathan Penslar, "Innovation and Revisionism in Israeli Historiography," *History & Memory* (Spring/Summer 1995), 134; Ratosh quoted in Amnon Rubinstein, *The Zionist Dream Revisited: From Herzl to Gush Emunin and Back* (New York: Schocken Books, 1984), p. 32.

47. As Jonathan Boyarin argues, however, the multiplicity of readings afforded by Exodus surpasses any attempt to contain the tale within the "modern world-system model of imperial, adventurist conquest versus autochthonous liberation." Boyarin rejects Said's reading of Exodus, which ignores the fact that the Jews in Egypt were forced into slavery, minimizes the Torah's commandments not to oppress the stranger, and misreads the Zionist longing for land as an expression of imperial intentions when it was, in fact, a longing for *any* land in which to exist as a people. Whatever argument might be lodged against Israel in its conflict with the Palestinians, the origins of West-

ern expansionism, not to mention the depredations of colonialism, can hardly be attributed to Jewish tradition. The fact that identity as a people already existed for Jews prior to the creation of modern Israel is also, in Boyarin's view, one of the principal links between Jews and African Americans, allowing blacks to embrace Zionism and anti-imperialism at the same time. Edward Said, "Michael Walzer's Exodus and Revolution: A Canaanite Reading," *Grand Street* 5 (Winter 1986), 86–106; Regina M. Schwartz, *The Curse of Cain: The Violent Legacy of Monotheism* (Chicago: University of Chicago Press, 1997), pp. 57–62; Jonathan Boyarin, "Reading Exodus into History," *New Literary History* 23 (Summer 1992), 524–31. See also the exchange between Said and Daniel and Jonathan Boyarin in *Critical Inquiry* 15 (Spring 1989), 626–38.

48. Wilson Jeremiah Moses, *Afrotopia: The Roots of African American Popular History* (New York: Cambridge University Press, 1998), pp. 44–95, quotation at p. 47. Cf. Paul Gilroy's analysis of the the double descent of African Americans as "children of Israel or children of the Pharaohs." Paul Gilroy, *The Black Atlantic: Modernity and Double Consciousness* (Cambridge, Mass.: Harvard University Press, 1993), p. 205.

49. Gloria Naylor, *Bailey's Cafe* (1992; rpt. New York: Vintage, 1993, p. 146).

50. Ibid., pp. 223, 220.

51. Jeffrey Melnick, *A Right to Sing the Blues: African Americans, Jews, and American Popular Song* (Cambridge, Mass.: Harvard University Press, 1999), pp. 205–6; Ethan Goffman, *Imagining Each Other: Blacks and Jews in Contemporary American Literature* (Albany: State University of New York Press, 2000), p. 197.

52. David M. Goldenberg, *The Curse of Ham: Race and Slavery in Early Judaism, Christianity, and Islam* (Princeton: Princeton University Press, 2003), pp. 26–29, 52–59.

53. Martin Delany, *The Origins and Objects of Ancient Freemasonry* (1853), quoted in Clarence E. Walker, *We Can't Go Home Again: An Argument about Afrocentrism* (New York: Oxford University Press, 2001), p. 8.

54. See, for example, Louis Farrakhan, speech of 1989, quoted in Mattias Gardell, *In the Name of Elijah Muhammad: Louis Farrakhan and the Nation of Islam* (Durham: Duke University Press, 1996), p. 258; and Khalid Muhammad, speech of 1993, quoted in Marc Kaplan, *Jew-Hatred as History: An Analysis of the Nation of Islam's "The Secret Relationship between Blacks and Jews"* (New York: Anti-Defamation League, 1997), p. 6.

55. Howard Brotz, *The Black Jews of Harlem: Negro Nationalism and the Dilemmas of Negro Leadership* (Glencoe, Ill.: Free Press, 1964), p. 98; Tudor Parfitt, *The Lost Tribes of Israel: The History of a Myth* (2002; rpt. London: Phoenix, 2003), p. 249.

56. E. U. Essien-Udom, *Black Nationalism: A Search for Identity in America* (1962; rpt. Chicago: University of Chicago Press, 1971), pp. 33–36; Richard Brent Turner, *Islam in the African-American Experience* (Bloomington: Indiana University Press, 1997), p. 93; Edward E. Curtis IV, *Islam in Black America: Identity, Liberation, and Difference in African-American Islamic Thought* (Albany: State University of New York Press, 2002), pp. 45–55.

57. The characterization of Blacks Jews in this discussion draws on Roi Ottley, *"New World A-Coming": Inside Black America* (New York: New World Publishing, 1943), pp. 137–50; Arthur Huff Fauset, *Black Gods of the Metropolis: Negro Religious Cults of the Urban North* (Philadelphia: University of Pennsylvania Press, 1944), pp. 31–40; Brotz, *Black Jews of Harlem,* passim; Moses, *Black Messiahs and Uncle Toms,* pp. 183–95; Elly M. Wynia, *Church of God and Saints of Christ: The Rise of Black Jews* (New York: Garland, 1994), passim; James H. Boykin, *Black Jews: A Study in Minority Experience* (Miami, 1996), pp. 32, 38; Yvonne Chireau, "Black Culture and Black Zion: African American Religious Encounters with Judaism, 1790–1930, an Overview," in

Chireau and Deutsch, *Black Zion*, pp. 23–8; Merrill Singer, "Symbolic Identity Formation in an African American Religious Sect," in Chireau and Deutsch, *Black Zion*, pp. 57–58; Roberta S. Gold, "The Black Jews of Harlem: Representation, Identity, and Race, 1920–1939," *American Quarterly* 55 (June 2003), 179–225; Parfitt, *Lost Tribes of Israel* pp. 193–228; and especially the comprehensive treatment in James E. Landing, *Black Judaism: Story of an American Movement* (Durham, N.C.: Carolina Academic Press, 2002). The winter 1977 issue of *Black Books Bulletin*, devoted to blacks and Jews, featured several essays on the African origins of Judaism.

58. Matthew quoted in Ottley, *New World A-Coming*, pp. 144–45.

59. Landing, *Black Judaism*, pp. 137–40, 205–38.

60. Wentworth Arthur Matthew, *New York Afro-American*, February 8, 1936, quoted in Landing, *Black Judaism*, p. 216.

61. Robert G. Weisbord and Richard Kazarian, Jr., *Israel in the Black American Perspective* (Westport, Conn.: Greenwood Press, 1985), p. 70; Michael Gelbwasser, "Organization for Black Jews Claims 200,000 in U.S.," *J, the Jewish News Weekly of Northern California*, April 10, 1998, http://www.jewishsf.com/content/2-0-/module/displaystory/story_id/8426/format/html/displaystory.html (accessed June 12, 2004).

62. B. Levitin, "These Negroes Say They Are the Real Jews," *Forward*, October 2, 1920, quoted in Landing, *Black Judaism*, p. 123.

63. Leslie Fiedler in "Negro-Jewish Relations in America: A Symposium," *Midstream* 12 (December, 1966), 25.

64. Rudolph R. Windsor, *From Babylon to Timbuktu: A History of the Ancient Black Races Including the Black Hebrews* (1969; Atlanta,: Windsor's Golden Series, 2003), pp. 33–36.

65. My summary is based on Israel J. Gerber, *The Heritage Seekers: American Blacks in Search of Jewish Identity* (Middle Village, N.Y.: Jonathan David Publishers, 1977), pp. 77–82; Louis Rapoport, *The Lost Jews: Last of the Ethiopian Falashas* (New York: Stein and Day, 1980); David Kessler, *The Falashas: A Short History of the Ethiopian Jews*, 3rd ed. (London: Frank Cass, 1996); Daniel Summerfield, "The Impact of the Italian Occupation of Ethiopia on the Beta Israel," in Tudor Parfitt and Emanuela Trevisan Semi, eds., *The Beta Israel in Ethiopia and Israel: Studies on Ethiopian Jews* (Surrey, England: Curzon, 1999,) pp. 50–60; Steven Kaplan and Chaim Rosen, "Ethiopian Jews in Israel," in David Singer, ed., *American Jewish Yearbook, 1994* (New York: American Jewish Committee, 1994), pp. 59–109. For coverage through the nineteenth century only, see Steven Kaplan, *The Beta Israel (Falasha) in Ethiopia: From the Earliest Times to the Twentieth Century* (New York: New York University Press, 1992).

66. Emanuela Trevisan Semi, "The 'Falashisation' of the Black Jews of Harlem," in Tudor Parfitt and Emanuela Trevisan Semi, *Judaising Movements: Studies in the Margins of Judaism* (New York: RoutledgeCurzon, 2002), pp. 87–110. Some contemporary commentators, such as Ben-Jochannan and Malcioln, do not distinguish between Falashas and Black Jews.

67. Parfitt, *The Lost Tribes of Israel*, p. 243.

68. On the etymological and scriptural origins of "Ethiopia," see Goldenberg, *The Curse of Ham*, pp. 17–25, 41–45, 125. On Ethiopianism and black Zionism generally, see Wilson Jeremiah Moses, *The Golden Age of Black Nationalism, 1850–1925* (New York: Oxford University Press, 1978), pp. 197–271, passim; Weisbord and Kazarian, *Israel in the Black American Perspective*, pp. 7–10; Robert A. Hill, "Black Zionism: Marcus Garvey and the Jewish Question," in V. P. Franklin et al., eds., *African Americans and Jews in the Twentieth Century: Studies in Convergence and Conflict* (Columbia: University of Missouri Press, 1998), pp. 40–53; V. Y. Mudimbe, *The Invention of Africa: Gnosis, Phi-*

losophy, and the Order of Knowledge (Bloomington: Indiana University Press, 1988), pp. 98–134; Sundquist, *To Wake the Nations,* pp. 551–63; Stephen Howe, *Afrocentrism: Mythical Pasts and Imagined Homes* (London: Verso, 1998), pp. 35–65; and John Cullen Gruesser, *Black on Black: Twentieth-Century African American Writing about Africa* (Lexington: University of Kentucky Press, 2000), pp. 1–49 passim.

69. See, e.g., George Shepperson, "Ethiopianism and African Nationalism," *Phylon* 14 (Spring 1953), 9–18; Thomas Hodgkin, *Nationalism in Colonial Africa* (New York: New York University Press, 1957), pp. 93–114; George Shepperson, "Notes on Negro American Influences on the Emergence of African Nationalism," *Journal of African History* 1 (1960), 299–312; Guenter Lewy, *Religion and Revolution* (New York: Oxford University Press, 1974), pp. 194–236; and Dickson D. Bruce, Jr., "Ancient Africa and the Early Black American Historians, 1883–1915," *American Quarterly* 36 (Winter 1984), 684–99. Early black studies that sought to counter standard racist views of Africa and outline a continuum with black America include George Washington Williams, *History of the Negro Race in America* (1883); William T. Alexander, *History of the Colored Race in America* (1887); Pauline Hopkins, *Primer of Facts Pertaining to the Early Greatness of the African Race* (1905); William Ferris, *The African Abroad* (1913); and Du Bois, *The Negro* (1915).

70. Emperor Menelik quoted in F. Nnabuenyi Ugonna, introduction to J. E. Casely Hayford, *Ethiopia Unbound: Studies in Race Emancipation* (1911; rpt. London: Frank Cass, 1969), p. xxv.

71. Brenda Gayle Plummer, *Rising Wind: Black Americans and U.S. Foreign Affairs, 1935–1960* (Chapel Hill: University of North Carolina Press, 1996), pp. 37–56; William R. Scott, *The Sons of Sheba's Race: African Americans and the Italo-Ethiopian War, 1935–1941* (Bloomington: Indiana University Press, 1993); Ibrahim Sundiata, *Brothers and Strangers: Black Zion, Black Slavery, 1914–1940* (Durham: Duke University Press, 2003), pp. 286–304.

72. James H. Meriwether, *Proudly We Can Be Africans: Black Americans and Africa, 1935–1961* (Chapel Hill: University of North Carolina Press, 2002), pp. 27–56, quotation at p. 56.

73. Curtis, *Islam in Black America,* pp. 21–43.

74. Edward W. Blyden, "Ethiopia Stretching Out Her Hands to God; or, Africa's Service to the World" (1880), in *Christianity, Islam, and the Negro Race* (1887; rpt. Edinburgh: Edinburgh University Press, 1967), p. 120.

75. Edward W. Blyden, "The Origin and Purpose of African Colonization" (1883), ibid., p. 108.

76. Edward W. Blyden, "The Jewish Question," in *Black Spokesman: Selected Writings of Edward Wilmot Blyden,* ed. Hollis R. Lynch (London: Frank Cass, 1971), pp. 209–14. Cf. Curtis, *Islam in Black America,* p. 40.

77. Blyden, "Ethiopia Stretching Out Her Hands to God," pp. 116–17, 120, 124–26. See also Gilroy, *Black Atlantic,* pp. 208–11.

78. W. E. B. Du Bois, *The Crisis* (March 1915) and (February 1919), also in *The Oxford W. E. B. Du Bois Reader,* ed. Eric J. Sundquist (New York: Oxford University Press, 1996), pp. 639–40. The seeming anti-Semitism of Du Bois's early nationalism derived from the strain present in the German nationalism he encountered during his graduate work in Berlin, in particular that of Heinrich von Treitschke. See Michael P. Kramer, "W. E. B. Du Bois, American Nationalism, and the Jewish Question," in Reynolds J. Scott-Childress, ed., *Race and the Production of Modern American Nationalism* (New York: Garland, 1999), pp. 169–94.

79. Henry M. Turner, "The American Negro and His Fatherland" (1895), in *Africa and the Negro: Addresses and Proceedings of the Congress on Africa* (Atlanta: Gammon Theological Seminary, 1896), pp. 195–98. On Turner, see in particular Edwin S. Redkey, *Black Exodus: Black Nationalist and Back-to-Africa Movements, 1890–1910* (New Haven: Yale University Press, 1969), pp. 24–46, 170–94.

80. Casely Hayford, *Ethiopia Unbound*, pp. 172–73.

81. Blyden, "Origin and Purpose of African Colonization," p. 100.

82. Marcus Garvey, "African Fundamentalism," in *Marcus Garvey: Life and Lessons,* ed. Robert A. Hill (Berkeley: University of California Press, 1987), p. 10. On Garvey's Ethiopianism and "black Zionism," see Edmund David Cronon, *Black Moses: The Story of Marcus Garvey and the Universal Negro Improvement Association* (Madison: University of Wisconsin Press, 1955), pp. 188–95; Tony Martin, *Race First: The Ideology and Organizational Struggles of Marcus Garvey and the Universal Negro Improvement Association* (Westport, Conn.: Greenwood Press, 1976), pp. 344–57; Randall K. Burkett, *Garveyism as a Religious Movement: The Institutionalization of a Black Civil Religion* (Metuchen, N.J.: Scarecrow Press, 1978), passim; Judith Stein, *The World of Marcus Garvey: Race and Class in Modern Society* (Baton Rouge: Louisiana State University Press, 1986), pp. 153–70; Moses, *Black Messiahs and Uncle Toms,* pp. 124–41; and Gregory Stephens, *On Racial Frontiers: The New Culture of Frederick Douglass, Ralph Ellison, and Bob Marley* (New York: Cambridge University Press, 1999), pp. 154–66.

83. Jeffrey Louis Decker, *Made in America: Self-Styled Success from Horatio Alger to Oprah Winfrey* (Minneapolis: University of Minnesota Press, 1997), pp. 53–62.

84. Marcus Garvey, "Declaration of Rights of the Negro Peoples of the World," in *Philosophy and Opinions of Marcus Garvey,* 2 vols. in 1, ed. Amy Jacques-Garvey (1925; rpt. New York: Atheneum, 1977), pp. 135–43.

85. Cronon, *Black Moses,* pp. 124–32; Sundiata, *Brothers and Strangers,* pp. 15–78.

86. A. Philip Randolph, "Black Zionism," *The Messenger* 4 (January 1922), 331–35.

87. Richard Wright, "How Bigger Was Born," introduction to *Native Son* (1940; rpt. New York: Perennial, 1966), pp. xviii–xix.

88. Garvey quoted in Robert A. Hill, introduction to *Marcus Garvey,* p. lx; Marcus Garvey, "Lessons from the School of African Philosophy," ibid., p. 194.

89. Marcus Garvey, speech of September 4, 1921, in *The Marcus Garvey and Universal Negro Improvement Association Papers,* ed. Robert A. Hill, 9 vols. to date (Berkeley: University of California, 1990), IV, 28. On Garvey, see also Robert A. Hill, "Black Zionism: Marcus Garvey and the Jewish Question," in Franklin et al., *African Americans and Jews in the Twentieth Century,* pp. 40–53.

90. The reference was to "Hatikvah," a Zionist song that was to became the Israeli national anthem. See Hasia Diner, *In the Almost Promised Land: American Jews and Blacks, 1915–1935* (1977; rpt. Baltimore: Johns Hopkins University Press, 1995), pp. 54–55, 76.

91. Essien-Udom, *Black Nationalism,* pp. 46–47; Landing, *Black Judaism,* pp. 99–107.

92. Although Garvey was mistakenly credited with predicting the coming of Selassie as a divine black king—Garvey was critical of Selassie and spoke of the movement with contempt—Rastafarianism, the foremost instance of contemporary Ethiopianism, sprang not directly from him but from an amalgam of sources, including one text known as the *Holy Piby* (the "Black Man's Bible"), compiled by Robert Athlyi Rogers of Anguilla between 1913 and 1917, another called the *Royal Parchment Scroll of Black Supremacy,* produced by the Reverend Fitz Balintine Pettersburgh of Jamaica in 1926, and a widely publicized statement now traced to James Morris Webb, rather than to Garvey: "Look to Africa, for the crowning of a Black King; He shall be the Redeemer."

Timothy White, *Catch a Fire: The Life of Bob Marley,* rev. ed. (New York: Henry Holt, 1998), pp. 7–10. On Garvey and the Rastafarians, see Barry Chevannes, *Rastafari: Roots and Ideology* (Syracuse: Syracuse University Press, 1994), pp. 37–42, 91–110.

93. George E. Simpson, "Political Cultism in West Kingston, Jamaica," *Social and Economic Studies* 4 (June 1955), 138.

94. Nathaniel Samuel Murrell and Burchell K. Taylor, "Rastafari's Messianic Ideology and Caribbean Theology of Liberation," in Nathaniel Samuel Murrell et al., eds., *Chanting Down Babylon: The Rastafari Reader* (Philadelphia: Temple University Press, 1998), 390–411; Joseph Owens, *Dread: The Rastafarians of Jamaica* (Kingston, Jamaica: Sangster, 1976), pp. 39–44, 224–30, Rastaman Teddy quoted at p. 40.

95. Stephens, *On Racial Frontiers,* pp. 182–87, 191–95.

96. Martin Luther King, Jr., quoted in David J. Garrow, *Bearing the Cross: Martin Luther King, Jr., and the Southern Christian Leadership Conference* (New York: Random House, 1986), p. 428.

97. Elijah Muhammad, *Message to the Blackman in America* (Chicago: Muhammad Mosque of Islam No. 2, 1965), pp. 115–16, 64–65.

98. Malcolm X, with Alex Haley, *The Autobiography of Malcolm X* (1965; rpt. New York: Grove Press, 1966), p. 278.

99. Curtis, *Islam in Black America,* p. 69; Turner, *Islam in the African-American Experience,* pp. 147–73.

100. Bernard Malamud, *The Tenants* (1971; rpt. New York: Penguin 1972), p. 101.

101. *Muhammad Speaks* (April 15, 1966), quoted in Gary T. Marx, *Protest and Prejudice: A Study of Belief in the Black Community* (New York: Harper and Row, 1967), p. 139n; Nathaniel Deutsch, "The Nation of Islam and Judaism," in Chireau and Deutsch, *Black Zion,* pp. 91–117.

102. Karl Evanzz, *The Messenger: The Rise and Fall of Elijah Muhammad* (New York Pantheon, 1999), pp. 74–77.

103. Muhammad, *Message to the Blackman in America,* p. 87.

104. Malcolm X, "God's Judgment of White America," in *The End of White Supremacy: Four Speeches,* ed. Imam Benjamin Karim (1971; rpt. New York: Arcade, n.d.), p. 127. This was the famous "chickens coming home to roost" speech, a phrase Malcolm used in answer to a question to suggest that the assassination of President John F. Kennedy was in some way a form of retribution for his policies, and for which Malcolm was rebuked by Elijah Muhammad and suspended from representing the Nation of Islam.

105. Leon Forrest, "Elijah," in *Relocations of the Spirit: Essays* (Wakefield, R.I.: Asphodel Press, 1994), pp. 67, 114.

106. Malcolm X, interview with Alex Haley (1963), in Alex Haley, *The Playboy Interviews,* ed. Murray Fisher (New York: Ballantine Books, 1993), p. 34.

107. Amiri Baraka, *A Black Mass,* in *Four Black Revolutionary Plays* (New York: Marion Boyars, 1998), pp. 46–49; Eldridge Cleaver, *Soul on Ice* (New York: McGraw-Hill, 1968), pp. 101–2.

108. Haley, *The Playboy Interviews,* p. 21.

109. Elijah Muhammad, *The Fall of America* (Chicago: Muhammad's Temple of Islam No. 2, 1973), pp. 66, 225.

110. Fauset, *Black Gods of the Metropolis,* passim; Mia Bay, *The White Image in the Black Mind: African-American Ideas about White People, 1830–1925* (New York: Oxford University Press, 2000), pp. 208–15.

111. Ellison, *Juneteenth,* p. 150.

112. Albert B. Cleage, Jr., *The Black Messiah* (New York: Sheed and Ward, 1968), pp. 39–46.

113. James H. Cone, *God of the Oppressed* (1975; rpt. Maryknoll, N.Y.: Orbis, 1997), pp. 91, 123–24.

114. James H. Cone, *Black Theology and Black Power* (1969; rpt. New York: HarperCollins, 1989), pp. 38, 89, 147.

115. Cleage, *The Black Messiah,* pp. 52–53. On other manifestations of the Black Christ and Black Theology, see, for example, Gayraud S. Wilmore, *Black Religion and Black Radicalism: An Interpretation of the Religious History of the Afro-American People,* 2nd ed. (Maryknoll, N.Y.: Orbis, 1983), pp. 167–241, passim; Smith, *Conjuring,* pp. 55–76; William L. Van Deburg, *New Day in Babylon: The Black Power Movement and American Culture, 1965–1975* (Chicago: University of Chicago Press, 1992), pp. 236–47; and Sundquist, *To Wake the Nations,* pp. 592–602.

116. Tananarive Due, *My Soul to Keep* (New York: HarperCollins, 1997), pp. 93, 57, 315–16, 343; idem, *The Living Blood* (New York: Pocket Books, 2001), pp. 188, 141.

117. Due, *The Living Blood,* pp. 271–72.

118. Alan Dundes, "The Ritual Murder or Blood Libel Legend: A Study of Anti-Semitic Victimization through Projective Inversion," in Alan Dundes, ed., *The Blood Libel Legend: A Casebook in Anti-Semitic Folklore* (Madison: University of Wisconsin Press, 1991), pp. 336–66. On medieval blood libel and ritual murder, see Joshua Trachtenberg, *The Devil and the Jews: The Medieval Conception of the Jew and Its Relation to Modern Anti-Semitism* (1943; rpt. Philadelphia: Jewish Publication Society, 1983), pp. 124–55.

119. Geneva Smitherman, *Black Talk: Words and Phrases from the Hood to the Amen Corner,* rev. ed. (Boston: Houghton Mifflin, 2000), p. 72.

120. Malcolm X, *The Autobiography of Malcolm X,* pp. 201–2.

121. Louis Farrakhan interviewed in William Pleasant, *Independent Black Leadership: Minister Louis Farrakhan, Dr. Lenora B. Fulani, Reverend Al Sharpton* (New York: Castillo International, 1990), pp. 43–44.

122. Jon Michael Spencer, *Tribes of Benjamin* (Richmond, Va.: Harriet Tubman Press), pp. 28, 50, 93.

123. *Ibid.* p. 26.

124. *Ibid.,* pp. 7, 192–93.

125. Windsor, *From Babylon to Timbuktu,* p. 134.

126. Ben Ammi Carter quoted in Gerber, *The Heritage Seekers,* p. 48.

127. Weisbord and Kazarian, *Israel in the Black American Perspective,* pp. 61–84, passim; Robert G. Weisbord, "Israel and the Black Hebrew Israelites," *Judaism* 24 (Winter 1975), 23–38; Gerber, *Heritage Seekers,* pp. 138–9, 144, 152, 169; Morris Lounds, Jr., *Israel's Black Hebrews: Black Americans in Search of Identity* (Washington, D.C.: University Press of America, 1981); Rapoport, *The Lost Jews,* pp. 212–15; Bill Kurtis, "Strangers in the Holy Land," in Maurianne Adams and John Bracey, eds., *Strangers and Neighbors: Relations between Blacks and Jews in the United States* (Amherst: University of Massachusetts Press, 1999), pp. 92–99; Merrill Singer, "Symbolic Identity Formation in an African American Religious Sect," in Chireau and Deutsch, *Black Zion,* pp. 55–72; Ethan Michaeli "Another Exodus: The Hebrew Israelites from Chicago to Dimona," in Chireau and Deutsch, *Black Zion,* pp. 73–87; and Landing, *Black Judaism,* pp. 325–28, 389–422.

128. Ben Ammi, *The Messiah and the End of This World* (Washington, D.C.: Communicators Press, 1991), p. 150.

129. Ben Ammi, *God the Black Man and Truth,* rev. ed. (Chicago: Communicators Press, 1985), pp. 95–96.

130. Louis Farrakahn, originally in E. Black, *Chicago Reader,* April 11, 1986, quoted in Landing, *Black Judaism,* p. 416.

131. Ben Ammi quoted in Landing, *Black Judaism,* p. 401.

132. Caryl Phillips, *The Atlantic Sound* (New York: Alfred A. Knopf, 2000), pp. 267–75.

133. Landing, *Black Judaism,* pp. 423–24; "Israel Gives 'Black Hebrews' Resident Status," Associated Press, July 28, 2003, http://www.foxnews.com/story/0,2933,93105,00.html (accessed December 1, 2003).

134. "Death Bridges Gap for Black Hebrews," *Chicago Tribune,* January 21, 2002, sec. 1, p. 4.

135. Phillips, *Atlantic Sound,* pp. 148–49.

136. On contemporary tourism to slave castles, see, for example, Edward M. Bruner, "Tourism in Ghana: The Representation of Slavery and the Return of the Black Diaspora," *American Anthropologist* 98 (June 1996), 290–304; and Sandra L. Richards, "Cultural Travel to Ghana's Slave Castles: A Commentary," *International Research in Geographical and Environmental Education* 11 (2002), 372–75.

137. Phillips, *Atlantic Sound,* pp. 216–22.

138. James Baldwin, *The Fire Next Time* (1963; rpt. New York: Dell, 1964), p. 100.

139. Roy Wilkins quoted in Meriwether, *Proudly We Can Be Africans,* p. 242.

140. Meriwether, *Proudly We Can Be Africans,* p. 181.

141. Albert Memmi, *The Liberation of the Jew,* trans. Judy Hyun(New York: Orion Press, 1966), pp. 292–94.

142. Zygmunt Bauman, *Modernity and the Holocaust* (1989; rpt. Ithaca, N.Y.: Cornell University Press, 1992), pp. 34–35.

143. George Steiner, *The Portage to San Cristobal of A. H.* (New York: Simon and Schuster, 1981), p. 170.

144. On the cult of the sabra, denoting not simply a native-born Palestinian Jew or Israeli but the "new Jew"—a bold, self-confident, idealistic Zionist whose labor in the land and whose courage in battle together created the state of Israel—see Oz Almog, *The Sabra: The Creation of the New Jew,* trans. Haim Watzman (Berkeley: University of California Press, 2000); and Tom Segev, *The Seventh Million: The Israelis and the Holocaust,* trans. Haim Watzman (New York: Hill and Wang, 1993), pp. 109–10, 179–83. For Zionists, writes Jerold Auerbach, "the sabra and the kibbutz, not the rabbi and the shtetl, were the shining symbols of Jewish redemption. Exile was a condition of weakness and subservience, inherent in the absence of national sovereignty." Jerold S. Auerbach, *Are We One? Jewish Identity in the United States and Israel* (New Brunswick, N.J.: Rutgers University Press, 2001), p. 122.

145. Jacob Klatzkin, *Boundaries* (1914), in Arthur Hertzberg, ed., *The Zionist Idea: A Historical Analysis and Reader* (1959; rpt. Jewish Publication Society, 1997), pp. 322–23.

146. David Ben-Gurion quoted in Howard M. Sachar, *A History of the Jews in America* (New York: Random House, 1992), p. 722; Golda Meir, "What We Want of the Diaspora," in Étan Levine, ed., *Diaspora: Exile and the Jewish Condition* (New York: Jason Aronson, 1983), pp. 223–25. See also Melvin Urofsky, *We Are One: American Jewry and Israel* (New York: Doubleday, 1978), pp. 288–89; and Monty Noam Penkower, *The Holocaust and Israel Reborn: From Catastrophe to Sovereignty* (Urbana: University of Illinois Press, 1994), p. 317.

147. Philip Roth, *Operation Shylock: A Confession* (New York: Random Houses, 1993), p. 170.

148. Cynthia Ozick, "Toward a New Yiddish" (1970), in *Art and Ardor: Essays* (1983; rpt. E. P. Dutton, 1984), p. 173.

149. For postwar refugees settling in Israel, said Aharon Appelfeld, their immersion in Zionism and their rebirth in a living Hebrew language expunged the past, as though it

were alien, while awakening a recognition of the "vast distances" to which "we had exiled ourselves, as though we had been imprisoned all those years by unknown enemies, who had forbidden us any contact with our own secrets." Hana Wirth-Nesher, "Language as Homeland in Jewish-American Literature," in *Insider/Outsider: American Jews and Multiculturalism,* ed. David Biale, Michael Galchinsky, and Susannah Heschel (Berkeley: University of California Press, 1998), p. 219; Aharon Appelfeld, "The Awakening," in Geoffrey H. Hartman, ed., *Holocaust Remembrance: The Shapes of Memory* (Cambridge, Mass.: Blackwell, 1994), pp. 151–52.

150. Mordecai M. Kaplan, *The Future of the American Jew* (New York: Macmillan, 1948), pp. 129–30; idem, *A New Zionism* (New York: Theodor Herzl Foundation, 1955), p. 41. Unlike Louis Brandeis, however, Kaplan concluded that there could be no complete amalgamation of Jewish and American identities—or, in Kaplan's terms, of the two distinct civilizations in which the American Zionist was compelled to live. See Mark A. Raider, *The Emergence of American Zionism* (New York: New York University Press, 1998), p. 160. Reconstructionism focused on Judaism as a civilization rather than a theology.

151. Marshall Sklare, *Jewish Identity on the Suburban Frontier* (New York: Basic Books, 1967), pp. 214–49, quotation at p. 223; cf. Steven T. Rosenthal, *Irreconcilable Differences?: The Waning of the American Jewish Love Affair with Israel* (Hanover, N.H.: Brandeis University Press, 2001), pp. 30–31.

152. Jonathan D. Sarna, "A Projection of America as It Ought to Be: Zion in the Mind's Eye of American Jews," in Allon Gal, ed., *Envisioning Israel: The Changing Ideals and Images of North American Jews* (Jerusalem: Magnes Press, 1996), pp. 57–59; Hertzberg, introduction to *The Zionist Idea,* p. 82. According to Tom Segev, the strength of the United States as a guarantor of Israel's economic and military security, as well as the fact that large numbers of American Jews were not going to emigrate, dissolved the "ingathering of all exiles" as the foremost goal of Zionism, and Israeli reference to "exile" was replaced by the more neutral term "diaspora." Tom Segev, *Elvis in Jerusalem: Post-Zionism and the Americanization of Israel,* trans. Haim Watzman (New York: Metropolitan, 2002), pp. 35–36. For an overview of recent American attitudes toward Zionism, see Arnold M. Eisen, "Reflections on the State of Zionist Thought," *Modern Judaism* 18 (October 1998), 253–64.

153. *The Chosen* tells an archetypal story of American transvaluation, as the heir to a rabbinic dynasty, Danny Saunders, renounces his calling (along with his gabardine and sidelocks) in favor of a secular career in psychology, while his best friend, the assimilated Reuven Malter, having reconciled the study of Talmud to secular American Zionism, opts for the rabbinate. The two boys' crossing of identities, set against the backdrop of the Holocaust and Israel's birth, reconciles Old World with New. Much as Danny, with his liberal education and his doctorate from Columbia, will become "a tzaddik for the world" rather than for his father's Williamsburg synagogue alone, so, says the novel, will the United States help to build Eretz Yisrael *without* emigration or the coming of the Messiah. Chaim Potok, *The Chosen* (1967; rpt. New York: Fawcett Crest, 1968), p. 267.

154. Marian Anderson, *My Lord, What a Morning: An Autobiography* (New York: Viking Press, 1956), pp. 259–62.

155. Paul Robeson, "I Want to Be African," in *What I Want from Life,* ed. E. G. Cousins (London: George Allen & Unwin, 1934), p. 72. On Robeson and the role of African survivals in African American identity, see also Sterling Stuckey, *Slave Culture: Nationalist Theory and the Foundations of Black America* (New York: Oxford University Press, 1987), pp. 327–36.

156. Paul Robeson, "Bonds of Brotherhood" (1954), in *Paul Robeson Speaks,* ed. Philip S. Foner (New York: Citadel Press, 1978), pp. 411, 481, 390–93.

157. George W. Harris quoted in Plummer, *Rising Wind,* p. 158.

158. W. E. B. Du Bois, "The Case for the Jews" (1948), in *The Oxford W. E. B. Du Bois Reader,* p. 463; Weisbord and Kazarian, *Israel in the Black American Perspective,* p. 23.

159. Weisbord and Kazarian, *Israel in the Black American Perspective,* pp. 29–31, 95; Plummer, *Rising Wind,* pp. 247–65; Melani McAlister, *Epic Encounters: Culture, Media, and U.S. Interests in the Middle East, 1945–2000* (Berkeley: University of California Press, 2001), pp. 85–91; Marguerite Cartwright, "Bandung—Israel, the Country That Wasn't There," *Negro History Bulletin* 19 (December 1955), 56–58.

160. Adeed Dawisha, *Arab Nationalism in the Twentieth Century: From Triumph to Despair* (Princeton: Princeton University Press, 2003), pp. 168–69, 181–85; Gamal Abdel Nasser quoted in Benny Morris, *Righteous Victims: A History of the Zionist-Arab Conflict* (1999; rpt. New York: Vintage, 2001), p. 301.

161. W. E. B. Du Bois, "Suez," in *Creative Writings: A Pageant, Poems, Short Stories, and Playlets,* ed. Herbert Aptheker (White Plains, N.Y.: Kraus-Thomson, 1985), p. 45.

162. Penny M. Von Eschen, *Race against Empire: Black Americans and Anticolonialism, 1937–1957* (Ithaca, N.Y.: Cornell University Press, 1997), pp. 145–59, 185–87, and passim.

163. Kenneth B. Clark, *Dark Ghetto: Dilemmas of Social Power,* 2nd ed.(1965; rpt. Hanover, N.H.: Wesleyan University Press, 1989), p. 219.

164. Roger Wilkins, "What Africa Means to Blacks," *Foreign Policy* 15 (Summer 1974), 131–32, 140–41. In "Nobody Knows My Name" (1959), Baldwin had written: "Negroes in the North are right when they refer to the South as the Old Country. A Negro born in the North who finds himself in the South is in a position similar to that of the son of the Italian emigrant who finds himself in Italy, near the village where his father first saw the light of day. Both are in countries they have never seen, but which they cannot fail to recognize." James Baldwin, "Nobody Knows My Name: A Letter from the South," in *Nobody Knows My Name: More Notes of a Native Son* (1961; rpt. New York: Dell, 1963), p. 86.

165. Albert Murray, *The Omni-Americans: Some Alternatives to the Folklore of White Supremacy* (1970; rpt. New York: Da Capo Press, 1990), pp. 183–88. In the reprint edition of *The Omni-Americans* the subtitle is *Black Experience and American Culture.* Compare the more characteristic argument about black vernacular culture made by William Melvin Kelley, who contrasted the inherited oral tradition of African Americans to the written tradition of Europeans. Because we were "torn only from spoken cultures," thus lessening the shock of separation, he said, "we are different." In America blacks thus improvised on English, on Christianity, and on European dress, instruments, and games. William Melvin Kelley, "Black Power: A Discussion," *Partisan Review* 35 (Spring 1968), 217.

166. Walter Mosley, *Fearless Jones* (New York: Warner Books, 2001), p. 301. Mosley is the son of a Jewish mother whose parents emigrated from Russia and an African American father, a World War II veteran. In *A Red Death* (1991), set in 1953, his detective hero Easy Rawlins is hired to spy on the First African Baptist Church and its Jewish communist labor organizer, Chaim Wenzler, for whom Rawlins has more sympathy than he does for the racist, anti-Semitic FBI agent who hires him to do the job after he has been arrested for tax evasion.

167. Ossie Davis quoted in Alan W. Miller, "Black Anti-Semitism—Jewish Racism," in Nat Hentoff, ed., *Black Anti-Semitism and Jewish Racism* (New York: Richard W. Baron, 1969), pp. 103–4, 106.

168. James A. McPherson, "To Blacks and Jews: Hab Rachmones," *Tikkun* 4 (September–October 1989), 17.

169. See, for example, Erich S. Gruen, "Diaspora and Homeland," and Howard Wettstein, "Coming to Terms with Exile," both in Howard Wettstein, ed., *Diasporas and Exiles: Varieties of Jewish Identity* (Berkeley: University of California Press, 2002), pp. 18–46, 47–59.

170. Yosef Hayim Yerushalmi, "Exile and Expulsion in Jewish History," in Benjamin R. Gampel, ed., *Crisis and Creativity in the Sephardic World, 1391–1648* (New York: Columbia University Press, 1997), p. 5; Michael Galchinsky, "Scattered Seeds: A Dialogue of Diasporas," in Biale, Galchinsky, and Heschel, *Insider/Outsider*, pp. 194–98.

171. Insofar as exile is not just an expression of gentile persecution but a way of being God's chosen people—a concept that "gives our history, our being, and our identity as a people its meaning," as Ben Halpern wrote—the fulfillment of political Zionism would not bring the end of exile for those Jews who awaited the Messiah, a task advanced but not completed by the recovery of the biblical homeland. Ben Halpern, *The American Jew: A Zionist Analysis* (1956; rpt. New York: Schocken, 1983), pp. 100–101. On changing meanings of Jewish "exile" in postwar America, see the essays in the symposium "The Meaning of *Galut* in America Today," *Midstream* 9 (March 1963), 3–45.

172. David G. Roskies, *The Jewish Search for a Usable Past* (Bloomington: Indiana University Press, 1999), pp. 161, 170.

173. Jon Stratton, "(Dis)placing the Jews: Historicizing the Idea of Diaspora," *Diaspora* 6 (Winter 1997), 304–15; Moshe Halbertal, *People of the Book: Canon, Meaning, and Authority* (Cambridge, Mass.: Harvard University Press, 1997), pp. 129–34.

174. See Joan Comay, *The Diaspora Story: The Epic of the Jewish People among the Nations* (Tel Aviv: Steimatsky, 1981).

175. Gilroy, *Black Atlantic*, pp. 1–40, passim; Khachig Tölölyan, "Rethinking Diaspora(s): Stateless Power in the Transnational Moment," *Diaspora* 5 (Spring 1996), 3–5; James Clifford, *Routes: Travel and Translation in the Late Twentieth Century* (Cambridge, Mass.: Harvard University Press, 1997), p. 269.

176. Eva Hoffman, "The New Nomads," in André Aciman, ed., *Letters of Transit: Reflections on Exile, Identity, Language, and Loss* (New York: New Press, 1999), pp. 44–45. See also Ian Buruma, "The Romance of Exile," *New Republic* 224 (February 12, 2001), 33–38.

177. George Shepperson, "African Diaspora: Concept and Context," in Harris, *Global Dimensions of the African Diaspora*, pp. 49–50; George Shepperson, introduction to Martin L. Kilson and Robert I. Rotberg, eds., *The African Diaspora: Interpretive Essays* (Cambridge, Mass.: Harvard University Press, 1976), p. 2.

178. George Shepperson, "The African Abroad or the African Diaspora," in T. O. Ranger ed., *Emerging Themes of African History* (Nairobi: East African Publishing House, 1968), pp. 152–76. For a good overview of contemporary uses of diaspora in the context of the postwar revival of earlier pan-Africanist impulses, see Brent Hayes Edwards, "The Uses of Diapora," *Social Text* 66 (Spring 2001), 45–73.

179. Nico Israel notes that the Hebrew *za'avah*, rendered *diaspora* in Greek, denotes "fleeing in terror." The usage is unusual, however, with *galut* appearing far more often in the Hebrew Bible. See Nico Israel, *Outlandish: Writing between Exile and Diaspora* (Stanford: Stanford University Press, 2000), p. 2.

180. Tölölyan, "Rethinking Diaspora(s)," 10.

181. E. Franklin Frazier, *The Negro Family in the United States* (Chicago: University of Chicago Press, 1939), p. 21.

182. Richard Roberts, "The Construction of Cultures in Diaspora: African and African New World Experiences," *South Atlantic Quarterly* 98 (Winter/Spring 1999), 177–90.

183. Marcus Garvey, "An Appeal to the Conscience of the Black Race to See Itself" (n.d.), in *Philosophy and Opinions of Marcus Garvey*, II, 23–24; Stokely Carmichael, "A New World to Build" (1968), in Stokely Carmichael, *Stokely Speaks: Black Power Back to Pan-Africanism* (New York: Random House, 1971), pp. 152–53.

184. Stuart Hall, "Cultural Identity and Diaspora," in Jonathan Rutherford, ed., *Identity: Community, Culture, Difference* (London: Lawrence and Wishart, 1990), p. 235.

185. Marek Kohn, *The Race Gallery: The Return of Racial Science* (London: Jonathan Cape, 1995), p. 153.

186. Malcolm X, letter to *Amsterdam News,* May 10, 1964, quoted in Katya Gibel Azoulay, *Black, Jewish, and Interracial: It's Not the Color of Your Skin, but the Race of Your Kin, and Other Myths of Identity* (Durham: Duke University Press, 1997), p. 136n. On Malcolm X's attitude toward Jews, see also V. P. Franklin, "The Portrayal of Jews in *The Autobiography of Malcolm X*," in Franklin et al., *African Americans and Jews in the Twentieth Century*, pp. 293–308.

187. Baldwin, *The Fire Next Time*, p. 81.

188. Don L. Lee [Haki Madhubuti], "Tomorrow Is Tomorrow If You Want One," in Floyd B. Barbour, ed., *The Black Seventies* (Boston: Porter Sargent, 1970); idem, *From Plan to Planet* (Detroit: Broadside Press, 1973), pp. 25–28.

189. Richard Gibson, "Israeli Threat to Africa," *Liberator* 7 (July 1967), 7.

190. Amira Baraka, "Black Nationalism: 1972," *Black Scholar* 4 (September 1972), 23–29; Stokely Carmichael, "Pan-Africanism—Land and Power," *Black Scholar* 1 (November 1969), 36–43.

191. John Henrik Clarke, "Reclaiming the Lost African Heritage," in LeRoi Jones and Larry Neal, eds., *Black Fire: An Anthology of Afro-American Writing* (New York: William Morrow, 1968), pp. 11–18 (originally in John Henrik Clarke, *The American Negro Writer and His Roots*); Arthur A. Schomburg, "The Negro Digs Up His Past," in Alain Locke, ed., *The New Negro* (1925; rpt. New York: Atheneum, 1992), p. 231.

192. Richard B. Moore, *The Name "Negro": Its Origin and Evil Use*, ed. W. Burghardt Turner and Joyce Moore Turner (1960; rpt. Baltimore: Black Classics Press, 1992), pp. 46–47. As Sterling Stuckey has shown, the "names" controversy dates back to the early nineteenth century, and generations of debate had proved mainly that more than a change of name or "complexional designation" would be required to "exorcise the demon of racism." Stuckey, *Slave Culture*, pp. 193–244, quotation at p. 243.

193. Malcolm X, speech at the London School of Economics, February 11, 1965, in Malcolm X, *The Final Speeches*, ed. Steve Clark (New York: Pathfinder, 1992), pp. 53, 55.

194. Jonathan Boyarin and Daniel Boyarin, *Powers of Diaspora: Two Essays on the Relevance of Jewish Culture* (Minneapolis: University of Minnesota Press, 2002), p. 11.

195. Renee Neblett, 1998 interview in Robert Johnson, Jr., *Why Blacks Left America for Africa, 1971–1999* (Westport, Conn.: Praeger, 1999), pp. 58, 75.

196. Margaret Walker, "Some Aspects of the Black Aesthetic" (1976), in *How I Wrote Jubilee and Other Essays on Life and Literature*, ed. Maryemma Graham (New York: The Feminist Press, 1990), p. 120.

197. Howe, *Afrocentrism* , pp. 215–29. In addition to its excellent history of the field, past to present, Howe's comprehensive book also contains chapters devoted to major Afrocentric figures, including Cheikh Anta Diop, Martin Bernal, and Molefi Asante.

198. Eddie Glaude characterizes such an approach to black identity as archaeological—a "project in which we uncover our true selves and infer from that discovery what we

must do" in order to "respond to collective humiliation" and determine how to act "like a true black person." In contrast to the archaeological approach, Glaude favors the "pragmatic historicist" approach, which recognizes black identity to be a consequence of the struggle to resolve "problematic situations, dispose of meddlesome circumstances, and surmount obstacles," a mode of solidarity arising from "the kinds of stories we tell about our beliefs, choices, and actions in the context of problem-solving activity." Frantz Fanon, *The Wretched of the Earth,* trans. Constance Farrington (1961; rpt. New York: Grove Press, 1968), p. 210; Eddie S. Glaude, Jr., "Pragmatism and Black Identity: An Alternative Approach," *Nepantla: Views from South* 2, no. 2 (2001), 100, 102, 112.

199. Wade Nobles quoted in Andrew Sullivan, "Racism 101," *New Republic* 203 (November 26, 1990), 20.

200. Although his claims about antiquity—as opposed to his demonstrations that modern scholarship itself has been racially biased—have been rebutted on linguistic, racial, archaeological, and historical grounds in considerable detail, Bernal is responsible for instigating a rich and productive debate. See Martin Bernal, *Black Athena: The Afro-Asiatic Roots of Classical Civilization,* 2 vols. (New Brunswick, N.J.: Rutgers University Press, 1987); Mary Lefkowitz, *Not Out of Africa: How Afrocentrism Became an Excuse to Teach Myth as History* (New York: Basic Books, 1996); Mary Lefkowitz and Guy MacLean Rogers, eds., *Black Athena Revisited* (Chapel Hill: University of North Carolina Press, 1996); and Martin Bernal, *Black Athena Writes Back: Martin Bernal Responds to His Critics,* ed. David Chioni Moore (Durham: Duke University Press, 2001). My account of the historical argument for Afrocentrism relies also on Wilson Jeremiah Moses, *Afrotopia: The Roots of African American Popular History* (New York: Cambridge University Press, 1998), pp. 18–43 passim, 226–41; Howe, *Afrocentrism,* p. 109; and Gilroy, *Black Atlantic,* pp. 189–90.

201. Muhammad, *Message to the Blackman,* p. 31; McAlister, *Epic Encounters,* pp, 94–101.

202. Asante's thesis is derived largely from two texts, George G. M. James's foundational *Stolen Legacy: The Greeks Were Not the Authors of Greek Philosophy but the People of North Africa, Commonly Called Egyptians* (1954), which proves to Asante that the ancient civilizations of Africa are responsible for "medicine, science, the concept of monarchies and divine-kingships, and an Almighty God," and from pan-Africanist Cheikh Anta Diop's *Civilization or Barbarism: An Authentic Anthropology* (1981), which makes Egypt the source of Judaism, Islam, and Christianity, and seeks to restore in the African a sense that he is "a Promethean carrier of a new civilization . . . perfectly aware of what the whole Earth owes to his ancestral genius in all the domains of science, culture, and religion." The steps of "constructing," "enabling," and "liberating" articulated by Asante self-consciously resemble a therapeutic process. Indeed, as he describes it, the "Afrocentric cultural project is a wholistic plan to reconstruct and develop every dimension of the African world from the standpoint of Africa as subject rather than object," leading blacks to "a deep, self-conscious, positive relationship with [their] own experiences." Molefi Kete Asante, *Afrocentricity* (Trenton, N.J.: Africa World Press, 1988), pp. 39, 103–6; Cheikh Anta Diop, *Civilization or Barbarism: An Authentic Anthropology* (1981), trans. Yaa-Lengi Meema Ngemi, ed. Harold J. Salemson and Marjolijn de Jager (New York: Lawrence Hill, 1991), pp. 3, 6.

203. Rather than dismiss them as part of a demented fringe, those who undertake extensive refutation of the theories set forth by Afrocentrists such as Jeffries, Martha Nussbaum points out, may make eccentric arguments seem paradigmatic and thus revive old bigoted views of Africa as a terrain of barbarism and irrationality. Howe,

Afrocentrism, pp. 221–22; Martha Nussbaum, *Cultivating Humanity: A Classical De-fense of Reform in Liberal Education* (Cambridge, Mass.: Harvard University Press, 1997), pp. 181–84.

204. Lefkowitz, *Not Out of Africa*, p. 52.

205. Cheikh Anta Diop, *The African Origin of Civilization: Myth or Reality*, ed. and trans. Mercer Cook (Chicago: Lawrence Hill Books, 1974), p. 235. *The African Origin of Civilization* is a compilation of chapters from *Nations nègres et culture* (1954) and *Antériorité des civilizations nègres: mythe ou vérité historique?* (1967).

206. Stanley Crouch, "Do the Afrocentric Hustle," in *The All-American Skin-Game, Or, the Decoy of Race: The Long and the Short of It, 1990–1994* (New York: Pantheon, 1995), pp. 42–43.

207. Ralph Ellison, "The Little Man at the Chehaw Station: The American Artist and His Audience" (1977), in *Going to the Territory*, p. 21; Clarence Walker, *We Can't Go Home Again: An Argument about Afrocentrism* (New York: Oxford University Press, 2001), pp. xxiv, 130; Gerald Early, "Malcolm X and the Failure of Afro-Centrism," in *The Cul-ture of Bruising: Essays on Prizefighting, Literature, and Modern American Culture* (Hopewell, N.J.: Ecco, 1994), p. 256.

208. Glenn C. Loury, "Pride and Prejudice," *New Republic* 216 (May 19, 1997), 25; Glenn Loury quoted in Adam Shatz, "About Face," *New York Times Magazine*, January 20, 2002, 22.

209. Eddy L. Harris, *Native Stranger: A Black American's Journey into the Heart of Africa* (1992; rpt. New York: Vintage, 1993), pp. 27–28, 137, 312–13.

210. Keith B. Richburg, *Out of Africa: A Black Man Confronts Africa* (New York: Basic Books, 1997), p. xiv, 162, 247–48.

211. Kelefa Sanneh, "After the Beginning Again: The Afrocentric Ordeal," *Transition* 87 (2001), 89.

212. The Exodus plays a role in several of Bell's parables, including "Space Traders" (see Chapter 4) and "Racism's Secret Bonding," where Bell suggests that, deluged with suf-ficient data on the disabilities caused by racism, white Americans might willingly enact reforms and laws to erase discrimination. Bell imagines that three renegade black scientists, beginning one Fourth of July, bombard the earth with "Racial Data Storms," a mysterious form of energy precipitation that saturates whites with histori-cal data about slavery, black unemployment and death rates, differential prison terms, and so forth: "Those newly soaked not only knew the statistics but experienced the horrified feelings of the subjects of those statistics." The epigraph for Bell's parable is drawn from Exodus, where Moses calls forth the plagues upon Egypt, leading eventu-ally to deliverance from bondage. The fact that Pharaoh's heart was hardened by the plagues, however, suggests that Bell's fantasy remains just that; deliverance will need to come some other way. Derrick Bell, *Faces at the Bottom of the Well: The Permanence of Racism* (New York: Basic Books, 1992), pp. 45–46, 147–50.

213. *Oreo*'s equal infusion of Yiddish and black vernacular is just one element in a rich pastiche in which low culture mixes with classical mythology and James Joyce, as though to say that any conception of self-discovery must account for the truly rau-cous, bastardized contents of real-life individual identity. Ross's title itself, of course, is a send-up of the straitjacket of identity politics. The epithet "Oreo" describes a black person with a traitor's white manners or soul, but in Ross's hands it becomes a figure for the liberating complexities of human identity freed from the narrow bounds of a singular devotion to race—and liberation, too, from the narrow bounds of the contemporary black-Jewish argument, in politics and literature alike. Aboard a

bus on Riverside Drive, Oreo notices a man with one bad eye leave the bus, followed by a "dapper young man in a camel's hair coat"—none other than Artur Sammler and the black pickpocket about to confront him in Bellow's famous scene of phallic exposure in *Mr. Sammler's Planet*. Fran Ross, *Oreo* (1974; rpt. Boston: Northeastern University Press, 2000), p. 111. For more on the linguistic games of *Oreo*, see the introduction by Harryette Mullen and her longer article "'Apple Pie with Oreo Crust': Fran Ross's Recipe for an Idiosyncratic American Novel," *MELUS* 27 (Spring 2002), 107–29.

214. Langston Hughes, "Promised Land," in *The Collected Poems of Langston Hughes*, ed. Arnold Rampersad and David Roessel (New York: Alfred A. Knopf, 1996), p. 592

3. Black Skin, Yellow Star

1. *Newsweek* 57 (January 9, 1961), 83.
2. Lee was born in 1926. Both her father and sister practiced law in her hometown of Monroeville, Alabama, and Lee herself attended law school at the University of Alabama from 1945 through 1950 (including a year abroad at Oxford University) but did not take a degree.
3. Diane McWhorter, *Carry Me Home: Birmingham, Alabama: The Climactic Battle of the Civil Rights Revolution* (New York: Simon and Schuster, 2001), p. 322; Zell Miller quoted in Celestine Sibley, "Miller Unfurls a Call for Justice and Honor," *Atlanta Constitution*, January 13, 1993, B2.
4. James Farmer, *Lay Bare the Heart: An Autobiography of the Civil Rights Movement* (New York: New American Library, 1985), p. 14.
5. Harper Lee, *To Kill a Mockingbird* (1960; rpt. New York: Warner Books, 1982), pp. 5, 3.
6. Allison Graham, *Framing the South: Hollywood, Television, and Race during the Civil Rights Struggle* (Baltimore: Johns Hopkins University Press, 2001), pp. 156–61.
7. Harvard Sitkoff, *A New Deal for Blacks: The Emergence of Civil Rights as a National Issue* (New York: Oxford University Press, 1978), pp. 102–215 passim; Morton Sosna, *In Search of the Silent South: Southern Liberals and the Race Issue* (New York: Columbia University Press, 1977), pp. 60–87.
8. Gunnar Myrdal, *An American Dilemma: The Negro Problem and Modern Democracy*, 2 vols. (1944; rpt. New Brunswick, N.J.: Transaction, 1996), II, 1016.
9. Hugo Black, majority opinion in *Griffin v. Prince Edward County* (1964), quoted in Peter Irons, *Jim Crow's Children: The Broken Promise of the Brown Decision* (New York: Viking, 2002), pp. 193, 290.
10. Langston Hughes, "Nazi and Dixie Nordics," *Chicago Defender*, March 10, 1945, rpt. in *Langston Hughes and the Chicago Defender: Essays on Race, Politics, and Culture, 1942–62*, ed. Christopher C. De Santis (Urbana: University of Illinois Press, 1995), p. 80.
11. Adolf Hitler, *Mein Kampf*, trans. Ralph Mannheim (Boston: Houghton Mifflin, 1971), p. 562.
12. Hugo Black quoted in James T. Patterson, *Brown v. Board of Education: A Civil Rights Milestone and Its Troubled Legacy* (New York: Oxford University Press, 2001), p. 54.
13. Lillian Smith, *Killers of the Dream*, rev. ed. (New York: Norton, 1961), pp. 121, 87; Lee, *To Kill a Mockingbird*, pp. 136, 93; J. Thomas Heflin quoted in Sitkoff, *A New Deal for Blacks*, p. 267. Accused by townsfolk of being a radical because he is defending Tom Robinson, Atticus Finch jokes that he is "about as radical as Cotton Tom Heflin" (p. 253).

14. See, for example, I. A. Newby, *Jim Crow's Defense: Anti-Negro Thought in America, 1900–1930* (Baton Rouge: Louisiana State University Press, 1965), pp. 92–140; Lawrence J. Friedman, *The White Savage: Racial Fantasies in the Postbellum South* (Englewood Cliffs, N.J.: Prentice-Hall, 1970), pp. 140–68; George Fredrickson, *The Black Image in the White Mind: The Debate on Afro-American Character and Destiny, 1817–1914* (New York: Harper and Row, 1971), pp. 256–88; and Joel Williamson, *The Crucible of Race: Black-White Relations in the American South since Emancipation* (New York: Oxford University Press, 1984), pp. 111–323. On the one-drop rule in the United States, see also F. James Davis, *Who Is Black? One Nation's Definition* (University Park: Pennsylvania State University Press, 1991); and David A. Hollinger, "Amalgamation and Hypodescent: The Question of Ethnoracial Mixture in the History of the United States," *American Historical Review* 108 (December 2003), 1363–90.

15. Claude G. Bowers, *The Tragic Era: The Revolution after Lincoln* (Cambridge, Mass.: Houghton Mifflin, 1929), p. 308.

16. William Hannibal Thomas, *The American Negro: What He Was, What He Is, What He May Become* (New York: Macmillan, 1901), pp. 407, 411; James D. Sayers, *Can the White Race Survive?* (Washington, D.C.: Independent Publishing Co., 1929), pp. 11, 171.

17. Tom P. Brady, *Black Monday: Segregation or Amalgamation . . . America Has Its Choice* (Winona Miss.: Association of Citizens' Councils, 1955), p. 45. On southern resistance to *Brown* and legislative attempts to counteract it, see also Numan Bartley, *The Rise of Massive Resistance* (Baton Rouge: Louisiana State University Press, 1969), pp. 3–120; J. Harvie Wilkinson, *From Brown to Bakke: The Supreme Court and School Integration, 1954–1978* (New York: Oxford University Press, 1979), pp. 61–127; Michal R. Belknap, *Federal Law and Southern Order: Racial Violence and Constitutional Conflict in the Post-Brown South* (Athens: University of Georgia Press, 1987), pp. 27–69; and Patterson, *Brown v. Board of Education*, pp. 86–117.

18. David R. Goldfield, *Black, White, and Southern: Race Relations and Southern Culture, 1940 to the Present* (Baton Rouge: Louisiana State University Press, 1990), p. 87.

19. *Loving v. Commonwealth of Virginia*, 388 U.S. 1 (1967).

20. Jack Greenberg, *Race Relations and American Law* (New York: Columbia University Press, 1959), pp. 341–54, 396–97; Robert J. Sickels, *Race, Marriage, and the Law* (Albuquerque: University of New Mexico Press, 1972), pp. 71–72; Joseph R. Washington, Jr., *Marriage in Black and White* (1972; rpt. Lanham, Md.: University Press of America, 1993), pp. 74–75, 93–97; Paul R. Spickard, *Mixed Blood: Intermarriage and Ethnic Identity in Twentieth-Century America* (Madison: University of Wisconsin Press, 1989), pp. 275–82, 288–305, 374–75; Peggy Pascoe, "Miscenegation Law, Court Cases, and Ideologies of 'Race' in Twentieth-Century America," *Journal of American History* 83 (June 1996), 44–69. On interracial marriage law, see also Werner Sollors, ed., *Interracialism: Black-White Intermarriage in American History, Literature, and Law* (New York: Oxford University Press, 2000). Those who predicted an "epidemic" of racial mixing once anti-miscegenation laws were abandoned were not entirely wrong. The number of intermarriages doubled from the 1950s to the 1960s and then increased fivefold in the 1970s.

21. Herbert Ravenel Sass, "Mixed Schools and Mixed Blood," *Atlantic Monthly* 198 (November 1956), 45–49.

22. Arthur Raper, *The Tragedy of Lynching* (Chapel Hill: University of North Carolina Press, 1933), pp. 59–65. But cf. Robin D. G. Kelley, *Hammer and Hoe: Alabama Communists during the Great Depression* (Chapel Hill: University of North Carolina Press, 1990), who identifies the man as Tom Robertson (p. 81).

23. In a less well known case coincident with the publication of *To Kill a Mockingbird*, a

black man found hanged in the woods of McDuffie County in Georgia in 1960 was implausibly judged a suicide after a cursory examination by the chief of the Georgia Bureau of Investigation. See James Allen et al., *Without Sanctuary: Lynching Photography in America* (Santa Fe, N.M.: Twin Palms, 2000), plate 19, p. 172.

24. W. J. Cash, *The Mind of the South* (1941; rpt. New York: Vintage, 1960), pp. 117–19.

25. This is Ralph Ginzburg's estimate for the years 1859–1961 in *100 Years of Lynchings* (1962; rpt. Baltimore: Black Classic Press, 1988), pp. 253–70. Ginzburg also cites a Tuskegee Institute study of 1959 that catalogued 4,733 lynchings in the years since 1882 (p. 244). On lynching in the Jim Crow era, see Leon F. Litwack, *Trouble in Mind: Black Southerners in the Age of Jim Crow* (New York: Alfred A. Knopf, 1998), pp. 280–325; and more generally Phillip Dray, *At the Hands of Persons Unknown: The Lynching of Black America* (New York: Random House, 2002). Although lynching would not seriously abate until the postwar era, a shift in national attitudes was signaled in a 1935 radio address by President Franklin Roosevelt before a conference of Churches of Christ in America, the strongest public statement to date by an American president: "Lynch law is murder, a deliberate and definite disobedience of the high command, 'Thou shalt not kill.'" Franklin D. Roosevelt quoted in Joe William Trotter, Jr., "From a Raw Deal to a New Deal, 1929–1945," in Robin D. G. Kelley and Earl Lewis, eds., *To Make Our World Anew: A History of African Americans* (New York: Oxford University Press, 2000), p. 417.

26. William Bradford Huie, "What's Happened to Emmett Till's Killers?" *Look* 21 (January 22, 1957), 64. See also Stephen J. Whitfield, *A Death in the Delta: The Story of Emmett Till* (Baltimore: Johns Hopkins University Press, 1988); Jacqueline Goldsby, "The High and Low Tech of It: The Meaning of Lynching and the Death of Emmett Till," *Yale Journal of Criticism* 9 (1996), 245–82; and the compilation of documents in Christopher Metress, ed., *The Lynching of Emmett Till* (Charlottesville: University of Virginia Press, 2002).

27. See Howard Smead, *Blood Justice: The Lynching of Mack Charles Parker* (New York: Oxford University Press, 1986).

28. Roi Ottley, *Chicago Defender*, October 8, 1955, quoted in Metress, *Lynching of Emmett Till*, p. 132.

29. Cleaver was one of many African Americans, from Muhammad Ali to Henry Hampton, producer of the documentary film *Eyes on the Prize*, who dated their civil rights activism—or, in the case of Cleaver, his outlaw radicalism—to the effect of Till's lynching. Medgar Evers, field secretary for the NAACP, risked his life to gather evidence and witnesses against Till's killers. Anne Moody remembered that Till's murder made her hate both the whites responsible for the crime (the murder *and* the trial) and the blacks who did not rise against such injustice, while Susan Brownmiller, in her acclaimed study of rape, made the case a point of departure for her critique of the conjunction of racism and sexism. Till's murder inspired Gwendolyn Brooks's famous narrative poem "A Bronzeville Mother Loiters in Mississippi. Meanwhile, a Mississippi Mother Burns Bacon," depicting the revulsion of the wife of one of the white killers as the terror of her husband's act overtakes her; Richard Wright's hallucinatory novel *The Long Dream* (to which we will return later in this chapter); and eventually Toni Morrison's only stage play, *Dreaming Emmett* (1986). Eldridge Cleaver, *Soul on Ice* (New York: McGraw-Hill, 1968), pp. 11–14; Anne Moody, *Coming of Age in Mississippi* (1968; rpt. New York: Dell, 1976), pp. 129, 187; Whitfield, *Death in the Delta*, pp. 58–59, 85–126; and Susan Brownmiller, *Against Our Will: Men, Women, and Rape* (1975; rpt. Ballantine, 1993), pp. 210–55.

30. Wilson Jeremiah Moses, *The Wings of Ethiopia: Studies in African-American Life*

and Letters (Ames: Iowa State University Press, 1990), p. 130; Cleaver, *Soul on Ice,* pp. 69, 82.

31. Calvin C. Hernton, "A Fiery Baptism," in John A. Williams and Charles F. Harris, eds., *Amistad 1* (New York: Vintage, 1970), p. 206.

32. James Baldwin, *Blues for Mister Charlie* (New York: Dell, 1964), pp. 98, 102. On the decline of Baldwin's influence and the emergence of those who attacked or ignored him, such as Cleaver and Amiri Baraka, see also Robert E. Washington, *The Ideologies of African American Literature: From the Harlem Renaissance to the Black Nationalist Revolt* (New York: Rowman and Littlefield, 2001), pp. 261–73.

33. LeRoi Jones [Amiri Baraka], "What Does Nonviolence Mean?" (1963), in *Home: Social Essays* (New York: William Morrow, 1966), pp. 149–50.

34. Dan T. Carter, *Scottsboro: A Tragedy of the American South,* rev. ed. (Chapel Hill: University of North Carolina Press, 1991), pp. 45–46, 221–22; *Powell v. Alabama,* 287 U.S. 52, 58, 69, 71 (1932).

35. Lee, *To Kill a Mockingbird,* pp. 192, 204, 90, 240. Emmett Till was rendered in similar terms by William Faulkner in a 1956 interview: "Maybe the purpose of this sorry and tragic error committed in my native Mississippi by two white adults on an afflicted Negro child is to prove to us whether or not we deserve to survive." In what way Till was "afflicted" or how his murder might be construed simply as an "error" Faulkner, with his characteristic mixture of sympathetic insight and reactionary detachment, did not explain. See William Faulkner, *Lion in the Garden: Interviews with William Faulkner,* ed. James B. Meriwether and Michael Millgate (Lincoln: University of Nebraska Press, 1968), p. 254. One possibility lies in the claim made by Till's mother, reported in the Jackson, Mississippi, newspaper where Faulkner certainly might have seen it, that her son had a speech impediment and that his fumbling words were misunderstood by Carolyn Bryant as a daring comment or a "wolf whistle." See Whitfield, *Death in the Delta,* p. 18.

36. Lee, *To Kill a Mockingbird,* pp. 247–50.

37. My summary relies on the following sources: Robert N. Proctor, *Racial Hygiene: Medicine under the Nazis* (Cambridge, Mass.: Harvard University Press, 1988), pp. 131–32; Robert Jay Lifton, *The Nazi Doctors: Medical Killing and the Psychology of Genocide* (New York: Basic Books, 1986), p. 77; Henry Friedlander, *The Origins of the Nazi Genocide: From Euthanasia to the Final Solution* (Chapel Hill: University of North Carolina Press, 1995), pp. 31–33; James M. Glass, *"Life Unworthy of Life": Racial Phobia and Mass Murder in Hitler's Germany* (New York: Basic Books, 1997), pp. 39–43; Klaus P. Fischer, *The History of an Obsession: German Judeophobia and the Holocaust* (New York: Continuum, 1998), pp. 214–15, 258–61; Claudia Koonz, "Genocide and Eugenics: The Language of Power," in Peter Hayes, ed., *Lessons and Legacies: The Meaning of the Holocaust in a Changing World* (Evanston, Ill: Northwestern University Press, 1991), pp. 155–77; "Law for the Protection of German Blood and Honor," in Paul Mendes-Flohr and Jehuda Reinharz, eds., *The Jew in the Modern World: A Documentary History,* 2nd ed. (New York: Oxford University Press, 1995), p. 646.

38. See Shmuel Almog, ed., *Antisemitism through the Ages,* trans. Nathan H. Reisner (New York: Pergamon Press, 1988), plate 23.

39. Anonymous figure cited in Sander Gilman, "Dangerous Liasons: Black Jews, Jewish Blacks, and the Vagaries of Racial Definition," *Transition* 64 (1994), 42.

40. Erich Goldhagen, "Nazi Sexual Demonology," *Midstream* 27 (May 1981), 7–15; George L. Mosse, *Toward the Final Solution: A History of European Racism* (Madison: University of Wisconsin Press, 1985), pp. 105–12; Sander L. Gilman, *Jewish Self-Hatred: Anti-Semitism and the Hidden Language of the Jews* (Baltimore: Johns Hopkins University

Press, 1986), pp. 7–10; idem, *The Jew's Body* (New York: Routledge, 1991), pp. 99–102, 171–76. See also Sander L. Gilman, *On Blackness without Blacks: Essays on the Image of the Black in Germany* (Boston: G. K. Hall, 1982).

41. Clarence Lusane, *Hitler's Black Victims: The Historical Experiences of Afro-Germans, European Blacks, Africans, and African Americans in the Nazi Era* (New York: Routledge, 2003), pp. 48–52, 129–39.

42. See Mosse, *Toward the Final Solution*, pp. 175–76; Lusane, *Hitler's Black Victims*, pp. 69–78.

43. Michael H. Kater, "Forbidden Fruit? Jazz in the Third Reich," *American Historical Review* 94 (February 1989), 11–43; Lusane, *Hitler's Black Victims*, pp. 201–8; Henry Ford, *The International Jew: The World's Foremost Problem*, abridged ed. (1921; rpt. Los Angeles: Christian Nationalist Crusade, 1948), pp. 163–74, quotation at p. 163. The predicament of black musicians in Nazi Germany has been treated in fictional form by John Edgar Wideman in "Valaida" (see Chapter 1) and John A. Williams in *Clifford's Blues* (see Chapter 7). For the memoir of a black man raised in Germany (son of a German mother and an African father) who escaped Nazi incarceration and went on to become an American citizen and the managing editor of *Ebony* magazine, see Hans J. Massaquoi, *Destined to Witness: Growing Up Black in Nazi Germany* (New York: William Morrow, 1999).

44. Or in another instance: "The contamination by Negro blood on the Rhine in the heart of Europe is just as much in keeping with the perverted sadistic threat of vengeance of this hereditary enemy of our people as is the ice-cold calculation of the Jew thus to begin bastardizing the European continent at its core and to deprive the white race of the foundations for a sovereign existence through infection with lower humanity." Hitler, *Mein Kampf*, pp. 383, 325, 624.

45. Wyn Craig Wade, *The Fiery Cross: The Ku Klux Klan in America* (New York: Simon and Schuster, 1987), pp. 266–73; Langston Hughes, "Beaumont to Detroit, 1943," in *The Collected Poems of Langston Hughes*, ed. Arnold Rampersad and David Roessel (New York: Alfred A. Knopf, 1996), p. 281.

46. Robert Singerman, "The Jew as Racial Alien: The Genetic Component of American Anti-Semitism," in David A. Gerber, ed., *Anti-Semitism in American History* (Urbana: University of Illinois Press, 1986), pp. 103–28; Edwin Black, *War against the Weak: Eugenics and America's Campaign to Create a Master Race* (New York: Four Walls Eight Windows Press, 2003), pp. 21–123, 247–60 passim; Christine Rosen, *Preaching Eugenics: Religious Leaders and the American Eugenics Movement* (New York: Oxford University Press, 2004); Proctor, *Racial Hygiene*, 174; Stefan Kühl, *The Nazi Connection: Eugenics, American Racism, and German National Socialism* (New York: Oxford University Press, 1994), pp. 40–63, 85, 101; Joseph L. Graves, Jr., *The Emperor's New Clothes: Biological Theories of Race at the Millennium* (New Brunswick, N.J.: Rutgers University Press, 2001), pp. 128–39.

47. Edward J. Larson, *Sex, Race, and Science: Eugenics in the Deep South* (Baltimore: Johns Hopkins University Press, 1995), pp. 83–84, 90, 139–54, Whitten quoted at p. 154.

48. Johnpeter Horst Grill and Robert L. Jenkins, "The Nazis and the American South in the 1930s: A Mirror Image?" *Journal of Southern History* 58 (November 1992), 667–94; Sitkoff, *A New Deal for Blacks*, p. 122.

49. Gabrielle Simon Edgcomb, *From Swastika to Jim Crow: Refugee Scholars at Black Colleges* (Malabar, Fla.: Krieger Publishing, 1993). See also the 1999 documentary film by the same name, directed by Lori Cheatle, Pacific Street Films.

50. Lee, *To Kill a Mockingbird*, p. 198; John Dollard, *Caste and Class in a Southern Town* (New Haven: Yale University Press, 1937), p. 359.

51. Améry's dictum appears within his account of resisting the abuse of Juszek, a Polish prisoner acting as a foreman in Auschwitz, by which he transcended his oblivion: "My body, debilitated and crusted with filth, was my calamity. My body, when tensed to strike, was my physical and metaphysical dignity. In situations like mine, physical violence is the sole means for restoring a disjointed personality." To flee in the face of this "death sentence," he adds, "would have been nothing but a disgrace, whereas acceptance was simultaneously the physical revolt against it. I became a person not by subjectively appealing to my abstract humanity but by discovering myself within the given social reality as a rebelling Jew and by realizing myself as one." Jean Améry, *At the Mind's Limits: Contemplations by a Survivor on Auschwitz and Its Realities* (1966), trans. Sidney Rosenfeld and Stella P. Rosenfeld (1980; rpt. New York: Schocken Books, 1990), pp. 90–91.
52. Lee, *To Kill a Mockingbird*, p. 147.
53. Anonymous speaker quoted in Thomas F. Pettigrew, "Parallel and Distinctive Changes in Anti-Semitic and Anti-Negro Attitudes," in Charles Herbert Stember et al., *Jews in the Mind of America* (New York: Basic Books, 1966), p. 377.
54. Cash, *The Mind of the South*, p. 342; Pettigrew, "Parallel and Distinctive Changes in Anti-Semitic and Anti-Negro Attitudes," pp. 390–92.
55. Seth Forman, *Blacks in the Jewish Mind: A Crisis of Liberalism* (New York: New York University Press, 1998), pp. 33–54; William Styron, *Sophie's Choice* (1979; rpt. New York: Vintage, 1992), p. 41.
56. Howard M. Sachar, *A History of the Jews of America* (New York: Random House, 1992), p. 803; Ed Koch quoted in Murray Friedman, *What Went Wrong? The Creation and Collapse of the Black-Jewish Alliance* (New York: Free Press, 1995), p. 183.
57. Jacob Rothschild quoted in Melissa Fay Greene, *The Temple Bombing* (New York: Fawcett Columbine, 1996), p. 183.
58. Theodore Bilbo quoted in Friedman, *What Went Wrong*, p. 146. On the pressure exerted on national civil rights organizations, see Sachar, *History of the Jews of America*, pp. 803–4; Allen Krause, "Rabbis and Negro Rights in the South, 1954–1967," in Leonard Dinnerstein and Mary Dale Palsson, eds., *Jews in the South* (Baton Rouge: Louisiana State University Press, 1973), pp. 360–85; Leonard Dinnerstein, *Antisemitism in America* (New York: Oxford University Press, 1994), pp. 175–96; Cheryl Greenberg, "The Southern Jewish Community and the Struggle for Civil Rights," in V. P. Franklin et al., eds., *African Americans and Jews in the Twentieth Century: Studies in Convergence and Conflict* (Columbia: University of Missouri Press, 1998), pp. 123–64; Deborah Dash Moore, "Separate Paths: Blacks and Jews in the Twentieth-Century South," in Jack Salzman and Cornel West, eds., *Struggles in the Promised Land: Toward a History of Black-Jewish Relations in the United States* (New York: Oxford University Press, 1997), pp. 275–93; Marc Dollinger, *Quest for Inclusion: Jews and Liberalism in Modern America* (Princeton: Princeton University Press, 2000), pp. 166–73; Debra L. Schultz, *Going South: Jewish Women in the Civil Rights Movement* (New York: New York University Press, 2001), pp. 92–100; Clive Webb, *Fight against Fear: Southern Jews and Black Civil Rights* (Athens: University of Georgia Press, 2001), pp. 42–219 passim; and Michael E. Staub, *Torn at the Roots: The Crisis of Jewish Liberalism in Postwar America* (New York: Columbia University Press, 2002), pp. 52–62, 88–92. For case studies of particular rabbis and particular southern cities, see Mark K. Bauman and Berkley Kalin, eds., *The Quiet Voices: Southern Rabbis and Black Civil Rights, 1880s–1990s* (Tuscaloosa: University of Alabama Press, 1997).
59. McWhorter, *Carry Me Home*, pp. 293, 382–84, 418, 475.
60. Novels that take up black-Jewish relations in the South to one degree or another in-

clude Irving Schwartz, *Every Man His Sword* (1951); Louis Rubin, *The Golden Weather* (1961); Noah Gordon, *The Rabbi* (1965); Jack Ansell, *The Shermans of Mannerville* (1971); Ronald L. Bern, *The Legacy* (1975); and Roy Hoffman, *Almost Family* (1983).

61. Regretting her nonviolence as a young civil rights activist, Walker wished in a contemporaneous essay that she had instead disguised herself as a maid and dropped hand grenades into the laps of "the Hitlers of our time," those who "attacked and murdered our children, called us chimpanzees from their judges' benches, and made life a daily ordeal for us." Alice Walker, *Meridian* (1976; rpt. New York: Pocket Books, 1977), p. 179; idem, "Reading the Seasons" (1976), in *In Search of Our Mothers' Gardens* (New York: Harvest Books, 1983), p. 225.

62. Marvin Braiterman, "Mississippi Marranos," *Midstream* 10 (September 1964), 34.

63. Alfred Uhry, *Driving Miss Daisy* (New York: Theatre Communications Group, 1987), p. 38; McWhorter, *Carry Me Home*, pp. 132, 362.

64. Anonymous Ku Klux Klan member quoted in Jack Nelson, *Terror in the Night: The Klan's Campaign against the Jews* (1993; rpt. Jackson: University of Mississippi Press, 1996), p. 219.

65. Robert G. Weisbord and Arthur Stein, *Bittersweet Encounter: The Afro-American and the American Jew* (Westport, Conn.: Negro Universities Press, 1970), p. xxv.

66. My account of the Frank case draws on Leonard Dinnerstein, *The Leo Frank Case* (New York: Columbia University Press, 1968); Nancy MacLean, "The Leo Frank Case Reconsidered: Gender and Sexual Politics in the Making of Reactionary Populism," *Journal of American History* 78 (December 1991), 917–48; Albert S. Lindemann, *The Jew Accused: Three Anti-Semitic Affairs: Dreyfus, Beilis, Frank, 1894–1915* (New York: Cambridge University Press, 1991), pp. 221–22, 240–46; Benjamin Ginsberg, *The Fatal Embrace: Jews and the State* (Chicago: University of Chicago Press, 1993), pp. 87–91; Matthew Frye Jacobson, *Whiteness of a Different Color: European Immigrants and the Alchemy of Race* (Cambridge, Mass.: Harvard University Press, 1998), pp. 63–68; Jeffrey Melnick, *Black-Jewish Relations on Trial: Leo Frank and Jim Conley in the New South* (Jackson: University Press of Mississippi, 2000); and Steve Oney, *And the Dead Shall Rise: The Murder of Mary Phagan and the Lynching of Leo Frank* (New York: Pantheon Books, 2003).

67. According to Michael Rogin's critique, Donnelly was unusual, and Populism was no more anti-Semitic than other political movements of the late nineteenth century. See Michael Paul Rogin, *The Intellectuals and McCarthy: The Radical Specter* (Cambridge, Mass.: MIT Press, 1967), pp. 172–74.

68. Ben Hecht, *A Jew in Love*, quoted in Sachar, *History of the Jews in America*, p. 415.

69. Dinnerstein, *The Leo Frank Case*, p. 41; Melnick, *Black-Jewish Relations on Trial*, pp. 70–87; Oney, *And the Dead Shall Rise*, pp. 241–42, 496, 501; David Mamet, *The Old Religion* (1997; rpt. Woodstock, N.Y.: Overlook Press, 2002), p. 103.

70. On Griffith's film and the Frank case, see Melnick, *Black-Jewish Relations*, pp. 114–19.

71. Watson quoted in Oney, *And the Dead Shall Rise*, pp. 399–400; Mamet, *The Old Religion*, p. 95. With respect to the ogre-like image of him constructed in the public mind, Frank might bear comparison to the character Popeye in William Faulkner's 1931 novel *Sanctuary*, a lowlife criminal apparently white but with the imputation of "blackness" shadowing him, who achieves sexual pleasure watching others fornicate while hanging on the bedstead whinnying like a horse.

72. Oney, *And the Dead Shall Rise*, p. 485.

73. Unnamed pastor quoted in Dinnerstein, *The Leo Frank Case*, p. 33.

74. MacLean, "The Leo Frank Case Reconsidered," p. 938; Watson quoted in Wade, *The Fiery Cross*, p. 144.

75. MacLean, "The Leo Frank Case Reconsidered," 940–41; Sachar, *History of the Jews in America*, pp. 303–8.
76. Eugene Levy, "'Is the Jew a White Man?': Press Reaction to the Leo Frank Case, 1913–1915," in Maurianne Adams and John Bracey, eds., *Strangers and Neighbors: Relations between Blacks and Jews in the United States* (Amherst: University of Massachusetts Press, 1999), pp. 261–82.
77. Dinnerstein, *The Leo Frank Case*, pp. 139–40, 149–50; Williamson, *The Crucible of Race*, pp. 468–72; Nancy MacLean, *Behind the Mask of Chivalry: The Making of the Second Ku Klux Klan* (New York: Oxford University Press, 1994), p. 12; Oney, *And the Dead Shall Rise*, pp. 560–71, 625–26, 605–7, 615–16.
78. Lee, *To Kill a Mockingbird*, p. 135.
79. Ibid., p. 162.
80. Francis A. Allen, "The Supreme Court and State Criminal Justice," *Wayne Law Review* 4 (Summer 1958), 192–95; William Beaney, *The Right to Counsel in American Courts* (Ann Arbor: University of Michigan Press, 1955), pp. 151–57; Anthony Lewis, *Gideon's Trumpet* (1964; rpt. New York: Vintage, 1989), pp. 112–13, 197–20; David Fellman, *The Defendant's Rights Today* (Madison: University of Wisconsin Press, 1976), pp. 211–12.
81. By comparison to the role of education in *To Kill a Mockingbird,* right to counsel seems an abstruse issue—and one not overtly racialized. More critical might appear the other major Supreme Court decision to come out of the Scottsboro cases, *Norris v. Alabama,* which again overturned the convictions on the grounds that eligible African Americans had been systematically excluded from the jury pool and further accelerated the reversal of the post-Reconstruction rulings that gave states immunity in determining civil rights protection. Because it was decided in April 1935, *Norris* would have been at hand had Atticus Finch chosen to challenge the composition of the Maycomb County jury, arguing, for example, that his housekeeper, Calpurnia, who teaches her son reading out of Blackstone's *Commentaries,* is a fit juror. Even though it has no such explicit racial dimension, *Powell* was nevertheless racialized in fact. The Court's opinion, written by George Sutherland, adverted to racial realism in its second sentence: "The petitioners, hereinafter referred to as defendants, are negroes charged with the crime of rape, committed upon the persons of two white girls." The Court recognized, as the opinion indicates in several other instances, that the South's "rape complex" was more than a minor factor in the denial of due process. See *Powell v. Alabama,* 287 U.S. 49 (1932).
82. A. Leon Higginbotham, Jr., *Shades of Freedom: Racial Politics and the Presumptions of the American Legal Process* (New York: Oxford University Press, 1996), pp. 160–61; Jessie Ames quoted in Sosna, *In Search of the Silent South,* p. 36.
83. James Goodman, *Stories of Scottsboro* (New York: Random House, 1994), p. 151.
84. Carter, *Scottsboro,* p. 235.
85. Quentin Reynolds, *Courtroom: The Story of Samuel L. Leibowitz* (New York: Farrar, Strauss, and Co., 1950), p. 274.
86. Carter, *Scottsboro,* pp. 81, 205.
87. Goodman, *Stories of Scottsboro,* p. 133; Carter, *Scottsboro,* pp. 344–46; *Weems v. State,* 224 *Alabama Reports* 526, 528, 536, 551 (1932); Reynolds, *Courtroom,* pp. 283–84.
88. Williamson, *Crucible of Race,* p. 470; Paul Buhle and Robin D. G. Kelley, "Allies of a Different Sort: Jews and Blacks in the American Left," in Salzman and West, *Struggles in the Promised Land,* pp. 207–8; and McWhorter, *Carry Me Home,* pp. 40–41, 54, 66.
89. Frank L. Owsley, "Scottsboro: Third Crusade; Sequel to Abolitionism and Reconstruction," *American Review* 1 (1933), 267; Kelley, *Hammer and Hoe,* p. 79; Reynolds, *Courtroom,* p. 273.

90. E.g., Thomas L. Shaffer, "The Moral Theology of Atticus Finch," *University of Pittsburgh Law Review* 42 (1981), 181–224; Timothy L. Hall, "Moral Character, the Process of Law, and Legal Education," *Mississippi Law Review* 60 (1990), 511–54; Monroe H. Freedman, "Atticus Finch—Right and Wrong," *Alabama Law Review* 45 (1994), 473–82; and Calvin Woodard, "Listening to the Mockingbird," *Alabama Law Review* 45 (1994), 563–84.

91. Lee, *To Kill a Mockingbird*, p. 244.

92. Reynolds, *Courtroom*, p. 275; Carter, *Scottsboro*, p. 244; Allan K. Chalmers, *They Shall Be Free* (New York: Doubleday, 1951), p. 51.

93. Lee, *To Kill a Mockingbird*, pp. 236, 76.

94. Among important investigations to date of the role played by "ordinary Germans" are Christopher R. Browning, *Ordinary Men: Reserve Police Battalion 101 and the Final Solution in Poland* (1992); and Daniel Jonah Goldhagen, *Hitler's Willing Executioners: Ordinary Germans and the Holocaust* (New York: Alfred A. Knopf, 1996). On "bystanders," see Michael R. Marrus, *The Holocaust in History* (New York: Penguin, 1987), pp. 156–83; and Raul Hilberg, *Perpetrators, Victims, and Bystanders: The Jewish Catastrophe, 1933–1945* (New York: HarperCollins, 1992), pp. 195–268.

95. See Neil R. McMillen, *Dark Journey: Black Mississippians in the Age of Jim Crow* (Urbana: University of Illinois Press, 1989), pp. 224–53; Orlando Patterson, *Rituals of Blood: Consequences of Slavery in Two American Centuries* (Washington, D.C.: Civitas, 1998), pp. 171–218; Leon F. Litwack, "Hellhounds," in Allen et al., *Without Sanctuary*, pp. 8–37; and Dray, *At the Hands of Persons Unknown*, pp. 344–54.

96. Lee, *To Kill a Mockingbird*, p. 201.

97. Ibid., pp. 157, 220, 244, 146.

98. Michael Staub, *Torn at the Roots*, pp. 8–10.

99. Peter Novick, *The Holocaust in American Life* (Boston: Houghton Mifflin, 1999), p. 128; David S. Wyman, "The United States," in David S. Wyman, ed., *The World Reacts to the Holocaust* (Baltimore: Johns Hopkins University Press, 1996), p. 721.

100. Richard L. Rubinstein, *After Auschwitz: Radical Theology and Contemporary Judaism* (Indianapolis: Bobbs-Merrill, 1966), pp. x, 152–54. On Rubinstein, see also Michael L. Morgan, *Beyond Auschwitz: Post-Holocaust Jewish Thought in America* (New York: Oxford University Press, 2001), pp. 91–108.

101. Even though the plot of *The Slave*, set against the backdrop of the Chmielnicki massacres of the seventeenth century and the cult of the false messiah the Shabbetai Tzevi, is perfectly coherent in its own historical moment, allusions to a twentieth-century world abound. Of the bloodshed on which his novel is based, Singer writes, "It was beyond the power of any man to contemplate all these atrocities and mourn them adequately," a statement all the more true of the Holocaust. Singer probes his hero's radical spiritual doubts, his increasing awareness of Jewish accommodation to corruption and anti-Semitism, and his revulsion against those who fail to resist: "Though for generations Jewish blacksmiths had forged swords, it had never occurred to the Jews to meet their attackers with weapons. . . . Must a man agree to his own destruction?" Because *The Slave* appeared in English translation the same year as *Eichmann in Jerusalem*, its concluding invocation of militant Zionism also added Singer's voice to the swelling argument over the issues of Jewish resistance and the "banality of evil," while substituting for the messianic nation one created through the force of military strength and political resolve. Isaac Bashevis Singer, *The Slave*, trans. Isaac Bashevis Singer and Cecil Hemley (New York: Farrar, Straus and Giroux, 1962), pp. 106, 268.

102. Or compare Theodor Adorno's more famous (and, for him, regretted) aphorism, "to

write poetry after Auschwitz is barbaric." Insofar as the immensity of the Holocaust made it inconceivable, it also made it fantastic. Its incredibility made it ripe for the perverse arguments of Holocaust deniers, even as it demanded a mode of remembrance continually defeated by the scale of the atrocity. As Omer Bartov writes in summary of this line of thought, "devastation of such proportions not only destroys the very mechanisms capable of measuring its scale, it annihilates the ability to imagine it." George Steiner, "K" (1963), in *Language and Silence: Essays on Language, Literature, and the Inhuman* (New York: Atheneum, 1966), p. 123; Theodor W. Adorno, "Cultural Criticism and Society," in *Prisms,* trans. Samuel Weber and Shierry Weber (1967; rpt. Cambridge, Mass.: MIT Press, 1983), p. 34; Omer Bartov, *Mirrors of Destruction: War, Genocide, and Modern Identity* (New York: Oxford University Press, 2000), p. 124.

103. Novick, *The Holocaust in American Life,* pp. 83–98, 109–16. On the rise of American consciousness of the Holocaust, see also Stephen J. Whitfield, "The Holocaust and the American Jewish Intellectual," *Judaism* 28 (Fall 1979), 391–401; and Jeffrey Shandler, *While America Watches: Televising the Holocaust* (New York: Oxford University Press, 1999), pp. 127–32. For a comparative look at Anglo-American responses to the Holocaust, see Tony Kushner, *The Holocaust and the Liberal Imagination* (Cambridge, Mass.: Blackwell, 1994), pp. 205–69.

104. As Tzuref, the yeshiva director, puts it to Eli Peck, the story's title character, in America "the law is not the law." Indeed, their own victory over restrictive covenants dissipates into the surburbanites' anxious attempt to use zoning laws to prohibit the yeshiva. The tale's conclusion finds Eli, in an act of madness verging on transfiguration, attending the birth of his son—which is coincident with the birth of Israel in May 1948—dressed in an Orthodox greenhorn's black suit and *tzitzit*. To his wife and friends in the aptly named town of Woodenton, Eli is having a nervous breakdown, but the drug he is given to forestall his apparent mental collapse, writes Roth, calms Eli's soul but does "not touch it down where the blackness had reached." The metaphoric blackness of Eli's soul signifies the community of observance from which he is estranged, the shame and guilt of Americans in the face of the Holocaust and its survivors, and more generally the price paid to modernity by Jews, for whom the ascendancy of political liberalism did not mitigate the dominating force of Christianity, certainly not in Europe nor even in the United States. Philip Roth, "Eli, the Fanatic," in *Goodbye, Columbus* (1959; New York: Bantam, 1973), pp. 202, 216.

105. Coupled with Israel Independence Day, the Yom Hashoah Law of 1951 and the Yad Vashem Law of 1953 mandated commemoration of the Holocaust and of those who rose up in resistance, in particular the heroes of the Warsaw Ghetto rebellion. But some native-born Israelis, the sabras, derided Holocaust survivors as weak and pathetic representatives of failed Jewish societies—"human debris," or "soap," to cite the epithet derived from the legend that the Nazis made soap from the burned bodies of Jews. Reevaluation was boosted further by the Six-Day War in 1967 and especially by the Yom Kippur War in 1973, when exposure of Israel's vulnerability cast the victims of the Holocaust in a new light. At length, the State Education Law was amended in 1980 to mandate "awareness of the Holocaust and its heroism" through instruction and examination. See Yael Zerubavel, *Recovered Roots: Collective Memory and the Making of Israeli National Tradition* (Chicago: University of Chicago Press, 1995), pp. 75–76, 192–94; Dalia Ofer, "Israel," in Wyman, *The World Reacts to the Holocaust,* pp. 860–61; Oz Almog, *The Sabra: The Creation of the New Jew,* trans. Haim Watzman (Berkeley: University of California Press, 2000), pp. 82–90; and Tom Segev, *Elvis in Jerusalem: Post-Zionism and the Americanization of Israel,* trans. Haim Watzman (New

York: Metropolitan, 2002), pp. 101–5. By the same token, the Eichmann trial stimulated new expressions of Arab anti-Semitism. The Jordanian English-language daily *Jerusalem Times,* for example, counseled Eichmann to "be brave" and "find solace in the fact that this trial will one day culminate in the liquidation of the remaining six million to avenge your blood," those people "who tortured and ejected a million or so [Palestinians] from their homes." "Open Letter to Eichmann," *Jerusalem Times,* April 24, 1961, quoted in Yehoshafat Harkabi, *Arab Attitudes to Israel,* trans. Misha Louvish (New York: Hart Publishing, 1972), p. 279.

106. Arendt was answered point by point in Jacob Robinson's *And the Crooked Shall Be Made Straight: The Eichmann Trial, the Jewish Catastrophe, and Hannah Arendt's Narrative* (New York: Macmillan, 1965), which employed a great deal of documentary evidence of Jewish resistance and was published to a chorus of praise. But Robinson, like some others who attacked Arendt, at times confused her views with those of participants in the Eichmann trial or even of Eichmann himself. On Arendt's effect and responses to her argument, see, for example, Henry L. Feingold, *Bearing Witness: How America and Its Jews Responded to the Holocaust* (Syracuse, N.Y.: Syracuse University Press, 1995), pp. 41–52; Jennifer Ring, *The Political Consequences of Thinking: Gender and Judaism in the Work of Hannah Arendt* (Albany: State University Press of New York, 1997), pp. 154–56; Novick, *The Holocaust in American Life,* pp. 136–40; and Bartov, *Mirrors of Destruction,* pp. 130–34. For Hilberg's recollections of the controversy that attended his own book, see Raul Hilberg, *The Politics of Memory: The Journey of a Holocaust Historian* (Chicago: Ivan R. Dee, 1996), pp. 123–75.

107. Ruth R. Wisse, *The Modern Jewish Canon: A Journey through Language and Culture* (New York: Free Press, 2000), pp. 193–94.

108. Emil L. Fackenheim, "Jewish Faith and the Holocaust: A Fragment," *Commentary* 46 (August 1968), 30–33. The argument was more fully spelled out by Fackenheim in *God's Presence in History: Jewish Affirmations and Philosophical Reflections* (New York: New York University Press, 1970). See also Lionel Rubinoff, "Jewish Identity and the Challenge of Auschwitz," in David Theo Goldberg and Michael Krausz, eds., *Jewish Identity* (Philadelphia: Temple University Press, 1993), pp. 130–52.

109. Michael Walzer, *Exodus and Revolution* (New York: Basic Books, 1985), p. 115. In Arthur A. Cohen's formulation, "It is mandatory that this real presence of all Israel in the death camps, experiencing the *tremendum,* enter the liturgy as surely as it entered the narration of the Exodus." Arthur A. Cohen, *The Tremendum: A Theological Interpretation of the Holocaust* (1981; rpt. New York: Continuum, 1993), p. 23.

110. Michael André Bernstein, *Foregone Conclusions: Against Apocalyptic History* (Berkeley: University of California Press, 1994), p. 90.

111. Novick, *The Holocaust in American Life,* pp. 167–69, 186–203 passim. Harold Kaplan takes Novick to task for treating American discourse about the Holocaust as though it were "chiefly part of a political campaign" designed to manipulate public opinion and government action and ignoring its educational legacies, such as "an enlightened understanding of the ideology and spirit of racism." Harold Kaplan, "The Americanization of the Holocaust," in John K. Roth and Elizabeth Maxwell, eds., *Remembering for the Future: The Holocaust in an Age of Genocide,* 3 vols. (New York: Palgrave, 2001), III, 310–14.

112. Alain Finkielkraut, *The Imaginary Jew* (1980), trans. Kevin O'Neill and David Suchoff (Lincoln: University of Nebraska Press, 1994), pp. 7–15.

113. Jacob Neusner, *Stranger at Home: "The Holocaust," Zionism, and American Judaism* (Chicago: University of Chicago Press, 1981), pp. 61–91, quotation at p. 85. See also Ismar Schorsch, "The Holocaust and Jewish Survival," *Midstream* 27 (January 1981),

38–42; Novick, *The Holocaust in American Life*, pp. 146–203; Tim Cole, *Selling the Holocaust: From Auschwitz to Schindler, How History Is Bought, Packaged, and Sold* (New York: Routledge, 1999), pp. 1–19. In response to liturgical admonitions to remember the Holocaust, Michael Goldberg has argued that one certain way for Nazis to triumph is for Jews to adopt their master story in place of Exodus. For example, placing the new holiday of Yom Hashoah between Passover and the Warsaw Ghetto uprising on one side, and Israel's Independence Day on the other, creates a new sequence of Holy Days that displaces God's role in Exodus with the sacralization of secular resistance. American Jews, argues Goldberg, "must restore the narration of the Jewish community's covenantal birth at Sinai to its rightful place in their recounting of the Exodus master story." Michael Goldberg, *Why Should Jews Survive? Looking Past the Holocaust toward a Jewish Future* (New York: Oxford University Press, 1995), pp. 12, 51, 130, 141, 146.

114. Novick, *The Holocaust in American Life*, p. 175.
115. Don DeLillo, *White Noise* (1985; rpt. New York: Penguin, 1986), p. 4.
116. Melvin Jules Bukiet, "In the Beginning Was Auschwitz," *Chronicle of Higher Education* 48 (March 8, 2002), B10; Norma Rosen, *Touching Evil* (1969; rpt. Detroit: Wayne State University Press, 1990), unpaginated.
117. Gerd Korman, "The Holocaust in American Historical Writing," *Societas* 2 (Summer 1972), 259–62; Leon A. Jick, "The Holocaust: Its Use and Abuse within the American Public," *Yad Vashem Studies* 14 (1981), 303–15.
118. Call for Papers, "Critical Holocaust Anthology," posted December 2002 by Robert Soza, University of California, Berkeley, and David Leonard, Washington State University, http://www.english.upenn.edu/CFP/archive/2002–11/0105.html (accessed January 20, 2003).
119. Primo Levi, *The Drowned and the Saved* (1986), trans. Raymond Rosenthal (1988; rpt. New York: Vintage, 1989), p. 21.
120. Henryk Broder, "We Invented the Holocaust!" *Transition* 89 (2001), 74.
121. Myrdal concluded that "the conservative Southerner is not so certain as he sometimes sounds. He is a split personality. Part of his heart belongs to the American Creed." On closer examination, "the Southern conservative white man's faith in American democracy, which he is certainly not living up to, and the Constitution, which he is circumventing, are living forces of decisive dynamic significance." Myrdal, *An American Dilemma*, I, 461–62.
122. David G. Roskies, ed., *The Literature of Destruction: Jewish Responses to Catastrophe* (Philadelphia: Jewish Publication Society, 1989).
123. Wentworth Matthew, *Philadelphia Tribune*, February 1, 1934, quoted in James E. Landing, *Black Judaism: Story of an American Movement* (Durham, N.C.: Carolina Academic Press, 2002), p. 214.
124. *Afro-American* editorial, February 22, 1936, quoted in Lunabelle Wedlock, *The Reaction of Negro Publications and Organizations to German Anti-Semitism*, Howard University Studies in the Social Sciences 3, no. 2 (1942), 111. In addition to Wedlock's early study, see also Robert G. Weisbord and Arthur Stein, *Bittersweet Encounter: The Afro-American and the American Jew* (Westport, Conn.: Negro Universities Press, 1970), pp. 50–64; and Lusane, *Hitler's Black Victims*, pp. 118–21. On Wedlock, see also Paul Gilroy, *Against Race: Imagining Political Culture beyond the Color Line* (Cambridge, Mass.: Harvard University Press, 2000), pp. 292–93.
125. Kelly Miller, writing in *Opportunity* in 1936, found little to choose between Nazi Germany and the United States: "Between Hitler's treatment of the Jews and America's treatment of the Negro, you pay your money and take your choice." Kelly Miller,

"Race Prejudice in Germany and in America," *Opportunity* 14 (April 1936), 105. George Schuyler wrote to Walter White in 1935 that, much to his surprise, he had found that a surprising number of blacks in Mississippi seemed "to derive a sort of grim satisfaction from the Nazi persecution of the Jews." George Schuyler quoted in Bat-Ami Zucker, "Black Americans' Reaction to the Persecution of European Jews," *Simon Wiesenthal Center Annual* 3 (1976), 183.

126. Dray, *At the Hands of Persons Unknown*, p. 372; "Kristallnacht," *Crisis* 53 (April 1946), 110; Roy Wilkins, *Crisis* 45 (December 1938), 393.

127. Melvin B. Tolson, *"Harlem Gallery" and Other Poems*, ed. Raymond Nelson (Charlottesville: University Press of Virginia, 1999), p. 101); Hughes, "Nazi and Dixie Nordics," p. 79.

128. A. Philip Randolph, "March on Washington Movement Presents Program for the Negro," in Rayford Logan, ed., *What the Negro Wants* (Chapel Hill: University of North Carolina Press, 1944), p. 157; Adam Clayton Powell, Sr., *Riots and Ruins* (New York: Ayer Publishers, 1945), p. 55.

129. S. A. Haynes, *Philadelphia Tribune*, July 26, 1934, quoted in Wedlock, *Reaction of Negro Publications and Organizations to German Anti-Semitism*, p. 75.

130. Marcus Garvey, "German Thoroughness Impresses Marcus Garvey," *Negro World*, August, 6 1928, in *The Marcus Garvey and Universal Negro Improvement Association Papers*, ed. Robert A. Hill, 9 vols. to date (Berkeley: University of California, 1990), VII, 214. On Garvey and fascism, see Ibrahim Sundiata, *Brothers and Strangers: Black Zion, Black Slavery, 1914–1940* (Durham: Duke University Press, 2003), pp. 304–9.

131. B. Z. Sobel and May L. Sobel, "Negroes and Jews: American Minority Groups in Conflict" (1966), in Peter I. Rose, ed., *The Ghetto and Beyond: Essays on Jewish Life in America* (New York: Random House, 1969), pp. 388–89; Zucker, "Black Americans' Reaction to the Persecution of European Jews," 179; H. George Davenport, *Dynamite*, quoted in Weisbord and Stein, *Bittersweet Encounter*, p. 58.

132. See in particular David S. Wyman, *The Abandonment of the Jews: America and the Holocaust, 1941–1945* (New York: Random House, 1984); and Feingold, *Bearing Witness*. For a contrary view, see William D. Rubinstein, *The Myth of Rescue* (New York: Routledge, 1997). America accepted some 200,000 Jewish refugees between 1933 and 1945, more than any other nation but only a fraction of those who might have been saved by more aggressive action.

133. George Schuyler quoted in Julius Lester, "The Outsiders: Blacks and Jews and the Soul of America," *Transition* 68 (Winter 1995), 66; Walter White quoted in Cheryl Greenberg, "Negotiating Coalition: Black and Jewish Civil Rights Agencies in the Twentieth Century," in Salzman and West, *Struggles in the Promised Land*, p. 157; W. E. B. Du Bois, "As the Crow Flies," *Crisis* 40 (September 1933), 197.

134. Joesph D. Bibb quoted in Arnold M. Rose, *The Negro's Morale: Group Identification and Protest* (Minneapolis: University of Minnesota Press, 1949), p. 134.

135. Adam Clayton Powell, Jr., quoted in Zucker, "Black Americans' Reaction to the Persecution of European Jews," p. 185; Adam Clayton Powell, Jr., *Marching Blacks: An Interpretive History of the Rise of the Common Black Man* (New York: Dial Press, 1945), p. 193. An ardent foe of racial mixing, Bilbo wrote that he would rather see the white race "blotted out with an atomic bomb than see it slowly but surely destroyed in the maelstrom of miscegenation, interbreeding and mongrelization." Theodore Bilbo, *Take Your Choice: Separation of Mongrelization* (Poplarville, Miss.: Dream House Publishing, 1947), p. ii.

136. Menachem Begin quoted in Robert G. Weisbord and Richard Kazarian, Jr., *Israel in the Black American Perspective* (Westport, Conn.: Greenwood Press, 1985), p. 22.

137. Deborah McDowell, introduction to Zora Neale Hurston, *Moses, Man of the Mountain* (1939; rpt. New York: Harper Perennial, 1991), pp. xiv–xvi; Mark Christian Thompson, "National Socialism and Blood-Sacrifice in Zora Neale Hurston's *Moses, Man of the Mountain*," *African American Review* 38, no. 3 (2004), 395–415. In her unfulfilled plan to write a play about the fall of Jerusalem in 70 CE, Hurston intended to portray "the struggle of a handful of Jews against the mightiest army on the earth, that they might be free to live their own lives in their own way." Hurston quoted in Robert Hemenway, *Zora Neale Hurston: A Literary Biography* (Urbana: University of Illinois Press, 1980), p. 343.

138. John Biggers quoted in Edgcomb, *From Swastika to Jim Crow*, p. 79.

139. W. E. B. Du Bois, *The World and Africa*, 2nd ed. (1965; rpt. New York: International Publishers, 1985), p. 23. The book originally appeared in 1947.

140. W. E. B. Du Bois, *Dusk of Dawn: An Essay toward an Autobiography of a Race Concept* (1940; New York: Schocken Books, 1968), p. 306; idem, "The Negro and the Warsaw Ghetto," in *The Oxford W. E. B. Du Bois Reader*, ed. Eric J. Sundquist (New York: Oxford University Press, 1996), p. 471. For the cold war interracial context of Du Bois's essay, see Michael Rothberg, "W. E. B. Du Bois in Warsaw: Holocaust Memory and the Color Line, 1949–1952," *Yale Journal of Criticism* 14 (2001), 169–89.

141. Dray, *At the Hands of Persons Unknown*, p. 409; Seymour Maxwell Finger, "The United Nations," in Wyman, *The World Reacts to the Holocaust*, p. 811.

142. "Convention on the Prevention and Punishment of the Crime of Genocide," in Lawrence J. Leblanc, *The United States and the Genocide Convention* (Durham: Duke University Press, 1991), p. 245. On the Genocide Convention and its interpretation, see especially ibid., pp. 18–115, 235–44; and Samantha Power, *"A Problem from Hell": America and the Age of Genocide* (New York: Basic Books, 2002), pp. 31–60. Lemkin's distinction has led Yehuda Bauer to accept the term "genocide" for acts of radical denationalization through murder, as in the case of the Nazis' attack on the Poles, while he reserves the term "Holocaust" for the achieved or intended complete annihilation of a people, as in the case of the Nazis' intended destruction of the Jews. Yehuda Bauer, *Rethinking the Holocaust* (New Haven: Yale University Press, 2001), pp. 8–13, 56–58.

143. Civil Rights Congress, *We Charge Genocide: The Historic Petition to the United Nations for Relief from a Crime of the United States Government against the Negro People* (1951; rpt. New York: International Publishers, 1970), pp. 181–82, 195–96. (Some editions use the shorter subtitle cited in my text.) See also Dray, *At the Hands of Persons Unknown*, pp. 408–411.

144. Civil Rights Congress, *We Charge Genocide*, p. 196; William L. Patterson, *The Man Who Cried Genocide: An Autobiography* (New York: International Publishers, 1971), pp. 176–79. Patterson would recall in his autobiography that the "genocidal racist policies" of the United States judicial system operated under the cover of law much as Hitler had in building his "massive death machine" (p. 170).

145. Raphael Lemkin quoted in Power, *"A Problem from Hell,"* p. 67.

146. Paul Robeson, "Genocide Stalks the U.S.A.," *New World Review* (1952), rpt. in *Paul Robeson Speaks: Writings, Speeches, Interviews, 1918–1974*, ed. Philip S. Foner (New York: Citadel, 1978), p. 309. In each instance Robeson refers to a case of extralegal justice that was not a lynching in the usual sense of the word. The Groveland case concerned the deaths of two black men who had been convicted of raping a white teenager but whose convictions were overturned on the grounds that no blacks had been included in the jury. When the county sheriff's car had a tire blowout while he was transporting the two men to a new hearing, he shot and killed them for trying to es-

cape. Although the men were handcuffed and unarmed, the sheriff was not prosecuted. The "Martinsville Seven" was a group of black men who were convicted of raping a white woman and sentenced to death. Although the evidence pointed to guilt on the part of only some of the men, no differences or mitigating circumstances were taken into account by the jury, which meted out the maximum allowable penalty for all seven. Despite groundbreaking appeals work by the Civil Rights Congress, all seven were put to death in the electric chair in 1951. Although they were not lynched, as Philip Dray concludes, the case "opened the eyes of legal rights crusaders to yet another way in which supposedly 'fair and proper' court proceedings 'lynched' minority defendants." It was of course not the first such instance. See Dray, *At the Hands of Persons Unknown*, pp. 395–96, 412.

147. Du Bois and others presented to the Commission on Human Rights of the United Nations "An Appeal to the World: A Statement on the Denial of Human Rights to Minorities in the Case of Citizens of Negro Descent in the United States of America and an Appeal to the United Nations for Redress." Although it gained little notice either at the United Nations or elsewhere and was overshadowed by President Truman's Civil Rights Commission, whose report *To Secure These Rights* (1947) appeared to much fanfare at the same time, the 155-page document catalogued the history of racial discrimination and violence against African Americans. Du Bois's introduction summarized the nation's oppression of blacks and argued that continued discrimination was incompatible with the United States' membership in the United Nations. African America is a "nation" larger than many represented within the UN, said Du Bois, as he put the issue of domestic civil rights on the same plane, even a higher plane, of importance as postwar global politics: "It is not Russia that threatens the United States so much as Mississippi . . . internal injustice done to one's brothers is far more dangerous than the aggression of strangers from abroad." For the "Appeal to the World," see Sundquist, *The Oxford W. E. B. Du Bois Reader*, pp. 454–61. See also David Levering Lewis, *W. E. B. Du Bois: The Fight for Equality and the American Century, 1919–1963* (New York: Henry Holt, 2000), pp. 528–30.

148. Malcolm X apparently never submitted his petition to the United Nations, but only presented it for support to a meeting of the Organization of African Unity (OAU) in Cairo, which he attended as an observer in July 1964. His appeal to the African heads of state, which was received warmly but brought about only a cautious public response from the OAU, detailed recent instances of racial violence in the United States; argued that the Civil Rights Act was inadequate to protect the rights of "your 22 million African-Americans brothers and sisters"; pointed out that if the United Nations could claim jurisdiction in South Africa, it could also do so on behalf of blacks in the United States; and stated that the confluence of the Negro problem in America and the colonial problem in Africa indicated that black liberation was a matter not of civil rights but of human rights, an argument he was to reiterate a number of times prior to his assassination in 1965. Malcolm X, "Appeal to African Heads of State," in *Malcolm X Speaks: Selected Speeches and Statements*, ed. George Breitman (New York: Grove Press, 1966), pp. 71–77. The argument reappears, for example, in Malcolm's speech at Corn Hill Church, Rochester, February 16, 1965, and is incorporated in the Organization of Afro-American Unity's "Basic Unity Program," which also called on American blacks to seek help from Africans to "mend the chain of our heritage." See Malcolm X, *The Final Speeches*, ed. Steve Clark (New York: Pathfinder, 1992), pp. 170, 267. See also Bruce Perry, *Malcolm X: The Life of the Man Who Changed Black America* (New York: Station Hill, 1991), p. 315; and Karl Evanzz, *The Messenger: The Rise and Fall of Elijah Muhummad* (New York: Pantheon, 1999), p. 293.

149. Huey Newton and Bobby Seale, "Petition to the United Nations," in *The Black Panthers Speak,* ed. Philip S. Foner (New York: Da Capo Press, 1995), p. 254–55; Ossie Davis, preface to Civil Rights Congress, *We Charge Genocide,* p. v.

150. Martin Luther King, Jr., *Where Do We Go from Here: Chaos or Community?* (Boston: Beacon Press, 1967), p. 70.

151. *Brown v. Board of Education,* 347 U.S. 494, 492 (1954); Andrew Kull, *The Color-Blind Constitution* (Cambridge, Mass.: Harvard University Press, 1992), pp. 151–63; Richard Kluger, *Simple Justice: The History of Brown v. Board of Education and Black America's Struggle for Equality* (New York: Random House, 1975), pp. 700–714; Mark V. Tushnet, *Making Civil Rights Law: Thurgood Marshall and the Supreme Court, 1936–1961* (New York: Oxford University Press, 1994), pp. 168–231; Lawrence M. Friedman, "*Brown* in Context," in Austin Sarat, ed., *Race, Law, and Culture: Reflections on Brown v. Board of Education* (New York: Oxford University Press, 1977), p. 60.

152. Stuart Svonkin, *Jews against Prejudice: American Jews and the Fight for Civil Liberties* (New York: Columbia University Press, 1997), pp. 34–40.

153. "Modal personality" is described as "those characteristics and patterns of personality that are shared by large numbers of individuals in any group and that may be typical of the group." Introduction to Stanley S. Guterman, ed., *Black Psyche: The Modal Personality Patterns of Black America* (Berkeley: Glendessary Press, 1972), pp. xiii, xv.

154. Clark's influence on Warren's opinion derived particularly from his experiments to see how children responded to dolls representing different races. Clark's study, commissioned in 1950 by the American Jewish Committee, hypothesized that prejudice was formed early in childhood and sought to demonstrate how easily black children absorbed prevailing racist attitudes with reference to themselves. Even though Clark himself had reservations about the accuracy of the study, it was still cited by Warren in his *Brown* opinion. For Clark's impact on *Brown v. Board of Education,* as well as critiques of his methodology (for example, that poverty or discrimination more generally, rather than school segregation, was responsible for the self-denigration of black children), see Sitkoff, *A New Deal for Blacks,* pp. 198–201; Patterson, *Brown v. Board of Education,* pp. 42–49; Kluger, *Simple Justice,* pp. 317–21, 353–56; Ben Keppel, *The Work of Democracy: Ralph Bunche, Kenneth B. Clark, Lorraine Hansberry, and the Cultural Politics of Race* (Cambridge, Mass.: Harvard University Press, 1995), pp. 97–131; Svonkin, *Jews against Prejudice,* pp. 66–67; and Daryl Michael Scott, *Contempt and Pity: Social Policy and the Image of the Damaged Black Psyche, 1880–1996* (Chapel Hill: University of North Carolina Press, 1997), pp. 121–36. On the psychological and spiritual harm done by segregation, including to the dominant race, see also George Kateb, "*Brown* and the Harm of Legal Segregation," in Sarat, *Race, Law, and Culture,* pp. 91–109.

155. Kenneth B. Clark, "Jews in Contemporary America: Problems in Identification" (1954), rpt. in Norman Kiell, ed., *The Psychodynamics of American Jewish Life: An Anthology* (New York: Twayne, 1967), pp. 111–12.

156. "Letter from Birmingham City Jail," in *A Testament of Hope: The Essential Writings and Speeches of Martin Luther King, Jr.,* ed. James M. Washington (San Francisco: Harper, 1986), p. 293; King, *Where Do We Go from Here,* pp. 119–20.

157. Lyndon Johnson, "To Fulfill These Rights," in Lee Rainwater and William L. Yancey, eds., *The Moynihan Report and the Politics of Controversy* (Cambridge, Mass.: MIT Press, 1967), pp. 125–32.

158. Elkins's conceptualization of Africans enslaved in America was revealing in its own right. Describing the shock of the experience of enslavement, he argued: "The new

adjustment, to absolute power in a closed system, involved infantilization, and the detachment was so complete that little trace of prior (and thus alternative) cultural sanctions for behavior and personality remained for the descendants of the first generation. . . . We do not know how generally a full adjustment was made by the first generation of fresh slaves from Africa. But we do know—from a modern experience [the Holocaust]—that such an adjustment is possible, not only within the same generation but within two or three years. This proved possible for people in a full state of complex civilization, for men and women who were not black and not savages." Stanley M. Elkins, *Slavery: A Problem in American Institutional and Intellectual Life* (1959), 3rd ed. (Chicago: University of Chicago Press, 1976), pp. 81–139, quotation at pp. 88–89.

159. Scott, *Contempt and Pity*, p. 114; Elkins, *Slavery*, pp. 20–23.

160. Hannah Arendt, "Social Science Techniques in the Study of Concentration Camps," *Jewish Social Studies* 12 (January 1950), 49–64; idem, *The Origins of Totalitarianism* (1951), 2nd ed. (1968; rpt. New York: Harcourt Brace and Co., 1979), p. 438.

161. See Richard Pollak, *The Creation of Dr. B: A Biography of Bruno Bettelheim* (New York: Simon and Schuster, 1997).

162. During the time he was writing "Individual and Mass Behavior in Extreme Situations," Bettelheim was employed by the American Jewish Committee in a study of American anti-Semitism that included comparison with prejudice against blacks, published in 1950 as *Dynamics of Prejudice*. In 1960 he predicted that black Africans could defeat apartheid by marching against the guns of a police state: "Even if hundreds of dissenters are shot down and tens of thousands rounded up in camps, their fight will sooner or later assure them of a chance for liberty and equality." See Emily Miller Budick, *Blacks and Jews in Literary Conversation* (New York: Cambridge University Press, 1998), pp. 80–83; Bruno Bettelheim, "The Ignored Lesson of Anne Frank" (1960), in *Surviving and Other Essays* (1979; rpt. New York: Vintage, 1980), p. 257.

163. Bruno Bettelheim, "Individual and Mass Behavior in Extreme Situations" (1943), in *Surviving and Other Essays*, p. 83. Although both Bettelheim's argument and Elkins's reinterpretation of it continue to be debated, Holocaust survivor testimonies have corroborated their theory of the death camps' capacity to render humans an anonymous mass of living dead—what Primo Levi and other witnesses referred to as *Muselmänner*, so called because their flattened, indistinguishable figures resembled Muslims at prayer—in whom trauma has deranged all bodily functions and crushed the will to live. Terrence Des Pres took issue with both Elkins and Bettelheim, arguing that a psychoanalytic approach was not applicable in conditions of extremity. The death camps no longer constitute a "civilized state," Des Pres contended, and the "covert behavior" in which psychoanalysis finds human meaning becomes "explicit, actual, necessary in an immediately practical way." See Primo Levi, *Survival in Auschwitz: The Nazi Assault on Humanity* (1958), trans. Stuart Woolf (New York; Collier Books, 1961), pp. 80–81; Terrence Des Pres, *The Survivor: An Anatomy of Life in the Death Camps* (New York: Oxford University Press, 1976), pp. 88–94, 153–61; and Kalí Tal, *Worlds of Hurt: Reading the Literatures of Trauma* (New York: Cambridge University Press, 1996), pp. 32–46. On the contrasting view of survivors in Bettelheim and Des Pres, see Herbert Hirsch, *Genocide and the Politics of Memory: Studying Death to Preserve Life* (Chapel Hill: University of North Carolina Press, 1995), pp. 56–72.

164. Orlando Patterson, "Toward a Future That Has No Past—Reflections on the Fate of Blacks in the Americas," *Public Interest* 27 (1972), 40–42.

165. Albert Murray, "The HNIC Who He" (originally "The Illusive Black Image," 1967), in *From the Briar Patch: On Context, Procedure, and American Identity* (New York: Pantheon, 2001), p. 80.

166. Charles Silberman quoted in Dollinger, *Quest for Inclusion,* p. 196. As Silberman pointed out in his widely read book *Crisis in Black and White,* moreover, Jews made their liberation from slavery, led by Moses, central to collective remembrance, whereas blacks, whose liberation was the by-product of a civil war between whites, would probably prefer to erase the memory of slavery, or so it seemed to him. Charles E. Silberman, *Crisis in Black and White* (New York: Random House, 1964), p. 78.

167. LeRoi Jones [Amiri Baraka], *"Dutchman" and "The Slave": Two Plays* (New York: William Morrow, 1964), pp. 29–30.

168. The report was misrepresented by the media and demagogues alike, the first because they turned it into clichés and the second because they found it a useful starting point for rhetorical attacks. Moynihan, in fact, stressed first of all that the socioeconomic system of the United States, inflected by decades of racism and prejudicial actions, official and unofficial, was responsible for the instability and poverty of black families. This condition in turn led to other forms of pathological behavior. See Rainwater and Yancey, *The Moynihan Report and the Politics of Controversy,* pp. 1–313 passim.

169. Donna Franklin, *Ensuring Inequality: The Structural Transformation of the African-American Family* (New York: Oxford University Press, 1997), pp. 153–81; Rainwater and Yancey, *The Moynihan Report and the Politics of Controversy,* pp. 267–68, 402–9.

170. George S. Schuyler, *Black and Conservative: The Autobiography of George S. Schuyler* (New Rochelle, N.Y.: Arlington House, 1966), p. 351.

171. Adolph Reed, Jr., *Stirrings in the Jug: Black Politics in the Post-segregation Era* (Minneapolis: University of Minnesota Press, 1999), p. 222; Scott, *Contempt and Pity,* pp. 75–81, 151–59.

172. William H. Grier and Price M. Cobbs, *Black Rage* (1968; rpt. New York: Bantam, 1969), p. 19. In Ralph Ellison's view, the white pathologists of liberalism and black pathologists of militant nationalism were equally mistaken in their view that African American life was nothing more than the "sum of its brutalization." Ralph Ellison, "A Very Stern Discipline" (1965), in *Going to the Territory* (New York: Random House, 1986), pp. 288, 300.

173. Major works of the period include David Brion Davis, *Slavery in Western Culture* (Ithaca, N.Y.: Cornell University Press, 1966), and *Slavery in the Age of Revolution, 1770–1823* (Ithaca, N.Y.: Cornell University Press, 1975); Winthrop D. Jordan, *White over Black: American Attitudes toward the Negro, 1550–1812* (Chapel Hill: University of North Carolina Press, 1968); John W. Blassingame, *The Slave Community: Plantation Life in the Antebellum South* (New York: Oxford University Press, 1972); Eugene D. Genovese, *Roll, Jordan, Roll: The World the Slaves Made* (New York: Random House, 1974); and Herbert G. Gutman, *The Black Family in Slavery and Freedom, 1750–1925* (New York: Random House, 1977). See also Ann J. Lane, ed., *The Debate over Slavery: Stanley Elkins and His Critics* (Urbana: University of Illinois Press, 1971).

174. As *Slavery* went through successive editions, Elkins remained an important interlocutor in the debate. On the one hand, he argued in an addendum to the third edition published in 1975 that any theory must allow for damage, that "culture" acquired under the conditions of slavery is "bound to contain more than the normal residue of pathology." On the other, he observed that Moynihan's report, a "relentless, insistent, dreary picture of unrelieved damage," had failed to realize that the civil rights movement—including, as it did, dawning recognition that African Americans had long

had a vital culture, that their definitions of black identity counted for something, and that oppression might breed resistance as well as accommodation—had made the damage argument "ideologically untenable." Nevertheless, damage theory continued to serve the needs of both liberal and conservative agendas. In the 1990s, neoconservatives continued to trace black "pathology" in part to the welfare state and race-based policy, bemoaning, as did Shelby Steele, the "specimenization" of African Americans as helpless racialized beings. But critics on the left, wielding multicultural theory to celebrate and legitimize difference, also discovered new strains of black pathology, as in Cornel West's vision of the perpetual "nihilism" of the black underclass, little different in its assumptions from Moynihan. In an argument that can be typecast as neither liberal nor neoconservative, Orlando Patterson resurrected a good deal of Moynihan's ill-starred argument in asserting that the "holocaust of slavery" produced an "ethnocidal assault on gender roles, especially those of father and husband, leaving deep scars in the relations between Afro-American men and women," and codified pathological patterns that still plague a large proportion of African American families. Hugh Pearson likewise charges that the radical left and the media enshrined one version of racial damage as a hip lifestyle by "elevating the rudest, most outlaw element of black America as the true keepers of the flame in all it means to be black." The commercial sensationalizing of black gang culture, argued Pearson, represented African Americans as "pathological outsiders to the American mainstream." Elkins, *Slavery: A Problem in American Institutional and Intellectual Life*, pp. 271–72, 301; Scott, *Contempt and Pity*, pp. 156–59, 190–91; Shelby Steele, A *Dream Deferred: The Second Betrayal of Black Freedom in America* (New York: HarperCollins, 1998), pp. 23–29; Cornel West, *Race Matters* (Boston: Beacon Press, 1993), pp. 11–20; Stephen Steinberg, "The Liberal Retreat from Race during the Post–Civil Rights Era," in Wahneema Lubiano, ed., *The House That Race Built: Black Americans, U.S. Terrain,* (New York: Pantheon Books, 1997), pp. 33–40; Patterson, *Rituals of Blood*, pp. 24–29, 163–67; Hugh Pearson, *The Shadow of the Panther: Huey Newton and the Price of Black Power in America* (Cambridge, Mass.: Perseus, 1994), pp. 338–40.

175. Lee, *To Kill a Mockingbird*, pp. 195, 148.
176. Ibid., p. 221.
177. Claudia Johnson, "The Secret Courts of Men's Hearts: Code and Law in Harper Lee's *To Kill a Mockingbird*," *Studies in American Fiction* 19 (Autumn 1991), 129–39.
178. *Brown v. Board of Education*, 493.
179. Lee, *To Kill a Mockingbird*, pp. 72, 116.
180. Smith, *Killers of the Dream*, pp. 122–23; Smith's ellipses.
181. Lee, *To Kill a Mockingbird*, pp. 13, 284.
182. Ibid., p. 144.
183. Daphne Merkin, "Dreaming of Hitler: A Memoir of Self-Hatred," in David Rosenberg, ed., *Testimony: Contemporary Writers Make the Holocaust Personal* (New York: Random House, 1989), pp. 26–27.
184. Ian Buruma, "The Afterlife of Anne Frank," *New York Review of Books* 45 (Februrary 19, 1998), 4.
185. Because of its extensive use as a school text, the *Diary* became a special target of Holocaust deniers dedicated to disproving its authenticity, with the result that, after forensic authentication of the book by the Netherlands State Institute for War Documentation, an elaborate seven hundred–page critical edition was published in 1986. See *The Diary of Anne Frank: The Critical Edition,* ed. David Barnouw and Gerrold Van Der Stroom, trans. Arnold J. Pomerans and B. M. Mooyart-Doubleday (1986;

New York: Doubleday, 1989); Gilman, *Jewish Self-Hatred,* pp. 351–53; and Deborah Lipstadt, *Denying the Holocaust: The Growing Assault on Truth and Memory* (1993; rpt. New York: Plume, 1994), pp. 229–35.

186. The stage play was written by Frances Goodrich and Albert Hackett (best known as the co-writers of *Easter Parade* and *It's a Wonderful Life*) and directed by Garson Kanin. The film adaptation, directed by George Stevens, starred Millie Perkins, an unknown actress with all-American looks, in the title role. For Brooks Atkinson, writing in an introduction to the published play, the dramatization perfectly captured the "bloom of [Anne's] adolescence and the bloom of her spirit." In the same vein, Eleanor Roosevelt, in an introduction to the English translation of the *Diary,* called it "one of the wisest and most moving commentaries on war and its impact on human beings that I have ever read" and referred to the "ultimate shining nobility" of Anne's spirit in the face of degradation. Although he made the *Diary* yet another vehicle for his convoluted attack on the passivity of the Jews ("they could have sold their lives for a high price, instead of walking to their deaths"), Bruno Bettelheim contended that the wide acclaim given the sanitized play and film could not be explained "unless we recognize within it our wish to forget the gas chambers." For "if all men are good at heart, there never really was an Auschwitz." Frances Goodrich and Albert Hackett, *The Diary of Anne Frank* (New York: Random House, 1956), p. 174, vii; Eleanor Roosevelt, introduction to Anne Frank, *The Diary of a Young Girl,* trans. B. M. Mooyaart-Doubleday (1952; rpt. New York: Bantam, 1993), p. xiii; Bruno Bettelheim, "The Ignored Lesson of Anne Frank," pp. 249, 255, 251. See also Alvin H. Rosenfeld, "Popularization and Memory: The Case of Anne Frank," in Peter Hayes, ed., *Lessons and Legacies: The Meaning of the Holocaust in a Changing World* (Evanston: Northwestern University Press, 1991), pp. 251–58; Edward Alexander, *The Holocaust and the War of Ideas* (New Brunswick, N.J.: Transaction, 1994), pp. 51–54; Judith E. Doneson, *The Holocaust in American Film* (Philadelphia: Jewish Publication Society, 1987), pp. 61–83; Cole, *Selling the Holocaust,* pp. 23–46; and Novick, *The Holocaust in American Life,* pp. 117–20.

187. Goodrich and Hackett, *Diary of Anne Frank,* p. 168; Yehuda Bauer, "The Significance of the Final Solution," in David Cesarani, ed., *The Final Solution: Origins and Implementation* (New York: Routledge, 1994), p. 307; Philip Roth, *The Ghost Writer* (1979; rpt. New York: Vintage, 1995), p. 144.

188. Frank, *Diary of a Young Girl,* p. 53.

189. Richard Wright, *The Long Dream* (1958; rpt. New York: Harper Perennial, 1987), p. 238.

190. Orlando Patterson, *Slavery and Social Death: A Comparative Study* (Cambridge, Mass.: Harvard University Press, 1982), pp. 35–51.

191. Michel Fabre, *The Unfinished Quest of Richard Wright,* 2nd ed. (1973; rpt. Urbana: University of Illinois Press, 1993), p. 466.

192. McMillen, *Dark Journey,* p. 229.

193. Among the growing number of publications in English devoted to the Nazi death camps was the shocking 1946 memoir of survivor Dr. Miklos Nyiszli, first published in English in 1960 as *Auschwitz: A Doctor's Eyewitness Account.* In addition to performing legitimate medical duties at Auschwitz, Nyiszli assisted in Josef Mengele's torturous medical experiments. A paperback version of Nyiszli's book issued in the wake of the Eichmann trial ignored the moral conundrum of Nyiszli's collaboration in terror while emblazoning its cover with promises of "the truth about Eichmann's inferno" and a rendering of the slogan "Never Forget" that crossed memorialization with gross sensationalism: "Six million? Ten million? The exact number of the slaughter will never be known. But Auschwitz was real—and this brutal account of

human depravity is beyond the reach of any fiction. What you read here you will never forget!" See Miklos Nyiszli, *Auschwitz: A Doctor's Eyewitness Account,* trans. Tibere Kremer and Richard Seaver (1960; rpt. New York: Fawcett, n.d.), front and back cover.

194. Ralph Ellison, "Richard Wright's Blues" (1945), in *Shadow and Act* (1964; rpt. New York: Vintage, 1972), p. 84.

195. Richard Wright, "The American Problem—Its Negro Phase," in *Richard Wright: Impressions and Perspectives,* ed. David Ray and Robert M. Farnsworth (Ann Arbor: University of Michigan Press, 1973), p. 16.

196. Trudier Harris, *Exorcising Blackness: Historical and Literary Lynching and Burning Rituals* (Bloomington: Indiana University Press, 1984), pp. 29–68.

197. Richard Powers's description of Till's corpse in his novel *The Time of Our Singing,* based on photos published in the September 8, 1955, issue of *Jet,* is grimly eloquent on this point: "The boy has his white Christmas shirt on again, starched smooth, with a black jacket pulled over the top. These clothes are the only clue that the photo shows a human being at all. That the undertaker survived the corpse's dressing is itself miraculous. The face is a melted rubber model, a rotting vegetable, bloated and disfigured. Below the midline, there's nothing but a single flattened bruise. The ear is singed off. The nose and eyes have been returned to the face by hesitant guess." Richard Powers, *The Time of Our Singing* (New York: Farrar, Straus, and Giroux, 2003), p. 102. In a grim irony, the facing page of the lead story about Till in *Jet* displays an ad for a skin bleaching cream whose use guarantees that "any miss can be a hit with a lovely, light complexion."

198. Wright, *The Long Dream,* pp. 64, 76–78.

199. Ibid., pp. 158, 180.

200. Isolated from other prisoners and deliberately consigned to destruction in their turn so that they might not survive to tell about the killing operation, the *Sonderkommandos* were afforded certain privileges and, indeed, in some ways entered onto the same footing as the SS, thus becoming the "bearers of a horrendous secret." Levi, *The Drowned and the Saved,* pp. 50–55; Otto Friedrich, *The Kingdom of Auschwitz* (New York: HarperCollins, 1994), pp. 31–32, 69.

201. Lee, *To Kill a Mockingbird,* pp. 218, 30

4. EXODUS I: A NEGRO-LESS WORLD

1. William Melvin Kelley, "On Racism, Exploitation, and the White Liberal," *Negro Digest* 16 (January 1967), 10–12.

2. William Melvin Kelley, *A Different Drummer* (1962; New York: Anchor, 1989), pp. 60, 188.

3. Orlando Patterson, *Slavery and Social Death: A Comparative Study* (Cambridge, Mass.: Harvard University Press, 1982), pp. 334–42. See Hegel: "But just as lordship showed that its essential nature is the reverse of what it wants to be, so too servitude in its consummation will really turn into the opposite of what it immediately is; as a consciousness forced back into itself, it will withdraw into itself and be transformed into a truly independent consciousness." G. W. F. Hegel, *Phenomenology of Spirit,* trans. A. V. Miller (New York: Oxford University Press, 1977), p. 117.

4. James Baldwin, *The Fire Next Time* (1963; rpt. New York: Dell, 1964), p. 20.

5. His expatriation gave Wright the idiosyncratic perspective necessary for his nightmare novel *The Long Dream,* whereas Baldwin, although he needed to go to Europe in order to understand his role in the drama of America, found something else as well: "I was released from the illusion that I hated America." James Baldwin, "The Discovery of What It Means to Be an American" (1959), in *Nobody Knows My Name* (1961; rpt. New York: Dell, 1963), p. 19. For relatively short periods of time in the 1960s, Kelley lived abroad in Rome and Paris.

6. Cf. Dean E. Robinson, *Black Nationalism in American Politics and Thought* (New York: Cambridge University Press, 2001), p. 2.

7. Ralph Bunche, *A World View of Race* (Washington, D.C.: Associates in Negro Folk Education, 1936), pp. 93–94.

8. See, for example, Rob Nixon, "Caribbean and African Appropriations of *The Tempest,*" *Critical Inquiry* 13 (Spring 1987), 557–78, who examines writers such as George Lamming, Roberto Fernández Retamar, Aimé Césaire, Edward Braithwaite, and Ngugi wa Thiong'o.

9. Kelley, *A Different Drummer,* p. 127.

10. Henry David Thoreau, "Resistance to Civil Government," in *Walden and Resistance to Civil Government,* ed. William Rossi (New York: Norton, 1992), p. 234. Kelley's title comes from a famous passage, particularly popular in the counterculture of the 1960s, that appears in the concluding chapter of *Walden:* "If a man does not keep pace with his companions, perhaps it is because he hears a different drummer. Let him step to the music which he hears, however measured or far away" (p. 217).

11. Martin Luther King, Jr., *Stride toward Freedom: The Montgomery Story* (1958; rpt. San Francisco: Harper and Row, 1986), p. 51; John Lewis quoted in Taylor Branch, *Parting the Waters: America in the King Years, 1954–63* (New York: Simon and Schuster, 1988), p. 279; Kelley, *A Different Drummer,* p. 130.

12. Robert Abbott quoted in Taylor Branch, "Blacks and Jews: The Uncivil War," in Jack Salzman, ed., *Bridges and Boundaries: African Americans and American Jews* (New York: George Braziller, 1992), p. 53. A key role in stirring the dreams of countless southern blacks was played by northern black newspapers, none more so than the *Chicago Defender,* which increased its circulation tenfold between 1916 and 1918 by vigorously promoting the migration in editorials and advertisements that proclaimed a new Exodus to the Promised Land. Some white southerners welcomed such a development, but others fought desperately—sometimes through economic intimidation and violence—to maintain their pool of cheap labor.

13. Adam Clayton Powell, Jr., *Marching Blacks: An Interpretive History of the Rise of the Common Black Man* (New York: Dial Press, 1945), pp. 183–88.

14. Langston Hughes, "My America," in Rayford W. Logon, ed., *What the Negro Wants* (Chapel Hill: University of North Carolina Press, 1944), p. 303.

15. Lillian Smith, *Killers of the Dream* (1961; rpt. New York: Norton, 1978), p. 253.

16. Henry Dumas, "The Marchers," in *Goodbye, Sweetwater,* ed. Eugene B. Redmond (New York: Thunder's Mouth Press, 1988), pp. 177–83.

17. Aldon D. Morris, *The Origins of the Civil Rights Movement: Black Communities Organizing for Change* (New York: Free Press, 1984), pp. 195–228; Franklin McLain quoted in Vincent Harding, Robin D. G. Kelley, and Earl Lewis, "We Changed the World, 1945–1970," in Robin D. G. Kelley and Earl Lewis, eds., *To Make Our World Anew: A History of African Americans* (New York: Oxford University Press, 2000), p. 481; Ella Baker, "Developing Community Leadership," quoted in Charles M. Payne, *I've Got the Light of Freedom: The Organizing Tradition and the Mississippi Freedom Struggle* (Berkeley: University of California Press, 1995), p. 93. As Payne observes, focusing on

the dramatic high points of civil rights history obscures the fortuitousness of King's leadership and undervalues the long, hard work of many unrecognized people whose activities made breakthroughs possible, "the network-building, the grooming of another generation of leadership, the sheer persistence. . . . The popular conception of Montgomery—a tired woman [Rosa Parks] refused to give up her seat and a prophet rose up to lead the grateful masses—is a good story but useless history" (pp. 417–18).

18. Martin Luther King, Jr., "I See the Promised Land," in *A Testament of Hope: The Essential Writings of Martin Luther King, Jr.,* ed. James Melvin Washington (San Francisco: Harper, 1986), p. 282; William L. Van Deburg, *New Day in Babylon: The Black Power Movement and American Culture, 1965–1975* (Chicago: University of Chicago Press, 1992), p. 45; John A. Williams, *The King God Didn't Save* (New York: Coward-McCann, 1970), p. 141; Martin Luther King, Jr., *Where Do We Go from Here: Chaos or Community?* (Boston: Beacon, 1967), pp. 23–32.

19. King, *Where Do We Go from Here?,* pp. 170, 12, 159, 124.

20. Michael Walzer, *Exodus and Revolution* (New York: Basic Books, 1985), pp. 5, 43–70.

21. Charles P. Henry, *Culture and African American Politics* (Bloomington: Indiana University Press, 1990), p. 74.

22. LeRoi Jones [Amiri Baraka], "'Black' Is a Country" (1962), in *Home: Social Essays* (New York: William Morrow, 1966), p. 85.

23. Kelley, *A Different Drummer,* pp. 111, 7.

24. William Faulkner to Malcolm Cowley, September 20, 1945, in Malcolm Cowley, *The Faulkner-Cowley File: Letters and Memories, 1944–1962* (1966; rpt. Baltimore: Viking Penguin, 1978), p. 32.

25. Arthur Huff Fauset, *Black Gods of the Metropolis: Negro Religious Cults in the Urban North* (Philadelphia: University of Pennsylvania Press, 1944); John Horshor, *God in a Rolls Royce: The Rise of Father Divine: Madman, Menace, or Messiah* (New York: Hillman-Curl, 1936); Kelley, *A Different Drummer,* pp. 178–79.

26. "The National Movement for the Establishment of a 49th State," in Herbert Aptheker, ed., *A Documentary History of the Negro People of the United States,* 4 vols. (1974; rpt. New York: Citadel, 1990), IV, 85–86.

27. George Schuyler, "Separate State Hokum," *Crisis* 42 (May 1935), 135, 148–49; Eric Hobsbawm, *Nations and Nationalism since 1870: Programme, Myth, Reality* (New York: Cambridge University Press), p. 156.

28. Michael C. Dawson, *Black Visions: The Roots of Contemporary African-American Political Ideologies* (Chicago: University of Chicago Press, 2001), pp. 93–100.

29. The name Blackstone Nation probably comes from two sources merged into one. It derives in Muhammad's usage first of all from the sacred Black Stone of the Kaaba in the Great Mosque of Mecca, where he had made a pilgrimage in 1959, but he also associated the symbol of the Black Stone with his mission among African Americans. In southside Chicago, the Nation of Islam's headquarters, the Black Stone Rangers were a violent and powerful street gang that periodically succeeded in styling itself a black nationalist youth movement. In 1967 they were the target of a federal anti-poverty program that dissolved in criminality and gang warfare; in 1969, renamed the Black P (for "prince" or "power") Stone Nation, they once more attempted to achieve respectability with federal assistance but again failed, charged with fraud. During the 1970s, the gang took on a more specific Black Muslim coloring under the name El Rukn (taken to be Arabic for "black stone"). See Karl Evanzz, *The Messenger: The Rise and Fall of Elijah Muhammad* (New York: Pantheon, 1999), pp. 157–58; Claude Andrew Clegg III, *An Original Man: The Life and Times of Elijah Muhammad* (New York: St. Martin's, 1997), pp. 141–42; Mattias Gardell, *In the Name of Elijah Muhammad: Louis*

Farrakhan and the Nation of Islam (Durham: Duke University Press, 1996), pp. 209–10; Nicholas Lemann, *The Promised Land: The Great Black Migration and How It Changed America* (New York: Random House, 1991), pp. 247–49. The gang's original name, however, in all likelihood derived more prosaically from Chicago's Blackstone Avenue, named for Timothy Blackstone, president of the Chicago and Alton Railroad and the first president, from 1865 to 1866, of the Union Stock-yards and Train Company. An interesting sidelight appears in the unrelated figure of Chicago real estate tycoon turned evangelist William Blackstone, author of *Jesus Is Coming* (1878) and proponent of a premillennialist view that Zionism was a necessary precursor to the Second Coming of Christ. His 1891 "Blackstone Memorial," signed by business leaders such as Cyrus McCormick, J. P. Morgan, and John D. Rockefeller, and presented to President Benjamin Harrison, urged United States support for a Jewish homeland in Palestine as a means of realizing the prophecy of God's promise to restore the Jews to the land of Israel. See Paul Boyer, *When Time Shall Be No More: Prophecy Belief in Modern American Culture* (Cambridge, Mass.: Harvard University Press, 1992), pp. 100, 185–87, 193–94.

30. Elijah Muhammad, speech of May 31, 1959, quoted in E. U. Essien-Udom, *Black Nationalism: A Search for an Identity in America* (Chicago: University of Chicago Press, 1962), pp. 257, 260; Malcolm X, "Harvard Law School Forum of March 24, 1961," in *Malcolm X: Speeches at Harvard,* ed. Archie Epps (New York: Paragon House, 1991), pp. 126–27.

31. Malcolm X, speech at Audubon Ballroom, Harlem, February 15, 1965, in Malcolm X, *The Final Speeches,* ed. Steve Clark (New York: Pathfinder, 1992), p. 117.

32. Malcolm X, "God's Judgment of White America" (1963), in *The End of World White Supremacy: Four Speeches,* ed. Imam Benjamin Karim (1971; rpt. New York: Arcade, n.d.), pp. 147–48. The speech was also reprinted in *Evergreen Review* 50 (December 1967). Based on the extemporaneous response that he gave to a question, this speech became best known for his observation that President John F. Kennedy's recent assassination was an instance of "the chickens coming home to roost," by which he meant that the nation's failure to address its racial problems inevitably produced political violence. Although he did not mean to ascribe the assassination to a racist plot—at least he had no evidence to support such a view—Malcolm in any event contravened Elijah Muhammad's orders that no minister should make any negative remarks about the late president. Muhammad took the occasion of this lapse to suspend Malcolm for ninety days, an act that resulted ultimately in his irreparable break with the Nation of Islam.

33. Milton R. Henry interviewed in Robert Sherrill, "We Want Georgia, South Carolina, Louisiana, Mississippi, and Alabama—Right Now . . . We Also Want Four Hundred Billion Dollars Back Pay," *Esquire* 71 (January 1969), 72–75, 146–48, quotation at p. 73. See also Theodore Draper, "The Fantasy of Black Nationalism," *Commentary* 48 (September 1969), 46–47; Van Deburg, *New Day in Babylon,* pp. 145–49; Stephen Howe, *Afrocentrism: Mythical Pasts and Imagined Homes* (London: Verso, 1998), pp. 95–96.

34. Cyril V. Briggs, "The African Blood Brotherhood" (1920), in William L. Van Deburg, ed., *Modern Black Nationalism: From Marcus Garvey to Louis Farrakhan* (New York: New York University Press, 1997), pp. 34–35; James S. Allen, *The Negro Question in the United States* (New York: International Publishers, 1936), p. 182; Robert S. Browne and Robert Vernon, *Should the U.S. Be Partitioned into Two Separate and Independent Na-*

tions—*One a Homeland for White Americans and the Other a Homeland for Black Americans?*, reissued a few years later under the less cumbersome title *On Black Separatism* (New York: Pathfinder Press, 1972), pp. 6–7; Nelson Peery quoted in Robin D. G. Kelley, *Freedom Dreams: The Black Radical Imagination* (Boston: Beacon Press, 2002), pp. 101–2.

35. LeRoi Jones [Amiri Baraka], "The Legacy of Malcolm X" (1965), in *Home*, p. 249.

36. Chester Himes, *Cotton Comes to Harlem* (1965; rpt. New York: Vintage, 1988), pp. 5, 56, 107, 26.

37. Ray Bradbury, *The Martian Chronicles* (1950; rpt. New York: Bantam, 1979), pp. 89–102.

38. Lenora Berson, *The Negroes and the Jews* (New York: Random House, 1971), p. 174.

39. Gerald N. Rosenberg, *The Hollow Hope: Can Courts Bring About Social Change?* (Chicago: University of Chicago Press, 1991), p. 52.

40. Kelley, *A Different Drummer*, p. 59.

41. Walzer, *Exodus and Revolution*, p. 135.

42. Ralph Ellison, *Invisible Man* (1952; rpt. New York: Random Vintage, 1981), p. 191. Bledsoe's eloquence is bluntly condensed in the engraved document the narrator dreams of finding in his briefcase: "Keep This Nigger-Boy Running" (p. 33).

43. David Bradley, foreword to Kelley, *A Different Drummer*, pp. xxi–xxii; William Melvin Kelley, "The Ivy League Negro," *Esquire* 60 (August 1963), 55.

44. Kelley, "The Ivy League Negro," 55, 109.

45. Irving Kristol, "The Negro Today Is Like the Immigrant of Yesterday," *New York Times Magazine*, September 11, 1966, 50. The judgment almost four decades later must still be negative. As Nathan Glazer points out, the fact that the black of today "is not the immigrant of yesterday, or even the immigrant of today—who is less segregated and isolated than American blacks," reflects a continued profound divide in American society." Nathan Glazer, *We Are All Multiculturalists Now* (Cambridge, Mass.: Harvard University Press, 1997), p. 142.

46. Kelley, "Ivy League Negro," 54; Hughes, "My America," p. 299.

47. William H. Grier and Price M. Cobbs, *Black Rage* (1968; rpt. New York: Bantam, 1969), pp. 28–29; Richard Wright, *The Long Dream* (1958; rpt. New York: Perennial, 1987), p. 32.

48. Melville J. Herskovits, *The Myth of the Negro Past* (1941; rpt. Boston: Beacon Press, 1958), pp. 1–2, 298–99; E. Franklin Frazier, *The Negro in the United States* (New York: Macmillan, 1949), p. 21; Ulrich B. Phillips, *Life and Labor in the Old South* (1929; rpt. Boston: Little, Brown, 1963), p. 160.

49. Kelley quoted in Jervis Anderson, "Black Writing: The Other Side," *Dissent* 15 (1968), 236; E. Franklin Frazier, *Black Bourgeoisie: The Rise of a New Middle Class in the United States* (1957; rpt. New York: Collier, 1962), pp. 27–28, 180–88, 193.

50. Frazier, *Black Bourgeoisie*, p. 13.

51. Norman Podhoretz, "My Negro Problem—and Ours" (1963), in Paul Berman, ed., *Blacks and Jews: Alliances and Arguments* (New York: Delacorte, 1994), p. 91.

52. A. Lawrence Lowell quoted in Laurence Mordekhai Thomas, *Vessels of Evil: American Slavery and the Holocaust* (Philadelphia: Temple University Press, 1993), p. 171.

53. Martin Luther King, Jr., "Letter from Birmingham City Jail," in *Testament of Hope*, p. 293; idem, *Where Do We Go From Here?*, p. 120; Kelley, "The Ivy League Negro," 109.

54. Aimé Césaire, *A Tempest* (1969), trans. Richard Miller (New York: Ubu Repertory Theater, 1992), p. 15.

55. Kelley, *A Different Drummer*, pp. 22–23.

56. William Faulkner, *Light in August* (1932; rpt. New York: Modern Library, 1968), p. 425; Kelley, *A Different Drummer*, pp. 25–26.

57. Kelley, *A Different Drummer*, pp. 50, 68.

58. One might compare here the allegory of cultural dispossession outlined in *The Piano Lesson* (1990), where August Wilson sets the black recovery of southern land, a source of economic stability, in wrenching juxtaposition to the heritage of slave culture. The black southerner Boy Willie, trying to get enough money to purchase land still held by a descendant of the whites who first owned his ancestors, wants his northern sister Berniece to sell the family's piano, an heirloom carved with the family's history, intimately interwoven with that of their owners. "You can sit up here [in Pittsburgh] and look at that piano for the next hundred years and it's just gonna be a piano," says Boy Willie, blind to the sacrifice of ancestral knowledge his choice entails. "As long as I got the land and the seed [for my crops] then I'm alright. . . . Cause the land give back to you. . . . But that piano don't put out nothing else." August Wilson, *The Piano Lesson* (New York: Plume, 1990), p. 51.

59. Gerald Early, "Notes on the Invention of Malcolm X," in *The Culture of Bruising: Essays on Prizefighting, Literature, and Modern American Culture* (Hopewell, N.J.: Ecco, 1994), p. 250; Kelley, *A Different Drummer*, p. 183.

60. Ralph Ellison, "What America Would Be Like without Blacks" (1970), in *Going to the Territory* (New York: Random House, 1986), pp. 104–7, 112.

61. Kelley, *A Different Drummer*, pp. 191–92, 199, 197.

62. George S. Schuyler, *Black No More: Being an Account of the Strange and Wonderful Workings of Science in the Land of the Free, A.D. 1933–1940* (1931; rpt. New York: Collier Books, 1971), p. 205; Kelley, *A Different Drummer*, p. 191.

63. Smith continues: "Sex and hate, cohabiting in the darkness of minds too long, pour out their progeny of cruelty on anything that can serve as a symbol of an unnamed relationship that in his heart each man wants to befoul. That, sometimes, the lynchers do cut off genitals of the lynched and divide them into bits to be distributed to participants as souvenirs is no more than a coda to this composition of hate and guilt and sex and fear, created by our way of life." Smith, *Killers of the Dream*, pp. 162–63.

64. Christopher R. Browning, *Ordinary Men: Reserve Police Battalion 101 and the Final Solution in Poland* (New York: HarperCollins, 1992); Daniel Jonah Goldhagen, *Hitler's Willing Executioners: Ordinary Germans and the Holocaust* (New York: Alfred A. Knopf, 1996). Browning and Goldhagen differ significantly in their analyses and conclusions about the complicity of "ordinary" Germans in violent anti-Semitism and genocide. A useful summary can be found in Inga Clendinnen, *Reading the Holocaust* (New York: Cambridge University Press, 1999), pp. 114–33.

65. Smith, *Killers of the Dream*, p. 71.

4. Exodus II: The Wounding Past

1. Paule Marshall, "Shaping the World of My Art," *New Letters* 40 (Autumn 1973), 106–7.

2. For representative studies of the novel in a Caribbean colonial context, see Edward Brathwaite, "West Indian History and Society in the Art of Paule Marshall's Novel," *Journal of Black Studies* 1 (December 1970), 225–38; Adam Meyer, "Memory and Iden-

tity for Black, White, and Jew in Paule Marshall's *The Chosen Place, the Timeless People*," *MELUS* 20 (Fall 1995), 99–120; Johanna X. K. Garvey, "Passages to Identity: Remembering the Diaspora in Marshall, Phillips, and Cliff," in Maria Diedrich et al., eds., *Black Imagination and the Middle Passage* (New York: Oxford University Press, 1999), pp. 255–70; and Rinaldo Walcott, "Pedagogy and Trauma: The Middle Passage, Slavery, and the Problem of Creolization," in Roger I. Simon et al., eds., *Between Hope and Despair: Pedagogy and the Remembrance of Historical Trauma* (Lanham, Md.: Rowman and Littlefield, 2000), pp. 135–51.

3. Paule Marshall, *The Chosen Place, the Timeless People* (1969; rpt. New York: Vintage, 1984), pp. 17, 64.
4. Ibid., pp. 13, 164.
5. Emma Lazarus, "1492," in *The Poems of Emma Lazarus*, 2 vols. (Boston: Houghton, Mifflin, 1899), II, 22. Because it followed upon a series of earlier expulsions from European countries, including France, England, and Central Europe, and would be followed by others less dramatic, writes Yosef Yerushalmi, the expulsion of 1492 was "the quintessential symbol of a process through which, step by step, the Jewish presence was virtually eliminated from Western Europe and the global locus of Jewish life shifted from West to East." Yosef Hayim Yerushalmi, "Exile and Expulsion in Jewish History," in Benjamin R. Gampel, ed., *Crisis and Creativity in the Sephardic World, 1391–1648* (New York: Columbia University Press, 1997), pp. 18–20.
6. Marshall, *The Chosen Place, the Timeless People*, p. 69.
7. Harold Cruse, *The Crisis of the Negro Intellectual: A Historical Analysis of the Failure of Black Leadership* (1967; rpt. New York: Quill, 1984), pp. 483–84.
8. Ibid., pp. 487, 490.
9. Marshall, *The Chosen Place, the Timeless People*, pp. 53, 58.
10. Ibid., pp. 287, 112, 5. When she later extracted parts of Merle's story from the novel to compose a novella titled "Merle," Marshall said of her character that she envisioned her moving throughout the hemisphere as a "Third World revolutionary spirit" helping "the poor and oppressed to resist, to organize, to rise up against the condition of their lives." See Paule Marshall, *Reena and Other Stories* (Old Westbury, N.Y.: Feminist Press, 1983), p. 109.
11. Marshall, *The Chosen Place, the Timeless People*, pp. 59, 99–100, 321. What Marshall depicts as the source of a stronger implied racial kinship between blacks and Sephardic Jews was also subject to more tendentious interpretation, as when some blacks argued that the comparative decline of Sephardic Jewish immigration to the United States and the rise of Ashkenazi immigration led to increased exploitation of blacks—this in keeping with the purported Zionist control of mainstream civil rights activism whereby blacks were duped into false beliefs in a racial alliance and the role of Jews in slavery was cleverly suppressed. Some Sephardic Jews in Israel have likewise found themselves at odds with Ashkenazim. Those arriving from Asian and Arab countries in the new state of Israel in the years after 1948, the Mizrahim, faced various kinds of economic and social discrimination. Although they appeared closer to the Hebraic precursors of modern Jews, their traditional culture and religious practices seemed alien and primitive to the largely secular Ashkenazim from Europe (see Chapter 5). See William H. Pritchard, "Blacks, Jews, and Negro Zionists: A Crisis in Negro Leadership," *Black Books Bulletin* 5 (Winter 1977), 18–23.
12. Marshall, *The Chosen Place, the Timeless People*, pp. 207–18.
13. Ibid., p. 469.
14. See Simon Gikandi, *Writing in Limbo: Modernism and Caribbean Literature* (Ithaca, N.Y.: Cornell University Press, 1992), pp. 175–86.

15. Malcolm X, speech at Corn Hill Church, Rochester, N.Y., February 16, 1965, in Malcolm X, *The Final Speeches*, ed. Steve Clark (New York: Pathfinder, 1992), p. 160.

16. Several of the novel's subsidiary scenes, for example, are set in a nightclub presided over by an expatriate American of indeterminate racial heritage—"all the colors known to man might have come together and been canceled out in him"—named Sugar, who appears to be a cross between an Episcopal sexton and a croupier, but whose very name, though it appears to be borrowed from his hero, the boxer Sugar Ray Robinson, tautologically summarizes the burden of empire. Housed in a former sugar warehouse, Sugar's nightclub previously had been "one of the most famous barracoons in the West Indies. The rusted remains of the iron manacles that had been fitted around the ankles and wrists, around the dark throats, could still be seen, some said, in the walls of the cellar. It had all begun there." Representing three incarnations of slavery—barracoon, sugar warehouse, neocolonial tourism and sex trade—Sugar's nightclub, both its patrons and the miscellany of its chaotic decor, stands for "all the discards of the nations, all the things that had become worn out over the centuries or fallen into disuse," none more so than the strippers and prostitutes whose dessicated labor is descended from the corrupt sexual exploitation and racial mixing of the islands' founding figures such as the Vaughans. Marshall, *The Chosen Place, the Timeless People*, pp. 82–83.

17. W. E. B. Du Bois, *The Suppression of the African Slave-Trade to the United States of America, 1638–1870* (1896; rpt. New York: Social Science Press, 1954), p. 28; Thomas C. Holt, *The Problem of Race in the Twenty-First Century* (Cambridge, Mass.: Harvard University Press, 2000), pp. 29–32.

18. The rise of mass consumption of sugar in Britain and continental Europe supported large-scale Caribbean plantations that far outlasted the British abolition of slavery in 1838. Slave populations in the colonies that became the United States were self-reproducing, importing only about 6 percent of the slaves brought to the New World, but those of the Caribbean depended on continual replenishment. At the time of emancipation, the slave population of the United States was more than six times the number imported, whereas that of Jamaica, with a life expectancy for slaves of only seven to ten years, was less than half the number it had imported. As a more specific example, between 1700 and 1774 some 500,000 slaves were brought to Jamaica, but the slave population grew by only 150,000. Sidney W. Mintz, *Sweetness and Power: The Place of Sugar in Modern History* (New York: Viking, 1985), pp. 43–53, 73, quotation at p. 43; Richard S. Dunn, *Sugar and Slaves: The Rise of the Planter Class in the English West Indies, 1624–1713* (1972; rpt. New York: Norton, 1973), p. 229; Robert L. Paquette, *Sugar Is Made with Blood: The Conspiracy of La Escalara and the Conflict between Empires over Slavery in Cuba* (Middletown, Conn.: Wesleyan University Press, 1988), pp. 51–80; Peter Kolchin, *American Slavery: 1619–1877* (New York: Hill and Wang, 1993), pp. 22–23; Robin Blackburn, *The Overthrow of Colonial Slavery, 1776–1848* (New York: Verso, 1988), p. 20.

19. Marshall, *The Chosen Place, the Timeless People*, p. 39.

20. Ibid., pp. 106–7.

21. A. Alvarez, "The Literature of the Holocaust," *Commentary* 38 (November 1964), 65; Robert Jay Lifton, *History and Human Survival* (New York: Vintage, 1971), pp. 19–20. Cf. Peter Novick, *The Holocaust in American Life* (Boston: Houghton Mifflin, 1999), p. 110–12.

22. Norman Mailer, "The White Negro: Superficial Reflections on the Hipster," in *Advertisements for Myself* (1959; rpt. New York: Signet, 1960), pp. 303–4; Richard Wright, *White Man, Listen!* (1957; rpt. New York: Harper, 1995), p. 42. Marshall might also have

had in mind James Baldwin's somewhat less hyperbolic observation in *The Fire Next Time:* "But, in the end, it is the threat of universal extinction hanging over all the world today that changes, totally and forever, the nature of reality and brings into devastating question the true meaning of man's history. We human beings now have the power to exterminate ourselves; this seems to be the entire sum of our achievement." James Baldwin, The *Fire Next Time* (1963; New York: Dell, 1964), p. 79.

23. According to current estimates based on historical records, admittedly inadequate, the figure of 9 million dead in the Middle Passage is too high, but Marshall may have intended in any event to include in her estimate some calculus of deaths in the barracoons of Africa and America, or plantation deaths by disease, punishment, or sheer duress. See Chapter 7.

24. Jean-Paul Sartre's prefatory gloss on Fanon, a poetic paean to the rebel's special humanity, was nearly as influential as Fanon himself: "This irrepressible violence is neither sound and fury, nor the resurrection of savage instincts, nor even the effect of resentment: it is man recreating himself. . . . When his rage boils over, he rediscovers his lost innocence and he comes to know himself in that he himself creates his self." Frantz Fanon, *The Wretched of the Earth,* trans. Constance Farrington (1961; rpt. New York: Grove Press, 1968), pp. 21–22, 36–37.

25. Ibid., pp. 101–2.

26. Ross Posnock, *Color and Culture: Black Writers and the Making of the Modern Intellectual* (Cambridge, Mass.: Harvard University Press, 1998), pp. 91–92.

27. Paget Henry, *Caliban's Reason: Introducing Afro-Caribbean Philosophy* (New York: Routledge, 2000), p. 83.

28. Roberto Fernández Retamar, "Caliban: Notes Toward a Discussion of Culture in Our America" (1971), in *Caliban and Other Essays,* trans. Edward Baker (Minneapolis: University of Minnesota Press, 1989), pp. 4, 14.

29. Eldridge Cleaver, "Psychology: The Black Bible," in *Post-prison Writings and Speeches,* ed. Robert Scheer (New York: Random House, 1969), pp. 18–20; William L. Van Deburg, *New Day in Babylon: The Black Power Movement and American Culture, 1965–1975* (Chicago: University of Chicago Press, 1992), pp. 60–61; Stephen Howe, *Afrocentrism: Mythical Pasts and Imagined Homes* (London: Verso, 1998), pp. 77–80.

30. Fanon, *The Wretched of the Earth,* pp. 311–13.

31. Marshall, "Shaping the World of My Art," 108. Larry Neal also cites the passage in "And Shine Swam On," his afterword to the Black Arts anthology *Black Fire.* For Neal, Fanon is placed among the pantheon of black heroes, past and present, who prophesy that "we must liberate ourselves, destroy double consciousness . . . understand that we have within ourselves a great vision, revolutionary and spiritual in nature, understand that the West is dying, and offers little promise of rebirth." LeRoi Jones and Larry Neal, eds., *Black Fire: An Anthology of Afro-American Writing* (New York: William Morrow, 1968), pp. 653–54.

32. Wilfred G. Cartey, "Earth Flow in Zionism and Negritude," *Negro Digest* 17 (August 1968), 54–62.

33. Derek Walcott, "The Muse of History" (1974), in *What the Twilight Says* (New York: Farrar, Straus and Giroux, 1998), pp. 44–45.

34. Derek Walcott, "North and South" (1981), in *Collected Poems, 1948–1984* (New York: Farrar, Straus and Giroux, 1986), p. 408. The Holocaust also provides Walcott a template for reflecting on European colonial rule in "A Far Cry from Africa" (1962) and "The Fortunate Traveller" (1981).

35. Marshall, *The Chosen Place, the Timeless People,* pp. 402, 160, 166.

36. Bernard Lewis, *Semites and Anti-Semites: An Inquiry into Conflict and Prejudice* (1986;

rpt. New York: W. W. Norton, 1999), pp. 83–84; George M. Fredrickson, *Racism: A Short History* (Princeton: Princeton University Press, 2002), pp. 32–40.

37. The connotation of "Marrano" was clearly derogatory, but some wore the designation as a badge of honor, and it most likely derived from a bastardized contraction of Hebrew words accidentally transmuted into the word meaning "swine". In the view of Benzion Netanyahu, moreover, the Inquisition did not persecute Marranos because they were still secretly practicing Judaism; rather, it persecuted them as Christians who were deemed *racially* still to be Jews. That is, the fiction of rooting out Judaizers authorized an anti-Semitic campaign designed not to eradicate heresy among Marranos but to eradicate Marranos among the Spanish people. See Judith Laikin Elkin, *Jews of the Latin American Republics* (Chapel Hill: University of North Carolina Press, 1980), pp. 3–23; Norman Roth, *Conversos, Inquisition, and the Expulsion of the Jews from Spain* (Madison: University of Wisconsin Press, 1995), pp. 271–316; Benzion Netanyahu, *The Marranos of Spain from the Late XIVth to Early XVth Century According to Contemporary Hebrew Sources*, 2nd ed. (New York: American Academy for Jewish Research, 1973), pp. 3–4, 59.

38. Holt, *The Problem of Race in the Twenty-First Century*, pp. 41, 55; Cecil Roth, *A History of the Marranos* (1932), rev. ed. (Philadelphia: Jewish Publication Society of America, 1947), p. 271.

39. Marshall, *The Chosen Place, the Timeless People*, pp. 163–64, 154.

40. Marshall, "Shaping the World of My Art," p. 111.

41. Lyndon B. Johnson, "To Fulfill These Rights" (address at Howard University, June 4, 1965), in Lee Rainwater and William L. Yancey, eds., *The Moynihan Report and the Politics of Controversy* (Cambridge, Mass.: MIT Press, 1967), p. 132.

42. Huey P. Newton, "In Defense of Self-Defense," in Philip S. Foner, ed., *The Black Panthers Speak* (New York: Da Capo Press, 1995), pp. 40–41; Don L. Lee [Haki Madhubuti], "No More Marching," in *Black Pride* (Detroit: Broadside Press, 1968), p. 34.

43. Eldridge Cleaver, "The Land Question and Black Liberation," in *Post-prison Writings and Speeches*, pp. 67–71.

44. Theodore Draper, "The Fantasy of Black Nationalism," *Commentary* 48 (September 1969), 41–43.

45. C. L. R. James, "The Making of the Caribbean People" (1966), in *Spheres of Existence: Selected Writings* (London: Allison and Busby, 1980), p. 177.

46. Taylor Branch, "Blacks and Jews: The Uncivil War," in Jack Salzman, ed., *Bridges and Boundaries: African Americans and American Jews* (New York: George Braziller, 1992), p. 57.

47. Alan W. Miller, "Black Anti-Semitism—Jewish Racism," in Nat Hentoff, ed., *Black Anti-Semitism and Jewish Racism* (New York: Richard Baron, 1969), p. 112.

48. Pierre Vidal-Naquet, "Reflections at the Margins of a Tragedy" (1970), in *The Jews: History, Memory, and the Present*, ed. and trans. David Ames Curtis (New York: Columbia University Press, 1996), p. 208.

49. Paule Marshall, "From the Poets in the Kitchen," in *Reena and Other Stories*, p. 11. The essay was originally published as "The Making of a Writer: From the Poets in the Kitchen" in the *New York Times Book Review*, January 9, 1983.

50. Marshall, "Shaping the World of My Art," p. 97–104.

51. Claude Brown, *Manchild in the Promised Land* (1965; rpt. New York: Signet, 1967), p. viii; Roi Ottley, *"New World A-Coming": Inside Black America* (New York: Literary Classics, 1943), p. 127.

52. Marshall, "Shaping the World of My Art," p. 104.

53. Antonio Benítez-Rojo, *The Repeating Island: The Carribean and the Postmodern Perspective*, trans. James E. Maraniss (Durham: Duke University Press, 1992), pp. 5, 24.

54. Paule Marshall, *Praisesong for the Widow* (1983; rpt. New York: E. P. Dutton, 1984), p. 8; LeRoi Jones [Amiri Baraka], *Black Magic: Collected Poetry, 1961–1967* (Indianapolis: Bobbs-Merrill, 1969), p. 217; Marshall, "Shaping the World of My Art," p. 104; Fanon, *The Wretched of the Earth*, pp. 212–13.

55. Larry Neal, "Some Reflections on the Black Aesthetic," in Addison Gayle, Jr., ed., *The Black Aesthetic* (Garden City, N.Y.: Doubleday, 1971), pp. 13–14.

56. Arthur A. Cohen, "Our Narrative Condition" (1980), in *An Arthur A. Cohen Reader: Selected Fiction and Writings on Judaism, Theology, Literature, and Culture*, ed. David Stern and Paul Mendes-Flohr (Detroit: Wayne State University Press, 1998), p. 427.

57. My account draws on Herbert S. Klein, *African Slavery in Latin America and the Caribbean* (New York: Oxford University Press, 1986), pp. 50–54; Dunn, *Sugar and Slaves*, pp. 48, 237, 257, 260–62; Eric Williams, *From Columbus to Castro: The History of the Caribbean* (New York: Harper and Row, 1970), pp. 136–37; Michael Craton, *Testing the Chains: Resistance to Slavery in the British West Indies* (Ithaca, N.Y.: Cornell University Press, 1982), pp. 108–110, 291–321; Eugene Genovese, *From Rebellion to Revolution: Afro-American Slave Revolts in the Making of the New World* (1979; rpt. New York: Vintage, 1981), pp. 15, 35–37, 101–4, 108; Melville J. Herskovits, *The Myth of the Negro Past* (1941; rpt. Boston: Beacon Press, 1958), p. 94.

58. The Jamaican maroons led by Nanny and her brother Cudjoe repelled all expeditions sent against them and in 1739 forced a treaty giving them the right to self-government and possession of the land they held, and guaranteeing cessation of British attempts to enslave them. (It is said that Cudjoe insisted the treaty be signed in blood, or, by another account, sealed with a blood and rum mixture drunk by both parties, according by Ashanti custom.) In turn, the maroons agreed to cease raids on plantations and stop harboring escaped slaves; at length, they became slave catchers for their former masters and played a role in suppressing later rebellions, including the large 1831 uprising. The maroons issuing from Cudjoe's leadership were thus powerful in their way, but they were reviled by slaves for their duplicity, while in turn they believed slaves to be weak, lacking the courage to fight for their freedom. Richard Price, ed., introduction to *Maroon Societies: Rebel Slave Communities in the Americas*, 2nd ed.(Baltimore: Johns Hopkins University Press, 1979), pp. 2–3, 7; Mavis B. Campbell, *The Maroons of Jamaica, 1655–1796: A History of Resistance, Collaboration, and Betrayal* (Granby, Mass.: Bergin and Garvey, 1988), pp. 46–50, 69–162 passim; Milton McFarlane, *Cudjoe the Maroon* (London: Allison and Busby, 1977); Craton, *Testing the Chains*, pp. 64–66, 81–96.

59. George Lamming, "Caliban Orders History" (1960), in *The Pleasures of Exile* (1960; rpt. Ann Anbor: University of Michigan Press, 1992), p. 119.

60. Marshall, *The Chosen Place, the Timeless People*, p. 130; Lamming, *The Pleasures of Exile*, p. 9.

61. George Lamming, "Ishmael at Home," in *The Pleasures of Exile*, p. 152.

62. Tudor Parfitt, *The Lost Tribes of Israel: The History of a Myth* (2002; rpt. London: Phoenix, 2003), p. 50.

63. See John W. Blassingame, *The Slave Community: Plantation Life in the Antebellum South* (New York: Oxford University Press, 1972); Eugene D. Genovese, *Roll, Jordan, Roll: The World the Slaves Made* (New York: Random House, 1974); Lawrence W. Levine, *Black Culture and Black Consciousness* (New York: Oxford University Press, 1977); Vincent Harding, *There Is a River: The Black Struggle for Freedom in America*

(1981; rpt. New York: Vintage, 1983); and Sterling Stuckey, *Slave Culture: Nationalist Theory and the Foundations of Black America* (New York: Oxford University Press, 1987).

64. Vincent Harding, "You've Taken My Nat and Gone," in John Henrik Clarke, ed., *William Styron's Nat Turner: Ten Black Writers Respond* (Boston: Beacon Press, 1968), p. 32.

65. On *marronage* in modernist African American literature, see also Houston A. Baker, Jr., *Modernism and the Harlem Renaissance* (Chicago: University of Chicago Press, 1987), pp. 75–79, 95.

66. Marshall, *The Chosen Place, the Timeless People*, pp. 283, 287, 288.

67. I am drawing here on Paul Connerton's interpretation of Bakhtin's influential comments on Carnival in *Rabelais and His World*. See Paul Connerton, *How Societies Remember* (New York: Cambridge University Press, 1989), p. 50.

68. Marshall, *Praisesong for the Widow*, pp. 240, 244–45, 250.

69. Marshall, *The Chosen Place, the Timeless People*, p. 297.

70. Ibid., p. 325.

71. Ibid., pp. 314–18, 360.

72. Marshall, "Shaping the World of My Art," p. 107.

73. Marshall, *The Chosen Place, the Timeless People*, p. 405.

74. Ibid., pp. 402–3.

75. Ibid., p. 402.

76. Ibid., pp. 430, 455, 471.

77. Ibid., p. 402.

78. William H. Grier and Price M. Cobbs, *Black Rage* (1968; rpt. New York: Bantam, 1969), pp. 32–45, 129–151 passim.

79. Orlando Patterson, *The Sociology of Slavery: An Analysis of the Origins, Development, and Structure of Negro Slave Society in Jamaica* (1967; rpt. Cranbury, N.J.: Associated University Presses, 1975), pp. 182–95; Margarite Fernández Olmos and Lizabeth Paravisini-Gebert, eds., introduction to *Sacred Possessions: Vodou, Santería, Obeah, and the Caribbean* (New Brunswick, N.J.: Rutgers University Press, 1997), p. 6.

80. Alan Richardson, "Romantic Voodoo: Obeah and British Culture, 1797–1807," in Olmos and Paravisini-Gebert, *Sacred Possessions*, pp. 171–94; Ivor Morrish, *Obeah, Christianity, and Rastaman: Jamaica and Its Religion* (Cambridge: James Clarke, 1982), pp. 40–43; Lucille Mathurin, *The Rebel Woman in the British West Indies during Slavery* (Kingston: Institute of Jamaica, 1975), pp. 34–37.

81. Amos N. Wilson, *The Falsification of Afrikan Consciousness: Eurocentric History, Psychiatry, and the Politics of White Supremacy* (New York: Afrikan World Infosystems, 1993), pp. 36, 120.

82. Paul Gilroy, *The Black Atlantic: Modernity and Double Consciousness* (Cambridge, Mass.: Harvard University Press, 1993), pp. 188–89, 199.

83. Morrish, *Obeah, Christianity, and Rastaman*, pp. 97–98.

84. Marshall, *The Chosen Place, the Timeless People*, p. 326.

85. Alfred Métraux, *Voodoo in Haiti* (1959), trans. Hugo Charteris (New York: Schocken Books, 1972), pp. 42–43.

86. Hortense J. Spillers, "Chosen Place, Timeless People: Some Figurations of the New World," in Marjorie Pryse and Hortense J. Spillers, eds., *Conjuring: Black Women, Fiction, and Literary Tradition* (Bloomington: Indiana University Press, 1985), pp. 163–65.

87. Marshall, *The Chosen Place, the Timeless People*, pp. 251–58.

88. Sidney Mintz and Michel-Rolph Trouillot, "The Social History of Haitian Vodou," in

Donald J. Cosentino, ed., *Sacred Arts of Haitian Vodou* (Berkeley: University of California Press, 1995), pp. 138–39.

89. Mechal Sobel, *Trabelin' On: The Slave Journey to an Afro-Baptist Faith* (1979; rpt. Princeton: Princeton University Press, 1988), p. 73.

90. On the Rara, see Elizabeth A. McAlister, *Rara! Vodou, Power, and Performance in Haiti and Its Diaspora* (Los Angeles: Fowler Museum at UCLA, 2002), pp. 113–33, quotation at p. 113. Further information on the figure of the Jew in Vodou and the Rara courtesy of Donald Cosentino.

91. Marshall, *The Chosen Place, the Timeless People*, p. 262.

92. Ibid., pp. 401–2.

93. Keorapetse Kgositsile, "For B. B. King and Lucille," in *The Present Is a Dangerous Place to Live* (Chicago: Third World Press, 1974), p. 32.

94. Wole Soyinka, *The Burden of Memory, the Muse of Forgiveness* (New York: Oxford University Press, 1999), pp. 38–39, 83, 91.

5. Black Power, Jewish Power

1. For Patterson, however, the implied threat remained real, along with its implications for social policy. With the Holocaust hardly a generation in the past, the reappearance of social analysis anchored in race-based genetic theory, such as Richard Herrnstein and Charles Murray's study *The Bell Curve* (1994), as well as the resurgence of white supremacist militia groups, led Patterson to wonder aloud whether blacks are well advised to support gun control: "It is not only Jews who are under an obligation never to forget." John A. Williams, "My Man Himes: An Interview with Chester Himes," in John A. Williams and Charles F. Harris, eds., *Amistad 1* (New York: Vintage, 1970), p. 61; Orlando Patterson, *The Ordeal of Integration: Progress and Resentment in America's "Racial" Crisis* (Washington, D.C.: Civitas/Counterpoint, 1997), pp. 133–34.

2. Robert S. Browne, "A Case of Separation," in Robert S. Browne and Bayard Rustin, *Separation or Integration: Which Way for America? A Dialogue* (New York: A. Philip Randolph Educational Fund, 1968), p. 7.

3. *Report of the National Advisory Commission on Civil Disorders* (New York: E. P. Dutton, 1968), pp. 1, 236. See also Robert M. Fogelson, *Violence as Protest* (New York: Doubleday, 1971), pp. 1–128 passim; and Jonathan Kaufman, *Broken Alliance: The Turbulent Times between Blacks and Jews in America* (1985; rpt. New York: Touchstone, 1988), pp. 83–84.

4. Larry Neal, "And Shine Swam On," in LeRoi Jones and Larry Neal, eds., *Black Fire: An Anthology of Afro-American Writing* (New York: William Morrow, 1968), p. 646. On Black Power, see, for example, Clayborne Carson, *In Struggle: SNCC and the Black Awakening of the 1960s* (Cambridge, Mass.: Harvard University Press, 1981); William L. Van Deburg, *New Day in Babylon: The Black Power Movement and American Culture, 1965–1975* (Chicago: University of Chicago Press, 1992); Manning Marable, *Race, Reform, and Rebellion: The Second Reconstruction in Black America, 1945–1990*, rev. ed. (Jackson: University of Mississippi Press, 1991), pp. 86–113; Dean E. Robinson, *Black Nationalism in American Politics and Thought* (New York: Cambridge University Press, 2001), pp. 88–117; and Michael C. Dawson, *Black Visions: The Roots of Contemporary African-American Political Ideologies* (Chicago: University of Chicago Press, 2001), pp. 85–91.

5. Malcolm X, "Declaration of Independence" (1964), in *Malcolm X Speaks: Selected Speeches and Statements*, ed. George Breitman (New York: Grove Press, 1966), p. 21.

6. SNCC, "Position Paper on Black Power," first published in the *New York Times*, August 5, 1966, rpt. in William L. Van Deburg, ed., *Modern Black Nationalism: From Marcus Garvey to Louis Farrakhan* (New York: New York University Press, 1997), pp. 125–26. See also Stokely Carmichael and Ekueme Michael Thelwell, *Ready for Revolution: The Life and Struggles of Stokely Carmichael* (New York: Scribner, 2003), pp. 532–36.

7. George M. Fredrickson, *Black Liberation: A Comparative History of Black Ideologies in the United States and South Africa* (New York: Oxford University Press, 1995), p. 295. See also Chapter 1.

8. Shlomo Katz in "Negro-Jewish Relations in America: A Symposium," *Midstream* 12 (December 1966), 3.

9. Kenneth B. Clark, *Dark Ghetto: Dilemmas of Social Power*, 2nd ed. (1965; rpt. Hanover, N.H.: Wesleyan University Press, 1989), pp. 234–40; Kirkpatrick Sale, *SDS* (New York: Vintage, 1973), p. 276.

10. *Jewish Currents* editorial quoted in Clayborne Carson, "Blacks and Jews in the Civil Rights Movement: The Case of SNCC," in Jack Salzman, ed., *Bridges and Boundaries: African Americans and American Jews* (New York: George Braziller, 1992), p. 41; Arthur Hertzberg in "Negro-Jewish Relations in America: A Symposium," 49; Jack Newfield, "Chicago, Honkies, and Camus," *Evergreen Review* 50 (December 1967), 59; Stokely Carmichael, *New York Times*, April 14, 1970, quoted in Dennis Prager and Joseph Telushkin, *Why the Jews? The Reason for Antisemitism*, rev. ed. (New York: Touchstone, 2003), p. 134.

11. Addison Gayle, Jr., *The Black Situation* (New York: Horizon Press, 1970), p. 47.

12. James Baldwin, "White Racism or World Community?" (1968), in *The Price of the Ticket: Collected Non-fiction, 1948–1985* (New York: St. Martin's, 1985), p. 439; Carmichael and Thelwell, *Ready for Revolution*, pp. 144, 557, 562; Clayborne Carson, "Black-Jewish Universalism in the Era of Identity Politics," in Jack Salzman and Cornel West, eds., *Struggles in the Promised Land: Toward a History of Black-Jewish Relations in the United States* (New York: Oxford University Press, 1997), p. 187.

13. Carson, "Black-Jewish Universalism in the Era of Identity Politics," pp. 187–88; idem, "Blacks and Jews in the Civil Rights Movement," pp. 36–49. See also Waldo E. Martin, Jr., "'Nation Time!': Black Nationalism, the Third World, and Jews," in Salzman and West, *Struggles in the Promised Land*, pp. 341–55.

14. H. Rap Brown, *Die Nigger Die!* (New York: Dial, 1969), p. 107.

15. Robert F. Williams, *Negroes with Guns* (New York: Marzani and Munsell, 1962); Hugh Pearson, *The Shadow of the Panther: Huey Newton and the Price of Black Power in America* (Cambridge, Mass.: Perseus, 1994), p. 109. President of the Monroe, North Carolina, NAACP, Williams was suspended from his position in 1959 for advocating (and practicing) armed struggle against white racism. Following a skirmish with police in 1961, Williams fled to Cuba, where he hosted the radio program "Radio Free Dixie." See Timothy Tyson, *Radio Free Dixie: Robert F. Williams and the Roots of Black Power* (Chapel Hill: University of North Carolina Press, 1999).

16. Norman Podhoretz, "A Certain Anxiety," *Commentary* 52 (August 1971), 4–10.

17. Pierre Vidal-Naquet, *Assassins of Memory: Essays on the Denial of the Holocaust* (1987), trans. Jeffrey Mehlman (New York: Columbia University Press, 1992), p. 130.

18. The Masada myth has been analyzed and challenged by Nachman Ben-Yehuda in two books, *The Masada Myth: Collective Memory and Mythmaking in Israel* (Madison:

University of Wisconsin Press, 1995) and *Sacrificing Truth: Archaeology and the Myth of Masada* (Amherst, N.Y.: Humanity Books, 2002).

19. David Ben-Gurion quoted in Steven T. Rosenthal, *Irreconcilable Differences? The Waning of the American Jewish Love Affair with Israel* (Hanover, N.H.: Brandeis University Press, 2001), p. 29.

20. Hafiz al-Assad quoted in Prager and Telushkin, *Why the Jews?*, p. 171.

21. Michael Oren, *Six Days of War: June 1967 and the Making of the Modern Middle East* (New York: Oxford University Press, 2002), pp. 305, 307.

22. Omer Bartov, *Mirrors of Destruction: War, Genocide, and Modern Identity* (New York: Oxford University Press, 2000), p. 128; Uri Ramon quoted in Tom Segev, *The Seventh Million: The Israelis and the Holocaust*, trans. Haim Watzman (New York: Hill and Wang, 1993), p. 392; Bernard Lewis, *Semites and Anti-Semites: An Inquiry into Conflict and Prejudice* (1986; rpt. New York: W. W. Norton, 1999), p. 41.

23. On the revival of the "new Jew" in the Six-Day War, see Paul Breines, *Tough Jews: Political Fantasies and the Moral Dilemma of American Jewry* (New York: Basic Books, 1990), pp. 52–73; for the appearance of "Rambowitz" fiction, a genre devoted to Israeli super-spies and heroic mercenaries, see pp. 175–230.

24. For Miller, however, the course of Israeli history has been unfortunate. For a time, as Israeli technical and military missions were spread across Africa, "[Israel's] example seemed about to become an inspiration for any poor country attempting to enter this century." But eventually, writes Miller, Israel went from being "a land settled by pastoral socialists and international soldier-farmers, into a bellicose armed camp." Arthur Miller, introduction (1984) to *Focus* (1945; rpt. New York: Penguin, 2001), pp. vii–viii.

25. Howard M. Sachar, *A History of the Jews in America* (New York: Random House, 1992), pp. 841–42; Peter Novick, *The Holocaust in American Life* (Boston: Houghton Mifflin, 1999), p. 158.

26. "Never again shall Masada fall!" derived from the 1927 poem "Masada" by Yitzhak Lamdan, which revived among Zionist settlers the mythic memory of the futile but heroic defense of Masada against the Romans in 73 CE. The motto outlived the popularity of the poem, and in postwar years the glorification of Masada was explicitly juxtaposed to the disgrace of Jews during the Holocaust. In memorial terms, the founding of Israel was predicated on the injunction to remember a history of destruction—the destruction of the two Temples, exile and pogroms, and the Holocaust—and to ensure that such events will never happen again. "Never again" is inscribed in many languages on Holocaust memorials in Europe, for example, on a monument at the Treblinka death camp, where the phrase appears in Yiddish, Russian, English, French, German, and Polish. See Yael Zerubavel, *Recovered Roots: Collective Memory and the Making of Israeli National Tradition* (Chicago: University of Chicago Press, 1995), pp. 70–76, 114–16; Bartov, *Mirrors of Destruction*, pp. 169–70.

27. The platform of Likud, which emerged in 1977, states: "The right of the Jewish people to the land of Israel is eternal and indisputable and is linked with the right to security and peace; therefore, Judea and Samaria will not be handed to any foreign administration; between the sea and Jordan there will only be Israeli sovereignty." "Platform of the Likud Coalition," in Walter Laqueur and Barry Rubin, eds., *The Israel-Arab Reader: A Documentary History of the Middle East Conflict*, 6th ed. (New York: Penguin, 2001), pp. 206–7.

28. Yehuda Amital quoted in Amnon Rubinstein, *The Zionist Dream Revisited: From Herzl to Gush Emunin and Back* (New York: Schocken Books, 1984), pp. 104–5.

29. Benny Morris, *Righteous Victims: A History of the Zionist-Arab Conflict* (1999; rpt.

New York: Vintage, 2001), pp. 335–36; Jeff Halper, "The Key to Peace: Dismantling the Matrix of Control," in Roane Carey and Jonathan Shainin, eds., *The Other Israel: Voices of Refusal and Dissent* (New York: New Press, 2002), p. 23.

30. David Ben-Gurion quoted in Morris, *Righteous Victims*, p. 136. The members of the Arab League rejected partition first in the Peel Plan in 1937, then on the occasion of the British White Paper in 1939, and then again in response to the United Nations resolution of 1947. Nor, when Jordan controlled the West Bank between 1948 and 1967, did Arabs propose an independent Palestinian state. The British Mandate for Palestine, which included the Balfour Declaration of 1917 and was formally accepted by the fifty-two members of the League of Nations in 1922, designated a territory of some 8,000 square miles for a Jewish National Home, 1 percent of the area liberated by the Allies in World War I, in contrast to the 1.2 million square miles in which six mandatory Arab states emerged. Moreover, Jewish settlement was barred in Transjordan, so that with Egypt's occupation of Gaza and Jordan's annexation of the West Bank following the 1948 war, Arabs controlled more than 80 percent of the former Palestine.

31. Fatah was founded in Kuwait in 1958 by a group of former University of Cairo students, including Arafat, some with links to the anti-Western Muslim Brotherhood (outlawed in 1956 for seeking to overthrow the Egyptian regime and replace it with an Islamic state). Espousing a revolutionary ideology compounded of Marxism, Third World nationalism, and radical Islam, Fatah remained a marginal but ever-growing force in Arab politics until the Six-Day War. The PLO and its military arm, the Palestine Liberation Army, were created in Cairo in 1964 as a means for Arab nations, Egypt in particular, to define Palestinian strategy and, in principle, draw together contending quasi-revolutionary organizations. At the time, Syria, where Arafat had been able to establish a base of operations after the Baath Party revolution in 1963, chose to support Fatah, which also operated out of Lebanon and Jordan. Following a surprisingly strong show of resistance against Israeli troops in March 1968 in Karameh—a Palestinian refugee camp in Jordan whose name means "dignity," coincidentally a watchword in Nasser's vocabulary of anti-imperialist Arab nationalism—Fatah emerged as the essential force of the PLO, rich in new recruits and weaponry supplied by Egypt, Iraq, and Syria. Rashid Khalidi, *Palestinian Identity: The Construction of Modern National Consciousness* (New York: Columbia University Press, 1997), pp. 176–86, 190–98; Adeed Dawisha, *Arab Nationalism in the Twentieth Century: From Triumph to Despair* (Princeton: Princeton University Press, 2003), pp. 149, 258; Yezid Sayigh, *Armed Struggle and the Search for State: The Palestinian National Movement, 1949–1993* (Oxford: Clarendon Press, 1997), pp. 179–84.

32. Baruch Kimmerling and Joel S. Migdal, *The Palestinian People: A History* (Cambridge, Mass.: Harvard University Press, 2003), p. 250; Barry Rubin, *Revolution until Victory? The Politics and History of the PLO* (Cambridge, Mass.: Harvard University Press, 1994), pp. 18, 24, 34.

33. Baruch Kimmerling, "The Power-Oriented Settlement: PLO-Israel—the Road to the Oslo Agreement and Back?" in Avraham Sela and Moshe Ma'oz, eds., *The PLO and Israel: From Armed Conflict to Political Solution, 1964–1994* (New York: St. Martin's, 1997), p. 225.

34. Morris, *Righteous Victims*, p. 254–63; Howard M. Sachar, *A History of Israel: From the Rise of Zionism to Our Time* (New York: Alfred A. Knopf, 1979), pp. 396–403; Cairo Radio quoted in Paul Johnson, *A History of the Jews* (New York: Harper and Row, 1987), p. 530; Khalid al-Azm quoted in Alan Dershowitz, *The Case for Israel* (Hoboken, N.J.: John Wiley & Sons, 2003), p. 84.

35. Sachar, *History of Israel,* pp. 440–41; Saul Bellow, *To Jerusalem and Back: A Personal Account* (1976; rpt. New York: Avon, 1977), p. 173.

36. Mahmoud Abbas quoted in Mitchell G. Bard, *Myths and Facts: A Guide to the Arab-Israeli Conflict* (Chevy Chase, Md.: American-Israeli Cooperative Enterprise, 2002), p. 132.

37. Khalidi, *Palestinian Identity,* pp. 178–79.

38. Even though under Turkish and then British rule Palestinian Arabs more often thought of themselves as part of Syria or an indivisible Arab whole, an Arab Palestine might eventually have flourished as naturally as in Syria, Iraq, Saudi Arabia, and other post-Ottoman states. And even though the doubling of the Arab population in Palestine between 1922 and 1947 was spurred by the economic growth made possible by Jewish agricultural cultivation and sanitary development, the Israeli myth of a "land without people" prior to its settlement by Jews, often promulgated by official discourse and early scholars in post-1948 Israel, can hardly be sustained. No doubt Jewish emigration and its resulting economic activity and infrastructure improved the region and attracted additional Arab settlement, even as the Jews acquired more and more land from willing Arab neighbors and absentee landlords. But many of the generation of 1948 had no illusions—nor did they have particular moral qualms, given the circumstances—about what had taken place. Contrary to Prime Minister Golda Meir's notorious 1969 assertion that there never had been any such people as Arab Palestinians, Minister of Defense Moshe Dayan remarked that same year of the ongoing replacement of Arab names and histories with Jewish names and histories, "There is not one single place built in this country that did not have a former Arab population." Dayan went on, prophetically enough, to say, "We are doomed to live in a constant state of war with the Arabs and there is no escape from sacrifice and bloodshed." Dayan quoted in David Hirst, *The Gun and the Olive Branch: The Roots of Violence in the Middle East,* 2nd ed. (London: Faber and Faber, 1984), p. 221.

39. Meir Litvak, "A Palestinian Past: National Construction and Reconstruction," *History and Memory* 6 (Fall–Winter 1994), 24–56; Abu Jihad (Khalil al-Wazir) quoted in Yehid Sayigh, "The Armed Struggle and Palestinian Nationalism," in Sela and Ma'oz, *The PLO and Israel,* p. 25.

40. "Palestine National Council: Declaration of Independence" (November 15, 1988), in Laqueur and Rubin, *Israel-Arab Reader,* pp. 354–56; Efraim Karsh, *Arafat's War: The Man and His Battle for Israeli Conquest* (New York: Grove Press, 2003), p. 196. The Arabs' intention to displace Israel, as Ruth Wisse has pointed out, was tactically reflected in their usurpation of Jewish symbols and history: refugee Arabs became a "diaspora"; the PLO issued a "Covenant" that promised them the land of Israel; they accused the Israelis of being Nazis and threatened them with a Holocaust; they initiated the United Palestine Appeal, with the map of Israel as its emblem; they deployed public relations symbols such as a ship called *Exodus* and the picture of a dead Arab girl, the "Palestinian Anne Frank." Ruth R. Wisse, *If I Am Not for Myself: The Liberal Betrayal of the Jews* (New York: Free Press, 1992), pp. 122, 130–33.

41. Anton La Guardia, *War without End: Israelis, Palestinians, and the Struggle for a Promised Land* (2001; rpt. New York: St. Martin's Griffin, 2003), p. 201; Karsh, *Arafat's War,* pp. 70–71; Leila Khaled, *My People Shall Live: The Autobiography of a Revolutionary,* ed. George Hajjar (London: Hodder and Stoughton, 1973), p. 150.

42. Khalidi, *Palestinian Identity,* pp. 182–83; Nasir ad-Din an-Nashashibi quoted in Christopher Dobson, *Black September: Its Short, Violent History* (New York: Macmillan, 1974), p. 10.

43. The Palestinians' use of terror can also be traced to the anti-Zionist, anti-Semitic ideology of Haj Amin al-Husseini, the Mufti of Jerusalem (and distant relative of Yasser Arafat), who instigated Arab riots against Jews in 1922 and 1929, and then again in the Arab revolt of 1936–1939, and whose alliance with the Nazis, which lasted throughout the war, set the tone for his aspirations, as well as those of Palestinians leaders, for a *judenrein* Palestine. Because of his collaboration with the Nazis, al-Husseini was declared a war criminal at the Nuremberg trials but lived out his days in Egypt (home also to other former Nazis). See Joseph B. Schechtman, *The Mufti and the Fuehrer: The Rise and Fall of Haj Amin el-Husseini* (New York: Thomas Yoseloff, 1965), p. 298; R. Melka, "Nazi Germany and the Palestine Question," and David Yisraeli, "The Third Reich and Palestine," both in Elie Kedourie and Sylvia G. Haim, eds., *Palestine and Israel in the Nineteenth and Twentieth Centuries* (London: Frank Cass, 1982), pp. 89–113; Dershowitz, *The Case for Israel*, p. 56.

44. Fatah Political Platform, Fourth Fatah Congress, May 1980, quoted in Barry Rubin and Judith Colp Rubin, *Yasir Arafat: A Political Biography* (New York: Oxford University Press, 2003), p. 27; Sayigh, *Armed Struggle and the Search for State*, pp. 84–91, quotations at p. 88.

45. PFLP statement quoted in Hirst, *The Gun and the Olive Branch*, p. 282.

46. Faced with the radical destabilization of his regime, King Hussein of Jordan struck back in September 1970 at both the PFLP and Fatah, by this point effectively indistinguishable from the PLO. Fatah then moved its base of operations to Lebanon by the summer of 1971, which in turn led to a large increase in terror operations against northern Israel in the next four years and the advent of Black September, which engaged in a two-year campaign of terrorism, including letter bombs addressed to prominent Israelis and Jews around the world, and culminating in the heinous attack that killed eleven Israeli athletes at the 1972 Munich Olympics. Financed by Libya, Syria, and Algeria, Black September, which took its name from the month of Hussein's crackdown, was also loosely allied with groups such as the German Baader-Meinhof Gang and the Japanese Red Army, and trained in China, Vietnam, North Korea, Pakistan, and India, as well as in Arab states. Although Black September as such ceased its major operations by 1973, Palestinian hijackings continued into the early 1980s, by which point twenty-nine airlines had been targeted and a number of planes brought down by bombs. John K. Cooley, *Green March, Black September: The Story of the Palestinian Arabs* (London: Frank Cass, 1973), pp. 26, 123–56; Dobson, *Black September*, pp. 1–6, 38–41; Morris, *Righteous Victims*, pp. 377–80; Rubin, *Revolution until Victory?*, pp. 24, 38–39; Rubin and Rubin, *Yasir Arafat*, pp. 60–68. On the origins of Black September in Hussein's crackdown, see also *Black September* (Beirut: PLO Research Center, 1971).

47. Rubin and Rubin, *Yasir Arafat*, pp. 40–41.

48. Arafat quoted in Alain Gresh, *The PLO: The Struggle Within* (1983), trans. A. M. Berrett (London: Zed Books, 1985), p. 105.

49. Arafat quoted in Cooley, *Green March, Black September*, p. 99.

50. Because Soviet anti-imperialism, dating back to Lenin, was often explicitly anti-Semitic, by an ideological sleight of hand the routine association between Jews and revolutionary bolshevism was now suppressed, with Nazism stripped of its historical specificity and made a generalized term of abuse such that Jews could be neatly classed as Nazis, racists, and imperialists. Yehoshafat Harkabi, *Arab Attitudes to Israel*, trans. Misha Louvish (New York: Hart Publishing, 1972), pp. 142–51, 174–80; Lewis, *Semites and Anti-Semites*, pp. 140–63; Johnson, *History of the Jews*, pp. 573–83; Seymour Maxwell Finger, "The United Nations," in David S. Wyman, ed., *The World*

Reacts to the Holocaust (Baltimore: Johns Hopkins University Press, 1996), pp. 828–29.

51. Yehoshafat Harkabi, "On Arab Antisemitism Once More," in Shmuel Almog, ed., *Antisemitism through the Ages,* trans. Nathan H. Reisner (New York: Pergamon Press, 1988), pp. 227–39; Lewis, *Semites and Anti-Semites,* pp. 192–235; Harkabi, *Arab Attitudes to Israel,* pp. 181–205, 229–37, 250–55, 270–76, 475; Robert S. Wistrich, *Anti-Semitism: The Longest Hatred* (New York: Schocken Books, 1991), pp. 240–67; Wisse, *If I Am Not for Myself,* pp. 33–42, 117–42.

52. To cite just one contemporary example: in the summer of 2003, Dr. Abd al-Aziz Al-Rantisi, a Hamas leader who would be assassinated by Israel in April 2004 in reprisal for his role in terrorist attacks, combined admiration for those who have "proved" that the Nazi gas chambers did not exist, the accusation that Zionists financed the Holocaust to advance their cause, and routine anti-Zionism in an anti-Semitic concoction of the kind that surged forth once again as an adjunct to the *intifada:* "When we compare the Zionists to the Nazis, we insult the Nazis. . . . The crimes perpetrated by the Nazis against humanity, with all their atrocities, are no more than a tiny particle compared to the Zionists' terror against the Palestinian people." La Guardia, *War without End,* p. 207; Karsh, *Arafat's War,* pp. 95–98; "Hamas Leader Rantisi: The False Holocaust—The Greatest of Lies Funded by the Zionists," *Middle East Media Research Institute* (August 27, 2003); http://memri.org/bin/articles.cgi?Page=archives&Area=sd&ID=SP55803 (accessed August 27, 2003).

53. By some accounts, "post-Zionism" means the triumph of political secularism over Zionist or religious Judaism, especially as it is manifest in the Jewish settlements in the West Bank and Gaza, and the creation of a liberal, democratic state for all its citizens. By others, it amounts to a "post-Jewish" condition that might lead, either by design or by inadvertence, to the dismantling of the Jewish state. "In the Diaspora," writes Jerold S. Auerbach, "it took nearly two centuries for emancipation to eviscerate Jewish life. In Israel, however, fifty years of statehood has sufficed." Jerold S. Auerbach, *Are We One? Jewish Identity in the United States and Israel* (New Brunswick, N.J.: Rutgers University Press, 2001), pp. 7, 200. On post-Zionism, see, for example, Anita Shapira, "Politics and Collective Memory: The Debate over the 'New Historians' in Israel," *History and Memory* 7 (Spring–Summer 1995), 9–40; Derek Jonathan Penslar, "Innovation and Revisionism in Israeli Historiography," *History & Memory* (Spring–Summer 1995), 125–46; Laurence J. Silberstein, *The Postzionism Debates: Knowledge and Power in Israeli Culture* (New York: Routledge, 1999); Yoram Hazony, *The Jewish State: The Struggle for Israel's Soul* (New York: Basic Books, 2001), pp. 3–73; Tom Segev, *Elvis in Jerusalem: Post-Zionism and the Americanization of Israel,* trans. Haim Watzman (New York: Metropolitan, 2002); and Alain Dieckhoff, *The Invention of a Nation: Zionist Thought and the Making of Modern Israel,* trans. Jonathan Derrick (New York: Columbia University Press, 2003), pp. 273–89.

54. Hirst, *The Gun and the Olive Branch,* p. 175; A. B. Yehoshua quoted in Victor Perera, *The Cross and the Pear Tree: A Sephardic Journey* (New York: Alfred A. Knopf, 1995), p. 174.

55. "The colonial and thereby total character of the conflict over Palestine," writes Dan Diner, "is the actual gate of entry through which images and metaphors from the extermination of the Jews in Europe flow." See Dan Diner, "Israel and the Trauma of the Mass Extermination," trans. John McCole, *Telos* 57 (Fall 1983), 41–52, quotation at p. 42. In a 1988 article, "In Praise of Forgetting," written in reaction to reports of Israeli soldiers' brutality toward Palestinians, the historian Yehuda Elkana questioned whether repeated exposure to images of the Holocaust and admonitions to "Remem-

ber" might have acted as a stimulus to blind hatred and a propensity toward violent antagonism against Arab enemies. See Segev, *The Seventh Million*, pp. 503–4; and Bartov, *Mirrors of Destruction*, pp. 183–84.

56. Yeshayahu Leibowitz quoted in Hazony, *The Jewish State*, pp. 6, 12–14; Nicholas Von Hoffman quoted in Conor Cruse O'Brien, *The Siege: The Saga of Israel and Zionism* (New York: Simon and Schuster, 1986), p. 634. The incursion into Lebanon was undertaken in an effort to drive the PLO out of its positions. Israel forces were assisted by Christian Lebanese Phalangists, who avenged the assassination of their newly elected president by a massacre of Palestinians in a suburb of Beirut. Israeli forces, then commanded by Ariel Sharon, were held responsible by many for failing to rein in the Lebanese, and Prime Minister Begin was forced to resign.

57. Raja Shehadeh, *The Third Way* (1982), quoted in David K. Shipler, *Arab and Jew: Wounded Spirits in a Promised Land* (1986; rpt. New York: Penguin, 1987), pp. 342–43.

58. Even as they promulgated an ideology of national unity, the Ashkenazi majority descended from the nation's pioneer generations, effectively absorbed the Jewish history of Asia and Africa into the official memory of European Zionism, cultivating the view that the Mizrahim were primitive and superstitious—unprepared for civilized life, they had to be raised up to a higher standard by the more advanced European Jews— and forcing them to think of Arabness and Jewishness as antithetical. The Mizrahim were also bitter that, despite their dedicated national service, particularly in the Six-Day War, those long resident in Israel had lower priority for new housing and jobs than recent immigrants from the Soviet Union. Some also claimed that the Ashkenazim were deploying memory of the Holocaust in such a way as to minimize Sephardic persecution. A contemporary group of academics and intellectuals refer to themselves as "Hakeshet Hamizrahi" (the Democratic Mizrahi Rainbow). See Erik Cohen, "The Black Panthers and Israeli Society," *Jewish Journal of Sociology* 14 (June 1972), 93–109; Ella Shohat, "Sephardim in Israel: Zionism from the Standpoint of its Jewish Victims," *Social Text* 19/20 (Fall 1988), 1–35; Perera, *The Cross and the Pear Tree*, pp. 176–84; Bartov, *Mirrors of Destruction*, pp. 135, 172; and Segev, *Elvis in Jerusalem*, pp. 34–35, 45, 64.

59. Arafat quoted in Rubin and Rubin, *Yasir Arafat*, p. 27.

60. Stokely Carmichael, "Free Huey" (1968) and "A New World to Build" (1968), both in *Stokely Speaks: Black Power Back to Pan-Africanism* (New York: Random House, 1971), pp. 122–23, 152–53.

61. George Schuyler quoted in Robert G. Weisbord and Richard Kazarian, Jr., *Israel in the Black American Perspective* (Westport, Conn.: Greenwood Press, 1985), p. 24. On Schuyler's harsh anti-Zionism, see also Arnold M. Rose, *The Negro's Morale: Group Identification and Protest* (Minneapolis: University of Minnesota Press, 1949), pp. 135–36.

62. Gary T. Marx, *Protest and Prejudice: A Study of Belief in the Black Community* (New York: Harper and Row, 1967), pp. 126–67; King quoted in Weisbord and Kazarian, *Israel in the Black American Perspective*, p. 40; Gary E. Rubin, "African Americans and Israel," in Salzman and West, *Struggles in the Promised Land*, pp. 362–63; BASIC statement of principles quoted in Weisbord and Kazarian, *Israel in the Black American Perspective*, p. 51, and Friedman, *What Went Wrong?*, p. 321; Rustin quoted in John D'Emilio, *Lost Prophet: The Life and Times of Bayard Rustin* (New York: Free Press, 2003), p. 483.

63. Weisbord and Kazarian, *Israel in the Black American Perspective*, pp. 32–43; Carson, *In Struggle*, pp. 267–69; Julius Lester, *Revolutionary Notes* (New York: Richard W. Baron, 1969), pp. 28–29.

64. Huey P. Newton, "On the Middle East" (September 5, 1970), in *To Die for the People: The Writings of Huey P. Newton* (1972; rpt. Writers and Readers, 1999), p. 195. In the early 1980s Newton and other Black Panthers, well past the prime of their revolutionary leadership, were sponsored on a tour of the West Bank by the PLO, desperate for American leaders who might present their cause in a more favorable light. Newton, who had a Jewish grandfather, refused to go unless he could also visit Israel and Lebanon so as to see both sides of the conflict. Whatever opinion he brought back, however, was no longer important enough to be reported. Hugh Pearson, *The Shadow of the Panther: Huey Newton and the Price of Black Power in America* (Cambridge, Mass.: Perseus, 1994), p. 292.

65. Malcolm X quoted in C. Eric Lincoln, *The Black Muslims in America*, 3rd ed. (Grand Rapids, Mich.: William B. Eerdmans, 1994), p. 161. Lincoln does not date the statement, made in an interview with him, but it would have occurred probably in 1959 or 1960.

66. Nasser quoted in Bard, *Myths and Facts*, p. 47; originally in *Middle Eastern Affairs* (December 1956), 461.

67. Syrian newspaper *Al-Baath* quoted in Shipler, *Arab and Jew*, pp. 334–35.

68. Stokely Carmichael, "The Black and Palestinian Revolutions" (1968), in *Stokely Speaks*, p. 137; idem, "A New World to Build," pp. 161–62.

69. Connie Matthews, "Will Racism or International Proletarian Solidarity Conquer?" *The Black Panther* (April 25, 1970), quoted in Tom Milstein, "A Perspective on the Panthers," *Commentary* 50 (September 1970), 43.

70. "The Seven Points" (January 1969), in Laqueur and Rubin, *Israel-Arab Reader*, pp. 130–31.

71. Zeev Schiff and Raphael Rothstein, *Fedayeen: Guerrillas against Israel* (New York: David McKay, 1972), p. 166; "Arab Guerrillas Seek Other Militants' Aid," *New York Times*, August 27, 1970, 3; Cleaver quoted in Cooley, *Green March, Black September*, p. 185; *The Black Panther* quoted in Weisbord and Kazarian, *Israel in the Black American Perspective*, p. 43.

72. Between 1958 and 1972, 3,017 Israeli technical experts served in short- or long-term missions in Africa (out of 4,882 sent to the Third World generally), while 7,199 African trainees were hosted by Israel, with several thousand more trained in Africa. Samuel Decalo, *Israel and Africa: Forty Years, 1956–1996* (Gainesville: Florida Academic Press, 1998), p. 109.

73. Colin Legum, "The Third World, Israel, and the Jews," in William Frankel, ed., *Survey of Jewish Affairs* (Cranbury, N.J.: Fairleigh Dickinson University Press, 1982), pp. 227–28.

74. A reader of *Ebony*, in 1968, dissected Black Power's identification with the Arabs more carefully. "For any black man to think of himself as a natural ally of the Arabs" is foolish, said the reader. In league with the Portuguese, Arabs were "the chief instigators and the main profiteers of the slave trade, the ones who set tribe against tribe in bloody massacre and then sat back and collected the human debris; the ones who raped and razed defenceless villages, enslaving men, women and children, after slaughtering the aged, infirm and those considered unsalable. . . . Indeed, it was the Arab who showed the white man what a fortune could be made in black flesh." Letter to the editor quoted in Robert G. Weisbord and Arthur Stein, *Bittersweet Encounter: The Afro-American and the American Jew* (Westport, Conn.: Negro Universities Press, 1970), p. 108.

75. In the cultivation of racial thinking within the context of African colonial rule, which would reach complete fruition under Nazism, wrote Arendt, race was "the emergency

explanation of human beings whom no European or civilized man could understand and whose humanity so frightened and humiliated the immigrants that they no longer cared to belong to the same human species." See Hannah Arendt, *The Origins of Totalitarianism*, 2nd ed. (1968; rpt. New York: Harcourt Brace and Co., 1979), p. 185. On African colonialism as a precursor of Nazism, see also Patrick J. Furlong, *Between Crown and Swastika: The Impact of the Radical Right on the Afrikaner Nationalist Movement in the Fascist Era* (Wesleyan, Conn.: University Press of New England, 1991), pp. 16–96; and Paul Gilroy, *Against Race: Imagining Political Culture beyond the Color Line* (Cambridge, Mass.: Harvard University Press, 2000), pp. 76–81.

76. John Henrik Clarke, "Some Scratches on a Time Bomb: Israel and South Africa: The Unholy Alliance against Black People," *Black Books Bulletin* 5 (Winter 1977), 12–17.

77. In the postwar era, Egypt became a center for Islamic anti-Jewish research and publication. The *Protocols of the Elders of Zion* was publicly recommended by both Nasser, himself a Holocaust denier, and Anwar Sadat, while the blood libel appeared in a variety of published forms, including an official 1962 United Arab Republic (Egypt and Syria) publication, *Talmudic Human Sacrifices*. A popular government pamphlet titled *Israel, the Enemy of Africa*, released in 1965, featured citations from the *Protocols* and Henry Ford's screed *The International Jew*. Especially in the wake of the 1967 and 1973 wars, there was an outpouring of depictions of Jews in government publications and textbooks as satanic contrivers of plots (including the assassinations of presidents Lincoln and Kennedy) and enemies of Muhammad determined to liquidate Arab culture in Palestine and advance Zionism's domination throughout the Arab world. By the 1980s and 1990s, such propaganda had evolved to include accusations that Jews, representatives of an inferior and despicable culture, were responsible for spreading cancer, AIDS, syphilis, drug addiction, genetically poisoned crops and poultry, pornography, prostitution, and abortion. Lewis, *Semites and Anti-Semites*, pp. 148–49, 160–62, 197, 208–19, 265–66; Avner Giladi, "Israel's Image in Recent Egyptian Textbooks," *Jerusalem Quarterly* 7 (Spring 1978), 88–97; Johnson, *History of the Jews*, p. 577; Rivka Yadlin, *An Arrogant Oppressive Spirit: Anti-Zionism as Anti-Judaism in Egypt* (New York: Pergamon Press, 1989), pp. 98–99, 117–20; Wistrich, *Anti-Semitism*, pp. 254–58.

78. Johnson, *History of the Jews*, pp. 537, 578; Irving Louis Horowitz, *Israeli Ecstasies/ Jewish Agonies* (New York: Oxford University Press, 1974), pp. 75–85; Weisbord and Kazarian, *Israel in the Black American Perspective*, pp. 93–119; Richard L. Sklar, "Africa and the Middle East: What Blacks and Jews Owe Each Other," in Joseph R. Washington, Jr., ed., *Jews in Black Perspectives: A Dialogue* (Cranbury, N.J.: Associated University Press, 1984), pp. 132–47; Joel Peters, *Israel and Africa: The Problematic Friendship* (New York: St. Martin's, 1992), pp. 43–61; Decalo, *Israel and Africa*, pp. 105–34; Sachar, *History of Israel*, pp. 790–91.

79. Peters, *Israel and Africa*, pp. 29–38.

80. Having been recognized by the Palestinian National Council meeting of 1974, with the blessing of the Soviet Union, as the "the sole, legitimate representative of the Palestinian people" and sporting a pistol in his belt, Arafat continued to express his unalterable opposition to Resolution 242. "Destitute, oppressed European Jews," he charged, had been made into "instruments of aggression" on behalf of "world imperialism and the Zionist leadership." Because Zionism is united with anti-Semitism "in its retrograde tenets" and is "another side of the same base coin," it was a "racist entity" that made war on Palestinian Arabs in 1947 and launched unprovoked wars in 1956 and

1967 in an expansionist policy that "endanger[ed] world peace and security." Praising those Palestinian martyrs who had offered their lives in the struggle against Zionism, Arafat called on Jews to turn away from the illusions of their leaders and their own "Masada complex." Following his speech, hijackings carried out by the PLO immediately resumed. Yasser Arafat, "Address to the UN General Assembly" (November 13, 1974), in Laqueur and Rubin, *Israel-Arab Reader,* pp. 171–73, 182. See also Rubin, *Revolution until Victory?,* p. 47.

81. Finger, "The United Nations," pp. 829–30; Peters, *Israel and Africa,* p. 77.

82. The blood libel continued to be presented as historical fact by Arab delegates to the UN through the 1980s, and the organization patronized events that singled out Israel for ostracism and obloquy, the most notorious being the UN-sponsored 2001 World Conference against Racism, Racial Discrimination, Xenophobia, and Related Intolerance, staged in Durban, South Africa. The conference's official agenda repeated the anti-Zionism of previous such forums held in 1978 and 1983 and took as its starting point a declaration, formulated at a preliminary meeting in Tehran, asserting not simply that Israel's control of Palestinian territories was a "foreign occupation founded on settlements, its laws based on racial discrimination with the aim of continuing domination of the occupied territory," but that its security practices "constitute a serious violation of international human rights and humanitarian law, a new kind of apartheid, a crime against humanity, a form of genocide and a serious threat to international peace and security." Nations joined in making such charges included some with the worst human rights records in the world, notably Iran, China, and Syria. "Report of the Asian Preparatory Meeting," Office of the United Nations High Commissioner for Human Rights (February 19–21, 2001), http://www.unhchr.ch/html/racism/02-allregional.html (accessed October 1, 2003).

83. Nathan Glazer, "The Exposed American Jew," *Commentary* 59 (June 1975), 27–28.

84. W. E. B. Du Bois, *Darkwater: Voices from Within the Veil* (1920; rpt. New York: Schocken Books, 1969), pp. 34, 41; Harold Cruse, "Revolutionary Nationalism and the Afro-American" (1962), in *Rebellion or Revolution?* (New York: William Morrow, 1968), pp. 74–96. For overviews of theories of colonialism within a black American context, see also Van Deburg, *A New Day in Babylon,* pp. 57–62; Stephen Howe, *Afrocentrism: Mythical Pasts and Imagined Homes* (London: Verso, 1998), pp. 87–100; Gary Peller, "Race-Consciousness," in Kimberle Crenshaw et al., eds., *Critical Race Theory: The Key Writings That Formed the Movement* (New York: New Press, 1995), pp. 127–58; and Ethan Goffman, *Imagining Each Other: Blacks and Jews in Contemporary American Literature* (Albany: State University of New York Press, 2000), pp. 3–12.

85. Fredrickson, *Black Liberation,* pp. 314–15; Albert Memmi, *The Colonizer and the Colonized,* trans. Howard Greenfield (1957; rpt. Boston: Beacon Press, 1991); Eldridge Cleaver, "Psychology: The Black Bible" (1967), in *Post-prison Writings and Speeches,* ed. Robert Scheer (New York: Random House, 1969), pp. 19–20.

86. Malcolm X quoted in Lincoln, *Black Muslims in America,* p. 161; Carmichael, "The Black American and Palestinian Revolutions," pp. 137–38; *The Black Panther,* May 19, 1970, quoted in Milstein, "A Perspective on the Panthers," 36.

87. Stokely Carmichael, "Pan-Africanism" (1970), in *Stokely Speaks,* p. 218; Brown, *Die Nigger Die!,* p. 130.

88. Eldridge Cleaver, "Stanford Speech" (1968), in *Post-prison Writings and Speeches,* p. 120; *The Black Panther,* August 25, 1970, quoted in Prager and Telushkin, *Why the Jews?,* p. 158.

89. Don L. Lee [Haki Maduhubti], "See Sammy Run in the Wrong Direction," in *We Walk the Way of the New World* (Detroit: Broadside Press, 1970), pp. 62–63.

90. Huey P. Newton and Bobby Seale, "What We Want, What We Believe" (1966), in Philip S. Foner, ed., *The Black Panthers Speak* (1970; rpt. New York: Da Capo Press, 1995), p. 2. See also the Black Panthers' petition to the United Nations to enforce the convention on genocide and pay reparations to those "who have suffered the damages of racist and genocidal practices." Huey Newton and Bobby Seale, "Petition to the United Nations" (1969), ibid., pp. 254–55.

91. James Farmer quoted in Daryl Michael Scott, *Contempt and Pity: Social Policy and the Image of the Damaged Black Psyche, 1880–1996* (Chapel Hill: University of North Carolina Press, 1997), pp. 148–49.

92. James Forman, "The Black Manifesto," in Floyd B. Barbour, ed., *The Black Seventies* (Boston: Porter Sargent, 1970), pp. 296–308. See also James Forman, *The Making of Black Revolutionaries* (Seattle: Open Hand, 1985), pp. 543–50; Gayraud S. Wilmore, *Black Religion and Black Radicalism: An Interpretation of the Religious History of the Afro-American People*, 2nd ed. (Maryknoll, N.Y.: Orbis, 1983), pp. 202–5; and Carson, *In Struggle*, pp. 294–95. Dick Gregory connected the demand for reparations from Christian churches to their distortion of the true identity and message of the Black Jesus: "What price would God demand from the churches for having the audacity to lighten the color of his son's skin, straighten out his nappy hair, and portray him as a clean white hippie in a suburban setting?" Dick Gregory, "Divine Libel," in Robert S. Lecky and H. Elliott Wright eds., *Black Manifesto: Religion, Racism, and Reparations* (New York: Sheed and Ward, 1969), p. 107.

93. The Synagogue Council of America and the National Jewish Community Relations Advisory Council, together representing about a dozen Jewish organizations, noted that even if the demands of the Black Manifesto were met, "inequities and injustices would not be rectified." They called for "massive government action in the areas of employment, housing, education, health and welfare. To say this is not to shirk personal or organizational responsibility, for such action can come about only if we as citizens declare and press our determination to pay the substantial costs that are involved." See "A Policy Statement by the Synagogue Council of America and the National Jewish Community Relations Advisory Council," in Lecky and Wright, *Black Manifesto*, p. 141.

94. Sachar, *History of the Jews in America*, pp. 737, 741; Menahem Kaufman, "Envisaging Israel: The Case of the United Jewish Appeal," in Allon Gal, ed., *Envisioning Israel: The Changing Ideals and Images of North American Jews* (Jerusalem: Magnes Press, 1996), pp. 231–33; Monty Noam Penkower, *The Holocaust and Israel Reborn: From Catastrophe to Sovereignty* (Urbana: University of Illinois Press, 1994), p. 317.

95. Martin Weil, "Can the Blacks Do for Africa What the Jews Did for Israel?," *Foreign Policy* 15 (Summer 1974), 128–29.

96. Roy Wilkins, "Whither 'Black Power'?" *Crisis* 73 (August–September 1966), 353–54, rpt. in August Meier et al., eds., *Black Protest Thought in the Twentieth Century* (Indianapolis: Bobbs-Merrill, 1971), pp. 596–98; Whitney Young cited in Weisbord and Kazarian, *Israel in the Black American Perspective*, p. 34.

97. Roy Innis quoted in Arnold Foster and Benjamin R. Epstein, *The New Anti-Semitism* (New York: McGraw-Hill, 1974), p. 185.

98. Hugh Pearson, "My Love/Hate Relationship with America's Jews," *culturefront* 5/6 (Winter 1997), 105.

99. LeRoi Jones [Amiri Baraka], "The Legacy of Malcolm X, and the Coming of the Black Nation" (1965), in *Home: Social Essays* (New York: William Morrow, 1966), pp. 248–50.

100. Marcus Garvey, Jr., "Garveyism: Some Reflections on Its Significance for Today," in John Henrik Clarke, ed., *Marcus Garvey and the Vision of Africa* (New York: Vintage Random, 1974), p. 387. On "One God, One Aim, One Destiny," see Ivor Morrish, *Obeah, Christianity, and Rastaman: Jamaica and Its Religion* (Cambridge: James Clarke, 1982), pp. 78–79; on "black fascism," see also Gilroy, *Against Race,* pp. 231–37.

101. Lucy Dawidowicz in "Negro-Jewish Relations in America," 13–17.

102. Kaufman, *Broken Alliance,* pp. 159–60; Julius Lester, *Lovesong: Becoming a Jew* (New York: Arcade, 1988), pp. 51–52.

103. Julius Lester, "A Response," in Nat Hentoff, ed., *Black Anti-Semitism and Jewish Racism* (New York: Richard W. Baron, 1969), p. 233.

104. Weisbord and Stein, *Bittersweet Encounter,* pp. 139, 152; Marie Syrkin, "The Hatchett Affair at NYU," *Midstream* 14 (November 1968), 3–9; Kaufman, *Broken Alliance,* pp. 127–64. For Lester's reassessment of the Ocean Hill–Brownsville events, specifically the Behran poem and his role in it, and his later radio show, see Lester, *Lovesong,* pp. 57–65.

105. Marc Dollinger, *Quest for Inclusion: Jews and Liberalism in Modern America* (Princeton: Princeton University Press, 2000), p. 202; Jerald E. Poldair, *The Strike That Changed New York: Blacks, Whites, and the Ocean Hill–Brownsville Crisis* (New Haven: Yale University Press, 2002), pp. 124–25; Jay Kaufmann, "Thou Shalt Surely Rebuke Thy Neighbor," in Hentoff, *Black Anti-Semitism and Jewish Racism,* pp. 57–58; "The Black and the Jew: A Falling Out of Allies," *Time* 93 (January 31, 1969), 55. The Ocean Hill–Brownsville dispute was not divided purely between black and white (or even between black and Jew). Bayard Rustin, for example, admired the organizational skills of the Jews, and both before and during the dispute supported Shanker and the rights of the union members, with the result that he was vilified by many blacks. Jervis Anderson, *Bayard Rustin: Troubles I've Seen, A Biography* (New York: HarperCollins, 1997), pp. 330–32.

106. Kaufman, *Broken Alliances,* pp. 127–64; Lester, *Revolutionary Notes,* p. 183. On Shanker's role in inflaming fears of black anti-Semitism, see also Weisbord and Stein, *Bittersweet Encounter,* pp. 170–71, 193–94. For views critical of the union and its supporters, and dismissive of black anti-Semitism as a major problem, see William H. Booth [then chairman of the New York City Commission on Human Rights], "Racism and Human Rights," and Walter Karp and H. R. Shapiro, "Exploding the Myth of Black Anti-Semitism," both in Hentoff, *Black Anti-Semitism and Jewish Racism,* pp. 117–41. For other documents related to the strike, see Maurice R. Berube and Marilyn Gittell, eds., *Confrontation at Ocean Hill–Brownsville: The School Strikes of 1968* (New York: Praeger, 1969). For a study sympathetic to the black activist position, see Jane Anna Gordon, *Why They Couldn't Wait: A Critique of the Black-Jewish Conflict over Community Control in Ocean Hill–Brownsville, 1967–71* (New York: RoutledgeFalmer, 2001).

107. Poldair, *The Strike That Changed New York,* pp. 60–70, 124–26, 143–44, 168–82, quotation at p. 126.

108. Gunnar Myrdal, *An American Dilemma: The Negro Problem and Modern Democracy,* 2 vols. (1944; rpt. New Brunswick, N.J.: Transaction Books, 1996), I, 28.

109. Kenneth B. Clark, "Candor about Negro-Jewish Relations," *Commentary* (1946), rpt. in Salzman, *Bridges and Boundaries,* p. 92.

110. Kenneth B. Clark, "Jews in Contemporary America: Problems in Identification," in Norman Kiell, ed., *The Psychodynamics of American Jewish Life: An Anthology* (New

York: Twayne, 1967), p. 121. Clark's essay appeared originally in *Jewish Social Service Quarterly* 31 (1954), 12–22.

111. Harold Cruse, *The Crisis of the Negro Intellectual: A Historical Analysis of the Failure of Black Leadership* (1967; rpt. New York: Quill, 1984), p. 147; Lawrence P. Neal, "White Liberals vs. Black Community," *Liberator* 6 (July 1966), 4–6.

112. Joel Carmichael in "Negro-Jewish Relations in America," 5–8.

113. Lincoln, *Black Muslims in America*, p. 162.

114. Philip Roth, *American Pastoral* (Boston: Houghton Mifflin, 1997), pp. 160, 164.

115. "The Black and the Jew: A Falling Out of Allies," 59.

116. I. F. Stone quoted in Seth Forman, *Blacks in the Jewish Mind: A Crisis of Liberalism* (New York: New York University Press, 1998), p. 164.

117. Tom Wolfe, *Radical Chic and Mau-Mauing the Flak Catchers* (New York: Noonday Press, 1970), p. 6. According to Michael Staub, the disintegration was significantly facilitated in the mainstream press by the anti-left New Journalistic accounts of Wolfe and Gail Sheehy, in which the Bernstein party was the centerpiece in a reactionary evisceration of both the Panthers and their liberal white supporters, the latter allegedly transfixed more by style—"radical chic"—than by the substance of political struggle. See Gail Sheehy, "Black against Black: The Agony of Panthermania," a 1970 *New York* magazine essay devoted to the New Haven trial of Black Panthers charged with murdering a fellow Panther, which was expanded the following year into *Panthermania: The Clash of Black against Black in One American City* (New York: Harper and Row, 1971); and Michael E. Staub, "Black Panthers, New Journalism, and the Rewriting of the Sixties," *Representations* 57 (Winter 1997), 52–72. On FBI surveillance, see Kenneth O'Reilly, *"Racial Matters": The FBI's Secret File on Black America, 1960–1972* (New York: Free Press, 1989), pp. 293–353.

118. Sachar, *History of the Jews in America*, p. 809; Cornel West and Michael Lerner, *Jews and Blacks: A Dialogue on Race, Religion, and Culture in America* (New York: Plume, 1996), pp. 39–40; J. J. Goldberg, "Is Zionism Compatible with Radicalism?" *The Activist* (Spring 1970), rpt. in Jack Nusan Porter and Peter Dreier, eds., *Jewish Radicalism: A Selected Anthology* (New York: Grove Press, 1973), pp. 80–81; Michael Lerner, "Jewish New Leftism at Berkeley," *Judaism* 18 (Fall 1969), 475–78.

119. Jerry Rubin, *Do It! Scenarios of the Revolution* (New York: Simon and Schuster, 1970), p. 200.

120. Ibid., p. 13; Abbie Hoffman, *Revolution for the Hell of It* (New York: Dial Press, 1968), pp. 51, 71–74.

121. Jerry Rubin, *We Are Everywhere* (New York: Harper and Row, 1971), pp. 68, 72, 74–75. Rubin's translation is an appropriate rendering of a phrase that is otherwise somewhat confusing. In its normal pronunciation, the Yiddish phrase "shande far di goyim" (without the accent on "far") means "disgrace for the goyim" (or "shame for the goyim"). But the clear sense of the phrase (with the accent on "far") is "disgrace before the goyim," meaning "this would disgrace us in the eyes of the goyim." Rubin's meaning is more like "doing something disgraceful or shameful on behalf of the goyim," and he means more specifically that Hoffman's conduct is a disgrace in the eyes of right-thinking Jews. Thanks to Janet Hadda and Hana Wirth-Nesher for this translation.

122. Arthur Waskow, *The Freedom Seder: A New Haggadah for Passover* (Washington, D.C.: Micah Press, 1970), pp. 11, 13, 16, 19, 22, 43–44; Eldridge Cleaver, *Los Angeles Sentinel*, January 29, 1976, quoted in Weisbord and Kazarian, *Israel in the Black American Perspective*, p. 54. On the Freedom Seders and Waskow's Haggadah, see also Weisbord

and Stein, *Bittersweet Encounter,* pp. 199–200; and Michael E. Staub, *Torn at the Roots: The Crisis of Jewish Liberalism in Postwar America* (New York: Columbia University Press, 2002), pp. 153–54, 163–67, 172–75. See also the various radical liturgies for Sukkot, Kol Nidre, Rosh Hashanah, Hanukkah, and Shabbat included among the chapters of Arthur Waskow, *The Bush Is Burning! Radical Judaism Faces the Pharaohs of the Superstate* (New York: Macmillan, 1971).

123. Walter Laqueur, "Revolution & the Jews 1: New York and Jerusalem," *Commentary* 51 (February 1971), 42–45.

124. Arnold Jacob Wolf, "The Negro Revolution and Jewish Theology" (1964), quoted in Forman, *Blacks in the Jewish Mind,* p. 67; Stanley Rothman and S. Robert Lichter, *Roots of Radicalism: Jews, Christians, and the New Left* (New York: Oxford University Press, 1982), pp. 125–43; Seymour Martin Lipset, *"The Socialism of Fools": The Left, the Jews, and Israel* (New York: Anti-Defamation League, 1969), p. 26.

125. Ben Halpern, *Jews and Blacks: The Classic American Minorities* (New York: Herder and Herder, 1971), pp. 168–71; Norman Podhoretz, "The Tribe of the Wicked Son," *Commentary* 51 (February 1971), 10; Max Geltman, *The Confrontation: Black Power, Anti-Semitism, and the Myth of Integration* (Englewood Cliffs, N.J.: Prentice-Hall, 1970), p. 179; Nathan Glazer, "Blacks, Jews & the Intellectuals," *Commentary* 47 (April 1969), 35–39; Carson, "Black-Jewish Universalism in the Era of Identity Politics," pp. 191–92. On the Jewish New Left and dissent from it, see also Forman, *Blacks in the Jewish Mind,* pp. 158–71; and Staub, *Torn at the Roots,* pp. 194–220.

126. Richard Elman, "Law 'N Order Day" (1969), in *Crossing Over and Other Tales* (New York: Charles Scribner's Sons, 1973), pp. 162–74.

127. Lipset, *"The Socialism of Fools,"* p. 8; Saul Bellow, *Mr. Sammler's Planet* (1970; rpt. New York: Penguin, 1977), p. 211.

128. Rubin, *We Are Everywhere,* pp. 76, 126, 152.

129. Percy S. Cohen, *Jewish Radicals and Radical Jews* (New York: Academic Press, 1980), pp. 21–35; Itzhak Epstein, "Open Letter to the Black Panther Party," *Jewish Liberation Journal* (September 1969), rpt. in Porter and Dreier, *Jewish Radicalism,* p. 70; Sol Stern, "My Jewish Problem—and Ours: Israel, the Left, and the Jewish Establishment," *Ramparts* (August 1971), rpt. in Porter and Dreier, *Jewish Radicalism,* p. 362; M. Jay [M. J.] Rosenberg, "My Evolution as a Jew," *Midstream* 16 (August–September 1970), 52–53.

130. M. J. Rosenberg, "To Uncle Tom and Other Jews," *Village Voice,* February 13, 1969, rpt. in Porter and Dreier, *Jewish Radicalism,* pp. 5–10.

131. Staub, *Torn at the Roots,* pp. 90–91, 134–36, Bisk quoted at pp. 209–10; Ismar Schorsch quoted in Forman, *Blacks in the Jewish Mind,* p. 177.

132. Meir Kahane, *The Story of the Jewish Defense League* (1975; rpt. Institute for the Publication of the Writings of Meir Kahane, 2000), pp. 100–104; *New York Times,* June 24, 1969, 31; Staub, *Torn at the Roots,* pp. 224–26; Sachar, *History of the Jews in America,* p. 817.

133. Meir Kahane, 1971 interview in Porter and Dreier, *Jewish Radicalism,* p. 287.

134. Meir Kahane, *Never Again! A Program for Survival* (1971; rpt. New York: Pyramid, 1972), pp. v, 256. For ways in which the myth of passivity was used to advance a Jewish power agenda by JDL and other groups, see Staub, *Torn at the Roots,* pp. 220–31.

135. Sachar, *History of Israel,* pp. 187–88; Morris, *Righteous Victims,* pp. 107–8. On Jabotinsky, see also Walter Laqueur, *A History of Zionism* (1972; rpt. New York: Schocken, 1989), pp. 338–83. Like Jabotinsky before him, and like Benjamin Netanyahu and Ariel Sharon after him, Begin prompted similar reactions. The Israeli and American left

were dismayed by the election of Begin, whom *Time* magazine, skirting anti-Semitism in its disdain, labeled a "terrorist" and "superhawk" whose name "rhymes with Fagin." *Time* quoted in Auerbach, *Are We One?*, p. 99.

136. Dieckhoff, *Invention of a Nation*, pp. 214–15.

137. Avi Shlaim, *The Iron Wall: Israel and the Arab World* (New York: W. W. Norton, 2001), pp. 16–22, 101–3, 565–75, Moshe Dayan quoted at p. 102. In a chapter titled "The Wall" in his 1993 volume *A Place among the Nations*, Netanyahu rejected "land for peace" and kept faith with Jabotinsky: "To achieve a sustainable peace, Israel must maintain a credible deterrent long enough to effect a lasting change in Arab attitudes. It is precisely Israel's control of this strategic territory [the West Bank] that has deterred all-out war and has made eventual peace more likely." Benjamin Netanyahu, *A Place among the Nations: Israel and the World* (New York: Bantam, 1993), p. 293.

138. Vladimir Jabotinsky, "On the Iron Wall (We and the Arabs)" and "The Morality of the Iron Wall," quoted in Shlaim, *The Iron Wall*, pp. 11–16.

139. Kahane, *Never Again!*, p. 255; idem, *Story of the Jewish Defense League*, pp. 85–86.

140. When the Knesset refused to consider the bills, Kahane went before the Supreme Court, where Justice Aharon Barak ruled that, despite the fact that the bills "awaken horrifying memories," the nation's strength lay in the "meticulous preservation of the rule of law and the legality of power, even when this means giving expressions to opinions we abhor." Here and elsewhere Kahane exploited the specter of excessively virile Arab men preying on defenseless Jewish women and provoked his followers to harass mixed couples. One of Kahane's adherents, Alan Goodman, single-handedly stormed the Dome of the Rock in 1982, spraying bullets and killing several Arabs, with the intent to "liberate" the Temple Mount from Arab control, while another, Baruch Goldstein, attacked Muslims praying in the Tomb of the Patriarchs in Hebron in 1994, killing twenty-nine before he was beaten to death by worshippers. Insofar as Goldstein acted on behalf of the right of Jews to settle the Land of Israel—that is, Judea and Samaria—the murders accelerated the recourse to violence by Hamas and Islamic Jihad. By this time, however, Kahane himself had been assassinated, in Brooklyn in 1990, by El Sayyid Nosair, an Egyptian-born Muslim. Segev, *The Seventh Million*, pp. 406–7; Barak quoted in Shipler, *Arab and Jew*, pp. 292–93.

141. Kahane, *Never Again!*, pp. 96–97.

142. Kahane, *Story of the Jewish Defense League*, pp. 121, 202, 133–35; Janet L. Dolgin, *Jewish Identity and the JDL* (Princeton: Princeton University Press, 1977), pp. 37–38; Kahane, 1971 interview in Porter and Dreier, *Jewish Radicalism*, p. 280.

143. Leon Wieseltier, "The Demons of the Jews," *New Republic*, November 11, 1985, 24–25.

144. Donald Goines, *Never Die Alone* (1974; rpt. Los Angeles: Holloway House, 1991), p. 33.

145. Ernest Tidyman, *Shaft among the Jews* (New York: Dial Press, 1972), p. 210.

146. Boyd Upchurch, *The Slave Stealer* (1968; rpt. New York: Signet, 1969), pp. 48, 368.

147. Daniel Stern, *The Suicide Academy* (1968; rpt. New York: Arbor House, 1985), pp. 7, 163–66.

148. Hal Bennett, *Lord of Dark Places* (1970; rpt. New York: Turtle Point Press, 1997), p. 204.

149. Ibid., pp. 283–84.

150. Ibid., p. 283.

151. Bellow, *Mr. Sammler's Planet*, pp. 48–49.

152. Frantz Fanon, *Black Skin, White Masks*, trans. Charles Lam Markmann (1952; New York: Grove Press, 1967), pp. 165, 170.

153. James Baldwin, "The Black Boy Looks at the White Boy" (1961), in *Nobody Knows My Name* (1961; rpt. New York: Dell, 1963), p. 172; Norman Mailer, "The White Negro: Superficial Reflections on the Hipster" (1957), in *Advertisements for Myself* (1959; rpt.

New York: Signet, 1960), pp. 306, 308, 319–20. See also Morris Dickstein's observation that Sammler is an inversion of Mailer's "White Negro." Morris Dickstein, *Leopards in the Temple: The Transformation of American Fiction, 1945–1970* (Cambridge, Mass.: Harvard University Press, 2002), p. 175.

154. Norman Podhoretz, "My Negro Problem—and Ours" (1963), in Paul Berman, ed., *Blacks and Jews: Alliances and Arguments* (New York: Delacorte, 1994), p. 88.

155. Eldridge Cleaver, *Soul on Ice* (New York: McGraw-Hill, 1968), pp. 162, 180, 189–92, 185; "Huey Newton Talks to the Movement" (1969), in *The Black Panthers Speak*, pp. 58–59.

156. Bellow, *Mr. Sammler's Planet*, pp. 42, 64.

157. Among others who have argued that Black Power's assertion of outsized masculinity is a substitute for a civic equality yet to be achieved, see, for example, Elisabeth Lasch-Quinn, *Race Experts: How Racial Etiquette, Sensitivity Training, and New Age Therapy Hijacked the Civil Rights Revolution* (New York: Norton, 2001), pp. 76–86, 115–19.

158. Bellow, *Mr. Sammler's Planet*, p. 149.

159. Philip Roth, *Shop Talk: A Writer and His Colleagues and Their Work* (New York: Random House, 2001), p. 184.

160. Bellow, *Mr. Sammler's Planet*, pp. 9–10.

161. K. Zetnick [Yehiel Dinur], quoted in Dalia Ofer, "Israel," in Wyman, *The World Reacts to the Holocaust*, p. 879.

162. Bellow, *Mr. Sammler's Planet*, pp. 84–86.

163. Isaac Bashevis Singer, *The Family Moskat*, trans. A. H. Gross (1950; rpt. New York: Noonday Press, 1992), p. 611.

164. Bellow, *Mr. Sammler's Planet*, p. 286.

165. Saul Bellow, *To Jerusalem and Back: A Personal Account* (1976; rpt. New York: Avon, 1977), p. 78; cf. Edward Alexander, *The Resonance of Dust: Essays on Holocaust Literature and Jewish Fate* (Columbus: Ohio State University Press, 1979), pp. 172–73.

166. Stanley Crouch, "Barbarous on Either Side: The New York Blues of *Mr. Sammler's Planet*," in *The All-American Skin Game, or, the Decoy of Race: The Long and the Short of It, 1990–1994* (New York: Pantheon, 1995), p. 107. For other analyses of Eisen's role, see, for example, Sander Gilman, *Jewish Self-Hatred, Anti-Semitism, and the Hidden Language of the Jews* (Baltimore: Johns Hopkins University Press, 1986), p. 371–73; Andrew Furman, *Israel through the Jewish American Imagination: A Survey of Jewish-American Literature on Israel, 1928–1995* (Albany: State University of New York Press), pp. 63–72; and Goffman, *Imagining Each Other*, pp. 135–40.

167. As Amy Hungerford remarks of the novel's preoccupation with the excess of symbolic meaning, "symbol-making becomes deadly when the vulnerable, embodied humanity of the person is reduced to symbol and thus is figuratively . . . bludgeoned by the symbol." See Amy Hungerford, *The Holocaust of Texts: Genocide, Literature, and Personification* (Chicago: University of Chicago Press, 2003), pp. 127–34.

168. Bellow, *Mr. Sammler's Planet*, p. 157.

169. Ibid., pp. 262–68; Kahane, *Never Again!*, p. 245.

170. Bellow, *Mr. Sammler's Planet*, p. 132; idem, "Israel: The Six-Day War" (1967), in *It All Adds Up: From the Dim Past to the Uncertain Future* (New York: Viking Penguin, 1994), p. 208.

171. Yaacov Lozowick, *Right to Exist: A Moral Defense of Israel's Wars* (New York: Doubleday, 2003), p. 149.

172. John A. Williams, *Sons of Darkness, Sons of Light* (1969; rpt. Boston: Northeastern University Press, 1999), p. 151.

173. Ibid., pp. 214–15.

174. Ibid., pp. 108–9, 151, 217.

175. Yigael Yadin, ed., *The Scroll of the War of the Sons of Light against the Sons of Darkness,* trans. Batya Rabin and Chaim Rabin (London: Oxford University Press, 1962), pp. 3–37, 234–43, 256–60; Geza Vermes, *The Dead Sea Scrolls in English* (1962; rpt. Baltimore: Penguin, 1965), pp. 122–24; Eli Barnavi, ed., *A Historical Atlas of the Jewish People: From the Time of the Patriarchs to the Present* (New York: Schocken Books, 1992), pp. 38, 43; James Vanderkam and Peter Flint, *The Meaning of the Dead Sea Scrolls: Their Significance for Understanding the Bible, Judaism, Jesus, and Christianity* (San Francisco: HarperCollins, 2002), pp. 219–21, 364–69.

176. Yadin, *Scroll of the War of the Sons of Light,* pp. 324–26. The popular edition edited by Geza Vermes uses the same translation and is perhaps more likely to have been Williams's source (later editions have a different translation).

177. Although Nasser temporarily managed to spin Egypt's swift defeat in the Six-Day War as a victory by the superpower United States, the nation's humiliation at the hands of Israel was profound. In less than three hours after launching a surprise attack, the IAF destroyed more than half of Egypt's fighter and bomber aircraft (most of them on the ground), killed one third of their pilots, and rendered thirteen bases and twenty-three radar and antiaircraft sites inoperable. By the end of the day, attacks on the smaller air combat forces of Jordan, Syria, and Iraq raised the total number of planes destroyed to 416 (393 of them on the ground), with Israel losing only twenty-six aircraft. A native of Kibbutz Degania who had smuggled Holocaust survivors into Palestine after the war, Hod was a skilled veteran of the 1948 and 1956 campaigns, known for resourcefulness and taciturn toughness. Said Chaim Weizmann of Hod: "He may not be able to quote Bialik or Shakespeare, but he will screw the Arabs in plain Hebrew." Chaim Herzog, *The Arab-Israeli Wars: War and Peace in the Middle East from the War of Independence through Lebanon,* rev. ed. (New York: Vintage, 1984), pp. 151–53; Sachar, *History of Israel,* p. 640; Oren, *Six Days of War,* pp. 173–76, Weizman quoted at p. 174.

178. Williams, *Sons of Darkness, Sons of Light,* p. 53.

179. Ibid., pp. 43, 149, 191. See Exodus 21:24.

180. Morris, *Righteous Victims,* pp. 148–49.

181. Sachar, *History of Israel,* pp. 265–66.

182. The Stern Gang supported Arab liberation as well, but in their principal quest to create a safe haven for Jews even went so far as to propose to Hitler in 1941 that they would help in the conquest of Palestine in exchange for German guarantees of a Jewish state and the transfer of European Jews to it, a seemingly mad notion but one attuned to the unfolding disaster. Sachar, *History of Israel,* pp. 247, 265; O'Brien, *The Siege,* p. 246.

183. Menachem Begin quoted in Sachar, *History of Israel,* p. 282.

184. Williams, *Sons of Darkness, Sons of Light,* p. 228.

185. Kimmerling and Migdal, *The Palestinian People,* pp. 158–67. Two of the principal antagonists in the scholarly debate over the idea of "transfer" are Benny Morris, whose major works, *The Birth of the Palestinian Refugee Problem, 1947–1949* (1987) and *Righteous Victims* (1999), sought to expose collusion among Israel leaders to expel Palestinian Arabs from the territory that became the state of Israel, and Efraim Karsh, whose *Fabricating Israeli History: The "New Historians"* (1997) took issue with Morris's use of archival sources. Both have published revised editions of their works, and Morris took a surprising turn in 2001 when he recanted much of his earlier argument and held the Arabs and Palestinians largely responsible for the refugee problem. For a critique of Morris's original argument, see Shabtai Teveth, "The Palestinian Arab Ref-

ugee Problem and Its Origins," *Middle Eastern Studies* 26 (April 1990), 214–49; and Efraim Karsh, "Revisiting Israel's 'Original Sin': The Strange Case of Benny Morris," *Commentary* 116 (September 2003), 46–50, as well as the exchange of letters between Morris and Karsh in *Commentary* 117 (March 2004), 3–12.

186. My account of Deir Yassin draws on Hirst, *The Gun and the Olive Branch*, pp. 123–30, 136–43; Benny Morris, *The Birth of the Palestinian Refugee Problem, 1947–1949* (New York: Cambridge University Press, 1987), pp. 110–15, 130, 288; Johnson, *History of the Jews*, p. 528; Morris, *Righteous Victims*, pp. 201–9; and La Guardia, *War without End*, pp. 195–200. In 1969 Joseph B. Schechtman published a pamphlet incorporating an Israeli Foreign Ministry document ("Background Notes on Current Themes," dated March 16, 1969), which charges that the Deir Yassin massacre was a "21-year-old blood libel," a figment of Haganah disinformation intended to discredit the Irgun and Lehi repeated ever since as fact. This view of Deir Yassin is at odds with scholarly opinion. See Joseph B. Schechtman, *Israel Explodes Dir Yassin Blood Libel* (New York: United Zionists Revisionists of America, 1969). For documents and essays related to the efforts of a group called Deir Yassin Remembered to build a memorial, which would stand within sight of Yad Vashem, see Daniel A. McGowan and Marc H. Ellis, eds., *Remembering Deir Yassin: The Future of Israel and Palestine* (New York: Olive Branch Press, 1998). Martin Buber was among the first who tried to place the event into Israeli history with a sobering memorial purpose, asking Ben-Gurion, without success, to postpone the resettlement of the village, renamed Givat Shaul Bet, in the aftermath of the war. See Marc H. Ellis, "Remembering Deir Yassin: A Reflection on Memory and Justice," in McGowan and Ellis, *Remembering Deir Yassin*, pp. 10–23.

187. Even if it did not evolve into stated policy, transferring Arabs out of Palestine was seen by some as a moral solution to an inevitable conflict grounded in the need to absorb more Jewish immigrants, coupled with the view that Arab Palestinians could easily relocate to Transjordan, Syria, or Iraq. See Morris, *Righteous Victims*, pp. 140–42, 252–54.

188. Menachem Begin quoted in Colin Shindler, *Israel, Likud, and the Zionist Dream: Power, Politics and Ideology from Begin to Netanyahu* (London: I. B. Taurius, 1995), p. 37; Menachem Begin, *The Revolt*, trans. Samuel Katz, ed. Ivan M. Greenberg (Jerusalem: Steimatsky's Agency Limited, 1977), pp. 163–65. Cf. Teveth, "The Palestinian Arab Refugee Problem and Its Origin," pp. 216–17.

189. Ahmed Shukeiry and Abd al-Rahman Azzam Pasha quoted in Morris, *Righteous Victims*, pp. 218–19.

190. Kimmerling and Migdal, *The Palestinian People*, p. 435; *L'Orient-Le-Jour* (Beirut), September 7, 1972, quoted in Hirst, *The Gun and the Olive Branch*, p. 310.

191. Sharif Kanaana quoted in La Guardia, *War without End*, p. 199.

192. Cruse, *Crisis of the Negro Intellectual*, p. 495.

193. Williams, *Sons of Darkness, Sons of Light*, p. 149.

194. Hirst, *The Gun and the Olive Branch*, pp. 269–70; Sayigh, "The Armed Struggle and Palestinian Nationalism," p. 26.

195. Williams, *Sons of Darkness, Sons of Light*, pp. 203–4.

196. Construction of the Dimona reactor was begun in 1957 with the assistance of France (part of its extensive military assistance to Israel in the aftermath of the Sinai campaign) and made public in 1960 after American spy planes had detected the reactor, hidden under the cover of a textile plant. Facing pressure from the Kennedy administration, Israel agreed to regular American inspections but continued to deny that it was involved in nuclear weapons production, an explanation the United States publicly accepted. At the same time, Moshe Dayan spoke of the "bomb in the basement,"

a way of saying that a weapon was being developed without being tested and thus without being openly acknowledged. When Egypt carried out uninterdicted reconnaissance over Dimona in May 1967 and radio signals implied an attack was imminent, it underscored the need for Israel to strike preemptively. Morris, *Righteous Victims*, p. 307; Oren, *Six Days of War*, pp. 76, 99; Shlaim, *The Iron Wall*, pp. 208, 298; Warren Bass, *Support Any Friend: Kennedy's Middle East and the Making of the U.S.-Israel Alliance* (New York: Oxford University Press, 2003), pp. 186–238.

197. Williams, *Sons of Darkness, Sons of Light*, p. 203.

198. Such Arab facts would include "large and steadily increasing numbers, their influence in the world, the oil reserves at their disposal, and so forth." Moshe Dayan, "A Soldier Reflects on Peace Hopes" (September 27, 1968), in Walter Laqueur and Barry Rubin, eds., *The Israel-Arab Reader: A Documentary History of the Middle East Conflict*, 5th ed. (New York: Penguin, 1995), p. 282; Morris, *Righteous Victims*, p. 679.

199. Williams, *Sons of Darkness, Sons of Light*, p. 204; Salah al-Din quoted in Prager and Telushkin, *Why the Jews?*, p. 165.

200. Amidst the burgeoning anticolonial movements of the day, remarked Marie Syrkin, it is "difficult to convince survivors of Hitler that Jewish nationalism is the only heretical specimen," that the Jews are "the only people with no national need." Marie Syrkin, "Who Are the Palestinians?," *Midstream* 16 (January 1970), 12.

201. Williams, *Sons of Darkness, Sons of Light*, p. 204.

202. Fred Powledge, *Black Power, White Resistance: Notes on the New Civil War* (Cleveland: World Publishing, 1967), p. 264; Williams, *Sons of Darkness, Sons of Light*, p. 269.

6. BERNARD MALAMUD'S DARK GHETTO

1. Bernard Malamud, *The Tenants* (1971; rpt. New York: Penguin, 1972), p. 173.

2. Frantz Fanon, *Black Skin, White Masks*, trans. Charles Lam Markmann (1952; New York: Grove Press, 1967), pp. 162–65; Leslie Fiedler, "Negro and Jew: Encounter in America," in *No! in Thunder: Essays on Myth and Literature* (Boston: Beacon Press, 1960), p. 237.

3. Malamud, *The Tenants*, pp. 9, 173.

4. Malamud, interview with Daniel Stern (1974), in *Talking Horse: Bernard Malamud on Life and Work*, ed. Alan Cheuse and Nicholas Delbanco (New York: Columbia University Press, 1996), p. 22.

5. Tamar Jacoby, *Someone Else's House: America's Unfinished Struggle for Integration* (New York: Free Press, 1998), p. 212.

6. "Jew-Land," *Black Power* 1 (June 1967), quoted in Robert G. Weisbord and Arthur Stein, *Bittersweet Encounter: The Afro-American and the American Jew* (Westport, Conn.: Negro Universities Press, 1970), pp. 72–73n. See also Tom Wolfe, *Radical Chic and Mau-Mauing the Flak Catchers* (New York: Noonday Press, 1970), p. 85.

7. Malamud, interview with Daniel Stern, in *Talking Horse*, p. 22; Bernard Malamud to Evelyn Avery, July 8, 1973, quoted in Evelyn Avery, "Remembrances of Malamud: 1972–1986," in *Conversations with Bernard Malamud*, ed. Lawrence M. Lasher (Jackson: University of Mississippi Press, 1991), p. 147.

8. Alvin Kernan, *The Imaginary Library: An Essay on Society and Literature* (Princeton: Princeton University Press, 1982), p. 79.

9. Malamud, *The Tenants*, p. 61.

10. Bernard Malamud, "Jewishness in American Fiction" (ca. 1965–66), in *Talking Horse,* p. 137.

11. Philip Roth, "Imagining Jews" (1974), in *Reading Myself and Others* (New York: Penguin, 1985), pp. 300–301.

12. Malamud, *The Tenants,* pp. 11–15, 150. On *The Tenants* as a commentary on literary tradition, see Steven G. Kellman, "*The Tenants* in the House of Fiction," *Studies in the Novel* 8 (Winter 1976), 428–67; Kernan, *The Imaginary Library,* pp. 66–88; and Ethan Goffman, *Imagining Each Other: Blacks and Jews in Contemporary American Literature* (Albany: State University of New York Press, 2000), pp. 113–25. Goffman writes: "Jew and Black inhabit this desolate tenement, struggling to create a literature, a cultural narrative, from their fragmented positions on the margins. They must build their own 'house of literature' from the skeletal structure of the tenement building, of European form, giving it flesh through the artistic labors of besieged minority experience" (p. 115).

13. Jacob Cohen in "Negro-Jewish Relations in America: A Symposium," *Midstream* 12 (December 1966), 12; Fiedler, "Negro and Jew," pp. 241, 249–50.

14. Malamud, *The Tenants,* pp. 9, 28, 72; Jean-Paul Sartre, *Anti-Semite and Jew: An Exploration of the Etiology of Hate,* trans. George J. Becker (1946; rpt. New York: Schocken, 1985), pp. 69, 83.

15. Malamud, *The Tenants,* p. 166.

16. James Baldwin, "Negroes Are Anti-Semitic Because They're Anti-White" (1967), in *The Price of the Ticket: Collected Non-fiction, 1948–1985* (New York: St. Martin's, 1985), p. 430.

17. Arthur A. Cohen in "Negro-Jewish Relations in America," 10.

18. "Mayn rasistishe biografye" appeared in *Gezangn fun rekhts tsu links* [Songs from Right to Left] (New York: Tsiko Bikher Farlag, 1971), pp. 121–24. Translation by Justin D. Cammy in "Oykh ikh zing amerike," unpublished paper; used by permission.

19. James A. Randall, Jr., "Jew," in *Don't Ask Me Who I Am* (Detroit: Broadside Press: 1970), p. 11.

20. See Leo Baeck, *This People Israel: The Meaning of Jewish Existence* (1955), trans. Albert H. Friedlander (New York: Holt, Rinehart and Winston, 1964), pp. 46–47.

21. Malamud, *The Tenants,* p. 25.

22. Martin Luther King, Jr., *Where Do We Go from Here: Chaos or Community?* (Boston: Beacon Press, 1967), p. 170. For Theophus Smith, King's "world house" is a version of Du Bois's double consciousness that prophesies postmodern global communities transcending ethnocentrism and built upon the composite heritage of many nations, a kind of Exodus without end in which the condition of exile is superseded by a continual dispersal and reconfiguration of cultures. See Theophus Smith, *Conjuring Culture: Biblical Formations of Black America* (New York: Oxford University Press, 1994), pp. 252–53. See also Lewis V. Baldwin, *To Make the Wounded Whole: The Cultural Legacy of Martin Luther King, Jr.* (Minneapolis: Fortress, 1992), pp. 19–24, 163–218.

23. Abraham J. Heschel and Martin Luther King, Jr., "What Happens to Them Happens to Me," *United Synagogue Review* 16 (Winter 1964), rpt. in Jack Salzman, ed., *Bridges and Boundaries: African Americans and American Jews* (New York: George Braziller, 1992), pp. 86–90.

24. Maurice Samuel in "Negro-Jewish Relations in America," 68.

25. King, *Where Do We Go from Here?,* pp. 110–11; W. E. B. Du Bois, *Dusk of Dawn: An Essay toward an Autobiography of a Race Concept* (1940; rpt. New York: Schocken, 1968), p. 131.

26. Tom Wicker, introduction to *Report of the National Advisory Commission on Civil Dis-*

orders (New York: E. P. Dutton, 1968), p. ix; Kenneth B. Clark, *Dark Ghetto: Dilemmas of Social Power,* 2nd ed. (1965; rpt. Hanover, N.H.: Wesleyan University Press, 1989), p. 240. I have also drawn here on Loïc Wacquant's observation that the ghetto is not simply a spatial entity or an aggregation of families at the bottom of a class structure but a "uniquely racial formation that spawns a society-wide web of material and symbolic association between color, place, and a host of negatively valued social properties." Loïc Wacquant quoted in Glenn C. Loury, *The Anatomy of Racial Inequality* (Cambridge, Mass.: Harvard University Press, 2002), p. 78.

27. C. Bezalel Sherman, *The Jew within American Society: A Study in Ethnic Individuality* (Detroit: Wayne State University Press, 1961), p. 148; Albert I. Gordon, *Jews in Suburbia* (1959), quoted in Howard M. Sachar, *A History of the Jews in America* (New York: Random House, 1992), p. 670.

28. Louis Wirth, *The Ghetto* (1928; rpt. Chicago: University of Chicago Press, 1956); Ben Halpern, *The American Jew: A Zionist Analysis* (1956; rpt. New York: Schocken, 1983), pp. 58–59.

29. Peter I. Rose, ed., *The Ghetto and Beyond: Essays on Jewish Life in America* (New York: Random House, 1969).

30. As one classic postwar account of romanticized shtetl life put it: "The life described here no longer exists. People and culture have been destroyed, and soon it will be too late to find the models for a living picture." Mark Zborowski and Elizabeth Herzog, *Life Is with People: The Culture of the Shtetl* (1952; rpt. New York: Schocken, 1962), p. 24. Especially for later generations who never knew it, writes Eva Hoffman, the shtetl is often conceived as the site of Jewish authenticity defined either as spirituality or as suffering, either a quaint place of "fiddlers on thatched roofs" or the epicenter of "peasant barbarism and pogroms." Eva Hoffman, *Shtetl: The Life and Death of a Small Town and the World of Polish Jews* (Boston: Houghton Mifflin, 1997), p. 11.

31. Once the state of Israel was secure and American Jews had declared their permanent home to be the diaspora of the United States, David Roskies has argued, the European shtetl could be reborn as a mythic protagonist in the "covenantal rediscovery of a vanished cultural homeland." David G. Roskies, *The Jewish Search for a Usable Past* (Bloomington: Indiana University Press, 1999), pp. 43–44.

32. Edward Lewis Wallant, *The Pawnbroker* (1961; rpt. New York: Harvest, 1989), pp. 19, 4, 258–59, 27.

33. Ibid., pp. 52, 269, 278.

34. Ibid., p. 247. On the novel's fusion of Christian redemption and anti-Semitism, see S. Lillian Kremer, *Witness through the Imagination: Jewish American Holocaust Literature* (Detroit: Wayne State University Press, 1989), pp. 77–79.

35. Stephen Steinberg, *The Ethnic Myth: Race, Ethnicity, and Class in America,* rev. ed. (Boston: Beacon Press, 1989), pp. 106–27.

36. Nathan Glazer, "Blacks and Ethnic Groups: The Difference and the Political Difference It Makes" (1971), in *Ethnic Dilemmas, 1964–1982* (Cambridge, Mass.: Harvard University Press, 1983), pp. 70–93; Fred A. Jones, president of the St. Louis Business League, quoted in Eugene P. Foley, "The Negro Businessman: In Search of a Tradition," in Talcott Parsons and Kenneth B. Clark, eds., *The Negro American* (Boston: Beacon Press, 1967), pp. 555–56. Foley's essay first appeared in *Daedalus* 95 (Winter 1966).

37. Malcolm X, with Alex Haley, *The Autobiography of Malcolm X* (1965; rpt. New York: Grove Press, 1966), p. 193; Imamu Amiri Baraka, "Newark—Before Black Men Conquered" (1967), in *Raise, Race, Rays, Raze: Essays since 1965* (New York: Random House, 1971), p. 68.

38. Malamud, *The Tenants,* pp. 36, 73–75.

39. Max Geltman, *The Confrontation: Black Power, Anti-Semitism, and the Myth of Integration* (Englewood Cliffs, N.J.: Prentice-Hall, 1970), p. 67.

40. Adam Clayton Powell, Sr., *Riots and Ruins* (New York: Ayer Publishers, 1945), p. 47.

41. Baldwin, "Negroes Are Anti-Semitic Because They're Anti-White," p. 428.

42. Clark, *Dark Ghetto,* pp. xxxi, 63–67, 76–81.

43. Elie Wiesel, 1970 interview with Yaacov Agmon, *Israel Magazine* (April 1970), rpt. in *Against the Silence: The Voice and Vision of Elie Wiesel,* ed. Irving Abrahamson, 3 vols. (New York: Holocaust Library, 1985), III, 202.

44. Leslie Fiedler, "The Jig Is Up!" (1963), in *Waiting for the End* (New York: Stein and Day, 1964), p. 129.

45. King, *Where Do We Go from Here?,* pp. 47, 19, 70, 113; Fanon, *Black Skin, White Masks,* p. 60.

46. Ralph Ellison, "A Very Stern Discipline" (1965), in *Going to the Territory* (1986; rpt. New York: Vintage, 1987), p. 276; Albert Murray, *The Omni-Americans: Some Alternatives to the Folklore of White Supremacy* (1970; rpt. New York: Da Capo Press, 1990), p. 42, 69, 75–77.

47. Stokely Carmichael and Charles V. Hamilton, *Black Power: The Politics of Liberation in America* (New York: Vintage Random, 1967), pp. 2–32, 35, quotation at p. 2; Poussaint quoted in William H. Grier and Price M. Cobbs, *Black Rage* (1968; rpt. New York: Bantam, 1969), p. 179. See also Robert M. Fogelson, *Violence as Protest: A Study of Riots and Ghettos* (Garden City, N.Y.: Doubleday, 1971); and Joe R. Feagin and Harlan Hahn, *Ghetto Revolts: The Politics of Violence in American Cities* (New York: Macmillan, 1973).

48. Whereas the ghetto's calcification as an abode of black authenticity dates to the 1960s, when the War on Poverty unleashed a horde of social scientists "with the zeal of colonial missionaries," Robin Kelley points out, it has been abetted more recently by ethnographers of hip-hop culture who, "looking for the 'real nigga,'" claim to have found in ghetto culture the authentic voice of black youth. As theories of pathology were tempered by the alluring commercialization of "gangsta" life, there emerged a neo-separatist mode of black authenticity captured in Geneva Smitherman's definition of the slang term "ghetto fabulous": "Describes a person or thing that is fantastic, the height of something, according to the authentic, natural, 'keepin-it-real' standards of Blackness that are believed to exist in ghetto communities." The potential harm of such self-conceptions is readily evident: a 1991 Gallup Poll, for instance, showed that half of African Americans thought that three out of four blacks lived in the ghetto, when the real number was more like one in five. Robin D. G. Kelley, *Yo' Mama's Disfunktional: Fighting the Culture Wars in Urban America* (Boston: Beacon Press, 1997), pp. 15–42, quotation at p. 19; Geneva Smitherman, *Black Talk: Words and Phrases from the Hood to the Amen Corner,* rev. ed. (Boston: Houghton Mifflin, 2000), p. 145; John McWhorter, *Losing the Race: Self-Sabotage in Black America* (2000; rpt. New York: Perennial, 2001), p. 9.

49. Nathan Hare, "Brainwashing of Black Men's Minds," in LeRoi Jones and Larry Neal, eds., *Black Fire: An Anthology of Afro-American Writing* (New York: William Morrow, 1968), pp. 179, 185. On Black Power as a cultural resistance movement, see in particular William L. Van Deburg, *New Day in Babylon: The Black Power Movement and American Culture, 1965–1975* (Chicago: University of Chicago Press, 1992), pp. 112–292 passim.

50. Alan W. Miller, "Black Anti-Semitism—Jewish Racism," in Nat Hentoff, ed., *Black Anti-Semitism and Jewish Racism* (New York: Richard Baron, 1969), p. 111.

51. L. D. Reddick, "Anti-Semitism among Negroes," in Salzman, *Bridges and Boundaries,* p. 81.

52. Norman Podhoretz, *Making It* (New York: Random House, 1967), pp. 339–46.

53. Harold Cruse, "My Jewish Problem and Theirs," in Hentoff, *Black Anti-Semitism and Jewish Racism,* pp. 143–88, quotations at pp. 151, 174. See also the further reply to Podhoretz, at the time of his 1993 postscript, by Joe Wood, "The Problem Negro and Other Tales," in Paul Berman, ed., *Blacks and Jews: Alliances and Arguments* (New York: Delacorte, 1994), pp. 97–128.

54. Shlomo Katz, "An Open Letter to James Baldwin," *Midstream* 17 (April 1971), 3–5; James Baldwin and Shlomo Katz, "Of Angela Davis and 'the Jewish Housewife Headed for Dachau': An Exchange," *Midstream* 17 (June–July 1971), 3–10.

55. John Murray Cuddihy, "Jews, Blacks, and the Cold War at the Top," *Worldview* 15 (February 1972), 31–39. The essay is reprinted in John Murray Cuddihy, *The Ordeal of Civility: Freud, Marx, Lévi-Strauss, and the Jewish Struggle with Modernity* (New York: Basic Books, 1974).

56. Robert G. Weisbord and Richard Kazarian, Jr., *Israel in the Black American Perspective* (Westport, Conn.: Greenwood Press, 1985), p. 66.

57. James Baldwin, *The Fire Next Time* (1963; rpt. New York: Dell, 1964), pp. 126–27; idem, *No Name in the Street* (1972), in *The Price of the Ticket,* p. 547, 449. Julius Lester likewise defined Black Power within the tradition of Nat Turner and Malcolm X by reference to the spiritual: "Now I got my way / And I'll tear this building down." Julius Lester, *Look Out, Whitey! Black Power's Gon' Get Your Mama!* (1968; rpt. New York: Grove, 1969), p. 80.

58. Derek Walcott, "The Muse of History" (1974), in *What the Twilight Says* (New York: Farrar, Straus and Giroux, 1998), pp. 54–56; Addison Gayle, Jr., *The Black Situation* (New York: Delta, 1970), pp. 84–87. As Michael Novak remarked in 1972, "no group of black militants today runs any city with the thoroughness, skill, and ruthlessness with which Al Capone, even at age twenty-nine, ran Chicago" in the late 1920s. See Michael Novak, *Unmeltable Ethnics: Politics and Culture in American Life,* 2nd ed. (New Brunswick, N.J.: Transaction, 1996), p. 198, originally published in 1972 as *The Rise of the Unmeltable Ethnics.* In a reassessment of his book, Novak contrasts his continued endorsement of pluralism and ethnic identity with what he considers the "nine perversions of multiculturalism": Anti-Americanism, Victimology, Ego-boosting [falsely constructed self-esteem], Evasion [of universal standards of morality], Tactical Relativism, Censorship [of open inquiry], Groupthink, Egalityrrany [outcomes confused with opportunity], and Double standards (pp. xvi–xvii).

59. Welton Smith, "malcolm," in Jones and Neal, *Black Fire,* p. 288.

60. Malamud, *The Tenants,* pp. 33, 60.

61. Seth Forman, *Blacks in the Jewish Mind: A Crisis of Liberalism* (New York: New York University Press, 1998); pp. 112–15.

62. Malamud, *The Tenants,* pp. 147, 151, 61.

63. Ibid., p. 45; Albert Memmi, *The Colonizer and the Colonized,* trans. Howard Greenfield (1957; rpt. Boston: Beacon Press, 1991), pp. 120–22.

64. In a metaphor that usefully illuminates the mental enclosure replicated by the novel's narrative style, Addison Gayle, Jr., remarked that black intellectuals exist in the white world's "cabinet of the mind" like expensive pieces of fragile glassware, assigned specific places and roles, while few whites see the black man in his modern representative posture: "He is more alienated than Dostoyevsky's underground man because he has known loneliness for a much longer period of time; he is more terrified than Kafka's Joseph K because for a much longer time he has been the victim of forces beyond his

control; he is more capable of murder than Richard Wright's Bigger Thomas because today the channels through which manhood is attained are more closed." Gayle, *The Black Situation*, pp. 51, 60.

65. Malamud, "Jewishness in American Fiction," pp. 141–42; idem, "On Subject Matter," in *Talking Horse*, p. 115.

66. Malamud, *The Tenants*, pp. 54, 60, 66–67.

67. Carmichael and Hamilton, *Black Power*, pp. 164–77; Larry Neal, "And Shine Swam On," in Jones and Neal, *Black Fire*, pp. 652, 655–56. Neal would later reverse his opinion of Ellison and write one of the best essays on him. See "Ellison's Zoot Suit," in Larry Neal, *Visions of a Liberated Future: Blacks Arts Movement Writings*, ed. Michael Schwartz (New York: Thunder's Mouth Press, 1989), pp. 30–56.

68. Imamu Amiri Baraka, "Nationalism vs. PimpArt" (1969), in *Raise, Race, Rays, Raze*, p. 129 (Sékou Touré was the first president of Guinea and Julius Nyerere the first president of Tanzania); idem, "Black Art, Nationalism, Organization, Black Institutions" (1969), ibid. p. 98. Cf. Maulana Karenga, "Black Art: Mute Matter Given Form and Function," (1968), rpt. in Abraham Chapman, ed., *New Black Voices: An Anthology of Contemporary Afro-American Literature* (New York: Mentor, 1972), pp. 478–79; and Stephen E. Henderson, "'Survival Motion': A Study of the Black Writer and the Black Revolution in America," in Mercer Cook and Stephen E. Henderson, eds., *The Militant Black Writer* (Madison: University of Wisconsin Press, 1969), pp. 128–29.

69. LeRoi Jones [Amiri Baraka], "What Does Non-violence Mean?" (1963), in *Home: Social Essays* (New York: William Morrow, 1966), p. 149; idem, "State/meant" (1965), ibid., pp. 251–52; idem, "The Black Aesthetic," *Negro Digest* 18 (September 1969), 5–6; idem, "The Legacy of Malcolm X, and the Coming of the Black Nation" (1965), in *Home*, pp. 248–49.

70. Melvin B. Tolson, *"Harlem Gallery" and Other Poems*, ed. Raymond Nelson (Charlottesville: University Press of Virginia, 1999), pp. 354, 457. The ellipses are Tolson's.

71. See Van Deburg, *New Day in Babylon*, pp. 12–17, 181–91, 216–24, 280–91. On the Black Arts movement, see also Philip Brian Harper, "Nationalism and Social Division in Black Arts Poetry of the 1960s," in Eddie S. Glaude, Jr., ed., *Is It Nation Time? Contemporary Essays on Black Power and Black Nationalism* (Chicago: University of Chicago Press, 2002), pp. 165–88.

72. Nikki Giovanni, "Poem (No Name No. 3)" (1968), in *Black Feeling, Black Talk, Black Judgment* (New York: Morrow Quill, 1979), pp. 24–25.

73. Don L. Lee [Haki Maduhubti], introduction to "For Black People," in *We Walk the Way of the New World* (Detroit: Broadside Press, 1970), pp. 15–16, 55, 58.

74. LeRoi Jones [Amiri Baraka], *Black Magic: Collected Poetry, 1961–1967* (Indianapolis: Bobbs-Merrill, 1969), pp. 8, 116, 205. "The Black Man Is Making New Gods" first appeared in *Evergreen Review* 50 (December 1967), 49. On Baraka's anti-Semitism, see also Jerry Gafio Watts, *Amiri Baraka: The Politics and Art of a Black Intellectual* (New York: New York University Press, 2001), pp. 225–58 passim.

75. Jay Kaufmann, "Thou Shalt Surely Rebuke Thy Neighbor," in Hentoff, *Black Anti-Semitism and Jewish Racism*, pp. 67–69.

76. LeRoi Jones [Amiri Baraka], "For Tom Postell, Dead Black Poet," in *Black Magic*, p. 154.

77. Bernard Malamud, "Source of *The Fixer*," in *Talking Horse*, pp. 88–89.

78. See Saul S. Friedman, *The Incident at Massena: The Blood Libel in America* (New York: Stein and Day, 1978); and Abraham G. Duker, "Twentieth-Century Blood Libels in the United States," in Alan Dundes, ed., *The Blood-Libel Legend: A Casebook in Anti-Semitic Folklore* (Madison: University of Wisconsin Press, 1991), pp. 233–60.

79. Malamud, "Source of *The Fixer*," pp. 88–89.

80. Bernard Malamud, *The Fixer* (1966; rpt. New York: Penguin, 1967), pp. 121, 117. On the Beilis case and its context, see *Blood Accusation: The Strange History of the Beiliss Case* (New York: Alfred A. Knopf, 1966) by Maurice Samuel, who frames his account with attention to the case's demonstration of the power of totalitarian states to govern public affairs by means of the "big lie"; and Albert S. Lindemann, *The Jew Accused: Three Anti-Semitic Affairs: Dreyfus, Beilis, Frank, 1894–1915* (New York: Cambridge University Press, 1991), pp. 129–93. On the role of the Catholic Church in inflaming anti-Semitic fears of ritual murder, see also David I. Kertzer, *The Popes against the Jews: The Vatican's Role in the Rise of Modern Anti-Semitism* (New York: Alfred A. Knopf, 2001), pp. 213–36.

81. Malamud, *The Fixer*, pp. 206, 299.

82. Malamud, "Source of *The Fixer*," p. 89. On *The Slave*, see Chapter 3.

83. H. Rap Brown, *Die Nigger Die!* (New York: Dial, 1969), p. 137; "Revolutionary Art/ Black Liberation" (1968), in Philip S. Foner, ed., *The Black Panthers Speak* (1970; rpt. New York: Da Capo Press, 1995), p. 18.

84. Iceberg Slim (Robert Beck), *The Naked Soul of Iceberg Slim* (1971; rpt. Los Angeles: Holloway House, 1986), pp. 178, 172; Chester Himes, *Plan B*, ed. Michel Fabre and Robert E. Skinner (Jackson: University Press of Mississippi, 1993), pp. 189, 200.

85. Fanon, *Black Skin, White Masks*, pp. 157–59, 165–67; LeRoi Jones [Amiri Baraka], "American Sexual Reference: Black Male" (1965), in *Home*, pp. 228–30; Calvin C. Hernton, *Sex and Racism in America* (1965; rpt. New York: Grove Weidenfeld, 1988), pp. 111–15.

86. Albert B. Cleage, Jr., "An Epistle to Stokely," in *The Black Messiah* (New York: Sheed and Ward, 1968), pp. 39–41; Malamud, *The Tenants*, pp. 129, 80. On Black Jews and Black Power theology, see Chapter 2.

87. Malamud, *The Tenants*, p. 45.

88. Brown, *Die Nigger Die!*, pp. 21, 26. On the dozens, see, for example, John Dollard, "The Dozens: Dialectic of Insult," and Roger D. Abrahams, "Playing the Dozens," both in Alan Dundes, ed., *Mother Wit from the Laughing Barrel: Readings in the Interpretation of Afro-American Folklore* (1973; rpt. Jackson: University Press of Mississippi, 1993), pp. 277–309.

89. Malamud, *The Tenants*, pp. 102–5. In the initial retort Harry borrows appropriately from Yeats's poem "Crazy Jane Talks with the Bishop" (*Words for Music Perhaps*): "But Love has pitched his mansion in / The place of excrement; / For nothing can be sole or whole / That has not been rent."

90. Malamud, *The Tenants*, pp. 42–43.

91. Ibid., pp. 122, 111–12.

92. Henry Dumas, "Cuttin Down to Size," in Jones and Neal, *Black Fire*, pp. 349–50.

93. Malamud, *The Tenants*, p. 127.

94. Leslie Fiedler in "Negro-Jewish Relations in America," 29.

95. Moses Maimonides, *The Guide for the Perplexed*, trans. M. Friedlander (1904; rpt. New York: Dover, 1956), p. 378. I am indebted here to Nathan J. Brown, "'Tell Me You Love Me': Circumcision and the Ethics of the Neighbor in Black-Jewish Relations," unpublished seminar paper, March 2003. See also Josef Stern, "Maimonides on the Covenant of Circumcision and the Unity of God," in *The Midrashic Imagination: Jewish Exegesis, Thought, and History* (Albany: State University of New York Press, 1982), pp. 131–54.

96. Saul Bellow, *Mr. Sammler's Planet* (1970; rpt. New York: Penguin, 1977), pp. 48–49, 149. For more on Bellow's novel, see Chapter 5.

97. Malamud, *The Tenants*, p. 169.

98. Irving Howe, "Black Boys and Native Sons," *Dissent* 10 (Autumn 1963), 354–55; Ralph Ellison, "The World and the Jug," in *Shadow and Act* (1964; rpt. New York: Vintage, 1971), pp. 122, 112, 117.

99. Ellison, "The World and the Jug," pp. 126, 143; Cynthia Ozick, "Literary Blacks and Jews" (1972), in *Art and Ardor: Essays* (New York: E. P. Dutton, 1983), pp. 96, 102, 106–11. Ozick had no reason to backtrack when her essay was reprinted in 1993. If anything, Malamud's parable of the future seemed even more apt, except that his forecast of equal culpability was disproved for Ozick by the black violence and anti-Semitism of the Crown Heights riot. See Cynthia Ozick, "Afterward," in Berman, *Blacks and Jews*, pp. 66–75.

100. Emily Miller Budick, *Blacks and Jews in Literary Conversation* (New York: Cambridge University Press, 1998), pp. 19–32, 51–60. I am indebted throughout to Budick's interpretation of the interplay between Malamud's novel and the several figures of Ellison, Howe, Baldwin, and Hyman. See also Budick's essay "The African American and Israeli 'Other' in the Construction of Jewish American Identity," in Emily Miller Budick, ed., *Ideology and Jewish Identity in Israeli and American Literature* (Albany: State University of New York Press, 2001), pp. 197–212; Forman, *Blacks in the Jewish Mind*, pp. 122–27; and Morris Dickstein, *Leopards in the Temple: The Transformation of American Fiction, 1945–1970* (Cambridge, Mass.: Harvard University Press, 2002), pp. 194–95, 200–201.

101. As Budick points out, Lesser's ascetic life, with his few possessions such as his Bessie Smith records and typewriter, seems to borrow directly from Baldwin's description of his retreat to the mountains of Switzerland after a psychological breakdown in Paris: "There, in that absolutely alabaster landscape, armed with two Bessie Smith records and a typewriter, I began to re-create the life that I had first known as a child and from which I had spent so many years in flight." See James Baldwin, "The Discovery of What It Means to Be an American" (1959), in *Nobody Knows My Name* (New York: Dell, 1961), p. 18. See also Baldwin's "Stranger in the Village" (1953), in *Notes of a Native Son* (1955; rpt. New York: Bantam, 1964), pp. 135–49. Both essays argue that the freedom of expatriate experience brings a crystallizing understanding of what it means to be an American. Budick, *Blacks and Jews in Literary Conversation*, p. 52.

102. Ellison, "A Very Stern Discipline," pp. 278, 282.

103. Ralph Ellison, *Invisible Man* (1952; New York: Vintage, 1989), p. 266.

104. Malamud, *The Tenants*, pp. 146–47.

105. Ibid., pp. 64, 165, 22, 10.

106. Ibid., pp. 147, 151.

107. Frank Kermode, *The Sense of an Ending: Studies in the Theory of Fiction* (New York: Oxford University Press, 1967), pp. 38–39. Kermode's interpretation of *King Lear* is important here as well. As he notes, the play's raging storm and its stripping of Lear to his bare nakedness are signs not of divine justice but of impending evil chaos: "We seem to be left at the end of the play not only with a mere remnant of the great men and women, just or unjust, who began it, but with a mere remnant of time. Before everything was annihilated, evil destroyed itself, and Edgar has a future to face; but it comes toward him desolate and drained of meaning." Frank Kermode, introduction to *King Lear*, in *The Riverside Shakespeare*, 2nd ed., ed. G. Blakemore Evans et al. (Boston: Houghton Mifflin, 1997), p. 1302.

108. *The Oratory of Classical Greece: Antiphon and Andocides*, trans. Michael Gagarin and Douglas M. MacDowell (Austin: University of Texas Press, 1998), pp. 44–45.

109. Ibid., pp. 7, 17.

110. Bernard Malamud, "Imaginative Writing and Jewish Experience," in *Talking Horse*, p. 187.
111. Frederick Douglass, "The Meaning of July Fourth for the Negro," speech of July 5, 1852, in *The Life and Writings of Frederick Douglass*, ed. Philip S. Foner, 5 vols. (New York: International Publishers, 1975), II, 201. Douglass actually said "your nation's bosom," since throughout this famous address he used the pronoun "your" rather than "our" to accentuate the fact that blacks did not yet belong to the American nation.
112. Elisa New, "Film and the Flattening of Jewish-American Fiction: Bernard Malamud, Woody Allen, and Spike Lee in the City," *Contemporary Literature* 34 (Fall 1993), 435–36.
113. Gershom Scholem, "Toward an Understanding of the Messianic Idea" (1959), trans. Michael A. Meyer, in *The Messianic Idea in Judaism and Other Essays on Jewish Spirituality* (1971; rpt. New York: Schocken, 1995), pp. 35–36.
114. Naomi W. Cohen, "Dual Loyalties: Zionism and Liberalism," in Allon Gal, ed., *Envisioning Israel: The Changing Ideals and Images of North American Jews* (Jerusalem: Magnes Press, 1996), pp. 323–24.
115. Elijah Muhhumad, *Message to the Blackman in America* (Chicago: Muhummad Mosque of Islam No. 2, 1965), pp. 270–76. Cf. Smith, *Conjuring Culture*, pp. 238–41; and Eugen Weber, *Apocalypses: Prophesies, Cults, and Millennial Beliefs through the Ages* (Cambridge, Mass.: Harvard University Press, 1999), p. 213.
116. Herbert Weiner in "Negro-Jewish Relations in America," 87–88. One may note that Kook's son, Rabbi Zvi Yehuda Hacohen Kook, spiritual leader of Israel's National Religious Party, appeared to have prophesied the return of Judea and Samaria to Israel in May 1967 when he lamented the sins of the nation for abandoning Hebron and Bethlehem to Arab rule. Under the covenant with Abraham, say those for whom Kook speaks, the right of the Jewish people to Judea and Samaria cannot be contested or negotiated. See Howard M. Sachar, *A History of Israel: From the Aftermath of the Yom Kippur War* (New York: Oxford University Press, 1987), pp. 16–17.
117. Malamud, *The Tenants*, p. 23.
118. Ibid., pp. 43, 154–55.
119. Ellison, *Invisible Man*, p. 9.
120. Malamud, *The Tenants*, pp. 156–64.
121. Fiedler, "The Jig Is Up," pp. 132–33. "The Jig Is Up" originally appeared as "Race—the Dream and the Nightmare" in *Commentary* (October 1963).
122. Malamud, *The Tenants*, pp. 165–66, 153–54.
123. Hidden in ten tin boxes and two milk cannisters, the six thousand documents collected and recorded by the historian Emanuel Ringelblum and his staff of writers, statisticians, and social scientists told the story of the Warsaw Ghetto and its coming liquidation. Under the code name "Oyneg Shabes" ("enjoyment of the Sabbath"), Ringelblum's archive was an underground social and cultural encyclopedia made up of historical monographs on Polish towns, songs, poems, essays, autobiography, letters, medical and economic documents—everything that could be collected to contribute to an archival record and eyewitness account of wartime Jewish life in Poland up to the liquidation of the ghetto—meant to save a people's story from extinction and, perhaps, bring their murderers to justice. See Emanuel Ringelblum, "Oyneg Shabbes," in David G. Roskies, ed., *The Literature of Destruction: Jewish Responses to Catastrophe* (Philadelphia: Jewish Publication Society, 1988), pp. 386–98. Both Ringelblum's own diary, published in English in 1958 as *Notes from the Warsaw Ghetto*, and the collection of materials written secretly in Lodz under the direction of Chaim

Rumkowski and later published in abridged form as the *Chronicle of the Lodz Ghetto*, were part of the inspiration for John Hersey's 1950 documentary novel *The Wall*, which purports to be based on the hidden Yiddish archive of one Noach Levinson, housed in Israel after being unearthed from the ruins.

124. Malamud, *The Tenants*, p. 136.

125. Malamud may have intended an echo of Allen Ginsberg's "Footnote to Howl" (1955), which begins with the enunciation "Holy! Holy! Holy! . . ." repeated fifteen times in introduction of an incantatory poem declaring all manner of phenomena—hipsters, beggars, cocks, angels, typewriters, miracles, the abyss—to be holy. Or, he may have meant to echo Cannonball Adderly's recently popular jazz-funk tune "Mercy, Mercy, Mercy," recorded in 1966. In his own survey of hostilities between blacks and Jews, James Alan McPherson makes the interesting revelation that Malamud asked his advice about the manuscript of *The Tenants*, worried that he had not done justice to Willie's black idiom and worried, too, about the rising state of tension between black and Jewish intellectuals. McPherson offered advice on several aspects of the novel, but he failed to persuade Malamud to replace the *hab rachmones*, in its manic repetition, with a classic novelistic ending and a period. "Rereading the book eighteen years later," McPherson wrote in 1989, "I now see that, even after the 115th plea for mercy by Levenspiel, there is no period and there is no peace." Malamud, *The Tenants*, pp. 169–73; Allen Ginsberg, "Footnote to 'Howl,'" in *Collected Poems, 1947–1980* (New York: Harper and Row, 1984), p. 134; James A. McPherson, "To Blacks and Jews: Hab Rachmones," *Tikkun* 4 (September–October 1989), 15.

126. Malamud, interview with Daniel Stern, in *Talking Horse*, p. 22.

7. HOLOCAUST I: NEVER FORGETTING

1. The self-dramatizing cult of the Holocaust, Lopate added caustically, makes it appear to be a "corporation headed by Elie Wiesel, who defends his patents with articles in the Arts and Leisure section of the Sunday *New York Times*." Philip Lopate, "Resistance to the Holocaust," *Tikkun* 4 (May–June 1989), rpt. in David Rosenberg, ed., *Testimony: Contemporary Writers Make the Holocaust Personal* (New York: Random House, 1989), p. 287.

2. Kevin Merida and Michael A. Fletcher, "Supreme Discomfort," *Washington Post*, August 4, 2002, W08; Randall Robinson, *The Debt: What America Owes to Blacks* (New York: Dutton, 2000), p. 51.

3. Betty Friedan, *The Feminine Mystique* (1963; rpt. New York: Dell, 1970), p. 294. Later in the century, once the Holocaust could be indiscriminately invoked as a means of establishing identity through vicarious suffering in a deracinated, morally numbed world, one find's Friedan's insight extended into a principle of consciousness in *Eve's Tattoo* (1992), by Emily Prager, whose gentile narrator acquires a concentration camp number in secret sympathy with those Aryan women who are presumed to be the archetypal victims of Nazism's hypermasculinist need to possess and disfigure the feminine. Ishmael Reed, as we will see later, parodies this idea in *Reckless Eyeballing*.

4. Alan W. Miller, "Black Anti-Semitism—Jewish Racism," in Nat Hentoff, ed., *Black Anti-Semitism and Jewish Racism* (New York: Richard W. Baron, 1969), p. 99; David Hilliard, "If You Want Peace You Got to Fight for It" (1969), in Philip S. Foner, ed., *The Black Panthers Speak* (New York: Da Capo Press, 1995), p. 129.

5. Cf. Norman Finkelstein's distinction between the "Nazi holocaust" as a historical

event and "the Holocaust" as an ideological representation, a valuable distinction despite his otherwise tendentious analysis. Ever since the Six-Day War, in Finkelstein's
view, "the Holocaust" has been deployed as an "invaluable chip in a high-stakes
power game" to deflect criticism of Israel, a military power with a "horrendous human rights record," sustain the fund-raising appeals of Jewish organizations, and secure American Jews, the most successful ethnic group in the nation, in their own status as victims. Norman G. Finkelstein, *The Holocaust Industry: Reflections on the
Exploitation of Jewish Suffering* (New York: Verso, 2000), pp. 3, 30, 34.

6. Gerald Early, "Who Is the Jew? A Question of African-American Identity," *CommonQuest* 1 (Spring 1996), 42.

7. Jacob Neusner quoted by Michael Marrus, "The Use and Misuse of the Holocaust," in
Peter Hayes, ed., *Lessons and Legacies: The Meaning of the Holocaust in a Changing
World* (Evanston, Ill.: Northwestern University Press, 1991), p. 108.

8. Peter Novick, *The Holocaust in American Life* (Boston: Houghton Mifflin, 1999), pp.
188–98, quotation at p. 195.

9. Morrison went on to itemize a set of charges that white America has demonized,
pathologized, and criminalized blacks; discredited black artists; subverted black political representation; and, through a fascistic corporate regime, created "the perfect
capitalist, one who is willing to kill a human being for a product—a pair of sneakers,
a jacket, a car." June Jordan quoted in John McWhorter, *Losing the Race: Self-Sabotage
in Black America* (2000; rpt. New York: Perennial, 2001), p. 39; Toni Morrison, "Racism and Fascism," *The Nation* 260 (May 29, 1995), 760.

10. Ruth Kluger, *Still Alive: A Holocaust Girlhood Remembered* (New York: Feminist Press,
2001), pp. 64, 94.

11. George M. Fredrickson, *Racism: A Short History* (Princeton: Princeton University
Press, 2002), p. 9.

12. Seymour Drescher, "The Atlantic Slave Trade and the Holocaust: A Comparative
Analysis," in Alan S. Rosenbaum, ed., *Is the Holocaust Unique? Perspectives on Comparative Genocide* (Boulder, Colo.: Westview Books, 1998), pp. 66–67, 78–79, quotation at
p. 78. In addition to the specific citations that follow, I have drawn in this discussion on Zygmunt Bauman, *Modernity and the Holocaust* (1989; rpt. Ithaca, N.Y.: Cornell University Press, 1992), pp. 89–94; Steven T. Katz, *Historicism, the Holocaust,
and Zionism: Critical Studies in Modern Jewish Thought and History* (New York: New
York University Press, 1992), pp. 120–23; Laurence Mordekhai Thomas, *Vessels of Evil:
American Slavery and the Holocaust* (Philadelphia: Temple University Press, 1993),
pp. 7, 10, 126, 138–44; and Clarence E. Walker, *We Can't Go Home Again: An Argument
about Afrocentrism* (New York: Oxford University Press, 2001), pp. 113–19.

13. Benjamin B. Ferencz, *Less than Slaves: Jewish Forced Labor and the Quest for Compen-
sation* (Cambridge, Mass.: Harvard University Press, 1979), pp. xvii, 13; Berel Lang,
Holocaust Representation: Art within the Limits of History and Ethics (Baltimore: Johns
Hopkins University Press, 2000), p. 151.

14. "The real horror of the concentration and extermination camps," wrote Arendt, "lies
in the fact that the inmates, even if they happen to keep alive, are more effectively cut
off from the world of the living than if they had died, because terror enforces oblivion." Hannah Arendt, *The Origins of Totalitarianism*, 2nd ed. (1968; rpt. New York:
Harcourt Brace and Co., 1979), pp. 443–44; Wolfgang Sofsky, *The Order of Terror: The
Concentration Camp* (1993), trans. William Templer (Princeton: Princeton University
Press, 1997), pp. 170–72.

15. Thomas Sowell, *Race and Culture: A World View* (New York: Basic Books, 1994),
pp. 186–223, quotation at p. 186.

16. Michael Walzer, *Exodus and Revolution* (New York: Basic Books, 1985), p. 30; Thomas, *Vessels of Evil*, p. 149.

17. William Styron, *Sophie's Choice* (1979; rpt. New York: Vintage, 1992), p. 255; Richard L. Rubenstein, *The Cunning of History: The Holocaust and the American Future* (New York: Harper and Row, 1975), pp. 45–46, 79; William Styron, "Hell Reconsidered," review of *The Cunning of History, New York Review of Books* (1978), rpt. in *This Quiet Dust and Other Writings*, rev. ed. (New York: Vintage, 1993), pp. 110–11. Rubenstein's book is quoted extensively in *Sophie's Choice*. Rubenstein returned the compliment by using Styron's review as an introduction to a new edition of *The Cunning of History* and writing an admiring essay on *Sophie's Choice*, in which he quotes Styron quoting him. See Richard L. Rubenstein, "The South Encounters the Holocaust: William Styron's *Sophie's Choice*," *Michigan Quarterly Review* 20 (Fall 1981), 425–42.

18. John P. Sabini and Mary Silver, "Destroying the Innocent with a Clear Conscience: A Sociopsychology of the Holocaust," in Joel E. Dimsdale, ed., *Survivors, Victims, and Perpetrators: Essays on the Nazi Holocaust* (Washington, D.C.: Hemisphere Publishing, 1980), pp. 329–30.

19. Miller, "Black Anti-Semitism—Jewish Racism," p. 98.

20. Neither would the discovery of equivalent events necessarily change the meaning of the Holocaust. As Berel Lang writes, it would not matter if it was the second or even the fifth time such an event had occurred: "The identity and the number of the victims would remain the same; the same intention and deliberation on the part of the murderers would have been responsible. Nor would such precedents diminish the importance of understanding in historical terms why the Shoah occurred when and as it did, with its specific agents and victims." Christopher Browning, "The Holocaust and History," in Peter Hayes, ed., *Lessons and Legacies: Memory, Memorialization, and Denial* (Evanston, Ill.: Northwestern University Press, 1999), pp. 24–25; Berel Lang, *The Future of the Holocaust: Between History and Memory* (Ithaca, N.Y.: Cornell University Press, 1999), p. 90. For other accounts of the "uniqueness" of the Holocaust, see Stephen T. Katz, *Post-Holocaust Dialogues: Critical Studies in Modern Jewish Thought* (New York: New York University Press, 1983), pp. 287–317; Gavriel D. Rosenfeld, "The Politics of Uniqueness: Reflections on the Recent Polemical Turn in Holocaust and Genocide Scholarship," *Holocaust and Genocide Studies* 13 (Spring 1999), 28–61; Kenneth Seeskin, "What Philosophy Can and Cannot Say about Evil," in Michael L. Morgan, ed., *A Holocaust Reader: Responses to the Nazi Extermination* (New York: Oxford University Press, 2001), pp. 321–33; and, for a harsh critique, Finkelstein, *The Holocaust Industry*, pp. 42–48.

21. John A. Williams, *Clifford's Blues* (Minneapolis: Coffee House Books, 1999), pp. 309, 157, 65, 163, 180. The references are to three ardent southern segregationists: Theodore G. Bilbo, Mississippi governor (for two separate terms in the 1920s) and senator (from 1934 to 1947); James K. Vardaman, also Mississippi governor (1904–08) and senator (1913–18); and Benjamin S. Tillman, South Carolina governor (1890–94) and senator (1894–1918).

22. Ibid., pp. 234, 211.

23. Judy Chicago, *Holocaust Project: From Darkness into Light* (New York: Penguin, 1993), pp. 154–55, plates 18–20.

24. Patricia J. Williams, *The Rooster's Egg: The Persistence of Prejudice* (Cambridge, Mass.: Harvard University Press, 1995), p. 32.

25. Ibid., pp. 208–9.

26. Octavia E. Butler, *Kindred* (1976; rpt. Boston: Beacon Press, 1988), pp. 28–29, 116–17. In another episode Dana carries a book on the heroes of black history—Frederick

Douglass, Nat Turner, Harriet Tubman—back into slave times. The book frightens Rufus, and lest it imperil them, Dana burns it, an act that reminds her of Nazi book burnings (p. 141).

27. Stanley Crouch, "Aunt Medea" (1987), in *Notes of a Hanging Judge: Essays and Reviews, 1979–1989* (New York: Oxford University Press, 1990), p. 205.

28. Malcolm X, speech at Ford Auditorium, Detroit, February 14, 1965, in Malcolm X, *The Final Speeches*, ed. Steve Clark (New York: Pathfinder, 1992), p. 92; H. Rap Brown, *Die Nigger Die!* (New York: Dial, 1969), p. 138; James Forman, "High Tide of Black Resistance" (1967), in *High Tide of Black Resistance and Other Political and Literary Writings* (Seattle: Open Hand, 1994), p. 137.

29. Sam Greenlee, *The Spook Who Sat by the Door* (1969; rpt. Detroit: Wayne State University Press, 1990), pp. 112, 117. Bontemps's lines actually read, "Is there something we have forgotten? some precious thing / We have lost, wandering in strange lands?"

30. Ben Caldwell, *Top Secret or a Few Million After B.C.*, Drama Review 12 (Summer 1968), 49.

31. Gregory's own response: "My answer to genocide, quite simply, is eight black kids— and another baby on the way." Dick Gregory, "My Answer to Genocide," *Ebony* 26 (October 1971), 66–72.

32. Gary Alan Fine and Patricia A. Turner, *Whispers on the Color Line: Rumor and Race in America* (Berkeley: University of California Press, 2001), pp. 157–66; Cecil Williams quoted in "Losing Ground," *Newsweek* 119 (April 6, 1992), 21.

33. Charles Johnson, *Being and Race: Black Writing since 1970* (Bloomington: Indiana University Press, 1988), p. 89.

34. Michael Lerner and Cornel West, *Jews and Blacks: A Dialogue on Race, Religion, and Culture in America* (New York: Plume, 1996), p. 255; Derrick Bell, "Nigger Free," in *Gospel Choirs: Psalms of Survival in an Alien Land Called Home* (New York: Basic Books, 1996), pp. 115–40.

35. Harold Cruse, *The Crisis of the Negro Intellectual: A Historical Analysis of the Failure of Black Leadership* (1967; rpt. New York: Quill, 1984), p. 482.

36. James Baldwin, *The Fire Next Time* (1963; New York: Dell, 1964), pp. 74–75, 113.

37. Ross Posnock, *Color and Culture: Black Writers and the Making of the Modern Intellectual* (Cambridge, Mass.: Harvard University Press, 1998), pp. 224–27.

38. Eddie Ellis, "Semitism in the Ghetto," *Liberator* 6 (January 1966), 6–7; (February 1966), 14–15; (April 1966), 14–16; James Baldwin, "Anti-Semitism and Black Power," *Freedomways* 7 (Winter 1967), 75–77.

39. James Baldwin and Margaret Mead, *A Rap on Race* (1971; rpt. New York: Dell, 1992), pp. 61, 191–92, 196. As he notes in his introduction to *The Price of the Ticket*, Baldwin was aided early on by Jewish editors at magazines strongly identified with Jewish intellectual culture, including Philip Rahv of the *Partisan Review*, Elliot Cohen and Robert Warshaw of *Commentary*, and Saul Levitas of the *New Leader*. James Baldwin, introduction to *The Price of the Ticket: Collected Non-fiction, 1948–1985* (New York: St. Martin's, 1985), p. xiii. See also Morris Dickstein, *Leopards in the Temple: The Transformation of American Fiction, 1945–1970* (Cambridge, Mass.: Harvard University Press, 2002), pp. 181–85.

40. James Baldwin, *No Name on the Street* (1972), in *The Price of the Ticket*, pp. 480, 546; idem, "Notes on the House of Bondage" (1980), ibid., p. 671.

41. James Baldwin, *The Evidence of Things Not Seen* (1985; rpt. New York: Henry Holt, 1995), pp. 85, 102, xv.

42. The Tuskegee experiment had received significant publicity in James H. Jones, *Bad Blood: The Tuskegee Syphilis Experiment* (1981). On the relationship between the Tus-

kegee experiment, the CDC, and the Atlanta murders, see also Bernard Headley *The Atlanta Youth Murders and the Politics of Race* (Carbondale: Southern Illinois University Press, 1998); and Fine and Turner, *Whispers on the Color Line*, pp. 127–31.

43. Baldwin, *The Evidence of Things Not Seen*, pp. 87, xv.

44. Ibid., pp. 45–46, 50.

45. Caryl Phillips, "James Baldwin: The Lure of Hollywood," in *New World Order: Essays* (New York: Vintage, 2002), p. 72. On Baldwin's decline, see, for example, Henry Louis Gates, Jr., "The Welcome Table," in *Thirteen Ways of Looking at a Black Man* (New York: Random House, 1997), pp. 3–20; Stanley Crouch, "The Rage of Race" (1988), in *Notes of a Hanging Judge*, pp. 231–36; and Will Walker, "After The Fire Next Time: James Baldwin's Postconsensus Double Bind," in Eddie S. Glaude, Jr., ed., *Is It Nation Time? Contemporary Essays on Black Power and Black Nationalism* (Chicago: University of Chicago Press, 2002), pp. 215–33. Conceivably, Baldwin's descent into paranoid speculation, as well as his implied identification with Wayne Williams, grew in part from his rejection and ridicule as a gay black man—a "faggot"—by Black Arts masculinists such as Baraka and Cleaver.

46. Baldwin, *Evidence of Things Not Seen*, pp. xiii–xiv.

47. Ibid., p. 78.

48. Toni Morrison, "A Bench by the Road," quoted in Nellie Y. McKay, introduction to William L. Andrews and Nellie Y. McKay, eds., *Toni Morrison's Beloved: A Casebook* (New York: Oxford University Press, 1999), p. 3.

49. Toni Morrison, *Beloved* (1987; rpt. New York: Plume 1988), p. 199.

50. Both books deal with a mother's guilt-ridden encounter with history through the resurrection of a dead daughter, each referred to as "beloved"; both explore the collapse of language, the capacity for representation, in the face of extreme trauma and do so by linking it to the collapse of maternal nurture, the capacity for human generation; and both introduce a scholarly analyst—Dr. Tree in *The Shawl* and Schoolteacher in *Beloved*—whose purportedly scientific paradigms of analysis, in each instance driven by the residue of scientific racism, belittle the tragedies they attempt to explain. As Emily Budick notes, *The Shawl*'s publication as a novella in 1989 may have been prompted in part by the appearance of *Beloved* in 1987, but the two parts of the novella, published in the *New Yorker* in 1980 and 1983, respectively, suggest also that Morrison may have borrowed elements of her novel from Ozick. See Emily Miller Budick, *Blacks and Jews in Literary Conversation* (New York: Cambridge University Press, 1998), pp. 209–11.

51. The story of Garner was published in the antislavery paper *The Liberator* under the title "A Visit to the Slave Mother Who Killed Her Child." Morrison apparently learned about the case while editing, at Random House, Gerda Lerner's documentary anthology *Black Women in White America* (1972), which, like *The Black Book* (1972) by M. A. Harris, reprinted the 1856 article about the case. See Samuel J. May, "Margaret Garner and Seven Others," from *The Fugitive Slave Law and Its Victims* (1856), rpt. in Andrews and McKay, *Toni Morrison's Beloved*, pp. 25–36; and Steven Weisenberger, *Modern Medea: A Family Story of Slavery and Child-Murder from the Old South* (New York: Hill and Wang, 1998), pp. 161, 288n.

52. Morrison, *Beloved*, pp. 62, 210–11.

53. The resonant description of Auschwitz as the *anus mundi*, used by keepers and prisoners alike, was coined by Heinz Thilo, a Nazi doctor, and appears to have sprung less from the camp's filth and stench, what Terrence Des Pres has characterized as its "excremental assault," than from the Nazi vision of extermination as the solution to a biomedical problem of racial pollution. In either case, however, it meant, in Primo

Levi's words, that Auschwitz was the "ultimate drainage site of the German universe." Terrence Des Pres, *The Survivor: An Anatomy of Life in the Death* Camps (New York: Oxford University Press, 1976), pp. 53–71; Robert Jay Lifton, *The Nazi Doctors: Medical Killing and the Psychology of Genocide* (New York: Basic Books, 1986), p. 147; Primo Levi, *The Drowned and the Saved* (1986), trans. Raymond Rosenthal (1988; rpt. New York: Vintage, 1989), p. 65.

54. The "drowned," said Levi in an earlier book, were "an anonymous mass, continually renewed and always identical . . . One hesitates to call them living: one hesitates to call their death death, in the face of which they have no fear, as they are too tired to understand." Levi, *The Drowned and the Saved*, pp. 83–84; idem, *Survival in Auschwitz: The Nazi Assault on Humanity* (1958), trans. Stuart Woolf (New York: Collier Books, 1961), p. 82. As Giorgio Agamben elaborates, the true witnesses are the "drowned," those who stood at the threshold between the human and non-human but "did not bear witness and cannot bear witness." The survivors speak in their stead, bearing witness to their "missing testimony." Giorgio Agamben, *Remnants of Auschwitz: The Witness and the Archive*, trans. Daniel Heller-Roazen (New York: Zone Books, 1999), pp. 34, 55.

55. George Jackson to Fay Stender, April 4, 1970, in George Jackson, *Soledad Brother: The Prison Letters of George Jackson* (Chicago: Lawrence Hill Books, 1994), pp. 233–34.

56. Marianne Hirsch, "Surviving Images: Holocaust Photographs and the Work of Postmemory," *Yale Journal of Criticism* 14 (Fall 2001), 8–10.

57. Unlike Morrison, Baraka captures the painful margin between dehumanization and dignity in a cacophonous mélange of sound—the "hummmmmmm" of African modal chanting, the beating of drums, children crying, elders calling on African gods, warriors calling for freedom—all of it a language of mourning and defiance beyond the comprehension of the white slavers. Amiri Baraka, *Slave Ship: A Historical Pageant*, in *The Motion of History and Other Plays* (New York: William Morrow, 1978), pp. 135–38.

58. Toni Morrison cited in Bonnie Angelo, "The Pain of Being Black" (1989), in *Conversations with Toni Morrison*, ed. Danielle Taylor-Guthrie (Jackson: University of Mississippi Press, 1994), p. 257.

59. "The Nazi revolution was an exercise in social engineering on a grandiose scale," argues Bauman. Like the Stalinists, but with a more precise design, the Nazis "attempted to reach the most ambitious aims of the civilizing process. . . . They showed what the rationalizing, designing, controlling dreams and efforts of modern civilization are able to accomplish if not mitigated, curbed, or counteracted." Bauman, *Modernity and the Holocaust*, pp. 66, 91–93.

60. Paul Gilroy, *The Black Atlantic: Modernity and Double Consciousness* (Cambridge, Mass.: Harvard University Press, 1993), pp. 221–22.

61. Toni Morrison, "Living Memory: A Meeting with Toni Morrison," in Paul Gilroy, *Small Acts: Thoughts on the Politics of Black Culture* (London: Serpent's Tail, 1993), p. 178; Ulrich B. Phillips, *Life and Labor in the Old South* (1929; rpt. Boston: Little, Brown, 1963), p. 160; E. Franklin Frazier, *The Negro Family in the United States* (Chicago: University of Chicago Press, 1939), p. 21; Morrison, interview in *The Economist* 347 (June 6, 1998), 83.

62. Geoffrey Hartman, "Public Memory and Its Discontents," *Raritan* 13 (Spring 1994), 35; Morrison, *Beloved*, p. 36.

63. S. E. Anderson, *The Black Holocaust for Beginners* (New York: Writers and Readers Publishing, 1995), p. 1.

64. Robinson, *The Debt*, p. 216.

65. Na'im Akbar, *Chains and Images in Psychological Slavery* (1984), quoted in Stephen Howe, *Afrocentrism: Mythical Pasts and Imagined Homes* (London: Verso, 1998), p. 266; *The Secret Relationship between Blacks and Jews* (Boston, Mass.: Nation of Islam Historical Research Department, 1991), p. vii.

66. Des Pres, *The Survivor*, pp. 49–50.

67. John Edgar Wideman, *Fatheralong* (New York: Random House, 1994), pp. ix–x.

68. Ibid., p. 106.

69. Police attempted to serve arrest warrants on four MOVE members. Rebuffed, they fired tear gas and smoke projectiles, and, when MOVE fired on police, ten thousand rounds of ammunition over a ninety-minute period from automatic weapons, machine guns, and antitank guns. Insertion teams failed to penetrate the heavily fortified house, at which point a helicopter dropped a satchel of explosives on the roof bunker, with the intent of dislodging it and opening the building to police penetration. The bunker, which held a five-gallon can of gasoline, ignited a fire that destroyed sixty-one homes and damaged more than one hundred others. Despite two grand jury investigations, no indictments were handed down against city officials, although the city eventually paid some $24 million in civil suits to MOVE members for the deaths of the children. See Hizkias Assefa and Paul Wahrhaftig, *The MOVE Crisis in Philadelphia: Extremist Groups and Conflict Resolution* (Pittsburgh: University of Pittsburgh Press, 1990); and Robin Wagner-Pacifici, *Discourse and Destruction: The City of Philadelphia versus MOVE* (Chicago: University of Chicago Press, 1994).

70. John Edgar Wideman, *Philadelphia Fire* (1990; rpt. New York: Vintage, 1991), p. 140.

71. Simba, whose first name means "lion" and whose last name is a Bantu word that may be translated, according to Janheinz Jahn, as "man" but more significantly embraces "living and dead, ancestors and deified ancestors: gods," is at once mythic and intimately personal. As a "wild animal," Simba is also reminiscent of "Wile Child" in Alice Walker's *Meridian* (1976), whose death is the catalyst for the protagonist's coming to political consciousness at the dawn of the civil rights movement; and he is a variation, looking ahead two years, on Bob Marley's "Iron Lion Zion" ("I have to run like a fugitive to save the life I live, / I'm going to be iron like a lion in Zion"). But his name most proximately recalls Simba Wachanga, the "Young Lions," the security force for Maulana Karenga's US Organization. Wideman, *Philadelphia Fire*, pp. 33, 88; Janheinz Jahn, *Muntu: African Culture and the Western World*, trans. Marjorie Grene (1961; rpt. New York: Grove Weidenfeld, 1989), p. 18; Bob Marley, "Iron Lion Zion," *Songs of Freedom* (Polygram Records, 1992); William L. Van Deburg, *New Day in Babylon: The Black Power Movement and American Culture, 1965–1975* (Chicago: University of Chicago Press, 1992), pp. 171–74.

72. Wideman, *Philadelphia Fire*, pp. 7–8.

73. Wideman, *Fatheralong*, p. 65.

74. H. Bruce Franklin, *Prison Literature in America: The Victim as Criminal and Artist*, rev. ed. (New York: Oxford University Press, 1989), pp. 233–76; Van Deburg, *New Day in Babylon*, pp. 106–11.

75. George Jackson to Fay Stender, April 1970, in *Soledad Brother*, p. 18; John Edgar Wideman, "Doing Time, Marking Race," in *Behind the Razor Wire: Portrait of a Contemporary American Prison System*, photographs and text by Michael Jacobson-Hardy, essays by Wideman et al. (New York: New York University Press, 1999), pp. 13–17.

76. Wideman, *Fatheralong*, pp. 75, 82. The allusion here is to Baldwin's *No Name in the Street* (1972), a book in which Nazi Germany serves as a prototype for America on a number of occasions and in which, as noted in the previous chapter, blacks are "the despised and slaughtered children of the great western house—nameless and un-

nameable bastards," and the nation is "one vast, howling, unprecedented orphanage." Baldwin, *No Name in the Streeet*, p. 547.

77. Irving Howe, *World of Our Fathers: The Journey of the East European Jews to America and the Life They Found and Made* (New York: Simon and Schuster, 1976).

78. John Edgar Wideman, 1991 interview with Rebekah Presson, in *Conversations with John Edgar Wideman*, ed. Bonnie TuSmith (Jackson: University Press of Mississippi, 1998), p. 110; Wideman, *Philadelphia Fire*, pp. 88, 163–65.

79. Wideman, *Philadelphia Fire*, pp. 165–66.

80. Ibid., pp. 93–94, 30, 88.

81. Wideman quoted on back cover of James Baldwin, *Evidence of Things Not Seen* (1985; rpt. New York: Henry Holt, 1995).

82. Wideman, *Philadelphia Fire*, pp. 155–59.

83. Baldwin, *The Fire Next Time*, p. 14; Frazier, "In the City of Destruction," in *The Negro Family in the United States*, pp. 269–351.

84. Bob Marley, "Jump Nyabinghi," *Confrontation* (Polygram Records, 1983). On Marley's usage, see Gregory Stephens, *On Racial Frontiers: The New Culture of Frederick Douglass, Ralph Ellison, and Bob Marley* (New York: Cambridge University Press, 1999), p. 212.

85. Glenn C. Loury, *On the Role of Black Intellectuals* (Claremont, Calif.: Center for Humanistic Studies, Monograph Series 8, 1996), pp. 14–15; Wideman, *Philadelphia Fire*, p. 5.

86. Wideman, *Philadelphia Fire*, p. 141.

87. Ibid., pp. 170, 177.

88. Ibid., p. 156.

89. Ibid., p. 49.

90. André Schwarz-Bart, *The Last of the Just* (1959), trans. Stephen Becker (New York: Atheneum, 1960), pp. 373–74. On the *Lamed-Vav* and Schwartz-Bart's novel, see also Gershom Scholem, "The Tradition of the Thirty-six Hidden Just Men," trans. Michael A. Meyer, in *The Messianic Idea in Judaism and Other Essays on Jewish Spirituality* (1971; rpt. New York: Schocken, 1995), pp. 251–56.

91. Wideman, *Philadelphia Fire*, pp. 188–99.

92. Schwarz-Bart, *The Last of the Just*, p. 174. I am indebted here to Theodore Solotaroff, "The Path to Auschwitz" (a review of *The Last of the Just*), *Commentary* 30 (December 1960), 548–51.

93. "Declaration and Recommendations for a Programme of Action," Africa Regional Preparatory Conference for the World Conference against Racism, Racial Discrimination, Xenophobia and Related Intolerance, Dakar, Senegal, January 22–24, 2001, in Raymond Winbush, ed., *Should America Pay? Slavery and the Raging Debate on Reparations* (New York: HarperCollins, 2003), p. 351.

94. Since 1995 the state of Florida has paid some $2 million to victims of the 1923 white race riot in Rosewood in which a community of two hundred blacks was destroyed, with an undetermined number of residents killed, the rest driven from town, and their property confiscated. The state paid $150,000 each to survivors, as well as compensation for lost property to other families and scholarships for descendants and other minorities. In a similar case, the Tulsa Race Riot Commission recommended compensation to survivors of that city's riot of 1921, in which up to three hundred black people may have been killed and thirty-five square blocks of the prosperous black community of Greenwood were burned to the ground. When the state legislature chose to ignore the recommendation, survivors sued. On Rosewood, see Michael

D'Orso, *Like Judgment Day: The Ruin and Redemption of a Town Called Rosewood* (New York: G. P. Putnam's Sons, 1996); on Tulsa, see James S. Hirsch, *Riot and Remembrance: The Tulsa Race War and Its Legacy* (Boston: Houghton Mifflin, 2002).

95. Founded in 2001 and building on the pioneering legal work of Deadria C. Farmer-Paellmann, the Reparations Coordinating Committee, which has included Harvard law professor Charles Ogletree and attorney Johnnie Cochran among others, began pursuing lawsuits that target corporations, insurance firms, banks, newspapers, and even universities that directly or indirectly profited from slave labor, the ownership of slaves, or the pursuit of runaway slaves. Statutes of limitation, the legality of slavery, and the difficulty of demonstrating harm to living descendants present formidable barriers, but as in the case of the compensation for Nazi slave labor, the litigants no doubt count on the willingness of parties to settle rather than face the spotlight of trial publicity. Those sued may likewise demonstrate an interest in redirecting legal responsibility toward government, in which case the suits might act as a prelude to a formal governmental apology and the authorization of reparations. As of late 2003, both Chicago and Los Angeles had enacted ordinances requiring companies bidding for city contracts to disclose if they had profited from slavery, and both Illinois and California required insurers to disclose if they issued policies to slaveholders. Under its African American president, Ruth Simmons, Brown University undertook a study in 2004 to determine whether reparations should be paid, and if so what kind and on what basis, for any enrichment of the university that could be traced to slavery or the slave trade.

96. House Resolution 40 (so numbered to evoke "forty acres and a mule," General William T. Sherman's unfulfilled 1865 promise to freed slaves of the South) would simply establish a "Commission to Study Reparation Proposals for African Americans," whose charge would be to recommend appropriate remedies, potentially including an apology and compensation. See John Conyers, "The Commission to Study Reparations Proposals," in Roy L. Brooks, ed., *When Sorry Isn't Enough: The Controversy over Apologies and Reparations for Human Injustice* (New York: New York University Press, 1999), pp. 367–69. For overviews, see Brooks, *When Sorry Isn't Enough,* pp. 317–438; Robin D. G. Kelley, *Freedom Dreams: The Black Radical Imagination* (Boston: Beacon Press, 2002), pp. 110–34; Elazar Barkan, *The Guilt of Nations: Restitution and Negotiating Historical Injustices* (New York: Norton, 2000), pp. 283–307; and Winbush, *Should America Pay?*

97. "Even though we (Caucasians) are dependent on the Blackman for his creativity and spiritual strength, we must accept separation as the inevitable result of slavery. Reparation and separation are the first step to a positive, healing, self-determining future of unlimited progress for the Blackman." Ida Hakim et al., *Reparations, the Cure for America's Race Problem* (Hampton, Va.: U.B. and U.S. Communication Systems, 1994), p. 32.

98. C[larence] J. Munford, "Reparations: Strategic Considerations for Black Americans," in Brooks, *When Sorry Isn't Enough,* p. 423. See also Clarence J. Munford, *Race and Reparations: A Black Perspective for the Twenty-First Century* (Trenton, N.J.: Africa World Press, 1996).

99. David Horowitz, *Uncivil Wars: The Controversy over Reparations for Slavery* (San Francisco: Encounter Books, 2002), p. 15.

100. In 2003 it was announced that Dr. Nabil Hilmi, the dean of the Faculty of Law at the University of Al-Zaqaziq in Egypt, along with a group of Egyptian expatriates in Switzerland, was preparing a lawsuit against "all the Jews of the world" seeking restitution

for the supposed theft of more than three hundred tons of gold and other property during the "so-called 'great exodus of the Jews from Pharaonic Egypt'" (the current value being equivalent, Hilmi was said to argue, to at least a thousand trillion tons of gold). See "Egyptian Jurists to Sue 'The Jews' for Compensation for 'Trillions' of Tons of Gold Allegedly Stolen during Exodus from Egypt," *Middle East Media Research Institute,* www.memri.org/bin/opener_latest.cgi?ID=SD55603 (accessed August 22, 2003).

101. Boris I. Bittker, *The Case for Black Reparations* (New York: Random House, 1973), pp. 27–29. For another contemporary response to the Black Manifesto, see Arnold Schuchter, *Reparations: The Black Manifesto and Its Challenge to America* (Philadelphia: Lippincott, 1970).

102. See www.ncobra.com (accessed June 30, 2003).

103. Horowitz, *Uncivil Wars,* p. 124.

104. Robert Westley, "Many Billions Gone: Is It Time to Reconsider the Case for Black Reparations?," *Boston College Law Review* 40 (December 1998), rpt. in Winbush, *Should America Pay?*, pp. 129, 134; Martha Minow, *Between Vengeance and Forgiveness: Facing History after Genocide and Mass Violence* (Boston: Beacon Press, 1998), p. 117. On remedy and injury, see also Carl Gutiérrez-Jones, *Critical Race Narratives: A Study of Race, Rhetoric, and Injury* (New York: New York University Press, 2001); and Nancy Rosenblum, ed., *Breaking the Cycles of Hatred: Memory, Law, and Repair* (Princeton: Princeton University Press, 2002).

105. John McWhorter, "Against Reparations," *New Republic* 225 (July 23, 2001), 36; Mari Matsuda, "Looking to the Bottom: Critical Legal Studies and Reparations," in Kimberle Crenshaw et al., eds., *Critical Race Theory: The Key Writings That Formed the Movement* (New York: New Press, 1995), p. 74; Leon Wieseltier, "Scar Tissue," *New Republic* 200 (June 5, 1989), 20.

106. Dan Pagis, *The Selected Poetry of Dan Pagis,* trans. Stephen Mitchell (Berkeley: University of California Press, 1989), p. 35.

107. Plans for a national museum of African American history and culture have been formulated and debated since early in the twentieth century. Thanks to the renewed efforts of congressmen John Lewis of Georgia, J. C. Watts, Jr., of Oklahoma, and others, in 2003 both the House and the Senate passed legislation authorizing a museum to be erected on or near the national mall, probably adjacent to the United States Capitol, which was itself built in part with the labor of black American slaves. "Long Quest, Unlikely Allies," *New York Times,* June 29, 2003, 1, 24. On failed plans for a "National African-American Museum," debated between 1984 and 1994, see Faith Davis Ruffins, "Culture Wars Won and Lost, Part II: The National African-American Museum Project," *Radical History Review* 70 (Winter 1998), 78–101.

108. Jewel Crawford, et al., "Reparations and Health Care for African Americans: Repairing the Damage from the Legacy of Slavery," in Winbush, *Should America Pay?*, pp. 276–78.

109. Bebe Moore Campbell, *What You Owe Me* (New York: G. P. Putnam's Sons, 2001), p. 443.

110. Tony Martin, *The Jewish Onslaught: Dispatches from the Wellesley Battlefront* (Dover, Mass.: Majority Press, 1993), p. 78.

111. Campbell, *What You Owe Me,* p. 533.

112. Ibid., pp. 110–11, 503.

113. Ibid., p. 295.

7. HOLOCAUST II: OTHER PEOPLE'S NIGHTMARES

1. Alfred Uhry, *Driving Miss Daisy* (New York: Theatre Communications Group, 1987), p. 47.
2. Richard Powers, *The Time of Our Singing* (New York: Farrar, Straus and Giroux, 2003), pp. 345, 304–5.
3. Ibid., pp. 476, 425.
4. Ishmael Reed, *Reckless Eyeballing* (New York: St. Martin's, 1986), p. 4.
5. Ibid., p. 44.
6. Ibid., pp. 5, 49.
7. Ibid., p. 104.
8. See, for example, Saul S. Friedman, *The Oberammergau Passion Play: A Lance against Civilization* (Carbondale: Southern Illinois University Press, 1984); and James Shapiro, *Oberammergau: The Troubling Story of the World's Most Famous Passion Play* (New York: Pantheon, 2000).
9. All quotations are from Darius James, *Negrophobia: An Urban Parable* (New York: St. Martin's, 1992), pp. 92–100.
10. Jeffrey Shandler, *While America Watches: Televising the Holocaust* (New York: Oxford University Press, 1999), pp. 10–15.
11. Paul Beatty, *The White-Boy Shuffle* (1996; rpt. New York: Picador, 2001), p. 40.
12. Paul Beatty, *Tuff* (New York: Alfred A. Knopf, 2000), pp. 95, 93, 48, 217.
13. Tony Kushner, *Angels in America, Part Two: Perestroika,* rev. ed. (New York: Theatre Communications Group, 1996), pp. 24, 75–7, 56–57.
14. Lore Segal, *Her First American* (1985; rpt. New York: New Press, 1990), p. 16, 142.
15. Ibid., p. 194.
16. Lore Segal, *Other People's Houses* (1963; New York: New Press, 1990), pp. 303–4.
17. Lore Segal, "The Bough Breaks," in David Rosenberg, ed., *Testimony: Contemporary Writers Make the Holocaust Personal* (New York: Random House, 1989), p. 248; Segal, *Her First American,* p. 264. On not remembering and misremembering, see also Lore Segal, "Memory: The Problems of Imagining the Past," in Berel Lang, ed., *Writing and the Holocaust* (New York: Holmes and Meier, 1988), pp. 58–65.
18. Segal, "The Bough Breaks," p. 246.
19. Segal, *Her First American,* pp. 29, 255.
20. Ibid., pp. 261–63.
21. Ibid., pp. 263, 273.
22. Ibid., p. 125.
23. Segal, *Other People's Houses,* p. xii; idem, *Her First American,* pp. 142, 151–53.
24. Segal, *Her First American,* p. 287.
25. Lenora Berson, *The Negroes and the Jews* (New York: Random House, 1971), p. 193.
26. Nelson was acquitted of murder in a state trial in 1992, then convicted in a federal trial in 1998. A new trial was ordered in 2002, when it was determined on appeal that the judge had improperly empaneled the jury in order to maintain a balance of Jews and blacks. Having finally confessed to the murder, Nelson was convicted in 2003.
27. Wendy Wasserstein, *An American Daughter* (New York: Harcourt Brace, 1998), pp. 8, 34.
28. Jonathan Rieder, "Reflections on Crown Heights: Interpretive Dilemmas and Black-

Jewish Conflict," in Jerome A. Chanes, ed., *Antisemitism in America Today: Outspoken Experts Explode the Myths* (New York: Birch Lane Press, 1995), pp. 348–84. According to one analysis, which runs contrary to other accounts, news coverage favored the black community, even though reports dwelled on blacks portraying the Lubavitchers as Ku Klux Klan and purveyors of apartheid, or asserting that Hitler had failed to "finish the job." See William McGowan, *Coloring the News: How Crusading for Diversity Has Corrupted American Journalism* (San Francisco: Encounter Books, 2001), pp. 61–62.

29. It is interesting to note, however, that in the 1980s the Hasidic Jews of Crown Heights had been denied eligibility by the Small Business Administration for participation in its minority business set-aside program on the grounds that granting them disadvantaged status, despite the support of influential Jewish members of Congress and despite the fact that they were demonstrably victims of anti-Semitism, and many of them Holocaust survivors, might establish an impermissible religious classification. The real opposition, however, came from blacks, likewise including influential members of Congress, who feared dilution of affirmative action benefits directed toward blacks. Hugh Davis Graham, *Collision Course: The Strange Convergence of Affirmative Action and Immigration Policy in America* (New York: Oxford University Press, 2002), pp. 147–48.

30. Ethan Goffman, *Imagining Each Other: Blacks and Jews in Contemporary American Literature* (Albany: State University of New York Press, 2000), p. 219.

31. Anna Deavere Smith, *Fires in the Mirror: Crown Heights, Brooklyn, and Other Identities* (New York: Anchor Books, 1993), pp. xxvii; xxxiii, xli. On Smith's strategies and her use of mirroring (facing) and disjunctive structures, see also Adam Zachary Newton, *Facing Black and Jew: Literature as Public Space in Twentieth-Century America* (New York: Cambridge University Press, 1999), pp. 158–68; and Kimberly Rae Connor, *Imagining Grace: Liberating Theologies in the Slave Narrative Tradition* (Urbana: University of Illinois Press, 2000), pp. 210–20.

32. Smith, *Fires in the Mirror*, p. 62. See also Letty Cottin Pogrebin, *Deborah, Golda, and Me: Being Female and Jewish in America* (1991; rpt. New York: Anchor, 1992), pp. 304–5.

33. Smith, *Fires in the Mirror*, pp. 54–55, 57–58.

34. Ibid., pp. 50–51.

35. Quoted in Rieder, "Reflections on Crown Heights," p. 374.

8. Spooks

1. Yiddish (and German) for "another" or "another thing," "*noch*" has the connotation in this case of "on top of everything else." Leo Rosten, *The Joys of Yiddish* (1968; rpt. New York: Pocket Books, 1970), pp. 269–70.

2. Julius Lester, *Lovesong: Becoming a Jew* (New York: Arcade, 1988), pp. 20.

3. Ibid., p. 22.

4. Ibid., pp. 1, 189.

5. "When we say that a people 'remembers' we are really saying that a past has been actively transmitted to the present generation and that this past has been accepted as meaningful." "Forgetting" occurs when groups, whether through an abrupt break or a process of erosion, fail to transmit what they know of their past to posterity. Yosef Hayim Yerushalmi, *Zakhor: Jewish History and Jewish Memory* (1982; rpt. New York: Schocken, 1989), p. 109.

6. Lester, *Lovesong*, pp. 161, 89, 123.

7. James McBride, *The Color of Water: A Black Man's Tribute to His White Mother* (New York: Riverhead, 1996), pp. 40, 80, 2, 218.

8. Ibid., pp. 85, 29, 31–32, 87, 21, 51.

9. Ibid., pp. 224, 87, 103.

10. Ibid., pp. 284, 274, 43.

11. Ibid., p. 277.

12. Ibid., p. 287.

13. Lester, *Lovesong*, pp. 45, 25.

14. At the least, Lester appears concerned about his masculinity. Following the circumcision he undergoes upon his conversion, he allows that it is "as if something within me has been set free." But he is greatly relieved, he reports, to find that he is still sexually functional. Indeed, in reporting emphatically that "IT WORKS BETTER THAN EVER!!," Lester seems to play comically upon the obverse stereotypes of Jewish and black masculinity that we have encountered in *Mr. Sammler's Planet* and *The Tenants*. Lester, *Lovesong*, pp. 215, 218.

15. Ibid., p. 33.

16. Ibid., pp. 61, 64. Cf. Julius Lester, "A Response," in Nat Hentoff, *Black Anti-Semitism and Jewish Racism* (New York: Richard W. Baron, 1969), p. 232.

17. Lester, *Lovesong*, p. 236. See Chapter 1 for further discussion of Lester's reaction to the event.

18. Ibid., p. 44.

19. Ibid., pp. 58, 30.

20. Ibid., pp. 37, 192, 244, 1, 225.

21. Daniel Bell, "Reflections on Jewish Identity," *Commentary* (June 1961), rpt. in Peter I. Rose, ed., *The Ghetto and Beyond: Essays on Jewish Life in America* (New York: Random House, 1969), p. 475.

22. Philip Roth, *The Human Stain* (Boston: Houghton Mifflin, 2000), p. 6.

23. Ibid., pp. 15–16.

24. Ibid., pp. 97, 131, 109, 131–32.

25. Bernard Malamud, *The Tenants* (1971; rpt. New York: Penguin 1972), p. 105; Roth, *The Human Stain*, pp. 155, 139; James Weldon Johnson, *Autobiography of an Ex-Coloured Man* (1912; rpt. New York: Hill and Wang, 1960), p. 211.

26. Philip Roth, "After Eight Books" (interview with Joyce Carol Oates, 1974), in *Reading Myself and Others*, new ed. (New York: Penguin, 1985), p. 109. Cf. Ada Savin, "Exposure and Concealment in *The Human Stain*," in Paule Lévy and Ada Savin, eds., *Philip Roth: Profils Américains* (Montpellier, France: Université Paul-Valéry Montpellier III, 2003), pp. 185–91.

27. Gunnar Myrdal, *An American Dilemma: The Negro Problem and Modern Democracy*, 2 vols. (1944; rpt. New Brunswick, N.J.: Transaction, 1996), I, 117.

28. Ralph Ellison, *Invisible Man* (1952; rpt. New York: Vintage, 1981), p. 3. On Fanon's thesis, see Chapters 1 and 6; on Fanon and *The Human Stain*, see Michael T. Gilmore, *Surface and Depth: The Quest for Legibility in American Culture* (New York: Oxford University Press, 2003), pp. 173–75.

29. Ralph Ellison, "Change the Joke and Slip the Yoke" (1958), in *Shadow and Act* (1964; rpt. New York: Vintage, 1971), p. 55.

30. Anatole Broyard, "Portrait of the Inauthentic Negro," *Commentary* 10 (July 1950), 56–59, 63.

31. As Gates puts it, "We give lip service to the idea of the writer who happens to be black, but had anyone, in the postwar era, ever seen such a thing?" Henry Louis Gates,

Jr., "The Passing of Anatole Broyard," in *Thirteen Ways of Looking at a Black Man* (New York: Random House, 1997), pp. 181, 208.

32. Roth's remarks were made at a 1963 conference in Israel, where he went on to assert that he had inherited "no body of law, no body of learning and no language, and finally, no Lord," which meant that, inheriting only "a psychology, and not a culture and not a history in its totality," he had to "invent the Jew." See Philip Roth, "Second Dialogue in Israel" (1963), quoted in Louis Harap, *In the Mainstream: The Jewish Presence in Twentieth-Century American Literature, 1950s–1980s* (New York: Greenwood Press, 1987), p. 136.

33. Jonathan Freedman, *The Temple of Culture: Assimilation and Anti-Semitism in Literary Anglo-America* (New York: Oxford University Press, 2000), p. 205; William Styron, *Sophie's Choice* (1979; rpt. New York: Vintage, 1992), p. 125.

34. Gershom Scholem quoted in David Remnick, "Into the Clear: Philip Roth Puts Turbulence in Its Place," *New Yorker* 76 (May 8, 2000), 85. Less forcefully, *Portnoy's Complaint* signaled to Irving Howe "an end to [the] philo-Semitism in American culture" created by guilt over the Holocaust. Irving Howe, "Philip Roth Reconsidered," *Commentary* 54 (December 1972), 69–77.

35. James E. Young, *Writing and Rewriting the Holocaust: Narrative and the Consequences of Interpretation* (Bloomington: Indiana University Press, 1988), p. 110.

36. Garson Kanin, the play's first director, ruminated in 1979 that Anne, like Peter Pan and Mona Lisa, "remains forever adolescent . . . she remains for us ever a shining star, a radiant presence who, during her time of terror and humiliation and imprisonment, was able to find it within herself to write in her immortal diary, 'in spite of everything I still believe that people are good at heart.'" Garson Kanin, *Newsweek* 93 (June 25, 1979), quoted in Alvin H. Rosenfeld, "Popularization and Memory: The Case of Anne Frank," in Peter Hayes, ed., *Lessons and Legacies: The Meaning of the Holocaust in a Changing World* (Evanston, Ill.: Northwestern University Press, 1991), p. 253.

37. Marie Syrkin quoted in Philip Roth, "Imagining Jews" (1974), in *Reading Myself and Others*, p. 300; Roth, interview with Hermione Lee (1984), ibid., p. 166. On Roth's treatment of Anne Frank sentimentality, see also Jeffrey Rubin-Dorsky, "Philip Roth's *The Ghost Writer*: Literary Heritage and Jewish Irreverence," *Studies in American Jewish Literature* 8 (Fall 1989), 168–85.

38. Dan Issac, "Roth's Fictive Imagination," *Midstream* 27 (March 1981), 48.

39. Philip Roth, "'I Always Wanted You to Admire My Fasting'; or, Looking at Kafka" (1973), in *Reading Myself and Others*, p. 315.

40. Ibid., pp. 312–13.

41. Roth, *The Human Stain*, p. 108.

42. Ross Posnock, "Purity and Danger: On Philip Roth," *Raritan* 21 (Fall 2001), 94; Roth, *The Human Stain*, pp. 334–35.

43. Roth, *The Human Stain*, p. 242.

44. Ibid., p. 108.

45. Roth, "Imagining Jews," p. 301.

46. Roth, "Writing about Jews," p. 220.

47. Roth, *The Human Stain*, p. 184.

48. Ibid., pp. 290, 336, 213. On Coleman Silk's secrecy as his identity, see Amy Hungerford, *The Holocaust of Texts: Genocide, Literature, and Personification* (Chicago: University of Chicago Press, 2003), pp. 144–45.

49. Peter Wood, *Diversity: The Invention of a Concept* (San Francisco: Encounter Books,

2003), pp. 118–20, 134–37. Cf. David Hollinger, *Postethnic America: Beyond Multiculturalism*, rev. ed. (New York: Basic Books, 1996), pp. 183–89.

50. Roth, *The Human Stain*, pp. 145, 328.

51. Ibid., p. 325.

52. Ibid., pp. 131–32.

53. Lani Guinier and Gerald Torres, *The Miner's Canary: Enlisting Race, Resisting Power, Transforming Democracy* (Cambridge, Mass.: Harvard University Press, 2002), p. 11.

54. Lawrence Levine, *The Opening of the American Mind: Canons, Culture, and History* (Boston: Beacon Press, 1996), p. 137.

55. Franz Boas, "The Problem of the American Negro," *Yale Review* 10 (1921), 395.

56. L. D. Reddick, "Anti-Semitism among Negroes," in Jack Salzman, ed., *Bridges and Boundaries: African Americans and American Jews* (New York: George Braziller, 1992), p. 79; Sanford Goldner, *The Negro People and the Fight for Negro Rights* (Los Angeles: Committee for Negro-Jewish Relations, 1953), pp 5, 53.

57. Ralph Ellison, "Perspective of Literature" (1976), in *Going to the Territory* (New York: Random House, 1986), p. 335.

58. Samuel G. Freedman, "An Unlikely Friendship, an Unusual Morning Show," *New York Times,* December 22, 2002, B48.

59. Tom Tugend, "One-Woman Bridge," *Los Angeles Times,* March 14, 2004, E4; Cookie Lommel, "Operation Unity's Kibbutz Program," California Association of Human Rights Organizations Newsletter (December 1997–January 1998), http://www.cahro.org/html/oppuntiy.html (accessed March 25, 2004).

60. Elie Wiesel quoted in Jervis Anderson, *Bayard Rustin: Troubles I've Seen, A Biography* (New York: HarperCollins, 1997), p. 341.

Acknowledgments

The dedication records my renewed debt to my most exacting and beloved reader.

I would also like to thank the following friends and colleagues for reading various parts of this book in manuscript. All gave me much think about and to correct, even those who responded to portions of a work in progress that did not find a place in the published book. None of these kind readers, of course, is responsible for the remaining mistakes and shortcomings in my arguments. Whether or not they agree with the final results, I am indebted to Carol Bakhos, Sara Blair, Emily Budick, William Cain, Sharon Cameron, Eric Cheyfitz, Gary Fine, Rena Fraden, Gregg Crane, Ernest Frankel, Jonathan Freedman, Keith Gandal, Allison Graham, Janet Hadda, Susan Herbst, Susannah Heschel, Peter Hayes, David Hollinger, Amy Hungerford, Greg Jackson, Michal Lemberger, Nancy MacLean, Wayne Mixon, Wilson Moses, Elisa New, Max and Estelle Novak, Sharon Oster, Ross Posnock, Murray Roston, Mark Seltzer, Carl Smith, Michael Staub, Mark Christian Thompson, Alan Trachtenberg, Alan Wald, Cindy Weinstein, Hana Wirth-Nesher, and an anonymous reader engaged by Harvard University Press. For good counsel, tips, and answers on one point or another, I also thank Amanda Busch, Justin Cammy, Michael Colacurcio, Donald Cosentino, Andrea Grossman, Milly Heyd, Michael Kramer, Jacob Lassner, John Lowe, Susan Mizruchi, Brook Thomas, and Richard Yarborough.

As this book unfolded, over a long period of time, I had the opportunity to present various parts of it to audiences at the following institutions: Arizona State University, Bar-Ilan University, the Bread Loaf School of English, the California Institute of Technology, Dartmouth College, Hampshire College, Indiana State University, Louisiana State University, National Taiwan University, Northern Illinois University, Northwestern University, Palacky University (Czech Republic), Scripps College, Stanford University, Tel Aviv University, the University of Arizona, the University of California at Irvine, the University of California at Riverside, the University of Illinois at Chicago, the University of Michigan, the University of Pennsylvania, the University of Southern California, Université de Versailles Saint-Quentin-en-Yvelines, West Virginia University, and Yale University. I am grateful for the responses and criticism I received, just as I am grateful for the research assistance I was provided at Vanderbilt University, Northwestern University, and especially the University of California at Los Angeles, and for the inspiration of graduate students at those institutions, whose work in seminars and whose conversation shaped my thinking in many ways. I would also like to express special thanks to the chair of the Department of English at UCLA, Thomas Wortham, and to the former Dean of Humanities, Pauline Yu, for their friendship and support.

At Harvard University Press, William Sisler and Lindsay Waters waited patiently for a book that turned out to be quite different from the one promised. I thank both of them for their good faith, just as I thank Donna Bouvier and Thomas Wheatland for ever responsive and tactful assistance, and Amanda Heller for expert copyediting.

I am grateful to the following publishers for their permission to reprint material that appeared in earlier and substantially different form: "Blues for Atticus Finch: Scottsboro, *Brown*, and Harper Lee," in Larry J. Griffin and Don H. Doyle, eds., *The South as an American Problem* (Athens: University of Georgia Press, 1995), pp. 181–209, © 1995 by the University of Georgia Press; "Promised Lands: *A Different Drummer*," *Triquarterly* 107–8 (Spring–Summer–Fall 2000), 267–83; and "Dry Bones," in Ross Posnock, ed., *Cambridge Companion to Ralph Ellison* (New York: Cambridge University Press, 2005), pp. 217–30, reprinted with the permission of Cambridge University Press.

In addition, I am grateful to the copyright holders for permission to reprint the following:

Langston Hughes, "Promised Land" from *The Collected Poems of Langston Hughes,* copyright © The Estate of Langston Hughes. Used by permission of Alfred A. Knopf, a division of Random House, Inc., and Harold Ober Associates, Inc.

Excerpts from "North and South" and from "The Sea is History" from *Collected Poems: 1948–1984* by Derek Walcott. Copyright © 1986 by Derek Walcott. Reprinted by permission of Farrar, Straus and Giroux, LLC, and Faber and Faber, Ltd.

James A. Randall, Jr., "Jew," *Don't Ask Me Who I Am*. Detroit: Broadside Press, 1970. Reprinted by permission of the author.

Nikki Giovanni, "Poem (No Name No. 3)" from *Black Feeling, Black Talk, Black Judgement* by Nikki Giovanni. Copyright © 1968, 1970 by Nikki Giovanni. Reprinted by permission of HarperCollins Publishers, Inc.

Amiri Baraka (LeRoi Jones), "The Black Man Is Making New Gods," "Citizen Cain," "Black Art," and "For Tom Postell, Dead Black Poet" from LeRoi Jones,

Black Magic; Amiri Baraka, "So the King Sold the Farmer #39" from Amiri Baraka, *Transbluency.* Reprinted by permission of SLL/Sterling Lord Literistic, Inc. Copyright by Amiri Baraka.

Lucille Clifton, "moses" from *Good Woman: Poems and a Memoir 1969–1980.* Copyright © 1987 by Lucille Clifton. Reprinted with the permission of BOA Edtions, Ltd., *www.BOAEditions.org.*

Melvin B. Tolson, "The Idols of the Tribe," "Babylon," and "Harlem Gallery" from *"Harlem Gallery" and Other Poems,* ed. Raymond Nelson. Charlottesville: University of Virginia Press, 1999. Reprinted with the permission of the University of Virginia Press.

Larry Neal, excerpt from "The Middle Passage and After" from *Hoodoo Hollerin' Bebop Ghosts.* Copyright © 1968, 1974 by Larry Neal. Reprinted with the permission of Howard University Press. All rights reserved.

Dan Pagis, "Draft of a Reparations Agreement," *The Selected Poetry of Dan Pagis.* Edited/Translated by Stephen Mitchell. Berkeley: University of California Press, 1996. Copyright © 1996 The Regents of the University of California.

Eldridge Cleaver, "To a White Girl" from *Soul on Ice.* New York: McGraw-Hill, 1968. Reprinted by permission of McGraw-Hill Companies.

Excerpt from "The Rabbi" by Frederick Glaysher, editor. Copyright © 1962, 1966 by Robert Hayden, from *Collected Poems of Robert Hayden* by Robert Hayden, edited by Frederick Glaysher. Used by permission of Liveright Publishing Corporation.

Excerpts from "See Sammy Run in the Wrong Direction" and "For the Black People," from Haki R. Madhubuti, *Groundwork: New and Selected Poems,* copyright © 1996 by Haki R. Madhubuti. Reprinted by permission of Third World Press, Chicago, Illinois.

Index

Abbas, Mahmoud (Abu Mazen), 325

Abbott, Robert, 244

Abernathy, Arthur T., 193

Ackerman, Nathan, 221

Adorno, Theodor, 221, 575n102

Affirmative action, 81–83, 223, 315, 436, 438, 476; and "color-blind" ideal, 5, 72, 75, 78, 221, 239, 286; Jews' dissent from, defined as racial preferences, 4–5, 22, 66, 76–78, 313, 336, 383. *See also* Quotas

Africa: as black homeland, 3, 120–128, 145–147, 154–156, 160–165, 258–259, 281, 286, 288, 291; as source of African American culture, 48–49, 162–164. *See also* Afrocentrism; Afro-Zionism; Black Jews; Ethiopianism; Israel: as Jewish homeland

African Americans. *See* Blacks

Afrocentrism, 53, 101, 121, 159, 160, 163–169, 497

Afro-Zionism, 8, 120–128, 133, 139, 145–147, 151, 155–158; in relation to Black Power, 161–162, 251–255, 341–342. *See also* Afrocentrism; Black Jews; Black Power; Ethiopianism; Rastafarianism; Zionism

Agamben, Giorgio, 632n54

Agus, Jacob, 21

Akbar, Na'im, 462

Ali, Noble Drew, 115

Allen, James, 254

Allen, Lewis (Abel Meeropol): "Strange Fruit," 27–28

Alliance, black-Jewish. *See* Civil rights: Jewish support for

Als, Hilton, 290n

Alvarez, A., 277

American Israeli Public Affairs Committee, 340

American Jewish Committee, 38, 76, 78, 81, 93, 196, 221, 340

American Jewish Congress, 31, 37, 54, 76, 81

"America's Jews": blacks as, 3, 10, 23–27, 36, 64, 258, 342, 343, 351, 386, 526

Améry, Jean, 189

Ames, Jessie, 198

Amital, Yehuda, 322

Anderson, Marian, 151, 482

Anderson, S. E., 440n; *The Black Holocaust for Beginners,* 461–463

Anderson, Sherwood: *Dark Laughter,* 67

Andy Griffith Show, The (television series), 172

Ansky, S. (Shloyme Zanvl Rappoport): *The Dybbuk,* 390n

Anticolonialism: in Africa and Third World, 148, 153–155, 264–265, 268, 279, 282, 286–288, 314, 318, 336, 391, 412; theories of, applied to black ghetto, 8, 286–288, 313–314, 319, 336–339, 398–399, 406, 407. *See also* Anti-Zionism; Israel: as model of anticolonial struggle; Zionism: as form of colonialism

Anti-Defamation League of B'nai B'rith, 21, 27, 43, 76, 81, 192, 196, 331, 340

Antin, Mary: *The Promised Land,* 25–26

Antiphon: *Tetralogies,* 427–428

Anti-Semitism, 9, 11, 21, 26, 50, 72, 335–336, 394–395, 412–414, 426–427, 475, 523, 608nn77,80, 609n82; among blacks, 8, 17, 22–23, 39–44, 48, 84–92, 101, 211–213, 318, 368, 387–388, 400, 402–412, 432–433, 510, 511, 546n195; and Christianity, 9, 28, 40, 58, 59, 85, 307, 394–395, 471; in Nation of Islam, 86–92, 396; in U.S., 6, 18, 20, 59, 65–66, 86–87, 531n4; in U.S. South, 189–198, 201–202. *See also* Anti-Zionism

Anti-Zionism, 86, 208, 331, 335; Arab, 312, 320, 323–328, 334–336, 351, 375, 380, 608nn77,80, 609n82; black, 8, 82, 109–110, 153–155, 160–162, 251, 312, 318–319, 331–339, 342, 346, 348–354, 377–380; in relation to anti-Semitism, 11, 22, 312, 328, 331–339, 348–354, 377–380, 383, 409, 608nn77,80. *See also* Anti-Semitism; Zionism

Aptheker, Herbert, 345

Arafat, Yasser, 85, 110, 323, 325, 327–330, 334–335, 376–377, 608n80

Arendt, Hannah, 206–207, 224, 228n, 335, 345n, 351, 370, 413, 442

Armstrong, Louis, 24–25

Asante, Molefi, 160, 165, 168, 565n202

Asher, Carol: *The Flood,* 64–65n

Asher, Lila Oliver: *Homage to Ben Shahn,* 32, 34, 401n

Ashkenazim (Ashkenazi Jews), 78, 116–117, 119n, 139, 274, 283, 330, 593n11, 606n58. *See also* Black Jews; Mizrahim; Sephardim

al-Assad, Hafiz, 320

Atlanta child murders, 453–456, 469

Auerbach, Jerald S., 605n53

al-Azm, Khalid, 325

Azoulay, Katya Gibel, 504n

Babylon: biblical, 53, 99n, 107, 123, 141, 156, 159n, 385, 416, 430; America or New World as, for blacks, 53, 99–100, 104, 115, 126–128, 132, 133, 145n, 282, 301, 337–338. *See also* Exile

Baker, Ella, 247

Bakke, Allan, 77–78

Baldwin, James, 53, 67n, 155, 248, 316, 343n, 401, 402–403, 407, 422, 424, 430, 460, 464, 471, 517, 562n164; "The Black Boy Looks at the White Boy," 69, 363; *Blues for Mister Charlie,* 179–180, 234, 235; *Evidence of Things Not Seen,* 453–456, 469, 484; *The Fire Next Time,* 161, 242, 385–386, 404, 422, 452, 459n, 468, 469, 595n22; *Go Tell It on the Mountain,* 397; "The Harlem Ghetto," 19, 41, 102; "Negroes Are Anti-Semitic Because They're Anti-White," 40, 48, 90, 388, 389, 397, 400; *No Name in the Street,* 404

Bambara, Toni Cade: *Those Bones Are Not My Child,* 454n

Barak, Aharon, 330n, 614n140

Baraka, Amiri (LeRoi Jones), 8, 73n, 86, 162, 180, 249, 348, 384, 403, 407, 415, 416, 420, 504n; "Black Art," 410; "The Black Man Is Making New Gods," 410–411; *A Black Mass,* 131; "Citizen Cain," 410; *Dutchman,* 225; "For Tom Postell, Dead Black Poet," 8, 410n, 411; "Leroy," 290; *Slave Ship,* 459; "Somebody Blew Up America," 411n; "So the King Sold the Farmer #39," 435

Barnett, Ross, 201

Barnstone, Willis, 504n

Bartov, Omer, 209–210n, 576n102

Bass, Leon, 215

Bates, Ruby, 199

Bauer, Yehuda, 233, 580n142

Bauman, Zygmunt, 459

Bayen, Malaku, 244

Beatty, Paul, 187n; *Tuff,* 488; *White-Boy Shuffle,* 253n, 488

Beckett, Samuel, 458

Begin, Menachem, 214, 322, 356, 372, 374–375

Beilis, Mendel, 205, 412–414

Belafonte, Harry, 31

Bell, Daniel, 65, 77, 512

Bell, Derrick, 168–169, 257, 451–452, 566n212

Bellow, Saul, 1, 55, 325, 350, 410, 517; "Israel: The Six-Day War," 367–368; *Mr. Sammler's Planet,* 10, 35, 282, 312, 353, 356, 362–368, 421, 483, 493

Ben Ammi (Carter), 95, 113, 126, 135, 141–145, 147, 151, 404

Benedict, Ruth, 62

Ben-Gurion, David, 149, 320, 322, 356

Benjamin, Judah, 122

ben-Jochannan, Yosef A. A., 115

Bennett, Hal: *The Black Wine,* 44, 361; *Lord of Dark Places,* 360–361

Bercovitch, Sacvan, 103

Bergman, Elihu, 74

Berlin, Irving, 165n

Berman, Paul, 2, 110

Bernal, Martin, 165

Bernstein, Leonard, 348

Bernstein, Michael André, 208

Bernstein, Vernon, 46–47

Berson, Lenora, 34, 38, 43, 259, 495

Bettelheim, Bruno, 61, 221, 224, 232, 235, 397, 466n

Bialik, Hayyim, 281

Bibb, Joseph D., 213

Bible: Acts 2, 304; Acts 9, 301; Daniel 3, 468; Daniel 5:24–27, 455n; Daniel 6, 102; Deuteronomy 6:4, 472; Deuteronomy 7:2, 110; Deuteronomy 10:19, 30n; Deuteronomy 25:17–19, 321; Deuteronomy 28:25, 158; Deuteronomy 28:64, 156; Deuteronomy 28:68, 142; Ephesians 6:5, 302; Exodus 2:21, 113; Exodus 3:14, 425; Exodus 6:5–7, 133; Exodus 13:21–22, 257n; Exodus 20:2, 103, 385, 388; Exodus 21:24, 372; Exodus 22:20, 30n; Ezekiel 1:4–28, 130n, 256; Ezekiel 37:11–14, 53n, 99n, 107, 123, 141, 159n; Genesis 9:4, 138; Genesis 9:25, 85n; Genesis 15, 133; Genesis 17:11–13, 420; Genesis 25:23, 38; Hebrews 11:1, 453; Isaiah 42:6–7, 134; Jeremiah 29:5–7, 385; Jeremiah 31:10, 156; John 6:53–56, 138; Leviticus 3:17, 138; Leviticus 11:7, 306n; Leviticus 17:11, 136; Leviticus 17:12, 138; Leviticus 19:16, 401, 534n42; Leviticus 19:17, 411; Leviticus 19:18, 390n; Leviticus 19:34, 3, 30n, 500; Leviticus 26:33, 156; Nehemiah 1:3, 469; Numbers 12:1, 114; Psalms 68:31, 120–121, 123; Psalms 137, 95, 104; Romans 11:26–31, 429; Romans 11:27, 302n

Biggers, John, 215–216

Bilbo, Theodore, 51, 124n, 192, 213, 445

Birth of a Nation, The (film), 175, 195

Bittker, Boris I., 475, 476n

Black, Hugo, 173, 174

Black Americans in Support of Israel (BASIC), 331

Black Arts movement, 384, 400, 404, 408–412, 418, 424, 466

Black Christ, 110, 113, 124, 132–135, 138–139, 247, 250, 289, 471. *See also* Black Theology; Moses: as Egyptian or black

Black fascism, 125, 166, 211–213, 214, 313, 341–342

Black Fire (anthology), 163

Black Hebrews. *See* Hebrew Israelites

Black holocaust, 6, 10, 35, 36, 90, 132, 152, 302, 378, 437–438, 452–453, 464, 473, 493. *See also* Genocide; Holocaust; Lynching; Nazism

Black Holocaust Museum, 438

Black Jews, 9, 110–120, 166, 416; as "true Jews," 113, 115–118, 126–128, 133–134, 139–140, 143–144, 484; distinguished from black Jews, 111n. *See also* Jews, black; Mizrahim; Sephardim

"Black Manifesto," 339–340, 473, 475, 610n93

Blackmun, Harry, 77

Black Muslims. *See* Nation of Islam

Black Panther (periodical), 334, 338, 415

Black Panthers (Black Panther Party), 82, 161, 179, 219, 239, 245, 253n, 282, 287, 311, 317, 331, 332, 333, 337, 339, 348, 350, 379, 383, 401, 407, 435, 483, 494, 612n117; as model for Jewish Defense League, 355, 358

Black Panthers (Israeli), 120, 329–330. *See also* Mizrahim

Black Power, 4–5, 55, 75, 86, 90, 106, 110, 132–135, 154–155, 160, 180, 218, 246, 286, 331–332, 334, 336, 342, 344, 356, 363, 369, 382, 385, 399, 418, 430, 466, 481; defined as a source of black identity, 79–80, 82, 313–316; in relation to "Jewish Power," 10, 82, 289, 312, 354–359, 362–368; Jewish support for, 69n, 315–316, 319, 348–355, 365n. *See also* Anti-Zionism

Black Power (periodical), 383

Blacks (African Americans): and concept of homeland in separate state, 241, 250–260, 287, 341; as "America's Jews," 3, 10, 23–27, 36, 64, 258, 342, 343, 351, 386, 526; as liberators of concentration camps, 214–215, 446; as source of sexual or "biological" danger, 60, 61, 170–171, 173–180, 360–361, 363–365, 382, 415–422, 445, 486–487, 515, 520; masculinity of, in relation to Jews, 68–69, 363–365, 401–402, 415–422; passing as Jewish, 503, 512–523; passing as white, 14, 67, 69–71; priority of, over Jews as Americans, 3, 51–53, 423–424, 492

Black September, 327, 369, 375, 604n46

Black Theology, 110, 124, 132–135, 247, 289, 421, 471. *See also* Black Christ; Moses: as Egyptian or black

Black Zionism. *See* Afro-Zionism

Blake, William, 386; "The Tyger," 431

Bland, Edward, 235

Blassingame, John, 296

Blauner, Bob, 87n

Bloch, Julius, 27

Blood: as figure of sacrifice, 136–137, 519–522; black fears about, based on AIDS rumors, 85, 138, 450–451; black fears about, based on Tuskegee syphilis experiment, 138, 445, 454; "one drop" of, in racial categorization of blacks, 61, 138, 175, 183, 186, 286, 519; purity of, as racial concept, 136, 138–139, 174–179, 183–184

Blood libel, 88, 90, 412–414, 471, 484–485, 609n82; related to Christian eucharist, 137–138, 307–308

Bloomfield, Arthur, 430n

Blyden, Edward, 110, 122–125, 137, 151, 161, 251

Boas, Franz, 71–72, 524

Bontemps, Arna: "Nocturne at Bethesda," 449

Bor, Joseph, 205

Borowitz, Eugene, 74

Boteach, Shmuley, 526

Bourne, Randolph, 57–58, 539n107

Bowers, Claude, 175

Boyarin, Daniel, 421

Boyarin, Jonathan, 163, 553n47

Boyer, Paul, 439n

Brackman, Harold, 439n

Bradbury, Ray: "Way in the Middle of the Air," 256–257

Bradley, David, 260; *The Chaneysville Incident*, 457

Brady, Tom P., 175

Braiterman, Marvin, 192

Branch, Taylor, 288

Brandeis, Louis, 7, 25; on Zionism and Americanism, 57, 125, 151, 164, 511

Briggs, Cyril V., 254

Broder, Henryk, 211

Brodsky, Joseph, 200

Brotz, Howard, 115

Brown, Claude: *Manchild in the Promised Land*, 42–43, 73n, 98, 289, 397, 407

Brown, H. Rap (Jamil Abdullah Al-Amin), 314, 317–319, 333, 337, 415, 417, 449

Browne, Robert S., 254, 313

Browning, Christopher, 267, 444

Brown v. Board of Education, 12, 31, 53n, 63–65, 76, 100, 107n, 172, 173, 174, 176, 180, 198, 226, 228n, 229, 235, 243, 259, 450n, 468, 515, 525; and theories of racial damage, 222, 225, 466n; cited by chief justice of Israeli Supreme Court, 330n; influenced by social science research, 218, 221, 582n154. *See also* Holocaust: effect of, on civil rights movement; Warren, Earl

Broyard, Anatole, 68–69n, 73; "Portrait of the Inauthentic Negro," 70–71, 516–517, 520

Bruce, Lenny, 66
Buber, Martin, 351, 381
Budick, Emily, 2, 422, 424, 425n
Bukiet, Melvin Jules, 209
Bunche, Ralph, 36, 214, 242, 251
Bundy, McGeorge, 38, 77, 544n166
Buruma, Ian, 233
Bush, George W., 451, 478n
Butler, Octavia: *Kindred,* 448–449

Cahan, Abraham, 540n113
Caldwell, Ben: *Top Secret or a Few Million After B.C.,* 450
Campbell, Bebe Moore: *What You Owe Me,* 478–481, 484
Carmichael, Joel, 40, 346
Carmichael, Stokely (Kwame Ture), 8, 133, 280, 407, 409; anti-Zionism of, 159, 160, 330–336; on Black Power, 314–319; on ghetto and colonialism, 337, 399; on Zionism as model for blacks, 162
Carper, Laura, 398n
Carroll, Charles, 175, 193
Carson, Clayborne, 29
Carter, Ben Ammi. *See* Ben Ammi
Carter, Jimmy, 82
Cartey, Wilfred, 281
Cartwright, Marguerite, 153
Casely Hayford, J. E., 123–125, 158
Cash, Wilbur, 173, 177, 190, 486
Caspary, Vera: *Thicker Than Water,* 44
Césaire, Aimé, 279n, 281; *The Tempest,* 264
Chaney, James, 31
Cherry, F. S., 115
Chesler, Phyllis, 36
Chesnutt, Charles: *The Marrow of Tradition,* 191
Chicago, Judy: *Holocaust Project,* 446–447
Chomsky, Noam, 352
Chosen people: blacks as, 14, 54, 111, 122, 128, 133–135, 269, 271, 281, 360, 421, 499; Jews as, 14, 34, 56, 102, 122, 149, 208, 269, 271, 281, 360, 420, 421, 430n, 451n 455, 499, 549n2. *See also* Covenant
Christianity, dominance of, in American culture, 6, 18, 19, 28, 40–41, 50, 52–53, 133, 361, 506, 507–509. *See also* Anti-Semitism: and Christianity; Black Christ; Black Theology
Churchill, Winston, 217
Circumcision, 114n, 195, 417–421; related to castration, 420, 421, 470. *See also* Covenant
Civil rights: and intimidation of Jews in South, 189–194, 482, 507–508; Jewish support for, 1–2, 4, 14, 17, 28, 29, 33–34, 75–76, 191–193, 269, 309–

311, 313, 352, 362, 383, 387, 479, 481, 482, 483, 525; northern Jews fight for, in South, 31–32, 37, 191, 315; sincerity of Jews' support for, doubted, 92–94, 489. *See also* Liberalism
Civil Rights Act (1964), 22, 93, 259, 313
Civil Rights Commission, 63, 81
Civil Rights Congress, 217–219, 494, 581n146
Clark, Kenneth B., 12–13, 40, 53n, 87n, 154, 316, 345, 468n; on ghetto, 337, 391–392, 395, 396, 397, 465–466; on racial damage, 222, 398
Clarke, John Henrik, 163, 335
Cleage, Albert, Jr., 128, 133–135, 247–248, 416, 421
Cleaver, Eldridge, 131, 148, 234, 235, 278, 280, 350, 351, 352, 466; and black masculinity, 179, 363–364, 418n; appears at Fatah rally, 334, 354; cited as model for Jewish Power, 357, 359; on ghetto and colonialism, 337–338; on Zionism as model for blacks, 161, 287, 331; *Soul on Ice,* 179, 357, 363
Cliff, Michelle: *Abeng,* 303n
Clifford, James, 157
Clifton, Lucille: "Moses," 101
Clinton, Bill (William Jefferson), 451, 520
Cobbs, Price M., 226, 261
Cochran, Johnnie, 97, 635n95
Cohen, Arthur A., 73, 291, 388
Cohen, Edward, 190
Cohen, Hettie. *See* Jones, Hettie Cohen
Cohen, Jacob, 23, 386
Cohen, Steven M., 92
Cokely, Steve, 85
Commandment Keepers of the Royal Order of Ethiopian Hebrews, 111, 112, 116, 141, 211
CommonQuest (magazine), 93–94
Communist Party, 29, 31, 198, 200, 206, 241, 345, 402, 473, 489
Cone, James H., 128, 133–135, 137, 280
Congress of Racial Equality (CORE), 172, 280, 314, 315, 339, 343
Connerly, Ward, 480n
Conyers, John, 474
Coughlin, Charles, 28
Covenant, Jewish concept of, 19, 74, 102, 113, 114n, 134n, 137, 156, 208, 286, 371, 418, 420, 421, 428, 431; relation of circumcision to, 114n, 195, 417–421. *See also* Chosen people: Jews as
Cox, Earnest, 124n
Cox, Oliver C., 40
Crouch, Stanley, 166, 366, 418–419n, 449
Crowdy, William S., 116
Crown Heights, 9, 86, 323n, 481, 496–502, 526
Cruse, Harold, 29, 76, 79, 84–85, 101, 253n, 272, 336, 345, 376, 402, 421, 422, 452

Cuddihy, John Murray, 403
Cullen, Countee: "Black Christ," 203
Cunard, Nancy, 163
Curse of Ham, 85, 167n, 486
Curtin, Philip, 439n

Daddy Grace, 132, 250
Davidson, Basil, 439n
Davis, Angela, 347–348, 402–403, 497
Davis, David Brion, 284n
Davis, Ossie, 155–156, 219
Davis, Sammy, Jr., 338
Dawidowicz, Lucy, 342
Dayan, Moshe, 328, 356, 378
deCoy, Robert H., 106
Defoe, Daniel, 386
DeFunis, Marco, 76
DeFunis v. Odegaard, 76
Deir Yassin, 373–378
Delany, Martin, 114, 251
DeLillo, Don: *White Noise,* 209
Des Pres, Terrence, 464, 583n163, 631n53
Dett, Nathaniel, 102
Dewey, John, 57
Diaspora: black, 14, 18, 49–50, 95, 98–99, 123, 156–162, 163, 240, 269–271, 281–283, 291–292, 304, 376, 478; Jewish, 14, 18, 123, 149–151, 156–162, 163, 240, 281–285, 379, 428. *See also* Exile
Dick, Philip: *The Man in the High Castle,* 524–525
Dickstein, Morris, 615n153
Dieckhoff, Alain, 356
Dillard, J. L., 83
al-Din, Muhammad Salah, 378
Diner, Dan, 605n55
Diner, Hasia, 34
Diop, Cheikh Anta, 114n, 166
Disney, Walt, 487, 488
Displaced Persons Acts, 63
Dixon, Thomas, 175, 184, 199, 202n, 226
Dollard, John, 173, 189, 437
Donat, Alexander, 205
Donnelly, Ignatius, 194
Dorsey, Hugh, 196
Douglass, Frederick, 23, 104, 106, 428
Drake, St. Claire, 42, 396
Drescher, Seymour, 441
Du Bois, Shirley Graham, 332
Du Bois, W. E. B., 8, 53, 63, 90, 113, 121, 152, 158, 161, 163, 275, 279, 336, 345, 378, 391, 408, 440n, 474, 494, 505, 511; *Dusk of Dawn,* 216, 391; on Jews under Nazism, 216; on Zionism, 123–124; petition to United Nations, 219; *The Souls of Black Folk,* 23, 53, 65, 102, 216; view of Israel after Suez War, 153–154
Due, Tananarive: *The Living Blood,* 135–139; *My Soul to Keep,* 135–139
Dumas, Henry: "Ark of Bones," 99n; "Cuttin' Down to Size," 420; "The Marchers," 246
Dundes, Alan, 137–138

Early, Gerald, 54, 164n, 167, 265, 346n
Eban, Abba, 321
Efroyin v. Rusk, 321
Egypt: as metaphor in black usage, 23, 101, 110, 132, 133, 245, 247, 249, 252, 266, 316; biblical, 4, 19, 30, 102, 107, 124, 125, 252, 351, 390, 416; black identification with, as enemy of Israel, 95, 110, 160, 162, 330–336, 371–372; in Afrocentrism, 160, 165–166, 168; in modern Middle East, 95, 153–154, 160
Eichmann, Adolf, 206, 321, 370, 413, 452
Eisen, Arnold, 92
Eisenhower, Dwight, 228n
Eliot, George, 122
Eliot, T. S., 386, 411, 424
Elis, Aharon Ben-Israel, 144
Elkana, Yehuda, 605n55
Elkins, Stanley, 223–226, 232, 235, 244, 296, 297, 398, 443, 466n, 584n174
Ellis, Eddie, 439n, 452
Ellison, Ralph, 1, 68n, 167, 228n, 235, 239, 242, 399, 407, 517, 526; "Change the Joke and Slip the Yoke," 71, 425n, 516; debate of, with Irving Howe, 422–426, 492; *Invisible Man,* 204, 260, 263, 408, 425, 431, 515–516; *Juneteenth,* 96, 111, 133, 159n; on Malamud, 424n; on Roth, 515–516; "What America Would Be Like without Blacks," 53, 105, 266
Elman, Richard: "Law 'N Order Day," 352–353
Epstein, Itzhak, 354
Epstein, Leslie: *San Remo Drive,* 214–215n
Equiano, Olaudah, 114
Ethiopia, 111, 119, 120, 128, 136–137, 162
Ethiopianism, 110, 120–128, 132, 135, 151, 157–158
Ethiopian Jews (Falashas), 111–112, 118–120, 139–141, 526
Eugenics, 129, 182, 186–188. *See also* Nazism: in relation to American segregation and racism
Exile: black, 10, 50, 99–100, 110–123, 156–162, 263–268, 425; Jewish, 10, 26, 50, 65, 149–151, 156–162, 428. *See also* Diaspora
Exodus: biblical, 5, 7, 38, 96, 114, 478n, 506; black use of, 5, 10, 19, 50, 96–101, 104–111, 122–128, 133–135, 139, 144, 168–169, 239–246, 256–260, 264–269, 316, 386, 404, 464; in relation to

Exodus *(continued)*
Holocaust, 5, 11, 50, 92, 240, 443, 464, 473; in relation to Middle Passage, 99–100, 104, 144, 282–284, 304. *See also* Moses

Fackenheim, Emil, 207–208, 309
Faitlovitch, Jacques, 119
Falashas (Falashim). *See* Ethiopian Jews
Fanon, Frantz, 60, 134, 145, 164, 189, 278–279, 280, 286, 291, 303, 309, 323, 327, 336, 381, 398; on blacks' "biological danger" and Jews' "intellectual danger," 61, 363, 382, 415, 421, 515
Fard, Wallace D., 114, 116n, 128
Farmer, James, 72, 172, 339
Farrakhan, Louis, 86, 143, 245, 257n, 483, 484, 499; anti-Semitism of, 88–91, 132; on blacks as "true Jews," 139; speech at Madison Square Garden, 88–89, 317n; speech at Million Man March, 91, 100, 169
Fast, Howard, 40; *Freedom Road,* 27
Fatah (Palestine National Liberation Movement), 323, 324, 326, 327, 333, 334, 354, 376, 377, 602n31, 604n46
Father Divine, 132, 250
Faubus, Orval, 201
Faulkner, William, 72, 570n35; *Absalom, Absalom!,* 271; *Go Down, Moses,* 265; *Light in August,* 203, 230, 250, 264, 514; *Sanctuary,* 573n71
Fauset, Arthur Huff, 250
Ferencz, Benjamin, 442
Fiddler on the Roof (stage play and film), 83
Fiedler, Leslie, 40, 47, 49, 55, 56, 74, 81, 118, 345, 382, 386–387, 398, 420, 431–432, 517
Finkelstein, Norman, 628n5
Fitzgerald, F. Scott: *The Great Gatsby,* 467
Ford, Arnold Josiah, 116, 118–119, 126
Ford, Henry, 90, 184; *The International Jew,* 28, 608n77
Forman, James, 280, 339, 355, 449, 473
Forman, Seth, 66
Forrest, Leon, 1, 16, 131
Frank, Anne, 39n, 54, 303n, 485, 510, 518; *The Diary of a Young Girl* (autobiography), 231–234; *The Diary of Anne Frank* (stage and film adaptation), 82, 231–234, 237
Frank, Leo, 6, 27, 193–197, 198, 202, 445, 484–485
Frankfurter, Felix, 30
Frankl, Victor, 397, 466n
Franklin, C. L., 247
Frazer, Chaim, 29
Frazier, E. Franklin, 49, 53, 124n, 158, 162, 226, 262, 460, 465, 469
Fredrickson, George, 62, 85n, 440
Freedman, Jonathan, 517

Freedman, Samuel G., 15
Freeman, Ellis, 56, 59
Freud, Sigmund, 95, 114n, 390
Friedan, Betty, 436
Friedman, Bruce Jay: *Stern,* 52–53
Friedman, Monroe, 337–338
Friedman, Murray, 21, 481
Fuchs, Lawrence, 88

Gaines, Ernest: *The Autobiography of Miss Jane Pittman,* 457
Galut. See Exile
Garnet, Henry Highland, 134
Garvey, Marcus, 85, 116, 132, 139, 155, 250, 251, 252, 408, 473; Afro-Zionism of, 110, 123–127, 147, 158–159, 161, 291; and fascism, 212; on Jews, 41, 41–42n, 88n
Garvey, Marcus, Jr., 342
Gates, Henry Louis, Jr., 90, 517, 639n31
Gavit, James A., 61
Gayle, Addison, Jr., 316, 404, 622n64
Geltman, Max, 352, 396
Genocide: as defined in United Nations Genocide Convention, 217; as problem of comparability, 7, 68, 202–203, 204–205, 310, 435–437, 443–444, 483–484, 493, 510; black fears of, 128–132, 398–399, 409, 448–452, 467, 471–473; integration as form of, 72, 128–132, 162, 313, 452, 483; invention of term, 216–217; lynching and racial violence as, 216–219, 234–237, 431, 438, 448–452. *See also* Black holocaust; Holocaust; Lynching; Nazism
Genovese, Eugene, 296
Ghetto, 42, 46, 385–386, 391–392; black, 41–47, 81, 336–339, 344, 350, 361, 391–400, 406, 407, 432, 467, 469–470, 480, 502, 621n48; charges of Jewish exploitation of blacks in, 8, 42–44, 88, 289–290, 337–338, 346–347, 393, 396, 467–468, 480–481, 484; Jewish, in Europe and under Nazism, 45–46, 48, 337, 339, 353, 393–394, 397, 432, 486; Jewish, in U.S., 41–44, 45–46, 55–56, 59, 80–81, 393–396, 502
Gibson, Richard, 162
Gideon v. Wainwright, 198
Gilroy, Paul, 157, 304, 459–460
Ginsberg, Allen, 73, 351, 627n125; "Kaddish," 66
Giovanni, Nikki: "Poem (No Name No. 3)," 234, 409
Gitlin, Todd, 84
Glatstein, Jacob: "Mayn rasistishe biografye" (My racist biography), 389
Glazer, Nathan, 52, 57, 74, 79–80, 83–84, 352, 353, 395, 541n128
Glicksberg, Charles, 32
Glissant, Edward, 291–292

Godbey, Allen, 115
"Go Down, Moses" (African American spiritual), 31, 96–97, 105, 152, 351
Goebbels, Joseph, 182, 184
Goffman, Erving, 400, 466n
Goffman, Ethan, 2, 497, 533n30
Goines, Donald: *Never Die Alone,* 359
Gold, Michael: *Jews without Money,* 26, 117n
Goldberg, J. J., 350
Goldberg, Michael, 578n113
Goldenberg, David, 85n
Goldhagen, Daniel Jonah, 267
Goldner, Sanford, 524
Goldstein, Israel, 31
Goodelman, Aaron, 27
Goodman, Andrew, 31, 32
Gordon, Albert I., 392
Gossett, Thomas, 540n120
Grant, Madison, 186, 187
Gratz v. Bollinger, 78
Greenberg, Cheryl, 21
Greenberg, Hank, 54–55
Greenberg, Irving, 206n
Greenberg, Jack, 31, 37, 37n, 401
Greenlee, Sam: *The Spook Who Sat by the Door,* 449
Gregory, Dick, 450, 454, 610n92
Grier, William H., 226, 261
Griffin, John Howard: *Black Like Me,* 69
Griggs, Sutton: *Imperium in Imperio,* 254
Grutter v. Bollinger, 78
Guinier, Lani, 93, 523
Guterman, Stanley S., 222
Gutman, Herbert, 227

Hacker, Andrew, 35, 40, 346n
Halevi, Kohain, 145–147
HaLevi, Shalomin, 117–118n
Haley, Alex, 132, 167; *Roots,* 82, 288, 457, 459
Halkin, Hillel, 150
Hall, Stuart, 160
Halpern, Ben, 59, 352, 392
Hamas (Islamic Resistance Movement), 328, 376n
Hamid, Sufi Abdul, 42
Hamilton, Charles, 337, 399, 407
Handlin, Oscar, 79
Hannerz, Ulf, 396
Harap, Louis, 17, 18, 400
Harding, Vincent, 296, 297
Hare, Nathan, 400
Harlan, John Marshall, 218
Harlem on My Mind (museum catalogue), 387–388n
Harris, Eddy, 168

Harris, George W., 152
Hartman, Geoffrey, 460
Hatchett, John, 343
Hayden, Robert, 510; "The Rabbi," 46n
Haynes, S. A., 212
Hebrew Israelites (Black Hebrews), 113, 141–147, 404
Hecht, Ben: *A Jew in Love,* 194
Heflin, J. Thomas, 174
Hegel, Georg W. F., 48, 241, 392, 587n3
Heimrich, Alan, 91
Hendrick, Burton J., 186
Henry, Aaron, 191
Henry, Milton R., 254
Henry, Paget, 280
Hentoff, Nat, 22, 352, 511; *Call the Keeper,* 362
Herberg, Will, 64n, 100, 550n15
Hernton, Calvin, 179, 415
Herrnstein, Richard, 78n
Herskovits, Melville, 48, 49, 262, 345
Hertzberg, Arthur, 55, 74–75, 86, 93, 316, 548n210
Hertzler, J. O., 59
Herzl, Theodor, 58, 120, 142, 148, 161, 287, 304, 334; *Old-New Land,* 161n
Heschel, Abraham, 32, 53; and Martin Luther King, Jr., 92, 106, 108–109, 248, 391, 401, 422
Heschel, Susannah, 526
Hester Street (film), 392
Higham, John, 62
Hilberg, Raul, 188n, 206, 207n, 209, 451
Hilliard, David, 436
Himes, Chester, 43, 242, 311; *Cotton Comes to Harlem,* 255–256; *Lonely Crusade,* 3, 39–40, 51, 52, 492; *Plan B,* 415
Himmelfarb, Milton, 77
Hitler, Adolf, 36, 47, 148, 207, 208, 278, 332, 356, 408, 413–14, 427, 435, 451, 485, 525; as "great man" for Nation of Islam, 88, 91, 132; cited in relation to American racism, 6, 45, 54, 65, 91, 108, 155, 173, 174, 178, 181, 188, 211, 212, 218, 219, 316, 337, 341, 344, 398, 386, 436, 449, 451, 465; *Mein Kampf,* 42, 173, 184, 186, 212, 328, 331, 414. *See also* Anti-Semitism; Black fascism; Nazism
Hobsbawm, Eric, 251
Hobson, Laura: *Gentleman's Agreement,* 66–67, 80, 201
Hochschild, Jennifer, 66
Hod, Mordechai, 371
Hoffman, Abbie, 350
Hoffman, Eva, 157
Hoffman, Julius, 338
Holiday, Billie: "Strange Fruit," 27
Hollinger, David, 20, 64n, 82
Holmes, Charles Henry, 121

Holocaust, 21, 34, 36, 47, 55, 181–186; American reactions to, 80, 204–211, 354–359, 365–367; as "sacrificial," 471–473; black reactions to Nazism and, 36, 108, 211–220; effect of, on civil rights movement, 65, 221–225; in American literature, 231–238; in relation to nuclear war and slavery, 68, 277–278, 279, 282; in relation to slavery and racism, 5–6, 35–36, 39n, 90–92, 99, 145–147, 168, 180, 214–215, 223–226, 234–237, 271, 283, 396, 398, 402–404, 439–447, 446, 448, 451–452, 455, 456–464, 484, 486–488, 494, 495, 498–500; in relation to Zionism, 7, 148–149, 154; meaning of term, 6, 209; "uniqueness" of, 7, 204, 210–211, 437, 438 441n, 444, 629n20. *See also* Black holocaust; Genocide; Nazism
Holocaust (television miniseries), 82, 209, 517, 545n180
Holocaust, black. *See* Black holocaust
Homeland. *See* Africa: as black homeland; Blacks (African Americans): and concept of homeland in separate state; Israel: as Jewish homeland; Palestinians: and homeland of "Greater Palestine"
hooks, bell, 40
Hooks, Benjamin, 77
Hopkins, Pauline, 121
Horowitz, David, 474, 475
Houston, Drusilla Dunjee, 121
Howe, Irving, 28, 55, 80, 205, 467, 517, 541n138; debate of, with Ralph Ellison, 422–426, 492
Howe, Stephen, 164
Hughes, Langston, 173, 179, 212, 245, 261, 505; "Beaumont to Detroit, 1943," 186; "Promised Land," 169, 260
Huie, William Bradford, 178
Hull, Cordell, 213
Hungerford, Amy, 615n167
Hunter, W. L., 124
Hurston, Zora Neale, 228n; *Moses, Man of the Mountain,* 95–96, 100–101, 133, 159, 214, 244; *Mules and Men,* 307
Hussein, King (Jordan), 153, 604n46
al-Husseini, Haj Amin, 375, 604n43
Hyman, Stanley Edgar, 425

Iceberg Slim (Robert Beck), 415
Immigration, of Jews, from Europe to America, 20, 25–28, 41–48, 50–51, 60–63, 491–492, 506–507. *See also* Israel: American Jewish emigration to *(aliyah)*; Migration
Innis, Roy, 280, 341
Intermarriage: and interracial sexuality, 45–46, 56, 72–74, 173–180, 197–204, 363–365; black-Jewish, 73, 359–361, 416, 431–432, 482–483, 507–508.

See also Blacks: as source of sexual or "biological" danger; Jews: as agents of racial pollution
Interreligious Foundation for Community Organization, 339, 340
Irgun (Irgun Z'vai Leumi: National Military Organization), 356, 367, 372–376
"Iron wall," concept of, 356–357, 362, 366–368, 372. *See also* Jabotinsky, Vladimir (Ze'ev); Jewish Defense League; Kahane, Meir
Isaacs, Harold, 49
Israel: American Jewish emigration to *(aliyah),* 149–151, 155, 321, 379; American Jewish support for, 75, 92, 149–151, 340–341; as Jewish homeland, 2, 147–162, 252–254, 268, 281, 288, 318, 371, 511, 512; as model of anticolonial struggle, 11, 154–155, 160, 161, 334–335, 372–376; black support for, 5, 109–111, 151–153, 154–156, 161–162, 287, 331, 351. *See also* Anti-Zionism; Palestinians; Zionism

Jabotinsky, Vladimir (Ze'ev), 356–357, 367
Jackson, George, 347, 403, 459, 466
Jackson, Jesse, 77, 85, 88n, 453, 511
Jackson, Robert, 218, 466n
Jacobson, Matthew Frye, 62
Jahoda, Marie, 221
James, C. L. R., 279, 288, 292–293, 295, 297
James, Darius: *Negrophobia,* 486–488
James, George G. M., 166
James, Henry, 12, 386
Janowitz, Morris, 61, 221
Jazz, as corrupting black-Jewish music, 184–185, 445
Jazz Singer, The (film), 67, 542n138
Jefferson, Thomas, 104, 436
Jeffries, Dexter, 40, 504n
Jeffries, Leonard, 85–86, 166
Jenkins, Jerry, 429; *Armageddon,* 430n
Jeremiah X, 346
Jeter, Mildred, 175
Jewish Defense League (JDL), 82, 144, 321, 344, 355–359, 382, 401
"Jewish Power," in relation to Black Power, 10, 82, 289, 312, 354–359, 362–368
Jews: as agents of racial pollution, 182–185, 193–197, 365n 441; as "black," 26, 62, 67–69, 138, 183–186, 193, 195, 445; as "intellectual" danger, 60, 61, 363–364, 382, 401–402, 415, 421, 515, 520; as killers of Christ, 9, 40, 85, 307, 471; as people of color (ethnic), 74, 79, 81–84, 353–355, 514, 522; as white, 14, 22, 58–60, 62, 65, 66–67, 72–74, 77, 81, 197, 332, 350, 370, 389, 405, 479, 480, 484, 491, 495, 497, 503, 514–516, 522; assimilation of, 21–22, 52, 56–59, 72, 74–79, 263, 345, 387, 392–394,

426, 503; assimilation of, as destructive of Jewish community, 73–80; assimilation of, as "Holocaust," 56, 72; black emulation of, 13, 23–25, 48, 66, 79, 161–162, 289–290, 484, 523; black objection to paternalism of, 13, 29, 225, 345–346, 352, 383, 402, 421; held responsible for slavery and slave trade, 89–90, 284–285, 499; racism among, 6, 17, 35, 39–41, 45–47, 348–359, 388, 507. *See also* Black Jews; Jews, black

Jews, black, 9, 48, 111, 112, 338–339, 503–504; distinguished from Black Jews, 111n. *See also* Black Jews

Johnson, Charles, 451

Johnson, Charles S., 173

Johnson, James Weldon, 102, 179, 242, 256n, 537n87; *Along This Way,* 512–513; *The Autobiography of an Ex-Coloured Man,* 67, 514

Johnson, Lyndon, 223, 286, 409, 415

Johnson-Reed Act, 61, 62

Jolson, Al, 67

Jones, Del: *Invasion of 'de Body Snatchers,* 450n, 454

Jones, Fred A., 395

Jones, Hettie Cohen, 73n, 410n, 416, 504n

Jones, James Howard, 445

Jones, LeRoi. *See* Baraka, Amiri

Jones, Lisa, 504n

Jordan, June, 438

Joyce, James, 240, 296; *Portrait of the Artist as a Young Man,* 295

Judgment at Nuremberg (film), 204

Jum'a, Sa'ad, 328

Kafka, Franz, 517; "The Burrow," 518–519; *The Trial,* 412

Kahane, Meir, 144, 355–358, 362, 367, 401n, 614n140

Kakungula, Semei, 119n

Kallen, Horace, 57–58, 539n108

Kanaana, Sharif, 375–376

Kaplan, Chaim, 205

Kaplan, Mordecai, 104, 150

Kardiner, Abram, 49, 63

Karenga, Maulana, 53, 91n, 93, 164, 280, 407, 549n211, 633n71

Katz, Moise, 36

Katz, Shlomo, 38, 315, 403, 422

Katz, Stephen, 439n

Kaufman, Alan, 187n, 402n

Kaufman, Donald, 80–81

Kaufman, Jay, 411

Kaufman, Jonathan, 31, 481

Kazin, Alfred, 55, 392

Kelley, Robin D. G., 621n48

Kelley, William Melvin, 239, 262, 562n165; *Dancers on the Shore,* 256; *dem,* 240; *A Different Drummer,* 11, 239–246, 249–251, 256–260, 264–269, 437, 483; *Dumsfords Travels Everywheres,* 240; "The Ivy-League Negro," 3, 260–265

Kennedy, Robert, 193

Kermode, Frank, 426–427

Kernan, Alvin, 384

Kgositsile, Keorapetse, 308

Khaled, Leila, 326, 353

Khalidi, Rashid, 325

King, Martin Luther, Jr., 5, 22, 25, 31, 37, 49, 50, 51, 90, 104, 110, 127–128, 131, 132, 180, 192, 202n, 226, 230, 239, 240, 244, 259, 323n, 351, 471, 487n; and Abraham Heschel, 92, 106, 108–109, 248n, 391, 410, 422; and anti-Zionism hoax, 109; assassination of, 92, 312–313, 404; Exodus or Promised Land in speeches and writings of, 96, 106, 247–249; on Black Power, 314–316, 398; on Jewish support for civil rights, 32, 54; on racial damage as genocide, 108, 219, 222–223, 263, 395; support for Israel of, 109, 331

King Alfred Plan, 450–451

Klatzkin, David, 149

Kluger, Ruth: *Still Alive,* 35–36, 55, 438

Koch, Ed, 191

Komunyakaa, Yusef, 30

Kook, Abraham Isaac, 430

Kosinski, Jerzy: *The Painted Bird,* 231–232

Kramer, Michael, 88

Kramer, Stanley: *Home of the Brave* (film), 80

Krim, Seymour, 69, 71

Kristol, Irving, 261, 345

Kubrick, Stanley: *Dr. Strangelove,* 250

Ku Klux Klan, 27–28, 62, 124n, 175, 184, 186, 189, 190n, 192, 193, 196, 198, 218, 230, 252, 257, 341, 446, 454, 469, 525

Kushner, Tony: *Angels in America,* 489–490; *Caroline, or Change,* 490n

Kwanzaa, 164

Lacy, Ed: *In Black and Whitey,* 362

LaHaye, Tim, 429; *Armageddon,* 430n

Lamming, George, 295–296

Landing, James, 116

Lang, Berel, 9, 629n20

Langbaum, Robert, 77

La Rose, John, 100

Larsen, Nella: *Passing,* 67

Lasch, Christopher, 22

Laurents, Arthur: *Home of the Brave* (stage play), 80

Lawrence, Jacob: *Migration Series,* 97–98

Lazarre, Jane, 504n

Lazarus, Emma: "1492," 270

Lee, Don L. *See* Madhubuti, Haki
Lee, Harper, 170; *To Kill a Mockingbird,* 11–12, 170–175, 181, 188–189, 197, 201–203, 220–221, 227231, 237–238, 240, 268, 482, 483, 490n
Lee, Robert E., 170, 504n
Lehi (Lohamei Herut Israel: Fighters for the Freedom of Israel), 372–376
Leibowitz, Samuel, 31, 193, 198–201
Leibowitz, Yeshayahu, 329
Lemkin, Raphael, 216–218, 436–437, 449
Lerner, Michael, 19, 350, 451, 481–482, 526
Lester, Julius, 48, 89, 93, 332, 342–343; *And All Our Wounds Forgiven,* 278n; *Lovesong,* 14, 343n, 505–506, 510–512, 523; "The Stone That Weeps," 39n
Levenson, Jon D., 552n37
Levi, Primo, 205, 210, 237, 458–459, 632n54
Levin, Ira: *The Boys from Brazil,* 485
Levin, Michael, 78n
Levine, Lawrence, 296, 523
Levison, Stanley, 31
Lévi-Strauss, Claude, 202n
Lewis, Anthony, 65
Lewis, Bernard, 320
Lewis, David Levering, 29
Lewis, John, 244
Lewis, Sinclair: *Kingsblood Royal,* 69
Lewis, William A., 116
Liberalism, 21, 22, 74–80, 83–84, 201, 312, 314–319, 385, 410, 436, 484, 527; Black Power critique of, 239–240, 345–346, 352–359, 363–364, 401–402, 416, 420–422, 522; in relation to Jewish neoconservatism, 13, 74–80, 167; in relation to Jewish New Left, 32, 55–56, 348–354; surveys of Jewish commitment to, 92, 548n209
Liebman, Charles S., 55, 92, 547n197
Liebow, Eliot, 396
Lifton, Robert J., 277
Lincoln, C. Eric, 346
Lindbergh, Charles, 36
Lindsey, Hal: *The Late Great Planet Earth,* 429
Lipset, Seymour Martin, 109, 352, 353
Locke, Alain, 24, 48, 163
Lomax, Louis, 75
Lommel, Cookie, 526
Long, Edward, 293n
Lopate, Philip, 435
Loury, Glenn, 93, 167, 469, 541n132, 544n166
L'Ouverture, Toussaint, 292–293, 295, 297–298, 305
Loving, Richard, 175
Loving v. Commonwealth of Virginia, 176, 221
Lowell, A. Lawrence, 263
Lowen, Marilyn, 351
Lowenfeld, Viktor, 216

Lucy, Autherine, 228
Lynching, 24–25, 177–179, 197, 213, 215, 217–219, 234, 415, 444, 445, 462, 468; and castration, 175, 382, 433, 454, 470, 514; as sacrificial rite, 202–203, 267–268; related to anti-Jewish pogroms, 27–28, 38–39, 267. *See also* Black holocaust; Genocide; Nazism

Macdonald, Andrew: *The Turner Diaries,* 86
Madhubuti, Haki (Don L. Lee), 29, 161–162, 440n, 476n; "For Black People," 409; "Mainstream of Society," 65–66; "No More Marching," 287; "See Sammy Run in the Wrong Direction," 338–339
Magnes, Judah, 57
Mailer, Norman, 55, 69n, 352, 365n, 410, 517; *Of a Fire on the Moon,* 364–365n; "The White Negro," 68–69, 71, 80, 277–278, 350, 363, 514
Maimonides, Moses, 140, 141, 420–421
Malamud, Bernard, 55, 350, 406–407, 410, 517; "Angel Levine," 384n; *The Assistant,* 385; "Black Is My Favorite Color," 384–385n; *The Fixer,* 205, 383, 412–414, 428; "The Jewbird," 384n; *The Tenants,* 11, 12, 129, 240, 282, 312, 347–348, 362, 363–364, 380–391, 396, 400, 403–407, 414, 416–434, 489–490, 495, 514
Malcioln, José V., 115, 440n
Malcolm X, 84, 89, 138, 163, 239, 259, 275, 291, 314, 330, 357–358, 407, 408, 409, 410n, 440n, 449, 466, 494; and foundational ideas of the Nation of Islam, 128–132; and idea of separate state, 252–254, 341; *Autobiography of Malcolm X,* 130, 357–358; on Jews, 24, 91, 332, 337, 396; on Pan-Africanism likened to Zionism, 8, 161; petition to United Nations, 219
Mamet, David: *Homicide,* 43n; *The Old Religion,* 195
Mandela, Nelson, 332n
March on Washington (1963), 245, 452, 482
Marcus, Paul, 91
Marcus, Stephen, 81
Mark, David: *The Neighborhood,* 44
Marley, Bob, 126–127, 469, 633n71; "Exodus," 127
Marranos, 192, 284, 285, 306–307, 596n37
Marshall, Louis, 30, 38–39, 48, 51, 196
Marshall, Paule: *Brown Girl, Brownstones,* 269, 290; *The Chosen Place, the Timeless People,* 11, 240, 243, 269–286, 292, 296–310, 362, 437, 449, 483; "From the Poets in the Kitchen," 289–290; *Praisesong for the Widow,* 269, 290, 291, 299; "Shaping the World of My Art," 280, 285, 289–290, 300
Marshall, Thurgood, 37n, 401
Martin, Tony, 29, 85, 479
Matsuda, Mari, 477

Matthew, Wentworth Arthur, 112–113, 116–118, 140, 211
Matthews, Connie, 333
Mayer, Milton, 67–68
Mayor, William, 158
McAlister, Elizabeth, 307
McBride, James: *The Color of Water,* 507–509
McCary, P. K., 105
McCoy, Rhody, 401
McGruder, Aaron, 164n
McKay, Claude, 42
McLain, Franklin, 246
McPherson, James Alan, 156, 627n125
McWhorter, Diane, 171
McWhorter, John, 78, 477
Mead, Margaret, 452
Meir, Golda, 149
Melnick, Jeffrey, 542n138
Melville, Herman, 103, 179, 431
Memmi, Albert, 148, 336–337, 406
Memory: of Holocaust, as part of Jewish consciousness, 168, 207–210, 291, 321, 355–359, 378, 472–473, 506, 576n105; of slavery, as part of black consciousness, 145–147, 168, 283, 290–292, 297–301, 308–310, 437–438, 447–449, 454–464, 506
Menelik I, 116, 119
Menelik II, 121
Meredith, James, 228, 245, 314
Meriwether, Louise: *Daddy Was a Number Runner,* 44
Merkin, Daphne, 232
Messianism, 131–132, 371, 427, 429–431, 434
Meyerson, Bess, 54
Michaels, Walter Benn, 460n
Middle Passage, 223, 259, 288, 299, 448, 470; in relation to Exodus, 99–100, 104, 144, 282–284, 304; in relation to Holocaust, 10, 91, 234, 277, 278, 311, 438, 440, 442, 449, 458, 459, 460, 461, 462, 464, 499, 506
Migration, of blacks, from South to North, 19–20, 26–28, 41–48, 50–51, 97–98, 241–245, 396–397, 509. *See also* Immigration
Milam, J. W., 177
Miles, Zears, 450
Miller, Alan W., 288–298, 400, 436, 444, 532n12
Miller, Arthur, 321; *Focus,* 515
Miller, Kelly, 211, 578n125
Miller, Zell, 172
Million Man March (1995), 91, 100, 245, 482, 483
Minow, Martha, 477
Mintz, Sidney, 276
Missouri ex rel. Gaines v. Canada, 198
Mitchell, Margaret: *Gone With the Wind,* 172

Mizrahim (Mizrahi Jews), 112–113, 120, 329–330, 332, 593n11, 606n58. *See also* Ashkenazim; Black Panthers (Israeli); Sephardim
Mohammad, Conrad, 498–500, 502
Montagu, Ashley, 62
Moore, Richard B., 163
Morel, Edmund, 184
Morris, Benny, 378
Morris, John William, 121
Morrison, Toni, 438, 456, 464, 500; *Beloved,* 10, 302n, 440n, 449, 456–459, 462
Morse, Arthur, 321
Moses, 8, 19, 99, 100, 108, 123, 124, 158, 425; as Egyptian or black, 95–96, 114, 129, 131, 133–134, 166, 214, 289, 307, 341, 359; in African American tradition, 105, 350, 353. *See also* Exodus: black use of; Hurston, Zora Neale: *Moses, Man of the Mountain;* King, Martin Luther, Jr.
Moses, Wilson Jeremiah, 100, 111, 179
Mosley, Walter, 93; *Devil in a Blue Dress,* 214; *Fearless Jones,* 147, 155; *A Red Death,* 562n166
Most, Andrea, 542n138
Moynihan, Daniel Patrick, 52, 57, 79–80, 226
Moynihan Report ("The Negro Family: The Case for National Action"), 226–227, 465–466, 584n168
Muhammad, Elijah, 100, 114–115, 116, 133, 147, 165, 166n, 226, 256–257, 314, 407, 422, 430, 466, 470, 473; and foundational ideas of the Nation of Islam, 128–132; and idea of separate state, 251–254; *The Fall of America,* 132; *Message to the Blackman,* 130, 131
Muhammad, Khalid Abdul, 91
Muhammad, W. Fard. *See* Fard, Wallace D.
Munford, Clarence J., 474
Murray, Albert, 53n, 155, 225, 399
Murray, Charles, 78n
"Muscle Jew," concept of, 320, 355, 366, 368
Myrdal, Gunnar, 60, 63, 70, 173, 211, 345, 491, 515

al-Nakba (the Palestinian "Catastrophe" of 1948), 323, 325n, 326, 327, 376
an-Nashashibi, Nasir ad-Din, 326–327
Nasser, Gamal Abdel, 153, 323, 333, 616n177
National Advisory Commission on Civil Disorders, 313
National Association for the Advancement of Colored People (NAACP), 38, 69, 77, 147, 191, 198, 213, 219, 247, 250, 314, 340; role of Jews in 4, 19, 29, 30–31, 37n; support for founding of Israel, 153
National Coalition of Blacks for Reparations in America (N'COBRA), 475, 476
National Conference on Religion and Race, 108

National Jewish Community Relations Advisory Council, 92–93
National Museum of African American History and Culture, plans for, 478
National Urban League, 30, 339
Nation of Islam (Black Muslims), 114–115, 165, 166, 245, 263, 282, 341, 346, 436, 511; advocacy of separate state by, 241, 251–254, 257, 287; anti-Semitism of, 88–91, 499–500; as "true Jews," 115–116, 128–131, 139–141, 333, 430; foundational ideas of, 128–132. See also Farrakhan, Louis; Malcolm X; Muhammad, Elijah
Naylor, Gloria: Bailey's Cafe, 10, 111–112, 119, 137, 139
Nazism: and the "blackness" of Jews, 62, 138, 183–186, 445; in relation to American segregation and racism, 12, 171, 173–174, 180, 184–189, 191, 198, 202–203, 211–220, 234–237, 438; Jews under, 17, 58–60, 61–63, 170, 181–189, 521. See also Genocide; Holocaust
Neal, Larry, 280, 291, 297, 313, 345, 384, 408, 424, 595n31; "The Middle Passage and After," 171–172
Neblett, Renee, 163
Neoconservatism. See Liberalism: in relation to Jewish neoconservatism
Netanyahu, Benjamin, 356, 614n137
Netanyahu, Benzion, 596n37
Neusner, Jacob, 208, 437
"Never again." See Memory: of Holocaust, as part of Jewish consciousness
"Never forgetting." See Memory: of slavery, as part of black consciousness
New, Elisa, 429
Newman, Israel Ben, 116n
Newton, Adam, 2
Newton, Huey, 253n, 286, 332, 338, 350, 364, 418n, 466
Nkrumah, Kwame, 147
Nobles, Wade, 165
Noel, Peter, 526
Nordau, Max, 320–321n
Norris v. Alabama, 574n81
Novick, Peter, 438
Nuremberg Laws, 37, 58, 214, 182–186, 357, 415, 445, 524
Nzingha, Yaa Asantewa, 476n

Ocean Hill–Brownsville, 342–344, 355, 382, 401, 405, 481, 496, 510
Offord, Carl Ruthven: The White Face, 44
Opatoshu, Yosef: "Lintsheray," 27–28
Oren, Michael, 319n
Organization of African Unity, 335, 581n148
Organization of Afro-American Unity, 161, 219

Osofsky, Gilbert, 225, 396
Ottley, Roi, 42, 178, 289
Ovesey, Lionel, 49, 63
Owsley, Frank, 200
Ozick, Cynthia, 149, 423; The Shawl, 457

Pace v. Alabama, 176
Pagis, Dan: "Draft of a Reparations Agreement," 477
Palestine Liberation Organization (PLO), 312, 322, 323, 327, 328, 333, 334, 351, 354, 375, 376, 377
Palestine National Liberation Movement. See Fatah
Palestinians, 8, 10, 153, 288, 314, 320, 326, 333–335, 337–338, 373–378, 429, 603n38; and homeland of "Greater Palestine," 324, 325, 327–328, 376–378; and right of return, 323–326, 375–377, 429. See also Arafat, Yasser; Deir Yassin; Fatah; Palestine Liberation Organization
Paley, Grace: "Dreamer in a Dead Language," 55; "The Long-Distance Runner," 47; "Zagrowsky Tells," 47–48, 73
Pan-Africanism. See Afro-Zionism; Ethiopianism
Parfitt, Tudor, 115
Park, Robert E., 52
Parker, Mack Charles, 177, 178, 180, 252
Parks, Paul, 215
Parsons, Talcott, 74
Pasha, Abd al-Rahman Azzam, 375
Passing. See Blacks: passing as Jewish; Blacks: passing as white; Intermarriage: black-Jewish; Jews: as white
Passover, 30, 137, 142, 309, 351, 412, 412, 493, 509; as American symbol, 96, 103–104; in relation to Holocaust, 208; in relation to Kwanzaa, 164. See also Exodus; Moses
Patterson, Haywood, 198
Patterson, Orlando, 202, 225, 235, 241, 311–312, 465
Patterson, William L., 217–218
Paul, Nathaniel, 102
Pearson, Hugh, 341, 585n174
Peck, Gregory, 201
Peery, Nelson, 254–255
Petry, Ann: The Street, 256, 397
Phagan, Mary, 194, 195, 196, 484
Phillips, Caryl, 41n, 100, 234n, 456; The Atlantic Sound, 144–147; black-Jewish scenarios in writing by, 145n
Phillips, Ulrich B., 224, 262, 460
Piazza, Thomas, 66
Plessy v. Ferguson, 23, 174, 176, 218, 221, 243
Podair, Jerald, 344
Podhoretz, Norman, 55, 75, 318–319, 345, 352, 366,

402; "My Negro Problem—and Ours," 72–73, 84–85, 263, 363, 401–402, 421, 422

Pogrebin, Letty Cottin, 498–500, 502

Popular Front for the Liberation of Palestine (PFLP), 327, 375, 379

Posnock, Ross, 519

Potok, Chaim: *The Chosen*, 151, 561n153

Poussaint, Alvin, 399

Powell, Adam Clayton, Jr., 213, 245, 315n

Powell, Adam Clayton, Sr., 397

Powell, Clarence, 198

Powell v. Alabama, 181, 197–199

Power, Samantha, 7

Powers, Richard: *The Time of Our Singing*, 482–483, 508, 587n

Powledge, Fred, 379

Prato, David, 356

Price, Victoria, 199, 201

Prinz, Joachim, 37

Promised Land, America as: for blacks, 3, 21, 97–99, 102, 104–109, 169, 240–246, 249, 386; for early colonists, 103–104; for Jews, 2, 21, 56–58, 149–151, 386, 403, 410. *See also* Exodus; Israel

Protocols of the Elders of Zion, 28, 130, 328, 430n, 491, 608n77

Pryor, Rain, 504n

Public Enemy: "Swindler's Lust," 43n

Quotas, racial, 77–79, 81, 318, 383. *See also* Affirmative action

Qu'ran, 130, 132, 139, 143

Raab, Earl, 90

Rabin, Yitzhak, 319n

Race, evolving concepts of, 13, 15, 61–64, 482–483

Racial damage, postwar theories of, 63–66, 174, 220–227, 234–237, 261–263, 397–399, 436, 443, 465–466. *See also* Holocaust: effect of, on civil rights movement

Racial preferences. *See* Affirmative action; Quotas

Rahv, Philip, 55

Ramon, Uri, 329

Randall, James, A., Jr.: "Jew," 389

Randolph, A. Philip, 29–30, 31, 125, 212, 245

al-Rantisi, Abd al-Aziz, 605n52

Raper, Arthur, 173, 177

Ras Tafari. *See* Selassie, Haile

Rastafarianism, 126–128, 136–137, 139–141, 146, 168, 307, 465. *See also* Ethiopianism; Marley, Bob

Ratosh, Yonathan, 553n46

Reagan, Ronald, 31, 347, 453

Reddick, L. D., 17, 18, 400, 404, 524, 525

Redding, Grover, 126

Reed, Adolph, Jr., 87

Reed, Ishmael, 87; *Reckless Eyeballing*, 188n, 346n, 484–486, 488

RemedyRoss: "Never Again," 83

Reparations, black, 7, 339–341, 369, 436, 438, 462, 473–481, 634n94, 635nn95,96

Republic of New Africa, 253–254, 287, 317, 407, 473, 476n

Retamar, Roberto Fernández, 280

Return: Law of (Israeli), 113, 119, 142, 148, 258, 268, 326; refugees' right of, Palestinian concept of, 323–326, 375–377, 429

Reuter, Edward, 61

Revolutionary Action Movement, 253n, 317

Richburg, Keith, 168

Ricks, Willie, 315n

Rivers, Larry, 403n

Roberson, Elder Warien, 118

Robeson, Paul, 31, 90, 505; on blacks and Jews, 151–152; on lynching in relation to Holocaust, 217–219

Robinson, Jackie, 54

Robinson, Randall, 436, 462

Roosevelt, Franklin, 31

Roosevelt, Theodore, 25, 125

Roots (television miniseries), 82, 209. *See also* Haley, Alex: *Roots*

Rose, Arnold, 43–44

Rosen, Norma: *Touching Evil*, 209

Rosenbaum, Thane: *Second Hand Smoke*, 488–489

Rosenberg, M. J., 354, 366

Rosenfeld, Isaac: *Passage from Home*, 26

Rosenwald, Julius, 31, 39n

Roskies, David, 157, 211, 393

Ross, Fran: *Oreo*, 169

Rosten, Leo, 80, 83

Roth, Dan, 518

Roth, Philip, 364, 385, 410, 520–521; *American Pastoral*, 347; "Eli, the Fanatic," 206, 576n104; *The Facts*, 55, 516n; *The Ghost Writer*, 234, 485, 517, 518, 519, 521; *Goodbye, Columbus*, 515, 516n, 518; *The Human Stain*, 2, 14, 70, 73, 81, 503, 513–523, 527; *Operation Shylock*, 54, 149, 519; *The Plot against America*, 36; *Portnoy's Complaint*, 56, 352, 518, 521; *Zuckerman Unbound*, 208

Rothschild, Jacob, 191

Rousset, David, 68, 318

Rubenstein, Richard, 279, 354, 358, 443

Rubin, Jerry, 56, 350, 353

Ruchames, Louis, 37

Rumkowski, Chaim, 353

Rustin, Bayard, 43, 79, 331, 526

Said, Edward, 110

Salzman, Jack, 481

Sanders, Ronald, 37
Sanford, John: *People from Heaven,* 27
Sanneh, Kelefa, 168
Saperstein, Rachel, 322n
Sarna, Jonathan D., 75
Sarna, Nahum, 96
Sartre, Jean-Paul, 50, 70, 387, 516, 595n24
Sass, Herbert Ravenel, 176–177
Sayers, James D., 175
Schenker, Avraham, 155
Schiffman, Lisa, 83
Schindler's List (film), 43n, 488
Schneerson, Menachem, 86, 496
Scholem, Gershom, 207n, 429
Schomburg, Arthur, 163
Schorsch, Ismar, 354
Schultz, Alfred A., 186
Schuyler, George, 211, 213, 226, 251, 331, 579n125;
    Black No More, 72, 267
Schwartz, I. J., 25
Schwartz, Regina, 110
Schwartz-Bart, André: *The Last of the Just,* 170,
    472–473
Schwerner, Michael, 31, 32
Scott-Heron, Gil: *The Nigger Factory,* 552n36
Scottsboro cases, 177, 180–181, 193, 196, 197–203, 220
*Scroll of the War of the Sons of Light against the
    Sons of Darkness, The,* 370–371, 373, 377, 379
Seale, Bobby, 338
Secret Relationship between Blacks and Jews, The
    (Nation of Islam publication), 89–91, 132, 346n,
    440n, 462–463, 481–482
Segal, Dovid, 25
Segal, Lore: "The Bough Breaks," 492–493; *Her
    First American,* 15, 484, 490–495, 502; *Other
    People's Houses,* 393, 492, 494
Segev, Tom, 561n152
Selassie, Haile (Ras Tafari), 116, 119n; as
    Rastafarian deity, 120, 126–127, 137, 140, 146
Semi, Emanuela Trevisan, 118
Senna, Danzy: *Caucasia,* 81
Sephardim (Sephardic Jews), 9, 112, 140, 270, 283–
    285, 302, 329–330, 593n11; expulsion of, from
    Spain, 9, 270, 283–285, 309. *See also* Ashke-
    nazim; Mizrahim
Shahn, Ben: *Identity,* 316n; *Thou Shalt Not Stand
    Idly By,* 31, 33, 401n
Shakespeare, William: *King Lear,* 425–427; *The
    Merchant of Venice,* 41n, 505; *Othello,* 495; *The
    Tempest,* 131, 243, 264, 296, 465, 470
Shakur, Sanyika (Monster Kody Scott), 253n, 358n
Shaler, Nathaniel, 51–52, 537n87
Shandler, Jeffrey, 215
Shanker, Albert, 343, 344, 401

Sharansky, Natan, 86
Sharon, Ariel, 323n, 357
Sharpton, Al, 28, 97, 497
Shehadeh, Raja, 329
Shepp, Archie, 403n
Shepperson, George, 100, 158
Sherrod, L. G., 476n
Shirer, William, 170, 204
Shitrit, Sami Shalom, 330
Sholem Aleichem: *The Bloody Hoax,* 412
Shufeldt, R. W., 175
Shukeiry, Ahmed, 375
Silberman, Charles, 32, 225
Silver, Abba Hillel, 21
Silvers, Robert, 352
Sinclair, Jo (Ruth Seid): *The Changelings,* 10, 44–
    46, 47, 50, 73, 389, 395–396
Singer, Isaac Bashevis, 55, 317, 517; *The Family
    Moskat,* 365–366; *The Slave,* 205, 414, 575n101
Six-Day War (1967), 150, 160, 207, 281, 312, 319–
    330, 331–332, 334, 367, 368, 371–379, 411, 429, 437,
    511, 616n177; American Jewish reaction to, 75,
    82, 92, 318–319, 340–341, 354; as factor in black-
    Jewish conflict, 10, 11, 22, 162, 452. *See also* Anti-
    Zionism; Palestinians; Zionism
Sklare, Marshall, 150
Skrentny, John, 82
Slavery: and racism, in relation to the Holocaust,
    5–6, 35–36, 39n, 90–92, 99, 145–147, 168, 180,
    214–215, 223–226, 234–237, 271, 283, 396, 398,
    402–404, 439–447, 446, 448, 451–452, 455, 456–
    464, 484, 486–488, 494, 495, 498–500; and slave
    rebellion, in relation to black consciousness,
    273–274, 292–301, 303–304. *See also* Black holo-
    caust
Smith, Anna Deavere: *Fires in the Mirror,* 86, 490
Smith, Bessie, 405, 426
Smith, Lillian, 174, 203, 230, 267–268
Smith, Rogers, 13
Smith, Welton: "malcolm," 405
Smith, William Gardner, 34
Smitherman, Geneva, 621n48
Sniderman, Paul, 66
Snow, Valaida, 60n
Sofsky, Wolfgang, 442
Sollors, Werner, 103
Southern Christian Leadership Conference
    (SCLC), 93, 108, 245, 247, 250, 314
Sowell, Thomas, 442
Soyinka, Wole, 309
Spencer, Jon Michael: *Tribes of Benjamin,* 10, 89–
    90, 135, 139–141
Spiegelman, Art: *Maus II,* 35, 47, 486n; Valentine's
    Day illustration for *New Yorker,* 500–501

Spingarn, Arthur, 30
Spingarn, Joel, 30
Spivak, John: *Georgia Nigger*, 27
Stampp, Kenneth, 224, 296
Stannard, David, 441n
Staub, Michael, 204, 612n117
Steele, Shelby, 84n, 585n174
Steiner, George, 205, 459n; *The Portage to San Cristobal of A. H.*, 148, 485
Stern, Daniel: *The Suicide Academy*, 360
Stern, Sol, 354
Sternberg, Harry, 27
Stern Gang. *See* Lehi
Stoddard, Lothrop, 186
Stone, I. F., 348
Stowe, Harriet Beecher: *Uncle Tom's Cabin*, 25, 67n, 104, 220, 233–234, 342n, 346n
Stranger, biblical concept of the, 2, 3–4, 23, 30, 32, 41, 47–48, 386, 387, 390, 424, 434, 500–502, 527
Strauss, Leo, 50, 54, 56, 167
Streicher, Julius, 182
Stringfellow, William, 338
Stuckey, Sterling, 296, 564n192
Student Non-Violent Coordinating Committee (SNCC), 245, 246, 247, 280, 314–316, 332, 333, 339
Students for a Democratic Society (SDS), 316, 354
Styron, William: *The Confessions of Nat Turner*, 209, 225–226, 291, 296–297, 362; *Sophie's Choice*, 190, 208–209, 279, 443, 517
Suberman, Stella, 190n
Suburbs, Jews' move to, 44, 46, 55–56, 79, 392, 394–395, 509
Suez War (1956), 153–154, 332, 334
Sun Ra, 166–167
Syrkin, Marie, 228n, 368n, 518

Taguieff, Pierre-André, 440
Tarr, Herbert: *Heaven Help Us!*, 117n
Taylor, Charles, 78
Terry, Wallace, 138
Thomas, Clarence, 435–436
Thomas, Hugh, 439n
Thomas, Laurence Mordekhai, 50, 443, 512
Thomas, William Hannibal, 175
Thoreau, Henry David, 243–245, 260, 265, 269, 351
Tidyman, Ernest: *Shaft among the Jews*, 359
Till, Emmett, 177–180, 193, 196, 202, 220, 234, 235, 236, 486, 587n197
Tolson, Melvin: "Babylon," 455n; "Harlem Gallery," 405, 408–409; "The Idols of the Tribe," 180, 212
Toomer, Jean, 179; *Cane*, 203
Torres, Gerald, 523

Trilling, Lionel, 55, 517
Truman, Harry, 63, 81
Tubman, Harriet, 97
Ture, Kwame. *See* Carmichael, Stokely
Turner, Henry McNeal, 123–124
Turner, Nat, 287, 291, 294, 295, 298
Turpin, Waters: *O Canaan!*, 44, 98
Twain, Mark, 386; *The Adventures of Huckleberry Finn*, 171, 432

Uganda, 273, 300; Abayudaya (Jews) of, 119n; as potential Jewish homeland, 148, 287, 304, 333
Uhry, Alfred: *Driving Miss Daisy*, 192, 193, 482, 483, 490n; *Parade*, 195
United Jewish Appeal (UJA), 192, 340–341
United Nations, 6, 63, 287; and partition of Palestine, 142, 154, 325, 326, 372; anti-Zionism among member nations of, 208, 331, 335; petitions to, by African Americans, 216–219, 494; sponsorship of World Conference against Racism, 474, 609n82
United Nations Genocide Convention, 6, 216–220, 287, 311, 339, 436, 441, 494
United States Holocaust Memorial Museum, 82, 457, 517
Universal Negro Improvement Association (UNIA), 124, 125, 126
University of California Regents v. Bakke, 76–78, 521
Upchurch, Boyd: *The Slave Stealer*, 359–360
Uris, Leon, 55; *Exodus*, 320, 512

VanDerZee, James, 116n, 117
Van Ellison, Candy, 388n
Van Vechten, Carl, 69
Vernon, Robert, 254
Vesey, Denmark, 105, 106, 287, 294
Vidal-Naquet, Pierre, 288, 319
Von Hoffman, Nicholas, 329
Vorspan, Albert, 38, 75
Voting Rights Act (1965), 22, 313, 314

Wacquant, Loïc, 620n26
Wakeman, Samuel, 103
Walcott, Derek, 404; "The Muse of History," 282, 295; "North and South," 283; "The Sea as History," 99
Walker, Alice, 504n; *Meridian*, 73n, 192, 416, 633n71
Walker, Clarence, 167
Walker, David, 104
Walker, Margaret, 318n; *Jubilee*, 164, 457
Walker, Rebecca, 234n, 504n
Wallace, George, 201, 415

Wallace, Michelle, 418n

Wallant, Edward: *The Pawnbroker,* 44, 393–395

Wallerstein, Pinchas, 323n

Walters, Ronald, 450

Walzer, Michael, 106, 248, 260, 443

Ward, Douglas Turner: *A Day of Absence,* 257

War of Independence, Israeli (1948), 149, 325, 329, 331, 332, 341, 369, 372–376, 378–380

Warren, Earl, 64, 66, 221, 229–230, 466n. See also *Brown v. Board of Education*

Warren, Robert Penn, 191, 228n

Wartofsky, Victor: *Meeting the Pieman,* 362

Washington, Booker T., 23–24, 25, 26, 143, 161, 191, 346n

Waskow, Arthur, 351

Wasserstein, Wendy: *An American Daughter,* 496

Watson, Tom, 194–196

al-Wazir, Khalil (Abu Jihad), 326

Webb, James Morris, 124

Weiner, Herbert, 430

Wells, H. G, 362, 363n, 365

Welsing, Frances Cress, 451

West, Cornel, 19, 93, 451, 481–482, 526, 585n174

Westley, Robert, 476–477

White, Walter, 69, 213

"White Negro," concept of, 66–71, 230, 350, 514. *See also* Jews: as white

Whitfield, Stephen, 54

Whitman, Walt, 506

Whitten, Benjamin O., 187

Wicker, Tom, 391

Wideman, John Edgar, 78, 243, 407; *Brothers and Keepers,* 465; *Fatheralong,* 246, 464, 466; *Philadelphia Fire,* 11, 464–473, 484; "Valaida," 60n

Wiesel, Elie, 207, 397–398, 526; *Night,* 205, 209, 231–232

Wieseltier, Leon, 359, 477

Wilkins, Roger, 154–155

Wilkins, Roy, 147, 172, 191, 211, 341

Wilkomirski, Benjamin, 232n

Williams, Cecil, 451

Williams, John A.: *The Angry Ones,* 368; *!Click Song,* 369; *Clifford's Blues,* 369, 445; *The Man Who Cried I Am,* 369, 450; *Sons of Darkness, Sons of Light,* 10, 282, 312, 356, 362, 368–373, 377–380, 449, 483

Williams, Joseph, 115

Williams, Patricia, 447–448

Williams, Robert F., 253n, 317–318

Williams, Wayne, 453n

Wilson, Amos N., 304

Wilson, August: *The Piano Lesson,* 592n58

Windsor, Rudolph, 141

Winthrop, John, 159

Wirth, Louis, 59, 392

Wise, Isaac Meyer, 103–104

Wise, Stephen, 30

Wisse, Ruth, 207, 210n

Wolf, Arnold Jacob, 352

Wolfe, Tom, 350

Wouk, Herman: *Marjorie Morningstar,* 55

Wright, Richard, 98–99, 407, 422, 517; *Black Boy,* 40, 235; *Black Power,* 315n; "Bright and Morning Star," 251; *The Long Dream,* 234–237, 240, 261, 437, 455; *Native Son,* 125, 179, 256, 397; *12 Million Black Voices,* 97–99; *White Man, Listen!,* 278

Yehoshua, A. B., 329

Yerushalmi, Yosef Hayim, 506, 593n5, 638n5

Yom Kippur War (1973), 119n, 312, 331, 332, 334, 335, 340, 341

Yossef, Ovadia, 119

Young, Andrew, 107, 335–336, 511

Young, Robert Alexander, 121

Young, Whitney, 339, 341

Youth International Party (Yippies), 350

Zangwill, Israel, 56–57

Zetnik, K. (Yehiel Dinur), 365

Ziegler, H. S.: "Entartete Musik," 185

Zionism, 7–8, 100, 120, 122, 123, 125, 132, 142, 149, 155, 156, 246, 271, 356, 366, 429; and Americanism, 7, 150–151, 164, 511; as form of colonialism, 110, 160, 161–162, 314, 317, 319, 324, 327–329, 332–334, 375–379; compared to apartheid in South Africa, 317n, 335; gives way to "post-Zionism," 328, 330, 373, 374; in relation to black nationalism, 161–162, 272, 288, 302, 330–333, 356–359, 372–374, 402. *See also* Anti-Zionism; Israel; Palestinians

Zionist Organization of America, 31, 57

CPSIA information can be obtained at www.ICGtesting.com
Printed in the USA
LVOW10s2257170214

374109LV00008B/134/P